Special Edition

USING
LOTUS NOTES
AND DOMINO 4.5

Written by

Cate Richards

with

Jane Calabria

Rob Kirkland

David Hatter

Roy Rumaner

Susan Trost

Tim Vallely

Mark Williams

QUe

Special Edition Using Lotus Notes and Domino 4.5

Library of Congress Catalog No.: 96-71454

ISBN: 0-7897-0943-0

99 98 97   6 5 4 3 2

Interpretation of the printing code: the rightmost double-digit number is the year of the book's printing; the rightmost single-digit number, the number of the book's printing. For example, a printing code of 97-1 shows that the first printing of the book occurred in 1997.

Screen reproductions in this book were created using Collage Plus from Inner Media, Inc., Hollis, NH.

Composed in *Stone Serif* and *MCPdigital* by Que Corporation.

Contents at a Glance

Notes Basics

Designing Applications

Working with LotusScript

Going Mobile

Advanced Notes Topics

Appendixes

Working with the Web

CD-ROM

Contents

4 Getting Started with Electronic Mail   135

6 Advanced Mail 217

15 Working with Functions and Commands   593

16 Buttons and Agents   611

III Working with LotusScript   645

17 LotusScript Basics   647

IV Going Mobile   789

20 Setting Up to Go Remote   791

21 Working Remote   825

V Advanced Notes Topics   871

22 Security and Encryption   873

23 Case Study: Taking Advantage of Lotus Notes Features   905

VI Working with the Web   975

25 Lotus Notes and the Web   977

26 Using the Web Navigator   989

27 Using Domino Server's HTTP Service   1029

Bonus Chapters on CD-ROM

3   Command Reference

4   @Functions

5   Remote Troubleshooting

Credits

President
Roland Elgey

Publisher
Joseph B. Wikert

Publishing Manager
Fred Slone

Senior Title Manager
Bryan Gambrel

Editorial Services Director
Elizabeth Keaffaber

Managing Editor
Sandy Doell

Director of Marketing
Lynn E. Zingraf

Acquisitions Editor
Al Valvano

Production Editor
Maureen A. McDaniel

Copy Editors
Juliet MacLean
Matthew B. Cox
Thomas Cirtin
Patrick Kanouse
Caroline D. Roop
Kelli M. Brooks
Kristin Ivanetich
Sydney Jones
Judith Goode
Bonnie Lawler

**Assistant Product
Marketing Manager**
Christy M. Miller

Strategic Marketing Manager
Barry Pruett

Technical Editors
Bob Cepican
Steve Kern
Debbie Lynd

Technical Support Specialist
Nadeem Muhammed

Acquisitions Coordinator
Carmen Krikorian

Editorial Assistant
Andrea Duvall

Book Designer
Ruth Harvey

Cover Designer
Dan Armstrong

Production Team
Marcia Brizendine
Maribeth Echard
Daryl Kessler
Darlena Murray
Julie Searls

Indexer
Chris Wilcox

To my parents, Ann and Bill Collins, you are the best friends and parents a gal can have—keep smiling! To my son, Robert, you are the sunshine that wakes me in the morning.

About the Authors

Cate Richards is a Senior Consultant for Bay Resources, Inc., a Lotus Business Partner in St. Petersburg, Florida. Her primary responsibility is to work with her clients to help automate and maintain their business systems using Lotus Notes as the platform. She also spends a great deal of her time training her clients in the use of Notes, assisting them with re-engineering their business processes, and working with them to document their policies, procedures, and systems. Cate has worked with Lotus Notes for over six years, and has been a beta test participant since version 2.0 of Notes. Cate holds an M.B.A. from the Roy E. Crummer Graduate School of Business at Rollins College in Winter Park, FL, and a B.A. in marketing from the University of South Florida in Tampa. This is Cate's fifth writing endeavor on Lotus Notes books for Que, and she is currently working on her sixth book—*Using Lotus Notes 4.5*—written for the beginning Notes user. Cate has also contributed time to Xephon as a technical editor for their *Notes Update* magazine. She is also an L-Team member, selected by Lotus, to assist users in the CompuServe Lotus Notes support forum (**GO LOTUSC**). You can find her there most days trying to assist other Notes users, and having a little fun at the same time! You can reach Cate via e-mail at **cate_richards@bay.com**, **102350,3042** (CompuServe), or **Cate Richards @ Bay Resources @ Notes Net**.

Jane "JC" Calabria is a Certified Lotus Notes Instructor (CLI), Certified Notes Consultant (CLP), and author of several Que books on Lotus Notes, including *10-Minute Guide to Lotus Notes Mail*, *Lotus Notes and the Internet 6-in-1*, and *10-Minute Guide to InterNotes Web Navigator*. She teaches classes on Lotus Notes, desktop applications, groupware, and Windows 95 for Rockey & Associates in Malvern, PA. As a consultant, she works with Lotus Notes planning and implementation, and Notes application development, and develops PC support organization models for large corporations. Jane is also a correspondent for Philadelphia's KYW News Radio 1060 AM where she broadcasts weekly as "JC on PCs" with her computer news and tips. She can be reached on CompuServe at **74754,3360**.

Rob Kirkland is a Certified Lotus Notes Instructor (CLI), a Certified NetWare Engineer (CNE), and a Microsoft Certified Product Specialist (MCPS) for Windows NT. He is a contributing author of several Que books, including *Using Windows NT Workstation*, *Intranet Publishing*, *Running a Perfect Intranet*, and *Intranet HTML*. He teaches classes on Lotus Notes, Novell NetWare, Windows NT, communications software, numerous application programs, and hardware management. Rob works for Rockey & Associates in Malvern, PA with his wife Jane. They are featured in two Lotus Notes training videos and CD-ROMs produced by LearnKey Inc. in St. George, UT entitled "Lotus Notes Application Development I" and "Domino Web Server." As a consultant, he sets up networks and designs applications, and subdues unruly hardware or software. In his spare time, Rob picked up a law degree. He can be reached on CompuServe at **74754,3360**.

Dave Hatter is a Groupware/Messaging Specialist with Entex Information Services, the largest PC systems integrator in the United States and is recognized as the leading provider of "Total PC Management" for large organizations. Dave has over five years of programming experience with a variety of tools and has been working with Lotus Notes for nearly three years. He is a Lotus Certified Notes Specialist (LCNS) for Notes R3.x, and a Certified Lotus Professional Developer and Certified Lotus Professional System Administrator for Notes R4.x. In addition, Dave teaches a wide variety of technology-related community education courses and appears monthly on a local cable TV show to discuss current technology and trends. He holds a B.S. in information systems from Northern Kentucky University. Dave lives in Ft. Wright, KY with his wife Leslee and his son Samuel. Dave can be reached via e-mail at **dhatter@one.net** or visit his Web page at **w3.one.net/~dhatter**.

Roy Rumaner is Senior Lotus Notes Consultant for Terasys, Inc., a Lotus Business Partner in Naperville, IL. He has over two years' experience with Lotus Notes and has been a beta test member for the past two versions of Notes. Roy has also contributed time to Xephon as a technical editor for their *Notes Update* magazine. He is also an L-Team member, selected by Lotus, to assist users in the CompuServe Lotus Notes support forum (**GO LOTUSC**). Roy is also the unofficial Lotusphere Party Chairman of the CompuServe Notes L-Team. Roy is a frequent speaker for many of the various Chicago-area Notes technical workshops. Roy lives in Aurora, IL with his wife Karen and his extensive collection of Tigger toys. Roy can be reached at **rrumaner@terasys.com**, **105073,2256** (CompuServe), and **Roy Rumaner @ Terasys @ Notes Net**.

Susan Trost is an independent Notes consultant and has been working with Notes since early 1992. She has worked internationally for Andersen Consulting and Lotus Development and was one of the first certified engineers for communications products at Lotus. Susan holds a B.S. from Towson State University in Maryland, and an M.S. in telecommunications from the University of Colorado in Boulder. She can be reached via e-mail on **100102,3500@compuserve.com**.

Tim Vallely holds a B.S. with honors in electrical engineering and computer science from the University of London and has over 12 years of development experience working for IBM, Nielsen International, and as an independent Lotus Notes Developer and Technical Architect. Tim has been working with Lotus Notes for over four years and specializes in complex development and programmability tools including LotusScript, HiTest Tools, MQ Series, and the Notes API. He is a Certified Lotus Professional and has extensive international Notes roll-out experience having worked for clients both in the USA and abroad. In true Lotus Notes fashion, Tim leads a mobile life and is best contacted via e-mail at **100434,774@compuserve.com**.

Mark Williams is a Senior Consultant with Bay Resources, Inc., a Lotus Business Partner, in St. Petersburg, FL. He has worked with Lotus Notes since version 2.0, and is responsible for system design and development. His primary responsibility is to work with Bay Resources clients to help automate and redesign their client server needs to use Lotus Notes and other third-party products. Prior to Bay Resources, Mark worked for JP Morgan, where he helped support their worldwide Lotus Notes infrastructure and develop Lotus Notes applications. Mark has been "in the business" for over 20 years. This is Mark's second endeavor with Que, and, contrary to popular belief, he is not a sheep farmer in Washington.

About the Tech Editors

Bob Cepican is a certified Lotus Notes Consultant in the Chicagoland area, and has worked for such companies as Waste Management, Inc., Andersen Consulting, and Terasys, Inc. He is also the author of *Yesterday Came Suddenly, The Definitive History of the Beatles*, published by Arbor House, 1985. Bob resides with his wife and children in Downers Grove, IL.

Steve Kern is a Certified Lotus Professional and the Senior Notes Consultant for LDA Systems, headquartered in Cleveland, OH. He works at the Columbus, OH branch. Before becoming a consultant, Steve spent 15 years in Business Management, and began working with PCs in the early 1980s. Steve received a B.S. in agriculture from The Ohio State University, and lives in Columbus, OH with his wife, two daughters, three fish tanks, and one Golden Retriever.

Debbie Lynd has 17 years of experience in the computer industry as a consultant and instructor. She is currently an independent consultant and certified instructor for both Lotus Notes and cc:Mail products. She has been involved with Notes from a systems perspective for the last five years, covering deployment, operations, applications development, and systems management.

The following people worked on the CD in the back of this book:

Craig Hensley is a Senior Consultant with Bay Resources, a Lotus Business Partner in Miami, FL. His primary responsibility is to work with clients in designing, planning, implementing, and documenting the Lotus Notes infrastructure. His role is to guide clients through the enterprise deployment of Lotus Notes, as well as help them define the way that Notes is administered, maintained, and scaled. Craig has worked with Lotus Notes since 1993, and also has a background in network administration with NetWare, Windows NT, and OS/2. He holds a B.S. in computer science from Marshall University in Huntington, WV, as well as several Lotus and Novell (CNA and LCNS) certifications.

Rafael Campos is a Senior Groupware Consultant at Bay Resources, Inc., a Lotus Business Partner in Miami, FL. His primary focus is the planning, development, and integration of document imaging technologies to workgroup applications, and utilizing LN:DI and other companion products. Prior to joining Bay Resources, Rafael worked in the mortgage banking field in a variety of information systems functions, which included system evaluations, acquisitions and installations, and the development and management of document management systems. Rafael lives in Greenacres, FL—"The place to be." He holds a B.S. degree in industrial design from the Illinois Institute of Technology.

Acknowledgments

When I first began using computers, I bought a few books and noted the authors' names on the cover (and then promptly forgot them). What I never took the time to do was flip the page and find out who "really" was responsible for getting this book out. To get this book together, a team of Lotus Notes professionals and Que editors banded together to get the job done in an extremely tight timeframe. My first and foremost thank yous go to this team! Not only have I been blessed with wonderful folks who really know what they are doing, but I have formed some lifetime friendships that span across the oceans! There would be no book without all of these folks, and I salute them! I encourage you to review their biographies and the credits in the preceding pages.

Next in line, but first in my heart, is my family. The hustle and bustle of writing this book is all-consuming, as the beta releases require rewrites upon rewrites of text you just submitted the day before for the previous beta release! My parents, Ann and Bill Collins, and my son, Robert Richards, have been my cheerleaders, dietitians, exercise monitors, sounding boards, housekeepers, back massagers, and all-around sanity checkers from day one! Mom and Dad, you are the greatest!! Without you, I couldn't have gotten through this! And Robert, what can Mommy say... "You are my life!" Mommy is very proud of you (and just has to brag about you winning at the Tae Kwon Do Junior Olympics and being the National Tae Kwon Do Champion in your division this year!) Brother Bill and Sister Shau Li, thank you for your support from afar—I promise to come see you at *your* house soon!

Heartfelt thanks go out to all of the folks at Lotus who have helped throughout the course of the development of this book. Special thanks go to Dick Alme and Landon Hunsucker, our Business Partner representatives in Atlanta, who have been fantastic in helping get the information we need for the book—as well as answering all of those pesky questions we always seem to come up with! Thanks also to Wizop Ildiko Nagy for her assistance and trust in the CompuServe LOTUSC forum!

Thanks to Master Hyun Park, my Tae Kwon Do instructor, friend, and role model for all of the encouragement and inspiration over the past few years. I will miss you greatly when I move, but will remember you always in my heart (and I'll see you often)! Thanks also to the folks at Master Park's Tae Kwon Do World school in Altamonte Springs for all of your cheers and encouragement over the years!

I would be remiss if I did not thank all of the folks at Bay Resources, (who are too many to name individually). Cass Casucci, Dan Baker, Bob Hamilton, and Rod Dunlap have been wonderful to work for since the day I started with Bay Resources (and I'm not just saying that to get a raise!). Your overwhelming encouragement in these "book things" is something I've never had before in a company, and it is greatly appreciated!

Thanks to all of the folks at Que who have helped make this book happen—Al (who picks the best time to take a vacation), Kelly (who has a special key chain with clip picked out just for her), and Maureen (who dares to get married during my deadline)—and all of the other editors who helped keep me on time! The folks at Que are THE BEST around—even if they do set a deadline that keeps you working all night and through the weekend! Salute!

I have been told that I will be in big trouble if I don't say thanks to all of the folks in the CompuServe Lotus Notes forum (**GO LOTUSC**) for all of the inspiration, fun, and answers they have provided over the past year! Deb, Roger, John, Raj, Chet, Peter, Ron, Gerald, Les "G," Steve(s), Lou, Carolyn, John, Zev & Zoe, Stuart, Kirstin, and the rest of the forum crew have provided great examples, ideas, and laughs throughout the year! LOTUSC is definitely the best (if not wackiest) forum going <CG>!

Personal thanks to my two mentors—Linda Metcalf (and Doug, too) and Gary Strack—for jump-starting me years ago into "doing what I want to do." And finally, thanks goes to my chiropractor, Dr. Kent Klonel, and the staff at Klonel Chiropractic and Rehabilitation Center in Altamonte Springs who kept me sitting upright without pain during the tight deadlines! My neck, back, and editors thank you dearly!

We'd Like to Hear from You!

As part of our continuing effort to produce books of the highest possible quality, Que would like to hear your comments. To stay competitive, we *really* want you, as a computer book reader and user, to let us know what you like or dislike most about this book or other Que products.

You can mail comments, ideas, or suggestions for improving future editions to the address below, or send us a fax at (317) 581-4663. Our staff and authors are available for questions and comments through our Internet site, at **http://www.mcp.com/que**, and Macmillan Computer Publishing also has a forum on CompuServe (type **GO QUEBOOKS** at any prompt).

In addition to exploring our forum, please feel free to contact me personally to discuss your opinions of this book: I'm **74671,3710** on CompuServe and **avalvano@que.mcp.com** on the Internet.

Thanks in advance—your comments will help us to continue publishing the best books available on new computer technologies in today's market.

Al Valvano
Acquisitions Editor
Que Corporation
201 W. 103rd Street
Indianapolis, Indiana 46290
USA

Introduction

In our daily work, many of us have been caught up in the eternal—and often infernal—chase of paper around the organizations in which we work and communicate. Coworkers send flyers reminding everyone of the company picnic. The Human Resource department modifies several policies in the HR manual and then reprints and ships the 3"-thick manual to all employees. You must order supplies, so you fill out a purchase request and forward it for approval to your manager, who forwards it to Accounting, which forwards it to be ordered by Purchasing, which then forwards the form back to you to let you know it has been ordered. Does any of this seem familiar? It is this chase after paper that companies have struggled with that has created the perfect environment for Lotus Notes to take hold, and quickly become the market leader in groupware technology.

Groupware is software designed to be used by groups of people sharing information and working together. It lets a group of people use the same information—but oftentimes in different ways, depending on their particular needs. Lotus Notes lets you perform many of the common activities you currently partake in during the workday: exchanging mail, sharing ideas, accessing information, and planning for the future. Notes endeavors to literally replace paper documents with electronic documents, but with a twist. You can create sophisticated workflow applications that automate—and often streamline—your business processes. Notes does not simply create a copy of a paper form; it "moves" it through the business process through the use of electronic signatures, status conditions, and other indicators. Notes lets you automate your workflow, re-creating the path your document takes, oftentimes improving it as unnecessary steps are made more visible for inspection or elimination.

What Is Lotus Notes?

If you ask anyone who works with Lotus Notes to define what it is, you are most likely going to get a different answer from each person you talk to. Lotus Development Corporation representatives themselves often struggle with defining Notes—because it can mean different things to each organization that uses it. Some refer to Lotus Notes as a document database—but don't let that simple definition fool you. Notes is more than a receptacle for storing documents, like many of the more traditional types of databases.

It's perhaps better to think of Notes as a way of organizing documents and making them available to groups of people. However, the word *document* can often be misleading, as many think only of text when they think of documents. With the rich text field capability of Lotus Notes, a document can contain just about any electronic object, which is why many refer to Lotus Notes as a storage container. You can embed or import graphics into documents, incorporate spreadsheets, insert video files that can be viewed straight from the document, insert voice messages that can be played with the click of a button, and attach any file in any format to a document for distribution to others.

With Notes' open, nonproprietary format, it can also serve as the "glue" that helps your other applications talk to each other. You can use Notes to gather and workflow information around your organization as a front-end, user-friendly GUI (graphical user interface), and then schedule the information to download into your more traditional legacy mainframe applications. You can also develop sophisticated applications in languages like Visual Basic and C, and then pass the information collected in those applications to Notes to be stored or workflowed around an organization. With Notes' new capability to work with information on the Internet through its family of products and the built-in Web browser, Notes now combines the rich text and security capabilities of its package with the vast frontier of information on the Internet—providing you with the best of both worlds.

Benefits of Notes

Notes' unique database structure lets you keep track of complex, relatively unstructured information (which is how you typically receive most information) and makes that information available to groups of users on a network—whether they are connected directly to the network, or are dialing in from remote locations. Notes helps eliminate much of the redundant paperwork and steps in your business processes by moving the flow of documents from paper format—where typically one person at a time reviews the information—to an electronically organized workflow in which many can review, approve, and communicate the information with the click of a button. In a world where companies must cut costs while increasing the speed in which people must communicate with one another to maintain a competitive presence, Lotus Notes can provide the companies using it a definite edge.

Who Should Use This Book?

This book is written for the "power user" and/or "new designer" of Lotus Notes—someone who wants to use Notes for more than accessing e-mail and a few databases that have already been designed. It is also a great resource for existing Notes users who need to get up and running on a much-enhanced, but significantly different, version of Lotus Notes. The user will, of course, receive guidance in all of the activities to get started using Notes R4—sending e-mail, composing documents, changing the way you view information, and so on—so the new user for Lotus Notes will benefit from this book, too!

The CD that accompanies this book contains text, applications, demos, screencams, white papers (research studies), adjunct product information, training information, and support numbers provided by Lotus Development and many of the third-party vendors to give you a feeling for many of the products and services available in the market, as well as to give you ideas on how you might want to use Notes in your organization. Also available on the CD are sample applications, a Database Icon Library, a Notes Architecture Guidebook, five bonus chapters, and an advanced Formula Catalog database, to name a few.

Finally, for those of you who would like to view this book on your computer, rather than always from the printed version, you can access the entire book in HTML format on the CD-ROM. There is an added bonus on the CD-ROM as well—included is a complete book on working with JavaScript titled *Special Edition Using Java Script*. This book will help teach you how to write JavaScript—which Lotus Notes 4.5 now supports—to help you enhance your new Web designs. Instructions for accessing these online books are provided in Appendix D, "Using the CD-ROM."

How to Use This Book

This book is divided into seven parts. The earlier parts are intended for a general audience, and the later parts depend on an understanding of the previous parts. You will also find a wealth of information in the appendixes and on the CD-ROM to help you further understand Notes. Even if you are an "old hat" to Notes, check out the beginning chapters to review many of the changes incorporated in Notes R4.

Part I—Notes Basics

Part I discusses the basic nature of Lotus Notes, and presents an overview of its capabilities. In this part of the book, you find out what has changed between Lotus Notes R3.x and Lotus Notes R4. This is light reading, but recommended for all readers, both new users and veterans of Lotus Notes.

In Chapter 1, "Getting Started with Lotus Notes," you are introduced to the concepts of working with groupware, understanding the Notes interface, and starting and exiting Lotus Notes. This chapter also highlights many of the new features available with Notes R4.

In Chapter 2, "Customizing Notes," you learn how to personalize your Notes setup, create custom SmartIcons, and work with your DESKTOP.DSK and NOTES.INI files.

Chapter 3, "Using Databases," provides the foundation for working with any database. You learn about the basic components of a Notes database and how to use them.

Chapter 4, "Getting Started with Electronic Mail," walks you through working with Lotus Notes' e-mail package.

To gain insight into how the Name & Address Book acts as the heart of the Lotus Notes system, read Chapter 5, "Using the Address Book." It provides instructions for using the

Name & Address Book when addressing e-mail, as well as creating group lists, person documents, and other functions available to you in working with the Name & Address Book.

Chapter 6, "Advanced Mail," continues the discussion of working with e-mail, covering such advanced topics as working with attachments, forwarding documents via mail, and many other tips for getting the most out of mail.

Chapter 7, "Working with Text," walks you through all of the commands and features available to enhance text in your documents. You learn how to change font attributes, control margin settings, use the Clipboard, and work with bullets and numbering.

In Chapter 8, "Working with Documents," you explore features available in Notes that add pizzazz to your documents. You learn how to create tables, hotspots, collapsible sections, links, and more. You also learn how to use the Lotus Notes spell checking feature.

Chapter 9, "Lotus Notes Group Calendaring and Scheduling," teaches you how to work with the new calendar feature located in your Mail database. You will learn how to create appointments, invite users to a meeting, schedule resources, and more in this chapter.

Part II—Designing Applications

In Part II, you learn the basic building blocks used in creating or redesigning a Notes database application. This part of the book also explores design, @function, and LotusScript terminology. If you are already an experienced Lotus Notes programmer, you may still want to skim through these sections because so much has changed in this recent release of Lotus Notes.

In Chapter 10, "Creating New Databases," you are introduced to the basic building blocks of application design, including learning how to create applications from templates, work with the design menus, and develop graphical navigators.

To take a deeper look into developing database forms, see Chapter 11, "Designing Forms." In this chapter, you learn how to create a form from scratch. This chapter provides a basic understanding of form design—as well as some tips on using some of the more advanced features available to you when creating forms.

Chapter 12, "Designing Views," delves further into application design by looking at how you design the views that report information. This chapter walks you through creating a view from the ground up. You will learn the basics of view design and many of the advanced features as well.

Chapter 13, "Integrating Notes with Other Applications," provides the basics for working with OLE2, FX (field exchange), and other methods that let you incorporate information from other applications into Notes databases.

Chapters 14, "Working with Formulas," and 15, "Working with Functions and Commands," provide you with a foundation for using Lotus Notes formula function programming. These chapters supplement the chapters on creating databases, forms, views, and other programmable objects by providing you the rules and explanations for writing formulas using Notes' functions.

Chapter 16, "Buttons and Agents," looks at designing and incorporating buttons and agents into your Notes application to enhance the design and user-friendliness of the application and to perform routine "housekeeping" features within an application.

Part III—Working with LotusScript

Chapter 17, "LotusScript Basics," provides the foundation for beginning to work with LotusScript. LotusScript is a basic compatible language (much like Visual Basic) that is used in developing applications in Lotus Notes.

Chapter 18, "Writing Scripts with LotusScript," takes you one step further into working with Notes LotusScript language. This chapter provides detailed examples in working with this programming language, and gives you a boost in becoming an expert programmer.

Chapter 19, "More LotusScript," shows that too much of a good thing sometimes isn't bad! This chapter gives you more advanced examples on working with LotusScript.

Part IV—Going Mobile

In Part IV, you will learn how to work with Notes remotely—not connected to a network. Remote users must set up their systems to prepare for working disconnected from the server, and then initiate communication with the server each time they are ready to send and receive information. This section provides users with the instructions to prepare and work off of the network with Notes. Even if you are not a Notes user, you may benefit from scanning these chapters as you may be communicating with remote users—and would therefore benefit from seeing Notes from their point of view.

In Chapter 20, "Setting Up to Go Remote," you learn what you will need to work with Notes when away from a network. You also learn how to set up Notes to go on the road.

Chapter 21, "Working Remote," walks you through the process of working remote, which is calling the servers and replicating (exchanging) information with the servers. You will also learn tips on keeping the size of your remote databases manageable.

Part V—Advanced Notes Topics

As you and your business become more experienced with Lotus Notes, you will undoubtedly want to really take advantage of the special features of the program. This part of the book delves further into these more advanced topics of Lotus Notes.

Chapter 22, "Security and Encryption," takes a look at the security features in Notes. Understanding your Notes ID and certificates, managing database access control, and working with encryption are just a few of the important topics in this chapter.

Chapter 23, "Case Study: Taking Advantage of Lotus Notes Features," discusses some more advanced application design techniques introduced in previous chapters. In this chapter, you will review many of the design tips used in creating the Sentinel application from Mayflower Software.

Chapter 24, "Notes: Under the Hood," explains the behind-the-scenes happenings of Lotus Notes from a high level. You gain an understanding into the role servers play, the platforms they work on, the new centralized Notes Administration interface, and other features that Notes uses to keep the people on your system communicating. This chapter is geared toward the user who needs to understand what is going on in the background so that applications are developed correctly, or to answer some of the "why is this happening?" questions that frequently occur when users work with Notes.

Part VI—Working with the Web

This section is dedicated to working with Lotus Notes' new Internet-enabled features. You will learn how to configure your workstation to browse the Internet using the Lotus Notes Web browser. You will also learn about working with Domino, and the Web Navigator. The author also provides you with insight into the direction Lotus is taking with the Internet.

Chapter 25, "Lotus Notes and the Web," discusses the new enhancements found in Lotus Notes. This chapter also discusses the reasoning behind the inclusion of the Internet capabilities found in Notes, and the future direction of Lotus with regard to Web communication.

Chapter 26, "Using the Web Navigator," teaches you how to configure your workstation and use the powerful features of the Lotus Notes Web browser. This chapter provides you with a soup-to-nuts explanation on working with this tool.

Chapter 27, "Using Domino Server's HTTP Service," shows you how to set up and work with the new Domino server add-on that is integrated into Lotus Notes 4.5. This powerful tool lets you publish Web databases directly to the Internet, work with mail and other databases from any Web browser, and much more.

Finally, Chapter 28, "Using Domino.Action," introduces you to Domino.Action, a Lotus Notes application that creates and maintains a whole, Domino-based Web site. Domino.Action lets you take advantage of Notes' workflow, security, and document-management features for your Web site. Learn all about it in this chapter.

Appendixes

You will also find a wealth of information in the appendixes and on the enclosed CD-ROM to further facilitate your understanding of Lotus Notes. The appendixes provide additional reference information that supports many of the chapters in this book.

Appendix A, "SmartIcons," provides you with a listing of all of the SmartIcons and their descriptions for quick reference.

Appendix B, "Database Templates," gives a brief description of the templates shipping with Lotus Notes R4. Use this appendix to quickly get an idea of what is available for your use.

Appendix C, "Special Characters," details the list of special characters available when working with Notes. Use this table as a quick reference when working with special characters (like the registered trademark).

Appendix D, "Using the CD-ROM," provides you with a brief insight into the contents of the enclosed CD, and provides you with the instructions on how to access the information.

Bonus Chapters on the CD-ROM

The CD-ROM provides screencams of add-on and third-party products, application demos, sample Notes databases, and additional technical and reference information. Also included is an electronic version of this book for your use. Refer to the detailed index at the back of this book to facilitate your location of information.

Also included on the enclosed CD are five bonus chapters.

Bonus 1, "ODBC and Lotus Components," takes a deep look into applications of LotusScript programming—building on what you learned in Part III, "Working with LotusScript."

Bonus 2, "Working with the Web Publisher," looks at how to use the Web Publisher to manage your Web sites. Though much of this technology is also available in the new release of Domino (discussed in Chapter 27), many companies still use the Internet Web Publisher to manage their Web sites—this chapter will show you how.

Bonus 3, "Command Reference," provides a detailed list of the Notes R4.5 menu commands—and their corresponding hot keys. Use this as a quick reference for finding those elusive commands while learning your way around Notes.

Bonus 4, "@Functions," provides you with a listing and description of all of the @functions available for you to use when you want to work with Lotus Notes' Formula programming language. This chapter supplements what you have learned in Chapters 14, "Working with Formulas," and 15, "Working with Functions and Commands."

Bonus 5, "Remote Troubleshooting," provides a list of problems and solutions for many of the most common problems experienced when working remote. Use this chapter in conjunction with the Mobile Survival Kit and Smartform Modem Doctor databases, also located on the CD-ROM, to help resolve remote troubles.

Conventions Used in This Book

Que has over a decade of experience developing and publishing the most successful computer books available. With that experience, we've learned what special features help readers the most. Look for these special features throughout the book to enhance your learning experience.

Several type and font conventions are used in this book to help make reading it easier:

- *Italic type* is used to emphasize the author's points or to introduce new terms.

- Screen messages, code listings, and command samples appear in `monospace typeface`.

- URLs, newsgroups, Internet addresses, and anything you are asked to type appears in **boldface**.

Tip

Tips present short advice on a quick or often overlooked procedure. These include shortcuts that can save you time.

Note

Notes provide additional information that may help you avoid problems, or offer advice that relates to the topic.

Caution

Cautions warn you about potential problems that a procedure may cause, unexpected results, and mistakes to avoid.

▶▶ See these cross-references for more information on a particular topic.

Sidebar

Longer discussions not integral to the flow of the chapter are set aside as sidebars. Look for these sidebars to find out even more information.

Troubleshooting

What is a troubleshooting section?

Troubleshooting sections anticipate common problems in the form of a question. The response provides you with practical suggestions for solving these problems.

Part I

Notes Basics

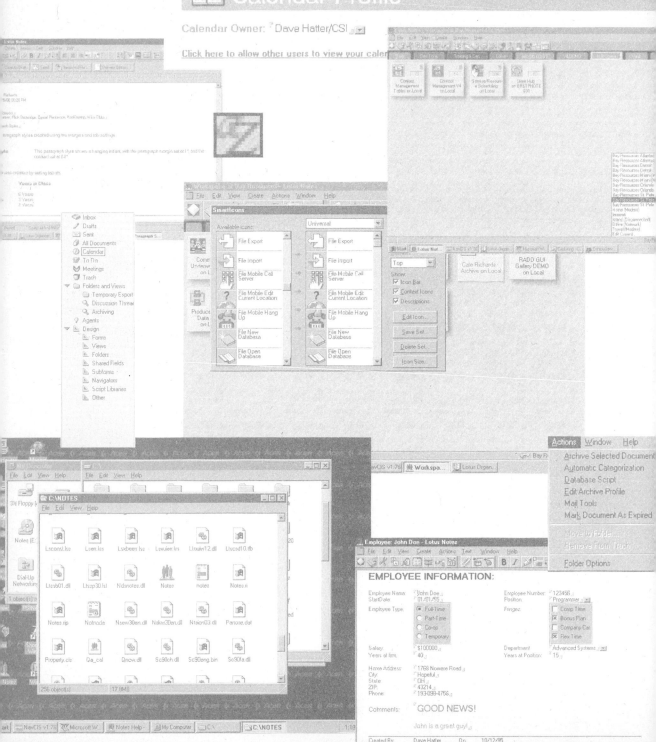

## Chapter 1

Getting Started with Lotus Notes

In this chapter, you learn about basic Notes concepts that will help you develop a good foundation for working with this software.

Welcome to Lotus Notes R4.5

The most difficult part of working with Lotus Notes is often trying to explain just what it is. The new users may think of Lotus Notes as electronic mail (e-mail) because that is often their first introduction to Notes. Others may call it a database software package, a workflow product, a document library, groupware, communication software, and so on. Notes is all of these things, and more. Essentially, Notes is a distributed client/server database application that enables users to organize, process, track, and share information. With Notes, users can access the same database at the same time and use the information to suit their individual needs. Notes consolidates the tools needed to effectively communicate and collaborate in an organization. Notes provides:

- E-mail
- Group Discussion
- Workflow
- Scheduling
- Document Management
- Application Development
- Web Publishing and Browsing
- Distributed Document Replication
- Centralized Directory Services (Address Book)

Notes can be used simply as an e-mail package that sends e-mail to other Notes users on your network. However, with the inclusion of some special software and gateways that can be installed by your Notes Administrator, your e-mail capabilities can be extended to let you send and receive faxes,

Some of the main topics in this chapter are

- Understanding Notes capabilities
- Learning new features in Release 4
- Working with views, panes, and folders
- Creating and editing documents
- Getting help

communicate with Notes users outside of your network, and even send mail and publish databases over the Internet to non-Notes users. If your network is set up to use these products and features available with Notes, it becomes the user-friendly, single source of access to multiple e-mail and other communication services.

Businesses benefit greatly not only from Notes' powerful e-mail capability, but from the ability to redefine and automate their business processes. Businesses using Notes, for example, have successfully automated their hiring and/or purchase approval process to include signature authorizations at each phase. Some companies run their entire business communications on Notes, often using Notes as a front-end, data-gathering tool for information that eventually ends up stored on a mainframe. Many companies also build reporting applications in Notes that import data from mainframe computers to report across a wide range of users in a corporation.

There are not many business applications that cannot use Notes 4. Many applications are simple, easy-to-develop databases that allow better communication among a group of users, whereas other applications are sophisticated business process programs developed with a combination of Lotus Notes and other programming languages and software tools. These applications can be designed by someone in your organization or by outside consultants. As you use this book, you learn about the tools, applications, and methods for successfully working with Notes 4.5. Throughout this book, tips and techniques used by expert Notes developers and administrators assist you. The CD-ROM accompanying this book provides you with example databases, tips, demos, and other information.

> **Note**
>
> While this book focuses on what Lotus Notes is, it would be prudent to briefly discuss what it isn't. Lotus Notes is not a relational database system, in which changes made to one record automatically update all instances of that entry throughout the system.
>
> For example, in the banking industry, an application may exist that tracks all of the information about a banking customer for each account held at the bank. If the customer changes his or her phone number, a relational system would update that change throughout every record in the system of that customer. In Lotus Notes, if the phone number changes in a customer record, code would have to be created to update all instances of that phone number in subsequent documents related to that client—or the records would have to be individually edited to make the change. Careful layout of the design of a database can overcome some of these limitations, but keeping this limitation in mind is warranted when deciding upon which system you need to resolve your business problems.
>
> Lotus Notes is also not meant to be a high volume transactional-based system where thousands of documents are accessed and created each day. While Notes can handle high volume tasks with some careful planning and development, the responsiveness and capacity of the system may suffer. Consider the transaction volume level when selecting what type of system best meets your business needs.

What's New in Notes R4?

For those of you who have worked with Lotus Notes in the past, some changes will further enhance your use of Notes. These changes have been brought about by the wealth of information provided by end users, Business Partners, and Lotus support desk information collected over the past few years.

Most of the changes in Lotus Notes 4.5 fall into one of the following categories:

- Messaging
- Internet server
- Internet client
- Scalability and manageability
- Security
- Programmability

> **Note**
>
> The features listed in this section are new to Lotus Notes 4.5. For a listing of features new to Lotus Notes 4, review the *Special Edition Using Lotus Notes and Domino 4.5* database document titled *Changes from Lotus Notes R3.x to Lotus Notes R4.*

Messaging. Notes provides many new features in R4.5 that facilitate your messaging infrastructure. Although applauded for the award-winning cc:Mail interface that was incorporated into the new Notes 4.0 mail database, Notes did not have sound calendaring and scheduling features to round out its messaging offering. New in R4.5 is the calendaring features that many users became accustomed to when using Lotus Organizer.

Lotus also delivers additional protocols and design elements in 4.5 to further enhance the programming and administering of Lotus Notes messaging.

Group Calendaring & Scheduling. Notes Release 4.5 also includes a rich set of calendaring and scheduling (C&S) functionality that's designed to be powerful and intuitive for end users. The new C&S features are flexible for application developers by letting developers incorporate the calendaring interface into their existing Notes applications. The C&S features are scalable even to the largest enterprise. Notable C&S end user features include the following:

- **Calendar views**—Based on the Lotus Organizer user interface, Notes C&S offers daily, weekly, biweekly, and monthly views of calendars.

- **Easy appointment/meeting creation**—Users can create appointments and schedule meetings of groups either by clicking an action bar button or clicking on a free time slot for a given day within a calendar view. By clicking date and time controls, users will be able to choose a different date, time, or meeting duration.

- **Meeting notification**—When a meeting is scheduled, each attendee is notified of the date, time, and place of the meeting. The person being notified can accept, delegate, reject the appointment, or easily add the meeting to their personal calendar with the click of a button.

- **Free time search**—Once meeting attendees are chosen, the Notes free time search system provides the user with a graphical representation of all attendees' availability and suggests a new time slot if the proposed one is not viable for all attendees.

- **Viewing other people's calendars**—Users can look at other people's calendars, as long as the owner of the calendar has granted them at least Reader level access.

- **Repeating appointments**—When creating an appointment, you can choose from various repeating rules (daily, weekly, monthly by date, and so on).

- **Room Reservations**—When scheduling an appointment, you can choose a meeting room directly from the appointment form and a search is made to a Room Resources database. You can also use this database to enter other resources, like audio visual equipment, as well.

- **Alarms**—You can set alarms for appointments, which provides a pop-up dialog box reminding you of the upcoming appointment. You will also hear a short beep when the dialog prompt appears. The alarm is activated only on your PC.

- **Conflict warning**—You can choose to be notified in the event a new appointment conflicts with an existing one. If you allow conflicting appointments, Notes indicates the conflict with a conflict flag (a red line) in the calendar view.

- **Moving appointments**—Drag-and-drop support lets you move existing appointments to a new date and/or time slot. If you move a repeating appointment, Notes prompts you to specify if you want to move all repeating appointments or just the selected one.

- **Calendar Profile**—You can specify preferences via a Calendar Profile. Such preferences can include free time options such as when your work week starts and allowable free times, default meeting duration.

- **Delegation Profile**—The Delegation Profile lets you specify who can view and/or manage your calendar entries. This Delegation Profile lets you specify who can view and/or manage your calendar independently from your mail file.

You also get to take advantage of the other Notes features when working with Notes Calendaring and Scheduling. For example, you can use the replication capabilities of Notes to keep your calendar synchronized while you're on the road and full text search to help you locate all entered training days in your calendar.

> **Note**
>
> The Freetime feature in Notes Calendaring and Scheduling supports a plug-in API that allows extensions to support free time searches in other calendaring systems such as IBM OfficeVision and Lotus Organizer.

You can extend the calendaring and scheduling functionality beyond managing your personal calendar and scheduling group meetings. Application developers can design

C&S features into other applications, for example, service desk call tracking and training schedules.

Calendar and Time controls can be used anywhere a Notes DateTime edit control currently exists in a form layout region. Using the Field InfoBox, designers can specify if they want a pop-up control to appear. By designing a field in a layout region and setting its type to Time *and* setting it to Show Date, the field displays as a DATE control (see Figure 1.1.)

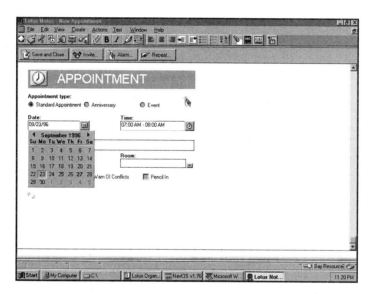

Fig. 1.1   The new Date control is a feature that can be programmed into any application.

By designing a field in a layout region and setting its type to Time *and* setting it to Show Time, the field displays as a Time control that looks something like Figure 1.2.

By designing a field in a layout region and setting its type to Time, selecting to allow Multiple values, and indicating to separate values with a Blank Line in the Options panel, the calendar displays as a duration control, which looks like Figure 1.3.

In addition to the calendar features discussed previously, Notes 4.5 also provides the following additional features:

- **@Functions** to access and store calendar profile information and to identify available free times.

- **NotesName**, a new LotusScript class, that facilitates handling of addresses and recipient names in mail-enabled applications.

- **Calendar style** views can be used to change any standard view in a database to display calendar information.

- **NotesSession.FREETIMESEARCH**, a new LotusScript method, allows access to the free time system via LotusScript.

■ **NotesName**, a new LotusScript class which facilitates the handling of addresses and recipient names in mail-enabled applications.

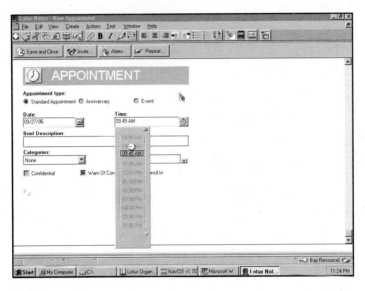

Fig. 1.2 You can program a Time control into any application that you want a user to select a date.

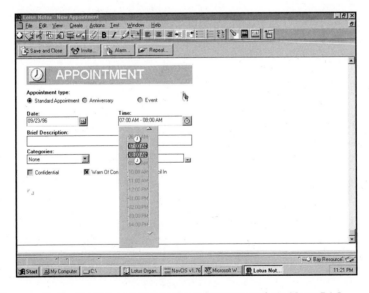

Fig. 1.3 You can display the Time control to show duration easily in Notes R4.5.

Additionally, new @functions have been added to access and store calendar profile information and to identify available free time.

Protocols and Standards. In addition to the new calendaring features, Notes includes additional support for Internet standards, protocols, directory support, and integration with other applications. Notes R4.5 provides the following:

- **Native SMTP/MIME MTA**—Notes Release 4.5 includes native support for the Internet mail standard, SMTP.

- **Integration with cc:Mail networks**—Notes Release 4.5 includes full-featured integration of cc:Mail and Notes messaging environments. The Notes cc:Mail MTA enables high-fidelity message and directory interoperability between Notes and cc:Mail networks.

- **POP3 Support**—The Notes Release 4.5 server provides POP3 mail support for POP3 clients (for example, Eudora, Netscape). Once POP3 clients download Notes Mail, they can save messages in a standard Notes Mail NSF file or delete them. Password level authentication that maintains a high level of security (that Notes users are used to) is included in Notes POP3.

- **Mobile Corporate Directory**—Notes Release 4.5 includes a new field-level replication option for Address Books to minimize the amount of disk space used by a local copy of the corporate Public Address Book.

Internet Server. Lotus Notes R4 had a Web Browser incorporated into the Notes client. Notes users could use the browsing capabilities of Notes and a Web server to publish and retrieve Web pages from the World Wide Web. During the first half of 1996, Lotus released Domino technology—free as a download Notes server task from the Lotus interactive Domino site. Lotus Notes R4.5 adds the Domino technology for even more support for Web users. The next few sections discuss some of the major features available for users wanting to work with the Web.

Domino. Domino is a Notes server task that makes it possible to use the application development environment of Notes to develop, manage, and host Web applications. Domino provides interactive Web client access to dynamic data and applications on a Notes Server. This means that Web clients may:

- Securely access a Notes server

- Access dynamic data and application based on time, database queries, and/or user identity

- Create, edit, and delete documents in a Notes database

- Use the full text search engine of Notes to search a Notes-hosted Web site

- View content in a Notes database with powerful Notes navigational capabilities such as the ability to expand and collapse views

- Receive enhanced support for @Functions and LotusScript (including @Db functions)

- Serve HTML files stored in the file system

- Run CGI scripts activated by Web clients

Domino also extends Notes Access Control to include Web clients:

- Updated template of Notes Public Address Book form includes new encrypted field to provide a web client password

- Web client authentication via Basic Web Authentication (name and password)

- Web user may be added to ACL lists and assigned a "role"

- Database to field-level access control for web clients

- SSL support for server authentication and encryption of data in secured sessions

Some of the new Domino functionality in Lotus Notes 4.5 includes the following:

- The ability to control the layout of views with greater flexibility

- The ability to attach files to Notes documents from a Web browser

- Support for many of the Calendaring and Scheduling features, to include the ability to schedule appointments, view your calendar, and use the calendar action bar

- Support for OLE2 and OCX/ActiveX object support, which lets Domino serve embedded objects to Web browsers, as well as allows the viewing of OCX/ActiveX components from a Web browser

- Support for DBColumn and DBLookup to allow access to Notes internal and non-Notes external databases

- Support for client-side SSL for even more secure Web communications

You will also notice more robust support for LotusScript, such as the ability to use a print statement to send back HTML to the Web browser, get context information, and return a "location" (URL) to the browser. Additional HTTP server enhancements have also been made to support multihoming and file system access control. Background imaging capabilities for forms and documents, cell background colors, and other table improvements also enhance the use of Domino with Notes. Finally, the integration of Domino into the Notes install program greatly simplifies the Web server setup.

Net.Action. Net.Action, the first of Lotus' Net.Apps, streamlines the creation, design, and content management of Web sites. Net.Action was designed to create both Internet (home page, company and product information, job postings), and intranet (policies manuals, suggestion box, approval processes) sites.

Net.Action works like a template to employ predesigned Notes forms, views, and databases as the foundation for Web content templates. It provides a library of layout options for content templates. You can customize the templates to construct unique site pages. Web sites created with Net.Action can range from the simple (few documents, static publishing) to the complex (thousands of documents, interactive applications).

Net.Action is free at the time of Notes 4.5 release, and can be downloaded from the Lotus Internet Applications' Web site at **http://www.net.lotus.com**.

Cross-Database, Cross-Server Full-Text Searching. Notes R4 users could only search indexed database for words and phrases, but Notes R4.5 enables both web browsers (via Domino) and Notes clients to perform full-text queries across multiple databases on multiple servers.

SOCKS Support. SOCKS version 4 support has been added to utilize a centralized SOCKS server to Notes R4.5 clients and servers running the IP protocol. This gives customers the ability to leverage new or existing SOCKS services to provide Internet access for Notes users. This feature is supported for Notes clients (including the Notes Web Navigator) and Notes servers.

HTTP Proxy Support. The Notes Web Navigator client (directly via the Internet) or the Notes server (via the server's Web Retriever process) can use the HTTP Proxy support to utilize new or existing HTTP Proxy servers to connect to the Internet.

Notes RPC Proxy (HTTP Connect Method). The Notes RPC Proxy (HTTP Connect Method) gives a native Notes client or server access to a remote Notes server through a standard HTTP proxy that supports the SSL Tunneling Specification (see: **http:// home.mcom.com/newsref/std/tunneling_ssl.html** for details on this specification). All native Notes RPCs (Remote Procedure Calls) are retained in this configuration and tunneled through HTTP. Similar to SOCKS support, customers can utilize new or existing HTTP Proxy servers to provide Internet access for native Notes users.

Internet Client. Since the release of Notes R4, the Notes client has the ability to access information from the Web. Any Notes application can contain actual Web pages or links to them. The InterNotes Web Navigator application serves as a repository for all cached pages and Web pages can be shared, ranked, annotated, or otherwise used as collaborative resources. This integration between Notes clients and the Web can link the wealth of information found on the Web with the collaborative applications hosted in Notes. Notes R4.5 expands the Internet functionality of the Notes client by combining enhanced support for Web client conventions with unique Notes features, to include:

- **Client-side retrieval of HTML over HTTP**—With this feature, users can directly retrieve Web pages by using the Notes client. Client-side retrieval results in faster access to Web pages. Of course, users may still fetch Web pages via their defined InterNotes server as they have been able to do since the release of Notes R4.

- **Personal Web database**—This is a Notes application customized for the individual Web user who wants to obtain and manage the information retrieved on the Internet. This application also includes the following agents:

  - **Page Minder**—With this agent, users can automatically keep on top of new information posted to their favorite Web sites. When a Notes user drags and drops a Web page into this graphical folder in the navigation pane, Notes goes to that URL and looks for updates to the page(s). Using the new Internet Options preferences form, users can indicate how often Notes should check for updates. When Notes determines that pages in the Page Minder folder have been updated, it automatically refreshes the page in the user's Personal Web Navigator folder and either forwards the individual pages or sends the user a news summary of the updates to the page(s).

- **Web Ahead**—With this agent, users retrieve multiple pages from a Web site via Web crawler-type functionality. Users simply drag-and-drop a page into the Web Ahead folder and Notes automatically retrieves all linked pages to the number of levels as predefined by the user. This feature is particularly handy for the mobile users who want to be able to access Web pages off-line without having to pre-surf all the pages manually.

■ **Java applet execution**—Notes clients can execute Java applets embedded in HTML pages from the web or Java applets embedded into Notes applications or documents with this feature. Notes 4.5 only has this feature on the Windows 95, Windows NT, and Sun Solaris (SPARC and x86) platforms. Support for Java applet execution for other Notes platforms will be included in future releases.

■ **Netscape Plug-in API support**—This feature enables Notes clients to use Netscape 2.0 plug-ins for the execution of plug-in files embedded into documents. This feature will be available on the Windows 95 and Windows NT platforms only in Notes 4.5. Support for the Netscape API for other Notes platforms will be included in future releases.

■ **HTML 3.2 support**—Notes Release 4.5 now supports the latest HTML release. Some of these enhancements include support for background bitmaps, transparent GIFs, and new table features.

■ **Progressive rendering of text and graphics**—This feature renders documents (in both HTML and the Notes document format) faster to the user.

■ **Page-centric Launch**—This feature enables Notes client users to directly launch into a Web page (or any Notes document) at the start of a Notes session.

■ **Single-click URL syntax**—With this syntax, users can use the standard single-click action to launch an URL or any Notes DocLink, view link, or database link.

■ **URL in search bar**—Users can toggle between using the Notes search bar to initiate full text searches and using it as an URL location field.

■ **Support for alternate browsers**—A user can define an alternate browser to be used for launching URLs when they are encountered in Notes.

■ **SSL support**—Notes clients can use connections secured by the Secure Sockets Layer (SSL) protocol when connecting to Web servers, using this protocol.

■ **SOCKS support, HTTP Proxy support, Notes RPC Proxy support**—See descriptions for these items in the Internet server enhancements section mentioned earlier.

Scalability and Manageability. Notes R4.5 builds on the gains in scalability and manageability realized by the release of Notes R4. Additional features added to the new release make it easier to manage Notes and make Notes more capable of satisfying a corporation's enterprise-wide communication needs. Notes R4.5 features include:

- **Notes server clustering**—Notes server clustering enables companies to cluster up to six Notes servers to provide load balancing and failover capabilities in the Notes environment. A real-time replication scheme ensures that applications hosted on servers in a cluster remain synchronized. *Load balancing* enables administrators to define a particular threshold that, when exceeded, automatically passes new sessions to another server in the cluster that has more resources at its disposal. Clustering also provides *failover,* that ensures that, in the event a Notes server fails, users accessing that server are switched to the same application on another server in that cluster.

- **Billing**—Billing lets customers build their own custom billing applications to do things like measure the amount of mail traffic from users or sites or measure the way specific applications are used. This capability is ideal for measuring and billing back internal costs for the use of Internet service providers (ISPs) and carriers, and internal resource allocations from the Information Systems group based on usage of the system, and determining the value of applications and content based on measurements of the way they are used—and who uses them.

- **Partitioned servers**—Partitioned servers let customers run several logical Notes servers on one physical machine. This is particularly useful for the ISP and carrier groups to allow them to reduce the overall investment they need to make in a Notes application (or in hosting mail services). This feature, at the initial release of Notes 4.5, will be available only for AIX, HP-UX, Solaris (x86 and SPARC), and NT/ Intel platforms.

- **Directory Assistance**—Directory Assistance enables Notes users and processes to easily search and browse for information in Address Books of Notes domains other than their own based on an administrator-defined set of Public Address Books to browse.

- **Admin Process enhancements**—The Administration Process was introduced in Notes Release 4 to streamline the process of managing server and user name changes. The Administration Process automatically updates user and server names in database access control lists and Public Address Book documents and recertifies server and user IDs. The Administration Process recertifies an ID, renames a user or server, and deletes a user, group, or server. Notes Release 4.5 is enhanced to enable the Administration Process to have even more granular name updates. This is in addition to the functionality mentioned previously and will automatically modify reader and author fields. In addition, the Administration process triggers the deletion of mail files for users who are no longer in the organization.

- **Database management tools**—New database management tools provide administrators more efficient ways to perform database management functions on multiple databases on the same server or across servers at the same time from a single location (the Administration Control panel introduced in Notes Release 4.0).

These new tools include:

- Setting the Administration server
- Analyzing the database
- Managing Notes server clusters
- Compacting databases
- Setting the Consistent ACL option
- Creating new replicas on several other servers at once
- Indexing full-text databases
- Setting the multidatabase search option for a database (for the cross-data base, cross-server, cross-domain searches already described in the Internet Server section)
- Moving databases to another server in a cluster

■ **NT Single logon, user management, and Event Logger integration—** Notes Release 4 included support for a number of Windows NT features such as the inclusion of Notes statistics in the NT Performance Monitor and being an NT Service. Notes Release 4.5 continues to build on this integration with the Windows NT operating system with the following features:

- **NT Single logon**—With a single logon, users only enter a single password once when logging into a Windows NT domain or Notes. This feature is only available to Notes clients running on the Windows NT platform for Notes Release 4.5.

- **Notes/NT user management**—Administrators can automatically create and delete Windows NT user accounts when they create or delete a Notes user in the Notes Public Address Book. They can also create or delete Notes user accounts when creating or deleting Windows NT users through the Windows NT User Manager for Domains.

- **Integration with the NT Event Logger**—Notes events can be redirected from the Notes Event service to the Windows NT Event Logger. This enables Windows NT administrators to use a single Event-tracking environment for both Windows NT and Notes operations for activities such as alarms or informational events.

■ **Apple Remote Access (ARA) support**—Notes Release 4 introduced support for Remote LAN Services. Workstations and servers can use remote LAN service connections to perform all Notes tasks, such as replicating and routing mail, as if they were directly connected to the network. Workstations also use Remote LAN Service connections to access network services (for example, printing.) Notes Release 4.5 expands the Remote LAN Service support to include Apple Remote Access (ARA). ARA support provides transparency to a Macintosh client who wants to connect to a Notes Server through a dial-up ARA connection without having to separately dial through ARA before entering Notes.

Security. Notes is widely respected for its robust, unmatched security model. Notes Release 4.5 further extends the Notes security model with the following features:

■ **Execution Control Lists**—The Execution Control List (ECL) enables users to protect their data against the threats of mail bombs, viruses, Trojan horses, or unwanted application intrusions encountered when navigating the Internet. Execution Control Lists provide a mechanism for managing whether such executable files should execute and at what level of access.

ECLs are managed on a per user basis (accessible via the User Preferences panel) and are controlled to a very granular level. For example, a user may stipulate that when a document is digitally signed by a certain trusted colleague, programs executed by that document can access documents and databases as well as modify environment variables but cannot access the file system or external programs.

■ **Password expiration and reuse**—Passwords protect and ensure the security of the Notes system by preventing other users from using a person's ID file. Lotus recommends that all users password protect their ID files and keep passwords private. The Password Expiration feature protects the Notes system from a malicious user who obtains the ID file and password of a user and impersonates that user. With this feature, Notes administrators specify and enforce an expiration period/date on passwords for user ID files. During the authentication dialog, users are notified if their passwords have expired and that new ones are required. A list of previous passwords prevents users from reusing any of their previous *n* passwords.

■ **Java applet source specification**—lets users determine from which locations Java applets can be brought to the Notes client, such as inside your firewall only, only from certain Internet hosts, or from all Internet hosts except certain specified hosts.

Programmability. In addition to the features listed in the Calendaring & Scheduling section, Notes Release 4.5 contains dozens of enhancements in the area of programmability. Some of these are:

■ **Script Libraries**—Script libraries build reusable LotusScript modules that can be invoked from multiple places within a Notes application. It is similar to the SubForm feature introduced in Notes Release 4.0 that enabled developers to build reusable Notes from code.

■ **OLE2 Support on the Macintosh**—Notes Release 4.5 now includes OLE2 support (out-of-place editing only) on the Macintosh 68K and PowerPC platforms.

■ **Extended OCX/ActiveX support**—Notes Release 4.5 extends the OCX/ActiveX support originally introduced in Notes Release 4.0 for OCX/ActiveX controls, such as the Lotus Components.

■ **LotusScript enhancements**—Many new LotusScript classes and events and other enhancements are added to Notes Release 4.5. Among these are the following:

- Database Scripts conditionally executes LotusScripts upon the opening of a Notes database.

- Database profiles handle global items within a database.

- Access to the new calendar and time controls implemented as part of the native Notes Calendaring and Scheduling functionality (described earlier in the Messaging section in more detail).

- With one function, one LotusScript agent can invoke another LotusScript agent.

- Enhanced LS:DO support. The LS:DO will now be available on the Notes/UNIX platforms as well, with full write capability.

■ **Integrated Development Environment (IDE) enhancements**—Several enhancements have been made to the Notes IDE in Notes Release 4.5, to include:

- Find and replace

- Context-sensitive help (F1 key)

- File import/export script

- Code colorization

- Table design enhancements

- New Text features

- Additional Auto Launch features

- Background graphic display features for forms

- Enhancements to Special Options in Notes Mail

Living and Working in a Notes Culture

As mentioned previously, some companies use Lotus Notes to run all of their business communications whereas others use it to automate specific tasks or processes in their organization. Some companies only use the e-mail capabilities with perhaps a few discussion databases. Regardless of the way(s) a company uses Notes, at least initially, Notes is change management—it changes the way users communicate and work within an organization. Individuals at lower levels of a company now have rapid access to information never before available, as well as the ability to funnel communication directly to management when necessary.

End users have more control over the look and feel of the databases they are using. Users of Notes R4.5 can easily display information in a format that makes sense to them rather than having to use the format developed by a programmer. Applications are typically built and modified much faster than in traditional database packages. This makes it easier for organizations to match their communication structures to the ever-changing business processes caused by the pressures of the industries they are operating in. The ease and speed with which applications can be built and altered—often referred to as Rapid Application Development, or RAD, in the industry—reduces development costs.

Fewer programmers are required for application development in Notes and this often leads to radical changes in the way information systems departments are organized and staffed. Because Lotus Notes is built to run on a wide variety of platforms within a company, information systems departments are finding it easier to network various departments and locations with one communications package. This task was tedious before, if not impossible. With the easy remote and Internet capabilities of Lotus Notes, many companies have moved toward creating virtual offices so the employee can work from home.

Recent trends show that companies are building more applications that link them with their clients and vendors, thus making Notes a means of commerce and revenue generation to their businesses.

Notes changes the way a company communicates. Managing this communication and the applications that support it, provides a significant challenge. In this book, you not only learn how to use Notes and begin developing applications, but you also gain insight into managing your own communications needs.

Starting Notes

To start Notes, locate the Lotus Notes icon on your Windows or OS/2 desktop. The placement of this icon depends on how your company installed Notes on your PC.

The person who installs Notes on your desktop can determine where the icon appears on your desktop. You may have a group, or menu option, called Lotus Notes that includes the Lotus Notes program. You may want to copy the icon automatically to your Windows or OS/2 Startup folder so that Notes starts automatically each time you start Windows or OS/2.

Start Notes as you would any other program. Put the mouse pointer on the Notes icon and double-click. As Notes starts, it briefly presents a start-up logo. Eventually, you see a screen similar to that shown in Figure 1.4.

Note

For those of you who are new to Windows 95, the start procedure for Notes may appear a little different. Simply select Start, Programs. Find the menu option where your Notes program is located (usually Lotus Applications). Click the Notes menu item to start Notes.

For other operating systems, follow your standard procedures for starting a program.

Understanding the Notes Workspace

As with any Windows or OS/2 program, learning the various parts of the screen is the key to learning how to use Notes. In this section, you learn about the different parts of the Notes screen and how to control them using the mouse and keyboard. Figure 1.4 shows a typical Notes screen and some of the many features of the program.

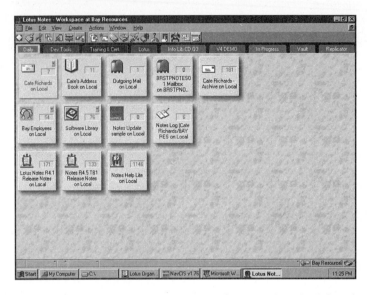

Fig. 1.4 There was little change made to the workspace for Lotus Notes R4.5, but if you are just upgrading from Notes R3.x, you will find new features to surprise you!

The Menu Bar

When you first start Notes, the menu bar is near the very top of the Notes screen and contains words such as File, Edit, View, Create, Actions, Window, and Help. Each word represents a menu of operations. Table 1.1 briefly summarizes the operations available through each menu on the menu bar.

Tip
Not all menu commands display in the menu bar when you first start Notes. Some commands are available only when performing particular functions.

Table 1.1	Menu Operations
Menu	**Operations Accessed**
File	Enables you to perform database operations, print, configure your environment, work remote (not connected to a network), manipulate attachments, bring information from word processors and other programs into Notes, and save information from Notes to other programs.
Edit	Contains functions for moving, copying, and making other changes to documents; checks spelling; linking; works with unread marks; searches for text; and undoes the last command you performed.
View	Enables you to determine what information you see on-screen.

Menu	Operations Accessed
Create	Formerly the Compose menu command in Release 3 of Notes, Create enables you to create messages, documents, folders, views, agents, database designs, sections, tables, objects, hotspots, and page breaks.
Actions	Enables you to perform functions on a document, text, or database. You can move documents to folders; categorize documents; enter, change, or delete field values; edit, send, and forward documents; and perform advanced features like truncating, untruncating, and resaving documents.
Text	Enables you to alter the size, color, and font style of text within your message and to set tabs and margins.
Window	Provides you with a list of open Notes windows and enables you to switch from one window to another. You can also elect to tile, cascade, minimize, and maximize windows with this menu item.
Help	Provides you with online help to all Lotus Notes functions and enables you to determine the version of Notes you are using.
Design	Provides you with menu selections available only when you are designing views, forms, subforms, navigators, fields, or agents. This menu command is only present when you are in design mode.
Table	Provides you with menu selections only when your cursor is located in a table.
Attachment	Available only when attachments are present in a document, this menu command provides actions you can perform on attachments—such as Detach selected documents.
Section	Available only when collapsible sections are present in a document. This menu gives you the ability to control attributes about a section, for example, renaming the section.

Note

There are additional menu commands, not listed here, that appear in the menu bar when special functions are applied in Notes. For example, if you insert a Lotus 1-2-3 Worksheet into a document, a 1-2-3 Worksheet command appears in the menu to provide you a quick way to manipulate the properties of the object.

Databases and Workpages

Even if you use Notes only for sending and receiving electronic mail, you still need to know how to manage databases because your mailbox is a database. However, if you use Notes to its fullest, you and your coworkers will store and share many different kinds of information: status reports, customer records, sales prospects, various kinds of paperwork, budgets, and so on. You may want to access dozens of different databases at different times. Organizing this information is the key to using Notes effectively.

Each database you work with is represented by an icon located on a workpage. When you first start up Notes R4.5, you see a set of six file folder tabs just below the SmartIcons, each representing a workpage. Think of workpages as categories of data. Just as you may use different drawers in a file cabinet to contain related files, workpages organize your databases into well-defined grouped sections. You can decide what to call each workpage and where to place the databases on each workpage.

In Notes R4.5, you can add or delete workspace tabs as you need them. You learn more about how to do this in the section "Customizing Your Workspace" in Chapter 2, "Customizing Notes."

Note

There is a seventh tab titled Replicator. This tab is predefined by Notes to replicate database information between your remote PC and a Notes server, run agents, and send and receive mail when working remote. You learn more about this tab in the section, "Setting Up the Replicator" in Chapter 21, "Working Remote."

You can display any workpage by clicking the tab associated with that workpage. Each database appears as a box containing a name and a small icon. The icon is usually a picture that you can associate easily with the topic of the database. A database of unsolved problems may have an icon of a question mark or a frowning face, for example. Sometimes each box displays other information about each database, depending on how you set up your preferences.

▶▶ See "Customizing Information Displayed on Database Icons," p. 53

If you use Notes exclusively for mail, this workpage may be the only one you use. Together, the six workpages are known as your workspace.

The organization of your workspace is completely up to you. Arrange your workpages in any convenient manner and place any database on any workpage. Notes does not require any particular arrangement.

The SmartStatus Strip

The SmartStatus strip appears at the bottom of the screen. The SmartStatus is a strip of icons and messages that displays information about network and hard disk activity, mail, database access levels, text attributes, and various status messages (see Figure 1.5). The strip is divided into segments that contain indicators. Table 1.2 describes the indicators in each segment.

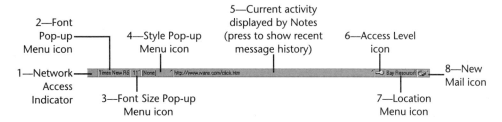

2—Font Pop-up Menu icon

4—Style Pop-up Menu icon

5—Current activity displayed by Notes (press to show recent message history)

6—Access Level icon

1—Network Access Indicator

3—Font Size Pop-up Menu icon

7—Location Menu icon

8—New Mail icon

Fig. 1.5 The Status Bar displays current activities performed by Notes so you can quickly access some of the most used features in Notes through pop-up menu selection lists.

Table 1.2 Understanding the Status Bar Icons	
Status Bar Icon	**Description**
1	The first segment indicates disk or network activity. If a lightning bolt appears, Notes is accessing data across the network. The segment is blank when Notes isn't performing network access.
2	The second segment shows the current font typeface you are using. This segment is used only when you're editing a document or designing a new form and your cursor is located in a Rich Text field (see Chapter 7, "Working with Text"). If you click this segment, Notes displays a list of available fonts from which you can select.
3	The third segment, the Font size segment (like the typeface segment), is available only during editing and displays the current text point size. Clicking this segment displays a list of the available point sizes. You can select a new point size by clicking one of the sizes in the list.
4	The fourth segment, the Style segment, presents predefined styles that you can select.
5	The fifth segment displays status, error messages, and Internet addresses if you are working with the Web features.
6	The sixth segment, the Access Level segment, indicates your permission level for the database you are accessing. In Chapter 22, "Security and Encryption," you learn about the various access levels and how to interpret the icon in this segment. If you click this segment, Notes displays a message explaining the meaning of the symbol.
7	The seventh segment, the Location segment, indicates how your machine is set up for working. For example, if your computer is connected permanently to a network, you see Office (Network) appear in the section. Other settings, such as Travel (Remote), Island (Disconnected), and Edit Current will be discussed in Chapter 2, "Customizing Notes," and in Part IV of this book, "Going Mobile."
8	The eighth segment displays an inbox icon with an envelope in it when new mail arrives; otherwise, it displays as an envelope. Clicking this segment pops up a list of options you can perform to create, scan, receive, and send mail from your mailbox.

Notes Basics

Context-Sensitive Menus

You can access context menus by clicking once with your right mouse button anywhere in the Notes workspace. A context-sensitive menu of available commands appears next to your cursor providing you easy access to the most commonly used functions performed in your current situation. The selections in this menu change as you perform different tasks in Notes. The context-sensitive menu in Figure 1.6 shows the commands available while you are entering text in a mail message.

Fig. 1.6 Context-sensitive menus help speed your work with Lotus Notes by placing some of the most common features you need at the click of a mouse button.

Working with SmartIcons

Notes provides yet another way to perform common functions. Arranged along one edge of the screen (usually the top) is a row of icons, known as SmartIcons, that represent common functions (see Figure 1.7). SmartIcons represent the same operations that you can access with the pull-down menus, but enable you to invoke these functions with a single click. For example, you can display the Notes ruler (explained in Chapter 7, "Working with Text") by clicking the SmartIcon that looks like a ruler, instead of choosing View, Ruler.

Notes provides a SmartIcon for almost every operation, but the entire collection of icons would fill the screen. After deciding which operations you perform most often, you can tell Notes which SmartIcons you want displayed.

▶▶ See "SmartIcons," p. 1113

Fig. 1.7 SmartIcons provide shortcuts for performing menu commands.

New to Notes R4.x is the ability for Lotus Notes to display context-sensitive SmartIcons—in other words, the icons displayed in the icon bar change according to where you are working at any given time.

Notes provides one set of SmartIcons, the universal set, for you to choose from. You can, however, add additional icon sets to the list of available SmartIcon sets. You can also customize the universal set to add new SmartIcons to it. You can also select the Context Icons option to have Notes automatically display different icons that are based on the tasks you are performing.

If you want to hide the SmartIcons from your workspace, choose File, Tools, SmartIcons and then deselect the Show Icon Bar option in the dialog box. Likewise, if you want to hide only those SmartIcons from the workspace that are context-sensitive, deselect Context Icons. If you want to hide the icon descriptions that display when you point to an icon, you can deselect Descriptions. If you later change your mind and want to display any of these features, return to this dialog box and reselect these options.

Note

You can also change the SmartIcon set by opening the SmartIcons dialog box and selecting the set you want to use from the drop-down list box. You learn more about this dialog box in the next section.

Changing the Position of SmartIcons. You can change the position in which your SmartIcon palette is located. To do so, perform the following:

Tip

If you are new to Windows 95, you can also reposition your Start menu by clicking anywhere within the bar and dragging it to a new position. This may make your workspace appear less cluttered at the bottom of your Notes windows.

---

1. Select File, Tools, SmartIcons and the SmartIcons dialog box appears (see Figure 1.8).

2. Click the down arrow in the Position list box.

3. Select the location in which you want the SmartIcons to be displayed: Left, Right, Top, Bottom, or Floating.

4. If you do not want to customize your SmartIcons further, select OK to save your settings and return to your workspace.

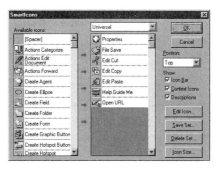

Fig. 1.8   Use the SmartIcons dialog box to add new icons to your SmartIcons bar, create custom SmartIcons, and change the position of the SmartIcons box.

Selecting Floating from the list of positions lets you display the SmartIcons in a box that can be repositioned in the window by dragging it (see Figure 1.9). You can resize the floating SmartIcons box by clicking any of the corners of the box and dragging its borders until the box is the length or height you want. Figure 1.10 illustrates the same set of Mail SmartIcons floating after resizing.

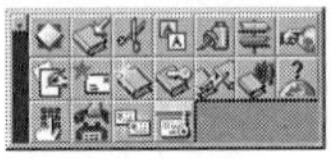

Fig. 1.9   You can elect to have your SmartIcons floating on the workspace so that you can position them near the section of the page in which you are working.

Fig. 1.10   You can resize your floating SmartIcons box so that it is not in the way of the work you are performing and is the shape you want.

If you want to close the floating SmartIcons set, click the Close box in the upper left corner of the window. To redisplay the window, select the SmartIcon indicator on the status bar and select a SmartIcons set.

Tip

If you select Left or Right as the position for the SmartIcons, keep in mind that the height of your screen will not accept as many SmartIcons to display as the width of your screen does. If you find that one of these settings frequently results in some of your SmartIcons being truncated from the set, you may want to select Top, Bottom, or Floating from the list, or customize the SmartIcon set you are using to display fewer icons.

Customizing SmartIcon Sets. Although Lotus constructed sets of icons that they thought would be useful, you are not locked into Lotus' choices. Within each set, you can add icons, remove icons, rearrange icons, or even create new sets.

To customize the SmartIcons, display the SmartIcons dialog box by choosing File, Tools, SmartIcons Setup (see Figure 1.11). The list box on the left displays all of the available SmartIcons that you can put on a SmartIcon bar. Next to each icon, Notes displays the menu selections you can make to perform the equivalent operation. (All these icons are described further in Appendix A.)

The list box in the center of the dialog box shows the icons that now make up one of the available SmartIcons set. (This section refers to this list box as the current set.) Select the set of icons you want to customize.

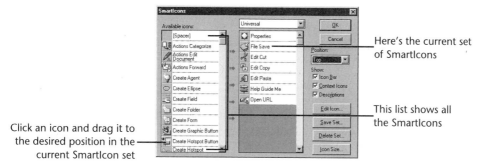

Here's the current set of SmartIcons

This list shows all the SmartIcons

Click an icon and drag it to the desired position in the current SmartIcon set

Fig. 1.11   In addition to selecting and positioning the desired SmartIcon set, you can use this dialog box to modify any set of SmartIcons.

To add a new icon to an existing set, find the icon in the list of available icons and drag it to the current set. Notes inserts it into the set. You can add the same icon to as many SmartIcon sets as you want. When you have added all of the SmartIcons you want to the current list, select <u>O</u>K to save your changes and return to the workspace.

> **Note**
>
> At the top of the list of available icons is a special item called Spacer. If you insert this item in an icon set, Notes inserts a small gap between icons.

To remove an icon from the current set, drag an icon from the current set off to one side, out of the current set list box. (It doesn't matter where you drag it, as long as it's out of the current set list box.) When you have removed all of the SmartIcons you want from the current list, select <u>O</u>K to save your changes and return to the workspace.

You can also add and remove icons from the universal set of SmartIcons. While the universal set of icons was predefined by Lotus, you may find that you want other icons to display throughout your work in Notes. Notes displays the icons in the universal set in conjunction with the context-sensitive icons wherever you are working in Notes. Context-sensitive SmartIcons do not display in the list of current SmartIcons in the dialog box, but will appear to the right of them in the workspace when the situation calls for them to be active. When you are adding icons to this icon set, keep in mind that if you add too many icons, you will most likely run out of display room. If you want to add many more icons to the set, you will most likely need to display the set as floating to be able to view them all.

To create a new set of SmartIcons, first display an existing set and choose <u>S</u>ave Set. Notes displays the Save Set of SmartIcons dialog box that enables you to assign a name to the new set. You also must provide a filename with an SMI extension. You can then customize the new set as needed by adding and removing icons.

To delete an existing set, choose <u>D</u>elete Set. Notes lists all the existing sets. Select one or more sets and then choose <u>O</u>K. Notes deletes the sets you selected.

Caution

You cannot delete the Universal set of SmartIcons from the Delete Sets dialog box, but it can be deleted using a File Manager program or your system operating commands if you are not careful. This SmartIcon set's filename is UNIVERSE.SMI, and it must be present in your SmartIcon subdirectory as defined in your NOTES.INI file (even if you do not use it) or you will not be able to use SmartIcons in Lotus Notes. If this file is not present, Notes prompts for the Icon subdirectory the next time you start Notes. You will need to select Cancel multiple times to continue the start up. You won't have access to SmartIcons if this file is not present, even if you have other SmartIcon files defined.

Make sure you do not accidentally delete this file when you are cleaning up your files on your hard drive. If you should accidentally delete it, you can either reinstall Notes, use your operating system or File Manager to rename another SMI file you have created UNIVERSE.SMI, or create a blank text file using any text editor and save the file with the name UNIVERSE.SMI. Notes can then start up without an error message, and provide you with the capability of using SmartIcons.

There may be times when you need to change the size of the SmartIcons displayed. For example, you may want to increase the size of your SmartIcons when giving a presentation so that the audience can see which SmartIcons you are selecting. With the SmartIcons dialog box open, select the Icon Size button. The Icon Size dialog box appears as shown in Figure 1.12.

Fig. 1.12   You can increase the size of SmartIcons so that they are easier to see by selecting Large in the Icon Size dialog box.

Select Small (the default) if you want to display the SmartIcons in their usual size. Select Large if you want to display large SmartIcons. Of course, you will not be able to display as many icons when you select Large. Large icons, however, are ideal if you are using Notes to make a presentation.

Editing and Creating SmartIcons. You can edit and create new SmartIcons—with limitations. The existing, defined SmartIcons that perform commands such as File, Print, cannot be edited. However, Notes provides several custom SmartIcons that you can use to create your own special SmartIcons to run macros easily. (Editing and creating a SmartIcon is easy, but you will need to understand formulas to do so. See Chapters 14, "Working with Formulas," and 15, "Working with Functions and Commands," for more information on writing formulas.)

Custom SmartIcons can be a real time-saver for commands frequently run or complicated tasks in which a macro is used. For example, if you frequently like to switch to the Calculator in Windows while you are working in Lotus Notes, you may want to add a custom icon to your SmartIcon set to automatically open it. To do so, follow these steps:

1. Select the <u>E</u>dit Icon button in the SmartIcon dialog box. The Edit SmartIcons dialog box appears.

2. Scroll through the list of Custom Icons available for you to edit. Highlight the icon you want to use.

3. Edit the icon's name in the <u>D</u>escription text box to describe the function it will perform. In this example, type **Calculator**. This is the name Notes displays in the bubble help that appears when you point to a SmartIcon on the workspace.

4. Select <u>F</u>ormula to open the SmartIcons Formula dialog box as shown in Figure 1.13.

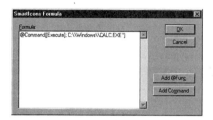

Fig. 1.13   You can enter formulas to customize the functions of SmartIcons.

5. Type the formula you want to apply to the Custom Icon. In this example, you would enter the formula as it is displayed in Figure 1.13. Note that the formula contains double backslashes between the drive and subdirectory names. When you write a directory path in Notes formulas, you must use double backslashes. You learn more about writing formulas like this one in Chapter 14, "Working with Formulas."

6. Select <u>O</u>K, and then <u>O</u>K again to save the formula.

7. Add the newly created SmartIcon to your SmartIcon palette as described in the previous section, "Customizing SmartIcon Sets."

You can now use the edited SmartIcon to run the command to open File Manager whenever it is selected. When you exit File Manager, you return to Notes exactly where you left it.

Opening and Viewing Databases

Note

If you are opening a database for the first time during your working session, you may be prompted for your Notes password. Simply type your Notes password in the dialog box provided and select <u>O</u>K. Notes passwords are case-sensitive, so you need to type the password exactly as your Notes Administrator set it up for you. You learn more about working with your Notes password in Chapter 2, "Customizing Notes."

It is quite easy to open a database. Simply double-click a database icon corresponding to the database you want to use. Database icons appear as squares on your workspace, with the name and location of the database printed on it. Notes opens the database to display navigators, views, panes, and folders, as illustrated in Figure 1.14. This section briefly describes how you move around a database to find the information you are looking for. If you have used a previous release of Lotus Notes before, you may still want to read this section because Notes has added many new features.

Note

If this is the first time you have opened the database, you will first see the About This Database document, which usually provides you with a summary of the purpose of the database, along with any rules for using it, and a contact name in case of problems. Take a moment to read the document and then press the Esc key to exit the document. You will only see this document in subsequent uses of the database if you select Help, About This Database, or if the designer of the databases elects to have the document display upon each opening or if it has been modified.

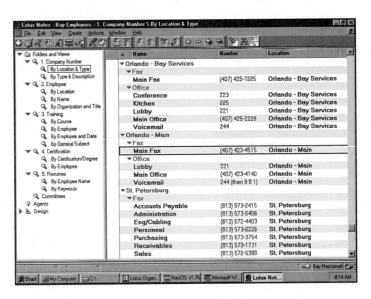

Fig. 1.14 Databases open to display navigators, views, panes, and folders, similar to those shown in your Public Name & Address Book.

Working with Panes

When you first open a database in Notes R4.5, you notice that the window is split into two panes. The left pane displays the default database Navigator (usually the Folder Navigator) that provides a graphical way to navigate through the documents in the database. A database designer can also build other navigators and assign one of them as the default navigator to be displayed when you open the database. Figure 1.14 displays the default folder navigator for Richard's address book.

The navigator contains symbols and text that guide you through working in the opened database. The symbols in Table 1.3 are present in most Folder Navigators. Database designers can incorporate additional symbols and graphics in navigators, as discussed in Part II of this book, "Designing Applications."

Table 1.3 Common Symbols Found in Most Database Navigators		
Symbol	**Represents**	**Description**
	Folders	Folders are used to store related documents or groupings of documents. Folders can contain documents, views, and other folders. You can drag documents from the view to the right of the navigator pane and drop them in folders to store related topics. You learn more about working with folders in Chapter 3, "Using Databases."
	Views	Views are represented by a small magnifying glass. Views contain listings of documents that are sorted according to criteria defined by you or the database designer. For example, Figure 1.12 shows the Locations view highlighted that displays the list of location documents to the right of the navigator pane. You learn more about views in the next section.
	Agents	Agents are represented by a small lightbulb. Agents are macros that are created to perform assigned tasks on documents in a database. You will learn more about agents in Chapter 16, "Buttons and Agents."
	Design	A small triangular ruler represents the design menu in the navigator. Selecting a design menu displays a list of designs in the view to the right (see Figure 1.15).
	Section Indicators	Small, solid triangles represent section indicators and appear next to items in views, panes, or documents that can be expanded. Click a section indicator pointing toward the right to expand the section. Click the section indicators going down to collapse the section.

Selecting the symbols next to the identifying text displays the corresponding information in the views to the right of the pane.

Working with Views

The person who designs the database decides how the documents are ordered, categorized, and what information displays about each document. A view is the way in which the list is presented. When the right side of a database is open, it displays the view pane. Figure 1.16 shows a sample view for the Richard's Address Book database. This view shows the Location documents used for network and remote connections with the server. You'll learn more about server connections in Part IV, "Going Mobile."

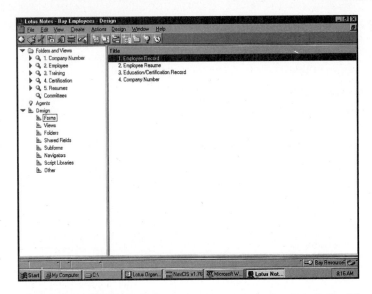

Fig. 1.15   Selecting the design menu displays a list of designs in the view to the right.

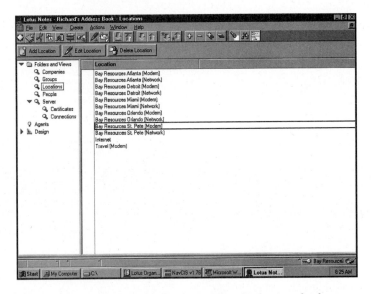

Fig. 1.16   Views list all, or a subset, of the documents that display in a database.

The database designer may have determined that the list can be presented in several useful ways and may have created several views. Consider a database that contains sales orders. A view called By Customer may present the documents (sales orders) strictly in alphabetical order by customer last name; another view, perhaps called By Sales Rep, may categorize documents by sales representative. By selecting a view, you can determine how Notes presents the list of documents.

Different views may display the documents in the same order, but show different information about each document. A view called Revenue, for example, may show each document's customer name, gross sales amount, profit, and commission. Another view, called Customer, may list the same documents, but show customer address and phone numbers as well.

A view may not list all the documents in a database. A view called Delinquent Accounts, for example, may list only documents that represent unpaid sales orders that are at least 90 days late.

The designer of a database selects one of the views in the database as the default view that Notes uses when you open the database for the first time. You can select another view at any time, as explained in the next section.

Selecting a View

When you open a database, Notes displays a view. If you are accessing this database for the first time, you see the predefined default view. Otherwise, Notes displays the last view you selected. After you select a different view, Notes always remembers the view you last selected, even when you exit Notes. In some databases, the database designer may have created only a single view, so your choice is limited to that view, unless you create a new view for yourself (discussed in Chapter 10, "Creating New Databases"). In other databases, some views are hidden by the designers so that access is granted only to particular users of the database, or through special actions programmed into the application, for example, from a navigator. In most databases, however, you can choose from among several views.

You can select views from the navigator pane by clicking the text displaying a small magnifying glass next to it. You can also select a view by selecting View and then choosing the title of the view you want to use (see Figure 1.17). Notice that the available views are listed in the drop-down menu and in the navigator. The active view has a checkmark next to it in the View menu and has a box surrounding the view title in the navigator.

Fig. 1.17   Available views in a database appear at the bottom of the View menu command list.

Expanding Categories in Views

Categories in views are represented by small triangles, plus signs, or other graphics chosen by the designer of a database to indicate that there are collapsible categories in the view. These category indicators appear to the left of a category title. For example, if you select the text marked by a category indicator that is pointing to the right, you will expand the category to view more documents or categories. If you select text marked by a category indicator that is pointing down, you will collapse the category. You can also expand and collapse views by using SmartIcons, as shown in Table 1.4. You will learn more about working with views in Chapter 3, "Using Databases."

Table 1.4   SmartIcons that Help You Collapse and Expand View Categories

Icon	Contents	Action
➕	Single plus sign	Expands one category level
➖	Single minus sign	Collapses one category level
➕	Multi-plus sign	Expands all categories
➖	Multi-minus sign	Collapses all categories

Working with Folders

Folders are similar to views but can store other folders as well as documents. Folders are a great tool to use when you want to sort related documents in a database according to criteria that you set. You learn more about creating and using folders in Chapter 3, "Using Databases."

When you select a folder icon in the navigator, documents stored in the folder display in the view to the right. If the folder is marked with a category indicator, selecting the indicator displays additional folders stored within the folder. For an example of a folder storing all location documents and subfolders sorting the same location documents by city, see Figure 1.18.

Secondary folders that store a subset of documents in the primary folder

Primary folder for a group of documents

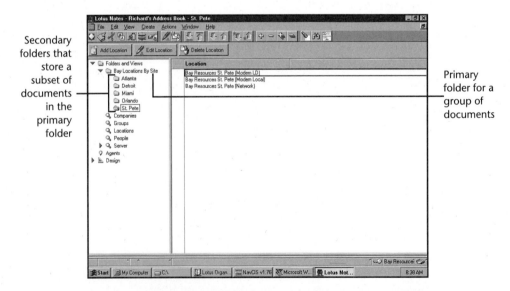

Fig. 1.18   You can store folders within folders to further organize your documents.

Understanding Documents

The building blocks for all databases are forms. A form is a template designed and stored in the database that users select to create a document that stores information. When you create a document in a database, you select from one of the forms created by the database designer. This form serves as a template for you to enter your information. When you save the information you have entered in the form, Notes displays it as a document in the database. This section quickly walks you through understanding documents. You learn, in detail, how to work with documents throughout all of Part I, "Notes Basics" of this book.

Opening Documents

Once you have located the document you want to read in the view, Lotus Notes provides several ways to open it:

- Double-click the document's title

- Highlight the document and press the Enter key

- Highlight the document and select File, Open

When the document opens, you may scroll through its contents using the scroll bars to the right and bottom of the document window.

Creating Documents

Each database design provides a wealth of forms to be created and each can be different. You may have forms to complete to enter time into a time-tracking database, or forms that order supplies from your purchasing department. The method to create a document is typically the same for all of them. Select Create from the menu commands while you are in the database (see Figure 1.19). Select the form name that represents the document you want to create. The document appears in edit form ready for you to enter information.

Note

Some designers may create databases in which you are prompted to create a new document by clicking a button, rather than selecting the form name from the Create menu. You learn more about creating new documents in Chapter 3, "Using Databases."

Fig. 1.19   To create a document in a Notes database, you may pick from the available list of documents displayed in the Create submenu.

To enter text in a document, the document must be in edit mode. In other words, the brackets surrounding the fields must be open as displayed in Figure 1.20. If you open an existing document and do not see the open brackets, double-click anywhere in the document, or select <u>A</u>ctions, Edit Document so it is placed in edit mode. Now you can enter or edit text as desired.

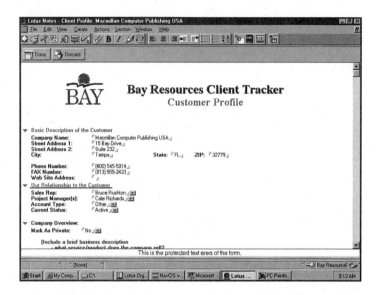

Fig. 1.20 A document in edit mode displays open brackets around the fields indicating that you can enter information into the fields.

Exiting a Document

When you are ready to close a document, perform one of the following:

- Double-click the right mouse button (if you have this option selected in your preferences. Refer to Chapter 2, "Customizing Notes").

- Select <u>F</u>ile, <u>C</u>lose.

- Press the Esc key.

- Press Ctrl+W (or Ctrl+S to Save).

Notes will close the document you are reading. If you entered or edited any information in the document, you will be prompted to save the document. Select <u>Y</u>es if you want to save the information, <u>N</u>o if you want to discard your entries and exit anyway, and <u>C</u>ancel if you want to return to the document before saving.

Caution

If you select <u>N</u>o when prompted to save your changes, Lotus Notes closes the document without saving any information you have added and you lose all entries made. Select <u>C</u>ancel if you want to go back and add or remove information before saving.

Getting Help

Notes includes an extensive online help system using many of the new Notes R4 features. The help system contains hundreds of documents, with each describing a Notes topic. You can access the help system at any time by pressing F1. Notes will take you to the Guide Me help panel that relates to your current tasks. You can follow through the various linked documents to learn about the task you are trying to perform, or you can select the Help Topics button to exit the Guide Me panel and open the Help view. You can also access help directly by selecting Help, Help Topics, or double-clicking the Notes Help database icon (see Figure 1.21).

Fig. 1.21 Notes ships with two Help databases: the full Notes Help database and the remote Notes Help Lite database.

> ### Tip
>
> For those who will be designing databases and would like to see examples on the use of many of the new features of Lotus Notes, the Notes Help database utilizes many of those features in its design. If the database is stored on your hard drive, you will be able to access the design of the database to see how it is put together. Pay a visit to the design of the navigators in the database to get an idea of how Lotus Notes panels and other navigators are put together. Do not change any of the design or your next help session may exhibit problems.

Lotus Notes provides context-sensitive help whenever you press F1. Notes looks at what you're doing and tries to select the panel from its help database that will offer you the most useful information. For example, if you are in the middle of sending a mail message, pressing F1 displays a document that offers you information on sending mail messages. You can also press the Help Topics SmartIcon, if available, to open the Notes Help database.

Figure 1.22 shows a typical Notes help document. For long help messages, you can press the Page Up and Page Down keys to move through the text of the help document.

In a book you often find cross-references in which one section of text makes references to another. For example, a printed book might contain a printed notation such as "See page xxx for more information." Lotus Notes includes the electronic equivalent, known as hotspots, which enable you to access related information in another help document.

In Figure 1.22, notice that the words "Editing a document" are underlined (on-screen, they're also displayed in green text)—these are hotspots. The presence of this text attribute tells you that you can get more information about this term. If you double-click the text, Notes displays a different document that contains information about ways to change how paragraphs look. This document, in turn, might contain other hotspot links that can guide you to other related sections. You learn more about hotspots in Chapter 8, "Working with Documents."

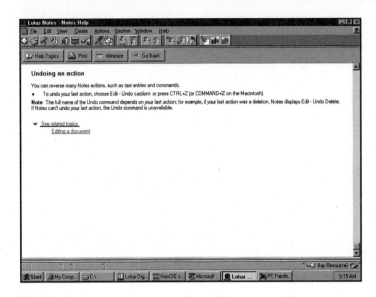

Fig. 1.22   Notes Help documents provide you with instructions on using Notes features and guide you through finding additional information on a related topic.

Some of the help articles also contain pop-up boxes, indicated by light green outline boxes that provide quick definitions for important terms. For example, the words edit mode in Figure 1.23 indicate the presence of a pop-up box. By pointing at the word in the box and holding the left mouse button, a box appears with a definition of the phrase within the box.

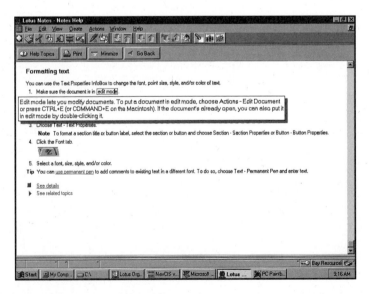

Fig. 1.23   Pop-ups in Help documents indicate additional information about a word or phrase. Click anywhere in the pop-up box to view the information.

At the top of the Help window, you find a series of buttons that enable you to use Help to your best advantage. These buttons include the following:

- The Help Topics button opens the Help Index view and displays a list of all documents in the database. The document you were viewing is still open and can be accessed by closing the current window or selecting the document from the Window menu. This provides you with a fast way to look up another document without having to close the current one.

- The Print button quickly prints the current help document.

- The Minimize button minimizes the Help window.

- The Go Back button goes back one window (it is the same as pressing the Esc key).

If you are reading an article that you accessed through a doclink or hotspot, you can press either the Esc key or click the Go Back button (if showing) to return to the Help document you were reading. A *doclink* is a link icon resembling a document that opens another document related to the topic when you double-click it. If you are reading a document that you invoked by pressing F1, pressing Esc closes the help system and returns you to your previous activity.

Using the Visual Index

New to the Notes 4 Help database is the Visual Index that takes advantage of new Notes features—hotspots and graphical navigators. You can open the Visual Index by clicking the Visual Index icon in the Navigator of the Notes Help database. The Visual Index, as shown in Figure 1.24, shows graphical representations of subjects covered in the Help database.

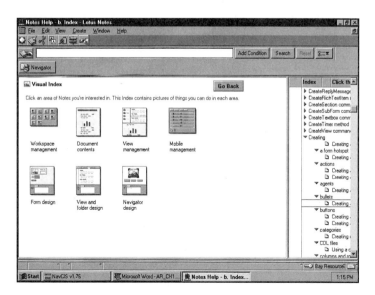

Fig. 1.24 The Visual Help Index displays graphical representations of the types of visual Help documents available in the database. Just click any picture to open a visual help document about that subject.

When you double-click one these graphics, a visual picture of a subject appears (see Figure 1.25). You will notice several yellow bubbles with question marks on them. When you double-click one of these bubbles, you learn how to perform the feature marked by the bubble. For example, double-clicking the yellow bubble positioned over the bullets in Figure 1.26 shows text indicating that the feature is a bullet and then leads you to the steps for creating the bullets. You learn even more about hotspots and graphical navigators in Chapter 8, "Working with Documents."

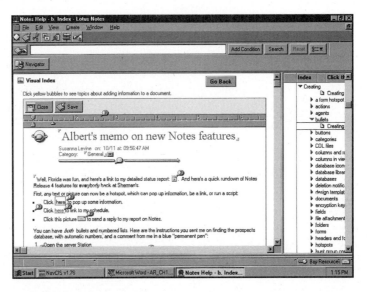

Fig. 1.25   Visual Index documents in the Help database provide quick, easy ways to learn about many of the features in Notes. Just click any of the question mark indicators to display additional information about a topic.

You can search for a particular help subject by using the Search Bar. To display the Search Bar, select View, Search Bar. The Search Bar appears directly above the Help view. You can type words in the text entry box and then click the Search button. Notes searches through all of the documents in the database and displays checkmarks next to the documents that meet your search criteria. You learn more about using the Search features of Notes in Chapter 8, "Working with Documents."

Storing Help Topics for Quick Reference

While you are viewing the Help database navigator pane, you notice a pink box surrounding the text, To store topics for quick access later, drag them into this folder. Beside this text, you see a small folder. As you read through Help documents, you may find a few that you want to reference frequently. Simply highlight the document you want to reference and drag it onto the small folder. To view the topics that you stored for quick access, select View, Navigators, Folders. Double-click the folder titled My Help Topics and then choose from the list of documents in the view.

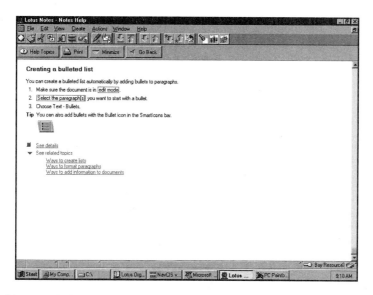

I

Notes Basics

Fig. 1.26 After you click a question mark indicator, Notes opens a document describing how to use the corresponding feature.

Using Notes Help Lite

Lotus Notes R4.x provides an abridged version of Notes Help called Notes Help Lite. This database installs on your hard drive when you install Lotus Notes R4.x. The purpose of the database is to provide mobile users with a Help database that minimizes the amount of hard drive space needed, while continuing to supply valuable help information when you are working remote. Essentially, Help Lite provides help on the features you use in working with Lotus Notes remote and excludes topics on design, administration, and LotusScript. The Visual Index is also excluded because the graphics take up more space.

If you look in Help Lite for topics that are not common to everyday use, Notes prompts you to access the network copy of the full Help database. If you elected to install both versions of Help during the installation of Notes R4.x, you can safely delete the Help Lite database because the documents are duplicates of the full Help database.

Getting Help for Notes 3 Users

If you were a Notes 3 user, you have noticed by now that many of the commands and actions you memorized have now all changed. Lotus Notes R4.x provides you with a quick way to discover the new command equivalents for Lotus Notes 3 commands. Select Help, Release 3 Menu Finder. The Release 3 Menu Finder window appears as shown in Figure 1.27.

Fig. 1.27   You can find the equivalent Notes R4 menu commands for tasks you used to perform in Notes R3 by selecting the R3 command you would use.

Select the menu command sequence you used to perform in Release 3 of Lotus Notes. The equivalent Release 4 commands appear in the window. Perform the commands listed in the window to perform the same task that you used to perform in Release 3.

Exiting Notes

Because Notes provides many ways to perform most operations, you can find several ways to exit Notes. You can exit Notes by performing any of the following:

- Press Alt+F4.

- Choose File, Exit.

- Click the Control-menu box in the upper-left corner of the Notes screen. The Control menu appears. Choose Close to quit Notes.

- Double-click the Control-menu box.

From Here...

This chapter showed you the basic terms that you will encounter throughout the book and when talking with other Notes users. You learned about the terms database and document and learned something about the way Notes works. You learned to start and exit Notes, open and close documents, and access Notes help.

For more information on the topics discussed in this chapter, refer to the following:

- Chapter 3, "Using Databases," teaches you how to work with Lotus Notes documents, views, and other features of a Notes database.

- Chapter 8, "Working with Documents," explains how to work with hotspots, doclinks, and other features that provide impact to your documents.

- Chapter 14, "Working with Formulas," shows how to create formulas that you can use to customize your SmartIcons.

Chapter 2

Customizing Notes

Many people who use Notes spend most of their day working with it. If your job involves a great deal of contact with other people, much of that interaction may involve exchanging messages through Notes. If you're going to work frequently with Notes, you will be pleased that you can customize most aspects of the program.

This chapter provides tips and techniques to use in customizing your Notes environment. In this chapter, you learn about arranging your workspace pages and icons, configuring Notes, and setting up your printer. You also learn a little bit about two special Notes files, DESKTOP.DSK and NOTES.INI, and the importance they play.

Customizing Your Workspace

Your workspace is the starting point for working with Notes. Even though organizing your workspace may not be as important to you as organizing the databases in which you work, it can help you quickly locate and work with the databases you need.

> **Note**
>
> As you work in Notes, you may be prompted for your Notes password. This usually happens when you first begin your session in Notes, try to make changes to the Access Control Lists (ACLs), or when you first try to access a database that is located on a server or one that enforces local security when you are working remote. You may also be prompted for your password even if you already entered it during the working session, if you try to access documents or a database that is encrypted on your hard drive, or if you try to change your password or call a server from a remote location.
>
> When you are prompted for your Notes password, type it in the Password dialog box exactly as your password states because Notes passwords are case-sensitive. For more information on Notes passwords, read Chapter 22, "Security and Encryption."

Some of the main topics in this chapter are

- Arranging your workspace

- Setting up your printer

- Changing your password

- Specifying your Notes preferences

- Working with your DESKTOP.DSK file

- Understanding the NOTES.INI file

Arranging Workspace Pages

Notes' workspace is initially divided into six workspace pages and each database you access appears as a box with an icon on one of the pages. When you add databases to your workspace and create your own databases, the first step is to select the page on which you want the database to appear.

When you start using Notes, you will probably work with only a few databases: your mailbox, the Name & Address database, and perhaps one or two information databases your department uses. Because the number of databases is small, you probably put all your databases on a single workspace page.

As your familiarity with Notes increases and your use of Notes expands, you will work with more and more databases. Eventually, you may want to use more databases than can fit on a single workspace page. You can fit a total of 99 database icons on a single workpage. Long before that happens, however, you will probably feel that your page is cluttered and will want to organize it.

Adding New Workpages

Notes R4.x lets you add additional workpage tabs to better organize your workspace. You can have up to 32 workspace pages, in addition to the workpage titled Replicator. Notes automatically adjusts the size of the tabs to accommodate the addition of extra tabs and the size of the words you are entering as tab titles. However, if you enter more text/tab combinations than Notes has room to display, the tabs on the right side of the workspace begin to disappear. If this happens, the only way you can move to those workpages is to highlight any workpage and press your right arrow key to view the contents of the hidden workpages. To add a new workpage, follow these steps:

1. Click a workspace tab to insert the workspace page to the left of the selected workspace page.

2. Choose Create, Workspace Page. If you haven't added a workspace page before, Notes asks if you want to upgrade your desktop file if you have upgraded from Notes R3.x to Notes 4.x.

3. Click Yes to add the workspace page and upgrade your desktop file, or click No to cancel adding the page.

> **Caution**
>
> When you add additional workpages to your workspace, you modify your DESKTOP.DSK file that stores your personal preferences and setup information. Once you modify this file in Notes R4.x, you cannot use the file with previous releases of Notes.

Deleting Workpages from Your Workspace

Just as you can add workpages to your workspace, you can also remove them. When you remove a workpage, however, you also remove any database icons you have positioned on the page. If you do not want to remove the icons from your workspace, you need to move them to another tab before following these procedures. To remove a workpage from your workspace, follow these steps:

1. Click the workspace page's tab.

2. Choose Edit, Clear or press Delete.

3. Click Yes to confirm the deletion or No to cancel it.

Note

Removing the database icon and deleting the database are not the same thing. Deleting the database is accomplished by selecting File, Database, Delete and will physically remove the database (if you have access permission to do so). Removing the database icon removes the icon only from your workspace. If the file is located on your hard drive or server, you simply need to again add the database icon to another workpage.

Naming Workpage Tabs

When you feel that your workspace is getting cluttered, you may want to use the other workpages. To name a workpage, follow these steps:

1. Double-click the workspace tab that you want to name, or click the workspace tab once and then select the Properties SmartIcon. The Workspace Properties InfoBox for the selected tab appears (see Figure 2.1).

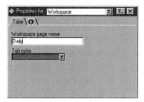

Fig. 2.1 You can name your workpages by opening the Workspace Properties InfoBox.

2. Type in the new name for the tab in the Workspace Page Name text entry box.

3. Select a color for the tab by choosing a color from the Tab Color list box.

4. Double-click the Control Menu box (in this example, it's the X in the upper right corner of the box) to close the InfoBox and accept your edits.

Moving Databases on the Workspace

You can move databases from one page to another at any time. Click the workspace page on which the database now resides and then drag the database from that page to the tab belonging to the page where you want to move the database. The Workpage tab displays a box around the title when the cursor is positioned correctly. You can move multiple databases by holding down the Shift key, clicking each of the databases you want to move, and then dragging the icons to the new page.

As you move icons from one workspace page to another, you may find that the icons on the pages become rather disorganized. You can tell Notes to straighten up a workspace page by selecting the page and choosing View, Arrange Icons. Notes arranges all the database icons on the current page starting from the top and moving down, with no gaps.

You can also move the icons on your Notes workspace without a mouse. To do so, follow these steps:

1. Select the icon you want to move.

2. Hold down the Shift and Ctrl keys at the same time.

3. Use the cursor arrows to reposition your icon.

4. Release the Shift and Ctrl keys.

5. Press Enter when you have completed the move.

The icons will now appear on the newly designated workpage.

Working with Stacked Icons

There are times when you may want to keep more than one copy of a database icon on your workspace. Perhaps you have access to the same database that is stored on more than one server on your network or you may be working remote and keeping a replica copy of a database that is stored on your hard drive as well as the icon pointing to the main database stored on your server. Your workspace may get too cluttered with all of the copies of the database icons displaying. You can set your workspace to show all database replicas as stacked icons. Stacked icons take up less room on your workspace and make it easier to work with all of the databases at once. When you stack icons, the topmost, leftmost icon appears at the top of the stack. Stacked icons appear with a stacked icon indicator in the upper right corner of the icon as shown in Figure 2.2.

Fig. 2.2   You can stack replica copies of icons so that they take up less space on your workpage.

Stacking Database Icons. If your duplicate icons do not appear to be stacked, select View, Stack Replica Icons. A checkmark appears that indicates the selection is active and Notes remembers this setting until you turn it off.

When you stack icons, Notes checks your location and displays whichever icon you last used when you were working using that location at the top of the stack. The icons automatically display the server name or Local in the title of the icon as they are brought to the top of the stack. This lets you quickly know which copy of the database you are using: a server (a network copy), or Local (a copy stored on your hard drive). For example, in Figure 2.2, you see Cate Richards' database located on the Local hard drive.

If a database has replicas on multiple servers, and all are added to your workspace, the top left icon on the workpage appears at the top of the stack when you elect to stack your icons.

Using Stacked Icons. Typically, you store replica copies of databases on your hard drive when you are working away from a network (refer to Chapter 20, "Setting Up to Go Remote," for more information on creating replica copies of databases). You may also keep replica copies of databases on your hard drive if you are making design modifications to a database and don't want to do so directly in the production server copy.

Regardless of the reason for having multiple replicas of a database on your workspace, you may often find the need to switch between the replica copies during your work session. Because the replica that is at the top of the stack is the database that Notes works on, you simply need to select a new replica to be placed on the top of the stack. To do so, follow these steps:

1. Click the database indicator (down arrow) in the upper right corner of the database icon. The database icon menu drops down (see Figure 2.3).

Fig. 2.3   Select the database indicator to choose between replica databases when their icons are stacked.

2. Select the copy of the replica that you want to work in. For example, in Figure 2.3, the Local copy of the database is currently at the top of the stack—the checkmark displays next to that location. To bring the network copy of the icon to the top of the stack, choose the server name in which the replica is stored. In this example, you would select BRSTPNOTES01/BAY RESOURCES.

> **Note**
>
> The Replicate option in the database location menu list is discussed in Chapter 20, "Setting Up to Go Remote."

If you decide you do not want to stack your replica icons anymore, select View, Stack Replica Icons to remove the checkmark. Your icons automatically unstack and arrange themselves on the workspace.

Customizing Information Displayed on Database Icons

In addition to arranging the workspace pages on which your databases reside, you can customize the appearance display of the database information. The simplest database icon (and the default) consists of a picture, relating to the content of the database and the title of the database. Figure 2.4 shows a sample workspace page with three databases.

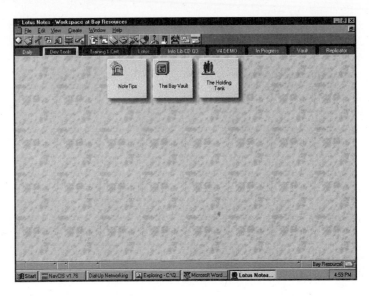

Fig. 2.4 These three databases show the default database information.

You can customize the icons to display additional information about each database. The View menu contains two options that prompt Notes to tell you more about each database on your workspace:

■ **Show Unread**—This tells Notes to display a tiny window next to each icon, showing the number of unread documents in the database. This number tells you if you need to allocate time to read the contents of the database. Be aware, however, that Notes doesn't update this number every time someone enters a new document into the database. The Show Unread window shows only the number of documents that were in the database the last time you opened the database. If you want Notes to update the number of unread documents for each database on your current workpage, exit all of your databases and then press F9 or choose View, Refresh Show Unread. Notes also updates the unread document counter the next time you start up Notes. The Unread count for the database you are working in updates when you exit the database.

> **Tip**
>
> Pressing Ctrl+Shift+F9 updates all databases on all Workpages on your desktop.

> **Note**
>
> You can scan databases for unread documents in Notes to quickly review new information stored in your databases. Read the section "Scanning Databases for Unread Documents" in Chapter 10, "Creating New Databases," for more information on this feature.

- **Server names**—This tells Notes to display the server name of each database under the database title. This information can be helpful if you need to know which server the database is located on. Local refers to databases that are stored on your local disk drive.

Tip

If you hold the Shift key as you select View, Show Server Names, Notes displays the filename for each database. Notes does not display the filenames without the server names on the icons.

Figure 2.5 shows the same workspace page shown in Figure 2.4, with the addition of the unread document counter, server name, and filename showing.

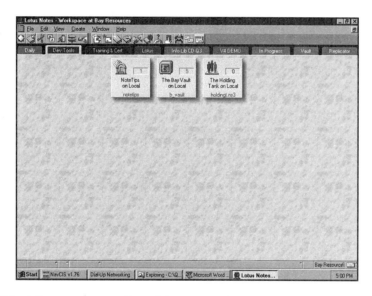

Fig. 2.5   If the full server name, or file path/name is too long to display on the database icon, you can find the same information by selecting File, Database, Properties.

You can also elect to enlarge the size of the database icon through the Notes Preferences settings as described in the next section. This enlarges the entire database icon, including the text size of the titles. This is great if you have difficulty reading the database titles. Keep in mind that you will see only a few icons in the workspace at a time and long database title names will be truncated.

Note

For OS/2 3.1.5 Notes users, the VGA fonts may appear too small when using IBM's S3, 32-bit, and 64-bit graphic chips. If you have this difficulty, you may want to increase the font size using File, Tools, User Preferences. You should also add this parameter to your NOTES.INI file:

(continues)

Notes Basics

(continued)

        DISPLAY_FONT_INCREASE=1

The display font options are 1, 2, and 3 with 1 as the best for the video chips mentioned here.

You will read more about modifying the NOTES.INI file later in this chapter.

Setting Up Your Printer

 You use your operating system software to tell your computer what kinds of printers are available. For example, in Windows 95, you use the Printer's Properties InfoBox. The only information Notes needs is the printer(s) you want to use.

Choose File, Print to open the File Print dialog box shown in Figure 2.6. Select the Printer button located in the upper left portion of the dialog box. Notes displays a list of available printers in the Print Setup dialog box (see Figure 2.7). If you only have a single printer available, Notes displays only that printer. Make your printer selection and then select OK. After you select a printer, Notes routes all printouts to that printer until you change your selection.

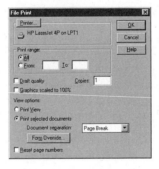

Fig. 2.6   Select the Printer button to switch printers or make changes to your printer setup in the File Print dialog box.

Note

The dialog box that appears when selecting and setting up printers will vary depending on the type of printer and the operating system you are working with. For example, the dialog boxes that appear in this figure are for an HP LaserJet 4P printer with a workstation running Windows 95. Your dialog boxes may vary slightly from those shown here.

The Print Setup dialog box also enables you to configure various options about how the printer works by selecting the Setup button. You should not have to modify any of these options often unless you are printing some custom work.

Fig. 2.7   Select the printer you want to use, or for which you want to make setup changes, from the list of printers you have available to you.

Perhaps the change most often made when changing printer setups is to switch between landscape and portrait printing. This change in paper orientation is made through your operating system printer setup but can be reached by selecting File, Print, Printer, Setup. The Printer Setup dialog box opens as shown in Figure 2.8.

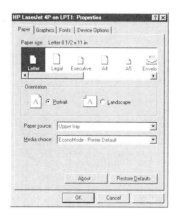

Fig. 2.8   If your printer supports landscape printing, you can switch between landscape and portrait printing in the Printer Setup dialog box.

Figure 2.8 shows the Printer Setup dialog box that displays when printing to the HP LaserJet 4P printer. This setup box, and the available options, is dependent upon the type of printer you have selected so you may see a slightly different setup printer dialog box for your printer. In the Orientation combo box, select the paper orientation that you want to use, select OK, and then select OK again to save your settings. Typically, the page orientation settings remain in effect until the next time you change them. However, some networks are set up and administered to always shift print settings back to their default. It all depends on how your PC is installed and what operating system you use.

If you have additional questions about the other options available for your printer, refer to your printer manual.

Changing Your Password

Notes maintains several important pieces of information about you. Some of this information, such as your user ID number, isn't of personal concern to you, but is vital to Notes. You can display some of the information by choosing File, Tools, User ID. When Notes prompts you for your Notes password, type your password and click OK. When you choose this command, the User ID Information dialog box appears (see Figure 2.9).

Fig. 2.9 The User ID dialog box provides you with a summary of your personal ID information. You can select the Set Password button to change your Notes password.

This dialog box provides the following information about your ID file:

- User name
- ID filename and location
- ID type
- Security (North American or International)
- License type
- ID number
- Software number
- Validation code
- Key

You also open this dialog box to do the following:

- Change your user name
- Work with certificates
- Configure for encryption
- Work with advanced options concerning your Notes ID

You learn more about managing your Notes ID in Chapter 22, "Security and Encryption." For now, we will only look at changing your password.

> ### Caution
> Changing your user name removes all the certificates from your ID and you will have to acquire new certificates before you can use any shared databases (databases not on your local drive). Contact your Notes Administrator before performing this function!

Perhaps the most important selection on the User ID dialog box enables you to change your password. Security experts say that you should change your password on a regular basis, but most people change their passwords only when they have a pressing need for a new password (for example, if a trusted friend who knows the old password turns out to be a snoop!).

> **Note**
>
> Though beyond the scope of this chapter, it is important to highlight a new feature in Lotus Notes 4.5. Beginning with Notes 4.5, Notes Administrators can set up an administrative task on the Notes server to enforce password aging of your Notes password. Whether this option is set or not is dependent upon the needs and policies of your company.

To change your password, choose File, Tools, User ID. Enter your current Notes password when prompted and then select the Set Password button. The Enter Password dialog box appears, and prompts you for your old password (see Figure 2.10). Enter your old password and then select OK.

Fig. 2.10   You must first enter your old Notes password in the Enter Password dialog box and then type your new password when prompted.

> **Note**
>
> You will notice that the hieroglyphic symbols next to your password change as you type each letter of your password. This is just an additional security feature of Notes to let you know that the letters and/or numbers you type are being recognized, without displaying your password to others around you.

Notes then prompts you with the Set Password dialog box shown in Figure 2.11. Type in your new password and then select OK. As is always true when you enter a password, your new password doesn't appear on-screen as you type. To ensure your security, avoid creating passwords that can easily be guessed by those who know you—like your child's or pet's name. Because passwords are case-sensitive, you can decrease the chance of someone guessing your password by varying the case of the letters that make up your password. For example, if you want to enter pluto3 as your password, try entering plutO3—capitalizing the O (or any other letter). Adding numbers to the password also helps discourage people from discovering your password.

Fig. 2.11   You can enter a new password in the Set Password dialog box, but take note of the minimum number of characters your Notes ID requires for a password.

Note

The minimum number of characters you need to type to enter a new password may vary, depending on the minimum character limit your Notes Administrator may have set when your Notes ID was issued. Typically, the minimum character limit is set at eight, as suggested by Notes, but could be as low as zero and anywhere in between. If you try to type a new password and Notes does not accept it, try typing a password with more characters.

Finally, Notes prompts you for your new password again. This is a safety feature to be sure that you typed the password correctly. Notes signals an error if you didn't type the same new password both times; otherwise, Notes accepts the new password. You must use it the next time you start Notes or clear your logon. Select Done to exit the User ID dialog box.

Caution

A Clear password button in the User ID dialog box can remove your password. If you value the security of your mailbox, do not use this option by selecting this button. With your password cleared, anyone who has access to your laptop or PC can access your Notes mailbox and even send mail under your name.

Specifying Your Notes Preferences

Through Notes Preferences, you can customize various aspects of Notes. Choosing File, Tools, User Preferences gives you the Preferences dialog box which provides a single location for customizing all of your global preference settings.

The Preferences dialog box is divided into the following four sections:

- **Basics**—Displays a panel that enables you to control startup options, the location of your Notes data directory, colors, and your User Dictionary.

- **International**—Displays settings that let you customize the way Notes translates particular international symbols, casing, and collation. You can also select which international dictionary you want to use.

- **Mail**—Displays settings that let you specify how you want your mail treated. You also define the location of your mail database and which mail program you are using.

■ **Ports**—Enables you to control the serial or network port that Notes uses to connect with the Notes server. Your system administrator can assist you with any changes you may want to make in this pane if you are unsure of the settings you need to make. If you are planning to work remote, read Chapter 20, "Setting Up to Go Remote," for more information on the Port settings you need to make.

Basic Settings

The Preferences dialog box always opens to the Basics settings as the default, as shown in Figure 2.12. Most of the settings you make in this section do not take effect until you restart Lotus Notes.

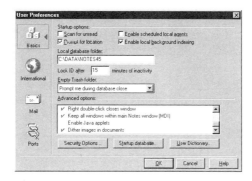

Fig. 2.12   The Basics settings pane lets you change many of the default startup settings in Notes.

The largest portion of the dialog box is devoted to the Startup options that consist of check boxes and text entry boxes that govern the actions Notes takes each time you start Notes. The following sections describe the options.

Scanning Unread Documents. If you choose the Scan for unread option, Notes scans some or all of your databases for unread documents each time you start Notes. You can determine which databases Notes scans in the Scan Unread dialog box (for more information, see Chapter 8, "Working with Documents").

Prompting for Location. The Prompt for location option causes Notes to display the Choose Location dialog box every time you start Notes. You might find this feature handy if you travel frequently with your laptop because you can select from any of the locations you have defined in your Name & Address book. The locations you define tell Notes whether it is on a network or is working remote. It also lets you tell Notes what phone numbers to call if working remote and what time zone you are working in. You can also change the date and time entries when prompted for your location. You learn more about this setting in Part IV of this book, "Going Mobile."

Starting the Agent Manager. If you want to automatically start the Agent Manager when you start Notes, select the Enable scheduled local agents option in the Preferences dialog box. With the Agent Manager, you can run agents (macros) in the background. This way, you can have Notes automatically perform tasks that you set up, such as filing documents, finding particular topics, or sending mail at particular times. You learn about working with agents in more detail in Chapter 16, "Buttons and Agents."

Indexing in the Background. The Enable local background indexing option lets you create full text indexes in the background, letting you continue to work while full text indexes create. A full text index is a collection of files that indexes the text in a database and lets you search for text anywhere in the database through queries. You learn more about full text indexes in Chapter 8, "Working with Documents."

Changing the Default Data Directory. The local database folder in the Preferences dialog box enables you to specify where Notes' data files (databases, desktop settings, and so on) are kept. `C:\NOTES\DATA` is the default. You can use this field to specify an alternate directory in which your local databases reside.

If you are upgrading from Notes 3 and did not store your databases in a subdirectory other than `C:\NOTES` (the default data directory for Notes 3), or you have otherwise specified `C:\NOTES` as your data directory, you can, and should, store your local databases in a directory other than `C:\NOTES` if possible. By storing the data files in a subdirectory other than `C:\NOTES`, you can get easier access to them and protect yourself against accidentally deleting important system files when you are housecleaning your data files.

If you leave the data directory as `C:\NOTES`, your data files store along with all of the program files. Not only is this inefficient, but it can be dangerous as well. It takes longer for you to hunt through several filenames to find your database files when they are not stored separately; and you may accidentally select a program file by mistake when copying, moving, or deleting files, which may cause problems in running Notes. Keep in mind that if you move your data files to a different directory, some Notes functions may be affected, such as the use of indexes created in R3, or any formulas you have in a database that reference a particular database by the filename and its path.

> **Note**
>
> Release 4.x of Notes uses `C:\NOTES\DATA` as the default data directory when the software is installed and is a change from Notes 3, which used `C:\NOTES` as the data directory. Unless you change your data directory, this is where Notes looks for all of your data files. You will find a list of the data files that should be stored in your data directory later in this section.

You can easily create a new data directory and move your data files to it. Usually, this subdirectory is within the Notes subdirectory, but it doesn't have to be. In fact, there are some circumstances in which you may want to specify a different drive name as well as subdirectory name. This is usually when you are working in a situation in which your hard drive space is limited, but you have plenty of file storage space on a network drive.

> **Note**
>
> If you work remote frequently, you will want to keep your data directory on your local hard drive because you will not always be connected to a LAN. This does not mean that you can't store databases on a network file server—it simply means that they will not be available to you when you are working remote.

To create a data directory other than `C:\NOTES`, follow these steps:

1. Change the data directory setup by selecting File, Tools, User Preferences and typing the new local database directory name in the text box. For example, type C:\NOTES\DATA (or substitute your new directory name for C:\NOTES\DATA).

Tip

Write the new data directory down exactly as it was entered in this step, or copy it to your Clipboard by highlighting it and then selecting Ctrl+C. When you create the new folder, you can either type the folder name or paste it in using Ctrl+V. Using the copy/paste method will help you avoid typographical errors. You may want to reference the full path and directory name in step 5.

---

2. Select OK to save the entry.

3. Close Notes and open File Manager or Explorer in Windows. If you are running a different operating system, follow your operating system's procedures for making subdirectories and moving files into them. You will need to close Notes to move the DESKTOP.DSK file because it otherwise will be in use.

   If you already have a C:\NOTES\DATA directory created, and just need to move your data files, skip to step 6.

4. Highlight the drive or directory folder where you want to locate the new data directory. For example, if you want the new data directory to be located within the Notes directory, highlight the Notes directory folder.

5. Select File, Create Directory (or File, New, Folder in Windows 95). In the Create Directory dialog box, type the name of the new data directory (in Windows 95, rename the Folder by clicking the folder name once to place it in edit mode). The name can contain up to eight characters (in our example, create a data directory in the C:\NOTES subdirectory named DATA).

6. Select File, Search (or Start, Find, Files or Folders in Windows 95). Type ***.NSF** in the Search For (or Named in Windows 95) text box (make sure you include the asterisk in this entry). Type **C:** in the Start From (In Windows 95, it's Look in) text box if you want to copy all databases on your hard drive to your new data directory, and then choose OK (or Find Now). Once you have located all of your .NSF files, select all of them by pressing the Shift key and clicking the first filename in the list and then the last filename in the list. All of the database files will be selected, and ready to move into the new data directory (DATA, in this example).

Note

If you have several subdirectories in which you store Notes databases and you only want to move the files in C:\NOTES, then you may want to type C:\NOTES in the Start From text box to move only the databases stored in the existing C:\NOTES subdirectory.

If your previous data directory was stored elsewhere and you want to move your files, type that subdirectory's path in the Start From text box.

Notes Basics

7. Select File, Move (not Copy, as that would leave a copy of the database files in the old directory and take up unnecessary hard drive space). Enter the entire path name in the To text box. For this example, type C:\NOTES\DATA as the path. In Windows 95, you need to select Edit, Cut to cut the files to your Clipboard and then open the new destination's folder and select Edit, Paste.

You must also move the following files to your new data directory following the same procedures in steps 4 and 5, and substitute the appropriate file extensions as needed:

- Any Version 2 databases stored with the .NS2 extension.

- Your DESKTOP.DSK file. You learn more about this file later in this chapter.

- Your CACHE.DSK file.

- Any character and language files that you have installed. These files end in the .CLS file extension.

- Your locally stored template files (.NTF files).

- Your personal dictionary file (where you have defined words in the spell checker) titled USER.DIC.

- If you work with OS/2, your NOTES.INI file.

You may also want to copy your Notes ID file to this subdirectory to simplify switching to it if you use more than one ID on a workstation.

8. Select OK to move the files.

9. Exit File Manager or Explorer and restart Notes.

You now have a new data directory in which your existing Notes databases are located. You may experience a slight delay the first time you open a database that has been moved into the new data directory. This is because Notes is updating its location information.

If you receive a prompt from Notes indicating that it cannot find a database in the new data directory, check to make sure that the file was moved, and that you correctly updated the Local database directory name in the Preferences dialog box.

If you experience any problems—for example, Notes will not start after you make these changes, or you discover that your desktop is blank when Notes starts—check to make sure you correctly moved your DESKTOP.DSK file, NOTES.INI file (if you use OS/2), and the other files listed above into your new data directory.

Setting the Automatic Log-Off Point. The Lock ID after minutes of inactivity option lets you specify the number of minutes you want Notes to keep your password active before logging you off when you haven't touched your keyboard or mouse. Notes will automatically logoff from Notes and you will have to reenter your Notes password the next time you begin to access your databases.

Tip

Don't make this setting so short that you do not have a chance to review a complex document, embedded chart, or spreadsheet. A setting between 15–30 minutes is usually sufficient to protect your Notes' security, while minimizing the number of times you spend typing your password during a Notes session.

Empty Trash Folder. Your mail database contains a trash folder that contains all of the mail you have marked for deletion during a session. You can tell Notes how to empty the trash folder with three options:

- Choose Prompt me during database close to have Notes ask you whether you want to clear the mail in the trash folder each time you close your mail database. This is the default selection.

- Choose Always during database close to have Notes automatically clear the mail in the trash folder each time you close your mail database.

Caution

Once you empty your trash folder, you cannot undo your deletion selection. You will not be able to get the mail back!

- Choose Manually to cancel automatic clearing of the trash folder. If you select this option, you must select Actions, Empty Trash to clear the mail in the trash folder.

Selecting Advanced Options. You can select from many advanced options to control many of Notes' options when it starts up. The list of options is summarized in the following sections.

Marking Previewed Documents as Read. Choose the Mark documents read when opened in the preview pane option if you want Notes to mark a document as being read when you preview it using the preview pane (even though you haven't opened it). You learn more about the preview pane in Chapter 3, "Using Databases."

Selecting a Font. Notes normally uses proportional fonts, where letters require varying amounts of screen space—a capital *M*, for example, takes up much more space than a lowercase *i*. The Typewriter fonts only option tells Notes to display all information (including database titles, views, and documents) in monospace fonts, in which all letters take up the same amount of space. You may find this option useful for checking the width of columns. If a column is wide enough in a monospace font to display the entire contents of the column, it will probably be wide enough when you switch back to a proportional (non-monospace) font.

The Large Fonts Option. The Large fonts option tells Notes to display text in large letters. This increases the font size that displays in the database icons (as well as the size of the database icon). It also increases the font in the views and forms as it displays on your workstation. It does not change the size that the font prints, or the size in which it displays to other users (unless they have also selected Large fonts). You may find this option handy if the regular characters are too small to read comfortably on-screen, if you need to view the screen from a distance, or if you give a presentation in which many people need to see the screen.

Caution

Selecting this option may cut off text in your database titles. This happens because the text becomes too large to fit in the small areas.

Make Internet URLs (http://.....) into Hotspots. You can select the Make Internet URLs (**http://...**) into hotspots option to have Notes automatically convert Internet addresses into hotspots if you are set up to have Notes interface with the Internet through the new Web browser feature of Notes R4.x. URL stands for *Uniform Resource Locator*, which is the World Wide Web name for a document, file, or other resource. It describes the protocol required to access the resource, the host where it can be found, and a path to the resource on that host. If you are configured to access the Web through Notes, you can click an URL hotspot and Notes takes you out to the referenced Web site.

Changing the Texture of Your Workspace. You can select to have Notes display the workspace with a 3-D, marbled look by selecting Textured workspace. When you click a database icon with this selection, it appears to flatten against the workspace to indicate that it is selected. You must have your display set to at least 256 colors to use this feature—otherwise, it does not appear in the list.

Keeping the Maximized Workspace in Back. The Keep Workspace in back when maximized option lets you automatically keep the Notes workspace behind other open windows when you have the Notes window maximized. This way, each time you close a window, Notes returns to the last window that was current instead of to the workspace.

Using Monochrome Settings. The Monochrome display option tells Notes to display everything in black and white (monochrome), even on a color monitor if you are using Windows-based operating systems, OS/2, or UNIX. You may find this option handy if you design databases and want to see how they would look on a monochrome monitor.

Closing Windows with Right Double-Click. The Right double-click closes window option lets you use your right mouse button to close any open window by double-clicking it while your cursor is anywhere within the window. If you were a former Notes 3 user, you will probably want to select this option immediately if you have gotten used to exiting Notes documents by right double-clicking the mouse.

Keeping All Notes Windows Within the Main Notes Window. You can select the Keep all windows within the Main Notes Window (MDI) option to have Notes windows maximize only as large as the main workspace window. This option is selected as the default option. If you deselect this option, Notes windows that are opened within the main Notes window can be maximized to fill the entire screen—even if the main Notes window does not.

Enabling Java Applets. You can tell Notes to enable Java applets so that you can view them with the Personal and/or Server Web Navigator. By default, this option is not selected. Even if you have this feature selected, you must also adjust the settings in the Java Applet Security section in your Location documents to use this feature.

Dithering Images to Match Your Display. Selecting Dither images tells Notes to use a particular pattern of pixels to convert the graphic to something more appropriate for your particular display. This selection's purpose is to attempt to fine-tune graphical images so that they appear sharper on your monitor.

Security Options. Select the Security Options button to make selections in the Execution Control List (ECL) to protect your data against the threats of mail bombs, viruses, Trojan horses, or unwanted application intrusions encountered when navigating the Internet. Execution Control Lists provide a way for you to manage whether such executable files are allowed to execute—and what level of access the program should be permitted. ECLs are specific to your PC and can be controlled to a very granular level, as displayed in Figure 2.13. For example, you may stipulate that when a document is electronically signed by a certain trusted colleague, programs executed by that document can access documents and databases as well as modify environment variables, but cannot access the file system or external programs. This is a new feature to Notes R4.5 and is put in place to protect your data when accessing documents from Notes and Web locations.

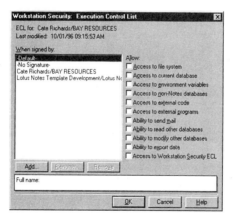

Fig. 2.13 Execution Control Lists (ECLs) let you indicate what types of executable files can execute—and what level of access the program should permit.

Choosing which Database to Automatically Open When Notes Is Launched. Select the Startup Database button to tell Notes which database, if any, you want to automatically open when you start Notes. Databases are listed according to the workpage they are on as shown in Figure 2.14. You can select one database title and then select OK to save your setting.

Fig. 2.14 Notes R4.5 allows you to select a particular database to automatically open when you first start Notes.

Changing the User Dictionary. Selecting the User Dictionary button causes Notes to display the User Spell Dictionary dialog box (see Figure 2.15). Through this dialog box, you can add, update, and delete words that you have defined in your personal data dictionary.

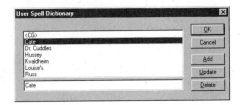

Fig. 2.15 You can define words, names, and phrases that you commonly use in your User Dictionary to facilitate the spelling checker.

To add new words to your dictionary, type the new word in the text entry box at the bottom of the dialog box and then click Add. To delete a word, select the word from the scrolling list box and then press the Delete button. To edit an existing word, select the word from the scrolling list box, edit the text in the text entry box, and then select Update. Select OK to exit the dialog box and save your changes or Cancel to exit without saving your changes.

Caution

Do not press Esc to exit this (or any) Notes dialog box. Doing so causes you to lose any setting changes you have made and is the same as clicking the Cancel button.

International Settings

To display the options for International settings, click the International icon in the Preferences dialog box. Notes displays the International settings panel shown in Figure 2.16. Through this dialog box, you can control characteristics that tend to vary from one country to another. These characteristics are described in the following sections.

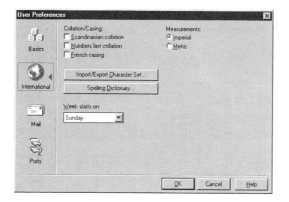

Fig. 2.16 You can change your dictionary, Import/Export character translation sets, and other settings that typically change based upon your international location.

> **Note**
>
> The International settings here do not change the currency denomination indicator, nor the date format used in many countries outside of North America. You make these changes in your operating system.
>
> For example, if you want to use British pounds Sterling, or the date format dd\mm\yy, you could open up the Control Panel in Windows and select the International icon. Change the Country setting to United Kingdom. The currency indicator and date format default would then be changed to reflect the common format used in the United Kingdom.
>
> Check your operating system information for additional information on changing the international default settings.

Controlling Collation and Casing. In Lotus Notes, database designers can specify that items listed in a view display in a particular sort order—ascending or descending. The Collation/Casing options let you tell Notes how to treat some of the characters when sorting. You can choose any or all of the options. If you choose Scandinavian collation, Notes puts accented characters at the end of the alphabet (which is where the Scandinavians put them). If you choose Numbers last collation, Notes considers numbers to come after letters (thus, part number 6X032 would appear after ZY512). If you choose French casing, Notes discards accent marks when you change lowercase letters to uppercase.

Notes uses Country Language Services files (.CLS files) to translate international currency symbols such as the pound £ and the yen ¥ symbols, and accented letters when you import or export data from Notes. Notes also uses .CLS files to determine the order in which characters are sorted.

The collation and casing options are turned off by default. If you choose these options, they don't take effect until the next time you start Notes. If you can't be sure that every user will set up the collation and casing options the way you want them to appear in a particular database, be sure to incorporate the necessary sort settings into your design.

Changing the Unit of Measurement. The Measurements radio buttons enable you to specify Imperial units of measurement (inches, the default) or Metric units (centimeters). Your choice determines whether you must specify margins and tabs in inches or in centimeters. If you have the ruler displayed, this option changes the unit of measurement to inches or centimeters.

Translating Files. The Import/Export Character Set button enables you to specify a file for translating foreign characters and symbols from a non-Notes file into Notes. When you press this button, you are greeted with the Choose Translation Table dialog box (see Figure 2.17).

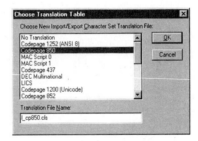

Fig. 2.17   The selection you make in the Choose Translation Table dialog box determines how Notes translates characters when you import or export documents.

You can either select an existing translation (.CLS) file from the Choose New Import/Export Character Set Translation File list box or type the path and filename of a .CLS file that you want to use that is not stored in your data directory. See Chapter 13, "Integrating Notes with Other Applications," for more information about importing and exporting data.

Selecting a Dictionary. The Spelling Dictionary button enables you to tell Notes which dictionary (such as French or British) to use, instead of the American dictionary. The following list shows the available dictionaries:

American English	Finnish
American Medical	French
Australian English	German
Brazilian Portuguese	German (ss)
British (ise) English	Greek
British (ize) English	Italian
British Medical (ise)	Norwegian
British Medical (ize)	Nynorsk
Canadian French	Polish
Catalan	Portuguese
Czech	Russian
Danish	Russian Jo
Dutch General	Spanish
Dutch Preferred	Swedish

The dictionary files selected here are not the same as your User Dictionary in which you add words when you select Define while using the spell checker. These files are located in your Notes program directories. The default file is English and denoted by the filename ENGLISH.DIC.

Tip

If you write documents that must be sent from your home office to an office in a different country, change the dictionary before running the spell checker. This is particularly helpful when sending/receiving documents between countries that vary in the use of British (ise) English and British (ize) English spellings.

Setting the Starting Day of the Week. You can specify which day of the week your week starts on by selecting Week starts on and then choosing the day of the week from the list. This setting is important if you use the Calendaring and Scheduling features as Notes will use this setting in identifying the layout of the calendar pages. The default setting for this option is Sunday.

Mail Settings

You can control how Notes accesses and processes your mailbox by selecting File, Tools, User Preferences, and then selecting the Mail icon in the left side of the dialog box. Notes displays the Mail setup options in the Preferences dialog box (see Figure 2.18).

Notes Basics

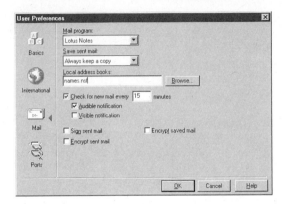

Fig. 2.18 You can customize the way Notes treats mail in the User Preferences Mail pane.

Specifying the Mail Program. The Mail program field identifies the mail system you are using and should be set to Lotus Notes, the default, unless otherwise specified by your Notes administrator.

Saving Sent Mail. The Save sent mail option tells Notes how you want to treat mail when you select the Send button (or select Actions, Send). If you want to Always keep a copy of a memo that you send, select this option. If you do not want to save a copy when you send a memo, select Don't keep a copy. If you want Notes to prompt you to save every time you send a message, select Always prompt.

Caution

If you select Don't keep a copy, you are not prompted to save a document when you select the Send button to send the message. Notes simply sends the document and closes it. If you later need to reference the document, you are not able to do so unless the recipient forwards it back to you. It is safer to select one of the other two options if you think you need to review any of the messages you send.

However, if you right double-click, or press Esc to exit and send the document (rather than clicking the Send button), your default selection for saving sent mail is highlighted in the checkbox. You are then able to deselect the option for that instance before you select Yes to send the mail message.

Selecting your Local Address Books. If you travel often, you may want to carry more than one Name & Address Book with you—like your company's Public Name & Address Book—so that you can select users' names from the list of available recipients while you are on the road. Your Personal Name & Address Book's filename is NAMES.NSF and is located in your Data directory.

To configure Notes to access any additional Name & Address book, you need to type or select the Name & Address Book's filename in the Local address book's text box. You can use the Browse button to select the filename (recommended) or type the filename directly in the text entry box using commas to separate each filename. You can select only one address book filename at a time if you use the Browse button. If you want to select more than one address book, simply press the Browse button again for each new selection. The Name & Address books entered here must be located in your data directory. The setting you make in this text box is saved to your NOTES.INI file (as discussed further in this chapter). When you select the Address button while composing an e-mail message, you are able to switch from one Address Book to the other.

> **Note**
>
> When you send mail or use the type-ahead feature in Notes to address mail, Notes looks in the first database you have listed in the Local address book's text box and then checks the next database, and so on. You should keep your Personal Name & Address book, NAMES.NSF, as your first entry and then each subsequent database listed in the order in which you want Notes to search them.

Checking for New Mail. As you learn in detail in Chapter 4, "Getting Started with Electronic Mail," Mail notifies you when new mail arrives. By changing the number of minutes in the Check for new mail every_minutes setting, you can control how often Notes checks the server to see whether new mail arrived in your mailbox. If you need to quickly know when new mail has arrived, enter a small number (perhaps 3 or 4). If you receive mail rarely, or if you do not need to be notified immediately, entering a larger number (15 or 20) saves your computer the work of frequent checking. If you uncheck the associated checkbox, Notes won't automatically inform you when new mail has arrived—you've got to check for yourself periodically.

You can also tell Notes how you want to be notified of new mail. If you select Audible notification, Notes plays a short tune whenever you have new e-mail delivered. Selecting Visible notification results in a small dialog box appearing to notify you that new mail has arrived. You need to select OK to clear this dialog box from your window.

Signing and Encrypting Sent Mail. If you select the Sign sent mail checkbox, Notes checks the Sign box when you mail a document. Chapter 4, "Getting Started with Electronic Mail," describes in more detail the Sign check box that electronically signs your mail messages.

Selecting the Encrypt sent mail option automatically checks the Encrypt box when you close a mail document. See Chapter 22, "Security and Encryption," for more information about encrypting messages.

Encrypting Saved Mail. If you check the Encrypt saved mail option, Notes encrypts mail stored in your mailbox on the server, and in your hard drive if you work remote and have a copy of your mail database there. Although you can generally assume that your mailbox is private and secure, a few people (such as your system administrator(s)), can access your mailbox without your permission. You can use this option if you are particularly concerned about keeping the messages in your mailbox secure.

Ports Settings

The Ports panel in the Preferences dialog box provides options and buttons that enable you or your system administrator to configure how your computer communicates with your server and what kind of network or modem your computer has. After your computer is set up, you normally do not have to adjust any of these options if you are working on the network. If you are not experienced with the requirements of your network, consult with your system administrator if you need to change your Ports setup.

If you are working remote, you may find that you use the Ports preferences quite frequently. If you want to learn more about this preference panel, read Chapter 20, "Setting Up to Go Remote."

Configuring Options Under Windows and OS/2

Many of the most important preference choices you can make are controlled not by Notes, but by Windows, Macintosh, UNIX, or OS/2. For example, through the Windows Control Panel or the OS/2 System Setup, you can specify the following parameters:

- Some screen colors (for example, the colors of borders and title bars)

- Available fonts and font sizes

- International settings (such as country name, currency symbol, and time and date formats)

- Types and configurations of printers

Consult your Windows, OS/2, or other operating system manual for more information about these parameters.

The *DESKTOP.DSK* File

When working with Notes, it is often helpful to understand a little something about the key files that are accessed in your daily use of the program. The DESKTOP.DSK file is one of the files that you should be familiar with. Information about your workspace is stored in your local data directory in a file named DESKTOP.DSK. This file stores the following information:

- The database icons you've added to your workspace

- The workpage tabs and names you've added to your workspace

- Settings made in the File Page Setup dialog box, such as headers and footers

- Design information about any private views or folders you may have

- The number of documents still unread in a database

Your DESKTOP.DSK tells Notes where it should display all of your database icons when you start up Notes. It also stores all of your private view definitions for all databases to which you have access. Private views are ones that you have designed for yourself that are not available to other users of a database. You learn how to design them in Chapter 12, "Designing Views."

Caution

If you delete the DESKTOP.DSK file, or it becomes corrupted for any reason, you lose all of the desktop settings (for example, database icons, tab names), and you lose all of your private views. Keep this in mind when working with this file. You should back up the DESKTOP.DSK file regularly, using your operating system, perhaps once a month.

The DESKTOP.DSK file can grow as large as 50M—a big file. The larger your DESKTOP.DSK file, the slower your response time can become—not to mention the amount of space it takes up on your hard drive. As you add private views and databases to your desktop, this file grows.

Note

You can compact the DESKTOP.DSK file just as you would any other database. Compacting your Workspace is covered later in this chapter.

When you delete database icons from your desktop, or private views from databases, the space that was taken up will become available but the size of the file is not reduced. When you add new database icons to the workspace, or private views to databases, they first take up the freed space before the file size grows. When you compact your DESKTOP.DSK, you decrease the white space.

Changing the Location of *DESKTOP.DSK*

By default, Notes looks for the DESKTOP.DSK file in the data directory (defined in the User Setup dialog box). The data directory is identified in the NOTES.INI file with the following parameter:

```
Directory=[drive]:\[directory]
```

If you want to locate the DESKTOP.DSK in a directory other than the data directory, add the following line to the NOTES.INI file:

```
Desktop=[drive]:\[directory]\DESKTOP.DSK
```

Whereas it is recommended that you keep your DESKTOP.DSK file in your data directory, you may find the need to locate an alternate DESKTOP.DSK file for when you perform demonstrations. For demonstrations, you don't want your normal desktop settings displayed.

For example, if you wanted to store a second copy of your DESKTOP.DSK file to be used when teaching a class, you could enter the following in the NOTES.INI file:

```
Desktop=C:\CLASS\DESKTOP.DSK
```

When you start Notes, Notes looks in the CLASS subdirectory for the DESKTOP.DSK file. When you no longer want to use the special DESKTOP.DSK file, you need to modify this line again to change where Notes looks for your DESKTOP.DSK file.

You also need to store your DESKTOP.DSK file in a separate directory if you are sharing your workstation with someone else. In this circumstance, consult with your Notes Administrator for assistance because special settings need to be made to your workstation in addition to locating your DESKTOP.DSK file in a separate directory.

Compacting Your *DESKTOP.DSK* File

As you work in Lotus Notes, you add database icons, workpages, private views, and other features whose definitions are stored in your DESKTOP.DSK file. As you remove some of these features, Notes leaves some white space in the database where the definition was stored. Over time, this white space builds up and takes up valuable disk drive space. You can, however, remove the white space by compacting your DESKTOP.DSK file. This recovers unused disk space by removing references to databases you no longer have on your workspace. To compact your DESKTOP.DSK file, follow these steps:

   1. Double-click any workspace tab and the Workspace Properties InfoBox opens, or select the Properties SmartIcon while viewing the Notes workspace and do not have any databases highlighted.

   2. Click the Information tab. The tab is marked with a bold, lowercased *i*. The Information tab will be displayed (see Figure 2.19).

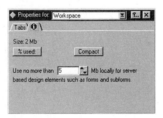

Fig. 2.19   The Information tab enables you to compact your DESKTOP.DSK file.

   3. Click the % used button.

   4. If the percentage is under 85 percent, click the Compact button. If the percentage is over 85 percent, there's no need to compact yet.

You are now working with a cleaner DESKTOP.DSK file that takes up less space on your hard drive. You should periodically check the size of your DESKTOP.DSK file, particularly if you are short on hard drive space.   •

> **Note**
>
> You may also want to limit the size of the CACHE.DSK file, which is used to cache server-based design elements to make them more readily available when you are working in Notes. To limit the size, choose the number of megabytes (normally from 1 to 16). Use no more than 1M locally for server-based design elements such as forms and subforms. When you limit the size of the CACHE.DSK file, Notes removes older, unused design elements to make room for new ones. If it appears that database design elements, such as subforms, are taking a long time to appear, then you may want to increase this setting and then recompact your workspace.

Handling a Corrupted *DESKTOP.DSK* File

If your DESKTOP.DSK file becomes corrupted, you need to close Notes and delete the DESKTOP.DSK file through your operating system commands. When you start Notes again, a new DESKTOP.DSK file is created. Of course, you lose all your workspace customization and private view information.

> **Tip**
>
> By having a backup copy of your DESKTOP.DSK file, you can quickly restore your workspace and private views without having to re-create the views from scratch. Simply copy the backup copy of the DESKTOP.DSK file over the corrupted file in your data directory.

The *NOTES.INI* File

The NOTES.INI file (also called the Notes Preference file on the Macintosh) is a settings file that Notes checks when you first start Lotus Notes. The NOTES.INI file resides in the Notes data directory for OS/2 Notes users and in the Windows directory for most Windows Notes users. If you upgraded from a Release 2 Notes to Release 3, your NOTES.INI file may be located in the Notes directory instead.

Information in the file comes from many sources, including installation choices, server console commands, and selections made in the Setup dialog boxes discussed previously in this chapter. Notes uses most of the variables in this file internally, and you can set those through the Notes user interface (File, Tools, User Preferences) rather than having to edit the NOTES.INI file using a text editor.

> **Note**
>
> When possible, make NOTES.INI settings by changing your User Preferences (File, Tools, User Preferences). It is safer to make changes using the Notes interface than by editing the file directly.

Each time Notes starts, the NOTES.INI file is used to check installation settings, Setup selections (mail, user, and location information, and your DESKTOP.DSK file), and other variables Notes uses.

This section covers just a few of the settings that can be made in the NOTES.INI file to give you an understanding of how the NOTES.INI file works, and to discuss a few of the settings that you may need to make directly in the file, rather than through the User Preferences dialog box.

Editing *NOTES.INI*

Before editing NOTES.INI, exit Notes because the changes you make to the NOTES.INI file do not take effect until the next time you start Notes. Edit the lines of text, insert new lines, or delete lines using a text editor, like the Notepad application found in Windows applications. Make sure, however, that your typing is exact, and that no blank spaces follow any of the lines of text, or you will experience problems.

> **Note**
>
> Macintosh users must edit the NOTES.INI file using a resource editor like ResEdit. Other Notes users can do so using any simple text editor, like the Notepad in Windows. Macintosh users should consult their system's documentation before trying to edit the NOTES.INI file.

When you exit the NOTES.INI document you are editing, save your changes and then restart Notes to have your changes take place.

> **Caution**
>
> Make sure you create a backup copy of your existing NOTES.INI file before you edit it.
>
> Editing the NOTES.INI file can be dangerous to your Notes' health if you are not used to editing these types of files. For example, even leaving a blank space after a line of text in the NOTES.INI file can cause trouble when you try to start Notes. If you have a choice, make Notes changes through the Notes selections or contact your Notes administrator for help.

Changing the New Mail Tune. You can change the tune Notes uses to signal you that new mail has been delivered by editing the NOTES.INI file to reference a new .WAV file—the sound file type used in Notes for the new mail tune. You may already have a few .WAV files available to you in your operating system's directory or in a special sound file directory if you have a sound board. You can also purchase new .WAV files at most software stores or even find many of them passed along as shareware.

For most users with .WAV files, it is a fun change to have your computer play the theme from "Leave It to Beaver" or to say "bummer" every time you get new mail.

For those who have computers that cannot adjust the sound for the new mail tune, the capability to change the new mail tune, and thus edit the sound volume as well, becomes a treat. This is particularly true if you are working close to others. Changing the new mail tune is also handy if you share an office with others and want a distinctive sound to let you know you have new mail.

You must have a sound driver installed to change the new mail tune. If you don't have a sound board installed and do not have a non-soundboard speaker driver, you need to consult with your network administrator or local software dealer. Follow your operating system's instructions for installing and changing the volume for sound on your system.

To change the New Mail Tune (for example, to have your computer say "bummer" each time you get new mail), insert the following line in your NOTES.INI file:

```
NewMailTune=drive:\directory\.WAV file name
```

For example:

```
NewMailTune=C:\WINDOWS\BUMMER.WAV
```

This tells Notes to reference the BUMMER.WAV file each time new mail is delivered to you.

You need to restart Notes to have this edit take effect.

Eliminating the Design Menu. This function generally is used by Notes administrators to keep users from being able to design new databases. However, you can also use this setting if you have no desire yourself to design databases or to manage a public workstation, but want it only to get mail or if you do not want anyone to design databases from your workstation.

Add this line to your NOTES.INI file:

```
NoDesignMenu=1
```

Where 1 means turn on the No Design Menu function to disallow this feature and remove the menu selection from the menu bar in the Notes window.

Protecting Against Mail-Bomb-Type Viruses. While the new ECL security settings in your User Preferences dialog box go a long way toward protecting your workstation, if you want to completely protect your workstation against Mail-Bombs—viruses sent to you via special attachments and features in your mail, enter the following line:

```
NoExternalApps=1
```

Where 1 turns on the No External Applications command and disallows the use of any applications outside of Notes.

When you indicate this setting, you turn off all external applications that are accessed while you are working with Notes; however, this means you are not able to use the following Notes features as long as this selection is made:

- DDE
- DIP
- @Command
- @DbLookup (when using non-Notes databases)
- @DbColumn (when using non-Notes databases)

- ■ @MailSend

- ■ @DDExxx

- ■ Object Linking and Embedding (OLE)

- ■ Launching of file attachments

- ■ Launch to edit (LEL)

- ■ Subscribe (on Macintosh workstations)

Turning Off the Mail Menu. You may want to turn off the ability for people to use the Mail menu commands—for example, if you are managing a public workstation for a group of people, and all you want them to access are project databases. This function would help keep the workstation free more often.

To disable the Mail menu, enter the following line in the NOTES.INI file:

```
NoMailMenu=1
```

Where 1 turns off the Mail menu in Notes. This selection not only eliminates the Mail menu from the workstation, but also sets the user's mail system to None.

> **Note**
>
> If you are having trouble using Mail, and you are meant to do so, you may want to check the NOTES.INI file of the workstation to make sure this setting has not been made. This setting overrides the setting made in the Setup Mail dialog box in Notes to specify which mail package you are using.

Changing the Location of Your ID File. Normally, your ID file is located in your Notes directory or wherever you specified when you set up Notes. If you want to change where your Notes ID file is located, specify it by entering the following:

```
KeyFilename=<location>
```

Where location specifies the drive and directory in which your Notes ID is stored.

This entry is usually used when more than one person is sharing a workstation and separate NOTES.INI and DESKTOP.DSK files are created and stored in personal subdirectories for each user. This option is also useful when administering OS/2 servers—when you specify your ID file. When you open the client on the server, your ID file is used rather than the server ID.

When Something Goes Wrong with *NOTES.INI*

If you have problems with your NOTES.INI file that cannot be resolved, you need to delete all but the first three lines in the NOTES.INI file, save it, and then restart Notes. Examples of problems could be: it is corrupted, you have made mistakes when editing it, the appropriate default information does not seem to be present, or you cannot seem to correct the problem.

The three lines that you must have in your NOTES.INI file to start Notes are the following:

```
[Notes]
KitType=1
Directory=<Notes data directory>
```

Where KitType indicates whether you are running the Notes workstation or server. A value of 1 indicates you are running a workstation. A value of 2 indicates that you are running both a workstation and server. Unless you are setting up a server, specify 1. The setting for your Directory indicates the location of your Notes' data directory and represents where your data files are located.

For example, the directory line could read:

```
Directory=C:\NOTES\DATA
```

You need to make your personal Setup selections again, but you are at least able to start up Notes with all of the default information present.

From Here...

In this chapter, you learned how to customize some of the characteristics of Notes to your tastes. This customization should make your work with Notes more pleasing. For more information on the topics discussed in this chapter, refer to the following:

- Chapter 4, "Getting Started with Electronic Mail," teaches you how to work with Lotus Notes Mail and the Name & Address Books.

- Chapter 12, "Designing Views," explains how to create private views that enable you to list documents in a database according to your own needs.

- Chapter 20, "Setting Up to Go Remote," shows how to configure your laptop for remote access to Notes.

Notes Basics

Chapter 3

Using Databases

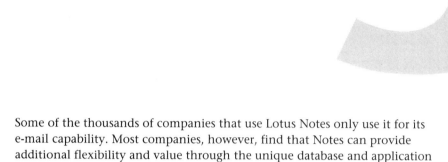

Some of the thousands of companies that use Lotus Notes only use it for its e-mail capability. Most companies, however, find that Notes can provide additional flexibility and value through the unique database and application development capabilities it provides. These capabilities allow companies to communicate, collaborate, and coordinate.

Lotus Notes databases can store, organize, and retrieve any kind of information (text, graphics, sound, and so on). Notes databases are easy to use, they enable local and remote end users to share information in a timely fashion, and they can be developed quickly.

Understanding Databases

Once you understand the architecture of Notes databases , you can begin to harness and apply the tremendous power of Notes. Notes databases, sometimes called *object stores* because they can store any kind of electronic information, are document-oriented.

Although this is not a direct correlation, it may help you to think of documents in a Notes database as records in a relational database. Each database can hold many documents, and each document can hold many fields, each with discrete information.

Because each document can store semi-structured and unstructured data (meaning that the type and amount of data can vary from document to document), Notes databases are versatile and flexible, allowing Notes applications to solve many business problems.

In addition to storing and organizing data, Notes databases accept imported data from external applications such as ODBC-compliant databases (Oracle, Sybase, Access) and Excel. Notes databases can create links to external applications for dynamic data sharing (OLE and Notes/FX) and can even have information e-mailed in. Notes also provides tight database security through access control lists (ACLs) and encryption to protect your data from prying eyes.

Some of the main topics in this chapter are:

- Parts and types of databases

- How an access control list (ACL) works

- Changing database settings

- Opening, saving, closing, and deleting documents and databases

- Using the universal viewer

- Working with file folders

- Printing documents and views

Notes databases are grouped loosely into the following categories:

- System databases
- Mail databases
- Help databases
- Discussion databases
- Document libraries
- Tracking databases
- Workflow databases

These categories show only the most common ways that Notes databases are used. The list is by no means inclusive of all the possible applications for Notes databases. In fact, many of the best Notes solutions are a mixture of different kinds of Notes applications that are linked to legacy systems.

> **Note**
>
> In Notes jargon, the terms *application* and *database* are used interchangeably because Notes databases hold the design elements that make up an application. You'll learn how to begin creating databases in Chapter 10, "Creating New Databases."

Internally, Notes does not classify databases in any way. In Notes 4.5, the interface has been standardized and you can use the same methods and commands to access and navigate all Notes databases.

The following sections describe each type of database.

Databases

System databases provide important information to Notes. System databases are especially important because they hold information that is needed for Notes to function correctly. Well-maintained system databases can make your Notes sessions much more productive and enjoyable. The following short sections describe the system databases.

Address Books. Your Public Address Book and Private Address Book hold information about Notes end users in your company. They also hold server connections, locations, groups, and many other kinds of Notes control documents.

Chapter 5, "Using the Address Book," describes the address books in vivid detail. They are absolutely essential for Notes to work correctly. They also provide directory services, verify database access, provide system management and control information, and do other important jobs. Figure 3.1 shows some typical address book icons.

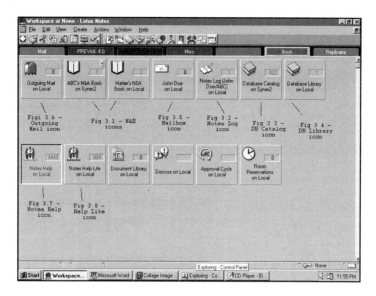

Fig. 3.1 The Public and Personal Name & Address Book icons—along with the other icons—have new R4.x graphics.

Notes Log. The personal Notes log database records information about system activity that takes place while you are using Notes. Some of the many things that are tracked in the Notes Log are replication events, phone calls (if you are working remotely), database usage, and other miscellaneous events.

Each Notes server also has a Notes Log database that tracks server activity. The Notes log database is an invaluable tool for troubleshooting problems.

Database Catalog. The database catalog provides information about databases that are available to you in your Notes network, including information such as the location of each database and the policy for using each database. The database catalog is automatically created when Notes is installed and is normally updated each night automatically by a server task on the Notes server.

Database Libraries. Database libraries make it easy for end users to find databases that interest them. Database libraries can be public (when they reside on a server) or private (when they reside on a workstation).

When the Notes 4 client software is installed, it automatically creates a database library for your workstation that keeps track of the databases on your workstation. In addition, database libraries for only a specific type of database can be created on the server. For instance, all the databases regarding sales might be "published" in the Sales Library database so that other end users can find them easily.

Mail Databases

Mail databases are used by the Notes mail system to store and route e-mail messages. (These databases are covered in detail in Chapter 4, "Getting Started with Electronic Mail," and Chapter 6, "Advanced Mail.")

Mailbox. Your mailbox, likely to be one of your most used databases, is where Notes stores your incoming mail, your outgoing mail, and your calendar. Chapter 4, "Getting Started with Electronic Mail," describes the basics of using your mailbox; Chapter 6, "Advanced Mail," has more advanced information.

Outgoing Mailbox. The outgoing mailbox automatically appears on your workspace when you are configured to use workstation-based mail. It is used to store all outgoing mail until you connect with the server and the router transfers the mail to the server. This database can be helpful when you are troubleshooting mail problems for a workstation configured to use workstation-based mail.

Tip

If you are set up to use workstation-based mail (this applies primarily to remote end users), you can open the Outgoing Mail database and select the Pending Mail view to examine mail that is waiting to be sent. If you decide, for instance, that you would rather not send that mail to your boss stating that you quit, you can delete it from Outgoing Mail and she'll never know the message was written.

Help Databases

In Notes R4.5, most of the documentation is online in Notes databases. This is particularly useful because you can install these databases on your machine and take them with you wherever you go (at the cost of considerable disk space).

Even better, you can create a Full Text Index to the Help databases so that you can find help on a given topic quickly and easily. Notes R4 ships with several Help databases, but the two that most end users find most useful are the Notes Help and Notes Help Lite databases.

Notes Help. The Notes Help database (HELP4.NSF) holds the full, end-end user, online documentation for Notes R4. Although this database can be useful, it is also large (4600+ documents for a total on-disk size of approximately 21 megabytes) and may be too much for end users whose hard disk space is at a premium.

If you have the space on your local workstation, it is highly recommended that you install this database and create a Full Text Index on the database for easy searching. Using the default settings, this will consume another six megabytes of disk space.

Notes Help Lite. The Notes Help Lite database (HELPLITE.NSF) is a much smaller subset (it is approximately six megabytes) of the full Help database designed with the mobile end user in mind.

Other Help Databases. Notes also includes many other useful online help databases that you may or may not be able to access (if you cannot find the following databases, see your administrator):

- Notes Administration Help (HELPADMN.NSF)—This database holds detailed information geared toward Notes administrators.

- Install Guide for Workstations (WRKINST.NSF)—This database holds detailed information for people responsible for Notes R4 workstation installations.

- Install Guide for Servers (SRVINST.NSF)—Much like the Install Guide for Workstations, this database is geared toward Notes server installations.

- Migration Guide (MIGRATE.NSF)—This database holds detailed information for end users migrating from older versions of Notes to Notes R4.

- R4 Features (R4FEAT.NSF)—This database highlights many of the new features of Notes R4.

- Lotus Notes R4.x Release Notes (README.NSF) — This database is invaluable for people migrating from one version of Notes to another. It quickly and concisely tells you about new features and functionality.

Sample Databases

Sample databases are developed by Lotus for you to use as learning tools when building your own databases.

If your workstation was set up with the default installation, these databases are in the C:\NOTES\DATA directory. The databases are called *templates* and have the extension NTF (Notes Template Facility).

You'll learn more about templates and how they can speed your application development in Chapter 10, "Creating New Databases." For example, RESERVE4.NTF is a sample database for tracking room and resource reservations that shows you how the components of a Notes database can be assembled when building database.

Note

If you are migrating from Notes R3.x to Notes R4.x, you might find a mixture of R3 and R4 templates. You can easily identify the R4 templates because Lotus has added the text "(R4)" to the title of each template.

Discussion Databases

Discussion databases are one of the most common uses for Notes databases. These databases facilitate timely communication and collaboration among groups of people.

A discussion database often has very little structure, so end users are free to use it as they want. Many companies developing and deploying databases "cut their teeth" on discussion databases because they are usually simple and can quickly provide a high return on investment.

An example of a discussion database is one that provides technical information and tips for end users of Lotus Notes. Lotus includes a discussion database template, titled Discussion (R4) (DISCUSS4.NTF is the filename) for you to use as a basis for designing discussion databases.

Document Libraries

Document libraries are an electronic repository for documents that remain relatively static but must be distributed to a large or geographically dispersed group of end users in a timely fashion. A document library holds product information brochures, sales literature, and electronic presentations for salespeople to share and use while on the road.

Lotus was kind enough to include the Document Library template, Document Library (R4) (DOCLIB4.NTF), which you can use to create simple document library databases.

Tracking Databases

Tracking databases are usually interactive with many end users contributing data. One example is a complaint-tracking database used by the customer service group to track complaints and progress toward resolution of the complaints.

Another example is a help-desk database in which trouble tickets are entered. After each problem is resolved, the solution is available to other technicians so they don't have to "reinvent the wheel" for common problems. Lotus has included the Room Reservations (R4) template (RESERVE4.NTF), which is useful for creating a tracking application.

Workflow Databases

Workflow databases automate routine tasks to compress cycle time and increase efficiency. A common application of this concept is an expense-reports database that electronically routes expense reports to the right managers for approval, and then to payroll for the payout.

Lotus has included a workflow database template, Approval Cycle (R4) (APPROVE4.NTF), that can be useful as the basis for a workflow database.

Template Overview

Notes R4.5 ships with other useful templates summarized in Table 3.1. For more information about using these templates, see the "About Notes Application Templates" in the Help Database. Or choose a template and click the About button in the New Database dialog box.

▶▶ See "Using Templates," p. 396

There are also advanced system templates, but these fall outside the scope of this chapter. For more information about these advanced templates, see "About Notes System Templates" in the Notes Help database.

Table 3.1 Useful Database Templates Included with Notes R4		
Template Title	**Template Name**	**Filename**
Approval Cycle	StdR4Approval	APPROVE4.NTF
Discussion (R4)	StdR4Disc	DISCUSS4.NTF
Document Library (R4)	StdR4DocLib	DOCLIB4.NTF
Lotus Smart Suite Library (R4)	StdR4DocLibLS	DOCLIBL4.NTF
Microsoft Office Library (R4)	StdR4DocLibMS	DOCLIBM4.NTF
Personal Journal (R4)	StdR4Journal	JOURNAL4.NTF
Room Reservations (R4)	StdR4Room	RESERVE.NTF

Accessing a Database

Before you can access the data in a Notes database, you must have a database icon for that database on your workspace. You can add to your workspace an icon for any database to which you have been granted access rights. (You'll learn more about access rights later in this chapter under "Understanding Access Control Lists.")

Tip

You can use the database catalog and libraries to quickly find databases you might be interested in and then add their icons to your workspace.

Adding a new database icon to your workspace is quite simple. Figure 3.2 shows you the menu options to do this. Just choose File, Database, Open (or press Ctrl+0).

Fig. 3.2 The File menu options are used to add a database icon to your workspace.

You see a dialog box like the one shown in Figure 3.3, giving you a list of the Notes servers available from your machine and a list of all Notes databases on that server.

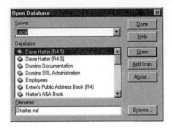

Fig. 3.3   The Open Database dialog box.

You can use the Server combo box to choose the server on which the database you want resides. When you select a server, the Database list box shows the title of each database on the server.

If the server you select is not local (for instance, you are working remotely), Notes will display a dialog box which asks you whether you'd like to call the remote server.

> **Note**
>
> The list of databases you see might not include every database on the server. This is because the designer or database manager may elect to hide certain databases from the Open Database dialog box, or some databases may reside in other Notes Named Networks. In addition, you do not necessarily have access rights to every database in the list.
>
> If you don't see a database listed but you know the filename of the database, you can type it into the Filename field and open the database. (You must have access rights to do this.) If you cannot find a database that you think should be listed, or you cannot access a listed database, see your administrator.

When you select a database from the list, the filename of the database is displayed in the Filename box below the Database list box. At this point, if you want to add a database icon to your workspace and open the database, click the Open button. This puts the icon on your workspace and opens the database.

If you only want to add the database icon to your workspace, click the Add Icon button. This is the best way to go if you are going to add several icons because opening each database is an unnecessary waste of time.

The About button can help you identify the use of a particular database. When you click the About button, the About document of the database (if one exists) is displayed. This should provide information regarding the use of a database.

As in all Windows applications, clicking the Help button at this location displays context-sensitive help about using the Open Database dialog. If you cannot find a database by its title, you can click the Browse button to display the standard File dialog box. This allows you to search for a database by its filename (see Figure 3.4).

Fig. 3.4 The Choose a Notes Database or Template File dialog box.

When you have created an icon for the database you want to access, you are ready to begin working with the database. Before you do so, you need to understand what the different parts of a database are and how those parts interact.

Parts of a Database

Each Notes database is a distinct, on-disk structure with a filename that must meet the operating system conventions and must be unique. For example, if you are using the Notes Windows 3.11 client, you are limited to the DOS naming standard, which is eight characters for the filename and three characters for the file extension.

If you have questions about valid filenames, consult the documentation for your operating system. By default, all Notes databases have the extension NSF.

Note

Although Notes databases normally end with the NSF extension, a Notes database is not required to have an NSF extension. If you use an extension other than NSF, the database does not appear automatically in the Open Database dialog box in the list of database files.

Besides its filename, each database has a database title that is displayed on the database icon. Each database title can have a maximum of 32 characters, allowing much more descriptive naming of the database.

For example, you might have a Notes database that holds information about your competitors. The filename could be COMPET.NSF and the database title might be ABC's Competitors' Information. Unless you create your own databases, the filename and database title for each database you access have already been assigned by someone else.

If multiple end users need access to a database, it must reside on the Notes server. If you are the only end user, you can store it on the Notes server or keep it locally on your hard disk.

One of the nicest features of Notes is that in most instances you do not need to know where the database physically resides. Notes keeps track of database locations, and all you need to do is double-click the database icon to access whatever data is in the database.

When you have access to a database, it is important to understand how information is structured and organized by Notes. The internal architecture of a Notes database is unique.

Like any database, a Notes database is a collection of related information. But unlike traditional relational databases, any kind of information can be stored in a Notes database. In fact, Notes is particularly well suited for storing semistructured information and unstructured information.

Lotus describes a Notes database as an *object store*. It can store, organize, and retrieve any kind of data object.

It might be helpful to visualize a Notes database as an open box. Just as you can put any real-world object into an open box (if you have enough room in the box to accommodate the object), you can put any kind of data object in a Notes database.

Each Notes database is made up of several building blocks:

- Documents
- Forms
- Subforms
- Navigators
- Views
- Folders
- Fields
- Shared forms
- Actions
- Layout regions
- Agents
- Access control lists

Understanding Documents

The basic data storage units in a Notes database are documents. These correspond loosely to records in a relational database (see the following note). Each document holds one or more items that store a variety of data types: text, numbers, dates, images, sound, and so on.

All the information that applies to one specific entry in the database is stored in a document. For example, if you are using a contact management database, one document in the database might hold information such as the company name, contact name, customer address, customer phone, and how many times you have contacted the customer. Each individual customer would have his or her own document.

Each document can hold virtually any amount of information, from a single character to several pages of text and graphics. The size is limited only by the amount of available disk space (up to 4G!). This practical lack of size limitations is in direct contrast to relational databases, where field and record sizes are strictly defined in the database structure.

> **Note**
>
> Relational databases store information by breaking it down into individual data elements and maintaining it in tabular fashion (think of a spreadsheet). Related data elements (fields) are grouped as rows in the table, and related rows (records) are stored in the same table (database).
>
> Because of this data-centric view, relational databases are transaction-oriented—meaning they reflect only the most current state of the data. For data in a relational database to be useful, the end user must be able to sort and query the data in various ways.

In conventional terms, a data-entry screen is called a *form* in Notes. Forms provide the structure of a document. For more information on documents, see Chapter 8, "Working with Documents."

Forms

Forms are templates that provide the format and layout when you enter data into new documents or when you display and edit data from existing documents. Each database must hold at least one form.

The designer decides which form will be used most and designates it as the default form. Each form is created by the designer and can hold static text, fields, graphics, buttons, hotspots, text links, and layout regions. You'll learn about these design elements in Chapter 11, "Designing Forms."

> **Note**
>
> It might be easier for you to understand Notes forms by thinking about preprinted paper forms. Each year, for example, the IRS has to collect certain information from you to guarantee that when April 15th rolls around, you have remitted the correct amount of income tax.
>
> To make it as easy as possible for you to give them this information and to ensure that they get this information, they provide the 1040 form. This form has instructions to help you fill in areas (fields) that group logically related information.
>
> If the IRS did not provide these structured forms, they would face total chaos because there would be no consistency between the information from one taxpayer and the next. Notes forms work exactly the same way.

When you choose the Create menu to create a new document, Notes presents a list of forms that are available in the selected database (see Figure 3.5). You must choose a form from that list before you can enter data. When a form is selected, it is displayed. You can begin to enter data into the fields on the form.

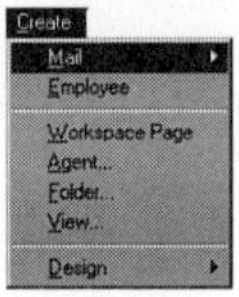

Fig. 3.5   The Create menu in the Employee database.

When you save the document, Notes stores the name of the form used to create the document in a special field named Form. The next time the document is accessed, Notes examines the contents of the Form field to determine which form should be used to display the document.

If no form name is found, the document is displayed using the default form. If no default document has been created and the form cannot be located, you get an error message and the document cannot be opened. In this case, contact your administrator.

> **Note**
>
> Documents can be displayed using any form in the database; however, this can cause a great deal of confusion because fields in the form might not align with items in the document. Data that the end user expects to see might not be displayed, and data the end user is not expecting might be displayed instead.

Subforms

Subforms are a new feature of Notes databases that make designing databases faster and easier. A subform is a mini-form that can be inserted into a form and can hold any valid Notes design element.

Because it can be shared among multiple forms in a database, the subform allows the designer to work from one location and avoid updating several elements. In addition, subforms can be dynamically inserted into forms, based on conditions a developer specifies.

For example, if an end user chooses certain values, you might display a subform with fields x, y, and z. Otherwise, the subform with fields 1, 2, and 3 would be inserted. The use of subforms makes Notes databases more flexible, modular, and maintainable, because you can keep the design elements in the subform from one place.

Layout Regions

Layout regions are a cool new feature of Notes databases that allow designers to build more intuitive, windows-standard databases. In a nutshell, a layout region can be put in a form or subform to provide a fixed region. This region can hold graphics, custom interface elements, and fixed fields. For more information on layout regions and their use, see Chapter 11, "Designing Forms."

Navigators

To make Notes databases more end user-friendly and visually appealing, Lotus added a new design feature called a *navigator*. A navigator is a tool that allows end users to graphically manipulate Notes databases.

If you have used Notes 4.x at all, you most likely have seen navigators. A good example is your mailbox (see Figure 3.6). In your mailbox, Lotus has built an intuitive navigator. This allows you to click icons representing the mailbox's views and folders so you don't have to use the View menu.

Fig. 3.6   The standard navigator for 4.x mailboxes.

By default, all databases have a navigator that displays all the non-hidden views and folders in the database. You should familiarize yourself with this format.

However, Notes designers can build custom navigators that better represent the use of a Notes database and are more visually appealing than the magnifying glasses and folders that Notes displays in the default navigator.

Note

In most databases, designers use navigators for two basic reasons. The first is to supplement or replace the View menu. Views and folders can be set to not display in the View menu and the user will only be able to access a view or folder for the navigator. If you can't find a view or folder that you expect to see, be sure to launch the default navigator and see whether it's shown there.

Second, navigators provide a main menu or menu system that allows end users to navigate through the entire database graphically.

Views

For the individual data elements in Notes documents to be useful information, they must be organized meaningfully for the end user and they must be easily accessible. Views and folders organize the data and allow you to navigate through it. (Folders are discussed in the following section.)

Each database must have a minimum of one view. The designer designates as the default whichever view is most likely to be used. This view is displayed the first time each new database is opened. The ability to build and use several views and folders gives the end-end user tremendous flexibility when working with Notes documents.

> **Note**
>
> Notes keeps track of the last view opened and displays this view each time the database is opened. This view is not displayed if you use the View menu to choose a different view before opening the database or if the designer has set the database to autolaunch a navigator that also displays a view.

If you have not yet opened the database, you can use the <u>V</u>iew menu to select any view created for the database you are using (see Figure 3.7). If you have opened the database, you can use the <u>V</u>iew menu or the Navigator to select a view. Keep in mind that like every element in Notes, views can be secured so that only users explicitly granted access can use them.

Fig. 3.7   The View menu for the Employee database before it has been opened.

Once you have opened a view, three things happen: The documents selected by the view are displayed in the view pane, the view title will have a checkmark displayed beside it in the <u>V</u>iew menu to show that it is in use, and in the navigator, the view in use is denoted by a blue magnifying glass rather than a yellow one.

> **Note**
>
> Be aware that as the database grows in the number and size of documents it stores, the views take more time to open.

Each view has a selection formula (created by the designer) that tells the view which documents to display. Some views have a selection formula to select and display all the documents in the database. Other views have selection formulas that select only a subset of the documents, based on some criteria.

For instance, a view in a sales tracking database might select only orders for which the total sale price is greater than $50,000. View-selection formulas allow the designer to create customized views.

Generally, each row in a view represents a document. However, this is not always the case. In order to help organize information in a view, some rows may be categories meaning that when you click a category, it will expand and show documents that fall into that category. Documents are categorized based on criteria that the view designer designates. In Notes 4.5, most developers use "twisties" (a small blue triangle) to indicate categories. We'll cover this in more detail later in this chapter. In addition, the enhanced features of Notes 4.5 views allow documents to span multiple rows so that more information can be displayed. Each column in the view can either display data from a field in the document or use a formula to compute a value to display.

As you can see in the view pane of Figure 3.8, several columns display data from each employee document in the database. The leftmost column in the view is a special feature in Notes views and folders called the *marker column*.

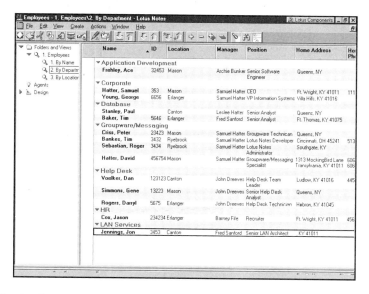

Fig. 3.8   The Employees by Department view.

The marker column displays a variety of system information and is separated from the other columns in the view by a thin gray line that extends the length of the view. If you delete a document, for instance, you see a small blue trash can icon in this column. If you have not read a document, a star is displayed in this column.

Note

The designer chooses the icons that are displayed in columns in the views and folders. The designer also chooses the colors that indicate different aspects of a view or folder, such as unread documents. The icons that appear in the view marker column cannot be changed in this version of Notes.

Table 3.2 summarizes the contents of the Employees by Department view.

Notes Basics

Table 3.2   Summary of the Employees by Department View in the Employee Database

Column	Description	Sorted	Categorized
Department	Displays the contents of the field Department.	Department	Yes
Name	Has a formula that puts the last name before the first name so that this column can be sorted by last name.	Last name	No
ID#	Displays the contents of the EmployeeIDfield.	No	No
Location	Displays employee's work.	No	No
Location.Manager	Displays the employee's manager.	No	No
Position	Displays the employee's title.	No	No
Home Address	A concatenated field that displays the contents of the Address, Apt#, City, State, and Zip code fields.	No	No
Home Phone/Fax	A concatenated field that displays the contents of the phone and fax fields.	No	No

An outstanding new feature of Notes 4.5 views and folders is the ability to dynamically resize columns, unless this feature has been explicitly disabled by the designer. To resize columns in any view or folder, simply click the line separating any two columns, drag it sideways until the column reaches the width you want, then release the mouse button.

Another great new feature available when you are designing views is the option to allow end users to dynamically change the sort order of a column. If a column has this feature enabled, you see either a small up arrow, a down arrow, or both in the column header.

The up arrow means that you can sort the column in ascending order. The down arrow means that you can sort the column in descending order.

If both arrows are present, you can toggle back and forth between ascending and descending order. To use this feature, simply click one of the arrows, and the view is re-sorted in the order you want.

Additionally, Notes views allow the designer to configure column headers to launch another view. If this feature is enabled, you see a long arrow pointing up. When you click this arrow, a new view is displayed.

Some other nice additions to 4.x views are Multi-line rows, Shrink rows to content, Alternate row colors, and Multi-line headings, among others.

Multi-line rows allow columns with large amounts of data to wrap on to the next line. When coupled with shrink rows to content, Multi-line rows make the rows only as large as needed to fit the data being displayed. This is an effective way to display data.

Alternate row colors can also help differentiate rows by displaying a different color for each row, dramatically increasing readability. Multi-line headings allow the designer to use much more descriptive column headings without sacrificing horizontal space in a view.

This is all very nice, but what can a view really do for you? A view allows you to find, organize, and manipulate documents. When you open a view, a document is automatically selected.

This is either the first document in the view, the last document in the view, or the document you last selected when using the view. The selected document is highlighted by the *selection bar.*

> **Note**
>
> The selection bar is usually black. The designer chooses the colors for various aspects of the view or folder such as the view or folder background, the text of each column, and unread documents. To make the information displayed in the view or folder easy to read, Notes automatically chooses a contrasting color for the selection bar.

You can use several methods to select a document in a view or folder. You can use the mouse and scroll bars to navigate through the documents, then click the document you want to use. You can also use the cursor keys to move the selection bar to the document you want, or you can use the navigation SmartIcons.

> **Tip**
>
> If the first column of a view or folder is sorted, you can just type in the first few characters of the item you want to find. Notes displays a Quick Search dialog box that allows you to find documents in the view. When you enter the search term, Notes moves to the first document that matches whatever characters you have typed in.
>
> For instance, if you are using a view that displays all of your customers' names sorted alphabetically by last name and you are looking for Philip Krezewicz, typing "Krez" should be enough to move you to the right document.

When you select the document you want, you can open the document (to read or edit), print the document, or delete the document. The next few sections cover each of these topics in detail.

The designer, with the system end users, decides which data elements from the underlying documents should be displayed and how they should be organized. In most databases, many views are created so that end users can easily navigate through the database using whatever information they find most useful.

For instance, in the contact management example, you might have the following three views:

■ **Contacts by Company**—Displays all the customer documents in the database, sorted and categorized by company name and contact name.

■ **Contacts by State**—Displays all the customer documents in the database, sorted and categorized by state and then by company name.

■ **Complaints by Customer**—Displays all the complaint documents in the database, sorted by customer.

By selecting different views, the end user can examine different "snapshots" of the data. In fact, a view need not display all the documents in the database. A view named Calls This Week might only display a subset of customers that you spoke to this week, whereas a view named Calls Next Week might display all your calls scheduled for next week.

After using a database for some time, you might find that additional views and folders that are not currently part of the database design would help you navigate and manipulate the database. If other end users might also benefit from the use of these new views, you can have the designer create these views for you in the server copy of the database.

If these are views that others are unlikely to use, you can build private views. Private views can sort and display the information you want to see. But these views are inaccessible by other end users.

Note

Shared and Shared Private on First Use views are stored as part of the database design. They can be replicated with other database design elements and data. Private views, on the other hand, are not stored as part of the database. They are stored in an individual end user's DESKTOP.DSK file. See Chapter 2, "Customizing Notes," for more details on DESKTOP.DSK.

Folders

Folders are a cool new feature of Notes 4.5 and are very much like views. The difference between folders and views is that folders do not need selection formulas. Instead, you move documents into and out of folders.

Folders are an easy way to organize documents by subject matter (or any other criteria) and allow you to maintain a much smaller subset of documents than you could in a categorized view.

For example, you are the manager of the Technical Services department. You often use a view that selects all 2,200 documents in an employee database and is categorized by the department field.

Even though you are only interested in the Technical Services employees, you still have to deal with other documents in the view. You could create a folder called Tech Services, select your employees in a view, and drag them into the Tech Services folder. This would be a smaller, faster, more manageable subset of data to work with.

In the view shown in Figure 3.9, a company's departments are organized into categories such as Application Development, Corporate, Help Desk, and Human Resources (HR). These categories are not documents and you cannot open them as you could open documents. You can, however, perform operations on them.

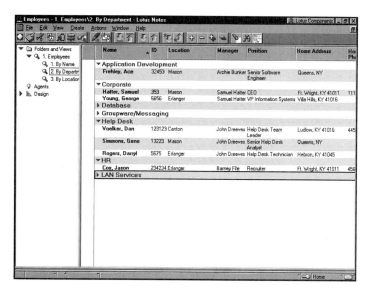

Fig. 3.9   The Employees By Department view categorized on Department.

Note

In most views, category titles stand out from document titles in boldface and are displayed with a *twistie* (small blue arrow) to indicate expandability/collapsibility. However, it is up to the designer to configure these options.

In Figure 3.9, you can see documents listed under each category. These categories are *expanded.*

Note

In Notes R3, most designers made the first column in a view display a plus sign (+) when the category is collapsed (when there are documents beneath the category that are not displayed) and a minus sign (–) when the category is expandable. In Notes R4.5, a twistie indicates a category.

You can click the twistie to expand and collapse the category. A twistie that points right rather than down indicates a collapsed category, whereas a twistie pointing down indicates an expanded category.

To help reduce information overload, you can temporarily limit the amount of information displayed in a view by collapsing a category. When you double-click the name of the category, all of the documents in that category disappear.

Alternatively, you can select the category and press the minus key (–). You can select the category and choose View, Expand/Collapse, Collapse Selected Level. Or you can use the View Collapse SmartIcon. The documents themselves aren't deleted from the database, but Notes stops displaying them while the category is collapsed.

> **Note**
>
> Categories are not documents—they act only as headings so that documents can be logically grouped together. If you click the twistie beside (or double-click) any of the categories in a view, you expand or collapse that category. Categorization is a feature that the designer builds into views and folders to increase their usefulness.

If you are only interested in employees in the Application Development department, for example, you can collapse the HR and Advanced Systems categories so that only employees in the Application Development department are displayed. You can later expand the other categories—that is, make the employees in other departments reappear—by double-clicking the other category names.

Alternatively, you can expand the other categories by selecting them and pressing the plus key (+). You can select them and choose View, Expand/Collapse, Expand Selected Level. Or you can use the View Expand SmartIcon.

If you are working with a view or folder that has dozens of categories and you're interested in only one, collapse all the categories. You can do this by choosing View, Collapse All; by pressing the Shift and minus (–) keys simultaneously; or by using the View Collapse All SmartIcon. Then double-click (or use any of the previously mentioned methods) the one category you want to expand.

Similarly, you can expand all the categories by choosing View, Expand All; by pressing the Shift and plus (+) keys simultaneously; or by using the View Expand All SmartIcon.

The capability to quickly expand and collapse categories in views and folders makes data much easier to work with.

Viewing the Database: Views, Folders, and Categories

As discussed briefly in Chapter 1, "Getting Started with Lotus Notes," the way you interact with Notes databases in Release 4.5 has been significantly overhauled. In Notes 3.x, when a database was opened, it immediately displayed a view window that showed either the most recently used view or the default view for the database if that was the first time the database was opened.

The new end user interface provides *panes*—a series of smaller windows that work together to provide easy navigation through views and folders. (Views and folders are discussed in more detail in the following sections.)

Figure 3.10 displays information from the Employee database. You can see that rather than one large view window, the screen is split into three window panes separated by gray lines. Each of these panes has a distinct and useful function:

- The leftmost pane on the top displays the navigator pane (a hierarchical structure of graphic objects that represent parts of the database), a feature that is new to Lotus Notes 4.x.

- To the right of the navigator pane, you can see the view pane, which is not new but has been redesigned and enhanced. The view pane displays data from documents in the database that are selected by folders and views (folders and views are covered in detail in the following sections).

- Below the navigator pane and the view pane, you can see the preview pane, another new feature of Notes 4.x. The preview pane enables you to view the contents of a document without opening it, which can save time and effort.

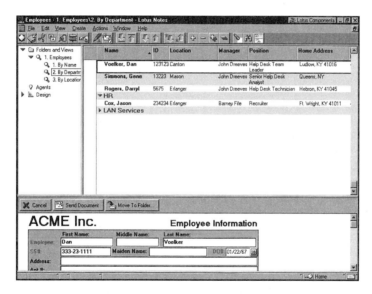

Fig. 3.10 The various panes of the Notes 4 database interface.

Each of these panes can be resized to suit your taste. The navigator and preview panes can be hidden if you don't find them useful, or want to use the screen in other ways.

Using the Pane Navigator. The default pane navigator is easy to use. It has graphical icons and presents your choices in a hierarchical structure that can be expanded or collapsed. The folder at the top of the tree represents folders and views.

You click this icon to expand a diagram of the folders and views available in the database. Each folder or subfolder is represented by a folder icon, and each view is represented by a magnifying glass. The currently selected icon turns blue; all other icons remain yellow.

Previewing Documents with the Preview Pane. The preview pane is another completely new feature of Notes. It allows you to select a document in a view or folder, and to save time by viewing the contents of the document without opening the document. You can scan through a database quickly using this tool.

The preview pane is flexible. It can be resized and placed in a variety of on-screen locations. To change the placement of the preview pane, choose View, Arrange Preview. Then click the button that corresponds to the placement you want.

Another database property can be used to set the preview pane location. Simply choose File, Database Properties (or right-click the database and choose Properties) to display the database Infobox. Click the Launch tab, and then click the Preview Pane Default button to change the default location.

> **Note**
>
> You can disable the preview pane if you don't find it useful. The View, Document Preview menu option works like a toggle switch to enable and disable the preview pane. If a checkmark is visible next to this menu option, the preview pane is displayed mid-screen. Alternatively, you can double-click the bar that separates the view pane and preview pane, or you can click and drag the separator bar to resize the preview pane to the desired size.

Fields

After you select a form using Create, Notes displays an empty document. Throughout the document, you see fields in which you can enter data. Most documents have several fields, which you can think of as the blanks on a paper form.

> **Note**
>
> The number, data type, and placement of fields within a form are determined by the designer.

On Notes forms, editable field boundaries are delineated by small, gray, square brackets. Normally, each field has a label that explains what data should be entered into the field.

> **Tip**
>
> If the designer has included field help (a useful feature to help guide end users when entering data), you might find additional information about the data expected in the field and the field's use by choosing View, Show, Field Help.

You can move the cursor from field to field using the directional arrows or the Tab key, or by clicking in whichever field you want the cursor located. If you are working in a rich text field, you cannot use the Tab key to move to the next field. See the later section "Rich Text Fields," for details.

Like most databases, Notes has a variety of data types for fields. You might encounter a mixture of different data types when working with fields inside a Notes form. Figure 3.11 shows a sample form named Employee Information. This form holds many different data types.

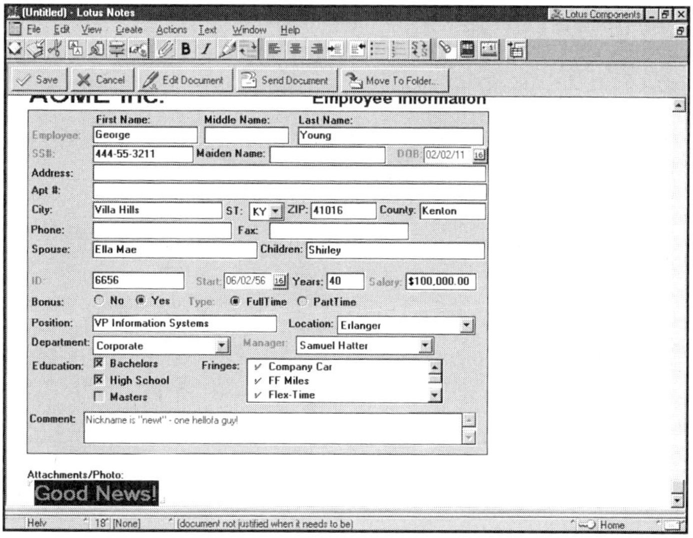

Fig. 3.11   Fields on the Employee form.

The available field types are described in the following sections.

Text Fields. The text data type can be used to store alphanumeric data (essentially any character) that will not be used mathematically. Text fields, the most common type, can hold a large amount of information (up to 15K). In the document in Figure 3.11, Employee Name, SS#, ID#, Home Address, City, State, ZIP, and Phone are all text fields, as are most of the fields.

Tip

Numeric fields are needed only when the data values will be used in mathematical calculations. Data such as ZIP codes and phone numbers need not be stored in number fields because they normally are not used in calculations.

In addition, Notes allows designers to easily convert between data types. For more information, see "Function Reference by Category" in Chapter 14, "Working with Formulas," or Chapter 17, "LotusScript Basics."

Rich Text Fields. The rich text field (RTF) data type is similar to the text data type in that it stores alphanumeric data that will not be used mathematically. However, RTF is more flexible because it allows you to format the data.

For instance, you can change font features such as style, size, or color. You can format text, insert objects from other applications, insert file attachments, and display graphics.

In Figure 3.11, Attachments/Photo is a rich text field. Notice that the phrase "Good News" is larger than the surrounding text.

Because they can display any type of information, rich text fields cannot be displayed in views. In most cases, they cannot be used in formulas. Chapter 11, "Designing Forms," discusses rich text fields in more detail.

> **Tip**
>
> According to the Lotus Notes Application Developer's Reference, you should use rich text fields when your data meets any of the following conditions: "includes pictures or graphs, pop-ups, buttons, or embedded objects; or if you want end users to use text attributes such as bold, italic, underlining, or color."

Keyword Fields. The keyword data type stores text but allows you to choose a value from a list of predefined choices. Generally, designers use a keyword field when they want to ensure that the data entered in a field is from an acceptable list of values or when they want to speed data entry.

Although keyword fields store the data as text, the items in the list do not have to consist of only text characters. For example, a list of possible household salary ranges could be <$10,000, $10,001-$20,000, $20,001-$40,000, $40,001-$60,000, >$60,000.

Three ways ways to present the list of keywords in a standard form are standard keywords, checkboxes, or radio buttons. If you are using a layout region, you can choose to display the list using a combo box, list box, radio buttons, or checkboxes. The following short sections describe each method.

> **Tip**
>
> Checkboxes are square; radio buttons are round. Checkboxes are not mutually exclusive: You can select as many checkboxes as you want. Radio buttons, on the other hand, are mutually exclusive: You can select only one button in a group of radio buttons.

Standard Keywords. When using a standard keyword field, which is not an option inside a Layout Region, you can choose only one of the values in the list. When the cursor is positioned on such a field, repeatedly pressing the space bar displays each possible value in turn.

You can also press the first letter of the item you want, such as P for Programmer, and Notes fills in the rest of the word. If you want to see a list of all possible selections in a keyword field, put the cursor in the field and press Enter.

Or if the designer has enabled it (the default setting), you can click the Entry Helper button (the small, gray down arrow button next to the field). Notes displays the Select Keywords dialog box.

If you want to change the field value to one of the values listed in the dialog box, you can select an item from the list and then press Enter (or choose OK).

> **Note**
>
> Most keyword fields present you with a fixed set of values and you are expected to choose one value from the list. The designer can, however, allow you to enter something other than one of the predefined selections or allow you to select multiple items from the list.
>
> If a keyword field has been designed to allow new values, the Keywords dialog box contains an input box into which you can enter new text. If the keyword field accepts multiple values, you can use the mouse to select several items from the list. Each is displayed in the field when the dialog box is closed.

Checkboxes. Fortunately, checkboxes work the same way regardless of their placement in a standard form or a Layout Region. If the designer has enabled the Checkbox option on a keyword field, you see a list of checkboxes.

Each checkbox represents one entry in the predefined list. By default, checkboxes are not mutually exclusive, so you can select one, several, or all of the boxes if you want them to apply.

For example, the Education field in Figure 3.11 lists four fringe benefits that the company provides. You can select whichever services the client uses.

An X appears in each box you select, indicating that the client uses that service. An empty checkbox indicates that the selection does not apply.

Radio Buttons. If the designer has enabled the Radio Buttons option, you see a list of radio buttons, so named because they work like the channel selector buttons on early car radios. Each button represents one item in the list, and you must choose one of several mutually exclusive items.

In the Type field in Figure 3.11, for example, you can specify the type of employee. Selecting a button causes a black dot to appear in the button, and whichever button was previously selected is automatically deselected (the black dot disappears).

List Box. List boxes should be familiar to Windows end users because they are common in Windows applications. A list box displays a scrollable box, holding the list of valid choices.

In some instances, you can choose more than one item. This is decided by the designer. The Fringes field in Figure 3.11 is an example of a list box.

Combo Box. A combo box control should also be familiar to most Windows end users. It is displayed as a text field and a small gray button with a black down arrow. When you click the button, a list of valid options "drops down," and the end user can select a value.

In addition, the end user positions the cursor in the field and types the first letter of any valid entry to index to the first entry in the list that begins with the typed letter. In Figure 3.11, the State, Department, Manager, and Location fields are examples of combo boxes.

> **Note**
>
> Combo boxes and List boxes are special new design elements that can be displayed only in Layout regions, which means that if the database designer elects not to use layout region, you'll never see these elements. For more information about layout regions, see that section earlier in this chapter, or see Chapter 11, "Designing Forms."

Time/Date Fields. The time/date data type enables you to enter a time or date in a field. If the value you enter is not a valid time or date value, Notes prompts you to enter a valid one. In Figure 3.11, the Hired field holds the date that employee was hired.

Numeric Fields. The number data type expects a numeric value (0–9) such as the number of employees in a company or the number of calls made to a customer. If a value entered in a number field is not a number, Notes prompts you to enter a valid value.

The form in Figure 3.11 has two number fields: Salary and Years. (The field with a phone number cannot be a number field because it has nonnumeric characters such as parentheses, spaces, and dashes.)

Names Fields. The three names data types are author names, reader names, and names. Each one has a special function when used on a Notes form, as explained in the following sections.

> **Note**
>
> Author names and reader names fields do not override the access control list (ACL) for a database. They can only refine it.
>
> For instance, if your name is in a ReaderNames field in a document but the ACL grants you "No Access," you can't read the document. Also, if you are in the Group "Testers" and have Editor access to a database but you are not in the ReaderNames field in a document, you can read it but not edit it.

Author Names. The author names data type has a text list of Notes names (end user names, group names, and access roles) that determine who can edit a document. When you use an author names field in a document, it creates a special field in the document named $UpdatedBy.

If you have a minimum of reader access to the database and your end user name appears in the author names field in a document, you can edit that document. Otherwise, you can read but not edit the document.

If an author names field is created and no one is named in the field, only those with editor access or higher can edit the document. Author names fields work with other Notes security features such as ACLs and reader names fields (discussed next) to provide additional database security.

In Figure 3.10, the document's Created By field is an example of an author names field.

> ### Tip
>
> You can click and hold an author names field in read or edit mode of any document to determine who has editor access to the document.

Reader Names. The reader names data type expects a text list of Notes names (end user names, group names, server names, and access roles) that determine who can read a document. If a document has a reader names field and no one is named in it, anyone with reader access or higher can read the document.

This is the opposite of the way author names fields work. If your end user name appears in the reader names field in a document, you can read that document.

Otherwise, you can't read the document, though it may still appear in categorized views. Reader names fields work with other Notes security features such as ACLs and author names fields to provide additional database security.

Names. The names data type can hold a text list of Notes names (end user names, group names, server names, and access roles). A names field is useful when you want to store or display a list of end user names but not to assign access rights to a document.

In a names field, end user names are displayed in abbreviated format—for example, Dave Hatter/Entex. But they are stored in canonical format—for example, CN=Dave Hatter/0=Entex.

Sections. The section data type specifies an area on a form that allows controlled access to an area of a form. For example, you might have a workflow application in which only certain end users should be able to read and edit certain data on the form.

With controlled access sections, you can determine which end users can do this. In Notes R4.x, you can now use collapsible sections. These allow designers to save space on a form by "hiding" information in a collapsible section so end users see the information only if they want to. This advanced field type is covered more in "Editable Field Formulas" in Chapter 11, "Designing Forms."

Field Types. When defining a field, you not only define the type of data it can hold. You also have the following choices for each field: editable, computed, noneditable, computed for display, and computed when composed. The following sections examine the benefits and drawbacks of each of these options.

Editable Fields. An editable field can be any data type. It is stored in the document when the document is saved. The end user enters the value for an editable field from the keyboard. Or the designer develops formulas (you learn more about formulas in Chapter 14, "Working with Formulas") to provide a default value that the end user can change.

When an editable field is displayed on a form, it is delineated with small gray brackets, unless the data type is set to RTF, in which case the brackets are red. An example of an editable field is a field named PhoneNumber in which the end user enters a phone number from the keyboard.

Computed Fields. The value of a computed field is calculated by formulas that the designer develops. The end user cannot change the value of a computed field (unless the formulas in the field are based on end user input data). But this value is recalculated each time a document is edited, refreshed, or saved.

Computed fields (those composed and computed for display fields) can be used with all data types except RTF. No brackets are shown around these fields because the end user cannot directly change the value. When the end user saves the document, the value of the computed fields is saved.

An example of using a computed field is a field that reads the end user name from your Notes ID and stores it in a field named ModifiedBy each time the document is saved. This tracks the person who last modified the document. Another example is a field named ModifiedDate that reads the system date and time the document was last modified and stores it when you save the document.

Computed for Display Fields. The value of a computed for display field is calculated by formulas that the designer develops. The end user cannot change the value of such a field, and its value is recalculated each time a document is edited or refreshed.

The difference between computed and computed for display fields is that the values in a computed for display field are not saved in the document (which means they cannot be displayed in views). You use a computed for display field to display data to the end user that can be easily computed, changes frequently, and does not need to be displayed in a view. If all of these conditions are true, there is no reason to save values so you save precious disk space.

Computed When Composed Fields. The value of a computed when composed field is calculated by formulas that the designer develops. The end user cannot change the value of such a field, and its value is calculated only when the document is composed. This value is never recalculated. When the document is saved, all computed when composed fields are also saved.

An example of a use for this type of field is a field named CreatedBy that reads the end user name from the Notes ID in use when a document is composed and stores that field when the document is saved.

Shared Fields

Shared Field is similar to fields, but allows you to make your applications more modular because you can create the field definition once and use it in any of the forms in a database. For example, you might create a computed when composed field named `CreatedBy` that stores the name of the user who created the document. You could then share the field and use it in every form in the database rather than record it for each form. For more information about shared fields, see Chapter 11, "Designing Forms."

Agents

For those of you familiar with Notes R3, you most likely have worked with macros. Agents are the new and improved version of macros in Notes R4.x. Agents can work in the background to make things happen.

For example, an agent might automatically send mail, move documents into a folder, or search a database for a particular topic of interest. Custom agents created by designers or end users can perform more powerful functions, such as manipulating field values or retrieving data from external applications.

Whether you are an end user or a designer, agents can help you work more effectively and efficiently. For more information on agents, see Chapter 16, "Buttons and Agents."

Actions

The best way to think of actions is as small "code snippets" that can automate tasks in Notes databases. Actions can be used in forms, views, folders, and navigators. They are easy to create (in fact, Lotus was kind enough to add a number of predefined Simple Actions) and they can make using a Notes database much easier. For more information on actions, see Chapter 16, "Buttons and Agents."

Understanding Access Control Lists

When working with a database, you might discover that you can't do all possible operations. Each database has a manager who is responsible for that database. One of the manager's responsibilities is setting an ACL so that data security and integrity are maintained.

ACLs are a powerful feature of Notes. In Notes 4.x, database ACLs can be enforced on local databases to ensure that data remains secure for remote users.

The ACL performs three functions related to database access:

- Defines who has access to a given database (the list can hold user names, server names, group lists, and database roles).

- Defines what the users can do to the database.

- Defines groups for refined access to specific forms and views.

Only the database manager (or any user with Manager access) can manipulate the ACL. On the list, the manager arranges all users into one of the seven access levels shown in Table 3.3.

Users at each level can do only certain tasks. The list can include group names so that the manager can assign the same access privileges to an entire department or workgroup with just one entry, which greatly reduces maintenance.

Note

Throughout this book, when you read instructions for performing operations, you should keep in mind that Notes may not allow you to proceed if the database manager hasn't placed you at the access level for that operation.

Table 3.3   Notes Access Levels

Category	Tasks Allowed
No Access	Cannot access the database.
Depositor	Can create new documents but cannot edit, delete, or read existing documents, even those you created.
Reader	Can read documents but cannot create, edit, or delete documents.
Author	Can create, read, edit, and possibly delete your own documents; can read documents created by other users.
Editor	Can create, edit, read, and possibly delete documents (this is a suboption that can be toggled off or on for each user), including those created by other users.
Designer	Has same access rights as the Editor level and can also create, edit, or delete design elements such as forms and views.
Manager	Has complete access to all facets of the database, including the ability to delete it from the hard disk and to change the ACL.

Your assigned access level can (and probably will) vary from one database to another, because the manager for each database decides what level you should have. Consider the following examples:

- For a database holding sales reports, you have Author access. This allows you to create new sales reports and to change them later. In addition, you can read sales reports entered by other users but you cannot edit them.

- For a database handling suggestions, comments, and complaints, you have Depositor access. You can add new suggestions to the database but cannot read or edit them once they have been saved, much like an anonymous comments box hanging on the wall.

- For a database holding technical support material, you have Editor access. This allows you to add new documents, edit documents that you have created, and also edit documents that others have created.

- For a strategic plans database, unless you are an executive, you might be assigned No Access. At this level, you cannot even open the database.

Notes also allows the designer to restrict access individually to particular forms, views, sections, and fields in a database. This allows a database manager to give you access to a database but to restrict you from accessing certain information. You learn more about this type of access control in Chapter 10, "Creating New Databases."

> **Tip**
>
> To find out what access level you have been granted to a specific database, open the database and look at the third block from the right on your status bar. It displays an icon representing your access level. You can click that area of the status bar for a textual description of your access level.

Changing the Database Settings

Notes allows you to fine-tune a database by manipulating the many "database" settings that you can access through the database property sheet of each database. For instance, you can compact the database and make it smaller, or you can create a full-text index so that searching the database is easier. By examining and learning the options available to you, you can exert a tremendous amount of control over each database.

To access the database settings for a database, choose File, Database, Properties; select a database by clicking it; click the Properties SmartIcon; or right-click and choose Database Properties. This displays the Database Properties InfoBox (see Figure 3.12).

Fig. 3.12   The Basics tab of the Database Properties InfoBox enables you to edit particular database information.

In Notes R4.5, this InfoBox allows you to use the tabs at the top of the box to select which settings you are interested in. The following sections describe the settings on each tab.

Basics Settings

The first tab, Basics, allows you to view and edit some primary database information, including the following:

- **Database Title**—This is the title displayed on the database icon and in the File Open dialog box. If necessary, you can change the title.

- **Database Filename**—This is the name associated with the database file at the operating system level.

- **Server**—This is the name of the server on which the database resides. This is basically an FYI.

- **Replication History**—Click the Replication History button to view or clear the replication history for the database. Each time a database replicates successfully, this log is updated (this is covered in Chapter 24, "Notes: Under the Hood").

- **Replication Settings**—Click this button to view or edit the replication settings for the database (this is covered in Chapter 24, "Notes: Under the Hood").

- **The Database Type**—Use this combo box (if you have Manager access) to change the database type from Standard, which is the default, to Library, Address Book Personal Journal. As mentioned earlier, library databases can be used to store information on other databases of interest.

  Use the Personal Journal type for databases created with the Personal Journal (R4) template (JOURNAL4.NTF). A journal doesn't allow shared agents, folders, or views, since the database is meant for personal use.

  Use Address Book if you are creating a database that will be used as an Address Book of some type.

- **Encryption**—Click the Encryption button to encrypt the local copy of this database and thereby enforce local security. Encryption provides very tight security but causes a modest performance hit. Encryption is covered in more detail in Chapter 22, "Security and Encryption."

- **Disable Background Agents for This Database**—This checkbox, when selected, disables and schedules agents for this database. If you create or enable any default agents in a database, they do not run when this option is turned on. You learn more about agents in Chapter 16, "Buttons and Agents."

- **Allow Use of Stored Forms in This Database**—This option allows you to determine whether you want documents that have forms stored in them to be displayed with the stored form (default action) or to be displayed with form resident in the database. This can be useful when documents are mailed into a database.

Information Settings

The Information tab displays the following information about the database (see Figure 3.13):

- **The size of the database in kilobytes.**

- **The number of documents in the database**.

- **The date the database was created.**

- **The date the database was last changed.**

- **The replica ID of the database.** This is a very important piece of information that you learn about later in this chapter and in Chapter 24, "Notes: Under the Hood."

- **% Used.** This button displays the amount of space in the database that is being used to store data. When this number drops below 100 percent (which it frequently does), "white space" or free space is not being used in the database. When this number drops below 90 percent, you should compact the database to free the white space.

- **Compact.** This button can free unused white space by compacting the database, thus freeing up valuable disk space.

- **User Activity.** This button allows you to enable activity tracking (to log reads, writes, and updates to the database) or to view each user's activity in the database if tracking has been enabled. This can be a powerful troubleshooting tool but does add overhead to the database.

And at the bottom of the property sheet, a message is displayed to indicate which Notes clients are legally authorized to use the chosen database and by whom they were authorized.

Fig. 3.13   The Information tab of the Database Properties InfoBox.

Print Settings

The Print tab (identified by the printer icon on the tab) allows you to set options for printing documents and views. These options apply globally across a database and do not replicate with other copies of the database (see Figure 3.14):

- **Header**—The Header radio button allows you to add a header to the top of each document when it is printed. You can select the text box below to enter a standard header. The graphic buttons below the text box allow you to insert a page number, date, time, tab, and document title (which defaults to the form name), respectively, so you can dress up the header.

- **Footer**—The Footer radio button works exactly like the Header except that a footer is added to the bottom of a document when printed.

- **Font, Size, and Style**—Each of these list boxes allow you to apply various formatting options to the header and footer.

- **Print header and footer on first page**—This checkbox does exactly what it says: It prints the header and footer on the first page.

Fig. 3.14   The Print tab of the Database Properties InfoBox.

For example, you can insert a header or footer (discussed in more detail later in this chapter), or change the header and footer fonts that are sent to the printer.

Design Settings

The fourth tab, Design, displays information that concerns designers, such as the Inherit design from templates checkbox and the Database is a template checkbox (see Figure 3.15). These settings are covered in detail in Chapter 10, "Creating New Databases."

> **Caution**
>
> You should not change any of these settings unless you are absolutely certain that you understand what you are doing. These settings can have deleterious effects on the selected database as well as on other databases!

- **Design is/is not hidden**—This is static text that tells you if the database design is locked out from changes. This is an advanced feature that allows designers to prevent changes to the underlying database code.

- **Inherit design from template**—When this option is enabled, you can use the Template Name text field immediately below to choose a database template on which the current database should base its design. This feature is covered in more detail in Chapter 10, "Creating New Databases."

- **Database is a template**—When this option is enabled, you can use the Template Name text field immediately to the right to enter a template name for this database so that the design of the database can be propagated to other databases. This is covered in more detail in Chapter 10, "Creating New Databases."

- **List as "Advanced Template" in new database dialog**—This option allows you to show a database as an advanced template and is covered in more detail in Chapter 10, "Creating New Databases."

- **List in database catalog**—This option allows you to have the current database included in the database catalog. When the option is enabled, you can choose from the Categories field below the categories under which the database is displayed in the database catalog.

- **Show in open database dialog**—When this option is enabled, the current database is displayed in the File, Open, Database dialog box. If this option is deselected, the database is displayed in the list, although users can still access it if they know the path and file name.

- **Include in multi-database indexing**—When this option is enabled, you can index the database with other databases for cross-database, full-text searching.

Fig. 3.15   The Design tab of the Database Properties InfoBox.

Launch Settings

The fifth tab, Launch, displays checkboxes offering choices that allow you to change what happens each time a database is opened (see Figure 3.16):

- **On Database Open**—Allows you to specify what happens when the user opens the database. The following table shows each option and a description of what it does.

Choice	Description
Restored as last viewed by user	Opens the database exactly as it was when the user last used it.
Open About database document	Opens the About document each time the database is opened.
Open designated navigator	Opens a selected navigator each time the database is opened.
Open designated navigator in its own window	Opens a selected navigator in its own window.
Launch 1st attachment in About database document	Launches or opens the first attachment stored in the About document.
Launch 1st doclink in About database document	Launches or opens the first doclink stored in the About document.

- **Show "About database" document is opened for the first time**—Allows you to decide if the About Database document is displayed upon the first opening of the database.

- **Show "About database" document if modified**—Allows you to automatically redisplay the modified About database document when the database is opened only if the About database document has been modified since the last opening of the database.

■ **Preview Pane Default button**—When you click this button, the resulting dialog box can be used to set the default location of the preview pane.

Fig. 3.16   The Launch tab of the Database Properties InfoBox.

Full-Text (Index) Settings

The Full Text tab provides the following buttons so you can create and change full-text indexes. These indexes help you search for information in the database (see Figure 3.17):

■ **Last Index Time**—Shows you the date and time the database was last indexed.

■ **Size**—Displays the size in kilobytes of the full-text index. Remember that this is additional disk space being used to store the full-text index.

■ **Update Index**—Allows you to create a new full-text index or update an existing index. If you are creating a new index, you are prompted for a variety of settings that allow you to control the size and effectiveness of the full-text index.

■ **Create Index**—Allows you to create a new full-text index.

■ **Delete Index**—Deletes a full-text index.

■ **Update Frequency combo box**—Allows you to choose how often server-based databases are reindexed. This setting only affects server-based databases. Local databases must be indexed manually.

■ **Count unindexed documents**—Displays the total number of documents in the database that have not been included in the index. You can use this statistic to determine when you need to update the index.

Fig. 3.17   The Full Text tab of the Database Properties InfoBox after you create an index.

In addition, this InfoBox displays other pertinent information about how the index was created, as described in the following table

Option	Description
Case-sensitive index	The first option allows you to create indexes that permit case-sensitive searches. However, this increases the size of the index and decreases the speed of the search.
Index Attachments	When enabled, this option allows you to index the contents of any attachments in any document so that you can search their contents as well. This is a powerful new feature but can add significantly to the size of the index.
Index encrypted fields	When enabled, this powerful new option allows you to index the contents of any encrypted fields.
Exclude words in "stop words" file	This option allows you to exclude from the index any words found in the stop words file. This greatly reduces the size of the index, speeds searches, and reduces the number of non-relevant hits. The stop words file contains common words such as "the" that could cause many hits you don't want. You can choose the default stop words file (default.stp) or a custom stop words file that you have built.
Index breaks	By default, "word breaks only" is chosen, which helps keep the size of the index down and allows you to search based on words found in documents. "Word, sentence, and paragraph" allows the additional flexibility to search for sentences and paragraphs as well as words, but adds significantly to the size of the database.

Working with Documents

Now that you know how to access a database and how its various parts work, you'll learn about creating, editing, and saving documents.

To open an existing document, simply select it in a view or folder, and double-click it. If you have Reader access to the database, the document is displayed on your screen in read mode.

This means you cannot edit it at this point (see Figure 3.18). An easy way to tell that a document is in read mode is that there are no brackets around fields or all the fields are grayed out, indicating that they are disabled.

In read mode, you can see all the data in the document, you can print the document, but you cannot edit it. To edit the document, press Ctrl+E. (You can use the Actions Edit Document SmartIcon if you have the appropriate access level.)

When the document is in edit mode, you can change any of the data elements to which you have access (see Figure 3.19). (You can see the small gray brackets around the editable fields in a standard form. In a Layout Region, all of the controls you are authorized to use will no longer be grayed out.)

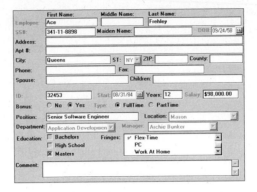

Fig. 3.18 An Employee document for Ace Frehley in read mode.

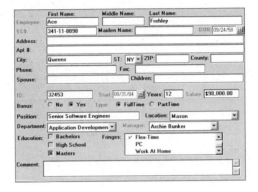

Fig. 3.19 Ace Frehley's employee document in edit mode.

To create a new document, choose <u>C</u>reate, which displays all available forms in the database (see Figure 3.20).

Fig. 3.20 A list of available forms for the Employee database.

As you can see from this figure, there is only one form in the Employee database: Employee. To create a new employee, choose <u>C</u>reate, Employee. A new document like the one shown in Figure 3.21 is created.

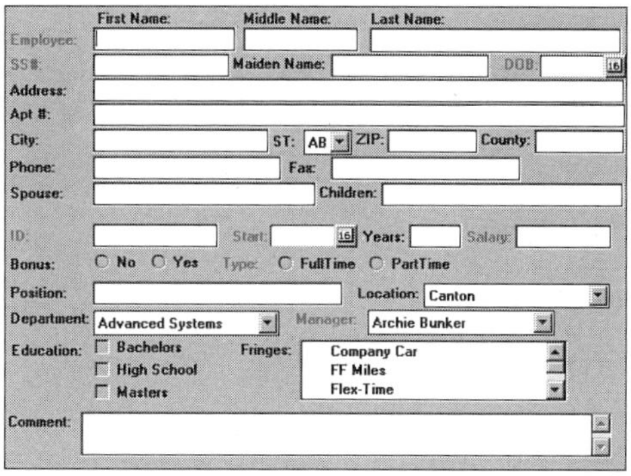

Fig. 3.21   A new Employee document.

Note

Remember that your ability to read and access documents is controlled by the ACL for each database. The ACL is set by the database manager.

You can now enter data in the document. Notice that the Created By and On fields have been set automatically by the system.

Saving and Closing Documents

Now that you know how to create and edit documents, you need to know how to save or cancel your changes. When you are finished reading or editing a document, you can save the document, save and close the document, or just close the document and discard the changes.

To save any Notes document, press Ctrl+S or use the File Save SmartIcon. This does not close the document but writes the data to disk.

To close a Notes document and return to the folder or view, do one of the following:

- Press Esc.

- Press Ctrl+W.

- Click the document window's Control-menu box and then choose _C_lose (the Control-menu box is the small application icon in the upper left corner of the window).

Note

You'll see two Control-menu boxes, one for Notes 4.x (in the upper left corner) and one for the window that is currently open in Notes, just below the program's Control-menu box. Make sure to click the view or folder's window. If you inadvertently click the Notes Control-menu box and then click Close, you will exit Notes.

■ Double-right-click anywhere in the document. This is a holdover from Notes 3.x and may not be enabled for your workstation. See Chapter 2, "Customizing Notes," to learn how to enable this feature.

Doing any of the actions listed previously causes Notes to check if you have made any changes to a document. If you have made changes, you are prompted with a dialog box like the one in Figure 3.22.

Fig. 3.22 The Notes File Save dialog box.

To save your changes, choose Yes. To close the document without saving changes, choose No. To avoid closing the document (and not saving the document), choose Cancel.

Closing a Database

To close a Notes database, first close any open documents by using one of the methods listed in the last section. Then follow the same steps you would use to close a document. Don't worry if you forget to save any changes you have made to open documents—you will be prompted to save the changes.

Copying a Database

You may need to make a copy of a Notes database. For instance, if you want to make an archive database that does not replicate with other databases (you learn about this in Chapter 24, "Notes: Under the Hood"), you need to make a new copy of the database. To do so, choose File, Database, New Copy.

Using this command to copy a database is like using the operating system to make a copy of the file, except that you get some additional choices about database elements you can copy to the new database. Figure 3.23 shows the dialog box you see after you choose to copy a database.

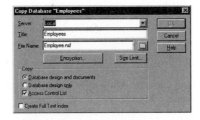

Fig. 3.23 The Copy Database dialog box.

You can choose a different server to get a copy of the database, give the copy a different title, and choose a filename for the new copy. In addition, you can copy all the documents and design elements (forms, views, and so on) or only the design elements.

You can also choose to copy or not to copy the ACL, regardless of the other selections you have made. Finally, you can secure local copies of the database and specify the maximum size of the database in kilobytes.

> ### Caution
>
> Each database has a replica ID, which is a unique identifier that allows it to replicate with other replica copies of the same database. (Replication is the process that synchronizes replica copies of Notes databases. You learn more about replication in "Understanding Notes Replication" in Chapter 24, "Notes: Under the Hood.")
>
> When you make a new copy of a database rather than a replica copy, the database gets a different replica ID, which means that the new copy will not replicate with other replica copies. If you want this new copy to replicate with other replicas of the same database, use the File, Replication, New Replica option rather than the New Copy option.

Deleting Database Icons and Databases

The two ways to delete a database from your workspace are

- Delete the database icon from your workspace.

- Delete the database permanently from your hard disk or server through Notes.

Anyone can delete a database icon from a work page, but only users with Manager access to a database can permanently delete a database from the hard disk. The following sections explain the differences between these two procedures.

Deleting Database Icons from Your Workspace

When you no longer need a database, you can delete it from your workspace without deleting the database file from the server or hard drive where it is stored. To do so, follow these steps:

1. Select the workspace on which the database resides, if it is not currently showing.

2. Click the database you want to remove. (Don't double-click or you'll open the database.)

3. To delete more than one database from the same workspace, Shift + click the other databases you want to delete (hold down the Shift key and then click the other database icons you want to select).

4. Press Del; or choose Edit, Clear; or click the Edit Clear SmartIcon.

5. Notes prompts you with a dialog box that asks if you are sure you want to delete these icons from your workspace (see Figure 3.24). If you are sure, choose Yes to delete the selected icon(s) from your workspace. If you have changed your mind, choose No.

Fig. 3.24   The Remove Database icon dialog box.

Deleting database icons does not actually delete the database file—it only removes the icon from your workspace. Any other users who access the database will still see the database icon on their workspaces and can still access the database. In fact, you can add the same database icon to your workspace again later.

Tip

After you delete database icons from your workspace, there are gaps where the icons used to be. You can fill in the gaps easily by dragging other database icons into these empty positions. Or you can choose View, Arrange Icons to have Notes rearrange the icons on that workspace so that all gaps are filled in.

Deleting a Database

If you have Manager access through the ACL for a given database, you can permanently delete the database file.

Caution

The following instructions tell you how to permanently delete a database and all its information from the hard disk where the file resides. If you do this on a database, all data in that database will be lost!

To permanently delete a database, do the following:

1. Click the database icon of the database you want to delete—this selects the database.

2. Choose File, Database, Delete. Notes prompts you with a dialog box informing you that you are about to permanently delete the database and asking if you are sure that's what you want to do (see Figure 3.25).

Fig 3.25   The Delete Database Warning dialog box.

3. Choose Yes to permanently delete the database from the server or hard drive, or choose No to cancel the deletion.

> **Caution**
>
> By default, you have Manager access to all Notes databases that are stored on your workstation. This includes important system databases such as your Mail database, your Notes Log database, and your Personal Name & Address Book database. You also have Manager access to your Mail database on the Notes server.
>
> There is no good reason to delete these databases because you will use these databases (particularly your Mail database) very often. You should not delete any of these databases without first seeking the advice of your Notes administrator.

Using the Universal Viewer

Notes 4.5 has a powerful and useful new feature named the Universal Viewer that allows you to view the contents of any file attachment, even if you do not have a copy of the application that originally created the file. In fact, you do not even need to know what application created the attachment. The Universal Viewer is smart enough to determine the file type (in most cases) and display it for you.

This can be handy when you get file attachments in a format you are unfamiliar with, when you don't have a licensed copy of the application that created the file, or when you want to quickly view or print the file without launching another application, which consumes memory and wastes time.

To invoke the Universal Viewer, double-click any file attachment. This displays the Attachment Properties InfoBox for the attachment (see Figure 3.26).

Fig. 3.26   You can choose one of five tabs in the Attachment Properties InfoBox.

Click the View button on the Information tab of the InfoBox to send the Universal Viewer into action. The file is displayed for you to look at. While the file is displayed, you can control a variety of display and print settings. To change any of the settings for the file, right-click to get a menu of options (see Figure 3.27).

Fig. 3.27   You have many options with the Universal Viewer.

The Print option displays a Print dialog box. From this dialog box, you can change various print settings and then send the document to the printer. The next menu section lists display options, which vary depending on the file format of the file being viewed.

For instance, when you right-click a Microsoft Word document, you see options that apply to the document display modes in Word. The Options option displays a cascading menu like the one shown in Figure 3.28, which allows you to change many aspects of how the file can be displayed, printed, and copied to the Clipboard.

Fig. 3.28 The Options menu of the Viewer pop-up menu.

If you choose Display, you see the Display Options dialog box, as shown in Figure 3.29. From there, you can change the default display font and decide how (or if) to display files that are unfamiliar to the Universal Viewer. You can choose More to reach additional options, such as how to display database and spreadsheet files.

Fig. 3.29 The Display Options dialog box.

The Print menu option displays the dialog box shown in Figure 3.30. This dialog box allows you to change a variety of printer output options, such as the printer font, the font used for the document header, whether or not a header prints, the page margins, and a name for the print job.

Much like the display options, you can choose More to reach additional options that control how certain types of files are printed. This causes the More Print Options dialog box to appear (see Figure 3.31).

For instance, you can print grid lines and cell headers for spreadsheets, grid lines and field names for databases, and borders for graphics files. In addition, when you print graphics files like bitmaps or drawings, they can be printed in their original size or scaled to fill the entire page.

Fig. 3.30   The Print Options dialog box.

Fig. 3.31   The More Print Options dialog box.

The Clipboard menu displays the Clipboard Option dialog box, which allows you to select a format to place on the Clipboard (see Figure 3.32). As you can see from the figure, there are a variety of format types for the Clipboard.

You can also change the Clipboard font. Choosing More displays another dialog box that allows you to change how database and spreadsheet files are copied to the Clipboard.

The Universal Viewer is a powerful utility that can save you time and effort when you need to deal with file attachments.

Fig. 3.32 The Clipboard Options dialog box.

Printing Documents and Views

Although Notes can bring the dream of a paperless office much closer, in reality we still need to print hard copies of information. Notes has flexibility when it comes to printing documents and views. You have several options for what should be printed:

■ Print a single document.

■ Print selected documents.

■ Print the entire view.

There are two ways to print a single document, each of which is slightly different:

■ Print a selected document from a view or folder.

■ Print an open document.

Printing a Selected Document from a View or Folder

If you are in a view or folder, you can select a document either by clicking it or by clicking in the view marker column (which puts a check in the view marker column). Then choose File, Print or click the File Print SmartIcon to display the dialog box shown in Figure 3.33.

Fig. 3.33 The File Print dialog box as displayed when a single document is chosen in a view.

The File Print dialog box allows you to control many aspects of printing, such as the following:

- Click <u>P</u>rinter to select a different printer from the one selected (this is displayed next to the printer icon) or to change the printer setup for a printer (the next section discusses specifying other printers).

- Choose Print range to set a range of pages in the document to be printed. This only applies to printing individual documents.

- Select the <u>D</u>raft quality checkbox to use lower-resolution printing, which speeds the printing process. This might be necessary if the selected printer does not have much memory.

- Use the <u>C</u>opies setting to indicate if you want multiple copies of the document printed.

- Select the <u>G</u>raphics scaled to 100% checkbox to print graphics at their original size.

The most important options in this dialog box are in the View options section and are described in the following text.

The selections in the View options section allow you to print only documents that you have selected or print the entire view. Notice that because only a single document was selected in the view, the Print selected documents radio button is selected by default. In addition, you can choose For<u>m</u> Override when printing documents to select a form for printing other than the form that the document was saved with.

Tip

The Form Override feature of Notes can be useful. For instance, if you use a database in which a form is designed to speed data entry but is not very attractive when printed, a separate form can be designed for printing. When you decide to print the document, use Form Override to select the form designed for printing, which ensures that the document is printed with the more attractive format.

Document separation allows you to choose from one of three options when printing multiple documents. The first option, Page Break between documents, allows you to eject a page and start printing the next document on a new page.

The second option, Extra Line, does not eject a new page. It inserts one blank line between each document to make the printout easier to read.

The final option, No Separation, provides no separation between documents. The next document in the queue will begin printing on the line immediately following the previous document. When you are printing only a single document, the Document separation options do not apply.

Finally, you can select the <u>R</u>eset page numbers checkbox, which works with the Page Break Document separation option to reset the page number to 1 for the first page of each document.

When you have made your selections, choose $\underline{O}$K to send the document to the printer.

> **Tip**
>
> If you want to see where the pages will break and words will wrap for a given document before you print, you can open the document and choose $\underline{V}$iew, $\underline{S}$how, Page $\underline{B}$reaks. A heavy black line is displayed wherever a page break will be inserted.

Printing the Open Document

The second way to print a selected document works for a document open in read or edit mode. Choose $\underline{F}$ile, $\underline{P}$rint, or use the File Print SmartIcon, and you get a slightly altered dialog box that has fewer choices than the dialog box you would see if you began in a view or folder (see Figure 3.34).

Fig. 3.34 The File Print dialog box for a single open document.

The dialog box in Figure 3.34 is essentially the same as the one you saw in Figure 3.33. The difference is that you are printing a single, open document rather than a document in a view or folder. As a result, there are no view options, you cannot select For$\underline{m}$ Override, and you cannot insert page breaks. Choose $\underline{O}$K to send the document to the printer.

Printing Selected Documents

Printing selected documents is like the first option for printing a single document. Open a view or a folder, then select multiple documents by clicking the view marker column next to each document you want to print (a small checkmark in the view marker column indicates that you have selected a document).

Once you have chosen all the documents to print, choose $\underline{F}$ile, $\underline{P}$rint, or use the File Print SmartIcon. You see the File Print dialog box (refer to Figure 3.34). Your options are the same as when printing a single document, but the View options and Document separation selections take on new importance.

Make sure that the Print selected documents radio button is selected and select Page Break as the document separator. You can also use For$\underline{m}$ Override to print each selected document with a form other than the form with which it was last saved.

When you have made all your printing choices, choose $\underline{O}$K to send the print job to the printer.

Printing a View

You may want to print the view instead of the documents displayed in the view. Notes makes it easy to do this. You open the view you want to print and then choose File, Print (or you can press Ctrl+P or use the File Print SmartIcon).

You arrive at the familiar File Print dialog box (refer to Figure 3.33). In the View options section, select the Print View radio button, which dims the document-specific print settings such as Form Override and Document separation. Set the other print options, such as Copies, and then choose OK to send the view to the printer.

Printing a List of Documents in a Folder

Printing documents from folders is much like printing documents from views. To print a list of documents from a folder, just select the documents you want to print, and choose File, Print, or click the File Print SmartIcon.

Specifying a Printer

When Windows was installed on your workstation, a default printer driver should have been installed and selected for the printer that you use most frequently. When you print from Notes, the program sends your output to the default printer unless you specify a different printer.

It is often helpful to have access to a printer other than your default printer. Having access to a printer with 8.5-inch by 14-inch paper is particularly helpful when printing wide views that scroll off the screen.

This way you can take advantage of some options that your default printer does not offer, such as an envelope feeder. Each time you print something from Notes, you see the dialog box from either Figure 3.33 or Figure 3.34, depending on what you are trying to print.

Each of these dialog boxes displays a Printer button above the selected printer (indicated by a printer icon). Click the Printer button or click the File Print Setup SmartIcon to change printer drivers.

After you click Printer, you see a dialog box that displays all the printer drivers installed on your workstation (see Figure 3.35).

Fig. 3.35 The Print Setup dialog box with installed printers shown.

Click to select a printer driver from the list and then click Setup to display a property sheet for the selected driver. Figure 3.36 shows the dialog box for the HP LaserJet 4M driver.

Fig. 3.36   The dialog box for an HP LaserJet 4M printer.

Using Headers and Footers

Another nice feature that Notes provides is the ability to set global headers and footers for all documents in a database. Headers and footers allow you to further identify documents when printing them.

A good example is the headers at the top of the pages of this book. In the header, you see information such as the title of the book and the page number.

To set a header or footer, choose the Print tab of the Document Properties InfoBox (see Figure 3.37). From this tab, select the Header radio button to create a header.

Fig. 3.37   The Print tab of the Document Properties InfoBox.

Then enter the text you want your header to display in the input box below the button. Type the text you want the header to display. Click the green check button to accept the changes or the red cancel button to reject the changes.

Choosing the Footer radio button allows you to enter text to print in the footer. It works just like the Header button.

You can see several icons immediately beneath the text box for the header and footer. These icons make it easy for you to automatically add additional information to the header or footer:

Inserts a page number, which is displayed in the text box as &P.

Inserts the current date, which is displayed as &D.

Inserts the current time, which is displayed as &T.

Inserts a tab, which is displayed as ¦.

Inserts the code &W, which tells Notes to print the Window title.

A header formula, for example, can print the date and time, insert a tab, print the text Test Header, insert another tab, and then print the current page. When printed, the header would look something like the following:

10/21/96@10:10PM Test Header   Page 1

From this Properties InfoBox, you can also adjust font settings such as typeface, size, and style for the header and/or footer. To change the typeface for the header or footer, select a new font from the Font list box.

To change the size of the font, select a font size from the Size list box. To change the font style, select the style from the Style list box.

Note

The font settings for the header and footer are mutually exclusive; that is, you can use different font settings for the header and footer.

From Here...

In this chapter, you learn the basics of using Notes databases: forms, data types, field types, and how to access databases. Now that you know the basics of using databases, Chapter 4, "Getting Started with Electronic Mail," teaches you how to use the NotesMail system.

Other chapters you might find useful at this point include the following:

- Chapter 8, "Working with Documents," explains how to use the many advanced features of Notes R4 such as hotspots and doclinks.

- Chapter 10, "Creating New Databases," shows you how to create and distribute new Notes databases.

- Chapter 11, "Designing Forms," explores creating Notes applications.

Chapter 4

Getting Started with Electronic Mail

Electronic mail (e-mail) is one of the most important and useful tools to come out of the information age, making it quick and easy to communicate with coworkers, regardless of geographical and time barriers. Although Notes provides many valuable services in addition to e-mail, e-mail is probably the single most used service.

The Notes e-mail system is a friendly, durable, client/server system modeled after their best-selling, stand-alone e-mail package, cc:Mail. NotesMail makes it easy to communicate with other Notes users and with other mail systems such as Microsoft Mail or Internet mail, if you have the proper hardware and software.

NotesMail is flexible. You can not only send messages to other users, you can send file attachments and embed objects such as spreadsheets or graphics in the e-mail. Understanding and using NotesMail is key to maximizing productivity when using Notes.

In this chapter, you learn the basics of sending and receiving mail. Later chapters explain the more advanced mail features and other features of Notes that help you and your coworkers work together more effectively.

Introducing E-Mail

Technological progress has a profound effect on the methods people use to communicate. As few as 30 years ago, the U.S. Postal Service was the way people sent messages to one another (paper-based mail is sometimes called *snail mail* because it is so much slower than e-mail). But as technology has advanced, new methods such as the fax machine and e-mail have made it easier, faster, and often less costly to send messages to other people.

Since the mid-1980s, the popularity of e-mail as a tool to send messages has grown exponentially. For proof of this trend, just look at the number of business cards you see with an e-mail address.

This chapter helps you understand the following:

- Advantages and disadvantages of using e-mail.

- How to work with your mailbox.

- Workstation-based mail versus server-based mail.

- Reading your incoming mail.

- Creating and sending mail.

- Forwarding, printing, deleting, and archiving messages.

- Using the status bar and SmartIcons to handle your mail.

E-mail has revolutionized internal communications for companies that use it. Many companies are now providing e-mail links to their customers and vendors, giving them a significant advantage over competitors who rely on paper-based mail.

If you ask people who have worked with e-mail for any length of time, most wonder how they ever got by without it because it makes their jobs easier, faster, and more fun. In fact, e-mail is rapidly becoming the preferred method of communication among technologically savvy professionals.

More and more ordinary people (not just techno-geeks, nerds, and dweebs like me) are beginning to use e-mail, too, because of the many advantages it provides. Before long, e-mail will most likely supplant the postal service for all messages except those that cannot be delivered by e-mail, such as that fruitcake your Aunt Bertha sends you every Christmas.

Some of the advantages of e-mail include the following:

- **Paperless Messaging**—Because e-mail messages are composed and delivered electronically and are generally read and stored electronically, you don't need to ever print out the message. All e-mail systems provide the option to make a hard copy of the mail message if you want.

- **Speed**—E-mail messages travel across the wire at the speed of light, which makes for quick delivery. Most businesses can immediately see a return on their investment. The time it takes for employees to communicate is drastically shortened, particularly in geographically dispersed companies.

- **Ease of Use**—Most common e-mail systems are easy to use and work much like a word processor. Once you start the mail software, you can address the mail by pulling up a directory of other e-mail users in your network. You type in your message, add any file attachments you want to send, and send the mail. Some e-mail systems even offer spell-checking, so you don't have to worry about typographical errors.

  Since most people would type the letter or memo they want to send, they can save a step by using the e-mail editor to both compose the message and send it in one step.

- **Message Organization**—Most e-mail systems offer power features that enable you to prioritize, sort, categorize, file, and search for your e-mail. This makes it much easier to manage your messages than with paper mail in traditional folders or filing cabinets.

  For example, think how handy it would be to search for an important memo from your boss simply by typing in his or her name rather than digging through all the papers on your desk for the paper version.

- **Flexibility**—E-mail makes it easy to work with your messages. You can delete mail you're not interested in, forward a message to others, reply to a message, or send the same message to a large number of users just by adding their addresses.

With electronic mail, you can do anything you can do with paper mail. Many e-mail systems have other advanced features such as "agents," which enable you to automate mail functions. For instance, you might want a special notification each time you get mail from your boss.

- **One-Stop Shopping**—Since you most likely use the computer for other jobs, having the mail available on your computer helps to eliminate redundancy. In addition, because the mail is an electronic file, you can export the information to other applications. For example, if I send you a picture of a new product our company makes, you can include that in a sales brochure that you are producing.

When compared with paper-based mail, e-mail has few disadvantages. The following are examples of disadvantages:

- **Expense**—The initial investment in hardware, software, and configuration for an electronic mail system can be large. Many of these systems, such as Notes, are expensive in themselves. The computers to use them are expensive and highly skilled people are needed to install and maintain the system.

  However, most modern offices have computers for their employees, and it is easy to show the advantages e-mail provides. The cost is outweighed by the productivity increase.

- **Facelessness**—Because most e-mail messages are just text, it's hard to convey personal feelings or warmth. Many people would rather get a handwritten note from a friend than an e-mail, even though they say the same thing.

To learn how to make text-based mail more friendly, see the section "E-Mail Etiquette" later in this chapter.

- As e-mail packages improve, it's getting easier to include graphics and sound for that extra touch. But some things still need to be written by hand, like a birthday card for your son or a get-well card for a friend.

Now that you have an overview of e-mail, let's see how NotesMail, the mail system integrated into Notes, works and how it can help you become a more productive Notes user.

Working with the Notes Mailbox

To use NotesMail, you must be familiar with your mailbox. Your mailbox is a Notes database (like what you read about in Chapter 3, "Using Databases") in which all your mail is stored. Figure 4.1 shows the database icon for a typical NotesMail user.

Fig. 4.1   A NotesMail database icon for Samuel Hatter's mailbox.

> **Note**
>
> Notes provides three core services: Document Databases, Application Development, and Messaging Services. The fact that your mailbox is actually a Notes database points to the tight integration of core services in Notes. Messaging is woven into the database structure so that any database can send and receive e-mail messages.

In most Notes installations, your mailbox is created for you at setup, and its icon is placed on a page in your workspace normally labeled Mail. (This is the normal configuration, but your configuration may be different. If you have trouble finding your mailbox, see your administrator.)

Because your mailbox is really just a Notes database, the procedures and techniques you use to read incoming mail and to create new mail are the same as those you use when working with other Notes databases (see Chapter 3, "Using Databases," for more information).

The only thing that makes your mailbox special is that the mailbox user interface resembles that of Lotus's cc:Mail product, which facilitates sending, storing, and organizing mail messages to and from other users and Notes now includes native Calendaring and Scheduling capabilities, which will be covered in depth in Chapter 9, "Lotus Notes Group Calendaring and Scheduling." As you read this chapter, keep in mind that many of the techniques you will learn for working with your mailbox and working with mail messages (documents) apply to all Notes databases.

Another important aspect of your mail database (hereafter called *mailbox*) is how you connect to the server to get your mail. If you are a mobile user with no ongoing connection to a server, you are probably set up for workstation-based mail.

If you have an ongoing connection to the server (usually via a LAN), you are probably set up for server-based mail. The type of mail you are currently using can be configured for each location.

To determine whether you are using workstation or server-based mail, edit your current location document and examine the Mail File Location setting. If it's set to Local, you are using workstation-based mail; if it specifies a server name, you are using server-based mail.

Server-Based Mail. If you spend most of your time using Notes connected to a Notes server via a LAN or WAN, you are probably set up to use server-based mail. When you are set up for server-based mail, you use your mailbox on the Notes server.

Each time you create and send a new mail document, it is immediately transferred to the Notes server's mailbox. If you also save it, a copy of the document is placed in your mailbox.

The Router process on the server resolves the address of the recipient or recipients and routes it to the intended recipient almost immediately. In addition, incoming mail is delivered to your mailbox shortly after it is delivered to your mail server.

Workstation-Based Mail. If you are a mobile user or don't have an ongoing connection to a Notes server (for instance, you might work in a remote office or at home), and if you connect to your Notes server occasionally via modem, you are probably set up for workstation-based mail.

When your workstation is set up for workstation-based mail, you work with a replica copy of your mailbox. A special Notes database titled Outgoing Mail is created on your workstation. The icon should look like Figure 4.2.

Fig. 4.2   The Outgoing Mail database icon for workstation-based mail users.

> **Note**
>
> The Outgoing Mail database (whose filename is MAIL.BOX) is created by default the first time you change your location to Travel, Island, or any custom location profile where workstation-based mail is specified. You learn more about location profiles in Chapter 5, "Using the Address Book," and in Chapter 20, "Setting Up to Go Remote."

Unlike server-based mail, when you compose and send a new mail message, it is not immediately sent to the server's mailbox. Instead, the mail message is temporarily stored in the Outgoing Mail database until your next connection to the server. If you save a copy of the mail, it is stored in your local mailbox, which is a replica copy of your mailbox on the server.

When you next connect to the server (if the send Outgoing Mail option is turned on, which it normally is by default), your outgoing mail is automatically transferred to the server. In addition, if you replicate during this connection, your local mailbox receives all incoming mail from the server.

To enable or disable the Send outgoing mail, click the Replicator workspace tab. On the Replicator page, there should be an entry for Send outgoing mail that displays the Outgoing Mail database icon and a small checkbox. If the checkbox has a check in it, the option is enabled and outgoing mail will be sent during each connection.

Figure 4.3 shows the Replicator page with the Send outgoing mail option turned on.

> **Note**
>
> The NotesMail system is flexible and you have considerable control over when messages get sent. For instance, you can tell Notes to make a connection immediately for High Priority mail.
>
> You can also tell Notes to make a connection when more than a given number of mail messages is pending in the Outgoing Mail database. You learn more about these options in Chapter 5, "Using the Address Book" and Chapter 20, "Setting Up to Go Remote."

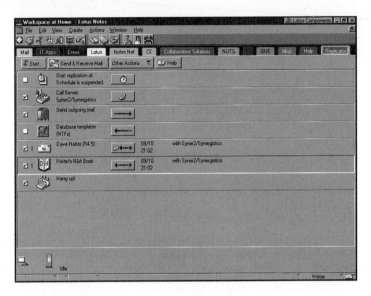

Fig. 4.3   The Replicator page shown with Send outgoing mail enabled.

If you don't have a temporary storage facility for outgoing mail, you need to make a connection to the server each time you send a mail message. Not only would this be a major hassle, it would severely limit your ability to use Notes on the road.

However, like other remote mail systems such as CompuServe, America Online, and Eudora, Notes provides this temporary storage facility, giving you tremendous freedom to create and send mail.

You can create a mail message in the plane on your way to a meeting and another while driving down the road to a sales call. When you next connect to the server, the Router transfers the mail messages from your Outgoing Mail database to the intended recipients.

> **Caution**
>
> The Outgoing Mail database is a critical component of the mail system for users who do not have an ongoing connection to a Notes server. Because your outgoing mail is stored in this database until your next connection, it is very important that you do not delete this database or delete it from your replicator page.

Mailbox Features

As with all Notes databases, to access your mail messages you must first open your mailbox. In most cases, your administrator has put your mailbox icon on your workspace for you. So just double-click the mailbox icon and the database opens.

Remember that if you don't see the database icon you want, check the other pages in your workspace to see whether the database resides on a different page. When you open your mailbox, you should see something like Figure 4.4.

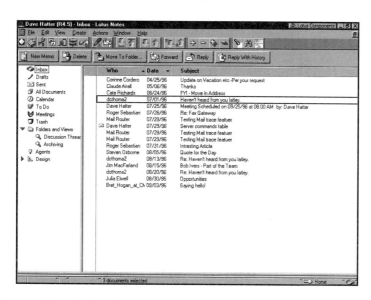

Fig. 4.4   The new NotesMail mailbox interface.

For those who have used NotesMail in older versions of Notes, you can quickly see from Figure 4.4 that the mail interface has changed somewhat from 4.0; it now includes new views for Group Calendaring and Scheduling (if you're upgrading from Notes 3.x, the changes are drastic). As mentioned earlier in this section, Lotus has made the look and feel of the new mail design very much like that of their award-winning cc:Mail.

If you have used cc:Mail before, you will have a leg up on other users who are converting from Notes 3.x. If you have not used cc:Mail, don't worry, Lotus has made the new mailbox much easier to use.

On the left side of the screen in Figure 4.4, you should see the navigator pane, which has been customized for the mailbox but works the same way in every database. As you know from Chapter 3, "Using Databases," the navigator provides a graphical representation of the elements of a database. Lotus has used this to their advantage in your new mailbox design.

To the right of the navigator is the view pane. It is like Notes 3.x views but provides more flexibility than the old R3/x views. The various views are discussed shortly.

One of the most useful new features of Notes 4.5 is the preview pane. Although you can enable this for any database, it can be particularly useful in your mailbox because it enables you to read your mail messages without opening the document. This can save you a lot of time.

To display the preview pane, choose View, Document Preview, which displays the preview pane in approximately 50 percent of the screen. Or you can simply click the thick gray line at the bottom of the view pane and drag up, which displays the preview pane.

Remember, the display of your mailbox at any given time may depend on any changes that a designer made to the database and changes you might have made, such as resizing the preview pane or changing its screen location. Notes 4.5 gives you flexibility and control when working with your mail.

To make the new format of the mailbox as useful and easy as possible, Lotus has designed several default folders and views that you can access by clicking icons from the Navigator. These are as follows:

- Inbox folder
- Drafts folder
- Sent folder
- All Documents view
- Calendar
- To Do view
- Meetings
- Trash folder
- Folders and views

The following sections examine each of these new items.

Viewing Inbox Messages. To quickly view the new mail you have received, click the Inbox icon, which opens the Inbox folder. Figure 4.5 is an example of the Inbox folder.

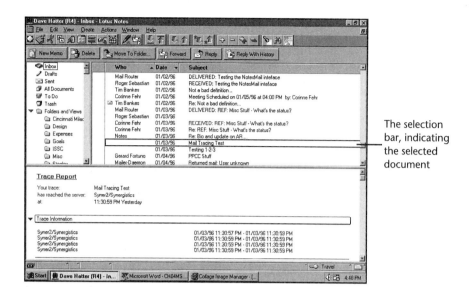

The selection bar, indicating the selected document

Fig. 4.5 In the Inbox folder, the view pane displays the currently selected document.

All incoming mail is stored in the Inbox folder until you move it elsewhere or delete it. (See "Moving Your Messages" later in this chapter for details on how to organize your mailbox contents.)

Viewing Draft Messages. For a view of your drafts, which are mail messages that you have saved but not yet sent, click the Drafts icon (see Figure 4.6).

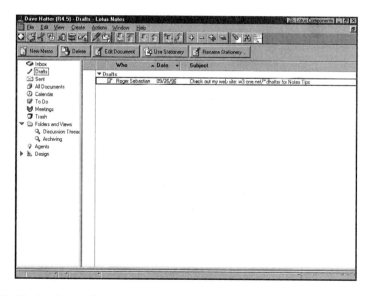

Fig. 4.6 The Drafts view in the new mailbox database.

When you send a draft, it is automatically moved from the Drafts folder to the Sent folder, unless you specify another folder.

Viewing Sent Messages. To see only the messages that you have sent, click the Sent icon, which launches the Sent view (see Figure 4.7).

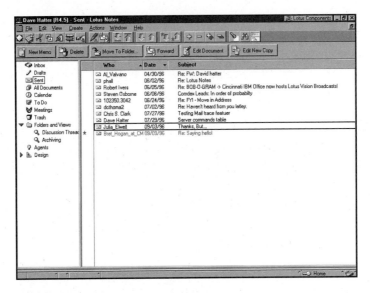

Fig. 4.7   The Sent view in the new mailbox database.

Viewing Your Calendar. Notes 4.5 has cool new added functionality that enables you you to do group Calendaring & Scheduling (C & S) through Notes. (Calendaring and Scheduling are covered in detail in Chapter 9, "Lotus Notes Group Calendaring and Scheduling.")

To view your appointments, anniversaries, and events, click the Calendar icon. This displays the new calendar view so you can see and edit your calendar (see Figure 4.8).

Viewing To Do Documents. In Notes 4.x, a new type of mail message has been added that enables you to keep track of tasks you need to do, as well as assign tasks to other NotesMail users. To view your To Do's, click the To Do icon, which launches a folder displaying only your To Do's sorted and categorized by their status. Figure 4.9 shows the To Do folder.

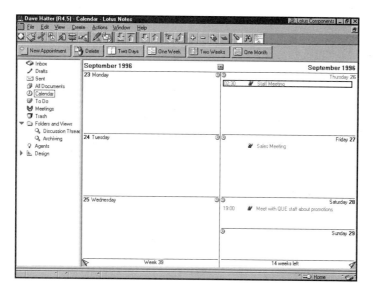

Fig. 4.8   The really cool and useful Calendar view in the new mailbox database.

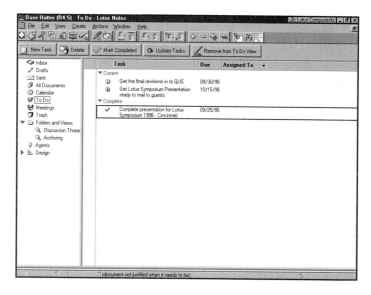

Fig. 4.9   The To Do Folder.

Viewing Your Meetings. Another new feature in the 4.5 mailbox is the Meetings view, which at a glance shows you all your scheduled meetings. Figure 4.10 shows the Meetings view with several meetings scheduled.

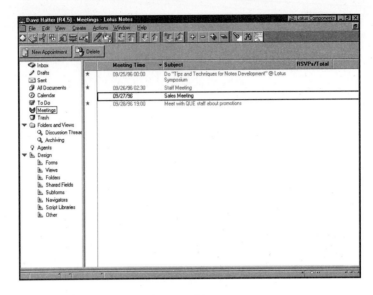

Fig. 4.10 The new Meetings view in the 4.5 mailbox.

Viewing All Documents. To see all the documents in your mailbox regardless of the folder they are in, you can click the All Documents icon. This launches a view of all the documents in the database, regardless of their status (see Figure 4.11). This view is sorted on the date column. You can, however, click the arrows on the Name and Date columns to change the sort order.

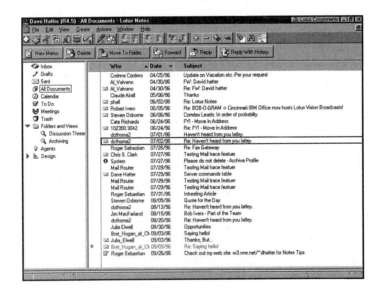

Fig. 4.11 The All Documents view in the new mailbox.

Viewing Deleted Messages (Trash). Documents in the Trash folder are marked for deletion but are not yet deleted. To see the documents you have selected to delete from your mailbox, you can click the Trash icon, which displays your Trash folder (see Figure 4.12). If you see documents in the trash folder that you don't want to delete, you can move them (using drag and drop) to another folder to prevent them from being deleted.

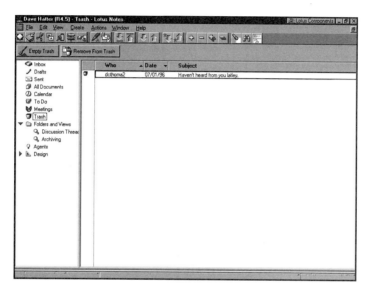

Fig. 4.12   The Trash (deleted mail) folder in the new mailbox.

Navigating the Mailbox. In addition to the special views and folders in the mailbox, private views and folders that you add help to organize your mailbox.

For instance, you can expand the Folder and Views icon by clicking it. This displays a list of other views and folders in the database. In Figure 4.13, you can see several other views in your mailbox, each one represented by a yellow magnifying glass and folders represented by a file folder.

These other views and folders are covered in detail in Chapter 6, "Advanced Mail." The currently selected view is represented by a blue magnifying glass and its title is displayed in the window title.

You might also be able to access these other views by choosing the View menu option and then selecting the specific view you are interested in from the menu. (This option can be disabled by a designer.)

Note

Although the screen shots used in this book are in black and white, we refer to the colors used in the views so you can identify them on your screen.

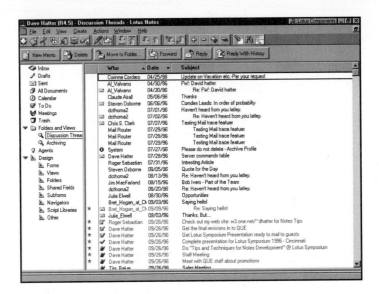

Fig. 4.13 Other views in the new mailbox.

The view pane has been enhanced in Notes 4.5 but works like Notes 3.x views. (See Chapter 3, "Using Databases," for more information about views and folders.) Mail messages in your mailbox are displayed in the view pane. (Remember that mail messages are just specialized Notes documents, and that *mail message* and *document* are frequently used interchangeably.)

Each column in the view pane displays either a field in a mail message or some computed value. Each row represents an individual mail message or document.

In many of the folders and views in the standard mailbox, the documents displayed are categorized. This means that documents with the same category are grouped together and are displayed beneath the category (which is displayed as a separate row) in the view pane (see Figure 4.13).

The following are several columns that display data from each mail message in the mailbox:

■ The leftmost column in the view pane is a special feature of Notes views and folders. It is called the Marker Column and is separated from the other columns in the view by a thin, vertical, gray line that extends the length of the view.

■ This column shows a variety of system information. For instance, if you delete a mail message, you see a small blue trash can icon in this column. If you have not read a mail message, a star is displayed in this column and the row text is red. For an example of this, look at the message from Roger Sebastian, which has a red star in the Marker Column in Figure 4.14.

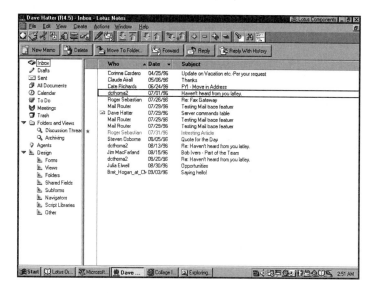

Fig. 4.14   The Inbox view showing sortable columns.

> **Note**
>
> The various icons that are displayed in these views and folders, as well as the colors that indicate different parts of the view or folder, are set by the designer. So your mailbox may look somewhat different from the screen shots shown here.

- The first column to the right of the Marker Column, the Who column, shows the name of the user who sent you the message. This column always shows a value because Notes mail messages automatically "stamp" the sending user's name into the message in the from field.

- In the Who column heading, you should see an up arrow, indicating that the column can be sorted in ascending order by clicking this arrow. By default, the mail messages in this view are sorted by the date the message was sent.

> **Note**
>
> Categories are not documents. They act only as headings so that documents can be logically grouped together. If you click any of the categories in a view, you can expand and collapse the categories.
>
> Categorization is a feature that the designer builds into views and folders. For more information on how categories work, see Chapter 3, "Using Databases."

- The second column, Date, shows the date the mail message was sent to you. Notes automatically date/time stamps all e-mail messages. You'll also see a down arrow in the column heading, telling you that you can resort the date column in descending order.

- The third and final column, Subject, shows the subject of the mail message. A subject is not needed in an e-mail message so this column may be blank. (Still, e-mail Netiquette dictates that you should always enter a subject in your mail messages.) In addition, if the mail has any file attachments, it also shows a paperclip icon to the left of the subject text.

> **Note**
>
> Notes allows you to place a copy of a file inside any Rich Text field on any document. Once a file has been attached to a mail message, it can be transferred along with the mail message to all the intended recipients. They can then detach the file and work with its contents. ("Working with File Attachments" in Chapter 6, "Advanced Mail," covers file attachments in more detail.)

Reading Incoming Mail

To access the data in a mail message, you must, as a minimum, select the document in a view or folder. Selecting mail messages is just like selecting documents in a regular Notes database. Choose the view or folder that is most useful and navigate to the message you want.

For instance, to reply to a message your boss sent to you today, the Inbox folder or the All Documents view would probably be the most helpful. When you have found and selected the message from the boss (put the selection bar on that document), you are ready to read the mail message and create a reply.

> **Tip**
>
> To save time, you might want to read only new mail messages. There are a couple of ways to do this. The first and easiest is to open the Inbox folder and then choose View, Show, Unread Only (see Figure 4.15) to display only the new mail messages.

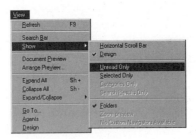

Fig. 4.15 The View menu options to show only unread mail messages.

Alternatively, you can click the All Documents view in the navigator (or choose View, All Documents) and then choose View, Show, Unread Only. When you select a mail message to read, you can enable the preview pane to scan the contents without opening it. Or you can double-click the message to open it in read mode.

Figure 4.16 shows a sample mail message. Notice that the format of the standard Notes mail message, called a *memo*, is somewhat like an interoffice memo or standard business letter.

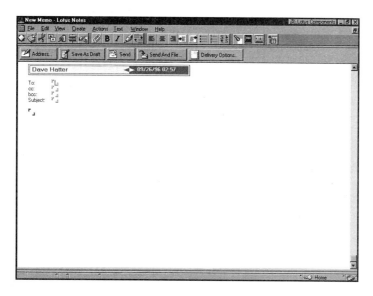

Fig. 4.16   The new Memo form shown in edit mode.

The first four lines (often called the *envelope*) provide the addressing information and the subject of the message. The parts of the envelope are as follows:

■ The To field displays the names of the primary recipients of the message. If you are reading a message you received, obviously your name appears in this field. If other names also appear in the To field, those people also got the mail.

> **Tip**
>
> When you address a Notes mail message, you can select individual user names, and group names (lists of users), or database names to send a mail message to. In most cases, you send mail to users or groups. This is covered in more depth in Chapter 5, "Using the Address Book."

■ The cc field displays the names of secondary recipients to whom the mail was sent. (*cc* is an abbreviation for *carbon copy*, a holdover from the days when carbon paper was used to make copies—some things just never die!)

■ The bcc field displays the name or names of other recipients to whom the mail was sent. If you send a mail message with names in the bcc field, the recipients in the To and cc fields do not know that the people in the bcc field also received the mail. (*bcc* is an abbreviation for *blind carbon copy*.)

- The From line (the colored bar at the very top of the envelope area) indicates the user name of the senders of the mail message. The names in this field are automatically generated by Notes, based on the user ID in use when a mail message is composed. In addition, the date and time the mail message was sent are normally displayed in this bar.

- The Subject line briefly tells you what the mail message is about. Although a subject is not required, when you send a message to another user, it is common courtesy (and good Netiquette, geek slang for Internet etiquette) to include a subject so that the user has an idea of what the message is about before opening it.

The envelope is followed by the text of the message, commonly called the *body*. The body of a NotesMail message can be any length and can hold embedded objects such as pictures, sound, charts, and so on. It can also have file attachments. You learn about these other features in Chapter 6, "Advanced Mail."

> **Note**
>
> The body field in a NotesMail message is a special field called a Rich Text Format field (RTF). You learn more about the powerful features of RTF fields in Chapter 3, "Using Databases," and in Chapter 11, "Designing Forms."

Moving Your Messages. One of the best new features NotesMail is the ability to create folders. This allows you to organize your mail based on criteria that you set.

For example, you might create a folder named Accounting to store all correspondence from the Accounting department and a folder named HR to store all mail messages about Human Resources. Once you have created a folder, you can move mail messages into it.

To move a message into or out of a folder, you can click the message you want to move. This should make your mouse pointer display a piece of paper with one edge folded down and a plus (+) symbol above it.

You can drag (hold down the left mouse key and move the mouse over another folder) it to another folder and drop it (release the left mouse key). You cannot drag a message to a view, only to a folder.

If you drag it to a view, the mouse pointer changes to a circle and diagonal line (the international symbol for No) that means you can't do that.

> **Tip**
>
> Remember that you can use the Marker column to select multiple mail messages and move them all at one time.

Alternatively, you can choose <u>A</u>ctions, Move to Folder, which displays the Move To Folder dialog box (see Figure 4.17).

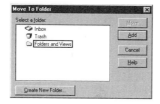

Fig. 4.17   The Move To Folder dialog box.

You can then select a folder to move the document into and click the Move button to move the document into the folder. You can also create a new folder from this dialog box by clicking the Add button.

Mail Notification. Most people want to know whether they have new mail as soon as possible. By default, when new mail arrives in your mailbox, Notes plays a short tune to indicate that you have new mail.

You can also set a user preference that pops up a small dialog box with a visual notification of new mail. (For more information on user preferences, see Chapter 2, "Customizing Notes.")

In addition, on the status bar is a small icon in the lower-right corner that gives you visual cues about new mail. A small dimmed envelope is displayed when you have no unread mail messages in your mailbox. If an inbox with a piece of paper is displayed, you have unread (possibly new) mail messages in your mailbox.

> ### Tip
>
> To quickly access your new mail, click the Inbox icon in the lower-right corner of the status bar and choose Scan Unread Mail from the list.

Like most things in Notes, you can control how often Notes checks for mail and if Notes should signal you audibly and/or visually when new mail arrives. If you disable the notification features of Notes, you need to check your mailbox from time to time to see if you have new mail. In Chapter 2, "Customizing Notes," you learn how to edit the default settings for mail notification and scanning.

To take advantage of the new mail notification features, you must leave Notes running constantly on your workstation, even if you are using other applications. You can minimize Notes if you need to run other applications.

But ending your Notes session prevents you from getting mail notifications although it does not stop you from getting mail. If Notes is minimized and you get new mail, the Notes icon displays an envelope in addition to its usual graphic.

Understanding the Mailbox Icons

To make the new NotesMail interface more intuitive, Lotus has added many new graphics that can be displayed in the mail folders and view. At a glance, you can identify certain kinds of messages and items with a graphic icon. Table 4.1 describes the most common icons you will see in your mailbox.

Table 4.1 Common NotesMail Graphics		
Icon	**Description**	**Location**
Yellow envelope	Sent Mail of Normal or Low importance	View or Folder Column
Red envelope	Sent Mail of High importance	View or Folder Column
Paper and pencil	Draft (unsent mail message)	View or Folder Column
Paper clip	Attachment icon	View or Folder Column
Torn sheet of paper	Truncated document	View or Folder Column
Trash can	Deleted message	View Marker Column
Star	Unread mail	View Marker Column
Checkmark	Selected document	View Marker Column
One piece of paper over another	Stationery	View or Folder Column

Creating Outgoing Mail

The Notes e-mail system is flexible and offers several different kinds of mail messages you can send and receive. To send a mail message, choose Create. This displays a menu listing all the forms available in your mailbox.

Figure 4.18 shows the default forms available in the standard mailbox.

Each of the default forms in the mailbox provides a function. Let's look at the most common and useful forms.

The Memo form is the standard form. You use it to send mail messages to other users. To create a new memo, choose Create, Memo. A new memo, like that shown in Figure 4.19, is displayed.

Fig. 4.18 The Create menu in the mailbox.

Fig. 4.19 A new memo in edit mode, ready to be completed and sent.

At the top of the Memo form, you see the envelope section and you can begin to address the mail. The colored bar at the top replaces the old From and Date fields (in Notes 3.x mail).

Notes supplies the user ID in use at the workstation (this should be your user name if you are sending mail) and the current date, time in this section. Because I composed the mail, you see my user name and the time and date the message was composed.

Addressing the Mail

You use the first editable field, To, to list the primary recipient of this message. If you know the exact user name of the recipient, you can type it in.

> **Note**
>
> Each Notes user must have an account and a Notes ID file with that Notes user name and password (among other information). Notes keeps a directory of each user name for security and to identify users to the mail system.
>
> The Public Name & Address Book is the repository for all user information and plays a critical role in the Notes e-mail system. Chapter 4, "Getting Started with Electronic Mail," covers the Public Name & Address Book in detail.

For example, if you want to send a mail message to Bob Dole, you could enter Bob Dole in the To field.

In Notes 4.x, the Memo form has a handy new feature: you can type the first few characters of a user's name in any of the address fields (To, cc, bcc) and Notes looks up the user's name in the Name & Address Book.

If a match is found, Notes completes the name for you. If a match is not found, the status bar displays the message that the name was not found in the Name & Address Book.

To send the message to several people, you can enter multiple recipients' names separated by commas. Figure 4.20 shows an example of multiple recipients on a memo.

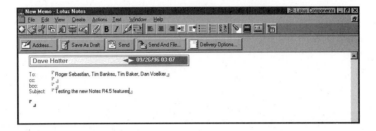

Fig. 4.20 A new memo with several (primary) recipients in the To field.

Tip

You can also list each name on a new line by pressing Enter after each name but the last. Each time you press Enter, Notes provides additional room for the next name.

When you have added the names of all of the primary recipients, you can press the Tab key to move to the cc field (or click the cc field). To send a copy of this message to other users, you enter those names in this field.

For example, if you want to send mail to Roger Sebastian but want Rick Flagg and Chris Clark to get a copy, you put Roger Sebastian in the To field, and Rick and Chris in the cc field (see Figure 4.21).

All three of the named users will get the mail, just as if you had included them all in the To field. However, by putting Roger in the To field and Rick and Chris in the cc field, you are indicating to Roger that the mail is primarily intended for him but that you also sent the information to other users. By copying Rick and Chris, you let them know what you sent to Roger.

In some cases, you might not want the primary recipient or recipients to know that you have sent a copy of the mail to another person. If so, you can use the bcc field to send a copy of the message to other users, but the recipients named in the To and cc fields are not notified that a copy was sent to someone else.

Figure 4.22 shows a message that is sent to Roger Sebastian, carbon-copied to Rick Flagg and Chris Clark, and blind carbon-copied to Tim Bankes.

The message sent to Roger Sebastian and the copy sent to Rick and Chris will not display the bcc field showing that Tim Bankes also received a copy. So unless Tim spills the beans, he'll be the surprise I'm bringing to lunch on the 16th.

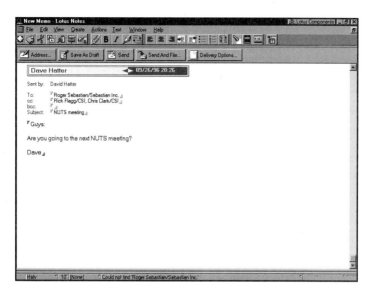

Fig. 4.21   A New Memo with both To and cc recipients specified.

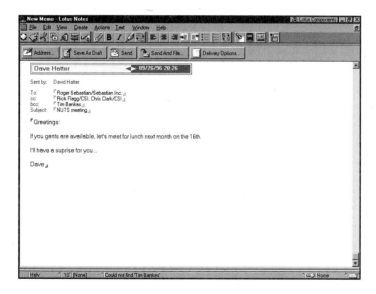

Fig. 4.22   A New Memo with To, cc, and bcc recipients specified.

In addition to the ability to type names into the address fields or use the dynamic lookup capability of the New Memo form, you can click the Address button on the Action Bar of the screen to display the Mail Address dialog box. This enables you to choose recipients directly from the Name & Address Book (see Figure 4.23).

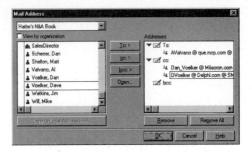

Fig. 4.23 The Mail Address dialog box.

Notes is smart enough to remember the last Name & Address Book you used in the dialog box and chooses it automatically each time you open this dialog box. To select a different Name & Address Book, click the down arrow to display the list of the Name & Address Books you can see from your workstation.

The Name & Address Book drop-down box selects your Personal Name & Address Book if you are configured for workstation-based mail and the Public Name & Address Book if you are using server-based mail. The Name & Address Books you can access depends on the configuration of your Notes network, of your local machine, and on the access levels you have been granted by your administrator.

When you select a Name & Address Book, the list box below the Name & Address Book drop-down box displays all the users and groups in that Name & Address Book.

A user is an individual Notes user, whereas a group is a collection of Notes users that can be addressed as one entity. Notes supplies the individual address of each person in the group and places each individual name in the field.

When you use the Mail Address dialog box, users are indicated by a small purple icon that looks like a person, and groups are indicated by a small multicolor icon that looks like a group of people standing together. This is covered in more detail in Chapter 5, "Using the Address Book."

You can use the mouse to scroll through this list to find the user or group you want to send a message to or you can type the first character of the user or group name you are searching for. Notes searches the list to find the first entry that begins with the character(s) you entered.

For instance, to find Roger Sebastian in the list, you could type S. Notes would move the selection bar to the first item in the list that begins with S, in this case, Roger Sebastian. This feature is particularly helpful when you are dealing with a large list of users and groups.

You can also select more than one user or group from the list. This works much like selecting multiple messages from a view or folder. Just click in the small empty column (view marker column) next to each name in the list and a small checkmark appears, indicating that you have selected that user or group.

On the right side of this dialog box, you see another list box titled Addresses. This list box displays small envelope icons representing each of the address fields. If any users or groups have been assigned to a particular field, they are displayed beneath the icon representing that field.

For example, in Figure 4.23, you can see that Al Valvano has been assigned to the To field. Like a view or folder, these lists can be collapsed or expanded by clicking the twisties to save space.

To add a user or group to the distribution list, select the user or group from the list of Name & Address Book entries. Click the button that corresponds to the address field you want to place this user name in.

For example, to add Mojo Nixon to the To field, you can choose Mojo from the list and press the To button. The Addresses list box immediately reflects the new item.

If you make a wrong entry, click the entry you want to remove from the Addresses list and press the Remove button. If you want to delete every entry in the Addresses list, press the Remove All button.

Tip

In large companies, there may be several users with similar names. When using the Mail Address dialog box, if you cannot distinguish one user from another or need more information about a particular user, click the Open button to open the selected user's person document. This should give you the information you need about a specific Notes user. This also applies to group documents.

The Copy to Local Address Book button enables you to copy group and user documents from the Public Name & Address Book and add them to your local Name & Address book. This is particularly useful if you are a mobile user. It allows you to address mail from your Personal Address Book, eliminating the need to know the exact address or to carry around a full replica of the Public N & A Book, which can get quite large.

Just select the entry you want to transfer and press the Copy to Local Address Book button. When you finish addressing the mail, click the OK button to update the mail message with the addresses. To discard your changes, click the Cancel button.

Specifying the Subject

When you have entered the address information, you can tab to the Subject field. This field allows you to enter a brief description of the contents of the message. It is displayed in the all default mail views and folders (see Figure 4.24).

Because the subject is the first thing the user sees regarding your message contents, it should be as explicit and concise as possible. Although you can enter up to 15K of data in the subject, most of the views and folders truncate the text in the display at 7K. (Not to worry, your subject is not affected; this is for display only.)

Notes Basics

Fig. 4.24 The new memo form with a completed subject.

   ▶▶ See "E-Mail Etiquette," p. 168

Creating the Body of the Message

After you enter the address information and a brief subject, you are ready to enter your actual message, called the *body*. Although this field looks small, you can enter just about as much text as you like; this is an RTF field.

You can also embed objects from other applications, such as a 1-2-3 spreadsheet, or include file attachments. Figure 4.25 shows the completed mail memo ready to send.

   ▶▶ See "Working with File Attachments," p. 225

Tip

Don't forget to use the integrated spell-check to make sure you don't have any spelling errors. When you are ready to spell-check your message, choose Edit, Check Spelling or use the Edit Check Spelling SmartIcon.

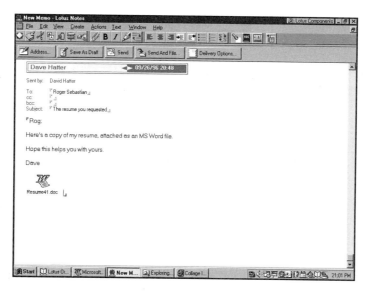

Fig. 4.25   A completed memo with file attachments ready to be sent.

Mailing Options

If you are familiar with the Notes 3.x mail system, you know that at the bottom of the old mail forms there were four fields that enabled you to set certain mailing options. The old fields were the following:

- Delivery Priority
- Receipt Report
- Delivery Report
- Personal Categories

Although these fields still exist in many of the new forms, the Memo form has been enhanced and presents these fields with more descriptive names and includes some additional fields to increase its usefulness.

Because of these differences, we cover each of these options briefly in the following sections and in more detail in later sections in this chapter.

To examine or change these options, click the Delivery Options button on the Action bar at the top of the form. The Delivery Options button launches the Delivery Options dialog box (see Figure 4.26).

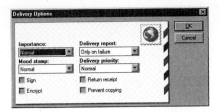

Fig. 4.26   The Delivery Options dialog box.

> ### Note
>
> Think back, way back, to Chapter 3 and the explanation of layout regions. The Delivery Options dialog box is an example of the effective use of layout regions and dialog boxes to enhance an application both functionally and visually.

Choosing a Mood. You can use the Mood stamp drop-down list to select a mood for your mail. A mood conveys the tone you want to the recipients, minimizing the faceless-ness problem we discussed earlier in this chapter.

This is a new field in Notes 4.x. The default mood is Normal, which indicates a neutral tone. You can also select one of any of the following moods. This inserts a graphic image between the envelope and the body to represent the tone:

Confidential tells the recipients that they should not share this information with others.

Flame indicates that you are angry about something.

FYI means that this mail message is For Your Information only and no action is needed.

Personal indicates that the mail is of a personal nature and should not be shared with others.

Private is like confidential; the information in the mail is for the distribution list only.

Thank You tells the recipients that you are showing your appreciation for something.

Good Job lets the recipients know that they are being commended for a job well done.

 Joke gives the message a light tone.

 Question tells the recipients that the message is a question that they need to answer.

 Reminder indicates to the recipients that they should not forget to do something. (NotesMail can be a great tool to jog people's memory!)

Generating a Delivery Status Report. In most cases, if your mail message cannot be delivered to your intended recipients, the Notes server sends you a message that it had a problem delivering the mail message with a suggested corrective action.

If you send a message and you don't get a Failure Report message, you can assume that your mail message was delivered. For very important messages, you may want to have the Notes server send you a Delivery Report to let you know that your mail was delivered successfully.

The Delivery Report drop-down list has four possible settings: Only on failure, Confirm delivery, Trace entire path, and None. The default setting is Only on failure. This sends a delivery report only if a routing error is encountered.

You can change the setting by typing the first letter of the setting you want (O, C, T, or N). Or you can click the down arrow and choose from the list.

If you change the Delivery Report field to Confirm delivery, in addition to sending you notification of the delivery failure, the Notes server notifies you when your mail is delivered. A Delivery Report from the server appears in your mailbox like any other NotesMail message. Figure 4.27 displays a Delivery Report.

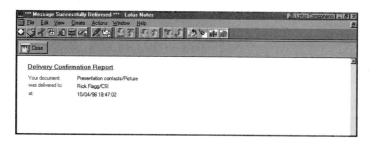

Fig. 4.27   A Delivery Report indicating that my mail was delivered to Rick's Mailbox.

> **Note**
>
> A Delivery Report does not indicate that the mail message recipient read the message. It tells you only that the mail message was successfully delivered to the recipient's mailbox.

The Trace Entire Path setting returns a confirmation message from each hop along the routing path between the sender and the recipient. If you are having trouble sending and receiving mail, this can be a valuable troubleshooting tool because you can see where the mail died on the routing path. If you communicate only with users on the same server, Trace Entire Path probably isn't useful.

If you change the Delivery Report field to None, you don't get a notification, even if the delivery fails. Though not often used, this setting can be helpful if you are sending an unimportant message to many people (called *spamming* on the Internet) and don't care if Notes cannot deliver the message to someone.

For instance, if you were going to send FYI mail to the whole organization, you might use this option.

Setting the Delivery Priority. The Delivery Priority field is like the old Delivery Priority field. This drop-down list enables you to choose from the following settings: Low, Normal, and High.

Each of these options has an effect on the speed and cost with which the mail is routed by the server. As you would expect, high-priority mail is fastest, regardless of the cost. Low-priority mail is the slowest and most economical. Normal priority is the default and is sufficient for most mail messages.

If you communicate with other Notes users only via a LAN connection (an ongoing connection to the network) or have only one Notes server, this setting has little effect on the speed or cost of routing.

If you communicate with other Notes users across leased-line or dial-up connections, this setting is more important because it can have a significant effect on the timeliness of delivery and the cost.

For instance, high-priority mail is routed immediately, regardless of the routing cost. Low-priority mail is sent only between 12:00 A.M. and 6:00 A.M. This is more cost-effective because connect charges are considerably less during the off-peak hours.

Normal mail is routed according to priorities set by the administrator. If you are cost-conscious and the timeliness of the mail is not important, use the Low setting. Conversely, if the mail is important and must be delivered as soon as possible, use the High setting.

 ▶▶ See "Advanced Connection Settings," p. 821

> **Note**
>
> The Notes server software enables the Notes administrator to set up scheduled connections to other Notes servers for routing and replication. As part of this process, the administrator can choose a routing cost to determine the most economical times and paths for mail routing and database replication.

Requesting a Return Receipt. Return receipt is used to indicate that you want to receive a message from the server when the recipient opens the mail message you have sent. This can be useful when you need to be sure that a user has received and read (or at least opened) your mail (see Figure 4.28).

To enable this feature, select the Return receipt checkbox in the Delivery Options dialog box. An x should appear, indicating that it is enabled. To disable this feature, click the checkbox a second time to remove the x.

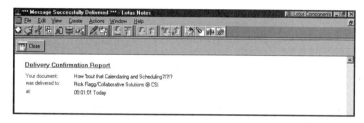

Fig. 4.28   A return receipt indicating that Rick read my mail message.

> **Tip**
>
> Many people are irritated when they frequently receive mail that generates a return receipt. It makes them feel pressured to respond to the mail immediately.
>
> A return receipt also uses extra system resources because a second mail message must be generated, delivered to you, and stored in your mailbox. Although this can be useful when necessary, you should use this feature sparingly.

Encrypting the Message for Security. The Encrypt checkbox enables you to encrypt your mail message with your private key. This provides additional security: Even though a user can receive this message, he or she cannot decrypt and read any of the encrypted fields unless he or she possesses a copy of your public key.

You learn more about encryption in Chapter 22, "Security and Encryption."

Adding an Electronic Signature. The Sign checkbox enables you to attach an electronic signature to your mail. An electronic signature is derived from your unique key stored in your Notes ID.

An electronic signature is impossible to duplicate and guarantees that any mail or document signed with your Notes ID came from you (or at least your Notes ID). Electronic signatures are discussed in more detail in Chapter 22, "Security and Encryption."

> **Tip**
>
> Electronic signatures and encryption are extremely secure methods for protecting mail messages (or any document, for that matter). But they depend on the physical security of your Notes ID.
>
> Anyone who can access your Notes ID and knows your password can impersonate you! The moral of this story is to keep your ID secure, your password to yourself, and change your password frequently.

> **Caution**
>
> All Notes encryption keys are based on the 64-bit Rivest Shamir Adleman (RSA) standard (named for the individuals who created it). This standard creates almost unbreakable encryption codes, and needs a public key and a private key. If you encrypt a mail message or a document and then lose your Notes ID file or even forget your password, chances are your information will be irretrievable! Use encryption only when security is paramount.

Disallowing the Printing or Copying of Your Mail Messages. Notes' new mail interface offers another great new security feature, Prevent copying. You can simply put a check in the Prevent copying checkbox of the Delivery Options dialog box to enable this feature.

When you enable Prevent Copying, recipients of the mail message cannot copy the message to the Clipboard, print the message, or forward the message to other users. This helps to ensure that confidential information isn't leaked to others through the NotesMail system.

Sending Your Message

After you select the settings you want, you are ready to save and/or send your mail message. Press Esc to close the message and display the Close Window dialog box shown in Figure 4.29. You can send the message in the following ways:

■ The S̲end and save a copy radio button tells Notes to send the mail and put a copy of the mail message in your mailbox. This is the default for this dialog box and is recommended for any mail that you might need to refer back to in the future (this is called *CYA—cover your a***).

■ The S̲end only radio button tells Notes to send the message but does not put a copy of the mail message in your mailbox. If you are sending mail that you don't need to keep, maybe a joke, you can use this option to save space in your mailbox.

■ The Sa̲ve only radio button tells Notes not to send the message but to save a draft of the mail message in your mailbox. All mail messages that you save without sending are considered drafts until sent and you can see them in the Drafts view. This is handy if you don't have time to finish a mail message and want to come back later and work on it.

- The Discard changes radio button tells Notes to ignore the changes in the mail message. If you are composing a new mail message, this option causes the new message to be neither sent nor saved. If you are editing a message, all edits are discarded and the saved mail stays the same.

When you have chosen the option you want, click OK. Choose Cancel to ignore the option and return to the mail message you are editing. Pressing Esc while this dialog box is displayed is equivalent to choosing Cancel.

> **Tip**
>
> You can also use the Send or the Send And File buttons on the action bar to send the mail. To send the mail and store it in your sent folder without saving a copy in your mailbox, click the Send button.
>
> To save a copy into a folder when the mail is sent, click the Send And File button. This sends the mail and launches the Move to Folder dialog box so you can choose the folder in which to store the mail.

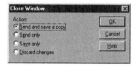

Fig. 4.29   The Close Window dialog box for mail messages.

How Notes Validates Mail Recipients

When you try to send mail, Notes compares each of the recipients' names you have entered in the address fields against the user names in your Personal Name & Address Book. If a match is found, the name is validated and searching stops.

If no match is found, the Public Name & Address Book is searched. If none of the recipient names in your memo matches any of the names in the Name & Address Book, Notes does a *soundex* search (a search based on items that sound similar) to show you a list of users with similar user names.

For example, if you enter the last name Jones but the user name is Will Jones, Notes finds all the people named Jones and displays them in the Ambiguous Name dialog box (see Figure 4.30).

Fig. 4.30   The Ambiguous Name dialog box.

If you see the name of the person you want, double-click the name, or use the arrow keys to select the name and click O̲K. Notes inserts the correct user name in place of the invalid user name.

If you don't see the right name in the dialog box, click the Cancel Sending button and use the Address button on the Action bar to pull up a list of valid names.

> **Tip**
>
> Because the Mail Address dialog box takes its information from the Notes Name & Address Books, using it to address your mail messages can save time and hassle by avoiding invalid user names.

E-Mail Etiquette

Now that you know how to use NotesMail, it's important to know a little about e-mail etiquette so as not to offend your colleagues. The following lists some tips and conventions you might want to follow when sending e-mail messages:

- Do not type your messages in all UPPERCASE. This is called *shouting* and makes people angry with you. Always use the proper case unless you want to imply that you *are* SHOUTING!

- E-mail is private information, just like the rest of a company's business correspondence, and security is important. You should never send an e-mail message with proprietary or confidential information outside the company without prior approval.

- E-mail may seem private but in most cases a business manager can read an employee's e-mail with impunity and without informing the employee and, tape-backups are often made of Notes servers, so your mail might be around for a long time. Before you send that juicy love note to your colleague, remember that others could read it.

- E-mail can be edited and forwarded without the originator's knowledge, unless you use the Prevent copying delivery option when you send your mail.

- Importance and Delivery priority on messages should be set to High only when essential.

- To give constructive criticism or to reprimand someone, it's better to do it in person. E-mail may not convey the tone or message you want.

- People who send frequent or unnecessary messages, or who write dissertations or diatribes, are eventually ignored, like the boy who cried "wolf."

- Subject lines should give the recipient some idea of the content of the message and should be brief.

- E-mail should be read and edited carefully and then spell-checked before you send it. Typos make you look foolish, or convey a misleading or wrong meaning.

- Cute or cryptic use of e-mail shorthand can cause miscommunication. The following lists many of the common e-mail shorthand and *emoticons* (e-mail shorthand is normally enclosed in quotes; for example, <g> which means grin):

BTW:	By the way
FYI:	For your information
LOL:	Laughing out loud
ROFL:	Rolling on the floor laughing
BRB:	Be right back
IMO:	In my opinion
IMHO:	In my humble opinion
CU:	See you...
PMJI:	Pardon me for jumping in
GD&R:	Grinning, ducking, and running
;-)	Wink
:-)	Smiling
:-(	Frowning
:-D	Big smile
:-O	Mouth open in amazement
8-)	Smile with glasses

Tip

Remember that the body of a NotesMail message is rich text, which means that you can include graphics, sounds, movies, or any other object to help liven up your mail. You are not limited to using the text-based shorthand and emoticons.

Using Other Mail Forms

Your mailbox has several forms other than the Memo that can be useful. After the Memo form, the forms you'd be most likely to use are the Appointment form, the Reply form and the Reply with history form, the Task form, and the Phone Message form, all of which are standard in the new NotesMail mailbox.

Creating Appointments

The Appointment form is a key component of group calendaring and scheduling. You can use the Appointment form to keep track of appointments for yourself and others, as well as list other people for an appointment. Figure 4.31 is an example of this form.

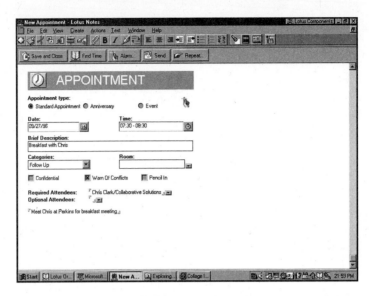

Fig. 4.31   A new appointment for me and Chris Clark from Collaborative Solutions.

For the most part, using the appointment form is easy. You enter the information about an appointment and it's mailed to the attendees. We cover creating and managing appointments in Chapter 9, "Lotus Notes Group Calendaring and Scheduling."

Replying to a Message

You often get a mail message that needs a reply. You can compose a new memo. But that doesn't necessarily reference the original mail, so you have to start from scratch. Notes has a much easier way to create a reply.

You can reply to a mail message with two types of reply forms in your standard mailbox: Reply and Reply with History. You create a reply that references the original mail by selecting the original mail message and choosing Create, Reply or by clicking the Reply button on the Action Bar.

This is a new reply, and the To and Subject fields already have the right values. The To field is set to the user name of the person who sent you the original mail.

The Subject field reflects the subject of the original mail and adds Re: before the subject to indicate that this is a reply. Enter the text of your reply and send the reply as you would any mail message (see Figure 4.32). When Notes sends the reply, it returns you to the original memo.

The Reply with History form is almost exactly like the Reply form, except that it copies in the body of the original mail message. This means you can reply to specific points raised in the original mail message, saving the time it would take to rekey the information (see Figure 4.33).

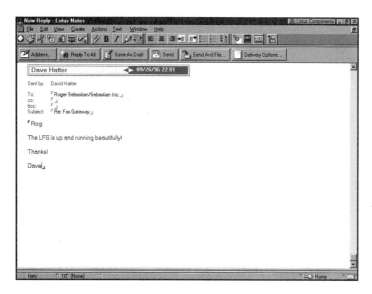

Fig. 4.32 A new reply mail message to a mail message from Roger Sebastian.

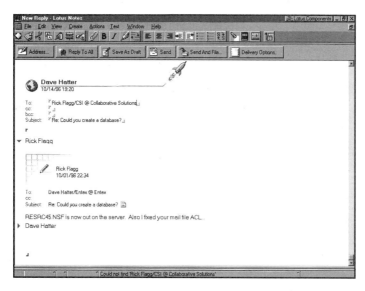

Fig. 4.33 A new Reply With History, showing the text of the original message from Rick Flagg.

To create a Reply With History message, select the mail message you want to reply to and choose Create, Reply with History or click the Reply with History button on the Action bar. As in the Reply form, the To and Subject fields are filled in and the body field holds an exact copy of the original mail message body. Notes also includes a doclink, enabling you to quickly access the original message, which creates a thread. You can edit this copy and insert your rebuttals.

Phone Messages

A phone message is a mail message with a format like the written phone memo pad. If you take a phone call for someone else, you can use the phone message to let her know she has a phone message via Notes mail.

This is not only faster but sets off the new mail indicators in Notes. To send a phone message, choose Create, Special, Phone Message.

Figure 4.34 shows a sample phone message. Your user name appears in the From field, just as it would on a real phone memo pad.

The phone message has additional fields that you can fill in, including Contact and Phone. The message also has check boxes for typical comments such as Telephoned and Please Call.

When you finish the phone message, send it as you would any other mail message.

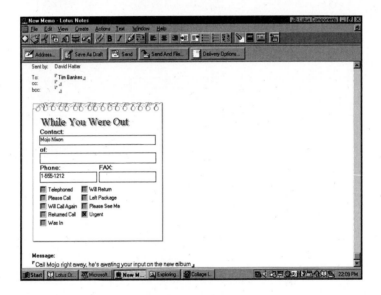

Fig. 4.34 The new Phone Message form in your mailbox.

Tasks

Those of you who have used Notes 3.x might have used the To Do forms in the old mail database. Notes 4.5 overhauls the Task form.

This form allows simple time management: you can assign action items, meetings, anniversaries, birthdays, and the like to you and others. You can see them in the Tasks view. To compose a new Task, choose Create, Task (see Figure 4.35).

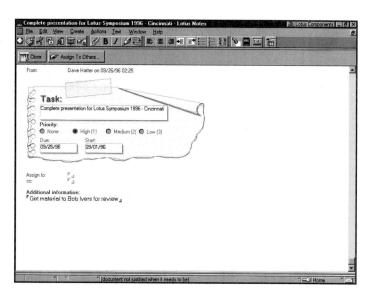

Fig. 4.35   The Task form to remind me to turn my presentation in for review.

The Task field enables you to enter a textual description of the task that needs to be done. The priority radio buttons can be used to assign a priority to the task so that you or the other assignees know the importance of the task.

None is the default setting for priority. The Start and Due fields enable you to enter dates to track when a task needs to be done and how many overdue tasks you have.

You can enter other comments in the Additional information field. To assign this task to others, click the Assign to Others button on the Action bar.

This displays the Assign to and cc fields, which work just like the To and cc fields in the Memo form. Any user or group names entered into these fields cause all the named individuals to get the task via mail.

Bookmarks

Bookmarks are another incredibly useful new feature of the new Mailbox design. A bookmark is a customized mail message that enables you to automatically create a doclink to any document.

An example of a typical use for a bookmark is if you're browsing the Technical Support database and find a document you want to share with your team. You can copy the document into a mail message and send it to everyone on the team.

But this would be redundant because the document already exists in the Technical Support database. You could instead send mail that tells the users where to find the document.

Or you could send them a bookmark. This is a dynamic link to the original document that takes the user there with a single click.

To compose a bookmark, open or select the document you want to link to and then, if you are not in your mailbox, choose Create, Mail, Special, Bookmark. If you are in your mailbox, choose Create, Special, Bookmark.

A new form that looks like Figure 4.36 is created with a doclink and some descriptive information that explains to the recipients what the doclink points to.

When you compose the bookmark, you add the address information as you would with any other mail form and send the bookmark. When the recipients get the bookmark, they follow the instructions beside the red arrow and click the link icon to open the linked document.

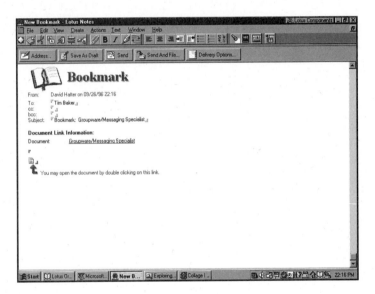

Fig. 4.36 The Bookmark form lets you create and mail a doclink to another document.

Forwarding a Mail Message

You often receive a mail message you want to send to other users who were not included in the original distribution list. To do so, select any mail message and choose Actions, Forward or click the forward button on the action bar.

You see a new Memo form that looks much like a regular memo, except that the body of the memo contains the whole mail message you were reading or had selected (see Figure 4.37). (This is like the Reply With History option but it doesn't put the sender's address into the To field and doesn't automatically fill in the subject field.)

You can address the message using the steps you learned earlier in this chapter. You can edit the body of the memo if you need to add to or change the original message, or to include additional information with the old message. Send the message as you would any other.

You can see from the figure that the original mail has been copied into the body of the new mail message and that other text has been added. Forwarding mail messages makes it easy to distribute information to other users.

> **Note**
>
> Remember that unless you enable Prevent Copying in the Delivery Options for your mail messages, any recipient can easily forward your mail messages to any number of other users without your knowledge.
>
> This includes Internet users if the appropriate Message Transfer Agents (MTAs) are in place. A major security breach could result, so keep this in mind when mailing confidential information.

Notes Basics

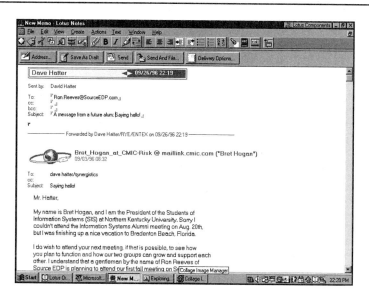

Fig. 4.37 A message forwarded from me to Ron Reeves.

Printing Messages

Even though you use your mail electronically 99 percent of the time, you may occasionally want to print a copy of a mail message you have sent or received. Printing a mail message is just like printing any Notes document.

Here is a reminder for printing documents:

1. Select the message you want to print. (Remember, if you are in a view or a folder, you do not have to open the message to print it.) To print the mail message you are reading, proceed to the next step.

2. Choose File, Print, or click the File Print SmartIcon. This causes the File Print dialog box to be displayed. (See Chapter 3, "Using Databases," for more information about this dialog box.)

3. Select the appropriate settings for this document in the FIle Print dialog box.

4. Choose OK to print your document.

5. Remember that users can disable the printing capability when they send you a message.

Closing Messages

When you are finished reading a mail message, you can close the message and return the folder or view you were in by doing any of the following:

■ Press Esc.

■ Press Ctrl+F4 or Ctrl+W.

■ Click the view or folder window's Control menu box and choose Close (the Control menu box is the small application icon in the upper-left corner of the view or folder window) or Select File, Close.

> **Note**
>
> You see two Control menu boxes, one for Notes R4 in the upper-left corner, and one for the view or folder window just below the program's Control menu box. Make sure you click the view or folder's window. If you inadvertently click the Notes Control menu box, you are prompted to exit Notes.

■ Double-click the right mouse button in the document. This is a holdover from Notes 3.x and may not be enabled for your workstation. See Chapter 2, "Customizing Notes," for more information on how to enable this feature.

Deleting Messages

As you accumulate mail messages in your mailbox, you'll probably decide you no longer need a number of messages. Unneeded mail messages clutter your mailbox, making it harder to find the important messages. They also occupy precious disk space and decrease the performance of your mailbox.

(If you keep every mail message you get, you'll consume a large amount of disk space and your administrator will probably call to tell you about it.)

Consider the following techniques for conserving disk space:

■ After you have read an incoming message, delete it unless it has information you really need to keep. Similarly, when you send a message to someone else, don't select the Save checkbox in the Document Save dialog box unless you really need to keep a copy of the mail message.

I

- You may often need to keep messages for a long time—for example, if you work in a legal department. You might also need to keep a message or a return receipt message as proof that you responded to a problem.

- You can print the message and delete the electronic copy. You can also move the message to an archive mailbox, which is discussed in the next section.

- Regularly scan your mailbox, at least once a month for unneeded messages. Take five minutes to examine your mailbox for messages that you no longer need. When you find these messages, delete them.

- You may get mail messages with file attachments you don't really need but you want to save the mail message. Deleting unneeded attachments can conserve significant space because the attachments are also stored in your mailbox.

▶▶ See "Deleting Attachments," p. 232

Deleting Mail Messages

Because of the way Notes allocates storage space for databases, your mailbox can eat up inordinate amounts of disk space if you don't delete mail messages frequently. This is important for remote users because disk space on most notebooks is usually at a premium.

The moral of this story is to delete your unneeded mail frequently. This makes it easier to find mail you need to keep, saves disk space, and increases the performance of your mailbox.

As in any Notes database, to delete mail messages, open your mailbox and choose the view or folder you find most useful for reading mail. Then, select the message or messages you want to delete and press the Delete key on your keyboard. Or click the Edit Cut SmartIcon to marks that message for deletion.

Notes does not delete the message immediately; it moves the message to the Trash folder. This is a useful feature because if you decide you really don't want to delete any of the marked documents, you can rescue them from the trash by opening the trash folder and moving the documents back out.

If you are sure you want to delete the documents in the trash folder, click the empty Trash button on the action bar, press the F9 key, or close the database. Any of these actions displays a dialog box warning you that you are going to permanently delete the documents and asking you to confirm the operation.

You can also delete a message while you are reading it by pressing Delete. Notes flags the message (with the trash can icon in the view marker column) for deletion and takes you to the next message in your mailbox. This works only when you're reading a message, however. The Delete key has a different effect when you are composing a message.

Exiting Your Mailbox

To exit your mailbox, use any of the following methods you learned earlier for closing a database:

- Press Esc.

- Press Ctrl+F4 or Ctrl+W.

- Double-click the control box for your mailbox view.

- Double-click the right mouse button (it doesn't matter what the mouse is pointing at). This method only works if the right mouse button option is enabled as a user preference on your workstation.

As in any database, if you have flagged messages for deletion, Notes gives you a prompt asking if you want to permanently delete the flagged documents. If you click <u>Y</u>es, the messages you have flagged are deleted permanently from your mailbox. If you click <u>N</u>o, the messages stay in your mailbox and the deletion flag is reset.

Handling Your Mail with the Status Bar and SmartIcons

As you are probably aware by now, Notes provides many ways to do the same task, particularly for e-mail. One of the most useful features is the mail section in the far right corner of the status bar.

When a dimmed Envelope icon is displayed, you have no new mail. When new mail is transferred to your mailbox, an in box with a piece of paper in it is displayed. Clicking this icon displays the menu in Figure 4.38.

Fig. 4.38   You can access the Mailbox feature from the status bar.

Choose one of the following options from this menu:

- You can select the Create Memo option to open your mailbox and create a new blank mail memo, just as if you had chosen <u>C</u>reate, <u>M</u>emo in your mailbox.

- Selecting the second option, Scan Unread Mail, opens your mailbox and opens the first unread mail message in your mailbox. You can then navigate between the unread documents until no more unread documents are left. If no unread mail messages are found, the status bar displays

```
There are no unread documents in your mail file.
```

> **Note**
>
> When you use this method to read the unread documents, you open the documents. This means that Notes no longer considers the mail message unread.

- You can select Receive Mail, the third option, to initiate a server connection and begin replicating your local mailbox with the server copy of your mailbox. Any new mail that is queued at the server mailbox is transferred to your local mailbox. Outgoing mail is not sent.

- The fourth option, Send Outgoing Mail, initiates a server connection and routes pending mail from your workstation to the server's mailbox. Incoming mail is not received.

- The fifth option, Send & Receive Mail, performs the actions of both Receive Mail and Send Outgoing Mail.

- The sixth and final option, Open Mail, opens your mailbox and displays the last view or folder you used.

When you open your mailbox, in addition to the status bar, Notes provides a context-sensitive set of NotesMail SmartIcons that can make your NotesMail sessions easier and more productive. Table 4.2 shows each of the default NotesMail SmartIcons and its function.

Table 4.2 The Default NotesMail SmartIcons

Icon	Name	Description
	Actions Edit Document	Opens the currently selected document in edit mode.
	Actions Forward	Forwards the currently selected document.
	Navigate Next Main	Goes to the next Main document in the current view or folder.
	Navigate Previous Main	Goes to the previous Main document in the current view or folder.
	Navigate Next	Goes to the next document in the current view or folder.
	Navigate Previous	Goes to the previous document in the current view or folder.
	Navigate Next Unread	Goes to the next unread document in the current view or folder.

(continues)

Notes Basics

Table 4.2 Continued

Icon	Name	Description
	Navigate Previous Unread	Goes to the previous unread document in the current view or folder.
	View Expand	Expands the current category.
	View Collapse	Collapses the current category.
	View Expand All	Expands the whole view (All Categories).
	View Collapse All	Collapses the whole view (All Categories).
	Edit Find Next	Launches the Search dialog box.
	View Show/Hide Search Bar	Toggles the full text search bar off and on.
	View Show/Hide Preview Pane	Toggles the document preview pane off and on.

From Here...

In this chapter, you learn how to work with your mailbox—reading, composing, addressing, printing, deleting, and archiving mail. You should now be able to use NotesMail effectively, increasing your ability to communicate with other e-mail users in your company.

For more information on using NotesMail, see the following chapters:

■ In Chapter 5, "Using the Address Book," you learn about the critical role the Name & Address Books plays in all Notes communications and how they make your NotesMail sessions much more productive and enjoyable.

■ Chapter 9, "Lotus Notes Group Calendaring and Scheduling," teaches you how to use the group calendaring and scheduling capabilities of Notes 4.5.

■ Chapter 6, "Advanced Mail," provides more information on advanced mailing techniques and on securing mail messages, as do Chapter 8, "Working with Documents," and Chapter 22, "Security and Encryption."

■ Chapter 20, "Setting Up to Go Remote," teaches you how to configure your machine to use NotesMail remote.

■ Chapter 21, "Working Remote," helps you get through using Notes from the road.

Chapter 5

Using the Address Book

Chapter 2, "Customizing Notes," briefly discussed the Public and Personal Name & Address Book databases and how important they are to Notes operation. In Chapter 3, "Using Databases," you learned how to address mail by using the names of users and groups from the Name & Address Book (N & A Book). This chapter goes further into the Name & Address Book.

Understanding the Personal Name & Address Book

Figure 5.1 displays a Public N & A Book icon for ABC Company and a Personal N & A Book icon for Dave Hatter. At first glance, the Personal N & A Book and the Public N & A Book seem very similar in form and function, but they are actually quite different in supporting the enhanced functionality of Notes R4.5. The Personal N & A Book database is a subset of the Public N & A Book, created on each user's workstation when the Notes client software is installed. It is essentially a directory service that you can use to store information that pertains only to you and your workstation. For instance, if you frequently send mail to a Notes user in another company, but no one else in your organization needs that e-mail address, then store the address in your Personal N & A Book.

The Public Name & Address Book has a much more important role and a larger scope than the Personal N & A Book. In fact, according to the Lotus documentation, the Public N & A Book is the "most important database in a domain." It is shared by all users in a domain and contains the same types of documents as the Personal N & A Book, but it also contains documents that are used by the server for server administration and maintenance.

From an end user perspective, the use of the Personal and Public N & A Books is similar, and many of the forms in each database are identical. Because much of the functionality of the Public N & A Book is administrative in nature and of little or no concern to end users, I will discuss the Personal Name & Address Book first.

Some of the main topics in this chapter are

- Differences between the Personal and Public Name & Address Books

- How these books work together to make your Notes sessions more productive

Fig. 5.1   The Public and Personal Name & Address Book icons.

> ### Note
>
> If you have used previous versions of Notes, you should be familiar with the Public and Personal N & A Book concept. In Notes 3.0, your Personal N & A Book was based on the same database template (the design of the database was the same) as the Public N & A Book, which meant that although your Personal N & A Book was not shared with other users, it contained the exact same forms and views as the Public N & A Book. In Notes R4.5, each of the databases is based on a different template.
>
> The Public N & A Book database is based on the StdR4PublicAddressBook template (PUBNAMES.NTF) and contains all of the server management forms and views. The Personal N & A Book is based on the StdR4PersonalAddressBook template (PERNAMES.NTF) and contains only forms and views that apply to the workstation. By eliminating forms and views that apply only to the server, the Personal N & A Book is smaller, less confusing, and yields better performance.

Figure 5.2 displays the Create menu of a standard Personal N & A Book. As you can see in Figure 5.2, the Personal N & A Book contains the following types of documents (described in the subsequent sections):

- Company
- Person
- Group
- Location
- Server Connection
- Certificates

Fig. 5.2   The Create menu in Notes R4.

> **Note**
>
> The word standard is used to describe the design elements, such as views, folders, and forms, in your N & A Book as they ship from Lotus. What you actually see might vary from the screens displayed in this chapter, because each of these design elements could be altered by Notes administrators or designers in your organization.

Company Documents

In Notes R4.5, the Personal N & A Book can serve as a makeshift contact manager. In fact, if you use Organizer or any other Personal Information Manager (PIM), you can easily import the "Address" section into your Personal N & A Book. For each company you do business with, you can create a Company document (see Figure 5.3).

> **Note**
>
> If you have used some other application to maintain a list of contacts, you can easily import them into your Personal Name & Address Book without programming if the software supports exporting data as either an ASCII text file (nearly every software package supports this) or a 1-2-3 spreadsheet. Once you have exported the data, the steps you follow next will depend on the type of file format you chose when you exported the data and which fields you want to import from your old PIM into Notes. In order to learn exactly how to do this for your particular data set, see the Lotus Notes Help Database or the Lotus Notes 4 Application Developer's Guide for the topic "Importing."

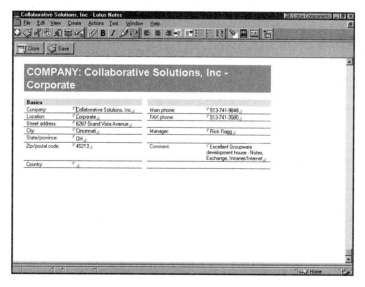

Fig. 5.3   A Company document for Collaborative Solutions, Inc.

The usage of this form is very straightforward; you simply fill in information on a company that you want to store in your Personal N & A Book. Company documents are not used by the system; they merely provide a convenient way for you to keep information about companies you commonly deal with in the same place you keep information regarding the specific people you deal with at a given company.

To create a new Company document, choose Create, Company, (alternatively, from the Companies view, click the New Company Action) then enter the information and press Ctrl+S or press Esc. When prompted to save the document, click Yes.

> **Note**
>
> The line that displays the company name and location immediately beneath the Company graphic on the form will not be displayed until you either save the document or press the F9 key to refresh the document. Each type of document in the N & A Book has this same functionality.

Person Documents

Person documents are one of the most important types of documents in the N & A Book and serve two fundamental purposes: security and directory services. Security is accomplished through the presence, or lack thereof, of Person documents in the Public N & A Book. Valid Notes users must have a Person document in the Public N & A Book, or must be cross-certified to gain access to the server. (For more information on cross-certification and certification in general, please see Chapter 24, "Notes: Under the Hood.") Person documents provide directory services in the sense that the Notes mail router uses Person documents in the Public N & A Book to identify Notes users and find the location of their mailbox.

As a Notes end user, you will have a Person document in the Public N & A Book that was automatically created for you when your administrator created your Notes account. Because of the importance of this document, you should not be able to edit it. If, however, you find that you can edit the document, you should NOT change any of the values it contains without first consulting with your administrator; otherwise, you might cause tremendous problems for yourself. Figure 5.4 displays a Person document in edit mode.

Name and E-Mail Information. The Name and E-Mail sections of the Person document contain important system information used by the Notes server for user authentication and mail routing.

At a minimum, each Person document should have the First name, Last name, Preferred mail, and Notes address fields completed. The First name, Middle initial (which is not required, but should be used because it helps to make a name unique), and Last name fields are the names entered by the administrator when a user is registered. This is the same name stored in the user's ID file.

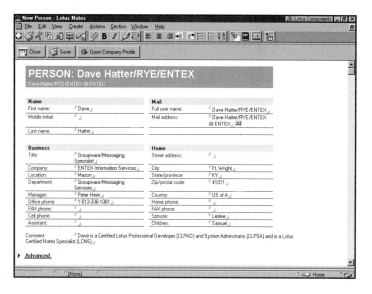

Fig. 5.4 A Person document for John Doe in edit mode.

> **Note**
>
> If the correct password is entered for the user ID in use at the workstation when a user attempts to log in to a Notes server, the server then authenticates the user ID by checking to see if that user exists in its Public N & A Book, or has a valid cross-certificate. If that user exists, it then checks the user's Private Key against the user's Public Key. If it finds a match, the user is authenticated and a communication session with the server is established.
>
> For more information on Public and Private keys, please see Part V, "Advanced Notes Topics."

The other fields in these two sections allow you to further describe the user and enter mail addressing information for users who will need to communicate with other mail systems, such as cc:Mail or MS Mail. They are as follows:

- **The Short name field**—This field can be used to enter a shorter name, such as a nickname, for the user. If a user's name is Jehosephat Van Rumplestiltskin, for example, you might want to give him the short name JVR.

- **The Comment field**—This field allows you to enter additional information that may be helpful when trying to identify an individual.

- **The Mail Address field**—This field is a standard keyword list that displays the Mail Address Assistant dialog box shown in Figure 5.5. The default value for this field is Notes (of course), but if this user employs another mail system, it can be indicated from this list, which will display a "helper" to help the user enter a valid e-mail address.

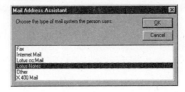

Fig. 5.5 The default value for this field is Notes, but if a user employs another mail system, it can be indicated on this list.

■ **The Notes Mail Address Assistant**—This feature provides some guidance when you enter the names and domain of a user. As you can see in Figure 5.6, the names referring to the user are displayed in the User name field, and the user's domain is displayed in the Notes domain field.

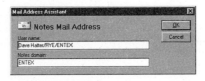

Fig. 5.6 The Notes Mail Address Assistant for Dave Hatter.

> **Note**
>
> Once you have entered the name of the user, you can press the F9 key to refresh the document and Notes attempts to plug in the e-mail address for you. You will need to check the address to ensure that it is correct.

■ **The cc:Mail Address Assistant**—This is a dialog box (shown in Figure 5.7) that can be used to guide you when entering cc:Mail addresses if you need to communicate with someone who uses cc:Mail.

Fig. 5.7 The Notes cc:Mail Address Assistant for Dave Hatter.

■ **The Internet Address Helper**— As you can see from Figure 5.8, the Internet Address helper guides you when entering an Internet Mail address. (Internet mail capability requires an SMTP gateway, or the enablement of the Notes R4 SMTP MTA, and a connection to the Internet through an ISP. See Chapter 25, "Lotus Notes and the Web," for more information on connecting Notes to the Internet.)

Fig. 5.8 The Notes Internet Address Assistant for Dave Hatter.

The X.400 Address Helper guides you when you are entering an address for users who use X.400-compliant mail systems. As you can see from Figure 5.9, X.400 naming can be quite complicated and confusing. In most cases, you will not be able to use X.400 mail unless you have the recipient's business card with his or her X.400 address on it, or the address has been written out for you, as it's highly unlikely that you could correctly guess it.

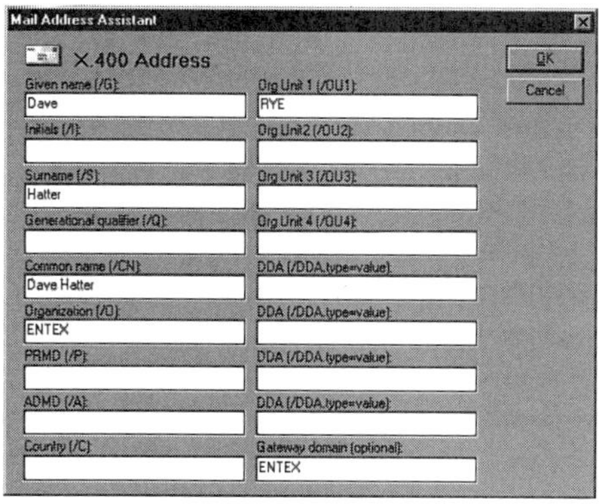

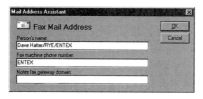

Fig. 5.9 The Notes X.400 Address Assistant for Dave Hatter.

The Fax Mail Address Assistant guides you when entering a fax address. You just enter the user's name, fax number, and the Notes domain that points at your fax gateway (in order to send a fax through Notes, you need either the Lotus Fax Gateway (LFS) or some third-party fax gateway). Figure 5.10 displays the Fax Mail Address Assistant.

Fig. 5.10 The Fax Mail Address Assistant.

The last choice, the Other Address Assistant, guides you when you need to enter an address for some other unlisted type of mail system that is connected to Notes through a gateway. As you can see from Figure 5.11, you just enter the user's mail address and enter the Notes domain that points at the other system.

Notes Basics

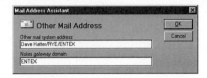

Fig. 5.11   The Notes Other Address Assistant for Dave Hatter.

The Distinguished Name

Each Notes user has a distinguished name that is based on the X.400 naming standard and is broken down into four components: the Common Name (CN), Organizational Unit (OUN, where N is the number of the organization unit), Organization (O), and Country (C). The following format is used:

```
CN/OU1/OU2/OU3/OU4/O/C
```

An example of a fully distinguished name is as follows:

```
Samuel Hatter/R&D/Tech Services/Help Desk/Notes/ABC Company/US
```

The following list explains each component in the name:

- **Common Name**—Each Notes user must have a Common Name, which can be up to 80 characters long. The common name is derived from the user's first and last names (and middle name if entered), as displayed in the Person document and stored in the Notes user ID. Examples are Samuel Hatter or Mojo Nixon. In this example, the common name is `Samuel Hatter`.

- **Organization**—The Organization component of a distinguished user name is typically the name of the company, institution, or organization that is installing Notes, although it can be anything that the administrator chooses to use when the first server is installed. Each Notes user must have an Organization specified as part of their fully distinguished name. Some examples are ABC Company and Mojo Nixon Fan Club. In the Samuel Hatter example, ABC Company is the organization component. At this point, Samuel's distinguished name would be `Samuel Hatter/ABC Company`.

- **Organization Unit**—Normally, the Organization Unit is a department or group name that is added to a distinguished user name to make it unique and to provide additional levels of security within the Notes installation. If two people named Bob Smith worked at ABC Company, for instance, Notes wouldn't know which one you were sending mail to. However, if one worked in the accounting department and the other in the manufacturing department, these department names could be added to their distinguished names as Organizational Units to further qualify each person and grant or deny access at different levels. For example, `Bob Smith/Accounting/ABC Company` might have access to all accounting related databases and servers, but have no access to the manufacturing related databases and servers.

  Although Notes users can have up to four Organization Units in their fully distinguished names, Organizational Units are not required. In the Samuel Hatter example, R&D would be OU1, Tech Services would be OU2, Help Desk would be OU3, and Notes would be OU4. Samuel's fully distinguished name at this point would be `Samuel Hatter/R&D/Tech Services/Help Desk/Notes/ABC Company`.

- **Country**—This is a two-letter abbreviation that identifies your country. The country codes are defined by CCITT. (CCITT, or The Consultative Committee for International Telegraph and Telephone, is a committee of the International Telecommunications Union, a United Nations treaty organization that studies, recommends, and develops standards for technical and operational telecommunications issues.) This component is optional and is only used when needed to uniquely identify a distinguished name worldwide. In the Samuel Hatter example, US is the country component that would yield the fully distinguished name. Samuel's fully distinguished name at this point would be `Samuel Hatter/R&D/Tech Services/Help Desk/Notes/ABC Company/US`.

Whenever you send a Notes mail message to another user, the Mailer module uses the address information that you have entered to look up the distinguished name from the N & A Book. The Router module of the server then uses the distinguished name to route the mail to its recipient(s). If the recipient is another Notes user, the mail will be delivered based on the mail priority and scheduled connections between servers. If the mail recipient is using another supported mail system such as cc:Mail, Internet, or X.400, you must have a connection to the other system for the mail to be routed. In other words, you must have an Internet mail connection for your Internet mail to be routed to the recipient.

Work and Home Information. The Work and Home sections of the Person document are not used by Notes; therefore, it is not necessary to enter information into these fields. However, this information can be a valuable resource for use within the company because it provides other Notes users within your domain access to important contact information that can be easily shared and maintained. If this information is known about each user, it is highly recommended that it be entered. For example, if you were trying to solve a critical customer service issue after-hours and needed a team member's home phone number, you could turn to the Public N & A Book to find it very quickly and easily.

Group Documents

Group documents are very useful because they can be used to refer to multiple users, servers, or even other groups, which can save you a significant amount of time when addressing mail messages and creating database ACLs. For example, you might need to mail the weekly sales numbers to your entire sales team. Rather than enter each of their names into the To field in a mail message (or choose each name from the Address dialog box), just create a group document that references each user, then reference the Group name in the To field of your mail message. Remember that as an end user, you most likely will not be able to add group documents to the Public N & A Book; however, you can request that your administrator add a group, or you can add the group to your Personal N & A Book. To add a group, simply choose Create, Group from the menu in the N & A Book or, from the Groups view, click the New Group button. Figure 5.12 displays the standard group document in edit mode with the Administration section expanded.

Fig. 5.12   A Group document for Dave's Discussion Group.

The first section, Basics, contains the fundamental fields needed to define a group—Group name, Group type, Description, and Members. The Administration section contains additional information that is useful for identifying who created the group and who maintains the group.

Basic Information. You use the Basics fields as follows:

- **The Group name field**—This field is required, as it is the name that Notes will use to find the group. A Group name might be Widget Sales Team or Accounting. Longer names are recommended because they are more descriptive and generally more unique (however, if you make a name really long, it will be cumbersome to use).

- **The Group type field**—This field is a standard keyword list that allows you to determine how a group list will be used (this field is really geared for use in the Public N & A Book). For instance, you can indicate that the group should only be used for database ACLs, which means when addressing mail, it won't be seen. You can set a group for use in mail addressing only, which means it can't be used in ACLs; or you can use a group to deny access, which means that users in a specific group will be denied access to the server. It can also be a multi-purpose group, meaning that it can be used for any of those functions. This field is not required and, in most instances, should be left on the default setting Multi-purpose.

- **The Description field**—This is an optional text field that you can use to add more detail to a Group document. For example, you might want to explain the purpose of a particular group so that other users and administrators understand the purpose of the group.

- **The Members field**—This is a multi-value list field that is used to name the members of the group. When you reference a group, it is this field that Notes uses to determine who or what is in the group. For a Group document to have any meaning, this field must be populated with the Notes usernames of the members of the group. You can click the down arrow button beside the field to launch the Names dialog box and add users or other groups to the list very quickly. Figure 5.13 displays the Names dialog box, which works exactly like the dialog box that is launched when you click the Address button in a mail Memo form. Simply choose the users or groups you want, and click OK.

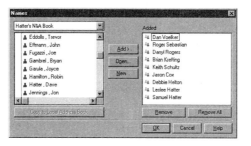

Fig. 5.13 The Names dialog box.

Administrative Information. The Administration section can be expanded and collapsed by clicking the twistie beside the title. Once the section is expanded, the Owners and Administrators fields can be accessed, as follows:

- The Owners field can be used to list the user or users who "own" the group. In most cases, this is the person who created the group and it should be left alone.

- Likewise, the Administrators field can be used to identify the administrator(s) of the group. The group documents found in your Personal N & A Book are identical in function and usage to those found in the Public N & A Book.

> **Note**
>
> Every N & A Book, when it's created, has two groups entered by default. They are the LocalDomainServers and the OtherDomainServers groups. These groups are also entered into every database ACL as Manager when a database is created. If each server in your domain is entered in the LocalDomainServers group, then the servers will be guaranteed access to the database. This ensures that the server can replicate with the local copies of a database.

Location Documents

Location documents are new to Notes R4 and are a very handy way to define location-specific setup information so that you can quickly change your configuration for access to your Notes network from any site. For instance, you might have a Location document for your office connection that enables the LAN port and disables the modem, and a Home location configured to disable the LAN port and dial-out to your Notes server by using the modem on COM2.

When the Notes 4.5 workstation software is installed on your workstation, six default Location documents will be created in your Personal N & A Book automatically. They are the Office, Internet, Home, Island, Travel1, and Travel2 documents. If you travel to other sites frequently and need to communicate with Notes from those locations, you can create Location documents that match the physical configuration that your PC will need to use to connect at each site.

To create a Location document, simply choose Create, Location from the Create menu or, from the Locations view, click the New Location button on the Action Bar.

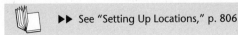 ▶▶ See "Setting Up Locations," p. 806

Figure 5.14 displays a Location document in edit mode. Location documents work hand-in-hand with Server Connection documents. Each Server Connection document contains information needed to connect to a server, such as the server's phone number if a dial-up connection is used. When you attempt to communicate with a Notes server, information from Location documents and Server Connection documents is used to make the connection.

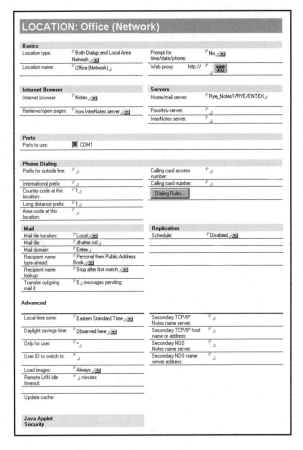

Fig. 5.14 A Location document for your office network.

The Location documents are primarily used when you work remote. See the section "Setting Up Locations" in Chapter 20, "Setting Up to Go Remote," for detailed explanations of the settings in the Location document.

> **Note**
>
> Chapter 20, "Setting Up to Go Remote," assumes that you will be working with a dial-up modem. If you will be connected to the Notes server via a LAN, choose Local Area Network in the Location type field of the Location document, which will tell Notes to use the LAN card in your workstation when looking for a Notes server.
>
> If you need to have LAN and dial-up connections available for a given location, select Both Dial-Up and Local Area Network, which will allow you to access your Notes server either way. The last choice, No Connection, can be used if you will have no connection to a Notes server, but you want to work with local databases on your workstation.

Understanding the Type-Ahead Feature. The Recipient name lookup field in the Location document can be used to enable and configure the type-ahead feature when addressing mail messages. When type-ahead is enabled, Notes will look into the specified N & A books to find a name based on the characters you have entered in the To, cc, or Bcc field of a message. For example, if you wanted to send a mail message to a user named Ace Frehley/KISS Inc., you could position the cursor in the To field and begin typing the first few characters in the recipient's name. In this example, you could type **Ace** and Notes will search the N & A Book for the first user with a name that begins with the characters *Ace*. It is best to enter enough characters to uniquely identify the name. For instance, in our earlier example, it would be better to enter **Ace** than **Ac**.

Although this feature can be very handy, it can be time-consuming if your N & A Book is very large. If you want to disable this feature when you are sending mail messages, select Disabled in the Recipient name type-ahead field of the Location document. If you only want to attempt to fill in the field from your Personal N & A Book, which can greatly reduce the lookup overhead, you can select Personal Address Book Only. If you want to have Notes search both your Personal and Public N & A Books for recipients' names, select Personal then Public Address Book. Notes will then look first in your Personal N & A Book for a match; if one is not found, it will then search the Public N & A Book.

The Recipient name lookup field works in conjunction with the Recipient name type-ahead field. If type-ahead is enabled, you can use the Recipient name lookup field to determine the scope of the search, as follows:

- **Stop after first match**—This setting tells Notes to stop searching when it finds a match for a user name.

- **Exhaustively check all address books**—This tells Notes to continue searching all N & A Books available from your workstation even after a match has been found. If you have many Notes users in your organization, this option can take some time, but may produce more accurate results.

Server Connection Documents

For each server that you communicate with, you must have a Server Connection document. These documents are used to provide specific connection information about each server and, as mentioned earlier, work hand-in-hand with Location documents. In order to create a new Server Connection document, choose Create, Connection from the Create menu. However, in most cases, your administrator should be involved in this process, as you may not necessarily know all the information you need to complete the document.

The type of connection that you use to access the server determines the specific information needed in the Connection type field, as follows:

- If you dial in to the server via modem, select Dialup Modem.

- If you access the server over a LAN connection, select Local Area Network.

- If you use a Notes passthru server, select the Passthru Server option.

- The Remote LAN Service option should only be used if you will be dialing in to a remote LAN service, such as AT&T Network Notes, to get connected to a server. This is similar to a passthru server.

Dial-Up Modem Connection. A dial-up connection document for the server Saturn is shown in Figure 5.15. For details on setting up Server Connection documents for remote access, see the section "Setting Up Connections Records" in Chapter 21, "Working Remote." The other types of connections are described in the following sections.

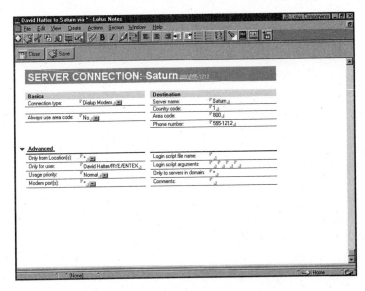

Fig. 5.15 A dial-up server connection document for the server Saturn.

LAN Connection. Figure 5.16 displays a Server Connection document for the server Uranus. In this example, the connection is via a LAN.

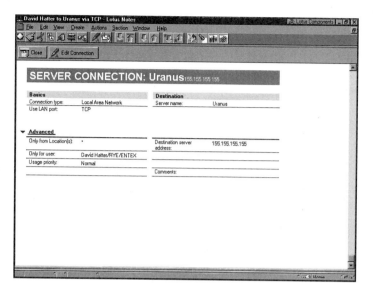

Fig. 5.16 A LAN Server Connection document for the server Uranus.

This document has only a few fields that require information (your system administrator will probably do this for you), as follows:

- **The Use LAN port field**—This is a standard multi-value keyword list field that displays the enabled ports on the system. Use this field to indicate which port to use when accessing the specified server.

- **The Only from Location(s) field**—This can be used in conjunction with specified location documents. This can be useful if you have a number of Notes servers and locations, but cannot access every server from every location.

- **The Only for user field**—This can be used to limit access to the server through the Server Connection document. To use this field, enter fully qualified user names. This is very beneficial when more than one user is using a particular workstation because this field can limit access to users or groups explicitly stated in the list.

- **The Usage priority field**—This is a standard keyword list field. The Normal and Low choices allow you to select the priority Notes uses when it searches for connection documents. Normal priority documents will be used before Low priority documents. If you generally want to replicate with a specific server, you could set it to Normal priority, and set other servers that you might use in the event the primary server is down as Low priority.

- **The Destination section**—Here you only need to enter the name of the server in the Server name field.

- **The Destination server address field**—If you are using the TCP/IP protocol, you should enter the server's IP address in this field.

Passthru Server Connection. Figure 5.17 displays a Server Connection document for the passthru server Pluto in edit mode. This document is nearly identical to the Local Area Network connection document. The special settings for this type of connection are as follows:

- **The Basics section**—Rather than defining a LAN port, you define the Passthru Server name here.

- **The Passthru Server name field**—This is used to define the name of the passthru server that you will connect with.

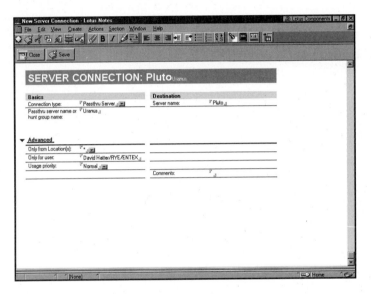

Fig. 5.17   A passthru Server Connection document for the server Pluto.

Remote LAN Service Connection. Figure 5.18 displays a Server Connection document for the remote LAN service server, Mars, in edit mode.

This document is nearly identical to the Local Area Network connection document. The only differences are as follows:

- **The Remote LAN Service field**—This is a standard keyword list field that allows you to select the type of remote LAN service you are using. If the service you are using is not displayed in the current list, you may add the name in the New Keywords input box at the bottom of the Keywords dialog box.

- **The Remote connection name field**—This value is used to give the remote connection a name to help identify this connection when displayed in views.

- **The Login name and Password fields**—These are text fields that work hand-in-hand to get you logged in to the remote access server. You should enter the login name and password that you use when accessing the remote access server.

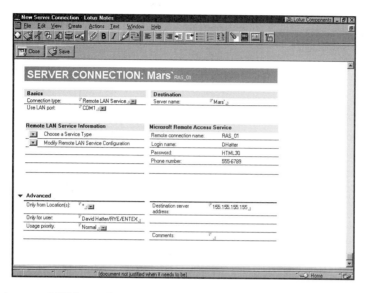

Fig. 5.18   A remote LAN Server Connection document for the server Mars.

Caution

Unless you secure your Personal N & A Book, someone could access your Remote LAN Service documents and learn your user ID and password for this service. There are two good solutions to protect the confidentiality of your Personal N & A Book.

The first method would be to encrypt the entire database, which would only allow access to someone with your ID and Notes password. This method adds some overhead in terms of performance and disk space, but is a reliable and secure method. To use this method, right-click your Personal N & A Book and choose Database Properties. You can then use the Encryption button to secure your database.

The second method will only secure specific documents. If you want to secure your Remote LAN Service document, right-click that document in a view and then choose Document Properties, which will launch the Document Properties InfoBox. Then click the tab that displays a small key. On this tab you may choose a list of people and groups that can access the document; you can also associate an encryption key with the document, which will protect the contents of your document from prying eyes.

- **The Phone number field**—This is a text field for storing the phone number used to connect to the remote LAN service.

Certificate Documents. Your Personal N & A books will also contain Certificate and Cross-Certificate documents. When you are certified to communicate with a server, you should receive a certificate or cross-certificate document—you must have one to be authenticated by the server.

 ▶▶ See "Understanding Certificates," p. 877

Creating New Documents

If you need to add users, groups, connections, and so on to your Personal N & A Book, complete the following steps:

1. Select your Personal N & A book.

2. Choose Create. (An alternative method is to open one of the views that contains the type of documents you want to create and use the Add button on the Action bar to create a new document.

3. Select the type of document you want to create from the following list:

   - Company
   - Group
   - Location
   - Person
   - Server Connection
   - Server Certifier

4. Fill in the information in the newly created document.

5. Press Ctrl+S, press Esc, and choose Yes, or use the File Save SmartIcon to save the document.

Tip

It's easy to add to your Personal N & A Book a user from whom you've received a mail message. Open the mail message and choose Actions, Add Sender to Address Book. This will automatically create a new Person document in your Personal N & A Book and copy the user's name, mail type, and Notes address into the appropriate fields. You can then add any additional information you have and save the new document. This method is very quick and easy and helps to ensure that the Person document contains valid information.

Editing and Deleting Documents

After you have been using Notes for some time, you will most likely realize the need to update and/or delete documents that exist in your Personal N & A Book. As you have probably guessed, this process works in exactly the same manner as every other Notes database. Simply open the view that displays the document(s) that you want to edit or delete.

For example, if you wanted to edit a Person document, you could open the People view and find the document you need to update. Simply select it in the view and either press Ctrl+E, or click the Edit button on the action bar, to open the document in edit mode. You can then make your changes and save the document. If you need to delete a Group document for a group that is no longer needed, simply select the group in the view and press your Delete key, or choose Edit, Clear, which will display the trashcan icon beside that document, indicating that it has been flagged for deletion.

Understanding the Public Name & Address Book

Although few users utilize the Public Name & Address Book for little more than mail addressing, it is much more than a simple user directory. When the first server in a domain is installed, Notes will automatically create a new Public N & A Book database in the Notes\Data directory (the actual filename defaults to NAMES.NSF) from the StdR4PublicAddressBook PUBNAMES.NTF template.

> **Note**
>
> In Lotus Notes, a domain is a group of users who share the same Public N & A Book, which controls mail routing. A company that has several locations can have one domain or many domains. The number of domains required is usually determined by security needs and the number of users in each domain. As a domain grows, so does its Public N & A Book, which decreases overall system performance because N & A Book searches take longer and consume more disk space. Each user's domain is determined by the server that his or her mailbox resides on. Don't get confused by this last sentence if you use workstation-based mail; even though you access your mail messages through a local database, it is merely a replica of your mailbox on the Notes server.

The Public N & A Book plays dual roles in every Notes installation. First, it provides Directory Services by acting as a central repository for user, server, and group names that can be accessed for communication with others. It also acts as a server management tool for Notes administrators by providing the Notes server with information on replication schedules, mail routing, automatic tasks, mail-in databases, certificates, and other important system information. Even if you don't use Notes Mail at your company, the Name & Address Book must exist for the Notes server(s) to operate properly.

Because the Public Name & Address Book plays such a crucial role in every Notes installation and can affect every user in a domain, access levels above Reader (which would allow changes to the database) should be limited to a select group of people who are very familiar with its operation. In most cases, you will not be allowed to create any type of document in the Public N & A Book. If you have an occasion to add a document, say a Person or Group document, to the Public N & A Book, you will probably need to send a request to your Notes administrator.

In order to make maintenance of the Public Name & Address Book easier and more secure, Lotus automatically adds a number of roles that can be used to refine the ACL and allow users or groups to perform very specific actions to certain types of documents. For example, you can assign the administrator who needs to certify users the Author access and the UserCreator and UserModifier roles to create and edit Person documents. He or she would not, however, be able to create, edit, or delete any of the other documents in the Public N & A Book.

Regardless of your access level (even if you have Manager access to the Public N & A Book), in order to create a document, you must be named in the appropriate Creator role. The Modifier roles only apply to users with Author access; users with Editor, Designer, or Manager access are automatically granted modifier rights. The following list shows the roles available in the Public N & A Book:

- **GroupCreator**—GroupCreator allows users or groups named in this role to create new groups, but not to modify or delete them.

- **GroupModifier**—GroupModifier allows users or groups named in this role to edit or delete groups, but not to create them.

- **NetCreator**—NetCreator allows users or groups to create all documents except Person, Group, and Server documents.

- **NetModifier**—NetModifier allows users or groups to edit or delete all documents except Person, Group, and Server documents.

- **ServerCreator**—ServerCreator allows users or groups to create Server documents.

- **ServerModifier**—ServerModifier allows users or groups to edit or delete Server documents.

- **UserCreator**—UserCreator allows users or groups to create Person documents.

- **UserModifier**—UserModifier allows users or groups to edit or delete Person documents.

In the first half of this chapter, I discussed how the Personal N & A Book contained only a subset of the functionality of the Public N & A Book, and this becomes readily apparent when you examine the Create menu in the Public N & A Book.

As you can see in Figure 5.19, many of the forms are the same as in the Personal N & A Book, but there are several additional forms available from the menu. These forms create documents that fall into two basic categories of services that the Public N & A Book provides: Directory Services and Server Management.

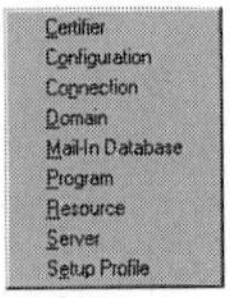

Fig. 5.19   The server forms available in the Public Name & Address Book.

Directory Services

Each time you send a mail message or open a database on a Notes server, you will come into contact with the directory services aspects of the N & A Book. Notes keeps track of users and servers in the Public N & A Book. Whenever a mail message is sent, the Notes server will look in the Public N & A Book in an attempt to find a document that corresponds to the user, server, or group names listed on the envelope of the mail message. If a match is found, then the message can be routed; if no match is found, then the server cannot route the message.

Likewise, when a user attempts to open a database on a server, the server examines the database's ACL. (Remember, if you are working with a local database, you have Manager access by default.) If a user is listed in a group in the ACL, the server must find that group in the Public N & A Book to determine if the user is in the group.

In the Public N & A Book, the following four forms fall into the directory services category:

- Person documents
- Server documents (these documents serve both roles—directory services and server management)
- Group documents
- Location documents

These forms are described in the following sections.

Person Documents. Each Notes user in a domain will be identified by a Person document in the Public N & A Book. A user's Person documents in the Public and Personal N & A Books are identical. The primary difference is that Person documents in the Public N & A Book are shared amongst all users in the domain.

A Person document is automatically created in the Public N & A Book for each user during the new user registration process (which also creates a certified user ID). Certain key fields in the Name and E-Mail sections are populated based on the registration information. If these users will be accessing Notes databases using Domino and the Web, there are additional fields that will be added. For more information about setting up Person documents for Web users, see Chapter 27, "Using Domino Server's HTTP Service."

Caution

In most instances, with the exception of your Person document, you will not have sufficient access to the Public N & A Book to make changes to any of the documents it contains. It is critically important that you do not make changes to any documents in the Public N & A Book without first speaking to your Notes administrator, as this can cause a wide variety of serious problems, such as mail not routing. In fact, in almost every instance, you should request that the Notes administrator make any required changes.

Server Documents. Each server in a domain has a Server document in the Public N & A Book (automatically created when a new server is installed).

Basic and Network Configuration Information. Like most forms, the server form is divided into logical sections. The following are the basic fields:

- **The Server name field**—This contains the name the server was given during the installation process, and is required. On the outside chance that you have edit access to server documents, do not change this field, unless you are absolutely certain that you must change it. Changing a server name requires updating every other document in the Public N & A Book that refers to that server (which could be every document).

- **The Server title field**—This is not required, but can be used to help identify a particular server when looking at server views and folders.

- **The Domain field**—This contains the domain name that was entered for a server during installation, and is required. The value in this field is critically important in the mail routing process and should not be changed without consulting your administrator.

> ### Caution
>
> In most cases, unless you are the Notes Administrator for your installation, you will not be able to edit any of the server documents. If, however, you can edit these documents, be especially careful not to change the server or domain names unless you are absolutely certain that you know what you are doing. If you inadvertently change either of these fields, you could cause the Notes server to have a variety of problems communicating with other servers and users and could possibly cause the entire Notes installation to fail.

- **The Administrators field**—This allows you to name users or groups of users who are responsible for the server. Users named in this field will be able to use the Remote Console, which means that they can administer your Notes server(s) from their workstations, or even remote locations. This lends a tremendous amount of power and flexibility to Notes administration, but also brings with it a certain level of danger. For instance, a Notes server can be shut down from a remote location, but cannot be restarted remotely.

The next section of the server document, called Network Configuration, is a table that defines network information about the server so that users and other servers can communicate with a given server. For example, you can define and enable a port so that it is seen in one Notes Named Network, but not in other Notes Named Networks. For more information on the meaning of each of these settings, see your Lotus Notes R4 documentation.

Restriction Information. The Restriction section of the document is very important because it enables you to limit users or groups of users to certain tasks, as follows:

■ **The Access server field**—This field allows the administrator to define users or groups who can access the server. If this field is left blank, then any user who has an ID that has been certified by the server in question can access that server. If any names are put in this field, then only those users named can access the server.

> **Tip**
>
> It can get very tedious and time-consuming to maintain these lists for many servers. The folks at Lotus were kind enough to provide the following shortcuts to make this easier. You can insert an asterisk (*) to allow access to everyone listed in the Public N & A Book. An asterisk followed by a view name allows access to everyone listed in that view of the Public N & A Book. An asterisk followed by a slash (/) and a hierarchical certifier's name allows access to everyone certified by that certifier.

■ **The Not access server field**—This field does the exact opposite of the Access Server field. Even if you have an ID that has been certified by the server, you will not be granted access to the server if your name is in this field (or in a group that is in this field).

> **Note**
>
> Lotus recommends that you create a group name such as Deny_Access or Terminations and put that group name in the Not access server field. You can then add users who leave the company to the group, and they will immediately be denied access to all servers that have that group specified.

■ **The Create new databases field**—This field can be used to define a list of users who can create databases on a given server. Again, if this field is left blank, any certified user can access the server and can create new databases on the server. If any names are defined in this field, then only those users can create new databases.

■ **The Create replica databases field**—This field works in a similar fashion to the Create new databases field, except it controls the ability to create replica databases. The one difference is that, if this field is left blank, no one can create replicas on the server.

> **Note**
>
> In Notes R3, many of the settings that you can now maintain in the Restrictions section of the server document had to be maintained manually in the NOTES.INI file. It is much easier to maintain these settings through the server document.

Contact Information. The Contact section allows you to define the following additional information about a server that helps others determine where a server is and whom it belongs to:

- **The Location, Department, and Comment fields**—These fields are not used by Notes and are not required but can be used to provide additional information.

- **The Detailed description field**—This field can be used to enter as much text as necessary to help identify the purpose and usage of a server. For example, if a server is used only as a replication hub, it might be helpful to note that in this field.

Statistics Reporting. The Statistics Reporting section allows the administrator to establish performance and error reporting for a server, as follows:

- **The Mail-In database address to receive reports field**—This allows the administrator to define a mail-in database that will have the server's reports mailed to it. This is particularly handy in large organizations with multiple servers, because these reports can be centralized in a database on one server.

- **The Collection interval field**—This allows the administrator to define how often the server's statistics should be reported. The default collection interval, 60 minutes, should be sufficient in most cases.

Group Documents. Group documents in both the Public and Personal N & A Books are identical and are used in the same way. The primary difference is that Group documents in the Public N & A Book are shared amongst all users in the domain.

Location Documents. Much like Group documents, Location documents in both the Public and Personal N & A Books are identical and are used in the same way. The primary difference is that Location documents in the Public N & A Book are shared amongst all users in the domain.

The rest of the documents in the Public N & A Book generally fall into the Server Management category.

Server Management Documents

The Public N & A Book contains the documents that are almost exclusively used by Notes Administrators; I will only briefly examine these documents. (For a more detailed explanation of the purpose and usage of these documents, please refer to your Lotus Notes Release 4.x Administrator's Guide.) They are the following:

- **Configuration documents**—These documents are used to control and monitor the Notes environment, reducing the workload on administrators. Examples of Configuration documents are the ACL Monitor, Event, Replication Monitor, and Statistics Monitor documents.

- **Certifier and Cross-Certifier documents**—These documents identify each certificate's ancestry. Certifier documents are crucial to the security of a Notes installation. For more information, refer to Chapter 22, "Security and Encryption."

- **Domain Documents**—These documents can be created to allow communication and mail routing to other Notes domains or to foreign domains, such as the Internet. There are two basic types—Foreign Domain documents and Non-Adjacent Domain documents. Foreign Domain documents are used to define a non-Notes domain, such as a cc:Mail domain, while Non-Adjacent Domain documents are used when you need to communicate with a Notes domain through an intermediary domain. For example, you want to send mail to Ace Frehley in the XYZ domain, but you don't have a connection to that domain; however, you do have a connection to the ABC domain, which communicates with the XYZ domain. A Non-Adjacent Domain document would specify the route to XYZ through ABC.

- **Connection Documents**—These are much like the Connection documents in the Personal N & A Book, except, rather than defining user-to-server connections, they define server-to-server communication and establish mail-routing and replication schedules.

- **Program Documents**—These can be used to automatically start server tasks, batch programs, or API programs. For example, if you wrote an API program to transfer data from an Access database to a Notes database and wanted it to run each night, you could create a Program document that would run the program at the specified interval.

- **Setup Profile Documents**—These documents allow the administrator to define a common set of setup elements that can then be applied to multiple users. Profile documents can make adding new users to the system significantly less complicated and time-consuming. For example, if you wanted everyone in a certain OU, such as Accounting, to be configured exactly the same, you could create a Profile document that would allow you to build a common set of configuration parameters for this group.

- **Mail-In Database Document**—These documents allow the administrator to configure a database to receive mail messages. For example, you might have a sales rep on the road compose an expense report form and mail it into a centralized expense report database.

Using Views in the Name & Address Books

Each of the Name & Address Books contains views and folders that can be very useful. Like the documents that each N & A Book contains, many of the views overlap and provide the same functionality, but on a different scale. In this section, I will examine the views that exist in the Personal N & A Book first and then the views that only exist in the Public N & A Book. When a view exists in both databases, I will point out any differences.

Companies View

The standard Companies view is found only in the Personal N & A Book (see Figure 5.20). This view is very straightforward. The first column, Name, displays the name of each company, sorted in ascending order. The second column, Telephone, displays the main phone number for that company.

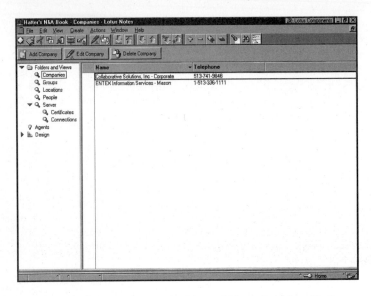

Fig. 5.20 The standard Companies view in the Personal Name & Address Book.

Groups View

The standard Groups view exists in both the Personal and Public N & A Books. The Group column displays the name of each group, sorted in ascending order. The next column, Description, displays the group's description if one was entered.

Locations View

The standard Locations view exists only in the Personal N & A Book. This view displays all of the Location documents that exist in your Personal N & A book, sorted by the first (and only) column, Location, which displays the name of the location (see Figure 5.21).

People View

The standard People view is the default view in both the Personal and Public N & A Book. The People view is very useful because it displays every Notes user in the domain if you are looking at your Public N & A Book, or every user you have defined if you are looking at your Personal N & A Book (see Figure 5.22). The following is the information available in this view:

- The first column in the view, Name, displays the name of the user, sorted in ascending order by last name.

- The next column, Telephone, is a multi-row column. This is another new and very useful feature of Notes R4, which displays the user's office and home phone number if this information has been entered into the document.

- The last column in the view, E-Mail address, is pretty much self-explanatory; it displays the user's Notes e-mail address.

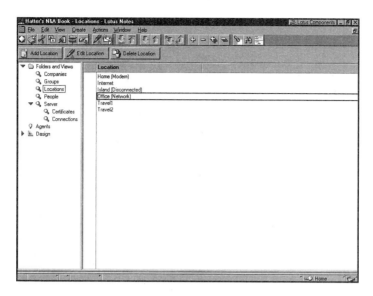

Fig. 5.21 The standard Locations view in the Personal Name & Address Book.

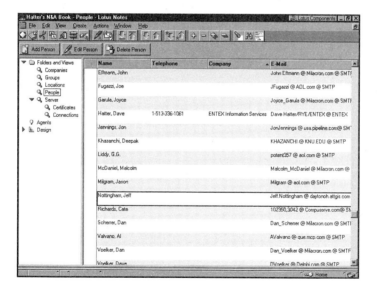

Fig. 5.22 The standard People view.

Server/Certificates View

The standard Server/Certificates view can be found in both the Personal and Public N & A Books. In the Public N & A Book, it displays all of the certificates and cross-certificates the servers in the current domain hold. In the Private N & A Book, it displays all of the certificates and cross-certificates that you hold.

Server/Connections View

The standard Server/Connections view in the Personal N & A Book is very similar to the Connections view in the Public N & A Book. In the Public N & A Book, it displays all of the connections for servers in the current domain. In the Personal N & A Book, it displays all of the connections you have configured. A sample of this view is shown in Figure 5.23.

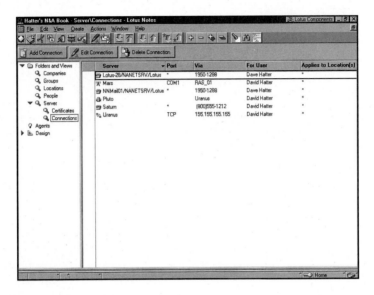

Fig. 5.23 The standard Server/Connections view.

This view shows all Server Connection documents in your Personal N & A Book, as follows:

- The first column, Server, displays the name of the server this connection document refers to. It is sorted in ascending order.

- The next column, Port, displays the port that the connection will attempt to use.

- The Via column displays the route the connection will take.

- The final column, Applies to Location(s), displays any location-specific information. An asterisk (*) indicates that this connection document can be used from any location.

Server/Clusters View

The standard Server/Clusters view in the Public N & A Book displays all of the server clusters in your domain (this is based on the cluster name field in the server documents).

This view shows all Server Clusters documents that are part of a Notes server cluster in your Personal N & A Book, as follows:

- The first column, Cluster, displays the name of the cluster this server is in. It is sorted in ascending order.

- The Server column displays the name of each server.

- The Title column displays the server's title if one is entered.

- The final column, Administrator, displays the name(s) of the server's administrators.

Server/Configurations View

The standard Server/Configurations view in the Public N & A Book displays all of the Server Configuration documents for the Domain.

This view shows all Server Configuration documents in your Personal N & A Book, as follows:

- The first column, Server Name, displays the name of the server using this configuration.

- The Parameters column displays all of the settings in this configuration.

- The Last Updated By column displays the name of the person who last updated the configuration.

Server/Deny Access Groups View

The standard Server/Deny Access Groups view in the Public N & A Book displays all of the groups in the domain that are defined as Deny Access Groups (see Figure 5.24). Remember that when you create a group, you can define the type of group from the following list: Multi-purpose, Access Control List Only, Mail Only, Deny List Only. This view provides administrators a quick and easy way to view just the groups configured as Deny List Only, rather than trying to find them mixed in with the other groups.

The columns display the following information:

- The Group column displays the name of each of the Deny Access Groups.

- The next column, Description, displays the group description if one was entered.

Server/Domains View

The standard Server/Domains view displays all of the Foreign and Non-Adjacent Domain documents in the Public N & A Book. A sample of this view is shown in Figure 5.25.

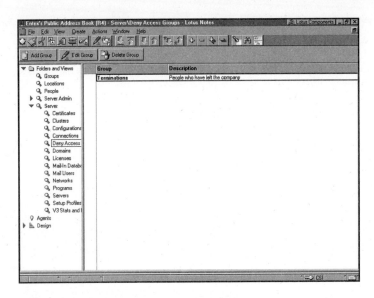

Fig. 5.24   The standard Server/Deny Access Groups view.

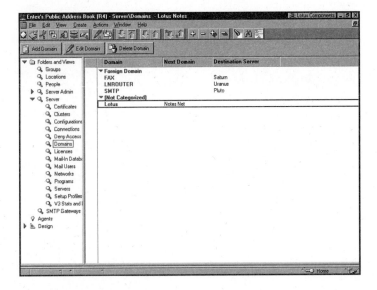

Fig. 5.25   The standard Server/Domains view.

This view shows all Server Connection documents in your Personal N & A Book, as follows:

- The first column, Domain, displays the name of the domain.

- The next column, Next Domain, displays the next connection for non-adjacent domains.

■ The Destination Server column displays the location of the final destination for the domain.

Server/Licenses View

The standard Server/Licenses view in the Public N & A Book displays a summary of all the various types of Notes licenses registered in your Notes installation, along with a count, providing an easy way to keep track of your Notes licenses (see Figure 5.26).

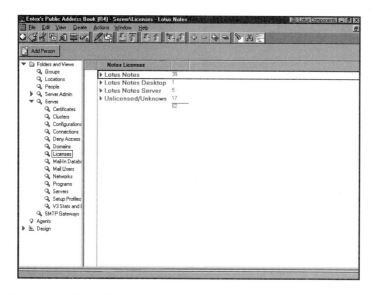

Fig. 5.26   The standard Server/Licenses view.

The columns display the following information:

■ The first column, Notes Licenses, displays the types of licenses registered.

■ The second column displays a count of each type of license.

Server/Mail-In Databases View

The standard Server/Mail-In Databases view in the Public N & A Book displays all of the mail-in database documents (see Figure 5.27).

The columns display the following information:

■ The first column, Name, displays the name used by the router for delivering mail into the database.

■ The second column, Server, displays the server the database resides on.

■ The Database column displays the actual path and filename of the database.

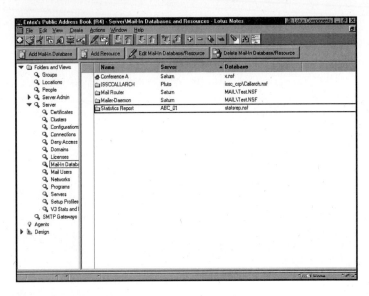

Fig. 5.27   The standard Server/Mail-In Databases view.

Server/Mail Users View

The standard Server/Mail Users view in the Public N & A Book displays a categorized list of all mail users based on their mail server. A sample of this view is shown in Figure 5.28.

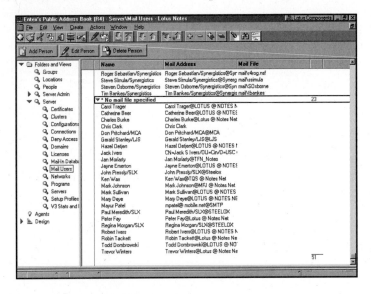

Fig. 5.28   The standard Server/Mail Users view.

The columns display the following information:

■ The first column is sorted and categorized based on the server name.

■ The second column, Name, displays the user's common name.

- The third column, Mail Address, displays the user's complete mail address.

- The fourth column, Mail File, displays the path and actual filename of the user's mail file.

- The fifth and final column displays a count of users on each server.

Server/Networks View

The standard Server/Networks view in the Public N & A Book displays all of the Notes Named Networks in your domain (see Figure 5.29).

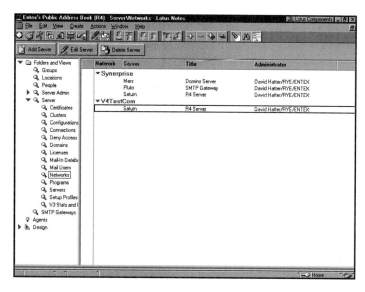

Fig. 5.29   The standard Server/Networks view.

The columns display the following information:

- The Network column is sorted and categorized based on the Notes Named Networks stored in the server documents in your domain.

- The second column, Server, displays each server in the Notes Named Network.

- The Title column displays the server title, if one was entered.

- The Administrator column displays the administrator(s) for each server.

Server/Programs View

The standard Server/Programs view in the Public N & A Book displays all of the program documents. A sample of this view is shown in Figure 5.30.

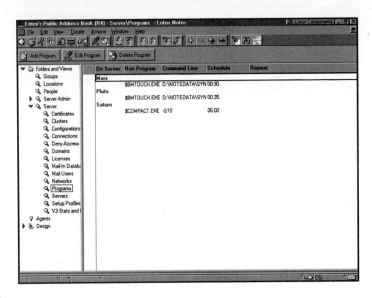

Fig. 5.30 The standard Server/Programs view.

The columns display the following information:

- The On Server column is sorted and categorized based on the name of the server on which the program will run.

- The Run Program column displays the name of the program that you want to run.

- The Command Line column displays the path and filename of the program to run.

- The Schedule column displays the time that the program is scheduled to run.

- The Repeat column displays the interval in which the program is designed to run.

Server/Setup Profiles View

The standard Server/Setup Profiles view in the Public N & A Book displays all of the server setup profiles.

The columns display the following information:

- The first column, Name, displays the name used by the router for delivering mail into the database.

- The Servers column displays the server the database resides on.

Replicating the Public Name & Address Book

If you are primarily a remote user (that is, you spend most of your time using Notes not connected to a LAN), you will probably want to create a replica of the Public N & A Book on your workstation so that you can take advantage of the user addresses and groups it contains, rather than rekeying or adding all of the users to your Personal N & A Book.

To do so, use the same steps you would use in creating a replica of any database. Select the copy of the Public N & A Book icon on the server and choose File, Replication, New Replica. The New Replica dialog box is displayed (see Figure 5.31).

Fig. 5.31 The New Replica dialog box.

The Server box should be set to Local and the Title box should display the title of your company's Public N & A Book. Enter a new filename for the replica of your Public N & A Book.

> **Caution**
>
> By default, the Public N & A Book on the server has the filename NAMES.NSF. Your Personal N & A Book on your workstation has the same name. If you choose to store a replica of the Public N & A Book on your workstation, you must change the default filename given to the replica; otherwise, you will overwrite your Personal N & A Book with your Public N & A Book.
>
> If you forget to change the filename, Notes will warn you that a file with that name already exists and will ask you if you want to overwrite it. Choose No and enter a new filename for the Public N & A Book replica. If no standard exists in your organization for naming local replica copies of the Public N & A Book, you might want to use PUBNAMES.NSF for the actual filename.

You can then use the other settings in the New Replica dialog box to set a size limit for the Public N & A Book replica, enter encryption settings, create a full text index, copy the ACL into the replica, and choose when to create the new replica. When you are sure all of the settings are correct, click OK and a New Replica stub icon will appear.

Once the replicator has initialized and copied all of the documents into your Public N & A Book replica, you can begin to use the replica as you would the original database on the server.

> **Note**
>
> Remember, by default, you have Manager access to all local databases, which means that you will be able to create and modify documents that exist in the replica of the Public N & A Book. However, if the Administrator has done his or her job properly, your changes will be overwritten by the data in the server copy. In short, don't add or change documents in your replica of the Public N & A Book because they will be overwritten. Make them in your Personal N & A Book. This brings us to another note; if you have many users in your company, your Public N & A Book could grow VERY large. If space on your computer is at a premium, you might want to copy documents from your Public N & A Book to your Personal N & A Book, rather than make a full replica copy.

Notes Basics

From Here...

In this chapter, you learned about the importance of, and the differences between, the Personal and Public N & A Books and how they are used by Notes. In the next chapter, "Advanced Mail," you will learn how to use the N & A Books to address mail and how to use other advanced features of the Lotus Notes mail system.

For more information on some of the topics discussed in this chapter, refer to the following:

- Chapter 4, "Getting Started with Electronic Mail," teaches you how to work with Lotus NotesMail and the mail forward feature.

- For more information on advanced mailing techniques and securing mail messages, refer to Chapter 6, "Advanced Mail," and Chapter 22, "Security and Encryption."

## Chapter 6

Advanced Mail

In Chapter 4, "Getting Started with Electronic Mail," you learned the basics of the Lotus Notes e-mail system. There are a number of additional features that you can use to extend the capabilities of NotesMail. In this chapter, we examine the advanced features that enable you to use NotesMail with maximum efficiency, effectiveness, and enjoyability.

NotesMail: Under the Hood

NotesMail is the leading client/server, store-and-forward mail system, with more than 4 million seats installed and a quickly growing base.

> **Note**
>
> Client/server is a major buzzword in the technology arena and deserves a clear definition. According to Gabor J. Toth's *Free Online Dictionary of Computing* (point your Web browser to **http://wagner.princeton.edu/foldoc/**), *client/server* means "a common form of distributed system in which software is split between server tasks and client tasks. A client sends requests to a server, according to some protocol, asking for information or action, and the server responds. There may be either one centralized server or several distributed ones. This model allows clients and servers to be placed independently on nodes in a network, possibly on different hardware and operating systems appropriate to their function, e.g., *fast*server/cheap client."

The following are some of the many reasons why NotesMail is so popular:

- **Intuitive User Interface**—NotesMail sports the award-winning, industry-leading cc:Mail user interface. Because it's easy to learn and intuitive to use NotesMail, users can become productive immediately.

- **Rich Text Support**—Because the body of the mail message is a Rich Text Field, any type of object can be put inside a mail message, including file attachments, OLE objects, graphics, and doclinks.

This chapter covers the following:

- Organizing your mail

- Working with file attachments

- Using mail-in databases

- Extending NotesMail with gateways and MTAs

- Working with Lotus cc:Mail

- Mail Tools

- Calendar Tools

- Other Useful Mail Tools

■ **Bidirectional, Field Level Replication**—Like all Notes databases, your mail database can be replicated. This allows you to keep multiple copies of your mail database in perfect synchronization, the ideal situation for remote users. Each time you connect to the Notes server, your local replica copy of your mail database will be synchronized with the copy on your server. If you delete mail in your local copy, it will be deleted on the server; if new mail is waiting on the server, it will be transferred to your local replica. For more information, see Chapter 24, "Notes: Under the Hood."

■ **Functionality**—NotesMail has a vast array of built-in functions that power e-mail users expect, such as Forwarding and Reply, folders, and Address Book-based addressing. Some of the additional power features are Letterheads, Stationery, Return Receipts, Mood Stamps, Delivery Reports, automatic reply capability, and archiving utilities.

■ **Security**—NotesMail offers two immensely powerful security features: encryption at both the message and database level, and digital signatures, which provide a level of security unmatched in other mail systems.

■ **Shared Mail**—Although shared mail is administrative (meaning that as an end-user, you need not concern yourself with it), it is a powerful new technology. Shared Mail allows the administrator to configure NotesMail so that when a message is sent to multiple recipients, the summary (envelope information) is stored in each user's mailbox, whereas the nonsummary (body) information is stored in the shared mail file on the server.

Each user has a link to the shared information, so when the message is accessed, the user sees the full message. This allows much better disk usage because large mail messages are not stored in each mailbox. It also helps reduce network traffic.

■ **Integration**—Messaging is one of Notes' core services. This means that NotesMail is tightly integrated into Notes, allowing mail messages to be sent from or to users, databases, and other systems.

■ **Extensibility**—NotesMail is easily extended to communicate with other enterprise-wide mail systems such as MS Mail or IBM's PROFS.

■ **Scalability**—NotesMail works well for 10 users or 100,000 users. This is because Notes server software can take advantage of multiple processors and because NotesMail uses the client/server architecture.

These are just some of the reasons that NotesMail is so powerful and popular. Before we delve more deeply into the advanced features of NotesMail, here is a quick refresher course on how it works.

Each Notes server has a Router task (a software router that runs on the server and routes mail messages from senders to recipients). For the following example, assume that the user is connected to a Notes server through a LAN, only one recipient is entered, and the recipient's address is valid.

When a user creates and sends a new mail message, the Router tries to verify the address of the recipient against the Name and Address Book. When the address is verified, the Router transfers the mail message to the Mail.box database on the user's mail server.

The Router then tries to determine whether the recipient is on the same mail domain (shares the same Public N & A Book). If so, the message is put into the user's mailbox almost immediately.

If the user is in another domain, the Router tries to make a connection to the user's domain via connection documents and foreign/nonadjacent domain documents in the Public N & A Book. When the proper route to the user's domain is determined, the Router makes a connection based on the priority of the message and the connection schedules in the Public N & A Book.

That, in a nutshell, is how NotesMail works. For more detailed information, see Chapter 24, "Notes: Under the Hood," or see the *Lotus Notes Release 4 Administrator's Guide*. Now that you understand the basics of how e-mail works, let's look at the advanced features of NotesMail.

Organizing Your Mail

The ability to quickly and easily find and manipulate mail messages is paramount for effective mail use and user satisfaction. The smart folks at Lotus realized this and have added a variety of powerful tools to help you effectively organize your mail messages.

In addition, like most things in Notes, your mailbox can be tailored to your specific needs. (See Chapter 2, "Customizing Notes," to learn more about Notes customization.)

You can add a certain amount of customization to most views and folders even if you are not a database designer—unless the database designer has disabled some of these features. In general, you have more control over folders than views.

In terms of customizing views, unless you have Designer or higher access to a database, the amount of customization you can lend to a view is somewhat limited compared to a folder. You can, however, create your own private views. (For more information on private views, see Chapter 12, "Designing Views.")

In the standard Notes R4 mailbox, you can make some simple changes to the shared views that provide greater usability. You can also put your mail into folders that simplify organizing and storing the volume of mail you receive.

Caution

Unlike most databases, you have Manager access (by default) to your mailbox, regardless of whether it resides on the server or is a replica on your workstation. This means that you have the highest level of access to the database and can change the database design. You can even permanently delete the database! This means that unless you have a backup, your mail is lost!

(continues)

(continued)

In almost every case, the mailbox should provide all the functions you would ever need. It is highly recommended that you do not try to make design changes to the mailbox other than those mentioned in this section.

You might also be using the NotesMail license or the Notes Desktop license, which do not allow you to make any design changes. Or, if you feel that changes are need, submit a request to the database design team to make the changes.

If you decide to make design changes to the database, you should be very careful. You might make changes that affect how your mailbox works and that cannot be easily corrected.

In addition, because your mailbox is based on a template, your changes may be overwritten. You learn more about this issue in Chapter 12, "Designing Views."

Changing the Mail View

In Chapter 4, "Getting Started with Electronic Mail," you learn that when you open your mailbox, Notes displays a list of incoming and outgoing messages in the view or folder that you last used. As with most databases, you can choose any of several different views and folders. Each of these presents your mail messages in a different way.

In the new mail template, the views are hidden from view menu and can only be accessed from the Navigator. If you expand the Folders and Views element in the Navigator, you'll see two additional views, Archiving and Discussion Threads.

Note

The design elements such as views and folders in your mailbox are standard. What you see in your mailbox, however, may vary from the screens in this chapter because each of these documents might be changed by Notes administrators or designers in your organization.

The following describes these standard views:

■ **Discussion Threads**—When someone starts an ongoing discussion that prompts responses and then responds to the responses, the collective body of related messages is called a *thread* (this is a very common term in Internet jargon, especially in UseNet, newsgroups, and e-mail).

The Discussion Threads view displays in a hierarchical manner all messages that are part of the same discussion. Any message that has a reply is displayed with the reply below it, and any replies to a reply are displayed below each reply. This view makes it easy to keep track of an ongoing e-mail discussion.

■ **Archiving**—This view enables you to see and edit your Archive Profile and Archive log documents for each archive session as well as set the location for your mail archive file. (This is much like the Notes Log.) You learn how to archive mail messages later in this chapter under "Archiving Your Mail."

Organizing Your Mail into Folders

If you are a Notes 3.x user, this section will be particularly important to you. In the old version of the mail database, each NotesMail message had a special field named Personal Categories. This field allowed you to specify categories so that you could logically group your mail messages.

When the category field was populated with data, NotesMail used this field to categorize the mail messages in views. For instance, if you often get mail from the Finance department, you might have categorized this mail as "Finance," whereas mail from Accounting you would categorize as "Accounting."

You could create as many categories as you needed to help organize your messages into groups and make the views more meaningful and less cluttered.

In the Notes 4.x mailbox, each document still has a Personal Categories field, but it is there only for backward compatibility with older e-mail messages. Lotus has added a much more powerful feature to the new mail database: folders. (For a brush-up on folders, see Chapter 3, "Using Databases.")

When you are trying to organize your mail messages, folders are useful because you can put messages in a folder that apply strictly to a specific issue, account, concept, and so on. For instance, you can create a folder called ABC Company and put all mail messages related to ABC Company into this folder.

This folder would hold only messages about the ABC Company, so the number of messages it holds would be much smaller than the number of messages that would show up in a categorized view. Searching, manipulation, and viewing are therefore quicker and easier. An additional benefit is that the folders are added into the standard Navigation pane, allowing you to find and manipulate them.

Notice that in my mailbox, shown in Figure 6.1, I have created several folders, such as the Lotus and ENTEX folders, to help organize my mail messages.

If the folders you want to store mail messages in already exist, click and drag documents to these folders. Or you can use <u>A</u>ctions, Move to Folder, or click the Move To Folder button on the Action Bar to display the Move To Folder dialog box, shown in Figure 6.2.

Notes Basics

Fig. 6.1   My user-defined folders for frequent communications in the new mailbox database.

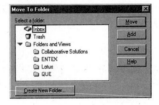

Fig. 6.2   The Move To Folder dialog box displays the list of folders in my mailbox.

From this dialog box, you can choose a folder from the graphical list displayed in the Select a folder list box. Once you have selected a folder, you can use the Move button to move the document from the folder it's in to the selected folder.

Or you can choose Add to add a document to the selected folder and leave it in its current folder as well. To create a new folder, click the Create New Folder button to launch the Create Folder dialog box, which is covered in the next section.

You can create as many folders as you need to organize your mail messages in your mailbox. To create a new folder, choose Create, Folder. The Create Folder dialog box is displayed (see Figure 6.3).

The Create Folder dialog box is easy to use. You enter a new folder name in the Folder name field and choose a location for the new folder from the hierarchy of folders shown in the Select a location for the new folder list box. (This list box displays all the folders and their hierarchy in your mailbox.)

Click the folder where you want to put the new folder and click OK. The new folder is added to your mailbox, and you can use it immediately.

Fig. 6.3 The Create Folder dialog box displays a list of existing folders in my mailbox so I can decide where to put the new folder.

To begin using your folders, select a mail message or messages the same way you would select any documents. Click and drag the messages to the proper folder. It's as simple as that!

Folders are a very powerful new feature of the new NotesMail interface. They can make your life easier when working in your mailbox. If you often get mail messages from another department or person, you might want to create a folder to organize those messages.

For instance, if you often communicate with several departments at the XYZ Company via e-mail, you might create a folder called XYZ for general mail messages from the company and create several subfolders under XYZ, such as Purchasing, Engineering, Marketing, and Sales, to store mail messages from those departments.

Remember, customize your folders to meet your needs. You can store a mail message in one or many folders. You can move it from one folder to another at any time.

Note

If you are upgrading from Notes 3.x to Notes 4.5, Lotus has included an agent that enables you to convert the categories stored in your old mail messages to folders, which can save you a considerable amount of time. (See Chapter 16, "Buttons and Agents," for more information.) To use this agent, open your mailbox and click the Agent icon (the small light bulb) in the Navigator.

Select the Convert Categories to Folders agent and right-click it to launch a pop-up menu. Choose Run to start the agent and create new folders for each category. When the agent is finished, Notes displays a brief summary of the actions done by the agent in the Agent Log dialog box. Your administrator may have already done this for you as part of the upgrade process if you are moving from Notes R 3.x. If you open your mailbox and see folders that correspond to the categories you had in your old mailbox, you won't need to do this.

Changing the Width of Columns in a View or Folder

In the view pane, the columns are separated by thin gray lines. Most columns in a view are resizable, much like the columns in an Excel or 1-2-3 spreadsheet. When you position your mouse pointer directly over any of the column separator lines, notice that the mouse pointer changes to a solid black line with an arrow on each side.

When your mouse pointer changes, you can "grab" (hold down the right or left mouse button) the column separator and drag it to the size you want. This can be handy since it allows you to dynamically determine how wide a column should be.

Note

The first nondata column in any view or folder is called the Marker column. It is easily identified by the thin, vertical gray line that extends the length of the view and separates it from the other columns. You cannot resize this column. See Chapter 3, "Using Databases," for more information on the special function of this column.

Changing the Sort Order

Many of the views in the mailbox, such as the All Documents view, enable you to change the sorted order of certain columns (see Figure 6.4). Any column heading that displays a small arrow pointing up, down, or both indicates that you can click in the column heading to change the sort order.

Sorts the column in ascending order

Sorts the column in descending order

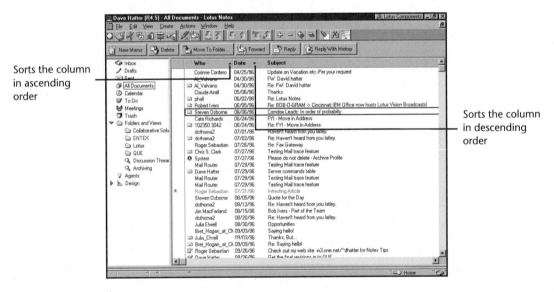

Fig. 6.4 You can change the sort order of columns in the All Documents view with a single click.

In Figure 6.4, the Who column displays an arrow pointing up. This means that when you click the Who column header, that column is sorted in ascending order.

The arrow changes color from black, meaning that the column is in its default order, to a shade of bright turquoise, meaning that the column is now sorted in ascending order. You can click again to return the column to its default sort order, which is unsorted.

The Date column is already sorted in ascending order (the oldest dates first). The column heading displays the down arrow, indicating that you can change the sort order from the default—ascending order—to descending order (most recent dates first). A second click on this column returns the messages to ascending order.

Another useful feature allows you to view only new messages. To enable this feature, simply choose <u>V</u>iew, <u>S</u>how Only Unread.

Without getting into the design of a view, these are the only view features that you as an end user can customize in your mailbox. Folders, on the other hand, can not only be customized in the same ways that views can, they can be created from scratch. This allows you to build your own folders to organize your mail messages.

Working with File Attachments

As a PC user, you probably need to share files with other users on many occasions. As you know, this is often much more easily said than done, particularly if you work for a geographically dispersed company.

Notes, however, makes it easy to e-mail a file as an attachment to your mail message to any other NotesMail user. Perhaps a coworker in Bangladesh needs a copy of the technical documentation you have prepared in Lotus Word Pro, or the plant in Düsseldorf needs your market analysis report created with Lotus 1-2-3.

Before e-mail (and particularly NotesMail), sharing files meant copying the files to a shared disk drive on the LAN. Or it meant copying them to a floppy disk and using "sneaker net" (you got up and ran the disk down to the colleague who needed it) if the colleague was in the office, or snail mail if he or she was at another location.

Notes simplifies the sharing of files by allowing you to attach a file to an e-mail message. The following sections explain how to work with attachments.

Note

Users new to e-mail are often confused by the concept of a file attachment, so I'll try to explain it here. When you attach a file (regardless of the original file format) to an e-mail message, Notes makes a *copy* of the whole file. It inserts the copy of the file into the body of the e-mail message, leaving the original file unchanged.

This is like using your OS to copy a file, except that now you can mail the file to other users and they can use the file just as if they had created it themselves.

Attaching Files

You can attach a file (or files) to any mail document. The first step is to create a new message. When the new mail message is on-screen, you work with it just as you would with any other mail message until you are ready to attach the file.

You can attach any file, regardless of its format, to a NotesMail message. For instance, if you have an office in Germany that needs the latest sales figures, you can attach the 1-2-3 spreadsheet to a mail message and send it to the German office. Likewise, you can attach the Access database with the latest inventory data and mail it to a colleague in a different office.

To attach one or more files, follow these steps:

1. Place the cursor in the body portion of the memo, and then choose File, Attach or click the File Attach SmartIcon. The Create Attachment(s) dialog box appears (see Figure 6.5).

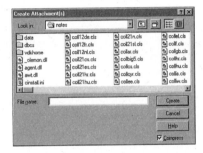

Fig. 6.5 The Create Attachment(s) dialog box is simple to use; just select the file(s) to attach.

You must be in the Body field to attach a file. File attachments can be attached only in Rich Text fields, and Body is the only Rich Text field in the mail message.

2. You can use the "look in" drop-down box to select the directory where the file(s) you want to attach reside. The listbox below will display all the files in the selected directory. By default, the Create Attachment(s) dialog box points at the last directory you accessed with this dialog box. If this is the first time you're using it, it should point at the Notes directory `C:\NOTES`.

3. Select all the files you want to attach by clicking the file in the list box (selected files are highlighted with a blue bar), and they will be displayed in the File name text box. To select more than one file, hold the Ctrl key down as you select files.

4. Click Create. Notes inserts an icon in your document that represents each of the attached files. Notes uses the file extension of each file you attach to scan the Windows Registry to try to identify the source application (the application that created the file) so that an icon representing the application that created the file can be displayed.

For example, if you insert an MS Word document, the MS Word icon is displayed in the mail message to represent the file attachment. If Notes cannot identify the file attachment (its ability to identify file attachments is based on your operating system), an icon that looks like a blank, gray piece of paper with the right edge folded over is inserted.

Figure 6.6 shows a sample memo with several different file attachments.

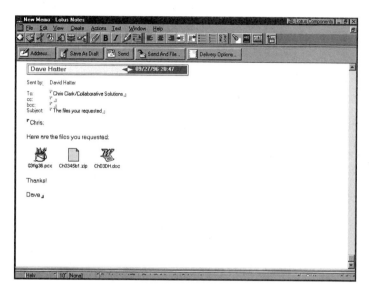

Fig. 6.6 A mail message displays the icons of known file types when they are attached.

When you have attached the files, address the mail as you normally would, enter the subject, and add any text to the message body that might help the recipient understand the attachment. Once the file is attached, you still have complete editing capability in the Body field.

You can insert text above, below, beside, or between the attachments and move the attachments as if they were text. After you finish the message and attach the files, send the message as you would any other.

◄◄ See "Sending Your Message," p. 166

A Word About Compression

The Compress checkbox in the Create Attachment(s) dialog box is enabled by default. In most instances, you should leave this option checked so that Notes will compress the file attachment(s).

During the compression, Notes searches for repeating patterns in the file. It codes these repeating patterns and strips them out, reducing the size of the file.

(continues)

(continued)

In many cases, a compressed file attachment is 80 to 90 percent smaller than the original file. Because the files are smaller, they can be transferred more quickly than the original file and consume less disk space on the server. The only disadvantage of compressing attachments is that the attach process takes slightly longer (the increased time is barely noticeable) because Notes must analyze and process each file attachment.

Certain types of files don't contain repeating patterns—for example, any file that has already been compressed by another compression utility such as PKZIP (the repeating patterns have already been stripped out) or certain graphics files that use a compression scheme by default, such as GIF and JPEG files. Having Notes compress these files won't cause any damage. But the space savings are negligible, and compression takes slightly longer.

When the recipient gets the mail message and tries to extract, launch, or view the attachments, Notes automatically decompresses the file into its original format. The recipient doesn't need to take any special actions if only the Notes compression method was used.

Detaching Attachments

When you open your mailbox, you should be able to immediately identify mail messages that have attached files. This is because all the standard views and folders display a paper clip somewhere in the view pane to indicate that a file has been attached, as Figure 6.7 shows.

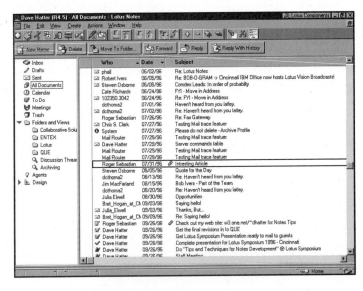

Fig. 6.7 The All Documents view displays messages with attachments with a paper clip icon.

> **Note**
>
> The position of the paper clip may vary from view to view and folder to folder, but it is displayed in all the standard views and folders that ship with Notes 4.0. Be aware that if custom view and folders have been specified for the database, the paper clip icon may not be displayed. This is at the discretion of the designer.

To detach (extract the file from the mail message and store it a file on your disk) one or more of the attached files, follow these steps:

1. Open the mail message that has attachments. You see the corresponding icons in the body.

2. When you select any or all of the attachments, a new menu, Attachment, appears between the Actions and Window menus (see Figure 6.8).

Fig. 6.8   The Attachment menu on the main menu bar mimics the features available by clicking the attachment.

3. From this menu, choose Detach (a bit of a misnomer because it does not detach the attachment from the message but saves the file separately). Notes displays the standard file dialog box, asking where you want to copy the file and what the file name should be.

4. The original file name of the attachment is the default value for the new file name, but you can give the file a new name. Pick any directory you want. Notes detaches the file from the message onto your hard disk.

   Or you can double-click any of the attachments to display the Attachment Properties InfoBox and view, launch, or detach the attachment (see Figure 6.9).

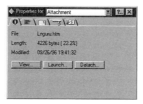

Fig. 6.9   The Attachment Properties InfoBox allows you to set a number of options for each attachment.

Attached files stay in a mail message even after you detach, launch, or view them (launching and viewing are described shortly). You can extract the attachment as many times as you want.

You can detach the file to your hard disk, for example, and then detach it again to a disk (specify A: or B: as the directory). If you forward the message to someone else, the attached file goes with it.

> **Tip**
>
> File attachments are often quite large and can quickly consume precious disk space. If you find yourself running low on space, you can open mail messages and delete their attachments while retaining the mail message itself. See "Deleting Attachments" later in this chapter for details.

Detaching Multiple Attachments

Many times, you will receive a mail message that has more than one file attached, and it can be more convenient to extract several at once. To detach more than one attachment, follow this procedure:

1. Select the attachments you want to detach (hold down the right mouse button and drag over the attachments; this highlights the icons with a black bar).

> **Tip**
>
> Notes doesn't care how much text you select in addition to the attachments, so don't worry about selecting only the attachments. In fact, if you want to detach all attachments in a message, you can select the whole document (and all the attachments in it) by selecting Edit, Select All. This is much faster.

2. Choose Attachment, Detach All.

3. Notes displays the standard file dialog box that enables you to select a directory in which to store the attachments. Choose a directory (all the attachments will be stored in the directory you select) and select OK. Notes detaches the selected attachments.

Viewing Attachments

Sometimes you get file attachments that you want to look at before you detach them onto your workstation's disk. To view only the contents of an attachment, you can select the attachment and open the Attachment property sheet by double-clicking the icon.

Click View to open the Universal Viewer and examine the file contents. Or you can select the attachment to view and choose Attachment, View.

As discussed in Chapter 3, "Using Databases," the Universal Viewer allows you to examine the most popular file formats, such as Microsoft Word, Microsoft Excel, Microsoft Access, Lotus 1-2-3, Lotus Word Pro, and many others. However, you might receive files that the Universal Viewer cannot understand.

For instance, many people use a compression utility such as PKZIP to compress files before they are attached because it provides superior file compression. Because the file is specially encoded, the Universal Viewer can't understand the contents of the file and can't display it correctly. If this is the case, you'll need to find the application that originally created the file to view it.

Launching Attachments

Not only can you extract the files to disk or view, and print the contents with the Universal Viewer, you can also launch (start) the application that created the file and begin editing the file immediately. But first, a few caveats.

For the Launch function to work correctly, the following must be true:

- Unless the attached file is an executable file, such as a Lotus ScreenCam movie, you must have access to the application that created the file attachment, either from the hard disk on your workstation or from a drive on a network server. In other words, you can launch 1-2-3 by double-clicking a file with a WK4 extension only if you have 1-2-3 available from your computer.

- The application that originally created the file must have been successfully installed and configured in the Windows Registry for your system. In the Registry, Windows maintains a database of applications it recognizes and the types of files that are associated with each application.

  When you launch a file, Windows examines the extension of the attached file and searches the Registry for a match. If a match is found, Windows starts the application and opens the attached file. For example, you receive a mail with the DOSINFO.SAM file (which is an Ami Pro 3.1 file) attached. Windows determines from the Registry that files with the extension .SAM are Ami Pro files, so it starts Ami Pro and the attached file is opened as an Ami Pro document.

This method is not foolproof because end users can name a file anything they want. And although a file might look like a 1-2-3 spreadsheet (has the extension WK4), it might be an ASCII text file, which means that file will not be launched correctly. If you cannot get a file to launch, consult your operating system manuals and your Notes administrator for more information.

> **Caution**
>
> Some malicious user could send you a virus or other harmful program as a file attachment that infects your computer when launched. If you get mail that has an executable file from a suspicious source or you are suspicious of an attached file, do not launch it! Scan the file with an antivirus program or consult your administrator to learn about the new Execution Control List feature of Notes R4.5. See Chapter 2, "Customizing Notes," for more information about Execution Control Lists (ECLs).

To launch an attachment in its associated program, select the file and open the property sheet by double-clicking the attachment's icon. You can then click the Launch button to open the file with the application that originally created it.

When you elect to <u>L</u>aunch, Notes starts the application that created the file and opens the file in that application. For example, if the file was created in 1-2-3, Notes starts 1-2-3 and loads the attachment into 1-2-3 for editing. If the file is an executable program, Notes executes the program.

Deleting Attachments

Normally, attached files stay in a message until the message is deleted. This can quickly consume an inordinate amount of disk space. You can, however, keep the mail message but delete the attachments to save disk space.

Some reasons for deleting attachments include the following:

■ The mail message has important information but you don't need the file attachments.

■ You detached the files or launched the files with the host application, and saved the file to disk. Either of these choices creates a copy of the attached files on disk, meaning that you now have redundant copies of the files on your workstation that consume disk space. By deleting the attachment from the mail, you free up this space.

■ Files were erroneously attached to the mail message. You don't want to send the files but you do want to send the mail message. If you delete the message, it deletes the attachments but you must retype the mail message.

To delete an attached file or files, the document must be opened in edit mode. If you are viewing the document in a view or have the document open in read mode, press Ctrl+E to switch to edit mode.

With the document open in edit mode, select the files you want to delete and press the Delete key or choose <u>E</u>dit, Clear. You could also click the Edit Clear SmartIcon.

Notes prompts you with a dialog box indicating that the delete operation cannot be undone. If you are sure you want to delete the attachment, choose Yes; otherwise, choose No to cancel the delete operation.

Working with Mail-In Databases

Because messaging is at the core of Notes, mail messages can be sent to any database if it is enabled. This feature can be especially handy if you need to share information between two databases that do not replicate.

For example, you can create a suggestion-box-type application in which users can mail documents to a database but they don't need the database available to them. Or the Mail-In database capability can be useful if you want to design a workflow application in which documents can be routed to individuals who are part of the business process.

A Statistics Collection application is a classic example of using a Mail-In database. For example, you have two Notes servers in your organization, each constantly generating server statistics. Rather than have to view two different databases on each server to see the statistics, you could create one database on one of the two servers and have the statistics for both servers mailed to this database.

Before a database can get messages, you or the Notes administrator must create a Mail-In database document in the Public N & A Book (see Figure 6.10). To do so, select the Public Name & Address Book and choose Create, Server, Mail-In Database. Remember, you must have Author access or better, and/or be in the (NetCreator) role to create a new document in the Public N & A Book.

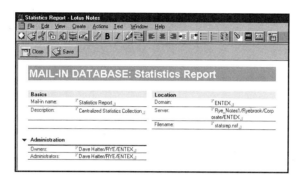

Fig. 6.10   A Mail-In database document for the Statistics Report database.

You must then enter a name for the database (this is the name users enter in the To field of a mail message), the domain of the server where the database is stored, the name of the server where the database is stored, and the file name of the database. Optionally, you may enter a description to help identify the purpose and use of the database.

Be sure to inform users that the new database is available. Explain that to send a message to the database, you must use the name in the Mail-In Database name field of the Mail-In database document.

Working with Custom Forms in Your Mailbox

As they begin to understand how Notes can increase productivity through workflow automation and information sharing, many companies expand the default capabilities of the Notes mailbox by adding Custom Forms. Custom Forms usually go hand in hand with Mail-In databases. They are Notes forms designed to provide added function to your mail system by automating manual processes.

For instance, most companies have a standardized expense report that must be routed to several people for approval before it can be processed for payment. In Notes, a Custom Form modeled from your company's standard paper expense report can be created and added to the mailbox so that the report can be filled out and mailed to the approving authority. If approved, the form is then mailed to the accounting or finance department for payment.

Another example of how Custom Forms can be useful is forms routing. Take the case where a sales representative in the field needs to request market development funds. The representative fills out a form that is snail-mailed or faxed to the manager, who must approve the funds and pass it off to the VP of Marketing.

If the VP of Marketing approves the request, it is forwarded to accounting so that a check can be cut. This may take several days or even weeks, and there is a good chance the form may get misplaced or overlooked.

In Notes, a Custom Form can be added to the mailbox that allows the sales representative to compose an MDF Request, which is then e-mailed to his or her supervisor. If the form is approved, it is e-mailed to the VP, and from the VP to accounting (digital signatures can be used as part of the approval process). Because the process is automated through NotesMail, the time and effort to process the request are minimized.

To access any Custom Forms that may be in your mailbox, select your mailbox and choose Create, Other. This displays the Other dialog box (see Figure 6.11). You can also choose Create, Mail, Other from the menu if you are not in your mailbox to get the same Other dialog box.

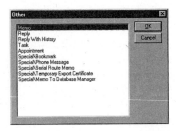

Fig. 6.11   All the forms in your mailbox are displayed by the Other dialog box.

The Other dialog box displays all the forms available from your mailbox. Select the form you want from the list and a new form opens. At this point, you handle this form as you would any other mail message form.

Although Custom Forms can be designed for any purpose, they are just special NotesMail messages. This means that to be delivered, the messages must be addressed to a Notes user, Mail-In database, or Notes server.

In most cases, the designer who creates the Custom Forms includes a SendTo field as a minimum. He or she may include the cc, bcc, and Subject fields as well. This way, when the document is delivered to a mailbox, it is displayed like other mail messages in the folders and views.

An example is a company-wide, peer-based awards program that allows management and employees to recognize others for doing a good job. In each employee's mailbox is a custom form named Good Job.

Anyone can recognize a colleague for doing a good job by composing and mailing a Good Job form, which is sent to every employee in the company. The form is also sent to a Good Job Mail-In database so a tally can be kept for each individual. Anyone who accumulates 10 awards gets a cash award.

The From field on the form is automatically calculated based on the Notes user ID of the person sending the award. The value in this field is used as the From field for mailing.

The Date field is automatically calculated as the Date field of the mail message. The Award radio buttons indicate an individual or team award. The Awardee field stores the names of the person being commended.

The person submitting the award chooses the name(s) of the individual(s) to receive the award. These names are used as the To field. The final step is for the person submitting the award to enter the description of the commendable activity.

The Award description is used as the Body of the mail message. A formula automatically enters "Good Job" for the Subject of the message. When the Award is saved, it is mailed to all the Awardees and to the Awards database.

In most organizations, all NotesMail mailboxes are based on a mailbox design template. When a database designer completes the testing of a new custom form, the form is put in the standard mailbox template. This automatically puts the new form in your mailbox on the server. If you use workstation-based mail, the form is placed in your local mailbox during your next replication.

> **Note**
>
> Remember that these are "Custom" forms; they have been added by a Database Designer and are not included in the Mailbox templates that Lotus provides. If you upgrade your version of Notes and refresh the design of your mailbox, your custom forms will be deleted, so make provision for this if you need the custom forms. For more information about templates, see Appendix B, "Database Templates."

Extending Notes Mail with Gateways and MTAs

NotesMail is very powerful and can meet the needs of most organizations, from the smallest to the largest. Still, it may be necessary to connect NotesMail to other mail systems such as IBM's PROFS mail, Novell's MHS-based mail systems, or even the Internet.

Lotus recognizes the need to allow NotesMail to easily integrate with these other systems. It has made much progress since the R3 days toward seamless connectivity for most major mail systems.

Lotus has done this in two ways: by developing internal gateways and message transfer agents (MTAs), and by encouraging Lotus Business Partners. There are now over 12,000 business partners to develop third-party solutions.

Before we look at two of the most popular and useful extensions, you need a better understanding of what gateways and MTAs do.

MTAs are new to Notes R4. They are integrated server tasks that, according to Lotus, "provide scalable, high-performance routing and relaying of messages in their native format." MTAs are completely integrated into the infrastructure of Notes. As a result, they are generally more reliable and give better performance with less cost.

In the context of NotesMail, gateways "move messages from one electronic mail system to another, acting as a protocol converter between different e-mail formats." (For a more generic definition, see the definition that follows.) Although not as tightly integrated as MTAs, gateways afford connectivity to most systems. Lotus provides a number of gateways, as do a number of third-party software vendors.

> **Note**
>
> According to the LAN Times Encyclopedia of Networking, a gateway "is a computer system or other device that acts as a translator between two systems that do not use the same communications protocols, data formatting structures, languages, and/or architecture."

With this knowledge under your belt, let's examine the Lotus Fax Server (a gateway) and the simple mail transfer protocol (SMTP) MTA.

Sending Faxes with Lotus Notes

The e-mail system in Lotus Notes is very flexible and, through the use of additional software, can be used to send faxes from Notes. If your company buys the Lotus Fax Server (LFS) and a machine to run the software on, you can fax any Notes document.

You can also fax documents created in other applications, such as Microsoft Word or Lotus 1-2-3. This benefits your company because it allows multiple users to share the resources of the fax server.

You can greatly reduce the need for paper because you can send and receive faxes electronically. In fact, if you couple the fax server with a scanner, you can completely eliminate the physical fax machine!

Your Notes administrator should install this software. It means the configuring a Foreign Domain document in the Public N & A Book, its own machine, and knowledge of your Notes installation.

When the Fax gateway is configured and running, you or your administrator need to install the Lotus Image Viewer software on your local machine. This software installs the printer drivers that allow you to fax documents other than Notes documents, and allows you to view incoming faxes.

Faxing a Message or File Attachment

After your workstation is configured, when you open your mailbox and choose Create, you see two new forms in your mailbox: Fax a File Attachment and Fax a Message. When you choose Fax a Message, the familiar Notes 3.x memo form appears with two new fields added—Cover page message and Include all names on cover page (see Figure 6.12).

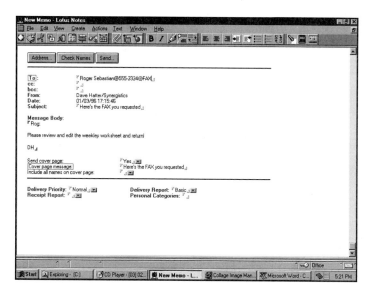

Fig. 6.12   The Fax a Message form for sending faxes through Notes.

Cover page message is a text field that you can use to enter a message that is displayed on the cover page of the fax. Include all names on cover page is a standard keyword field that allows you to display the recipients' names on the cover page if there is more than one recipient. If you want all the fax recipients to be aware of the others who have received this document, choose Yes; otherwise, choose No.

The Fax a File Attachment form, shown in Figure 6.13, is almost identical to the Fax a Message form, except that it has an additional field, FAX File Attachments. FAX File Attachments is a Rich Text field that allows you to attach files, such as Microsoft Word or Lotus Word Pro, that you want to fax.

This can be useful because you don't have to open the application that created the file and print the file to the Fax gateway. The Fax gateway converts the file to graphics and sends it as part of the fax.

When you Fax a File Attachment, the Lotus Fax software converts the attached file into graphics that can be sent to the receiving fax machine. Because each file must be converted from its original format, not every type of file can be faxed (most common file types are accepted).

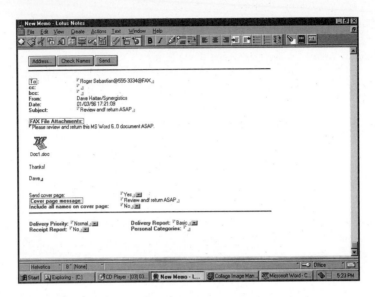

Fig. 6.13 The Fax a File Attachment form with an MS Word file attached.

For instance, a file that was compressed with PKZIP does not fax correctly because the file is specially encoded and the fax software cannot convert it. For a list of files that can be faxed as attachments, consult the Lotus Fax Server manuals.

To tell Notes that this is a fax message and not a regular mail message, you address it in a slightly different way than you would a regular mail message. If your organization uses the standard settings in the SendTo field, you would enter the address in the following format:

    User Name@Phone Number@FAX

For example:

    Dave Hatter@1-555-555-1212@FAX

The User Name portion of the address is for information only and has no bearing in the delivery of the fax. The Phone Number portion of the address is the phone number of the recipient's fax machine.

The Fax portion is the name used to tell Notes that this message should be passed on to the fax gateway (a foreign domain) for transmission to the recipient's fax machine. The address you enter here is not case-sensitive.

> **Note**
>
> To send the same message to multiple users, separate each address with a comma, as you would in a regular e-mail message. The Fax Server software faxes the message to each listed addressee.

Once you have addressed your fax message, send it as you would any e-mail message. The router takes over from there. When the router sees the foreign domain FAX, it transfers the mail to the fax gateway's outgoing mailbox.

The Lotus Fax Server (LFS) periodically polls the LFS mailbox. When a new outbound fax is found, the LFS software renders the message as a graphic image and sends the fax.

Note

The name of the Foreign Domain used to point to your LFS does not have to be FAX and it is not case-sensitive. This name is determined arbitrarily by your administrator. For instance, it might be called "LFS" or "Fax Gateway" or "fax server." To use this correctly, be sure to get the LFS' foreign domain name from your administrator.

Faxing Documents from Other Applications

Another way to take advantage of the Fax Server is to redirect the output of an application, such as Microsoft PowerPoint or Lotus Organizer, to the Fax Server. For instance, you might type up a quick letter with Lotus WordPro and fax it to a colleague at another company.

When you finish the letter, change your printer driver to Lotus Print to Fax and print your document. Your output is redirected to the Lotus Fax Server, which launches the Lotus Print-to-Fax dialog box (see Figure 6.14).

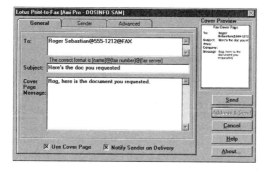

Fig. 6.14 The Lotus Print-to-Fax dialog box for an Ami Pro document.

As you can see in Figure 6.14, the Print-to-Fax dialog box sports a tabbed interface that allows you to set various faxing parameters. In most cases, you only need to use the settings in the General tab.

The first field, To, works just like a NotesMail message: you enter the address (a fully qualified phone number such as 1-888-555-1212) of the recipient's fax machine in the standard Notes Fax format. The next field, Subject, is self-explanatory: enter the subject of the fax.

The Cover Page Message field allows you to enter text to print on the cover page, just like a regular fax. The Use Cover Page checkbox acts as a toggle: if it's checked, a cover page that looks like the one in the Cover Preview box is sent with the information you have entered in the aforementioned fields; otherwise, no cover page will be sent.

The Notify Sender on Delivery checkbox is like a return receipt. When your fax server gets an acknowledgment from the recipient's fax machine, you get a mail message that the fax was delivered.

When you have set the appropriate options, click Send. Your fax is queued at the server until a fax/modem is available to deliver the fax.

> **Tip**
>
> Remember that messaging is one of the core services of Lotus Notes: you can mail any Notes document. This also applies to faxing. For example, you have a lead in your Lead Tracking database who is interested in a service that your friend at another company provides and you want to fax the information to her.
>
> To do so, open the document you want to fax and choose Actions, Forward. A new Memo is created and the lead document is copied into the Body field. In the SendTo field, you enter the recipient's name and fax number in the *User Name@Phone Number*@Fax format mentioned earlier. The router sends the message to the Fax gateway for faxing.

The Lotus Fax Server, though not cheap, is a powerful and worthy addition to any Notes installation. If your company does not have this capability, it is certainly worth investigating. It can be a powerful addition to your office environment.

Accessing Your Mailbox from Another PC on the Network

If you use Notes for any length of time, sooner or later (probably sooner) you'll want to use Notes from someone else's PC. For instance, your PC might be down and you need to check your mail to see whether you got that big promotion. Or you might be in a different location for the day and need to check your mail.

Accessing Notes from another PC in your company is easy, but you must be prepared in advance. The following sections explain what you need to do to use Notes from any PC.

> **Tip**
>
> You should do the following sometime in the very near future. You never know when your PC might crash, leaving you unable to get your mail or access your databases.

Creating an ID Disk

When Notes is first installed on your computer, a Notes ID file is created for you. This file holds the information Notes needs for you to access to the Notes server, such as your user name and password. You can think of your ID file as a key that allows you to unlock the door of the Notes server.

Your ID file, which is normally stored in your Notes data directory (`C:\NOTES\DATA\`), has the extension ID. Normally, the first part of the file name is part of your real name.

For instance, Darryl Rogers may find a file called `DROGERS.ID` in his Notes directory. If you cannot locate your ID file, choose File, Tools, User ID, which displays the User ID dialog box, like the one in Figure 6.15.

Fig. 6.15   The User ID dialog box for my personal ID file.

As you can see in Figure 6.15, the second line, ID file, displays the full path to the file and the file name.

Because you must have this file to use Notes, the best plan for using Notes from other PCs is to copy this file to a disk. You can use the same method that you would to copy any file to a disk.

> **Note**
>
> If you don't know how to copy a file to disk, contact your Notes administrator or your Help Desk.

After you copy the file to the disk, put a label on the disk as soon as possible. On the label, identify the disk as your Notes ID and be sure to write down the file name of the ID file. In addition, write down the name of the mail server on the disk (I explain how to get it shortly). You use this information to access Notes from the other PC.

> **Tip**
>
> Your Notes ID file is critically important to your success in using Notes. Without an ID file, you can't use Notes. If you lose or corrupt your ID file, or forget your password, you *cannot* access Notes. Although a new ID can be created, this can cause problems if you have encrypted any documents.

(continues)

(continued)

Make several backup copies of this file and keep them in a secure place. (Remember, if someone else can get your ID file and knows your password, he or she can pass as you!) In addition, make backup copies of this file regularly since information stored in the file can change.

You can save yourself a lot of pain by making regular backups of this file. If you change your password in your current ID and then have to use a backup copy of your ID file, it may have an old password. The moral of this story is to back up your ID file often!

You need one more piece of information to access your mailbox from another PC. You must know the name of your mail server (the server where your mailbox database is stored). To find the name of your mail server, choose File, Mobile, Locations. Note the Locations view in your Name & Address Book.

Open any of the location documents and you see the Home/Mail Server field in the Servers section in the upper-right corner of the form (see Figure 6.16). Or click the second box in the status bar (which displays the name of your current location setup) and select Edit Current. This also opens the current location document in your Personal N & A Book.

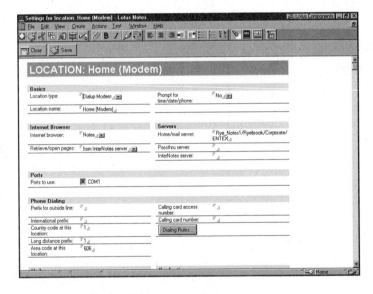

Fig. 6.16 A location document for the Home location.

When you have your ID file on a diskette and know your mail server, you can use Notes from another PC. To access your mailbox from someone else's PC, do one of the following:

- Log into Notes.

- Add the icon for your mailbox to the workspace of the workstation you are using.

The next two sections cover the steps to do this.

> **Note**
>
> Because Notes is a truly cross-platform application, you can easily move between workstations that have different operating systems. Notes has the same look and feel on all platforms.
>
> You may, however, have trouble if you try to use a UNIX or Macintosh workstation. Those machines may not be able to read a disk that was formatted by DOS, Windows, or OS/2. If you need to use one of these workstations, consult your Notes administrator or Help Desk for advice on creating a cross-platform Notes ID disk that can be read by these machines.

Logging On to Notes with Your ID Disk

To log on to a Notes server with your ID disk, follow these steps:

1. If Notes is running on the workstation, go to step 2. If Notes is not running, start it. You may be asked for a password. If so, choose Cancel and go to step 2.

2. Insert your ID disk in the machine.

3. Choose File, Tools, Switch ID.

   Notes displays the Choose User ID to Switch To dialog box that shows the file name of the ID file in use on the workstation. This is the ID of the last person to log on to Notes from this workstation (see Figure 6.17).

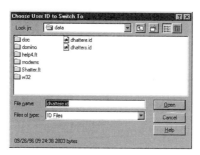

Fig. 6.17   Use the Choose User ID to Switch To dialog box to use a different ID.

4. Click the down arrow of the Look in box and select the drive that you inserted your disk into.

5. In the File Name list, choose your ID file and click OK. Or you can click the File Name box and type the drive letter you put the disk into, followed by a colon and the name of your ID file (this method is slightly faster if you know the name of your file). For example, if you are switching to Samuel Hatter's ID, you would type:

   `A: SHATTER.ID`

6. You are prompted for your Notes password. Enter your password and click Enter. Notes displays the User ID dialog box with key information about your Notes user

ID. This includes your user name, type of license, and your internal Notes ID number (refer to Figure 6.15).

7. Choose <u>O</u>K.

At this point, you are logged in to Notes. You can do anything you can do on your workstation, unless you have databases on your machine that are not on this machine. You could, however, open them on this workstation.

Remember, though, that workspace on this computer is arranged by the user and you may not find things the way you have them on your workstation. For instance, you won't find your mailbox on any of these workpages (unless you added the icon previously). You must add it. The next section explains how to access your mailbox when you are logged on.

Tip

It's considered bad form to rearrange the workspace on another person's workstation without explicit permission. If you do, you should try to put it back the way it was.

Adding Your Mailbox Icon to the Workspace

After you have logged in and are using someone else's workstation, you can access your mailbox. But you must add an icon for the mailbox first. Adding your mailbox is exactly like adding any other database icon.

 ◀◀ See "Accessing a Database," p. 89

To add a mailbox icon to your workspace, follow these steps:

1. Select a workpage on which to add your mailbox. (Courtesy dictates that you ask the owner of the workspace before you arbitrarily add the icon.)

2. Choose <u>F</u>ile, <u>D</u>atabase, <u>O</u>pen, or press Ctrl+O.

3. Select the name of the server that houses your mailbox. (You wrote the name of your mail server on the disk label, didn't you? If not, you need to know the name of your mail server before you continue.)

4. When you select a server, the Database displays a list of the databases on the specified Notes server. You probably won't see your mailbox in the list. But if you scroll through the list, near the end of the list you should see the entry [MAIL] (the square brackets indicate that this is a directory rather than a database).

This is the MAIL subdirectory on the server, where mailboxes are stored by default. Like most things in Notes, the mail databases can be stored elsewhere, and it's up to the administrator where the mail databases are stored.

If you can't find the mail subdirectory, contact your administrator for the location of your mail file. When you have the appropriate directory, select it and click Open, or double-click the [MAIL] entry.

> **Tip**
>
> You can type *M* to index down to the first entry that begins with M, which is slightly faster than using the scroll bars. This works in all list boxes.

5. The Database list displays the mailboxes in the MAIL directory. Each mailbox is identified by the name of the user to whom the mailbox belongs. Scroll through the list of names until you find your own name and select it. (Remember, you can type the first letter in your name to index to the first mailbox that begins with that letter.)

To add the icon and open the database in one fell swoop, click the Open button. This puts the icon on the current workpage and opens the mailbox. Or double-click the entry in the Database list. To add the icon without opening the mailbox, click the Add button.

You now can access your mailbox from this workstation as you would from your own workstation. Your mailbox is available until you or the owner of the workstation remove the icon from the workspace.

If you plan to use this workstation to access your mailbox often, leave your mailbox icon on the workpage to save time. But if you don't plan to use this machine again or if you use it infrequently, remove the icon from the workspace when you have finished reading your mail. To do so, select the icon and press the Delete key.

◀◀ See "Deleting Database Icons from Your Workspace," p. 123

When you open your mailbox on this new workstation, all your mail messages appear as Unread messages, even if you have read them. This is because Notes tracks the "read marks" in the desktop.dsk file on each workstation. Similarly, if you read messages while using another workstation, Notes displays those messages as unread when you return to your own PC.

Logging Off the Other Workstation

When you finish using another workstation, be sure to clear your user information. If you don't clear your user information or switch back to the owner's ID, you stay logged in to Notes as long as that session remains active.

This means that anyone can access your mailbox and read your mail, or worse—send mail as you. Just imagine, your boss gets a mail from you detailing what a jerk she is—you get the picture, right? In addition, anyone may have access to any of the databases that you have access to.

To maintain security (and your job), always do one of the following to make sure that you are logged off the system:

- **Exit Notes**—If you did not copy your ID file to the workstation's hard disk but just used it from the floppy disk, there is absolutely no way anyone can access your information. If you did copy your ID to the workstation's hard disk, the user must know your password to log in as you (and you'd never tell your password to anyone else, would you?).

- **Press F5**—This key tells Notes to clear all private user information, logging you off the system. Anyone trying to access a mailbox must enter your password.

- **Ask the workstation's owner to log on while you watch**—When the owner of the workstation uses File, Tools, Switch ID to select his ID file and log on to his account, you are automatically logged out.

Logging On After Someone Uses Your Workstation

As soon as someone else logs on at your workstation, your Notes session ends. When you are ready to use Notes again on your workstation, you log on to Notes again. The following procedure is almost identical to the one you used to log on to someone else's workstation:

1. If Notes is still running, go to step 2. If Notes is not running, restart it. If Notes prompts you for the last user's password, select Cancel and go to step 2.

2. Choose File, Tools, Switch ID. Notes asks for the location of your ID file. The File name box displays the file name of the ID last used on your workstation.

   Your ID file should be in the C:\NOTES\DATA directory on your local hard disk. If the path does not point to this directory, change the Drive and Directory boxes to point to this directory. The File Name box should display your ID file. (As a shortcut, if you know the path and name of your ID file, you can type this into the File Name box and click the OK button.)

   For example, if your user name is Roger Sebastian, your ID path and file name probably is C:\NOTES\DATA\RSEBASTI.ID. If you cannot find your ID file, contact your Notes administrator or your help desk. You cannot reestablish a Notes session without your ID file.

   When you identify your ID file, you are prompted to enter your password. After you have done this successfully, Notes acknowledges that you are logged on and you can begin to use Notes as usual.

> **Note**
>
> You can also use Notes via a dial-up connection from outside your company. See Chapter 20, "Setting Up to Go Remote," for more information on how to work with Notes remote.

Sending Mail Outside Your Company

Many companies that use Notes need to send mail to other Notes users outside their company or to users that use other mail systems such as the Internet. As more companies discover the benefits of e-mail, the need to link similar and dissimilar mail systems is growing.

In fact, there is a growing market of add-on products to enable Notes to communicate with other mail systems. Within the next decade, you should be able to communicate with almost anyone via e-mail. As of this printing, Notes can be connected to the following e-mail systems. The next three sections tell you how to send NotesMail to other companies that use Notes, how to send NotesMail to Internet e-mail users through an SMTP gateway, and how to send mail to users of other mail systems such as Microsoft Mail.

Sending NotesMail to Other Notes Users

Exchanging NotesMail between companies that use Notes needs coordination and cooperation between the Notes administrators of the companies, but needs no additional hardware or software.

For mail to be exchanged, the following must be in place:

- Each company must have at least one server set up to communicate with a server at the other company. Each of these servers must be cross-certified so that they can communicate. Your Notes administrator should do the cross-certification to enable access for the other server.

- At least one of the servers must call the other servers to make a connection through which mail messages can be transferred. This dictates a Connection document in the Public N & A Book for the server that makes the calls.

◄◄ See "Server Connection Documents," p. 193

- Calling times should be scheduled in the Connection document so that mail is exchanged in a timely, cost-effective manner.

> **Note**
>
> This is only a brief overview of the steps required to exchange mail between organizations. To exchange mail with another company that uses Notes, see your Notes administrator.

When this setup is in place, sending mail to outside people is only slightly more complex than sending mail to your coworkers. Users in another company are outside your domain and do not appear in your Public N & A Book.

This means that you must provide more routing information to Notes. When you address a message to someone outside the company, you include their domain (which is almost always the company name; your contact at the other company should provide this information for you), preceded by an "at" sign (@).

For example, to send a message to Dan Voelker at ABC Company, you would address the message as follows:

```
To: Dan Voelker/ABC Company@ABC Company
```

This notation tells Notes that Dan Voelker is not in your domain (your company's N & A Book) but is outside your organization and that this message should be forwarded to the ABC Company server on the next connection. When the mail message is delivered to the mailbox on the ABC company server, it is routed to Dan Voelker's mailbox by their server.

If you often communicate with people in other companies, you can make it much easier on yourself by adding their addresses to your Personal N & A Book. To do so, you must add a Person document for each person your want to communicate with, just as you would for people in your own company who are not in your domain.

The difference for people outside your company is that you must put the person's full mail address in the Forwarding Address field. When Notes sees an address in this field, it knows that the person specified is in another domain or organization, and that the mail must be transferred outside the current domain.

Figure 6.18 shows a Person document configured to send mail to Dan Voelker at the ABC Company.

 ◄◄ See "Person Documents," p. 184

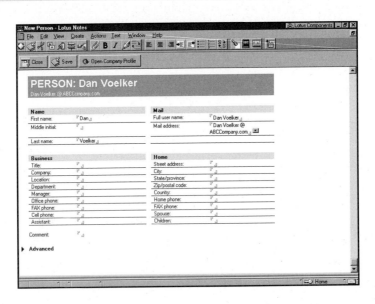

Fig. 6.18 A person document for Dan Voelker @ ABCCompany.com.

> **Tip**
>
> If you have previously received mail from someone outside your company who is not in either of your N & A books, you can easily add them to your Personal N & A Book for future use. Select the mail message you received and choose Actions, Mail Tools, Add Sender to Address Book. This creates a new Person document and automatically copies the sender's information into the Person document.

As the popularity of Notes continues to grow, the ability to communicate with other Notes users becomes increasingly important. In fact, many third-party service providers such as CompuServe have seen the potential for Notes. These companies have developed large Notes networks that allow you to transfer messages from your company to other Notes users easily for a small monthly charge. If your company uses Notes but can't afford the additional support to enable and maintain external connections, these services are an attractive alternative.

Sending Notes Mail Messages to Internet Users

Unless you have been living under a rock for the past five years, you must have at least heard of the Internet and might possibly use it. The Internet is a vast worldwide network of networks that allows millions of people to communicate electronically without regard to geography or time.

Lotus realized the tremendous potential of the Internet and how it can extend Notes capabilities early on. Notes now provides software for Notes users to send and receive Internet mail messages from within Notes.

To enable this, the Lotus SMTP MTA must be configured on a Notes server in your organization and your company must have a connection to the Internet. If both of these conditions are met, all you need to send mail to someone over the Internet is an Internet address.

When the Notes administrator installs and configures this software, a foreign domain is created, much like the Lotus Fax Server software, so Notes knows that this message is to be forwarded to the Internet. To send a mail message over the Internet, the SMTP domain should be appended to the user's Internet address, or with Notes R4.5 it can be configured so that any mail sent to an unrecognized domain is forwarded to the SMTP MTA, which eliminates the need to append the foreign domain name.

For example, you have a friend, Rose Wezel, who works at XYZPDQ Manufacturing, which has an Internet account. You want to send a message to her so you create a new mail message and address it as follows:

```
Rose Wezel@XYZPDQ.com
```

When the NotesMail router sees this message, it reads but does not recognize the domain XYZPDQ.com and transfers it to the SMTP agent for conversion to the Internet format.

> **Note**
>
> If you often communicate with Internet users via NotesMail, you can add these people to your Personal N & A Book to make it easier to address mail messages. Once you have received and read an Internet mail, you can choose Actions, Mail Tools, Add Sender to Address Book to add the user to your Personal N & A book.

Sending Notes Mail to Users of Other E-Mail Systems

Many large companies have a mixture of e-mail systems, such as Microsoft Mail on one LAN and cc:Mail on another. In most cases, this lack of standardization is because when LANs and e-mail were first introduced, each department chose the system it found most suitable.

If your company uses other e-mail systems in addition to NotesMail, you can buy software products that allow Notes to send and receive messages from most popular mail systems.

Some of the mail gateways and MTAs available for Notes are the following:

- **cc:Mail MTA**—Allows seamless message transfer and directory synchronization with Lotus cc:Mail, the leading files-based messaging system.

- **SMTP/MIME MTA**—Lotus now provides SMTP/Multipurpose Internet Multimedia Extensions (MIME), which allow file attachments to be sent over the Internet, and MTA for native Internet mail connectivity.

- **X.400 MTA**—Provides native connectivity to x.400 environments.

- **MHS gateway**—Provides seamless connectivity between Notes and Novell's Message Handling System.

- **SMTP gateway**—Provides Internet connectivity for R3 users.

- **Pager gateway**—Provides the capability to send NotesMail messages to alphanumeric pagers.

- **MBLink**—Provides connectivity to MS Mail and many others. For information, contact FHS at 703-883-9090.

For an inclusive listing of third-party gateways and MTAs, visit the Lotus Web site at **www.lotus.com**, or pick up a copy of the Lotus Notes & cc:Mail guide from your Lotus representative.

Working with cc:Mail

Lotus cc:Mail is the number one e-mail system, with over ten million seats. Naturally, Lotus makes it easy to use cc:Mail as an alternative messaging system to NotesMail or to integrate Notes with cc:Mail.

If your organization already has a large number of cc:Mail users, it's easy to use cc:Mail in place of NotesMail. You tell Notes that you want to use cc:Mail instead of NotesMail through the configuration of your user preferences.

However, there are limitations to using cc:Mail instead of NotesMail. To enable cc:Mail, select File, Tools, User Preferences, and then click the Mail icon.

From the Mail Program combo box, choose cc:Mail. This displays a path to the cc:Mail executable. If this is right, leave it. Otherwise, type the correct path or use the browse button to search for the cc:Mail executable.

You are also prompted to enter or browse for the local of your cc:Mail address book. Now you see the limitations of NotesMail mentioned previously: many of the NotesMail options are disabled.

Also, you'll notice that the NotesMail menu system is replaced by one with the more limited function of cc:Mail. The new commands are as follows:

- **Open**—Runs cc:Mail's client program.

- **Forward**—Renders the contents of the open or selected document(s) to text and sends the text as a cc:Mail message.

- **Forward as attachment**—Converts the open or selected document(s) to an encapsulated Notes database and attaches the database to the message you are sending. The recipients of the message *must* have Lotus Notes to read the attached file.

- **Send**—Converts the open or selected document into the format in the MailFormat field of the document. If none exists, the document is converted into an encapsulated Notes database. The names of the recipients are taken from the SendTo, CopyTo, and BlindCopyTo fields in the document.

As you can see, it's easy enough to use cc:Mail as an alternative mail system. But with NotesMail's new, more friendly interface and powerful client/server technology, NotesMail is a much better choice.

Working with the Mail Trace Feature

Mail Tracing is a new Notes 4.x feature that allows the route of a mail message to be traced from sender to recipient. This can be a useful tool when mail is routing incorrectly because it tells you how far along the route a message went before failing.

Mail Tracing can be configured so that the router at each "hop" along the path sends a verification or just sends a verification at the final destination. This allows the user or administrator to see the exact route a mail message took on the way to its destination.

To enable Mail Tracing for a mail message, choose the Trace Entire Path for the Delivery Report Delivery option.

The Mail Tools Menu

Notes 4.0 has a flexible e-mail interface that can be customized by end users to make NotesMail more productive and enjoyable. A good example of this is the folders feature that allows you to specify folders to sort and organize your e-mail messages, based on your own criteria.

This section explores several additional features that enable you to add your own distinctive flair to your mail messages and make your NotesMail sessions easier and more productive. Figure 6.19 shows the options on the <u>A</u>ctions, <u>M</u>ail Tools menu. This menu is context-sensitive: it is available only when you are in your NotesMail mailbox.

Fig. 6.19   The Actions, Mail Tools menu in the NotesMail mailbox.

As you can see from Figure 6.19, six of the seven options in this menu are:

- <u>A</u>dd Sender to Address Book
- A<u>r</u>chive Selected Documents
- <u>C</u>hoose Letterhead
- <u>C</u>reate Stationery
- <u>D</u>elegation Profile
- <u>O</u>ut of Office

The rest of this section covers each of these six options.

Add Sender to Address Book

As mentioned earlier, when you receive a mail message, you can easily add the sender's address to your Personal N & A Book for future use. Just choose <u>A</u>ction, <u>M</u>ail Tools, <u>A</u>dd Sender to Address Book, and a new person document will be created in your address book for this person.

Archiving Your Mail

Although it's a good idea to delete mail messages that are no longer needed, many jobs require that you keep some mail messages for long periods of time. For instance, if you work in a purchasing department and do electronic commerce with your suppliers via e-mail, you might need to keep copies of these e-mail messages for legal reasons.

If this is the case, you can improve the response time of your mailbox and make it more manageable from an organizational perspective by creating an Archive mailbox and storing old mail messages there.

> **Note**
>
> An Archive mailbox can be useful to store e-mail messages for long periods of time when you don't want to incur the overhead for doing so in your mailbox. But you consume more disk space because you are storing more mail messages.

To create an Archive mailbox, first decide where it will be stored: on your local machine or on the Notes server.

If you decide to store the Archive mailbox on the Notes server, common courtesy (and the possible wrath of the Notes administrator) dictates that you speak to the Notes administrator of your server before you put the database on the server. In fact, in most Notes installations, only administrators can put new databases on the server. So you may *have* to consult the Notes administrator for help.

When you decide where the Mail Archive database should be stored, it's easy to create the archive. You can select the Archiving view and click the Setup Archive button, or select your mailbox (if you are not using your mailbox) and choose <u>A</u>ctions, <u>M</u>ail Tools, <u>A</u>rchive Selected Documents. If this is your first time making an archive, a new Archive Profile document is created, as shown in Figure 6.20.

Fig. 6.20   An Archive Profile for my local mailbox.

As you can see from Figure 6.20, the Archive Profile form is straightforward. The first checkbox, Archive Expired documents, enables Archive Expired documents and displays the after ___ days field when checked. You can enter a value for the number of days you want to elapse before inactive documents are archived.

> **Note**
>
> Any document can have an expiration date—a date after which the author of the document thinks it will no longer be valuable. To set an expiration date for a mail message, choose <u>A</u>ctions, <u>S</u>pecial Options and enter an expiration date in the Special Options Dialog box.

Notes Basics

The next checkbox, Archive documents which have no activity, when you check it, displays the after ___ days. This allows you to enter the number of days to wait before an inactive document (a document that has not be edited and saved) is archived.

To generate an archive log each time you archive messages (an archive log is a summary what the archive action did), you can check. An Archive Log will be generated each time an archive occurs to create a log entry that you can look at in the Archiving view.

If you check archive logging, you see the next checkbox—the Archive Log will include a doclink to each archived document. If you want to be able to open the archive log and quickly jump to any archived document, enable this feature.

By default, Notes fills in the file name of your mailbox and uses the extension ARC.This information is needed. You can change the file name if you want, but it is recommended that you go with the default value that Notes plugs in.

The Archive Profile editors field lets you define a list of users that can edit this Archive profile; it defaults to your distinguished username.

When you have configured your Archive Profile, you are ready to begin archiving your mailbox.

Storing Mail in the Archive

You can archive mail messages in one of two ways. The first is through the use of an agent. Lotus provides an archiving agent, Periodic Archive, that by default runs on a weekly schedule and archives your mail messages based on the criteria you set in the Archive Profile.

This schedule can be changed. For more information on agents, see Chapter 16, "Buttons and Agents." To enable the Periodic Archive agent in your mailbox, click the Agents icon in the Navigator. This displays all the agents in your mailbox (see Figure 6.21).

On your screen, you can see the Periodic Archive agent with a small empty checkbox on the left. The checkbox is not checked because this agent is not set to run by default. To enable the agent, click the checkbox. This launches the Choose Server To Run On dialog box shown in Figure 6.22.

Click the drop-down list and choose the server on which this agent should run. If the archive file is stored on your workstation, choose Local. Otherwise, choose the name of the server where the archive file is stored. When you enter this information, the check box is checked and periodic archiving begins.

The second option needs some user interaction. You can at any time select mail messages in your mailbox and choose <u>A</u>ctions, <u>M</u>ail Tools, <u>A</u>rchive Selected Documents to move the selected mail messages into the archive file. This is useful if you get many mail messages and don't want to wait for the agent to run.

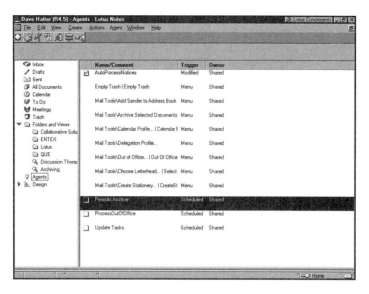

Fig. 6.21 The Agents view lets you add, update, and delete agents.

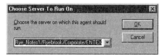

Fig. 6.22 The Choose Server To Run On dialog box lets you tell the agent where to run.

Note

Remember that your new Mail Archive database is only a copy of your mailbox, not a replica. This means the archive gets only new messages when the Periodic Archive agent runs or when you use the Actions, Mail Tools, Archive Selected Documents Menu option.

As you use your Mail Archive database, it grows quickly. You should periodically check for mail messages you no longer need to keep in the archive and can permanently delete.

Using the Archive

Occasionally, you'll need to use the mail archive file to refer to old mail or delete messages from it. To access mail messages stored in your archive, you can either follow a doclink from the Archive Log or open the archive database by double-clicking it.

Delegation Profile

The Delegation Profile is also new to Notes R4.5 and is another key component of Group Calendaring and Scheduling. This form allows you to define who can access your mailbox to see your calendar and schedule appointments for you. In addition, it allows you to determine whether other users can read and manage your mail and even send mail on your behalf. This could be a very handy option if you are a busy executive. Because this is primarily used for C & S, it will be covered in detail in Chapter 9, "Lotus Notes Group Calendaring and Scheduling." Figure 6.23 shows the new Calendar Profile form.

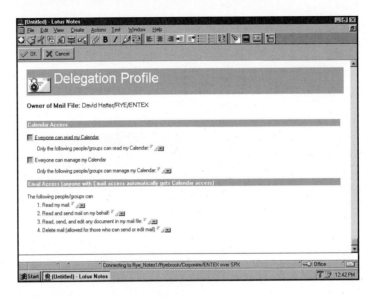

Fig. 6.23   Here is the new Delegation Profile form.

Out Of Office Profile

If you have used e-mail before, particularly if you work for a large organization, you are probably aware of what happens when you go on vacation or must be out of the office for an extended period. People keep sending you e-mail because they don't know you are gone. When you return, your mailbox is full, and people are angry because you have not answered their mail messages.

NotesMail provides a simple way to solve this problem. If you are going to be out of the office for an extended period, you can create an Out Of Office Profile so users are notified of your absence (see Figure 6.24).

You can enter a Leaving Date and a Returning Date in the Out Of Office Profile. Notes fills in a default subject and message, which you can edit to say whatever you want.

Any mail messages that are sent to you within the time specified in this document causes a return mail to be generated to the senders. This return mail tells them that you are out for the specified time period, as well as any other information you put in the My Out of the Office Message for Most People section.

In addition, you can put a special message for certain people in the People/Groups folder. These are people who should receive a special message. You can also make a list of people and groups who get no message.

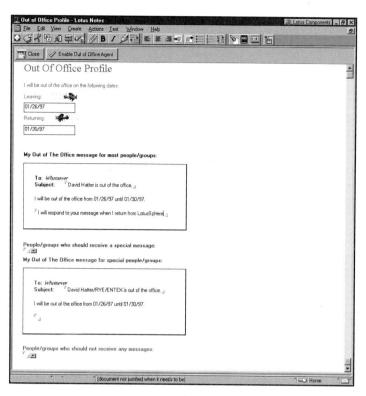

Fig. 6.24 The Out Of Office Profile helps you notify coworkers of your absence automatically.

When you have entered the appropriate information, click the Enable Out Of Office Profile button; you are asked which server to run this agent on. Be sure to put it in your Home/Mail server. (See the earlier section "Creating an ID Disk" for information on how to determine your Home/Mail server.)

On your scheduled return, you get a "Welcome Back!" message and the Out Of Office Profile is disabled.

> **Note**
>
> For the Out of Office profile to run correctly, you must be granted the ability to run agents on your server. Be sure that the administrator has enabled this for you.

Creating Letterhead

In Notes 4.x, you can select from several letterhead styles to display at the top of your mail messages. In the standard mail Memo form, the letterhead is the multicolored bar that displays your user name, and the time and date the mail was composed.

This new capability allows you to add a personal flair to your mail messages. To change your letterhead, open your mailbox and choose Actions, Mail Tools, Select Letterhead. This displays the Choose Letterhead window (see Figure 6.25).

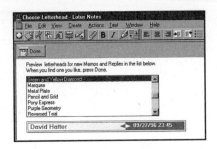

Fig. 6.25 The Choose Letterhead window.

The Choose Letterhead window displays a list of all the available letterheads in your mailbox. Select one of them from the list, and this new letterhead is applied to all your mail messages. The From the Desk Of letterhead is the default letterhead used in all NotesMail forms.

Creating Stationery

Notes also allows you to create stationery, a mail message whose format and recipients' list you can use again. This is very useful if you often send a mail message to the same people.

For instance, if you send a weekly sales report to your sales team, you could create stationery for this purpose that specifies the recipient list. Use this stationery to send the weekly mail.

To create stationery, open your mailbox and choose Actions, Mail Tools, Create Stationery. This launches the Create Stationery dialog box (see Figure 6.26).

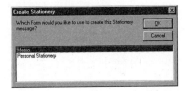

Fig. 6.26 The Create Stationery dialog box displays the existing Stationery forms.

This dialog box displays a list of the stationery you can use. Choose one and click OK, which will display the selected Stationery so you can edit it. When you finish editing, complete the recipient list, add whatever text you need, and send the message.

When the message is sent, you are asked whether you want to save the message as stationery. If you choose Yes, you are prompted for a name for the new stationery. Enter a name and click OK. The Save Stationery dialog box appears (see Figure 6.27).

Fig. 6.27 The Save Stationery dialog box.

Notes tells you that the new stationery has been saved in the Drafts folder. To compose a new mail message with this stationery, open the Drafts view and open the stationery you want to use.

The Calendar Tools

Notes 4.5 now includes a very powerful Group Calendaring and Scheduling capability that is accessed through your mailbox and comes with several tools that make it easy to use. Because Group Calendaring and Scheduling is such a powerful new feature, it is covered in detail in its own chapter, "Lotus Notes Group Calendaring and Scheduling" (Chapter 9), and will be discussed only briefly here. Figure 6.28 shows the options on the Actions, Calendar Tools menu. Like the Mail Tools menu, this menu is also context-sensitive and will be displayed only when your NotesMail mailbox is open.

Fig. 6.28 The Calendar Tools menu allows you to configure and work with your Calendar.

As you can see from Figure 6.28, the three options in this menu are:

- Calendar Profile
- Delete Repeating Appointment(s)
- Open Another Calendar

Calendar Profile

The Calendar Profile is new to Notes R4.5 and is an essential component of Notes' cool new Group Calendaring and Scheduling capabilities. This form is used to configure your personal Calendar and will be covered in detail in Chapter 9, "Lotus Notes Group Calendaring and Scheduling." Figure 6.29 displays the new Calendar Profile form.

Delete Repeating Appointment(s)

The Delete Repeating Appointment(s) option allows you to select a repeating appointment in your calendar and have Notes delete all instances of it, rather than you delete each one individually. This will also be covered in more detail in Chapter 9, "Lotus Notes Group Calendaring and Scheduling."

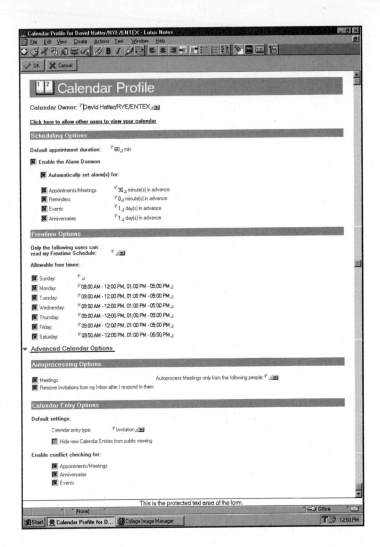

Fig. 6.29 The Calendar Profile is your "one-stop" configuration tool for your personal calendar.

Open Another Calendar

The Open Another Calendar option allows you to open another user's calendar. When you choose this action, it displays the dialog box shown in Figure 6.30.

From the Open Calendar dialog box, you can choose which Name and Address Book to use and then select the server where the other user's mailbox resides so that you can view their calendar. Remember that you won't be able to view another user's calendar unless they have given you access to it. Like the other topics it this section, this will be covered in detail in Chapter 9, "Lotus Notes Group Calendaring and Scheduling."

Fig. 6.30 The Open Calendar dialog box allows you to easily select another user's calendar.

Other Useful Mail Actions

Five other mail actions can be useful: Resend, Convert To Task, Delivery Information, Special Options, and Save as Stationery. The first, Resend, is context-sensitive and can be used from mail views and folders but not from documents.

If you get a delivery failure, you can use Resend to correct the address and resubmit the mail for delivery. This way, you don't have to re-create the mail message with a corrected address. To use the Resend action, from the main menu choose Actions, Resend.

The second, Convert To Task, is not context-sensitive. You can use it from views or inside documents. It allows you to convert any mail message into a task. To do this, choose Actions, Convert To Task.

Action three, Delivery Information, is also context-sensitive and it works only for opened documents. When you use Delivery Information, it displays the dialog box shown in Figure 6.31.

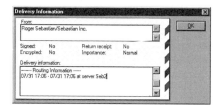

Fig 6.31 The Delivery Information dialog box is a new Notes R4.x feature that shows you mail routing information.

The Delivery Information dialog box shows you who sent the message, the delivery options, and the mail-routing information in one convenient, visually appealing place.

The fourth, Save As Stationery, is context-sensitive and allows you to convert an open mail message you have composed into stationery.

The last action, Special Options, is context-sensitive and works only for open messages not yet sent. When you select Special Options, the dialog box shown in Figure 6.32 is displayed.

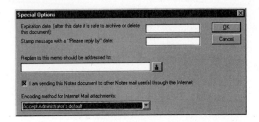

Fig 6.32 The Special Options dialog box helps you manage advanced mail options.

Using the Special Options action is easy. The first field, Expiration Date, allows you to enter the date used by the Archive macro to determine that a document is safe to archive.

The second field, Stamp Message with a "Please reply by" date, allows you to enter a date, from which Notes generates a Please reply by message in the mail message.

The Replies to this memo should be addressed to field allows you to have replies to your mail message routed to another user. You can even use the address helper to choose the user, so you don't need to know the user's address.

The I am sending this Notes document to other Notes mail user(s) through the Internet checkbox is used to tell Notes to encapsulate the message so that Rich Text items will be retained when received at the other end.

Finally, the Encoding method for Internet Mail attachments combo box allows you to choose a number of standard mail-attachment transfer protocols such as UUENCODE or MIME. For more information on Internet mail transfers, consult your Notes administrator.

From Here...

In this chapter, you learn how to use some of the more advanced functions of the Notes e-mail system: attaching files to mail messages, using different mailbox views, and customizing mail views, folders, and custom mail forms.

See the following chapters for information you might find useful when using NotesMail:

- Chapter 3, "Using Databases," covers Notes databases in detail. Remember, your NotesMail mailbox is just a Notes database.

- Chapter 7, "Working with Text," shows you how to make your text aesthetically pleasing.

- Chapter 8, "Working with Documents," shows you tips and tricks for working with Notes documents. NotesMail messages are documents, and any database can send and receive mail, not just your mailbox.

- Chapter 9, "Lotus Notes Group Calendaring and Scheduling," covers the cool new Group Calendaring and Scheduling capabilities and options in detail.

- Chapter 20, "Setting Up to Go Remote," covers topics such as location and connection documents, and workstation-based mail. This is helpful for mobile users.

Chapter 7

Working with Text

In earlier chapters, you learned how to compose simple documents. Although the techniques you learned are adequate for getting information across to your coworkers, you can communicate much more effectively by using the wealth of enhanced features that Notes offers. These features add emphasis to your writing and facilitate communication as you work with Notes.

Editing Text Fields

If you have used a word processor before—anything from Ami Pro to WordPerfect—you're used to rearranging, highlighting, and manipulating text. Notes includes a sophisticated text processor that provides many of the same features you have come to appreciate in word processors. If you're familiar with Windows-based word processors such as Microsoft Word for Windows, Word Pro, or WordPerfect for Windows, you will find that many of the keystrokes are the same.

Even if you haven't used a word processor before, by now you probably have done some experimenting in Notes and have discovered that you can make some simple corrections by performing the following basic actions:

- Pressing the arrow keys enables you to move up, down, left, and right within your document. The arrow keys also let you move from field to field.

- Pressing the Home key positions the insertion point at the beginning of the line.

- Pressing the End key positions the insertion point at the end of the line.

- Pressing the Page Up and Page Down keys scrolls one screen up or down, respectively.

Some of the main topics in this chapter are:

- Add color to your documents

- Use different font styles and sizes

- Use the permanent pen

- Work with styles

- Work with bulleted and numbered lists

- Work with tabs, margins, and other page settings

■ Pressing Ctrl+Home positions the insertion point at the beginning of the document; pressing Ctrl+End moves it to the end.

■ Pressing Ctrl+left arrow moves the insertion point back a word; pressing Ctrl+right arrow moves it forward a word.

■ Pressing the Delete key deletes the character just to the right of the insertion point.

■ Pressing the Backspace key deletes the character just to the left of the insertion point.

■ You can reposition the insertion point by clicking anywhere within the text.

As you read through this chapter, keep in mind that Notes provides you with a quick mouse trick to bring up a list of some of the most popular formatting selections, as well as the Text Properties InfoBox—which provides you with a wealth of text and paragraph settings to enhance your documents. To use this shortcut, click your right mouse button one time anywhere in the Notes document. Notes displays the context-sensitive menu box shown in Figure 7.1.

Fig. 7.1 You can make quick formatting selections by right-clicking your mouse button anywhere in the document.

In the following sections, you learn about more powerful editing commands.

Selecting Text

Some of the most powerful editing and formatting operations involve a two-step process. You first must identify the text that you want to do something to, and then tell Notes what to do with that text. As you read through the next few sections and learn how to perform editing tasks such as copying, changing text styles, and many others, you first must select the text as a way of telling Notes that this is the text you want to work with.

> **Note**
>
> If you have not typed text yet, you can set font attributes for the new text first. After setting the font attributes (such as style, size, and color), all of the text you type appears with those attributes until you change them or exit the document.

To select a section of text, place the pointer at the beginning of the text you want to work with, hold down the left mouse button, move the mouse pointer to the end of the text, and release the mouse button. If you prefer to use the keyboard, position the insertion point at the beginning of the text you want to select, hold down the Shift key, and move the insertion point to the end of the text using the directional arrows on your keyboard. By using either method, you can select any amount of text.

After you select the text, it appears in reverse video—that is, the text appears as a lighter color with a dark box surrounding it (see Figure 7.2).

> **Tip**
>
> You can select just one word quickly by double-clicking your mouse while the pointer is on the word. This is a great time-saver if you want to check the spelling or change the font attributes of just that one word.

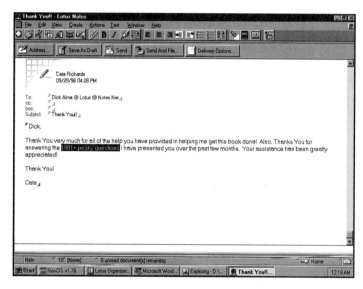

Fig. 7.2   You can select text in documents by clicking and dragging your mouse cursor over it.

After you select the text, you can tell Notes what you want to do to that text.

One of the simplest and most common operations is deleting the selected text, which you can do by pressing the Delete key. Other ways to delete selected text include selecting Edit, Clear, clicking the Edit Clear SmartIcon, or simply pressing the spacebar.

Another common operation is typing over a selected section of text with new text. After you select the text, start typing new text to replace the old text. The instant you start typing, Notes deletes all the selected text and begins inserting the new text that you type.

Caution

Be careful that you don't accidentally type text while you have text selected. If you type new text while old text is selected, Notes thinks that you want to replace the old text with the new text. Many users have experienced a momentary panic at seeing a large block of selected text disappear because their finger accidentally brushed a letter or a digit. If you make such a mistake, select Edit, Undo Typing before you type anything else, or perform any other function.

Using the Clipboard

The Clipboard is a storage area shared among Notes and other Windows, Macintosh, and OS/2 applications. It serves as a temporary holding location for data that you are moving or copying between Notes and other word processors, spreadsheets, and many other programs. You can use the Clipboard to cut text, bitmaps, or other inserted objects (like spreadsheets and other graphic files) from a Notes document—for example, switch to a Windows word processor such as Microsoft Word for Windows or Word Pro—and paste them into a Word or Word Pro document. You can also use the Clipboard (also referred to as the Clipbook in Windows for Workgroups) to cut and paste a document(s) from one database to another. (You learn more about cutting and pasting documents in Chapter 8, "Working with Documents.")

Note

You can use the Clipboard to copy data between any applications that are designed to work with the Clipboard.

The Clipboard is a temporary storage location. You can store data there only during a single Windows or OS/2 session. If you turn off your PC or exit Windows or OS/2, the Clipboard is cleared and the data is permanently lost.

Caution

Copying something else to the Clipboard will erase whatever you currently have stored there, unless you are appending text to the Clipboard (discussed in a moment). You will lose the old data when you copy new data to the Clipboard.

The following sections explain how to use the Clipboard as a means for copying and moving data with Notes and between Notes and other applications.

While this section discusses the copying, cutting, and pasting of text, these procedures also apply to all objects found in Notes documents. For example, follow these same procedures to copy attachments, graphics, and other objects stored in the database.

Moving Text. As you type your text, you may decide that your thoughts make better sense in a different order, and you may want to move text from one place to another. This process—known as cutting and pasting—comes from the days when editors cut snippets of text from a paper document and pasted them elsewhere in the document. As the technique's name implies, cutting and pasting is really a two-step process: You remove the text from its old location (cut it) and insert it into its new location (paste it).

You must be in edit mode to cut and paste data. To enter edit mode, double-click anywhere within a document that is in read mode to open for editing—the field brackets will appear to indicate that you are in edit mode.

To cut and paste text, follow these steps:

1. Select the text you want to move.

2. Press Ctrl+X; choose Edit, Cut, or click the Edit Cut SmartIcon.

Notes removes the text from your document.

3. Position the insertion point where you want to paste the text.

4. Press Ctrl+V; choose Edit, Paste; or click the Edit Paste SmartIcon. Notes copies whatever text is in the Clipboard into your document wherever the insertion point is.

Copying Text. Copying text is very similar to moving text. As with moving, you want to put the text somewhere else in your current document or another document; but with copying, you also want the text to remain at its current location. You can be in read or edit mode to copy text, but you must be in edit mode to paste it.

Like the procedure to move text, copying text is a two-step process using the Clipboard as an intermediate holding place. Only the second step is different, as you can see in the following steps:

1. Select the text you want to copy.

2. Press Ctrl+C; choose Edit, Copy; or click the Edit Copy SmartIcon.

The text remains where it is, and nothing seems to have happened. Notes, however, has copied the selected text onto the Clipboard.

3. You now can move the insertion point to a new position and paste as described in the preceding set of steps or by using any of the other methods described earlier. Notes copies the text from the Clipboard to the document in the new location.

Tip

If you prefer to use the keyboard whenever possible, you can press Shift+End to highlight all text to the right of the insertion point on a line. Or, you can press Shift+Page down to copy everything from the insertion point to the bottom of the page. Holding the Shift key down while pressing the directional arrows will highlight everything in the direction of the arrow you press until you release the directional arrow key. However, be careful! If you accidentally press Shift+Insert instead, Notes will copy whatever is on the Clipboard into your document. If this happens, select Edit, Undo Typing immediately to remove the mistake.

Notes Basics

Many applications provide cut, copy, and paste operations but use a different set of shortcut keys. Lotus Notes supports two sets of shortcut keys, shown in Table 7.1. If you choose to use the keyboard for editing operations, you can use either set of keys. Keep in mind that the Macintosh uses the Command key—rather than the Ctrl key—when working with the keyboard commands.

Table 7.1 Shortcut Editing Keys		
Operation	**Standard Keys**	**Alternative Keys**
Cut	Ctrl+X	Shift+Delete
Copy	Ctrl+C	Ctrl+Insert
Paste	Ctrl+V	Shift+Insert
Undo	Ctrl+Z	Alt+Backspace

Copying Multiple Pieces of Data. You may find yourself in a situation where you want to copy several different pieces of text from several different documents and paste them all into a new document. By using the copy-and-paste technique described above, you must copy each piece to the Clipboard, and then paste it into the new document before copying the next piece of text. Each new copy operation replaces what is already on the Clipboard.

Notes, however, provides an operation just for this situation:

1. Use the usual key combination—Ctrl+C—to copy the first piece of text to the Clipboard.

2. For a subsequent piece of text, press Ctrl+Shift+Insert. Notes copies the selected text to the Clipboard; but rather than replacing the Clipboard's existing contents, Notes appends the new text so that the Clipboard contains both pieces of text.

   You can also hold down the Shift key and choose Edit, Copy or Edit, Cut for each piece of text you want to add to the Clipboard.

Note

When you copy more than one noncontiguous section to the Clipboard, Notes does not put a space between the last character of the first section copied and the first character of the next, unless you copy a space or blank line at the same time you copy the text. Rather, it simply adds the text at the end of the section you have previously copied.

This may create a messy copy on the Clipboard, in which you will have to spend time "cleaning up" when you paste the information into a new document. If keeping paragraphs, sentences, or words separate is important to you, make sure you highlight the spaces you want copied as well.

By repeating step 2 for additional text, you can accumulate as much text as you need on the Clipboard. Place your cursor in the location in which you want the copied text to appear, and then press Ctrl+V, (or Edit, Paste). Notes pastes the entire contents of the Clipboard into the new location.

More About Moving and Copying Text

After you cut or copy text to the Clipboard, you don't have to paste it into its new location immediately. The text remains on the Clipboard until you cut or copy something else (or until you exit Windows or OS/2). If you need to perform other operations at the location where you cut or copied the text, feel free to as long as you don't cut or copy other text. However, to avoid accidentally losing your data, it is best if you paste the data on the Clipboard into its new location as soon as possible—particularly if you are busy or often distracted and run the risk of forgetting where you left off in your work.

Pasting copies text from the Clipboard into your document, but the text remains on the Clipboard too. If you want to place another copy of the same text elsewhere, you need only to move the insertion point to the new location and paste again. Thus, from a single cut or copy you can perform as many paste operations as you like.

You need not cut (or copy) and paste within the same document. After you cut or copy text to the Clipboard, you can close the current document, open another document, and then paste the text into the second document.

In fact, you need not even paste within the same application or database. You can cut or copy a section of text in Lotus Notes, switch to another application that is designed to use the Clipboard, and then perform a paste into a word processing document, spreadsheet, or other file in that application. Similarly, you can perform a cut or copy in other applications, switch to Notes, and perform a paste. This capability to move and copy from one application to another is one of the most important advantages of using applications that support the Clipboard.

Pasting Text into Dialog Boxes. Often, you may want to copy (or cut) and paste information into a dialog box, but the Cut, Copy, and Paste commands are not available to you when you choose Edit. Don't worry, you can use Ctrl+C to copy (or Ctrl+X to Cut) the information to the Clipboard, and then Ctrl+V to paste the information. This is particularly helpful when you are trying to enter information into a dialog box—where the Edit, Copy and Edit, Paste commands are not available from the menu bar.

For example, you can use this tip when you are trying to fill the contents of a formula box when designing a field in a document. As shown in Figure 7.3, the formula in the formula definition box is quite long and would take the designer a good bit of time to write. However, if the designer already has this formula designed elsewhere, he or she can copy the formula from there and paste it into the field. The designer is now free to customize the formula as needed.

Tip

Often, designers use Notes databases to store copies of formulas—particularly complicated ones, in simple text fields. Then, when the formula is needed, the designer simply opens the database document referencing the type of formula needed, copies the formula text, and pastes it into the field formula definition box currently being defined. The designer might need to customize the formula—editing references to other fields, forms, or views, for example—but the formula, with its particular syntax, provides a great template to work from.

Often, this database is stored on a server, and all database designers can contribute and use the formulas. This lets companies maximize the use of database design using the trusted *CASE* method of Notes development—*Copy And Steal Everything*! You can use the CASE method with the Notes Formula Catalog database included on the CD-ROM accompanying this book. In this database, you will find numerous formulas that you can copy directly into the design of your application!

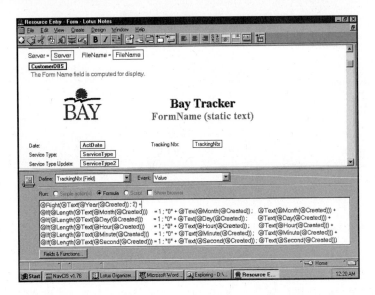

Fig. 7.3 You can easily paste text into a formula dialog box by copying from one location using Ctrl+C, and then pasting it into the new formula entry field using Ctrl+V.

Undoing Changes

Everybody presses the wrong key or chooses the wrong menu option occasionally, and you may wind up cutting when you meant to paste, or deleting when you meant to copy. Fortunately, with Notes all isn't lost.

Whenever you perform an operation that modifies a section of text—such as delete, cut, copy, or paste—Notes offers you a chance to change your mind. You can reverse the effects, or undo, the last operation by choosing Edit, Undo; pressing Ctrl+Z; or clicking the Edit Undo SmartIcon.

The exact wording of the first option on the Edit menu varies depending on the last operation you performed. If you last did a cut, the first item on the menu is Undo Cut; if you last did a paste, the command is Undo Paste. If you choose the command, Notes undoes the last operation by restoring the deleted text, removing the pasted text, or reversing whatever action you performed.

Notes also lets you change your mind about Undo—if you undo an operation, like boldfacing text, and you decide you want to perform that function anyway, choose Edit, Redo. The bold text will reappear. Like the Undo menu command, the Redo menu command will change depending on what action you are performing.

Undo is useful only if you realize immediately that you have made a mistake because you can undo only the most recent operation. Suppose that you delete a piece of text and then perform another operation (for example, type another character, or copy another piece of text to the Clipboard). If you realize then that the deletion was a mistake, you're out of luck—it's gone for good.

> **Caution**
>
> The Undo command cannot be used to bring back entire documents that have been deleted from a database.

Understanding Rich Text Fields

The most common type of field you encounter in most Notes documents is a text field. You can enter any kind of text into such a field—words, sentences, names, and so on. In Notes, however, you encounter two types of text fields: plain text fields and rich text fields.

> **Note**
>
> The body of your Notes e-mail memo is an example of a rich text field, while the Subject field in the memo is a text field.

A rich text field is so called because you can enter text, objects, and formatting information. Associated with any portion of rich text is a particular color, type style, justification, line spacing, and many other characteristics. By changing the characteristics for any portion of rich text, you can tell Notes to display (and print) that portion in any one of various colors, sizes, and type styles. You also can enter tables, graphics, document links, buttons, and other objects in rich text fields.

In the following sections, you learn how to make the most of text attributes. In Chapter 8, "Working with Documents," you will learn how to insert objects like tables, document links, and buttons.

> **Note**
>
> Rich text fields are the only fields in which you can change the font attributes, format paragraphs, insert graphics, embedded objects, attachments, tables, document links, pop-up boxes, and other special inserts. They are also the only fields in which you can import data from other applications. If you are trying to use one of these features and the menu command is not available to you, your cursor is not located in a rich text field.
>
> Information entered in rich text fields, however, will not be displayed in views. Text (and other field types) is used when the information needs to be displayed in a view.

Spotting Rich Text Fields

How can you tell whether a field is plain text or rich text? You cannot tell by looking at an empty field, but you can try to use some of the features described in this section. If you try to change the style of the field—by adding color or changing the type style—and Notes will not let you, the field is not a rich text field. Also, with your cursor located in the field, you can look at the Text section of the status bar at the bottom of the Notes window. If the type and size of the font appear, you are in a rich text field; otherwise, you are not.

Finally, you can distinguish between the two types of text fields by placing the insertion point anywhere within the field and pulling down the Text menu. If the insertion point is on a plain text field, most of the menu choices, such as Bold, Italic, and Underline, are grayed out, indicating that they are not available.

Generally, rich text fields are fields in which you may have good reason to use different fonts and type styles, such as the description of a customer problem or notes about a meeting with a client. Other fields that contain simple pieces of data, such as an author's name or the subject of a meeting, are plain text fields.

As you become acquainted with various databases, you may notice that plain text fields tend to contain small amounts of data—name of an addressee, a ZIP code, or a Social Security number, for example—whereas rich text fields tend to include much longer amounts of text, such as a description of a meeting or the body of a memo.

Many documents consist of a few short plain text fields and a single potentially long rich text field. A memo, for example, has several short plain text fields (To:, Cc:, Bcc:, Subject:) and a single rich text field (the body of the memo), which can contain thousands of lines of text and other objects.

Some database designers will exclude rich text fields from documents to keep users from attaching files in the document. This is the designer's way of trying to minimize database size or maximize the speed in which documents are replicated from one copy of the database to another. If you are using a database in which attaching documents is necessary, then you must contact the database manager to see whether the field type can be changed.

Changing the Appearance of Text with the Text Menu

The Notes Text menu provides control over text characteristics, such as text attributes (boldface, italic, underline), fonts, justification, spacing, and others (see Figure 7.4). You can use a single set of procedures to manipulate any of these characteristics. Many of the selections in the Text menu, such as Italic, Bold, and Underline, are quick selections for options that are also available in the Text Properties InfoBox. You will learn about those features when you work through the attribute settings found in the Text Properties InfoBox.

Fig. 7.4 You can change text attributes from the Text menu one at a time, or open the Text Properties InfoBox to change them all at the same time.

You must be in edit mode to type text and change the font attributes. If you do not see open brackets positioned around each field in the document to signify the document is in edit mode, right double-click anywhere in the document. You can use the Actions Edit Document SmartIcon if you have it available in your set of SmartIcons. If you are composing a new document, it is already in edit mode.

Selecting Text to Modify

To control the characteristics of new text that you are about to type, follow these steps:

1. Position the insertion point where you want to type the new text if the insertion point isn't already in the proper location.

2. Choose Text, Text Properties, or press Ctrl+K.

3. Choose the characteristic you want to change (such as Font or Size).

The new text you type at that location will take on the characteristics you selected.

Suppose that you are about to type the phrase "This task is critical to our success," and you want the word "critical" to appear in bold and in red. Type the first part of the sentence (This task is). Next, change the text color to red and then change the style to bold by following these steps:

1. Choose <u>T</u>ext, Text <u>P</u>roperties (or select the Text Properties SmartIcon).

2. Choose <u>R</u>ed in the Text Color drop-down list, and choose Bold from the Style list box.

3. Whatever you type now appears in bold red. Type **critical**.

Before you finish the sentence, you need to switch back to plain (nonbold) black, which you can do by following the preceding steps, but choosing Black rather than Red, and Normal rather than Bold, in step 2. Then, finish the sentence by typing "to our success."

You also can change characteristics for existing text. Suppose that you already have typed the sentence "This task is critical to our success," and then decide that you want "critical" in bold red. Follow these steps:

1. Select the text you want to change—in this example, the word *critical*.

2. Choose <u>T</u>ext, Text <u>P</u>roperties.

3. The Text Properties InfoBox appears. Choose Red and Bold.

The word "critical" changes from black to red. The surrounding text remains normal black. The text you have highlighted remains in reverse video when you select <u>O</u>K to change the font attributes. Simply click the mouse button once anywhere in the document to view your font changes.

Even if you know as you type the sentence that you want the word "critical" in bold red, you may find that typing the complete sentence and then changing the color and style for the word "critical" is easier.

Tip

When you are changing fonts and font sizes, keep in mind that some fonts naturally appear smaller to the reader. For example, Helv 10 font is the default and is relatively easy to read on-screen. If you change the font type to Script, and leave the font size 10, you will notice that it is quite difficult to read the text. You will need to increase the font size for the Script font to be readable on-screen.

Also, while Helvetica 10 font is easy to read on-screen, it is often difficult for some to read text with this font size when it is printed. You may want to increase the font size to 12 or greater if you are printing this document, or if you are fairly sure the reader will want to print the document.

Working with the Text Properties InfoBox

The first selection from the <u>T</u>ext menu, Text <u>P</u>roperties, lets you control the appearance of the characters that make up a section of text. The Text Properties InfoBox lets you control the characters' size, color, type style, and other attributes (see Figure 7.5). The Text Properties InfoBox is made up of the following five tabs:

Font—Controls the font sizes, styles, and colors. The font attributes used by the Permanent Pen are also adjusted through this tab.

 Alignment—Controls how the text in a paragraph aligns in relation to the left margin. The options on this tab also include automatic bulleting and numbering for text and the line spacing for the text in a paragraph.

 Pages/Tabs—Controls the pagination and tab settings for the paragraph. This tab also contains the right margin setting for printing purposes.

 Hide—Controls when Notes displays a paragraph. Notes lets you hide text based on numerous conditions.

 Style—Allows users the ability of defining frequently used paragraph styles. The styles defined through this tab are available for selection in the Style section of the status bar at the bottom of the Notes window.

Fig. 7.5 The font panel of the Text Properties InfoBox is used to change font style, height, color, and other attributes.

Each of the settings on these tabs is discussed in detail in the following sections.

Note

If you do not have a mouse and need to select a tab in the Text Properties InfoBox that is not currently displayed, use the right and left arrow keys to cycle through the five tabs until the tab you want to work with is visible. If you press the right or left arrow keys and nothing happens, try pressing the Tab key until you notice a dotted-line box surrounding the current tab's icon. Then press the right or left arrow keys until the tab you want appears.

Font Settings. In the Font tab of the Text Properties InfoBox you can select the font type (Figure 7.5 shows Helv selected), the size of the font, the color, and the type style.

For many common characteristics, Notes provides menu commands and shortcut keys that you can use instead of the Text Properties InfoBox (see Table 7.2). You can access the menu commands using the Text menu. When you choose Text, Notes shows you the shortcut keys opposite their corresponding characteristics. Rather than choose Text, Bold, for example, you can press Ctrl+B and skip the menu altogether (refer to Figure 7.4).

Table 7.2 Text Quick Command Reference

SmartIcon	Command	Shortcut
	Text, Text Properties	Ctrl+K
	Text, Permanent Pen	
	Text, Bullets	
	Text, Numbers	
N	Text, Normal Text	Ctrl+T
I	Text, Italic	Ctrl+I
B	Text, Bold	Ctrl+B
U	Text, Underline	Ctrl+U
	Text, Shadow	
	Text, Emboss	
	Text, Extrude	
AA	Text, Enlarge Size	F2
AA	Text, Reduce Size	Shift+F2
	Text, Color (select color from the list)	
	Text, Align Paragraph, Center	
	Text, Align Paragraph, Full	
	Text, Align Paragraph, Left	
	Text, Align Paragraph, Right	
	Text, Align Paragraph, No Wrap	
	Text, Spacing, Single	
	Text, Spacing, One and a half	
	Text, Spacing, Double	
	Text, Spacing, Other (opens the Properties InfoBox)	

SmartIcon	Command	Shortcut
⭲	Text, Indent	F8
⭰	Text, Outdent	Shift+F8
	Text, Named Styles	F11 (to use Cycle list)

You can change the text style to highlight portions of your text in various ways. The style includes characteristics such as text color and font and attributes such as boldface, emboss, shadow, extrude, and italic. Different text styles can add emphasis to important phrases, add interest to your document, and draw your reader's attention to crucial passages.

The following sections show the different text attributes available in the Text Properties InfoBox and some suggested uses.

Change the Fonts. You can choose one of many fonts. Helv 10pt is the default font used by Notes (except in Macintosh, in which Geneva is the default font). The following are three examples of typefaces:

Helv

`Courier`

Times Roman

You can also view fonts as Typewriter fonts. The Typewriter fonts option in File, Tools, User Preferences tells Notes to display all information (including database titles, views, and documents) in monospace fonts, in which all letters take up the same amount of space. You may find this option useful for checking the width of columns. If a column is wide enough in a monospace font to display the entire contents of the column, it will probably be wide enough when you switch back to a proportional (non-monospace) font. This is a particularly useful feature when you are designing export views.

Change the Point Size. You can choose from any of the font sizes in the Size list box or type an entry in the box below the list. Clicking the up and down arrows next to the Size text box will cause the text size to increase or decrease one step for each click.

Change the Color. When you click the down arrow next to the Text color selection box, Notes presents a list of 16 colors. Colors are especially helpful in headings and important passages.

Change the Text Style. You can choose from any of the following text styles:

- **Boldface** causes text to stand out from the surrounding text. Typing key points or names in boldface helps your reader spot the topic of a paragraph instantly.

- *Italic* puts extra emphasis on text. Use italic to highlight especially important words or phrases or for foreign phrases.

- Underline also adds emphasis.

- ~~Strikethrough~~ puts a line through the text you have selected. Using strikethrough helps your reader immediately identify areas of the text that you want removed from a document or that you don't agree with.

- Superscript is used to slightly raise text above the preceding text and make it smaller. This attribute is used in mathematical equations as in 2^2, and with some symbols like copyright or registered trademarks. You can also use it to show degrees.

- Subscript lowers one or more characters below others, as in chemical symbols like H_2O.

- Shadow creates a gray shadow effect behind each letter. This feature typically is used in form or section titles to jazz up the look of the document. Be careful with this feature, however. If your font size is small, then using the shadow attribute can cause the letters to look blurry on the screen. This attribute is not applied to text when it is printed—it is used to view text on-screen.

- Emboss creates a three-dimensional raised effect that highlights the text with which you are working. Be careful with this feature, however. If your font size is small, then embossing it will cause it to look blurry. This attribute is not applied to text when it is printed—it is used to view text on-screen. This attribute is especially appealing to use on text that is shown in three-dimensional layout regions.

- Extrude creates a three-dimensional sunken look to your text. As with embossing and shadowing, applying this attribute to text with a small font size may cause it to look blurry. This attribute is not applied to text when it is printed—it is used to view text on-screen. This attribute is especially appealing to use on text that is shown in three-dimensional layout regions.

You can also enlarge and reduce the size of text one point size at a time through the <u>T</u>ext menu commands or by using the following function keys:

- **Enlarge Size**—Press F2 or choose <u>T</u>ext, <u>E</u>nlarge to enlarge text by one point size. Pressing F2 repeatedly makes the text repeatedly larger.

- **Reduce Size**—Press Shift+F2 or choose <u>T</u>ext, Reduce Si<u>z</u>e to reduce text by one point size. Pressing Shift+F2 repeatedly makes the text smaller.

You can also change fonts and font sizes quickly by clicking the font name or font size portions of the status bar at the bottom of the Notes window. The font types and sizes available will appear as a pop-up list when you choose the status bar option. The selection of fonts available to you may appear differently—it depends on what fonts are installed on your PC.

Working with Strikethrough. The Text Properties InfoBox offers a selection called strikethrough, which is very useful, but often overlooked, if you are responsible for editing someone else's documents. For example, if you are reviewing a memo listing the anticipated price on a contract, and you determine that the dollar amount is incorrect, you can simply change it and then save the document. However, this does not leave a "flag" to let the author easily know what has been changed in the document. You can, however, strike through the original figure (and even make the change red), and then enter the new figure to the right of the entry (see Figure 7.6). The author can then review the changes and delete the strikethrough if in agreement.

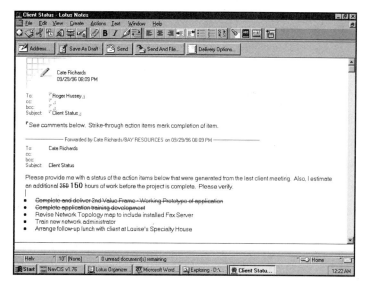

Fig. 7.6 Using the strikethrough command helps you highlight changes you have made to a document.

Another use for the strikethrough feature is in "To-Do" lists in documents. You can use the strikethrough to indicate to others who read the document that an item in the list has been completed, or to indicate edits made to a document (like all of the changes the editors of this book have requested during author review). An example of this application of the strikethrough feature appears in Figure 7.6 as well.

Working with Font Attributes. Avoid using characteristics that you cannot print if you are unsure of the audience that is reading the document. You can choose different colors for your text, for example, but most people don't own color printers, and thus cannot print in color. However, using color in documents that will be published to the Web is important to attract the reader's interest. Although using color to add pizzazz and emphasis to your document isn't wrong, don't depend solely on the color to convey crucial information. You shouldn't include an instruction that says all steps in red are mandatory, for example, because some people may print your document and cannot tell from the printed copy which text was originally red. Similarly, laptop users often have a monochrome display and cannot easily differentiate colors—particularly those colors in the lighter shades. In cases like these, you may want to use font size or bold text to convey your message. These will print, and display on monochrome screens.

Figure 7.7 shows a sample document that uses several different text styles.

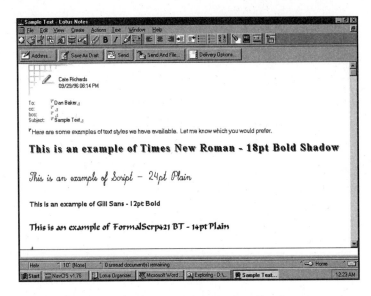

Fig. 7.7 You can highlight your text by using different types of styles.

Don't get carried away with using typefaces, color, sizes, and other attention-grabbing characteristics. Bright colors, large type, and attributes such as boldface and italic are meant to emphasize and draw attention. If every paragraph in your document is a different color, size, and style, you may have created a work of abstract art, but you will give your reader a headache trying to find the important parts of the document.

You may find that responding to another user's message by using the Text options is helpful. For example, in Figure 7.8, Larry Cook received a memo from Kelly Sloan requesting some information on an upcoming meeting. Larry chose Actions, Forward (or the Forward button in the mail database, as discussed in Chapter 3, "Using Databases") to return the message to Kelly, indicating his responses in bold red and indented. Kelly then elected to respond further by forwarding the memo back to Larry again, typing her response using a different font attribute. This technique allows individuals to respond to each other's questions while leaving the question in the memo for easy reference. At the end of the "discussion," Larry and Kelly only have to reference the last memo if they want to review all of the material at a later date.

Tip

Other ways to respond to a message and include the original text with it include using collapsible sections to display the original message (see Chapter 8, "Working with Documents"). Your e-mail database will do this if you use the Reply with History button when responding to a message. You can also use paragraph indenting to emphasize your answer to a message.

A common method in many Internet discussion groups is to use the symbols ">>" and "<<" before and after the message you are responding to. Any of these methods will help the reader see the original message along with any corresponding feedback to make the communication much more effective.

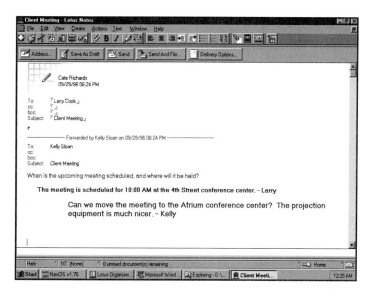

Fig. 7.8 You can use text-formatting options to help you communicate with others in a forwarded message.

Paragraph Justification Settings. As with any good word processor, you can set margins if you want part or all of your document to have margins different than the one-inch default. You can also use tabs to indent text to predefined positions that you select. The following sections explain how to set margins.

Although some characteristics, such as type style or size, can apply to any portion of text, other characteristics, such as justification, apply only to whole paragraphs—that is, a section of text that ends with a carriage return. You cannot have part of a paragraph with one kind of justification while another part of the same paragraph has a different type. If you change the justification of any portion of a paragraph, the whole paragraph changes.

For these paragraph-only characteristics, Notes provides a shortcut. If you want to adjust a characteristic for a single existing paragraph, you don't have to select the paragraph; just place the insertion point anywhere within that paragraph. Then from the Alignment tab in the Text Properties InfoBox, choose the characteristic you want to adjust. If you want to adjust more than one paragraph, however, you must select the paragraphs as you do any section of text.

To change the attributes for paragraphs, you can open the Text Properties InfoBox by choosing Text, Text Properties, or the menu commands and bullets as described in Table

7.2. To set paragraph alignment, bullet lists, number lists, margin settings, and line spacing, click the Alignment tab (see Figure 7.9). The following selections are available:

- Alignment

- First line

- List

- Left margin

- Spacing

Fig. 7.9   You can change paragraph settings in the Text Properties Alignment InfoBox.

Alignment. Alignment controls how each line of text is aligned along the left and right margins. To set alignment, select the text alignment icon in the InfoBox representing the type of alignment you want to use. The types of alignment are as follows:

 Left Alignment—Notes aligns each line of text at the left margin. This style—the same type you see in typewritten text—is especially appropriate for memos. Because the text isn't aligned along the right margin, the right side of the text has a staggered appearance; as a result, this style of alignment sometimes is known as ragged right.

 Center Alignment—Notes centers text between the left and right margins. You may want to use this kind of alignment for headings.

 Right Alignment—Right alignment causes Notes to align each line against the right margin, but not the left, resulting in a ragged left paragraph. This is beneficial if you are trying to align numbers, particularly in column design, but otherwise, this alignment option tends to have little use for the average user.

 Full Alignment—Notes aligns each full line of text along the left and right margins. By adding tiny amounts of space almost imperceptibly between words, Notes manages to make each line exactly the same length. For partial lines, such as those at the end of a paragraph, Notes aligns only the left margin.

Newspapers and many books use this type of alignment, which tends to give your document a more professional, pleasing appearance. Many people dislike editing a document with full alignment, however, because Notes' constant changing of the spacing between words during editing distracts them.

None—Notes displays each paragraph as a single long line. If a paragraph is longer than Notes can display on the screen, you must use the scroll bars or left and right arrow keys to view the rest of the line.

> ### Tip
>
> If you need to edit text that has been fully aligned, you can change the alignment to left alignment, edit the text, and then change the alignment back to full. This will make it easier for you to edit the paragraph as you won't have to work around Notes' continuous adjustment of the font alignment as you are editing.
>
> You can also set alignment by using the SmartIcons.

First Line Settings (Indent/Outdent). The First Line group of icons tells Notes how to treat the first line of text in a paragraph. You use these settings to indent or outdent the paragraph as the following list describes:

■ **Standard**—Notes does not indent or outdent the paragraph; rather, Notes aligns the first line of text with the rest of the paragraph alignment setting.

■ **Indent**—To indent the first line of the paragraph, select the Indent button and then type in the amount you want to indent the text in the text box that appears to the right. The default setting is .25".

■ **Outdent**—To outdent the first line of the paragraph, click the Outdent button and then type in the amount you want to outdent the text in the text box that appears to the right. The default setting is .25".

You can see an example of these settings in Figure 7.10.

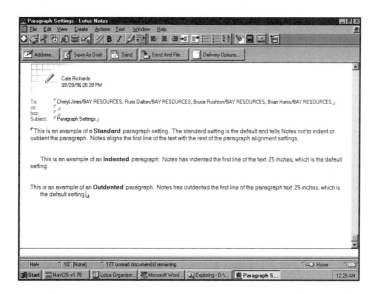

Fig. 7.10 You can add pizzazz to your documents by indenting or outdenting paragraphs.

Bullets and Numbers. Notes will automatically indent and insert bullets and numbers in documents when you select the Bullets and Numbers buttons in the List section of this tab.

You may also insert bullets and numbers by selecting Text, Bullets and Text, Numbers as needed from the menu command list (see Figure 7.11).

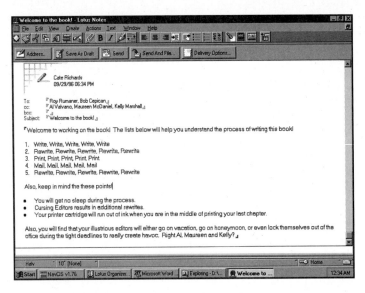

Fig. 7.11   You can add impact (and sometimes fun) in your documents by using the bullet and numbering features.

Setting the Left Margin. Enter the left margin setting for the paragraph. You can use whole numbers and decimals to indicate your setting. The standard paragraph left margin setting is 1". The maximum limit for this setting is 22.75"—but you should take care to ensure that the margins are displayed on-screen so that readers of the document are able to see the paragraph.

You can select the Top, Bottom, Left, and Right margin settings for the entire document by choosing File, Page Setup. The Page Setup dialog box appears. Here is where you can alter global document settings. You learn about these settings in Chapter 8, "Working with Documents."

Line Spacing. The spacing options in Notes control the amount of spacing between paragraphs and between the lines of text in a paragraph. The following selections are available:

- Interline—How many blank lines Notes inserts between lines within each paragraph.

- Above—How many blank lines Notes inserts before each paragraph.

- Below—How many blank lines Notes inserts after each paragraph.

When clicking the down arrow next to each of these options, Notes displays a selection list asking for the number of blank lines. Notes uses the same type of notation you may have encountered when adjusting the spacing setting on a typewriter:

- Single (no extra blank space)

- 1 ½ (half a line's worth of blank space)

- Double (a full line's worth of blank space)

If you choose Below and then Double, for example, an extra line of blank space follows each paragraph.

> **Caution**
>
> Be mindful that if you select options for both Above and Below for a paragraph, you may be left with up to four lines between paragraphs. If this is not your intention, pick one option or the other.

Pages/Tabs Settings. As you work with Notes, you will have some instances when you want to set the pagination so that Notes inserts a page break where you want it rather than when Notes fills up a page with text. You may also want to adjust tab settings and set the right margin for printing purposes. To perform any of these functions, highlight the paragraph you want to "control" and then open the Text Properties InfoBox. Click the Pages/Tabs tab so that it appears (see Figure 7.12).

Setting Pagination. The first section on the tab controls pagination. In this section, you can specify the following:

- **Page Break before Paragraph**—Notes inserts a page break before the selected paragraph. This setting is ideal if you want to insert a page break to ensure that a particular paragraph is printed at the top of the following page. For example, you are writing sections within a proposal document, and you want the heading of each section to begin at the top of a page.

This setting can also be used with your e-mail if you want to print the body of the memo but do not want to include the To, From, Date, and Subject fields. Place your cursor on the first line in the body of the memo, and then select this option. Notes prints the address information on one page, and the remainder of the memo starts at the top of the second page.

■ **Keep Paragraph on One Page**—Notes keeps the lines of text highlighted together when printing. Notes breaks the page either before or after the selected paragraph but not within the text. This is ideal if a user wants to make sure that an entire paragraph prints on the same page to make reading easier.

■ **Keep Paragraph with Next Paragraph**—Notes keeps the selected paragraph on the same page as the following paragraph. Notes breaks the page before the selected paragraph if it does not fit on the same page as the following paragraph. This is ideal for users who are providing an example and want the descriptive paragraph below the example to print on the same page.

Fig. 7.12   The Pages/Tabs section of the Text Properties InfoBox lets you specify settings that affect your document when it is printed.

Tip

You can also set a page break by choosing Create, Page Break. This option acts as a toggle for setting page breaks; selecting Create, Page Break once will enter a page break, while selecting it again will remove the page break.

A line appears across the page to indicate any page breaks that you specify.

Removing a Page Break. If you decide that you want to remove a page break before a paragraph, place your cursor in the first line of the paragraph immediately following the page break and choose Create, Page Break. Notes will remove the page break.

Setting the Right Margin for Printing. Use the Right Margin (for Printing) field to specify the right margin. This option applies only to the printed document; the right side of the screen is always the right margin when you display a document, so make sure that you specify this setting based on the paper size. Keep in mind that many printers, (like lasers) will not print any closer than $1/4$ of an inch from the edge of the paper—regardless of the margin you specify.

The default is traditionally 1" to 1.25"—but is dependent upon your specific printer's capabilities. If you select Other from this setting, you must enter a value in the text entry box that appears. When you specify settings for Other, make sure you do so in relation to the paper size. For example, to display a 1" right margin setting on the standard 8.5×11-inch paper, type **7.5** in the text entry box. This tells Notes that you want the margin to begin 7.5" from the left side of the paper.

Setting Tabs. You can set tab spacing for your text by using the Pages/Tabs settings in the Text Properties InfoBox. You can set tab stops for one or more paragraphs by entering specific tab stops in the text entry box provided. Setting tab stops is a two-step process. You must first indicate how you want the tab stops to be set, and then specify the factor Notes will use in setting the tab. Follow these steps to set tabs:

1. Select the down arrow next to the Tabs text box. You have two options to choose from:

   - **Individually Set**—This lets you enter the places you want tab stops to occur. You can enter numbers in inches or centimeters (for example, .5" or .5 cm). If you enter more than one tab stop, separate them with semicolons (for example, .5"; 1.35"; 4").

   - **Evenly Spaced**—Notes evenly spaces tab stops, based on an interval setting you provide. For example, you can tell Notes to set a tab stop every .45".

   There are four types of Tab stops in Notes that can be set by typing their corresponding letter before the tab stop, or by using the mouse to set the tab stop using the ruler (see "Setting Margins and Tabs with the Ruler" later in this chapter for more information on using the mouse). The following list describes the type of tab stop, its corresponding letter, and the corresponding tab indicator that is displayed in the ruler:

   - **Right**—This is represented by the letter R before the Tab stop in the Tabs entry box. Right tabs cause text to be aligned flush right at the tab stop. You often use this setting if you are trying to align currency values.

   - **Left**—This is represented by the letter L before the Tab stop in the Tabs entry box. Left tabs cause text to be aligned flush left at the tab stop. You often use this as the standard tab entry.

   - **Decimal**—This is represented by the letter D before the Tab stop in the Tabs entry box. Decimal tabs cause text to be aligned according to the decimal point location in the text. This setting is ideal if you are trying to align numbers in a list.

   - **Center**—This is represented by the letter C before the Tab stop in the Tabs entry box. Center tabs cause the text to be centered on both sides of the tab stop. This option is ideal if you are trying to display a list of items to a reader.

2. Once you have made your Tabs type selection, specify the interval for the tab settings. If you are individually specifying the tab stops, type in the exact location for each tab, using semicolons to separate multiple entries. If you are telling Notes to evenly space the tab stops, type in the interval space between each tab setting.

> **Note**
>
> You do not have to enter semicolons to separate multiple entries (as illustrated in the following example). If there is a space between the number settings, Notes will insert the semicolon when you save your selections. However, inserting the semicolon helps delineate the individual tab stops when you review your settings—decreasing the chance of you "running" your numbers together and ending up with an incorrect setting.

You have flexibility when setting tab stops. To set tabs at 1.5, 2, and 4 inches, for example, type the following:

```
1.5 2 4
```

You don't need to type the quotation mark (or double prime, ") after the number; Notes adds it to all numbers that represent inches.

> **Note**
>
> Notes always displays the current tabs in this box using semicolons, even if you entered the tabs using spaces.

If you prefer to measure a specific tab stop in centimeters, you can type cm after a number. For example:

```
1 2.3 10cm 15cm 6
```

In this example, Notes will set five tabs. The 1, 2.3, and 6 represent inches, but the 10 and 15 represent centimeters.

If you have chosen Metric measurements as your default measurement (see Chapter 2, "Customizing Notes"), Notes assumes that all measurements you enter are in centimeters unless you enter a double prime (") to indicate that a measurement is in inches. If you have your default set to Metric and set tabs at the following positions:

```
10 20 6"
```

Notes sets a tab at 10 and 20 centimeters and at 6 inches.

After you set tabs, you can press Tab to move to the next tab stop in your document. If the insertion point is already past the last tab stop, pressing Tab causes Notes to beep and produces an error message.

Hiding Text. Notes allows you to hide text within a document during particular functions. While this feature is typically used by database designers when designing the forms that will be used, it is discussed briefly here. You will find more information on hiding fields in the database design sections in Chapter 11, "Designing Forms."

With the Text Properties InfoBox open, click the Hide tab. The Hide tab appears as displayed in Figure 7.13.

Fig. 7.13 You can hide text in documents depending on how you are working with the document. You make the hide-when selections in the Hide tab of the Text Properties InfoBox.

Notes provides the following options:

- **Previewed for Reading**—The hidden information isn't visible when users read documents in the preview pane. Users can, however, read the text if they open the document for reading, or have Editor level access and place the document in edit mode from the preview pane—unless additional restrictions are selected as described later.

- **Opened for Reading**—This option hides any text selected when users open a document to read it. Users can, however, read the text if they have Editor-level access and place the document in edit mode—unless additional restrictions are selected as described later. This option is ideal in designing documents if the designer wants to provide instructions on completing a field when a user is composing a document but doesn't want the user to be bothered with the instructions when reading the document.

- **Printed**—This tells Notes to print everything but the highlighted text. You can use this option when you want to omit portions of sensitive text when printing a document for someone else to read or otherwise limit the text that prints.

- **Previewed for Editing**—This option lets readers of the document see the text when reading (unless additional restrictions are selected) but not when composing or editing a document when they are viewing the document in the preview pane.

■ **Opened for Editing**—This option allows readers of the document to see the text when reading a document (unless additional restrictions are selected) but not when composing or editing a document. This option is usually used by designers who have fields displaying information in a format that is different than when the document is composed. For example, the user selects a keyword series that identifies the product name, price, and catalog number while composing a document, which is easier than having to make three separate selections in three separate fields. The database designer, however, elects to hide that keyword field when someone is reading the document and sets up separate fields to display this information for ease of reading and editing at a later date.

■ **Copied to the Clipboard**—This tells Notes to ignore this text when copying text to and from the Clipboard. It is a handy command when you want to copy all but a part of a document or when the database designer has set security in the fields that should not be overridden if a text is copied to the Clipboard. This setting also affects text when a document is forwarded from a database—the text marked for hiding will not appear in a message forwarded from the database. This setting does not affect entire documents that are copied and pasted at the view level.

■ **Hide Paragraph if Formula Is True**—By entering a qualifying formula in the Formula window, the database designers can set conditions for when the text is hidden. For example, if a designer wants only the author of the document to be able to see the text in the field, then an author formula can be written to provide this criteria for viewing the text. You will learn more about writing formulas in Chapters 14, "Working with Formulas" and 15, "Working with Functions and Commands."

Style Settings. You can define and save combinations of paragraph and text properties that you use regularly as named paragraph styles. This is a handy way of defining particular styles that you use frequently so that you do not have to continuously set the attributes individually through the Text Properties InfoBox. To set up a named paragraph style, follow these steps:

1. Place the document you are working on in edit mode by double-clicking anywhere within the document.

2. Select a paragraph and make all of the attribute settings you want. This is the paragraph style that you will save in the following steps. For example, if you want to create a style to use as a response to other memos in which the text is indented, bold, and red, create these settings for the existing paragraph.

3. Select <u>Text, Text <u>P</u>roperties, and then click the Style tab. The Style tab appears (see Figure 7.14).

Fig. 7.14 You can create Styles that can be reused by highlighting a paragraph whose style you want to copy, and then opening the Style tab of the Text Properties InfoBox.

4. Select Create Style. The Create Named Style dialog box appears (see Figure 7.15).

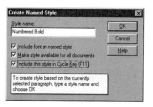

Fig. 7.15 Provide descriptive names in the Create Named Style dialog box to make it easier to remember what the style is used for.

5. Enter a name for the paragraph style in the Style name text box. For example, name the style Bold Red Response.

6. Check Include font in named style, which is the default, if you want to include all font settings, as well as paragraph settings.

7. Check Make style available for all documents if you want to have this style setting available regardless of the document you are working in. Selecting this option adds the style name to the status bar pop-up selection list at the bottom of the Notes window.

8. Check Assign Styles to Cycle List if you want this style to appear when you cycle through the available styles with the F11 key.

9. Select OK.

Once you have defined the style name, you may highlight a paragraph and select the setting by returning to the Text Properties Style tab or by selecting Text, Named Styles, and then clicking the name of the style you want to apply. If you elected to display the style when pressing F11 to view the cycle key, you will be able to select the style through those options as well. You can also select styles by clicking the Styles option on the status bar to display the list of currently defined styles, as shown in Figure 7.16.

Notes Basics

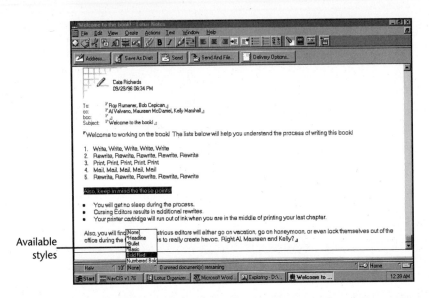

Available
styles

Fig. 7.16 You can quickly change the style of a paragraph by clicking the Style option of the status bar, and then selecting one of the defined styles in the pop-up menu.

Notes R4 predefines the following three styles for you that can be selected from the Text, Named Styles menu:

- **Headline**—This displays the selected text in bold, purple, Helvetica 12pt font.

- **Bullet**—This displays the selected font in bullet style.

- **Basic**—This changes the selected font size to Helvetica 10pt, but maintains any other text formatting options previously defined.

You can use the Redefine Style button in the Text Properties InfoBox to redefine a named style based on the current paragraph selection, or you may want to "clean house" periodically and get rid of old styles by pressing the Delete Styles button and then selecting the style to delete.

Setting Margins and Tabs with the Ruler

Notes provides two methods for indicating how you want to set the margins and tabs: you can access the Text Properties InfoBox as discussed earlier in this chapter or use the ruler. Whether you use the ruler method for setting margins and tabs or the Text Properties InfoBox, you may want to have the ruler present to guide you in making your settings.

Displaying the Ruler. When controlling margins and tabs, you may find displaying the Notes ruler helpful. The Notes ruler is a bar near the top of the screen marked off in inches like a ruler but with special marks indicating your margins and tab settings (see Figure 7.17). The ruler helps you visualize distances in your document and provides a simple means for setting margins and tabs.

Ruler—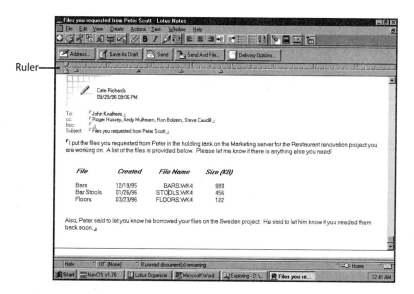

Fig. 7.17   Use the ruler to help guide you in setting margins and tabs.

To display the ruler, choose <u>V</u>iew, <u>R</u>uler (or select the View Ruler SmartIcon if it is present in your current SmartIcon group). Along with measuring the document in inches, the ruler shows margins and tabs. Notes displays tabs as arrows pointing up, and the left margin as a pentagon arrow. Choosing <u>V</u>iew, <u>R</u>uler again causes the ruler to disappear.

Note

Table column settings are represented in the ruler by a mark that looks like a T. You will learn more about creating tables in Chapter 8, "Working with Documents."

In addition to changing margins, you can use the ruler to set tabs, as explained in the next section.

Changing Margins and Tabs with the Ruler. To change the left margin of the first line using the ruler, click the top pentagon arrow, and drag it to its new location. If you want to adjust the left margin of the paragraph to indicate a setting other than the one set for the first line, click the bottom pentagon arrow, and drag the bottom portion of the arrow to a new location.

By specifying a different left margin for the first line and all other lines, you can create the paragraph styles shown in Figure 7.18.

Top
pentagon
arrow

Bottom
pentagon
arrow

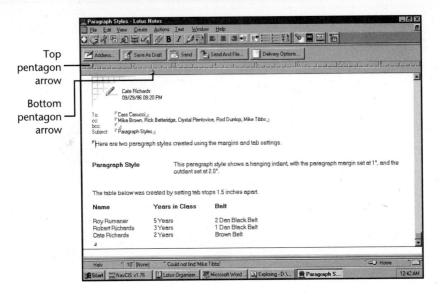

Fig. 7.18   You can use the ruler to define margin settings in your documents.

You can also set tabs using the ruler. Display the ruler if it isn't showing, and then select the paragraphs you want to change. You can then change the position of a margin by dragging the corresponding triangle to a new position. Recall that the upward pointing triangles are tabs. Figure 7.19 shows all four types of tabs you can define.

Fig. 7.19   You can define tab stops by clicking directly on the ruler. But, if you want to use the special tab attributes like Right align, Left align, and Decimal Point align, you must use the Text Properties InfoBox or right-click your mouse button once on the tab stop to open a pop-up menu box with the four tab stop styles available for selection.

To set a new tab, place the mouse pointer on the ruler at an empty position and click once with the left mouse button. A tab arrow appears to mark the tab stop. To change the tab setting, click and drag the corresponding tab arrow to a new position and release the mouse button. To clear an existing tab, click the corresponding tab arrow a second time.

As discussed earlier, you can place four types of tabs in your documents. To place these tabs using the ruler, perform one of the following:

- **Left tab**—Left-click at the tab location.

- **Right tab**—Right-click at the tab location.

- **Center tab**—Shift+right-click at the tab location.

- **Decimal tab**—Shift+left-click at the tab location.

(Refer to Figure 7.19 for examples of each of these tab settings.)

> **Note**
>
> Setting margins and tabs by using the ruler is one of the few Notes operations that require a mouse; there are no corresponding hot keys. If you don't have a mouse, you must choose Text, Properties and use the Pages/Tabs pane of the InfoBox to set margins and tabs.

Setting Margins Fast with the Keyboard

Notes provides several keystrokes for quickly changing margins. After selecting the paragraphs you want to affect, you can do the following:

- Press F7 to indent the first line by a quarter of an inch. By pressing this key several times, you can indent the first line by any multiple of a quarter of an inch. Press Shift+F7 to outdent the first line by a quarter of an inch.

- Press F8 to indent every line by a quarter of an inch. Shift+F8 unindents every line by a quarter of an inch.

You can create a hanging indent (that is, paragraphs in which the first line is further to the left than the other lines) by indenting all lines one or more times by pressing F8 and then unindenting the first line by pressing F7.

Working with the Permanent Pen

The Permanent Pen option lets you use revision marking to quickly add comments that stand out in a document. When you use the Permanent Pen, you don't have to reset the font every time you move somewhere different in the document. For example, if you are answering questions in a document and want to write all of your answers in bold, red font, you can set up your Permanent Pen to use these font attributes. Then, you can type text in multiple places in the document without having to redefine the font attributes each time you move to a new location.

Before you use your Permanent Pen, you may want to change the font attributes. To do so, select Text, Properties, and select the font, size, style, and color you want to assign to the Permanent Pen in the Text Properties InfoBox. Once you have made your settings, press the Set Permanent Pen font button to save your selections.

To use the Permanent Pen, use the following steps:

1. Select Text, Permanent Pen.

2. Click once at the beginning of the section you want to add a comment.

3. Type your text. The text you type will be in the style, size, and color you specified for the Permanent Pen.

4. Reposition your cursor in the next position where you want to use the Permanent Pen and type your comments.

5. Continue using the Permanent Pen until you have completed all of your comments.

6. Deselect the Permanent Pen by selecting Text, Permanent Pen to disable this option.

> **Note**
>
> If you want to change the font characteristics for the Permanent Pen, choose Text, Text Properties. In the Text Properties InfoBox, make all of the necessary font, size, style, and color selections you want to use and then select the Set Permanent Pen font button. Notes will redefine the Permanent Pen font characteristics until you repeat this process again.

Using Special Characters

Occasionally, you may have to use special characters that don't appear on your keyboard, such as currency, copyright, and trademark symbols or other special characters. Notes lets you enter hundreds of special characters into a document by pressing special key combinations.

To type a special character, press Alt+F1 followed by the code that represents the special character. Each code, consisting of one or two keys, is selected to remind you of the special character. To type the symbol for the Japanese yen (¥), for example, press Alt+F1, Y, =. Appendix C, "Special Characters," lists more characters available.

Using this feature, you can enter letters that belong to non-English alphabets, fractions, international currency designations, and so on.

> **Note**
>
> Not all printers can print all special characters, and Notes may have to drop some special characters when printing documents. In particular, most daisywheel printers are limited in their selection of characters. Keep this limitation in mind when composing documents if you are sharing information with people who use older printers or daisywheel printers.

From Here...

In this chapter, you learned how to create attractive documents by using different colors, text styles, margins, and other text characteristics. In the next chapter, you learn even more Notes features that will add pizzazz and increase functionality when you learn about working with documents.

For more information on some of the topics discussed in this chapter, refer to the following:

- Chapter 2, "Customizing Notes," shows how to change your ruler's units of measurement.

- Chapter 4, "Getting Started with Electronic Mail," teaches you how to work with Lotus Notes Mail and the mail forward feature.

- Chapter 8, "Working with Documents," teaches you more ways to add pizzaz to the documents you are working with by adding tables, hotspots, and other more advanced Notes features. You will also learn to run spell check!

- Chapter 11, "Designing Forms," explains how to create hidden fields based on formulas, and further utilizes the text attributes described in this section.

Chapter 8

Working with Documents

Lotus Notes 4.5 has a wide variety of features that help make it a robust environment for communicating with others. These features can be added, or applied, directly to a rich text field within a document that has already been designed. You can also build some of these features, as you will learn in this chapter, into the design of the database forms. In Chapter 7, "Working with Text," you learned how to use text to enhance your use of Lotus Notes. This chapter covers features that enable you to use the power of Notes to enhance your documents.

Checking Your Spelling

No matter how professional your document appears or how insightful your message is, you will not impress readers if misspellings litter your document. And if you are like many who have used word processing software for quite some time, your ability to spell even the simplest words has somehow disappeared! Notes includes a spelling checker that looks for misspelled words and other common mistakes.

Some of the main topics in this chapter are

- Search for text and phrases

- Work with unread marks

- Copy and paste documents

- Insert objects, such as links, hotspots, and tables, into your documents

- Insert sections into your documents

- Use folders to organize your documents

> **Tip**
>
> As discussed in International Settings in Chapter 2, "Customizing Notes", you can select from one of 28 dictionaries by selecting File, Tools, User Preferences, clicking the International icon, and then selecting the Spelling Dictionary button.
>
> Switching from one dictionary to another is a big plus in organizations that work internationally. A proposal can be written in the U.S., for example, forwarded to the U.K., and spell-checked there using the British (ise) dictionary to pick up on differences in spelling between the two countries. (For example, organization is spelled organisation, with an s instead of a z, in the U.K.)

To check the spelling of a document, position the insertion point at the top of the document then choose Edit, Check Spelling. If Notes finds a misspelled

word or detects some other irregularity that it regards as a mistake, it displays the dialog
box shown in Figure 8.1. In this example, the word developed was misspelled.

Fig. 8.1 Use Spell Check to find misspelled words and other common errors in documents.

> ### Tip
>
> You can check the spelling of just one word or a group of words without having to check the
> spelling of the entire document. To do so, highlight the word(s) and then select Edit, Check
> Spelling.

At the bottom of the dialog box, you will see the status field that will tell you the problem Notes finds with each word or phrase it highlights. For example, in Figure 8.1, the
status field displays Unknown Word (that is, the word isn't one that Notes recognizes as
correctly spelled). The offending word is highlighted within your document and displayed in the Replace text box. At this point, you must decide what to do among the
following options:

- If the word is misspelled, as in the example here, you can fix the word in the Replace box and then choose Replace. Notes replaces the misspelled word in the
  document with the fixed word. If you misspelled the same word in the same way
  elsewhere in the document, Notes fixes only the word in one location at a time and
  will ask you what to do each time it encounters the misspelled word.

- If you agree that the word is misspelled but don't know how to spell it correctly,
  you can view the guesses that Notes makes. Notes searches its dictionary for words
  similar to the misspelled word and displays them in the Guess list box. Figure 8.1
  shows the guesses Notes produced for developed.

  Often, the first word in the Guess list box is the correct spelling, and in this example, Notes guessed the correct spelling as developed. Select the correctly spelled
  guess and then choose Replace. Alternatively, you can double-click the correctly
  spelled word. Notes replaces the misspelled word in the document with the correctly spelled word.

> ### Note
>
> Notes cannot always guess the correct spelling. If too many letters are wrong or if you
> transpose letters, Notes may not be able to produce the correct word.

- You may want to prompt Notes to accept an incorrectly spelled word or phrase
  deliberately. For example, if you intentionally misspell a word or phrase, such as

Ye Ol' Shoppe, but you want Notes to point out similar misspellings later that may be unintentional, then you can choose <u>S</u>kip to skip just this one incidence of the spelling, or Skip <u>A</u>ll to always skip this misspelling during this spell checking session.

This feature is most useful for acronyms, names, and technical words that occur several times throughout the document that you know are correct but that you don't want to add to your dictionary.

- If you know the word is spelled correctly and is a word you use often, choose <u>De-fine</u>. Notes adds the word to your personal dictionary so that Notes will consider the word valid any time you check spelling in the future, whether in this document or another. This feature is most useful for technical terms or proper names that you use often.

- If you want to exit Spell Check before Notes prompts you that it is completed, select the <u>D</u>one button. Notes will halt the spell checking process at that point and return you to your document.

> **Note**
>
> Words that you define during spell checking sessions are entered into your personal dictionary (USER.DIC). For more information on adding or removing words to or from your personal dictionary, refer to Changing the User Dictionary in Chapter 2, "Customizing Notes."

Along with catching misspelled words, Notes watches for other common errors, such as unusual capitalization and repeated words (such as "I saw the the dog"). As with misspelled words, you can tell Notes to ignore the problem or how to fix it.

After Notes displays all the questionable words, it displays a final dialog box telling you that spelling is complete. Choose OK to close this dialog box.

> **Caution**
>
> Although the spell check is a wonderful aid for producing error-free documents, it cannot replace proofreading. The spell check cannot catch grammatical errors or incorrectly used words. Worst of all, it doesn't catch words that you misspell if they happen to be different words that are spelled correctly. For example, if you meant to write "I hear that we have hired ten new people" but mistakenly omit the *a* in *hear*, Notes will not catch the resulting *her* as a misspelled word. Likewise, if you spelled the word *here*, Notes won't see it as an error, even though it's not the correct usage.

Searching for Text

No good word processor is complete without the capability to locate text wherever it occurs within a document. Notes includes features to enable you to search for text strings and replace one phrase with another. Notes also enables you to search entire databases for text strings so you can quickly locate documents that relate to the same topic in some manner. Notes contains several ways to search for information in databases. If the database has a full text index, you can do more advanced searches than if the database does not. All Notes databases provide the following capabilities:

- You can search for text in a document that you are reading. If your document is in edit mode, you can also elect to replace the text you find with new text.

- You can search for text in document titles that appear in a particular view. Notes will find and highlight the first document in a view whose title matches your word or phrase.

- You can find all documents that contain a word or phrase anywhere in the document. Using this search method will show the documents in the view, with a checkmark placed next to them. The words within the document that match the search criteria will not be highlighted, however, as they will be if the database is indexed for full text search as described as follows.

If a database has a full text index, you can enhance the capabilities of your search as follows:

- You can find all documents that contain a word or phrase anywhere in the document and have Notes outline the search words with red boxes in the document to highlight them.

- You can use the Search Builder feature to help you quickly create search formulas to find documents.

- You can save search formulas to reuse at a later date.

- You can define your search in the following ways:

  - Make your search case-sensitive.

  - Include synonyms of search words.

  - Search for words that are located near one another in a document.

  - Include variations of the same word in your search.

  - Customize the way your search results are displayed.

  - Search for documents in multiple databases at the same time.

In the following sections, you will learn about all of these features.

Performing General Searches for Text

This section will walk you through searches you can perform whether or not your database is indexed. As you will see, the general search capabilities on any database are pretty powerful!

Searching for Text in a Document You Are Reading. Notes makes it simple to find (and replace if you're in edit mode) a word or phrase in a document whether you are reading or editing the document. You can search for a word or phrase anywhere within a field by choosing <u>E</u>dit, <u>F</u>ind/Replace. Notes displays the Find and Replace dialog box (see Fig. 8.2). In the Find and Replace text boxes, enter the word or phrase you want to find.

Fig. 8.2   Finding and replacing text is easy when you use the Find and Replace feature in Notes.

Tip

If the phrase you want to find or replace is now on-screen, you can select the phrase so that it appears as the phrase to find when you perform a find or replace operation. Suppose that on-screen you now see a paragraph discussing money market funds and you want to find other places in the document that also discuss them. Select the phrase "money market fund," and when you choose <u>E</u>dit, <u>F</u>ind/Replace (or <u>E</u>dit, Find Ne<u>x</u>t), the phrase "money market fund" already appears in the phrase to find.

After you enter the search phrase (if different from the one Notes displays), you can choose any of the following checkbox options in the Match section of the dialog box to change the way Notes performs its search.

- **<u>W</u>hole Word.** Normally, Notes looks for the search phrase without regard to word boundaries. If you ask Notes to find cat, for example, it stops not only on the word cat, but also on scat and catalog because they both contain the letters cat. If you are searching for especially short phrases, however, you can choose <u>W</u>hole Word to tell Notes that you are interested only in the word cat, not these three letters within any word.

- **Accen<u>t</u>.** Normally, when Notes searches text, it ignores diacritical marks when finding phrases. If you choose this option, Notes considers diacritical marks when searching for text. Suppose that you are writing a document that includes the name Björn. If you want to search for this word and you don't check Accen<u>t</u>, Notes finds the word if you enter only Bjorn. If you check Accen<u>t</u>, however, Notes will find only Björn if you enter it with its umlaut. (See Using Special Characters in Chapter 7, "Working with Text," for information about entering special characters.)

- **Ca<u>s</u>e.** When you choose this option, Notes looks only for phrases capitalized exactly the way you typed the search phrase. During a search for cat, for example, Notes won't stop on Cat or CAT.

Choose Find Ne<u>x</u>t to begin the search. Notes searches for the phrase from the current insertion point position and repositions the insertion point on the next occurrence of the phrase. If Notes reaches the end of the document without finding the phrase, it displays a dialog box telling you that it cannot find the phrase.

Often, the first occurrence of your phrase that Notes finds isn't the one you want. Choose Edit, Find Next, or press Ctrl+G to repeat the last search. Notes searches for the same phrase, using the same combination of selected options. By pressing Ctrl+G enough times, you can find each occurrence of the phrase throughout the document.

> ## Tip
>
> You also can search for phrases that include tabs and that are separated by a hard right carriage return by typing \t and \n, respectively. (The \n stands for new line.) If you want to find the words cat and mouse separated by a tab, for example, enter cat\tmouse as the search phrase.

Replacing Text. On occasion, you may need to change a phrase that occurs several times throughout a document. For example, a particular function formerly performed by your Denver office may have been transferred to Atlanta, and you need to find all instances of Denver within a document and change them to Atlanta. You can use the Find feature to find and change each occurrence individually, but Notes provides a related feature, Replace, that makes this kind of wholesale replacement easier.

To perform a replace, you must be in edit mode. Press Ctrl+E to switch to edit mode if you're now in read mode (brackets appear around each field if you are in edit mode). Position the insertion point at the top of your document and choose Edit, Find and Replace. Notes displays the Find and Replace dialog box (see Figure 8.3).

Fig. 8.3   To quickly find and replace text, use the Find and Replace dialog box, but make sure you are in edit mode first.

The Find and Replace dialog box offers exactly the same checkbox options as the Edit Find dialog box, and you use them in the same way. After you enter the phrase to find and the replacement phrase, choose any options that apply and then choose Find Next. Notes locates the first occurrence of the search phrase from the point at which your cursor was located when you began the search, highlights it, and waits for you to choose one of the following buttons:

- If you choose Find Next, Notes leaves the current occurrence of the phrase unchanged and finds the next one.

- If you choose Find Previous, Notes searches for the occurrence directly before the current one (or the cursor location if you are just beginning your search).

- If you choose Replace, Notes replaces the current occurrence with the replacement phrase.

- If you choose Replace All, Notes replaces every occurrence of the search phrase with the replacement phrase.

> **Caution**
>
> Think carefully before using Replace All. If you make a mistake, you cannot undo the operation with the Edit, Undo command. It is much too easy to make incorrect changes to your document that will take you hours to fix. If, for example, a female replaces your male personnel manager, you may want to revise a certain memo by changing he to she. If you forget to check Whole Word, however, Notes changes other to otsher, there to tshere, and similarly messes up all other words that have the letters he in them.

■ If you choose Done, Notes stops the search, leaving the current occurrence of the search phrase as is.

> **Tip**
>
> Save your document (choose File, Save) before using Replace All. If you make an error in your editing, you can always exit the current document without saving and then reopen the document from its saved version.

Searching for Documents in a View. Not only can you search for a phrase within a single document, but Notes also enables you to search in other useful ways when you are looking at a view. You can search for documents within a view to have Notes highlight documents that contain your search word or phrase anywhere within view columns (any of the text showing in the views).

To perform a search within a view, complete the following steps:

1. While in a view, select Edit, Find Next. The Find dialog box appears, as shown in Figure 8.4.

Fig. 8.4 To search for a word or phrase within a view, type the text you want to search for in the Find dialog box.

2. In the Find text box, type the text you want to find. As an option, you can select Whole word, Accent, and/or Case. (See "Searching for Text in a Document You Are Reading" earlier in this chapter for information on these features.)

3. Select Find Next or Find Previous. If you select Find Next, Notes highlights the first title that contains the text after the location of the cursor. If you click Find Previous, Notes highlights the first title that contains the text before the location of the cursor.

4. Repeat step 3 until you are through with your search for documents.

5. Click Done when you are through with your search.

Full Text Searching in Databases

Notes provides a more powerful search mechanism known as a full text search. Using this search feature, you can search for documents that contain several phrases rather than a specific single phrase. Perhaps you want to find documents that discuss stock prices and quarterly earnings, for example. This type of search also enables you to search an entire database or even more than one database at a time, displaying all of the documents that meet your search criteria in a view.

To use a full text search, the database must have been indexed for full text searches. The indexing process creates a special file that enables Notes to determine quickly which words or phrases a document contains. If a database isn't indexed, you can perform only limited searches by choosing Edit, Find, or using the Search bar without an index as previously discussed.

Indexing a Database. You can index any databases that you create on your local hard disk, unless the database is enforcing a consistent access control list and you are not the manager or designer. Only someone with Designer or higher access can index a database that is shared with other individuals on a server. You can index a database in one of the two following ways:

- Choose File, Database, Properties to bring up the Properties InfoBox. Select the Full Text tab and then select Create Index to bring up the Full Text Create Index dialog box shown in Figure 8.5. This dialog box controls how the database will be indexed.

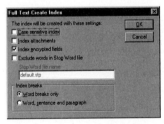

Fig. 8.5 To index a database, open the Full Text Create Index dialog box in the Database Properties InfoBox.

- You can also tell Notes you want to index a database by selecting View, Search Bar while in a database that is not indexed already. Notes will open the Search Bar and provide you with a button to Create Index. If you click this button, the display in Figure 8.5 will appear to begin the process.

> **Note**
>
> As you are the manager of your e-mail database located on the server, you can index that database if you want to. If your server capacity is low, however, indexing your mail database may overburden your server as it produces the index and keeps it updated. If your Notes administrator indicates that you should not index your mail database located on the server, then it is usually a sign that the server does not have enough memory or space.

You can create an archive e-mail database using the archiving capabilities within mail, which allow you to periodically move documents to the archive file. The archive is typically stored on your hard drive. Notes users often prefer this process as there is less need to index the active mail databases where so many changes are taking place every day and requiring continuous updates of your index. Most often, you are trying to search through older memos to find this information, and you can search for this kind of information easily in the archive copy of the e-mail database.

In the Full Text Create Index dialog box, you should normally accept the default selections, as shown in Figure 8.5. These selections provide you with the most compact (small) index possible. The following sections describe the indexing options.

Case Sensitivity. The Case Sensitive Index option enables you to indicate whether you want Notes to distinguish between upper- and lowercase letters. For example, it will treat cat, Cat, and CAT as different entries. If this is unnecessary, which is usually the case, then don't select this option—it can greatly increase the size of the index and may exclude documents that you really want to find. Use this option only if case-sensitive searches are required, for example, if you index a database full of C programming concepts and structures.

Indexing Attachments. With the Index Attachments option, you can indicate whether you want Notes to index any attachments containing text that you inserted in a document. If you select this option, you will be able to search the database for words or phrases stored in Notes documents and any files attached to the documents. For example, if you attached a Word Pro document to a document stored in a database that maintains this selection in its indexing setup, you will be able to search the Notes text and the Word Pro text when you query the database. Choosing this option may significantly increase the length of time it takes to index the database, however, as well as the amount of space the index takes up on the hard drive. Notes is also unable to highlight the words in the search phrase in the attached document. Instead, it highlights the attachment icon in the document.

Indexing Encrypted Fields. If you want to include text in encrypted fields in a full text index, choose Index Encrypted Fields. You can index encrypted fields only if you have the appropriate encryption key, and only people with the encryption key can search the fields. Using this option increases the size of an index by the number of encrypted fields in a database and the amount of text they contain. See Chapter 22, "Security and Encryption," for more information on working with encryption.

Using Stop Word Files. The Exclude Words in Stop Word File option tells Notes not to search for words that are extremely common (the, and, if, it, and so forth). These common words are called stop words and are defined in the field following this selection. You will probably want to select this option as it reduces the number of documents selected to only those that match the remainder of your search criteria.

If your database is local, however, and you find that you need to keep a word in the search, such as off, so that a search for articles on Off Broadway, for example, can be run successfully, then you will need to edit the Stop Word file to remove the word off. The default Stop Word file, named DEFAULT.STP, is located in your Notes directory. Although it can be edited using any ASCII text editor, you can make a copy of the file and then edit the copy. That way, you can revert to the original file when needed.

> **Tip**
>
> The line '[0-9]+ in DEFAULT.STP tells Notes not to index numbers. You may want to create a Stop Word file with only this line in it and give it a name that reminds you of its purpose, such as NUMBERS.STP. You can then select this file when users don't need to search for numbers.

You can also create additional Stop Word files and customize them for specific local databases. For example, if you have a local database for computer topics, you can create a Stop Word file for the database to include words, such as computer, keyboard, mouse, and so on, that appear so frequently in documents that they're not useful in searches.

If you create an additional Stop Word file, you must do so before you create the index that uses it. Once you create the Stop Word file, you can select it when you create the index. The filename must be eight characters or less and use the extension STP, for example, COMPUTER.STP. The Stop Word file must be located in the program directory, typically in C:\NOTES.

> **Tip**
>
> In large databases, a Stop Word file can reduce the index size by about 20 percent (on average), according to indexing dynamics. Of course, don't bother searching for "To be or not to be" in a Shakespeare database!

> **Note**
>
> Indexes created with customized Stop Word files do not replicate along with the database, either from server to server or from server to workstation.

Working with Index Breaks. The Index Breaks section has two options: Word breaks only and Word, sentence and paragraph. You will normally use the Word breaks only unless you are trying to perform fancier searches. If you select Word, sentence and paragraph, Notes enables you to perform more complex searches that specify that the search words have to all be in the same sentence or paragraph. This can lengthen the time of your search and also can take up a large amount of space. As most documents you search are fairly short, particularly in your e-mail database, selecting Word, sentence and paragraph is not necessary.

Completing the Indexing Process. When you have completed making your selections, Notes tells you that the indexing of the database has been queued if the database is located on the server. If you index a database on your hard drive, Notes will inform you that it is performing a local index. If the database is located on the server, you can continue working in other databases while the database is being indexed, but you won't be able to work in the database the server is indexing until it is finished. You will not get a message that the indexing is completed—you will know it is done when you can open the database. If the database is local, you will not be able to continue working in Notes until the indexing is complete, unless you have elected to Enable local background indexing in the User Preferences dialog box (File, Tools, User Preferences). This is selected by default. In local indexing, you will know the indexing is complete when the Indexing Database status box disappears or your status bar indicates that the process is complete.

When you create a full text index, Notes creates a subdirectory and stores the index files there. Notes names this subdirectory according to the name of the indexed database with the file extension FT. For example, if you index a database named MARKET.NSF, Notes creates the subdirectory MARKET.FT and places it in the same directory as the database—usually the Notes data directory.

> ### Caution
>
> If you are running short on hard disk space, don't index your database. If you begin indexing a database and run out of disk space before the indexing is complete, you will not be able to use the index. You will need to delete the index, clean up space on your hard drive, and then create a new index on the database.

Updating the Index. If you add, delete, or change any documents in a database that has been indexed, the index will no longer accurately reflect the database; new words will have been omitted and words no longer in any document will continue to remain in the index. This causes your searches to behave unexpectedly if you are searching for words that have changed. You will have to periodically update a database index.

If the database is on a server, updating the index occurs automatically, though you can "force" the update as well by selecting Update Index from the Full Text tab of the Database Properties InfoBox. You control how often an index update occurs automatically by editing the information in this tab of the Database Properties InfoBox (see Figure 8.6). Open this InfoBox by selecting File, Database, Properties and selecting the Full Text tab. Select the arrow next to Update frequency (servers only) selection box and choose between Immediate (the default), Daily, Scheduled, and Hourly, depending on how often you want the database to be indexed. Because setting indexing options affects server resources, you should contact your Notes administrator before performing this function.

Fig. 8.6 Update database indexes in the Full Text tab of the Database Properties InfoBox. Also, specify the frequency in which a server copy of a database index should be updated with this tab.

Tip

If you are unsure of which setting to select for scheduling indexing, select Immediate. If you discover, or if users report, that the database's response time is very slow, then reduce the frequency of the updates.

If users access a database on the server infrequently or if the database is not modified often, select Daily, which will update the index at night based on the server task Updall runs. (Updall settings are made by the Notes administrator.) This will help conserve server resources, making everyone very happy with you!

You can also schedule the updates for an off-peak time to reduce the drain on server resources when many people are trying to use the server. Selecting Scheduled updates the index according to a schedule in the Public Address Book Program document for the Updall server task (a task set by your Notes administrator). If you select this option and no Program document for Updall exists, then scheduled updates don't occur. Check with your Notes administrator if you are unsure of this option.

If you are working with a database index on your hard drive, you must "force" the indexing by selecting File, Database, Properties and selecting the Full Text tab. Click the Update Index button. Notes immediately updates the index, presenting you with a status box to show how many documents it is indexing. When the Database Properties InfoBox disappears, you can resume working in Notes with a newly indexed database.

Note

The larger the database and the more complicated the index selections, the larger the file space and memory it will take to maintain. Make sure that you will really use the indexing feature in a database before you index it.

Indexing in the Background. As mentioned earlier, you can enable background indexing at startup, creating full text indexes in the background. With this feature set, you can keep working in Notes without having to wait until Notes completes the indexes. To do this, follow these steps:

1. Select File, Tools, User Preferences.

2. Select Enable local background indexing and click OK.

3. Click OK when Notes tells you that some preferences will not take effect until you restart Notes.

If background indexing is enabled when you replicate databases, Notes automatically updates each database's full text index and views in the background after replication is completed.

Deleting an Index. You can delete a full text index if you no longer want a database indexed. You should also delete the index and then re-create it if you are experiencing full text index problems or if you want to change index options. In the latter two cases, create a new index after deleting the original. Do not delete the index from the index subdirectory directly; rather, use the following procedure when you delete an index:

1. Select the database and select File, Database, Properties.

2. Select the Full Text tab in the Database Properties InfoBox.

3. Select the Delete Index button. Notes displays the dialog box shown in Figure 8.7.

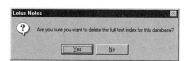

Fig. 8.7 You can delete database indexes that you no longer use to conserve disk space.

4. Select Yes when prompted to delete the index.

Notes deletes the index for the database and removes the subdirectory created for this index from your hard drive. If you want to re-index the database after selecting new indexing options or if the index was experiencing problems, follow the procedures to create a full text index described in the previous section, "Indexing a Database."

Performing a Full Text Search. If a database has been indexed for full text searches, choosing View, Search Bar causes Notes to display the Search Bar dialog box across the top of the document window, as shown in Figure 8.8, which is quite different from the Find dialog box you saw earlier. The Search Bar consists of two areas into which you can enter one or more phrases.

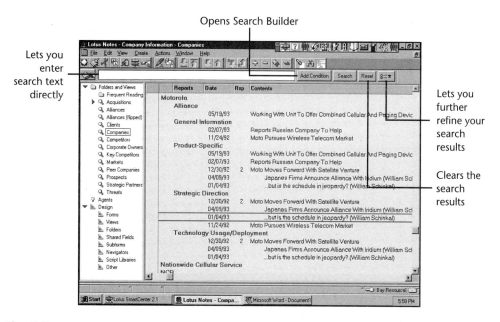

Fig. 8.8 Use the Search Builder to perform queries against indexed databases.

If you are performing a simple search for just a word or phrase, you can type it in the text entry box to the left of the Search Builder and click Search. Notes will perform a search on the documents of a database and display the results in the view according to how you elect to see them. You can work with the documents displayed in the view, but if you exit the database, you will clear the results of your search. You can also elect to clear the results of the search by selecting the Reset button in the Search Bar. (You will read more about how Notes displays query results in the next few sections.)

If you want to perform a more detailed query, you can select the Add Condition button to add further detail on the query you want to build in the Search Builder. When you are finished building a query, you can select Search, and Notes will display the results of your query in the view according to how you elected to see them. This section will walk you through building a query, selecting viewing options, and interpreting your view results.

> **Tip**
>
> You can create complicated, extensive search queries by using any of the search techniques described in the following sections. You can also use a combination of any of these search methods to further refine your search query. For example, you can define a search for a particular author's documents by selecting the By Author search, making your selections, and then selecting OK to save your entry. You can then select another condition and input words or phrases that you want the document to contain to further enhance your query.

Searching for Specified Text. In the previous examples, you learned how to search for a single word or phrase in a database. If your database is full text indexed, however, you can use Search Builder to find documents that contain the words and phrases in a list.

Before you conduct the search, be sure that the database is open to the view you want to search, and then perform the following steps:

1. If the Search Bar is not visible, choose View, Search Bar.

2. Click the Add Condition button.

3. In the Condition drop-down list, leave the default value Words and Phrases.

4. Click All to have Notes display only documents that contain all of the words or phrases you enter into the Search Builder. Selecting Any, as described later in this chapter, will display documents that contain any of the words or phrases you type.

5. Type a word or phrase in as many of the numbered text boxes as you want. Search Builder searches for documents that contain all of these words and phrases (see Figure 8.9).

6. Click OK. Notes displays the query you have built in the text box of the Search Builder. Entries you created in the fields are separated by AND to signify that these words and phrases must all be in the document for it to be displayed in the results.

7. Click the Search button in the Search Bar.

Fig. 8.9 By typing words or phrases into each of the entry boxes, you can narrow your search results by selecting only those documents that meet all of the criteria.

> **Tip**
>
> If you need to include more than eight words and phrases in your search, repeat steps 2 through 6 until all of your criteria have been entered.

For example, Figure 8.9 shows a query that has been built to search a company information database for all documents that contain the words telecommunications, RBOC, wireless, and the phrase new legislation.

The results from this query would be any documents in the database that contained all of the words and phrases listed in the example shown in Figure 8.9. In this example, only one document, as shown in Figure 8.10, contained all of these words and phrases.

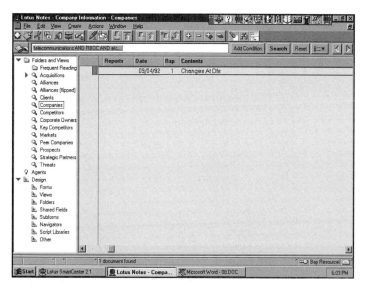

Fig. 8.10 The view will display the results of a full text query against a database.

Opening the document displayed in the view will show all of the words and phrases defined in the query highlighted with red boxes, as shown in Figure 8.11.

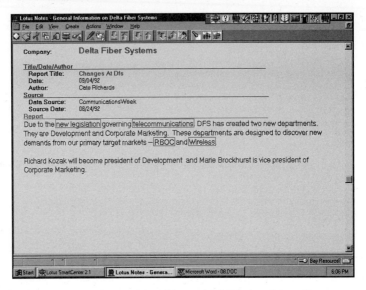

Fig. 8.11 Words and phrases appear with red boxes highlighting them when you open a document displayed after a query when the database is indexed.

If you want to find documents containing any of the words or phrases you have specified, choose <u>A</u>ny in step 4. Entries you created in the fields are separated by OR to signify that at least one of these words or phrases will be displayed in the results for the document.

Notes will display the results of this query in the current view, as shown in Figure 8.12. In this example, several documents meet the criteria defined in the query.

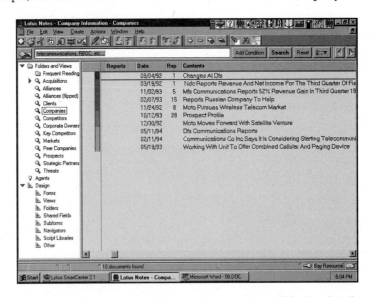

Fig. 8.12 If two or more documents meet the search query, they will be listed in the view according to the criteria you defined.

Searching Multiple Databases. You can search more than one database at a time, if necessary. To do so, complete the following steps:

1. Select the database icon for each of the databases you want to search (they must all be on the same workpage) by holding down the Shift key and clicking each database icon once.

2. While holding down the Shift key, double-click any of the database icons you selected.

3. A view will open in which the titles of the selected databases appear in the navigator (almost like category titles in a database view), as shown in Figure 8.13.

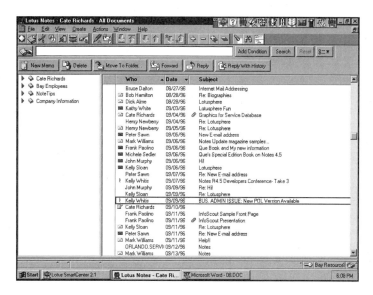

Fig. 8.13 When searching multiple databases for text, the database titles appear in a temporary navigator when they are selected for query.

4. Perform a full text search as usual.

5. To see the results of the search in each database, click the small triangle to the left of each database title in the view. That database title will open to display all of the documents found to contain your search criteria. Switch between views and folders as usual in the database to see all documents.

Searching by Author. If your database is indexed, you can define a query to search a database to display all documents composed by a specific author or group of authors.

Before you conduct the search, be sure that the database is open to the view you want to search then perform the following steps:

1. If the Search Bar is not visible, choose View, Search Bar.

2. Click the Add Condition button and the Search Builder appears (see Figure 8.14).

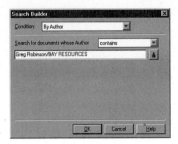

Fig. 8.14 When you query a database for documents By Author, Notes changes the appearance of the dialog box.

3. In the Condition drop-down list, select By Author.

4. In the Search for documents whose Author drop-down list, select contains if you want documents created by the authors you select or does not contain if you want to exclude documents created by a specific author.

> **Note**
>
> In any query you build, if you elect to exclude an entry based on a selection or term that you enter, Notes will insert NOT before the phrase to indicate that Notes should exclude any documents that contain that entry. You can also type this entry directly before any word or phrase to get the same effect. For example, if you want to exclude documents authored by anyone named Larry, enter NOT Larry in the search formula by author.
>
> This principle works for all searches you build, not just searches by author.

5. Perform one of the following:

- Type the name of an author in the text box. To include more than one name, separate the names with commas.

- Click the Author icon (it appears as an icon of a person) and select the names of the authors you want from the Name & Address Book displayed (see Figure 8.15). If you are working on the network, Notes will display the Public Name & Address Book. If you are working remote (off the network), Notes will display your Private Name & Address Book. If you have more than one Address Book available to you, you can switch between them as usual.

To select a name from the address list, highlight the individual's name (group names have no effect in this search), and then click Add. Notes will add the name you have selected to the list on the right side of the dialog box. Continue to select names until all of the authors you want to include in your query are selected.

6. Click OK in the Names dialog box and again in the Search Builder dialog box.

7. Click the Search button on the Search Bar.

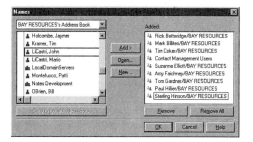

Fig. 8.15 You can select the author(s) you want to search for from your Address Book to make sure you have the correct spelling for your query.

Note

You can search by author in all databases created using Notes Release 4.x as long as there is an author field in the design of the database. You may experience difficulty searching databases created in versions earlier than Release 4, however. You will not be able to search by author in anonymous databases (databases meant to hide the identity of the author of a document).

Searching by Date. If your database is indexed, you can search for documents based on the date they were created or modified. Before you conduct the search, be sure that the database is open to the view you want to search and then perform the following steps:

1. If the Search Bar is not visible, choose View, Search Bar.

2. Click the Add Condition button.

3. In the Condition drop-down list, select By Date. Notes will alter the dialog box to appear as shown in Figure 8.16.

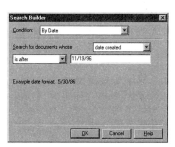

Fig. 8.16 This query searches for documents created after 11/19/96.

4. In the Search for documents whose drop-down list, select date created or date modified.

5. In the next drop-down list, select how the date for which you are searching is re-lated to the documents for which you are searching.

6. Type a date in the date text box. If there are two text boxes, type dates in both of them. Make sure you use the format displayed below the list box when typing your dates. The date format is typed according to the format used by your operating system.

7. Click OK. (Repeat steps 2 through 7 if you need to include more dates in your search.)

8. Click the Search button on the Search Bar.

Notes will search the database for all documents that meet your date criteria and display them in the view.

Searching by Field Contents. If a database is indexed, you can search for documents that have a specific entry in a particular field. For example, in a Marketing database, you may want to find documents that contain the word Competitor in the ClassificationR field.

Before you conduct the search, be sure that the database is open to the view you want to search and perform the following:

1. If the Search Bar is not visible, choose View, Search Bar.

2. Click the Add Condition button.

3. In the Condition drop-down list, select By Field. Notes displays the dialog box shown in Figure 8.17.

Fig. 8.17   This query looks for the word Competitor in the ClassificationR field of the database.

4. In the Search for documents where field drop-down list, select the field you want to include in the search. This drop-down list box contains a list of all of the fields contained in the design of the database.

5. In the last drop-down list, make a relationship choice: The field either contains the entry or does not contain the entry.

6. In the text box (or text boxes), type the text, dates, or number for which you want to search. For example, type Competitor.

7. Click OK. (Repeat steps 2 through 7 if you need to include more fields in your search.)

8. Click the Search button on the Search Bar.

If you are not familiar with the design of the database and do not know the name of the field you want to use in your query, you can review the field design information by highlighting a document in the database view you are searching and selecting Edit, Properties. Notes will display the Document Properties InfoBox for the document. Select the Fields tab. A list of all of the fields will appear in the left list box, as shown in Figure 8.18. As you select a field name, Notes displays in the right list box the design and contents of the field for the document you selected. Reviewing this information should assist you in finding the appropriate field to use in this query.

Fig. 8.18   You can view the form's field design in the Fields tab of the Document Properties InfoBox for the document.

Searching by Criteria in a Form. If your database is indexed, you can search for documents by entering criteria into any database form, as long as the database designer indicated that the form could be displayed in Search Builder.

Before you conduct the search, be sure that the database is open to the view you want to search, and then complete the following steps:

1. If the Search Bar is not visible, choose View, Search Bar.

2. Click the Add Condition button.

3. In the Condition drop-down list, select By Form. Notes will display the dialog box shown in Figure 8.19.

Fig. 8.19   This query checks for the word WorldCom in the Subject field of the memo.

4. In the Forms drop-down list, select the form you want to use in the search. All forms in the database will appear in the drop-down list unless the database developer designed the forms to not appear. See Chapter 11, "Designing Forms," for more information on form design.

5. In the form you selected, type entries (text, numbers, and so on) in as many fields as you want to include in the search in the fields defined in the database form. What you type in each field is what you search for. Type your entries into the fields that appear in the form just as if you were typing in a regular Notes document.

6. Click OK.

7. Click the Search button on the Search Bar.

Notes will search for documents that include all of the entries you make.

Searching for Documents Created with a Certain Form. If a database has been indexed, you can use the Search Builder to find documents that were created using a specific form. For example, you can create a query in a Marketing database to show only documents created using the Company form. Typically, you use this type of search when you know that a particular word or phrase appears in many different documents in a database and when you are interested in information that would be contained in only one particular type of form. For example, the word hotel may appear many times in a company travel database, but if you are preparing a report on all problems with hotels reported by employees you are interested only in the instances of the word appearing in a Trouble Report form in the database.

Before you conduct the search, be sure that the database is open to the view you want to search and complete the following steps:

1. If the Search Bar is not visible, choose View, Search Bar.

2. Click the Add Condition button.

3. In the Condition drop-down list, select By Form Used. Notes will display the dialog box shown in Figure 8.20.

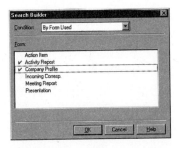

Fig. 8.20 This selection indicates that you want to search in the Activity Report and Company Profile forms.

4. In the Forms list box, select one or more forms; a checkmark will appear next to each form selected.

5. Click OK.

6. Click the Search button on the Search Bar.

Refining Your Search Results. Notes provides you with many ways to view and alter the results you receive when you run a search query. You can alter the order in which documents are displayed, use synonyms in your search, change the maximum number of entries displayed, and save a search formula. You make these settings with the Options button. When you refine your searches by selecting the Options button on the Search Bar before running the query, the menu in Figure 8.21 is displayed.

Fig. 8.21 By selecting the Options button, you can change the way Notes displays your results.

Your options from which to select in this drop-down menu are as follows:

- **Include Word Variants.** This option tells Notes to include any words in which the base part of the word you are looking for is present. For example, if you enter training as the search criteria, documents containing "train" would also be selected. If you select train, Notes will also display training, trained, and so on.

- **Use Thesaurus.** With this option, you can include synonyms of search words in your search. For example, if you search for documents that contain the word doctor, Notes also finds documents that contain the word physician. This selection will remain active until you reset the Search Builder or exit the database.

- **Sort by Relevance.** By default, the search results in databases queried with the Full Text Search feature are displayed in the order of significance, which means that the more times the word or phrase is found in a document, the higher up in the list the document will be displayed. You can ascertain the significance of the document in the search by looking to the left of the documents in the view. A vertical bar is displayed to indicate the relevance of each document to the search criteria (see Figure 8.22). The darker the portion of the bar, the more relevant the document.

- **Sort by Oldest First.** This option displays the documents found in the search according to their compose date, with the oldest documents displayed first. This sort order is ideal if you are trying to follow a discussion on a topic and want to read the discussion from beginning to end.

- **Sort by Newest First.** This option displays the documents found in the search according to their compose date, with the newest documents displayed first. This sort order is ideal if you are looking for the latest information regarding a particular topic; for example, if you are reviewing a database of customer contact reports and want to see what is current for a particular topic.

- **Maximum Results.** This option enables you to determine the maximum number of documents you will accept in the results of a search. The default setting is 250 documents, which is usually adequate for your needs. If you are interested only in receiving those documents that best suit your query and want to speed up the search process, then reduce this setting.

- **Save Search As.** This option enables you to save a search formula so that you can use it whenever you use the database in which you created it. If you have Designer or Manager access to the database on a server, you can also make the search formula available to anyone who uses the database by selecting Shared search in the Save Search As dialog box, as shown in Figure 8.23. Saved search formulas appear at the bottom of the Options menu in the Search Bar, as shown in Figure 8.24.

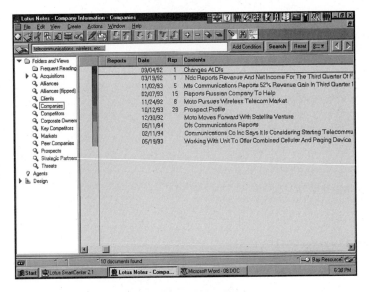

Fig. 8.22   By default, search results are displayed in the view according to relevance.

Fig. 8.23   You can save search formulas in the database in which you used them.

- **Delete Saved Search.** With this option, you can remove saved search formulas. When you select this option, Notes displays the Delete Saved Search dialog box (see Figure 8.25). Select the saved search name you want to remove and then select Delete.

Notes will display a checkmark next to selected items to tell you what options you have selected. Once you have made your selections, you can press the Search button on the Search Bar to begin searching the database.

Fig. 8.24 Saved searches are displayed at the bottom of the Options menu in the database in which you saved them.

Fig. 8.25 You should delete old, saved queries that you will no longer use to keep your menu list from becoming cluttered.

In addition to the methods of refining your queries that you have learned in the preceding sections, you can also use the following terms in your query field entries to further enhance your query capabilities.

If you selected Word, sentence and paragraph as Index breaks when you created the full text index, you can use the proximity operators to increase the relevance ranking of words that are close to each other. The following proximity operators are available to you:

- **Near.** The closer the words or phrases are to each other, the higher Notes will rank their relevance in the sort view. For example, if you entered Competitor near Threat in a query field exactly as shown here, Notes will sort those documents in which these terms are closer to each other at the top of the view.

- **Sentence.** This option works much the same as near, but all of the words or phrases must be in the same sentence. For example, if you entered Competitor sentence Threat in a query field exactly as shown here, Notes will sort the documents with both of these terms in the same sentence at the top of the view.

- **Paragraph.** This option works much the same as near, but the words or phrases must all be in the same paragraph. For example, if you entered Competitor paragraph Threat in a query field exactly as shown here, Notes will sort the documents with both of these terms in the same paragraph at the top of the view.

You can also use wildcard characters in place of other characters when you search for text, such as the following:

- Use a question mark (?) for a single character. For example, typing owe? will return documents containing words such as owed and owes.

■ Use an asterisk (*) for multiple characters. For example, typing fl* will return documents containing words like Florida, Floridians, flow, and flop.

Wildcard characters work only in text fields; they will not work in fields that contain dates or numbers.

You can also perform a second search on the results of the first search to further refine your query. For example, if your first search against a company information database for company names considered threats to your organization provided so many documents that it was ineffective, you may want to refine the search to include only those companies that are threats and whose product line focuses on the same target market as yours.

You can do this by performing the first query on the database to find those companies that are considered threats, and then with that query's results still displayed, perform another query on documents containing target market names the same as yours. Notes will search only those documents listed in the first query for matches to the second.

Working with Document Read Marks

You have seen that Notes displays a star next to documents that you haven't read. In databases such as your mailbox, these markers can serve as important reminders that you need to read certain documents. Sometimes, however, you may decide that you don't want to read certain documents in a database or in your mailbox at a particular time.

Suppose that your company maintains a database of important scheduled events that you want to keep abreast of. Someone in your company routinely adds notices about the company softball team, however, which just doesn't interest you. After a long vacation, you return to your desk and find 14 softball announcements in the database. You really don't want to read them, but they all have the stars next to them, screaming, "Pay attention to me!"

You can use the Unread Marks operation to tell Notes to remove the stars and make the documents appear as though you have read them. To mark documents as read, open the database and choose Edit, Unread Marks. The Unread Marks submenu appears, enabling you to select one of the following four options (see Figure 8.26):

■ **Mark Selected Read.** This option marks all selected documents as read.

■ **Mark All Read.** This option marks all documents in the database as read.

■ **Mark Selected Unread.** This option marks all selected documents as unread.

■ **Mark All Unread.** This option marks all documents in the database as unread.

Note that the last two choices enable you to mark read documents as unread; that is, you can read a document and then tell Notes to mark it as though you hadn't read it. At first glance, this capability may seem like a feature in search of a use, but you actually may find it useful, especially if you keep old memos in your mailbox that you think may be important later.

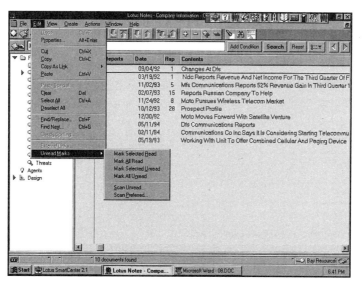

Fig. 8.26   You can mark documents as read to indicate that you have already read them or as unread to draw your attention to those documents at a later date.

When you open your mailbox, you probably look for the stars that call attention to newly arrived mail. Suppose you read a message just before quitting time one afternoon, however, and realize that the memo will require significant attention tomorrow. If you close the message, Notes now considers it one of the many previously read messages and removes its attention-grabbing star. You can put the star back by marking the document as unread, however, so that it will again attract your attention the next time you read your mail.

> **Tip**
>
> You can now open documents directly from the preview pane rather than just through the view. If you want to make sure that documents you read in the preview pane are also marked as being read, then select File, Tools, User Preferences. In the Basic settings, select Mark documents read when opened in preview pane in the Advanced options section. Notes will mark any documents you open through the preview pane as well as those you open directly through the view as being read.

Scanning for Unread Documents

Many people work with several different databases and must constantly be on the look-out for new documents showing up in those databases. Suppose that your company has several databases that contain status reports from different departments, and one of your jobs is to monitor those status reports for customer problems. You may find it cumbersome to check each database several times a day to see whether new documents have appeared. Instead, you can use the Scan Unread feature in the Edit, Unread Marks submenu to tell you about new documents.

Scanning Preferred Databases. You can use the Scan Unread feature in several ways, but the most common—and most useful—method involves a two-step process. In the first step, tell Notes which databases you want to watch for unread documents; these databases are known as your preferred databases. Then, at any time, you can ask Notes if there are any unread documents in any of your preferred databases.

To supply Notes with your list of preferred databases, select Edit, Unread Marks, Scan Preferred. The Scan Unread dialog box appears, as shown in Figure 8.27. Select Choose Preferred and the Scan Unread Preferred Setup dialog box appears (see Figure 8.28).

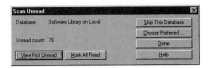

Fig. 8.27   You can use the Scan Unread dialog box to begin set up preferred databases to scan.

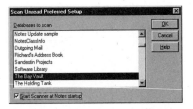

Fig. 8.28   You must select each database you want to mark as preferred individually from the list. Workpage names are indicated with a hyphen before and after the name—you cannot select workpage names.

Notes lists all the databases on all of your workpages. The workpages themselves are identified with names surrounded by dashes, such as the following:

    - Misc -

Select the databases that you want scanned for unread documents. You must click each database title individually. Select OK to save your selections.

Note

The Scan Unread Preferred Setup dialog box includes a checkbox labeled Start Scanner at Notes startup. If you check this box, Notes will automatically scan your preferred databases for unread documents each time you start Notes.

When you have selected your preferred databases, you can scan them for unread documents by making sure no databases are selected on the workspace (click anywhere in the blank gray portion of the workspace) and choosing Edit, Unread Marks, Scan Preferred. Notes displays the Scan Unread dialog box (refer to Figure 8.27).

The dialog box displays the name of the first of your preferred databases and shows the number of unread documents in the database. You can choose any of the following actions:

- **View First Unread.** Notes opens the first document in the first database. You can then read the unread document. Press Tab to move to the next unread document in the database, and press Esc to exit the current document and open the database view.

- **Mark All Read.** Notes assumes that you don't want to read the documents and marks them as read from this database only. All other databases you are scanning will not be affected by this selection.

- **Skip This Database.** Notes displays the name of the next preferred database and the number of unread documents in that database.

After Notes scans all databases, it loops back to the first and begins scanning again. When you see the same databases appearing again, choose <u>D</u>one to exit scanning.

Scanning a Single Database. To scan a single database for unread documents, highlight the database you want to scan by clicking once on the database icon. Select <u>E</u>dit, Unread <u>M</u>arks, <u>S</u>can Unread. Notes will open the first unread document in the database. Press Tab to open the next unread document. Press Esc to end the scan and exit the document and you will be returned to the database view.

Scanning Multiple Databases. You can select multiple databases and then scan them. To do so, press the Shift key and then select each of the databases you want to scan. Select <u>E</u>dit, Unread <u>M</u>arks, <u>S</u>can Unread. Notes opens the Scan Unread dialog box. Follow the procedures listed in "Scanning Preferred Databases" in this section to scan the databases you have selected.

Copying and Pasting Documents

Not only can you use the Clipboard to copy pieces of text from one document to another as described in the section "Copying and Pasting Text" in Chapter 7, "Working with Text," but you also can use almost the exact same technique to move or copy documents from one database to another. Do the following:

1. Open the database in which the documents now exist.

2. Select one or more documents by clicking in the left margin next to each. A checkmark will appear next to selected documents as shown in Figure 8.29.

3. If you want to copy the documents, choose <u>E</u>dit, <u>C</u>opy, press Ctrl+C, or click the Copy SmartIcon. If you want to move the documents, choose <u>E</u>dit, Cu<u>t</u>, press Ctrl+X, or click the Cut SmartIcon.

4. Close the current database and open the database in which you want to place the documents.

5. Choose <u>E</u>dit, <u>P</u>aste, press Ctrl+V, or click the Paste SmartIcon.

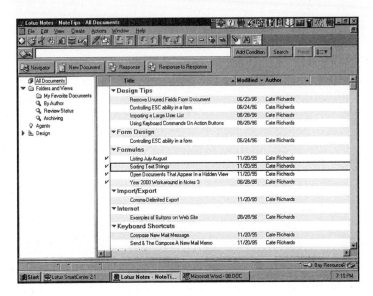

Fig. 8.29 Selecting documents in a view allows you to perform a function—such as copying—on all of them at one time.

Notes inserts the documents into the new database. This procedure works best if both databases contain the form that you used to compose the documents. If, for example, the documents were composed with a form called Client Information and both databases contain forms by that name, Notes can perform the move or copy easily. Otherwise, Notes will display the document using the database's default form, which may not contain the same field names. In that case, you may see a blank document when you open it using the default form, only some of the fields in the document, or you may not see the document in the view at all, if the view is using a selection formula based on the form or other field contents.

Caution

Trying to copy documents into a database that does not contain a copy of the form in which they are created can result in Notes being unable to display any of the information in the form or displaying only a small portion of the information. Read Chapter 11, "Designing Forms," for information on working with form design.

Applications of Copying and Pasting Documents

The ability to copy text, fields, or even entire documents is a Notes feature that is often overlooked but that contains a great deal of power. Some excellent applications of the capability to copy (or cut) documents to the Clipboard are the following:

- Though Notes provides you with an automatic archival agent for your e-mail, which is date-driven if activated, sometimes you might simply want to archive specific documents out of your e-mail database on demand. You can cut documents from your active mail database and store them in an e-mail "archive" database for safekeeping. With this archive, you can keep your active mail database relatively small as well as have the capability to keep important documents in case you need to get to them quickly at another time. As mentioned before, make sure that the document's form design is also present in the archive database to ensure that you can read the documents clearly. It is best if your archive mail database is a copy of your active database design. Read Chapter 10, "Creating New Databases," for more information on database design.

■ You can temporarily protect against losing documents while you perform other functions in the database. For example, if you are getting ready to run an agent against several documents in a database to replace some text but want to make sure the documents are protected against errors, such as being deleted, before you do so, you can copy them to the Clipboard, run your macro, and then verify that your results appear as you expected in your original documents.

If something went wrong when you ran the macro, you can always delete the modified documents and paste the documents from the Clipboard back into the database so that the information is restored to its original condition (before you began the agent).

■ Copying and pasting documents within the same database is a time-saver if you want to edit small portions of a document but want to keep the old, unedited document intact, such as a large proposal that someone else in your organization wrote. Copy the document to the Clipboard and then repaste it into the database by selecting Edit, Paste. Open the copy of the document and edit it. Your document will contain the edits without disturbing the original document.

Often, depending on the design of the database, your copy of the document will appear slightly indented below the original document as a response document if you highlighted the original document before pasting. (Your database designer may have bypassed your need to do this by selecting one of the following options: New versions become responses, Prior versions become responses, or New versions become siblings in the Form Property InfoBox during the creation of the form design. See Chapter 11, "Designing Forms," for more information on the Form Property InfoBox.)

Linking Documents

Often, you will want to guide readers to other areas where there is information related to the topic they are currently reading about. Perhaps a document that you are composing discusses a topic that is mentioned in another document.

For example, if you are discussing the health benefits of broccoli, you may want to create a link to another document that contains a recipe for actually making the stuff edible! The link need not even be in the same database as the document you are reading.

You can create links to the following:

■ Documents

■ Views

■ Databases

Links appear as pages of paper with their corners folded down, as shown in Figure 8.30. Associated with each link is a location, called the link pointer, within the link document. When the user double-clicks the link, Notes displays the link document showing the section of text containing the link pointer. When the user closes the link document, Notes returns to the original document that contained the link.

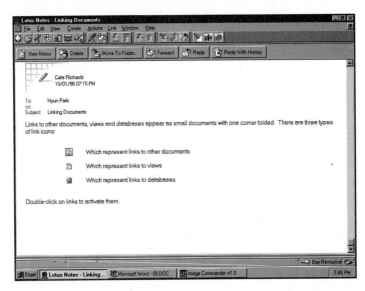

Fig. 8.30 Notes can link a document to other documents, views, or databases.

To create a link, complete the following procedure:

1. Start with one of the following:

- Open the link document (the document you want to link to—it does not have to be in the same database) and select a link point by clicking the position within that document that you want Notes to display when the doclink is activated. Note that if you open the document in read mode, the insertion point flashes only momentarily on-screen, but Notes still knows where it is.

- Open the view in which you want to link (the view does not need to be in the current database). Press F6 and select the view or folder you want to link to in the navigator pane.

- Highlight the database you want to link to by clicking its icon once.

2. Choose Edit, Copy as Link.

Select whether the link you are creating is a Document Link, View Link, or Database Link. Notes puts a link on the Clipboard that corresponds to the link point that you selected. Notes will indicate that the link has been copied to the Clipboard in the Status Bar at the bottom of your Notes window.

3. Open the document in which you want to insert the link. You must open the document in edit mode.

4. Paste the link into any rich text field in the document just as you would a section of text. (Choose Edit, Paste or press Ctrl+V.)

Caution

The following circumstances may keep the links from working for someone trying to use them:

- If the database ID or document ID referenced in the doclink is changed, you will have to make the link again. This often happens when the database is copied to another server (as opposed to making a replica copy) and the original database is deleted. It can also happen if the document is cut out of the linked database and stored in another database.

- The user does not have access to the database, server, or directory on the server in which the referenced database is located. The user must have at least Reader access.

- The user does not have form access to read the document referenced in the link. Form access is assigned when the form is created by the database designer—the default is All Users (who have access to the database).

- The user does not have view access necessary to read the view that is linked. The access level for reading a view is created by the database designer—the default is All Users (who have access to the database).

- Remote users will not be able to use the link unless the referenced database is located on their hard drive or they are dialed out to a server hosting a copy of the database.

If you are working on the network and double-click a link and the referenced database is not located on your workspace, Notes will search the servers to which you have access and add the database icon to your workspace, opened to the link point.

Because links are simply a set of numbers referencing the database ID and document ID, you can use them in messages to users to have them add a new database to their desktop and open the database to the referenced link point. When you close the database to which you have been linked, you will notice that the database icon has been added to your desktop. The database icon will remain on the workpage until the reader removes it.

This is an ideal way for database managers to assist users in accessing a new database. There is another way: using buttons that specify exactly which server you should access as well as the name of the database (and possibly the document). You will learn more about buttons in Chapter 16, "Buttons and Agents."

Tip

You can use links in designing databases to guide users automatically to referenced information. For example, if you have a discussion database, you can create a link in the form design of the response documents to always link back to the parent document, should the reader want to review the original topic. You will learn more about designing forms and views in Chapter 11, "Designing Forms," and Chapter 12, "Designing Views."

Adding Hotspots to Your Documents

Hotspots enable you to communicate additional information. Depending on its type, a hotspot may display pop-up text, switch to a linked destination, or perform a Notes action. For example, a pop-up hotspot displays pop-up text, as shown in Figure 8.31.

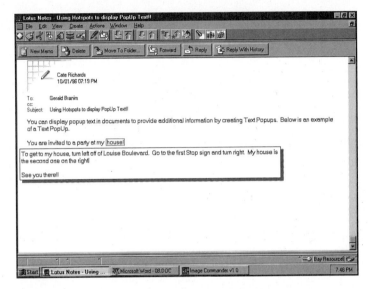

Fig. 8.31 Pop-up hotspots are handy when you want to display information in a document that only some readers will be interested in seeing, such as directions to your house.

Notes also can use hotspots to link to another document. For example, the document displayed in Figure 8.32 shows a document with underlined text. The author of the document created a hotspot for this text so that when users double-click the text, they will open up a related document. You will see many examples of this use of text hotspots in the online Lotus Notes Help database. (The text hotspots appear as underlined green text in the help documents to link you to information related to that help topic.)

Finally, Notes can use hotspots to perform actions. For example, you can define an action to compose a document titled "Registration" whenever someone clicks a hotspot called Register (see Figure 8.33).

> **Note**
>
> To create a hotspot, your cursor must be located in a rich text field and your document must be in edit mode. You must be in read mode to display or activate a hotspot.

> **Note**
>
> There is one final type of hotspot—buttons that you can create in documents as well as in the design of a form. Button hotspots are covered in detail in Chapter 16, "Buttons and Agents."

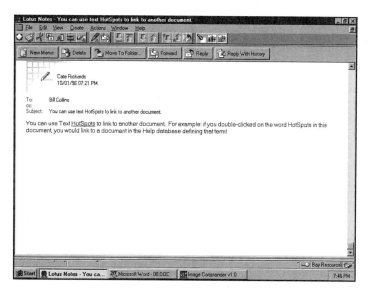

Fig. 8.32 You can use text hotspots to link readers to a related text.

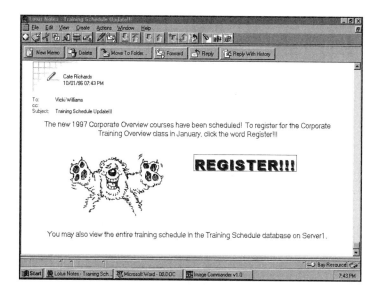

Fig. 8.33 You can use action hotspots to perform functions—such as compose a new form—whenever someone clicks them.

Pop-Up Hotspots

To define a text pop-up hotspot, in which text pops up whenever the user clicks and holds the left mouse button on a particular hotspot, complete the following steps:

1. Make sure the document is in edit mode.

2. Select the area to which you want to add the hotspot. This area can be text that you have typed or a graphic that you have copied to the Clipboard.

3. Perform one of the following:

   - Choose <u>C</u>reate, <u>H</u>otspot, <u>T</u>ext Popup and enter the text you want the popup to display. For example, you can type help information about a particular form in the text box to provide help information, particularly when the instructions are too long to fit in the field help line displayed at the bottom of the window.

   - Choose <u>C</u>reate, <u>H</u>otspot, <u>F</u>ormula Popup and enter a formula in the programmer's pane that will set the text you want the popup to display. For example, you can set a formula that looks up a list of current products in a product database whenever someone clicks the hotspot. You will learn more about writing formulas in Chapter 14, "Working with Formulas," and Chapter 15, "Working with Functions and Commands."

Tip

If the text you want to enter has already been typed in another Windows or OS/2 document, you can highlight the text and select <u>E</u>dit, <u>C</u>opy to copy the text to the Clipboard. Then with your cursor in the pop-up text field, press Ctrl+V to paste the text from the Clipboard. (The <u>E</u>dit, <u>P</u>aste function is not available to you because you are in a dialog box.) This is a quick way to put a large amount of text in a popup. The formatting and font attributes will not be present in the popup, however.

As mentioned previously, database designers most often use popups to include additional help or reference information in the design of a form. You, too, can use the popup feature in the body of documents for limiting the amount of information a reader has to filter through to get to the information needed in the document you are creating.

For example, if you are working with a team on a proposal and have been exchanging information about it (close dates, dollar amounts, and so forth) but also want to provide the readers with the definition of some of the terms within the contract, you can create a popup around the terms. If the readers need the definition, it can be accessed; otherwise, the reader does not need to waste time reading through the definition and can continue through the rest of the document.

You can also copy information from a previous memo and paste it into a pop-up box when links are not applicable. The reader then has the option of reading previous information, if needed, by clicking the popup that you created or just the current information. To paste text from the Clipboard into a pop-up box, create the pop-up box as usual, and then select Ctrl+V to paste the text from the Clipboard into the dialog box.

One last example of using Formula popups is to display editing information about the particular document you are reading. The developer of the application can provide a pop-up hotspot (perhaps in a graphical format) with a Notes formula that tracks the history of the original author and any editors of the document. Folks interested in seeing that information can click the graphic to display it—otherwise, the information is tucked out of sight from the main body of the document.

> **Tip**
>
> The Online Help database provides some great examples of the use of pop-up hotspots in documents and navigators.

Link Hotspots

You can add a hotspot that enables users to switch to another document, view, folder, or database. This is an example of a link hotspot that leads to another document (much as you learned in the "Linking Documents" section earlier in this chapter). The difference between creating a link and creating a link hotspot is in the appearance of the "trigger" that initiates the link.

In creating links, you paste an object that looks like a document into a document. In creating link hotspots, any area that you highlight will serve as the "trigger" for making the link. For example, you could highlight a graphic of an airplane to have Notes link you to a policy on airline travel in another database.

To create a link hotspot, complete the following steps:

1. Begin by choosing any of these options:

    - In the view pane, click the document to which you want to link.

    - In the navigation pane, click the view or folder to which you want to link.

    - In the workspace, click the database to which you want to link.

    - In a document, click the area of the document to which you want to link.

2. Choose Edit, Copy as Link.

3. Open the document to which you want to add the hotspot in edit mode.

4. Highlight the area to which you want to add the hotspot. (This area can be text or a graphic.)

5. Choose Create, Hotspot, Link Hotspot.

Action Hotspots

You can add a hotspot to an area of a document (such as text or a graphic) that enables users to perform a Notes action. For example, you can add a hotspot that creates a document that you can type in and send, such as a registration form in a training database. A good example of action hotspots can be found in many of the new V4 navigators, in which clicking a graphic opens a navigator, view, or document for you to read. Other examples in the Help database include the action hotspots that are programmed around each of the book icons in the navigator pane. Clicking a book opens another navigator and view for quick access to the information you need the most.

To create an action hotspot, do the following:

1. Make sure the document is in edit mode.

2. Select the area to which you want to add the hotspot by highlighting it. The area can be text or a graphic.

3. Choose <u>C</u>reate, <u>H</u>otspot, <u>A</u>ction Hotspot. The programmer pane will appear as shown in Figure 8.34.

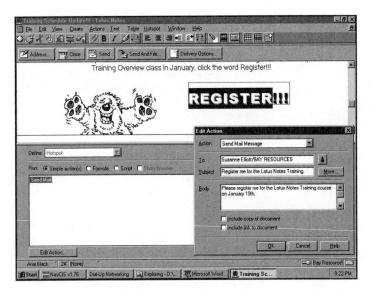

Fig. 8.34   To create action hotspots, you will need to work in the programmer pane.

4. In the programmer pane, do one of the following:

   - Specify a preprogrammed action that Notes includes by selecting Simple action(s) and clicking Add Actions. Then select an action, specify any settings Notes needs to perform the action, and click <u>O</u>K.

   - To enter a formula that performs an action, select Formula and enter the formula. The formula you use can be a simple formula, such as telling Notes to close the database, or can be quite complicated.

   - To enter a script that performs an action, select Script and enter the script. The script you use can be a simple script, such as composing a document, or can be quite complicated.

> **Note**
>
> You will learn about programming simple actions, formulas, and scripts in Part II, "Designing Applications."

5. Click anywhere within the document to close the programmer pane and continue working.

You can remove the green border that surrounds a hotspot by highlighting the hotspot while you are in edit mode or in the design pane and selecting Edit, Properties. The Properties InfoBox will appear, as shown in Figure 8.35.

Deselect the Show border around hotspot checkbox. You can also hide the hotspot, change fonts, colors, and other text attributes as well as perform any paragraph formatting options by making the appropriate selections in the hotspot's Properties InfoBox.

Fig. 8.35 Use the HotSpot Button Properties InfoBox to control how the hotspot is displayed in the document or form.

To use a hotspot, double-click anywhere within the border of the hotspot, with the exception of pop-up hotspots. To use a pop-up hotspot, click anywhere within its borders and hold the left mouse button down. The text will be displayed as long as you press the mouse button.

Using Tables in Your Documents

As you use Notes to compose documents, you may find tables handy for representing data. Tables consist of data arranged into rows and columns in any manner you choose. The intersection of each column and row is a cell. Most often, lines surround each cell so that the table forms a grid. Like most other advanced formatting features, tables can appear only in rich text fields.

You can include tables in the design of your database forms by following the instructions for creating tables provided in the next section. Rather than entering text into all the cells, however, you will define fields instead. An example of a form using a table as part of its design is found in Figure 8.36 (in design mode). See Chapter 11, "Designing Forms," for additional information.

In the following sections, you will learn how to create tables in documents, add data to the tables, and change the tables' characteristics.

Creating Tables

To create a new table, position the insertion point where you want the table to appear then choose Create, Table. Notes opens the dialog box shown in Figure 8.37.

Enter the number of rows and columns you want for this table. Notes immediately creates a table in your document with the numbers of rows and columns you specified.

Notes will also add a new menu command to the menu bar at the top of the Notes window: Table. You can use this menu command to control the attributes of the table with which you are working.

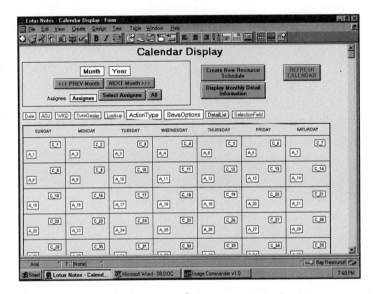

Fig. 8.36 You can create tables as part of the form design. Each cell can contain static text or a separate field design.

Fig. 8.37 Enter the number of rows and columns for your table.

You can add and delete columns and rows from a table, change the cell widths, change the cell borders, and change other attributes of a table at any time. The following sections provide details.

Adding and Deleting Columns

To add a new column to your table, click where you want to add the column. Select Table, Insert Column. Notes adds another column to your table to the left of your cursor location.

If you want to add multiple columns to your table, click where you want to add the columns and select Table, Insert Special. Notes displays the Insert Row/Column dialog box (see Figure 8.38).

Type the number of columns you want to add in the text box provided, and then select Column(s). Next, select from the following options:

- **Insert.** Inserts the number of columns specified to the left of the current location of the cursor

- **Append.** Adds the number of columns specified to the far right side of the table

- **Cancel.** Enables you to exit without adding any columns

- **Help.** Accesses the online help in Notes

Notes adds the columns to your table.

Fig. 8.38   By selecting Table, Insert Special, you can add multiple columns or rows to your table at once.

You can also delete columns from your table by placing your cursor in the columns you want to remove and selecting Table, Delete Selected Column(s). Notes will prompt you if you want to delete the column; click Yes. You can also delete multiple columns by placing your cursor in the first column in the table you want to delete and then selecting Table, Delete Special. Select Column(s) and specify how many columns you want to remove. When you have made your selection, click Delete. Notes removes the current column and any additional columns to the right of the current one, according to the number of columns you specified.

Adding and Deleting Rows

To add a new row to your table, click where you want to add the row. Select Table, Insert Rows. Notes adds another row above your current cursor location.

If you want to add multiple rows to your table, click where you want to add the rows and select Table, Insert Special. Type the number of rows you want to add in the text box provided, and then select Row(s). Next, choose from the following options:

- **Insert.** Inserts the number of rows specified above the current location of the cursor

- **Append.** Adds the number of rows specified to the bottom of the table

- **Cancel.** Enables you to exit without adding any columns

- **Help.** Accesses the online help in Notes

Notes adds the rows to your table.

You can delete rows from your table by placing your cursor in the rows you want to remove and selecting Table, Delete Selected Row(s). Notes will prompt you if you want to delete the row; click Yes. You can also delete multiple rows by placing your cursor in the first row in the table you want to delete and then selecting Table, Delete Special. Choose

Notes Basics

I

Row(s) and specify how many rows you want to remove. When you have made your selection, click Delete. Notes removes the current rows and any additional rows below the current one, according to the number of rows you specified.

Changing Table Attributes

You can change the way your table looks by changing border attributes, column width, space between the columns and rows, cell colors, split cells, join cells, and select margin settings. To change these attributes, place your cursor in the first column or row that you want to modify—or if you want to modify multiple cells, select the first cell, click and hold your left mouse button, and drag the cursor over all of the cells you want to modify—and select Table, Properties. The Table Properties InfoBox appears with the Cell Borders tab displayed, as shown in Figure 8.39.

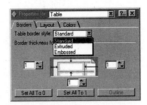

Fig. 8.39 You can change the borders for your table in the Table Properties InfoBox to add pizzazz to your table and highlight important information.

You can specify border widths ranging from 0 (no border) to 10 (thickest border) for each side of the cell's border. You can also specify whether you want the table border to be

- **Standard**: a plain black line

- **Extruded**: a "pushed-in" 3-D effect

- **Embossed**: a raised 3-D effect

To change border settings (the thickness of the lines and appearance surrounding your table's cells), complete the following steps:

1. With the Table Properties InfoBox opened to Cell Borders, do one of the following:

   - Change the Table border style. Click the drop-down arrow selection indicator and pick from standard, extruded, or embossed. This selection affects all cells of the table, not just the cell(s) you have highlighted.

   - Set the border on one or more sides. Select the up/down arrow next to each border thickness for the current selection setting option and increase/decrease the width of each border.

   - Set the border on all sides to single. Click Set All To 1.

   - Remove the border from all sides. Click Set All To 0.

   - Set the outline of the cells you have highlighted to a particular thickness or style. Click Outline and then select any of the other options available to you.

2. If necessary, select another cell in the table and repeat step 1 until all of the cell's borders are set as you would like them.

3. Close the dialog box.

Tip

To change borders only for the outer sides of the table, select the entire table by dragging your mouse over it and click Outline in the Table Properties InfoBox. Then select the border styles and settings for each side of the table. This feature makes framing your table with a special border setting easy.

You can also highlight the entire table and remove the border or select border styles that affect the entire table, including each individual cell's borders.

To make adjustments to the margins, column width, and spacing between rows and columns, select the Layout tab while viewing the Table Properties InfoBox. Notes displays the InfoBox shown in Figure 8.40.

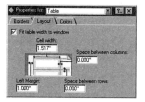

Fig. 8.40 Adjusting margins, spacing, and column width helps add impact to your tables.

You can control the following settings:

- **Fit to window.** This setting tells Notes always to adjust the column widths proportionately to fit within the current size window. This way, those who read the table can easily see all columns of the table regardless of the size of their monitor or window.

Note

Large tables sometimes can be difficult to read if Fit to window is not selected, as the user will have to scroll back and forth in the window to see all of the information.

Also, tables sometimes can be difficult to read on different platforms, screen sizes, and/or resolutions. Keep your user in mind when you create tables in documents.

- **Left Margin.** To indent the table, enter a larger number than the default (1.25") in this field. Notes will move the left margin of the table accordingly.

- **Space between rows and Space between columns.** With these options, you can specify how much blank space Notes displays between the text and the cell's borders. The default is zero.

■ **Cell width.** This setting enables you to specify the width of the cells in each column in inches. You can set the current cell's column and then click in another cell and adjust its width. Notes records which cell you are adjusting next to the Cell width text entry box.

New to Notes R4.5 is the capability to highlight particular cells with color. To add color to any of the cells in your table, highlight the cell(s) and select the Color tab in the Table Properties InfoBox. The Color settings will appear as shown in Figure 8.41. Select the color from the Background color selection drop-down box. Notes will fill the cell(s) with the color you have selected. Select the Apply to Entire Table button if you want the selected color to fill all of the cells in the table. You can also select Make Transparent to remove the color from any cell(s) you have selected.

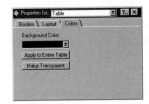

Fig. 8.41 The top row of cells in the table will be filled with black to emphasize the column headings of the table. This is just one use for adding color to your tables.

When you have made all of your adjustments, close the Table Properties InfoBox to continue working with your table.

> **Note**
>
> Large tables in documents tend to slow down the PC's response time when it reads and prints documents. Keep this in mind when you decide to insert a table.

Merging and Splitting Cells

New to Lotus Notes R4.5 is the capability of merging and splitting cells. Merging and splitting cells provides you with an enhanced way of drawing focus to your form and communicating information to your readers. It also enables you to duplicate the design of many simple paper forms more accurately in Notes.

To merge cells, follow these steps:

1. Highlight the cells you want to merge, as shown in Figure 8.42.

> **Note**
>
> You must highlight more than one cell before the Merge Cells menu command is available for you to use. However, as of this writing, merging cells can throw off the width of the columns dramatically.

Fig. 8.42   You can merge cells in Notes R4.5 to change the size and shape of areas of a table.

2. Select Table, Merge Cells.

Notes merges the cells into one. If you have text in any of the cells, Notes will display the combined text from the single cells in the new cell created.

To split cells, follow these steps:

1. Place your cursor in the cell you want to split.

> **Note**
>
> The cell you want to split must be a previously merged cell before the Split Cells command is available for you to use.

2. Select Table, Split Cell.

Notes splits the highlighted cell into the original number of cells and copies any text in the merged cell into one of the new cells.

Entering Data in the Table

Suppose that you need to represent revenue figures for the fourth quarter in each of your company's three business units, along with totals. At first, you may think you want a table with four columns and four rows, but an extra row and column would enable you to label each month and business unit. So enter **5** as the number of rows and **5** as the number of columns. When you choose OK, Notes creates the table.

You can enter data in the new table just as you can anywhere in the document. Figure 8.43 shows what the table may look like after data is typed into the cells (but before its characteristics are adjusted to enhance its attractiveness). In this example, the data was typed individually into each cell, including the totals. If the table had been part of the design of the form, then you can design a formula to add the numbers automatically in the Totals row. You will read more about creating formulas in Chapter 14, "Working with Formulas."

Once you have set the design of the table, you can adjust the borders, cell widths, and other text formatting characteristics to add impact and highlight information to attract the reader's attention. Figure 8.44 displays the same table shown in Figure 8.43 but is formatted to enhance the presentation of information. As you enter data into a table, keep the following points in mind:

■ You can move around within a table using the arrow keys just as you can move anywhere within the document. Within a table, however, you also can press Tab to move from one cell to the next and Shift+Tab to move to the preceding cell (that is, the cell to the left or the last cell on the preceding row if you are at the beginning of a row).

■ If you enter text that is too wide for the cell, the cell extends to as many lines as necessary to hold the text.

■ If you enter a single word that is too long to fit in a cell, Notes extends the height of the cell and splits the word. Notes never increases the width of the cell to accommodate long words. If a word is too long to fit, type a hyphen and then press Enter to divide the word correctly. When you press Enter, Notes adjusts the height of the cell to accommodate the additional line.

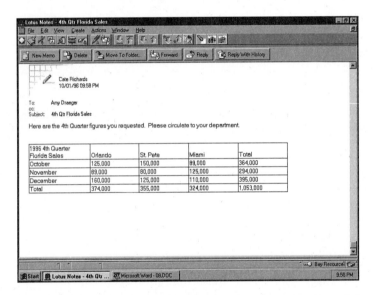

Fig. 8.43   Tables, such as the one shown here, communicate information correctly but are bland and do not highlight important information.

Creating a One-Cell Table

You can highlight text in a document to emphasize a point by creating a table that has one cell and one column, as shown in Figure 8.44. In this example, the author created a one-cell table with the right and bottom borders defined as double, while the top and left borders were left as single. This provides a shadowing effect that adds some pizzazz to your documents.

Once you have created the one-cell table, you can enter text into the box. Notes will not let you put a box around text that has already been typed, so if you want to try this feature with previously entered text, you will need to create the box and then cut and paste the text into it.

Fig. 8.44   You can use table settings to highlight text in a document.

Changing Table Text Characteristics
You can change many characteristics of the table text at any time, just as you would any text. You can use the Text menu settings and Text Properties InfoBox to change the color, size, and other font attributes for the text in the table.

You can also change the justification of an entire column or row. Highlight the columns or rows for which you want to set justification and select Text, Align paragraphs. You can specify whether the entire column or row should be left, right, centered, or full (you cannot specify none in tables). In Figure 8.45, the columns of numbers have been right-justified so that the numerals align properly.

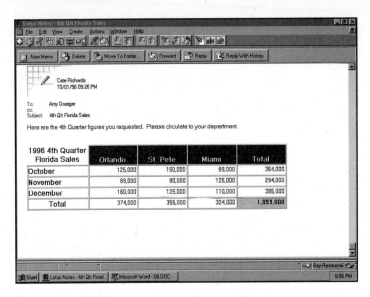

Fig. 8.45 You can align text in tables and modify table settings to enhance its readability. This is the same table shown in Figure 8.43, but it is now formatted to enhance its presentation.

Creating Sections in Documents

You can use sections to collapse one or more paragraphs in a document into a single line, referred to as the Section Title. The reader can see more detail than that displayed on the Section Title by clicking the section indicator (down arrow) next to the Section Title to expand the section to reveal more information. Sections make navigation in large documents easier.

Readers can expand a section when they want to read its contents or ignore the section if it does not apply to them. In designing forms, database designers can create hide-when formulas to provide logic to determine when a particular section can be seen. In this section, you will learn how to create sections in documents. You will learn more about designing forms in Chapter 12, "Designing Views."

> **Note**
>
> You must be in a rich text field to create a collapsed section.

Figure 8.46 illustrates a document about an upcoming meeting in which sections have been created. One section, "Directions to Roy Rogers," has been expanded to display further information. You can tell there is a collapsible section by the twistie located to the left of the section title.

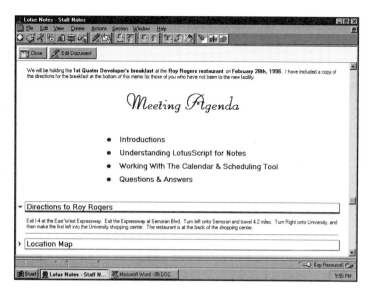

Fig. 8.46 Collapsible sections can make navigating through documents easier for the reader.

To create a section, perform the following steps:

1. Highlight the paragraphs, graphics, and other information you want to collapse into a section.

2. Choose Create, Section. Notes will immediately collapse the section and display the title of the section as the first line of text in the paragraphs that you selected. If the first line that you had highlighted was blank, your section heading will be blank.

Changing the Title of a Section

If you want to edit the title of a collapsed section after it is created or change any of its other attributes, click anywhere within the collapsed section and select Edit, Properties. Notes displays the Section Properties InfoBox, as shown in Figure 8.47.

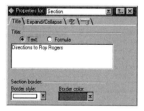

Fig. 8.47 You can change collapsible section titles in the Section Properties InfoBox.

In the Title tab of this InfoBox, you can change the section title by clicking in the title text entry box and typing the title of your section. You can also select the Formula option and have Notes compute the title of the section based on a formula you enter. After you have entered the title of the section, you can select the border style and color from the drop-down selection boxes at the bottom of the InfoBox.

Controlling How Notes Displays the Sections

In Notes, you can control the way the collapsible sections are treated when you first open the document as well. With the Section Properties InfoBox open, select the Expand/Collapse tab as shown in Figure 8.48.

Fig. 8.48   You can control how Notes displays the collapsible sections when you open and print the document.

In the Expand/Collapse tab, the following options are available to you for each mode the document is in—Previewed, Opened for reading, Opened for editing, and Printed:

- Don't auto expand or collapse indicates that the section will appear in the state that it was left in the last time you opened the document.

- Auto expand section tells Notes always to expand this section when you open the document.

- Auto collapse section tells Notes always to collapse this section when you open Notes.

You may also select Hide title when expanded if you don't want to display the section title when the section is expanded, which can help conserve space in the document. You can select Preview only if you want the section feature active only when you are previewing a document. In any other mode, the expand/collapse capability will not be available, and the section title will not be displayed.

> ### Tip
>
> It is often useful, regardless of how you want documents to be viewed online, to tell Notes to Auto expand section when printing to make sure you see all of the data on the form in the printout. Also, it is a good idea not to include required fields (fields into which you require users to enter data before they can save the form) in sections that are automatically collapsed. Hiding the field from display in that manner may frustrate users when they try to save the form and discover required fields that they could not see.

Changing Section Fonts and Hiding Sections

In Chapter 7, "Working with Text," you learned how to change the fonts and to hide text that you were working with. Likewise, Notes provides you with the capability to change the font color, size, and style of the section title by clicking the Font tab in the Section Properties InfoBox. Make the necessary settings just as you would for regular text. Likewise, you can hide the section based on the status or condition of the document by clicking the Hide when tab of the sections Properties InfoBox. You learned about this feature in Chapter 7, "Working with Text," and will learn more about it in Chapter 11, "Designing Forms."

You can create nested collapsible sections by highlighting more than one collapsed section and then selecting Create, Sections again. Figure 8.49 displays multiple layers of collapsible sections for an account profile document.

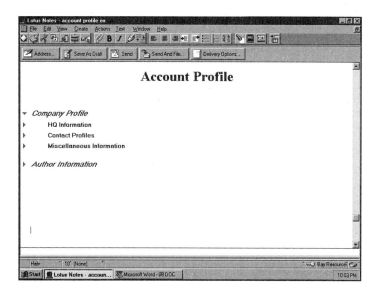

Fig. 8.49 You can create multiple layers of collapsible sections.

> **Note**
>
> You can incorporate sections into the design of your form and control access to those sections so that only particular readers can see the section. You will learn more about controlling access to sections of a form in Chapter 11, "Designing Forms."

Deleting Sections

Sometimes you may not want to keep the section setting in your document. For example, some people don't want to keep the collapsible section created when you elect to reply with history in your e-mail database—they would rather see just the contents of the section. If you decide you don't want a collapsible section in your document, you can easily remove it, as long as it is not part of the design of the form. To remove a section, click the section title and select Section, Remove Section. Notes will remove the section but leaves all of the text, graphics, and other objects in the document.

Using Folders to Organize Your Documents

You can use existing folders in a database—or design your own—to organize your documents in a manner that makes sense to you. For example, in your e-mail database, you may want to create a folder titled Hot Topics to store memos on issues of great importance to you. (This is similar to selecting a category for the mail memo in Lotus Notes 3.x.) When you find a document in a view that you want to store in your folder, simply click the document title and drag it to the folder. When your mouse pointer is located over the appropriate folder (the folder will be highlighted with a box when it is selected), you can release the mouse button. The document will move into the folder. When you click the folder, you will see your document located in it.

Creating Folders

Folders can take on the characteristics of views in that you can copy the column design of the views so that they appear the same in the folder. For example, you can create a folder titled Executive Correspondence and base the folder design on the People view in the database, which sorts documents according to people's names.

To create a new folder, do the following:

1. Select or open the database where you want to create the folder.

2. Choose Create, Folder to show the Create Folder dialog box (see Figure 8.50).

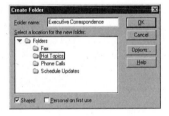

Fig. 8.50   You can enter or edit the name of a folder in the Create Folder dialog box.

3. Enter a name for the folder in the Folder name box. The name length should be descriptive and can contain any characters. The name is limited by the number of characters you can type in the Folder name box (between 14 and 26 characters, depending on capitalization). If you want to place the folder inside another existing folder, click the existing folder title in the Select a location for the new folder list. This list will vary depending on whether you create a Private folder (the default) or select Shared, as discussed in step 4.

4. If you have at least Designer-level access to a database and the database manager has granted you permission, you can click Shared to tell Notes that this is a folder that you want everyone who uses the database to have access to.

5. Click OK.

Notes creates the folder and it appears in the navigator according to the options you selected.

If you want to select a view or folder on which to base the folder's design, follow these steps:

1. In the Create Folder dialog box, click Options to display the Options dialog box (see Figure 8.51).

Fig. 8.51 Select the view design that you want the design of your folder to inherit.

2. Click a view or folder in the Inherit design from list. If you want to change the design of the folder as soon as the folder is created, select the Design now option. When you click OK to create the folder, Notes will automatically open its programmer pane. You will learn more about designing folders and views in Chapter 13, "Integrating Notes 4.0 with Other Applications."

3. Click OK.

Deleting Folders

Occasionally, you may find that you no longer have a need for a particular folder in your database and you don't want it to clutter up your navigators. You can easily delete a folder by performing the following:

> **Note**
>
> You must have Designer- or Manager-level access to delete, rename, or move shared folders (those used by everyone) in a database.

1. Select the folder you want to delete from the navigator pane.

2. Select Actions, Folder Options, Delete Folder.

3. Select Yes when prompted to delete the folder. Notes removes the folder from your navigator.

The documents displayed within the deleted folder have not been deleted, however. You can switch to any view designed to display the documents to see them.

> **Tip**
>
> You can also delete a folder by highlighting the folder's name in the navigator and pressing F6, and then the Delete key. Select Yes when prompted to delete the folder.

Renaming Folders

Sometimes you might want to rename a folder to further define its contents. Do this by selecting the folder you want to rename then selecting Actions, Folder Options Rename. The Rename dialog box appears, as shown in Figure 8.2. Type the new folder name in the Name box then select OK.

Fig. 8.52 You can also open the Rename dialog box by selecting the folder you want to delete, pressing F6, and selecting Actions, Rename.

Moving Folders

Just as you might want to rename a folder, you might also want to move the folder to display within another folder or move a folder out of another folder. To move a folder, highlight the folder you want to move and select Actions, Folder Options, Move. The Move dialog box appears, as shown in Figure 8.53. Highlight the location where you want to relocate the folder and then select OK. Notes will move the folder to the new location.

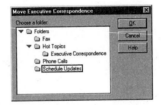

Fig. 8.53 You can also open the Move dialog box by highlighting the folder you want to move, pressing F6 and selecting Actions, Move.

Moving Documents In and Out of Folders

You can move documents to folders by clicking the document title in the view and dragging it to the folder in which you want to store the document. Alternatively, you can select all of the documents you want to move to the folder by placing a checkmark next to each document title and selecting Actions, Move to Folder. Notes will prompt you to select the folder into which you want to move the documents. Moving documents to a folder does not move the document out of a view—rather, it works somewhat like creating a category sort for the document. If you return to the view that originally displayed the document, you will still see it displayed there.

You can remove documents from a folder by clicking the document title (or selecting multiple documents by placing a checkmark next to each name) in the folder and selecting Actions, Remove from Folder. Notes will remove the selected documents from the folder. This does not delete the document from the database, however—you can still see the documents if you switch back to a view designed to display those documents.

> **Caution**
>
> Do not select the documents and press the Delete key, send the documents to the Trash, or select Edit, Clear unless you want to permanently delete the document from Notes. Unlike selecting Remove documents from folder, these actions permanently delete the documents from the database.

From Here...

In Part I, you learned to work with many of the advanced options available when you are working with documents. You have learned to search text, insert options that enhance your communication, work with tables, create folders, and create sections. You will learn more about many of these features and their use in designing applications in Part II, "Designing Applications."

For more information on the topics discussed in this chapter, refer to the following:

- Chapter 10, "Creating New Databases," teaches you the basics of designing a Lotus Notes database.

- Chapter 12, "Designing Views," teaches you how to design views, and more about creating folders within the design of a database.

- Chapter 14, "Working with Formulas," shows how to create formulas that you can use to customize your hotspots and folders.

Chapter 9

Lotus Notes Group Calendaring and Scheduling

For years, stand-alone *Personal Information Managers* (*PIMs*) such as Lotus Organizer have helped people better organize and schedule their time and priorities. However, the fundamental problem with these tools was their inability to share information in a workgroup. If you've ever tried to schedule a meeting with a group of people—particularly in a large company or one for which people are on the road frequently—I'm sure you know the frustration of not being able get in touch with key people.

In recent years, many vendors have made progress toward group scheduling, for instance, MS Schedule + or the latest release of Organizer. But the problem with these tools is their dependence on the file-system model of sharing information. Users must be connected to the LAN to access the schedules of their team members. Not only does this model not scale well, it's slow and is not effective for supporting remote/mobile users. What is needed is a client/server-based tool that supports mobile users.

This chapter introduces you to the concepts of Group C & S and shows you how to use Notes for C & S in your workgroup.

An Overview of Group Calendaring and Scheduling

As more and more companies of all shapes and sizes begin to understand the synergy and tremendous return on investment that can be realized by implementing collaborative technologies, such as Lotus Notes, they demand more functionality of the underlying architecture. In its usual fashion, Lotus has risen to the occasion by delivering a very powerful, user-friendly Group Calendaring and Scheduling (C & S) based on its award-winning Organizer Personal Information Manager (PIM).

On the outside chance that you haven't had the opportunity to work with one of the user-friendly C & S tools, such as Organizer, Goldmine, or MS Schedule +, we should probably briefly explain what C & S is and does.

Some of the main topics in this chapter are

- An overview of Group C & S
- Enabling and configuring Notes C & S
- Getting started with Notes C & S
- Managing Calendar Entries
- Resource Reservation
- Notes C & S Under the Hood

In a nutshell, Calendaring and Scheduling enables you to schedule and track appointments, events, and anniversaries for you as well as members of your workgroup, team, or organization. In addition, you can send invitations to meetings, view your colleagues' free time, and even schedule company resources, such as conference rooms, auditoriums, training rooms, and A/V equipment. The best part is that—because it's Notes-based—it replicates! This gives you the capability to schedule meetings, send invitations, and reserve resources even as a remote user.

Let's walk through a possible scenario. While flying to the fall Comdex, Samuel Hatter, President of Hatter Enterprises, needs to schedule a meeting with several key members of his team as well as some key business partners with whom his company works closely to discuss technological trends for 1997.

Somewhere in Illinois, Sam launches Notes and opens his mailbox to the Calendar view. He quickly sees that on December 21, 1996, his whole day is open, so he sets out to schedule a meeting. Sam creates a new Appointment and invites Rick Flagg and Chris Clark from Collaborative Solutions as well as Dan Voelker, Jason Cox, John Mason, and Darryl Rogers from Hatter Enterprises. When Samuel saves the Appointment, Notes checks the invitees' free time for conflicting appointments. If no conflicts exist, each of the invitees will receive an invitation (including Rick and Chris who are outside the company); otherwise, Samuel will be notified of a scheduling conflict so he can adjust the schedule. When Sam gets to his hotel room, he simply plugs his machine into the phone line and replicates with his Notes server, which sends out the invitations.

When the invitees to Samuel's meeting receive their invitation, they can accept or decline the invitation; they can even suggest an alternate time or delegate the meeting to someone else. As invitees accept or decline, Samuel will be notified of their status and can plan accordingly.

When the invitees show up on December 21, they score big points with Sam because they are using Notes C & S to track appointments, anniversaries, and events, and they remember to wish him happy birthday.

For those of you who have used Organizer, you're going to love the powerful new group C & S capabilities of Notes. (This even includes remote dial-up users!) For those of you who haven't used Organizer, be prepared for a real treat: The user-friendly, easy-to-use interface makes organizing your time a piece of cake.

For several years, Lotus has enjoyed a large market share in the C & S market with Organizer. By joining forces with IBM, its total market has grown significantly, as IBM has been a player in this arena for years with such products as Office Vision and Time and Place/s. In fact, it is estimated that Lotus and IBM combined currently have over 10,000,000 C & S seats, counting only existing products.

In short, Lotus set out to make Notes *the* client for enterprise-wide, cross-platform C & S by building Notes C & S around its proven technologies and enabling seamless integration into existing groupware and messaging infrastructure. The following are some of the primary benefits of the new group C & S capabilities:

- Integration with NotesMail with access through mailbox

- Legacy system migration and/or coexistence

- Remote/mobile access to schedules, free time, and resources

- Extensibility through programming

- Tight security through Notes native security

- Real-time access to scheduling information

- Scalable calendar store

- Delegation of authority for reading mail and scheduling appointments

- Ease of use and accessibility based on the award-winning Organizer interface

- Access to C & S data through Web client with Domino

- Can be woven into existing applications, increasing their effectiveness

Notes' group C & S capabilities can be a tremendous asset to your organization and will make your users much more effective. Let's learn how to use Notes C & S.

Enabling and Configuring Notes C & S

Before you can begin actually using Notes C & S, your Notes Administrator must do a number of things to set up C & S. If you have been using an older version of Notes, your mailbox will need to have its design upgraded to the new NotesMail 4.5 design before you'll be able to access the C & S elements. Likewise, the design of the Public Name & Address Book must be updated so that it contains some new and revised forms and views.

The Domain form has a new section, Calendar, that contains two new fields, which are used to tell Notes how to look up free time.

Note

In a group Calendaring & Scheduling system, *free time* is any user's availability. It is absolutely critical to be able to determine when other users are available so that you can schedule meetings with and for them. If you don't know when other users are available (that is, when they have *free time*), how can you effectively schedule activities for them?

Figure 9.1 displays the modified Domain document.

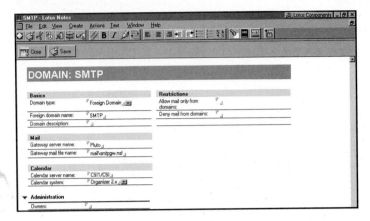

Fig. 9.1   The Domain document in Notes 4.5 has been modified significantly to provide new functionality such as a Global Domain for Internet mail.

The Calendar server name field is used to tell Notes which server is used as the Calendar server so that it knows where to go to find free time information about a user whose home server is different than your own server. The Calendar system field is a keyword list that enables you to choose from the two currently supported formats other than the native Notes format: Lotus Organizer 2.x and IBM Office Vision. Once this document has been completed, Notes will know how to handle freetime lookups.

Additionally, a new document, Resource, enables you to define resources, such as rooms and equipment, in the Public N & A Book so that they can be found and managed easily. The new version of the Administration task (Adminp) will create Resource documents in the Public N & A Book for each Resource document it finds in the Resource reservation database. Figure 9.2 displays the new Resource document.

> **Note**
>
> If you are not running the Administration task on your server, you'll need to create resources manually in the Public Name and Address Book. However, Resources you enter in the Public Address Book won't be available for free time queries unless you make a corresponding entry in the Resource Reservations database; the Administration task will not coordinate resource information entered into the Public Address Book with the Resource Reservations database.

The first section of the form, Basics, contains fields that define the resource. The first field, Resource Type, is pretty much self-explanatory: It enables you to choose the type of resource you are defining. The Resource Name enables you to give the resource a name that Notes will use to reference it. The Capacity field is also self-explanatory.

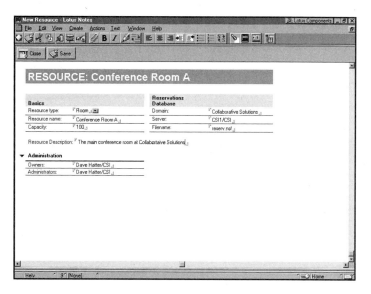

Fig. 9.2 The Resource document is a useful new feature that allows you to define "resources" that can be scheduled and managed.

The Reservations Database section contains fields that tell Notes where to find the actual database in which the resources are stored and shared. The Domain field tells Notes which domain the Resource Reservations database can be found in. The Server field enables you to specify the server where the database resides. The Filename field should contain the actual filename of the Resource Reservations database, for example, Resource.nsf. The Resource Description field can be used to add additional information to help describe the resource.

The last section, Administration, contains fields that enable you to define the owner of the resource and who can administrate it. This is standard on all of the other documents in the Public N & A Book. As you might expect, there is also an updated view, Server\Mail-In Database and Resources, that provides an easy way to view and manage these resources.

Furthermore, the administrator will need to ensure that new server tasks (Schedule Manager and Calendar Connector) are running on the Notes server. For more information on server tasks, see Chapter 24, "Notes: Under the Hood."

Note

The Free Time system is comprised of two new server tasks: Schedule Manager (SCHED.EXE) and Calendar Connector (CALCONN.EXE). When you install Notes, both of these tasks are added to the Notes INI file so that they are loaded by default.

Schedule Manager

When the Schedule Manager task is first loaded on a Notes 4.5 server, it creates a new free time database (BUSYTIME.NSF) on the server. Then for each Person document in the Public Name & Address Book, it creates an entry in the free time database for each user whose MailServer field is set to that server name. Schedule Manager runs in the background constantly; each time users change to their calendars, Schedule Manager enters the change in the free time database automatically.

Note

Because of the sensitive nature of the information in the Free Time database, only the Schedule Manager has access to it by default.

Calendar Connector

The final step involves creating a new Resource Reservation database from the Resource Reservations template (RESRC45.NTF) and configuring it for use. This new database has three new forms: Resource, Site Profile, and Reservation. Resources and Site Profiles are covered in this section. Because they are created and used by end users as normal parts of Calendaring & Scheduling, Reservations will be covered in their own section. The Site Profile form, displayed in Figure 9.3, is used to define a site where resources can be allocated and managed.

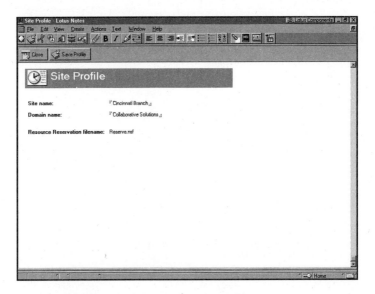

Fig. 9.3 The new Site Profile document allows you to define "sites" that contain resources that can then be scheduled and managed.

Tip

The default access granted to the Resource Reservation database is "Author." However, in order to create Resource and Site Profile in this database, users must be assigned to the [Create Resource] role. For more information on Access levels and Roles, please see Chapter 3, "Using Databases," and/or Chapter 22, "Security and Encryption."

The Site name field is used to give the site a name that Notes will use to refer to it. The Domain name field tells Notes which domain it can find this site in. The Resource Reservation filename field enables you to specify the actual database file name in which the room reservations can be found. In addition, if the database is on a Notes server (rather than a local copy), Notes will compute the server's name and display it in the Resource Reservation server field. This field will only display if the database is on a server.

Once you have defined your sites, you can begin to define resources at each site. This is accomplished by composing Resource documents for each resource you want to manage through the C & S interface. Figure 9.4 displays the Resource document.

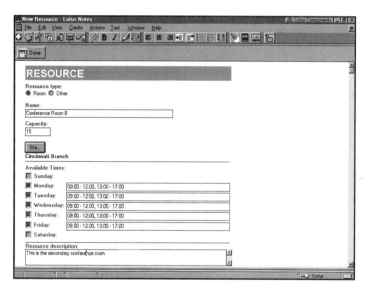

Fig. 9.4   The Resource document allows you to create a resource as a site that can then be scheduled and managed through Notes Group C & S.

Note

You must define at least one Site document before you'll be allowed to create Resource documents in the Resource Reservations database.

The Resource document is very simple. The Resource Type checkbook is used to tell the system whether this resource is an actual room or is a resource such as an overhead projector or multimedia PC. The Name field is used to define the name you want Notes to use when referring to this resource. The Capacity field enables you to define the total number of users/people that can be facilitated by the resource. You can click the Sites button to launch a dialog box that displays all of your currently configured sites. You can then pick the site this resource belongs to.

The fields in the Available Time section enable you to define the days and times that the resource is available. To enable the availability for a given day, just click the checkbox next to the day. You can then enter a time or a range of times that a resource is available for each day. That's all there is to it. The final field, Resource Description, can be used to enter any additional information needed to identify this resource.

Once these tasks have been completed, you are ready to begin using Notes C & S.

Getting Started with Notes C & S

To use Notes C & S, you begin in your mailbox. When you open your Notes 4.5 mailbox, you'll see a number of new items you'll need to become familiar with. Right away, you'll notice two new views in the default navigator: Calendar and Meetings. Figure 9.5 displays the new 4.5 NotesMail navigator.

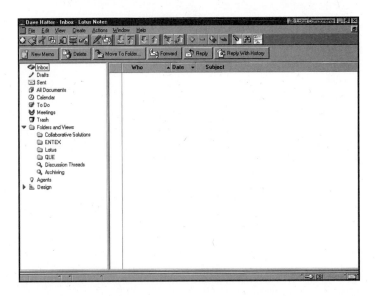

Fig. 9.5 The 4.5 NotesMail navigator has new views to support the Group C & S Capabilities.

In addition, you find a new form, Appointments, and several new actions that are used to configure your C & S options. The Appointments form is used to create Standard Appointments (Meetings), Anniversaries (no longer can you use the excuse, "I'm sorry, honey; I've been so busy and stressed out at work that I just forgot our anniversary."), and Events, such as the monthly alumni club meeting that you always forget to go to. (We'll cover these items in detail throughout the rest of this chapter.) But before you start creating and managing your appointments, you'll need to configure your Calendar Profile and, if necessary, your Delegation Profile.

Creating a Calendar Profile

In order to maximize the usefulness and functionality of Notes C & S, you must create a Calendar Profile for yourself that defines how you want to use C & S. In order to create a Calendar Profile, open your NotesMail mailbox and choose <u>A</u>ctions, Calendar Tools, Calendar Profile. Figure 9.6 displays a Calendar Profile document.

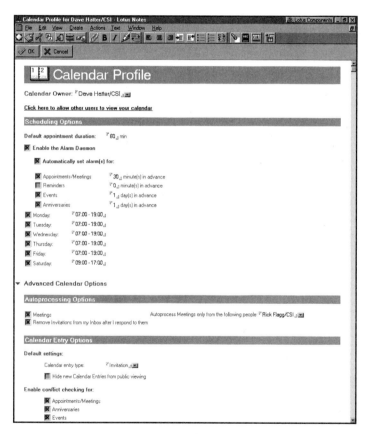

Fig. 9.6   The new Calendar Profile allows you to configure your Calendaring defaults.

The first field on the form, Calendar Owner, is used to tell Notes to whom this profile belongs. It defaults to the user name on the ID in use when the form is composed and enables you to choose a different user from the Public Name & Address Book.

> **Note**
>
> Allowing others to see your calendar is very different than allowing others to see your free time. Be careful with this selection. If you allow others to see your calendar, they will see appointments you've entered into your calendar, except for those you specifically mark as "Not for public viewing." You can also give people access to your mail, which also dictates that you should carefully consider who can do this.

The Scheduling options section contains a number of fields that enable you to configure your scheduling defaults. The first field, Default Appointment Duration, is used to set a default value for meeting length in minutes, meaning that for each new appointment you create, its length will be set to the default value you enter here. It defaults to 60 minutes. The next field, Enable the Alarm Daemon, is a checkbox that acts as a toggle switch for setting Alarms. When this feature is checked, it tells Notes to scan your calendar for appointments that have alarms so you can be notified. If you have enabled Enable the Alarm Daemon, the Automatically Enable Alarms option becomes enabled so that you can set alarms and set default values for each type of appointment. The usage of these fields is self-explanatory.

The Freetime Options section enables you to define who can access your free-time information and what days and time ranges should be considered when calculating your free time.

The first field, Only the following users can read my Freetime Schedule, is a keyword field that pulls up a dialog box displaying users from your N & A Book. Just select the users who should be able to access your free time information. The rest of this section is pretty simple; to enable a day, simply check its box and then enter the times that should be considered available.

The expandable section, Advanced Calendar Options, contains two additional sections, Autoprocessing Options and Calendar Entry Options, each of which allows you to enable settings that can make Group C & S more productive for you.

The Autoprocessing Options section contains options that allow you to automatically processes items in your calendar. Currently, you can autoprocess only meetings. If you want to do so, simply check the Meetings checkbox and then choose the people whom you want to autoprocess from the keyword list that the Autoprocess meetings only from the following people field option presents. You can click the Remove Invitations from my Inbox after I respond to them checkbox to tell Notes to automatically delete invitations from your mailbox once you have accepted the invitation to a meeting, saving you the time of having to look for invitations and delete them.

The final section, Calendar Entry Options is subdivided into two categories: Default Settings and Enable Conflict Checking For:. In the Default Settings options, the Calendar Entry Type field allows you to choose from the different appointment types so that each time you create a new appointment, it will be set to the type chosen here. The Hide new Calendar entries from public viewing checkbox tells Notes to only allow users explicitly named in your Delegation Profile to view your Calendar entries.

The Enable Conflict Checking For section contains a series of checkboxes that allow you to tell Notes to check for conflicts on certain types of appointments. Your choices are: Appointments/Meetings, Anniversaries, and Events. To enable any of the options, simply place a check in the respective box and Notes will then check for scheduling conflicts when you create any of these types of appointments.

Once you have set your desired options, save the document and your Notes client will begin using your new configuration.

Creating a Delegation Profile

If you travel a lot, or work as part of a very closely knit team, it may often be necessary to have someone else read and respond to your mail and schedule. Notes now adds this capability through Delegation. Delegation is the ability to allow access to your mailbox to a user or group that you specify.

To enable delegation, you must create a Delegation Profile, which is done by opening your NotesMail box and choosing Actions, Mail Tools, Delegation Profile. Figure 9.7 displays a Delegation Profile.

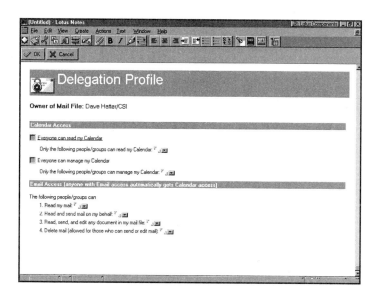

Fig. 9.7   The Delegation Profile is a powerful new tool that allows you to delegate access to your mailbox and Calendar.

As you can see, the Delegation Profile is relatively simple to complete. The first field, Owner, tells Notes to whom this Delegation Profile belongs. When a new Delegation profile is created, this field defaults to the user name of the Notes ID in use.

The first section, Calendar Access, contains Calendar delegation options. If you'd like everyone to be able to read your Calendar, click the Everyone can read my Calendar checkbox, which will hide the Only the following people/groups can read my calendar field. If you want only specific users to access your calendar, you can use the Only the following people/groups can read my calendar to select people or groups that should have access. As you might expect, the Everyone can read my Calendar and the Only the following people/groups can read my calendar fields are mutually exclusive.

You can also allow other Notes users to manage your Calendar. If you'd like everyone to be able to manage your Calendar (this is not recommended), click the Everyone can manage my Calendar checkbox, which will hide the Only the following people/groups can manage my calendar field. If you want only specific users to access your calendar (this is the better choice), such as an assistant, you can use the Only the following people/groups can read my calendar to select people or groups that should have access. As you might expect, the Everyone can manage my Calendar and the Only the following people/groups can manage my calendar fields are mutually exclusive.

> **Note**
>
> There is a BIG difference between read and manage access to your calendar. If you grant manage access to everyone, anyone can add, edit, or delete your appointments. You should use that level of access judiciously.

The second section, E-mail Access, allows you to define people and/or groups that can access your mailbox. The first thing you should notice is that anyone you grant E-mail Access to will automatically have Calendar access. You can use the following four fields in this section to control a number of e-mail access options:

- **Read my mail**—This field can be used to select a list of users who can read mail in your mailbox.

- **Read and Send mail on my behalf**—When users or groups are named in this field, they will be allowed to not only read mail, they will be able to send mail on your behalf; this means that they can send mail for you, but it will be denoted on the mail that *they* sent, if for you.

- **Read, send and edit any document in my mail file**—This field allows any users named in the this field to not only read and send mail, but to edit any type of message in your mailbox. This is a very powerful delegation and should be given judiciously.

- **Delete Mail**—This field allows you to name users that can delete mail from your mailbox; notice that if you have given people/groups read or edit access, they get this access by default.

> **Note**
>
> As long as your mailbox's Access Control List is set correctly, you will have no worries: Only the people that you name in the E-Mail Access section will have access. If you don't specify any users, only you will be able to read your mail.

If you want or need to have the capability to allow other Notes users to access your mail and take actions on your behalf, the Delegation Profile will provide this functionality.

Once you have created a Calendar Profile and a Delegation Profile (if necessary), you are ready to begin using Notes Calendaring and Scheduling to manage your time and the time of your colleagues.

Managing Your Calendar

Everyone—no matter what the size of the organization—occasionally must attend a meeting. Notes native C & S capability makes it easy to manage your schedule because you can create meetings, reserve resources, and even invite others to your meetings electronically whether you are a local or remote user!

Creating a Calendar Entry

When you are ready to schedule a meeting, you simply open your mailbox and choose Create, Calendar Entry or from the Calendar view, click the New Entry button on the Action Bar. This launches a new Calendar Entry form, as shown in Figure 9.8.

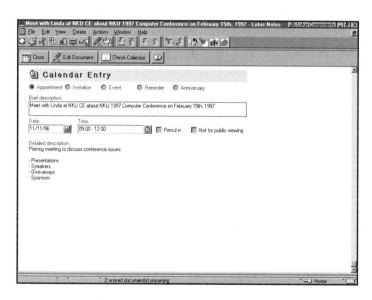

Fig. 9.8   The new Calendar Entry form is a powerful and versatile tool for managing your calendar.

The first thing you'll notice about this form is a series of five radio buttons that you can use to choose the type of entry you'd like to create. As you work with the Calendar Entries, you notice that each of the five form types has many overlapping fields, but each has fields specific to the purpose of the form. Since there are differences between the forms, we'll examine each one individually. Your choices are the following:

- **Appointment**—As you'd expect, appointments are used to add meetings to your schedule.

- **Invitation**—Invitations allow you to create an appointment and invite other people/groups to the meeting.

- **Event**—Events are used to denote special meetings—a trade show or a presentation—to your schedule.

- **Reminder**—Reminders are just that; they are added to your Calendar to help you remember to do something. They can work hand-in-hand with Anniversaries, for example, to help you remember to purchase an Anniversary present for your spouse.

- **Anniversary**—Anniversaries are used to enter recurring things such as birthdays, wedding anniversaries, and holidays to your schedule.

Appointments

Creating an Appointment is simple. Just click the Appointment radio button and the Calendar Entry form will display the fields shown in Figure 9.9.

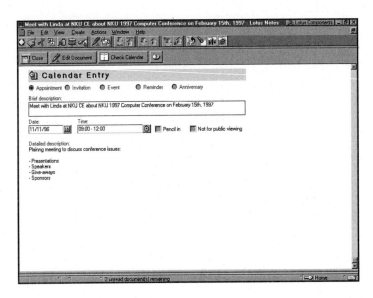

Fig. 9.9   The Appointment form.

The first field, Brief Description, is used to enter the text that describes the appointment. It will be displayed like a mail message subject in the views and folders in your mailbox, so it's important to enter a description that makes sense.

The Date and Time fields are pretty much self-explanatory: They are used to store the date and time of the Appointment. The Date field will default to the current date as will the Time field default to the current time. However, special attention should be paid to these fields, as they implement two of the cool new controls that Lotus has added to Notes 4.5, the Date control and the Time control, which are "borrowed" from the award-winning Lotus Organizer.

Notice that beside the date field is a small button with a calendar graphic. When this button is clicked, it launches a graphical calendar control. You can move forward and backward a month at a time by clicking the small, black arrows in the upper corners of the control. When you find the date you want, simply click it, and it will be inserted into the Date field. Figure 9.10 displays the calendar control.

Fig. 9.10 The new calendar control in Notes allows you to easily select date values.

You'll also notice that beside the Time field is a button with a clock graphic. Much like the new calendar control, when clicked, this button displays a graphical time bar so that you can select the time range for your appointment. To select a time range, you can click and drag the clocks at either end of the time bar to the appropriate start and end times. If you need to see more of the time control, just click on the up and down arrows to scroll through the times. Figure 9.11 displays the new time control.

Note

Both the Date and Time controls are now standard design elements that are available to Notes application developers for use in their applications. Kudos to Lotus, as this functionality has been needed for a long time. For more information on using these controls in your application, see Chapter 11, "Designing Forms."

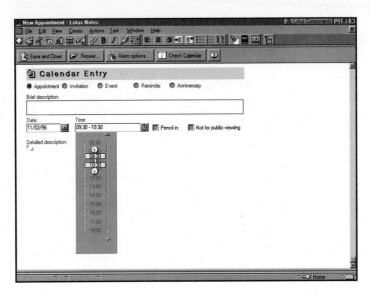

Fig. 9.11 The new time selection control in Notes allows you to point-and-click your way to setting the time of your appointment.

The Not for Public Viewing field is a checkbox that acts as a toggle to enable you to indicate that this appointment is confidential and should not be displayed to other users.

The Pencil In checkbox, when checked, is just like "penciling in" something in your day timer. It just indicates that this appointment is tentative.

The final field, Detailed description (indicated by the gray angle brackets) is a Rich Text field that can be used to enter a detailed description, add file attachments, and/or insert objects that help to additionally describe the Appointment.

You'll also notice the Save and Close, Repeat, Alarm Options, Check Calendar, and Help buttons on the Action Bar. These two action buttons extend the functionality of C & S. The Saved and Close button, when clicked, will save the appointment and close the current window.

If you'd like to make the appointment repeat without rekeying the information, you can click the Repeat button, which will launch the Repeat Rules dialog box shown in Figure 9.12.

Fig. 9.12 The Repeat option allows you to quickly and easily schedule recurring appointments.

The Repeat Rules dialog box allows you to easily choose the repeat options. You can use the Repeat drop-down field to tell Notes how often this Appointment will repeat from the following choices:

- **Weekly**—Choosing Weekly will tell Notes to create an entry in your calendar each week on the dates and times you specify. An example would be your weekly staff meeting every Friday at 9:00 A.M.

- **Monthly by Date**—Choosing Monthly By Date tells Notes to create an entry in your calendar each month on the dates and times you specify. For example, you attend the monthly Notes user's group on the 10th of each month.

- **Monthly by Day**—Choosing Monthly By Day tells Notes to create an entry in your calendar each month on a specific day rather than on a date. For example, you can watch me on TKR Channel 6 in Northern Kentucky on the 2nd Thursday of each month.

- **Yearly**—Choosing Yearly tells Notes to create an entry in your calendar each year on the date and time that you specify. For example, an annual Jaycee convention that you attend.

- **Custom**—Custom is the most powerful option; you tell Notes to enter entries based on the criteria that you specify.

Once you have made a choice for repeating your entry, use the other fields to define the specifics of the repeating appointments. For example, if you choose monthly on the 2nd and that falls on a weekend, you have the option to move the meeting forward or backward on that one specific instance. This is a very powerful tool that can make scheduling recurring appointments easy.

The Alarm button launches the dialog box shown in Figure 9.13. From this dialog box, you can set the alarm parameters for this entry. The first field, When, is static text that displays the time and date of the entry.

Fig. 9.13 The Set Alarm dialog box is very handy when you need to remember important appointments.

> **Note**
>
> If you have not enabled Alarms in your calendar profile, you will be prompted to enable this before the Set Alarm dialog box is displayed.

The next two fields work together to determine when the alarm process will notify you. The minutes field enables you to enter a time in minutes that, when the Before, After, or On option button is set, will cause you to be notified before, after, or on the appointment time and date.

The Alarm Message field enables you to enter a message that will be displayed when the alarm is kicked off. This value defaults to the value of the Brief Description field, but you can enter any value you like.

The final field, Turn Alarm Off, is a checkbox that toggles the individual alarms off or on.

> **Note**
>
> If you enabled alarms in your Calendar profile, the Minutes and Before/After/On fields will default to the values you entered for the Automatically Set Alarm for Appointments. You can override this on an individual basis by entering a new time for the alarms. To change this value permanently, just edit your calendar profile.

Once you have enabled an alarm for an entry, you will see a dialog box pop up on your screen at the designated time to remind you that you are scheduled to attend this appointment.

The Check Calendar button will open your calendar view so that you can quickly check your schedule for available times. When you are finished, you simply press ESC to return to your Appointment. The final button on the Action Bar is the Help button. When clicked, it displays a context-sensitive dialog box that explains how to complete the Calendar Entry you are creating.

> **Note**
>
> In order to make the C & S process as easy as possible, Lotus made the usage of the Brief Description, Not for Public Viewing, Pencil In, and the Detailed Description fields consistent throughout the five types of Calendar Entries, as is the usage of the new date and time controls, which helps to decrease the learning curve and make Notes C & S more user-friendly and useful. In addition, the Alarm and Repeat, Check Calendar, and Help action buttons are consistent across all of the Calendar Entries.

Now that you know how to create an Appointment, using the other Calendar Entry forms is easy because of the overlapping fields. Rather than reiterate the same information for each of the forms, we'll examine the divergence from the Appointment form in the remaining four forms.

Invitations

If you work in an organization with more than one person, you'll often want to schedule other individuals to attend a meeting, and that's where the Invitation comes into play. To create an Invitation, just create a new Calendar Entry and click the Invitation radio button. Notice that in Figure 9.14, an Invitation contains all of the same information as an Appointment but adds a subsection that allows you to define the invitees.

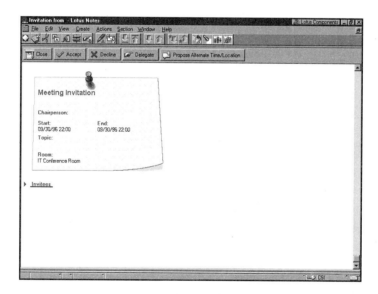

Fig. 9.14 The Invitation form provides the ability to schedule other users/groups to attend your meetings.

Because the Invitation is identical to the appointment other than the Invitation section, we'll examine only the invitation here. The first field, Send Invitations to, is a keyword list that allows you to select a list of users or groups that you'd like to send an invitation to from the Name and Address Book. The next field, optional Attendees is identical to the Send Invitations To field, except that people and groups selected here are not required to be in attendance, but could benefit from attendance.

Click here to find free time for all invitees is a hotspot that will allow you to search the Freetime database for each of the named recipients to ensure that they are available at the designated time. The I don't want responses from the Invitees checkbox allows you to tell Notes not to have the recipients send you mail responses in regard to the invitation.

If you want to reserve rooms and/or resources for your meeting, you can click Reservations. Reservations is an expandable section that contains three Hotspots links: Click here to reserve any available room, Click here to select and reserve a specific room, and Click here to select and reserve resources.

Click here to reserve any available room allows you to search the Resource Reservation database for any room that is available during the time and date you have specified for the Appointment. Click here to select and reserve a specific room launches a dialog box that displays a list of available resources. When you select a room, Notes will check to see if it is available at the specified time and date; if so, it will be reserved for your meeting. The last option, Click here to select and reserve resources works in a way that is very similar to Click here to select and reserve a specific room; you can choose a resource from the list and Notes will check to see if it is available. If it is, it will be reserved for your meeting.

The final field, Chairperson, is a display only field that when the document is saved, will display the common name of the Notes ID in use.

Events

If you'd like to schedule an event, such as a trade show or conference, simply create a new Calendar Entry and click the Event radio button, which will change the appearance of the form slightly as shown in Figure 9.15.

The primary difference between an Event and an Appointment or Invitation is the fact that events are entered on a daily basis rather than an hourly basis, which is why you have a Duration field in which you can indicate the number of days the event lasts. Notes will create an Event in your schedule for each of the days you indicate in the Duration field. For example, if you were going to LotusSphere, you might enter a date of January 26th, 1997, and a duration of six days. Notes would then create an event for January 26th and for each of the next five days.

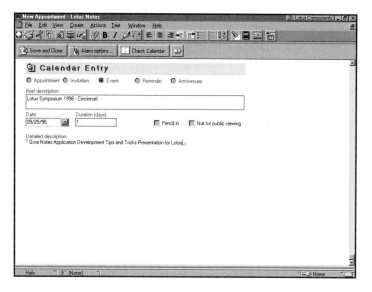

Fig. 9.15 Events allow you to schedule multi-day entries easily.

Reminders

Reminders are almost identical to Appointments, except that the Time field expects a discrete time rather than a time range. Figure 9.16 displays a Reminder.

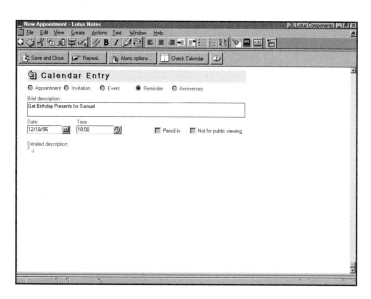

Fig. 9.16 You can create Reminders to help keep yourself out of trouble.

Anniversaries

The last type of Calendar Entry, Anniversary, can be very useful. If you want to denote special dates so that you don't have problems with schedule conflicts or to help you remember a special date, such as someone's birthday, you can create an Anniversary. Figure 9.17 displays an Anniversary.

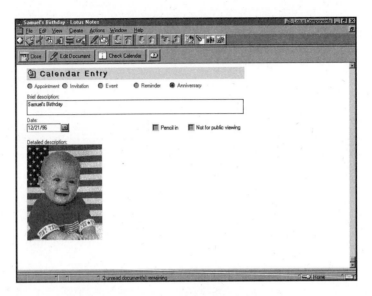

Fig. 9.17 Never miss a birthday again; use Anniversary to keep track of important dates.

Viewing Your Calendar Entries

Once you have created Calendar Entries, or been invited to appointments, you obviously need to be able to view, edit, and delete them, and Lotus has made it easy to do so. To find your Standard Appointments, you can use the Meetings, Calendar, or All Documents view.

The Meetings View. The Meetings view, shown in Figure 9.18, displays all of your appointments, and is a quick and easy way to manage your schedule.

The first column, Meeting Time, is sorted in ascending order based on the meeting time and date. Notice the down arrow on the column header, which indicates that the column can be resorted in descending order.

The second column, Subject, displays what the user entered for the brief description of the meeting.

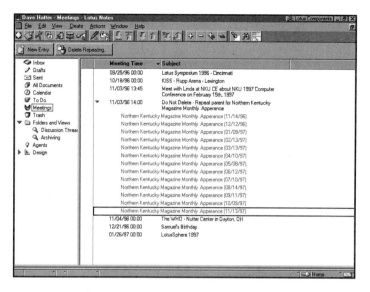

Fig. 9.18   The Meetings view displays all of your Calendar Entries in a utilitarian format for ease of use.

The Calendar View. The Calendar view is a very powerful new feature of Notes 4.5 that brings the award-winning look and feel of Organizer to Lotus Notes. It enables you to view your Appointments through a Calendar metaphor so that it's easy to manage your schedule. Because this is such a powerful new feature that can be used by application developers in their own applications, it warrants its own section where it's covered in detail in "The New Calendar Style View" section later in this chapter. Figure 9.19 displays the Calendar view.

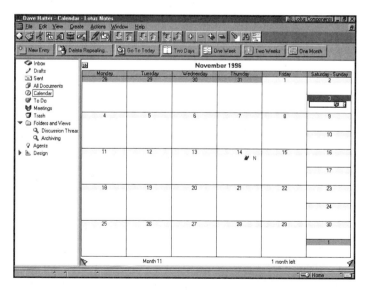

Fig. 9.19   The Calendar view displaying a month's worth of my Calendar Entries.

As you can see in Figure 9.19, this is a killer new feature of Notes. It enables you to view your schedule "At a Glance" and see all of your appointments. Notice the new Calendar-related action buttons on the action bar. Each of these buttons enables you to change the views of your calendar so that you can display as much data as needed to suit your personal preferences—from two days at a time to up to a month's worth of data.

The All Documents View. By now, the All Documents view is probably old hat to you, but it can be used for C & S as well because it displays your appointments (see Figure 9.20). However, because it does not discriminate toward the documents it displays, it can be somewhat overwhelming.

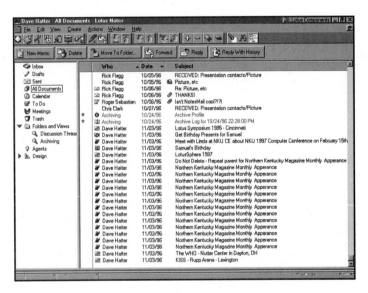

Fig. 9.20   The All Documents displays special icons for Calendar Entry documents.

As you can see in Figure 9.20, there are a lot of different types of documents displayed in this view. Lotus did, however, add several new icons to the view to indicate that a document is an appointment.

> **Tip**
>
> Remember that you can create folders in which to store your schedule items and make them easier to work with. For example, you might create an Anniversaries folder so that you can quickly and easily view only your anniversaries, or a High Priority Appointments folder to store the appointments that are very important.

Once you have learned how to use the views, you can quickly find your appointments and begin to edit and delete them.

Editing a Calendar Entry. To edit an existing entry, you use the same techniques that you would use to edit any Notes document. Using one of the C & S views or the All Documents View, find the document and then open it by double-clicking it and pressing Ctrl+E, or by choosing File, Edit Document. Once you have opened it, make the appropriate changes and save the document. Notes will then examine the document and recompute the scheduling information to see if a conflict exists for any of the invitees. If not, the invitees will be notified of the new date, time, and location. If a conflict exists, you'll be notified so you can take the appropriate action.

Deleting a Calendar Entry. Again, you can find an appointment that you want to delete by using the C & S views. Then, you can select the document and press the Delete key. When the document is deleted, Notes will remove it from the schedule of all of the invitees.

Resource Reservations

Often you'll need to reserve a room and that is where the Reservation form in the Resource Reservation database comes in handy. The Reservation form does just what is says; it allows you to reserve a resource and works somewhat differently depending on whether you elect to reserve a Room or a Resource.

Reserving a Room

To create a Room reservation, open the Resource Reservation database and choose Create, Reservation, which will display a new Reservation form as shown in Figure 9.21.

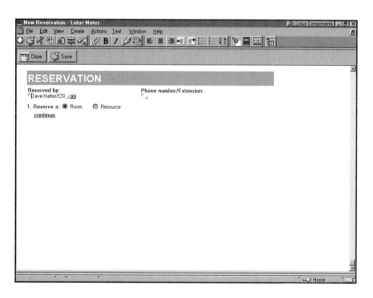

Fig. 9.21   The Reservation form allows you to quickly and easily find an available resource and schedule it.

When you create a new Reservation, the Reserved By field is defaulted to your username, but you can choose another user from the addressbook by clicking the entry helper for the Reserved by field. You can use the Phone number/extension field to enter the phone number of the person who reserved the resource, making it easy to get in touch with him or her quickly. You then begin to answer a series of questions that will define the actions Notes will take. If you click the Room radio button and then click the Continue button, Notes will then display the fields shown in Figure 9.22.

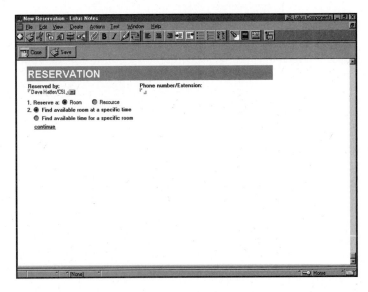

Fig. 9.22   The Reservation form, displaying the options that pertain to reserving a room.

You then have the option to Find available room at a specific time, or you can do the converse—Find available time for a specific room.

Finding a Room at a Specific Time. If you choose Find an available room at a specific time, and click Continue, the fields shown in Figure 9.23 will be displayed.

You can then enter or select a date in the Reservation date field, enter or select a time in the Time field, choose a site from the defined sites in the Site field, and then enter a valid number for the Number for Attendees field and click Click here to find an available room, which will search the resources database for conflicting room reservations. When a room that meets your criteria is found, it will be displayed as shown in Figure 9.24. If no rooms are available, Notes will display an error message indicating that no room could be found.

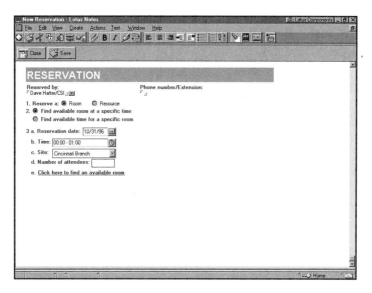

Fig. 9.23 Reserving a room at a specific time.

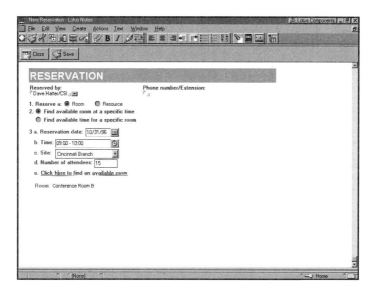

Fig. 9.24 The reservation form displaying an available room.

You can then click the Save button, press Ctrl+S or choose File, Save to add your reservation to the database and effectively block out that room for the date and time you've indicated.

Finding a Time for a Specific Room. Alternatively, when you want to reserve a room, you can elect to have Notes find a time for a specific room you choose from the available resources. For example, you might have 50 people coming in for a presentation and only your largest conference room can support that many people. In this case, you want to find a time when that room is available.

To do this, just click the Find Time for a Specific Room radio button, which will display the Rooms dialog box shown in Figure 9.25.

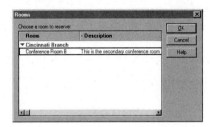

Fig. 9.25 The Rooms dialog box allows you to choose a room from the resource database to reserve.

Once you select a room from the Rooms dialog box, additional fields will be added to the Reservation form as shown in Figure 9.26.

You then enter the Reservation Date and the Duration in hours for which you want to reserve the room and click Click here to find an available time, which will launch the Find Time dialog box so that you can see the free times for this room and select the appropriate time. Once you have made a selection, the time range will be displayed on the reservation form and you are finished, just save the document.

Reserving a Resource

Creating Resource Reservations is very similar to Room reservations. Just choose the Resource Reservation database and choose Create, Reservation which will open a new Reservation form. Just click the Resource radio button and Notes will display the Find available resource at a specific time and Find available time for a specific resource radio buttons. Because, like the Room reservation options, this form displays different fields based on the choice you make, we'll examine these options independently.

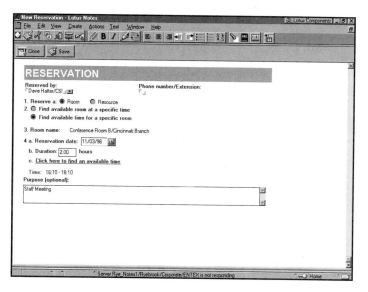

Fig. 9.26 The Reservation form when finding a time for a specific room.

Finding a Resource at a Specific Time. If you choose Find available resource at a specific time, and click Continue, the fields shown in Figure 9.27 will be displayed.

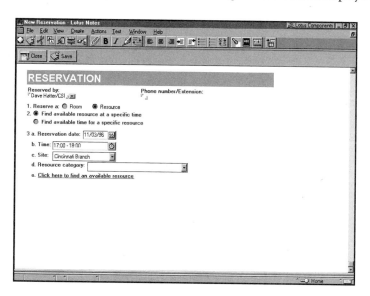

Fig. 9.27 The Reservation form makes reserving a resource at a specific time easy because it uses the free time database.

You can then enter or select a date in the Reservation date field, enter or select a time in the Time field, choose a site from the defined sites in the Site field, and then choose a Resource Category from the list. Once you have entered the requested information, just click the Click here to find an available resource hotspot which will search the resources database for conflicting reservations for the resource you requested. When a resource that meets your criteria is found, it will be displayed as shown in Figure 9.28. If no resources are available, Notes will display an error message indicating that no resource could be found.

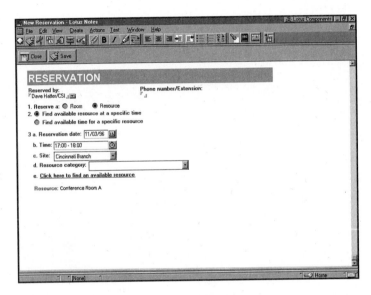

Fig. 9.28   The reservation form displaying an available resource.

If you were able to schedule a resource, you are ready to save the document. You can click the Save button, press Ctrl+S, or choose File, Save to add your reservation to the database and effectively block out that resource for the date and time you've indicated.

Finding a Time for a Specific Resource. Just like the Room reservation process, you can also choose to have Notes find a time for a specific resource.

To do this, just click the Find Time for a Specific Room radio button, which will display the Resources dialog box shown in Figure 9.29.

Once you select a resource from the Resources dialog box, additional fields will be added to the Reservation form as shown in Figure 9.30.

You can then enter the Reservation Date and the Duration in hours for which you want to reserve the resource and click Click here to find an available time, which will launch the Find Time dialog box so that you can see the free times for this room and select the appropriate time. Once you have made a selection, the time range will be displayed on the reservation form and you can save the reservation.

Fig. 9.29   The Resources dialog box allows you to choose a resource from the resource database to reserve.

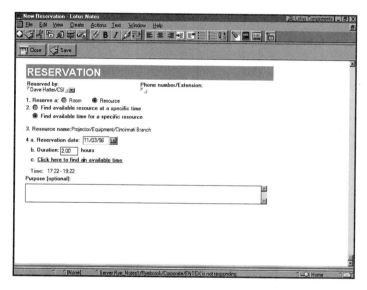

Fig. 9.30   The Reservation form when finding a time for a specific resource.

The New Calendar Style View

The new Calendar style view is an incredibly cool new feature that enables you to graphically display your schedule in a planner metaphor, much like a Franklin Planner. In fact, each view looks similar to an actual piece of paper. You navigate through the calendar by clicking the "dog-eared" edges of the page. You can also print the view to have a nice copy of your schedule.

Note

The best thing about this new view style is that it is not limited to your schedule; your developers can use this style of view in any Notes database.

The calendar view can be configured to display data in several ways: two days at a time, one week at a time, two weeks at a time, or one month at a time. The Two Days at a time view displays the most detailed information and looks similar to a page from a Franklin Planner (see Figure 9.31). It includes the appointment's time of day and the description of the appointment.

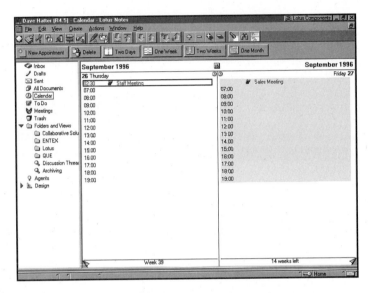

Fig. 9.31 The two-day version of the Calendar view displays detailed information about your schedule.

The view is very easy to use. When opened, it defaults to today and tomorrow. To view the preceding or the following day, simply click the "upturned edges" of the page to move through your schedule one day at a time. You'll also notice a small white calendar icon. This can be clicked to display a calendar control to enable you to move through your schedule in much bigger chunks. In addition, the bottom of each "page" displays the day number (out of 365 days) and how many days are left in the current year.

To access any scheduling information, simply double-click it to open the appointment. If you want to add a new appointment, find an open time and double-click it. It will launch a new Appointment form.

The one-week version of the view works exactly like the two-day view, except that it displays slightly less detail (see Figure 9.32). It shows you only the description for any appointments you have scheduled within a given week. By default, it displays the current week. At the bottom, it displays the week number (out of 52) and the number of weeks left in the year.

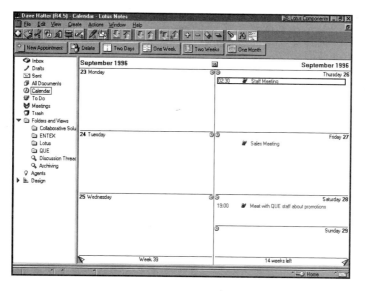

Fig. 9.32   The one-week version of the Calendar is very useful; it gives you a week-at-a-glance view of your schedule.

The two-week version of the view (shown in Figure 9.33) also works exactly like the other views, but it displays even more of your schedule with less detail. Each of the two pages displays a week's worth of your data, and it defaults to the current week and the following week. At the bottom, it displays the weeks' numbers (out of 52) and the number of weeks left in the year for each of the two weeks displayed.

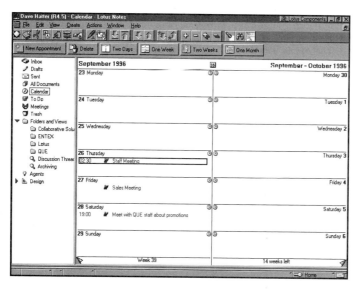

Fig. 9.33   The two-week version of the Calendar view can be useful to see the current week's schedule and to plan for the next week.

The one-month version of the view is probably the most useful for a quick "one-stop shopping" view of your schedule (see Figure 9.34). It displays an entire month of your schedule at one time with minimal detail. For each day that you have something scheduled, you'll see an icon (the same one used in the standard views) that indicates you have appointments on a particular day. At the bottom of the view, it displays the number of the month (out of 12) and the number of months left in the year.

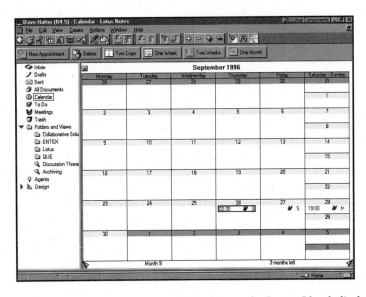

Fig. 9.34 The one-month version displays your schedule on the "macro" level, displaying very little detailed information.

How Notes C & S Works

The new Notes Group C & S functionality is based on a number of new infrastructure elements that must be in place before Group C & S can be used. You'll need administrator access to the server to perform many of the tasks, so this section serves only as an overview of the Group C & S architecture. For more detailed information, consult the Lotus Notes Administrator's Guide and the Notes Help database.

Before Notes Group C & S can be used, the following must happen:

- Each Notes user's mailbox design must be upgraded to the design of the 4.5 mail template (MAIL.NTF).

- The Notes Public Name & Address Book for your domain must have its design upgraded to the 4.5 Public N & A template (PUBNAMES.NSF).

- The Calendar section of the Domain document must be completed. You must tell Notes where to find the users' calendar information.

- The administrator must create a new database for Resource Reservations on your server from the Resource reservations template (RESRSV45.NTF).

- The administrator must create a new Freetime Database to store users' free time and make that free-time information available to other users (BUSYTIME.NTF).

Once all of the configuration items are out of the way, the fun can begin.

Let's follow the scheduling of a Standard Appointment for three invitees from start to finish. The process begins when a user, Leslee Hatter, composes an Invitation. She chooses to invite Dan Voelker. She also chooses to reserve the Management Conference Room, which is pulled from the list of available resources in the Resource Reservation database, and sets the date for 10/31/96 from 1:00 to 3:00 P.M.

In order to save time and ensure that the date and time she selected is open for the invitee, Leslee elects to determine the invitee's free time by clicking Click here to find free time for all invitees, which will display the Find Time dialog box. Notes will then send a query to Leslee's mail server, "Ace." Ace will then look for Dan Voelker's Person document in the Public Name & Address Book and, depending on whether or not Dan's Person document is found, will do two very different things.

If Dan's Person document is found, Server Ace will examine Dan's Mail Server field. If Dan's MailServer is also Ace, Notes will examine Bob's free time in the Free Time database and will display this information to Leslee. If Dan's MailServer is another server in the same domain, Notes will forward the query to Dan's MailServer and look up his free time for Leslee. If Dan's MailServer is outside the Domain, Notes will use the Calendar Domain field to determine where Dan's free time information resides.

If the Free Time system cannot find Dan's Person document in the Public N & A Book, it has no choice but to assume that Dan's mailbox is in a different domain. If Leslee appends the domain name to Dan's address or if Dan's hierarchical name has enough information to tell the Free Time system where Dan's domain is, the Free Time system will attempt to search the Public Address Book for a domain document for Dan's domain and take one of the following actions based on what it finds.

If an adjacent domain document is found by the Free Time system, it looks at the CalendarServer field for the name of a server that accepts Free Time requests for Dan's mail domain. If the data in this field has been entered correctly, the Free Time system will open the Free Time database on Dan's MailServer and then return Dan's information to Leslee. If the CalendarServer field is incorrect or empty, the free time request fails and the Find Time dialog box indicates that Dan's information is unavailable.

If a Foreign Domain document is found by the Free Time system, it knows that Dan is using a different scheduling application such as Organizer. The CalendarServer field in the Foreign Domain document identifies the name of a server that processes free time requests for Dan's domain. The CalendarSystem field identifies the name of the plug-in program that will perform the free time lookup on Dan's server. The Free Time system forwards the query to Bob's server for processing and if successful, will return the results to Leslee.

If no Domain documents are found by the Free Time system, Leslee's request fails and the Find Time dialog box indicates that Dan's information is unavailable by displaying all of Dan's time as a solid gray bar.

Note

A free time query will fail if the invitee's home server is down or any of the links that are used to get from your server to the invitee's server are down. If this happens, you'll receive an error message indicating that the server is down, and the find time dialog box will indicate that the user's time is unavailable.

If no conflicts exist, Leslee can use the Find Time dialog box to select a different time; otherwise, when she saves the form, an invitation is generated and mailed to each of the invitees, and the appointment is added to Leslee's schedule—which updates her Free Time database and puts a Reservation in the Resource Reservation database to inform other users that the Management Conference Room is booked on October 31.

When the invitees receive their invitations, they can check their schedules. (They should be free because Leslee elected to check for conflicts.) When Dan Voelker receives the invitation, he accepts and his schedule is updated to reflect the meeting with Leslee.

Barring natural disasters or a higher priority event popping up, Dan should show up at 1:00 P.M. on October 31, 1996, for Leslee's meeting because they have their schedule to remind them every day. (They could even set an alarm!) In addition, when other users try to schedule Dan, they will see that Dan is booked on that date.

From Here...

Now that you've had a chance to see the awesome power of Notes C & S, you'll probably want to start using it right away because it can improve your efficiency and effectiveness tremendously. If, however, you want to learn more about NotesMail or how you can use C & S to extend your applications, take a peek at the following chapters:

- Chapter 4, "Getting Started with Electronic Mail," explains how to use the NotesMail interface.

- Chapter 5, "Using the Address Book," explains the functions of both the Public and Private Address Books.

- Chapter 24, "Notes: Under the Hood," explains how Notes works its wonders.

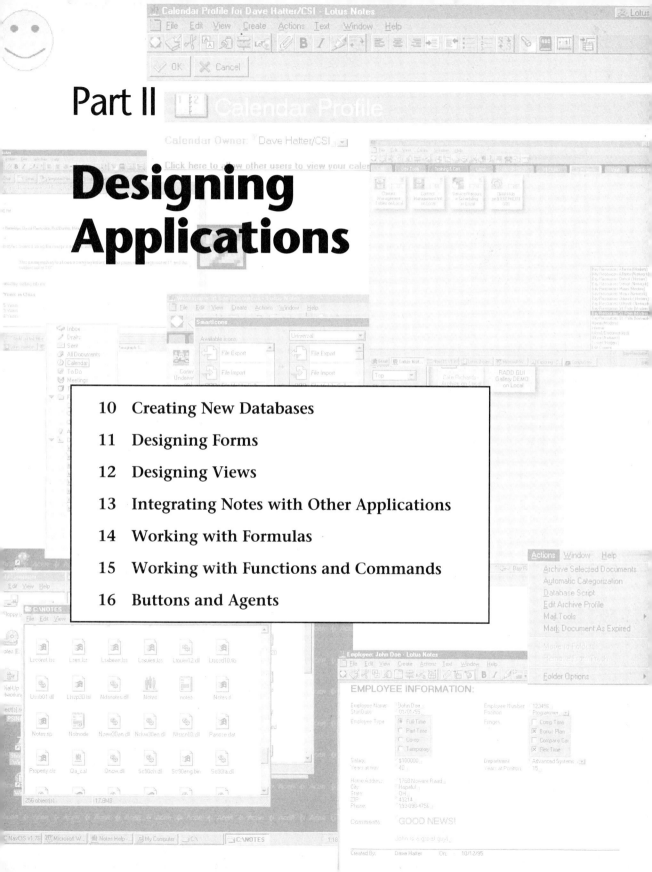

Part II

Designing Applications

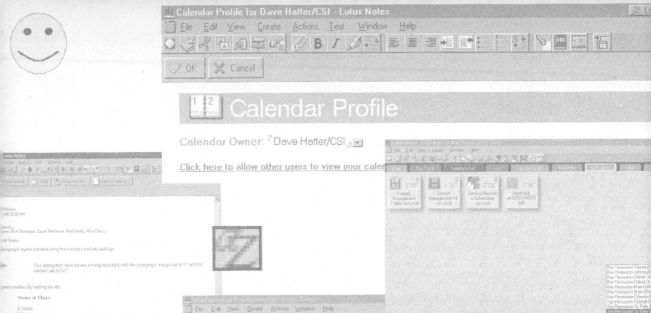
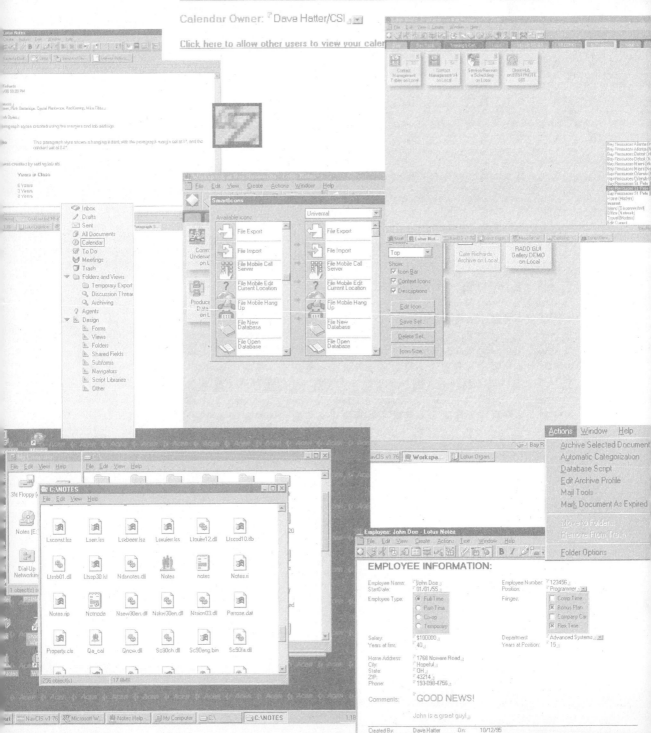

Chapter 10

Creating New Databases

Throughout this book, you read about the databases that others have created—the Mail database, the Address Book, and so on. In this chapter, you learn how to create your own customized databases, which you can use to store and share almost any kind of data you can imagine.

Users of many skill levels can design and build Notes databases. Even beginners with very little computer knowledge and even less Notes experience can learn to build simple-but-useful databases for many purposes, because Notes comes with many helpful templates. Experienced users, especially programmers, find in Notes a wealth of powerful features that enable such users to showcase their programming prowess and generally dazzle others with their database skills. Whatever your skill level, however, building databases in Notes is fun and useful.

Throughout this chapter, you will learn about the various features for designing and building databases. As you build databases, you might not perform these actions in exactly this order, although creating the database obviously comes first! You might customize an existing form and then customize a view, only then deciding to create a new form. As you read through this chapter, you learn how to perform these steps, which you can perform in the order best suited to your own needs.

Some of the main topics in this chapter are

- Create a database from a template

- Use the design menu/navigator to create and edit forms, views, subforms, navigators, and agents

- Control security to your database

- Create a database icon

- Create custom navigators

II

Designing Applications

> **Note**
>
> Lotus Notes comes in several different flavors designed for varying levels of users. Some Notes clients do not have the capabilities to create and modify Notes databases. If the menu commands described in this chapter are not available, contact your system administrator and ask how you can upgrade your version of Notes to one with design capabilities.

Using Templates

Notes comes with a collection of templates—ready–made databases—that you can use as a starting point for creating your own databases. A template is a special type of Notes database from which other databases are modeled. You use templates to serve as a guideline when you start creating new databases.

The first step in creating a database is deciding which template should serve as the starting point for your new database. In many cases, you might find that one of the supplied templates meets your needs exactly and you might need to do little more than create the database with that template. If none of the templates matches your needs exactly, a certain template still might contain many of the forms and views you require and therefore can serve as a starting point for creating your new database.

Before you begin to create a new database, think about how you or others are likely to use this database. Are you creating a database to serve as a central storage location for some type of document? Is the database to serve as a discussion group for sharing ideas? Consider the information you want to store in the database and give some thought also to the various ways you want the data displayed and printed.

After you have a clear picture of the purpose of your database, you might be pleasantly surprised to discover that Lotus has anticipated your needs and that one of the templates is exactly what you need to build your database. In the following sections, you learn how to create a database by using a template. Later in this chapter, you learn how to customize databases to match your precise needs and how to create new databases from scratch.

Reviewing the Notes Templates

Notes comes with more than a dozen templates. A few in particular are extremely useful and can be used to create your own databases with little or no customization on your part. If you design new databases often, you will find that you keep coming back to these few templates over and over as starting points. Other templates are useful only to system administrators or for use in system databases such as mailboxes. Table 10.1 lists and summarizes several of the Notes templates.

 ▶▶ See "Database Templates," p. 1123

Table 10.1 Standard Templates Available with Notes	
Template Name	**Description**
Approval Cycle	Used to create sets of databases which will track and follow issues through a cycle of approvals.
Discussion	Enables you to create a Notes discussion database. Discussion databases are informal databases where users can ask questions or post comments that others will find useful. They are a means of sharing and storing knowledge.
Document Library	Used for storing and describing documents. Also allows you to set up document approval cycles. Can be modified for describing a collection of almost anything.

Template Name	Description
Microsoft Office Library	The same as the Document Library template except you can store copies of documents created with any of the Microsoft Office applications—using OLE2.
Personal Address Books	Used to create multiple Personal Address Books. The template is the same one used for your Personal Address Book.
Personal Journal	Enables you to keep a diary or journal and to categorize entries into folders.
Room Reservations	Used to manage and track room reservations. It can be easily modified to track reservations for almost anything.

Creating a Database from a Template

Once you decide on a template, follow these steps to create your database:

1. Select the workpage on which you want to create the database.

2. Select File, Database, New; or press Ctrl+N. Notes displays the New Database dialog box shown in Figure 10.1.

Fig. 10.1   The New Database dialog box.

The top half lets you set the database's location, name, and other options. The bottom half of the dialog box contains a list of available templates.

3. In the Server list, select the server on which you want your database to reside.

> ### Note
>
> When you choose to create a database on Local, you are telling Notes to place the database in your Notes Data directory located on your personal computer. It's a good idea to start your databases locally and transfer them to the server when you are ready to test and pilot the database.
>
> In addition, sometimes Notes will not permit you to create a database on a specific server. That's because the Notes administrator has control over who is and is not permitted to place databases on a Notes Server. If Notes forbids you to create a database on a server, contact your system administrator for more information.

4. In the Title box, enter a descriptive title for the database—up to 32 characters long—such as Legal Contract Library or Equipment Requests.

> **Tip**
>
> This title is an easy way to quickly identify this particular Notes database from your workspace and appears in the title bar at the top of the screen when it is opened. It is also the title that appears in the database list when a user selects File Database Open. Your database will be much easier for users to find if the title is descriptive and complete.
>
> Notes does not require unique database titles, but you should avoid duplicate titles to reduce confusion among users.

5. In the File Name box, enter the name of the database file. The name should have an NSF extension, such as CONTRACT.NSF or REQUESTS.NSF. (Notes automatically adds the extension if you leave it out.) Notes does support extended filenames (for Windows 95); and, by default, the database filename is the same as the title you just typed.

6. To encrypt a local database, choose Encryption, select Locally encrypt this database using, and then choose an encryption type (see Figure 10.2).

> **Note**
>
> If you encrypt a local database, anyone who uses your computer must enter your password to access the encrypted database. This is especially useful if you have a laptop computer and are worried about someone taking your computer and possibly accessing sensitive information in your Notes database.
>
> Desktop security is also useful in an office environment because it helps ensure the confidentiality of the data stored on your personal machine.

 ▶▶ See "Understanding Database Security," p. 879

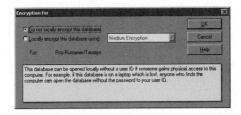

Fig. 10.2   Locally encrypt a database using the Encryption For dialog box.

7. To set a size limit for your database, select Size Limit. The default size limit of 1G is probably enough for most Notes databases, but the limit can be increased to as much as 4G.

8. To create a full text index for the database, click <u>C</u>reate Full Text Index For Searching.

◀◀ See "Full Text Searching in Databases," p. 308

9. From the template list, select the template you want to use to create your database. When specifying a template, keep the following notes in mind:

- If you select Blank from the template list, Notes creates an empty database with no forms or views. Use this to create a database from scratch.

- The template list contains a list of templates available locally on your computer. To select a template located on a server, select Template Se<u>r</u>ver and choose the server on which the template is located. The template list will update to list the templates available on the server you selected.

- Templates may or may not be installed on your personal machine, depending on how the Notes installation was performed. If you do not have templates available on your machine, make sure you look for them on your Template Server.

- If you click Show Advanced Te<u>m</u>plates, the template list will include system templates such as the Notes Log and Mail Router Mailbox, as well as any other templates marked as advanced templates. In most cases, you will not need to create databases with these templates. If you have upgraded your machine from Notes 3.x to 4.0, other, older templates may also appear in this list. The templates with [R4] in their titles are specifically geared to take advantage of Notes 4.0 features.

> **Tip**
>
> For more information about a particular Notes template, click the About button from the New Database dialog box.

10. By default, Notes checks the <u>I</u>nherit Future Design Changes check box. Deselect this option if you do not want design changes to be inherited. Keep these issues in mind:

- When this box is checked, the design of your database is automatically synchronized with the design of the template. This is useful if your database will be based exactly on the design template. If you have several databases based on a single template—for example, you have several document library databases—you can change the single underlying template and those changes will propagate out to all databases based on that template. If you are using the template only as a starting point for your database, you should deselect this checkbox.

- If you click Inherit Future Design Changes and later make design changes to your database, you might be surprised to find that your changes were overwritten by the design in the template.

- When a database inherits design changes from a template, it inherits the design from the template on the workstation or server on which the database resides. This means that if you create a database using a template on your workstation and later move the database to a server, you should make sure that the template on the server matches the one on your workstation. Otherwise, the design of your database could be changed without your knowing it—with potentially disastrous results.

11. Click the OK button to create your database. Notes will think for a few moments, create a new file in your Data directory, add a database icon onto your workspace, and open the new database automatically for you.

12. Notes displays an About document, which briefly describes the database. Close the About document by pressing Esc or by double-clicking with the right mouse button anywhere within the document.

After you complete these steps, you see your newly created database, which doesn't contain any documents yet. If the template exactly matched your needs, you are ready to begin entering documents and using your database.

More often than not, however, you must customize the database for it to meet all of your needs. Throughout the rest of this book, you will learn all you need to know to customize your database designs.

Selecting a Location for Your Database

As you create a database, you must select a server from the New Database dialog box's Server list and then enter a filename for the database. Together, these two pieces of information determine where the database resides. The location you select for your database will depend on who accesses your database and what directories are on your server.

Note that you should not use network drives to share databases with other people. If multiple people access a database without going through a Notes server, the database could become corrupted.

In the Server list box, you have the following options:

- **Local**—You can select the first entry in the Server list—Local—and the database will be created on your PC's hard drive. Because it is local to your PC, users cannot access the database unless they are using your computer.

- **Server**—You can select a server name from the Server list and the database will be created on the selected Notes server. Since it is on the server, it will be available to everyone on your Notes network, assuming they are given access in the database Access Control List.

Once you have selected a server, enter a filename in the File Name box. You have three options for the filename:

- You can enter a filename such as PROBLEMS.NSF. The database will be put into the default data directory for the selected server. For example, if the data directory is C:\NOTES\DATA, the full path and filename will be C:\NOTES\DATA\PROBLEMS.NSF.

- You can enter a directory and filename such as DATABASE\PROBLEMS.NSF. The database will then be put into C:\NOTES\DATA\DATABASE\PROBLEMS.NSF, if C:\NOTES\DATA is the data directory.

- If you selected Local as your server, you can enter a full path and filename for your database, such as D:\DATABASE\PROBLEMS.NSF. This is useful if you want to put your database on another disk drive or a network drive.

Adding and Changing Design Elements in the Database

Now that you have created your database, you are ready to customize its design to fit your needs. You do this by adding, deleting, or changing its design elements. Notes databases have six main design elements that you will use:

- Forms define the data that will be entered into a document. They consist of static text, fields, and actions. The forms are the meat of an application. They are the primary user interface for entering data into your database and contain many of the actions that users invoke while using the application.

- Views are a list of documents that includes specific information about each document. Views are indexes to the information in your databases. A single database usually has many views that list different subsets of documents or different information, or sort the documents in different orders. A well-designed set of views makes information in your databases easy to find and more useful.

- Subforms are reusable groups of fields and other form design elements. They are somewhat of a form within a form. Subforms can include the same elements that are placed on forms. You should use them if you have a part of a form that is common to several forms. By using them, you do not have to add the design elements individually to each form; you can just insert the subform. Also, if you need to make changes to the subform, you can make your change once—in the subform— and it will propagate to all forms using the subforms.

- Navigators are graphical interfaces to your databases. They can contain icons, buttons, bitmaps, hotspots, and static text. Clicking an element on a navigator can execute Simple Actions (such as opening a view or another navigator), @function formulas, or LotusScript programs. Navigators make your applications more intuitive and easier for your users.

- Script Libraries allow Notes developers to build reusable LotusScript modules, which can be invoked from multiple places within a Notes application. It is similar to the SubForm feature in Notes Release 4.0, which allowed developers to build reusable Notes forms.

■ Agents are macros written in either LotusScript or @functions. You can run them at predetermined intervals from a menu selection or event. Agents can be either private (created by a user and used only by that user) or shared (created by the database designer and used by all users). Some good uses for agents include archiving a set of documents, categorizing documents into folders, or updating groups of documents.

You will access these design elements through the navigation pane and the <u>C</u>reate menu.

Accessing Existing Elements with the Folders Navigator

The navigation pane, shown in Figure 10.3, enables you to access all existing design elements of your database with just a few clicks. When you are designing a database, the first thing you should do is display the folders navigator if it is not already shown. If another navigator is currently selected, select <u>V</u>iew, Show, <u>F</u>olders.

Fig. 10.3   Access existing design elements of a database with the folders in the navigation pane.

The following headings are under the Design category in the navigation pane:

■ Forms

■ Views

■ Folders

■ Shared Fields

■ Subforms

■ Navigators

■ Script Libraries

■ Other

Clicking any of these displays a list of the corresponding existing elements in your database where the current view is normally displayed. For example, selecting Forms lists all of the forms in your database (see Figure 10.4).

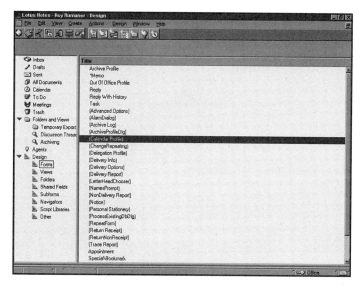

Fig. 10.4 Selecting Forms displays all existing forms.

If you click a form name, you are put into design mode for the selected form (see Figure 10.5). Likewise, if you click views, folders, or any other heading, you will get a list of views, folders, and so on.

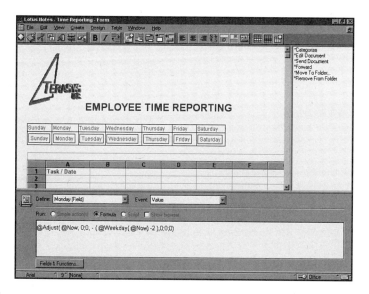

Fig. 10.5 The form design screen.

Creating New Elements with the Create Menu

The folders navigator allows you to edit existing elements; but suppose you want to create a new form, view, and so on? You use the Create menu (see Figure 10.6).

Fig. 10.6   Create new elements using the Create menu.

Table 10.2 lists each design element and its corresponding item on the Create menu.

Table 10.2   Creating Elements with the Create Menu

Element	Create Menu Selection
Agent	Create, Agent
Folder	Create, Folder
View	Create, View
Form	Create, Design, Form
Shared Field	Create, Design, Shared Field
Subform	Create, Design, Subform
Navigator	Create, Design, Navigator
Script Library	Create, Design, Script Library

You will learn more about each element listed previously and how to create them in the following sections.

Deleting Design Elements

You can also easily delete design elements from your Notes database. First, choose the type of element you want to remove from the navigation pane on the left side of the screen.

For example, you can select Forms to get a list of forms saved within the database. Then choose the actual element (in this case, form) you want to erase from the list on the right by selecting it with your mouse. Next, press the Delete button from your keyboard; choose Edit, Clear from the menu bar; or use the Edit Clear SmartIcon.

Understanding Database Access

Now that you have created a database, you need to decide who should access it. Once you put your database on a server, it is out there for everyone on your Notes network to see. However, you most likely want only certain people to access your database. Even if you want everyone to see the data in your database, you will want to restrict certain functions from users. For example, you probably want only one person, or a group of people, to be able to change the design of your database (chances are, you will be part of the group of people). You will probably want only certain people to edit existing documents, while others will only enter new documents, and still others will only be able to read documents. If you did not restrict these functions to specific people or groups, your data and database design would be in jeopardy because anyone could make changes to your database. This is why controlling access to your database is vitally important.

The key to controlling access is your database's Access Control List (ACL). Within your ACL, you define what people or groups of people have access to your database and what functions they can perform. Additionally, the ACL defines what servers can access your database and what they can replicate.

Note

By default, the database Access Control List (ACL) affects only databases stored on a server. If the property Enforce Consistent ACL Across Replicas is selected, the ACL is enforced locally. The local enforcement of the ACL is not a security measure; it can be bypassed.

To provide this security, choose File, Database, Access Control from the menu bar. Click the Advanced tab that appears and select the Enforce a consistent Access Control List across all replicas of this database option.

To gain a better understanding of how the Access Control List affects security, we should step back and take a quick look at the entire Notes security framework.

Notes has four layers of security:

- **Server-level security**—Before users can access a database on a server, they must have access to the server. Server access is controlled by the server administrator through the use of certificates attached to users' ID files and server access lists. This is the first and most general layer of security.

- **Database-level security**—Database security for any database on a server is handled by the database Access Control List. The ACL lists users and servers and assigns them rights to the database. Access levels range from Manager, who has total access to the database, to No Access. The database manager creates and controls the ACL. An additional database-level security feature is Local Encryption, which causes local databases to be encrypted, so that only the user who set Local Encryption can access them.

■ **Document-level security**—Document security consists of the document's Read Access list. The Read Access list is defined by the form's Read Access list, any Reader Names fields in the document, and the Read Access list in the Document Properties dialog box. The Read Access list refines the ACL for that document, meaning that if someone has Reader access or above in the ACL but is not listed in any Read Access list, he or she cannot read the document. If a person is not a reader in the ACL, he or she cannot read the document even if he or she is listed in the document's Read Access list.

■ **Field-level security**—Certain fields on a form can be encrypted using encryption keys, so that only users with the correct key can read those fields. The database designer specifies which fields are encryptable; and when a key is associated to the document, all encryptable fields are encrypted with the key.

One good way to think of the various levels of Notes security is as a funnel. At the top level, the administrator controls who has access to a particular server. Then the next level is access to a particular database. Database ACLs can work only within the constraints of what security the administrator has set. All the security options work like a funnel, where you can control access to a particular level of security based only on what the previous level allows you to do.

Within this framework, the ACL is the highest level of security that a database designer can use to control access to a database. Therefore, it is very important that you give serious thought to who will access your database and set up the ACL correctly.

Assigning Access Levels

When planning your Access Control List, you will decide who gets what level of access. There are seven levels you can assign:

■ Manager

■ Designer

■ Editor

■ Author

■ Reader

■ Depositor

■ No Access

In the Access Control List, you list users and servers who need access to your database. In the ACL, users and servers are listed together and are given one of the same seven access levels listed above. The access levels have a slightly different, but similar, connotation, depending on if they are given to a person or a server. For a person, the access levels define what actions the user can perform on the database. For servers, access levels define what information the servers can replicate. The access levels for users and servers are outlined in Tables 10.3 and 10.4.

Table 10.3 Access Levels for People

Access Level	Description
Manager	Users with Manager access can modify the ACL, modify replication settings, set a database for local encryption, and delete the database. A Manager also can perform tasks of lower access levels—Designer, Editor, Author, Reader, and Depositor. Every database should have at least one Manager (usually you have two or more so there is a backup) so that someone is always around to make necessary changes to a database.
Designer	Users with Designer access can change any design elements of a database, modify replication formulas, and index a database for full text searching. Designers also can perform the tasks of lower access levels—Editor, Author, Reader, and Depositor. Normally the person who designed the database has Designer access at the very least unless design responsibility was given to another person.
Editor	Users with Editor access can create documents and edit all documents in the database. Editors also can perform the tasks of lower access levels. Normally you should limit Editors to those who must edit all documents; too many Editors increases the risk of replication or save conflicts.
Author	Users with Author access can create documents and edit documents they created, if there is an Author Names field in the document with the author's name in it. Authors also can perform the tasks of lower access levels. Author access is the most common level given to users who need to create documents.
Reader	Users with Reader access can read documents in the database. Give Reader access to users who need to read the database but don't need to create new documents or edit existing documents. You want to set the default ACL level for this database to be Reader or better if you are performing an @DbLookup command on the information stored within this database.
Depositor	Users with Depositor access can create new documents, but they cannot see any documents in the database. To a Depositor, the database is like a sealed box that they can only put things into but not take anything out.
No Access	Users with No Access cannot compose or read documents. They cannot even open the database or add its icon to their desktop. Often you will set a database's default access to No Access.

Replication Conflicts

Replication conflicts occur when a document is edited in multiple replicas between replication. When a database replicates, the replicator does not know how to resolve changes to both documents, so it creates a conflict document as a response to the other. The main document is the one which has been edited more recently or which has been saved more times.

Tip

It is useful to create a group in your Public Name & Address Book containing the names of all administrators and provide that group's Manager with access to all databases.

Likewise, you can create a group containing all developers and provide that group's Designer with access to all databases. Using a group, it is easy to control and add people to a database ACL because they are stored in the shared Name & Address Book.

II

Designing Applications

Table 10.4   Access Levels for Servers

Access Level	Description
Manager	A server with Manager access can send ACL changes to replica databases as well as changes allowed by lower access levels. If you want to centrally administer ACL changes from a single server, you should give only that server Manager access to the database and have it replicate with all replica databases.
Designer	A server with Designer access can send changes to design elements and replication formulas to replica databases as well as changes allowed by lower access levels. You can centralize design changes by giving only one server Designer access and having it replicate with all replicas. Keep in mind that if servers do not have at least Designer access to all replicas and the design is changed, it will not be changed in all replicas.
Editor	A server with Editor access can send new documents and changes to existing documents to replica databases. Deletions will be sent only if the Delete Documents box is checked in the Access Control dialog box.
Author	A server with Author access can send new documents to replica databases. It will send only updates to existing documents if the documents have an Author Names field containing the server name, which is usually not the case. If you want updates to replicate, you should use Editor access.
Reader	A server with Reader access cannot send changes to replica databases. However, it can receive documents from the replica on another server if the other server has at least Author access. For example, if server X has Editor access and server Y has Reader access, new documents and changes on server X will replicate to server Y but no changes on server Y will replicate to server X. Be aware that for a server to receive changes from a replica, the server must have at least Reader access (a server cannot receive changes that it cannot read).
Depositor	A server with Depositor access can send new documents to replica databases. This is an unusual access level to give to servers; if you want to send only new documents, you should give the database Author access.
No Access	A server with No Access cannot send or receive anything from replica databases, regardless of the access level assigned to the other server.

Names, Servers, and Groups in the ACL

Now that we have looked at the access levels you can assign in the Access Control List, we should look at how people and servers are listed in the ACL. Each entry in the ACL is one of the following:

■ User Name

■ Server Name

■ Group Name

■ Databases Replica ID

User names in the ACL should be entered exactly as they appear in the user's ID file. If your organization uses hierarchical names, you should enter the fully distinguished hierarchical name; for example, Jane Doe/Marketing/Standard. If the server your database is on and the person you are adding are in the same organization, you can enter just the common name in the ACL, but the fully distinguished name is more secure, since two people cannot have the same fully distinguished name.

Server names are entered in much the same way as user names. You should use the server's fully distinguished name—for example, Server1/Marketing/Standard. But you can use the common name if the servers are in the same organization.

Note

Notes allows you to use the asterisk wildcard (*) to replace any component of a hierarchical name below the organization. Using wildcards, one ACL entry can grant access to everyone within a single organization or organizational unit. For example, the entry */Terasys gives access to any-one in the organization Terasys (including Greg Sutton/Terasys or Erik Johnson/Graphics/Terasys). The entry */Graphics/Terasys applies to anyone with an organizational unit Graphics and an organization Terasys (including Erik Johnson/Graphics/Terasys but not Dave Haas/Terasys).

Group names in the ACL can be any group of people or servers that is defined in the Public Name & Address Book. Using group names in your ACLs has several advantages over individual names, including the following:

- One group representing many users keeps the number of entries in the ACL low. This makes keeping track of the ACL much easier.

- If a group of people needs its access changed, you only need to change the access for a single group rather than several individual users.

- A single group can be in the ACL in several databases. Simplify administration by centralizing changes within the Public Name & Address Book.

- Using groups, you can list a descriptive name that makes up a set of people, so you don't have to worry about typing in each individual entry, just the group name.

Whenever a background agent acts on a database (either by changing documents or reading documents via an @DbLookup or @DbColumn), the database replica ID should be listed in the ACL with the appropriate access level. The database replica ID is a unique number that Notes assigns to every database created. You can find a database replica ID by clicking the database and selecting File, Database, Properties.

Standard ACL Entries

There are four standard entries that should be in the ACL for every database: Default, LocalDomainServers, OtherDomainServers, and database creator (the user name of the individual who creates the database). They are created by default in every new database. When you plan the ACL for your database, you should first assign access levels to these four entries. You do not have to include all four of the standard ACL entries, but using them makes your ACLs across databases uniform, making the ACL easier to administer and more secure. The following list describes each entry:

- The Default entry defines the access level for anyone who is not listed anywhere else in the ACL. It is recommended that Default be either No Access, Reader, or

Author. Your selection depends on the purpose and content of the database. A database with confidential information, such as a human resources database, has a Default of No Access. One with general enterprise-wide information, such as a company policy database, has a Default of Reader. One in which everyone composes documents, such as a discussion database, has a Default of Author.

■ LocalDomainServers is a group that is in every domain's Name & Address Book that contains the names of all the servers in your domain. Normally you give this group Manager access, so that replicas of the database on all servers can replicate the entire database, including changes to the ACL. There are two cases in which you do not give this group Manager access:

  • When you want to control ACL or design changes from a central server. In this case, you will give the group a lower access level (probably Editor) and the central server a Manager access.

  • When you do not want your database replicated to all servers in your domain. In this case, you will give the group No Access.

■ OtherDomainServers is also a group in every domain's Name & Address Book. It contains the names of servers in other domains within your organization with which you regularly replicate. This group typically has Designer access if the database is replicated to other domains (to keep the designs in sync among replicas). If the database is not replicated to other domains, the group has No Access.

■ The database creator is put in the ACL with Manager access. You do not have to keep this person in the ACL, but Notes does require that at least one person be given Manager access to the database. If there is no Manager, it is possible that everyone could be locked out of a database with nobody able to add people to the ACL.

Caution

Notes will allow you to give the Default group any access level, all the way up to Manager. But you should never set it higher than Author for a database in production; this poses a serious security threat. Even Author access should be used sparingly. In fact, many organizations impose a standard that Default is given only Reader or No Access.

If you need to give a large group a high access level, you are better off leaving Default no higher than Reader; create a group in the Public Name & Address Book that you can grant a higher access level.

Note

If you replicate with servers in other domains outside your organization, those servers are usually listed in the ExternalServers group in the Name & Address Book. OtherDomainServers should only refer to servers in other domains within your organization.

Beyond these standard entries in the ACL, you will add additional entries for users, servers, and groups of users or servers. These additional entries will affect the bulk of the database users.

Creating the ACL

In the previous sections, you learned about the access levels and entries that make up the Access Control List. Now it is time to put that knowledge to work and actually create an ACL.

The first step you take in creating the ACL is to plan who needs access to your database. As part of this process, you collect all the names of your users and organize them into any necessary groups. If you use any groups, now is the time to either create the groups yourself or ask the administrator to create them for you.

The groups you create should have descriptive names. You can describe either the tasks of the group (e.g., PO Approvers) or the members of the group (e.g., Account Managers). A descriptive name tells you who belongs in a certain group when ACL changes are made, possibly months or years down the road.

If you have an administrator create the groups for you, make sure he or she includes you as a group owner. As an owner, you can add or remove people from the groups you use. Therefore, if an administrator is not available, you can make access changes immediately.

Table 10.5 lists a sample ACL. It contains the standard server groups (LocalDomainServers and OtherDomainServers), two individual names, two groups of users, one name using wildcards, and the Default entry.

Table 10.5   Sample ACL Entries

Entry	Access Level
LocalDomainServers	Manager
OtherDomainServers	No Access
Roy Rumaner/NotesAdmin/Terasys	Manager
Bill Harris/Development/Terasys	Manager
Document Editors	Editor
Account Managers	Author
*/Executives/Terasys	Reader
Default	No Access

Once you have defined who needs access to the database, you are ready to create the ACL. You create the ACL using the Access Control List dialog box. To display the dialog box, follow these steps:

1. Click the database icon for which you want to set up an ACL and select File, Database, Access Control. Or right-click the database and select Access Control (see Figure 10.7).

Designing Applications

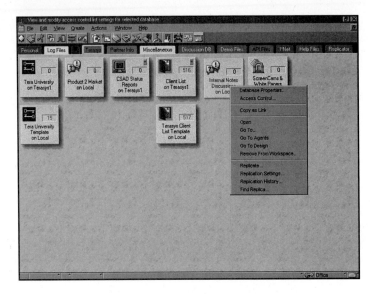

Fig. 10.7 Right-click a database to view its pull-down menu.

2. Notes prompts you for your password if you have not already entered it and then displays the Access Control List dialog box (see Figure 10.8).

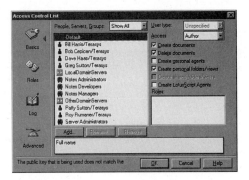

Fig. 10.8 The Access Control List dialog box.

People, Servers, Groups lists all the entries in the ACL. You can add, delete, or update entries in the list. Use the following procedure to add names to the list:

1. Click the Add button (located below the list of people, servers, and groups). Notes displays the Add User dialog box (see Figure 10.9).

Fig. 10.9 Enter names into the Add User dialog box.

2. Enter a single name in the Person, server, or group box. Or click the Person button in the Names dialog box, which is used for looking up names in a Name & Address Book (see Figure 10.10). This dialog box is very similar to the one you use to address NotesMail. You can select names from the list on the left and click Add to add them to the list on the right. In addition, you can also select groups of individuals from the Name & Address Book.

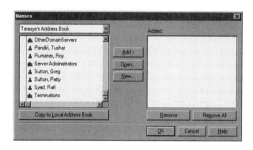

Fig. 10.10 Add names from an Address Book in the Names dialog box.

3. When you have added all of the names, click OK. The names will now show up in the People, Servers, Groups list.

To rename an item in the list, follow these steps:

1. Select the name you want to rename and click Rename. The Rename User dialog box appears (see Figure 10.11).

Fig. 10.11 The Rename User dialog box.

2. From this point on, the procedure is the same as for adding new names, except that the name you enter will replace the one you selected. Notes tries to reconcile a name in the ACL with one in your Name & Address Book and looks for spelling and phonetic matches.

To delete a name from the list, select the name you want to delete and click Remove.

Once you have entered the correct names, you can assign access levels to those names using the following procedure:

1. Select a name from the list of People, Servers, Groups listbox.

2. If you want, select a user type from the User type pull-down list (see Figure 10.12).

3. Select the appropriate access level from the Access pull-down list (see Figure 10.13).

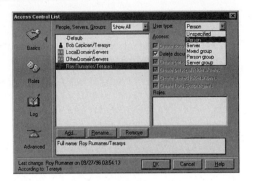

Fig. 10.12 Selecting a user type.

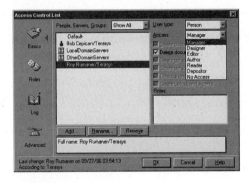

Fig. 10.13 Selecting an access level.

4. Below the Access list are six checkboxes that you should check to further refine a user's actions. The actions available for selection depend on the access level you assigned the user. For example, the Create Documents box is unavailable for a user with Reader access because a reader, by definition, cannot create documents. Any unavailable items are grayed out.

5. Finally, you can select any roles assigned to this user, if any are defined, in the Roles list box.

You can also set other ACL-related options by clicking the icons on the left side of the Access Control List dialog box. Figure 10.14 shows the advanced options you can set.

With these advanced options, you can control whether this database's ACL can be updated by an agent automatically and enforce the ACL for databases on local workstations:

- **Basics**—This option is used to set up names and access levels.

- **Roles**—This option allows you to set up roles for the database. Roles let you define more specific security entries for a database. Roles are used in the lower levels of security, like Readers fields and Authors fields.

- **Log**—This option displays a history of changes to the ACL.

- **Advanced**—This option allows you to select advanced options, such as selecting the Administration Server or Enforce a consistent Access Control List across all replicas of this database.

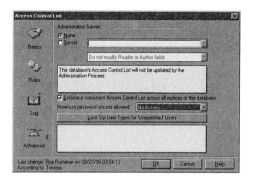

Fig. 10.14   Setting other ACL-related options.

Customizing Database Icons

An icon (a tiny picture that Notes displays on your workspace to help you spot the database at a glance) is associated with each database. Most database templates have a default icon associated with them that the Lotus designers considered appropriate for that type of database. Sometimes the icons are clever, sometimes they are not. Figure 10.15 shows the icon that Notes assigns to a database created from the Document Library template as described earlier in this chapter.

Fig. 10.15   The Document Library icon.

> ### Tip
>
> You should create at least a simple icon for every database to help users distinguish databases on the desktop.
>
> Having common icons for similar databases can cue the user to the type or purpose of the database.

Using the Icon Editor

You can modify the icon as you want or even create new icons. To edit or create a new icon for your database, double-click it from your Notes workspace. Once opened, click Design in the navigation pane on the left hand side of the screen and then select Other. Notes displays several unique aspects of the database you can change in the view pane on the right side of the screen. Double-clicking Icon opens up the Design Icon dialog box, the built-in icon editor (see Figure 10.16).

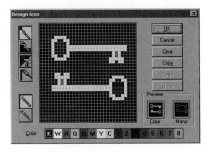

Fig. 10.16   The Design Icon dialog box.

If you want to showcase your originality and creativity, you can change the current icon by choosing a Color from the colored squares at the bottom of the dialog box and clicking points in the large icon image. You can experiment with the various tools on the left side of the Design Icon dialog box; the tools enable you to fill large areas of the icon with certain colors and perform other special editing.

You can draw an entirely new icon by first clicking the Clear button, which erases the current icon and gives you a clean drawing area. When you are finished making changes, click the OK button to save your changes.

Copying and Pasting Icons from Another Source

Even if you are not artistic, you still can add more interesting icons to your databases. If you know of another database that has an interesting icon, for example, you can "borrow" that icon for your database. To copy another database's icon, follow these steps:

1. Open the database that has the icon you want to use.

2. Click Other under Design on the folders navigator and select Icon. The Design Icon dialog box appears.

3. Click the Copy button. Notes copies the icon to your computer's Clipboard.

4. Click Cancel to close the dialog box, ensuring that you have not made any changes to this icon, and then press Esc to close the database.

5. Open the database for which you want to use the icon.

6. Again, click Other under Design on the folders navigator and select Icon to access the Design Icon dialog box.

7. Click the Paste button. The icon you copied from the other database appears in the icon editor area of the dialog box.

8. Click OK to close the dialog box. Your new icon is in place.

You can use icons from other sources also. If you have access to Windows and OS/2 icons and can copy them to the Clipboard, you can paste them into the icon editor of the Design Icon dialog box. You might also have access to an icon library database that contains all kinds of icons that others have created, and you can use them for your databases.

Remember that when an icon is changed for a database on a server, people won't see the new icon until the next time they access that database on their PC.

Creating Standard Help Documents

Every database has two standard help documents, an About document and a Using document. These standard help documents will help your users by telling them the purpose of your database and how to use it. Also, they eliminate some of the questions asked of you. You should therefore take some care in creating these documents before deploying your database.

The user can access these documents from the Help menu. If, for example, the user is reading the Company Procedures database, the Help menu will show two items, About Company Procedures and Using Company Procedures.

Creating an About Document

A database's About document tells people about the database; that is, what kind of information the database contains, who should use the database, and how to get the most benefit from that particular database. If you create a database for your private use, you probably will not create an About document. However, if your database will be used by others who might not be familiar with it, you should always create an About document that includes a brief description of the database, who should use it, and the names of the database managers.

The About Document can also display default information, your company logo, or perform automated events when a database is opened, propagating information to all database users in a simple way.

To create or modify an About document, open the database. Click Design in the navigation pane, and then select Other. Now select the About Database Document from the view pane on the right side of the screen.

Notes displays the current About document, or a blank screen if no About document exists, and enters an edit mode very similar to the one used to edit forms (see Figure 10.17). You can type new text, delete existing text, or perform almost any editing function on your About document.

After you complete your About document, close the window. When Notes asks if you want to save your changes, select Yes.

Designing Applications

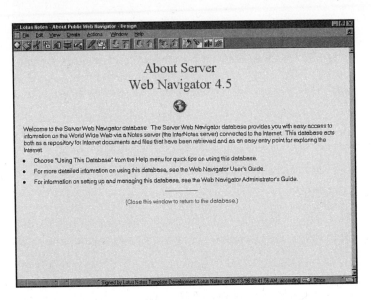

Fig. 10.17 Sample About document for the Company Procedures database.

> **Tip**
>
> You should list any important database contacts, such as the database owner or manager, in the About document. That way, the users will know who to contact if they have any problems.

Creating a Using Document

A Using document is very similar to an About document except it describes how to use the database. It usually describes the forms and views in the database and how they function.

> **Tip**
>
> The Using document is also useful if you use doclinks. Many designers create a form with a name such as Help Document, which they use to compose many documents, each describing some facet of working with the database. These designers then insert doclinks into the Using document that reference these other documents. This technique creates a very powerful help system, but complicates the database views because each view must include a specific selection formula so that the Using documents don't appear in any of the views. That selection formula might appear as follows:
>
> ```
> SELECT Form != "Help Document"
> ```

Figure 10.18 shows how a portion of the database Using document might appear.

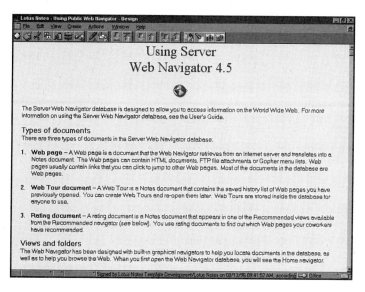

The Server Web Navigator database is designed to allow you to access information on the World Wide Web. For more information on using the Server Web Navigator database, see the User's Guide.

Fig. 10.18 Sample Using document.

Creating Graphical Navigators

Once you have created forms and views for your database, you will want to build a user interface that helps users maneuver around it. Graphical navigators are that interface. Navigators provide a graphical way for users to do such things as switch views, open documents, file documents into folders, and just about any other action you can program in Notes.

Navigators are made up of objects (text, pictures, or shapes) that cause actions to occur when they are clicked. One common use for navigators is a graphical table of contents. The Notes Help Database uses this style of navigator (see Figure 10.19).

You have already worked with at least one navigator, the default navigator. Each database automatically has a navigator that splits up your screen into two different panes, which allows easier access to your Notes information.

Even though the navigator provides a good interface to a database, you undoubtedly are going to want to create your own specialized navigators.

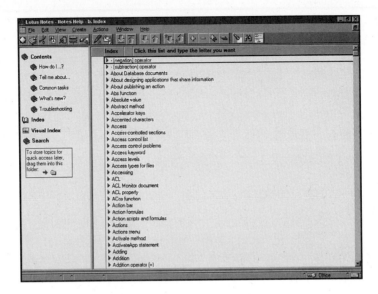

Fig. 10.19   A table of contents navigator from the Notes Help Database.

Working with Navigator Objects

Navigators are a collection of navigator objects that are graphical shapes and images that can have actions assigned to them. To work with these objects, choose Create, Design, Navigator from the Notes menu or use the Create Navigator SmartIcon. All of these objects can be added to a Navigator by using the Create menu.

There are six types of navigator objects:

- **Graphic Backgrounds**—A graphic background is a bitmap that is pasted into the navigator. Each navigator has only one background, and you cannot attach actions to it. In fact, a graphic background is the only element that cannot perform an action. You can think of a graphics background as wallpaper behind the information that appears on the screen.

> **Note**
>
> Graphical backgrounds cannot be resized once they are pasted into a Navigator.
>
> Use a graphics design program such as *PC Paintbrush Pro* to size your graphic. This will allow you to size the graphic and paste it into the Navigator.

- **Graphic Buttons**—Graphic buttons are small images that can be pasted into a navigator. They can appear like icons on-screen and perform specific actions when clicked.

- **Graphical Shapes**—Similar to buttons, graphical shapes can be rectangles, polygons, polylines, or ellipses. They are drawn using Notes drawing tools and can be any shape you choose. Like graphic buttons, you can assign Notes tasks to be performed when they are clicked.

- **Hotspots**—Hotspot are extremely similar to graphical shapes except they are displayed on-screen in a more discreet manner. For example, a hotspot might be a green pop-up box that appears around text. When clicked, additional information might appear. They are transparent so that they don't take up a lot of room on-screen.

- **Textboxes**—Textboxes are simply blocks of text that can be placed on the navigator that also can have actions associated with them.

- **Command Buttons**—Command buttons are normal buttons with a text caption on their face. Command buttons are useful for initiating any actions that do not have graphical depictions.

Tip

Navigator buttons cannot be used with Domino at this time.

Navigator objects can be created or drawn within the navigator design space using the Create menu. Table 10.6 shows the procedure to create each type of object.

Table 10.6   Creating Navigator Objects

Object	Procedure
Graphic Background	Create a picture in any drawing program, copy the picture to the Clipboard, and select Create, Graphic Background. The graphic will be pasted into the navigator. You can also set the background color of the Navigator by editing its properties (choose Design, Navigator Properties).
Graphic Button	Create a picture in any drawing program, copy the picture to the Clipboard, and select Create, Graphic Button.
Graphical Shapes	From the Create menu, select the type of shape you want to draw. Then use the mouse to draw the shape.
Hotspots	Select Create, then either Hotspot Rectangle or Hotspot Polygon. After drawing the hotspot, double-click it to display its Properties InfoBox. Select the HiLite tab. In this box, you can specify if the hotspot should highlight when touched or clicked.
Textbox	Select Create, Text and draw a box using the mouse. After you draw the box, the Text Box Properties InfoBox opens. Enter the text you want to display in the Caption box and close the Properties InfoBox.
Command Button	Select Create, Button and draw the button with the mouse. The Button Properties InfoBox will appear. Enter the text for the face of the button in the Caption box and close the Properties InfoBox.

Tip

Use the Lotus Color Palette that is available on the CD accompanying this book or the Lotus Web Page at **www.lotus.com**.

Working with Navigator Actions

> **Tip**
>
> To make sure that your Navigator is fully displayed, use the Auto Adjust option and place a small (1 space) hidden object just to the right edge of the completed Navigator.
>
> You might find it helpful to use a transparent rectangle 1 character wide.

Up to this point, we have referred to objects having actions associated with them. But what can these actions do? An action can be one of three types:

- A simple action
- A formula
- A script

You define actions in the bottom portion of the navigator design screen, as in Figure 10.20.

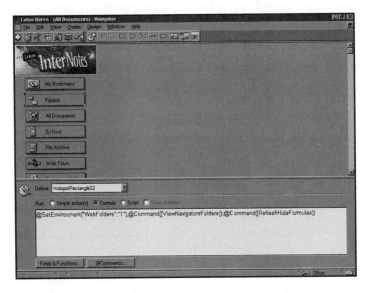

Fig. 10.20 The navigator design screen.

To define an action for an object, you should first click the object. This activates the bottom portion of the design screen. Then click the radio button corresponding to the type of action you will define, either Simple action(s), Formula, or Script.

If you select Simple action(s), you must select an action from the Action pull-down list. Table 10.7 describes the type of simple actions you can select.

Table 10.7   Types of Simple Actions

Simple Action	Description
Open another Navigator	This action causes the current navigator to close and another to open in its place. When you select this option, another list box opens from which you select the navigator to which you want to switch.
Open a View	This action switches the user to the specified view. When you select it, another list box opens from which you select the view to which you want to switch.
Alias a Folder	This action causes any documents dragged from the view pane onto the object to be placed in a specified folder (like your mail database). When you select this, a list box opens from which you select the folder you want to alias.
Open a Link	This action opens a specified document. Before selecting this option, go to a document and select Edit, Copy as Link. The object will link to the specified document.
Open an URL	This action switches the user to a specified URL. The user must be connected to a Domino server that has access to the WWW in order for this option to work.

If you select either a Formula or Script, a box opens where you can write any @function formula or LotusScript program, respectively. Formulas are described further in Chapter 14, "Working with Formulas," and LotusScript is discussed in Chapters 17 and 18.

Displaying a Default Navigator When Your Database Opens

Once you have created several navigators, you might want to select one navigator and have it open every time the database opens. Setting a default navigator in this way ensures that the same screen will always display on startup. By creating a default navigator, you can link to different views, documents, and other navigators, creating a graphical user interface to your Notes database.

To select a default navigator, open the Database Properties InfoBox (from the workspace, right-click the database icon and select Database Properties) and select the Launch tab (see Figure 10.21).

Fig. 10.21   Select a default navigator in the Database Properties InfoBox Launch tab.

II

Designing Applications

There are two options you can select in the On Database Open pull-down list regarding navigators:

- **Open Designated Navigator**—This option opens the designated navigator within the normal three-paned window (the navigator is on the left, the view is on the right, and the preview is on the bottom).

- **Open Designated Navigator In Its Own Window**—This option displays only the navigator when the database is opened; the three-paned window won't appear until the navigator is closed.

A new feature in 4.5 allows the developer to force the database to open in one of the three Preview Pane modes (see Figure 10.22).

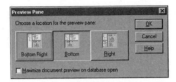

Fig. 10.22   Choose a location for the Preview Pane.

Tip

Opening a navigator in its own window is a convenient way to display a welcome screen each time the database is opened.

From Here...

Now that you know how to create a Notes database, the next several chapters further explore creating forms and views, followed by chapters that cover writing formulas and LotusScript programs. For more information on the topics discussed in this chapter, refer to the following:

- Chapter 11, "Designing Forms," describes how to create and design custom forms for your database.

- Chapter 12, "Designing Views," shows how to create views to display the documents created from your forms.

- Chapter 17, "LotusScript Basics" teaches the basics of the powerful LotusScript programming language, which can be used to manipulate objects and links.

- Chapter 27, "Using Domino Server's HTTP Service," shows you how to publish your Web pages to the Internet.

- "Working with the InterNotes Web Publisher" on the CD-ROM shows you how to set up a Web page in Notes.

Chapter 11

Designing Forms

Now that you have learned how to create a new database, you're ready to create a form. Forms contain the fields you will use in your application. Lotus Notes uses forms for data entry, displaying data, and controlling the field structure in documents. When users open documents, they see the data "through" the form. A database may have a variety of forms used for displaying different data, or even for displaying the same data in different formats.

The form can contain fields, static text, tables, graphics, buttons, pop-ups, and other objects such as subscriptions or OLE links. When you design a form, you place these objects where you want them displayed; you can also select formats to control how the data appears on the screen.

What's Contained in a Form?

A form contains multiple components that define the structure of your database. These components could be fields, static text, graphics, buttons, pop-ups, layout regions, tables, and objects (OLE, Subscriptions, FX fields) that link Notes to other products and a variety of other components.

Following is a list of the most widely used components for designing forms:

- **Fields**—You can place fields anywhere you want on a form. A field can be unique to that form, shared among forms within a database, or based upon a design template and used in multiple databases. Fields are the basis for how data is stored and displayed from within Notes. Besides storing data you can use fields to calculate data and even add LotusScript programs that run when users move to or from certain fields. Text attributes, such as bold type or color, applied to fields are reflected in the way data is displayed in the finished document. Fields can also be Notes/FX fields that exchange information with other products.

Some of the main elements in this chapter are

- Define your database structure through Create Design Form

- Create forms by defining static text and form attributes

- Create fields to be utilized on the form

- Designate the data and field types for the fields

- Use field formulas to manipulate data

- Format the fields to display on the form

- **Text**—You can place static (unchanging) text anywhere on a form, and you can apply any text attributes to it—color, size, different typefaces, and so on. You generally want to label fields with text that helps users understand the purpose of each field.

- **Graphics**—You can place a decorative graphic anywhere on a form, and it will appear on every document created with the form. For example, if you are designing a form for correspondence, you can place your company logo at the top of the form to create a letterhead.

- **Actions and hotspots**—Form actions and hotspots allow users to click them to accomplish simple tasks that mimic the Notes menus or complex tasks that are defined by formulas or a LotusScript program. Form actions can be displayed on the action bar and the Actions menu. Hotspots are placed directly on the form. Hotspots, in the form of pop-up text, actions, links, and formulas, are a useful way to automate static text and decorative graphics.

- **Tables**—Tables are useful for summarizing information or lining up fields in rows and columns. A table placed on a form appears in every document created with the form. You can disable the cell borders (lines that surround each table cell) if you want to create an "invisible" table.

- **OLE objects**—A form that has an Object Linking and Embedding (OLE) object enables you to use a Notes document to view and update data created in another product. For example, an Employee Information form can include an OLE object that links to a Word Pro file where the employee annual performance reviews are stored. See Chapter 13, "Integrating Notes with Other Applications," for details on using OLE with Notes.

New Design Logistics in Notes 4.5

If you have previously developed in Notes 3.x or earlier, you will notice a profound change in the appearance of Notes 4.5, especially when first developing a database. Don't worry, Lotus has actually made your life easier. Though the menu and options have changed for accessing and designing a form, the basic principles of database design have not. As a developer, you still need to define your form types, fields, field types, static text, objects, and the formulas within the fields.

Designing forms in Notes 4.5 is now easier, more accessible, and more visually appealing. If you are designing or modifying forms, always verify that the Design options are displayed by selecting View, Show, Design. Figure 11.1 shows a sample database in design mode, which was created using the sample discussion (DISCUSS4.NTF).

Notice that in the navigation pane you see the various components of the database, such as the folders and views, agents, and design. Click Design to expand the design components. This displays the views, forms, folders, shared fields, subforms, navigators, and other components that exist in the database.

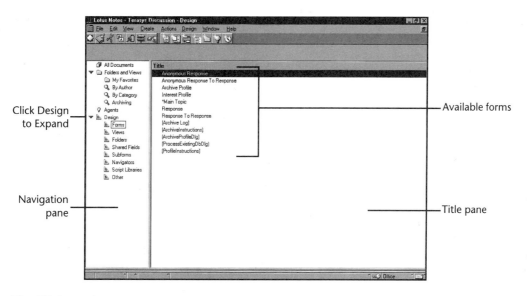

Fig. 11.1 In design mode, the navigation pane displays the design objects that currently exist in the database, whereas the title pane displays the individual design components.

When you double-click Forms in the navigation pane, the title pane on the right displays all of the forms that exist in the database. You can now double-click one of these forms to go into edit mode. Figure 11.2 displays the Response form in edit mode. (Page down in the form pane to skip over the hidden fields.) Once in form design mode, you can show up to three different window panes.

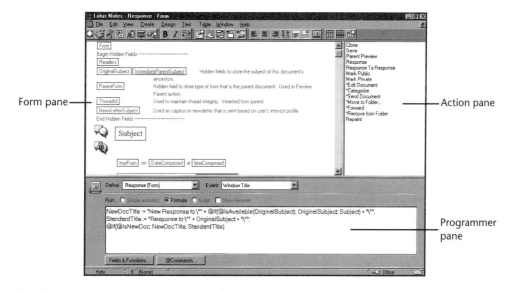

Fig. 11.2 While editing a form, you can easily maneuver between panes to design the form and its attributes.

On the top-left, the form itself is displayed in the Form pane. This is where you can enter static text, fields, and objects. On the top-right is the action pane, which allows you to define various actions that can be performed on the database. This pane may be hidden. To open it, choose View Action Pane from the menu. On the bottom center is the design pane, which allows you to define the formulas, scripts, and actions for all of the design elements associated with the form.

Now that you are aware of the new features and logistics that are encountered when designing a form, you can begin creating a form. The next few sections detail how to define a form and its attributes.

Understanding Form Hierarchy and Types

Before jumping in and selecting <u>C</u>reate, <u>D</u>esign, <u>F</u>orm to create a new form, you need to understand the structure or hierarchy of a Notes database. Each form created for any application has a form type associated with it. The following three types of forms can exist in a Notes database, and they follow a hierarchical order:

- Document
- Response-to-document
- Response-to-response

Document is the default form type and the highest-ranking form in the form hierarchy. If you create only one form in the database, it should be of document type.

Response-to-document and *Response-to-response* type forms are used to create responses to documents and other responses. It is important to remember that the relationship between the document and the response is created by highlighting the appropriate document before composing the response. Also, when building views, Notes distinguishes between these three types of documents by indenting the responses beneath their parent and by creating the appropriate column formulas and attributes to enable Notes to thread discussions correctly. Figure 11.3 shows an example of response documents in a hierarchical view.

Note

Response-to-response type forms provide the user with more flexibility when composing documents because they can be associated with either a document or any response-type document.

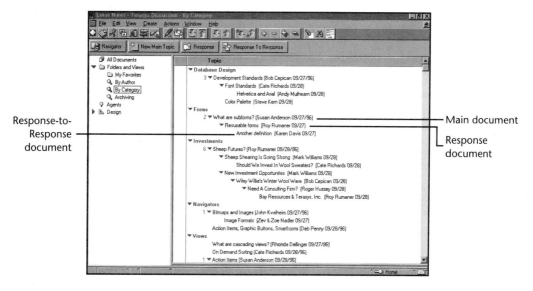

Response-to-
Response
document

Main document

Response
document

Fig. 11.3 Response documents create a hierarchy in a view where the responses and response-to-response appear below the main document, indented three spaces.

Table 11.1 summarizes the three different form types.

Table 11.1	The Three Form Types
Form Type	**Description**
Document	Used to create any main document. Independent of all other documents.
Response-to-document	Used to create responses associated to a main document. Dependent upon the main document. In a view that uses a response hierarchy, a response document appears underneath the main document that is highlighted when the user chooses Compose, and is indented three spaces under a main document. You can display 32 levels of responses.
Response-to-response	Used to respond to either a main document or another response document. Indented under another response document. Multiple levels are allowed.

Planning and Formatting a New Form

When laying out a form, you should always attempt to think the way a user would when inputting data. Your goal is to make the form appealing and the data entry logical and free-flowing. Developers in a company should focus on using their company's defined formatting standards to increase their organization's corporate identity; e.g., logo in the left corner, a specific font size, and color).

Keep in mind the following tips when designing your forms:

■ You should always try to keep a standard or consistent look and feel in your forms, especially if you are developing applications for a company that wants to maintain a corporate image.

- Sketch the form on paper before you actually create it on-screen. Your sketch should indicate static text, graphics, field names and placement, field data types, whether the field value is calculated or entered by the user, default values, keyword lists, graphics, and help text.

- Look at other databases' forms to discover and learn new form design techniques. Open them up and learn. If appropriate, copy and paste desired parts of other forms.

- You should consider how your forms will appear when used in various screen size resolutions and attempt to use light-colored backgrounds for easy viewing.

- Utilize tab settings for consistent alignment and do not use too many fields, as users become frustrated when forced to enter large amounts of data.

Creating a New Form

When first designing a new form, you can define the fields, graphics, text, margins, and tabs because Notes does not create any predefined structure on the form. To create a form, you need to perform the following steps:

1. Select the database you want to add the form to.

2. Choose Create, Design, Form to create a blank, untitled form as displayed in Figure 11.4 (or you can choose the Create Form SmartIcon).

Fig. 11.4   Selecting Create, Design, Form enables you to begin designing a new form. The Form's InfoBox allows you to define the form's properties.

3. To define the form properties for a form, you need to select Design, Form Properties to display the Form Properties InfoBox. Notice in the Properties For list box that Form is automatically selected. The Form Properties InfoBox enables you to modify the settings for your form, such as its name, what to do when the document is opened or closed, and other default options.

> **Tip**
>
> Right-click the form pane and select Form Properties for quick access to the Form Properties InfoBox.

4. Lay out the form by placing fields, text, graphics, and other objects on the form as needed.

5. Save the form by choosing File, Save (Ctrl+S). If you have not named the form in the Form Properties InfoBox, you will be prompted to name the form before saving. The form name is significant because Notes can reference it from within field formulas, form formulas, selection formulas, and view column formulas.

Adding Static Text to a Form

All forms need field labels. Field labels are static text that describes the field. You can add static text to a form in design mode the same way you type characters into any Notes document: type directly on the form exactly where you want the text to appear. Figure 11.5 shows a form in design mode with static text.

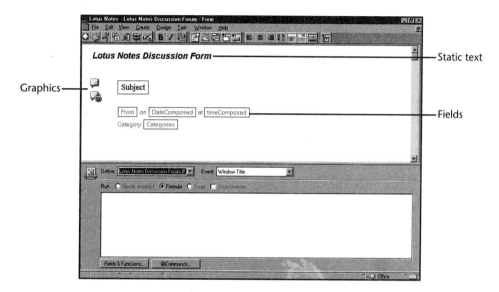

Fig. 11.5 Static text identifies and labels your fields.

> ### Tip
>
> Information entered into a field is usually of variable lengths. For example, a customer name field would be variable, while a Social Security number field would be of constant length. Therefore, place fields of variable lengths where they could enter more than one line of data on a line by themselves, since Notes will move any fields to the right of the data as data is entered.

The default font and color for static text on new forms is Helvetica 10-point in black. Usually, you should create static text with a different color or size, or use boldface, to set it off from the field contents.

Choose Text, Text Properties; press Ctrl+K; press the Text Properties SmartIcon; or right-click and select Text Properties to change the size, color, and other attributes of static text. Table 11.2 shows some of the most common text attributes and the different methods you can use to apply them.

◀◀ See "Changing the Appearance of Text with the Text Menu," p. 275

Table 11.2 Methods to Achieve Text Attributes

SmartIcon	Command	Keyboard	Description
B	Text, Bold	Ctrl+B	Boldfaces selected text or turns on boldfacing
U	Text, Underline	Ctrl+U	Underlines selected text or turns on underlining
I	Text, Italic	Ctrl+I	Italicizes selected text or turns on italics
AA	Text, Enlarge Size	F2	Enlarges selected text one point size
A·A	Text, Reduce Size	Shift+F2	Reduces selected text one point size

Tip

Add tabs by using the ruler to align fields. To toggle the ruler display, choose View, Show Ruler or press the View Ruler SmartIcon. To set margins and tabs using the ruler, you must use a mouse.

 ◀◀ See "Setting Margins and Tabs with the Ruler," p. 294

Copying a Form from Another Database

Occasionally, you may want to copy a form from one database and use it in another, possibly modifying it to meet the new application's needs. This procedure can save you a lot of development time, especially if you begin using consistent formatting standards in your databases.

 ▶▶ See "Database Templates," p. 1123

To copy and paste a form, complete the following steps:

1. Select the database containing the source form.

2. Verify that you are in design mode (View, Show, Design).

3. In the navigation pane, click Design to expand the design components.

4. Click Forms to display the available forms in the database in the Title pane.

5. Select the form you want to copy from the Forms list.

Tip

You can select a range of forms by clicking and holding down the Shift key or the Ctrl key to select individual forms.

6. Select Edit, Copy, or click the Edit Copy SmartIcon.

7. Switch to the database where you want to paste the form and click Design in the navigation pane, and then click Forms to display the list of forms.

8. Select Edit, Paste, or click the Edit Paste SmartIcon. The new form's name will appear in the Forms list.

Caution

If you are copying and pasting a form from the same database, the form is pasted into the list of forms but is renamed by changing the name to "Copy of" and the original form name.

▶▶ See "Naming a Form," p. 434

Form Properties

Adding static text is just the initial step in creating a form. You also need to define the form's overall attributes, such as its name, the type, read access, compose access, whether to hide the form, whether to make it the default form in the database; and then you will be ready to add the fields. Form attributes are defined in the Form Properties InfoBox, which is accessed by selecting Design, Form Properties. See Figure 11.6. The following sections describe how to use the settings on the various tabs in the InfoBox.

Fig. 11.6 The Form Properties InfoBox enables you to define the properties of a form. Each tabbed section enables you to define different attributes.

Note

You must be designing or editing a form to select Form Properties.

Basic Settings

The Basics tab in the Form Properties InfoBox for a form is the default tab, which you will always encounter first. In this section, you can name the form, select the form's hierarchy in the database structure, and decide whether to include it in the Create menu.

The following sections explain in more detail the available options that can be used to define a form's properties or attributes in the Basics tab.

Naming a Form. In the Form name box, enter a name for this form. The name can be any combination of characters, including spaces, and it is case-sensitive. A name can have as many characters as you want, but only the first 32 will appear on menus and characters in dialog boxes.

Keep the following items in mind when naming a form:

- **Use descriptive names**—The form names appear on the Create menu. Essentially, the form name is the Create command to create a specific document, so its name should indicate its purpose. For example, if it's a response form, try to use the word "Response" in its name. I like to precede form names by "frm" (though not necessary) to clearly identify the form name, which is especially useful if the form name is used in formulas. For example, frmResponse, frmMainDocument, frmLoan, and so on.

- **Use accelerator keys**—The first unique letter in the form name is used as the form's accelerator; the accelerator is underlined in the Create menu. To force Notes to use a different letter as the accelerator, insert an underscore (_) before that letter. For example, to force the letter "A" to be the accelerator key for a form named Loan Analysis, enter the name as Loan _Analysis. Even though you can designate the same letter multiple times as an accelerator key, it is good practice to use a different letter for each form that will appear under the Create menu.

- **Use cascading form names**—Enter the top-level form name, followed by a backslash (\) and the additional form name. For example, entering Loan Analysis\Initial Review causes the name Loan _Analysis to appear on the Compose menu and the Initial Review form to cascade from it, as shown in Figure 11.7. Notes allows one level of cascades.

Cascading menu —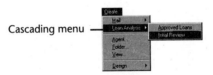

Fig. 11.7 Cascading form names are useful for organizing your forms under the Create menu.

- **Use synonyms**—Synonyms enable you to change the form's name on the Create menu without tracking down and rewriting formulas that reference the original form name, which is a great time-saver. For example, if you changed the Loan Analysis\Initial Review form to Loan Analysis\Initial Loan Review, you would attain errors in various formulas that reference that form.

To use synonyms, enter the form name, followed by a vertical bar (|) and the synonym's name. The synonym is only used internally in the Form field; the first name in the Name box is the name that appears on the Create menu. If you're using both a cascade and a synonym, put the cascade name before the synonym. By using the synonym in a form name, you can easily change the name that appears on the create menu without affecting the internal name or synonym.

> **Note**
>
> To save yourself a lot of agony, you should get in the habit of using synonyms when naming forms. In the previous example, the form name should be something like:
>
> ```
> Loan Analysis\Initial Review ¦ frmInitialReview.
> ```

Specifying the Form Type. As mentioned before, three types of forms are in a Notes database: Documents, Responses-to-documents, and Responses-to-responses. In the Form type drop-down list box, you can select the desired form type (see Figure 11.8). The default form listed is Document.

Fig. 11.8 Select the desired form type in the Form type drop-down list box. To fully understand the hierarchy of forms, see the earlier section "Understanding Form Hierarchy and Types."

Including the Form in the Create Menu. Select the Include in Menu option if you want to display the form in the Create menu. If you deselect this option, the form is effectively hidden from the database's users. For example, your Notes mail database has several hidden forms that are used only for displaying information. Developers use this feature to prevent users from composing a certain form, but to enable them to use the form for reading documents. This is also useful when you want to control what forms are used through navigators.

> **Tip**
>
> If you want a limited number of users to use the form, keep it in the Create menu, but then create an access list for the form.

> **Caution**
>
> Deselecting Include in Menu does not guarantee that the form is truly hidden. This is because users could use it in form formulas (to select which form will be used in a particular view) and print it by choosing File, Print, Form Override. To permanently hide a form, you can place parentheses around the form's name in the Form Name box (form name). Using parentheses not only hides the form on all menus, but prevents users from using Form Override to print the document. The form, however, can still appear in form formulas. Developers like to use this technique to hide an old form that they want to store for future use or backup.

You could select the Include in Menu option and then choose the Create—Other dialog box option in the displayed list box. This removes the form from the Create menu and moves the form to the Other menu dialog box, which is accessed from the Create menu (see Figure 11.9). This is useful if you don't expect a form to be used frequently, but want to shorten the list of forms shown in the Create menu.

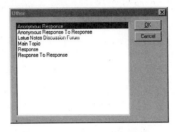

Fig. 11.9   The Other dialog box is accessed by selecting Create, Other.

Including the Form in the Search Builder. If a database manager has created a full text index for a database, the Include in Search Builder option enables you to use the form in a Search Builder for full text search. In a full text search, users can select a form to use in a search and enter search criteria in the fields on the form (see Figure 11.10). This option even enables users to search for text in attachments and embedded objects.

Fig. 11.10   The Search Builder enables you to select the condition By Form and then the desired form to be used in conducting a query.

 ◄◄ See "Full Text Searching in Databases," p. 308

Tip

If the form is used to display documents, it generally should be made available for queries so that users can attempt a full text search using a familiar layout versus having to enter more complex query commands when a form is not made available.

Tracking the Version. Normally, every time you save an updated document, it replaces the original document, which is lost forever. With the versioning option, you can allow this to happen or force a saved update to become a new response document. Figure 11.11 displays the available options that would enable you to begin version tracking, meaning that when a user creates a response to the current document, the new document can become either.

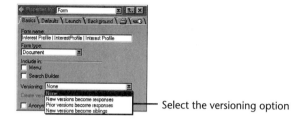

Select the versioning option

Fig. 11.11 Versioning enables you to incorporate whether documents become responses or siblings upon being updated. This is a great way to track who and how often documents are being used.

The following options are available for incorporating versioning into your database:

- **None**—This is the default option that designates no versioning to occur.

- **New versions become responses**—This enables you to incorporate document version control in your application. If a document created with this form is modified, the original remains intact and all updated copies are stored as responses to that original, providing a history of changes. This method of version control is immune to replication and save conflicts. For example, if users on different servers modify and save the same main document, their versions are treated and displayed as two separate response documents when the databases replicate.

  A replication conflict occurs when two or more users edit the same document in different replicas between replications. A save conflict occurs when two or more users edit the same document in a database on a server at the same time. At the next replication, after two users edit and save the same document, Notes designates as the main document the document that has been edited and saved the most frequently and displays the other(s) as responses to the main document labeled "[Replication or Save Conflict]" with a diamond symbol in the left margin.

- **Prior versions become responses**—This is another method of version control, except in this case if a document created with this form is modified, the updated copy replaces the original main document, which is then stored as a response to the new version. Again, this gives an application the ability to maintain a history of changes.

- **New versions become siblings**—In this situation, the original document is listed first, and all successive versions or siblings follow as additional main documents. You should choose this option if you want to leave the original document as a main document without introducing the risk of replication or save conflicts, which can occur if the database resides on multiple servers.

Tip

Distinguish sibling and response documents from their main parent documents by adding labels such as "New Version:" or "Revised:" to the column formula that is displayed in a view column.

◄◄ See "Understanding Form Hierarchy and Types," p. 428

Selecting a Background Color. The Background Color option enables you to select the form's background color. Notes R4.5 offers a larger variety of colors than previous versions of Notes. Keep in mind that monitor resolution and size affect color, and that background color affects the visibility of text. Select light colors such as white, light blue, and yellow for easier viewing.

Note

Be especially careful when choosing form colors if you have mobile users who still use laptops with monochrome screens.

Troubleshooting

I have attempted to order these three non-alphabetically but have been unsuccessful. How can this be done? The three forms are currently named Weekly Timesheet, 401K Enrollment, and Expense Reimbursement.

The trick is to rename the forms by preceding the existing form names with a number. For example, rename each form listed above to the following: "1. Weekly Timesheet," "2. 401K Enrollment," and "3. Expense Reimbursement." Then, they are listed in numerical order in the Create menu.

After creating a new form, I noticed that it is not appearing in the Create Menu. Why?

Make sure that you did not deselect the option Include in Menu in the Form Properties InfoBox. Also, verify that you did not use parentheses around the form name. For example, naming the form "(Expense Reimbursement)" would not display the form in the Create menu.

Default Settings

In the Defaultstab of the Form Properties InfoBox, you can select options that enable you to define a form for specific actions. Some of these options are familiar to Notes 3.x developers, such as designating default forms, storing the form in the document, and automatically refreshing fields; but developers will be excited about several new options, such as automatically enabling a document in edit mode and inheriting the whole document into one rich text field. Figure 11.12 displays the Defaults tab options for the Form Properties InfoBox.

Fig. 11.12   The Defaults tab in the Form Properties InfoBox enables you to specify the default characteristics for how your form acts.

The following sections describe the options that are available in the Defaults tab.

Specifying the Form as the Default Form. Selecting the Default database form option makes the current form the default form for the database. A database must have exactly one default form. Figure 11.13 displays the list of available forms in the database with the default form designated by an asterisk.

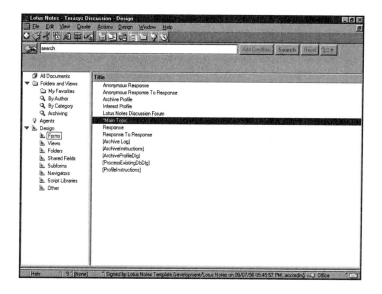

Fig. 11.13   The default form in the current database is always indicated by an asterisk (*) in the Title pane.

Caution

When you designate a form as the default form, another form in the database that might already have that designation loses default form status. The new default form setting takes precedence.

Using a default form ensures that if a form is renamed without a synonym or is deleted from the database, users can still view documents created with that form through the default form. Anytime

(continues)

(continued)

Notes cannot find the form used to create a document, it always reverts to the default form for the database. This may not always display the information contained in the document, as the document must contain the fields that are in the form design.

Automatically Refreshing Fields. The Automatically Refresh Fields option recalculates all of the form's computed fields (fields are described later in this chapter) every time the user moves the mouse pointer to the next field during data entry. This allows you to update calculated fields for users automatically as they move through the document during data entry. By default, this option is not enabled which means that the calulated fields in the form will be updated only when the document is saved or refreshed.

Caution

If the form contains many computed fields, constant recalculation will slow data entry and irritate the user. Use this option sparingly or only when it is necessary to see the result of a calculation when proceeding to the next field.

Tip

The user can always update the fields manually by pressing F9.

Storing Forms in Documents. Normally, only the data entered in the fields of a form are stored within a document. The Store Form in Document option, when selected, automatically stores the form with each document allowing you to retain the layout of that form with that document. This is a relatively significant setting because documents that are created with a form using this setting are not updated if the form is changed, the form stored with the document is stored only when the document is created, and the design is never updated. It also causes the database to become very large because the entire form design is stored with each document.

You should use this option if you are intending to mail documents from the database to users' mail files because the mail file would not contain the form design.

Caution

Use this option sparingly, as it requires a lot of overhead in disk space and memory to store the form in each document. If you expect the documents to be used in other databases, you might want to store a copy of the form itself in those databases.

Enabling Field Exchange. With the Enable Field Exchange option, you can enable field exchange to occur between a Notes document and fields from another application that supports Notes/FX technology such as a Lotus 1-2-3 spreadsheet. Notes/FX uses OLE technology to enable Notes and any OLE server application to share data fields. The contents of fields in an OLE server application file can automatically appear in a corresponding field in a Notes document and vice versa. Furthermore, depending on the type of field, the contents of the field can be updated from either direction.

Inheriting Default Field Values. In the On Create section of the Defaults tab, select the Formulas Inherit values from selected document option if you want documents created with this form to inherit or copy values from the highlighted document when the user chooses the form from the Create menu. An example of inheriting field values would be if a document were created where the field CustomerName contained "ABC Company, Inc." and a response to that document were then created, and the Customer Name appears in the response document's CustomerName field upon creation.

This option is very useful in discussion databases where you utilize the three different types of forms (Document, Response-to-document, and Response-to-response) and want to have similar information filter down to the child documents. For example, you may want to copy relevant information, such as the subject from a main discussion document to a Response document in the discussion database. The Discussion template (DISCUSS4.NTF) has two forms, Response and Response-to-response, that utilize this option and is an excellent starting point in learning this Notes development technique.

From a developer's standpoint, inheriting fields from parent documents is useful for making a Notes database more closely associated to a "relational" database rather than the general "flat-file" Notes database. This technique helps significantly when designing views because associated main documents, responses, and responses-to-responses have data that is the same in all three because of the designated inheritance feature. Inheritance happens only when a document is first created. If the parent's information changes, the child will not re-inherit the data, however, there are programmable workarounds for this.

Turning a Response Document into Rich Text. A new feature in Notes R4.5 for developers is the Inherit entire selected document into rich text field option. If selected, you can choose how you want the response document to appear: as a link, collapsible rich text, or rich text. For instance, a new response document can automatically inherit the contents of its main document. Just make sure that you have created a rich text field to store the inherited document. After selecting Inherit entire selected document into rich text field, you can select the rich text field you created. Then select one of the following full document display options:

- **Collapsed rich text**—This option displays the parent document as a collapsed section and gives users the opportunity to review the parent document, but it doesn't clutter the form.

- **Rich text**—Rich text inherits the fully expanded contents of the parent document.

- **Link**—This creates a doclink to the original parent document.

Figure 11.14 displays an example of a document if Link was selected as the inherit option.

Designing Applications

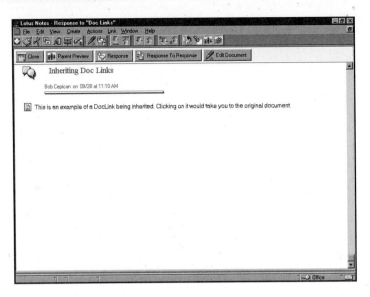

Fig. 11.14 Doc Links allow users to quickly navigate between documents in databases. The Link option allows developers to automate the creation of doclinks.

Automatically Opening a Document in Edit Mode. Your users will appreciate this new feature in Notes R4.5. If the Automatically enable Edit Mode option is selected, an accessed document is placed in edit mode. Earlier versions of Notes opened the document only in read mode upon double-clicking.

You can also govern how a document appears when it is open by selecting the Show Context pane option and its associated appearance option, either Doclink or Parent. For example, Figure 11.15 displays how the context pane for a Contact Profile response document appears when opened if the Parent option is selected for the Show Context pane option.

Mailing Documents When Saving. Did you know that any document can be mailed to a fellow user by choosing Forward from the Mail menu? Occasionally, in applications that require workflow procedures, you may want to automate this procedure.

To facilitate document mailing, you could include a Text field called SendTo on the form. Then, if the Present mail send dialog box option is selected in the On Close section of the Form Properties InfoBox, and a SendTo field exists on the form with an individual's name, Notes will prompt the author of the document to mail, save, or discard the document, as shown in Figure 11.16.

This is a great feature if you want to mail-enable forms in your databases and is especially useful for creating workflow type applications, such as sending approvals. Remember, though, that if you choose to use this, you must either choose to Store the form with the document, or copy the form to the user's mail file.

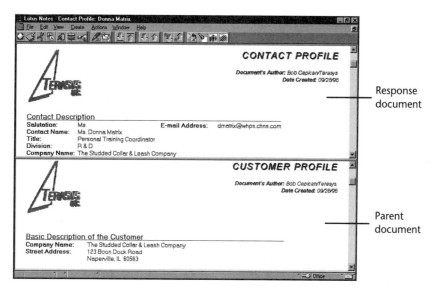

Fig. 11.15 Selecting Parent in the Show Context pane option enables you to see a clear association between a main document and a response document by viewing both simultaneously.

Fig. 11.16 The Close Window dialog box appears automatically when saving a document if a SendTo field exists on the form.

Settings for Launching Objects

The Launch tab in the Properties InfoBox for a form initially displays only Auto Launch drop-down list box with a default to None. Here, you can select the object type or application that you want to launch from within your form and any associated actions. These actions are covered in more detail in Chapter 13, "Integrating Notes with Other Applications."

Printing Options

The Print tab, which displays a printer icon, enables you to define a header and/or footer in your form and to set its corresponding font, size, and style attributes (see Figure 11.17).

◀◀ See "Using Headers and Footers," p. 132

Tip

To specify a multiline header or footer, press Enter at the end of each line of the header or footer.

II

Designing Applications

Fig.11.17 It is easy and flexible to set the Header and Footer options for your form when printing. Unfortunately, these options are not WYSIWYG and you are forced to print out the header and footer to see how they print.

Security Settings

At times, you will want to restrict who can create or read specific documents. The Security tab, which displays a key icon in the Form Properties InfoBox, enables you to establish whether a user can read or create a certain document with this form (see Figure 11.18). The following sections describe these options.

Fig. 11.18 The Security tab in the Form Properties InfoBox enables you to define who can and cannot see specific documents using this particular form.

Restricting Read Access. By default, anyone with at least Reader access to the database can read all documents. You can define a read access list that restricts the form so that documents created with the form are available only to a limited list of people. Then, every document created with the form receives this list.

Follow these steps to define the list of users allowed to read documents composed with this form:

▶▶ See "Working with the Access Control List," p. 742

1. Deselect All readers and above in the Default read access for documents created with this form section.

2. Select each user, group, server, or access role you want to include.

> **Note**
>
> The database ACL and any access roles should already be defined by the manager using File Database Access Control.

3. If a person does not exist in the ACL, you can click the Person icon to select a name from a Public or Private Address Book.

Repeat steps 2 and 3 for each name that you want added to the list. To remove a name, click the name again to remove the checkmark.

4. Save the form.

> **Note**
>
> The read access list refines the ACL, it cannot override the ACL. If a user does not already have Reader access to the database, he or she will not be able to read the documents created with this form, even if you list them in the read access list.

Create Access. You can restrict the form to a limited list of people for creating documents. The create access list is designed just like the read access list. By default, anyone with at least author access to the database can create documents with any of the database's forms. To define the subset of users who will be needing a specific form, perform the following steps:

1. Deselect All authors and above in the Who can create documents with this form section.

2. Select each user, group, server, or access role you want to include.

3. If a person does not exist in the ACL, you can click the Person icon to select a name from a Public or Private Address Book.

Repeat steps 2 and 3 for each name that you want added to the list. To remove a name, click the name again to remove the checkmark.

4. Save the form.

Other Methods of Securing Forms. The Security tab in the Form Properties InfoBox also enables you to select the following options:

- **Disable printing/forwarding/copying to Clipboard**—This option prevents users from printing, forwarding, or copying restricted information. This feature greatly helps to prevent accidental or intentional distribution of confidential information. This does not prevent a user from using a screen capture program, however.

- **Default encryption keys**—This option enables you to select and associate any defined encryption keys for the form. To use this feature, you must define one or more fields on the form as encryptable. Every document created with the form will automatically have its encryptable fields encrypted, using the keys you specify here. Be sure to distribute the keys to people who will be using the form.

Adding Fields to a Form

Once you have defined a form, you can add fields to it. Fields are the means by which you enter data into Notes and display the data stored in Notes. A form can accept and display only data for which there are fields; for example, if you want users to enter their employee ID numbers on the form, you must add the EmployeeID field to the form layout.

You create a field by giving it a name and selecting some attributes for it, such as the data type, field type, and format. Notes then places the field on your form.

The following sections explore the various types of fields you can use in your forms.

Single-Use and Shared Fields

Notes supports two types of fields: single-use and shared. A single-use field is a normal field. You define it, select attributes for it such as its data type, and then place it on a form. If you want to use it again in a different form, you can define a new field using the same name and define the attributes or copy the field from the existing form and paste it in the new form, but in both cases, the new field has no relation to the original. Single-use fields are stored within the form itself and are available only on that level.

Shared fields are fields that are to be used in multiple forms in the database and require the same attributes and formulas in each form. These fields are stored as separate entities in the database design and are accesible from any form design. A shared field is accessed through the Insert Shared Field dialog box, which lets you place the shared field at the insertion point for any form in the database. Every time you update one instance of the shared field, all other instances are automatically updated, too, because they use the same field definition. If you make a shared field a text field instead of a number field, for example, all instances of that shared field are updated automatically to reflect your changes.

Shared fields are useful when you want to use the same field in multiple forms, and want to make sure that the exact same definition is used everywhere. For example, your database might use the InterestRate field in three different forms. To make sure that all the forms use the same field definition, you define a single shared field called InterestRate, and then "use" it in each form.

To create a new field, follow these steps:

1. Place your mouse pointer on the form where you want the field to appear.

2. Select Create, Field, or press the Create Field SmartIcon to insert a single-use field. Notes inserts a new field called Untitled on your form and displays the Field Properties InfoBox, as in Figure 11.19. You can now rename the field and change other properties of the field.

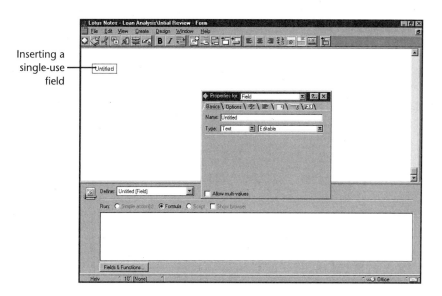

Inserting a
single-use
field

Fig. 11.19   Inserting a new field onto a form. A single-use field is identified by its light rectangle outline.

3. Select Create, Insert Shared field, or press the Create Insert Shared Field SmartIcon to display the Insert Shared Field dialog box, as shown in Figure 11.20. Select the shared field and then click OK to insert the field onto the form (see Figure 11.21).

Fig. 11.20   Inserting a shared field called ReviewDate onto a form.

If you have not defined a shared field, this dialog box will be blank. To define a shared field, you must return to the navigation pane, select Create, Design, Shared Field, and then name and define the shared field. Once saved, this newly named shared field will appear in the Insert Shared Field dialog box for reuse.

> ### Tip
>
> You can copy and paste fields between forms by using the Clipboard. However, shared fields will revert to single-use fields when copied and pasted because its definition is not stored with the field.

If you define a shared field and then place it in a form that has the Store Form in Documents option selected, that instance of the field is automatically converted to a single-use field whenever a document is created and saved using that form. This ensures that if the document is mailed or pasted into another database, the field will be accessible even if the new database does not contain a copy of the shared field's definition (this is true of any field not just shared fields).

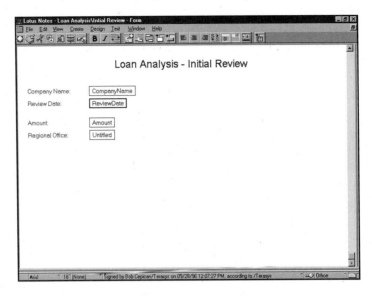

Fig. 11.21   The shared fields are designated by a heavy bold rectangle.

If you delete a shared field from a form, the data entered through that field cannot be displayed. There is no message, and the data itself cannot be altered; but it can still be displayed by adding the field to another form. The contents of the field are still considered part of the document; but because there is no field to display them in, they are displayed on the form itself as text. You cannot edit or delete this text.

Note

You could use another form or create a new field to write a formula to see the contents of that deleted shared field.

Defining Fields

Once you've chosen whether the field on the form is single-use or shared, you must define the field's characteristics; e.g., its data type, field type, format, paragraph attributes, and so on. This is accomplished in the Field Properties InfoBox.

Tip

Double-click an existing field, select Design, Field Properties, or press the spacebar while a field is selected to display its Field Properties dialog box.

Basic Settings. Use the Basics tab section to name the field, select the data type, and then select the field type. Figure 11.22 displays the Basics tab of a Field Properties InfoBox.

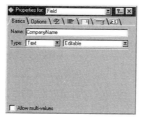

Fig. 11.22   The Properties InfoBox for a field enables you to define the attributes for the fields in your form.

The following options appear in the Basics tab section of the Field Properties InfoBox when defining a field:

- **Name**—Name the field first. The field name must begin with a letter, but it can include numbers and the symbols _ and $. Fields beginning with $ are internal type fields used by Notes that you usually will not have to focus upon unless you begin more complex Notes database programming. You should never begin the name of your fields with $ unless you are using an internal field. When naming a field, remember that it may be used in a formula, so you should try to pick a short name that is easy to remember. There are about a dozen field names, such as Categories, SendTo, and Sign, called Reserved Fields, that hold a special meaning in Notes. Fields that have these reserved field names behave in a predefined way. Field names may contain up to 32 bytes (if you are using multibyte characters, 32 bytes is different from 32 characters).

- **Type**—Notes supports nine data types for fields. Select a data type to indicate how this data will be stored and used. These data types are discussed later in the next section.

- **Allow multi-values**—If multiple values will be accepted in a field, select the Allow multi-values checkbox. Multi-value fields are useful if you have a field that can contain more than one value. For example, you may want to have a field where someone can enter names of people who can edit a document, or where they can assign multiple dates or numbers.

Choosing Options. In the Options tab, you can define help descriptions, address security issues, and define multiple-value separators (see Figure 11.23). The following list details those options:

- **Help Description**—If provided, the optional Help description appears as a one-line prompt at the bottom of the form window when the mouse pointer is placed in that field. For example, "Enter the date the loan closed" is a poor example of field help description because it fails to inform the user how to enter the date. A better example would be "Enter the date the loan closed using the format MM\DD\YY."

Fig. 11.23 The Options tab section in the Field Properties InfoBox is where you supply help instructions and apply multi-value features.

> ### Tip
>
> Try to make the Help Description useful and indicate the field's general purpose. Use a pop-up on the form if you cannot fit all the information into this Help. To toggle Display field help, select View, Show, Field Help.

- **Give this field default focus**—This is a great feature new to Notes developers. It enables you to automatically move the mouse pointer to a particular field location when the document is created or opened in edit mode. If not selected, the cursor moves to the first editable field on the form.

- **Multi-value options**—This section enables you to handle multi-values in a field. You need to define either Separate values or Display separate value with and then the corresponding separator value (Space, Comma, Semicolon, New Line, or Blank Line).

  The Separate values when a user enters an option allows you to give users choices for entering text. If the field is editable, it's best to allow several kinds of separators so users can separate entries as they want, and Notes can still identify the following individual entries:

  > Europe, Asia, North America

  If you allow only one separator, such as a comma, users must use that separator to prevent Notes from reading multiple entries as a single entry.

  The Display separate value with option allows you to define how the multi-value entries appear. To align and separate multiple values on the form, use the ruler (Ctrl+R) to create a hanging indent where the field begins. Selecting New Line for both the input and display separator.

- **Security Options**. Here, you can select Sign if mailed or saved in section, Enable encryption for this field, and Must have at least Editor access to use to enable security features for particular situations.

  Select Sign if mailed or saved in section to determine whether mailed documents are signed or encrypted automatically during mailing. These override the users' settings in the Document Save dialog box. Select the Enable encryption for this field option to activate the encryption of a field when it is saved. Selecting the

Must have at least Editor access to use allows you to define if a user with at least Editor access can modify the field.

Setting the Font. The Font tab displays an icon with the letters A and Z in custom fonts (see Figure 11.24). The options on this tab enable you to easily set or modify the field's font, size, style, and text color. You can also set the permanent pen font for adding comments to a document in a different font.

Fig. 11.24   The Font tab section in the Field Properties InfoBox.

Alignment Settings. The Alignment tab section permits you to define how a field appears. Figure 11.25 displays the available alignment options on the Alignment tab (the tab sports an icon with left-aligned rows of text). You can specify the field's alignment, where the first line begins, whether the field is displayed within a list using bullets or numbers, where the left margin begins, and the desired spacing of lines.

Note

Make sure these alignment settings work in tight conjunction with your static text fonts and alignment settings.

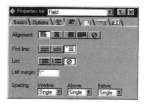

Fig. 11.25   The Alignment tab section in the Field Properties InfoBox.

Pagination Settings. In this section, you can specify how a form is paginated. A form could have a Page break before a paragraph, Keep paragraph on one page, or Keep paragraph with next paragraph. The Page break before a paragraph option allows you to keep all the lines in one paragraph on the same page. The Keep paragraph on one page and the Keep paragraph with next paragraph options enable you to keep consecutive paragraphs on the same page.

You can also specify the right margin, when printing, and the spacing of tabs. Figure 11.26 details the available pagination options. The Pagination tab icon looks like a page with the number 1 displayed.

Fig. 11.26   The pagination tab has features that are very useful when printing documents.

Options for Hiding Fields. The options on the Hide tab, displaying a window shade icon as shown in Figure 11.27, are used a lot by Notes developers to hide data when users are either reading or editing a form. Developers usually have fields on a form that they use for calculations or storing information that the user does not need to see. This information is generally stored at the bottom of a form and hidden from the users. You can hide such fields in the form layout.

Fig. 11.27   You can hide lines of your form depending on whether a user is reading, editing, previewing, or printing a form.

> ### Caution
>
> Hiding fields is more useful as a formatting option than as a security measure. Hidden data, such as Salary, could always be seen by a user who selects File, Document and then the Fields tab in the Document Properties InfoBox when a document is selected. If you want to ensure that data is hidden from users, you should encrypt those fields.

The following options for hiding fields are available in the Hide tab of a Field Properties InfoBox:

- **Previewed for reading**—This option hides the text or field when the document is being read in a preview pane. It can still be seen when being read or edited.

- **Opened for reading**—This hides the text or field when the document is being read. Whenever you hide information in read mode, it is automatically hidden during printing, too.

- **Printed**—This hides the text or field when the document is printed. The data is not hidden when the document is being read unless you also select Opened for reading.

- **Previewed for editing**—This option hides the text or field when the document is being edited in a preview pane.

- **Opened for editing**—Hides the text or field when the document is being edited.

- **Copied to the Clipboard**—Hides the text or field when the document is copied, so that the hidden information is not copied to the Clipboard.

- **Hide paragraph if formula is true**—You must provide the formula. For example, the following formula would hide the paragraph that contains the Categories field if it contained the keyword "General:"

    `@If(Categories = "General";1;0).`

> **Note**
>
> If you select Opened for reading, Notes automatically selects Previewed for reading and Printed. If you select Opened for editing, Notes automatically selects Previewed for editing.

To hide a field or paragraph using any of these options listed, perform the following steps:

1. Select the paragraph(s) or field(s) you want to hide. You can hide only entire lines or paragraphs (delimited by a hard return).

2. Select the Hide tab and in the Hide paragraph when document is section, you can select any of the options detailed previously.

> **Tip**
>
> Some developers like to place all of their hidden fields that are only to be displayed when edited at the very bottom of the form with a "Hidden Fields" label. This makes the hidden fields easy to locate if the form has to be modified. With that said, read the following caution.

> **Caution**
>
> Notes calculates fields from top to bottom, left to right in a document. Thus, beware of placing all of your hidden fields at the bottom if it is required to complete a calculation in another field above it because the hidden field must be encountered before the field that uses its data.

Saving Paragraph Properties as Styles. You can use the Style tab to save combinations of paragraph properties that you use regularly, such as alignment, indentation, and margins, as a named paragraph style. These named styles can then be used to quickly format existing paragraphs.

Suppose that you often write financial reports in italic text with a 2.25" left margin. You could save the italic and left margin paragraph properties as a named style called Reports. Then, when you write financial reports, you could format them with Reports without having to specify the italic and left margin properties individually each time. You could select Reports from the Text, Named Styles menu, or you could assign Reports to the cycle key F11, which enables you to cycle through each of the named styles you have created and assigned to the key.

To create a named style, perform the following steps:

1. Create and customize a paragraph to your liking. With the paragraph selected choose Text, Text Properties to display the Text Properties InfoBox.

2. Select the Style tab and choose Create Style to display the Create Named Style dialog box.

3. Enter a name for the paragraph style as shown in Figure 11.28.

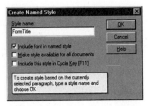

Fig. 11.28 Creating a named paragraph style is a great time-saving tool for quickly formatting lines in a form.

4. (Optional) Deselect Include font in named style if you don't want to save the selected paragraph's font in the named style.

5. (Optional) Select Make style available for all documents to make the style available when you format paragraphs in other documents in the database.

6. (Optional) Select Include this style in Cycle Key [F11] to make the style available when you press F11 to cycle through named styles.

7. Click OK to save your style.

After you create named styles, you can format paragraphs with those styles. To format a paragraph with a named style follow these steps:

1. Make sure the document is in edit mode.

2. Select the paragraph(s).

3. Perform one of the following:

   - Choose Text Named Styles and select a style from the menu Notes displays.

   - Click the Named Styles indicator on the status bar and select a style from the list Notes displays.

4. Press F11 or click the Text Style Cycle Key SmartIcon to cycle through the named styles when you format paragraphs.

Understanding the Data Types

Nine data types are available when creating a field. The data type definition enables you to define what type of data can be entered into the field. In most cases, you will be dealing with Text fields that can accept alphanumeric data such as phone numbers or regional offices names. However, you will encounter situations in which your form will require use of the other data types, such as Time, Number, Rich Text, Reader, Author, and Keyword type fields.

It's easy to select and format these field types; but once you begin developing more complex formulas that manipulate the entered data, you will want to know how each data type is stored. The following sections explain in further detail each of the available data types.

▶▶   See "Working with Formulas," p. 555

Text. Text consists of letters, punctuation, spaces, and numbers that are not used mathematically. Company names, addresses, and phone numbers with hyphens are all good examples of the Text data type. Individual text within a Text data type field cannot be styled by the user (bold, color, and so on); it can only be plain. The developer of the form, however, can globally change the format for all of the data contained in the field.

> **Note**
>
> To allow a user to change individual pieces of text in a field, you should use rich text as the data type. Here a user can designate bold, underline, and color for various texts, lines, and paragraphs.

> **Caution**
>
> Carefully consider the need to use Rich Text fields versus Text fields, which are easier to manipulate in formulas. Rich text fields cannot be evaluated for content. For example, if the field BodyText is a rich text field, you cannot display its contents or convert it to plain text by specifying @Text (BodyText). However, you can test for the availability of the field. The following formula tests for the availability of a rich text field:
>
> ```
> @Prompt([OK]; "Is BodyText Available"; @If(@IsAvailable(BodyText);
> "Yes"; "No"))
> ```

Time. The Time data type is comprised of both the time and the date; it is made up of letters, numbers, and punctuation. You must use the Time data type if you want Notes to recognize a value as a time-date value; otherwise, it is treated as text.

The following are examples of valid Notes time formats. When the Time data type is selected, the Field Properties InfoBox changes to display the available time and date options. See Figure 11.29.

Dates can range from 1/1/1000 through 12/31/9999, whereas times can range from 00:00:00 through 23:59:59 in the 24-hour format and from 12:00:00 A.M. through 11:59:59 P.M. in the 12-hour format.

Fig. 11.29 Notes can format time data in several different time, date, and overall time formats. It's as simple as selecting the displayed option.

Note

You can use formulas to convert text fields to date fields or vice versa. For example, @TextToTime("07/31/64") converts the text string "07/31/64" to the date 07/31/64. On the other hand, @Text(@Today) converts the value of today's date to text.

See Chapter 14, "Working with Formulas," for details on writing formulas to convert data types.

Numbers. The Number data type is used to represent all numbers that need to be displayed or calculated mathematically. It can include any of the ten numerals (0 to 9), the minus and plus signs (– and +), the decimal point (.), scientific notation (E), and the constant (e).

When the data type Number is selected, the Field Properties InfoBox displays the available number options, as shown in Figure 11.30.

Fig. 11.30 The number section on the Basics tab enables you to define the format for your number field, which is how it will be displayed in Notes.

The available Number formats are as follows:

- **General**—Displays numbers as they are entered, with zeroes being suppressed.

- **Fixed**—Displays numbers with a fixed number of decimal places as specified in the Decimal Places list box.

- **Scientific**—Displays numbers using exponential notation.

- **Currency**—Displays values with a currency symbol and two digits after the decimal point.

You can also choose whether to display percentages, parentheses, and punctuation at thousands. Table 11.3 summarizes the available number formats.

Table 11.3 Number Formats	
Format	**Examples**
Integers	123, –123
Decimal fractions	1.23, 0.12, –.123
Scientific notation	1.23E4, 1.23E-4, –1.23E4
Currency	$1.23, ($1.23)

Keywords. Keywords are a list of predefined values for a field that a user can select from. For example, you may want the user to select from a list of keywords for a field named BranchOffice. Notes stores keywords as text, but the keywords do not have to be made up of text characters. Using keywords lends consistency to the values that appear in the database documents because each user has the same set of values to choose from when entering information into a keyword field.

To create a Keyword list, follow these steps:

1. After creating the field, select Keywords as the data type in the Type list box.

2. In the Choices list box, select one of the following:

   - **Enter Choices (one per line)**—This is the most widely used option when building keyword lists.

   - **Use Formula for choices**—Developers like to use this technique to query other databases (mainly Notes) and bring in a view column of key words. This can be accomplished using @DbLookup or @DbColumn.

   - **Use Address dialog for choices**—This enables you to use the Address book as the keyword list, which is convenient to use if building a keyword list of names contained in your Address book.

   - **Use Access Control List for choices**—This enables you to pull in the predefined Access Control List for the current database to build the keyword list. This is a handy new feature that Notes developers will appreciate because now you can build more flexible security features into a database, such as possibly allowing users to choose who can access a document that they create. This may not be as useful if you have defined groups in the ACL instead fo actual user names.

   - **Use View dialog for choices**—This allows you to select a database, view, and column in the view to display choices from.

3. Select whether the field is to be editable or computed. Keyword files are editable because you want the user to choose the desired keyword from the list you are providing. If you want the value calulated, make the field a text field instead.

4. In the keyword text section, enter each keyword followed by a hard return. Figure 11.31 displays a "one per line" keyword list using Florida, Illinois, New York. You can sort the lists after entering by clicking the Sort button.

Fig. 11.31 Creating a simple keyword field will enable the user to select from predefined lists of data when entering data.

5. Select Allow values not in list if you want users to be able to enter additional keywords to your list. You can also select Allow multi-values to enable a user to select multiple entries from the keyword list.

Tip

Select Allow multi-values when you want to associate a document to multiple keywords. This is very useful when building views that require a document to be shown in multiple categories.

Caution

Any keywords entered by users will be accepted in the field, but will not be added to the list permanently. The newly added keyword will appear in the keyword list only for that document.

To determine how you want the keyword list to be displayed, select the Display tab (second tab) in the field's Properties InfoBox to select an interface style for displaying the keywords (see Figure 11.32). You can choose from three methods for displaying the list of keywords to users, plus designate the frame type and number of columns:

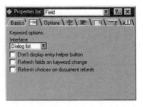

Fig. 11.32 Selecting the interface style for your keyword list enables you to creatively display your available options when a user inputs the data.

■ **Dialog list**—Presents a standard field interface. Users can press the spacebar to cycle through the list, type the first letter of the appropriate item to display it, or if there are multiple items with the same first letter, they can begin to type the first few letters of the word to display the appropriate choice, or press Enter to display the keyword dialog box listing all the items. This interface gives you the option of allowing users to enter items not included on the list (select Allow values not in this list); however, the additional items are not added to the list for future use.

■ **Checkboxes**—Presents a vertical list of checkboxes, each representing one list item, as shown in Figure 11.33. Users can select more than one of the available keywords.

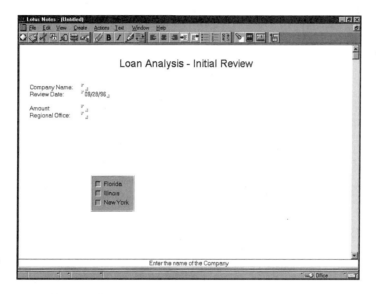

Fig. 11.33 Keywords can be formatted with checkboxes using a 3-D frame with one or more columns. Checkboxes enable users to select multiple keywords.

■ **Radio buttons**—Presents a vertical list of radio buttons, each representing one list item. Users can select only one item. Figure 11.34 displays how radio button keywords will appear.

Select Don't Display entry help button if you do not want to display the entry help button (see Figure 11.35). This is available only for dialog box list keywords. I like to keep this button to help the user easily identify keyword lists when inputting data; and it allows them to enter the data with only the mouse instead of hitting a key in the field.

You can also select Refresh fields on Keyword Change to automatically change other fields within the document that may be using that keyword selection in a formula. This is important if other fields are based upon the current keyword selection because you want them to be updated to display the correct information.

After you finish setting up the keyword field, apply any formatting options desired, close the Field Properties InfoBox, and save the form (or press Ctrl+S or the File Save SmartIcon).

Designing Applications

II

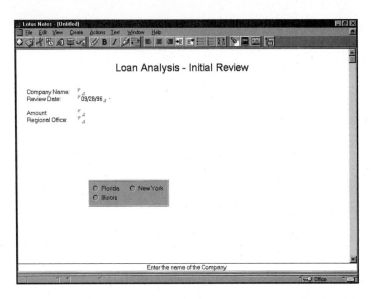

Fig. 11.34 Keywords can be formatted with radio buttons using a 3-D frame with two columns. Radio buttons enable users to select only one keyword.

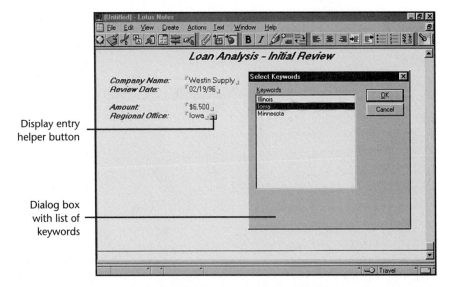

Display entry helper button

Dialog box with list of keywords

Fig. 11.35 The display entry help button displays the dialog box list of keywords when clicked.

> **Note**
>
> Always test out your keyword list by selecting the saved form from the Create menu and verify its interface style and the list of options.

You can also create synonyms for your keywords, which allows you to display one set of keywords to a user while storing another in the document. Keyword synonyms are designated by using | followed by the synonym. The following shows a keywords list for a Type of Loan field with synonyms:

- Commercial | C

- Private | P

- Real Estate | R

The leftmost name is displayed within the document, while both the name and the synonym (the rightmost name after |) are stored internally. If you categorize a view based on a keywords field, the keyword synonyms will be used as the category names.

Rich Text. Rich text information may contain text, tables, embedded or linked objects, file attachments, or graphics. The text in a rich text field can be individually styled (bold, color, and so on) with the Text Font command. Text fields cannot be individually styled and all of its contents are the same font and size.

Rich text fields are more versatile than Text fields, but they have two limitations: They cannot be combined with other data types in an @function, and they cannot be displayed in a view.

Authors. Authors is a data type that contains a list of user names (group names and access roles may also be used) that indicates who can edit a given document (see Figure 11.36). The user names should always be entered as a Notes user name. For instance, if a user's name in Notes is Jim Brown/ABC Corp, then his name should be entered the same way in an Authors field. The name entered is stored in the document as a fully distinguished name in hierarchical format. Authors fields are an interesting and integral part of security in Notes applications and documents because they provide another level of security beyond the ACL.

Fig. 11.36 An Authors field enables you to indicate who can edit a given document.

The database ACL will refer to the Authors field(s) in a document to determine who the Author is when you have assigned Author access to the database and will allow editing of the document based on the contents of that field. If there is no Author field and you have given the users of the database Author level access, they will not be able to edit their own documents. Since very few applications should allow anyone to edit all of the documents in a database (Edit level access), an Authors field should be included in all of your forms.

In most situations, you will want the user who originally composed a document to be able to edit the document later. To enable this, include at least one field that is an Authors data type. This field should be Computed when a composed field that has @UserName as the default field formula.

A document can contain multiple Authors fields; this is useful when you want to display the name of the document's original author in one field, and then designate Editor access to additional users with another field. Any user listed in any of a document's Authors fields can edit the document.

 ▶▶ See "Working with Formulas," p. 555

▶▶ See "Working with Formulas," p. 555

> **Caution**
>
> If the Authors field on a document is blank, it acts as if the field is not there. The original author, unless he/she has Editor access or above in the ACL, will not be able to edit the document. This can occur quite often (if you do not include a formula, it still calculates the username) if you allow the field to be editable and the user accidentally removes his/her name as the author.

> **Tip**
>
> Click and hold the Authors field in the read or edit mode to display the contents of the $UpdatedBy field.

> **Note**
>
> If a user says he or she cannot edit his or her own documents, verify that an Authors field exists and that it contains the user's name.

If you choose to make the Authors field editable, you can generate the list of choices in the Authors field by choosing one of the following options in the Choices list box on the Basics tab:

- **None**—In this situation, you must rely on a formula or on the authors to create the list of names.

- **Use Address dialog for choices**—This option displays the Names dialog box so users can select names from a Personal or Public Address Book. Select Look up names as each character is entered to help users fill in a name quickly. Notes looks up a match for the character in the open Address Book.

- **Use access control list for choices**—This option brings up a list of people, servers, groups, and roles in the access control list, which is a smaller subset than the Address book.

- **Use View dialog for choices**—This option brings up a dialog box containing entries from a column in a Notes database view. Select the database to look up, select a view, and select a column number. This is similar to using @DbColumn formula to bring in a list of users.

> **Note**
>
> You must select Allow multi-values for an Authors field to store a text list with multiple names. Concatenate the names in the formula with colons.

Readers. Similar to the Authors data type is Readers, which contains a text list of user names (group names and access roles may also be used) that determines who can read documents.

If provided, users can control read access to a particular document. If the document also contains a read access list, the two lists are combined. If a Readers field does not exist, the ACL defines who can read the documents. Users not included in a Readers field (regardless of ACL rights) cannot see the document in any view and therefore cannot read the document. In fact, if a user who is not listed in the Readers field makes a local replica of the database, the document will not be replicated. This includes database Managers. This does not, however, include servers that replicate the database, as long as the server is defined as User Type Server or Server Group in the ACL.

A Readers field has available the same choices to generate a list of readers as an Authors field. See the previous section, "Authors," for an explanation of these choices.

> **Note**
>
> Readers is similar to Authors, except that it limits read access to a document instead of granting edit access. It is important to remember that Readers and Authors fields can further restrict, but cannot extend a user's capabilities.

Names provides a means of displaying distinguished names in various formats. Distinguished names are always stored internally in their canonicalized format, listing all components of the name along with their labels. The Names field displays only the Common Name component of a distinguished name; that is, the person's first name and last name.

A Names field converts hierarchical names to a cleaner, abbreviated form, such as:

    Roy Rumaner/Management/US

instead of:

II

Designing Applications

```
Roy Rumaner=CN/Management=O/US=G
```

Use this type of field when you want to show user names as they appear on Notes IDs.

Use the Names field to display a list of user names or server names where an Author Names or Reader Names field is inappropriate because you are not trying to assign any type of read or write rights, such as when using a SendTo field in a workflow application.

Field Types

The field type determines whether the data is user entered or calculated. Not all field types are available for all data types, so be sure your selection makes sense. The four field types are: Editable, Computed, Computed for display, and Computed when composed.

All three of the Computed field types are non-editable, meaning the developer supplies the data or value automatically via a formula; the user cannot modify it. The purpose of Computed fields is to automatically generate data, such as time and author names, and then protect that information from being updated by the user.

Editable

Every form will contain some editable fields because you usually want the user to enter some data. After the user enters data, it is stored with the document. As part of an editable field you can optionally define a default value formula that forces an initial value to appear when the user composes the document, or utilize an input translation formula which converts the date the user enters or an input validation formula which checks the validity of the user's input, or even begin utilizing the LotusScript programming language to create an event to run when the user enters or exits a field.

Computed

Computed fields are automatically calculated upon composing and can be used with any data type except rich text. Computed fields allow only one formula. This formula is entered in the programmer pane by selecting the event Value. As a developer, you supply the value by either a constant or a formula that calculates the value.

Computed fields are used to provide field data based on calculations and manipulation of entered data. It is important to remember that this value is recalculated every time the document is refreshed and saved. A perfect example of the use of Computed fields is to capture the name of the document's Author in an Authors field and the date the document was created in a date field (see Figure 11.37).

▶▶ See "Working with Formulas," p. 555

Computed When Composed

This field is very similar to a computed field, except as the type states, the field value is only computed when the document is first created. This field type can be used with any data type except rich text. Fields that inherit information from another document are often Computed when composed fields, since inheritance also only happens when a document is first created as shown in Figure 11.38. See the earlier section in this chapter, "Understanding Form Hierarchy and Types," detailing response documents. These values are not permanently locked because these and other fields can still be changed through other field formulas or agents that are contained in the document.

Fig. 11.37   The formula for this simple Computed field will capture the author's name.

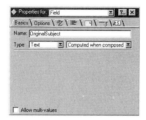

Fig. 11.38   This field in a Response document would inherit the Subject field from its parent document. The field name Original Subject dictates that the form will inherit the Subject data in the parent document.

Computed for Display

The value of a Computed for Display field is determined when the document is retrieved. The value is not stored in the document. Instead, the value is recalculated for display every time the document is opened for reading or editing. You can use this with any data type except rich text.

A good example of its use is to display the current time or the date the document was created as these values are automatically stored internally with each document. Developers also use Computed for Display field to present information contained in another field in a different format.

Caution

You cannot display the contents of a computed-for-display field in a view because it is not a value stored in the document. Also, it is not a good idea to use a lot of these field types on a form because they can slow down performance when opening a document.

> **Note**
>
> For computed or computed-when-displayed fields you can delay computing until after input validation formulas have been run by selecting Compute after validation. Input validation formulas are used to verify that the information entered in a field meets specific criteria or to verify that a required field has been filled in. This can help you speed up data entry.

Editable Field Formulas

Every field type accepts at least one formula, as described herein. Editable fields can accept up to three formulas for the field, while Computed (non-editable) can contain one formula. The three field formulas for editable fields are Default Value Formula, Input Translation Formula, and Input Validation Formula.

The formulas are optional, meaning you do not have to supply a formula for any of the three; but if you want to manipulate or automate data entry you will have to provide formulas. For example, after the user enters his data, you could convert the entry to uppercase letters and then validate the entry to make sure it meets certain requirements.

Formulas are written in the programmer pane, which is located at the bottom of the screen when editing a form. This is displayed by selecting <u>V</u>iew, <u>D</u>esign Pane. You can easily switch between the various fields by selecting the desired field in the Define list box to display the field's corresponding events, such as Default, Input Translation, and Input Validation formulas, in the Event list box.

When building formulas, you can also easily click the Fields & Functions button in the programmer pane to display a list of available Fields and Notes programming functions.

Default Value Formula

Default Value Formulas provide an initial value for the field, which the user can either accept or edit. Providing a default value ensures that the field gets filled in, and often removes the need for users to enter data such as their names or the date.

You can supply a constant such as "U.S.A." for a text field or 0.05 for a number field, or a formula that resolves to an appropriate value, such as Subtotal * 1.05. To construct the default formula, just write the expression; no assignment statement is needed (see Figure 11.39). However, if the Subtotal field used in the formula Subtotal * 1.05 is blank, an error will occur.

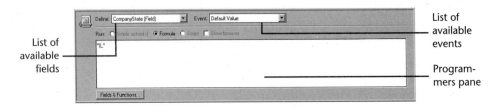

Fig. 11.39 Supply the constant "IL" for the text field CompanyState.

Note

The default field value is calculated only once when the document is first created.

Tip

If you want a text string in the formula entered as text (literally), you must enclose it in quotation marks (""). For number fields you need to enter the number; for example, 100 enters the number 100. You may want to have the default formula use another field and its value; for example, entering Price in the formula enters the value of the field named Price. Field names don't need quotation marks.

Troubleshooting

After double-clicking a field in design mode, I cannot see where to enter the default formula for the field.

You need to open the design pane for the field by selecting View, Design Pane. This will display the design pane that allows you to enter any formulas for the selected field.

Input Translation Formula

An input translation formula converts information entered by the user to adjust the field value or make the field conform to a specific format. Developers generally use them to convert text to proper case or capitalization, or to trim out blank spaces. It is important to remember that this formula executes when the document containing the field is saved or refreshed, and it must evaluate to a value suitable for storage in the current field.

When constructing the formula, be sure to reference the field name. For example, an input translation formula for the State field might convert its text to proper case (see Figure 11.40), and for the phone field, remove any spaces.

Fig. 11.40 @UpperCase(CompanyState) in the Input Translation Formula converts the CompanyState field to uppercase.

Input Validation Formula

The Input Validation Formula compares the data entered by the user with criteria specified by you in the formula. If the data satisfies the criteria, it is accepted; otherwise, a message is displayed. For example, an input validation formula for the CompanyName field might ensure that a value exists, as shown in Figure 11.41. The important point to remember is that this formula executes after the input translation formula, and when the document is saved or refreshed.

Fig. 11.41 The formula in this example verifies that a CompanyName exists; if it doesn't, a message is displayed.

Tip

Be careful not to use a lot of validation formulas on one form because the messages tend to annoy users when entering data.

An input validation formula usually uses the following three @functions:

- ■ `@If`—This enables you to test a condition and perform actions based on the result.

- ■ `@Success`—This instructs Notes to accept the value if the condition is true.

- ■ `@Failure`—This instructs Notes not to accept the value if the condition is false and to prevent the user from saving the document. This displays the message that you supply as an argument in this @function. Be sure to display a message that clearly indicates what is wrong and how the user can correct it.

Tip

If a field is required, you should indicate this in the field's Help description.

Layout Regions

Notes R4 has added a great new design feature called layout regions, which enables you to more easily design visually enticing forms. In earlier versions of Notes, forms designers had to insert fields, objects, tables, and so on, in one region, the form itself. With layout regions in Notes R4.5 you can now have regions within the form, allowing for more graphical features. The Personal Journal template (`JOURNAL4.NTF`) has an excellent example of a layout region in the Docinfo form. Figure 11.42 displays the Docinfo form being used in the database, while Figure 11.43 displays the layout region for that form in design mode.

Follow these steps to create a layout region:

1. Select the database and choose View, Design.

2. In the navigation pane, click Design, Forms.

3. Double-click the form you're designing.

4. Move the mouse pointer to the location where you want to place the layout region and choose Create, Layout Region, New Layout Region. This inserts a frame representing the layout region.

5. Add the desired text, fields, and objects in the region. You can add the following to a layout region, just as you can with forms and subforms: static text, graphics (either in the background or as selectable objects), hotspots for graphics and text, all fields (with greater numbers of display options) except rich text, buttons, and graphic buttons.

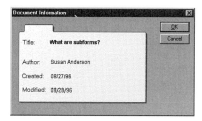

Fig. 11.42 Clicking the DocInfo button on the Journal Entry form opens the DocInfo form. Notice the folder graphic, static text, and fields. These have been placed in a layout region.

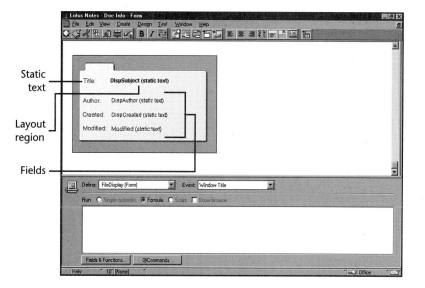

Fig. 11.43 Editing the DocInfo forms reveals how the layout region has been constructed with a graphic, static text, and the fields.

> **Note**
>
> Layout regions cannot contain rich text, so you cannot add the following to a layout region: links, tables, objects, attachments, pop-ups, sections, and rich text fields.

When creating layout regions, you will need to define the properties for the region in the Layout Properties InfoBox (see Figure 11.44). This can be accessed by selecting the layout region and then selecting Design, Layout Properties. Here you can define margins, widths, 3-D effects, borders, snapping to grid, and hiding options.

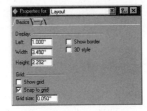

Fig. 11.44 The Layout Properties Infobox allows you to choose various options for your layout region.

6. Save the form.

Subforms

A subform is an excellent form-building shortcut that enables you to store often-used fields and other form elements together. In an earlier version of Notes, you needed to add fields individually; now, you can place subforms that consist of group fields on the form. Subforms are very similar to shared fields because they allow you to use fields in multiple forms within the database, except subforms are like groups of fields.

The Microsoft Document Library (DOCLIBM4.NTF) provides an excellent example of using a subform numerous times in the many forms contained in the database. Figure 11.45 displays the subform Document Workflow and its elements. Figure 11.46 shows this subform inserted in another form within that same database. This development technique will save you a lot of time.

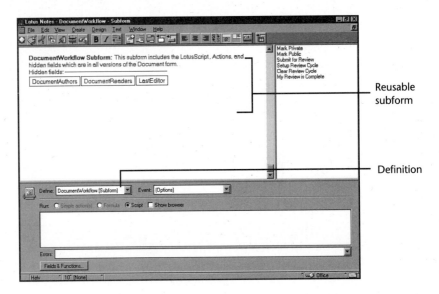

Fig. 11.45 The subform Document Workflow is used multiple times in other forms in the Microsoft Document Library database.

> **Note**
>
> Previously created subforms can be edited by clicking them directly in a form or by selecting Design Subforms in the navigation pane.

> **Caution**
>
> You cannot add other fields to the form that have the same name as those on the subform because this would be an attempt to have two fields with the same name on one form.

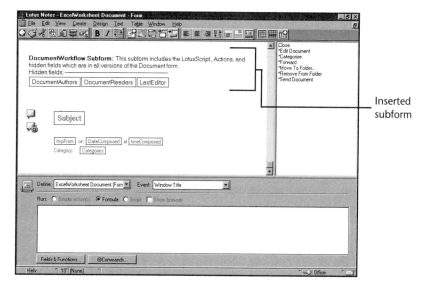

Fig. 11.46 Here's the subform being utilized in the MS Office/Excel Worksheet form.

The subform, which stores a group of form elements as a single design element, must have been created in advance. Subforms can contain the same components as regular forms. To create a new subform, perform the following steps:

1. Select the database that will have the new subform and choose Create, Design, Subform.

2. Choose Design, Subform Properties.

3. Give the new subform a name using the same rules as for forms.

4. In the Basics tab, choose the desired options for the subform: Include in Insert Subform dialog, Include in New Form dialog, or Hide Subform for R3 users.

5. Save the Subform.

II

Designing Applications

To insert a previously created subform, perform the following steps:

1. Open the desired form in edit mode and place the insertion point where you want to paste the subform and choose <u>C</u>reate, Insert S<u>u</u>bform. The Insert Subform dialog box is displayed, as shown in Figure 11.47.

Fig. 11.47   The Insert Subform dialog box enables you to place previously created subforms into your forms. Think of subforms as libraries of grouped fields that can be reused.

2. Select the subform you want to use and click OK to insert the subform into your form.

3. Save the form.

> **Note**
>
> Just as a form formula attached to a view changes how a whole document is displayed, a subform formula can be attached to a form to change how a portion of the document is displayed under different circumstances.

    ▶▶ See "Working with Formulas," p. 555

Tables

Tables are useful for summarizing information or lining up fields in rows and columns. A table placed on a form appears in every document created with the form. You can use tables to organize information or line up fields in rows and columns. Tables within forms can contain text, buttons, objects, or graphics. You can even omit the cell borders if you want to create an "invisible" table.

To create a table on a form, perform the following steps:

1. In the selected form, move the mouse pointer to the location where you want to place the table.

2. Choose <u>C</u>reate, Table.

3. Specify the starting number of rows and columns for the table and click OK. Figure 11.48 displays a 3-row, 2-column table.

Use the Table Properties InfoBox to change border styles and spacing for the high-lighted area or even highlight the table or individual rows or columns and choose Text, Text Properties to change the style of text or to hide text for the highlighted area.

Notes 4.5 allows you to merge cells either horizontally or vertically to allow you to use one table with various size rows and columns.

You also can now set the background color of any, or all, cells in a table.

4. Click the form; then save it.

Sections

Sections are useful for organizing documents that contain a lot of information. You can use sections to collapse one or more paragraphs in a document into a single line or to limit access to specific areas of a form. Sections make navigation in large documents easier. Readers can expand a section when they want to read its contents. Developers like to group related information in a large document into different sections.

◀◀ See "Creating Sections in Documents," p. 348

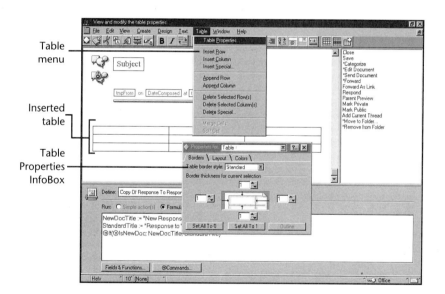

Fig. 11.48 Tables in forms are great for organizing and aligning fields. Use the Table menu or the Table Properties InfoBox to modify your tables.

To create a collapsible or controlled access section, perform the following steps:

1. Open the desired form in edit mode.

2. Select and highlight the paragraph(s) you want to collapse into a section.

3. Select <u>C</u>reate, Section, <u>S</u>tandard or <u>C</u>reate, <u>S</u>ection, <u>C</u>ontrolled Access.

Tip

Notes uses the first paragraph as the section title by default. To change a section's title, you must use the Section Properties InfoBox.

Hotspots

Hotspots are very useful for displaying pop-up text, using buttons to invoke a formula process, switching to linked destinations, or activating a Notes action.

 ◄◄ See "Adding Hotspots to Your Documents," p. 334

You can add a hotspot to an area of a document, such as text or a graphic. To create a hotspot, perform the following steps:

1. Open the desired form in edit mode.

2. Select the area you want to add the hotspot to.

3. Choose <u>C</u>reate, <u>H</u>otspot. You can now select either of the following:

- **Link Hotspot**—This enables you to link to a specific document, such as a Help document designed for your database. You must first use <u>E</u>dit, Copy as Li<u>n</u>k a portion of text on a target document prior to selecting this hotspot option.

- **Button**—Use this option to create a button and corresponding formula to perform some type of task.

- **Text Popup**—This enables you to enter the text you want the popup to display.

- **Formula Popup**—This enables you to enter a formula in the programmer's pane that will set the text you want the popup to display.

- **Action Hotspot**—Use this option to create an action hotspot that performs a specific action defined in the database.

Figure 11.49 displays the available hotspots.

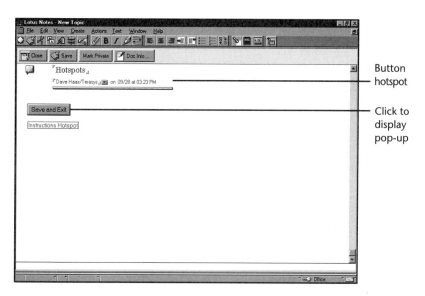

Button hotspot

Click to display pop-up

Fig. 11.49 Hotspots are useful for displaying help information, switching to linked destinations, and performing Notes actions.

From Here...

This chapter taught you how to begin creating forms. Forms are the building blocks and the basic structure of your database because it is the forms that contain the general layout, the field names, the field data types and formats, and any formulas that the field needs to calculate information. To learn more about how Notes uses the forms that you create, read the following chapters:

- Chapter 8, "Working with Documents," covers how to edit existing documents that could contain objects.

- Chapter 12, "Designing Views," shows how to create views to display the documents that store your objects.

- Chapter 17, "LotusScript Basics," teaches the basics of the powerful LotusScript programming language, which can be used to manipulate objects and links on your forms.

Designing Views

The secret to developing and building views in Notes is knowing the database's structure and having a vivid understanding of what you want to accomplish with the view. You need to understand what fields, data types, and forms exist in your database. Once you know that information, creating views is very easy.

In a Notes database, a view lists documents and provides a means of accessing them. Views are essentially tables of contents listing the documents in a Notes database. Unlike most printed books, a database can have many tables of contents, each of which selects, sorts, or groups the documents in the database in a specialized way.

Every database must have at least one view; most have multiple views. A view may display all of the documents in the database or show only a subset of existing documents. Often, you may want to view the same information in different ways. For example, you may want to see the information in a Contact or Address database organized and listed by Last Name, by State, by the date they were created, or by who created them, just to name a few of the possibilities.

Notes enables you to create multiple views for each database. You can design views that display only those documents that you want to see and sort the documents in a way that makes it easy to interpret the information.

The Logistics of Views

As previously mentioned, views are lists of documents in a Notes database. Depending on how they're designed, views can select, sort, or categorize documents in a variety of ways. Views can also show many types of information about the documents listed in them, such as author's name or date of creation. It is important to remember that views may show all documents in a database or only a selection of documents. You can split a view into three panes: the navigation pane, the view pane, and the preview pane.

This chapter discusses the following:

- Creating the view

- Assigning the view attributes

- Creating and formatting the view columns

- Using the selection formula to select documents to include in the view

- Using form formulas to select the form with which to display documents in the view

Designing Applications

Tip

Select View, Document Preview to toggle the preview pane.

Note

If the database's design allows for it, you can resize columns by dragging, or change the sorting in a column by clicking its title.

The views are created by the designer of a database. Users can customize panes and columns to some extent, but they cannot affect a view's design. Each view consists of one or more columns, each of which displays a field or the results of a formula. Think of views as a form of a report with each column in the report displaying the field information for the individual documents (rows).

Each line (row) in a view usually represents a single document. Notes R4 allows for multiple rows for a single document or word wrapping. Columns represent one type of information (field) available in the document. The developer writes a selection formula for each view, which picks what documents will be displayed in that view. The formula can select all the documents in the database, or select only those that meet certain criteria.

As a user, you can perform several tasks in a view. You can open a document, navigate between documents, find unread documents, forward documents (mail) to other Notes users, select documents to act upon (print, export, refresh fields, and so on), delete documents, copy documents, and refresh the view.

Views can either be shared or private. Shared views are available to all database users, unless restricted by a read access list assigned to the view. Private views can be seen only by the person who creates it. Private views are useful when a user wants to see the documents organized in a particular way. Think of private views as predetermined queries created by the user. However, a user's private view can display only those documents to which the user already has access; encrypted data and documents that the user does not have read access for will not be displayed.

Planning a View

Before creating a view in Notes, you should sketch the idea on paper. Your sketch should include the following information and should answer questions that may arise when creating views:

- Identify and state the purpose of each view. If the database is made up of main and response documents, it is a good idea to have at least one view of the database that shows each main document associated with its response documents. It is also a good idea to have a flat, nonhierarchical view that sorts documents by date.

- Which subset of documents will be displayed? Do you want to see all of the documents or just a subset?

- Decide how to sort documents in the view. To reduce the number of views, use columns that users can sort themselves.

- Try to visualize the columns of information (fields). Do you want to include all of the fields in columns or just some specific fields?

- Will unread markers be displayed? Do you want unread documents to appear in a different color and/or be marked with a star?

- Will the column display the field data or be manipulated in a column formula? Sometimes developers combine two fields, such as City and State, into one column using a column formula like City + ", " + State.

- Should Responses be indented beneath the parent document to display the hierarchy relationship? Indenting enables you to organize your related parent/child documents for easier viewing.

- Do you want to include any view statistics? For example, you may want to indicate whether a contact entry has had five call reports (responses).

- Do you want to categorize any columns? Categorization enables you to sort and organize your data to locate data.

- Decide if access to read the documents in each view is restricted. For tighter security, you can add access lists to forms rather than views.

- Decide if any shared or private-on-first-use folders are needed.

- Identify any hidden columns that are needed for special sorting or for other applications' lookups.

- Decide on the view style, such as colors for view elements, and the view background and the number of lines per row.

- Decide on column colors, type styles, and widths (either resizable or set).

Creating Views

After designing and planning the view, you can create a view in Notes by performing the following steps:

1. Select Create, View or press the Create View SmartIcon to display the Create View dialog box, as displayed in Figure 12.1. The Select a location of the new view list box defaults to creating a Private view.

Fig. 12.1   The Create View dialog box enables you to name and select the type of view that you want.

2. In the Ⅴiew name box enter a name for the view. This can be left as Untitled and changed from within the View Properties Info box.

    ▶▶ See "Naming the View," p. 483

3. Click Sha**r**ed if you want to create a Shared view. This can be further defined by selecting Ⲣersonal on first use. Notice that the Ⲥelect a location for the new view list box changes to display the current view folders (see Figure 12.2).

Fig. 12.2   Notice how the Create View dialog box changes to reflect a Shared view.

> **Note**
>
> A Ⲣersonal on-first-use View combines the attributes of the shared and private views. It is created as a shared view; but after it is used by an individual user for the first time, it becomes a private view. Developers use this option when they want to create specialized private views for each user, but they don't want to have each user's name on the View menu.

4. Click OK to create and save the view. The newly created view appears in the design pane when Design Views is selected in the navigation pane, as shown in Figure 12.3.

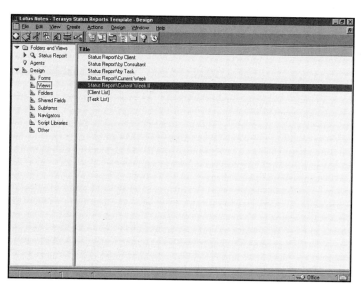

Fig. 12.3 The view, Untitled, appears in the design pane after being created and saved. If you named the view, its name would appear.

Double-click the new view to open the view in design mode, as shown in Figure 12.4.

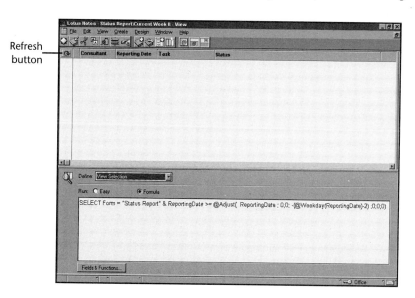

Fig. 12.4 The newly created untitled view is opened in edit mode. Here is where you begin defining the structure of the view.

The new view is identical to the view that is designated as the default design view. Figure 12.5 shows an example of a view based upon a default design view. Notice that there are preexisting columns. Otherwise, if no view has been designated as the default design view, the new view contains only one column that displays the document number (@DocNumber).12.

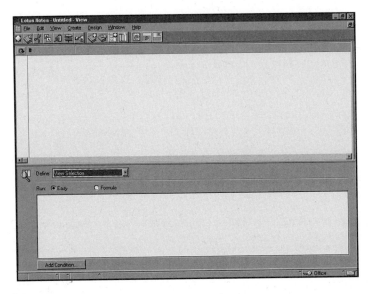

Fig. 12.5 This is an untitled view opened in edit mode that has not been based upon a default design view. Notice that the new view contains only one column to display the document number.

At this point, you can now modify the view by adding and modifying columns and their corresponding attributes.

Copying a View

Occasionally, you may want to copy a view from one database and use it in another, possibly modifying it to meet the new application's needs.

▶▶ See "Database Templates," p. 1123

To copy and paste a view, perform the following steps:

1. Select the database containing the source view.

2. In the navigation pane, select Design Views to display the available list of views in the Title pane.

3. Select the view you want to copy from the Views list.

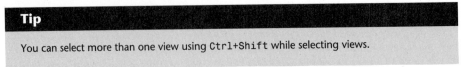

Tip

You can select more than one view using Ctrl+Shift while selecting views.

4. Select Edit, Copy or press the Edit Copy SmartIcon.

5. Switch to the database where you want to paste the form.

6. Select Edit, Paste and the new view's name will appear in the views list.

Caution

If you are copying and pasting a view from the same database, the view is pasted into the list of views but is renamed by changing the view name to "Copy of" viewname. This can be renamed using the View Properties InfoBox.

▶▶ See "Naming the View," below

Defining View Attributes

Before you begin laying out columns in the view, you will need to define some basic attributes, such as the view's name, styles, and default options, in the view's Properties InfoBox.

To open this InfoBox, perform the following steps:

1. Open the desired view in design mode.

2. Select Design, View Properties, or right-click and choose View Properties.

The Basics tab in the View Properties InfoBox, as shown in Figure 12.6, essentially enables you to supply a name, alias, and comment for the view.

▶▶ See "Using Aliases (Synonyms)," p. 485

Fig. 12.6. The Basics tab in a view's Properties InfoBox is used to define the Name, Alias, and any Comments for a view.

Naming the View. The name you type in the Name text box can be any combination of characters including spaces, and it is case-sensitive. A name can have up to 255 characters , but only the first 32 will appear on menus and in dialog boxes. View names appear on the View menu; thus, when you name a view, you are giving it the title that the user will choose. The name should be logical and indicate the criteria or sort order; for example, View By Contact. The following sections describe in more detail the specifics of naming a view.

Specifying Accelerator Keys. When naming a view, you should also use accelerator keys. The first unique letter in the form name is used as the view's accelerator. To force Notes to use a different letter as the accelerator, insert an underscore before the desired letter. In By _Contact, for example, the underscore forces the letter C to be used as the accelerator.

Ordering View Names. Consider how the views are ordered on the View menu. The View menu automatically sorts names in alphabetical order. If you want more highly used views to appear first, you can use numbers as the first character. For example:

```
1. Current Week
2. by Task
3. by Client
```

> **Tip**
>
> View names with numbers provides easy accelerators for users, because the numbers are unique and become the accelerator keys.

Grouping Views with Cascading Menus. You can use cascading views to group a series of views in a cascading submenu under a single name. This shows the user that the views are related and can save space on the menu. You define a cascading view by entering the top-level view name, followed by a backslash (\) and the additional view name. Notes allows one level of cascade. For example, these two view names would appear under View, By Contact:

```
By Contact \ Last Name
By Contact \ Company Name
```

When the user chooses View and highlights 1. By Contact, a cascading menu appears, as displayed in Figure 12.7.

Fig. 12.7   Cascading view names enables you to organize your views for quick, easy access. Views can also be accessed in the navigation pane.

Hiding a View. Occasionally, you may want to "hide" a view from the database's users by not displaying it on the View menu. Developers like to hide views for keyword look-ups or to save views for future use. To hide a view, enclose the view name in parentheses. For example:

```
(Client List)
```

> **Caution**
>
> Hidden views usually exist for use with formulas or LotusScript and Agents. Hiding a view is not a security measure. Users can still make a private view and see its data if they have Reader access to the database and have been given permission to create private views.

Using Aliases (Synonyms). Aliases (also called synonyms) in views work exactly like using synonyms in forms. Aliases enable you to change the view's name on the View menu without tracking down and rewriting formulas that reference the original name. If you didn't use aliases, these formulas and even doclinks from other databases would generate errors. Figure 12.8 displays an example of naming a view with an alias.

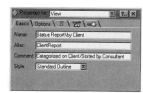

Fig. 12.8   You should use logical names for your views, plus use aliases to prevent any future programming agony.

> **Caution**
>
> If you want to rename a view, be sure to keep the original name as a synonym so any doclinks pointing to that view can still be opened.

Setting the View Options. The Options tab in the view's Properties InfoBox as shown in Figure 12.9 enables you to further define the properties of your view12. You can designate the view to be the default view, how view opens (expanded or collapsed), whether response documents will appear in a hierarchy, and even whether the view will appear in the View menu. The following list details the specifics of the available selections in the Options tab:

Fig. 12.9   The Options tab displays various default options for your view.

■ **Default when database is first opened**—This designates the view as the default view; and when the database is first added and opened by a user, this view will appear. Only one default view is allowed per database. The default view is marked with a star in the list of views in the Title pane. Your default view should not place restrictions on who can access the view since it is the first view shown to users when they open the database.

> **Note**
>
> Selecting this option in one view automatically deselects this option for another view because there can be only one default view.

■ **Default design for new folders and views**—This enables the developer to use the view as the default view when the designer or a user is designing other views and folders in the database. If selected and creating new views, the new view will initially be identical to this view. The view used for this purpose should be one which displays all documents in the database so that users who create folders with this view are not excluding documents that they move to a folder.

■ **Show response documents in a hierarchy**—You can indent response documents and response-to-response documents under their parent documents. This option enables you to indent response documents an additional three spaces under main documents. A response hierarchy is useful when readers want to see the progression of a discussion or want to see related topics grouped together. Discussion databases often use this format in a main view. Figure 12.10 shows a view where the option Show response documents in a hierarchy has been selected.

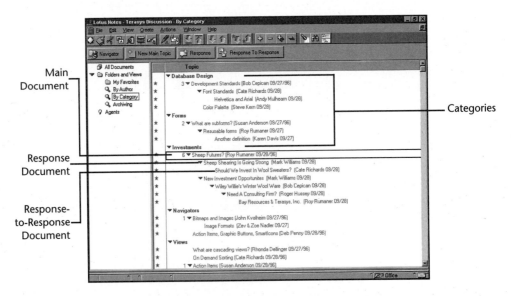

Fig. 12.10.   A hierarchical view indents and associates response documents under corresponding main documents.

A flat, nonhierarchical view doesn't distinguish between main and response documents. This is useful when the listing isn't focused on topics, such as in a By Author view or where there are no response documents, as shown in Figure 12.11.

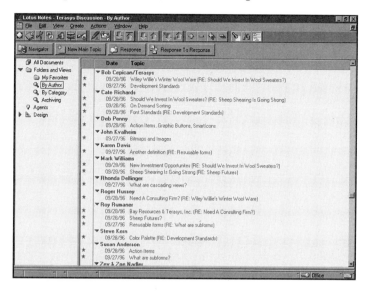

Fig. 12.11 A nonhierarchical view does not indent response level documents under their corresponding main parent documents. This view is categorized by Author Name and sorted by descending Date.

To indent response-to-response documents, create a column immediately to the left of the column that contains your main documents, such as the one shown in Figure 12.12.

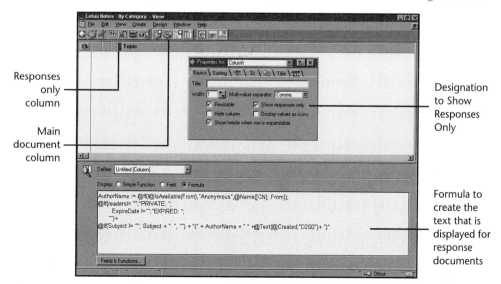

Responses only column

Main document column

Designation to Show Responses Only

Formula to create the text that is displayed for response documents

Fig. 12.12 Creating a hierarchical view requires two columns of importance: one to display the main-level documents and one to the left of that for displaying response-level documents.

▶▶ See "Showing Responses Only," p. 495

This new column will need to have Show Response Only selected and a formula written to display the response documents:

- **Show in View menu**—This option displays the view in the View menu. Deselecting this is synonymous with adding () around a view name and hiding the view, but in this case the name does not contain (). The major difference is that when formulas refer to the hidden view using parentheses, they need to include the parentheses.

- **On Open**—Here you can control when the user is in a view each time it is opened. Go to the last opened document, Go to the top row, or Go to the bottom row.

- **On Refresh**—A view that's ready to be refreshed has the refresh icon in the top-left corner of the view pane. This enables you to display the refresh indicator button when a refresh is needed for the view as shown in Figure 12.13.

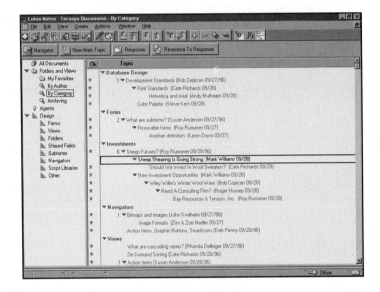

Fig. 12.13 The refresh indicator is displayed when the view needs to be refreshed to display any new documents that have been created.

- **Collapse all when database is first opened**—This initializes the view to collapse the existing documents into their categories when the view is opened.

Tip

I like to use this option to allow users to easily locate categorized documents in a very large view.

Setting the Style for the View. Notes R4.5 has dramatically improved upon how a view can appear. These new features can be found in the Styles tab of the View Properties InfoBox, as shown in Figure 12.14.

Fig. 12.14   The Styles tab enables you to set properties, such as color, and whether to use multiple rows for headings and rows. Some are new features to Notes R4.5.

Developers can find a variety of options in the Styles tab that enable them to affect how a view appears. In the Styles tab of the View Properties InfoBox, you can define the color of the following:

- **Background**—Generally, a light-colored background is easier to view data. White is the default.

- **Unread Rows**—This indicates by its color whether a document in a view has been read. Black is the default.

- **Column Totals**—This enables you to have column totals stand out from the other data. Gray is the default.

- **Alternate Rows**—This is a new feature that enables developers to interchange row colors and highlights for easier reading. For example, one row might be highlighted in yellow, the next row white, the next yellow, and so on.

- **Show Selection Margin**—The selection margin is used for selecting documents. If you need a clean space that shows only documents without other identifier information, you can remove the document selection margin at the left. Only in rare development situations would you deselect this option to prevent the users from marking or selecting documents to copy or refesh. Readers can still select documents by holding Shift as they click document names, but they won't be able to see which documents are selected.

- **Show Column Headings**—If deselected, the view's column headings will be hidden.

- **Beveled or Simple Headings**—In the Show Column Headings list box, you can indicate how you want the column headings to appear. The Beveled option is the default option that bevels the appearance of view columns. In Figure 12.15, you can see that the simple headings option displays the view columns without column separators using black text on white background.

Fig. 12.15 Use the Simple headings option to display the column headings.

- **Lines per heading**—You can now select the number of rows (1-5) the column heading can have. This is a great feature for using long column heading names, as shown in Figure 12.16.

Fig. 12.16 You can increase the size of your column headings; this example uses two lines. You can even hide the selection margin on the far left. This improves how views can be viewed and printed.

- **Lines per row**—Another new feature is the ability to have multiple rows in the view. This gives you the opportunity to use word wrapping and improve the reporting capabilities of Notes, as shown in Figure 12.17.

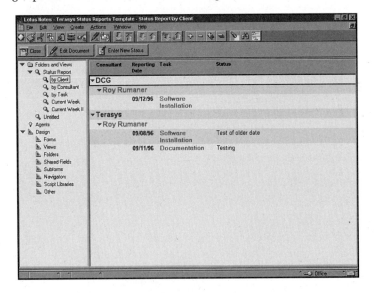

Fig. 12.17 The capability to designate multiple rows for each row in the view enables you to use word wrapping.

> **Note**
>
> Since rich text fields cannot appear in a view and they normally contain long strings of text that you would want to word wrap, you may want to convert the rich text field to a text field prior to attempting to use the word wrapping feature for a field in view column.

- **Shrink rows to content**—This essentially eliminates any extra rows that are not used by a document if you have indicated the Lines per row option to be more than one, thus saving view and reporting space.

- **Spacing**—Spacing, which is the vertical space between documents, can be specified as either single, $1\,^1/_4$, $1\,^1/_2$, $1\,^3/_4$, or double.

Advanced Features. The Advanced tab (with the beanie hat icon) enables you to select more advanced view features, as shown in Figure 12.18. This section enables you to specify when Notes should refresh or discard the view index, how to display unread marks, and which forms to use when a document is opened in this view. The attributes you can designate are described in the following sections.

Fig. 12.18   The Advanced tab enables you to establish when to refresh or discard the view index, plus designate a Form formula.

Refreshing the View. In the Refresh Index list box you can select Auto, after first use; Automatic; Manual; and Auto, at most every use. A view index, unrelated to a full text search index, is an internal filing system that lets Notes create the most current list for a view. When documents change, the view index must be refreshed to display the changes. To improve performance time, you can change how frequently the view index is refreshed by selecting one of the following options:

- **Auto, after first use**—The default option, this updates the view every time the view is opened after the first time by adding changes incrementally to the view index. Users never need to be concerned about whether the view displays the latest changes, but it takes a little longer for a view to display the first time the view is opened.

- **Automatic**—This option keeps the view updated whether or not users ever open the database, by adding changes incrementally to the view index. Users never need to be concerned about whether a view displays the latest changes, and views open more quickly.

- **Manual**—This option relies on the user to refresh the view. This option is useful with large databases, if it isn't critical for the view to be kept up-to-date, because it enables large databases to open faster. If users want to look for a new document, they can refresh the view by clicking the refresh indicator.

- **Auto, at most every**—This option enables you to specify how frequently the view index should be updated. This is also a good compromise between Automatic and Manual Indexing for large databases that change fairly often. The view's index is updated automatically only at the specified interval. If a user opens a database in which changes have been made since the last indexing, a yellow question mark appears at the top left of the view to indicate that changes have been made that are not visible in the view. Users have the option of manually refreshing the view to see the updates.

Discarding the Index. Change Discard index from Never to one of the other choices to save disk space, if slower view displays are acceptable. If the view index is deleted, users have to wait for the view index to be re-created. You have the following options:

- **Never**—This option preserves the view index permanently; updates are added to the existing index. The view index never has to be re-created, but this option takes up more disk space than the other options. Use this for views that users frequently need, so they don't have to wait for a new view index to be created when they open the database. For large databases, this can take several minutes.

- **After each use**—This option deletes the view index as soon as the database is closed. This option saves the most disk space, but the index must be rebuilt the next time the view is opened. Select this option when the view is used infrequently, but on a predictable basis; for example, only on Friday afternoons when an agent is run.

- **If inactive for _n_ days**—This option deletes a view index only if the view hasn't been used in the specified number of days. If the view is deleted, the view index is rebuilt the next time the database is opened. (This option doesn't affect local databases.) Select this option when a database is used infrequently on an unpredictable basis as a compromise between the Never and After each use options.

Displaying Marks for Unread Documents. In the Unread Marks list box, the Standard compute in hierarchy option displays asterisks for unread main documents and response documents, and for any collapsed categories containing unread main or response documents. Because this choice displays unread marks for every level, it displays the view the slowest, but gives the readers the most information about documents they need to read. You also have the following choices:

- **Unread documents only**—This option displays asterisks only for unread main documents. Unread marks do not appear next to response documents or collapsed categories. This choice displays the view faster than the Standard display and is a good compromise between showing unread marks at every level and not showing them at all.

■ **None**—This option does not display unread marks; it displays the view fastest, but doesn't help users see which documents they haven't read. Use this only if users don't need to see asterisks next to new or modified documents they haven't read, or if this is a reference type of database, where the users will never read all of the documents. Users can still navigate to the next unread document by using SmartIcons.

Security Options. You can select the Security tab (with the key icon) to define a limited list of users who can access this view. Figure 12.19 shows the Security options for a view. The default option is All readers and above, which utilizes what has been defined in the ACL for the current database. This is not a true security measure, however, as users can create private views to mimic any view you have created.

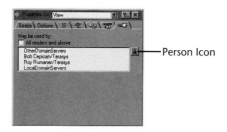 ——Person Icon

Fig. 12.19   The Security tab enables you to decide who (users and groups) can access the view. The initial list shown resides in the ACL; however, you can refine the list using the Address Book.

To refine this list further, follow these steps:

1. Deselect All readers and above.

2. Click the Person icon to select a name or group from a Personal or Public Address Book.

Creating Columns in a View

To fully create a view, you need to create columns. A column displays the contents of a field or the result of a formula, which may involve one or more fields. A new view always includes a column labeled # (using the formula @DocNumber to number the documents in the display) or columns that were included in the default design view which you may or may not want to keep. Keep the following tips in mind when creating columns:

■ Delete any columns that you do not want to use by selecting them and hitting the Delete key or by choosing Edit, Cut if you want to reuse and paste the column in another location.

■ You can add up to 255 columns as you desire.

■ It is advisable to fit the columns on the screen so the user is not forced to horizontally scroll the display to see them.

■ Always place the categorized columns in the leftmost position of the view followed by sorted columns, then unsorted columns.

To create a column, perform the following steps:

1. Click where you want the column to appear.

2. Choose Create, Insert, New, Column to insert a column to the left of the currently highlighted column. If you want to add another column to the right of the last column in the view, choose Create, Append New Column instead.

3. Double-click the new column header to display the column's Properties InfoBox, as shown in Figure 12.20.

Fig. 12.20 The column's Properties InfoBox enables you to establish how the column will appear.

Tip

Right-click the column header and select Column Properties to display the Properties InfoBox.

Caution

If you are editing a view that contains documents and you change the view by adding a column or modifying an existing column, you should click the Refresh indicator button to update the view.

Basic Settings

In the Basics tab of the column's Properties InfoBox you can enter the name of the column, set the width of the column, decide whether to hide the column, and several other options. Figure 12.20 in the preceding section displayed the basic options that are available for a column. The following sections describe these options.

Adding a Column Title. In the Title box, enter a title to be displayed at the top of the column; using a title is optional. If the title is longer than the defined column width, it will be truncated to fit the width unless you have designated multiple rows for the column header. See "Setting the Style for the View" earlier in this chapter for more information about the Lines per Heading option.

Note

Columns that are only one or two characters wide should not contain titles. Generally, these types of columns are categorized, and the categories themselves are self-evident for naming purposes.

Determining the Column Width. Enter the desired width of the column, in characters, in the Width box. Notes assigns a default width of ten characters to new columns, but you can make a column as narrow or as wide as you want. Depending on the font name and size, a variable amount of characters will fit in the length, not just ten characters.

Tip

TipDrag the column header lines with the mouse to size the column.

Choosing a Separator for Multiple Values. If the column shows several values (usually generated by a multi-value field), you can specify how you want to separate the values with the Multi-value separator field. If None is selected, the multiple value field is displayed as a single text string.

◀◀ See "Keyword Fields," p. 106
◀◀ See "Basics Settings," p. 113

Controlling Column Resizing. Select the Resizable option if users have the capability of adjusting the column header themselves as they use the database. The width reverts to the design setting when the database is closed.

Hiding Columns. The Hide column option is useful for columns that do not display information needed by users, but that are needed by the view's design, such as a column used only for sorting purposes. Figure 12.21 shows an example of a hidden sort column using the CreationDatefield. The column is sorted in ascending Date order.

Note

Hidden columns are not hidden when designing a view in design mode. They are hidden only when viewed in the view pane, and the width of a hidden column does not affect the view size on the screen.

Showing Responses Only. Select the Show responses only option to display the column only if the contents of the columns will display documents of the response or response-to-response document type. All response documents are displayed under their corresponding main documents; each level of response is indented an additional three spaces. This option is widely used in discussion databases or databases where you will want to show the parent (main document) to child (response) relationship. See "Setting the View Options" earlier in this chapter for more information on the Show response documents in a hierarchy option. You can define only one column as a responses only column in a view.

Hidden sort column

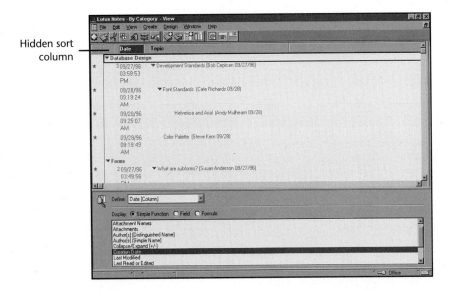

Fig. 12.21   A hidden sort column is used to force a sort on preexisting fields.

Caution

Why do you place a Show response only column to the left of columns that display only main document information? Because all columns defined after the responses only column will display data for main documents only.

Normally, Notes allows for information to be displayed only within the limitations of a column's width. But when Show Responses Only is selected, that restriction is bypassed.

To see the difference, use Ctrl+X to cut the column containing the Show responses only and re-fresh the view. Notice how the view changes? Now, Paste (Ctrl+V) the column back into the view.

Displaying Values as Icons. Select the Display values as icons option to display one of over 300 predefined icons in the column to graphically represent special values, such as attachments. Write a formula for the column; the result of the formula determines which icon is displayed. The following formula determines whether a document has an attachment and, if so, displays the appropriate attachment icon:

```
@If(@TextToNumber(@Version) > 122;
    @If(@IsDocTruncated;
        30;
    @IsAvailable($ContentIcon);
        $ContentIcon;
```

```
    (@Contains(@LowerCase(From); " pager ") ¦ @Contains(@LowerCase(SendTo); "
pager "));
        46;
    @Attachments;
        @If(@Contains(@LowerCase(@AttachmentNames); "message.wav" :
"vmsg_hdr.wav");
            44;
        @Contains(@LowerCase(@AttachmentNames); ".wav");
            15;
        @Contains(@LowerCase(@AttachmentNames); ".tif");
            47;
        5);
    0);
@IsAvailable($ContentIcon); $ContentIcon; @Attachments; 5; 0)
```

Use 0 as the false case when you want to leave the column blank. The formula above returns 0 when the document has no attachments, so nothing is displayed. Figure 12.22 displays a view using this formula.

Attachment icon

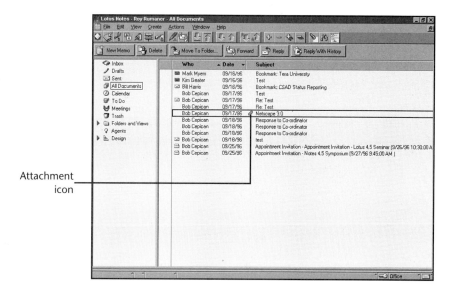

Fig. 12.22 The attachment icon (miniature paper clip) appears in the third column using the preceding formula.

Indicating Expandable Rows. The Show twistie when row is expandable option displays a green triangle that users can click to see categorized documents within a collapsed view or folder as shown in Figure 12.23.

Sorting Options

Sorting and categorizing is the fun and exciting part of building views. It enables you to be creative in how you will display your documents to users. You should always sort the view on at least one column; otherwise, documents and responses appear in the order they were composed.

The Sorting tab in the column's Properties InfoBox, displayed in Figure 12.24, enables you to define how the column will be sorted and categorized. The options available are described in the following sections.

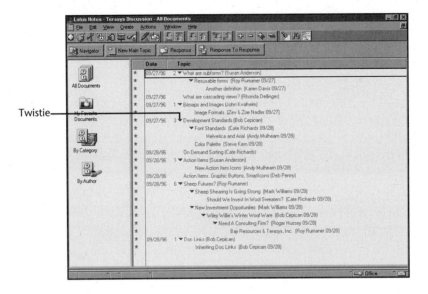

Twistie

Fig. 12.23.   The twisties enable users to quickly navigate views by expanding and collapsing categorized columns.

Fig. 12.24   The Sorting tab enables you to specify the sorting and categorization attributes for your view.

Sort Order. In the Sort section, select None, Ascending, or Descending. For alphabetical listings, ascending order is usually preferred. However, for Date columns, descending is preferred to display the most recent documents first. Figure 12.25 shows a view that sorts the Document Title in ascending order and then the Creation Date in ascending order. You can sort views in multiple ways and combinations. However, remember that columns are sorted from left to right.

Sort Type. In the Type section, choose Standard or Categorized. Standard is the default option, but you should select Categorized if the view will contain categories. Figure 12.26 contains a view with categories.

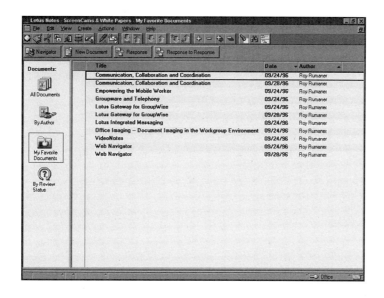

Fig. 12.25   This view is sorted first by the Document Title and then the Document Creation Date. Notice there is no categorization of columns.

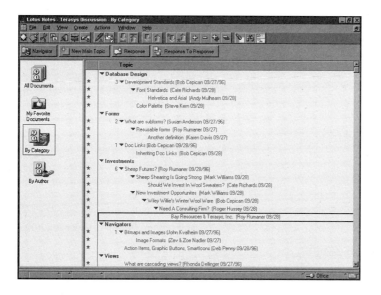

Fig. 12.26   This view has been sorted by the Category field and then subcategorized by the Document Type (Main Document, Response Document, or Response-to-Response Document). Each category enables users to drill down on information.

> **Note**
>
> If sorting a view by chronological order, you must design a column and sort using a formula with @Created. The formula function @Created returns the date the document was created. Using this time value, you can sort the column in ascending or descending order.

Sorting on Demand. You can designate one or more columns in a view as sortable on demand. Users click these special columns and see the documents in the order defined by the column.

To establish this feature select the Click on Column Header To Sort option. You can choose between Ascending, Descending, Both, or Change to view. The Change to view option lets you select a view that Notes will switch to when the user clicks the column. In the column header, the Ascending option is represented by an upward pointing arrow, the Descending option displays a downward pointing arrow, the Both option displays both arrows, while the Change to view option displays a curved arrow. Figure 12.27 shows a column heading with the Click on Column Header to Sort option selected using Change to view.

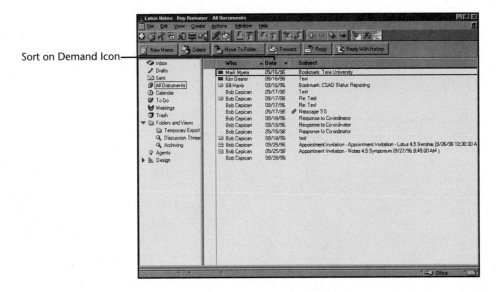

Fig. 12.27 Users click these special columns and choose a sorting method to see the documents in the order they choose. You can designate one or more columns in a view as sortable on demand.

If Ascending, Descending, or Both is selected, you can select the Secondary Sort Column to display option to list boxes that enable you to designate a second column and its sort order to automatically sort upon.

> **Note**
>
> Use the column heading title text to warn users what will happen if they use the Change to view option. For example, you might title the column "Click here to switch to the By Author view." Plus, the view they switch to should probably have this same option specified to return to the original view to prevent the user from getting lost.

Case-Sensitive and Accent-Sensitive Sorting. Deselect the Case-Sensitive Sorting option if you do not want the sort to be case-sensitive. Deselect Accent-sensitive sorting if you do not want the sorting for this column to be accent-sensitive.

Displaying Totals. The Totals option enables you to specify how you want totals to appear. The options are None, Total, Average per document, Average per subcategory, Percentage of parent category, and Percentage of entire view. You can click Hide details to hide the details row but show the totals for the categories.

Defining the Style for the Column

The Styles tab (its icon shows A and Z) in the Column Properties InfoBox enables you to define the style attributes for the selected column. Figure 12.28 displays the Styles tab options available in the column's Properties InfoBox. Here you can define the following attributes to improve the appearance of your view:

- Font

- Size

- Style (Select any predefined styles)

- Text Color

- Justification (Align the data in your column to be Left, Right, or Center)

Fig. 12.28   The options in the Styles tab are very logical. You can select font, size, color, and so on to make your view stand out when viewing and printing.

II

Designing Applications

> **Tip**
>
> Select Left when working with text and time-date values, Right when displaying numbers (especially numbers with decimal places), and Center when working with small values that you want to stand out (such as Yes and No).

One new feature developers will appreciate is that style changes are automatically reflected in the view. This saves an immense amount of time, since you don't have to close a dialog box to preview any changes. Also, you can click Apply to All to apply any changes made to all of the existing columns in the view, so you don't have to individually change each column.

Displaying Numbers

The Numbers tab in the column's Properties InfoBox (its icon is a large 2 and a small 1, as shown in Figure 12.29) enables you to define how columns with numbers will appear. You can choose among the following four number formats:

- **General**—This option displays numbers as they are entered. Zeroes to the right of the decimal point are suppressed; for example, 8.00 displays as 8.

- **Fixed**—This option displays numbers with a fixed number of decimal places; for example, 8 displays as 8.00. You can select the desired number of places from the Decimal Places list.

- **Scientific**—This option displays numbers using exponential notation; for example, 80,000 displays as 8.00E+04. You can select the desired number of decimal places from the Decimal Places list.

- **Currency**—This option displays values with a currency symbol and two digits after the decimal point; for example, $8.00.

Fig. 12.29 The Numbers tab enables you to define the numbering format for the column.

After choosing the numbering format, you can also set the following options:

- **Percentage (value * 100)%**—This displays values as percentages; for example, displays .80 as 80%.

- **Parentheses on negative numbers**—This displays negative numbers enclosed in parentheses; for example, (8) instead of –8.

■ **Punctuated at thousands**—This displays large numbers with the thousands separator; for example, 8,000.

Time and Date Settings

The Time and Date tab in the column's Properties InfoBox, displaying a clock and calendar icon as shown in Figure 12.30, enables you to define the following time and date attributes:

■ **Show**—You have four choices for controlling combinations of time and date: Date and time, Date only, Time only, and Today and Time. If you select the last choice, values indicating the current date will display Today instead of the date. Values indicating the previous day will display Yesterday instead of the date. All other values will display the date.

■ **Date format**—You can select MM/DD, MM/YY, and MM/DD/YY.

■ **Time format**—You can select HH:MM or HH:MM:SS to display the time using a 12-hour or 24-hour clock format.

■ **Time zone**—You can select Adjust time to local zone, Always show time zone, or Show only if zone not local. Adjust all times to local zone displays the time relative to the time zone of the reader. For example, a document created at 3:00 P.M. in New York that is read by a user in Los Angeles adjusts to Pacific Standard Time; the creation time is displayed as 12:00 P.M.

The Always show time zone displays the time zone where the document was created. With this option, the creator's time zone is always shown. The Show Only If Zone Not Local option displays the time zone where the document was created only when the document is read by someone in a different time zone.

Fig. 12.30   Here you select the date, time, and time zone formatting attributes.

Changing the Style of the Column Title

This is one of the most desired design features that developers have been wanting incorporated into views. Previously, column headings were not editable. Now, using the Title tab in the column's Properties InfoBox, you can modify how the column headings appear.

II

Designing Applications

The available options are identical to the styles tab, except that any changes made are reflected in the column title. You can also use multiple rows in the header by switching to the view's Properties and selecting the Style tab. See "Setting the Style for the View" earlier in this chapter for more information on the Lines per heading option.

Defining Column Formulas

Column formulas specify what information should be displayed in this column of the view. Usually, the formula is a field name if you want to display the data for a particular field. However, developers do require more complex formulas than just the field name.

To start writing a column formula, open the desired view in edit mode. Display the programmer pane if necessary.

Then select the column heading you want to write the formulas for. You can also click the Define list box in the programmer pane to select the desired column. Figure 12.31 displays the first column in the selected view and its corresponding formula.

Entering the formula into the Formula box is easy. You must select one of these Display options to enter your formula—Simple function, Field, or Formula. These options are described in the following sections.

Note

A column formula must evaluate to a text string.

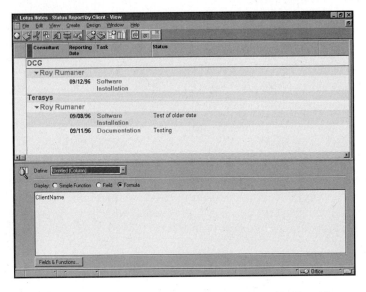

Fig. 12.31 This column formula specifies the column contents to be ClientName.

Simple Functions

Selecting the Simple Function option displays a list of multiple, simple, often-used functions that save you time in writing formulas from scratch. These functions let the columns you design display information about authors, attachments and documents, time and date, responses, the view, or folder. Figure 12.32 displays a column using the simple function Creation Date. This quick shortcut is identical to selecting Formula as the display option and writing the formula @Created in the formula window.

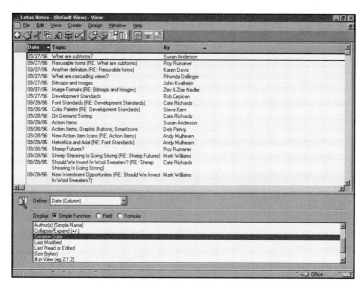

Fig. 12.32   Simple functions are a great development time-saver when creating formulas for columns. Notes displays a list of predefined simple functions.

The following is a list of available simple functions:

- **Attachment Lengths**—Uses @AttachmentLengths to return the size(s) of the document's attachment(s). The data type is a number list.

- **Attachment Names**—Uses @AttachmentNames to return the file names of the document's attachments. The data type is a text list.

- **Attachments**—Uses @Attachments to return the number of files attached to the document. The data type returned is a number.

- **Author(s) (Distinguished Name)**—Uses @Author to return the names of the document's author(s) in fully distinguished format, as in Amanda Lauster/ Marketing/IBM.

- **Author(s) (Simple Name)**—Uses @Name([CN];AUTHOR) to return the author's name without its fully distinguished format, as in Michael Solger.

- **Collapse/Expand (+/-)**—Uses @IsExpandable to return a plus symbol (+) if the view entry has descendants that are not visible because the main document or category is collapsed or a minus symbol (-) if there are no subordinate documents, or if subordinate documents are currently visible.

- **Creation Date**—Uses @Created to display the time and date a document was created. The data type is a time-date.

- **Last Modified**—Uses @Modified to determine when a document was last saved. The data type is a time-date.

- **Last Read or Edited**—Uses @Accessed to determine the last time and date a document was read or edited. The data type is a time-date.

- **Size (bytes)**—Uses @DocLength to return the size of the active document in bytes. The data type returned is a number.

- **# in View (e.g., 2.1.2)**—Uses @DocNumber to display a number for each document indicating its order in the view. Responses are numbered in outline style under Main documents; for example, the first response to the first main document would be 1.1.

- **# of Responses (1 Level)**—Uses @DocChildren to return the number of direct descendant (response) documents for a document or next-level subcategories for a category. The data type returned is Special text.

- **# of Responses (All Levels)**— Uses @DocDescendants to return the total number of descendant (response and response-to-response) documents for a document or subcategories for a category.

 ▶▶ See "Working with Formulas," p. 555

Fields

Selecting the Field option in the programmer pane displays a list of the fields currently available in the database. This is a great time-saver if you are not sure of the field names or their correct spellings. Figure 12.33 displays the TOPIC1 field being selected from the list of available fields for the second column of this view.

Formulas

Choosing the Formula option is the traditional Notes 3.x way to enter a column formula. You will encounter situations where the Simple Function and Field display are not enough to perform detailed column formulas, as shown in Figure 12.34.

Once in the formula window, you can enter the formula. You can even click the Fields & Functions button to display a list of available fields and functions that can be pasted into the formula.

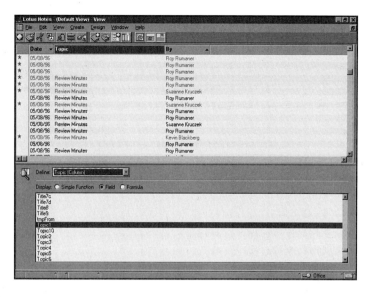

Fig. 12.33 You can choose from the list of available fields. This quick shortcut is the same as selecting Formula as the display and typing the field name.

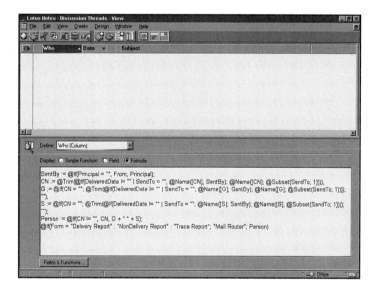

Fig. 12.34 The Formula option enables you to create broader and more detailed formulas to capture the column contents that you desire.

The following formula specifies the column contents as the Subject field followed by a blank (or nothing, if the Subject field is empty), followed by the From field in parentheses. By default (the first line), the From field contains the name of the author of the document:

```
DEFAULT From := @Author;
@If(Subject != ""; Subject + " "; "") + "(" + From " ")"
```

The following formula specifies the column contents as the number 1 for fields with a Status "Closed" and 2 for all other Status designations. This type of formula is useful to force sorting in a hidden column:

```
@If(Status = "Closed"; 1; 2)
```

The following formula reformats the contents of From to put the last name first followed by a comma, a space, and the first name. (e.g., Solger, Michael):

```
@If(@Contains(From; " "); @Right(From; " ") + ", " + @Left(From; " "); From)
```

The following formula is useful for a categorizing column that displays each month as a category name. Dates need to be converted to a text value to be displayed in a view:

```
m :=@Text(@Month(Date));
@If(m = 1; "January"; m = 2; "February"; m = 3; "March";m = 4; "April";m = 5;
"May"; m = 6; "June";m = 7; "July";m = 8; "August";m = 9; "September"; m =
➥10;
"October"; m = 11; "November"; m = 12; "December"; "")
```

To show people's names and phone numbers together in one column, create a column that is sorted in ascending order. The following formula separates the two field values with a blank space:

```
Name + " " + Phone
```

The following example joins the fields City, State, and Zip into one column.

```
City + ", " + State + " " + Zip;
```

Defining Selection Formulas

Usually, in each database you design a main view that displays all of the documents. However, it is often useful to have one or more selective views that include only those documents that are relevant to a particular topic or meet certain criteria. The view's selection formula selects which documents are displayed in a view.

Note

Every view has a selection formula. If you do not define one, Notes defaults the formula to SELECT @All, which selects every document in the database.

To create a selection formula, perform the following steps:

1. Open the desired view in edit mode.

2. In the programmer pane, select View Selection from the Define list box.

3. Write the selection formula in the formula box and refresh the view to see whether your formula evaluates correctly. Figure 12.35 shows a sample selection formula that selects only those documents where the field From author equals Cate Richards.

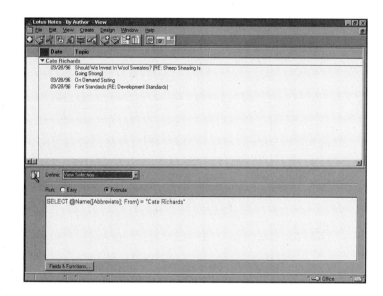

Fig. 12.35 Selection formulas enable you to eliminate extra forms and documents that you do not want to display.

Using Form Formulas

What would you do if you wanted to have users compose a document using one form, but then have them view the data entered in an entirely different form? You could use Form Formulas.

The form formula decides which of a database's forms is used for composing and displaying documents, depending on the conditions. This enables you to display the same information in different ways, order fields differently, or omit some fields in the alternate form. For example, the Address Label view of a Contact Information database could use the form formula frmAddressLabel to display documents using the Address Label form. The frmAddressLabel form could be a shortened version of the Contact Information form that includes only the Name and various Address fields.

The form formula is optional. If you do not create one, Notes will either display the documents in the view using the default form designated in the database (Design, Form

Properties), the form used if the Store form in document option was selected when the document was created, or the form with which the document was created.

Note

If a document is created with a form that has the option Store form in Document selected, the form formula is ignored and the document is displayed using the stored form. Storing the form in documents allows documents to display correctly even in databases where the form has not been defined, or where the form has been renamed or deleted. One note of caution, however: Storing the form with the document increases the size of the database.

To create a form formula, perform the following steps:

1. Open the desired form in edit mode and select Design, View properties to display the view's Properties InfoBox.

2. Click the Advanced tab.

3. Click Formula Window, which displays the Design Form Formula dialog box, as shown in Figure 12.36.

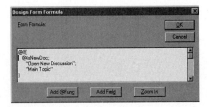

Fig. 12.36   This formula creates new documents using the Open New Discussion form and accesses existing documents using the Main Topic form.

4. Write the form formula and then click OK. A form formula must evaluate to the name of a form.

Caution

Why do you get an error in your keyword field called Loan Type that your Loan Type Lookup view says does not exist? You are using an @DbColumn formula to build the keyword list.

Make sure that you have not renamed the view. For instance, you may have hidden the view by placing parentheses around the name, or you may have modified the name. You should use an alias name and then refer to that alias in your @DBColumn formula. This prevents future errors if the view names change.

After creating a Form Formula for your view that uses the New Loan form if a new document is being composed and then uses the New Loan for Viewing if it's being loaded, why doesn't the New Loan for Viewing form get used when opening a previously created document?

Make sure that the New Loan form does not have the option Store form in Document selected. If it does, you need to remove this option. Any new documents created will display the viewing form; however, existing documents will still not be displayed. Either re-create these documents to remove the stored form, or run a macro on them that refreshes the fields and their contents.

Using Folders

Folders are very similar to views. In fact, you design a folder nearly the same way you design any Notes view. Why create folders? Designing a folder is useful when none of the existing views of a database shows information the way you want to see it. Folders let you store and manage related documents without putting them into a category, which would require a categories or keyword field in the form used to create the documents. In fact, you can easily add and remove documents from folders by dragging selected documents. Figure 12.37 displays the Discussion template database with the folder "My Favorite Documents," which displays documents that have been selected and moved into this folder.

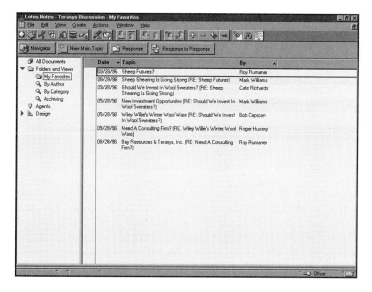

Fig. 12.37   Folders enable you to organize selected documents. This is especially useful if an existing view does not display the desired information.

When you create a folder, its design is automatically based on the design of the default view of the current database. You can choose to base the folder's design on a different existing view, or to design the folder from scratch. After you create a folder, it appears in the navigation pane until you delete the folder.

Designing Folders

You can keep a folder private, or share it with other users of a database. No one else can read or delete your private folders. To create private folders in a database, you must have at least Reader access to the database. To create shared folders in a database, you must have at least Designer access.

 ▶▶ See "Understanding Database Security," p. 879

When you create a private folder, Notes stores it in one of two places:

■ If the manager of the database has allowed it, your folder is stored in the database, letting you use the folder at different workstations.

  To see whether a database allows storage of folders, select the database, choose File, Database, Access Control, and see whether Create personal folders/views is turned on as shown in Figure 12.38.

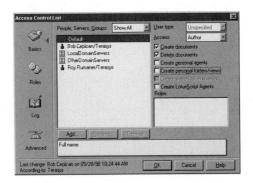

Fig. 12.38   The Access Control List dialog box enables you to see whether you can create personal folders/views.

■ If the manager has not allowed storage of folders in the database, Notes stores your folder in your desktop file (DESKTOP.DSK).

Creating a Shared Folder. If you cannot find a folder that is similar to the one you need, create a new folder. Its initial design is copied from the default design, or from the default view if you haven't set a default design. Follow these steps:

1. Select or open the database where you want to create the folder and choose Create, Folder. The Create Folder dialog box appears.

2. Enter a name for the folder in the Folder name box.

3. Select Shared. See Chapter 10, "Creating New Databases," to learn more about creating private folders.

4. Click Folders to store this folder at the top folder level, or click the name of another folder to place this new folder inside another existing folder.

5. Select <u>P</u>ersonal on first use if this is a private folder that you're distributing to multiple users.

6. (Optional) To select a view to base the folder's Inherit design on, select <u>O</u>ptions. This will enable you to choose the desired folder or view.

7. Click <u>O</u>K to create the folder.

If a view or folder already exists in the database that is similar to the one you need, you may be able to use it with only minor modifications. To copy a folder, perform the following steps:

1. In the selected database, choose <u>V</u>iew, <u>D</u>esign.

2. In the navigation pane, click Design, Folders.

3. Click the folder you want to copy and choose <u>E</u>dit, <u>C</u>opy (or press Ctrl+C).

4. Choose <u>E</u>dit, <u>P</u>aste or Ctrl+V. This will automatically create a copy of that folder starting with the name "Copy of." If no existing view or folder suits your purpose, create a new one. Its initial design is based on the default design you have set for new views and folders, or on the default view if you haven't set a default design. You could also copy a folder from another database.

Folder Properties. After creating the folder, you may want to further define its properties. Using the Properties InfoBox, you will be able to define basic properties like the folder name and alias, and the more advanced properties like its style and security levels. To do so, perform the following steps:

1. In the selected database, choose <u>V</u>iew, <u>D</u>esign.

2. In the navigation pane, click Design, Folders, and then double-click the desired folder. This opens the folder in design mode.

3. Click the right mouse button and choose Folder Properties or select <u>D</u>esign, Folder <u>P</u>roperties. This will display the Folder Properties InfoBox as shown in Figure 12.39.

Fig. 12.39 The Folder Properties InfoBox enables you to select and define the attributes for your folder.

While designing a folder, you can also create more advanced options using actions and navigators that will enable the user to automate moving documents between folders. Folder actions enable users to perform specific tasks on documents without having to open them, whereas navigators enable the user to switch and move easily between folders.

Renaming and Deleting Folders. You can rename or delete any private folder and any public folder to which you have Designer or Manager access. To rename a folder, follow these steps:

1. In the navigation pane, select the desired folder.

2. Choose Actions, Folder Options, Rename to display the Rename dialog box.

3. In the Name box, enter a name of up to 60 characters.

4. Click OK.

To delete a folder, perform the following:

1. In the selected database, choose View, Design.

2. In the navigation pane, click Design, Folders.

3. Highlight the folder you want to remove.

4. Choose Edit, Clear, or hit the Delete key.

5. Click Yes to confirm the deletion.

Moving Folders. You can move the folders under Folders and Views in the navigation pane into other unrelated folders but not into its parent folder, any of its children, or itself. To do so, perform the following steps:

1. Display the navigation pane.

2. If Folders and Views is collapsed (its triangle is pointing to the right), click the triangle.

3. Drag the folder you want to move into the folder you want to move it to.

4. Using the menu, select the folder you want to move.

5. Select Actions, Folder Options, Move.

6. In the Choose a folder list, click the folder into which you want to move the selected folder.

7. Click OK to move the folder.

From Here...

Views are lists of documents in a Notes database. This chapter discussed how to create views that can be used to select, sort, or categorize documents in different ways to make documents easier to locate. After a view has been designed, your users could open documents, copy and paste documents, delete documents, print documents or the view, forward selected documents to other Notes users, refresh the view to see new documents, and even search for documents containing specific text. To learn more about using the views that you create, review the following chapters:

- Chapter 8, "Working with Documents," covers how to edit existing documents that could contain objects.

- Chapter 11, "Designing Forms," describes how to create and design forms in Notes R4.

- Chapter 14, "Working with Formulas," covers how to write formulas using the available @functions and @commands in Notes.

- Chapter 17, "LotusScript Basics," teaches the basics of the powerful LotusScript programming language that can be used to manipulate objects and links.

II

Designing Applications

Chapter 13

Integrating Notes with Other Applications

With Notes, workgroup members can attain great productivity by using discussion databases, exchanging information via electronic mail, and managing a variety of documents. But workgroup members can also use Notes to share documents and data created in other applications and use those documents to collaborate on ideas, issue reports, track clients, monitor projects, and customize workgroup processes.

I like to think of Notes as a network enabler. It enables you to integrate data from other programs by importing, exporting, linking, and embedding the information. Once you have integrated your data with Notes, you can use the power of Notes—and its great security and replication features—to manage your documents. This is more powerful, secure, and manageable than saving files to a shared group network drive.

This sharing concept is enhanced by a technology called Notes/FX (Application Field Exchange) to share information between Notes document fields and OLE-embedded applications. With Notes/FX and OLE, you can create stunning work-together applications.

Importing and Exporting Data with Other Applications

Lotus Notes provides several ways to import information from other programs into Notes documents or views. Conversely, Notes data can be exported to other software programs and file formats.

In Notes, the File, Import and File, Export commands enable you to transfer information through a variety of standard file formats. Whether you want to exchange data with a Windows, OS/2, or DOS application or with your company's mainframe, you'll discover an easy way to do it with Notes.

Transferring data to and from Notes is performed from a view or from within a specific document. Views are used to exchange tabular information between the Notes database and another application. You use documents only when

Some of the main topics in this chapter are

- Importing and exporting data

- Linking data files to Notes documents

- Embedding OLE 2.0 objects in rich text fields

- Creating useful integrated applications with Notes/FX

II

Designing Applications

you want to transfer data from a specific document. In most cases, you probably will import or export large numbers of records and, therefore, will need to work from a view.

To import or export tabular data from the view level, switch to the desired view, select File, Import or File Export, choose the desired file format, and name or select the file to be imported or exported. Notes supports the following file formats when exporting or importing tabular data at the view level:

- Lotus 1-2-3 worksheet (WKS, WK1, WRK, WR1, WK3, and WK4 extensions)

- Structured text

- Tabular text

When exporting or importing rich text data at the document level, Notes supports the following file formats:

- Lotus Ami Pro (1.x or later)

- ASCII text

- Binary with text

- BMP image

- GIF image

- JPEG image

- Lotus 1-2-3 worksheet

- Lotus Pic

- Microsoft Word RTF

- Microsoft Word for Windows 6.0

- PCX image

- TIFF image 5.0

- WordPerfect 5.0, 5.1, 6.0/6.1

Importing a File into a Document

You can easily convert data from another application so that a Notes document can use the data. To import a file from another document, perform the following steps:

1. Open the document in edit mode; then click where you want the imported data to appear. You must be in a rich text field to import.

2. Choose File, Import or click the File Import SmartIcon to display the Import dialog box (see Figure 13.1).

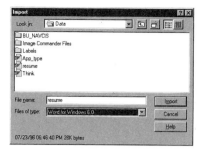

Fig. 13.1 Use the Import dialog box to specify the file to import into your Notes document.

3. In the Files of type list box, select a file type. Locate the desired file using the Look in list box, and then select the file; alternatively, just enter the path and filename in the File name box.

4. Click Import to import the file. Figure 13.2 displays a file imported into a rich text field.

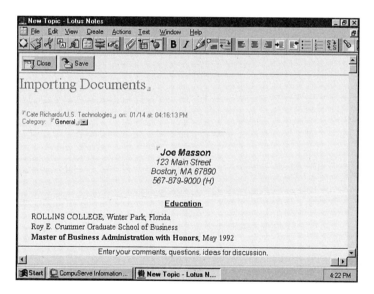

Fig. 13.2 The file is imported into the Notes document. You may need to adjust the margins and tab settings to align some portions of your imported file.

Importing Pictures

You can use the Clipboard to copy pictures into a document. You can also import picture files into a document using File, Import.

To copy a picture or graphic object into a document, perform the following steps:

1. Copy the picture in the source application (choose Edit, Copy or press Ctrl+C).

2. Switch to Notes and open in edit mode the document you want to add the picture to (press Ctrl+E or choose File, Open).

3. Click where you want to place the picture.

4. Choose Edit, Paste, press Ctrl+P, or click the Edit Paste SmartIcon.

It is important to note that you can only paste and import pictures into a rich text field. To import a picture file into a document, perform the following steps:

1. Open the Notes document in edit mode (press Ctrl+E or choose File, Open).

2. Click where you want to place the picture.

3. Choose File, Import or click the File Import SmartIcon to display the Import dialog box (see Figure 13.3).

Fig. 13.3 The Import dialog box is used here to import a BMP image file. You can select from a variety of image file types when importing into a Notes document.

4. Specify the file type and name of the picture file; then click Import. The image is inserted into Notes (see Figure 13.4).

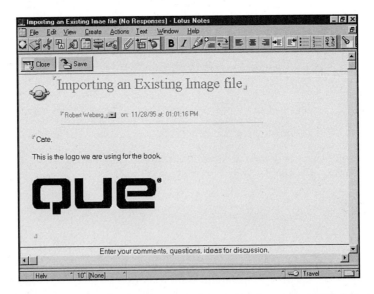

Fig. 13.4 The image is imported into your Notes document where you specified. You must import an image into a rich text field; otherwise, the Import menu is unavailable.

> **Note**
>
> If the file type for your image file does not appear, open the image in its source application and use a copy/paste procedure to copy the image into Notes.

Sizing Graphics for Rich Text Fields and Navigators

Two questions typically come up when working with importing pictures:

Q. The pictures that I import come in very large. How can I change their appearance in Notes?

A. Once a picture file has been imported into Notes, you can easily adjust or resize the graphic. To do so, click the picture once and then drag the box in the picture's lower right corner in the desired direction to resize. Notes treats the picture as one unit, so you must resize the entire picture. To help you gauge the picture's dimensions, Notes displays the picture's current width and height as a percentage of its original width and height above the status bar.

Q. After resizing a picture, I discovered the original dimensions of the imported picture was more appropriate. How do I return a picture to its original size?

A. Open the document containing the picture in edit mode and click the picture. Next, choose Picture, Picture Properties to display the Properties infobox. Click the Basics tab and then click the Reset width and height to 100% button.

It is important to note that Notes treats the graphic images and backgrounds you paste into navigators in a different manner than pictures imported into rich text fields. You must size all graphics you plan to paste into navigators before you paste them into Notes. You cannot size them once they are pasted into the navigator. This can be quite frustrating for users, who must continuously return to a graphics package to resize a graphic on the off-chance that they get the size correct after many attempts. Using a graphics package like PC Paintbrush, which lets you specify the exact size of the graphic in inches (or pixels) before you copy it to the Clipboard to paste into Notes, is often the best solution to sizing graphics. Packages like PC Paintbrush (which sells for less than $15 at most software dealers) also provide fast ways to convert a lot of the graphics from formats Notes does not use, .BMP formats that navigators require, or other graphic formats Notes rich text fields will accept.

Importing Structured Text Files

Importing data from ASCII files is relatively painless, and with a little preparation and setup, Notes can offer quite a bit of flexibility. For example, if your company's MIS reporting department provides your group with customer mailing lists in ASCII file format (generally mainframe downloads are in ASCII or tabular-text format), you can set up Notes to make importing the data a simple matter. The important step to remember when importing data into Notes is that you will be importing from the view level.

Choose File Import, and then in the Import dialog box you can select from three basic types of data files:

- ■ Structured Text

- ■ Tabular Text

- ■ 1-2-3 Worksheet

If you are working with ASCII text files, you must select either the Structured Text or Tabular Text type. A structured text file is an ASCII text file that contains labels that identify each field. It retains its structure in fields and values when imported into Notes. Generally, records and fields in structured text files are separated by a form-feed ASCII character or delimiter. The following example displays a comma-delimited text file:

```
"Joe Lotus","123 Main Street","Bartlett","IL","60103"
"Mary Smith","456 Oak Street","Streamwood","IL","60107"
```

When you import a structured text file into a view, the field names in the text file must correspond to the field names in the Notes document. To do this, you create a form that contains the names of the fields you're importing. Figure 13.5 shows an example of a structured text file that imports data into a contact list database.

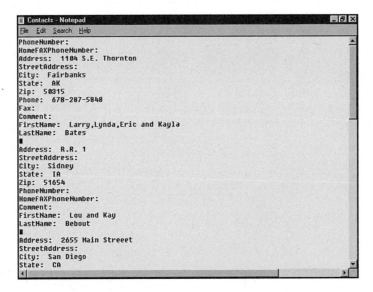

Fig. 13.5   You can import a structured text file into a Notes view. The field labels in the structured text file must correspond to the fields in your Notes database.

To import structured text files into Notes, follow these steps:

1. Choose File, Import or click the File Import SmartIcon. The Import dialog box appears (see Figure 13.6).

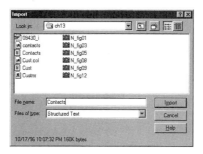

Fig. 13.6 This example displays the structured text file, CONTACTS.TXT, being imported.

2. In the Files of type list box, select Structured Text as the file type. Then select the path and name of the structured text file.

3. Choose Import. Notes displays the Structured Text Import dialog box (see Figure 13.7).

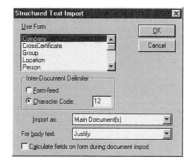

Fig. 13.7 The Structured Text Import dialog box specifies how to import the CONTACTS.TXT file into your Notes database.

4. Select in the Use Form list box the desired form into which you want the data imported. This list displays all the available forms in the database.

5. Select an interdocument delimiter to indicate how to separate the records—either Form-feed or Character-Code.

> **Note**
>
> The order of the labeled fields does not have to match the order of the fields in your Notes form. Each record could have fields of various sizes. You must separate records with a specific delimiter, however, such as ASCII Code 12 (the form-feed character).

6. Leave Main Document(s) selected in the Import As list unless you are creating Response documents. For example, if you have a Notes database that has contact information contained in main documents and call report information contained in response documents, you would select this option to import call report data into a corresponding call report response document.

7. Leave Justify selected in the For <u>b</u>ody text list to wrap text to fit the Notes window, or you can choose to maintain the existing line breaks in the source file by adding a return character at the end of each line of text.

8. If you want the imported documents to contain every field of the form you selected, select Cal<u>c</u>ulate fields on form during document import. This will create any of the calculated fields that exist on the form in the document, even if you are not importing them.

9. Click <u>O</u>K. Notes imports the data into the fields in your Notes database using the selected form (see Figure 13.8).

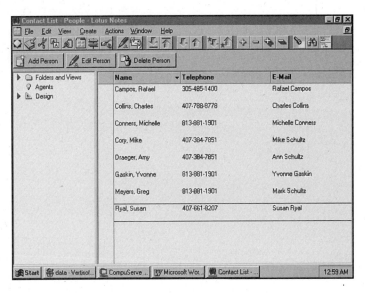

Fig. 13.8 Using the selected form, import the records into the view. Opening the individual documents would reveal that the data was imported into the appropriate fields.

You can now use existing views or design new views to display the imported data in any desired way. For example, you could design a view that sorted the contact information alphabetically that included contact name and address information. This view could then be exported to an external application for printing mailing labels.

◀◀ See "Adding Fields to a Form," p. 446
◀◀ See "Designing Views," p. 477

Importing Tabular-Text Files

Reports from mainframes or client/server databases are downloaded in the format of tabular-text files. Tabular-text files contain data in distinct rows and columns because records and fields are separated with equal amounts of tabs, spaces, or other delimiters.

If you have a Notes database with a view that exactly matches the contents of the tabular view in terms of both field names and widths, you might be able to import it directly into the view with little trouble. The tabular-text file doesn't always provide data for all the target fields, however, and also might not properly identify to Notes the contents of each field. Situations like this arise if you are attempting to import a file that has not been parsed. A nonparsed file is an ASCII file in which delimiters or tabs have not been defined.

Therefore, if you are frequently importing one type of file into a view or if the ASCII file and Notes view have a different format, create a column format descriptor file (COL file) to parse the ASCII file so its individual components correspond to columns in the Notes view or document fields. Notes uses A COL file to specify and map how a comma-delimited or tabular-text file is imported into a Notes database.

Suppose that you have a file containing a listing of customer information from your company's customer contact system that must be downloaded in comma-delimited format (see Figure 13.9). Each field in a comma-delimited file is surrounded by quotes and each field is separated by a comma. Each record must contain the same number of fields or items.

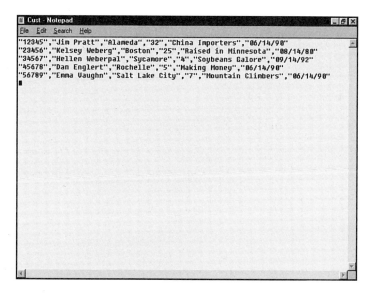

Fig. 13.9 The comma-delimited file CUST.TXT shows records as rows; the field data is separated by commas.

Next, suppose that you want to import this file into a Notes database you have designed. The Customer Profile form you are importing into the database should contain the fields listed in the CUST.COL file shown in Figure 13.10. You can create a COL file with any ASCII text editor and give it the extension .COL. The target form can contain more fields than the tabular-text or comma-delimited file and the fields can be in a different order.

II

Designing Applications

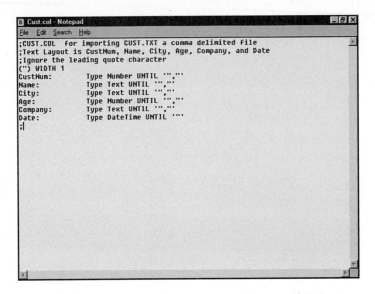

Fig. 13.10 The CUST.COL file tells Notes how to interpret the contents of the comma-delimited text file (shown in Figure 13.9) into documents, using a specified form in the database.

After creating the COL file, switch to Notes and the desired database that will receive the imported data. Then perform the following steps:

1. Choose File, Import or click the File Import SmartIcon to display the Import dialog box.

2. Select the Files of type list box and select the text file that will be imported in the File name list box, using the Look in list boxes if necessary.

3. Click Import to display the Tabular Text Import dialog box (see Figure 13.11).

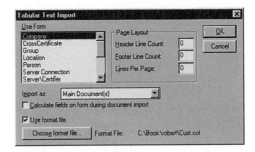

Fig. 13.11 With the Tabular Text Import dialog box, you can choose various options you need to import the comma-delimited file.

4. Select the desired form in the Use Form list box.

5. Select Use format file and then click Choose format file to display the Choose an Import Format File dialog box to select the COL file that you created.

6. Click <u>O</u>K to import the data based on the COL file.

Figure 13.12 displays the sample CUST.TXT file that was imported into a Notes database.

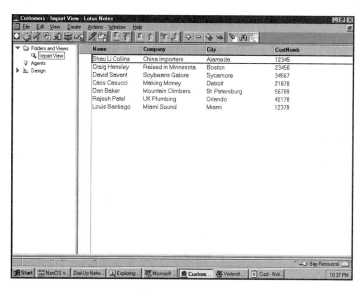

Fig. 13.12   The CUST.TXT file has been imported into the database.

Tip

To quickly see whether the data was imported in the correct fields, open a document or choose <u>F</u>ile, Docume<u>n</u>t Properties, and the Fields tab.

Using Notes with Spreadsheet Programs

Occasionally, you might need to extract Notes data into a format that enables you to perform what-if analysis or to build graphs for financial analysis. To meet that need, you can export the Notes data to a spreadsheet program. Because Notes can export and import data to and from Lotus 1-2-3 worksheet file format, any program that can read or write a WK* file can effectively share data with Notes.

Note

To export Notes data into Microsoft Excel for Windows, you must export the view data into Lotus 1-2-3 format and then use 1-2-3 to save the data as an Excel spreadsheet.

Exporting Notes Data to a 1-2-3 Worksheet. To export data from Notes to a 1-2-3 worksheet file, you must first start from a view because you can't export to a worksheet file from within an open document. When you export a view to a worksheet, each document becomes a worksheet row and each field becomes a worksheet column, with field contents becoming cell contents. The view does not need to display all the fields available in the Notes database, but it must contain all the fields you want to export.

◀◀ See "Creating Views," p. 479
▶▶ See "Working with Formulas," p. 555

Suppose that you want to export the sales information from the view shown in Figure 13.13.

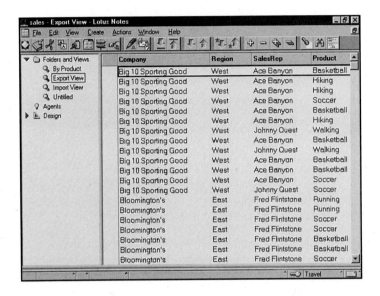

Fig. 13.13   This database contains sales information. A view named Export View has been created to prepare Notes data for export. You can export any view that exists in the database.

With the desired view selected, perform the following steps:

1. Choose File, Export or click the File Export SmartIcon to open the Export dialog box (see Figure 13.14).

2. Enter a filename in the File name box then choose Lotus 1-2-3 Worksheet in the Save File as Type list box.

3. Specify the drive and directories where you want to save the file in the Save in list boxes, and then click the Export button. The 1-2-3 Worksheet Export dialog box appears (see Figure 13.15).

4. Select All Documents if you want to export all the documents appearing in the view or Selected Documents if you have preselected a subset of the available documents.

5. Select the Include View Titles checkbox if you want to export the column titles along with the data.

6. Click <u>O</u>K. The view information is imported into 1-2-3 worksheet format.

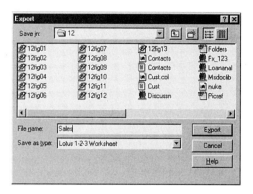

Fig. 13.14 In the Export dialog box, you can enter a filename and extension for the export file, choose the appropriate file type, and specify the drive and directory where you want to save the file.

Fig. 13.15 In the 1-2-3 Worksheet Export dialog box, you can specify how you want to export the data.

If you open the exported file in 1-2-3, you will see something like Figure 13.16.

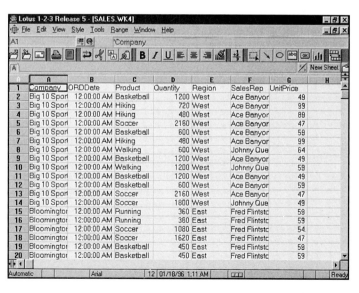

Fig. 13.16 The exported data from the Notes view is now displayed in 1-2-3. The fields in the original view have become columns and every document has become a row.

> **Caution**
>
> When you export a view to a new spreadsheet file, Notes exports the file as plain worksheet data without any formatting or styles, regardless of the file extension you specify. When you open the exported file in 1-2-3, you may receive the message `File or extension converted`, indicating that the worksheet has been converted to the appropriate format for the 1-2-3 version that you're using. Also, you may need to reformat data like time values into the desired format. Reformatting will be necessary when working with other programs such as Excel, Word, and Quattro Pro.

Importing Spreadsheet Data. Importing data into Notes from a spreadsheet file requires more preparation than exporting from Notes because when importing, you should assign a range name to the data range in the file that you want to import and you might need to build a view to receive the spreadsheet data. When you import a spreadsheet into a view, each spreadsheet row becomes an individual document and each spreadsheet column becomes a field, with the cell contents becoming field contents. You must create both a form and a view before you import a spreadsheet file into a view.

> **Caution**
>
> Notes only imports the first sheet in a multiple-sheet worksheet/workbook/notebook or a specified range in the first sheet.

> **Tip**
>
> Don't include any column headings in this range name because Notes imports the column headings as a document.

To understand how to import a spreadsheet, let's import the data SALES.WK4 we just exported (refer to Figure 13.16). This worksheet data will be imported into a view designed to receive the worksheet data. Follow these steps:

> **Tip**
>
> Before importing large amounts of data, always import small test files. Before importing an entire spreadsheet, for example, you might want to import a named range of several rows and columns.

1. Create and save the view that will import the spreadsheet data. Figure 13.17 displays a view in which columns are ordered and fields are designated to accept the data. The columns in the receiving view should not be categorized and must exactly match the columns in the worksheet. For example, if the first column in the worksheet's range contains a name, you should set the first column of the view to contain those names.

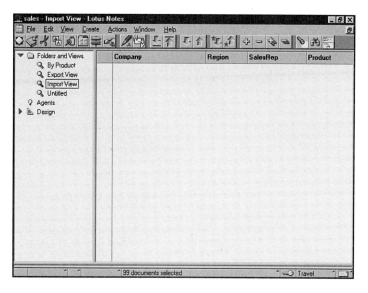

Fig. 13.17 The Import View has been designed to receive the worksheet data. Notice that the columns in the view are ordered exactly as the worksheet is ordered.

◀◀ See "Creating Views," p. 479

◀◀ See "Sorting Options," p. 497

   2. Switch to the view into which you'll be importing the data. Choose File, Import to display the Import dialog box (see Figure 13.18).

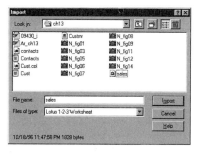

Fig. 13.18 The Import dialog box is similar to the Export dialog box. Use it to select the file type and filename to import.

   3. Specify 1-2-3 Worksheet in the Files of type list box.

   4. Select the file in the File name box using the Look in list box if necessary.

   5. Click Import to open the Worksheet Import Settings dialog box (see Figure 13.19).

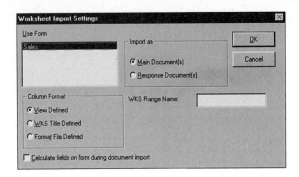

Fig. 13.19 In the Worksheet Import Settings dialog box, choose the appropriate Notes form and other options to use for importing the data.

6. In the Use Form list, choose the form that will receive the data. This form should be the one that contains the fields that exactly match the data you are importing.

 ◀◀ See "Creating a New Form," p. 430

7. Next, select the desired column format. This example uses View Defined because you're mapping the columns in the spreadsheet to the Notes view. The following list describes when to use the different column format options:

- **View Defined.** Select this option if the format of the worksheet columns exactly matches the format of the columns in the view. The columns in the view must contain the field name; otherwise, the data will appear in the view after the import but will not be contained in the corresponding field.

- **WKS Title Defined.** Select this option if the cell contents in the first row of the worksheet file are to become column headers in the database. These cell contents must be labels or text. Field names will be created from the column titles and can be used in the database forms.

- **Format File Defined.** Select this option (the most reliable import method) if you have created a separate column format descriptor file (COL file).

8. In the Import As section, select the desired option. Generally, you want to import each worksheet row as a main document, so leave the Main Document(s) option selected. If you need to, however, you can import the spreadsheet data into Response Document(s).

9. If you're importing the whole worksheet, leave the WKS Range Name box blank. Otherwise, enter the name of the named range you want to import. A named range is a name assigned to a range of cells or a single cell in a worksheet.

10. If you are importing data that needs to be calculated, select Calculate Fields on Form during Document Import. This option enables Notes to calculate any computed fields on the form during the import procedure. For example, if you have a computed field called "Region" that contains the following formula:

```
@If(State = "IL";"Midwest";State = "CA";"West";State = "OH";
"Mideast"; State = "NY";"East";"")
```

this would calculate the Region field based on this formula.

> **Caution**
>
> Notes imports information more quickly when you do not select Calculate Fields on Form because it is not required to calculate each field on the form when importing.

11. Choose OK or press Enter to import the data into the Notes database.

Understanding Object Linking and Embedding (OLE)

Notes enables you to copy and paste data from other Windows applications. You can paste text into any standard editable field. Pasting text is a great time-saver, but with today's Object Linking and Embedding (OLE, pronounced oh-lay) technology, you can do so much more—like pasting and embedding rich text, pictures, and bitmap objects—to make your Notes documents more robust. You could embed objects, such as a 1-2-3 worksheet, Word 6.0 document, Word Pro document, or Freelance presentation.

OLE 2.0, which is supported by Notes R4, is the second generation of OLE. OLE facilitates integrating and linking data between different Windows applications. OLE information generally can be linked, embedded, or both.

To use OLE 2.0, customers must have two OLE 2.0-compliant applications: a server and a client. The server application contains the source data while the client application is the recipient of the source data. For example, if you embed a 1-2-3 worksheet object into a Notes database, 1-2-3 is considered the server application and Notes the client application. Linking an OLE object means getting a copy of the object or data from the server, placing it in the client and maintaining a link to the server application so that the client is kept up-to-date.

> **Note**
>
> OLE linking is similar to Dynamic Data Exchange (DDE) linking in that the link is dynamic because the data updates when the original file changes. Unlike DDE, however, users can double-click an OLE link and load the server application to modify or update information. With a DDE link, you would need to first load the source application and locate and open the file to modify the data. Check your source application to determine whether it is DDE or OLE 2.0 capable.

Embedding an object means placing the entire object into the client application. Unlike linking, the connection is not dynamic. There is no continuing link to the server application. As a result, if a user changes data in the server application, it will not change in the client application; an embedded object immediately becomes a physical, static part of the client application.

II

Designing Applications

Linking an Object

A linked object is a pointer to data in another file. If you make any changes to the original source file, those changes are automatically reflected in the Notes document containing the linked object because of the link that was created. To link a file created with another application to a Notes document, perform the following steps:

1. Select the desired data in the file and copy it to the Clipboard using Edit, Copy (or Ctrl+C).

> **Caution**
>
> If the application is a DDE server but not an OLE server, make sure that you keep the server application and linked file open when updating a link between the DDE server and the Notes document containing the linked object.

2. Switch to Notes and open in edit mode the document to which you want to add the linked object (press Ctrl+E to place the document in edit mode).

3. Position the cursor where you want the object to appear.

4. Choose Edit, Paste Special or click the Edit Paste Special SmartIcon to display the Paste Special dialog box (see Figure 13.20).

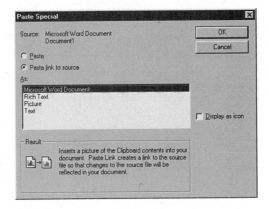

Fig. 13.20 In the Paste Special dialog box, you can link an object in a Notes document to the object's source file.

5. Select Paste link to source to create a linked object. You also could select the Paste option to paste the object without any linking features (see Figure 13.21).

6. In the As list box, select a display format for the object. The options available in the As list box will change, depending on the type of source data.

7. If available and desired, select Display as Icon to display an icon instead of the linked data. To display a different icon, click Change Icon and choose a different one. You may want to choose this option if you do not want to display all that is copied or don't want the object to take up a lot of space in your Notes document.

8. Click OK.

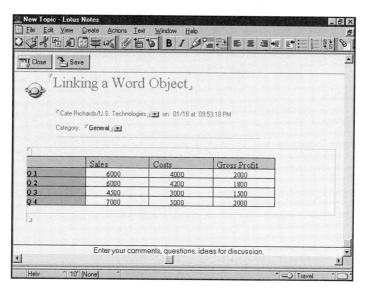

Fig. 13.21   The linked Word 6.0 object (in this case, a table) is inserted into the Notes document.

This process inserts a picture of your Clipboard contents into your document. Paste link to source creates a link to the source file so that any changes to the source file will be reflected in your Notes document. If you make any changes to the source file, Notes prompts you to update the linked object when you open the document (see Figure 13.22).

Fig. 13.22   Notes detects whether the object is linked and prompts you to update the object in the Notes document, if desired.

You can update linked objects automatically on activation or update them manually. To change a linked object's update type, perform the following:

1. With the document in edit mode, click the object.

2. Select Edit, External Links to display the External Links dialog box. This lists the links that are currently available in your document and enables you to edit the link, update the link, open the source, or break the link.

3. Select Automatic to update the object each time you activate it or Manual to update the object as needed.

4. Click OK to save your changes.

> **Tip**
>
> It's useful to manually update objects that take a lot of time to update, such as large bitmaps, by pressing F9 each time you edit them.

> **Tip**
>
> To display or edit an object's data when the object is displayed as an icon, double-click the icon.

When you link a file to a Notes document, keep the following in mind:

- You must be in a rich text field to add an object.

- You must save the source file. Without a filename, Notes does not know what file to link to.

- If the server application is an OLE server, Notes creates an OLE object. If the server application is a DDE server but not an OLE server, Notes creates a DDE object. When you create or activate a DDE object in Notes, you must have both the server application and Notes open.

- In Notes, you can display objects in four display formats (rich text, bitmap, picture, and text) as well as a format corresponding to the server application (for example, Word Pro document). The server application determines which display formats are available, however. If you select a display format the server application does not provide, Notes displays the object in picture format instead.

- Notes displays an icon instead of linked data if you select bitmap format, picture format, or the Display as Icon option or if the data in the original file uses multiple display formats.

- If you select the Display as Icon option, Notes displays the server application's icon by default. To display a different icon, click the Change Icon button, which appears when you select Display as Icon. This displays the Change Icon dialog box, with which you can choose between the current and various default icons available for that application or even choose a different file to select another icon.

Embedding Part or All of a File

Recall that an embedded object is basically a copy of data from another file. Changes made to the original source file are not reflected in the Notes document.

To embed a portion of a file, perform the following steps:

1. In the source application, select the data you want to embed and then copy it to the Clipboard by choosing Edit, Copy (or pressing Ctrl+C).

2. Switch to Notes and open in edit mode the document to which you want to add the embedded object (do so by choosing File, Open or pressing Ctrl+E).

3. Position the cursor where you want the object to appear.

4. Choose <u>E</u>dit, Paste <u>S</u>pecial or click the Edit Paste Special SmartIcon to display the Paste Special dialog box (refer to Figure 13.20).

5. Select <u>P</u>aste.

6. In the <u>A</u>s list box, select how you want the pasted data to appear.

7. If available and desired, select <u>D</u>isplay as Icon for Notes to display an icon instead of the embedded data.

◀◀ See "Linking an Object," p. 534

8. Click OK.

This procedure inserts an embedded picture of your Clipboard contents into your document. It looks the same as a linked object, but it acts differently in that any changes you make to the source file will not be reflected in your Notes document. In fact, double-clicking the object activates a new file based on the original object that you can modify and save back to Notes. Embedding files is ideal for document versioning applications.

When you embed an object in a Notes document, keep the following in mind:

■ You must be in a rich text field to add an object.

■ If you select the <u>D</u>isplay as Icon option, Notes displays the server application's icon by default. If <u>D</u>isplay as Icon is selected, you can click Change <u>I</u>con to choose a different icon to be displayed.

■ If Notes cannot determine the format of the data in the original file, it will display the server application's icon instead of the data.

■ If you embed a blank object using a server application that can also serve as a client application, then you can embed other objects into the object you're creating. For example, you could embed a Word 6.0 document into a Notes document and then within that same Word 6.0 document you could embed an Excel 5.0 object. In this way, you can build compound documents using different source applications.

To embed an entire file in a document, perform the following steps:

1. In Notes, open in edit mode the document to which you want to add the embedded object (press Ctrl+E).

2. Click to position the cursor where you want the object to appear.

3. Choose <u>C</u>reate, <u>O</u>bject, or click the Create Object SmartIcon to display the Create Object dialog box (see Figure 13.23).

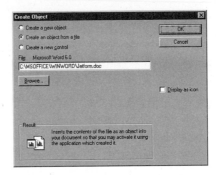

Fig. 13.23 With the Create Object dialog box, you can select the object type and file to insert.

4. Select Create a new object to display the available options. Notes displays the object types that have been registered to your operating system.

5. Optionally, select Create an object from a file and then in the File text box, enter the path and filename; alternatively, you can click the Browse button and select the desired file.

> **Note**
>
> You can also select Create a new control from the dialog box to select a new control that you have created to insert into a Notes document. For example, you may have created a .DLL or .OCX control that you want to insert into a document in Notes. You will also see these controls appear in the Create a new object list—flagged by a symbol with a yellow background. Selecting the control from either location is an acceptable way to work with these controls.
>
> You will learn more about working with controls in the LotusScript chapters and in the Designing Forms chapter of this book, as it is typically the Notes application developer that works with this feature of Notes.

6. If desired, select Display as Icon to have Notes display an icon instead of the embedded data.

7. Click OK to insert the object file, as shown in Figure 13.24. Double-click the embedded file to activate it for editing. If the application that created the embedded file is not currently running, Notes starts the application.

This is a new and separate object that is not related or linked to the existing object. Any changes or updates made in the original file will not be incorporated into this object.

Embedding a Blank Object in a Document

You can embed a blank object in a Notes document. Embedding blank objects is useful when you want to insert a new object not based on any preexisting data. Also, if you embed a blank object using a server application that can also serve as a client application, then you can embed other objects into the object you're creating.

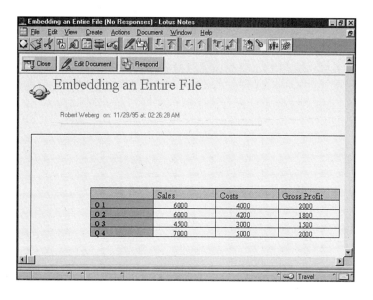

Fig. 13.24 This is the SALES.DOC file inserted as an object in a Notes document.

> **Note**
>
> Notes will display only the object types that have been installed on your system. For instance, Lotus Approach would not be shown as an object type option if it was not installed or registered. Check your WIN.INI and REG.DAT files for more details.

When you add a blank object, Notes opens a blank work file in the application you select so you can enter data. After selecting File, Save within the server or source application, the data and embedded object will be saved in Notes. Follow these steps:

1. In Notes, open in edit mode the document to which you want to add the embedded object (press Ctrl+E).

2. Click to position the cursor where you want the object to appear.

3. Choose Create, Object, or click the Create Object SmartIcon to display the Create Object dialog box.

4. Select Create a new object to display its available options (see Figure 13.25).

5. In the Object type list box, select the desired object type.

6. Select an object type that corresponds to the application you want to use (for example, Freelance Presentation or 1-2-3 Worksheet).

7. If desired, select Display as Icon to have Notes display an icon instead of the embedded data.

8. Click OK to insert the selected object into your Notes document.

II

Designing Applications

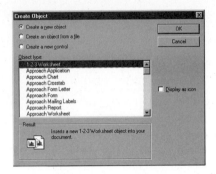

Fig. 13.25 Here, you can select a 1-2-3 worksheet object to insert into the current document. This activates 1-2-3 for Windows, with which you can enter desired data then update and save the object inside Notes.

9. You now can create new data in the blank work file.

   After working with the file and if the embedded object is OLE 2.0-compliant, you can click anywhere on the Notes document to save the object data and return to Notes. You can easily double-click the object to activate the object to edit and modify.

Using the OLE Launch Features in a Form

You can design document management databases that automatically open blank embedded objects when you create a new document. This type of Notes database is more ideal for organizing and managing databases than using a network drive because users may not have access to your network drive or may not know the correct path in which the files are located. Using Notes, any user with the appropriate access (designated in the Access Control List) can locate documents using the views in the database. The Microsoft Library template, MSOFT4.NTF, is an example that uses this workflow.

To create a form that automatically launches another application, perform the following steps:

1. In the database where you want this to happen, create a new form or edit an existing one. Add fields to store the desired information (for example, AuthorName, Category, Title, DateCreated, and Body).

2. Choose Design, Form Properties to display the form's Properties InfoBox or click the Design Form Properties SmartIcon.

3. Click the Launch tab to designate the launching properties for this form (see Figure 13.26).

4. In the Auto Launch drop-down list box, Notes will display the available applications installed on your PC that your operating system recognizes. You can select the application that you want to launch automatically. Also, Notes will display the following three options if an object or attachment already exists on your form:

- **First Attachment.** Automatically launches the first file attachment contained in the form.

- **First Document Link.** Automatically launches the first linked document contained in the form.

- **First OLE Object.** Automatically launches the first OLE object contained in the form. Selecting this option will display more options to further define how this object will launch.

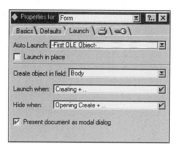

Fig. 13.26 The MS Office/Excel Worksheet form in the NISCUSS4.NTF template database provides an excellent example of using the Launch options.

5. You can select from the following options if you previously selected First OLE Object in the Auto Launch drop-down list box:

◀◀ See "Settings for Launching Objects," p. 443

- **Launch in Place.** Launches the object in place, enabling the user to edit the object directly within Notes. This is called in-place editing because the menu in Notes changes to adapt to the corresponding application versus having to launch the embedded object's application and then having Notes switch to that application.

- **Advanced Options.** Displays additional options such as hiding and creating when the object is selected.

- **Create Object in Field.** Enables you to select either None or First Rich Text Field. If another rich text field is available in the form, you could select it here. This will save the object in the indicated field.

- **Launch When.** Instructs Notes when to launch the indicated object. You can activate the object when Creating, Editing, or Reading. The Creating option launches the embedded object when the document is created. The Editing option launches the object when the user edits a document that was created with this form. The Reading option launches the object when the user opens a document created with this form and uses it in read mode.

II

Designing Applications

- **Hide When.** Instructs Notes when to hide the object. You can hide the object when you select the following options: Opening Create, Opening Edit, Opening Read, Closing Create, Closing Edit, and Closing Read. Some of these options will be grayed out depending on the setting for Launch when. You can design a form that hides the Notes document during any of these activities, and you can select more than one available option.

  Opening Create hides the Notes document when the user creates the document, Opening Edit hides the document when the user edits a document, Opening Read hides a document when the user reads a document, Closing Create hides a document when the user closes a document after creating it, Closing Edit hides a document after the user closes a document after editing it, and Closing Read hides a document after the user closes a document after reading it.

- **Present Document as Modal Dialog.** This option displays a dialog box with the form when returning from the object; otherwise, the form is presented in a full pane. Figure 13.28 shows an example of this option. The user can also select actions not shown in the modal dialog box by clicking the Action button.

6. Save the form.

Depending on what options you selected, you can now create a new form by selecting it from the Create menu. Figure 13.27 displays a Microsoft Word document object that is launched automatically when the user selects the form from the Create menu. The user can enter data into the document and then save the data and switch back to Notes.

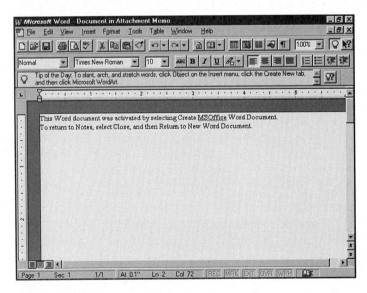

Fig. 13.27 This figure displays the automatic launching of a Word 6.0 object. The user enters the data and then returns to Notes.

In this example, the Document Info dialog box appears when the user returns to Notes, prompting the user for the document title and category (see Figure 13.28). Once it is saved, the document appears in the database's views, as shown in Figure 13.29.

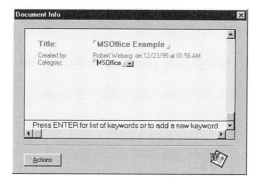

Fig. 13.28 The Present document as modal dialog option was selected in this example, so the user is prompted to enter a title and category.

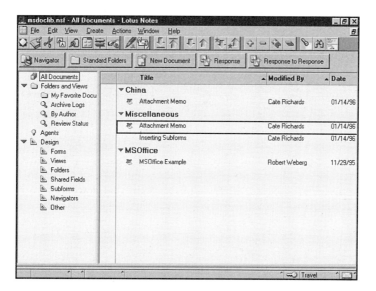

Fig. 13.29 The Notes document containing the embedded Word document is now displayed in the database. In this example, opening the document automatically launches the stored Word document.

New Features of OLE 2.0 Available in Notes R4

OLE 2.0 offers several enhancements to OLE 1.0 and provides for more versatility in Notes R4. For example, if a user double-clicks an object that was created by an OLE 1.0-compliant application though that object is contained within an OLE 2.0-compliant application that supports in-place editing, a new editing window is activated in the OLE 1.0 style.

II

Designing Applications

> **Note**
>
> OLE 2.0 is backward-compatible with OLE 1.0, which means that programs written to the OLE 1.0 specification can interact with OLE 2.0-compliant applications (and operating systems) as if both used OLE 1.0.
>
> If, however, you want to use OLE technology in your Notes applications and are working with non-Notes applications that do not support OLE 2 technology (or all of the special features of OLE 2 used by Notes)—at the time of this writing, Microsoft applications did not support the new functionality added in Notes that uses OLE 2—then you will need to install the 16-bit version of the Notes client on workstations that use this feature to be able to successfully use OLE.

The following list describes some new features of OLE 2.0 that are available in Notes R4:

- **In-place activation.** Enables users to directly activate objects within documents without switching to a different window. The menus, toolbars, palettes, and other controls necessary to interact with the object temporarily replace the existing menus and controls of the active window.

  For example, double-clicking the Word 6.0 object displayed in Figure 13.30 shows an in-place activation window within Notes R4.

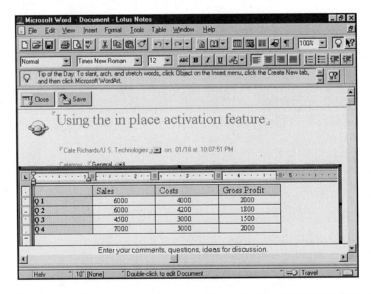

Fig. 13.30 This example displays an object being edited using the OLE 2.0 in-place activation feature.

- **Nested object support.** Enables users to directly manipulate objects nested within other objects and establish links to nested objects. Essentially, this means you can have embedded objects within other embedded objects.

- **Drag-and-drop.** Enables users to drag objects from one application window to another or drop objects within other objects.

For example, you can drag an illustration from a Word 6.0 application window and drop it into a Notes document (see Figure 13.31).

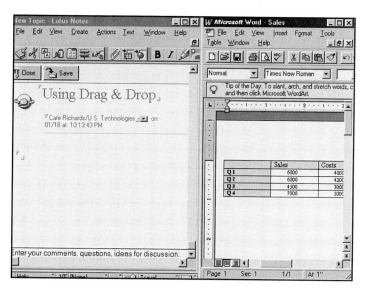

Fig. 13.31   You can drag and drop a Word 6.0 object into a Notes document and the object will then be embedded.

- **Storage-independent links.** Allows links between embedded objects that are not stored as files on disk but within Notes documents. In other words, embedded objects within the same or different documents can update one another's data, whether or not the embedded objects are recognized by the file system.

- **Adaptable links.** Maintains links between objects in certain move or copy operations, which means that if you move a linked object to a new file path, the link will be maintained and recognized in its new location.

- **Programmability.** Enables the creation of command sets that operate both within and across applications. For example, a user could use LotusScript to invoke a command from Notes R4 that sorts a range of cells in a spreadsheet created by Excel.

- **Logical object pagination.** Allows objects to overlap page boundaries and break at logical points.

- **Version management.** Enables objects to contain information about the application in which they were created, including what version of the application was used. This feature gives programmers the ability to handle objects created by different versions of the same application.

- **Object conversion.** Enables an object type to be converted so that different applications can be used with the same object. For example, an object created with one brand of spreadsheet can be converted so that it is interpretable for editing by a different spreadsheet application.

Designing Applications

The following sections describe in more detail some of the new OLE 2.0 features in Notes R4 that enable you to create remarkable compound documents using the power of Notes/FX.

Using Application Field Exchange

The latest releases of most productivity applications—1-2-3, Ami Pro, Word Pro, Freelance, Word for Windows, PowerPoint, Excel, and so on—support a powerful feature of application integration called Notes Field Exchange (Notes/FX).

Notes/FX uses OLE technology to enable Notes and any OLE server application to share data fields or to swap information. The contents of fields in an OLE server application file can appear automatically in a corresponding field in a Notes document and vice versa. Furthermore, depending on the type of field, you can update the contents of the field from either application.

> **Note**
>
> Lotus SmartSuite products use Notes/FX 1.1, the latest version, which includes enhancements to the handling of OLE objects. Microsoft Office products still use Notes/FX 1.0, an older version, however.
>
> If you install the 32-bit version of Notes on your client workstations, you may experience problems using FX between Notes and other applications. The 32-bit version of Notes supports OLE 2 technology—the technology used by FX. At the time of this writing, Microsoft did not support all of the additional functionality added in Notes OLE 2 technology. Therefore, if you want to use FX, you may need to install the 16-bit Notes client.

This Notes-driven technology greatly extends the application potential of Notes. For example, you can use 1-2-3 to create sophisticated worksheets or use Word Pro to create robust documents, and then users can save, categorize, and view these worksheets or documents in a Notes database. By working within Notes, you leverage the information stored in Notes and exploit the workgroup collaboration services of Notes. Why is Notes/FX more useful than just using object linking and embedding documents? Notes/FX expands the capabilities of OLE by enabling you to build fields of information that can be shared between a Notes document and the object. These fields can then be shown easily in either application.

From the desktop perspective, you now have a powerful way to store, browse, organize, share, and collaborate on desktop documents throughout an organization. There will be no more "Here's a disk with marketing files" or "The financial spreadsheets are somewhere on drive G."

Benefits of Notes/FX Applications

Notes/FX provides workgroup applications seamless integration with Notes by extending Notes to use the powerful editors and features provided by other applications. Designing a Notes/FX application yields the following benefits:

■ Documents and templates are replicated throughout the company.

- You can use security and access control features from Notes to regulate data access.

- You can use version control to implement and maintain documents.

- Approval management can be automated.

- You can build groupware applications quickly by using existing desktop applications, thereby facilitating rapid application development.

- Desktop documents can be categorized and sorted.

- Search and retrieval occurs quickly.

You can build a variety of business applications using Notes/FX. Table 13.1 lists a few potential business applications that could be used in developing a Notes/FX application.

Table 13.1   Business Applications of Notes/FX

Application	Examples
Managing workflow	Travel planning, expense authorization, customer support, call tracking
Collaboration and review	Budget planning, sales projections, contract management, document versioning
Sharing documents	Presentation libraries, form letters, marketing materials, corporate policies

How Does Notes/FX Exchange Data?

Notes/FX uses OLE embedded objects to exchange information with fields in a Notes form. For example, if you embed a 1-2-3 worksheet document in a Notes database using OLE, then 1-2-3 makes data in cells and ranges available to Notes, along with some document information. Notes can use these fields in views or calculations and can return new values to the 1-2-3 worksheet.

> **Note**
>
> For Notes/FX to exchange data with an OLE-enabled server application, the field names in the embedded file (server) must correspond exactly to the field names in the Notes form being used.

> **Note**
>
> For more information about fields in any other application that exchanges data with Notes, see the Help documentation for that application.

> **Caution**
>
> Make sure that SHARE.EXE (the DOS Share program) has been loaded in your Windows session; otherwise, Notes/FX will not work. You might need to add the following line to your AUTOEXEC.BAT file:
>
> ```
> C:\DOS\SHARE
> ```

Using Application Field Exchange

Three major steps are involved in setting up a Notes/FX application:

1. Create the application document that will be used with Notes; then copy a portion or all of the document to the Clipboard using Edit, Copy.

2. Embed the application in a Notes document or form. By embedding the object, you are initializing a live OLE link that enables the field exchange.

3. Define the user-defined fields that will be used to exchange information (as described by your application's Help instructions).

The following example creates a Notes/FX application using 1-2-3 and Notes that tracks expense reports. The expense reports are created in a 1-2-3 worksheet and then stored in Notes for easy document management and categorization.

All you must do is to identify and match Notes field names with 1-2-3 range names or cell addresses. To exchange data between 1-2-3 and Notes, a 1-2-3 worksheet object must be embedded in a Notes form. In the worksheet object, you need to create a two-column table of data you want to exchange.

Preparing the Notes Form. The Notes form must be designed to store the fields that will exchange data with the object (in this case, a 1-2-3 worksheet) and to store the 1-2-3 worksheet object itself. To create such a form, do the following steps:

1. In Notes, select or create a new database. Choose Create, Design, Forms or edit an existing form if desired.

◀◀ See "Creating a New Form," p. 430

2. Create and name fields to contain text and numbers from the 1-2-3 worksheet object (see Figure 13.32). Use descriptions and instructions to inform database designers how the form is designed to work.

3. Choose Design, Form Properties to display the form's Properties InfoBox; then click the Launch tab to reach the options shown in Figure 13.33.

4. Select First OLE Object in the Auto Launch drop-down list box. Doing so indicates that you want Notes to launch the first OLE object encountered on the form. (You will embed this object in the next section.)

5. Save the Notes form.

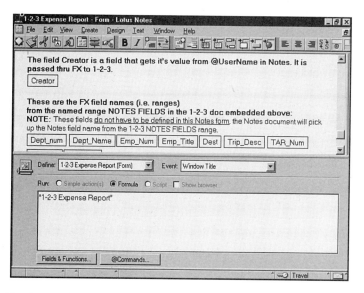

Fig. 13.32 The design of this Notes form will contain the necessary fields to exchange data with the object.

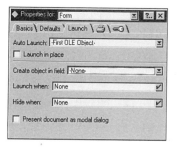

Fig. 13.33 The form's Properties InfoBox enables you to select the available Auto Launch option.

Preparing the Embedded Object. To create a Notes/FX application using 1-2-3 and Notes, perform the following steps:

1. Open the desired 1-2-3 worksheet or create a new file. Figure 13.34 displays the 1-2-3 worksheet object that will be embedded into a Notes form.

2. Create the fields to exchange data with Notes. This is a two-column table in the worksheet (see Figure 13.35). The first two columns are essential for Notes/FX to work. The first column lists the field names in the Notes form that will receive and send 1-2-3 data. The second column defines the range names of the corresponding information in the 1-2-3 worksheet. This range of field names is then named with the range name Notes Field, which enables FX to find and exchange the field information.

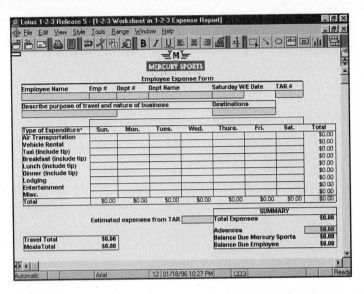

Fig. 13.34 You will use the 1-2-3 expense worksheet that is in the Notes/FX application.

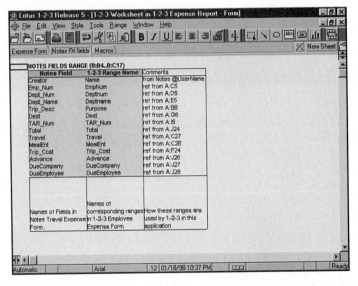

Fig. 13.35 The Notes Field range is required for Notes to exchange data with a 1-2-3 object.

> **Note**
>
> The headings in the first row are not part of the Notes Field range—these are for reference only. They are not necessary for Notes/FX to occur and should not be included in the Notes Field range.

> **Tip**
>
> Use Range, Name, Add in 1-2-3 Release 5 to name the two-column table Notes Field.

3. Arrange and position your worksheet area. Highlight a portion or all of the document and then choose Edit, Copy to copy the part of the worksheet that you want to display in the Notes form (see Figure 13.36). The selected range does not have to display the information that you want to exchange, but it is easier to recognize in Notes if the copied range is displayed.

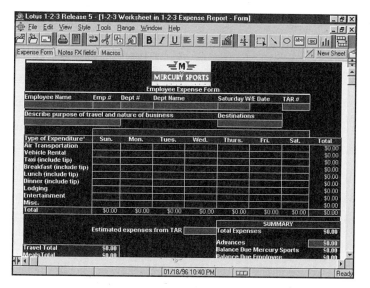

Fig. 13.36   Copy a range of data to display in Notes.

4. Switch to your Notes form and then click to position the cursor where you want the object to appear.

5. Choose Edit, Paste, Special to display the Paste Special dialog box.

6. Select Paste and then 1-2-3 Worksheet in the As list box to embed the 1-2-3 worksheet object in the form.

7. Save the Notes form.

Using the Notes/FX Application. You now can begin using your Notes/FX application designed in the preceding section. To create a new Notes document using the embedded 1-2-3 worksheet object, perform the following steps:

1. Choose Create and then select the name of the form that you just created. If you selected First OLE Object in the Properties InfoBox, Notes creates a new 1-2-3 worksheet document based on the embedded object.

2. Edit the data in the 1-2-3 expense worksheet.

3. Choose <u>F</u>ile, Update to update the worksheet object.

4. Choose <u>F</u>ile, <u>E</u>xit & Return to have Notes close 1-2-3 and return to Notes or choose <u>F</u>ile, <u>C</u>lose to close the worksheet object without exiting 1-2-3. The fields in the Notes document that match the 1-2-3 data are updated.

5. Your new document appears in the view, including the new data entered in the 1-2-3 expense report template (see Figure 13.37).

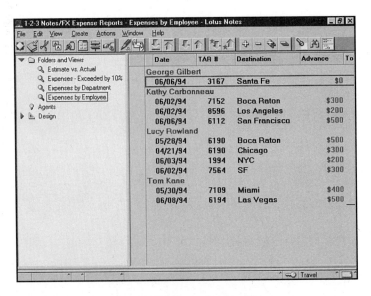

Fig. 13.37   The 1-2-3 expense report templates are saved in Notes.

Note

You can update the existing templates by opening the document that launches the 1-2-3 object. In 1-2-3, make any necessary changes then update the document and return to Notes. The fields you modified in 1-2-3 are reflected thereafter in Notes.

From Here...

This chapter discussed how to begin integrating Notes R4 with other applications. You can easily export and import data to and from external data sources and applications; you also can use OLE 2.0 to increase the functionality of your Notes documents. With Notes/FX, you can interchange data between Notes and other applications. To learn more about building Notes applications and working with Notes documents that can contain OLE objects, turn to the following chapters:

- Chapter 8, "Working with Documents," covers how to edit existing documents that can contain objects.

- Chapter 11, "Designing Forms," describes how to create and design forms in Notes R4.

- Chapter 12, "Designing Views," shows how to create views to display the documents that store your objects.

Chapter 14

Working with Formulas

Lotus Notes has four different ways to program custom features for a Notes database. You can use simple actions, simple functions, formulas, or LotusScript. Simple actions and simple functions are just that; you can select from a small range of actions from a predefined list of commands. Formulas enable you to define variables and use limited control logic, all of which is accomplished through calls to @functions. LotusScript goes one step beyond formulas—you can create procedures and functions.

What Is a Formula?

Simply put, a formula is an expression that Notes evaluates to find a value. This value is then used in whatever context is appropriate at the time of evaluation. A lot of formulas are simply evaluated and have no side effects. For example, the following is a simple formula:

```
100 + 100
```

It adds 100 to 100 which, of course, equals 200.

However, some of them do have side effects. For example, a formula might use the @Prompt function, which will cause a message box to appear:

```
@Prompt([Ok];"Reminder";"Don't forget to run backup tonight.")
```

When this formula is evaluated, the result is a dialog box that displays the message Don't forget to run backup tonight.

Taking the side effects even further, formulas can also be a sequence of expressions which comes close to being a program—in essence, all side effect and little evaluation. If fact, some people would argue that they are little programs in their own right.

Some of the main topics in this chapter are

- The concept of formulas and how they are evaluated

- How constants, operators, remarks, and functions are used in formulas and what each is

- Where formulas can be used and some examples

II

Designing Applications

▶▶ See "Understanding Function Basics," p. 593

So, writing a formula is a type of programming. Through formulas, you instruct Notes to accomplish some task. If you happen to be a programmer, you will find similarities between formulas and programming languages with which you are familiar. In fact, you might be more comfortable using LotusScript. If you're not a programmer, don't panic; you don't need a computer science degree to use formulas.

 ▶▶ See "What Is LotusScript?," p. 647

As mentioned in the introduction of this chapter, you can create variables and use control logic in formulas. Most of the complicated tasks that formulas do require use @functions. These functions like @Today, @If, or @SetField are discussed in Chapter 14, "Formula Functions." This chapter, while using @functions in examples, is more concerned with the basics.

Notes formulas perform calculations according to strict instructions you provide. In almost any situation where Notes needs to use or display a value, you can provide a formula that tells Notes what steps to take to calculate the value. They also let you express relationships between fields, cause Notes to choose between courses of action based on the values of fields, calculate values, and perform other complex actions.

One of the most common uses for formulas—and probably the easiest to understand—is using formulas in the columns of a view. Each column is usually set to a field name, and therefore, the value of that field is displayed. Simply by specifying the field name, you have created an extremely small formula. A more complicated formula might be computing a Total column by adding up a series of columns. Figure 14.1 shows the Total column in a view.

Tip

By taking advantage of Notes' built-in formatting, you can make columns more readable with very little work. The columns are right-aligned and two of the columns display dollar signs to indicate that they represent currency information.

When editing a column formula in Notes, you can see the whole view in the top section of the Notes window. This makes checking your formulas very easy.

 ◀◀ See "Creating Columns in a View," p. 493

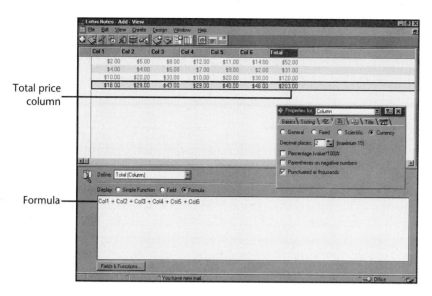

Total price column

Formula

Fig. 14.1 An example of a View Column formula.

The following are some other situations where formulas can be useful:

- When you define a view, you can define a formula that selects which documents Notes displays in the view.

- When you design a view, you create columns where Notes displays information about each document. When you create a column or edit the definition of an existing column, Notes enables you to enter a formula that tells how to compute the value you want to display.

- When you define a form, you can define a formula that specifies the title bar text that Notes displays when someone reads or composes a document. For example, the title bar text of the dialog box in Figure 14.1 is Example One - View.

- When you design a form, you create fields in which to store information. For each field, you can use a formula to define the default value for the field in the Default Value Formula box.

- For each field, you can provide an input translation formula that tells Notes to perform some type of automatic conversion each time the user enters a value into the field. For example, you could write a formula to change all the characters in a field to uppercase—"Roy and Karen Rumaner" could be changed to "ROY AND KAREN RUMANER."

- For each field, you can provide an input validation formula that enables Notes to determine whether data entered by the user is acceptable. If you expect the user to enter a number representing a month, for example, an input validation formula enables Notes to verify that the user entered a number between 1 and 12.

This short list does not describe all of the ways that you can use formulas in Notes. Later in this chapter, the section "Where Are Formulas Used?" details every formula type in Notes and gives examples of each.

Evaluating Formulas

When you use a formula in a view, the value Notes displays isn't stored in the document or database. Notes calculates the value of the formula each time it is displayed, using other information in the document.

The most basic formula is a simple expression. For example, the following formula:

```
"This is an expression"
```

consists of a single string constant (an unvarying text item). Expressions can also consist of a field name or variables interspersed by operators. For example, the following formula:

```
storeCost * 1.2
```

shows how to calculate a 20 percent markup on the original price of some item. The operator, in this case *, or multiplication, serves to connect the variable and a numeric constant. Operators are discussed in the "Using Operators" section later in this chapter.

Notes formulas can also consist of multiple expressions. When this happens, the last expression evaluated becomes the value of the entire formula. This is where some programming comes into play because variables are usually involved. For example, a two-step process might be involved in determining some total cost column:

```
customerCost := customerPrice * 1.2;
taxToAdd := customerCost * .06;
customerCost + taxToAdd
```

The first line uses customerCost as a temporary variable to simplify the calculation. It also helps to isolate the different parts of a formula. If the customerCost expression needs to change in the future, only one line needs to be changed. Temporary variables last only as long as the formula does. When the formula is finished, the temporary variables vanish.

Notice that the := sign is used to assign a value to a temporary variable. It is also important to note that a semicolon ends each line. The semicolon tells Notes that the expression is complete and that it should be evaluated before continuing. However, sometimes when you write formulas, you might want to break up the formulas for readability, and a semicolon actually is part of an expression even though it is at the end of a line.

The last line is used to give a value to the entire formula. Whatever it evaluates to is what Notes will display in the column.

Every formula must evaluate to some value; and every value must be one of the following five data types:

- ■ Numeric values—These are numbers and include fields that you define as numbers. The example of storeCost * 1.2 used previously would evaluate to a number.

- Time/Date values—These values represent a time or date and include fields that you define as time or date. Formulas that evaluate to Time/Date values are useful in column formulas. For example, you can use the @Adjust function to calculate when an invoice should be paid. The @Adjust function can add 14 days to the invoice date to arrive at the due date.

- Logical values—These values don't correspond to fields you define in a document. They always represent the answer to a question that can be expressed as "true" or "false." For example, when database replication is controlled by a formula, it must evaluate to true for those documents that get replicated and false for those documents that are left behind.

- Text values—These values include most other types of fields, including those you defined as text, rich text, or keyword. Because Notes is document-oriented, you will probably find yourself using text values quite often. For example, you might want to change a person's name to all uppercase characters to make searching easier. You could use the @Uppercase function to do this.

- List values—These values contain more than one element. The elements can be either number, text, or Time/Date value. However, usually each list contains only one type—for example, a list of cities or a list of birthdates. Notes provides special functions that let you perform different types of list processing. You could also think of Lists as an array.

As you write formulas, you will discover that some calculations make sense only when you apply them to certain types of data. To multiply two fields together, for example, both fields must be numeric—multiplying an interest rate by a principal amount makes sense, but multiplying a name by an address doesn't. Similarly, asking Notes what day of the week the number 437 falls on doesn't make sense; such a question is meaningful only when you apply it to a date. Essentially, all of the items in a single expression must have the same data type.

▶▶ See "Converting Data Types," p. 602

Now, let's discuss constants and how they can be used in formulas.

Using Constants

Constants enable you to specify values that never change. For example, a formula that computes average monthly sales may sum the sales of each month and divide by 12 (the number of months in a year). Because the number of months in a year won't change, a constant can be used.

In the next few sections, you will read about number, text, date, and list constants.

Number Constants. Perhaps the most familiar constants are numeric. If you see the number 3.1415, you might recognize it as Pi—one of the most famous numeric constants. When constants are used in formulas, nothing special is done; you just type in the number—for example, 36.23 or 4. Notes also recognizes a style of writing numeric constants called scientific notation; see the sidebar "Understanding Scientific Notation" for more information.

One of the simplest formulas is one that simply consists of a constant. For example, the default value of a state tax field might be 0.06, which represents six percent. As you design the field, you might create a default value formula of:

```
0.06
```

From then on, Notes will set that field to 0.06 each time a new document is composed. The user can change it as needed.

Text Constants. You can also specify constant text. This is done by surrounding a group of characters with quotation marks (""). Suppose that you are defining a city field in a form, and you expect that in most cases the user wants to enter Naperville. Specify the default value for the field as the following:

```
"Naperville"
```

The quotation marks are crucial to a proper text constant; without the marks, Naperville looks like a field name. If you omit the quotes, Notes thinks that you want to initialize the city field with the value in the Naperville field, and you will get an error if your document doesn't have a Naperville field.

Tip

If you are having trouble with a formula, check to make sure that the quotes are correct. You might be referencing a field name when you meant to use a text constant.

Time/Date Constants. The Time/Date constant is probably the least used. It is specified by enclosing a time or date in brackets ([ ]). Times can include AM or PM, and can include a time zone. For example, suppose you have a database in which you track company meetings. Most meetings begin at 8:30 A.M., so you might initialize the field that contains the meeting start time with the following time constant:

```
[8:30 AM EDT]
```

You can write dates as numbers, separated by slashes or dashes, depending on whether your computer is running Windows or OS/2. If you're using Windows, use slashes for dates:

```
[11/9/96]
```

If you're using OS/2, use dashes:

```
[11-9-96]
```

> **Note**
>
> When using Date/Time constants in formulas, you need to be aware of where the formula is being evaluated—the server or the workstation. For instance, Date/Time constants in views are executed by the server. If these fields are editable, computed, and computed for display, @Created, @Modified, @Accessed come from the server; @Now, @Today, @Yesterday, @Tomorrow are calculated at the workstation; and @Modified is computed at the workstation the first time it is executed. Fields that are computed when composed, the server computes @Created, while the workstation computes @Now, @Today, @Yesterday, @Tomorrow, and @Modified. @Accessed does not display.
>
> Use the Date/Time format (slashes or dashes) associated with the operating system of the machine that evaluates the formula.

List Constants. List constants are the most powerful and complicated type of constant. A list constant consists of one or more elements of the same data type. If the list constant has more than one element, the elements are separated by a list concatenation operator (:). For example, the following is a list containing the names of four cities:

```
"Boston" : "New York City" : "Orlando" : "Naperville"
```

Notice that each element is a text constant. You could also use number or date constants to form a list. For example, the following might be a list of quarterly billing dates:

```
[03/15/96] : [06/15/96] : [09/15/96] : [12/15/96]
```

To summarize, you write text constants surrounded by quotes, date and time constants surrounded by brackets, and number constants surrounded by nothing; and, list constants are combinations of other constants connected by the list concatenation operator.

Understanding Scientific Notation

To express very large and very small numbers, Notes supports scientific notation, which most often is used by scientists and engineers. A number expressed in scientific notation consists of a number (technically called the mantissa), the letter E, and one or two digits called the exponent, representing a power of 10:

```
1.73E14
```

You can read this number as "1.73 times 10 to the 14th power," which in turn is 173,000,000,000,000. (In general, don't type commas in numbers; Notes will not recognize them.)

You can also use negative exponents to represent numbers that are smaller than 1. For example, the following:

```
1.73E-4
```

is equal to 0.0173.

People who must deal with very large or very small numbers appreciate this notation because you can tell at a glance how large the number is. Unless you are involved in some type of scientific endeavor, you're not likely to run into this notation.

Performing Calculations

Most formulas perform simple calculations—adding, subtracting, multiplying, and dividing numbers to compute values. The following sections explain how to use operators.

Using Operators. Notes provides symbols, called operators, that represent actions that Notes can perform on data. Four of the most common operators, shown in Table 14.1, represent the basic arithmetic operations.

Table 14.1 The Four Most Common Arithmetic Operators	
Operator	**Description**
+	Addition
–	Subtraction
*	Multiplication
/	Division

Notice the symbols for multiplication (*) and division (/). You must use these symbols for these operations. You cannot, for example, use * for multiplication as you would if you were writing a formula on paper.

Suppose that your database contains documents which contain information about a sale your company made last month. In each document is a field called `customerPrice`. Normally, this field is displayed without a shipping charge. However, in one view's column, you need to display the price including a $6.00 shipping charge.

When you define the Total Price column, you can enter:

```
customerPrice + 6
```

as the default value formula. Yes, this default value formula is a bit overworked as an example—but you will use it a lot in real life also.

The first operand of the expression, `customerPrice`, represents the value of the `customerPrice` field in a document. The 6 is a numeric constant. The plus sign (+) tells Notes to add two values together—the value in the `Price` field and the number 6—for each document and display the resulting value in the column.

You also can perform calculations that involve several fields. Suppose you have the fields shown in the following table:

Field	Description
productCost	The amount you paid for the product
laborCost	Your cost for getting the product set up and ready for delivery
customerPrice	The price the customer paid for the item

In one column of the view, you might want to display the profit for each sale. When you define the column, however, you cannot enter a simple field name as the formula, because no field in the documents contains the profit on the sale. Instead, you can enter a formula that calculates the amount of the profit by subtracting the cost of the product and the labor from the price, as follows:

```
customerPrice - productCost - laborCost
```

As Notes reads this formula from left to right, it takes the value of `customerPrice`, subtracts `productCost`, and then subtracts `laborCost`. The result of this expression is the value Notes displays in the profit column, using the appropriate values for each document.

To take this example one step further, perhaps you want to display the preferred customer's price, which reflects a discount off the customer price. The discount percentage isn't contained in any of the fields in the document, but is always 85 percent of the regular customer price. So, the formula for the `discountPrice` column would be as follows:

```
customerPrice * 0.85
```

Notes evaluates this formula and then displays the resulting value in the column.

Suppose you had a `Discount Price` column that also showed a `Profit After Discount` column. This column uses the following formula:

```
(customerPrice * .85) - productCost - laborCost
```

Notice that the discount price formula is simply embedded into the profit formula by enclosing it in parentheses. More information about how to use parentheses and what they mean can be found in the next section.

Operator Precedence. As Notes computes the value of a formula, it usually reads the formula from left to right. For example, if you write the following:

```
fudgeFactor + increaseAmt - decreaseAmt + otherAmt
```

Notes takes the value of the `fudgeFactor` field, adds the value of the `increaseAmt` field, subtracts the value of the `decreaseAmt` field, and adds the value of the `otherAmt` field.

The operator precedence, or the order in which the operators are evaluated, is the same for addition and subtraction.

If a formula uses addition or subtraction mixed with multiplication or division, however, Notes does the multiplication and division first. This means that multiplication and division have a higher precedence than addition or subtraction.

Let's look at the evaluation order more closely. Suppose that a document contains information about an employee's pay, and one of the formulas looks like this:

```
empBonus + hoursWorked * hourlyRate
```

If you read this formula strictly left to right, you may think that Notes adds empBonus and hoursWorked, and then multiplies the result by hourlyRate. But Notes does the multiplication first, computing the value of hoursWorked times hourlyRate, and then adding the result to empBonus.

Thus, the order of operations is multiplication first and then addition. This order of operations can be seen in Table 14.2. You can see that multiplication has a precedence level of 3 and addition has a precedence level of 4. A precedence level of 1 is considered the highest. Therefore, the multiplication operation is performed first.

Table 14.2 Notes Operators and Their Precedence Levels

Operator	Operation	Precedence
:=	Assignment	N/A
:	List concatenation	1
+, −	Positive, Negative	2
*	Multiplication	3
**	Permuted multiplication	
/	Division	
*/	Permuted division	
+	Addition, Concatenation	4
*+	Permuted addition	
−	Subtraction	
*−	Permuted subtraction	
=	Equal	5
*=	Permuted equal	
<>	Not equal	
!=	Not equal	
=!	Not equal	
><	Not equal	
*<>	Permuted not equal	
<	Less than	
*<	Permuted less than	
>	Greater than	
>*	Permuted greater than	
<=	Less than or equal	
*<=	Permuted less than or equal	
>=	Greater than or equal	
*>=	Permuted greater than or equal	
!	Logical NOT	6
&	Logical AND	
|	Logical OR	

▶▶ See "The *@If* Function," p. 595

▶▶ See "Logical Operators," p. 598

The assignment operator does not have a precedence level because it is used only in assignment statements. The permuted operators are used for list operations. Both of these topics will be covered in a moment.

The Assignment Operator. It is sometimes convenient to break a formula into smaller parts. This is usually done to make the formula more understandable and easier to document.

The assignment operator is used to assign parts of a formula to a variable. For example:

```
empWage := hoursWorked * hourlyRate;
empWage + empBonus
```

This two-statement formula shows the assignment operator being used to calculate an employee's wage. Compare this example to the following:

```
(hoursWorked * hourlyRate) + empBonus
```

Using the variable empWage makes the formula easier to understand because it reduces the complexity of the formula's statements.

The next section shows you how to use parentheses to explicitly change the order of operations. They are also useful as an aid to documentation to show future users of your formulas that you intended the formula to be evaluated in a certain way.

Using Parentheses to Prioritize Operations. Usually, Notes performs arithmetic left to right, except when the order of precedence dictates otherwise. However, you can force Notes to perform specific operations first by surrounding portions of a formula with parentheses. In essence, the parentheses are telling Notes that the operators inside have a higher priority and need to be evaluated first.

Suppose that you want to display a discount price in a column, and you compute the discount price by adding the item cost and the item profit and multiplying by 90 percent. You might try to create a formula like the following:

```
itemCost + itemProfit * .9
```

If you have an itemCost of $10 and an itemProfit of $2, then this formula would be $10 + $2 * .9 or $8.20.

However, this is not correct. Notes performs multiplication first; therefore, it multiplies itemProfit by .9, and then adds the itemCost. To get the results you want, you need to explicitly tell Notes what to evaluate first, like this:

```
(itemCost + itemProfit) * .9
```

When the same values as before (an itemCost of $10 and an itemProfit of $2) are used, this version of the formula becomes ($10 + $2) * .9 or $7.20.

II

Designing Applications

Surrounding the addition portion of the formula with parentheses forces Notes to add first, and then multiply.

You can also nest parentheses if needed. Here is a contrived example simply to show you the technique. If you consistently get a two percent reduction in the `itemCost` because you pay your bills in cash, you might represent the fact in the formula as follows:

```
((itemCost * .98) + itemProfit) * .9
```

In this formula, the `itemCost` is multiplied by `.98` to reflect the two percent reduction for cash payment. This is enclosed in parentheses so that it will be the first operation performed. Then Notes will add the result to `itemProfit` and multiply that result by `.9`.

Using the previous values (an `itemCost` of `$10` and an `itemProfit` of `$2`) the formula becomes `(($10 * .98) + $2) * .9` or $7.02.

Concatenating Text

Concatenate means to connect end to end, an operation you often want to perform on text. When the plus sign (+) appears between two text values, it tells Notes to concatenate two pieces of text. By using plus signs interspersed between text or fields, you can concatenate as many pieces of text information as you need.

Suppose that a form contains two fields that contain a person's first name and last name, respectively. And, in a view, you want to display the last name, a comma, and the first name. You can use the following formula to define the column:

```
lastName + ", " + firstName
```

This formula evaluates to a single text value that contains the last name, followed by a comma and a space, and then the first name.

> **Note**
>
> Remember that using quotes in a formula causes Notes to use the text inside the quotes exactly as is. In the case of lastName, however, you don't actually want it to use the word "lastName" in constructing the person's full name; instead, you want it to access the value of the lastName field and use the field value. If you used quotes, it would print the literal word lastName.

> **Reusing Operators (or Overloading)**
>
> Notes uses the plus sign (+) to represent two different operations—addition and concatenation. Computer scientists like to call the dual use of a symbol operator overloading. This is done a lot in the C++ language.
>
> When you enter a plus sign between two numbers, Notes adds them; when you write a plus sign between two text values, Notes concatenates them. The data types determine the operation.
>
> This dual meaning for the plus sign is similar to the English language. A single group of letters, for example, can have more than one pronunciation and more than one meaning. Consider the dual meaning of lead in the sentence, "You can lead a horse to water by chasing him with a lead pipe."

You learn to look at the other words to distinguish between the various meanings of lead; Notes looks at the types of values on each side of the plus sign to determine whether it represents addition or concatenation.

List Operations

Earlier in the chapter, you saw that list constants looked like the following:

```
"Boston" : "New York City" : "Orlando" : "Naperville"
```

Each city is an item in this four-element list. In Notes, the colon (:) acts as a list concatenator in the same fashion that the plus sign (+) acts as a text concatenator.

You can use the assignment operator to store this list into a variable:

```
destinationCities := "Boston" : "New York City" : "Orlando" : "Naperville"
```

Now, the variable `destinationCities` has a list with four elements. If you needed to expand this list, you could do the following:

```
expandedList := destinationCities : "Roseland"
```

The `expandedList` variable holds a five-element list. This formula shows that the list concatenation operator works on list variables as well as list constants.

This section will look at the different operations that you can perform on lists. List operations fall into the following types:

- **Pair-Wise**—These operators act on two lists in parallel fashion. The first element in list A pairs with the first element in list B. If one list is shorter, the last element in the shorter list is repeated for each remaining element in the longer list.

- **Permuted**—These operators act on two lists by pairing each element in list A with every element in list B. Thus, every possible combination of values (all permutations) is used.

Of the four basic arithmetic operators, only the addition operator will be discussed since the addition, subtraction, multiplication, and division operators all work on lists in a similar fashion.

List Addition. The addition operator works differently depending on whether the lists being added are numeric or text. The numeric lists act as you probably would expect them to. The following formula:

```
listOne := 5 : 10;
listTwo := 1 : 2;
listOne + listTwo
```

will result in a list consisting of the following:

```
6 : 12
```

which is 5 + 1 and 10 + 2.

If one of the lists is longer than the other, the last element of the shorter list is repeated as many times as needed to make up the difference. For example, the following:

```
listOne := 5 : 10 : 20 : 30;
listTwo := 1 : 2;
listOne + listTwo
```

will result in a list consisting of the following:

```
6 : 12 : 22 : 32
```

which is 5 + 1, 10 + 2, 20 + 2, 30 + 2. Notice that the 2 in the listTwo variable is repeated twice.

Text lists, when added, result in the concatenation of an element in list A to an element in list B. For example, the following:

```
listOne := "A" : "B";
listTwo := "1" : "2";
listOne + listTwo
```

will result in a list consisting of the following:

```
A1 : B2
```

which is A + 1 and B + 2.

Again, if one of the lists is longer than the other, the last element of the shorter list is repeated as many times as needed to make up the difference.

Permuted List Addition. Let's use the previous examples to show permuted addition. The following example:

```
listOne := 5 : 10;
listTwo := 1 : 2;
listOne *+ listTwo
```

will result in a list consisting of the following:

```
6 : 7 : 11 : 12
```

which is 5 + 1, 5 + 2, 10 + 1, and 10 + 2. All possible combinations of values are used.

Lists with mismatched lengths do not need any special consideration when doing permuted operations. For example, the following:

```
listOne := 5 : 10 : 20 : 30;
listTwo := 1 : 2;
listOne *+ listTwo
```

will result in a list consisting of the following:

```
5 : 6 : 11 : 12 : 21 : 22 : 31 : 32
```

which is 5 + 1, 5 + 2, 10 + 1, 10 + 2, 20 + 1, 20 + 2, 30 + 1, and 30 + 2. Again, all possible combinations of values are used.

Permuted text list addition worked exactly as you might expect. For example, the following:

```
listOne := "A" : "B";
listTwo := "1" : "2";
listOne *+ listTwo
```

will result in a list consisting of the following:

```
A1 : A2 : B1 : B2
```

which is A + 1, A + 2, B + 1, and B + 2.

Note

The elements from the first list control the ordering of the resulting list. The first element of the first list is matched against the first element of the second list, and then the second element of the second list, and so on.

This may be important if you need to know the order of the list. I don't know of any situation where this is critical but you never know when a fact like this might save you a couple of hours of frustration looking for a bug in your formula.

Formula Keywords

You have read about the basics so far; let's look at some more complicated things. There are several things that make formulas into little programs—the temporary variables and the multiple expressions might be the most important.

However, Notes also has keywords that can be used in formulas. These statements are more executed than evaluated, and so might also fuel the "formulas are small programs" argument. No values are associated with keywords, just actions.

There are five keywords that are used with formulas:

- DEFAULT
- ENVIRONMENT
- FIELD
- REM
- SELECT

The next five sections discuss each of them.

The *DEFAULT* Keyword. This keyword lets you assign a default value to a field. It will also let you create a temporary field (which lasts while the formula is being evaluated) with a default value. And, since you can use the statement more than once in the same formula, you can have dynamic defaults.

The syntax of the DEFAULT keyword is as follows:

```
DEFAULT variableName := value ;
```

The Notes online help has a great example of how this statement might be used. You can use the following column formula:

```
@If(@IsAvailable(keyThought); keyThought; topic);
```

to display the topic field if the keyThought field is not available.

▶▶ See "The @If Function," p. 595

You can perform this same task by using the DEFAULT statement:

```
DEFAULT keyThought := topic
keyThought
```

You might consider the second method easier to understand and less error-prone. It says if the keyThought field does not exist, temporarily create it, using the topic field as the default value. If the field also exists and has a value, the DEFAULT keyword is ignored.

The *ENVIRONMENT* Keyword. This keyword is used to create and/or set environment variables in the NOTES.INI file under the Windows, OS/2, and UNIX operating systems and the Notes Preferences file under the Macintosh operating system. This means that each machine (and each user) can have different values for the same environment variable.

The syntax of the ENVIRONMENT keyword is as follows:

```
ENVIRONMENT variable := textValue ;
```

Notice that environment variables must be text values. If you need to use numbers with environment variables, check out the @Text and @TextToNumber functions in Chapter 15, "Working with Functions and Commands." They can be used to convert between text and number data types.

> **Note**
>
> The @Environment function can retrieve the value of an environment variable. It can also be used, along with the @SetEnvironment function, to set the value. Both of these functions are discussed in Chapter 15, "Working with Functions and Commands."

Environment variables are frequently used to create sequential numbers for Notes applications. The idea is that the first time you access the variable, it does not exist. So you create it with a value of 1. The next time you need a sequential number, read the value, increment it, set the environment with the new value, and use the new value in your document as needed.

Environment variables are also used to personalize databases since each user can have a different value. For example, if your company uses regional sales offices, the address of the local sales office can be stored in an environment variable and used in default value formula in fields. For example:

```
@Environment("salesOfficeAddress")
```

You also need to be aware of where the formula is being evaluated. Some formulas are evaluated at the server and the NOTES.INI or Notes Preferences file will be different than the one on the client workstation.

The Notes online help topic "Examples: @Environment, @SetEnvironment, and ENVIRONMENT" does a good job of explaining the details and intricacies of this keyword.

The *FIELD* Keyword. The FIELD keyword is used to assign a value to a field. It is also used to tell Notes which fields will be assigned values later in the formula. Before using the @SetField function, you need to use the FIELD keyword to tell Notes about the field before you try to set its value.

Before you use @SetField in your formula, the field receiving the assignment must have already been declared within the same formula. One way to do this is to declare it at the beginning of your formula:

```
FIELD Fieldname:=Fieldname;
```

The syntax of the FIELD keyword is as follows:

```
FIELD Fieldname:=Fieldname;
```

> **Caution**
>
> If Fieldname does not already exist in the document, it will be created. Make sure that you want a permanent field and not a temporary field when using the FIELD keyword. Also, when you use FIELD intending to create a new field, make sure that you are not overwriting an existing field by accident.

When using the FIELD keyword to tell Notes that you might set its value later, you can use this form of statement:

```
FIELD myField := myField;
```

This formula sets myField to the value stored in myField. In other words, the value does not change. You can blank out a field by using the following:

```
FIELD myField := "";
```

If you are not certain that the value of the field will be changing in your formula, set the field equal to itself. Only set the field equal to blank text if you intend to never use its value again.

The FIELD statement can also be used to delete fields by combining it with the @DeleteField function:

```
FIELD myField := @DeleteField;
```

II

Designing Applications

This keyword does not work in column, selection, hide-when, window title, or form formulas.

The *REM* Keyword. Remarks, also known as comments, are notes that you make, as part of your formula, to explain to yourself or others how your formula works. Lotus Notes completely ignores remarks but keeps them as part of your formula so that you can see them when you examine your formula.

If you become very proficient with formulas, someday you may work on a very complex formula for hours before getting it to work just right. If you—or worse, someone else— needs to make a change six months later, the nuances of the formula may have been forgotten. Perhaps you had the foresight to jot down a few notes about what your formula does in some internal documentation. But, of course, those are gone also. Adding comments to your formulas will avoid this problem.

The syntax of the REM keyword is as follows:

```
REM " [remark text] ";
```

For example:

```
REM "This formula selects only dogs without rabies vaccine";
REM "Written 08-12-96 by Waswaldo, Head Programmer";
```

Good programmers know that no matter how fresh your thoughts are in your mind today, six months from now they may be stale. You may not have the slightest idea why you wrote a formula the way you did.

In complicated formulas, you can use remark statements to separate different sections of the formula. For example:

```
REM "-----";
REM "Setup the first list";
REM "-----";
listOne := 5 : 10;
REM "                    ";
REM "********************";
REM "Setup second list   ";
REM "********************";
listTwo := 1 : 2;
REM "                    ";
REM "-----";
REM "Add the two lists.  ";
REM "-----";
listOne + listTwo
```

Of course, you use any character to create the line; some people use underscores, some use asterisks. It all depends on what you find readable. Both dashes and asterisks are used in the previous example. You should be consistent and always use the same character.

The *SELECT* Keyword. The SELECT keyword is used to target specific documents. When used, only those documents that match its criterion will be seen by the formula. The SELECT keyword is used before the expression that changes the documents.

The SELECT keyword defines criteria for the selection of documents in an agent that runs a formula, in a view, or during replication. You use a SELECT statement before an expression to define the set of documents that you want to change, see in a view, or replicate.

The syntax of the SELECT keyword is as follows:

```
SELECT expression ;
```

You can use the formula:

```
SELECT @All;
```

to have your formula see all of the documents in the database. Or you can have a complex expression, as in the following:

```
SELECT Form = "myForm";
```

This SELECT statement ensures that only documents created using the form named myForm will be seen by the formula.

> **Note**
>
> The Form field is a field that Notes automatically adds to each document. Its value is the name of the form used to create the document.

This keyword does not work in column, hide-when, section editor, window title, hotspot, field, form, or form action formulas.

Where Are Formulas Used?

One of the things that makes Notes so powerful and flexible is that there are so many different ways to customize your databases using formulas. Notes has almost 30 different types of formulas that can be used.

This section describes each formula type. This brief description lets you know the context in which this type of formula is found. For example, Column formulas can only be found in the View design mode.

You also see an example of each formula type. This small example gives you an idea of how each formula type can be used and what data type the formula needs to return. Some formula types, like a Replication formula, must return only a true or false value. SmartIcon, Agent, Action, Button, and Hotspot formulas do not require any return value. Instead, they are designed to do something.

The description also points out any @functions that are designed to work well with that particular formula type. For example, the @All function can be used only in Replication, Agent, and View selection formulas.

Another important consideration is where the formula will be evaluated. If the formula is evaluated on the server, you will not be able to access information stored in INI files as environment variables at the client.

Designing Applications

Formulas can be generally assigned to categories such as workspace formulas, form formulas, and so forth. However, some formulas fit in multiple places. We'll look at these first.

Action Buttons

Action buttons enable a user to perform tasks with the click of a mouse. Each action button is associated with either a view or a form and is displayed in the area just below the SmartIcons palette. This action bar area is nonscrollable vertically so users can look at long documents and still be able to access an action button. Figure 14.2 shows you what action buttons look like.

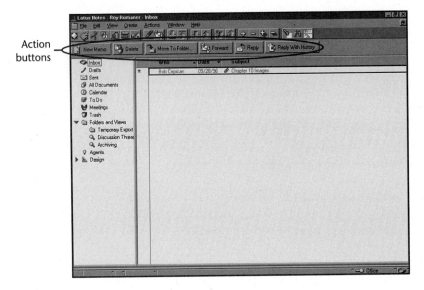

Fig. 14.2 The Inbox with six action buttons in view mode.

There are six predefined actions to which you can attach buttons:

- Categorize
- Edit Document
- Send Document
- Forward
- Move to Folder
- Remove from Folder

Each of these actions is automatic. You can't add anything to them and you can't change them. If the action does not do what you want, you can't use them and you will need to define your own custom action instead.

The next section on action button formulas shows you how to create custom actions.

Action Button Formulas. In addition to the six predefined actions, you can create your own custom actions. The Personal Journal template that comes with Notes shows a good use of action button formulas.

Figure 14.2 showed three action buttons from the InBox view of the Mail file. Now let's take a look at one of the definitions. In the navigator pane, select Design, Folders and then double-click ($Inbox). This puts you into design mode. Now choose View, Action Pane and then double-click the New Memo action in the action pane that appears. This screen should look similar to Figure 14.3.

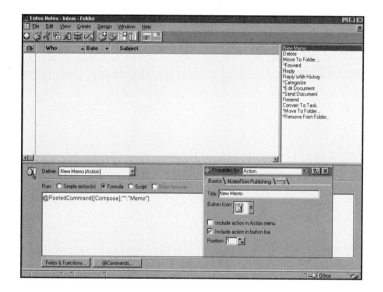

Fig. 14.3 The ($Inbox) view in design mode with the Infobox and action and programmer panes displayed.

This is a really busy figure. At the top left, the columns for the view are displayed. The top right holds the action pane. The bottom half holds the programmer pane with the action button formula. And lastly, the InfoBox at the bottom right is where you can decide the various options that affect the action buttons. You'll notice that the Include action in button bar option has been checked.

The New Memo action, the selected one in the action pane, has the following formula:

```
""@PostedCommand([Compose];"":"Memo")
```

When the action button is pushed, Notes evaluates the formula, which results in the creation of a new Memo. The @PostedCommand function is used to invoke a menu option from inside a formula.

You can also create action buttons—and their formulas—that are associated with a given form. When a given form is displayed, only the action buttons that are a part of that form are displayed.

> **Tip**
>
> When creating Actions, try not to duplicate a command found on the SmartIcon bar, or display an Action to which the user does not have access rights (i.e., displaying an edit Action to a user who has reader access). Actions should be context-sensitive.

Form action formulas are a good place to automate some tasks for the user, or to control field values. A simplistic example of this might be to use a form action formula to control a status field. For example, consider the following lines of code:

```
FIELD docStatus := docStatus;
question := "Has account been verified?"
response := @Prompt([YESNO]; "Caution"; question);
fld := "docStatus";
@if(response; @SetField(fld ; "OK"); @SetField(fld; "unknown"));
```

This formula asks the user whether an account has been verified. If it has, the status field is changed to OK. When controlling field content like this, you might want to change the field type to computed.

 ◀◀ See "Fields," p. 506

Notice that the FIELD statement is needed in this formula. Before passing a document field to the @SetField function, you need to declare it with the FIELD statement. You could assign any value you'd like to the field in the FIELD statement. In this example, we leave the value unchanged.

The @Command, @PickList, @PostedCommand, @Prompt, and @SetField functions and the FIELD statement are designed to work well in action button formulas.

The @IsDocBeingEdited, @IsDocBeingLoaded, @IsDocBeingMailed, @IsDocBeingRecalculated, and @IsDocBeingSaved functions can't be used in an action button formula.

Hide Action Button Formulas. The hide action button formulas are used to control when actions are shown to the user, either in the Action menu or the Action bar. When the Hide Action formula evaluates to true, the actions will be displayed.

> **Tip**
>
> If you want to hide a button from users who have read access, but display the button to users who can edit a document, enable the Hide Action if formula is true option in the Action Properties InfoBox, and use the following formula: !@Contains(@UserRoles; "Revisions").
>
> For this formula to work, in the ACL create a Role called Revisions, highlight the person(s)or group(s)defined in the ACL, and click the Role. Under Advanced, enable the Enforce a consistent Access Control List across all replicas of this database option.

This ability might come in handy if your weekend staff has a different set of tasks to perform than your weekday staff. The following formula:

```
day := @Weekday(@Now);
@If(day = 1 ¦ day = 7; 0; 1)
```

displays a given action only on Sunday (day equals 1) and Saturday (day equals 7).

Figure 14.4 shows the Hide tab of the Action Properties InfoBox for the action. When the formula shown in the InfoBox is true, the action will be hidden if the checkbox is checked.

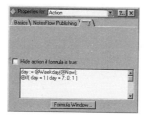

Fig. 14.4 An InfoBox showing a Hide When formula.

You can display the Action Properties InfoBox by double-clicking the action in the action pane or selecting the <u>D</u>esign, View <u>P</u>roperties menu option.

Each view or form action button also has an associated hide action button formula that you can set.

Hotspots

A hotspot is a highlighted object that does some task when clicked. A hotspot can display text in a pop-up window, execute a hypertext link, or perform an action. Hotspot formulas can be added to words in rich text fields, rectangles and polygons in Navigators, and buttons in layout regions.

The next section discusses how hotspots can perform actions and display pop-up windows.

Hotspot Formulas. Hotspot formulas are evaluated when the hotspot is clicked. The formula must evaluate to some text suitable for displaying in a pop-up window.

You might want to use a hotspot to let your user get some commentary or you might link the hotspot to a field on the document. Figure 14.5 shows how to use a corporate logo as an *action hotspot* to connect to a WWW site.

You can also use a hotspot formula to display a dialog box to request additional details. For example, your main form might be an inventory control form. If you need to display additional information about a supplier or detailed information about stock on hand in a particular warehouse, you can use a layout region and a dialog box to display the additional information. More information can be found in the topic "Showing users a dialog box instead of a document" in the HELP4.NSF database that comes with Notes.

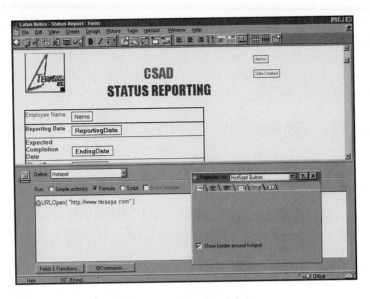

Fig. 14.5 A Hotspot action formula to connect to a WWW site.

You can create hotspot formulas for rectangles and polygons in Navigators. Their use in a Navigator is unrestricted. Whatever you can dream up, you can do. For example, you might create a Navigator to act as a graphic-based menu. In this case, each menu item might have a hotspot rectangle formula to execute whatever menu option is selected.

Hotspot formulas also come in handy when editing a document. You can create a hotspot formula simply by selecting words in a rich text field and then choosing Create, Hotspot, Formula Popup. The most common formula to add is probably a text constant that could act as commentary to the normal text. For example, the following formula:

```
"World Wide Web"
```

could be linked to the abbreviation "WWW." Later, readers of the document could click the hotspot to see an expansion of the abbreviation.

If the hotspot is already defined, the programmer pane is reached through the Hotspot, Edit Hotspot menu option.

The @Command, @DbColumn, @DbLookup, @DialogBox, @Platform, @Prompt, @Return, and @SetField functions are designed to work well in hotspot formulas. The SELECT statement can't be used in hotspot formulas.

Buttons

A button is a clickable object that you can add to a form. A Notes user can also add buttons inside a rich text field. When the button is clicked, Notes executes the actions, formula, or script associated with it. You look at button formulas in the next section.

Button Formulas. A good use of a button might be to automate switching to another form. For example, the following formula:

```
@Command([ViewSwitchForm]; "Medical Info")
```

could be used to look at the medical information form. This technique is useful when the main document is long or complicated. The second form would simply focus on one part of the information.

This might be a good time to pause a moment and reflect that this new version of Notes lets you perform a task many different ways. This example could also be used in an action button formula or as an agent. You could also create the medical information as a subform. There is no one right way to program in Notes. It all depends on the style that you are comfortable using.

The @DbColumn, @DbLookup, @IsDocBeingMailed, @IsDocBeingRecalculated, @IsDocBeingSaved, @IsNewDoc, @MailSend, @Platform, @Prompt, @Return, and @SetField functions and FIELD statements are designed to work well in button formulas.

If you want to use the @Command function in a button formula, you must make sure that the formula switches to the right context. For example, view-level menu options won't work unless Notes is in view mode.

Workspace Formulas

Formulas that act at the workspace level are global to all databases. They can perform any menu command and manipulate databases.

SmartIcons. A SmartIcon is a customizable button that performs actions. It acts just like the buttons on toolbars that you see in many Windows applications. Each SmartIcon has a formula associated with it. There are over 100 predefined SmartIcons, with formulas that map to one of the menu commands. Many people find that clicking a SmartIcon is faster than selecting menu options and easier than recalling keyboard shortcuts. You can create your own SmartIcon by choosing File, Tools, SmartIcons and clicking the Edit Icon button. Then select one of the customizable icons from the list, enter a description, click Formula, and enter a formula.

For instance, the following formula, when used in a SmartIcon, will format text in a Rich Text Field:

```
@Command([EditSelectAll]);
@Command([TextAlignLeft]);
@Command([TextSetFontFace];"Arial");
@Command([TextSetFontSize]; "9")
```

SmartIcons come in sets. Among others, there is a set for editing a document and a set for designing a form. When you create a SmartIcon, you need to assign it to an existing or new set.

▶▶ See "SmartIcons," p. 1113

Designing Applications

Figure 14.6 shows the SmartIcons dialog box, the Edit SmartIcons dialog box, and the SmartIcons Formula dialog box. The formula shown will open a dialog box to allow the user to enter a WWW site URL.

Fig. 14.6 A SmartIcon formula to connect to an URL.

The @Command, @DbColumn, @DbLookup, @IsNewDoc, @MailSend, @Platform, @Prompt, @Return, @SetField, and @ViewTitle functions are designed to work well in SmartIcons formulas.

Database Formulas

There are two types of formulas that act at the database level. One type, the Replication formula, controls replication. The other type, an agent, replaces the macros used in R3 of Notes.

Replication Formulas. A replication formula controls which documents will be replicated. It is applied to each document in the database. The formula is evaluated wherever the database is located, usually at the server.

You might use a replication formula to replicate all client documents that came from IBM or Compaq, as in the following:

```
SELECT Form="Client" & (Source="IBM" ¦ Source="Compaq")
```

If the formula evaluates to true, then the document is replicated.

By using @IsResponseDoc in a replication formula, you cause all response documents in a database to replicate, not just those that meet the selection criteria. To avoid this, use @AllChildren or @AllDescendants instead.

The @All, @AllChildren, and @AllDescendants functions and the SELECT keyword are designed to work well in a replication formula. In fact, all replication formulas must end with a SELECT statement.

The @DbLookup, @Environment, @Now, and @UserName functions can't be used in a replication formula.

Agent Formulas. An agent is a procedure that can be made of simple actions, a formula, or a script. You can have the agent triggered manually, from another agent, when new mail arrives, when documents are created or changed, when documents are pasted, or on a preset schedule.

Formula-based agents can be run on all documents in a database, all new or modified documents since the last run, all unread documents, all documents in a view, all selected documents, or the current document. In addition, you can use a SELECT statement to determine which documents will be looked at. The formula is applied to each document, one at a time.

The agent is run at the client if the agent is triggered manually, when documents are created or changed, and when documents are pasted. The agent is run at the server when the trigger is new mail or a preset schedule.

You might use an agent to set the status of a field. For example, let's say that your organization needs to highlight valued customers for a beginning-of-the-month sales promotion. You could create an agent triggered monthly that looks at new or changed documents since the last run, and the formula might look like the following:

```
SELECT monthlySales > 200000;
FIELD promoStatus := "Valued";
```

This formula sets the promoStatus field to Valued for any customer with monthly sales over $200,000.

The @All, @Command, @DbColumn, @DbLookup, @DeleteDocument, @DeleteField, @DocMark, @MailSend, @Platform, @Prompt, @Return, @SetField, @Unavailable, and @ViewTitle functions and the SELECT keyword are designed to work well in agent formulas.

View Formulas

Formulas that operate at the view level are used to control what information is seen in each view column, which documents are seen, and which forms are used to display information.

Column Formulas. A column formula controls what information is shown in a view column and must evaluate to a value that can be converted into text. It is evaluated either at the client or the server, depending on the database's location.

The column formula may be the most-used type of formula because views are built from columns. And views are the way that information is communicated most frequently in Notes.

◀◀ See "Creating Columns in a View," p. 493

Columns are very versatile in Notes. Here is a simple column formula that will let you know whether a document was created on a weekend or a weekday:

```
day := @Weekday(@Created);
@If (day = 1 ¦ day = 7; "WeekEnd"; "WeekDay")
```

The @Created function has a value that represents the time/date when the document was created.

The @Weekday function looks at a time/date value and indicates which day of the week the time/date value falls on. A value of 1 represents Sunday, 2 represents Monday, and so on. This value is then assigned to the day variable.

The second line, with the @If function, looks at the value of the day variable and decides between two text constants, WeekEnd or WeekDay. If the day variable is equal to Sunday (1) or Saturday (7), then the value of WeekEnd is selected; otherwise, the value of WeekDay is used.

The @DocChildren, @DocDescendants, @DocLevel, @DocNumber, @DocParentNumber, @DocSiblings, @IsCategory, @IsExpandable, and @Platform functions are designed to work well in column formulas. In fact, the @IsCategory and @IsExpandable functions can only be used in column formulas.

The @Command, @DeleteDocument, @DeleteField, @DialogBox, @Do, @DoesDbExist, @GetDocField, @IsAgentEnabled, @IsDocBeingEdited, @IsDocBeingLoaded, @IsDocBeingMailed, @IsDocBeingRecalculated, @IsDocBeingSaved, @MailDbName, @MailSend, @NewLine, @PickList, @PostedCommand, @Prompt, @SetDocField, @SetField, @Unavailable, @UserPrivileges, @UserRoles, @Version, @ViewTitle, and @WhatIsUserAccess functions and the FIELD statement can't be used in a column formula. In addition, none of the DDE functions can be used.

The @IsNewDoc function always has a value of false or 0 in a column formula.

Form Formulas. A form formula controls which form is used to display the document information and must evaluate to the name of an existing form. The formula is evaluated on the client. A form that is stored in the document will take precedence over the form formula.

> **Tip**
>
> You can store the form used to create each document inside the document. This, of course, will probably eat up a lot of disk space. But, if you avoid changing the form after creating a document, this might be a good option.
>
> This feature is turned on by selecting Design, Form Properties while editing a form, and then selecting the Defaults tab in the InfoBox. Check the Store form in document checkbox.

One of the most common uses for a form formula is to display a different form when an existing document is viewed versus when a document is being created (see Figures 14.7 and 14.8). The following two formulas, when used in Action buttons, set up Environment variables that will allow the Form Formula to open one of two possible forms.

The New Course and New Company action buttons have formulas that set up environment variables and open a specific form. The first formula is for the New Course button and the second is for the New Company button:

```
" " " "
NEW COURSE
@Environment( "Option" ; "Course");
@Command([Compose]; "Course")
.
NEW COMPANY.
@Environment( "Option" ; "Company Info");
@Command([Compose]; "Company Info")
```

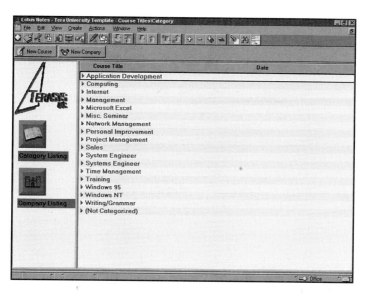

Fig. 14.7 A view that uses action buttons and a form formula to open different forms.

A form formula might also come in handy if you want to run some functions (perhaps to display some message) when a new document is composed, but not for existing documents. You can do this with the following formula:

```
msg := "Check all information before saving.";
@If (@IsNewDoc; @Prompt([OK];"Warning"; msg); "");
Form
```

You can use the Zoom In button to display a larger dialog box to make editing easier. In addition, you can use the Add @Func and Add Field buttons to select from lists of functions and fields.

The Form Formula in Figure 14.8 checks the Environment variable "Option" and opens the appropriate form when the Action button is pressed.

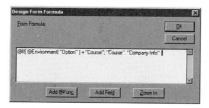

Fig. 14.8 A form formula to open one of two forms.

The @Environment and @IsDocBeingLoaded functions are designed to work well in form formulas.

The @Command, @IsDocBeingEdited, @IsDocBeingMailed, @IsDocBeingRecalculated, @IsDocBeingSaved, @Modified, @NewLine, @Now, @PickList, @PostedCommand, @SetField, and @Unavailable functions and the FIELD statement can't be used in form formulas.

Selection Formulas. A selection formula controls which documents appear in a view. The formula should begin with the keyword SELECT and be followed by a condition expression. The condition expression must evaluate to either true or false and is applied to each document in the database. Any document where the expression evaluates to true is included in the view. Selection formulas are evaluated at the database's location, either at the client or at the server.

You might use a selection formula that lists all customers with a negative account balance. For example, consider the following statement:

```
SELECT accountBalance < 0
```

If you have a database that includes several different forms, you might decide to show only a single form in a view. For example, in a database of veterinarian patients, you can select only cats—composed with the Feline Profile form—with this formula:

```
SELECT Form = "Feline Profile"
```

> **Tip**
>
> The special field, Form, is a part of every document and contains the name of the form used to compose that particular document.

If you don't specify a selection formula, Notes will use a default formula of:

```
SELECT @All
```

Form Formulas

Formulas that work at the form level have an effect when a form is being viewed. They help you to control actions, buttons, events, hotspots, paragraphs, subforms, and titles.

Event Formulas. Event formulas are evaluated whenever a specific event happens. There are seven different events for which you can create formulas: Queryopen, Postopen, Postrecalc, Querysave, Querymodechange, Postmodechange, and Queryclose. Table 14.3 lists these events and tells you when they will be run.

Table 14.3 When Are the Event Formulas Run?

Event	Formula Is Run...
Postmodechange	...after changing into or out of edit mode
Postopen	...after a document is displayed
Postrecalc	...after a document has been refreshed
Queryclose	...just before a document is closed
Queryopen	...just before a document is displayed
Querymodechange	...just before changing into or out of edit mode
Querysave	...just before a document is saved

Most of the time, you want to use an Event formula to do validation of field values or to display information automatically. For example, the `Postmodechange` Event formula can be used to reset some field information when going into edit mode. You do this with the following formula:

```
FIELD custDiscount := "unknown";
select @all
```

This formula automatically changes the customer discount to `unknown` when the form is in edit mode. You may want to do this so that no discount is given accidentally when a document is changed. A `Queryclose` Event formula may check the discount against other field values to make sure that it is being updated correctly.

Hide Paragraph Formulas. The Hide Paragraph formula can be used to hide individual paragraphs depending on a given set of conditions. For example, you could hide paragraphs depending on which state is being viewed. This can be very useful for an employee handbook where the rules in California are different from those in New York. One source document could serve both states. Paragraphs that are unique to New York might have the following Hide Paragraph formula:

```
@Environment("State") != "New York"
```

and paragraphs that are unique to California would use:

```
@Environment("State") != "California"
```

These formulas assume that some setup procedure created the `State` value in the `NOTES.INI` file. Notice that these formulas use the not equals operator (`!=`) so that the unique paragraphs are hidden if not displayed in that state.

You can also make paragraph visibility depend on a value in fields on the same document. For example, if someone over 65 is filling in a form, additional medical information may be needed. One possible hidden paragraph formula might be:

```
applicantAge <= 65
```

Again, the condition might be the opposite of what you expect to see. Remember that the formula evaluates to `true` if the paragraph is hidden. In this case, if the applicant is 65 or under, the paragraphs will not be seen.

> **Tip**
>
> Users can also hide paragraphs inside of Rich Text fields, if needed.

Insert Subform Formulas. Subforms are a good way to group a bunch of related fields together so that multiple forms can access them. This helps to keep form designs consistent. At times, you might want to dynamically determine which subform(s) to use with a given form. This is when the Insert Subform formula comes in handy.

An Insert Subform formula lets you dynamically determine the name of a subform to display in your form. It must evaluate to the name of an existing subform or a runtime error will result. This formula is run on the client.

Designing Applications

Continuing with the inventory control system for your examples, you can use subforms to display different information depending on the inventory type. Your formula may look like:

```
@If(invType = "Medical"; "Medical Detail"; "Standard Detail")
```

Insert Subform formulas are only evaluated when the document is opened. If the basis for the condition (such as the inventory type) changes, you must close and reopen the document to reevaluate the Insert Subform formula.

Section Access Formulas. Sections let you group portions of a document together. When a section is collapsed, only a title shows. When expanded, the section contents are readable. Sections are a good way to organize information because you can group related information into one section.

In addition to a standard section, you can create an access-controlled section to limit who can edit the information in the section. This type of section uses a Section Access formula to control access.

> **Note**
>
> The Session Access formula specifies who can edit the section, not who can read it. In addition, the formula will not override the access control list of the database.

Section Access formulas must evaluate to a name or list of names. This formula will run on the client.

You can simply specify names explicitly in the formula, like this:

```
"Jane Doe" : "John Doe"
```

which restricts edit access to just those two users. Or you might want to use a view and the @DbColumn, like this:

```
@DbColumn(""; ""; "(View of Section Readers)"; 1)
```

which looks at the list of names in the first column of the View of Section Readers view in the current database.

The @Command, @IsDocBeingLoaded, @Modified, @PostedCommand, and @ViewTitle functions and the SELECT statement can't be used in Section Access formulas.

Section Title Formulas. A Section Title formula is used to determine what is displayed as the section title. The formula must either be a single field or evaluate to a text or numeric value.

If you use sections to collapse a series of fields, perhaps the education information in a personnel form, you could use a Section Title formula to display some key information in the title. For example, examine this formula:

```
"Education: (" + yrGraduated + ") " + @Left(collegeName; 25)
```

This formula might display Education: (1964) Rutgers University when evaluated. Pulling out the most important information in this way can make your forms easier to understand and appear less cluttered.

Window Title Formulas. Window Title formulas determine the text that is displayed as the title for each document that is viewed. The formula is evaluated on the client.

You might use a Window Title formula to display one title for new documents and another for existing documents. For example, if your database describes an animal patient at a veterinarian's clinic, you might want to use the title New Patient when the document is first composed, and then use a title with the pet's and owner's names when read later. The following formula accomplishes this task:

```
@If (@IsNewDoc; "New Patient"; patientName + " (" + ownerName + ")")
```

You can also make very complicated window title formulas. The next example will display New Patient for new documents, patient (Owner) for existing documents, and patient (Unknown Owner) for existing documents whose owner is unknown. It's a contrived example, but the technique is useful nonetheless:

```
isFldThere = @IsAvailable(ownerName) & ownerName != ""
ifFldYes = patientName + " (" + ownerName + ")"
ifFldNo = patientName + " (Unknown Owner)"
@If(@IsNewDoc; "New Patient"; @If(isFldThere; ifSFldYes; ifFldNo))
```

The key element in this example is the first line:

```
isFldThere = @IsAvailable(ownerName) & ownerName != ""
```

which sets the variable isFldThere to true or false. The last line actually determines which text is displayed in the title.

Like Section Title formulas, the Window Title formula must either be a single field (except for rich text fields) or evaluate to a text or numeric value.

Field Formulas

Field level formulas are used to control what happens when buttons are clicked; they also determine default values, check for valid input and, in general, deal with things that happen when users are actively entering information into a document.

Default Value Formulas. Default value formulas enable you to specify the value that appears automatically in a field when a user composes a document.

A good example of a default value is a field that represents the current user's name. You could create a field called lastEditor with a default value formula of:

```
@UserName
```

The @UserName function equates to the name of the user reading or editing the document. Each time the document is edited, Notes inserts the user's name. If you want to keep the name of the original, make the field computed-when-composed.

Another example of a default value that is often used is a field that holds the current date. This is done by using the following function:

```
@Today
```

The @Today function returns the current date. When used in field level formulas, it is evaluated at the client.

Input Translation Formulas. Input translation formulas let you tell Notes to perform some type of automatic conversion on the information in a field. Notes executes the formula when the document is saved.

For example, you might want to make sure that all supervisors' names start with a capital letter and that the rest of the letters are lowercase. Notes has a function called @ProperCase that does this for you. Using it in an input translation formula would look like the following:

```
@ProperCase(supervisor)
```

When a user enters a value into this field in lowercase letters, @ProperCase provides the correct capitalization as the document is saved. For example, if the user enters the text "felemid mcfal," the above formula would convert it to "Felemid Mcfal."

If you requested a user to consecutively enter all nine digits of his Social Security number, an Input Translation formula, used in a text field, would add the hyphens in the appropriate place:

```
@If(SSN = ""; ""; (@IsDocBeingRecalculated ¦
@IsDocBeingSaved) & @Length(SSN) = 11; SSN; @Left(SSN; 3) +
"-" + @Middle(SSN; 2; 2) + "-" + @Right(SSN; 4))
```

Input Validation Formulas. Input validation formulas enable you to explain to Notes how to determine whether or not data entered by the user is valid. These formulas differ from other kinds of formulas because they answer only a yes or no question: Is the data valid?

Almost all input validation formulas contain an @If function that determines whether the field contains valid data. Two special functions, used exclusively in conjunction with input validation formulas, tell Notes whether the data is valid: @Success means the value in the field is acceptable; @Failure means that the value isn't acceptable.

Suppose that you have a field called ClientName, which must contain a name. You can use the @Length function to determine the length of the field, so the entire validation formula for the field may look like the following:

```
@If( @Length( ClientName ) = 0;
    @Failure( "Client Name cannot be blank" );
    @Success )
```

The @If function determines whether the ClientName field is blank; if so, it signals to Notes (through the @Success function) that the data is valid. Otherwise, it uses the @Failure function to signal that the data is invalid. @Failure requires you to provide a description of the problem, which Notes displays as an error message (see Figure 14.9). Further, Notes doesn't let the user save the document until he or she fixes the problem (in this example, the user needs to fill in the Client Name).

Fig. 14.9 This sample error message is produced through a validation formula.

The "Examples: @Environment, @SetEnvironment, and ENVIRONMENT" and the "Examples: @SetDocField" topics in the Notes online help system have more good examples of input validation formulas.

Computed Field Formulas. Document fields can be editable, computed, computed for display, and computed when composed. All of the computed field types need to have a formula associated with them. When evaluated, the result data type must agree with the data type of the field. A text value needs a formula that evaluates to the text string. A date field needs a formula that evaluates to a date.

For example, you might want a computed numeric field that calculates the sum of other document numeric fields. You could do this with the following formula:

```
monRevenue + tueRevenue + wedRevenue + thuRevenue + friRevenue
```

Unlike spreadsheets, there is no function to sum a series of numeric fields. You simply list each numeric field and add them together.

Keyword Field Formulas. Keyword fields are used to display a list from which a user can select the information that will be used in a field. The list can be explicitly created by the form designer or a formula can be used that will evaluate to a list.

One of the most common @functions used in keyword field formulas is @DbColumn, which is used to get a list of keywords from a column in a view. For example, to get a list of all clients in your database you might use this formula:

```
"""""" @DbLookup( "":"NoCache"; ""; "Client List";  Name; 2)
```

Figure 14.10 shows this formula in use in an InfoBox that is reached by choosing Design, Field Properties when a field is selected.

If you check the Allow values not in list checkbox in the Field Properties InfoBox, then the user can add information to the list as needed. Otherwise, you'll need to create another way to update the view to add selections.

Fig. 14.10   The Field Properties InfoBox shows the keyword value formula and its options.

> **Tip**
>
> These dynamic lookups are very powerful and make creating lookup tables very easy to do. At least, they'll be easy once you get the hang of it. However, dynamic lookups are slow. Don't use too many of them or your users will complain about poor response time.

Figure 14.11 shows the result of using this formula. Notice that to the right of the Dog Breed input field, there is a little down arrow button (immediately above the mouse pointer). When you click it, the Select Keywords dialog box is displayed.

Fig. 14.11   An example of a keyword field formula.

From the Select Keywords dialog box, the user can select from the list or type a new one in the box at the bottom of the dialog box.

From Here...

In this chapter, you learned about formulas. You saw that a formula can be a numeric or string constant, a field name, or an expression. Formulas can have variables and keywords and consist of multiple lines.

A great deal of discussion was spent on where formulas can be used and examples of how to use them. This chapter, of course, just skims the surface of what you can do with formulas. When used creatively, there seem to be few limits.

To continue your exploration of formulas and Notes programmability, consider the following:

- Chapter 11, "Designing Forms," and Chapter 12, "Designing Views," refresh the basics if some of the examples were confusing.

- Chapter 15, "Working with Functions and Commands," discusses all of the @functions that you can use in formulas.

- Chapter 18, "Writing Scripts with LotusScript," talks about the next level of Notes programming.

- The Notes online help has good examples of each type of formula and keyword. Take advantage of the full text search capability to look for specific information that you need.

II

Designing Applications

Chapter 15

Working with Functions and Commands

Although you can do a lot with the constants, operators, and keywords discussed in Chapter 14, "Working with Formulas," the real power of formulas is in Notes' collection of functions. A function is a Notes operation that processes data and provides a value that you use in some way. Notes has numerous functions that can process data in many different ways, as you will learn in this chapter.

Some of the main topics in this chapter are

- A description of functions and commands and how they are used

- @Functions broken up into categories

- @Commands broken up into categories

> **Tip**
>
> A complete reference to all @functions and @commands is included on the CD included with this book.

Quite frequently, programmers find it useful to be able to browse the function reference without being tied to a computer. This chapter will give you that chance. You can look through the lists and get a feel for the vast amount of control that the @functions and @commands give to you.

Understanding Function Basics

When you ask Notes to find the value of a field, it will go look for that value in the database. When you ask Notes to find the value of a function, it will need to perform some task associated with that function. The @Today function requests Notes to find the current date. In order to determine the current date, Notes does not need to reference the database.

> **Tip**
>
> Function names are easy to distinguish from field names because all function names begin with an at sign (@), as in @Success or @Year.

II

Designing Applications

Let's look at another example. Suppose that you defined a column with the formula

```
effectiveDate
```

which consists of a single field name. For each document, Notes fetches and displays the value of the `effectiveDate` field.

Compare that with the formula

```
@Created
```

which consists of a single function name. You can tell that `@Created` is a function because its name starts with @. `@Created` causes Notes to find the date that the document was created. So if you use this function in a column formula, Notes displays the date that each document was created. If you use this function in a default value formula, the creation date becomes the value of the field.

Function Arguments

Most functions require you to specify information with which they can work to produce a result. For example, if you want a function to determine what day of the week a certain date falls on, you must tell Notes exactly which date you are interested in.

The `@Weekday` function calculates the day of the week on which a date occurred; in order for this function to do its work, you must give it a date. Pieces of information that are required by functions are called arguments. Some functions, such as `@Created`, don't require any arguments, but most functions require a specific number and types of arguments, which you must provide in parentheses after the name of the function. In the case of `@Weekday`, you need to provide a single date argument. Consider the following formula, which might appear in the definition for a column:

```
@Weekday(effectiveDate)
```

The data in parentheses—the value of the `effectiveDate` field—is the data that `@Weekday` uses. `@Weekday`, in return, provides a number from 1 through 7, indicating a day of the week (Sunday through Saturday, respectively).

If a function requires more than one argument, you must list all the arguments inside the parentheses, separated by semicolons. Suppose that your documents contain a `homePhone` field, which you use to store home phone numbers with area codes. Suppose next that you want a column to display just the area code for each person. The `@Left` function enables you to extract characters from the left end of a text field. You must provide `@Left` with a text field and the number of characters you want. To display the leftmost three characters, for instance, enter the following:

```
@Left(HomePhone; 3)
```

Nesting Functions

You can use the result provided by one function as the data for another function to process, a technique called *nesting*. You have already seen that `@Created` gives you the date that a document was created, and `@Weekday` takes a date and tells you on what day of the week that date occurred. Thus, to display a number that represents the day of the week on which the document was created, you can write the following:

```
@Weekday(@Created)
```

Notes starts inside the parentheses and works its way out. @Created tells Notes to compute the date that the document was created; then @Weekday uses that date to compute the day of the week on which the creation occurred.

The *@If* Function

One of the most widely used functions is @If, which enables you to write a formula that chooses between several possible values based on the outcome of a question.

In its simplest form, the @If function returns one of two values. You supply a condition expression, a true expression, and a false expression. The first step that Notes takes is to evaluate the condition expression—it must evaluate to true or false. Next, one of the two other expressions is evaluated and its value becomes the return value of the @If function. If the condition evaluates to true, then the truth expression is evaluated. If the condition evaluates to false, then the false expression is evaluated.

For example, suppose that each document in a customer database contains a field named creditRating, which contains an A or B value. The A customers have credit limits of $10,000; the B customers have $3,000 limits. The following formula defines a column that displays the customer's credit rating:

```
@If(CreditRating = "A"; 10000; 3000)
```

Notice the three required parts:

- The first part is a condition that can be true or false; in this case, the condition asks whether the creditRating field is equal to A.

- The second part is the expression used if the condition is true; in this case, the value is 10000.

- The third part is the expression used if the condition is false; in this case, the value is 3000.

In effect, this function says if the value of the creditRating field is A, display the value 10000; otherwise, display 3000.

Now, suppose that each document in a database describes one of your customers, and has a field named areaCode that contains a customer's area code. Your courier considers every destination with an area code that starts with 328 to be local; all other destinations are long-distance calls, and thus are more expensive. In a column, you want to display either *Local* or *Long Distance*. Consider this function:

```
@If(@Left(areaCode; 3) = "328"; "Local"; "Long Distance")
```

This example is much trickier than the preceding example. The condition asks whether the first three digits of the area code are 328. If so, Notes displays Local; otherwise, it displays Long Distance.

The text constants in this example could be replaced with any Notes expression. This means that you could use field names, operators, and @functions to accomplish different tasks. For example:

```
localCost := .10
longCost := .30
@If(@Left(areaCode; 3) = "328";
callTime * localCost;
callTime * longCost)
```

In this example, the text constants have been replaced with expressions that represent the total cost of the phone call to the customer. If the phone call is local, then the first expression is evaluated. If the phone call is long distance, then the second expression is evaluated.

The Conditional Operators

Notes provides operators that you can use in the @If condition expression for comparing values. These are summarized in Table 15.1.

Table 15.1   The Conditional Operators

Operator	Description
=	is equal to
!=	is not equal to
=!	is not equal to (same as !=)
<>	is not equal to (same as !=)
><	is not equal to (same as !=)
<	is less than
<=	is less than or equal to
>	is greater than
>=	is greater than or equal to

You can also use predicate functions and logical operators in conditional expressions. See the "Predicate Functions" and "Logical Operators" sections that follow for more information.

For example, you can use the following formula in a column formula to alert you to customers who have spent too much:

```
@If (currentBalance > creditLimit; "Over Limit"; "")
```

This formula decides which of two values to display in the column. The formula asks whether the value of the currentBalance field is greater than the value of the creditLimit field. If so, Notes displays the value Over Limit; otherwise, Notes displays nothing, specified as two adjacent quotes with nothing in-between.

> **Note**
>
> The true expression and false expression can include any functions or combination of functions that you need. You are not limited to using constants as we have done in most of these examples.

The *@If* function has a related format that enables you to select from any number of values. In this format, the *@If* function includes any number of pairs of conditions and values. Notes begins checking conditions. As soon as Notes finds a condition that is true, the *@If* function selects the value that follows that condition.

Suppose that your company manufactures cameras. Throughout the course of its existence, the company has manufactured cameras with three different kinds of focusing mechanisms. All the cameras made before March 1981 were manual focus. After that date, manual cameras were discontinued, and all your factories produced cameras with fixed focus, except the Cleveland factory, which produced auto-focus cameras.

If each document in the database describes a camera and includes fields for the date and place of manufacture, you can define a column formula that displays the type of focus mechanism the camera uses:

```
@If (mfgDate < [3/1/81]; "Manual"; mfgSite != "Cleveland"; "Fixed"; "Auto")
```

This formula gives Notes the following orders: If the manufacture date is before 3/1/81, display Manual; otherwise, check the manufacture site—if it's not Cleveland, display Fixed; otherwise, display Auto.

Predicate Functions

Many Notes functions don't manipulate data, but instead examine data, testing for the existence of some condition. These functions—called predicate functions—are meant to be used with the *@If* function so that you can take some action if a specific condition exists.

For example, suppose that you want to change the title of a document to read:

```
Customer Complaint Meeting (James Owens)
```

when a user reads or edits a document. The first part of the title will be pulled from the document's subject field, and the name in parentheses will be the document author's name.

When a user first creates a document, however, the document doesn't have a subject, so a better title might include the words *New Document* with the author's name, as follows:

```
New Document (James Owens)
```

You can use the predicate function @IsNewDoc to distinguish between an existing document and one that is in the process of being created. By using the @IsNewDoc function as the condition of an *@If* function, you can construct one Notes formula to display either of the needed titles. The window title formula might look like this:

```
@If (@IsNewDoc; "New Document"; Subject) + " (" + @Author + ")"
```

Designing Applications

This formula tells Notes to determine whether this document is new, and to display the phrase New Document if it's new, or the value of the Subject field if it isn't new. Onto that value, Notes should concatenate an opening parenthesis, the author's name, and a closing parenthesis. The resulting text becomes the title of the document window.

Logical Operators

In some situations, you may need to test for combinations of conditions. You can test for these combinations by combining individual conditions with one of two special operators.

The And operator (&) enables you to determine whether all of two or more conditions are true. For example, let's say that you want to determine which magazine subscribers are eligible for renewal so that you remember to contact them. One way to do this is to create a column formula that displays "Renewal" if their subscription expires this month and they have a good credit rating. The column formula might look like this:

```
@If (@Month(@Today) = renewalMonth & creditRating = "Good";
"Renew";
"")
```

This @If function has two conditions separated by the And operator. When evaluated, Notes selects one of two values to display: Renew or "" (nothing). The @Today function returns today's date; the @Month function determines what month that date occurs in. Notes determines whether that month is equal to the value in the renewalMonth field. It also checks whether the creditRating field contains the value Good. For Notes to display Renew, both conditions must evaluate to true; otherwise, Notes displays nothing.

The Or operator (¦) enables you to determine whether any of two or more conditions are true. Suppose that your rental car fleet database contains documents describing vehicles in your corporate fleet, and you want to display an asterisk (*) in a column if the vehicle is due for maintenance. Vehicles are scheduled for maintenance every 3,000 miles or if the driver complained of a problem during his last run. The column formula might look like this:

```
@If (currentMiles > lastServiceMiles + 3000 ¦ complaint = "Y";
"*";
"")
```

This @If function selects between displaying an asterisk or displaying nothing. If the value in currentMiles is greater than lastServiceMiles plus 3000, or if the complaint field is equal to Y, Notes uses the asterisk—only one of the conditions has to be true.

The Not operator (!) changes true values to false and false values to true. Continuing with the rental car fleet example, let's say that you have a very rich, peculiar customer who insists that her rented car be red in February and December and blue in all other months. The following formula will evaluate to either Blue or Red:

```
@If (customerName = "Morganna" &
!(rentalMonth = "February" ¦ rentalMonth = "December");
"Blue" :
"Red")
```

When trying to understand a complex statement like this, always start with the inner-most parentheses. In this case, it means looking at the part about the rental months:

```
(rentalMonth = "February" ¦ rentalMonth = "December")
```

This formula clause or fragment will evaluate to true if the rental month is either February or December. However, the original formula has a Not (!) operator directly in front of this clause:

```
!(rentalMonth = "February" ¦ rentalMonth = "December")
```

This reverses the value of the clause so that it will be true only if the rental month is not February or December.

Now, you can look at the next larger clause which checks the customer name. If the customer name is Morganna and it's not February or December, then the whole formula will evaluate to Blue—otherwise, it will evaluate to Red.

Conditional expressions can get pretty complicated. But if you start in the middle and work your way outward, they can be understood one bit at a time.

Function Reference by Category

Notes includes more than a hundred functions. To help you organize them, this section groups the functions into different types. For example, some functions deal with text manipulation and others are mathematical.

In order to save space, only the function names are listed here. The syntax and a brief description of each function is listed in the "Alphabetical Function Reference" section later in this chapter.

The User Environment

The user environment is the client computer unless the formula is being evaluated in the following situations: replication formula, agent whose trigger is If New Mail Has Arrived or On Schedule, selection formula, or column formula.

The following functions are useful when dealing with the user environment:

@MailDbName	@Name	@OptimizeMailAddress
@Password	@UserName	@UserRoles
@Version	@V3UserName	

Defining Columns

Because column formulas and views can make up a large part of a Notes application, there are quite a few functions that are useful in defining columns:

@Begins	@IsCategory	@DbCommand
@DbLookup	@DocChildren	@DocDescendants
@DocLength	@DocLevel	@DocNumber

@DocParentNumber	@DocSiblings	@DocumentUniqueID
@Elements	@Ends	@If
@InheritedDocumentUniqueID	@IsAvailable	@IsCategory
@IsExpandable	@IsNotMember	@Keywords
@Length	@Matches	@NoteID
@Subset	@Unique	@UserRoles
@Word	@DbColumn	

Manipulating Dates and Times

Notes has several functions that let you manipulate date and time values. Functions such as @Month and @Day enable you to determine the parts of a date or time. @Adjust enables you to compute a time or date in the future or past—for example, you can compute the date 30 days from today. Most useful of all is @Today, which gives you today's date. This function is especially helpful as the default value formula of a date field, because it enables you to specify the current date as the initial value for a field when the user creates a document.

The following functions also are useful in dealing with dates and times:

@Accessed	@Adjust	@Created	@Date
@Day	@Hour	@Minute	@Modified
@Month	@Now	@Second	@Text
@Time	@Today	@Tomorrow	@Weekday
@Year	@Yesterday	@Zone	

Working with the Selected Document

When writing formulas that act on the selected document, the following functions are useful:

@All	@AllChildren	@AllDescendants
@AttachmentNames	@AttachmentLengths	@Author
@Attachments	@DeleteDocument	@DeleteField
@DocLength	@DocMark	@DocumentUniqueID
@InheritedDocumentUniqueID	@IsAvailable	@IsDocBeingEdited
@IsDocBeingLoaded	@IsDocBeingMailed	@IsDocBeingRecalculated
@IsDocBeingSaved	@IsNewDoc	@IsResponseDoc
@IsUnavailable	@MailSend	@NoteID

| @Responses | @SetField | @Unavailable |
| @SetDocField | @Set | @IsDocTruncated |

The DEFAULT, FIELD, and SELECT statements also are important when working with a selected document.

Manipulating Lists

The following functions are useful when dealing with lists:

@Elements	@Explode	@Implode
@IsMember	@IsNotMember	@Keywords
@Member	@Replace	@Subset
@Unique		

Manipulating Numbers

Manipulating numbers is done by mathematical functions. For example, the @Max function returns the largest number from a list of parameters that you pass it.

Here is a list of the functions that are useful in dealing with numbers:

@Abs	@Acos	@Asin
@Atan	@Atan2	@Cos
@Exp	@Integer	@Log
@Ln	@Min	@Modulo
@Max	@Pi	@Power
@Random	@Round	@Sign
@Sin	@Sqrt	@Sum
@Tan	@Text	

Manipulating Text

Text functions enable you to manipulate text in various ways, and to convert data from text to another type, or vice versa. The @Left function, which enables you to extract the beginning portion of a text value, is one such example of a function that can manipulate text. Other text functions enable you to check for the length of a field, manipulate text in various ways, and extract any portion of the field.

Suppose that a document requires the user to enter a part number in a field named partNumber. Letters in this field always are supposed to be in uppercase, but you want the user to be able to enter them in uppercase or lowercase. You can specify the following input translation formula:

```
@UpperCase (partNumber)
```

The following functions allow various types of text manipulation:

@Abstract	@Begins	@Char
@Contains	@Date	@Ends
@Explode	@Implode	@Left
@LeftBack	@LowerCase	@Middle
@MiddleBack	@NewLine	@ProperCase
@Replace	@Right	@RightBack
@Trim	@UpperCase	

WWW Access

The following functions enable applications to access the World Wide Web:

@URLGetHeader

@URLHistory

@URLOpen

Converting Data Types

When working with different data types, you frequently need to convert from one data type to another. For example, let's say that you have a time/date field that holds the order date of an invoice, and you would like to create a window title formula that shows the customer name and the year of the invoice. The window title, when finished, should look like this:

```
John Doe - 1996
```

Here is the formula that will accomplish this:

```
@ProperCase(customerName) + " - " + @Text(@Year(orderDate))
```

You've seen the @ProperCase function before—it makes sure that each word is capitalized. Let's concentrate on the right side of the formula. The @Year function looks at the orderDate field and extracts the year as a number date type. In order to concatenate it to the customerName field and the text constant, the year needs to be changed into a text data type. The @Text function does this for you.

> **Note**
>
> In order to create or edit a window title formula, you must first edit the associated form. Then in the programmer pane, select the form name in the Define drop-down list and the window title in the Event drop-down list.

The following functions allow various types of data-type manipulation:

@Explode	@Implode	@Text
@TextToNumber	@TextToTime	@Time

The following functions allow various types of list-type manipulation:

@Contains	@Elements	@Explode
@GetPortsList	@Implode	@IsMember
@IsNotMember	@Keywords	@Member
@PickList	@Replace	@Subset
@Unique		

Command Reference by Category

Notes includes more than 350 commands for use in formulas and functions. They are used in buttons, agents, and action items. In this section, the commands are grouped by type. For example, some commands deal with Administration issues while others deal with form and view design and manipulation, text editing, and replication.

In order to save space, only the command names are listed here. The syntax and a brief description of each command are listed in the "Notes Formula Catalog" included on the CD.

All commands use the same syntax, as follows:

```
@Command([commandname]; parameters )
```

Therefore, the @Command portion in the listings isn't repeated.

Administration

AdminCertify	AdminCreateGroup	AdminCrossCertifyIDFile
AdminCrossCertifyKey	AdminDatabaseAnalysis	AdminDatabaseQuotas
AdminIDFileClearPassword	AdminIDFileExamine	AdminIDFileSetPassword
Administration	AdminNewCertifier	AdminNewOrganization
AdminNewOrgUnit	AdminOpenAddressBook	AdminOpenCatalog
AdminOpenCertLog	AdminOpenGroupsView	AdminOpenServerLog
AdminOpenServersView	AdminOpenStatisticsView	AdminOpenUsersView
AdminOutgoingMail	AdminRegisterFromFile	AdminRegisterServer
AdminRegisterUser	AdminRemoteConsole	AdminSendMailTrace
AdminStatisticsConfig	AdminTraceConnection	RenameDatabase
PublishDatabase	SetCurrentLocation	

Agents

AgentEdit	AgentEnableDisable	AgentLog
AgentRun	AgentSetServerName	AgentTestRun

Attachments

AttachmentDetachAll	AttachmentLaunch	AttachmentProperties
AttachmentView		

Calendar

CalendarFormat	CalendarGoTo	FindFreeTimeDisplay

Create

CreateAction	CreateAgent	CreateControlledAccessSection
CreateEllipse	CreateFolder	CreateForm
CreateLayoutRegion	CreateNavigator	CreatePolygon
CreatePolyline	CreateRectangle	CreateRectangularHotspot
CreateSection	CreateSubForm	CreateTextform
CreateView		

Design

DesignDocumentInfo	ChooseFolders	RemoveFromFolder

Forms-Related Commands.

DesignFormAttributes	DesignFormFieldDef	DesignFormNewField
DesignForms	DesignFormSharedField	DesignFormUseField
DesignFormWindowTitle	DesignHelpAboutDocument	DesignHelpUsingDocument
DesignIcon	DesignMacros	DesignRefresh
DesignReplace	DesignSharedFields	DesignSynopsis

Views-Related Commands.

DesignViewAppendColumn	DesignViewAttributes	DesignViewColumnDef
DesignViewEditActions	DesignViewFormFormula	DesignViewNewColumn
DesignViews	DesignViewSelectFormula	
PasteBitmapAsBackground	PasteBitmapAsObject	
DatabaseReplSettings	DebugLotusScript	
DesignDocumentInfo	InsertSubFormPictureProperties	

Edit

Compose	EditBottom	EditButton
EditClear	EditCopy	EditCut
EditDeselectAll	EditDetach	EditDocument
EditDown	EditEncryptionKeys	EditFind
EditFindInPreview	EditFindNext	EditGotoField
EditHeaderFooter	EditHorizScrollbar	EditIndent
EditIndentFirstLine	EditInsertButton	EditInsertFileAttachment
EditInsertObject	EditInsertPageBreak	EditInsertPopup
EditInsertTable	EditInsertText	EditLeft
EditLinks	EditLocations	EditMakeDocLink
EditNextField	EditOpenLink	EditPaste
EditPasteSpecial	EditPhoneNumbers	EditPrevField
EditProfile	EditResizePicture	EditRight
EditSelectAll	EditSelectByDate	EditShowHideHiddenChars
EditTableFormat	EditTableDeleteRowColumn	EditTableInsertRowColumn
EditTop	EditUndo	EditUntruncate
EditUp		

File

FileCloseWindow	FileDatabaseACL	FileDatabaseCompact
FileDatabaseCopy	FileDatabaseDelete	FileDatabaseInfo
FileDatabaseRemove	FileDatabaseuseServer	FileExit
FileExport	FileFullTextCreate	FileFullTextDelete
FileFullTextInfo	FileFullTextUpdate	FileImport
FileNewDatabase	FileNewReplica	FileOpenDatabase
FileOpenDBRepID	FilePageSetup	FilePrint
FilePrintSetup	FileSave	FileSaveNewVersion

Folder

Folder	FolderCollapse	FolderCustomize
FolderExpand	FolderExpandAll	FolderExpandWithChildren
FolderMove	FolderProperties	FolderRename

II

Designing Applications

Form

FormActions   FormTestDocument

Help

Help   HelpAboutDatabase   HelpAboutNotes

HelpFunctions   HelpIndex   HelpKeyboard

HelpMessages   HelpTableOfContents   HelpUsingDatabase

HotSpot

HotSpotClear   HotSpotProperties

Layout

LayoutAddGraphic   LayoutAddText   LayoutElementBringToFront

LayoutElementProperties LayoutElementSendToBack LayoutProperties

Mail

MailAddress   MailComposeMemo   MailForward

MailForwardAsAttachment MailOpen   MailRequestCrossCert

MailRequestNewName   MailRequestNewPublicKey   MailScanUnread

MailSend   MailSendCertificateRequest MailSendEncryptionKey

MailSendPublicKey

Navigate

NavigateNext   NavigateNextHighlight   NavigateNextMain

NavigateNextSelected   NavigateNextUnread   NavigatePrev

NavigatePrevHighlight   NavigatePrevMain   NavigatePrevSelected

NavigatePrevUnread   NavigateToBackLink

Navigator

NavigatorProperties   NavigatorTest

Object

ObjectDisplayAs   ObjectOpen   ObjectProperties

Open

OpenDocument   OpenNavigator   OpenView

Replicator

ReplicatorSendReceiveMail   Replicator

ReplicatorReplicateHigh   ReplicatorReplicateNext

ReplicatorReplicateSelected ReplicatorReplicateWithServer

ReplicatorSendMail   ReplicatorStart

ReplicatorStop

Section

SectionCollapse   SectionCollapseAll   SectionDefineEditors

SectionExpand   SectionExpandAll   SectionProperties

SectionRemoveHeader

ShowHide

ShowHideLinkPreview   ShowHideParentPreview   ShowHidePreviewPane

Show

ShowProperties

Text

TextAlignCenter   TextAlignFull   TextAlignLeft

TextAlignNone   TextAlignRight   TextBold

TextBullet   TextCycleSpacing   TextEnlargeFont

TextFont   TextItalic   TextNormal

TextNumbers   TextOutdent   TextParagraph

TextParagraphStyles   TextPermanentPen   TextReduceFont

TextSetFontColor   TextSetFontFace   TextSpacingDouble

TextSpacingOneAndAHalf TextSpacingSingle   TextUnderline

Tools

ToolsCall   ToolsCategorize   ToolsHangUp

ToolsMarkAllRead   ToolsMarkAllUnread   ToolsMarkSelectedRead

ToolsMarkSelectedUnread ToolsRefreshAllDocs   ToolsRefreshSelectedDocs

ToolsReplicate   ToolsRunBackgroundMacros ToolsRunMacro

ToolsScanUnreadChoose   ToolsScanUnreadPreferred ToolsScanUnreadSelected

ToolsSetupLocation   ToolsSetupMail   ToolsSetupPorts

ToolsSetupUserSetup   ToolsSmartIcons   ToolsSpellCheck

ToolsUserLogoff

User

UserIDCertificates   UserIDClearPassword   UserIDCreateSafeCopy

UserIDEncryptionKeys   UserIDInfo   UserIDMergeCopy

UserIDSetPassword   UserIDSwitch

II

Designing Applications

View

ViewArrangeIcons	ViewBelowFolders	ViewBesidesFolders
ViewCertify	ViewChange	ViewCollapse
ViewCollapseAll	ViewExpand	ViewExpandAll
ViewExpandWithChildren	ViewHorizScrollBar	ViewMoveName
ViewNavigatorsFolders	ViewNavigatorsNone	ViewRefreshFields
ViewRefreshUnread	ViewRenamePerson	ViewShowFieldHelp
ViewShowObject	ViewShowOnlyCategories	ViewShowOnlySearchResults
ViewShowOnlySelected	ViewShowOnlyUnread	ViewShowPageBreaks
ViewShowRuler	ViewShowSearchBar	ViewShowServerNames
ViewShowUnread	ViewSwitchForm	

Window

WindowCascade	WindowMaximize	WindowMaximizeAll
WindowMinimize	WindowMinimizeAll	WindowNext
WindowRestore	WindowTile	WindowWorkspace

Workspace

WorkspaceProperties	WorkspaceStackReplicaIcons

Other

RefreshHideFormulas	ZoomPreview

Compatibility Commands

HelpRelease3MenuFinder	V3EditNextField	V3EditPrevField

> **Note**
>
> A complete alphabetical function reference can be found on the CD.

> **Note**
>
> A complete @command list can be found in the Help Files provided with Lotus Notes.

@Command and *@PostedCommand* Action List

In addition to the functions already discussed, you have a couple of other functions at your disposal. You can access any of Notes' menu options through the @Command and @PostedCommand functions.

Both @Command and @PostedCommand can handle the same actions—the key difference is when the actions are performed. @Command performs an immediate action in the Notes environment, whereas @PostedCommand defers actions until the end of the formula.

From Here...

This chapter discussed function basics, including how functions operate, how to call functions, and what arguments to pass to specific functions. The chapter also suggested broad categories of functions so that you could begin to make sense of the large numbers of @functions available in Notes.

Any true Lotus Notes guru spends much time learning formulas and functions. The wealth of @functions and @command actions that Notes provides can keep you busy learning them for months. Don't try to memorize the list, though—you'll find that learning as the need arises allows you to view Notes as a less intimidating environment.

When you are ready to tackle some more challenging stuff, take a look at the following:

- Chapter 17, "LotusScript Basics," gives you more information about programming with LotusScript.

- Chapter 24, "Notes: Under the Hood," provides an understanding of what happens internally when you run Notes.

II

Designing Applications

## Chapter 16

Buttons and Agents

Our world is filled with buttons. The idea of user programmable buttons has spread from TVs and VCRs to computer programs. While buttons aren't new to Notes, the way they're programmed and the things you can do with them have been enhanced with a new interface and LotusScript functionality.

In Notes Release 4.5, there's more flexibility than ever before in defining tasks or executing script programs. Behind a button may be some quite complex code, yet the user is presented with a simple, non-intimidating interface. But programmability can have a downside, which we'll discuss in this chapter.

Agents allow you to automate daily tasks or to build powerful tools that you may use to execute complex programs. Users of previous versions of Notes will recognize the similarity of the Agent Builder window with that of the Macro Design window from Notes 3.x. Basically, agents are macros, but more powerful and updated to include the new LotusScript capabilities.

Tip

If you've recently migrated to Release 4.x of Notes, you may want some assistance in converting your knowledge of Release 3.x menus to the current version. Choosing Help, Release 3 Menu Finder will activate a stay-on-top window showing the conversions in a display window as you click the familiar Release 3 menu interface.

Don't be intimidated by the idea of automating your database applications. After working with buttons and agents for a while on local databases, you'll be ready to begin adding them to some production databases. In this chapter, you'll learn basic concepts and some advanced tips that you can begin using today.

Understanding Agents

Thirty years ago, the media was full of predictions about the future. We were supposed to be flying around with jetpacks while machines took care of those pesky manual tasks like cooking dinner and cleaning the house. Computers were going to make work easy and paperless, remember? I don't have a

---

Some of the main topics in this chapter are

- Creating and naming agents
- Programming agents
- Selecting documents
- Running agents
- Building search queries
- Buttons and hotspots
- Testing your creations

Designing Applications

II

jetpack yet and still cook and clean for myself. Although my computer is helping me do more work, I'm still buried in paper.

Perhaps programmable agents are the beginning of that future. Agents can automate daily tasks, help you organize yourself, and keep you better informed. Agents carry out your instructions, pull information from other sources, and file it away until you need it. You can use them to answer mail and let others know you're flying off on your jetpack for a few days of rest and relaxation.

Agents can be run manually from the Notes menu, can be scheduled to execute on their own, can run in response to a database event (such as new mail being received), or can run at the touch of a button.

The type of agent that a user creates depends upon their access level (determined by the database's ACL) and their intended audience.

Public Agents

Public, or shared, agents are meant to be run by other users and are typically created by administrators and application designers. An example might be an agent that automatically searches a sales contract database, sending to the appropriate salesperson a reminder of clients with an approaching contract renewal date.

To create a public agent, you must have at least Designer access to the database. In order to run an agent, you must have at least Reader access. Agents are sensitive to the access level of the user and do not allow them to perform tasks they wouldn't be able to do manually.

Agents are stored within the database in which they are created. In order for Notes to activate an agent, the database must be stored in the Notes data directory (usually C:\NOTES\DATA) or one of its subdirectories on the computer where the database is kept. Directory links, which are text files pointing to data storage locations other than the Notes data directory, can be utilized; however, that link file must be stored in the Notes data directory.

> **Note**
>
> Once an agent is designated as public or private, that designation cannot be changed. If you create a private agent and want to make it public (or shared) later, you'll need to create a new agent and designate it as shared. A public agent is designated by selecting the Shared Agent checkbox in the Agent Builder window.

Private Agents

Users with ACL access below Designer can create agents for their own use. These private agents are stored in the database and may act on their own computer or on public databases.

You might want to create a private agent, for example, to organize your mail database or copy documents from a public database to a newsletter database.

A user must have at least Reader access to a database to run an agent. Private agents can't carry out a task that the user wouldn't be able to do manually in a given database. For example, an agent cannot update a document if the user doesn't have, at least, Editor access to the database.

Creating Agents

With Designer or better access to a database, you can create both public and private agents. If you have Editor, Author, or Reader access, you are limited to creating private agents. Agents can be created in one of three ways:

- You can copy an agent that performs a function similar to the one you require from the same database you're designing.

- You can copy an agent from another database.

- You can create an agent from scratch using the Agent Builder window reached through the Create, Agent menu choices. Again, you need Designer or better access to create public (or shared) agents and at least Reader access to create agents for your own use.

The following sections cover each method.

Copying an Agent in the Current Database

To copy an agent from the current database, follow these steps:

1. Choose View, Agents and highlight the agent you want to copy.

2. Choose Edit, Copy; press Ctrl+C, or use the Edit Copy SmartIcon.

3. Choose Edit, Paste; press Ctrl+V; or use the Edit Paste SmartIcon. Notice that the copied agent will have the name "Copy Of agentname."

4. Double-click the newly pasted agent to open the Agent Builder window. Edit the agent to fit your needs. If you have Designer level access and want to create a shared agent, select the Shared Agent checkbox in the Agent Builder window.

5. Press Esc and choose Yes to save your changes.

Copying an Agent from Another Database

To copy an agent from another database, follow these steps:

1. Highlight the icon of the database containing the agent you want to copy and choose View, Agents.

2. Highlight the agent you want to copy and choose Edit, Copy; press Ctrl+C; or use the Edit Copy SmartIcon.

3. Press Esc to close the database.

4. Open the database you want to paste the agent into.

5. Choose View, Agents.

II

Designing Applications

6. Choose <u>E</u>dit, <u>P</u>aste; press Ctrl+V; or use the Edit Paste SmartIcon.

7. Double-click the newly pasted agent to open the Agent Builder window. Edit the agent to fit your needs. If you have Designer level access and want to create a shared agent, select the Shared Agent checkbox in the Agent Builder window.

8. Press Esc to close the database and choose Yes to save it.

If you copy an agent from a database that is a design template, you'll be asked if you want to accept future design updates (see Figure 16.1). Choose <u>Y</u>es if you want to receive design updates from the original template. Choose <u>N</u>o if you want to update it yourself. See Chapter 10, "Creating New Databases," for more information on working with database template files.

Fig. 16.1   Agents copied from databases designated as a template can be updated automatically when those in the template are changed or updated.

It is possible to change this option later. To accept or deny changes to an agent after it has been created, follow these steps:

1. Click the agent name.

2. Choose Agent, Agent <u>P</u>roperties; or right-click the agent name and choose Agent <u>P</u>roperties. The Agent Properties InfoBox appears.

3. Click the Design tab in the InfoBox (see Figure 16.2).

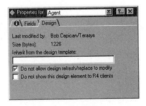

Fig. 16.2   Choose the Design tab in the Agent Properties InfoBox to change template update choices.

4. Choose the Do not allow design refresh/replace to modify option.

Note

You may also want to erase the template name from the Inherit from the design template field to ensure the reference is gone.

---

5. Close the Agent Properties InfoBox.

In Chapter 10, "Creating New Databases," you learned that Notes ships with example databases that can be used as templates for new databases. These databases are also an excellent place to find agents that you can use in other databases you create.

To access the template databases that are available to you, choose File, Database, New from the menu or press Ctrl+N. Notes will display the New Database dialog box, which allows you to choose the destination of the new database as well as designate a Title and File Name (see Figure 16.3). You can also choose templates from another server if there isn't one available locally that appears useful. Enable the Show advanced templates checkbox in the New Database dialog box to see additional template files.

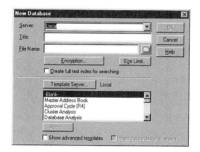

Fig. 16.3   Choose the destination of the new database in the New Database dialog box.

You may want to make a separate Workspace Page by choosing Create, Workspace Page from the menu, and place icons for template databases there. This way, you'll have a ready reference library to explore for ideas.

For example, an employee responsible for collecting articles for a monthly newsletter might want to advise people sending items to be included in the next newsletter that they will be on vacation for two weeks. This user can do one of the following:

- Add the Mail (R4) database template to their workspace.

- Copy the Out Of Office form as well as the Mail Tools\Out of Office and ProcessOutOfOffice agents to the newsletter database.

This will create a Mail Tools menu choice under the Actions menu. By choosing Mail Tools, the employee can complete an Out Of Office form. The way the form is completed determines the message that someone submitting a newsletter item receives as a reply.

The employee can choose to send a general message, a special message to certain users, or no message at all in response to a submission.

The ProcessOutOfOffice agent will send the appropriate responses once each day. The employee can schedule this agent to run weekly, or even hourly, if desired.

Creating an Agent from Scratch

You can build an agent from scratch if you cannot find one suitable to copy and edit. Keep these tips in mind when building agents from scratch:

- Write down the steps you'd follow if you were going to proceed manually. This will help you get the basic steps in the right order. Next, consider making a flowchart of the agent. This can help you to identify any holes or gaps in the process.

- Consider creating a "library" database to store copies of agents that you find useful. Agents can be copied here for later reference by you or other developers. This can be a big time-saver, especially when using complex formulas and LotusScript programs!

Before building an agent, consider the following:

- **What do I want the agent to do?** The things that agents can do have greatly increased with this version of Notes. Simple Actions enable users to create agents even without knowledge of Lotus' @functions. The addition of LotusScript lets you answer this question in ways users of previous versions only dreamed about. Have a clear idea of the tasks the agent should accomplish and how to have Notes do it.

- **What should I name the agent?** What you name a Notes agent matters. If you're creating public agents for others to use, you'll want to think about using descriptive names. Your users will thank you and you'll spend less time answering questions about why you named an agent X when it obviously should be called Y!

  Users who create private agents have only themselves to consider here. The workday can be frustrating enough without adding complications yourself. Do yourself a favor and use descriptive names so you don't have to remember exactly what "Delete" is going to do when you run it.

- **When do I want the agent to run?** For planning purposes, consider the time(s) that your agent will run. Are there periods during the day that you use your computer more than others? Are there times when the server you're using is busier than others, or perhaps unavailable? Consider scheduling agents that are resource-intensive (those requiring more time or processing power to complete) at times when resources are least strained.

  The details of scheduling your agent will be covered in the "Choosing When to Run the Agent" section later in this chapter. Right now, be aware that agents can be scheduled to run manually, in response to a database event (such as received mail), at a particular time, or repeatedly. For example, agents that archive public databases should be run when those databases aren't in use. Mail agents should run at least daily. You may want some agents only to be run manually.

- **Which database elements should it act on?** The scope of the actions for your agent should be considered. Agents can be run against an entire database, selected documents, or a single document. It is important to understand and plan your agent so that it affects only those database elements you desire. Otherwise, you could lose important information or negatively affect other people's jobs or your own!

By thinking about these questions before you begin, you'll find that you have the necessary elements in your grasp to easily create a useful agent.

Using the Agent Builder Window

To build an agent, follow these steps:

1. Highlight the icon of the database you want to design the agent in.

2. Choose <u>C</u>reate, <u>A</u>gent. The Agent Builder window opens (see Figure 16.4).

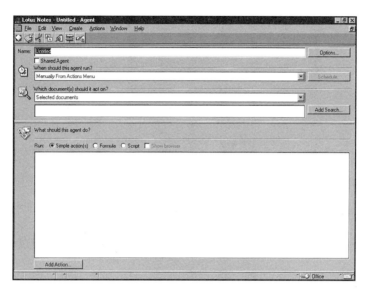

Fig. 16.4   Open the Agent Builder by choosing <u>C</u>reate, <u>A</u>gent from the menu or double-clicking the name of an existing agent to edit choices for that agent.

3. Choose the desired options in the Agent Builder window. If you have Designer level access and want to create a shared agent, select the Shared Agent checkbox in the Agent Builder window.

4. Specify the action, formula, or script for the agent. Check the format of your formulas by clicking the green checkmark to the left of the programmer pane. If there is an error in the format, a pop-up window will appear with text summarizing the problem. Make the necessary changes to the formula and click the checkmark again to verify that at least the formula is valid.

5. Press Esc.

6. Make sure you test the formula before allowing it to be used on live data. Use the simulated run option to verify that the agent will select the intended documents and act the way it's intended. You may place important data at risk, otherwise. Refer to the section "Testing Your Creations" later in this chapter for more details on testing agents.

Some options in the Agent Builder window are not available for all agents. Agents that are run manually from the Actions menu present the greatest number of options to the creator. Agents that run in response to defined actions like new mail or pasted documents are more limited since they run only on the documents that have changed.

As you may suspect, there are four elements required of an agent:

- Name
- Schedule
- Document selection
- Actions

The following sections describe the options for these required elements.

Simple Actions and @function formulas can be combined using the @function Simple Action. @Function formulas cannot be combined with LotusScript programs. However, you can create agents that trigger other agents, so it is possible to link components to accomplish a task.

> **Note**
>
> A comprehensive explanation of @functions and LotusScript are outside the scope of this chapter. See Chapters 13, "Integrating Notes with Other Applications," and 14, "Working with Formulas," for more information on @functions, and Chapter 17, "LotusScript Basics," for information on LotusScript programming.

Choosing a Name

First, give your agent a name so users can refer to it. Naming it first lets you refer to the agent by name as you work. If you save an agent without a name, it will appear as Untitled in the menu. Naming conventions aren't as innocuous as you might suspect.

> **Tip**
>
> Use the Options Button to the right of the Name field on the Agent Builder window to add a comment about the agent, its function, and so on. There are also checkboxes to control the way Notes displays the results of searches done by agents.

Using Descriptive Names. An agent's name should be descriptive of its actions—for example, "Save to Newsletter folder."

A descriptive name will help users decide which agent to run from the Actions menu. Since your agent names can contain up to 32 alphanumeric characters (including spaces and punctuation), you should be able to create names that describe the function of an agent. This can reduce mistakes and user anxiety. The function of an agent named Send article to Sales team is easy to understand.

Descriptive names reduce the work of users building their own agents. They'll have an easier time determining that an agent performs a task similar to the one they need, enabling them to copy that agent into another database and edit it for their purposes.

Naming Conventions. Standardized naming conventions help users to work efficiently since agents with similar functions will have similar names in all of the databases they use. It also provides a more cohesive look and feel to your company's Notes environment. This is especially important if you're considering publishing databases on the Internet.

Specifying Name Order. Notes will sort agent names, on the Actions menu, in alphabetical order (see Figure 16.5). If you want your agents to appear in a particular order on the menu, you'll have to name them appropriately. For example, if tasks are carried out in a particular order, you'll want to set the order of agent names accordingly.

Fig. 16.5   Agent names sorted alphabetically.

You can use numbers to name your agents. However, Notes will sort the numbers as text so 10 will be listed before 1, not after 9 as you might expect (see Figure 16.6). Circumvent this problem by using 01, 02, 03, and so on when naming instead of 1, 2, 3. Notes will then list the agents in "numeric" order (see Figure 16.7).

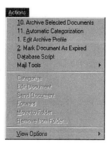

Fig. 16.6   Agent names numbered conventionally.

Specifying Accelerator Keys. Windows, OS/2, and UNIX users can select an agent by typing the first letter of its name or the underlined letter in the agent's name. These are referred to as accelerator keys and can be programmed by the agent's creator. To do so, place an underline character (_) in front of the letter you want to use as the accelerator key when naming the agent.

Fig. 16.7   Agent names numbered with preceding 0.

If you do not specify one, Notes will create a default accelerator key for you. Since the first unique letter in the agent's name will be used, the program's choice may not be intuitive to the user. For example, if you have two agents whose names begin with Copy, the first will use C as its accelerator key and the second will use O.

Naming agents alphabetically will allow users to select an agent by simply typing that letter. If two agent names begin with the same letter, the default accelerator key will be the first unique letter in the name of the second agent (see Figure 16.8).

Fig. 16.8   Note that the accelerator key for the first agent is D, followed by N for the second and X for the third.

Consider renaming agents alphabetically so that the first letter in each name is unique. If this isn't possible, force Notes to use a more intuitive choice by using an accelerator key.

Grouping Agents with Cascading Menus. If a database contains several agents that perform similar functions, consider creating a cascading menu. This presents a more cohesive and efficient menu to the user by grouping agents together by function. When you click the first level, a submenu appears with additional choices. This option is helpful in reducing clutter on the Action menu.

To set up a cascading menu, first decide on a descriptive name for the top level menu the user will see. For example, if there are several agents that copy selected documents to different folders, place them under one menu item with a name such as Copy To Folder.

When naming the agent, begin with the name from the preceding step followed by a backslash (\). Next, type the agent name the user will see in the submenu. For example, to create the menu shown in Figure 16.9, name the agents as follows:

```
Copy \ Documents to Finance folder

C           o           p           y                                   \
D           o           c           u           -
m           e           n           t           s
t           o                       M           a           r           -
k           e           t           i           n           g
f           o           l           d           e           r

Copy \ Documents to Sales folder
```

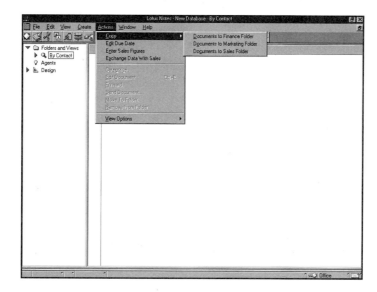

Fig. 16.9   Agents grouped by function.

Notes will support one level of cascaded names. These appear on a submenu. Each agent name cannot contain more than 64 bytes. Multi-byte characters (such as the \ character in the cascading name) will limit the number of characters, as opposed to bytes, the name may contain. The name of the top menu can be up to 32 bytes in length and the cascaded names can be up to 30 bytes.

Choosing When to Run the Agent

Some agents require user intervention to run. These manual agents are useful for tasks that are run at the user's discretion. Agents can also be set to run on a schedule or in response to certain database events. Let's look at how to create these agents and consider some examples of situations where they might be useful in your day-to-day work. The following choices are available in the field When Should This Agent Run?:

- Manually From Actions Menu

- Manually From Agent List

- If New Mail Has Arrived

- If Documents Have Been Created or Modified

- If Documents Have Been Pasted

- On Schedule Hourly

- On Schedule Daily

- On Schedule Weekly

- On Schedule Monthly

- On Schedule Never

Tip

If you're a laptop user and choose to receive truncated documents during replication (see the Receive summary and 40K of rich text only option under replication), agents will not run against these documents.

You may also choose not to receive agents when replicating a database. If you don't want agents to replicate to a local copy of a database, follow these steps:

1. Click the icon of the replica database.

2. Choose File, Replication, Settings, Advanced.

3. Under the Replicate incoming field, clear the checkmark from the Agents option.

Running Manually from the Actions Menu. Database designers who create public agents for use by others will find the Manually From Menu option the most useful. This allows users to run an agent by highlighting a database icon, clicking the Actions menu, and choosing an agent by name (see Figure 16.10).

Fig. 16.10 Choosing Actions in the menu displays a list of available agents.

This option can be useful when testing the component pieces of a complex agent before changing its run option to Manually From Agent List. Checking the function of component agents can save you from repairing the damage caused by unexpected results.

Hiding Agents/Running Agents from Other Agents. You may choose to hide an agent so that it doesn't show up in the Actions menu. Hidden agents can be run from another agent or by highlighting it in the Agents view and selecting Actions, Run. To hide an agent, choose Manually From Agent List in the When Should This Agent Run? field in the Agent Builder window. Keep the following in mind:

- Use the <u>A</u>ctions, Run option to test hidden component agents when creating large or complex agents. The Agent Log will appear after the hidden agent runs using the <u>A</u>ctions, <u>R</u>un menu options while in the Agents view.

- Use the Run Agent action in the programmer pane to combine existing agents. (If you want to run an agent from another database, you'll have to copy it into your database.) Use this technique to combine component agents using Simple Actions, @function formulas, or LotusScript into a single agent.

- Actions will be carried out sequentially, in the order in which they occur in the agents. Document selection is performed by the primary agent. The main agent (perhaps one chosen from the <u>A</u>ctions, <u>R</u>un menu) runs and passes the resulting information to a secondary agent for its processing. For example, the first component agent searches for all documents within a folder for a particular author name and marks them unread. The next component agent performs the programmed action on all of the documents selected by the first agent.

Scheduling Agents. Scheduled agents require no user intervention to run. They do exactly what their name implies. This also makes them one of the most useful tools in the never-ending battle to stay informed in a constantly changing market.

In the When Should This Agent Run? section of the Agent Builder window, choose the desired schedule:

- On Schedule Hourly

- On Schedule Daily

- On Schedule Weekly

- On Schedule Monthly

- On Schedule Never

A Daily agent can be used, for example, to run periodic checks of published databases that you subscribe to. This might be useful if you need to keep informed of your competitor's movement within a given market. Several companies now publish news and information databases for users of Notes. Lotus' Newsstand and WorldCom provide a source for published databases.

Perhaps you are responsible for the department newsletter or a weekly meeting. You might use a weekly agent to remind others to submit an article or complete an action item (or just to show up for a meeting).

Tip

If you are responsible for the company newsletter and you're one of the millions of people surfing the Web nowadays, check out Lotus' Newsstand. There's a neat list of published databases you can subscribe to providing industry and special interest information. For an up-to-date list, point your Web browser at **http://www.lotus.com/newsstand/**.

Designing Applications

An agent that runs monthly might be useful for copying documents more than six months old to an archive database for storage and reference. This could also serve to keep the size of a production database smaller, thus reducing the need for disk space on remote servers in branch offices.

The On Schedule Never option is reserved for background macros from Notes 3.x that were scheduled to run Never. If you want one of these to run, change the schedule to one of the Release 4 options.

Keep in mind that an agent runs on the computer where the database is stored. If you're running an agent from a database on your local machine, you can do more since you have Manager access, unless Local Security is enabled. Running an agent from the server requires you to pay closer attention to the user's Access Control rights.

To run scheduled agents when you start Notes, follow these steps:

1. Choose File, Tools, User Preferences.

2. Select Enable scheduled local agents.

3. Click OK when you get the message that some changes won't take place until Notes is restarted.

4. Click OK.

Using the Schedule button on the Agent Builder window, you can do the following (see Figure 16.11):

- Decide which server or workstation an agent runs on.

- Set the starting and ending dates.

- Set the frequency and starting and end times of hourly agents.

- Set the start time for a daily agent.

- Set the day of the week and time of day a weekly agent runs.

- Set the day of the month and starting time of monthly agents.

These options will be handy for agents that run time- or system resource-intensive tasks, such as archiving large databases or compiling a report. You can choose when you can afford to dedicate those resources. Some tasks lend themselves to being run during off hours.

A salesperson who's on the road visiting a customer may want his computer to dial into his home server at night, while the phone rates are less expensive, and pull all the orders he wrote for a client between the 1st and 20th of the month from the company's Projected Sales database, for example. Perhaps he also wants those orders that mention a certain part or product. Agents can also be set to query other databases for documents by certain authors, dates, even those including or excluding certain keywords. Look at the "Building Search Queries" section later in this chapter.

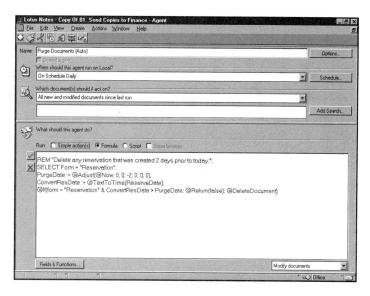

Fig. 16.11 Click the Schedule button in the Agent Builder window to choose the times this agent will run. Note that the agent in the example can be found in the Room Reservation template file.

Triggering Agents with Events. An agent that is set to activate whenever new mail arrives in the database might, for example, check the user name and Delivery Priority fields and forward any High Priority item from the District Vice President to your assistant for action while you're on vacation. To activate the agent with e-mail, choose If New Mail Has Arrived in the When Should This Agent Run? section of the Agent Builder window.

Agents may also be set to activate when a document is modified or if a document has been pasted into a database. Any important document from an employee work schedule to a customer contract might need to be sent to a Person or Group defined in the Name and Address Book if it were modified. To choose one of these options, select If Document Has Been Modified or If New Documents Have Been Pasted in the When Should This Agent Run? section of the Agent Builder window.

Specifying Documents Affected by the Agent

Deciding which documents within a database an agent will act upon is required for the successful creation and execution of any agent:

■ Manual agents present the greatest number of selection options. They will allow the agent to select a single document, folder, view, or the entire database.

■ Scheduled agents can be run against all documents in the database or on documents that were added or modified since the agent last ran.

■ Change-activated agents present the user with the fewest selection options because they will run only against those documents specified by the type of change that occurred—for example, new mail items, pasted documents, or documents modified since the agent was last run.

To specify what documents will be affected by the agent, select one of the following options in the Which Document(s) Should It Act On? section of the Agent Builder window:

- **All documents in the database**—The agent will attempt to modify all of the documents within the database.

- **New and Modified documents**—Only documents which have been created or modified since the agent last ran will be processed.

- **All unread documents**—The agent will run against documents marked as unread. You may use another agent to select documents by author, for example, and mark those unread before triggering a secondary agent.

- **Selected documents in the open view**—This option may be most useful to process documents selected by another agent or you may select documents manually and then run the agent from the Actions menu.

- **All documents in the open view**—This choice instructs the agent to run against all documents within the view that is currently open.

- **Current document**—The agent will make changes only to the document currently open.

- **Pasted documents**—Documents that are pasted into the database will be acted upon when the agent runs.

Building Search Queries. The use of search queries allows you to fine-tune document selection by agents. This section will introduce you to the options available using search queries.

The Add Search button in the Agent Builder window allows you to define search parameters for an agent (refer to Figure 16.11). This feature enables you to, more specifically, define criteria to select which documents should or shouldn't be acted upon by your agent.

Clicking the Add Search button displays the Search Builder dialog box, in which you can choose search options for documents including author names, dates, field values, or forms used (see Figure 16.12). You can build compound searches by adding parameters to more than one of the option fields in the Search Builder window.

For example, you may want to search a folder for documents by a particular author, created in a given date range. To do this, just complete the necessary fields in the By Author, By Date, and In Folder options in the Condition field. The resulting query will be shown in the field to the left of the Add Search button in the Agent Builder window.

Notes allows searches of encrypted fields and file attachments as long as the database is full-text indexed and the index was created to include these items. If it does not, contact the Manager of the database and ask for a new index to be created that includes attachments and encrypted fields.

Fig. 16.12 Use this dialog box to target all documents, for example, by a given user or all but those authored by the specified user.

> **Note**
>
> If the database is full-text indexed, make sure that it is current—otherwise, your results might not be accurate. Databases that are full-text indexed will produce better results than those that aren't.

To check the criteria used for the database's full-text index, follow these steps:

1. Highlight the database icon on the workspace.

2. Right-click your mouse on the icon.

3. Choose Database Properties.

4. Select the Full Text tab.

Databases that are stored on a server can use scheduled updates of full-text indexes. Contact your Notes Administrator for assistance in setting up a schedule that meets your needs. Remember that full-text indexes require both disk space and processor resources. The administrator can help balance the need for indexing with the resources available on the server.

The following sections describe each type of search.

Searching by Author. Any document that contains an Author Names field can be searched. You may specify documents that were either created by or not created by a specific author. You may also access either a Public or Private Name & Address Book to search for the author's name to ensure accuracy. In the example shown in Figure 16.12, the agent will search for documents authored by Bob Hamilton. This type of search is very useful if you remember who authored a document.

Searching by Date. You can search for any documents that were (or were not) either created or modified on or within a certain date range. The example shown in Figure 16.13 will search for any documents created on September 20th of 1996. Using this parameter, you can narrow your search to a specific timeframe. Used in conjunction with other search parameters, this is useful in large databases.

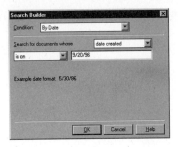

Fig. 16.13   Use the By Date parameter to target all documents by the date(s) they were created or modified.

Searching for a Field Value. You can search any field within the given form, via a pull-down menu, for the presence or the absence of a certain value. The example shown in Figure 16.14 will search documents with the CompanyName field for the occurrence of the term Worldwide Enterprises, Inc.

Fig. 16.14   Use the By Field parameter to target terms either contained or not in a specific field on a database form.

Searching Multiple Fields on a Form. You can search multiple fields on a particular form with the By Form option (see Figure 16.15). The forms available in the database are selectable from a pull-down menu. A representation of the form you choose will appear in the bottom portion of the Search Builder dialog box. Type the values you want to search for in the fields on the form.

Fig. 16.15   Use the By Form parameter to search for specific values in single or multiple fields on a selected database form.

> **Note**
>
> Problems with the By Form type of search include misspellings and values in fields Computed for Display, because the values are not stored within the form but computed when the document is opened.

Searching by Form Used. You can search by the form used in a database. Multiple forms can be selected. Clicking the name in the list of database forms creates a checkmark next to the form name. Notes will search the selected forms for documents meeting your selection criteria. This is a useful search parameter to isolate forms with similar fields and data. The example in Figure 16.16 will search any document created using the indicated forms.

Fig. 16.16   Use the By Form Used parameter to target specific forms within the database.

Searching for Words and Phrases. You can search for documents that contain either any or all of the words entered in the fields in the lower part of the Search Builder window. Up to eight words and/or phrases may be entered.

The example shown in Figure 16.17 will search for documents containing any of the words shown. This parameter is useful for selecting documents to be acted upon by a second agent.

Fig. 16.17   Use the Words and Phrases parameter to search for documents containing either any or all of the listed terms.

Programming the Agent's Function

Up to this point, you've learned the details to consider when naming an agent. You've considered, in general terms, when it should run and on which elements of the database it should act. Now you'll look at the how part of agents. Using the programmer pane, you'll define the specific functions that an agent actually carries out (see Figure 16.18).

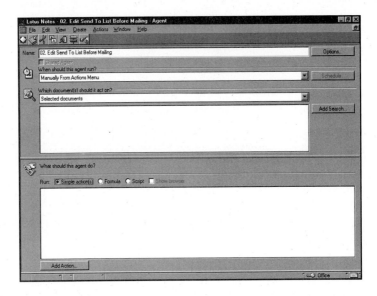

Fig. 16.18 The programmer pane is the portion of the screen that asks the question: What should this agent do?

An agent doesn't have to be complex to be useful. There are three ways to program an agent's function:

- Using Simple Actions (predefined Notes functions), a user can create an agent with no programming experience. Simple Actions are discussed in the following section.

- Using @function formulas, you can select and process documents. Agents that use @function formulas require an understanding of the @function commands but allow more flexibility than Simple Actions.

- Using LotusScript, Lotus' BASIC-compatible scripting language, you can interact with other scripting languages, such as Visual Basic.

Agents using LotusScript are the most complex of the three methods. LotusScript allows creation of powerful programs that can manipulate databases in ways not possible with Simple Actions or @functions.

Using Simple Actions. Simple Actions are predefined Notes functions that can be strung together to carry out a desired task. These allow manipulation of documents, fields, mail, and folders. You can use Simple Actions to trigger other agents, allowing you to combine component parts into a larger, complex agent.

To program the agent with Simple Actions, follow these steps:

1. With the Agent Builder window open, click Simple action(s) in the programmer pane.

2. Click the Add Action button on the bottom of the programmer pane. The Add Action dialog box appears on-screen (see Figure 16.19).

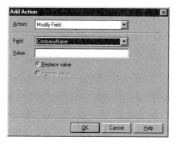

Fig. 16.19 Clicking the Add Action button in the programmer pane allows you to program one of Notes' predefined functions.

3. Click the arrow on the right side of the Action field to see a drop-down list of the actions available. You can choose from these 15 Simple Actions available in Notes 4:

Copy to Database	Move to Folder
Remove from Folder	Copy to Folder
Reply to Sender	Delete from Database
Run Agent	Mark Document Read
Send Document	Mark Document Unread
Send Mail Message	Modify Field
Send Newsletter Summary	Modify Fields by Form
@Function Formula	

> **Note**
>
> You can combine Simple Actions and @functions by choosing the @Function Formula action and writing an @function formula.

4. Note that the fields in the lower part of the Add Action dialog box change, depending upon the Action that you choose. Complete the fields in the lower part of the dialog box.

5. Press OK to save or Cancel to close the box without saving your choices. The resulting command will be shown in the programmer pane.

Notes will carry out multiple Simple Actions in the order listed in the programmer pane. To program an agent to carry out multiple Simple Actions, repeat steps 2 through 5. Each command you add will be shown in the programmer pane next to the preceding command (see Figure 16.20).

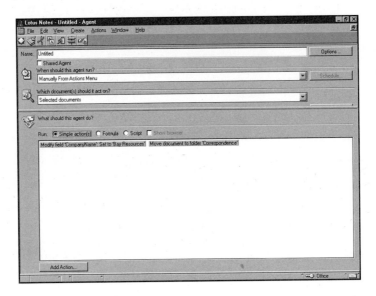

Fig. 16.20 Programmer pane shows the multiple Simple Actions selected.

Using @Function Formulas. Using @functions, you can do the following:

- Modify and save existing documents.

- Create new documents by making a copy of an existing document and modifying the copy, preserving the original.

- Select documents in a view but not process them. Use this option to test your selection formula before actually processing documents.

> ### Note
>
> Use of the @command functions are limited within agents. @Command and @PostedCommand can be used only with agents that act upon the currently selected document. Scheduled agents cannot use @DbColumn or @DbLookup to access information in databases on another server. They may, however, be used to access other databases on the same computer that the agent resides on.

Agents defined as formulas in the Run field on the programmer pane cannot be combined with Simple Actions or LotusScript programs in a single agent. Refer to Chapters 13, "Integrating Notes with Other Applications," and 14, "Working with Formulas," for detailed information on working with @functions.

Use @function formulas to select and process documents within a database. To program an agent using @functions, follow these steps:

1. Choose Formula in the Run field on the programmer pane.

2. Click the Field & Functions button. The Fields and Functions dialog box appears on-screen (see Figure 16.21).

Fig. 16.21 Select the Fields & Functions button to display a list of @functions and field names to add to your formula.

3. Choose either the Functions or Fields button:

   Selecting Functions will show a list of @function commands that can be pasted into the programmer pane. The keywords `Environment`, `Field`, `Rem`, and `Select` are also available. These must be the first word used in a formula statement. Highlight the desired selection and click Paste to add it to your formula.

   Selecting Fields will show a list of the fields defined in the database. Highlight the desired selection and click Paste to add it to your formula.

4. Write an @function formula in the programmer pane. As you enter parameters in the programmer pane, you'll note the appearance of a green checkmark and a red X to the left. Clicking the green checkmark allows you to check the format of the @function formula you've written. If the formula's format is incorrect, clicking the checkmark will produce a dialog box with a summary of the problem. Clicking the red X will clear the programmer pane.

5. On the bottom right side of the programmer pane is a pull-down menu; open the menu and select one of the following options:

   - Modify Documents will modify the original and save the new document.

   - Create New Documents will make a copy of an existing document and modify the copy, preserving the original.

   - Select Documents In View will mark documents with a checkmark but not process them. Use this option to select documents to be processed by an agent or to test your selection formula before actually processing documents.

Using LotusScript Programs. Agents defined as Script in the Run field on the programmer pane cannot be combined with Simple Actions or formulas in a single agent. Refer to Chapter 17, "LotusScript Basics," for detailed information on working with LotusScript.

Use LotusScript to create sophisticated programs that can process database documents, act on the database ACL, or interact with other programming languages.

II

Designing Applications

To program an agent using LotusScript, follow these steps:

1. Choose Script in the Run field on the programmer pane.

2. Write or copy-and-paste a LotusScript program that selects the documents you want to process and performs the actions you desire. You can check the Show browser checkbox to show a list of LotusScript commands that can be pasted into the programmer pane (see Figure 16.22).

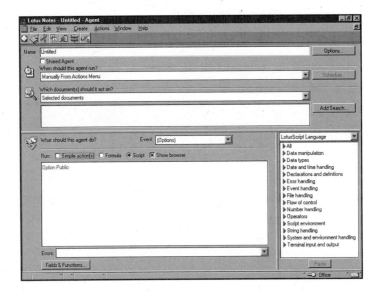

Fig. 16.22 Enable Show Browser to display a list of LotusScript programming parameters.

Completing the Agent

After you finish specifying what you want the agent to do, save the agent. Then test it to be sure it works as expected. Begin writing agents in local database copies so you won't corrupt important data. Begin testing your agent with the Simulated Run option, which identifies the changes that would occur if you actually ran the agent.

> **Tip**
>
> Refer to the "Testing Your Creations" section of this chapter for information on how to test your agent before running it on live data. The more complex an agent is, the more places things can go wrong. Consider creating several subagents that may be tested individually and linked together after the bugs are ironed out. This can make troubleshooting any problems easier.

Using Buttons and Hotspots

A button is a graphical representation of a push-button that you can place in a Rich Text field to carry out Notes commands or run a script (see Figure 16.23). Buttons allow users to run agents, formulas, or scripts from the form or document level by double-clicking. Again, users may complete only actions allowed by their access level defined in the ACL.

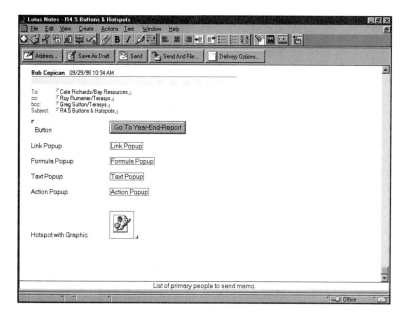

Fig. 16.23   This button will open the Year-End-Report document database.

The button interface has been updated in Notes R4. You have more options than with previous versions for creating and displaying the button itself, as well as the underlying code. From the Button Properties InfoBox, you can determine if a button appears on a form and format the text, alignment, and style.

Notes 4 adds a new design element called a *hotspot*. While a button is an independent graphic, a hotspot usually appears as text or a graphic, with a green border around it.

Like a button, users can click a hotspot to perform Notes actions or run scripts. You can use hotspots, like hypertext, to link documents together. For example, if a memo mentions a corporate policy, consider using a link hotspot to allow the user to read the policy document for clarification (see Figure 16.24). Hotspots can be used to annotate phrases and graphics, test formulas, or carry out a script.

Fig. 16.24   Hotspots can be linked to text or graphics. They carry out Notes' commands and actions much like buttons. Although they usually appear as a green border around text or a graphic, their power depends on the underlying code.

Creating and Removing Hotspots

Hotspots can execute Simple Actions, @functions, and LotusScript just like buttons. The presentation is the major difference between a hotspot and a button. While a button appears as a graphical object, a hotspot can appear as a bordered area of text—and even the border can be removed! In essence, a hotspot can do what a button can without taking up additional space in the document.

To add a hotspot, follow these steps:

1. Open the document or form you want to add the hotspot to.

2. When adding a hotspot to an existing document, choose Actions, Edit Document. While in edit mode, select the area in the Rich Text field where you want the hotspot. When creating a hotspot in a new form, highlight the Rich Text field where you want the hotspot to appear.

3. Choose Create, Hotspot.

4. Choose the type of hotspot to be created:

Link Hotspot	Formula Popup
Text Popup	Action Hotspot
Button	

5. If you choose a Formula Popup or Action Hotspot, you need to write a formula in the programmer pane that appears on-screen. Format the hotspot as desired, and close the Properties InfoBox for the hotspot. Test your formulas to ensure the actions taken are what you want before using them on live data.

6. Save the form.

To remove a hotspot, right-click the hotspot while in edit mode and choose Remove Hotspot from the menu.

Link Hotspots. Link hotspots can be used to create a link to another document or database—these are similar to doclinks. To create the link, follow these steps:

1. Go to the document or graphic object you want to link to this hotspot.

2. Choose Edit, Copy As Link.

3. Close the object.

4. Open the document or form you want the hotspot in.

5. Highlight the area of the Rich Text field you want to link. This can be text or even a graphic.

6. Choose Create, Hotspot, Link Hotspot.

Note

When you create a link hotspot, Notes doesn't copy the object into the field but uses a pointer to the destination. If the object you link to is not reachable due to ACL levels or if the server the object resides on is unavailable, Notes will present a menu asking where it should search for the object. For this link to function properly, ensure that the object will be available to the intended user.

You can find the object linked to a hotspot by double-clicking the hotspot. Clicking once and holding the left mouse button down will show the destination of the linked object.

Text Pop-Up Hotspots. Text pop-ups display text when the left mouse button is clicked once and held down while on the hotspot. This can be used to provide commentary or explanation for the text. To create a text pop-up hotspot, follow these steps:

1. Highlight the area of the rich text field you want the text to appear by when the hotspot is activated.

2. Choose Create, Hotspot, Text Pop-up. The HotSpot Pop-up Properties InfoBox appears (see Figure 16.25).

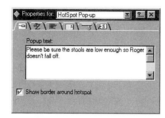

Fig. 16.25 The text entered into the HotSpot Pop-up Properties InfoBox appears when the hotspot is activated.

3. In the Properties InfoBox, enter the text you want to appear when the hotspot is activated.

4. Click the green checkbox in the left border to accept the text as entered. Click the red X in the left border to clear the text box.

Formula Pop-Up Hotspots. Formula pop-up hotspots will allow programming of an @function formula in the programmer pane. A user will see the result of this formula by clicking and holding the left mouse button down on the hotspot. The result of the hotspot formula must be a text string, such as True or False.

To create a formula pop-up hotspot, follow these steps:

1. Highlight the area of the rich text field you want the result of the @function formula to appear by when the hotspot is activated.

2. Choose Create, Hotspot, Formula Hotspot. The HotSpot Pop-up Properties InfoBox appears along with the programmer pane.

3. Enter an @function formula in the programmer pane.

Figure 16.26 shows a formula hotspot in progress, while Figure 16.27 shows the result of the formula when the hotspot is activated.

Fig. 16.26 Formula hotspot in progress.

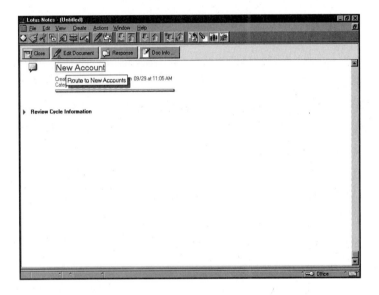

Fig. 16.27 The result of the formula is displayed when a formula hotspot is activated.

Action Pop-Up Hotspots. Action pop-up hotspots allow a user to execute an @function or @command when the hotspot is double-clicked, provided he or she has adequate ACL access to the necessary functions.

The following steps show how you create them:

1. Highlight the area of the rich text field you want the hotspot to appear.

2. Choose Create, Hotspot, Action Hotspot. The HotSpot Properties InfoBox appears on-screen along with a programmer pane.

3. In the programmer pane, enter Simple Actions, an @function formula, or a LotusScript program to control the hotspot.

> **Tip**
>
> Be aware that a hotspot that may contain code that executes another program using the @Execute command. If you are unsure what a hotspot is going to do, make sure that the Execution Control List Default options are all unchecked. See Chapter 22, "Security and Encryption," for a complete explanation of the ECL.

Making a Hotspot Invisible

You can remove the green border from around the hotspot, making it "invisible" to the user. To do so, follow these steps:

1. Click the inside of the hotspot.

2. Choose Hotspot, Hotspot Properties. The HotSpot Properties InfoBox appears.

3. Deselect Show Border around Hotspot. You'll see that the border disappears.

4. Close the HotSpot Properties InfoBox and save the form or document.

Editing a Hotspot's Function

You can edit the function of a formula or action hotspot, replacing or editing the underlying actions or formula. Button formulas are edited in a similar fashion:

1. Open the document or form in edit mode.

2. Click the hotspot (or button).

3. Choose Hotspot, Edit Hotspot from the main menu. (If editing a button, use the Button, Edit Button menu choice.) The HotSpot Properties InfoBox appears along with the programmer pane.

4. Make your changes to the code.

5. Save the changes and close the document.

Creating Buttons

Buttons manually execute Simple Actions, @functions, or LotusScript programs with the double-click of a mouse. They add automation to the database. Users don't have to use the menus to choose commands or the name of the agent necessary to carry out the actions programmed into a button.

To create a button, follow these steps:

1. Open the document or form you want to add the button to.

2. While in edit mode, place the cursor in the Rich Text field where you want the button to appear.

3. Choose Create, Hotspot, Button. A small button will appear on the form at the point you selected with your cursor. The Button Properties InfoBox and programmer pane will appear on the screen (see Figure 16.28).

Fig. 16.28 The Button Properties InfoBox.

4. Click the first tab of the Button Properties InfoBox (it looks like a button on a document).

5. In the Button label text box, type the label you want the user to see on the button.

6. The formatting options for buttons are the same as those for normal text. (These were discussed in greater detail in Chapter 7, "Working with Text.") With the formatting options in the Button Properties InfoBox, format the button as desired:

   Click the Fonts tab to format the attributes of the font used for the button's label.

   Click the Alignment tab to format the alignment and spacing used for the text in the button's label.

   Click the Pagination tab to format pagination, printing margins, and tab spacing for the text in the button's label.

   Click the Style tab to choose or manage the style of the button's text.

7. When you have finished selecting options for the button, close the Button Properties InfoBox.

8. In the programmer pane, program the actions the button will carry out. As with agents, program the buttons using Simple Actions, @function formulas, or LotusScript. Again, the code doesn't need to be complex in order to be useful. Buttons that transport users to a related document or add a database icon are relatively easy to create, and save time over completing the same action manually.

The default button settings create a functional button. To edit the properties of an existing button, follow these steps:

1. Open the document in edit mode by pressing Ctrl+E or selecting Actions, Edit Document from the menu.

2. Right-click the button and select the Button Properties option to bring up the Button Properties InfoBox. (Alternatively, you can choose Button, Edit Button from the menu.)

3. Select the tab of the property you want to edit (button title, text, and the rest).

4. Make the desired changes. As you make changes, they are reflected in the button on-screen. If you edit the button label, a green checkmark appears next to the Button Label field. Click the checkmark for the changes to the label to take effect.

5. Close the InfoBox.

Hiding Buttons and Hotspots

The Properties window has an additional choice that allows control over the display of a paragraph, including buttons, hotspots, sections, or attachments.

You might want to hide a paragraph due to either formatting or security concerns. For example, when a form is printed, buttons and other graphic objects may detract from its aesthetic appeal. Humans are visual creatures. The way a form looks often affects whether or not it even gets read! You may also want to hide sections with confidential or non-essential information. Refer to Chapter 14, "Working with Formulas," and Chapter 15, "Working with Functions and Commands," for more ideas on using this option.

You may choose to hide a paragraph under conditions defined here. The options in the Button Properties InfoBox are relatively self-explanatory. You can hide a paragraph while the form is being read, printed, edited, or copied.

In the InfoBox, you'll notice the option to Hide paragraph if formula is true. Below this is a formula window that allows you to enter an @function formula. By clicking the Formula Window button at the bottom of the InfoBox, a larger window is displayed.

The Field and Functions button on the bottom allows selection of @functions and field names. You might want to utilize this capability, for example, to hide the button/hotspot from certain users or groups.

Testing Your Creations

In this chapter, we've learned that agents, buttons, and hotspots can automate Notes databases. What you might have realized by now is that, improperly programmed, they could potentially cause a good deal of grief as well!

Think about what would happen if you created an agent on a Sales Commission Reports database that erased documents or worse, deleted the file. How many other files or records can you think of that would have disastrous results if they were to be lost or altered erroneously?

To save yourself and others a lot of grief, think about ways to test your agents, buttons, and hotspots before they're used on live data. Following are some ways to accomplish safe testing without pain.

Use Local Databases

When you're starting out with a new development project, consider using copies of the database(s) you're developing agents for on a local workstation instead of a server. This will limit your exposure if an error should occur. This is especially true with vital databases such as the server's Name & Address Book.

Considering the functionality of LotusScript or the inexperience of a new developer, it's a good safeguard.

Protect Server Data

If your agents are acting upon mailed documents, the test database needs to be on a server. Anytime you test on a server, take precautions to protect your investment. The first precaution should be involving your Notes administrator. He or she can advise you on server resources, data availability, index issues, and the best time to conduct testing.

Using these steps on your workstation or server will protect your data:

- Perform a clean backup of the server prior to testing agents that will interact with the Public Name & Address Book or other databases that are likely to be open when the server is running.

- Create a non-replica copy of the database you're affecting and rename it. Have the agent interact with the renamed database instead of that containing your live data.

- If possible, choose an execution time that will affect the fewest users if the unthinkable happens.

Tip

You can turn off all scheduled mail or change activated agents within a database by following these steps:

1. Choose File, Database, Properties.
2. Select the Disable agents for this database option.

This may prove to be useful while troubleshooting problems with agents on workstations or servers.

Simulation—Test Option

Notes provides a feature that will let you simulate the execution of an agent. To simulate an agent, follow these steps:

1. Highlight the database to be tested.

2. Highlight the agent to be tested.

3. Choose Actions, Test.

4. Look at the Test Report, which shows the number of documents that would be processed and describes the actions that would be taken if the agent were actually run.

5. Fix any problems encountered in the agent's code and test again.

6. Repeat until everything checks out. Close and save the agent.

Testing Complex Agents

When testing complex agents or scripts, break them apart into component parts and execute each in the order they will execute when run as a single agent or action. You can use the simulated run option to test individual components. Check the test log to identify problems with each component. This will enable you to easily and quickly isolate the problems that occur.

From Here...

This chapter has shown you how to create your own agents, buttons, and hotspots. Automating databases with these techniques can either save users time or cripple their ability to perform their jobs. Making life easier is the whole idea of database automation! Keep it simple and protect your company's investment in its people and data.

Other chapters you should read to enhance your ability to create effective automation include the following:

- Chapter 15, "Working with Functions and Commands," discusses all of the @functions that you can use in formulas.

- Chapter 17, "LotusScript Basics," teaches the basics of the powerful LotusScript programming language, which can be used to manipulate objects and links.

- Chapter 18, "Writing Scripts with LotusScript," talks about the next level of Notes programming.

II

Designing Applications

Part III

Working with LotusScript

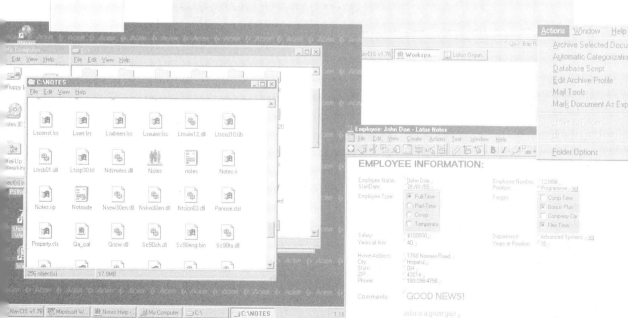

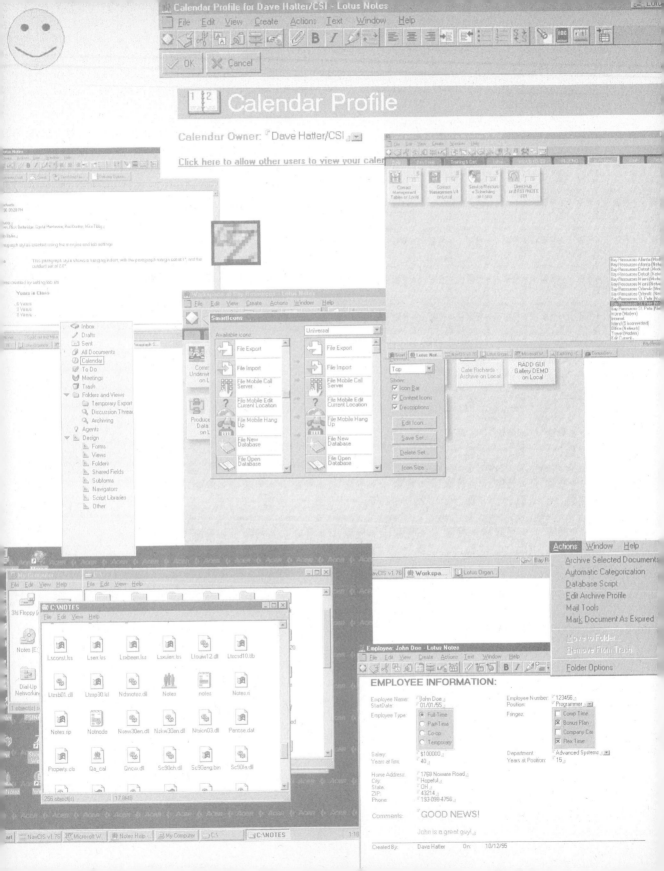

Chapter 17

LotusScript Basics

In previous chapters, you learned how to use Lotus Notes @functions and @commands. In this chapter, you learn about LotusScript, the cross-platform programming language used in Lotus products. The chapter covers the basics of LotusScript—its syntax and structure. What you learn in this chapter can be applied to any product that uses LotusScript. We'll look at the way LotusScript is used in Lotus Notes in Chapter 18, "Writing Scripts with LotusScript."

This chapter also assumes that you are not new to programming and already have some experience with scripting languages such as Visual Basic or REXX.

Some of the main topics in this chapter are

■ The basics of the LotusScript language

■ The syntax used when working with LotusScript

> **Note**
>
> Don't be tempted to cut and paste or type the example code fragments contained within this chapter directly into Lotus Notes, as their sole purpose is to demonstrate LotusScript syntax. You will have the opportunity to try LotusScript within the Lotus Notes environment in Chapter 18.

What Is LotusScript?

LotusScript is a BASIC compatible embedded scripting language with object-oriented extensions. LotusScript first appeared in Lotus Improv, the innovative dynamic spreadsheet product which was released for Windows in 1992. Gradually, more Lotus products were shipped with LotusScript, including Lotus Forms and Lotus Notes ViP (which was subsequently sold to Revelation). LotusScript Release 3 is available in Lotus Notes Release 4.

In this chapter, we investigate the major elements of the LotusScript language from a practical point of view, looking at everything from comments to data types, functions, and error-handling. We start with how to add comments to your code.

III

Working with LotusScript

Adding Comments to Your Code

The first and most important set of statements to learn in any new programming language is the one that enables you to put comments into your code—you'll surely agree if you have ever had to modify someone else's uncommented code (or even the code that *you* wrote three months ago and never quite got around to commenting!).

In LotusScript, a comment line begins with the apostrophe character. In fact, anything after an apostrophe is considered a comment, so you can easily add comments to the ends of lines. You can also use %REM and %END REM to comment blocks of lines, as in the following example:

```
' A single line comment . . .
' . . . and another
%REM
The first line in a multi-line comment
.
.
.
The last line in a multi-line comment
%END REM
```

Tip

Be kind to maintenance programmers (and yourself) by commenting your code as you go. I tend to write my code first as a series of comments, and only then do I write the actual LotusScript. This avoids the chore of having to add comments to your code after it has been written.

Understanding LotusScript Variables

In LotusScript, as with all programming languages, variables are used to store and manipulate data. While you may use variables in the same way in other programming languages, there are a few things you should be aware of when naming variables in LotusScript:

- The first character must be a letter.

- The other characters must be letters, numbers, or underscore characters.

- Variable names can contain a maximum of 40 characters.

- Variable names are not case-sensitive. For example, COUNT and count are the same variable name.

In fact, these rules apply to all names within LotusScript, such as the names for:

- Constants

- Types

- Classes

- Procedures such as functions, subroutines, and properties

LotusScript Constants

Several constants are built into LotusScript to make your programming life easier. They are shown in Table 17.1.

Table 17.1	LotusScript Built-In Constants
Constant	**Description**
FALSE	The Boolean value false. Represented by 0.
TRUE	The Boolean value true. Represented by –1.
NULL	For variables of type Variant, NULL indicates that the variable does not have a value.
NOTHING	For variables that can refer to objects, NOTHING indicates that the variable does not currently refer to an object.
PI	The ratio of the circumference of a circle to its diameter, if I can still remember my math!

Additional programming constants are defined in special files that you can include in your scripts. The files are known as *include files* and have a file extension of .LSS that indicates a LotusScript Source file. Use the %INCLUDE directive in the Declarations section of a script to include a .LSS file—for example, the following:

```
%INCLUDE "LSCONST.LSS"
```

These constants make your scripts more readable. For example, MB_OK and MB_OKCANCEL can be used with the LotusScript MsgBox function.

Tip

In a standard Notes installation, all of the .LSS files are stored in the Notes program directory. To find out more about these files and the constants they define, view them using a text editor, such as Notepad.

You can define your own constants using the Const statement. This is a useful way of making your code more readable. For example, to define constants to represent product sizes, you could use the following code fragment:

```
Const SIZE_SMALL  = 1
Const SIZE_MEDIUM = 2
Const SIZE_LARGE  = 3
```

As a general convention, constants are always given names in uppercase.

Understanding Data Types

All variables in a LotusScript program have a type associated with them. The type essentially defines two things:

- How much storage LotusScript should reserve for the data to be stored by the variable
- The types of statements in which you can use the variable

For example, once you declare a variable of type Integer, LotusScript reserves two bytes of storage for the value to be stored by the variable, and checks that the variable is only used in statements applicable to integer values.

LotusScript supports the data types shown in Table 17.2.

Table 17.2 LotusScript Data Types		
Data Type	**Number of Bytes Stored**	**Suffix**
Integer	1	%
Long	4	&
Single	4	!
Double	8	#
Currency	8	@
String	2 per character	$
Variant	16	None

Declaring LotusScript Variables

Strictly speaking, you don't have to declare variables in LotusScript because the first time you use a new variable, LotusScript automatically declares it for you. If you don't declare a variable, LotusScript automatically assigns it a type of Variant.

> **Tip**
>
> Always use the LotusScript Option Declare statement in the general declarations section of the code. This forces you to explicitly declare all of the variables you use. You will save a lot of debugging time and effort by using Option Declare. If you don't use it, you could waste time tracking down an error, only to find that you have misspelled a variable name, which LotusScript has then treated as a new variable.

You declare LotusScript variables using the Dim statement. For example, the following code fragment declares three variables: iCount as an integer, strName as a string, and curPrice as a currency value:

```
Dim iCount As Integer
Dim strName As String
Dim curPrice As Currency
```

You can add any of the suffixes shown in Table 17.2 to a variable declaration to declare a variable of the corresponding type. For example, the following lines of code declare a single and a double value:

```
Dim sRatio!
Dim dLimit#
```

> **Tip**
>
> As a rule, don't use suffixes when declaring variables. It makes your code harder to understand for someone who doesn't immediately know, for example, that ! means a single value.

If you don't explicitly give a variable a type, LotusScript treats it as a `Variant`. The following two lines of code both declare variables of type `Variant`:

```
Dim varFontType As Variant
Dim varFontName
```

> **Tip**
>
> It is good programming practice to always declare variable types, even when optional. It removes any doubt about the type that you intend to use and makes your program easier to maintain.

Notice the prefixes used as part of the variable names. Although they are not strictly necessary, it's a good idea to prefix your variable names, so that you can work out their types from the names. This helps you check that you're working with the correct type of variable in an expression. For example, just by looking at the variable names in your code, you should be able to see whether you are using values of different types in the same statement.

People use many different naming conventions. I tend to use the prefixes shown in Table 17.3.

Table 17.3   Suggested Prefixes for Variable Names

Data Type	Prefix	Example
Integer	i	iDocsDeleted
Long	l	lFileLength
Single	s	sWeightCoefficient
Double	d	dAcceleration
Currency	cur	curSalaryIncrease
String	str	strDocTitle
Variant	var	varName

You can easily extend this naming convention to include additional types and procedure names. For example, if I use an integer as a Boolean value, I prefix its name with f (for flag), or if a function returns an integer, I prefix its name with i. This can be useful as it clearly shows what type of value the function returns.

Converting Data Types

In many cases, when you assign data of one type to a variable of a different type, LotusScript automatically converts the data for you. In general, LotusScript converts data of different types using the following sequence:

- ■ Integer

- ■ Long

- ■ Single

- ■ Double

- ■ Currency

That is, if you mix a long value and a single value in an expression, LotusScript converts the long value into a single value before evaluating the expression.

LotusScript has a range of functions that lets you convert between variables of different types. The functions are listed in Table 17.4 and enable you to do the following:

- ■ Convert data from one type to another

- ■ Convert a number into a string

- ■ Convert a string into a number

- ■ Check the data type of a variable

Table 17.4 LotusScript Data Conversion Functions

Statement or Function	Description
Bin$	Converts the supplied number to a string representing its binary value.
CCur	Converts the supplied value to Currency data type.
CDat	Converts the supplied value to Variant of type Date.
CDbl	Converts the supplied value to Double data type.
CInt	Converts the supplied value to Integer data type.
CLng	Converts the supplied value to Long data type.
CSng	Converts the supplied value to Single data type.
CStr	Converts the supplied value to its string representation.
DataType	Returns an integer representing the data type of the supplied value.
Hex$	Converts the supplied number to a string representing its hexadecimal value.
Oct$	Converts the supplied number to a string representing its octal value.
Str$	Converts the supplied number to a string.
TypeName	Returns a string representing the data type of the supplied value.
Val	Converts the supplied string into a number of type Double.

Converting Data from One Type to Another

Use CCur, CDat, CDbl, CInt, CLng, CSng, and CStr to convert data from one type to another. You typically do type conversions to make sure that the result of a calculation is a certain type. For example, the following code fragment shows how to make sure that the price calculation is returned as a Currency value:

```
Dim iQuantity As Integer
Dim curPrice As Currency
Dim curTotal As Currency

curTotal = CCur(iQuantity * curPrice)
```

Converting a Number into a String

There are times when you need to convert a number into its string representation. LotusScript has a number of functions that enable you to do this. Str$ converts the numeric value you supply into its string representation, prefixing the resulting string with a space if the number is positive. For example, the following code prints " 143":

```
Print Str$(143)
```

If you don't want the leading space, use CStr instead. Bin$ takes the number you supply and converts it into a string containing its binary representation. For example, the following code prints "101":

```
Print Bin$(5)
```

Similarly, Hex$ and Oct$ convert numbers into their hexadecimal and octal representations.

Converting a String into a Number

Use the Val function to convert a string into a number. You supply Val with a string, and provided that the string can be converted to a number, Val returns a Double value containing the numeric representation of the string.

Checking the Data Type of a Variable

If you need to check the data type of a variable or an expression, you can use either the DataType or TypeName function. DataType returns an integer representing the data type of the variable or expression being checked. The LSCONST.LSS contains a set of predeclared constants that you can use to interpret the value returned by DataType. TypeName is similar to DataType except that instead of returning an integer, it returns a string describing the data type. For example, the following code prints "STRING":

```
Dim strName As String
Print TypeName(strName)
```

LotusScript Data Structures

LotusScript supports the common programming data structures of arrays and lists. It also supports object-oriented constructs; for example, you can create your classes, methods, and properties. You can also use LotusScript to work with OLE and ActiveX objects. Let's start simple and look at arrays first.

III

Working with LotusScript

Arrays

In LotusScript, you can declare two types of arrays: static and dynamic. A *static* array is an array of fixed size, containing a fixed number of elements. You can't add or delete elements. A *dynamic* array can be resized at any time; you make it larger or smaller by adding or removing elements. See Table 17.5 for the LotusScript functions you can use to work with arrays.

Table 17.5 LotusScript Array-Handling Functions	
Statement or Function	**Description**
Dim	Declares a static array and initializes its elements.
Erase	For fixed arrays, reinitializes each array element. For dynamic arrays, removes all elements from the array.
IsArray	Given a variable name or expression, returns True if the supplied expression is an array.
LBound	Given an array name and an optional dimension of the array, returns the lower bound of that dimension of the array.
ReDim	Declares a dynamic array and allocates storage for its elements or changes the size of an existing dynamic array.
UBound	Given an array name and an optional dimension of the array, returns the upper bound of that dimension of the array.

You declare a static array using the Dim statement. You specify the following:

- The number of dimensions for the array

- The subscript bounds for each dimension

- The type of data to be stored

Dim allocates storage for the array and automatically initializes each element of the array to a default value. Unless you specify otherwise, the first element of an array has an index of 0. If needed, you can change this default to 1 using the Option Base 1 statement. The following declarations declare static arrays:

```
Dim strPrinterNames(9) As String        'Declares 10 elements, bounds are 0
                                          to 9
Dim strQueueNames(19) As String * 32     'Declares 20 elements, bounds are 0
                                          to 19
Dim iRoutingMatrix(9, 9) As Integer      'Declare 100 elements
Dim iPrintJobIDs(1 To 50) As Integer     'Declares 50 elements, bounds are 1
                                          to 50
```

You can also use Dim to declare dynamic arrays. However, when you declare a dynamic array using Dim, you specify only the type. You don't specify the number of elements in the array and no storage is allocated for the array. Before you can use a dynamic array, you have to use the ReDim statement to allocate some storage for its elements. For example, the following code shows how to declare a dynamic array and then allocate some storage for it:

```
Dim iDatabases As Integer          ' Declare the number of elements to
                                     use
Dim strDatabaseNames() As String   ' Declare a dynamic array
iDatabases = 25                    ' Initialize the number of elements
ReDim strDatabaseNames(iDatabases) ' Allocate storage for this number
                                     of elements
```

You can also declare and initialize an array using ReDim. For example, to declare an array containing six elements of type Integer and initialize each element to 0, use the following:

```
Option Base 1                ' Specify that the first element of any
                               array has an index of 1
ReDim varWidgets(6) As Integer ' Declare a dynamic array with elements with
                               indices 1 to 6
```

You can use ReDim to change the size of a dynamic array with the option of preserving the existing contents of the array or reinitializing all elements. For example, if you have a dynamic array, iCustomerIDs, containing 50 elements and you need to increase its size to 100 elements while preserving its current contents, you can use the following code:

```
ReDim Preserve iCustomerIDs(99)
```

If you need to find the size of a dynamic array at runtime, you can use the LBound and UBound functions. You supply these functions with the name of an array, and (optionally) with the dimension whose bounds you are seeking. LBound returns the lower bound of the specified array dimension, and UBound returns the upper bound. For example, after resizing the iCustomerIDs array, LBound(iCustomerIDs) is 0, and UBound(iCustomerIDs) is 99.

You can use the Erase statement to delete all of the elements in a dynamic array and free up the storage the array uses. With a static array, you can use Erase to reinitialize each element.

You can assign an entire array to a variable of type Variant. Consequently, you may need to check whether a variable contains an array, using the IsArray function. If the variable or expression you supply to IsArray is an array, the function returns True. For example:

```
Dim varIcons As Variant
Dim lIconIDs(255) As Long
Print IsArray(varIcons)      'False
varIcons = lIconIDs
Print IsArray(varIcons)      'True
```

Lists

A *list* is similar to an array in that it contains a set of elements. It differs from an array in the way you identify and work with its elements. With arrays, you identify the element you are working with using an index. With lists, you identify elements using a list tag. A *list tag* is simply a string used to uniquely identify a particular element in the list. See Table 17.6 for the LotusScript functions used with lists.

Table 17.6 LotusScript List-Handling Functions

Statement or Function	Description
Dim	Declares a list.
Erase	For lists, removes all elements from the list. For list elements, removes the element from the list.
ForAll	Loops through the elements of a list.
IsElement	Given the name of a list and a string, returns True if the string is a list tag for any element in the list.
IsList	Given a variable name or expression, returns True if the supplied expression is a list.
ListTag	Can only be used inside a ForAll block and returns the name of the element in the list that is currently being processed.

You use Dim to declare an empty list, as in the following:

```
Dim curAmountOutstanding List As String
```

When you declare a list, it has no elements and no storage is allocated for it. You add elements to the list by assigning new list tags. For example, you can create two new elements in the list, with list tags ABC and XYZ, using the code shown below:

```
curAmountOutstanding("ABC") = 12.99
curAmountOutstanding("XYZ") = 52.00
```

You use the tag to refer to a list element in much the same way as you use an index to refer to an array element. For example, to add the two list elements we just created, use the following:

```
Dim curTotal As Currency
curTotal = curAmountOutstanding("ABC") + curAmountOutstanding("XYZ")
```

Use Erase to delete specific elements from the list, or to delete all elements. For example:

```
Erase curAmountOutstanding("ABC")
```

removes the ABC element from the list, while:

```
Erase curAmountOutstanding
```

erases all elements from the list.

If you need to check whether you have already added an element to a list, you can use the IsElement function. You supply the list tag for the element you are looking for, and the function returns True if the tag belongs to an element in the list. Continuing this example:

```
IsElement(curAmountOutstanding("XYZ"))
```

returns True.

In a similar way, you can use IsList to check whether a variable is a list. For example, the following:

```
IsList(curAmountOutstanding)
```

returns True.

To process elements in an array, you typically use a loop to step through each index in the array. When using lists, the only way to identify an element is by its list tag. So how do you loop through all elements in a list? The answer is to use a ForAll loop together with the ListTag function. For example, the following code prints out all the elements in our example list:

```
ForAll varElement In curAmountOutstanding
    Print ListTag(varElement); " owes ";  varElement
End ForAll
```

There are a few points to note when using ForAll. In the example, the variable varElement is known as a *reference variable*. A reference variable is a special kind of variable used by LotusScript when processing ForAll loops. In the body of the loop, each element in the list is assigned to the reference variable. You never have to declare a reference variable; LotusScript takes care of that for you and declares all reference variables to be of type Variant. In fact, if you do declare a reference variable, you'll get an error when you try to compile your script.

Inside a ForAll loop, you can use the ListTag function to find the list tag corresponding to the current element. ListTag only works inside a ForAll loop.

> **Caution**
>
> LotusScript only supports arrays and lists of up to 64K in size. Be aware of this limitation when allocating large arrays and lists.

User-Defined Types

You can define your own data types in LotusScript using the Type statement. You give your new type a name, and then define one or more member variables for the type.

> **Note**
>
> The term *member variable* is used to refer to any variable included in a user-defined type.

For example, to declare a new type with three member variables, suitable for holding a customer ID and name, you could use the following type declaration:

```
Type Customer
    lCustID As Long
    strCustFirstName As String
    strCustSurname As String
    curBalance As Currency
End Type
```

You can then use `Dim` to declare new variables of this type; for example:

```
Dim custNew As Customer
Dim custMailingList As List Customer
Dim custMostFrequentBuyers(99) As Customer
```

You refer to member variables using the form *VarName.MemberName* where *VarName* is the name of the variable of user defined type and *MemberName* is the name of the member variable.

```
custNew.lCustID = 14829
custNew.strCustFirstName = "Chris"
custNew.strCustSurname = "Edwards"
custNew.curBalance = 100.00
```

User-Defined Classes and Objects

You can define your own classes and objects within LotusScript. The `Class` statement is similar to the `Type` statement, except that in addition to defining member variables you can also define member procedures. You can define two special procedures within a class: New and `Delete`. You define New to initialize the member variables for an object of the class. You define Delete if you need to do any special processing when an object of the class is deleted. The following example shows a simple class with four member variables and four member procedures:

```
Class custObject

    ' Declare member variable
    lCustID As Long
    strCustFirstName As String
    strCustSurname As String
    curBalance As Currency

    ' Define constructor
    Sub New(lID As Long, strFirstName As String, strSurname As String,
    curBal As Currency)
        lCustID = lID
        strCustFirstName = strFirstName
        strCustSurname = strSurname
        curBalance = curBal
    End Sub

    ' Define destructor
    Sub Delete
        Print "Customer ";strCustFirstName;" ";strCustSurname; " deleted."
    End Sub

    Sub SetBalance(curBal As Currency)
        curBalance = curBal
    End Sub

    Function curQueryBalance As Currency
        curQueryBalance = curBalance
    End Function

End Class
```

As with other variables, you use `Dim` to declare object variables. When you use `Dim` with a class name, you are actually declaring a reference to an object. You then use `New` to create a new object, and `Set` to assign the object to the reference variable, as follows:

```
Dim custNew As custObject
Set custNew = New custObject(14829, "Chris", "Edwards", 100.00)
```

By default, the member variables you declare are private to the class, while the member functions are public. That is, you cannot refer directly to member variables using dot notation, but you can use dot notation to refer to member function. For example, to update a balance you use:

```
custNew.SetBalance(50.00)
```

instead of:

```
custNew.curBalance = 50.00
```

which would give you an error, because `curBalance` is private to the class. Similarly, to query a balance you would use:

```
curCurrentBalance = custNew.curQueryBalance
```

instead of:

```
curCurrentBalance = custNew.curBalance
```

The `With` statement gives you a shorthand way of accessing public procedures and member variables within an object. You use `With` to point to a particular object, then you use dot notation to refer to the object. The following example shows how to use With to set and query a customer balance:

```
With custNew
    Call .SetBalance(50.00)
    curCurrentBalance = .curQueryBalance
End With
```

When you are finished with an object, you can delete it using the `Delete` statement as shown:

```
Delete custNew
```

If you have defined a `Delete` subroutine within your class, it is executed before the object is deleted. For example, when you delete the customer object in our example, the `Delete` subroutine prints `"Customer Chris Edwards deleted"`. See Table 17.7 for the statements and functions related to working with classes and objects.

Table 17.7 LotusScript User-Defined Object-Handling Functions

Statement or Function	Description
Class	Used to declare a user-defined object class.
Delete	Executes the `Delete` subroutine for a user-defined object.
IsObject	Returns `True` if the supplied expression is an object.

(continues)

Table 17.7 Continued	
Statement or Function	**Description**
New	Used to create a new user-defined object.
Set	Associates an object with a variable.
With	Used to access public procedures and variables within an object using a dot notation.

OLE and ActiveX Objects

You can access the classes, methods, and properties of OLE and ActiveX objects using LotusScript and Notes. This means that you can use Notes to transfer data to applications such as Microsoft Excel and Lotus WordPro, then work with the data using the object classes within the application. You can also program ActiveX objects such as Lotus Components directly from LotusScript. See Table 17.8 for the LotusScript functions that deal with working with objects.

Table 17.8 LotusScript OLE and ActiveX Object-Handling Functions	
Statement or Function	**Description**
CreateObject	Given the name of an OLE object class, creates an OLE object of that class.
GetObject	Given a path to a file and the name of an OLE class, opens the OLE object contained within the file.
IsObject	Returns True if the supplied expression is an object.
Set	Associates an object with a variable.

You can create a new OLE or ActiveX object using the CreateObject function. You supply the name of the class of object you want to create, and LotusScript creates the object. If necessary, LotusScript will start the application required to create the object. The following example shows how to create a new WordPro document from a SmartMaster and save it:

```
Dim objDoc As Variant
Set objDoc = CreateObject("WordPro.Application")
objDoc.NewDocument "", "", "C:\DOCS\EBS.MWP", "" "" ""
' Update the document here . . .
objDoc.SaveAs "C:\DOCS\REPORT.LWP", "", "", False, True, False
Call objDoc.Close(False)
```

To open an existing object, use GetObject. You supply the path to the file containing the object, and optionally the name of the class. LotusScript finds and opens the object. The following example shows how to open a WordPro object:

```
Dim objDoc As Variant
' Open a WordPro Document
Set objDoc = GetObject("C:\DOCS\REPORT.LWP")
```

Understanding LotusScript Operators

In LotusScript, operators are used to perform the following types of function:

- Arithmetical
- Logical
- Comparison
- String concatenation

The arithmetical operators are shown in Table 17.9.

Table 17.9   LotusScript Arithmetical Operators

Operator	Description	Example	Result
–	Negates a number	–34	–34
–	Subtracts two numbers	7–5	2
+	Adds two numbers	5+9	14
*	Multiplies two numbers	7*6	42
/	Divides two numbers	16 / 5	3.2
\	Performs integer division on two numbers	16 \ 5	3
Mod	Performs modulo division on two numbers	16 Mod 5	1
^	Raises a number to a power	5 ^ 2	25

Table 17.10 shows the LotusScript comparison operators.

Table 17.10   LotusScript Comparison Operators

Operator	Description	Example	Result
=	Returns True if two values are equal	5 = 6	False
<> ><	Returns True if two values are not equal	5 <> 6	True
<	Returns True if one value is less than another	7 < 9	True
>	Returns True if one value is greater than another	7 > 9	False
>= =>	Returns True if one value is greater than or equal to another	8 >= 8	True
<= =<	Returns True if one value is less than or equal to another	8 <= 8	True
Is	Returns True if two object references refer to the same object	objA Is objB	True if objA and objB refer to the same object.

Table 17.11 shows the logical operators that you can use in LotusScript.

Table 17.11	LotusScript Logical Operators		
Operator	**Description**	**Example**	**Result**
Not	Logical Negation	Not B	True if B is False; False if B is True
And	Logical And	A And B	True if both A and B are True; False otherwise
Or	Logical Or	A Or B	True if either A or B is True; False otherwise
Xor	Exclusive Or	A Xor B	True if either A or B is True, but not both; False if A and B are both False or both True
Eqv	Logical Equivalence	A Eqv B	True if A and B are both False or both True; False if either A or B but not both is True
Imp	Logical Implication	A Imp B	True if A is False or both A and B are True; False if A is True and B is False

Table 17.12 shows the available string operators.

Table 17.12	LotusScript String Operators		
Operator	**Description**	**Example**	**Result**
&	Concatenates two strings	"AB" & "CD"	"ABCD"
+	Concatenates two strings	"AB" + "CD"	"ABCD"
Like	Returns True if a string matches a supplied pattern	"ABC" Like "A*"	True

Using Functions and Subs

In LotusScript, you can define functions and subs that you can call from within a script to perform specific functions. For example, you could define a function to convert a date with a two-digit year into a date with a four-digit year and keep your boss happy well into the next century! The main difference between a function and a sub is that a function returns a value and a sub does not.

Declaring Functions and Subs

You declare a function using the Function keyword, as follows:

```
Function fIsWeekend(iDay As Integer) As Integer
```

You give it a name, then define the list of arguments you are going to pass to it; finally, you define the type of value it is going to return. To set the return value, assign a value to the function name, as shown in the following example:

```
Function fIsWeekend(varDate As Variant) As Integer
    If Weekday(varDate) = 1 Or Weekday(varDate) = 7 Then
        fIsWeekend = True
    Else
        fIsWeekend = False
    End If
End Function
```

You define subs in much the same way using the Sub keyword. The only thing to remember is that you can't return a value from a sub, so you don't have to declare a return type. A typical sub declaration is shown below:

```
Sub GoToBeach(strResort As String, iMilesToResort As Integer)
```

Calling Functions and Subs

To call a function, you simply assign it to a variable. For example:

```
Dim fGoToWork As Integer
Dim varToday As Variant
' Use the built in function Today to get today's date
varToday = Today
' Use the fIsWeekend function
fGoToWork = fIsWeekend(varToday)
```

To call a sub, you can use any of the following methods :

```
Call SubName(Arg1, Arg2 ...)
```

or

```
Call SubName arg1, arg2
```

or

```
SubName(Arg1, Arg2 ...)
```

For example:

```
If fIsWeekend(varToday) Then
    Call GoToBeach("Maui", 4000)
End If
```

When you pass values to subs and functions, you need to be aware of the two following different ways that LotusScript can pass arguments:

- **By reference**—LotusScript passes a reference to the argument. The function works with the argument. Any changes that the function makes to the argument are reflected in the original.

- **By value**—LotusScript passes a copy of the argument to the function. The function works with the copy. Any changes to the copy do not affect the original.

Some arguments, such as arrays, lists, and objects, are always passed by reference. With other arguments, you have a choice. If you always want an argument to be passed by value, use the ByVal keyword when you declare that argument in the function or sub declaration. In the following example, the second argument is always passed by value:

```
Sub DeleteDocument(iDocNumber As Integer, ByVal strDocTitle As String)
```

Looping and Branching

LotusScript provides a variety of ways to control the flow of execution in a script. You can use loops to repeatedly execute a set of statements based on certain conditions being met. You can use branches to execute different parts of a script, based on the results of comparisons or the value of variables. Let's look at loops first.

For...Next Loops

You use the For...Next loop to execute a set of statements a specified number of times. You specify the following:

- A control variable for the loop

- A start value for the variable

- An end value for the variable

- Optionally, a step value to add to the control variable after each execution of the loop. If you don't specify a value, the default is 1.

The first time the loop is executed, the control variable has the start value. After each execution of the loop, the control variable is updated by adding the step value to it. If you use a positive step value, the loop finishes when the control variable is greater than or equal to the end value. The following example shows a typical For...Next loop.

```
Dim iCount As Integer
For iCount = 1 To 10 Step 2
   ' Do something . . .
Next
```

In this example, the loop is executed five times, with iCount having the values 1, 3, 5, 7, and 9.

ForAll Loops

We've already had a sneak preview of this type of loop when we looked at using lists in LotusScript. However, you aren't restricted to using ForAll loops with lists. You can also use them with arrays and object collections. For example, you can use a ForAll loop to loop through all views in a Notes database:

```
Dim session As New NotesSession
Dim db As NotesDatabase
Set db = session.CurrentDatabase
ForAll varView In db.Views
   ' Do something ...
End ForAll
```

Do...While Loops

Use a Do...While loop to repeatedly execute a block of statements while a specified condition is true. Before the loop is executed, the condition you specify is tested; if it evaluates to True, the block of statements within the loop is executed. If the condition evaluates to False, the loop is not executed, and control passes to the next statement after the loop. For example, the following loop executes three times and prints 17, 18, and 19:

```
Dim iCount As Integer
Dim iMax As Integer
iMax = 20
iCount = 17
Do While iCount < iMax
    Print iCount
    iCount = iCount + 1
Loop
```

An alternative form of the Do...While loop tests the condition after the loop is executed, as shown:

```
Dim iCount As Integer
Dim iMax As Integer
iMax = 20
iCount = 17
Do
    Print iCount
    iCount = iCount + 1
Loop While iCount < iMax
```

The main difference between the two loops is that you can guarantee that the second loop is always executed at least once.

Do...Until Loops

A closely related type of loop is the Do...Until loop. With this kind of loop, the set of statements in the loop is executed until the loop condition evaluates to True. For example, if we change the first of the Do...While loops to a Do...Until loop,

```
Dim iCount As Integer
Dim iMax As Integer
iMax = 20
iCount = 17
Do Until iCount < iMax
    Print iCount
    iCount = iCount + 1
Loop
```

the statements inside this loop are never executed, because the condition iCount < iMax is True before the loop is entered.

The Do...Until loop also has an alternative form that checks the condition at the end of the loop.

```
Dim iCount As Integer
Dim iMax As Integer
iMax = 20
iCount = 17
Do
    Print iCount
    iCount = iCount + 1
Loop Until iCount < iMax
```

This loop is executed only once and prints 17.

If...Then...Else Branches

You can use `If...Then...Else` statements to select which statements are executed based on a condition you specify. If the condition is `True`, one set of statements is executed; if the condition is `False`, a different set is executed. For example:

```
If iCount > iMax Then
    Print "Too many items!"
Else
    Print "Processing "; iCount; " item(s) . . ."
End If
```

You can omit the `Else` part of the statement if you only want to execute a set of statements when a condition is `True`. For example:

```
If iDaysOverdue > 14 Then
    Print "Time to send a nastygram!"
End If
```

Select...Case Branches

The `Select...Case` statement lets you select a block of statements to execute based on the value of an expression. For example:

```
Select Case iBoxesOrdered
    Case Is <= 0  : Call ProcessInvalidOrder(iBoxesOrdered)
    Case 1        : Call ProcessSmallOrder(iBoxesOrdered)
    Case 2 To 15  : Call ProcessMediumOrder(iBoxesOrdered)
    Case 16 To 31 : Call ProcessLargeOrder(iBoxesOrdered)
    Case Else     : Call ProcessHugeOrder(iBoxesOrdered)

End Select
```

GoSub and On...GoSub

Within a sub or function, you can use `GoSub` and `On...GoSub` to branch to a specific label within the procedure. A label is simply a way of identifying a place in your code. The code at the label can execute a `Return` statement, to branch back to the statement following the `GoSub`. For example, the following code branches to the label `lblLogError` if the order quantity is negative:

```
Sub ProcessInvalidOrder(iOrderQuantity As Integer)
    If iOrderQuantity < 0 Then
        GoSub lblLogError
    End If

    Exit Sub

lblLogError:
    Call LogError
    Return
End Sub
```

You can use `On...GoSub` to branch to one of a number of labels based on a supplied value. For example, when the following statement is executed:

```
On iErrorNumber GoSub lblA, lblB, lblC
```

If iErrorNumber is 1, the program branches to lblA; if iErrorNumber is 2, the program branches to lblB; and if iErrorNumber is 3, the program branches to lblC. If iErrorNumber is 0 or greater than 3, the On...GoSub statement is ignored.

GoTo and On...GoTo

GoTo and On...GoTo are similar to GoSub and On...GoSub in that they let you branch to specific labels. However, GoTo statements are one-way branches. You cannot use a Return statement to return control back to the statement after the GoTo.

Working with Strings

LotusScript has a rich set of functions that you can use to manipulate strings. In this section, we'll look at the following:

- Creating strings

- Creating substrings

- Formatting strings

- Finding and comparing strings

See Table 17.13 for a list of statements and functions you can use to manipulate strings.

Table 17.13   LotusScript String-Handling Functions

Statement or Function	Description
Asc	Given a string, returns the character code for the first character in the string.
Chr	Given a character code, returns the character corresponding to that code.
Format	Given an expression and a format string, evaluates the expression and formats the result according to the format string.
InStr, InStrB	Given two strings, returns the position of the character (InStr) or byte (InStrB) where one string first occurs within the other.
LCase	Converts a supplied string to lowercase.
Left, LeftB	Given a string and a number, returns that number of characters (Left) or bytes (LeftB) from the left of the string.
Len, LenB	Given a string or a number, returns the number of characters (Len) or bytes (LenB) used to store the string or number.
LSet	Assigns one string to another and left aligns the result, padding with spaces if necessary.
LTrim	Removes the leading spaces from the supplied string.
Mid	Given a string, a start position, and a length, returns the sub-string of the specified length that starts at the specified position.

(continues)

Table 17.13 Continued

Statement or Function	Description
Right, RightB	Given a string and a number, returns that number of characters (Right) or bytes (RightB) from the right of the string.
RSet	Assigns one string to another and right aligns the result, prefixing with spaces if necessary.
RTrim	Removes the trailing spaces from the supplied string.
Space	Given a number, returns a string containing that number of spaces.
StrCompare	Given two strings and a comparison method, compares the two strings according to the supplied comparison method.
Trim	Removes the leading and trailing spaces from the supplied string.
UCase	Converts a supplied string to uppercase.
UChr	Given a Unicode character code, returns the character corresponding to that code.
Uni	Given a string, returns the Unicode character code for the first character in the string.
UString	Given a length, and either a Unicode code or a character, returns a string of the specified characters of the supplied length.

Creating Strings

You use `Dim` to declare string variables. You can declare strings as variable or fixed length, as follows:

```
Dim strVariableLength As String
Dim strFixedLength As String * 20
```

As declared, `strFixedLength` contains 20 characters. If you want to set a string to a particular length after it has been declared, you can use the `Space$` function to set the string to a specified number of spaces. For example, the following code sets `strName` to 32 spaces:

```
Dim strName As String
strName = Space$(32)
```

Alternatively, you can use the `String$` function to set a string to any number of a specified character. You supply the number of characters, and either the character or ASCII character code of the character to use. For example:

```
strName = String$(32, "x")
```

sets `strName` to contain 32 'x' characters, as does:

```
strName = String$(32, Asc("x"))
```

If you are working with Unicode character codes you can use UString$ to do the same thing, provided you supply the Unicode character code:

```
strName = UString$(32, Uni("x"))
```

> **Note**
>
> The Asc function returns the ASCII character code corresponding to the character you specify. Similarly, the Uni function returns the Unicode character code for a character. If you already know the appropriate code, you can find the corresponding character using Chr for ASCII codes and UChr for Unicode codes.

Creating Substrings

Once you have a string, you can use any of the following functions to create substrings from it. With Left or Left$, you can create a substring consisting of a specified number of characters from the left of the string. The following example shows how.

```
Dim strName As String
Dim strFirstName As String
strName = "John G Testar"
strFirstName = Left$(strName, 4)    'strFirstName is set to 'John'
```

Similarly, you can use Right or Right$ to extract characters from the right of the string, for example:

```
strSurname = Right$(strName, 6)     'strSurname is set to 'Testar'
```

Use Mid or Mid$ to extract characters from anywhere in a string. You supply the start position and the number of characters, as shown:

```
strMiddleInitial = Mid$(strName, 6, 1)    'strMiddleInitial is set to 'G'
```

To find the length of a string, you can use Len. For example:

```
Dim iLength As Integer
iLength = Len(strName)    'iLength is set to 13
```

> **Note**
>
> Many LotusScript functions have two versions, one that ends in a $ and one that doesn't. If you use the version that ends in $, the return data type is String. If you use the version without a $, the return data type is Variant.

You can remove leading and trailing spaces from strings using Trim, LTrim, and RTrim. As their names suggest, Trim removes both leading and trailing spaces, LTrim removes leading spaces, and RTrim removes trailing spaces.

> **Caution**
>
> Several of the string-handling functions have one version that works with characters, such as Left, and another version that works with bytes, such as LeftB. This is fine where one character is stored in one byte. However, because the Unicode encoding scheme used by LotusScript represents each character with a two-byte character code, you should be wary of using the byte-oriented string functions LeftB, LenB, MidB, and RightB. They may give unexpected results with Unicode strings. Use Left, Len, Mid, and Right instead.

Formatting Strings

You can change the case of a string to lowercase using LCase, or to uppercase using UCase. For more advanced formatting, use the Format function. You can use this function to format a string, date/time, or number according to a format string. If you need to make sure that strings are correctly aligned, you can use the LSet and RSet statements. Use LSet to assign and left align a string. RSet is similar, except that the string is right-aligned. For example:

```
Dim strLabel As String
strLabel = Space$(8)
LSet strLabel = "ABC"    'Sets strLabel to 'ABC     ' because the current
                          length of strLabel is 8'
RSet strLabel = "XYZ"    'Sets strLabel to '     XYZ'
strLabel = "ABC"         'Sets strLabel to 'ABC'
```

Finding and Comparing Strings

If you need to find a string contained within a string, you can use InStr to find the position of the first character of the embedded string. You supply the following:

- Optionally, the position in the string to be searched at which to start searching. The default is the start of the string.

- The string to look for

- The string to be searched

- Optionally, a number to indicate whether the search is case-sensitive or not. 0 for case-sensitive, 1 for case-insensitive.

For example, the following code shows how to find the position of the first occurrence of one string within another, irrespective of case:

```
Dim strMain As String
Dim strSearch As String
Dim iPos As Integer

strMain = "Hello world!"
strSearch = "wor"
iPos = InStr(1, strMain, strSearch, 1)  ' Look for 'wor' within 'Hello
world!'
```

You can compare two strings using StrCompare. With StrCompare, you supply the following:

■ The two strings to compare

■ Optionally, a number to indicate how to compare the strings. For example, you can specify that the comparison is case-sensitive.

StrCompare returns the following:

■ –1 if the first string is less than the second

■ 0 if the strings are equal

■ 1 if the first string is greater than the second

Date and Time Handling

The LotusScript functions that you can use to manipulate dates and times are shown in Table 17.14.

Table 17.14 LotusScript Date and Time-Handling Functions

Statement or Function	Description
Date	Returns the current system date as a date/time value or sets the current system date to a specified value.
DateNumber	Given a year, month number, and day of the month, returns the corresponding date/time value.
DateValue	Given a string representing a date, returns the corresponding date/time value.
Day	Given a date/time value, returns the day of the month.
Hour	Given a date/time value, returns the hour.
IsDate	Given an expression, returns True if the supplied expression represents a date.
Minute	Given a date/time value, returns the minute.
Month	Given a date/time value, returns the month.
Now	Returns the current system date and time as a date/time value.
Second	Given a date/time value, returns the second.
Time	Returns the current system time as a date/time value.
TimeNumber	Given an hour, minute, and second, returns the corresponding date/time value.
Timer	Returns the number of seconds that have elapsed since midnight.
TimeValue	Given a string representing a time, returns the corresponding date/time value.
Today	The same as the Date function.
Weekday	Given a date/time value, returns an integer representing the day of the week. Day 1 is Sunday.
Year	Given a date/time value, returns the year.

III

Working with LotusScript

To find the current date, use either the Date or Today function. Both return a date/time value containing the current system date. You can find the current time using the Time function to return a date/time containing the current time. If you want both the date and time, use Now. To set a date to a specific value, you can use either DateNumber or DateValue. DateNumber returns a date value when supplied with a year, month, and day. DateValue returns a date value when supplied with a string representing a date. For example:

```
Print DateNumber(1992, 5, 29)      ' Prints 5/29/92
Print DateValue("May 29, 1992")    ' Prints 5/29/92
```

DateNumber is also useful in date calculations. For example, to find the date two years, three months, and twelve days before May 29, 1992, you could use:

```
Print DateNumber(1992 - 2, 5 - 3, 29 - 12)    ' Prints 2/17/90
```

There are two similar functions you can use to set a time to a specific value. TimeNumber returns a time value when supplied with an hour, minute, and second. TimeValue returns a time value from a string representing a time. For example:

```
Print TimeNumber(20, 40, 3)    ' Prints 8:40:03 PM
Print TimeValue("20:40")       ' Prints 8:40:00 PM
```

You can find the number of seconds since midnight by calling the Timer function.

Tip

You can use the Timer function to time parts of your program. For example, to check how long it takes to read a large file from a network file server, call Timer before and after reading the file and subtract the two values. Timer is accurate to the nearest hundredth of a second.

Once you have a date/time value, you can use Year, Month, Day, Hour, Minute, and Second to extract its constituent parts. You can use Weekday to return an integer representing the day of the week.

Working with Files

There are many ways you can work with files using LotusScript. Table 17.15 lists the functions available to you.

Table 17.15 LotusScript File-Handling Functions

Statement or Function	Description
Close	Closes one or more open files.
EOF	Indicates whether the end of a file has been reached. The exact condition used to determine the end of file depends on the type of file being read.
FileAttr	Given a file number and a flag, returns either the access type for a file, or the operating system file handle for the file.

Statement or Function	Description
FileCopy	Copies a file.
FileDateTime	Given a filename, returns a string containing the date and time that the file was created or modified.
FileLen	Given a filename, returns its length in bytes.
FreeFile	Returns a file number you can use to open a file.
Get	Used to read data from a binary or random file.
GetFileAttr	Given a file or directory name, returns its file system attributes.
Input #	Given a file number, reads data from a sequential file into a list of variables.
Input	Given a file number, reads a specified number of characters from a sequential or binary file into a String variable.
InputB	Given a file number, reads a specified number of bytes from a sequential or binary file into a String variable.
Kill	Deletes a file.
Line Input #	Given a file number, reads a line from a sequential file into a String or Variant variable.
LOC	Given a file number, returns the current position of the file pointer in a file.
Lock	Given a file number, locks the file, or optionally, a record or range of bytes within the file, so that other processes cannot update it.
LOF	Given a file number, returns the length of the file.
Name	Renames a file or directory.
Open	Opens a file.
Print #	Prints a list of variables to a file.
Put	Writes data to a binary or random file.
Reset	Closes all open files.
Seek	Given a file number, returns the current file pointer position. Or, given a file number and a position, sets the current file pointer position.
SetFileAttr	Sets the file system attributes for a file.
Spc	Inserts a specified number of spaces into a Print or Print # statement.
Tab	Moves the print position to a specified column.
Width #	Used to specify the line length of a sequential file.
Write #	Writes a list of variables to a file. Similar to Print #, except that delimiter characters are automatically written where necessary.
Unlock	Unlocks a file previously locked using Lock.

Types of Files

LotusScript can work with the three types of files shown in Table 17.16.

Table 17.16 LotusScript File Types	
File Type	**Description**
Sequential	A text file.
Random	A file consisting of a series of formatted records.
Binary	A file with a program defined structure.

Getting File Information

If you know the name of a file, you can use GetFileAttr, FileDateTime, and FileLen to access file information. Use GetFileAttr to check the attributes for a file. The FileDateTime function returns the date when the file was last modified, and FileLen returns the length of the file in bytes. For example, the following code checks whether a file is Hidden, and if it is, sets its Hidden attribute:

```
%Include "LSCONST.LSS"
Dim iAttributes As Integer
iAttributes = GetFileAttr("C:\TEMP.TXT")
If (iAttributes And ATTR_HIDDEN) Then
    Call SetFileAttr("C:\TEMP.TXT", ATTR_READONLY)
End If
```

Creating and Opening Files

To open a sequential file, use the FreeFile and Open statements. Use FreeFile to allocate a new file number for the file. You then use this file number in the Open statement. For example, to open a new sequential file for output, use

```
Dim iFileNumber As Integer
iFileNumber = FreeFile
Open "C:\RESULTS.TXT" For Output As iFileNumber
```

You can open a sequential file for Input, Output, or Append. Once you have opened a file, you use the file number to refer to it thereafter.

To open a random file, you also use FreeFile and Open, but this time, specify the Random option on the Open statement. For example:

```
Dim iFileNumber As Integer
iFileNumber = FreeFile
Open "C:\RECORDS.DAT" For Random As iFileNumber Len = 80
```

The Len option is used to indicate the number of bytes per record in the file.

Use the Binary option on the Open statement to open a binary file. For example:

```
Dim iFileNumber As Integer
iFileNumber = FreeFile
Open "C:\RECORDS.DAT" For Binary As iFileNumber
```

Once you have opened a file, you can use LOF to check the number of bytes in the file.

Reading Files

You can use the `Line Input #` and `Input #` statements, or the `Input` function, to read data from an open sequential file. `Line Input #` reads one line of data from the file. For example:

```
Do Until EOF(iFileNumber)
    Line Input #iFileNumber, strInputLine
Loop
```

The `EOF` function returns `True` when the end of file has been reached.

Use `Input #` to read data from a line in a file into a set of variables. For example, if your input file contains lines of the format:

```
14829, "Chris", "Edwards", 100.00
25674, "Marlene", "Metcalfe", 850.00
```

you could use the code below to read a line from the file:

```
Dim lID As Long
Dim strFirstName As String
Dim strSurname As String
Dim curBalance As Currency
'  . . . Open the file as in previous examples
Input #iFileNumber, lID, strFirstName, strSurname, curBalance
```

The `Input` function is another option for reading data from a sequential file. With `Input`, you supply the number of characters to read. For example, you could read the ID number from the beginning of a line in the file using the following code:

```
strID = Input$(5, iFileNumber)
```

When you are working with random or binary files, use `Seek` and `Get` to find and read records from the file.

Writing Files

You can use `Write #` to write the contents of a set of variables to a sequential file. For example, to write a line to an open file:

```
Dim lID As Long
Dim strFirstName As String
Dim strSurname As String
Dim curBalance As Currency
'  . . . Open the file for output or append as in previous examples
'  . . . Assign values to variables
Write #iFileNumber, lID, strFirstName, strSurname, curBalance
```

`Write #` automatically adds formatting characters to the output line, such as quotation marks around strings, or commas between values. Notice the similarity between `Write #` and `Input #`. They are designed to work in conjunction with each other to write and read lines in the same format. You can also use the `Print #` statement to write data to a sequential file. However, when you use `Print #`, you have to add your own formatting characters. There are a couple of functions you can use with `Print #` to help format the line. Use `Spc` to add a specified number of spaces to the line and `Tab` to move the print position to a specified position within the line. For example, the following code:

```
strFirstName = "Pat"
strSurname = "Green"
Print #iFileNumber, "*"; Tab(4); strFirstName; Spc(2); strSurname; "*"
```

prints:

```
*    Pat  Green*
```

Use Put to write data to random and binary files.

In some cases, you may want to block access to the file until your program has finished with it. LotusScript provides the Lock and Unlock statements to enable you to do so.

Closing Files

Once you have finished with a file, you can close it using the Close statement. If you want to close all the files that are open, you can use Reset.

Deleting Files

To delete a file use the Kill statement. You supply Kill with the name of the file to be deleted, as follows:

```
Kill "C:\TEMP.TXT"
```

Input/Output

When you are using LotusScript within Notes, you often use Notes forms to get information from users, and to display results. But sometimes you need to use different methods to communicate with a user. The LotusScript functions shown in Table 17.17 offer you some alternatives.

Table 17.17 LotusScript Input/Output Functions

Statement or Function	Description
Beep	Beeps the speaker.
InputBox	Displays a dialog box in which a user can enter a value.
MessageBox	Displays a message box to a user.
Print	Writes some text to the Notes status bar.

Use InputBox to display a dialog box with an entry field. A user can enter a string into the entry field and click an OK button. You can then access the string they typed from your script, as follows:

```
strName = InputBox$("Please enter your name")
```

If you want, you can specify a title for the dialog box, and a default value. For example:

```
iOrderQuantity = CInt(InputBox$("Enter the order quantity",
"Order Quantity", "10")
```

You can display values from your script using either MessageBox or Print. Use MessageBox to display a dialog box containing a message of your choice. For example, if you wanted to display a message to confirm this order you could use:

```
MessageBox("You are about to order " & CStr(iOrderQuantity) &
" widgets.  Is this correct?", MB_YESNO, "Confirm Order")
```

The `MB_YESNO` is one of several constants relating to the `MessageBox` function, defined in the LSCONST.LSS file. Additional constants are available that you can use to add icons and buttons to the message box. See the "MsgBox parameters" section in the `LSCONST.LSS` file for more details.

In Notes, the LotusScript `Print` function displays a line of text in the Notes status bar. This can be very useful if you are writing a LotusScript agent that may take some time to execute, because it gives you an easy way to keep the user informed about its progress. For example, in an agent that processes documents in a database, you could use

```
Print "Processing document " & CStr(iCurDoc) & " of " &
CStr(iTotalDocs) & " . . ."
```

inside the main processing loop to display a constantly updated status message to the user. To top it off, why not let them know when you're done by using `Beep` to wake them up!

The LotusScript Mathematical Functions

The LotusScript mathematical functions are shown in Table 17.18.

Table 17.18 LotusScript Mathematical Functions

Statement or Function	Description
Abs	Given any number, returns its absolute value.
ACos	Given a number between –1 and 1, returns its arccosine in radians.
ASin	Given a number between –1 and 1, returns its arcsine in radians.
ATn	Given a number, returns its arctangent in radians.
ATn2	Given the coordinates of a point in the Cartesian plane, returns the polar coordinate angle in radians.
Cos	Given an angle in radians, returns its cosine.
Exp	Given a number, returns the exponential of the number.
Fix	Returns the integer part of a number.
Fraction	Returns the fractional part of a number.
Int	Returns the nearest integer that is less than or equal to the supplied number.
Log	Given a number, returns the natural logarithm of the number.
Round	Rounds a number to a specified number of decimal places.
Sgn	Identifies the sign of the supplied number. Returns –1 for negative numbers, 0 for zero, and 1 for positive numbers.
Sin	Given an angle in radians, returns its sine.
Sqr	Returns the square root of the supplied number.
Tan	Given an angle in radians, returns its tangent.

Handling Errors at Runtime

LotusScript detects two types of errors:

■ Compiler errors

■ Runtime errors

Compiler errors are due to mistakes in your LotusScript code. You cannot run your code until you have fixed any compiler errors LotusScript has detected. We'll look at the Notes' Integrated Development Environment (IDE) in the next chapter, and explore some of the features that help reduce the number of compiler errors you'll have to fix.

Runtime errors are errors that occur when LotusScript attempts to run a script. For example, a runtime error occurs when a script attempts to open a file that has been deleted. LotusScript identifies many runtime errors, and assigns each one an error number and an error message describing the error. You can add code to your programs to provide special handling for any or all of these errors. You can even define your own errors if you want, and assign them error numbers and messages. Table 17.19 shows the LotusScript functions that relate to error-handling.

Table 17.19 LotusScript Error-Handling Functions

Statement or Function	Description
Erl	Returns the LotusScript line number of the most recent error.
Err	Either returns or sets the current error number depending on how it is used.
Error	Either returns an error message or signals an error depending on how it is used.
On Error	Sets up error-handling for a procedure.
Resume	Determines where a LotusScript program resumes execution after an error.

Whenever LotusScript detects an error at runtime it stores the following information:

■ The line number in the LotusScript source file where the error occurred

■ The error number

■ The error message

You can use the Erl function to get the line number for the most recent error. The Err function returns the most recent error number, and Error$ returns the associated error message.

Once LotusScript has stored this information, it looks for an On Error statement in the current procedure that can handle the error. If it can't find one, it checks in the procedure that called the current one, and so on until it has checked all of the calling procedures. If a suitable On Error statement isn't found, LotusScript displays the error message associated with the error and stops execution of the script. If an On Error statement is found, LotusScript transfers control to the On Error statement.

The On Error statement can do either of the following:

- Ignore the error. If you specify `On Error Resume Next,` LotusScript ignores the line that caused the error and executes the line immediately after it.

- Specify a label to go to. If you specify `On Error GoTo` followed by the name of a label, LotusScript transfers control to the code at that label. The code should handle the error. Use a `Resume` statement to restart the script.

The following example shows how to define your own error and set up an error handler to process it. The example `Sub` defines an error with error number 600, and then initializes an error handling routine to process errors with this number. It then forces the error to occur. Control is passed to the error handling routine, which prints the error number and line number of the statement where the error occurred. Control is then returned to the statement following the one that forced the error:

```
Sub ErrorTest
    ' Define an error
    Const ERR_MY_ERROR = 600

    ' Set up error handling to detect this type of error
    On Error ERR_MY_ERROR GoTo lblHandleError

    ' Force an error to occur
    Error ERR_MY_ERROR

    ' After the error is handled, control returns here . . .
    Print "Finished."

    Exit Sub

lblHandleError:
    Print "Error number "; Err; " occurred on line "; Erl
    Resume Next
End Sub
```

From Here...

In this chapter, we covered LotusScript the language. We looked at its syntax and structure, and at some of its main features.

In the next chapter, you'll learn how LotusScript fits into Notes, and how to use LotusScript and Notes to develop great Notes applications.

For information on related topics, see the following chapters:

- Chapter 18, "Writing Scripts with LotusScript," shows you how to use LotusScript within Notes.

- Chapter 19, "More LotusScript," looks at how to work with Lotus Notes Object Classes.

- "ODBC and Lotus Components" on the CD looks at how you can use the ODBC LotusScript extensions and Lotus components in your database designs.

Chapter 18

Writing Scripts with LotusScript

Chapter 17, "LotusScript Basics," introduced you to LotusScript and explained some of its basic features and syntax. In this chapter, you build on these basics and learn how to use LotusScript within Notes.

LotusScript extends the Notes programming interface beyond @functions and @commands. You use LotusScript to write scripts to perform various functions and tasks in Notes. You attach scripts to various objects in Notes, depending on what you need to accomplish. For example, you might use LotusScript to create an agent to update documents at a scheduled time. LotusScript provides some capabilities that Notes formulas do not, such as the ability to manipulate a Notes database's ACL, and the ability to print a list of all databases that reside on a server or local hard disk. You enter LotusScript code into Notes using the Notes Integrated Development Environment (IDE). Notes contains an integral LotusScript compiler that translates your code into executable LotusScript.

The Notes Integrated Development Environment

The Integrated Development Environment (IDE) in Notes lets you design forms, views, and agents in a consistent way. However, for each form, view, or agent that you design, you will use a different IDE. Although each IDE is different, they also share many common features, such as the script editor and debugger features. We'll focus on the *Forms* IDE, but the Script Editor and debugger work similarly in the other IDEs. The Forms IDE is displayed as shown in Figure 18.1.

Some of the main topics in this chapter are

- Learn how to use the Notes Integrated Development Environment to write LotusScript

- Learn how to use the script editor

- Learn how to use the LotusScript debugger

- Look at techniques for debugging LotusScript

- Understand how to access dynamic link libraries from within LotusScript

- Learn how to include LotusScript extensions in your scripts

III

Working with LotusScript

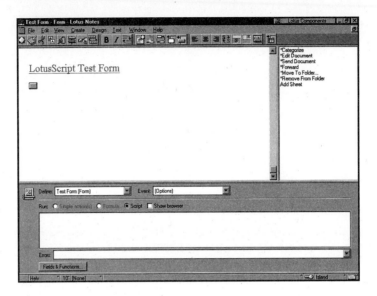

Fig. 18.1 Here is an example of the Forms IDE.

The screen is divided into three areas or *panes*.

The Form Layout Pane

The large pane at the top left of the screen is the *Form Layout pane*. You use this pane to design and lay out your form. You can add fields, static text, graphics, and layout regions to the form.

The Action Pane

The small pane at the top right of the screen is the *Action pane*. You use this pane to define the actions that are associated with the form. By default, the Action pane is not visible when you first open the IDE. To display the Action pane, select View, Action Pane from the Notes menu bar, or drag the vertical bar at the right edge of the screen to the left until the Action pane is the size that you want. Finally, if you're a SmartIcon fan, you can click the View Show/Hide Action Pane SmartIcon.

To hide the Action pane, either select View, Action Pane again to uncheck the menu option; drag the vertical bar to the right edge of the screen; or click the View Show/Hide Action Pane SmartIcon.

The Design Pane

The *Design pane* is the pane displayed at the bottom of the screen. This is where you write your LotusScript code. By default, the Design pane is visible. If you want to hide it, select View, Design Pane from the Notes menu bar, or drag the horizontal bar (the one that separates the Design pane from the rest of the window) down to the bottom of the screen.

The Design pane consists of a number of components that you use to write the LotusScript code. Let's look at each in turn.

The Define Box. The Define box, shown in Figure 18.2, is a drop-down combo box that you use to select the object or action that you want to program.

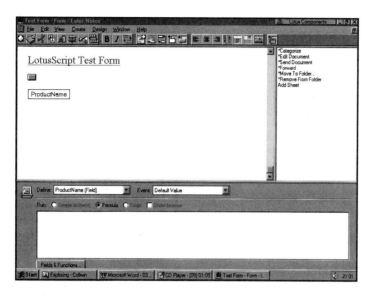

Fig. 18.2   The Define box shows the name of the object or action you are programming.

For example, Figure 18.2 shows that the ProductName field is currently being programmed. You can use the Define box to quickly switch to another object or action. To program a different object, click the arrow on the Define box. A list of the objects and actions that you can program is displayed as shown in Figure 18.3. Then, select the object or action that you want to program.

Fig. 18.3   Using the Define box to select an object to program.

The Event Box. The Design pane contains a second drop-down combo box, the Event box, as shown in Figure 18.4.

Fig. 18.4   The Event box shows the name of the event you are programming.

The Event box shows all of the events that are associated with the currently selected object or action. The Event box shows the event currently being programmed. For example, in Figure 18.4, the event being programmed is the form's QueryModeChange event. To program a different event, simply select it from the list in the Event box.

If the selected object or action has no events associated with it, such as one of the standard form actions, the Event box is not displayed. Figure 18.5 shows how the Design pane looks when the standard `Edit Document` action is selected.

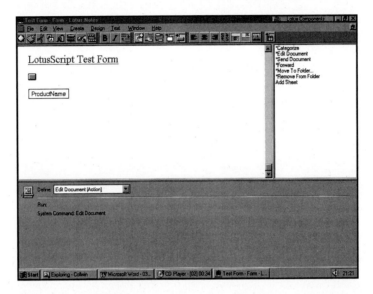

Fig. 18.5   This is how the Design pane looks when a standard form action is selected.

> **Note**
>
> If you add your own LotusScript functions and subs to a form, they are shown in the Event box when you select the `Globals` object for the form.

The Run Radio Buttons. Depending on the type of object you have selected in the Define box, you can use the Run radio buttons to select the type of programming for the object (see Figure 18.6). You have three choices:

- Simple Action(s)
- Formula
- Script

Select Script to program using LotusScript.

The Script Browser. After you have selected the Script radio button, you can display the Script Browser by checking the Show Browser check box. The Script Browser is shown in Figure 18.7.

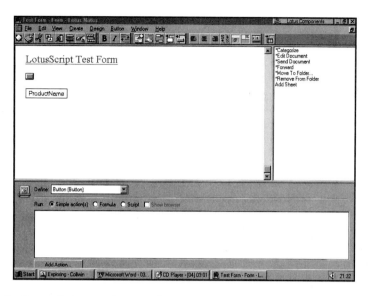

Fig. 18.6 The Run radio buttons let you select LotusScript as a programming option.

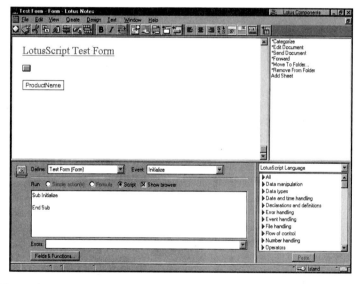

Fig. 18.7 This is the Script Browser.

The browser lets you display the following:

- A list of the functions and features available in LotusScript.

- All of the Notes classes and their associated methods, properties, and events. (We'll cover these in detail in the next chapter.)

- All of the OLE2 and ActiveX classes that are available to you.

You select what you want to display using the browser combo box. You can select the following:

- LotusScript language
- Notes classes
- Notes constants
- Notes subs and functions
- Notes variables
- OLE2 classes

For example, if you want to see what functions LotusScript has available for Error Handling, follow these steps:

1. If it is not already selected, select LotusScript Language in the browser combo box. A list of categories of functions is displayed.

2. Click the twistie next to Error Handling. The names and syntax of the LotusScript Error-Handling functions are shown (see Figure 18.8).

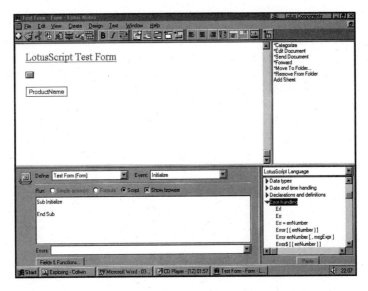

Fig. 18.8 The LotusScript error-handling functions shown in the Script Browser.

If you want to add an item from the browser to the code, (such as a function name), follow these steps:

1. Position the cursor in the LotusScript code where you want to insert the item.

2. In the Script Browser, double-click the item you want to insert. The item is inserted into the code where you placed the cursor.

The browser can be very useful when you want to do the following:

- Check for availability of a specific function.

- Check the parameters for a function.

- Check the properties, methods, and events of a Notes, OLE2, or ActiveX class.

The Script Editor. You will type your LotusScript code in the area of the Design pane called the *Script Editor*. The Script Editor understands LotusScript syntax and helps you by reviewing the script as you enter it. The Script Editor:

- Checks for syntax errors as you enter the script.

- Automatically capitalizes LotusScript key words.

- Formats the script by automatically indenting blocks of code.

- Completes certain types of LotusScript statements, such as If...Then statements and For...Next loops.

- Provides colors to display different types of statements in your script.

We'll look at how to use the Script Editor in more detail later in the chapter.

The Errors Box. The *Errors combo box* is used to display syntax and compilation errors. For example, Figure 18.9 shows how a simple syntax error is detected and reported.

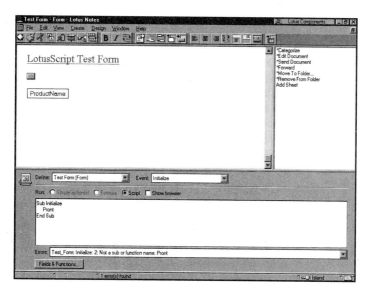

Fig. 18.9 How a syntax error is displayed.

III

Working with LotusScript

Using the Script Editor

If you can use a text editor, you can use the Script Editor! It works just like most text editors and supports the familiar key combinations for moving the cursor and for cutting, copying, and pasting text. For example:

- **Home** moves the cursor to the start of the current line.

- **End** moves the cursor to the end of the current line.

- **Ctrl+C** copies the selected text to the clipboard.

- **Ctrl+V** pastes text into the Script Editor from the Clipboard.

> **Caution**
>
> The Script Editor does not have an Undo feature, so be careful when you are editing!

Configuring the Script Editor

New to the Script Editor in Release 4.5 of Notes is its capability to choose the font used by the Script Editor, and to display different types of statements in different colors. You can choose color for:

- Identifiers

- Keywords

- Comments

- Directives

- Errors

To define the font and colors, follow these steps:

1. Right-click the Script Editor. A pop-up menu is displayed.

2. Select Design Pane Properties. The Design pane properties are displayed in the Properties InfoBox as shown in Figure 18.10.

Fig. 18.10   You use the Design Pane Properties InfoBox to configure the Script Editor.

3. Select the Script radio button.

4. Select the font type and size you want to use.

5. Choose a color for each type of statement.

Entering Code

Follow these steps to enter code:

1. Select the object or action with which you will work.

2. Select the event to which the code will be attached.

3. Type the code into the Script Editor.

You may select the object or action to be programmed in different ways. For example, to select an object you may do one of the following:

- Select its name from the drop-down list in the Define box.
- Click the object in the Form Layout pane.

To select an action to program, you can do one of the following:

- Select its name from the drop-down list in the Define box.
- Click the action in the action pane.

The Script Editor automatically checks the syntax of your code as you enter it. For example, as soon as you make a typing mistake, the Script Editor lets you know by displaying an error in the Errors Box. If you have configured the colors for the Script Editor, the error is highlighted in the color you chose for errors. Keywords, identifiers, comments, and directives are also highlighted when the Script Editor identifies them.

The code you enter using the Script Editor is stored in a LotusScript module. Notes stores a separate module for each form, view, and agent that you design. Some of the names listed in the Define box refer to parts of the LotusScript module rather than to objects or actions. The parts of the module that you use are:

- The (Options) part of the (Globals) section.
- The (Declarations) part of the (Globals) section.

You use the (Options) part to define options that affect the entire LotusScript module that you are writing. For example, if you want to use the Option Declare statement to make sure that all variable names are declared, you add it to the (Options) part of the (Globals) section. The (Declarations) section is where you define the data types and variables used by your module.

The Script Editor attempts to complete blocks of code and moves them to the correct location. For example, if you begin a Type statement on a new line in your script by entering **Type MyTypeName** and pressing Enter, the Script Editor automatically moves it to the (Declarations) part and adds the matching End Type statement. The Script Editor automatically moves the following blocks of code to the correct location:

- Type—Enter **Type** followed by the name of the type and press Enter. The Script Editor creates an empty Type...End Type block and adds it to the end of the (Declarations) section.

- Dim—If you type a Dim statement anywhere outside of a sub or function, the Script Editor moves the Dim statement to the end of the (Declarations) section.

- Function—Type **Function** followed by the name of the function and press Enter. The Script Editor creates an empty Function...End Function block and adds the name of the Function to the Event box.

- Sub—Type **Sub** followed by the name of the Sub and press Enter. The Script Editor creates an empty Sub...End Sub block and adds the name of the Sub to the Event box.

- Option—Type any of the LotusScript Option statements, such as Option Declare or Option Base and the Script Editor moves the statement to the end of the (Options) section.

- Class—If you begin a class definition by typing **Class** followed by a class name and pressing Enter, the Script Editor moves the definition to the (Declarations) section and adds an End Class statement for you.

- Property—For either Property Set or Property Get, the Script Editor automatically creates a new block for the property and adds its name to the Event box.

The Script Editor also completes the following blocks of code for you:

- **For loops**—Type in the first line of the loop and press Enter. The terminating Next is automatically added for you.

- **Forall loops**—The terminating End Forall is added when you press Enter after typing the first line.

- **If statements**—The End If is added for you.

- **Select statements**—The End Select is automatically added.

- **Do While loops**—The terminating Loop statement is added.

- **While statements**—The terminating Wend is added.

Compiling a Script

The Script Editor automatically compiles your LotusScript code for you. It does so at the following times:

- As you enter the script, the Script Editor partially compiles the script. This is how it detects syntax errors and knows when to complete blocks of code.

- When you save the script or when you click outside of the Script Editor, the Script Editor compiles the entire LotusScript module. It finds those errors that it cannot detect during the partial compilations. For example, this is the time that it can detect a call to a non-existent sub or function.

You cannot save a script that contains compile errors; you must correct them all *before* you save the script.

> ### Tip
>
> If you want to save a script containing errors, you can put %REM and %END REM directives around the part of the script that contains the errors. This comments out the entire section and hides the error so that you can save the script.

Using LotusScript Within Notes

Notes uses an object-oriented, event-driven programming model. The interface between LotusScript and Notes is via a set of object classes—the Notes object classes. Objects of each class generate and respond to different events. For example, a button object can respond to being clicked, or a field object can respond to the cursor being placed in the field. When you program using LotusScript in Notes, you write LotusScript that responds to these events.

You can attach LotusScript to events in the following types of objects:

- Buttons
- Actions
- Hotspots
- Fields
- Forms
- Views and folders
- Databases
- Agents

For each object, you need to know the events that it responds to.

Buttons, Actions, and Hotspots

Buttons, actions, and hotspots respond to the events shown in Table 18.1. The Click event is the one that you will use most often. It is generated whenever the button, action, or hotspot is clicked. The ObjectExecute event is designed so that an OLE2 server application can use NotesFlow to execute Notes actions.

Table 18.1 Button, Action, and Hotspot Object Events

Event	Trigger
Click	When the button, action, or hotspot is selected.
ObjectExecute	When the action is activated by an OLE2 server that is FX/NotesFlow enabled.

The following example shows how to add a button and write some LotusScript to handle the Click event.

1. Create a new blank database.

2. Create a new form in the database. The Forms IDE is displayed.

3. Select Create, Hotspot, Button. A button is added to the form and its Properties InfoBox is displayed.

4. Give the button a label by typing "Hello World!" in the Button label field in the InfoBox.

5. Click the Script Editor pane.

6. Select the Script radio button. By default, the Formula setting is selected for a new button.

7. Add the following code to the `Click` event:

```
Messagebox "Hello World!", 0, "Button Test"
```

8. Select Design, Test Form. You are asked to enter a name for the new form.

9. Enter **Test** as the form name and click OK. The new form is saved and displayed.

10. Click the "Hello World!" button. Your Hello World message box is displayed.

Fields

You can attach LotusScript to the Field object events shown in Table 18.2.

Table 18.2   Field Object Events

Event	Trigger
Entering	When a user places the cursor in the field.
Exiting	When the cursor is moved out of the field.

The `Entering` event is useful for responding to the user placing the cursor in the field. For example, as soon as a user tabs into a field you can enter some data into the field or clear its contents. You may use the `Exiting` event to see if a field has been correctly filled as soon as the user moves the cursor out of the field, rather than waiting until the document is saved. The following sample shows how to use Exiting to help validate a field:

1. Create a new blank database.

2. Create a new form in the database. The Forms IDE is displayed.

3. Select Create, Field. A field is added to the form and its Properties InfoBox is displayed.

4. Use the InfoBox to give the field the name "ProductID."

5. Click the Script Editor pane.

6. In the Event box, select the `Exiting` event.

7. Enter the following script:

```
Sub Exiting(Source As Field)
     Dim uiWorkspace As New NotesUIWorkspace
     Dim uiDoc As NotesUIDocument
     Dim strProductID As String

     Set uiDoc = uiWorkspace.CurrentDocument

     strProductID = uiDoc.FieldGetText("ProductID")
     If Len(strProductID) <> 5 Then
        Messagebox "Please enter a five character product ID", 0, "Re-
                    enter
          Product ID"
          Call uiDoc.GotoField("ProductID")
     End If
     Call uiDoc.FieldSetText("ProductID", strProductID)
End Sub
```

8. Save and test the form. Place the cursor in the ProductID field and press tab to move to the ProductName field. A message box displays to tell you to enter a five-character ID. Click OK and the cursor goes back to the ProductID field.

Forms

The form object (NotesUIDocument) responds to the events listed in Table 18.3. The QueryOpen event occurs when a request has been made to open a document. You can use it to set default values in the document—for example, looking up a set of keyword values from an external database. You can also use QueryOpen to see whether you should allow a document to be opened. For example, you can see who is trying to open the document or its current status before allowing it to be opened. Just after the document has been opened, the PostOpen event occurs. PostOpen keeps a history of who has read a document by adding his or her name to a list each time a PostOpen event occurs.

Table 18.3 Form Object Events	
Event	**The Event Is Triggered...**
PostModeChange	After the form is changed to or from edit mode.
PostOpen	After the form is opened.
PostRecalc	After the form has been refreshed.
QueryClose	Before the form is closed.
QueryModeChange	Before the form is changed to or from edit mode.
QueryOpen	Before the form is opened.
QuerySave	Before the form is saved.

When a document is open, the QueryModeChange and PostModeChange events let you respond to the document being switched to and from edit mode. QueryModeChange occurs just before the document changes mode (either from edit to read mode, or read to edit mode) and PostModeChange occurs just after. You can use QueryModeChange to decide if a user should edit a document. For example, if a document in a workflow system has been marked as an approved document, QueryModeChange can stop it from being edited.

III

Working with LotusScript

The PostRecalc event occurs after all of the formulas on a document's form have been recalculated. QueryClose and QuerySave let you respond to a user's request to close or save a document. For example, you can use QuerySave to check that all of the fields in a document have been filled in correctly.

The following example shows you how to use the PostOpen event to keep a list of the people who have edited a document:

1. Create a new blank database.

2. Create a new form in the database. The Forms IDE is displayed.

3. Select Create, Field. A field is added to the form and its Properties InfoBox is displayed.

4. Use the InfoBox to give the field the name "DocEditors."

5. Click the Script Editor pane.

6. In the Define box, select Untitled (Form), then select Postopen in the Event box.

7. Enter the following code:

```
Sub Postmodechange(Source As Notesuidocument)
    Dim s As New NotesSession
    If Source.EditMode Then
        Call Source.FieldAppendText("DocEditors", s.CommonUserName &
        Chr(10))
    End If
End Sub
```

8. Save the form.

9. Create a document using the form and save it.

10. Edit the document. Your name is automatically added to the DocEditors field each time you edit the document.

Views and Folders

The view and folder object (see the NotesUIView class in Chapter 19) is new to Release 4.5 of Notes. It responds to the events listed in Table 18.4. The QueryOpen occurs just before a view is opened. PostOpen occurs just after a view has opened. When a user attempts to open a document displayed in the view, the QueryOpenDocument event occurs. You can use this event to see whether a document should be opened, or to ask the user to enter some information before he or she can look at the document.

Table 18.4	View and Folder Object Events
Event	**The Event Is Triggered...**
PostDragDrop	After a drag-and-drop operation (Calendar views only).
PostOpen	After the view has opened.
PostPaste	After a document has been pasted into the view.
QueryAddToFolder	Before a document is added to a folder.

Event	The Event Is Triggered...
QueryClose	Before the view is closed.
QueryDragDrop	Before a drag-and-drop operation (Calendar views only).
QueryOpen	Before the view has opened.
QueryOpenDocument	Before a document is opened from the view.
QueryPaste	Before a document is pasted into the view.
QueryRecalc	Before the view is recalculated.
RegionDoubleClick	After a region has been double-clicked (Calendar views only).

There are two events that you can use to process documents that are pasted into the view. QueryPaste occurs just before a document or set of documents is pasted into a view; PostPaste occurs just after. You can use PostPaste to trigger specific processing of the documents that have just been pasted into the view. For example, you can store the date and time that the documents were pasted into the view. The QueryAddToFolder event occurs just before a document is copied to a folder. You can use it to check whether to allow the document to be added to the folder, or to ask the user to enter some filing information about the document. QueryRecalc occurs just before a view is recalculated and gives you the opportunity to stop the recalculation. The QueryClose event occurs just before the view is closed.

There are three events that are designed for use with the new calendar type of view. QueryDragDrop and PostDragDrop occur just before and just after a drag-and-drop operation. You can use them to decide whether to allow the drag-and-drop operation to continue or to perform some processing after the operation has completed. RegionDoubleClick occurs when a user double-clicks a date region in a calendar view.

The following steps show how to use the PostPaste event to store the date and time that a document is pasted into a folder:

1. Create a new discussion database from the Discussion (R4) template.

2. Select <u>D</u>esign, <u>F</u>olders and open the My Favorites folder in design mode. The Views IDE is displayed.

3. Select the PostPaste event in the Event box.

4. Enter the following code:

```
Sub Postpaste(Source As Notesuiview)
    Dim iDoc As Integer
    Dim doc As NotesDocument

    For iDoc = 1 To Source.Documents.Count
        Set doc = Source.Documents.GetNthDocument(iDoc)
        doc.PasteTime = Now
        Call doc.Save(True, True)
    Next
End Sub
```

5. Save the folder.

6. Create a new Main Topic document and save it.

7. Switch to the All Documents view, select the document you just created and copy it to the Clipboard.

8. Switch to the My Favorites folder and paste the document.

9. Check the Properties InfoBox for the document. The date and time that you pasted the document are stored in a new field called `PasteTime`.

Databases

Databases (see the `NotesUIDatabase` class in Chapter 19) respond to the five events shown in Table 18.5. The `PostOpen` event occurs after the database is opened.

> **Note**
>
> The `PostOpen` event for the database occurs after the `QueryOpen` and `PostOpen` events for view open.

Table 18.5   Database Object Events

Event	The Event Is Triggered...
PostDocumentDelete	After a document has been deleted from the database using Cut or Clear.
PostOpen	After the database has been opened.
QueryClose	Before the database is closed.
QueryDocumentDelete	Before a document or group of documents is deleted from the database.
QueryDocumentUndelete	Before a document or group of documents is undeleted.

The `QueryDocumentDelete` event occurs just before a document or documents are deleted from the database. `PostDocumentDelete` occurs just after the documents have been deleted. The `QueryDocumentUndelete` event occurs when a document or set of documents (that have been marked for deletion) are unmarked. `QueryClose` occurs just before the database is closed.

The following steps show how you can use the `PostDocumentDelete` message to automatically mail someone when documents are deleted from a database:

1. Create a new discussion database from the Discussion (R4) template.

2. Select <u>D</u>esign, <u>O</u>thers and open the Database Script.

3. Select the `PostDocumentDelete` event in the Event box.

4. Enter the following code:

```
Sub Postdocumentdelete(Source As Notesuidatabase)

    Dim db As NotesDatabase
    Dim doc As NotesDocument
    Set db = Source.Database
```

```
        Set doc = New NotesDocument( db )
        doc.SaveMessageOnSend = False
        doc.Form = "Memo"
        doc.SendTo = "Tim Vallely"
        doc.Subject = CStr(Source.Documents.Count) & " documents deleted at "
    & CStr(Now) & "."
    Call doc.Send( False )

        End Sub
```

5. Save the script.

6. Exit from the database and reopen it.

7. Create a new Main Topic document and save it.

8. Switch to the All Documents view, select the document you just created and mark it for deletion.

9. Exit from the database and delete the newly created document.

10. A mail message is automatically created and sent.

Agents

An agent is a user procedure that you can use to automate many tasks within Notes, such as the archiving of old documents, or the automatic generation of replies to mail messages. An agent can be triggered in a number of ways, including a menu command, a predefined schedule, the arrival of mail, or the pasting of documents. You can write LotusScript programs to create agents, and you can also use Notes-supplied agents.

Agents run at either of the following locations:

- The user workstation, if the agent's trigger has been set to any of the following: Manually from Actions Menu, Manually from Agent List, If Documents have been Created or Modified, or If Documents have been Pasted.

- The server or workstation containing the agent, if the agent's trigger has been set to either If New Mail Has Arrived or On Schedule.

Whenever an agent is executed, it runs the code attached to the `Initialize` event, so this is where you should put your agent code (see Table 18.6).

Table 18.6   Agent Object Events

Event	Trigger
Initialize	When the agent is started.
Terminate	When the agent is finished.

Using the Debugger

The debugger lets you check how a script is executing, line by line if you like. You can start and stop the script at any time and check the values that have been assigned to specific variables or properties. This can help you to quickly find errors in those scripts that are behaving improperly. The debugger displays its own window showing the script being executed. An arrow indicates which line of script is about to be executed and as lines are executed, the arrow moves to the next line. You can use the debugger to do the following:

- Step through a script a line at a time.

- Set breakpoints in the script so that the script temporarily stops executing at each breakpoint.

- Examine and modify the value of variables and properties.

Enabling the Debugger

When you want to start debugging, you enable the debugger by selecting File, Tools, Debug LotusScript from the Notes menu bar as shown in Figure 18.11.

Fig. 18.11   This figure shows how to enable the debugger.

To disable the debugger just select File, Tools, Debug LotusScript again.

Once the debugger is enabled, it starts automatically when you run any LotusScript. When the debugger starts, it will do the following:

- Display the debugger window (see Figure 18.12).

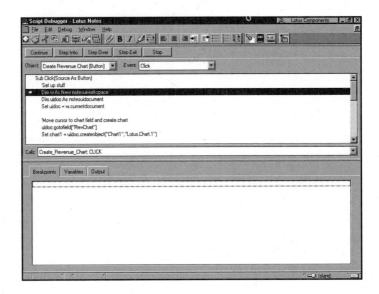

Fig. 18.12   Use the debugger window to find errors in your scripts.

- Highlight the first line in the script.

- Pause execution of the script at the first line.

The debugger window contains a number of areas that we will look at in turn.

The Button Area

You can control how the debugger steps through a script using the five buttons at the top of the screen. The buttons work as follows:

- **Continue**—Continue execution of the script until you reach a breakpoint or the end of the script.

- **Step Into**—Execute the current statement and stop at the next one. If the current statement is a sub or function call, stop at the first executable statement in the sub or function. In addition to clicking the button, you can use Step Into by selecting Debug, Step Into, or pressing F8.

- **Step Over**—Execute the current statement. If the current statement is a call to a sub or function, execute the sub or function and stop at the first statement immediately after the call. If the statement is not a sub or function call, execute the statement and stop at the next statement. You can click the Step Over button, select Debug, Step Over, or press Shift+F8 to use Step Over.

- **Step Exit**—Continue execution of the current sub or function until the end of the sub or function is reached, then stop at the statement immediately following the one that called the sub or function. Use Step Exit by clicking the Step Exit button, selecting Debug, Step Exit, or pressing Ctrl+F8.

- **Stop**—Stop executing the script.

The Object Box

The Object box displays the name of the object containing the script now running. For example, Figure 18.12 shows that the current script is attached to the Create Revenue Chart button. In order to see the code attached to any other objects, select the specific object(s) by using the Object box drop-down list.

The Event Box

The Event box shows the name of the event that the script is attached to. Similar to the Object box, the Event box drop-down list can be used to examine the code attached to any events within the current object. Figure 18.12 shows that the code displayed is attached to the Click event.

The Debug Pane

The Debug pane displays the LotusScript that you are debugging. An arrow points to the line about to be executed.

The Calls Dialog Box

The Calls Dialog box lets you trace the route your script has taken to the current line. Every time a sub or function calls another sub or function, its name is added to the Calls

III

Working with LotusScript

Dialog box, and a history of calls is built up. The subprogram that is being executed is displayed at the top of the list.

The Breakpoints Tab

The breakpoints tab displays any breakpoints that you have set. You can double-click a breakpoint to have the line displayed in the Debug pane. We'll look at breakpoints in more detail later.

The Variables Tab

Figure 18.13 shows the Variables tab, one of the most useful features of the debugger. It shows all the defined variables and lets you examine and change their current value. The Variables tab shows the variable name, its current value, and its type. Twisties are shown next to variables that represent objects or complex data structures. You can use the twisties to expand a variable, showing its properties or component values. You can change the value of a variable by typing a new value into the New Value field.

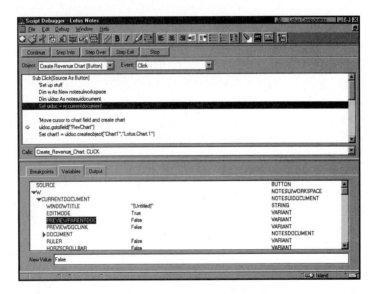

Fig. 18.13   Click the variables tab to display LotusScript variables.

The Output Tab

The Output tab is used to display the output from Print statements in your script.

Using Breakpoints

Breakpoints are a way of interrupting the execution of the script at a specific line. When the script has been interrupted, you may examine the current value of variables and properties. You may use the debugger to do the following:

■ **Set or clear a single breakpoint**— To set a breakpoint, double-click in the debug pane the line that you want to be a breakpoint. A red stop sign appears to the left of the line to show that it is a breakpoint, and the new breakpoint is added to the list of breakpoints shown on the Breakpoint Tab.

- **Clear all breakpoints**—To clear a breakpoint, double-click the line containing the breakpoint you want to clear.

- **Temporarily enable or disable a single breakpoint**—To temporarily disable a breakpoint, select the breakpoint in the Debug pane and select Debug, Disable Breakpoint from the Notes menu bar. The stop sign changes to a yellow slash, indicating that the breakpoint is disabled. To re-enable the breakpoint, select Debug, Enable Breakpoint.

- **Temporarily enable or disable all breakpoints**—To temporarily disable all breakpoints, select Debug, Disable All Breakpoints from the Notes menu bar. You can re-enable all breakpoints by selecting Debug, Enable All Breakpoints.

> **Note**
>
> You can also set and clear breakpoints by selecting Debug, Set/Clear Breakpoint from the Notes menu bar or by pressing the F9 key.

Additional Debugging Techniques

You can use a variety of techniques to test your scripts besides stepping through the code using the debugger.

Using *Messagebox*

You can test your scripts by using the Messagebox statement to display debugging messages. Simply define a debug sub that uses Messagebox to show text that you supply to indicate the progress and status of your script. Then call the debug sub when you need to show debugging information. A debugging sub example is shown below:

```
Sub ShowDebugMsg(strMsg As String)
    Messagebox strMsg, MB_OK, "Debug Message"
End Sub
```

Using *Print*

You may also use the LotusScript Print function. If you are testing a script that runs on a client, Print writes its messages to the Notes status bar. If the script is running on a server, the messages are written to the Notes server log database. When you are debugging your script, the output from Print statements is shown on the debugger output tab.

Using an Error Handler

You may want to define an error-handling routine to catch the error, display some details about it, and continue executing the script, because when the debugger detects an error, it stops executing the script. Include the handler in all event routines that you use so that every error is detected. LotusScript specifies a standard set of errors, and corresponding error numbers (as constants), in the file LSERR.LSS, so remember to use %Include to include this file in your script if you want to use the constants.

The following sample handler pops up a message box to show the error details. If an error occurs anywhere in the script, the code after the lblShowError label is executed, then control is returned to the statement following the one that generated the error. You can easily modify the code to write the error details to a log file for a permanent record of each error.

```
Sub Click(Source As Button)
' Set up the error handler
On Error Goto lblShowError

' Put your button code here . . .

Exit Sub

lblShowError:
    Messagebox "Line: " & CStr(Erl) & " - " & Error(Err), MB_OK,
 "Error: " & CStr(Err)
Resume Next
End Sub
```

Using Dynamic Link Libraries

With LotusScript, you can call functions and subroutines in external function libraries such as dynamic link libraries. You can use the features and functions of the underlying operating system via its programming interface, or you can call functions in your own libraries. For example, when running on Windows 95, you can use LotusScript to call external C language functions in the Windows 95 dynamic link libraries (DLLs). You can call external functions on all of the following platforms:

- Windows 3.1

- Windows 95

- Windows NT

- OS/2

- UNIX

- Macintosh

> **Note**
>
> The functions available and the calling conventions you use differ from platform to platform. If you need to write LotusScript to run on different operating systems, use the %IF directive to check the platform type on which your script is running; then call the appropriate function for that platform. See the LotusScript documentation on %IF for details.

To call a function in an external DLL, follow these steps:

1. Use the LotusScript `Declare` statement in the `Declarations` section of your script to declare a reference to the routine as either a sub or as a function.

2. When the routine has been declared, call it as if it were a LotusScript sub or function.

For example, the following script shows you how to declare and use the external func-tion `GetFreeSystemResources`. This function is available only in Windows 3.1 and returns system information about how Windows is managing its memory. When you run the script on a Windows 3.1 Workstation, it displays the available system resources in the Notes status bar:

```
Sub Click(Source As Button)
    Declare Function GetFreeSystemResources
    Lib "User" (ByVal iFlag As Integer)

    Dim iSystemResources As Integer
    Dim iGDIResources As Integer
    Dim iUserResources As Integer

    Const GFSR_SYSTEMRESOURCES = 0
    Const GFSR_GDIRESOURCES    = 1
    Const GFSR_USERRESOURCES   = 2

    ' Get the available Memory, GDI and User resources
    iSystemResources = GetFreeSystemResources(GFSR_SYSTEMRESOURCES)
    iGDIResources = GetFreeSystemResources(GFSR_GDIRESOURCES)
    iUserResources = GetFreeSystemResources(GFSR_USERRESOURCES)

    ' Display them on the Notes status bar
    Print "System Resources =" & Str$(iSystemResources)
    Print "GDI Resources =" & Str$(iGDIResources)
    Print "User Resources =" & Str$(iUserResources)
End Sub
```

Tip

LotusScript automatically converts the function name in a `Declare` statement to uppercase. This is fine in Windows 3.1; however, the function names used by Windows 95 and Windows NT are case-sensitive. So, if you call external functions in Windows 95 and Windows NT, you should al-ways use the `Alias` part of the `Declare` statement to specify the function name with the correct case.

By default, arguments are passed to external functions by reference. You can override this for certain types of data and have the argument passed by value using the `ByVal` keyword. For example, the following declarations pass both arguments by value:

```
Declare Function iMax Lib "MYFUNCS" Alias "iMax"
(ByVal iX As Integer, ByVal iY As Integer) As Integer
```

Using *Evaluate* and *Execute*

The LotusScript `Evaluate` and `Execute` functions let you compile and execute Notes @functions and LotusScript programs "on-the-fly." Use `Evaluate` to calculate an @func-tion formula. You supply two arguments, both the @function formula and the object used to execute that formula. For example, you can run the @function shown in the next example against a particular Notes document to display the total size of all attached files:

```
Sub Click(Source As Button)
    Const STR_FORMULA = "@if(@Attachments > 0; @Sum(@AttachmentLengths); 0)"
    Dim varTotalSize As Variant
    Dim uiWorkspace As New NotesUIWorkspace
    Dim uiDoc As NotesUIDocument
    Dim doc As NotesDocument

    Set uiDoc = uiWorkSpace.CurrentDocument
    Set doc = uiDoc.Document
    varTotalSize = Evaluate(STR_FORMULA, doc)
    Messagebox "Total size of all attached files is
" & CStr(varTotalSize(0)) & " bytes."
End Sub
```

Note

You must define a formula to Evaluate when the LotusScript is compiled, so you can't use a variable to define the formula. However, after we've looked at the Execute function, we'll look at a way of fooling LotusScript so that you can define a formula at runtime to use with Evaluate.

Using the Execute function, you can compile and execute a text string as a LotusScript program. LotusScript takes the contents of the string, compiles it, and runs it as a separate program. If you want to pass data between your main program and the program created by the Execute function, you can declare variables as Public. In this way, both programs have access to the variable and can use it to pass data back and forth between them. The following example uses a separate script to add the number "one" to another number.

First, in the (Declarations) section of the script, declare a Public variable to pass the number to and from the script being run by the Execute function:

```
Public piTempNumber As Integer
```

Tip

As a convention, consider starting the names of Public variables with the letter *p* so that it's easy to tell that they are public.

Then, declare a sub to build a mini-program and call Execute to run the mini-program and display the results:

```
Sub Increment(iNumber As Integer)
    Dim strScript As String
    piTempNumber = iNumber
    strScript = ¦piTempNumber = piTempNumber + 1¦
    Execute(strScript)
    Messagebox CStr(piTempNumber)
End Sub
```

Finally, create a button on the form in order to call the new sub:

```
Sub Click(Source As Button)
    Dim i As Integer
    i = 3
    Increment i
End Sub
```

When you click the button, the `Increment` sub is called and the mini-program (which will add "one" to the supplied number) is compiled and executed.

Although this is a simple example, it demonstrates how powerful this feature is. You can use `Execute` to compile and run any text as a LotusScript program. For example, you can combine `Evaluate` and `Execute` to avoid the problem of supplying the formula to `Evaluate` as a constant. You will first need to declare a `Public` variable to get the resulting formula:

```
Public pvarResult As Variant
```

Then, create a sub that creates and executes a mini-program using the supplied string as a formula:

```
Sub ExecuteFormula(strFormula As String, varResult As Variant)
    Dim strScript As String

    ' Create a mini-program with the supplied formula and
    ' assign the result to a Public variable so that the
    ' main program can get at it.
    strScript = ¦Const STR_FORMULA = "¦ & strFormula & ¦"
                Dim uiWorkspace As New NotesUIWorkspace
                Dim uiDoc As NotesUIDocument
                Dim doc As NotesDocument
                Set uiDoc = uiWorkSpace.CurrentDocument
                Set doc = uiDoc.Document
                pvarResult = Evaluate(STR_FORMULA, doc) ¦

    ' Run the mini-program
    Execute(strScript)

    ' Save the result returned by the formula
    varResult = pvarResult
End Sub
```

To call the new sub, add a button to a form and use the following script to pass a formula to the new sub:

```
Sub Click(Source As Button)
    Dim strFormula As String
    Dim varResult As Variant
    strFormula = Inputbox$("Enter a Notes formula to
    calculate for the current document:")
On Error Goto lblExecutionError
    Call ExecuteFormula(strFormula, varResult)
    Messagebox "The result of calculating " &
strFormula & " is " & CStr(varResult(0))
```

```
lblExit:
    Exit Sub

lblExecutionError:

    Messagebox "Unable to calculate the formula for this document."
    Resume lblExit
End Sub
```

To test the new sub, following these steps:

1. Click the button.

2. Type a formula, such as **@attachments**, into the input box and click OK.

3. A message box is displayed as shown in Figure 18.14.

Fig. 18.14 A message box showing the results of executing a Notes formula.

LotusScript Extensions

LotusScript extensions, or LSXs, are just that—extensions to LotusScript. A software developer or tools vendor can use them to add extra classes to Notes. For example, IBM has produced a set of LotusScript extensions for MQ Series Link for Lotus Notes that lets you access transactions and data on other systems. Lotus has used LSXs to add three classes to Notes that you can use to access ODBC data sources.

> **Note**
>
> For more information on MQ Series Link for Lotus Notes, point your Web client to **http://www.hursley.ibm.com/mqseries**.

To use a LotusScript extension, include the UseLSX statement in the (Options) part of the (Global) section of a script. For example, to use the ODBC LotusScript Extensions in a script, add the following line to the (Options) part:

```
UseLSX "*LSXODBC"
```

The command loads the DLL that contains the three classes that form the ODBC extensions to LotusScript.

From Here...

This chapter has shown you how to use LotusScript within Notes. You should now be familiar with the Notes Integrated Development Environment (IDE), the script editor, and the debugger. You have learned how to use dynamic link libraries from within LotusScript and taken a quick look at LotusScript extensions. Now that you know about writing LotusScript in Notes, it's time to look at how you can access all of the functionality of Notes from within LotusScript. To learn more, read the following:

- Chapter 19, "More LotusScript," covers all of the Notes object classes and describes how and where to use them in your LotusScript programs.

- "ODBC and Lotus Components" on the CD-ROM describes how to use the ODBC LotusScript extensions and how to work with the recently available Lotus components.

Chapter 19

More LotusScript

In previous chapters, you learned about the basics of the LotusScript language, the nuts and bolts needed to start building simple LotusScript programs. In this chapter, we look at the Lotus Notes Object classes and how you can use them to build more sophisticated Notes applications that exploit the full power of both LotusScript and Notes. The key to building these applications is a good understanding of the Lotus Notes object classes.

Understanding the Lotus Notes Object Classes

The Lotus Notes object classes let you use LotusScript to access databases, views, documents, and items. For example, from your LotusScript programs, you can use the Notes object classes to create, open, or delete databases and add, modify, or delete documents in those databases. In this chapter, we take a detailed look at each of the Notes object classes and see how each one can best be used from LotusScript. But before that, we need to differentiate between the different class types.

There are two types of classes that let you work with Notes objects: front-end, or user interface (UI) classes, and back-end classes.

> **Note**
>
> The two types of classes we look at in this chapter are not the only classes available to you from LotusScript. Other types of classes can be added as LotusScript extensions, such as the Open Database Connectivity (ODBC) classes explained in more detail on the CD.

The UI classes let you work with databases, views, and documents that are displayed in the active Notes window. For example, you can work with the document that is currently on-screen using the NotesUIDocument class. The methods and properties of the UI classes let you work with views and documents in the same way a user can. You can type text into fields, move the cursor around, use the Clipboard, and refresh views.

Some of the main topics in this chapter are

- The difference between front-end and back-end classes

- The 25 Lotus Notes object classes

- How to use the properties and methods of each class in your LotusScript programs

III

Working with LotusScript

There are four UI classes that are represented:

- The Notes Workspace

- The current document

- The current view

- The current database

We cover these classes first when we look at the classes in detail.

The second type of class, the back-end classes, represents the constituent parts of Notes. They include some obvious elements such as databases, views, documents, fields, and some more abstract concepts, such as sessions and collections of documents.

You need to understand the difference between the two types of classes mainly because they are interlinked. For example, a document displayed on-screen has two different representations: the UI document and the back-end document. When you type data into the UI document, the corresponding back-end document is not updated until you save your changes. Conversely, if an agent updates the back-end part of a document, the UI document does not display the changes until it is refreshed. We'll look at some of the methods you can use to keep both parts of the document in step.

The rest of the chapter looks at each class in detail. Let's start at the Notes workspace by looking at the NotesUIWorkspace class.

NotesUIWorkspace

The NotesUIWorkspace class represents the current Notes workspace window. It lets you use LotusScript to perform some of the actions that you normally perform from the Notes workspace, such as opening databases or creating and editing documents. If a document is already displayed in the active window or highlighted in a view, you can use this class to work with the document.

The class has only one property, CurrentDocument, which you use to get the current document. After you have the document, you typically use the properties and methods of the NotesUIDocument class to work with it. For example, the following script finds the current document and displays the value of a field called 'Title' in a message box:

```
Dim uiWorkspace as New NotesUIWorkspace
Dim uiDoc as NotesUIDocument
Set uiDoc = uiWorkspace.CurrentDocument
MessageBox(uiDoc.FieldGetText("Title"))
```

The NotesUIWorkspace class has ten methods that let you open databases and URLs, create and edit documents, check for alarms, and refresh views. You add a database to your workspace using the AddDatabase method. You supply the server and filename for the database, and it is added to the current workspace tab. You open a database by using the OpenDatabase method, the LotusScript equivalent of the @command, FileOpenDatabase. If you compare the OpenDatabase method with the FileOpenDatabase @Command, you see that their parameters are very similar. The FileOpenDatabase method accepts up to six parameters. The first two parameters specify the server and file name of the database to open. You use the remaining parameters to specify how to open the database. You can open the database at a specific view or navigator.

For example, you can supply the name or alias of a view as the third parameter to have the database open at that view. If the first column in the view is sorted, you can supply a key as a fourth parameter. In this case, the database is opened at the view you specify and the first document matching the key is highlighted. Alternatively, you can use the third and fourth parameters to open a navigator. You supply the name of a navigator as the third parameter and True or False as the fourth parameter to indicate whether the navigator should be opened in its own window. The fifth parameter specifies whether the view or navigator is opened in a new window, even if there is already an open window that contains the view or navigator. Specify True to have a new window opened, or False to use an existing window. The last parameter is used to indicate whether the database should be opened without adding it to your workspace. Specify True to open the database temporarily or False to add the database to your workspace.

So, to open a database from a button, use the following LotusScript:

```
Sub Click(Source As Button)
  Dim uiWorkspace As New NotesUIWorkspace
  Call uiWorkspace.OpenDatabase("Emerald", "Sales\Quota.nsf", "Weekly
Totals", "Northern", True, False)
End Sub
```

This opens the database QUOTA.NSF in the SALES directory on server Emerald at the Weekly Totals view and selects the Northern region sales totals document. The last two parameters ensure that a new window is opened for the view and that the database is always added to the user's workspace.

You can also use the FileOpenDatabase method to open a navigator. Instead of a view name you supply the name of a navigator, and instead of a key you supply True or False to specify whether the navigator should open in its own window. The other parameters are the same as for opening a view. For example, the following script opens a navigator called Main Navigator in its own window:

```
Sub Click(Source As Button)
  Dim uiWorkspace As New NotesUIWorkspace
  Call uiWorkspace.OpenDatabase("Emerald", "Sales\Quota.nsf", "Main
Navigator", True, True, False)
End Sub
```

After you select a document in a view, you can open it by using the EditDocument method. So, to have the button open the Northern sales totals document in edit mode, use the following updated script:

```
Sub Click(Source As Button)
  Dim uiWorkspace As New NotesUIWorkspace
  Dim uiDoc as NotesUIDocument
```

```
   Call uiWorkspace.OpenDatabase("Emerald", "Sales\Quota.nsf", "Weekly
Totals", "Northern", True, True)
   Set uiDoc = uiWorkspace.EditDocument(True)
End Sub
```

To open the document in read mode, specify `False` as the parameter to `EditDocument`.

You can create new documents in a database by using the `ComposeDocument` method. For example, the following script creates a sales totals document for the Eastern region whenever the button is clicked:

```
Sub Click(Source As Button)
   Dim uiWorkspace As New NotesUIWorkspace
   Dim uiDoc as NotesUIDocument
   Set uiDoc = uiWorkspace.ComposeDocument("Emerald", "Sales\Quota.nsf",
"Sales Totals")
   Call uiDoc.FieldSetText("Region", "Eastern")
End Sub
```

A new method in Release 4.5 is `EditProfile`. You can use `EditProfile` to create or edit a hidden profile document in the current database. A profile document lets you store and update database specific information. You open a World Wide Web page by using the `URLOpen` method. You can specify the URL along with some parameters that specify whether to find the latest copy of the Web page. Alternatively, if you don't supply any parameters, `URLOpen` displays the Open URL dialog box for you to enter the URL you want to open.

`EnableAlarms` and `CheckAlarms` let you use the alarm feature of the new Release 4.5 calendar. `EnableAlarms` starts the process that monitors alarms. Then, after this process is running, `CheckAlarms` lets you check whether any alarms are scheduled.

You can use the `DialogBox` method to really spice up your user interfaces. It displays the current document in a dialog box by using the form you specify. This is really useful when the form contains a single layout region because, in this case, the form behaves just like a standard dialog box. You fill in the fields and press OK or Cancel when you're done. The neat part is that if the form you specify has any field names in common with the current document, the contents of those fields are displayed in the dialog box. If the user changes the contents of any of the fields and clicks OK, the corresponding fields in the current document are updated.

To see a good example of how a form is displayed in a dialog box, create a new memo in your Mail database and click the Delivery Options button. The Delivery Options form is displayed in a dialog box, and any of the values you enter are updated in the Memo when you click OK.

The last method in the `NotesUIWorkspace` class is `ViewRefresh`. You use `ViewRefresh` to refresh either the view that is currently displayed or, if a document is currently displayed, the view from which the document was selected. Refreshing a displayed view is straightforward; just call `ViewRefresh` and you're done. Things get a little more complicated when you want to refresh a view from within a newly created document because you first need to refresh the back-end view, using the `Refresh` method of the `NotesView` class, so that the new document is included in the view. Then you need to refresh the front-end view by using the `NotesUIWorkspace ViewRefresh` method so that the updated view is displayed.

Table 19.1 lists all properties of `NotesUIWorkspace`, and Table 19.2 lists the methods.

> **Note**
>
> The properties and methods shown in the tables in italics are new in Release 4.5.

Table 19.1 *NotesUIWorkspace* **Properties**

Property	Description	Data Type	Usage
CurrentDocument	The document that is currently being displayed.	NotesUIDocument	Read Only

Table 19.2 *NotesUIWorkspace* **Methods**

Method	Description	Return Data Type	Return Value
AddDatabase	Add a new database to the workspace.	None	None
CheckAlarms	Check for new alarms in the mail database.	None	None
Compose Document	Create a new UI document in a specified database by using a specified form and display it in edit mode.	Notes UIDocument	The new UI document
DialogBox	Display a dialog box with OK and Cancel buttons that contains the current document displayed by using a form you specify.	Boolean	True if the user selects OK on the dialog box
EditDocument	True to open the current document in edit mode. False to open it in read mode.	Notes UIDocument	The UI document just opened
EditProfile	Create a new profile document or open an existing profile document in edit mode.	None	None
EnableAlarms	Set to True to start the background process that checks for alarms.	Boolean	True if the process is enabled.
OpenDatabase	Open a database at a specified view and optionally highlight a specific document.	None	None

III

Working with LotusScript

(continues)

		Return Data	
Method	**Description**	**Type**	**Return Value**
URLOpen	Open a Uniform Resource Locator (URL).	None	None
ViewRefresh	Refresh the current view.	None	None

NotesUIDocument

The NotesUIDocument class lets you work with the active document—that is, the document that is currently open on your workspace or highlighted in a view. You use this class to do the following:

- Update the contents of the fields in a document

- Position the cursor within a document

- Create and manipulate objects

- Change how a document is displayed

- Mail, forward, or delete a document

Let's look at these options in more detail. Table 19.3 lists all properties of the NotesUIDocument class, and Table 19.4 lists its methods.

Table 19.3 *NotesUIDocument* **Properties**

Property	**Description**	**Data Type**	**Usage**
AutoReload	Set to True to automatically update the currently displayed document to reflect any changes that have been made to its associated back-end document. Read to check the current setting.	Boolean	Read/Write
CurrentField	The name of the field that the cursor is in.	String	Read Only
Document	The back-end document associated with the current UI document.	NotesDocument	Read Only
EditMode	Set to True to put the current UI document into edit mode or read to check whether the current UI document is in edit mode.	Boolean	Read/Write

Property	Description	Data Type	Usage
FieldHelp	Set to True (when the UI document is in edit mode) to display field help. Read to check whether field help is currently displayed.	Boolean	Read/Write
HiddenChars	Set to True (when the UI document is in edit mode) to display hidden formatting characters. Read to check the current setting.	Boolean	Read/Write
HorzScrollBar	Set to True to display the horizontal scroll bar. Read to check whether the horizontal scroll bar is shown.	Boolean	Read/Write
InPreviewPane	True if the document is currently displayed in the preview pane.	Boolean	Read Only
IsNewDoc	True if the document has never been saved.	Boolean	Read Only
PreviewDocLink	Set to True to display the preview pane for a link. Read to check whether the preview pane is shown.	Boolean	Read/Write
PreviewParent Doc	Set to True to display the parent of the current UI document in the preview pane. Read to check whether the preview pane is shown.	Boolean	Read/Write
Ruler	Set to True to display the ruler. Read to check whether the ruler is shown.	Boolean	Read/Write
WindowTitle	The window title for the current displayed document.	String	Read Only

Table 19.4 *NotesUIDocument* **Methods**

Method	Description	Return Data Type	Return Value
Categorize	Put the document into a category.	None	None
Clear	In edit mode only, delete the currently selected text, graphics, or object.	None	None

(continues)

III

Working with LotusScript

Table 19.4 Continued

Method	Description	Return Data Type	Return Value
Close	Close the current UI document.	None	None
CollapseAll Sections	Collapse all the sections in the currently open UI document.	None	None
Copy	Copy the currently selected text, graphics, or object to the Clipboard.	None	None
CreateObject	For a UI document in edit mode with the cursor in a rich text field, create an OLE or ActiveX object.	Variant	A handle to the newly created object
Cut	In edit mode only, cut the currently selected text, graphics, or object from the document and place it on the Clipboard.	None	None
DeleteDocument	In read mode only, mark the document for deletion and then close the document.	None	None
DeselectAll	Deselect any currently selected text, graphics, or objects.	None	None
ExpandAll Sections	Expand all the sections in the currently open UI document.	None	None
FieldAppend Text	In edit mode only, append the supplied text to the contents of a named field (or the current field if no name is supplied).	None	None
FieldClear	In edit mode only, clear the contents of a named field (or the current field if no name is supplied).	None	None
FieldContains	True if a named field (or the current field if no name is supplied) contains the specified text.	Boolean	True if the field contains the text you specified.

Method	Description	Return Data Type	Return Value
FieldGetText	Get the contents of a named field (or the current field if no name is supplied). Convert the contents into a text string.	String	The contents of the field converted into a text string
FieldSetText	In edit mode only, set the contents of a named field (or the current field if no name is supplied) to the supplied value. Automatically convert the supplied value to the correct type for the field.	None	None
FindFreeTime Dialog	Display the Free Time dialog box.	None	None
Forward	Create a mail memo containing the currently open UI document.	None	None
GetObject	Given the name of an OLE or ActiveX object, return a handle to the object found.	Variant	A handle to the object
GotoBottom	In edit mode only, put the cursor in the last editable field.	None	None
GotoField	In edit mode only, put the cursor in the named field.	None	None
GotoNextField	In edit mode only, put the cursor in the next editable field below and to the right of the current cursor position.	None	None
GotoPrevField	In edit mode only, put the cursor in the next editable field above and to the left of the current cursor position.	None	None
GotoTop	In edit mode only, put the cursor in the first editable field.	None	None
InsertText	In edit mode only, insert the supplied text at the current cursor position.	None	None

III

Working with LotusScript

(continues)

Table 19.4 Continued

Method	Description	Return Data Type	Return Value
Paste	In edit mode only, paste the contents of the Clipboard at the current cursor position.	None	None
Print	Print the current document. Optionally display the File Print dialog box.	None	None
Refresh	In edit mode only, compute all the formulas for the computed fields in the document.	None	None
RefreshHide Formulas	Compute all the hide-when formulas in the document.	None	None
Reload	In edit mode, update the UI document with any changes that have been made to the associated back-end document.	None	None
Save	In edit mode only, save the document.	None	None
SaveNewVersion	In edit mode only, save the document as a new version (provided the document's form has the appropriate version-ing options enabled).	None	None
SelectAll	In edit mode, select the contents of the current field. In read mode, select the contents of the entire document.	None	None
Send	Mail the document.	None	None

Updating Fields

The NotesUIDocument class lets you access the data stored in the fields within a document. Depending on what you want to do, there are two groups of methods that you can use: those starting with Field and those starting with Goto. The Field methods are most useful when you need to refer to a field by name. If you know the position of the field within the document or want to move the cursor within the document, use the Goto methods.

Let's look at the `Field` methods first. There are five of them, and each expects you to supply a field name as its first parameter. A nice twist is that, if you supply a blank field name, the method assumes you're referring to the current field. You can find the name of the current field by querying the `CurrentField` property. After you've identified a field, you can get its contents with the `FieldGetText` method. This returns the contents of the field you specify, converted to a text string. If you want to change the contents of a field, use `FieldSetText`, `FieldAppendText`, or `FieldClear`. `FieldSetText` replaces the current contents of the field with the text you supply. `FieldAppendText` is similar, but it appends the text to the current value of the field rather than replace it. `FieldClear` deletes the contents of the field. If you need to check whether a field contains a specific text value, use `FieldContains`. You supply the field name and a value to look for, and the method returns True if the value occurs anywhere within the field. For example, when added to the `QuerySave` event of a form containing two editable text fields, `Title` and `Priority`, the following script checks whether the `Title` field contains the word `Urgent` and, if it does, sets the field `Priority` to `High`:

```
Sub QuerySave(Source As Notesuidocument, Continue As Variant)
    If source.FieldContains("Title", "Urgent") Then
        Call source.FieldSetText("Priority", "High")
    End If
End Sub
```

The other way of working with fields is to move the cursor into a field and then work with its contents. There are five methods that let you do this. If you know the name of the field where you want to put the cursor, use the `GotoField` method. You supply the name of the field, and the method places the cursor in that field. `GotoTop` moves the cursor to the first editable field in the document, while its companion, `GotoBottom`, places the cursor in the last editable field. If you want to navigate through the fields in a document, use `GotoNextField`; use `GotoPrevField` to move the cursor from field to field.

> **Tip**
>
> The document must be in edit mode for these methods to work.

After the cursor is in a field, you can use any of the `Field` methods with a blank field name to work with the field contents. Alternatively, you can use `InsertText`, or a combination of the `SelectAll` method and the Clipboard methods `Cut`, `Copy`, `Paste`, and `Clear`.

Use `InsertText` to add some text into a field at the current cursor position. To copy the contents of the current field to the Clipboard, use `SelectAll` to highlight the field contents, and then use `Cut` or `Copy` to copy the contents to the Clipboard. After you have some data on the Clipboard, you can use `Paste` to paste the Clipboard data into a field. If you want to delete the contents of the field, use the `Clear` method.

The following button script, when executed in a form containing two fields, `Title` and `History`, selects and then copies the contents of the first editable field, `Title`, to the `History` field and then appends the current date to the `History` field. Make sure that you enter some text into the `Title` field; otherwise, there is nothing to select, and you'll get an error.

III

Working with LotusScript

```
Sub Click(Source as Button)
    Dim uiWorkspace As New NotesUIWorkspace
    Dim uiDoc As NotesUIDocument
    Set uiDoc = uiWorkspace.CurrentDocument
    Call uiDoc.GotoTop
    Call uiDoc.SelectAll
    Call uiDoc.Copy
    Call uiDoc.GotoField("History")
    Call uiDoc.Paste
    Call uiDoc.InsertText(" " & Date$)
End Sub
```

Working with Objects

A powerful feature of the `NotesUIDocument` class is its capability to work with OLE objects. When a document is in edit mode with the cursor in a rich text field, you can use the `CreateObject` method to create and insert a new OLE object. If you don't supply any parameters to the method, Notes displays the Create Object dialog box so you can choose the type of object to create from the list. Alternatively, you can supply parameters to define the type of object to create. The first parameter is the name of the new object. You can use this name later to refer to the object from within a script. Then, depending on the type of object you want to create, you specify either the type of object, or the path to a file containing the object.

For example, to automatically create a new Lotus Project Scheduler Component whenever a new document is created, use the following:

```
Sub PostOpen(source As NotesUIDocument)
    Dim objNewSchedule As Variant
    If source.IsNewDoc Then
        Set objNewSchedule = source.CreateObject("Project Schedule",
"Lotus.Project.1")
    End If
End Sub
```

This automatically creates the new scheduler component in the first rich text field in the document.

To create an Excel Spreadsheet object from an existing file, in a rich text field called Sheet in an open document, use the following button script:

```
Sub Click(Source As Button)
    Dim uiWorkspace As New NotesUIWorkspace
    Dim uiDoc As NotesUIDocument
    Set uiDoc = uiWorkspace.CurrentDocument
    Call uiDoc.GotoField("Sheet")
    Call uiDoc.CreateObject("Expenses", "", "C:\EXPENSES.XLS")
End Sub
```

Note

With `CreateObject`, you supply either the object type or the file name, not both.

If a document contains an object, you can get the OLE handle to the OLE object by using the `GetObject` method. You supply the name of the object; the method returns either the handle to it or `Nothing`, if it cannot find the object.

For example, to get the handle to the Excel Spreadsheet created in the last example, use the following:

```
Dim uiWorkspace As New NotesUIWorkspace
Dim uiDoc As NotesUIDocument
Dim objSheet As Variant
Set uiDoc = uiWorkspace.CurrentDocument
Set objSheet = uiDoc.GetObject("Expenses")
```

Changing How the Document Is Displayed

You can set a number of properties to change how the current document is displayed. You can turn field help on or off by using the `FieldHelp` property. Set the `Ruler` property to show or hide the ruler, and `HorzScrollBar` to add or remove the scroll bar at the bottom of the document. When you need to show or hide the preview pane, you can use either `PreviewDocLink` or `PreviewParentDoc`, as appropriate. You can check whether the document is displayed in the preview pane by checking its `InPreviewPane` property.

> **Note**
>
> The `PreviewParent` property has a corresponding @command, `ShowHideParentPreview`, that lets you show and hide the preview pane.

If you need to switch the document from read to edit mode, or vice versa, set the `EditMode` property. After the document is in edit mode, you can use the `HiddenChars` property to have fields display their formatting characters, such as carriage returns and tabs.

You can also set the title that Notes displays for the document by using the `WindowTitle` property.

Several of the `NotesUIDocument` properties and methods deal with how and when the document is updated. The `AutoReload` property is used to make sure that the displayed document is always refreshed whenever its corresponding back-end document changes. The default for `AutoReload` is True, so unless you change it, your document is always kept in step with its back-end document. If you set `AutoReload` to False, you need to use the `Reload` method to update the displayed document to include any changes that have been made to its back-end document.

> **Note**
>
> `Reload` does not update the look of any rich text items that were changed in the back-end document until you close and reopen the document.

The Refresh method recalculates all the computed fields in the document, just as if you'd pressed F9. The RefreshHideFormulas method recalculates all of the hide-when formulas for the current document. You typically use RefreshHideFormulas when a value has changed in the document that may affect how you want to display the document. For example, you may want to show or hide a section within a document, depending on the value of a field. When that field value changes, call RefreshHideFormulas to make sure that the section is shown or hidden, as appropriate.

While we're on the subject of sections, you can change the way all sections within the current document are displayed by using the CollapseAllSections and ExpandAllSections methods. No prizes for guessing what these methods do!

Working with the Document

After you have an open document in front of you, what can you do with it? For a start, you can check whether it's a new document or not using the IsNewDoc property. The property returns True if the document has never been saved to disk. You can print the document by using the Print method. You can have Notes display the File Print dialog box by calling the method with no parameters. Alternatively, you can supply parameters for the number of copies to print, the start and end pages, and whether to print in draft mode. If you use these parameters, Notes prints your document without displaying the File Print dialog box.

You can categorize the document by using Categorize. You supply the name of a category, and the method places the document in that category. If the document is mail-enabled—that is, it contains a SendTo field—you can use Send to mail it to the list of recipients in the SendTo field. If the document contains a CopyTo or BlindCopyTo field, the recipients named in these fields are also mailed a copy of the document. You can forward a copy of the document by using the Forward method. Forward creates a new mail memo containing the document, and you complete and mail the memo as you would any other mail memo.

After you're done with the document, you can close it by calling the Close method. If you've made any changes to the document, Notes asks whether you would like to save your changes. If you're *really* done with document, provided that the document is in read mode, you can delete it by using the DeleteDocument method. This method closes the document and marks it for deletion, the same way you mark documents for deletion in a view. The document is deleted only when you refresh the view, or exit from the database and choose to delete marked documents.

Saving Your Changes

After you have finished making changes to a document, there are two methods that let you save your changes. The Save method saves the document to disk in exactly the same way as choosing File, Save from the menu. The SaveNewVersion method saves a new version of the document. For SaveNewVersion to work, the document's form must have the following settings:

■ Versioning must be switched on—that is, the Versioning setting for the form must be one of the following:

New versions become responses
Prior versions become responses
New versions become siblings

■ Versions must be created manually—that is, the Create Versions setting must be Manual—File, New Version.

If both of these conditions are met, SaveNewVersion creates a new version of the appropriate type.

NotesUIView

The NotesUIView class is new in Release 4.5 and represents the currently displayed view. There are no methods associated with the class. Its three properties are shown in Table 19.5.

Table 19.5 *NotesUIView* Methods

Property	Description	Data Type	Usage
CalendarDateTime	Only applicable in calendar views. The date and time of the selected area.	String	Read Only
Documents	A collection of all of the documents in the current view.	Notes Document Collection	Read Only
View	The back-end view that corresponds to the current view.	NotesView	Read Only

CalendarDateTime is designed to be used with the new Release 4.5 calendar view. It returns a string containing the date and time associated with the area that is currently selected in the calendar view. The Documents property returns a NotesDocumentCollection object that contains all of the documents in the view. You use the View property to access the back-end NotesView object that corresponds to the view you are working with.

NotesUIDatabase

The NotesUIDatabase class represents the Notes database that is currently open. Its two properties and one method are shown in Tables 19.6 and 19.7.

Table 19.6 *NotesUIDatabase* Properties

Property	Description	Data Type	Usage
Database	The back-end database that corresponds to the current database.	NotesDatabase	Read Only
Documents	A collection of all the documents in the current database.	NotesDocument-Collection	Read Only

Table 19.7 *NotesUIDatabase* **Methods**

Method	Description	Return Data Type	Return Value
OpenView	Given the name of a view in the current database, open the view.	None	None

The Database and Documents properties let you access some of the back-end objects that correspond to the current database. OpenView lets you open a view in the database.

NotesSession

Enough of the UI classes! Let's take a look at our first back-end class, NotesSession. The NotesSession class is the parent of all the back-end classes and represents the environment of the current script.

You can use NotesSession classes to answer the following questions about the current script:

- In which database is the script running?
- Is the script running on a Notes server or workstation?
- If running on a server, what is the server name?
- If running on a workstation, who is the current user?
- On what version of Notes is the script running?
- On what platform is it running?
- For agents, when was the agent last run, what happened, and was any data saved?

Table 19.8 lists all properties of the NotesSession class, and Table 19.9 shows its methods. You can use NotesSession methods to do the following:

- Read and write to environment variables in the NOTES.INI file
- Open databases
- Create other Notes objects such as NotesDateTime, NotesLog, NotesNewsletter, and NotesDBDirectory
- Mark documents as having been processed by an agent

Let's look at how to find the current database.

Table 19.8 *NotesSession* **Properties**

Property	Description	Data Type	Usage
AddressBooks	The address books that are available to the current script.	Array of Notes Databases	Read Only
CommonUserName	The common name part of the person or server running the script.	String	Read Only
CurrentAgent	The agent, if any, that is currently running.	NotesAgent	Read Only
Current Database	The database in which the script is located.	Notes Database	Read Only
Document Context	For agents that have been started via the Notes API and have created a document, this property returns the newly created back-end document.	Notes Document	Read Only
EffectiveUser Name	If on a workstation, the fully distinguished name of the person running the script. If on a server, the fully distinguished name of the person who last edited the script.	String	Read Only
International	The international settings for the machine on which the script is running.	NotesInternational	Read Only
IsOnServer	True if the script is running on a server. False if the script is running on a workstation.	Boolean	Read Only
LastExitStatus	For agent scripts only. The status code with which the agent ended the last time it ran.	Integer	Read Only
LastRun	For agent scripts only. The date when the agent last ran.	Variant of type DATE	Read Only
NotesVersion	The release of Notes on which the script is running.	String	Read Only
Platform	The type of operating system on which the script is running.	String	Read Only

(continues)

III

Working with LotusScript

Table 19.8   Continued

Property	Description	Data Type	Usage
SavedData	For agent scripts only. A Notes document stored within the database that can be used to store data between executions of the agent.	Notes Document	Read Only
UserName	If on a workstation, the common name of the person running the script. If on a server, the common name of the person who last edited the script.	String	Read Only

Table 19.9   *NotesSession* Methods

Method	Description	Return Data Type	Return Value
CreateDate Range	Create a new NotesDateRange object.	NotesDate Range	The newly created NotesDateRange object
Close	Close the current session.	None	None
CreateDateTime	Given a string representing a valid date and time, create a new NotesDateTime object.	NotesDate Time	The newly created NotesDateTime object
CreateLog	Given a string used to give the log a name, create a new NotesLog object.	NotesLog	The newly created NotesLog object
CreateNews letter	Given a NotesDocument Collection object, create a new Notes Newsletter object.	Notes Newsletter	The newly created NotesNewsletter object
CreateTimer	Create a new NotesTimer object.	NotesTimer	The newly created NotesTimer object
FreeTime Search	Search for free time slots for calendaring and scheduling.	Array of NotesDate Range	An array of NotesDateRange objects representing the available free slots

Method	Description	Return Data Type	Return Value
GetDatabase	Given the server and file name for a database, create a new NotesDatabase object that can be used to access the database and, if possible, open the database.	Notes Database	The newly created NotesDatabase object
GetDbDirectory	Given the name of a server, create a new NotesDbDirectory object that can be used to list the databases on the server.	NotesDb Directory	The newly created NotesDbDirectory object
GetEnvironment String	Given the name of a string environment variable, get its value. When running on a server, get the value from the server's NOTES.INI. When running on a workstation use the current user's NOTES.INI.	Variant	The value of the environment variable
GetEnvironment Value	As in GetEnvironmentString but for a numeric environment variable.	Variant	The value of the environment variable
SetEnvironment Var	Given the name of an environment variable and a new value, store the new value in the appropriate NOTES.INI file. When running on a server, use the server's NOTES.INI. When running on a workstation, use the current user's NOTES.INI.	None	None
Update ProcessedDoc	For agent scripts only, mark a document as having been processed by an agent.	None	None

Finding the Current Database

One of the most common uses of the NotesSession class is to get the name of the current database—that is, the one in which the script is running. The CurrentDatabase property returns a NotesDatabase object representing the database in which the script is running.

The following example displays the name of the database in which the script is run:

```
Dim s As New NotesSession
Dim db as NotesDatabase
Set db = s.CurrentDatabase
MessageBox("This script is running in the database " & db.Title)
```

Using `CurrentDatabase` is a useful technique because it means that you don't have to hard-code the name of the database into your script.

Finding Where a Script Is Running

Use the `NotesSession` class `IsOnServer` property when you need to know whether your script is running on a server or a workstation. If your script is running on a server, `IsOnServer` returns True.

For example, if an agent must be run on a server, the following code displays an appropriate message if you attempt to run it on a workstation:

```
Dim s As New NotesSession
Dim db as NotesDatabase
If Not s.IsOnServer Then
    MessageBox("This script must be run on a server.")
End If
```

Checking Who Is Running the Script

The `NotesSession` class gives you three slightly different ways to find out the name of the person or server running a script.

The `UserName` property returns the fully distinguished name of the current user. For scripts running on a workstation, the current user is the person currently logged on to Notes at the workstation. For scripts running on a server, the current user is always the server. Use this property when it is important that you have the fully distinguished name of the current user.

For example, when I run an agent script manually from the agent menu on my workstation, `UserName` returns `Tim Vallely/EBS`. If I change the script so that it is triggered on schedule hourly and, therefore, runs on the server, `UserName` returns `EBS_N1/EBS`.

When you need only the common name part of a user's name, use the `CommonUserName` property. As its name suggests, this property returns just the common name part of the current user's name. When I run an agent manually from the agent menu on my workstation, `CommonUserName` returns `Tim Vallely`; when I run the same agent on a server, it returns `EBS_N1`.

The third property that gets you a user name is the `EffectiveUserName` property. For scripts running on workstations, this returns exactly the same value as the `UserName` property. The difference occurs for scripts running on servers where `EffectiveUserName` returns the fully distinguished name of the last user to edit the script.

Checking How Notes Is Set Up

You can find out both the type of operating system and the release of Notes on which your script is running. The `Platform` property lets you find the type of operating system. As with many of the other `NotesSession` properties, `Platform` gives you a different answer depending on where the script is running. For scripts running on a workstation, `Platform` returns the type of the workstation operating system. For scripts running on a server, the type of server operating system is returned.

Note

`Platform` does not return the full details of the operating system. For example, `Platform` returns UNIX for all flavors of UNIX: AIX, Sun, HP-UX, and SCO.

Use the `NotesVersion` property of `NotesSession` to find out on which release of Notes the script is running. For example, the following script sets `strVersion` to 'Notes Release 4.5 (International)' when run on my server:

```
Sub Click(Source As Button)
      Dim s As New NotesSession
      Dim strVersion As String
      strVersion = s.NotesVersion
      Messagebox(strVersion)
End Sub
```

You can use the `International` property to check the current international settings, such as the currency symbol and date/time format.

Reading and Writing to Environment Variables

The `NotesSession` class contains three methods to give you access to Notes environment variables stored in the `NOTES.INI` or Preferences file. If your script is running on a server, the server's `NOTES.INI` is used; otherwise, the current user's `NOTES.INI` is used.

You get an environment variable by using either `GetEnvironmentString` or `GetEnvironmentValue`. Use `GetEnvironmentString` to return a string environment variable and `GetEnvironmentValue` to get a numeric environment variable. With each method, you supply the name and type of the environment variable, and the method returns the value. There are two types of environment variables: user variables and system variables. User variable names start with a dollar sign; system variable names don't.

Use `SetEnvironmentVar` to create a new environment variable or change the value of an existing one. You supply the name of the variable and its new value, which must be a string, an integer, or a date. The method converts the supplied value into a text string and writes the text string to the `NOTES.INI` with the name you supplied.

Opening Databases

Use the `GetDatabase` method with a server and file name to open an existing database. Provided the database exists on the specified server with the correct file name, a new `NotesDatabase` object is created and opened. If, for any reason, the database cannot be found, the method returns a closed `NotesDatabase` object. The `GetDbDirectory` method is useful when you need to process a set of databases in the data directory. When supplied with the name of a server, the method returns a `NotesDbDirectory` object, which points to the Notes data directory on that server. You can then use methods in the `NotesDbDirectory` and `NotesDatabase` classes to process the databases in the directory.

Working with Agents

One of the really useful features of the `NotesSession` class is its capability to store information from the last time an agent ran. In this way, you can build up a history of what an agent has done.

There are three properties that you can use from a LotusScript agent to get information about the last time the agent ran.

The `LastRun` property returns the date the agent was last executed, or 11/30/1899 if the agent has never been run before. The following script checks whether an agent has been run before:

```
Sub Initialize
    Dim s As New NotesSession
    Dim datLastRun as Variant
    datLastRun = s.LastRun
    If datLastRun = CDat("11/30/1899") Then
        MessageBox("This agent has not been run before.")
    Else
        MessageBox("This script was last run on " & CStr(datLastRun))
    End If
End Sub
```

The `LastExitStatus` property is the exit code that the Agent Manager returned the last time the current agent ran. If the agent ran without any errors, `LastExitStatus` is 0.

The `SavedData` property returns a `NotesDocument` object that the current agent can use to store data. This is how you save information between runs. For example, suppose that an agent runs every night to check whether anyone has been added to or removed from the ACL for a database. The names of the people in the ACL can be stored in the SavedData document each time the agent runs so that it can then check the saved names against the current names.

There is also one agent-related method in `NotesSession`—the `UpdateProcessedDoc` method. This is used with some of the methods and properties of the `NotesDatabase` class to ensure that documents get processed only once by an agent. We look at an example of how to use `UpdateProcessedDoc` later in the "NotesDatabase" section.

Working with Other *Notes* Objects

You can create several other `Notes` objects by using methods in the `NotesSession` class. Use `CreateDateRange`, `CreateDateTime`, `CreateLog`, and `CreateNewsletter` to create `NotesDateRange`, `NotesDateTime`, `NotesLog`, and `NotesNewsletter` objects. We cover these objects in more detail later in the "NotesDateRange," "NotesDateTime," "NotesLog," and "NotesNewsletter" sections.

NotesDbDirectory

This is one of the easiest of the classes to understand, with just one property and three methods. It represents the Notes data directory on a specific server or workstation, and its main use is for looping through a set of databases of a specific type or that meet certain criteria. For example, you can loop through all the databases on a server that are available for replication.

You create a new NotesDbDirectory object in one of two ways. You can use the GetDbDirectory method of NotesSession, as we saw in the last section, or you can use the New method. You specify the type of database that you are looking for; see Table 19.10 for details.

Table 19.10 Base Types for *NotesDbDirectory*	
To Find This Type of Database...	**Use This Constant...**
Any Notes database	DATABASE
Any Notes database template	TEMPLATE
All Notes databases available for replication	REPLICA_CANDIDATE
All Notes databases that can be a template	TEMPLATE_CANDIDATE

After you have a NotesDbDirectory object, you can access the databases in the directory by using GetFirstDatabase and GetNextDatabase. You can use the Name property to find out the name of the server whose directory you are accessing. For example:

```
Sub Click(Source As Button)
    Dim uiWorkspace As New NotesUIWorkspace
    Dim uiDoc As NotesUIDocument
    Dim DbDir As NotesDbDirectory
    Dim db As NotesDatabase
    Dim strDbsAvailToReplicate

    Set uiDoc = uiWorkspace.CurrentDocument
    Set DbDir = New NotesDbDirectory("Ruby")
    Set db = DbDir.GetFirstDatabase(REPLICA_CANDIDATE)
    Do While Not (db Is Nothing)
        strDbsAvailToReplicate = strDbsAvailToReplicate + db.Title +
Chr(10)
        Set db = DbDir.GetNextDatabase
    Loop
    Call uiDoc. FieldSetText("ServerName", DbDir.Name)
    Call uiDoc. FieldSetText("DbsAvailToReplicate", strDbsAvailToReplicate)
End Sub
```

The preceding script uses New to create a new NotesDbDirectory object for server Ruby. It then opens each database on the server that is available for replication and stores its name in the DbsAvailToReplicate field in the current document. It also uses the Name property to store the name of the server in the ServerName field. Tables 19.11 and 19.12 show the properties and methods of the NotesDbDirectory class.

III

Working with LotusScript

Table 19.11 *NotesDbDirectory* **Properties**

Property	Description	Data Type	Usage
Name	The name of the server on which this directory is located	String	Read Only

Table 19.12 *NotesDbDirectory* **Methods**

Method	Description	Return Data Type	Return Value
GetFirst Database	Given a type of database to search for, return the first database of that type. You can search for any database, any template, any database that is allowed to replicate, or any database that can be a template.	Notes Database	The first database of the type you specified
GetNext Database	Provided you have already used the Get FirstDatabase method, return the next database of the type you specified.	Notes Database	The next database of the type you specified
New	Create a new Notes DbDirectory object.	NotesDb Directory	The newly created object

NotesDatabase

The NotesDatabase class represents a Notes database. You use the class to do the following:

- Create, modify, and delete databases

- Create copies and replicas of databases

- Modify access control lists

- Create documents

- Find documents

The class also gives you access to other classes, such as NotesDocumentCollection, NotesView, and NotesDocument. See Table 19.13 for a list of the properties of the NotesDatabase class. Its methods are listed in Table 19.14.

Table 19.13 *NotesDatabase* **Properties**

Property	Description	Data Type	Usage
ACL	The ACL for the database.	NotesACL	Read Only
Agents	All of the agents defined in the database.	Array of NotesAgents	Read Only
AllDocuments	A collection containing all the documents in the database.	NotesDocument Collection	Read Only
Categories	All the categories to which a database belongs.	String	Read Only
Created	The date the database was created.	Variant of type DATE	Read Only
CurrentAccessLevel	The ACL access level for the current user.	Integer constant	Read Only
DelayUpdates	True if multiple updates to documents on a server are processed together for better performance.	Boolean	Read/Write
DesignTemplate Name	The name of the design template for the database.	String	Read Only
FileName	The file name and extension of the database.	String	Read Only
FilePath	The full path and file name of the database including drive letter, directory, file name, and extension.	String	Read Only
Forms	The forms in the database.	Array of NotesForm objects	Read Only
IsFTIndexed	True if the database has a full text index.	Boolean	Read Only
IsMultiDBSearch	True if the database can search multiple databases.	Boolean	Read Only
IsOpen	True if the database is currently open.	Boolean	Read Only
IsPrivate AddressBook	True if the database is a Personal Address Book.	Boolean	Read Only
IsPublic AddressBook	True if the database is a Public Address Book.	Boolean	Read Only

(continues)

III

Working with LotusScript

Table 19.13   Continued

Property	Description	Data Type	Usage
LastFTIndexed	For databases with a full text index, the date that the index was last updated. 12/30/1899 for databases with no full text index.	Variant of type DATE	Read Only
LastModified	The date the database was last modified.	Variant of type DATE	Read Only
Managers	All the people, groups, and servers who are managers of the database.	Array of strings	Read Only
Parent	The Notes Session that contains the database.	NotesSession	Read Only
PercentUsed	The percentage of the database that is currently in use.	Double	Read Only
ReplicaID	The 16-character replica ID for the database.	String	Read Only
Server	The name of the server on which the database is stored.	String	Read Only
Size	The size, in bytes, of the database.	Double	Read Only
SizeQuota	The maximum size, in bytes, to which the database is allowed to grow.	Long	Read/Write
TemplateName	For databases that are templates, the name of the template. If the database is not a template, returns an empty string.	String	Read Only
Title	The title of the database.	String	Read/Write
Unprocessed Documents	All the documents that are considered to be unprocessed by the script.	Notes Document Collection	Read Only
Views	All the public views and folders within the database. If the database is stored locally, personal folders are included.	Array of NotesViews	Read Only

Table 19.14 *NotesDatabase* **Methods**

Method	Description	Return Data Type	Return Value
Close	Close the database.	None	None
Compact	Compact a local database. Note that you cannot use this method to compact the database that the script is running in.	Long	The number of bytes recovered by compacting the database
Create	Given a server and file name, create a new database on disk.	None	None
CreateCopy	Given a server and file name, create a copy of the database. Give the copy the same title and ACL as the original.	Notes Database	A NotesDatabase object representing the newly created copy
CreateDocument	Create a new, empty document in the database. Note that you must save the document before you close the database; otherwise, the document will be lost.	Notes Document	The newly created document
CreateFrom Template	Given a server, file name, and the name of a template, create a new database based on the template.	Notes Database	A NotesDatabase object representing the newly created database
CreateReplica	Given a server and file name, create a replica copy of the database. Give the replica the same title and ACL as the original.	Notes Database	A NotesDatabase object representing the newly created database
FTSearch	Given a string representing a valid full text query, full text search the database.	Notes Document Collection	A collection of documents matching the query sorted so that the most relevant documents are first in the collection
GetAgent	Get an agent given its name.	NotesAgent	The agent
GetDocument ByID	Given a document's NoteID, find the document.	Notes Document	The document

(continues)

Table 19.14   Continued

Method	Description	Return Data Type	Return Value
GetDocument ByUNID	Similar to GetDocumentByID but uses the UNID.	Notes Document	The document
GetDocument ByURL	If the database is a Notes Web Navigator database, return the Notes document that corresponds to the Web page with the URL you specify. If required, you can force the Web Navigator database to reload the Web page.	Notes Document	The document corresponding to the URL
GetForm	Get a form given its name or alias.	NotesForm	The form
GetProfile Document	Get a profile document from the database.	Notes Document	The profile document
GetURLHeader Info	For Web Navigator databases, given an URL and header string, return the requested URL header information.	String	The header information
GetView	Given either the name or the alias of a view or folder, return the view or folder.	NotesView	The requested view or folder
GrantAccess	Change the ACL for the database to give a person, group, or server a specified access level.	None	None
New	Create a new Notes Database object. Note that this method does *not* create a new database on disk.	Notes Database	The newly created object
Open	Given a server and file name, open an existing database.	Boolean	True if the database was found and successfully opened
OpenBy ReplicaID	Similar to Open, but use the supplied server name and replica ID to find the database.	Open	True if the database was found and successfully opened

Method	Description	Return Data Type	Return Value
OpenIfModified	Given a server, file name, and date, open an existing database, provided it has been modified since the date you specified.	Boolean	True if the database was found and successfully opened
OpenMail	Opens the current user's mail database.	None	None
OpenURLDb	Opens the default Web Navigator database.	Boolean	True if the database was found and successfully opened
OpenWith Failover	Given a server and file name, attempt to open the database. If the database cannot be opened and the server is in a server cluster, attempt to open a replica of the database on another server in the cluster.	Boolean	True if the database was found and successfully opened
QueryAccess	Given the name of a person, group, or server, return their access level to the database.	Integer constant	The access level
Remove	Delete the database.	None	None
Replicate	Given a server name, replicate the database with its replica copy on that server.	Boolean	True if the database replicated successfully
RevokeAccess	Remove a person, group, or server from the ACL for the database.	None	None
Search	Given a Notes selection formula and a cut-off date, search the database for all documents that match the formula.	Notes Document Collection	All the documents that match the formula and have been modified since the cut-off date
Unprocessed FTSearch	For agent scripts only, the same as FTSearch, except that only those documents that the agent considers unprocessed are searched.	Notes Document Collection	The documents

(continues)

	Table 19.14 Continued		
Method	**Description**	**Return Data Type**	**Return Value**
Unprocessed Search	For agent scripts only, the same as Search except that only those documents that the agent considers unprocessed are searched.	Notes Document Collection	The documents
UpdateFTIndex	For any database with a full text index, up-date the index. For local database, create the index, if necessary.	None	None

Creating a Database

The `NotesDatabase` class gives you several methods with which you can create a new database on disk. The most straightforward is `Create`, which creates a new blank database. You specify the server and file name to use and whether to open the database after it has been created.

> **Note**
>
> A database has to be open before you can use the majority of its properties or methods.

After you create a new database or open an existing one, you can use any of the following methods to create new databases based on the original: `CreateCopy`, `CreateReplica`, or `CreateFromTemplate`.

Use `CreateCopy` to create a copy of the current database. The copy contains all the forms, views, and agents of the original, and has the same ACL and same title. You can create a replica of the current database by using the `CreateReplica` method. You supply a server and file name, and the method creates a replica copy of the database at the new location. If the current database is a template, you can create a new database based on the template by using `CreateFromTemplate`. As with the other methods, you supply a server and file name for the new database. You can also specify that the new database is to inherit future design changes from the template. The following example uses these methods to create new databases:

```
Dim s As New NotesSession
Dim db As NotesDatabase
Dim dbTemplate As New NotesDatabase("Sapphire", "report.ntf")
Dim dbReplica As NotesDatabase
```

```
Dim dbCopy As NotesDatabase
Set db = s.CurrentDatabase
'Create a replica of the current database on a different server
Set dbReplica = db.CreateReplica("Diamond", "stock.nsf")
'Create a backup copy of the current database
Set dbCopy = db.CreateCopy("Diamond", "backup\stock.nsf")
dbNew.Title = "Backup of New Stock Control Levels"
'Create a new database based on a template
Set dbNew = dbTemplate.CreateFromTemplate("Diamond", "report.nsf", True)
```

Tip

Scripts running on a server can only create or access databases on that server.

Opening, Closing, and Deleting a Database

Before you can access any of the properties or methods of a database, the database must be open. After you have opened the database, all of its properties and methods are available to you.

You can use the IsOpen property to check whether a database is open. If the database is not open, the simplest way to open it is to use the Open method. You supply a server and filename and the database is opened—provided it exists—and the script has at least reader access to it. If you know the replica ID of the database, you can use the OpenByReplicaID method. This works the same way as the Open method, but you supply the replica ID instead of the server and file name. OpenIfModified is useful for agents that must periodically check for updates to databases. You supply a server and file name as for Open, but, in addition, you supply a NotesDateTime object. The database is opened only if it has been modified since the date represented by the NotesDateTime object. If your Notes servers are configured as part of a server cluster, you can use the new OpenWithFailover method to attempt to open a database on one server and, if unsuccessful, automatically try to open a replica of the database on another server in the cluster.

There are also a couple of specialized Open methods. OpenMail finds and opens the mail database for the current user. As with some other methods, OpenMail behaves differently when run on a workstation than when run on a server. On a workstation, it finds the mail database for the current user. On a server, it finds the mail database for the last person who modified the script.

If a Notes Web Navigator database has been set up at your location, you can use OpenURLDb to find and open it.

All the open methods return True if the specified database was successfully opened and False if the database could not be opened for any reason.

> **Tip**
>
> To open a database, your script must have at least reader access to the database. So, if the script is running on your workstation, you must have reader access to the database you want to open. If the script is running on a server, the server must have reader access to the database.

When your script finishes running, Notes automatically closes all the databases that the script has opened. If you need to explicitly close a database, use the Close method. After you have closed a database, you cannot access its properties and methods. Use the Remove method if you want to delete a database.

Working with a Database

After you have opened a database, a wealth of information is available to you about it. There are properties that tell you when it was Created or LastModified. You can get the database's server, filename, and replica ID by using the Server, FilePath, FileName, and ReplicaID properties. You can find its title by using the Title property and check what categories the database is in by using the Categories property. The Parent property of a database returns the NotesSession that contains the database.

If you are working with full text indices, you can check that the database is indexed by using the IsFTIndexed property; or use LastFTIndexed to find the date and time when the index was last updated. You can use the new IsMultiDbSearch method to check whether the database contains a multi-database full text index. If you need to update the index, you can call the UpdateFTIndex method. You can also use UpdateFTIndex to create a full text index for a database, provided that the database is stored locally on a workstation. If you try to use UpdateFTIndex on a server-based database that has no full text index, you get an error. The following example checks whether a database has a full text index and creates one if necessary. If the database already has a full text index, the script updates it only if the database has been modified since the last time the full index was updated:

```
Sub Click(Source As Button)
      Dim s As New NotesSession
      Dim db As NotesDatabase

      Set db = s.CurrentDatabase

      If (Not db.IsFTIndexed) Then
            Print "Creating Full Text Index ..."
            Call db.UpdateFTIndex(True)
      End If

      If (db.LastModified > db.LastFTIndexed) Then
            Print "Updating Full Text Index ..."
            Call db.UpdateFTIndex(False)
      End If
      Print "Done."
End Sub
```

You can track the size of the database by using the Size, SizeQuota, and PercentUsed properties. Size gives you the size of the database in bytes, and PercentUsed gives you the percentage of this size that contains data (versus empty space). SizeQuota returns the maximum bytes that your Notes administrator has allowed for this database. For example, you can use Size and SizeQuota to monitor a database and issue a warning if its size approaches the quota limit. Or, if the PercentUsed is higher than a certain percentage, you can use the Compact method to reclaim the empty space.

> **Tip**
>
> You can compact local databases only by using the Compact method. So if you run a script on your workstation, you can compact databases only on your workstation. If you need to compact server databases, make sure that you run the script on the server.

If the database is a template, you can find the name of the template by using the TemplateName property. Similarly, if the database inherits its design from a template, you can find the name of the template from which it inherits its design by using the DesignTemplateName property.

If you are interested in Notes Address Books (well, who isn't!) and have used the AddressBooks property of NotesSession to get the currently available Address Books, you can check whether each is a Public or Private address book. IsPublicAddressBook and IsPrivateAddressBook return True if the database is of the appropriate type. For example, the following script counts the number of public and private address books currently available:

```
Sub Click(Source As Button)
    Dim s As New NotesSession
    Dim AddressBooks As Variant
    Dim iPublicAddressBooks As Integer
    Dim iPrivateAddressBooks As Integer

    AddressBooks = s.AddressBooks
    Forall Book In AddressBooks
        If Book.IsPublicAddressBook Then
            iPublicAddressBooks = iPublicAddressBooks + 1
        End If
        If Book.IsPrivateAddressBook Then
            iPrivateAddressBooks = iPrivateAddressBooks + 1
        End If
    End Forall

    Messagebox "This session has" & Str$(iPublicAddressBooks) & " public
address book(s) and" _
& Str$(iPrivateAddressBooks) & " private address book(s).", 0, "Address
Books"
End Sub
```

You can get a list of all the agents in a database by using the Agents property. Actually, what you get is an array of NotesAgent objects. You can then use the properties of the NotesAgent class to display information about each agent. If you know the name of an agent, you can get its corresponding NotesAgent object by using the GetAgent method. In a similar way, you can use the Forms property and the GetForm method to work with forms in the database.

III

Working with LotusScript

You can force a database to replicate with a specified server by using the `Replicate` method. You supply the server name, and the method initiates replication and returns True if the replication was successful.

Working with the Access Control List

The `NotesDatabase` class gives you several methods and properties to let you examine and modify ACL settings for the database. You can get the ACL for the database by using the `ACL` property. This returns a `NotesACL` object representing the current ACL. You can then use the properties and methods of the `NotesACL` and `NotesACLEntry` classes to read and modify the ACL.

Even if you don't use a `NotesACL` object, you can still work with the ACL for the database. You can use the `QueryAccess` method to check the access level for a person, group, or server. Give the method a person, group, or server name, and it returns an integer constant representing the current access level to the database for the name you specified; see Table 19.15 for details.

Table 19.15	Access Level Constants for *NotesACL*
Access Level	**Constant**
No access	ACLLEVEL_NOACCESS
Depositor	ACLLEVEL_DEPOSITOR
Reader	ACLLEVEL_READER
Author	ACLLEVEL_AUTHOR
Editor	ACLLEVEL_EDITOR
Designer	ACLLEVEL_DESIGNER
Manager	ACLLEVEL_MANAGER

You can use `QueryAccess` to check whether a user is allowed to perform certain tasks on the database. For example, the following script checks that the current user has at least Editor access to the database:

```
Sub Click(Source As Button)
    Dim s As New NotesSession
    Dim db As NotesDatabase
    Dim iAccessLevel As Integer

    Set db = s.CurrentDatabase

    iAccessLevel = db.QueryAccess(s.UserName)

    Select Case iAccessLevel
    Case ACLLEVEL_MANAGER
        Print "You have Manager access to this database."
    Case ACLLEVEL_DESIGNER
        Print "You have Designer access to this database."
    Case ACLLEVEL_EDITOR
        Print "You have Editor access to this database."
```

```
        Case Else
            Print "You do not have Editor access to this database."
        End Select

    End Sub
```

You can find the access level for the current user by using the `NotesDatabase` `CurrentAccessLevel` property. This returns the same set of integer constants as `QueryAccess`. You can also get a list of the name of the people, groups, or servers who have Manager access to the database by using the `Managers` property. This property returns a list of the names of the managers of the database.

If you need to alter someone's access level, you can either use the `ACL` property to get the `NotesACL` object and then use its methods; or you can use the `GrantAccess` and `RevokeAccess` methods of `NotesDatabase`. Use `GrantAccess` to give a person, group, or server a specified access level. Use `RevokeAccess` to remove a name from the ACL.

Creating a Document

Use `CreateDocument` to create a new document in the database. This method returns a `NotesDocument` object, which you can then use to add data to and save the new document. We cover `NotesDocument` in detail later in the "NotesDocument" section.

Finding a Document

All documents in Notes databases have two unique numbers that can be used to identify them. The Note ID is an 8-character ID that uniquely identifies a document within a particular database. The Note ID is specific to the database—that is, a copy of the document in a replica database may have a different Note ID. The Universal ID for a document is a 32-character ID that uniquely identifies the document in all replica copies of the database. The `NotesDatabase` class has methods that let you find a document by either its Note ID or its Universal ID.

Use `GetDocumentByID` when you know the Note ID and `GetDocumentByUNID` if you're using the Universal ID.

If the current database is a Web navigator database, you can find a document by its uniform resource locator (URL) when using `GetDocumentByURL`. For example, to get the latest update of the Lotus home page from the Web Navigator database, you can use the following:

```
    Dim s As New NotesSession
    Dim dbWebNavigator As NotesDatabase
    Dim LotusHomePage As NotesDocument
    'Assume that the current database is the Web Navigator
    Set dbWebNavigator = s.CurrentDatabase
    Set LotusHomePage = dbWebNavigator.GetDocumentByURL("http://www.lotus.com",
    True)
```

If you need to do fancy things with the HyperText Transport Protocol (HTTP) header information for a Web page, you can use `GetURLHeaderInfo` to get a specified header value. Supply the URL and the name of the header value you want; the method returns that header value. If the Web page doesn't contain the requested header, the method returns a null string.

III

Working with LotusScript

Finding a Group of Documents

You can find every document within a database by using the `AllDocuments` property. `AllDocuments` returns a `NotesDocumentCollection` containing all the documents in the database. If you want to find a subset of the documents in the database, you can use two different methods: `Search` and `FTSearch`.

If you want to select the documents by using a Notes selection formula, you can use the `Search` method. You supply `Search` with the following three parameters:

- A Notes selection formula, such as `Form = "Main Topic"`.

- A `NotesDateTime` object. Only documents that have been modified since the date specified by the date-time object are included in the search results.

- The number of documents to return (or 0 for all documents).

The method returns a `NotesDocumentCollection` containing all the documents that match the selection and date criteria.

If the documents you are after are better searched for by using a full text query, use the `FTSearch` method. With `FTSearch`, you supply two parameters: a Notes full-text query and the number of documents to return. The method searches the database and returns a `NotesDocumentCollection` containing the matching documents, sorted in order of relevance. Don't worry if the database you want to search isn't full text indexed; the method still works, albeit much more slowly than if the database is full-text indexed.

When you're working with agents and want to further restrict the set of returned documents to include only those the agent hasn't already processed, you can use the `UnprocessedDocuments` property and the `UnprocessedSearch` and `UnprocessedFTSearch` methods. Exactly which documents an agent defines as unprocessed varies depending on how the agent is set up. See the Notes Help database for details of how an agent defines an unprocessed document.

You can also use the `GetView` method to find a specific view with the database. After you have the view, you can use the search methods in the `NotesView` class to find documents within the view—which leads nicely to the next class...

NotesView

The `NotesView` class lets you work with Notes views and folders and the documents they contain.

By using `NotesView` properties and methods, you can do the following:

- Examine view attributes

- Navigate up and down a view hierarchy

- Search for documents within a view

- Delete a view

See Table 19.16 for all the properties of the NotesView class. Its methods are listed in Table 19.17. Note that you can't create new views within a Notes database from LotusScript; you can only access existing views. You can get a specific view by using the GetView method of NotesDatabase, or you can get all the views in a database via its Views property.

Table 19.16	*NotesView* **Properties**		
Property	**Description**	**Data Type**	**Usage**
Aliases	The aliases for the view.	Array of strings	Read Only
AutoUpdate	Set to True to have the front-end view automatically updated if the back-end view changes.	Boolean	Read/Write
Columns	All the columns in the view or folder.	Array of NotesView Columns	Read Only
Created	The date and time when the view or folder was created.	Variant of type DATE	Read Only
IsCalendar	True if the view is a calendar view.	Boolean	Read Only
IsDefaultView	True if the view is the default view for the database.	Boolean	Read Only
IsFolder	True if the view object represents a folder.	Boolean	Read Only
LastModified	The date and time when the view or folder was last modified.	Variant of type DATE	Read Only
Name	Depending on how you accessed the view object—either its name, its alias, or its name and alias.	String	Read Only
Parent	The database that contains the view or folder.	Notes Database	Read Only
ProtectReaders	Set to True to protect the $Readers item during replication.	Boolean	Read/Write
Readers	The names of the people, groups and servers that can read the view.	Array of strings	Read/Write
UniversalID	A 32-character ID that uniquely identifies the view or folder in all replicas of a particular database.	String	Read Only

Table 19.17 *NotesView* **Methods**

Method	Description	Return Data Type	Return Value
Clear	If a view has been filtered by using a full-text search, reset the view so that all documents are displayed.	None	None
FTSearch	Given a string representing a valid full-text query, full-text search the database and display in the view only those documents that match the query.	Integer	The number of documents that match the query
GetAll DocumentsByKey	Given a key, find all documents in the view that match the key.	Notes Document Collection	A collection of documents that match the key
GetChild	Given a document within the view, find the first response to the document.	Notes Document	The first response to the document
GetDocument ByKey	Given a key, find the first document in the view that has the supplied key.	Notes Document	The first document with the key
GetFirst Document	Get the first document in the view.	Notes Document	The first document in the view
GetLast Document	Get the last document in the view.	Notes Document	The last document in the view
GetNext Document	Given any document in the view, find the next document.	Notes Document	The document
GetNextSibling	Given any document in the view, find the next document at the same level as the supplied document.	Notes Document	The document
GetNthDocument	Given an index into the view, find the document at that position.	Notes Document	The document
GetParent Document	Given any response document in the view, find its parent document.	Notes Document	The parent document
GetPrev Document	Given any document in the view, find the previous document.	Notes Document	The document

Method	Description	Return Data Type	Return Value
GetPrevSibling	Given any document in the view, find the previous document at the same level as the supplied document.	Notes Document	The document
Refresh	Update the view to show any changes.	None	None
Remove	Delete the view from the database.	None	None

Working with View Properties

You can find the name of a view by using the Name property. If you need to find the aliases for the view, you can get them by using the Aliases property.

You can check whether you are working with a view or a folder by reading the IsFolder property.

Use Created and LastModified to find out when a view was created and the last time its design was modified. You can check whether a view is the default view in a database by using the IsDefaultView property.

The Columns property gives you access to all the columns within a view or folder. When you read the property, you get an array containing a NotesViewColumn object for each column in the view. You can use Columns in a loop to get all columns, or specify an index into the array to get a specific column.

Navigating a View Hierarchy

After you have a view, you can navigate through the documents in the view by using a variety of methods. Use GetFirstDocument and GetNextDocument, or GetLastDocument and GetPrevDocument to step through all the documents in the view in the order in which they are displayed. If you want to skip to a document based on its position within the view, use GetNthDocument.

If you're working with documents in a response hierarchy, you can use methods to get documents at different levels in the hierarchy. After you have found a document, you can use GetChild to get the first response to the document or GetParentDocument to get its parent. To get documents at the same level, use either GetNextSibling or GetPrevSibling.

Finding a Document in a View

Use GetDocumentByKey to find a document based on the column values that are displayed in a view. You supply a key in the form of an array of strings—one string for each column value you want to compare. The first string in the array is compared with the contents of the first sorted or categorized column, the second string with the next sorted or categorized column, and so on for each string you supply. If all the strings match the column values, the document with those column values is returned.

> **Note**
>
> If your key consists of more than one string, each column you compare must be sorted and categorized.

Searching for Documents in a View

You can use the power of Notes' full-text queries to find a set of documents within a view. The FTSearch method lets you execute a full-text search query on the view. The view is filtered to include only those documents that match the query. You can then use any of the NotesView navigation methods to process documents in the view. To reset the view so that all documents are included, use the Clear method.

Updating a View

Changes to a view—for example, new documents or deletions—are not automatically reflected in the NotesView object. To get the most up-to-date view contents, use the Refresh method.

Deleting a View

You can use Remove to delete a view permanently from a database.

NotesViewColumn

The NotesViewColumn object represents a column in a view or folder. Its properties are listed in Table 19.18.

Table 19.18 *NotesViewColumn* **Properties**

Property	Description	Data Type	Usage
Formula	If the column uses an @function or a simple function to calculate the value to display, the textual representation of the formula.	String	Read Only
IsCategory	True if the column is categorized.	Boolean	Read Only
IsHidden	True if the column is hidden.	Boolean	Read Only
IsResponse	True if the column is a responses-only column.	Boolean	Read Only
IsSorted	True if the column is sorted.	Boolean	Read Only
ItemName	If a column displays a field value, the name of the field.	String	Read Only
Position	The position of the column in its view. Column numbers start at 1.	Integer	Read Only

Property	Description	Data Type	Usage
Title	The title of the column, if it has one.	String	Read Only

You can't directly update any of the columns, but you can query their properties. You can check the position of a column within a view by using the `Position` property.

> **Note**
>
> All column positions start at 1, whereas by default, LotusScript array indices start at 0. Remember to add 1 to the array index to get the column position.

The `Title` property returns the column title, and you can check whether the column is visible by using the `IsHidden` property. You can check whether the column is sorted or categorized by using `IsSorted` and `IsCategory`.

You can check how the column calculates the values it displays by using either `Formula` or `ItemName`. Only one of these properties is valid for any particular column. If the column uses a Notes formula to calculate its value, `Formula` returns the formula as a string. If the column displays the contents of a field, `ItemName` returns the name of the field.

> **Note**
>
> `NotesViewColumn` represents the design of a column. To get the contents of the column for a document, use the `ColumnValues` property of `NotesDocument`.

NotesDocument

Notes is all about working with documents, and the `NotesDocument` class is all about working with documents by using LotusScript. The class is rich in function and large in terms of the number of properties and methods it contains, but after you gain a good knowledge of how the class works, you're on your way to understanding how to work with Notes documents. Table 19.19 lists the properties for the `NotesDocument` class, and Table 19.20 lists its methods.

Table 19.19 *NotesDocument* **Properties**

Property	Description	Data Type	Usage
Authors	The names of the people who have saved the document.	Array of strings	Read Only
ColumnValues	For documents retrieved from a view, the values that appear in each view column for the document.	Array of variants	Read Only

(continues)

III

Working with LotusScript

Table 19.19   Continued

Property	Description	Data Type	Usage
Created	The date the document was created.	Variant of type DATE	Read Only
Embedded Objects	All of the OLE or ActiveX objects within a document.	Array of NotesEmbedded Objects	Read Only
EncryptionKeys	The keys used to encrypt the document.	String or array of strings	Read/Write
EncryptOnSend	True if the document is to be encrypted when it is mailed.	Boolean	Read/Write
FTSearchScore	If the document was retrieved by a full-text search, the relevance score.	Integer	Read Only
HasEmbedded	True if the document contains at least one embedded or linked object or file attachment.	Boolean	Read Only
IsNewNote	True if the document has never been saved.	Boolean	Read Only
IsProfile	True if the document is a profile document.	Boolean	Read Only
IsResponse	True if the document is a response to any other document.	Boolean	Read Only
IsSigned	True if the document contains at least one signature.	Boolean	Read Only
IsUIDocOpen	True if this document was accessed from a NotesUIDocument.	Boolean	Read Only
IsUnread	True if this document is marked as unread by the current user.	Boolean	Read Only
Items	All the items stored within a document.	Array of NotesItems	Read Only
Key	For a profile document, the key for the document.	String	Read Only
LastAccessed	The date the document was last read or modified.	Variant of type DATE	Read Only
LastModified	The date the document was last modified.	Variant of type DATE	Read Only

Property	Description	Data Type	Usage
NameOfProfile	For a profile document, the name of the profile document.	String	Read Only
NoteID	An 8-character ID that uniquely identifies the document within a particular database.	String	Read Only
ParentDatabase	The database that contains the document.	Notes Database	Read Only
ParentDocument UNID	For response documents, a 32-character ID that uniquely identifies the document's parent.	String	Read Only
ParentView	For documents retrieved from a view, the view from which the document was retrieved.	NotesView	Read Only
Responses	The immediate responses to the document.	Notes Document Collection	Read Only
SaveMessage OnSend	True if the document is to be saved when it is mailed.	Boolean	Read/Write
SentByAgent	True if the document was mailed by a script. False if the document was mailed by a person.	Boolean	Read Only
Signer	If a document has been signed, the name of the person who signed the document.	String	Read Only
SignOnSend	True if the document is to be signed when it is mailed.	Boolean	Read/Write
Size	The size of the document in bytes (including any file attachments).	Long	Read Only
UniversalID	A 32-character ID that uniquely identifies the document in all replicas of a particular database.	String	Read Only
Verifier	If a document has been signed, the name of the certificate that verified the signature.	String	Read Only

III

Working with LotusScript

Table 19.20 *NotesDocument* **Methods**

Method	Description	Return Data Type	Return Value
AppendItem Value	Either create a new item in the document and set its value, or append a value to an existing item.	NotesItem	The new item
ComputeWith Form	Execute all of the default value, input translation, and validation formulas for the document by using its form.	Boolean	True if all formulas executed successfully
CopyAllItems	Copy all items from the document to another document.	None	None
CopyItem	Copy an item into the current document.	NotesItem	The new item
CopyToDatabase	Copy the document into a database.	Notes Document	The new document
CreateReply Message	Create a new document, formatted as a reply to the current document.	Notes Document	The new reply document
CreateRich TextItem	Create a new rich text item in the document.	NotesRich TextItem	The new rich text item
Encrypt	Encrypt the document.	None	None
GetAttachment	Get a named file attachment from the document.	Notes Embedded Object	The file attachment
GetFirstItem	Get the first item with the supplied name from the document.	NotesItem	The item
GetItemValue	Get the value of the item with the supplied name from the document.	String for Rich Text items. Array of strings for Text or Text List items. Array of doubles for Numbers, Number Lists, or DateTime items	The value
GetNextItem	Get the next item with the same name as the supplied item from the document.	NotesItem	The item
HasItem	True if the document has an item with the supplied name.	Boolean	True if the item exists.
MakeResponse	Make the current document a response to the supplied document.	None	None

Method	Description	Return Data Type	Return Value
PutInFolder	Put the document into the specified folder. Create the folder, if necessary.	None	None
Remove	Delete the document.	Boolean	True if the document was deleted
RemoveFrom Folder	Remove the document from the specified folder.	None	None
RemoveItem	Delete all items with the specified name from the document.	None	None
RenderToRTItem	Create a picture of the document and store it in a rich text field.	Boolean	True if the picture was created
ReplaceItem Value	Replace all items with the specified name with a new item, then assign the new item a value.	NotesItem	The new item
Save	Save any changes to the document. Any of the changes you make to a document take effect only after the document has been saved.	Boolean	True if the document was saved
Send	Mail the document to the specified recipients.	None	None
Sign	Add the current user's signature to the document.	None	None

Creating a Document

You create a new document by using either the CreateDocument method in NotesDatabase or the New method.

Finding a Document

There are many ways to find an existing document. You can use methods in the NotesView and NotesDatabase classes to find documents. Use methods in NotesView to do the following:

- Find a document based on its position within a view

- Use methods in NotesDatabase to:

   Find all documents in a database
   Find documents based on their Note ID or Universal ID
   Find documents which match a Notes full text query
   Find documents selected by a Notes selection formula

If the current document was found by using a Notes full-text search, the FTSearchScore property is set to the relevance score calculated by the search. If the document was retrieved from a view, you can use the ParentView property to find the view that contains the document. Another property that gets set only if the document was found in a view is the ColumnValues property. This returns an array representing the values that appear in each column of the parent view for this document.

See the "NotesView" and "NotesDatabase" sections earlier in this chapter for more details on finding documents.

The NotesDocument class also has properties that let you find of the responses to a document or the parent of a document. We take at look at these later in "Working with Response Documents."

Working with Document Properties

After you have a document, you can use some of the many properties of the NotesDocument class to examine it in detail. You can tell whether the document has just been created by using the IsNewNote property. If the document has never been saved, the property returns True. Created tells you when the document was created, and, if the document has been saved, you can use LastAccessed and LastModified to see when it was last updated. You can use the new Release 4.5 IsUnread property to check whether the current user has read the document. If you need to know how big a document is, the Size property gives you its current size in bytes.

The NoteID and UniversalID for the document are also available to you as properties.

You can check whether a document contains an electronic signature by using the IsSigned property. If IsSigned is True, the Signer property contains the name of the person who signed the document, and Verifier stores the name of the certificate used to verify the signature. If the document isn't signed, you can use the Sign method to sign it. The following example shows how to sign a document:

```
Sub Click(Source As Button)
        Dim s As New NotesUIWorkspace
        Dim uiDoc As NotesUIDocument
        Dim doc As NotesDocument

        Set uiDoc = s.CurrentDocument
        Set doc = uiDoc.Document

        If (Not doc.IsSigned) Then
                Call doc.Sign
                Call doc.Save( False, True )
                verifyName = doc.Verifier
                Messagebox("Document signed by " & doc.Signer & " and verified by
 " & doc.Verifier & ".")
        Else
                Messagebox("Document is already signed.")
        End If
End Sub
```

If security is important, you can also encrypt the document by using the `Encrypt` method. Be sure to set the `EncryptionKeys` property to the names of the encryption keys you want to use before encrypting the document. You can also check who has edited the document by reading the `Authors` property.

> **Caution**
>
> Mail encryption works differently from document encryption, so if you want to mail an encrypted document, set the `EncryptOnSend` property to True, and then mail the document by using the Send method.

If you are searching for embedded objects or file attachments within the document, you can use the `HasEmbedded` property to check whether any exist. You can get some, but not all, embedded objects by using the `EmbeddedObjects` property. Use `GetAttachment` to get a file attachment, given its filename.

> **Caution**
>
> The `EmbeddedObjects` property does not return any file attachments or OLE/1 objects created in Notes Release 3. If you need to get at these objects, use the `NotesRichTextItem` version of `EmbeddedObjects`.

Working with Profile Documents

Profile documents are new to Release 4.5. They are documents that you can create from LotusScript to store database specific items. For example, you may want to store some parameters that define how and when documents should be archived from a database. You use the `EditProfile` method of the `NotesUIWorkspace` class to create new profile documents. You can check whether a document is a profile document by using the `NotesDocument` `IsProfile` property. After you have a profile document, you can get its name from the `NameOfProfile` property and its key by using the `Key` property.

Creating and Modifying Document Items

Although we've already looked at quite a few of a document's properties, we still haven't looked at one of the most important ones—the `Items` property. You can use `Items` to get a list of all the items stored in a document. The property returns an array of `NotesItem` objects, which you can then examine by using the properties and methods of the `NotesItem` class. You can use `GetFirstItem` to get the first item in the document with the name you specify.

> **Note**
>
> The `GetNextItem` method that you may have used in Release 4.0 is no longer available in Release 4.5.

If you're looking for a particular item, you can see whether it exists by using `HasItem`. You supply the name of an item, and `HasItem` returns True if the document contains that item. You can get the contents of an item in several different ways. Either use `GetItemValue` and supply the name of the item as a parameter, or use what's known as *extended class syntax*, which lets you access the item as though it is a property of the document. For example, the following two scripts both get the contents of the `Quantity` item. The following script uses `GetItemValue`:

```
Sub Click(Source as Button)
    Dim uiWorkspace As New NotesUIWorkspace
    Dim uiDoc As NotesUIDocument
    Dim doc As NotesDocument
    Dim varQuantity As Variant

    Set uiDoc = uiWorkspace.CurrentDocument
    Set doc = uiDoc.Document

    varQuantity = doc.GetItemValue("Quantity")
End Sub
```

The following script does the same as the previous one, but uses extended class syntax:

```
Sub Click(Source as Button)
    Dim uiWorkspace As New NotesUIWorkspace
    Dim uiDoc As NotesUIDocument
    Dim doc As NotesDocument
    Dim varQuantity As Variant

    Set uiDoc = uiWorkspace.CurrentDocument
    Set doc = uiDoc.Document

    varQuantity = doc.Quantity
End Sub
```

> **Note**
>
> Extended class syntax lets you treat an item within a document as though it is a property. The items within a document, in effect, become extra properties of the document. You can read and set them the same way as any other property. For example, if a document contains an item called DocAuthor, you can access its value by using the same syntax as for a property.

> **Tip**
>
> GetItemValue always returns an array even if the item contains only one value. If the item contains a single value, it is stored as the first element of the array.

You can use `AppendItemValue` and `ReplaceItemValue` to create a new item or update the contents of an existing one. If an item of the name you supply doesn't exist, a new one is created. The following script uses the two methods to create new items in a document:

```
Sub Click(Source as Button)
    Dim uiWorkspace As New NotesUIWorkspace
    Dim uiDoc As NotesUIDocument
    Dim doc As NotesDocument
    Dim itmTitle As NotesItem
    Dim itmPrice As NotesItem

    Set uiDoc = uiWorkspace.CurrentDocument
    Set doc = uiDoc.Document

    Set itmTitle = doc.AppendItemValue("Title", "The Quest for Knowledge")
    Set itmPrice = doc.ReplaceItemValue("Price", 50)
    Call doc.Save(True, True)

End Sub
```

You can also create Rich Text items by using the CreateRichTextItem method.

Using the *ComputeWithForm* Method

The methods we've just looked at let you bypass the Notes user interface and create documents directly from a LotusScript program. Usually, you create documents by completing a form in the Notes user interface. When you save the document, the field validation formulas on the form are computed, and, if any of the field values are incorrect, the field validation formulas tell you and you can't save the document. By bypassing these validation formulas and creating documents in the background, we can create documents that would not pass the field validation tests. If it is important to check that the document you have created meets the field validation criteria for a form, you can use the ComputeWithForm method to force the validation formulas to be executed.

This can be useful if you've changed the design of a form to include new validation code, and you need to test whether the existing documents are still valid. You can check each document by using ComputeWithForm and update those that no longer meet the new validation criteria.

Copying and Deleting Document Items

There are two methods that let you copy items between documents. CopyItem copies a single item from one document to another, while CopyAllItems copies every item in the document.

To delete an item from the document, call RemoveItem.

Working with Response Documents

It's really easy to find all of the immediate responses to a document. Just look at the Responses property. This returns a NotesDocumentCollection containing all responses to the current document. If you need to check whether the current document is a response document, that's easy, too. Check the IsResponse property. If it's True, then you're working with a response document. You can then use the ParentDocumentUNID property to find the Universal ID of the document's parent.

Sometimes you need to change a document's position in a view hierarchy—for example, to make one document a response to another. Use the MakeResponse method to make this change. You call the MakeResponse method in one document to make that document a response to another.

Moving and Copying Documents

Not only can you alter a document's position in a hierarchy, you can also copy the document between databases. The CopyToDatabase method creates a new copy of the document in the database you specify.

You can also move documents between folders within the database. Use PutInFolder to add a document to a folder and RemoveFromFolder to take it out of a folder.

Mailing a Document

One of the great features of Notes is its tight integration with the mail system. All documents are potentially mail messages. The NotesDocument class lets you exploit this by making it very easy to mail-enable your documents. You can mail any document by using the Send method. Simply supply a list of recipients, call the Send method, and the document is mailed to those recipients. If the document contains a SendTo field, your list of recipients is ignored and the document is mailed to the recipients listed in the SendTo field. If you set the SaveMessageOnSend property, the document is automatically saved after it is sent. You can also specify some mail options such as SignOnSend and EncryptOnSend.

A useful method to use when you are mailing documents is the RenderToRTItem method. This creates a picture of a document and places it into a rich text field, just the same way as when you use Mail, Forward to forward a document.

You can also create a reply to the current document by using CreateReplyMessage. This method creates a new document that is formatted as a reply to the original. This can be useful for automatically generating and sending acknowledgments when you're designing a workflow application. For example, you could automatically acknowledge the receipt of an expenses claim form.

Saving and Deleting a Document

None of the changes you make to a document have any effect until it is saved. If you don't save your document, all of your changes are lost when you close the database. Use the Save method to save your changes. You supply Save with two or three parameters. Set the first parameter to True to save the document, even if someone else has edited a copy of it while you've been working with it. If you use this parameter, your copy of the document overwrites the original. If you set the first parameter to False, what happens when you save the document is decided by the second parameter.

If you set the second parameter to True, your document becomes a response to the original. If you set this parameter to False, the document is not saved and your changes are discarded.

The optional third parameter is new to Release 4.5 and you use it to indicate whether the saved document should be marked as read. Set this parameter to True to mark the document as read or False to mark it as unread.

You can delete a document from the database by using the Remove method.

NotesForm

The NotesForm class is new in Release 4.5. It lets you examine and work with form properties. You can also use the class to delete a form from a database. The class properties and methods are shown in Tables 19.21 and 19.22.

Table 19.21 *NotesForm* **Properties**

Property	Description	Data Type	Usage
Aliases	The aliases for the form.	Array of strings	Read Only
Fields	The names of the fields on the form.	Array of strings	Read Only
FormUsers	The names of the users that can use the form. (The contents of the $FormUsers field.)	Array of strings	Read/Write
IsSubForm	True if the form is a subform.	Boolean	Read Only
Name	The form name.	String	Read Only
ProtectReaders	Set to True to protect the $Readers item during replication.	Boolean	Read/Write
ProtectUsers	Set to True to protect the $FormUsers item during replication.	Boolean	Read/Write
Readers	The names of the users that can read the form. (The contents of the $Readers field.)	Array of strings	Read/Write

Table 19.22 *NotesForm* **Methods**

Method	Description	Return Data Type	Return Value
Remove	Delete the form from the document.	None	None

NotesItem

The NotesItem class lets you work with the contents of a Notes document. When you enter a value into a field on a form and save the document, Notes stores the value you enter as an item within the document. NotesItem lets you examine and modify these items. You can use the properties and method within NotesItem to do the following:

- Examine item properties
- Create items within a document
- Modify items within a document
- Delete items

See Table 19.23 for the NotesItem class properties and Table 19.24 for the methods.

Table 19.23	*NotesItem* **Properties**		
Property	**Description**	**Data Type**	**Usage**
DateTimeValue	For date-time items only, a NotesDateTime object representing the item.	NotesDate Time	Read/Write
IsAuthors	True if the item is an Authors item.	Boolean	Read Only
IsEncrypted	True if the item is encrypted.	Boolean	Read Only
IsNames	True if the item is a Names item.	Boolean	Read Only
IsProtected	True if the item can be modified only by users with at least Editor access.	Boolean	Read Only
IsReaders	True if the item is a Readers item.	Boolean	Read Only
IsSigned	True if the item contains an electronic signature.	Boolean	Read Only
IsSummary	True if the item is a summary item. Only summary items can be displayed in views and folders.	Boolean	Read Only
LastModified	The date that the item was last modified.	Variant of type DATE	Read Only
Name	The name of the item.	String	Read Only
Parent	The document containing the item.	Notes Document	Read Only
SaveToDisk	True if the item should be written to disk when the document containing it is saved.	Boolean	Read/Write
Text	A textual representation of the item. List items are separated by semicolons.	String	Read Only

Property	Description	Data Type	Usage
Type	The type of item.	Integer constant	Read Only
ValueLength	The size, in bytes, of the item.	Integer	Read Only
Values	The values stored within the item.	String for Rich Text items. Array of strings for Text or Text List items. Array of doubles for Numbers, Number Lists, or DateTime items.	Read/Write

Table 19.24 *NotesItem* **Methods**

Method	Description	Return Data Type	Return Value
Abstract	Abbreviate the text of the item.	String	The abbreviated text
AppendToText List	For a text list item, add another value to the end of the list.	None	None
Contains	For items containing lists, check whether the value you supply is one of the values in the list. You can search text lists, number lists, or date lists.	Boolean	True if the value is in the list
CopyItem ToDocument	Copy the item to a document.	NotesItem	The new item
New	Create a new item.	NotesItem	The new item
Remove	Delete the item from the document.	None	None

Examining Item Properties

Use the Name property to find the name of an item. You can find out what type of item you are working with by examining its Type property. For example, Type lets you know whether an item is a text item. You can find more out about the item by using IsNames, IsAuthors, and IsReaders to see whether it is one of these special types. The LastModified property returns the date when the item was last updated.

You can check the item's security settings by using IsEncrypted, IsProtected, and IsSigned.

Creating and Modifying Items

Use the New method to create new items within a document. You supply the document, the name of the new item, and its initial value. If you're creating a text item, you can optionally set it to be a Names, Readers, or Authors item. You can also create a new item by copying an existing item from one document to another by using CopyItemToDocument.

You can read or modify the contents of an item by using its Values property. When it is read, Values returns the item contents in the appropriate format—for example, as an array of string for a text or text list item. Similarly, when you use Values to modify the contents of an item, you must supply the values in the correct format—for example, an array of doubles for a number or number list item. Alternatively, you can use the Text property to convert an item value into its textual representation—for example, the Text property of a number field containing 42 is the string "42".

If you're working with a text list item, you can use the AppendToTextList method to add new values to the end of the list.

Finally, you can use the Abstract method to abbreviate the contents of a text item. You specify the maximum number of characters to return and information on how to abbreviate the text. The method returns the abbreviated contents of the item.

Deleting Items

To delete an item from a document, use the Remove method. Remember to save the document so that your changes take effect.

NotesRichTextItem

The NotesRichTextItem class lets you create and modify rich text fields within documents. You can do the following:

- Add text, formatting characters, and doclinks to a rich text field

- Combine rich text fields

- Import a Rich Text Format file into a rich text field

- Find the embedded or linked objects or file attachments that are contained in a rich text field

The class properties are listed in Table 19.25 and the methods are shown in Table 19.26.

Table 19.25	*NotesRichTextItem* **Properties**		
Property	**Description**	**Data Type**	**Usage**
Embedded Objects	All the OLE or ActiveX embedded and linked objects and file attachments in the rich text item.	Array of NotesEmbedded Objects	Read Only

Table 19.26 *NotesRichTextItem* **Methods**

Method	Description	Return Data Type	Return Value
AddNewLine	Append one or more new lines to the rich text item.	None	None
AddTab	Append one or more tab characters to the rich text item.	None	None
AppendDocLink	Given a database, view, or document, create a link to the supplied object and append the link to the rich text item.	None	None
AppendRTFile	Given a file in Rich Text format, append its contents to the rich text item.	None	None
AppendRTItem	Append one rich text item to another.	None	None
AppendText	Append the supplied text to the rich text item.	None	None
EmbedObject	Given the name of a file or application, create an embedded object, link, or file attachment and store it in the rich text field.	NotesEmbedded Object	The newly created object
GetEmbedded Object	Given the name of an embedded object, link, or file attachment within the rich text item, return the corresponding NotesEmbeddedObject.	NotesEmbedded Object	The object
GetFormatted Text	Return the contents of the rich text item as a text string.	String	The text of the rich text item
New	Create a new rich text item.	NotesRich TextItem	The newly created rich text item

Creating and Modifying a Rich Text Item

As with many of the other classes, you can create objects in the NotesRichTextItem class
in different ways. If you have a NotesDocument object, you can use its CreateRichTextItem
method to create a new NotesRichTextItem object. Alternatively, you can use New in the
NotesRichTextItem class.

To find and use rich text fields that already exist in a document, use the `GetFirstItem` and `GetNextItem` methods of `NotesDocument`. The following script shows how to find a rich text item called `Body`:

```
Dim doc As NotesDocument
Dim varItem As Variant
'... Set value of doc ...
Set varItem = doc.GetFirstItem("Body")
If (varItem.Type = RICHTEXT) Then
   'The item is a rich text item, so you can use the NotesRichText item
   methods
   End If
```

When you have created or found a rich text item, you can add text to it by using the `AppendText` method. You can also add any number of tabs and new lines by using `AddTab` and `AddNewLine`, or append the contents of one rich text field to another by using `AppendRTItem`.

You can create embedded objects or file attachments in a rich text field by using `EmbedObject`.

Caution

You can attach files on any supported Notes platform, but you can create embedded or linked objects only on platforms that support OLE.

One of the most useful methods supported by the class is `AppendDocLink`. This method lets you create any of the three types of Notes links—a database link, a view link, or a document link—and append it to a rich text field. This is great for creating summary documents. For example, you can create a script that searches all of your organization's newswire databases for new documents and mails you a summary document containing database links to the databases you should check.

Reading a Rich Text Item

You can get the text of a rich text item in a couple of ways. If you want to reformat the text, you can use the `GetFormattedText` method. This gives you the option of removing any embedded tab characters and wrapping the text after a specified number of characters. If you just want the text and don't care about the formatting, just access the rich text item the same way you access a plain text item.

You can get a named embedded object from a rich text field by using `GetEmbeddedObject`. You supply the name of the object, and the method returns a `NotesEmbeddedObject` representing the object. You can then use the properties and methods of `NotesEmbeddedObject` to work with the object.

NotesEmbeddedObject

The `NotesEmbeddedObject` class can represent either a file attachment, an embedded object, or a linked object. You use this class to do the following:

- Find the OLE class and properties of an embedded object

- Find the OLE verbs that the object supports

- Activate any of these OLE verbs

The properties for the class are shown in Table 19.27 and the methods are shown in Table 19.28.

Table 19.27 *NotesEmbeddedObject* **Properties**

Property	Description	Data Type	Usage
Class	The name of the application that created the object.	String	Read Only
FileSize	The size, in bytes, of the object.	Long	Read Only
Name	The name used to refer to the object.	String	Read Only
Object	The OLE handle to the object.	Variant	Read Only
Parent	The rich text item that contains the object.	NotesRich TextItem	Read Only
Source	For file attachments, the name of the file. For other object types, an internal name used by Notes.	String	Read Only
Type	Whether the object is an embedded object, linked object, or file attachment.	Integer constant	Read Only
Verbs	For OLE2 objects, the verbs that the object supports.	Array of strings	Read Only

Table 19.28 *NotesEmbeddedObject* **Methods**

Method	Description	Return Data Type	Return Value
Activate	For embedded or linked objects only, load the object and activate its OLE server application.	Variant	A handle to the object
DoVerb	For embedded objects only, execute the supplied verb.	None	None
ExtractFile	For file attachments only, copy the file attachment to the supplied file name.	None	None

III

Working with LotusScript

Method	Description	Return Data Type	Return Value
Remove	Delete the supplied embedded or linked object or file attachment.	None	None

Table 19.28 Continued

Creating an Embedded Object

You create embedded objects in a rich text field within a document by using the EmbedObject method of the NotesRichTextItem class.

Finding an Embedded Object

You can find all the embedded and linked objects within a document by using the EmbeddedObjects property of NotesDocument. If you need to look only in a particular field, you can use the NotesRichTextItem property, EmbeddedObjects, to get all the embedded objects in the field. Both properties return an array of NotesEmbeddedObjects. When you know the name of the rich text field and the name of the object, use GetEmbeddedObject in NotesRichTextItem to get the object.

Getting the Properties of an Embedded Object

After you have an object, you can use the properties in this class to get its details. Use Type to check whether the object is an embedded object, linked object, or file attachment.

Then, for embedded objects you can use Class to get the OLE name of the application that created the object. Use Name to get the name of the object. If the object were created by using the Notes Create Object dialog box, this is the name that appears in the Object Type list in the dialog box. Object gets the object's OLE handle, and Verbs gets a list of all the OLE verbs the object supports. For file attachments, use Source to get the file name of the attachment. For all object types, the FileSize property gives you the size in bytes of the object or attachment.

Activating an Embedded Object

You can load an OLE embedded or linked object by using the Activate method. You can optionally show or hide the user interface of the OLE server application. The method returns the OLE handle for the object, which you can then use to access the object's methods.

You can also execute any of the verbs supported by the object by using the DoVerb method.

Extracting a File Attachment

If you are dealing with a file attachment object, you can copy the file attachment to disk by using ExtractFile. You supply a path for the file, and the method copies the file to disk.

Deleting an Embedded Object

You delete an embedded object by calling its Remove method. As with the other methods that delete items from documents, you must save the document for your change to take effect.

NotesDocumentCollection

The NotesDocumentCollection class lets you work with a subset of the documents in a database. You have a lot of flexibility in how you select the documents in the collection. For example, you can get the following:

- All the documents in a database

- Those documents found by a full-text query of a database

- Those documents selected by a Notes selection formula

- All documents that have not been processed by an agent

- All the responses to a document

See Table 19.29 for the class properties and Table 19.30 for the methods.

Table 19.29 *NotesDocumentCollection* Properties

Property	Description	Data Type	Usage
Count	The number of documents in a collection.	Long	Read Only
IsSorted	Whether the collection is sorted. Only collections produced by full-text searching a database are sorted.	Boolean	Read Only
Parent	The database that contains the collection.	NotesDatabase	Read Only
Query	If the collection was produced by a search, the query that was used.	String	Read Only

Table 19.30 *NotesDocumentCollection* Methods

Method	Description	Return Data Type	Return Value
GetFirst Document	Get the first document in the collection.	Notes Document	The first document
GetLast Document	Get the last document in the collection.	Notes Document	The last document
GetNext Document	Given any document in the collection, get the next one.	Notes Document	The document

(continues)

		Table 19.30 Continued	

Method	Description	Return Data Type	Return Value
GetNthDocument	Given an index into the collection, find the document at that position.	Notes Document	The document
GetPrev Document	Given any document in the collection, get the previous one.	Notes Document	The document

> **Note**
>
> Collections are not as efficient as views for accessing documents because collections have to be created for you, whereas views are already built into the database. So if you can get the documents you want by using a view, use the view instead of a collection.

Creating a Collection

You use properties and methods in the NotesDatabase and NotesDocument classes to get a collection of documents. The simplest collection is all the documents in a database and is available by using the AllDocuments property of NotesDatabase. You can restrict the documents that are included in the collection by using either the FTSearch or Search methods in the NotesDatabase class. You supply the FTSearch method with a Notes full-text query and a maximum number of documents to find, and the method returns a collection of all documents that match the query. For example, to find the first 10 documents containing the words Holly and Bracken, use the following:

```
Sub Click(Source As Button)
     Dim s As New NotesSession
     Dim db As NotesDatabase
     Dim coll As NotesDocumentCollection
     Set db = s.CurrentDatabase
     Set coll = db.FTSearch(¦"Holly" & "Bracken"¦, 10)
End Sub
```

To find all documents that match the query, specify 0 as the number of documents to return.

> **Tip**
>
> Use the vertical bar to delimit the search string. If you use quotation marks as string delimiters, you have to double up any quotation marks in the search string, which soon makes it hard to read.

Use the Search method when you want to select documents by using a Notes selection formula. For example, to select all the Server documents in the current database that have been modified in the last week, use the following:

```
Sub Click(Source As Button)
    Dim s As New NotesSession
    Dim db As NotesDatabase
    Dim coll As NotesDocumentCollection
    Dim dtLastWeek As New NotesDateTime("Today")
    Set db = s.CurrentDatabase
    Call dtLastWeek.AdjustDay(-7)
    Set coll = db.Search(¦Form = "Server"¦, dtLastWeek, 0)
End Sub
```

If you are using an agent to access the collection, you can use the `UnprocessedDocuments` property or the `UnprocessedFTSearch` and `UnprocessedSearch` methods to further limit the collection by including only those documents the agent considers to be unprocessed.

If you use one of the full-text search methods to create a collection, the documents are sorted with the most relevant documents first. All the other methods return unordered collections. If you need to check whether a collection is ordered, you can use the `IsSorted` property to find out.

Finding Documents in a Collection

After you have a collection, you can use the `Count` property to check how many documents were returned. You can refine the documents in the collection by performing a full-text query on the returned documents. Use `FTSearch` to specify the query, and the method modifies the collection to contain only those documents that match the search criteria.

You then have several methods of finding documents in the collection. You can use `GetFirstDocument` and `GetNextDocument` to step through all the documents. If you want to step through the collection in reverse order, use `GetLastDocument` and `GetPrevDocument`. You can get a specific document in the collection by using `GetNthDocument`.

Working with Documents in a Collection

Release 4.5 introduces several new methods that you can use to work with document collections. You can add all the documents in a collection to a specified folder by using the `PutAllInFolder` method, or remove them with `RemoveAllFromFolder`. You can delete all the documents in a collection, using `RemoveAll`. If you want to add or update a specific item in all the documents in a collection, you can use `StampAll`. You supply the name of the item and its new value and `StampAll` updates it in every document in the collection. If the item doesn't exist, `StampAll` adds it. When you're working with agents, you can use `UpdateAll` to mark all the documents in the collection as having been processed by the agent.

NotesAgent

The `NotesAgent` class represents any public or private Notes agent or Notes Release 3.x macro. Agents let you automate tasks within Notes, such as archiving documents, sending mail messages, or routing documents through a workflow system. You can create shared agents as a database designer and make them available to users of your database. You can also create personal agents to help automate routine tasks.

III

Working with LotusScript

> **Note**
>
> You must have at least designer access to a database to be able to create shared agents. To create personal agents in a database, the Create personal agents option in the ACL must be selected for your name or for a group that you belong to. For server-based databases, you must also be included in the group of people allowed to create personal agents on the server. See the Agent Manager Restrictions section of the server documentation for details about who can create personal agents.

You can use NotesAgent to examine the properties of an agent or delete it from the database.

The NotesAgent class properties are listed in Table 19.31, and the methods are shown in Table 19.32.

Table 19.31 *NotesAgent* **Properties**

Property	Description	Data Type	Usage
Comment	The comment associated with the agent.	String	Read Only
CommonOwner	The common name of the person who last edited the agent.	String	Read Only
IsEnabled	True if the agent is enabled.	Boolean	Read Only
IsPublic	True if the agent is available to all database users.	Boolean	Read Only
LastRun	The date that the agent last ran.	Variant of type DATE	Read Only
Name	The name of the agent.	String	Read Only
Owner	The fully distinguished name of the person who last edited the agent.	String	Read Only
Parent	The database in which the agent is stored.	Notes Database	Read Only
Query	The text of the query used to select the documents on which the agent runs.	String	Read Only
ServerName	For server-based agents, the fully distinguished name of the server on which the agent runs. For workstation-based agents, the fully distinguished name of the current user.	String	Read Only

Method	Description	Return Data Type	Return Value
Remove	Delete the agent from the database.	None	None
Run	Run an agent.	None	None

Table 19.32 *NotesAgent* **Methods**

NotesACL

The NotesACL class represents the Access Control List for a database. You can use the NotesACL class to do the following:

- Create new entries in the ACL
- Examine existing entries in the ACL
- Modify ACL settings
- Add, rename, or delete roles in the ACL

See Table 19.33 for the class properties. The class methods are shown in Table 19.34.

Table 19.33 *NotesACL* **Properties**

Property	Description	Data Type	Usage
Parent	The database that contains the ACL.	NotesDatabase	Read Only
Roles	All of the roles defined within the ACL.	Array of strings	Read Only

Table 19.34 *NotesACL* **Methods**

Method	Description	Return Data Type	Return Value
AddRole	Given the name of a role, add that role to the ACL.	None	None
CreateACLEntry	Given a person, group, or server name and an access level, create a new ACL entry.	NotesACL Entry	The newly created ACL entry
DeleteRole	Given the name of a role, delete that role from the ACL.	None	None
GetEntry	Given a person, group, or server name, find the corresponding ACL entry.	NotesACL Entry	The ACL entry for the person, group, or server
GetFirstEntry	Find the first entry in the ACL.	NotesACL Entry	The first entry in the ACL

(continues)

Table 19.34   Continued

Method	Description	Return Data Type	Return Value
GetNextEntry	Given any ACL entry, find the next one.	NotesACL Entry	The next early in the ACL
RenameRole	Given the name of a role, find that role and rename it.	None	None
Save	Save any changes that have been made to the ACL.	None	None

Creating ACL Entries

The CreateACLEntry method lets you create a new ACL entry for a person, group, or server. You specify the name and the level you want to assign, and the method creates a new entry in the ACL.

Finding ACL Entries

You can get a specified ACL entry from the ACL by using the GetEntry method. You supply the name of the person, group, or server, and the method returns you a NotesACLEntry object containing the ACL details for that name. You then use the NotesACLEntry properties to examine or modify the entry. You can also loop through all the ACL entries by using GetFirstEntry and GetNextEntry.

Modifying ACL Settings

New to Release 4.5 is the ability to modify the ACL setting: Enforce a consistent Access Control List across all replicas of this database. Set the UniformAccess property to True to do this.

Modifying Roles

You can find all the roles that have been defined in the ACL by using the Roles property. You can also add, rename, or delete roles from the ACL by using AddRole, RenameRole, and DeleteRole.

Saving Your Changes

Any changes you make to an ACL take effect only after you have saved the NotesACL object by using the Save method. If you close the database before calling Save, any changes you have made are lost.

NotesACLEntry

The NotesACLEntry class represents an individual entry in the ACL for a database. You can use the NotesACLEntry class to do the following:

■ Add or delete names in the ACL

■ Change some of the actions that a user can perform in the database

■ Change the roles assigned to a name in the ACL

See Tables 19.35 and 19.36 for the properties and methods for the class.

Table 19.35 *NotesACLEntry* **Properties**

Property	Description	Data Type	Usage
CanCreate Documents	True if the ACL entry can create documents in a database	Boolean	Read/Write
CanCreate PersonalAgent	True if the ACL entry can create personal agents in the database	Boolean	Read/Write
CanCreate PersonalFolder	True if the ACL entry can create personal folders in the database	Boolean	Read/Write
CanDelete Documents	True if the ACL entry can delete documents from the database	Boolean	Read/Write
Level	The access level for this ACL entry	Integer constant	Read/Write
Name	The name associated with the ACL entry	String	Read/Write
Parent	The ACL that contains the entry	NotesACL	Read Only
Roles	The roles that are defined for this ACL entry	Array of strings	Read Only

Table 19.36 *NotesACLEntry* **Methods**

Method	Description	Return Data Type	Return Value
DisableRole	Given the name of a role, remove that role from the ACL entry	None	None
EnableRole	Given the name of a role, add that role to the ACL entry	None	None
IsRoleEnabled	Given the name of a role, check whether the ACL entry has that role enabled	Boolean	True if the role is enabled
New	Create a new ACL entry	NotesACL Entry	The newly created entry
Remove	Delete the supplied ACL entry from the ACL	None	None

Creating and Deleting ACL Entries

In addition to using the CreateACLEntry method of the NotesACL class, you can use New to create new entries in an ACL. For example, the following button script creates a new entry in the ACL for the group SupportTeam, and gives the group reader access to the database:

```
Sub Click(Source As Button)
     Dim s As New NotesSession
     Dim db As NotesDatabase
     Dim acl As NotesACL

     Set db = s.CurrentDatabase
     Set acl = db.ACL
     Dim aclGroup As New NotesACLEntry(acl, "SupportTeam", ACLLEVEL_READER)
     Call acl.Save
End Sub
```

If you need to delete an entry from an ACL, use the Remove method.

Modifying ACL Entries

You can find the name associated with an ACL entry by using the Name property, and the current level of access by using the Level property.

You can examine or modify the actions that are available to the ACL entry by using the following four properties: CanCreateDocuments, CanCreatePersonalAgent, CanCreatePersonalFolder, and CanDeleteDocuments, The properties correspond to the Create documents, Create personal agents, Create personal folders, and Delete documents settings in the ACL.

Modifying Roles

The NotesACLEntry class contains a similar set of methods and functions to the NotesACL class for working with roles. As you would expect, the methods in NotesACLEntry refer only to the roles for the entry you are currently working with. For example, the Roles property lists the roles that are enabled for the current ACL entry. You can add the current entry to a role by using EnableRole or remove it by using DisableRole. Use IsRoleEnabled to test whether a specific role is enabled for the current entry.

Saving Your Changes

After making any changes to an ACL entry, you must save your changes by calling the Save method in the parent NotesACL object. If you don't, you lose your changes when you close the database.

NotesLog

The NotesLog class lets you keep track of what your scripts are up to. You have several options for how you record your script's progress. You can log messages to a Notes database, which is useful when you want to keep a rolling history of what your script has done. Alternatively, you can store messages in a mail memo and automatically send the memo when your script has finished doing whatever it is that it does. This is useful to alert people when an script has something useful to tell them, like, "I know I was supposed to copy all those documents last night, but it was late, the server was running slowly, and...." You get the idea. A third option, if your script is running locally, is to write your log messages to a file. For scripts that are agents, you have an additional choice. Each agent has a log associated with it, and you can write messages to that log. You can display the log for an agent by selecting the agent and then selecting Agent, Log from the Notes main menu.

You can use the NotesLog class to do the following:

- Open a database, mail, or file log

- Log actions or errors to the log

- Send Notes events over the network

See Table 19.37 for a list of the NotesLog class properties and Table 19.38 for its methods.

Table 19.37 *NotesLog* **Properties**

Property	Description	Data Type	Usage
LogActions	True if actions should be logged.	Boolean	Read/Write
LogErrors	True if errors should be logged.	Boolean	Read/Write
NumActions	The number of actions that have been logged so far by the script.	Integer	Read Only
NumErrors	The number of errors that have been logged so far by the script.	Integer	Read Only
OverwriteFile	If the log is being written to a file, whether an existing log file should be overwritten or appended to.	Boolean	Read/Write
ProgramName	A name that identifies the script and is used to identify the log entries.	String	Read/Write

Table 19.38 *NotesLog* **Methods**

Method	Description	Return Data Type	Return Value
Close	Close a log.	None	None
LogAction	Write an action message to a log.	None	None
LogError	Write an error message to a log.	None	None
LogEvent	Generate a Notes event.	None	None

(continues)

Table 19.38   Continued

Method	Description	Return Data Type	Return Value
New	Create a new log.	NotesLog	The newly created log
OpenAgentLog	Open a log for an agent.	None	None
OpenFileLog	Given a file name, open the file and write any subsequent action or error messages to the file.	None	None
OpenMailLog	Create a new mail memo addressed to the recipients you specify. Write any subsequent action or error message to the memo and mail the memo when the log is closed.	None	None
OpenNotesLog	Given a server and file name, open the specified log database. Write any subsequent action or error messages to the database.	None	None

Creating a Log

You create a new log by using either the CreateLog method in NotesSession or the New method. With either method, you supply a name to identify the new log. You can access this name later by using the ProgramName property.

Opening a Log

You have four options for the type of log you want to create, and each type of log has a method to open it. OpenNotesLog opens a specified Notes database as the logging database. The database must be based on the StdR4AgentLog template, which comes with Notes. If you look at the design of the template, you see that it is designed to store and display log entries. You can create one log database for all your agents, or individual log databases for heavily used agents. When you log messages to the database, a new Log Entry document is created for each message.

> **Tip**
>
> If you're going to open a log database from a server-based script, make sure that the log database is on the same server. Scripts that run on servers can't open databases on other servers.

To open a mail log, use OpenMailLog. You supply the method with the names of the people or groups to receive the mail memo and optionally the subject line for the memo. Any log entries you write are stored in the mail memo until you close the log. The mail memo is then mailed to the list of recipients. The third open method is `OpenFileLog`. With this method, you supply fully qualified path and file name where you want to store your log messages. The last open method is `OpenAgentLog` and you use this method to log messages to the log associated with an agent.

Specifying What to Log

By default, actions and errors are written to the log. If you don't want to log either of these, set the `LogActions` or `LogErrors` property to False. You can check how many actions and errors have been logged so far by reading the `NumActions` and `NumErrors` properties. These properties are useful if you want to limit the size of a log to a specified number of log entries. If you're using a log file, you can set `OverwriteFile` to True to overwrite any existing file with the same name as your log file. If `OverwriteFile` is False, your log messages are appended to the log file.

Writing to a Log

When you want to write a log message to your log, call one of the `LogAction`, `LogError`, or `LogEvent` methods.

`LogAction` does one of the following, depending on the type of log you've opened:

- If you're logging to a Notes Database, `LogAction` creates a new Log Entry document in the database containing the text you supply to the method.

- If you're using a Mail log, the method writes the current date and time, followed by your log message to the Body of the mail memo.

- For file logs, `LogAction` writes the current date and time, followed by your log message as the next line in the file.

`LogError` is similar, except that you supply the method with an error code and a description, which is then written to the log the same way as in `LogAction`.

`LogEvent` is different in that it sends a Notes event message over the network. You can use `LogEvent` to send alerts to systems management software such as NotesView.

Closing a Log

When you are finished logging messages, you close the log by using the `Close` method. If you are using a mail log, `Close` sends the mail memo to its intended recipients.

NotesDateTime

One of the potentially confusing things about working with dates and times in LotusScript is that you have to deal with two different date-time formats: the Notes date-time format and the LotusScript date-time format. The `NotesDateTime` object represents a date and time in Notes format. As such, it has a date component, a time component, a time zone component, and a daylight savings time adjustment. It stores times to an accuracy of hundredths of a second. Contrast this with the LotusScript date-time variant, which has only a date component and a time component that stores times to the nearest second.

When you get a date-time value from a Notes document, you get it as a NotesDateTime object. You can use the NotesDateTime object to do the following:

- Convert between the Notes date-time format and the LotusScript date-time format
- Convert between the Notes date-time format and text strings
- Modify the date and time components of a Notes date-time

See Table 19.39 for the class properties and Table 19.40 for its methods.

Table 19.39 *NotesDateTime* Properties

Property	Description	Data Type	Usage
GMTTime	The date-time coverted to Greenwich Mean Time.	String	Read Only
IsDST	True if the computer running the script is set to observe daylight savings time, and daylight savings time is currently in effect.	Boolean	Read Only
LocalTime	The date-time in the local time zone.	String	Read/Write
LSGMTTime	The date-time converted to Greenwich Mean Time.	Variant of type DATE	Read Only
LSLocalTime	The date-time in the local time zone.	Variant of type DATE	Read Only
TimeZone	The current time zone.	Integer	Read Only
ZoneTime	The date-time adjusted for the TimeZone and IsDST properties and returned as a string.	String	Read Only

Table 19.40 *NotesDateTime* Methods

Method	Description	Return Data Type	Return Value
AdjustDay	Add or subtract the number of days you specify from the date-time.	None	None
AdjustHour	Add or subtract the number of hours you specify from the date-time.	None	None
AdjustMinute	Add or subtract the number of minutes you specify from the date-time.	None	None

Method	Description	Return Data Type	Return Value
AdjustMonth	Add or subtract the number of months you specify from the date-time.	None	None
AdjustSecond	Add or subtract the number of seconds you specify from the date-time.	None	None
AdjustYear	Add or subtract the number of years you specify from the date-time.	None	None
ConvertToZone	Convert a date-time to a specified time zone.	None	None
New	Create a new date-time object.	NotesDate Time	The newly created date-time object
SetAnyDate	Set the date part of the date-time so that it matches any date. The time part of the date-time is not changed.	None	None
SetAnyTime	Set the time part of the date-time so that it matches any time. The date part of the date-time is not changed.	None	None
SetNow	Set the date-time value to today's date and the current time.	None	None
TimeDifference	Given two date-time values, return the time difference in seconds between them.	Long	The number of seconds between the two date-times.

Creating a *NotesDateTime* Object

To create a new NotesDateTime object, you can use either the CreateDateTime method of NotesSession or the New method. You supply a string representing a date and time, and the methods return a new NotesDateTime object representing that date. You can specify the date and time in many different formats. Following are some of the formats:

- MM/DD/YYYY HH:MM:SS PM—For example, '05/29/1992 14:30:00 PM'

- MM/YYYY—For example, '12/2001'

- MM/DD HH:MM:SS—For example, '07/27 17:04:00'

By the way, you *are* using four-figure dates in all your LotusScript programs, aren't you? It's not that long to the year 2000!

After you have a NotesDateTime object, you can set it to the current date and time by using the SetNow method. You can also use SetAnyDate and SetAnyTime to set the date and time parts of the object to match any date or time.

Converting a Date to and from LotusScript Format

There are two properties that let you convert between the different date-time formats. LSLocalTime lets you convert a Notes date-time format to its equivalent LotusScript date-time format. You can also set the LSLocalTime property to convert a LotusScript date-time into a Notes date-time. The following example shows how to convert a Notes date-time format date and time into a LotusScript date-time:

```
Dim dtNotes As New NotesDateTime("07/27/1996 11:03 PM")
Dim datLotusScript As Variant
datLotusScript = dtNotes.LSLocalTime
```

In this example, the LotusScript date-time is set to represent 07/27/1996 11:03 PM, irrespective of the time zone setting for the computer.

You can also set the LSLocalTime property to convert a LotusScript date-time into its Notes date-time equivalent.

The second method, LSGMTTime, not only converts the Notes date-time into LotusScript format, it also converts the time component into Greenwich Mean Time. In the preceding example, if you replace the call to LSLocalTime with a call to LSGMTTime and run the script on a computer set to Eastern Standard Time, the LotusScript date-time is set to 07/28/1996 04:03 AM.

If you need to find the time zone setting for a Notes date-time, use the TimeZone property. The property returns an integer representing the time zone. When you need to know whether daylight savings time is in effect for a Notes date-time, you can use the IsDST property to check. If the computer on which you run the script is set to observe daylight savings time and daylight savings time is currently in effect, IsDST returns True.

Converting a Date to and from a Text String

If you need to convert a date-time between a Notes date-time value and a text string, you have two properties to help you. LocalTime and GMTTime work in a similar way to their LotusScript equivalents, except that they translate Notes date-time values to and from plain old text strings. You can also use the new ZoneTime property to get a date-time value displayed in its original time zone.

Modifying a Date and Time

You can modify parts of a date-time by using the AdjustYear, AdjustMonth, AdjustDay, AdjustHour, AdjustMinute, and AdjustSecond methods. For example, to calculate the date two weeks ago, use the following script:

```
Dim dtNotes As New NotesDateTime("Today")
Call dtNotes.AdjustDay(-14)
```

The methods are smart enough to adjust any parts of the date-time that need to be updated. For example, if the script runs on 2 July, the month part of the date-time is automatically changed to June. You can convert a date-time from one time zone to another by using `ConvertToZone`.

Performing Date and Time Calculations

Use the `TimeDifference` method to calculate the number of seconds between two Notes date-time values.

NotesDateRange

`NotesDateRange` is one of the new Notes classes introduced with Release 4.5. You use `NotesDateRange` objects to represent a time span. See Table 19.41 for the class properties.

Table 19.41 *NotesDateRange* **Properties**

Property	Description	Data Type	Usage
EndDateTime	The end of the date range.	NotesDate Time	Read/Write
StartDateTime	The start of the date range.	NotesDate Time	Read/Write
Text	The date range as a string.	String	Read/Write

Set the `StartDateTime` property to a `NotesDateTime` object representing the beginning of the time span and set the `EndDateTime` property to another `NotesDateTime` object representing the end of the span. You can then read the start and end dates by using the `Text` property. For example, the `Text` property of a `NotesDateRange` object could be `10/01/96 11:15:00 AM—10/03/96 11:15:00 AM`.

NotesName

`NotesName` is another of the new Release 4.5 classes. It represents a user or server name within Notes and lets you access the various components of hierarchical names. For example, you can use a `NotesName` object to extract the organization component of a user's name.

> **Note**
>
> All of the properties of the `NotesName` class are Read Only, so you can't use this class to update user or server names.

The class properties are listed in Table 19.42, and its one method is shown in Table 19.43.

Table 19.42 *NotesName* **Properties**

Property	Description	Data Type	Usage
Abbreviated	The abbreviated form of a hierarchical name.	String	Read Only
ADMD	The administration domain name part of a hierarchical name.	String	Read Only
Canonical	The name in canonical format.	String	Read Only
Common	The common name (CN) part of a hierarchical name.	String	Read Only
Country	The country (C) part of a hierarchical name.	String	Read Only
Generation	The generation part of a name.	String	Read Only
Given	The given part of a name.	String	Read Only
Initials	The initials of a name.	String	Read Only
IsHierarchical	True if the name is hierarchical.	Boolean	Read Only
Keyword	The name in keyword format.	String	Read Only
Organization	The organization (O) part of a hierarchical name.	String	Read Only
OrgUnit1	The first organizational unit (OU1) part of a hierarchical name.	String	Read Only
OrgUnit2	The second organizational unit (OU2) part of a hierarchical name.	String	Read Only
OrgUnit3	The third organizational unit (OU3) part of a hierarchical name.	String	Read Only
OrgUnit4	The fourth organizational unit (OU4) part of a hierarchical name.	String	Read Only
PRMD	The private management domain name part of a name.	String	Read Only
Surname	The surname part of a name.	String	Read Only

Table 19.43 *NotesName* **Methods**

Method	Description	Return Data Type	Return Value
New	Create a new NotesName object.	NotesName	The new NotesName object

NotesInternational

The NotesInternational class is new to Release 4.5 and gives you access to the international settings on the machine running a script. For example, on a machine running Windows, you can access the international settings that have been configured by using the Control Panel.

Note

If any of the international settings are changed, Notes recognizes the change immediately.

The class properties are shown in Table 19.44.

Table 19.44 *NotesInternational* **Properties**

Property	Description	Data Type	Usage
AMString	The string that indicates a time before noon in the local language.	String	Read Only
CurrencyDigits	The number of digits after a decimal point.	Integer	Read Only
CurrencySymbol	The currency symbol.	String	Read Only
DateSep	The character used to separate the year, month, and day in a date.	String	Read Only
DecimalSep	The character used to separate the parts of a decimal number.	String	Read Only
IsCurrency Space	True if there is a space between the currency symbol and the amount.	Boolean	Read Only
IsCurrency Suffix	True if the currency symbol is displayed after the amount.	Boolean	Read Only
IsCurrency Zero	True if a fraction has a leading zero when displayed as a decimal number.	Boolean	Read Only
IsDateDMY	True if the date format is day-month-year.	Boolean	Read Only
IsDateMDY	True if the date format is month-day-year.	Boolean	Read Only
IsDateYMD	True if the date format is year-month-day.	Boolean	Read Only
IsDST	True if daylight savings time is in effect.	Boolean	Read Only
IsTime24Hour	True if the time format is 24-hour.	Boolean	Read Only

(continues)

III

Working with LotusScript

Table 19.44	Continued		
Property	**Description**	**Data Type**	**Usage**
PMString	The string indicating a time after noon in the local language.	String	Read Only
ThousandsSep	The thousands separator character for numbers.	String	Read Only
TimeSep	The character used to separate the hours, minutes, and seconds in a time.	String	Read Only
TimeZone	The time zone setting.	Integer	Read Only
Today	The string that means today in the local language.	String	Read Only
Tomorrow	The string that means tomorrow in the local language.	String	Read Only
Yesterday	The string that means yesterday in the local language.	String	Read Only

NotesNewsletter

Suppose that you have a collection of Notes documents, perhaps the results of a full-text search of a database or a set of documents that haven't been processed by an agent. Wouldn't it be great if you could create a summary document containing doclinks to all the documents in the collection? Well, by using the NotesNewsletter class you can.

The class lets you create two types of summary document. The first type is based on all documents in the collection; the second type includes information from just one of the documents in the collection.

See Table 19.45 for the class properties and Table 19.46 for its methods.

Table 19.45	*NotesNewsletter* Properties		
Property	**Description**	**Data Type**	**Usage**
DoScore	For newsletters created by using the FormatMsgWithDoclinks method, True if the relevance score for each document should be included.	Boolean	Read/Write
DoSubject	For newsletters created by using the FormatMsgWithDoclinks method, True if the subject of each	Boolean	Read/Write

Property	Description	Data Type	Usage
	document should be included. (Use SubjectItemName to define which field to use as the subject.)		
SubjectItem Name	For newsletters created by using the FormatMsgWithDoclinks method, the name of the field to treat as the subject or title of the document.	String	Read/Write

Table 19.46 *NotesNewsletter* Methods

Method	Description	Return Data Type	Return Value
FormatDocument	Given the position of a document within the newsletter, create a picture of that document. Then create a new document in the supplied database and store the picture as the body of the new document.	Notes Document	The newly created document
FormatMsg WithDoclinks	Given a database, create a newsletter document in the database.	Notes Document	The newsletter document
New	Create a new newsletter.	Notes Newsletter	The new newsletter

Creating a Newsletter

You have two ways to create a new NotesNewsletter. You can use the CreateNewsletter method of NotesSession or the NotesNewsletter New method. With both methods, you supply a document collection containing the set of documents you want to include in the newsletter.

Formatting a Newsletter

After you have created a Newsletter object, you have two options for how to create a summary document from it. You can use the FormatMsgWithDoclinks method to create a document containing links to all the documents within the collection. You supply the method with the database in which to create the new document.

The new document has a summary line for each document in the collection. By default, each line contains the relevance score for the document, followed by a doclink to the document. If you don't want to include the relevance score, set the DoScore property to False. You can also include a title for each document by using the DoSubject and SubjectItemName properties. You set SubjectItemName to the name of the field that contains the text you want to use as the title. You then set DoSubject to True to include the title in each line of the newsletter. For example, suppose that the documents in the collection all contain a field called DocTitle, which stores the subject of the document. If you set SubjectItemName to DocTitle and DoSubject to True, each line in the newsletter consists of the relevance score for the document, a doclink to the document, followed by the text from the DocTitle field.

You can use the FormatDocument method to create a new document containing a picture of a particular document from the collection. This is similar to forwarding a document, where the new mail memo displays a picture of the forwarded document. You supply the method with the database in which to create the new document and a number to indicate which of the documents to include from the collection. The method creates the new document containing a picture of the document from the collection.

Saving or Mailing a Newsletter

The document you create by using the NotesNewsletter methods is, in Notes terms, the same as any other document. You can call the document's Save method to save the document, or you can use the Send method to mail the document.

NotesTimer

The NotesTimer object lets you set up a timer that you can use to trigger an event. You specify a time interval and each time the time interval has passed, an Alarm event is triggered. Its properties and methods are listed in Tables 19.47 and 19.48.

Table 19.47 *NotesTimer* Properties			
Property	**Description**	**Data Type**	**Usage**
Comment	A comment to identify the timer.	String	Read/Write
Enabled	Set to True to enable the timer. By default, a timer is enabled.	Boolean	Read/Write
Interval	The number of seconds to wait before triggering an Alarm event.	Integer	Read/Write

Table 19.48 *NotesTimer* Methods			
Method	**Description**	**Return Data Type**	**Return Value**
New	Create a new timer.	NotesTimer	The newly created timer

To use a timer, do one of the following:

- Declare a NotesTimer object in the (Declarations) or (Options) part of a script.

- Create a NotesTimer object by using New or the CreateTimer method of NotesSession. You supply a time interval and an optional comment.

- Use the `On Event Alarm` statement to define a sub to call each time the time interval has passed.

You use the `Interval` property to set the time interval for the timer and the `Comment` property to add an identifying comment to the timer. You can enable and disable the timer by using its `Enabled` property.

For example, to set up and use a timer to call a sub every minute, you first declare the timer in the `(Options)` or `(Declarations)` section as follows:

```
Dim tmrMinute As NotesTimer
```

Then, in part of your script, you create the timer and define the sub to call when the timer time period has expired:

```
Set tmrMinute = New NotesTimer(60, "One minute timer")
On Event Alarm From tmrMinute Call DoOneMinuteProcessing
```

Because, by default, the timer is enabled, the `DoOneMinuteProcessing` sub will be called approximately every minute.

Caution

Don't rely on the accuracy of the timing too much, as other events can delay the time at which the Alarm event is triggered.

From Here...

In this chapter, you learned about the Notes object classes. You have looked at the properties and methods of each class in detail and seen some examples of how to use them from LotusScript.

For information on related topics, see the following chapters:

- Chapter 17, "LotusScript Basics," discusses the basic features and syntax of LotusScript.

- Chapter 18, "Writing Scripts with LotusScript," shows you how to use LotusScript within Notes.

- "ODBC and Lotus Components" on the CD looks at how you can use the ODBC LotusScript extensions and Lotus components in your database designs.

III

Working with LotusScript

Part I

Notes Basics

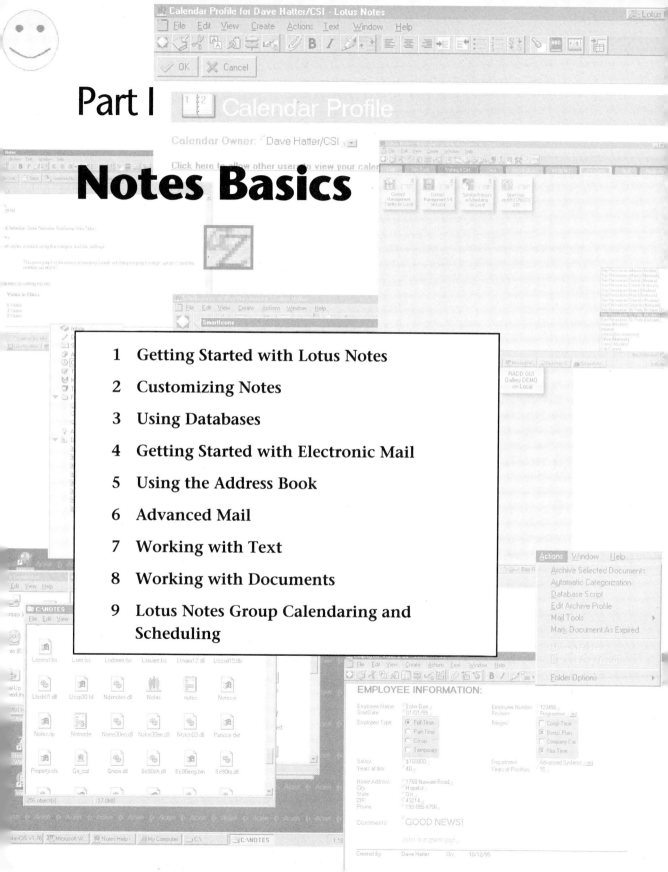

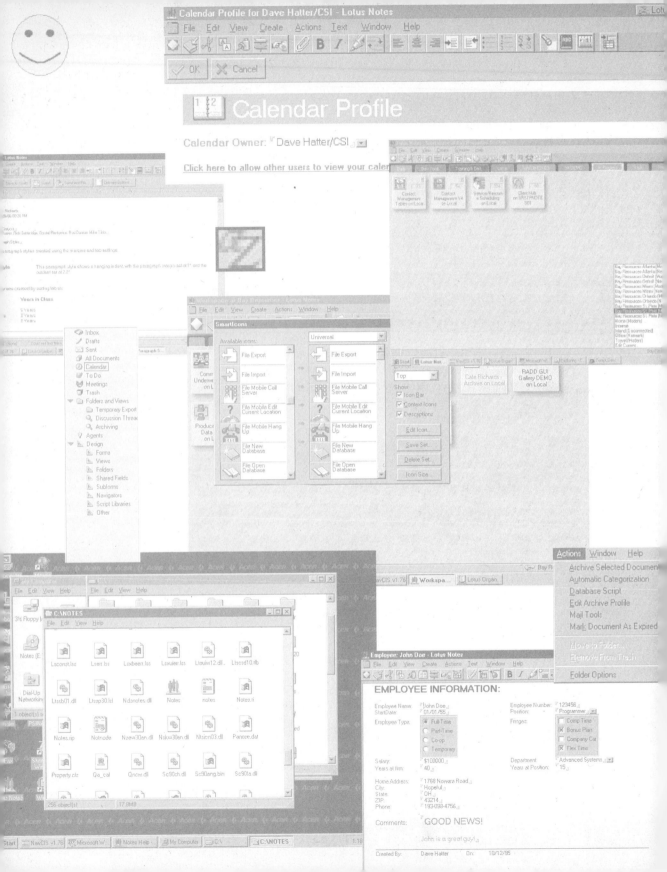

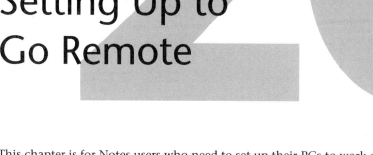

Chapter 20

Setting Up to Go Remote

This chapter is for Notes users who need to set up their PCs to work on Notes away from the office—that is, users who aren't connected to a Notes server through a local area network. You can work remote all the time (referred to as remote only) or part of the time (referred to as network/remote). With Lotus Notes' remote capability, you can easily send and receive mail, use public databases, and participate in Notes discussions as though you are working on-site.

This chapter will take you further into the world of working remote by walking you through setting up your Notes Mail to work off (and on) the network, connecting to a server via telephone lines, creating replica copies of your databases, exchanging information remotely, and tips on working smart while away from the office.

> **Note**
>
> As you will learn in Part VI, "Working with the InterNotes Family," you can also work with databases and get your e-mail using an Internet Browser if Lotus' Domino server is set up in your company to allow access in this manner. This chapter, and Chapter 21, "Working Remote," however, focus on remotely connecting directly from your Notes client to your Notes server through a dial-up connection. To learn how to access Notes' database via the Internet, check out Part VI of this book!

What Does It Mean to Work Remote?

When you connect to a Notes server through a local area network, your PC, whether it is a desktop or a laptop, is connected by cables directly through a LAN to one or more servers. You have direct access to databases on the servers in your network. Usually, you also have access to printing resources and other file servers (servers used to store files and applications for you). This access often enables you to work with a large amount of information without having to have a large hard disk to store it all. You also can work with the current database information and send and receive e-mail instantly.

Some of the main topics in this chapter are

- What Notes needs to work when you are not connected directly to a server

- How to set up your network ports for re-mote usage

- How to set up your modem to work remote

- How to set up your location and server connections so that you can make contact with your Notes server(s)

Notes works quite differently, however, when you work remote. When you set up Notes on your remote PC, you must use a modem to connect to a Notes server through a telephone line connection. You create copies of all the databases you want to use and store them on your PC's hard disk (unless you are working strictly through Interactive Connection, which Chapter 21 discusses). If you are using a printer, then you typically have the printer cables attached directly to your PC. In other words, you have to be in physical possession of just about everything you need to work with when you are off the network; you control the times when information is passed between you and others on the network because you must initiate the call to the server to begin the communication process.

Most often, a remote PC is a laptop that you use when you travel. You also can work remote with Notes on a desktop PC at home or in another office. Regardless of the type of equipment you use, keep in mind that you will require more disk space when working remote because you will have to store replica copies of databases on your hard drive. You will learn more about replica copies as you read through the rest of this chapter, and Chapter 21, "Working Remote."

The size of these copies depends on the amount of information the databases store and how much of the information you elect to carry with you remotely. In Release 4.x, the maximum size a database can grow to is four gigabytes. Although most databases will not grow to their maximum allowable size, they can be quite large and can require a significant amount of space. The minimum recommended amount of free hard disk space for running Notes, and working with the databases you need on your remote PC, is 100M—and that may be cutting things close if you are accessing multiple databases! You will find tips on minimizing your hard disk space usage in Chapter 21, which explains how to make and use databases while working remote.

Considering Disk Space When Going Remote

If you are getting ready to work remote, but have not yet purchased the PC that you will use, talk with your Notes administrator to find out how much disk space you will need to successfully work remote and access all of the applications you will require within your company. If you install the full version of Notes on your PC (all of the operating files, Help files, documentation files, sample databases, and so on), you are looking at using at least 55M of disk space before you make the first copy of a database you will use from the server! Keep in mind that most operating systems do not perform efficiently if you don't allow for at least 5M of free disk space to be used as swap file space while you are working.

You can elect to install Notes without all of the documentation and sample databases to minimize the disk space used. This type of installation is recommended if you are working only part of the time away from the office and you have access to these files when you are on the network if you need them. Typically, individuals who are planning to design (or customize) new databases and want to have an example of a database to use for ideas or as a template use the sample databases stored in a subdirectory titled EXAMPLES.

If you're not planning to design databases, you can safely elect not to install these databases on your hard drive. Documentation databases, which are stored in a directory titled DOC, are online copies of Notes documentation. You may want to install the documentation databases, and then delete the databases you don't find useful for your needs.

The Notes Help database (HELP4.NSF) is very large, but it provides online help for most Notes questions. When you were installing Notes 4.x, you or your Notes administrator also installed a database titled Notes Help Lite, unless you deselected this option during the installation. The file name for Notes Help Lite is HELPLITE.NSF, and it is stored in your C:\NOTES\DATA subdirectory (unless you specified a different data directory during setup).

Help Lite contains a subset of the Notes Help documents. It provides help while you travel, but it uses less disk space than the full Help database. Help Lite contains information you are more likely to need when you use Notes away from the office, such as information on working remote. It does not contain a lot of information on non-remote topics, such as database design.

If you work remote all of the time, you may want to delete the Help Lite database (by highlighting its icon and selecting File, Database, Delete, Yes) and keep the full Notes Help database, because you will most likely need to access help information on topics not covered in Help Lite. You can conserve some disk space by not carrying two copies of the same information on your hard drive.

However, if you typically work remote only a part of the time, you may want to delete the full Notes Help database from the hard drive of your PC and carry only the Help Lite database on your hard drive to conserve disk space. You can always access the full version of the Notes Help database from the network when you are working in the office.

Your Notes administrator can help you decide which of these databases you need while working remote. It is always recommended that you consult with your Notes administrator to ensure that you are working within the standards set for your company.

What You Need to Work Remote

To work remote, you need the following:

- A PC with Notes 4.x installed

- A modem connected to your PC with an asynchronous (serial) port enabled and a modem (MDM) file that's compatible with your modem

- The exact name of the Notes server(s) you will access

- The phone number(s) for the modem connection to the Notes server(s)

- The Notes server(s) name(s)

- A direct-dial, analog phone line

- A certified Notes User ID

Your Notes administrator also must do the following:

- Grant you appropriate access to the Notes server(s)

- Set up the Notes server(s) to receive incoming calls through a modem

- Enable network ports on the Notes server

In the following sections, you learn about modems and phone lines. The remainder of this chapter walks you through configuring your PC to work remote.

Using Modems

Modems, which are the most common type of communications processor, convert the digital signals from your computer at one end of a communications link into analog frequencies, which can travel over ordinary telephone lines. At the other end of the communications line, a modem converts the transmitted data back into digital form that the receiving computer can process.

You can buy several types and speeds of modems today. An internal modem (located inside your PC) is certainly more convenient when you travel with a laptop, but it is not always the recommended type of modem for your needs and is not supported in some older laptops. An external modem connects through a port outside your PC. External modems are now available in desktop models (meant for stationary use) and pocket models, known for their compact, lightweight, portable features.

Note

Most new laptops support PCMCIA cards—often referred to as PC cards—which are about the size of a credit card, and fit into small slots on the side of your laptop. One of the most popular PCMCIA cards is the modem card. These small, credit card-size modems are very popular due to their high-speed data transmission capabilities—typically 14,400 baud to 28,800 baud—and their lightweight, compact features (which helps keep the laptop weight down when you are lugging around a PC all day!). They are also popular because they are easy to take in and out of a laptop.

When you choose a modem, one of the most important factors is the modem's speed, which is measured in bits per second, also known as the baud. A higher baud means your PC and the server can exchange information more quickly, which results in a shorter (and cheaper) phone call. In business settings today, most users use 9,600 to 28,800 baud modems. The least expensive modems in use today are 2,400-baud modems, which have longer exchange times and higher phone costs. Several popular modem models on the market today offer speeds from 9,600 baud to 28,800 baud. Recent modems have speed capabilities even greater than 28,800 baud.

Paying attention to what type of baud the modem speed is manufactured for is also important. Fax modem speed refers only to the speed that a fax can be transmitted through the modem; data modem speed refers to how fast data can be transmitted through the modem. A 9,600/2,400 fax data modem, for example, enables you to transmit faxes at

9,600 baud and data at 2,400 baud. Lotus Notes transfers data (the information you are exchanging when you work in databases). Therefore, you must pay attention to the data baud that your modem supports. You should try to get a modem that supports at least 14,400 baud to help keep your phone calling costs down, as well as to keep the server from being tied up for lengthy periods of time. Table 20.1 illustrates just three average times for data transmission based on the baud of the modem you and the server are using.

Table 20.1   Comparison Transmission Times for Three Baud Values

Time	Baud Values
25 minutes	9,600
15 minutes	14,400
7 minutes	28,800

> **Note**
>
> When working with Lotus Notes remotely, you will be prompted when you have connected with the remote server and be told at which speed you have connected. The prompt information tells you the port connection speed, which is the speed at which your port is transmitting data to the port on the server.
>
> However, in many cases, this speed is not the actual speed at which data is being transmitted. The speed in which the carrier can successfully transmit data is also a factor. For the purposes of using Notes remote, think of a carrier as everything in between your modem and the server's modem, including the phone lines, hotel switchboards, and so on.
>
> When connecting internationally, through old phone systems or even through hotel switchboards, the carrier speed may be greatly reduced. You may receive a prompt that you have connected to the server at a port rate of 9,600 baud, for example, but everything will seem to be happening in slow motion. This problem is most likely due to the slow carrier speed for the transmission.

Notes can work with all the many different makes and models of modems that you can find, as long as you can locate or create a modem command file for your modem (see the following paragraph). Many manufacturers sell modems that are known as Hayes compatible, indicating that software can control them using commands that were standardized by a company called Hayes. Notes works well with these types of modems.

Notes comes with files called modem command files, which have MDM file extensions. These files provide the commands PCs need to use your modem. If you use a non-Hayes compatible modem, you need to search for a modem command file configured for your modem or spend time editing a modem command file to meet your needs. Editing a modem command file can be a considerable chore, and it's best done by an expert or at least, with assistance from one.

Caution

Before you buy a modem, check with your Notes administrator to make sure that your modem is compatible with the server's modem. Otherwise, you may experience problems with your modem connections, have to connect only at very low speeds, or sacrifice some of the special functionality of your modem in order to talk with the Notes server. Typically, Hayes-compatible modems are your best bet because Notes runs very well with them.

Note

If you purchase a new modem, and find that your particular modem's file is not currently available in Notes, you can check with your modem's manufacturer to see whether they have an updated file, or check the Internet services (such as CompuServe), which often have modem files stored in libraries by their manufacturers. You can also check out the Mobile Survival Kit, which houses many of the latest modem files available. You can find this database in CompuServe by entering **GO LOTUSC** and checking out the Library in this forum, or accessing the database from Lotus' Web site: **www.lotus.com**. You will find the Mobile Survival Kit in the Notes support section.

Getting Help with Your Modem Setup. If you have trouble with your modem, you have resources to turn to for additional help. Your Notes administrator is the first resource available to you for assistance with modem installation and troubleshooting.

The modem's manufacturer and the documentation that accompanied your modem may also provide the key to getting your modem set up properly. Look for a section in your modem documentation that indicates the appropriate modem files that may be compatible with your modem, as well as any special settings that may be required.

Also available from Lotus is the Mobile Survival Kit database, which provides debugging information for problems with modems, as well as additional modem files that may work better with your particular modem. A copy of this database is on the CD that accompanies this book. You will find it as an attachment in the Using Lotus Notes 4.5 database.

This database, if it's available to your company, will most likely be installed on a Notes server(s) on your network. Check your network's Database Catalog to see whether this database is available to you. If you do not see it listed, ask your Notes administrator if this database was acquired for use by your company through partnership agreements. As indicated in the preceding Note, you can also find this database on the Lotus Web site. It is updated weekly, so you will find the most up-to-date files there. Finally, several other outside resources, bulletin boards, and help services may be available to you if you have substantial trouble with your modem.

Phone Line Requirements

When you communicate with a server remotely, the modem you are using converts the data signals sent from your PC into analog signals that can be sent over a telephone line. The modem on the server then converts the analog signals back into digital form that your PC can understand. Having the proper type of phone line to transmit the signals being sent from your modem is therefore important.

To work with a modem, you need a direct-dial analog phone line, also referred to as a voice line. Most residential locations have an analog line into the house. Digital lines transmit digital signals that your modem cannot interpret—you typically find digital lines in office buildings.

You also must make sure that special telephone services such as call waiting and call park (similar to putting a call on hold), which may interrupt communications on your line, are discontinued or disabled when you work with your modem. Even a split-second interruption in the phone signal can cause your modem connection to be terminated. Contact your local phone company for details on the specific services they offer that may interfere with your modem.

Tip

If you can temporarily disable a special telephone service by pressing a particular number/character sequence (*70 on a touchtone phone or 1170 on a rotary phone in most North American areas), you may also be able to disable this service through Notes each time you dial the server. Enter the number sequence as part of the prefix number when you call a server. You may need to experiment or contact your phone company for additional information. More information on how to enter phone numbers is provided in the section titled "Setting Up Connections Records" later in this chapter.

Ideally, you would have a dedicated phone line to use if you are planning to work a great deal with Notes from your home. If you want to install a phone line, specify to the phone company that you want a POTS (plain old telephone service) line. This request ensures that you receive the type of line you need to work remote. You may also consider getting Integrated Services Digital Network (ISDN) service—particularly if you are planning to communicate a lot of data back and forth with a server(s). ISDN sends digital signals, which are more compatible with computer systems than analog systems, and the speed in which the data is transmitted is much greater. However, this type of service is more expensive, and you will need to get a special modem to use it.

Getting Started

Although Lotus Notes provides you with all the software capability you need to work remote, you first need to set up your system before you can work away from the network. Each step is discussed in detail later, but the following list gives you an overview of the steps you must perform on your PC:

1. Enable a port.

2. Enable your modem.

3. Create a location(s).

4. Create a server connection(s).

The remainder of this chapter discusses these steps in more detail. An additional step, setting up Notes for remote mail, is covered in Chapter 21 because the settings you make will depend on how you elect to work with the Notes server.

Enabling a Port

Before you can work with Notes remote, you must make sure that the proper communications ports are set up correctly on your system. Communications ports serve as a gateway through which your PC can "talk" with other hardware through special connections. To use Notes on a network, you enable a LAN port, which is denoted by the letters LAN and a number (such as LAN0). When you are working remote, you use a communications port, which is denoted by the letters COM and the number of the port (such as COM1). Notes makes setting up the type of communications ports you need to work with easy.

> **Tip**
>
> If you use your computer to work on a LAN at one site and to work remote at another, you can enable the LAN port and the COM port at the same time. Notes switches to the appropriate port as necessary based on the location you select for your working session. You will learn more about setting up locations shortly.

Follow these steps to verify, change, or set up your network port(s):

1. Choose File, Tools, User Preferences to open the User Preferences dialog box.

2. Select the Ports icon to display the Ports Setup panel, as shown in Figure 20.1.

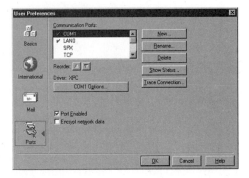

Fig. 20.1   To set up your communication ports, you use the Ports Setup panel of the User Preferences dialog box.

> **Note**
>
> You may not see as many ports listed in your Ports Setup pane as shown in Figure 20.1. The number of ports displayed is dependent on the setup of your computer.

3. In the Communication Ports scroll box, select the COM port attached to your modem. (COM2 often is used with modems for portable PCs, particularly internal modems. COM1 is often used for external modems. Check your PC's user manual to determine which COM port you need to choose.)

4. To see the status of the COM port you have selected, select the COM port in Communication Ports scroll box, and then select Show Status (see Figure 20.2). If you see any message indicating that the COM port is performing a function, select another COM port for your modem. The Port Status dialog box in Figure 20.2 indicates that no activity is taking place. Select Cancel to close this dialog box and return to the Ports Setup panel.

Fig. 20.2 Opening the Port Status dialog box is a fast way of determining whether another device is utilizing the port you have selected.

5. Select Port Enabled so that a check mark appears in the check box and next to the selected COM port in the Communication Ports scroll box.

6. If you need to encrypt the data as it's sent over the modem, choose Encrypt Network Data. (This selection slows down the transmission of data by turning off the ability to use data compression. It is really not recommended unless you are transmitting highly sensitive data or suspect that someone is tapping into your transmissions.)

Encryption causes Notes to encode data in such a way that anyone wiretapping a phone line cannot read the data. Notes encodes the data before transmitting it over the phone line and decodes it at the other end. Eavesdroppers see meaningless data if they try to analyze the line.

Leave the Ports Setup dialog box open. You need it to set up your modem in the next section.

Tip

You can reorder the way the ports are sorted in the Communication Ports scroll list by highlighting the COM or LAN port name you want to reorder and clicking the up or down arrow next to the Reorder option below the Communication Ports scroll list. Clicking a Reorder arrow causes the highlighted port to move up or down in the list of ports. Use this technique to move the port names you work with frequently to the top of the list for easier reference.

Defining a New COM Port

If you do not see any COM ports listed in the Port List scroll box, you must define one before you can move forward. This procedure is very simple. When you add a port, you are telling Notes what communications port on your PC to use and specifying what driver and buffer size to use. With the Port Setup dialog box open, follow these instructions to define a port:

1. Select New to display the New Port dialog box.

2. Enter the following information in the appropriate text fields:

   - Name—Enter the COM port that you want to set up. For example, enter COM1. If you are unsure of which port you need to activate, consult your PC and modem documentation.

   - Driver—Select XPC to specify the driver for dial-up use.

   - Select which location(s) will use this port name in the Use Port at the following locations list box. (You learn more about locations later in this chapter in the "Setting Up Locations" section.)

     Your new port setup should look similar to the example in the preceding figure if you are setting up a COM1 port.

3. Click OK to return to the Port Setup panel.

Setting Up Your Modem

Before you can use your modem, you need to specify the particular modem command file to work with your modem, the modem speed (baud) for your modem, and whether your dial setup is pulse or tone. You also may want to customize some additional settings. To set up your modem, follow these steps:

1. If you are not already in the Port Setup panel of the User Preferences dialog box, select File, Tools, User Preferences, and then select the Ports icon; otherwise, skip to step 2.

2. Choose the port's Option button. You will find this button located below the Driver information label in the center of the dialog box. The title of this button changes, along with the defined driver based on the port you have highlighted in the Communication Ports list box. The Additional Setup dialog box appears (see Figure 20.3).

3. From the Modem type list box, choose the type of modem you are using.

   If your exact modem type isn't available, choose the closest compatible type. Refer to your modem's user's guide to determine modem compatibility. If your modem type is not listed, see the next section, "What to Do If Your Modem Is Not Listed."

Fig. 20.3   You can adjust modem settings in the Additional Setup dialog box.

4. Adjust the remaining modem settings, if necessary. (The settings are described in later sections.)

> **Note**
>
> Ignore the buttons labeled Acquire Script and the Log script I/O checkbox. Script files are written and managed by Notes administrators on the Notes servers and are not covered in this book. Script files are similar to modem command files in that you use both to set up communications equipment to work in your environment. For example, if you try to connect to CompuServe's Lotus Notes server to send e-mail out to non-Notes users, you will need a script file provided by CompuServe to log on and navigate you through its complex services to reach the Lotus Notes servers. Your Notes administrator will contact you if you need to make adjustments to these features.

5. Choose OK, and then choose OK again to save your modem and network ports selections.

What to Do If Your Modem Is Not Listed

If your modem type is not listed in the Additional Setup dialog box, choose Auto Configure (for unlisted modems only). Notes will usually be able to adapt to the modem connected to your PC. If you later change your modem type, Notes automatically tries to adapt to the new modem if this file is selected.

If your modem type isn't listed, and the Auto Configure (for unlisted modems) MDM file does not allow your modem to connect with the server, try selecting modem files that may be similar to your modem. If you still cannot get your modem to work with an existing MDM file, you will need to create or edit an existing modem command file. You can do so by choosing one of the generic or null modem files to use as a template, and then selecting the Modem File button. Editing or creating a modem command file is not an easy task for most users; consult your modem's user guide or your Notes administrator for the technical assistance you need.

Choose a modem file specifically designed for your modem when possible. Often, when you use a modem file that is close to the type you need, but is not quite like it, you experience some problems, or lose some of the features of your modem. Refer to "Remote Troubleshooting" on the CD-ROM if you have problems making connections with your modem.

Note

If you cannot see any modem files listed when you open the Additional Setup dialog box, you may have a line missing from your NOTES.INI file. Exit to your command prompt and edit the NOTES.INI file to include the following line:

    ModemFileDirectory=C:\Notes\Data\Modems

If you specified a different data directory when you installed Notes, you will need to modify the entry above to show the path to your MODEMS subdirectory (or wherever you have your .MDM files stored). Save your new NOTES.INI file and exit. You must restart Windows and Notes before the edits will take effect. For more information on editing your NOTES.INI file, read Chapter 2, "Customizing Notes."

Port Speed

In the Additional Setup dialog box, the Maximum Port Speed option specifies the fastest speed at which transmission can take place, depending on the type of modem you use. If you chose Auto Configure as the modem type, choose 19,200; Notes automatically adjusts to the appropriate speed during each session for your particular modem.

Lotus Notes uses data compression when passing information across the phone lines, unless the data you are sending is encrypted. Data compression, for the most part, effectively doubles the speed at which the data is passed across the connection. For example, a modem with a maximum baud of 9,600 can transfer data at the relative speed of 19,200 baud with data compression because twice the amount of data is being passed within the same amount of time.

The speed actually used will be the lesser of the maximum speed you select in this setting and the maximum speed specified in the MDM file you have selected. For example, if you selected 19,200 bps in the Maximum Port Speed option, and the MDM file limits your modem to 9,600 bps as the maximum, you will see a warning like the one shown in Figure 20.4.

Fig. 20.4   This sample error message signals an incompatible modem speed.

If you dial from a hotel or on noisy phone lines, you may need to choose a slower speed than the maximum allowed by your modem to improve your connection. The large amount of electronic noise being processed by your modem at the same time as it is trying to process the data can cause connection problems, and the hotel's PBX switch may not be able to handle high-speed transmissions. Lowering the baud helps your modem to distinguish between what is data and what is noise.

Speaker Volume

The Speaker Volume option in the Additional Setup dialog box determines what you can hear when you dial the server. To hear the modem as it dials, choose any option except Off. If you listen to the modem, you can determine whether your modem is dialing, whether the carrier connection is established, and whether the server's modem and your modem are "shaking hands" (sort of a "Darth Vader with a cold" sound). Hearing the modem is also useful if you manually dial into the server. Choose to hear the modem tones unless you are scheduling your PC to call the server during times where you need quiet, like during the night in your hotel room!

Dial Mode

Use the Dial Mode option in the Additional Setup dialog box to specify what mode of dialing you should use: Tone (as used in a touchtone phone) or Pulse (as used in a rotary phone). The mode of dialing refers to how you dial to make a phone connection, not how the data is transferred (see the earlier discussion on analog signals). If you use a rotary phone, or have a modem style that does not support touchtone dialing, select Pulse under Dial Mode.

Tone is the most common selection in most North American countries. You may need to experiment if you are working internationally or on old phone systems. To verify a tone line, lift the receiver of the telephone connected to the analog phone line and enter a phone number. If the tones on the line vary depending on the numbers you have pressed, you are working in tone mode. If the tones for all of the numbers sound the same, you are working in pulse mode.

> **Note**
>
> Keep in mind that if you travel, you may need to make changes to the dial mode based on where you are trying to dial from. If you try to dial a server, and you receive an error message indicating that a dial tone cannot be found or another strange error message, try changing the dial mode. Typically, locations with relatively modern phone systems support a tone mode for dialing.

Dial Timeout

The Dial Timeout option in the Additional Setup dialog box sets the number of seconds to wait for a connection to a server before canceling the call. The default setting is 60 seconds. If you have problems connecting to a busy server, are dialing overseas, include a calling card number in your dialing, or find that your modem is particularly slow, increase the Dial Timeout setting. You can also increase the Dial Timeout setting for a particular session in the Call Server dialog box. You will learn more about this setting in Chapter 21, "Working Remote."

Notes uses this setting to determine how much time it will spend trying to successfully dial and connect (log on) to the server. Don't increase this setting to too high of a number, or you will find yourself waiting for long periods of time if there is an error in trying to dial a server. Also, don't set it too short, or you will rarely connect to the server in the time allotted! You may need to adjust this setting a few times if you experience problems connecting with the server within the default 60 seconds. Typically, a setting of 60 will work, and a maximum setting of 90 seconds is usually the upper limit you will need.

Hang Up/Idle Time Setting

Use the Hang Up If Idle For option in the Additional Setup dialog box to set the number of minutes your system stays connected to the server without any activity taking place against the server. The default time is 15 minutes. Increase the setting if you need more time. Decrease the amount of time if you don't need a long waiting period. You save in telephone costs and tie up the server for less time if you keep this setting low.

The Hang Up If Idle For setting is based on activity with the server, not activity being performed solely on your hard drive. For example, if you are reading a document in a server copy of a database while connected from a remote location, Notes does not count the time spent reading the document as performing a function against the server because the document is local to your workstation once you open it. Notes begins the idle count-down from the time you open the document until you perform another activity that accesses the server, such as indexing the database, opening another document, saving the document, and so on. You will know the server is being accessed when you see the green and red lights flashing in the modem icon in the lower left corner of the Notes window. Two non-blinking green lights displayed on the modem icon indicate that you are connected, but not actively performing a function with the server.

> ### Caution
>
> If you set up your PC to perform any selection that "talks" to the server while you are connected at least once during the time that is specified in the Hang Up If Idle For section, you will not be disconnected after the Hang Up If Idle time is met, even if you leave the room or otherwise stop working on the server.
>
> Three direct examples come to mind: if you have set up your Mail Preferences to check for mail in the File, Tools, User Preferences, Mail panel more often than the time set in the Hang Up If Idle For setting; if you have set up a macro that accesses a server database to perform its task while you are working on the server as well; and, if you set up your locations to replicate with the server more often than the time set in the Hang Up If Idle For setting.

The server also has a Hang Up If Idle setting, and the shorter of the two times is used. If increasing the Hang Up If Idle time on your system doesn't keep you from disconnecting from the server before your work is finished, contact your Notes administrator.

Logging Modem Input/Output

The Log Modem I/O setting in the Additional Setup dialog box enters modem responses in your system's log entries. Under normal circumstances, you don't need this option, but it can help if you need to troubleshoot modem problems.

If you select Log Modem I/O, each time you try to make a call (or perform just about any function in which your modem is involved), a document will be written in your Notes

Log database, which is stored on your hard drive. After a while, this database becomes quite large, depending on how often you call your server.

▶▶ See "Working Smart Remote," p. 862

Using Log Entries

Notes provides a special template that creates a Notes log on your PC that records all modem activity if you choose Log Modem I/O. (Your server also has a Log database that logs all of the activity—calls, replications, database access, and so on.) When Notes logs a modem activity, it creates a document that lists the details about the call. The log reports successes and failures in dialing remotely and provides you with a record of what occurred during communication with the server.

To view this information, add the Notes log from your C:\NOTES\DATA directory to your desktop (the log file name is always LOG.NSF), and then open the modem log as you would any other database. The Notes log is very beneficial in helping you troubleshoot problems while working remote.

Hardware Flow Control

The Hardware Flow Control option in the Additional Setup dialog box specifies what Notes should do if more data exists than can fit in your system buffer when receiving and transmitting. (In Notes 3.0, this option was called RTS/CTS Flow Control.) Choose this option unless your modem or serial card cannot support flow control. (Consult your modem/serial card documentation.) Activating this setting is especially recommended for transmission speeds of 9,600 baud or greater in order to protect against impaired performance.

Editing the Modem File

You can edit your modem command file, if necessary. For example, if you are receiving a large number of errors indicating that the modem cannot detect a dial tone (perhaps Notes does not recognize an international dial tone, or you are trying to dial through or out of a PBX system, which can be found in many offices and hotels), and Notes does not recognize its dial tone, you may want to edit the modem command file you are using.

To edit your modem file, highlight it in the Additional Setup dialog box, and select the Modem File button to open the Edit Modem Command File dialog box displayed in Figure 20.5. Scroll through the settings you want to change and edit them as you would any other text in Notes.

For this example, you would scroll down to the section headed [commands] and look for a line that starts with SETUP and contains the string of characters X4. You may need to look closely because this string is often hidden in a cluster of command strings. In Figure 20.5, the I-beam pointer is next to the appropriate character string for this modem file.

Fig. 20.5 Use this dialog box to change your modem file to deal with special circumstances.

Change the X4 command to X1. This command tells Notes to ignore listening for dial tones, ringing, and so forth, and continue to try to make a connection with the server. You will not need to change the command file back to its original state once you can make connections successfully. Notes will continue to function well with the change in any situation.

A great application for this edit is when an individual is overseas and wants to use the company's 800 phone number or other corporate phone access to connect to a Notes server through its internal phone mail system (provided that the company's PBX system will allow this situation to happen). This individual can then take advantage of cheaper rates and possibly have a direct connection to the server. Keep in mind that in some countries, such as Mexico, special arrangements may need to be made with the local phone company to set up connections to 800 phone numbers.

Select Save to save the new settings, Save As to save the new settings under a different name that you specify, or Done to exit the dialog box. If you try to exit the dialog box and have not already saved any changes you have made, Notes prompts you to do so. Select No if you do not want to save your settings, Yes to save your changes, or Cancel to return to the dialog box.

> **Caution**
>
> If you are editing a command file, make a backup copy of the file, or save the edited file under a different name. This copy will allow you to easily return to the original modem command file if you have made errors in the edited one or switch to a new modem that requires the original configuration. If you have never edited a modem command file, you may want to get assistance from someone experienced in doing so before attempting it yourself.

Setting Up Locations

A location is a place where you work with Notes using specified communication settings. For example, you may use a network port when you work in the office and are connected to a network, and you may use a remote port (COM) when you are disconnected from the network and are working remote.

Notes lets you create location documents in your Personal Name & Address Book to store specific communications settings for each location in which you work. You can create as many location documents as you want, and then switch to those locations when you want. The location document tells Notes how you are working in Lotus Notes (remote or network-based), how to call the server, how to treat mail during your work session, and many other communication details as discussed later in this chapter. The location document you select when you begin your work session also defines the databases you elect to replicate. In the location document, you specify the following items:

- The Location Type (Local Area Network, Dial-Up Modem, Both Dial-Up and Local Area Network, or No connection)

- Phone information (such as dialing prefixes)

- Ports to use

- Replication information

- Servers

- Mail information

When you first installed Notes, you automatically created the following five location documents in your Local Name & Address book:

- Island (Disconnected)

- Office (Network)

- Travel (Modem)

- Home (Modem)

- Internet

You can edit these documents and customize them, or create your own. You can then choose between the different locations you have defined to tell Notes how it will work with the server and mail the work session.

> **Note**
>
> An occasional problem when editing existing documents may occur, particularly if you are not the original "owner" of that document. Notes may not see the edited location as being available to you when you try to select it. If this happens and you review your entries and do not discover any errors, simply create a new Location document with the correct information to identify your location. Notes should be able to "see" that location when you want to switch to it.

With locations, a remote user can easily define multiple types of location connections to use while working away from the network, and then quickly switch back to the network when in the office by selecting a network-defined location. Some suggested tips for location settings include the following:

- If your home and office are typically in different area codes, create a location called Home, and specify a 1 and your office's area code as a dialing prefix. When you use the Home location to call a server, Notes automatically dials 1 and the area code before it dials the server's phone number.

- If you work in an office that is disconnected from a network and is located in a different area code, create a location called My Office, and specify a 1 and your office's area code as a dialing prefix. When you use the My Office location to call a server, Notes automatically dials 1 and the area code before it dials the server's phone number.

- If you are working from a hotel room, and typically use a calling card when you make long-distance calls from hotel rooms, create a location called Hotel and specify your calling card number. Then when you use the Hotel location to call a server, Notes automatically uses your calling card number. You may also want to specify a prefix for gaining an outside line when calling from a hotel room.

Entering a New Location

Location documents are stored in your Personal Name & Address Book, which is usually defined as your last name followed by the words address book. You can view your current location documents by opening your personal address book and selecting the Locations view from the navigator as shown in Figure 20.6 or by selecting the File Mobile Locations SmartIcon.

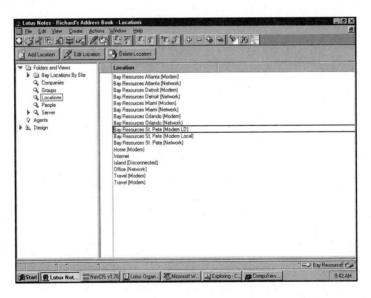

Fig. 20.6 Check out your defined location documents in your Personal Name & Address Book.

Figure 20.6 shows the four default locations created when you first install Notes 4.x along with several locations created by the user of this workstation. You can customize the default locations, or create new ones. To create a new location, follow these steps:

1. While viewing the Locations view, select <u>C</u>reate, <u>L</u>ocation or press the Add Location action button. The New Location document will appear as shown in Figure 20.7.

Fig. 20.7   Use this document to define a new location.

2. Specify that you are setting up for remote use by entering the information as described in the following sections. The Location form shows nine sections for this type of setup: Basics, Internet Browser, Ports, Phone Dialing, Mail, Servers, Replication, Advanced, and Administration. Make the appropriate entries. (Entries for each section are discussed as follows.)

3. When you have completed your entries, press Esc to exit the document, and then Yes to save it. You will see your new location document appear in the view.

To edit an existing location document, open the location document you want to edit, and then double-click anywhere within the body of the document. Notes will place the location document in edit mode for you to make the necessary changes. Exit and save the document as described in the preceding Step 3.

Note

The New Location document uses a new Notes 4 technique called Hide-When. The sections and field entries for this form change as you enter information into the preceding fields. This section discusses those options available to you when you select that you are working as a dial-up modem location. For additional information on the personal address book, read Chapter 5, "Using the Address Book."

Basic Location Settings. The first section of the location document, Basics, controls the basic information Notes uses to determine how you are working. The following are your options:

- **Location Type**—Select Dialup Modem to tell Notes that this location is used when you are disconnected from the network.

- **Location Name**—Type in the name of the location. This name can be anything you want to use that is descriptive of the location in which you would want to use this profile. For example, you could type **Hotel (Calling Card)** to define a location document that you plan to use when staying at hotels where you want to have the call billed to your calling card. You could enter another location document called Hotel (Direct Dial) to use when you stay at hotels that do not accept calling cards for dialing long distance.

- **Prompt for time/date/phone**—Select Yes if you want Notes to prompt you for these settings each time you start up Notes. If you select Yes, the dialog box shown in Figure 20.8 appears whenever you switch to this location or start Notes with this location defined. This option is recommended if you frequently work from different locations, particularly if you frequently work on and off the network, or if you frequently cross time zones.

Internet Browser. These settings indicate which Internet browser you want to use, and where you want to retrieve/open Web pages. You learn more about these settings in Chapter 26, "Using the InterNotes Web Navigator."

Fig. 20.8 The Location Setup dialog box appears if you tell Notes to prompt for time, date, time zone, and phone prefix information in the New Location document.

Ports. Select the Ports to use for this location. The available selections are determined by the ports you defined when you set up your modem. To select a port, click in the box located to the left of the port's name. For example, Figure 20.7 indicates that the port COM 1 will be used to connect to the server from this location. If you do not see the port you want to use in the available options, then that port has not been enabled in Notes. Refer to "Enabling a Port," earlier in this chapter for information on setting up a port for remote use.

Phone Dialing Information. The Phone Dialing section of the location is used to enter the phone dialing information you will use in conjunction with the phone number defined in the connections record. (You will learn about the connections record in the next section.) Notes adds the information you specify to a server's phone number as a prefix (outside line prefix, country code, area code, and calling card access number) or as a suffix (calling card number). In the Phone Dialing section, you set up the dialing instructions to connect with the server, as well as modify any server numbers that you may call when working from your particular location:

- **Prefix for outside line**—Enter any dialing prefix you must use to get an outside line when dialing the server from this location. For example, if you are in a hotel and must dial a 9 to get an outside line before you can call the server, enter 9 in this field. (See the later sidebar "Entering Prefixes and Suffixes" for more details.)

- **International prefix**—Enter any international prefix you need to use when dialing to another country from your location. For example, from the United States, it's 011.

- **Country code at this location**—Enter a country code if you always call the same country from your same location.

- **Long distance prefix**—Enter the prefix you must dial to make a long distance call. For example, to direct dial in the U.S., it is 1.

- **Area code at this location**—Enter the area code for this location if you did not enter this information directly with the phone number in the connections record. Typically, if you define a connections record for access to a server that is always outside your area code, you will enter **1**, the area code, and the remainder of the number in the connections document.

- **Calling card access number**—If you plan to use a calling card when using this location, and your phone long distance calling card plan requires you to enter an access number before dialing the phone number, enter that number in this field. You may want to include a comma or two after this number to have Notes pause to give time for the long distance access number to register. You may need to experiment with the number of commas you use to reach your long distance service.

- **Calling card number**—If you plan to use a calling card when using this location, enter the calling card number you would normally dial after you have dialed the phone number. You may want to add a comma or two before this entry to have Notes pause between dialing the server number and entering your calling card number. You may need to experiment with the number of commas you use to successfully enter your calling card number.

- **Dialing Rules**—Select the Dialing Rules button to open the Dialing Rules dialog box, as shown in Figure 20.9. This dialog box displays the list of all of your connections records and the phone numbers defined for each of those records. Select the server names to view the phone numbers that will be dialed when working from this location. You may want to edit these phone numbers for dialing from this location only to meet your needs. You will learn more about defining server phone numbers in the later section, "Setting Up Connections Records." Select <u>O</u>K to save your changes and return to your locations document.

Fig. 20.9   Check out your connections records in the Dialing Rules dialog box.

> **Note**
>
> An occasional problem may occur when you are trying to select a server to call when you press the Dialing Rules button (or when selecting <u>F</u>ile, <u>M</u>obile, <u>C</u>all Server), particularly if you edited an existing connections document when setting up your Notes workstation. Notes may not see the connection as being available to you when you try to select it. If this happens and you review your server connection entries and do not discover any errors, simply create a new Connection document with the correct server information. Notes should be able to "see" that server connection when you want to select it. You will learn how to create a Connection document in the later section, "Setting Up Connections Records."

Entering Prefixes and Suffixes

When you are entering dialing instructions, keep in mind that the phone number can include any numbers that you normally dial before or after a phone number, including calling card numbers. Insert commas after the prefix and before calling card numbers for each two seconds you normally would pause between dialing the phone number and entering your card number:

```
,,calling card number
```

Two commas are usually adequate before the calling card number, but you may need to experiment. It is best that you be able to hear your modem dialing when trying to work with calling card numbers to help you determine whether the entry is correct.

If you dial out of a hotel, and an operator comes on the line to ask for the calling card number you are dialing, you most likely need to increase or decrease the number of commas between the server phone number and the credit card number. If the pause between these numbers is too long, an operator will come on to ask you what number you want to dial before Notes dials the credit card number. You will need to hang up, remove a comma, and try again. If the pause is too short, your modem will try to enter the card number before the phone system is ready for it, and then an operator will come on the line to try to assist you. You will need to hang up, add a comma or two, and then try again.

If your modem is an older model, check the modem's documentation to determine the maximum number of digits it can dial. To fit as many numbers as possible into the sequence, don't use any hyphens in the phone number defined in the connections document or prefix and suffix entries in this document, and use as few commas as possible.

Some hotel phone systems may not enable you to use your calling card number for remote dialing. If not, you may need to dial directly and charge the call to your hotel room bill. Also, pay attention to the calling information in your hotel. Some hotels are set up to have you enter a 9 when making some outside calls and an 8 when making others. If you are unsure of which prefix to use, contact your hotel operator.

Finally, some hotels are using an older PBX system that will not allow you to use your modem, or let you use your modem only at very slow speeds. Though this situation is rare in North America, it can be quite common elsewhere. Refer to "Remote Troubleshooting" on the CD for additional help before you give up completely!

Mail Settings. The Mail section of the location document identifies how Notes treats your mail when you are working remote. Make the following entries when setting up your locations records:

- **Mail file location**—Select Local if you want Notes to use the copy of your mail file stored on your hard drive; choose On Server if you plan to work interactively with your Mail database file that is located directly on the server.

> **Note**
>
> When you select Local, Notes stores all of the mail you send in your Outgoing Mail database, which acts as a holding tank for your outgoing mail until you call the server and replicate your mail to pass it on to the recipients. When you select On Server, Notes immediately transfers the mail to the recipients when you send it, so you must be directly connected to the server to use this selection. It is recommended that you select Local for this option when working remote. You will read more about how mail is used in Chapter 21, "Working Remote."

■ **Mail file**—Specify the exact path and file name of your mail file. If you selected Local for your mail file location, you need to specify the path and file name of the mail file on your hard drive. Typically, your mail file is located either in the mail subdirectory of your data directory or in the data directory itself and is titled with the first initial of your first name, followed by the first seven letters of your last name. For example, the mail file name for Robert Richards would typically appear as mail\Rrichard.NSF.

If you selected On Server for your mail file location, you need to specify the path and file name of your mail file on your mail server. Typically, this mail file is also located in the mail subdirectory on your server and appears similar to the preceding example.

> **Tip**
>
> When possible, it is best to always name and store your mail file on your hard drive exactly as it is stored on your mail server. This setup makes it easy to change the mail file location without having to edit the mail file name.

■ **Mail domain**—Enter the mail domain to be used for this location. This entry is not required. If you are unsure of your mail domain, contact your Notes administrator.

■ **Recipient name type-ahead**—Select where you want Notes to look for address names when using the type-ahead feature of Notes R4 (see Chapter 5, "Using the Address Book"). You can specify one of the following:

- Selecting the Personal Address Book Only option means that Notes looks only in your Personal Address Book for entries. If a match is not in the Personal Address Book, Notes quits trying to use the type-ahead feature and accepts whatever you type in the recipient fields of a memo.

- Selecting the Personal then Public Address Book option means that Notes looks first in your Personal Address Book for entries, and if a match is not found there, Notes searches the Public Address Book. To use this entry, you must be connected to the server when addressing a memo or have a replica copy of the Public Name & Address Book stored in your local data directory and identified in your File, Tools, User Preferences setup, as discussed in Chapter 2, "Customizing Notes."

- In the Recipient name lookup field, select Stop after first match to have Notes find only the first name that matches the recipient name when you send mail from the location. Select Exhaustively check all address books to have Notes find all of the names that match the recipient name when you send mail.

- Selecting the Disabled option causes Notes to disable the type-ahead feature completely. If you don't have any names listed in your Personal Name & Address Book, and do not have a copy of the Public Name & Address Book stored on your hard drive, you may want to select this option so that Notes does not bother to look for the spelling when you mail a document.

■ **Transfer outgoing mail if**—Enter the number of outgoing mail messages you want to automatically initiate a call to the server. For this feature to work, your modem must be connected to a phone line, and you must have background replication running for this location. (You will learn more about setting up background replication later in this chapter in the "Meeting the Requirements for Background Replication" section.)

Server Settings. The Servers section of the location document specifies your Home/mail server, as well as passthru and InterNotes servers, if applicable. Make the following entries in the Servers section:

■ **Home/mail server**—Specify the exact name of your Mail server (often referred to as your Home server). This is the server in which your mail file is located. If you are unsure of your Mail server name, highlight the network copy of your Mail database and select <u>V</u>iew, Show <u>S</u>erver Names (a checkmark appears when this option is highlighted). The server name displayed in the icon of your network mail icon is the entry you must make in this field.

■ **Passthru server**—A passthru server configuration enables you to dial into one server location and access any other servers defined in the network through that dial-up connection. If your company uses this configuration, enter the server's name exactly as it is defined by the Notes administrator in the Public Name & Address Book. If you do not know your passthru server name, contact your Notes administrator for assistance before you make an entry in this field.

■ **InterNotes server**—If your company uses the Lotus InterNotes product, you can define the InterNotes server in this field. Contact your Notes administrator for particulars about this entry. You will learn more about working with the Internet features of Notes in Chapter 25, "Lotus Notes and the Web."

Replication. You can create entries that tell Notes how often you want to replicate with your server(s) when you are set up for a particular location. Replication is the process of calling the server and exchanging information. You learn more about replication in Chapter 21.

To use these settings, you must be set up for background replication. You will learn how to set up for background replication later in this chapter in the "Meeting the Requirements for Background Replication" section. To set up a replication schedule, make your entries in the following fields:

- **Schedule**—Select Enabled if you want Notes to perform background replications with the server at set times during the day. Select Disabled if you want to prompt Notes each time you want to perform a replication with a server.

- **Replicate daily between**—Specify the time frame in which you want Notes to try to call the server. Notes will try to dial the server during this time frame, based on the settings you make below this entry.

  You can enter a range of numbers by placing a hyphen between the start and end times, as follows:

  `08:00AM - 10:00 PM`

  You can also enter specific time(s) by separating the entries with commas, as follows:

  `08:00 AM, 01:00 PM, 05:00 PM`

- **Repeat every**—Specify how often you want Notes to repeat its replication with the server. For example, if you specify 60 minutes, Notes will try to replicate every 60 minutes during the time frame specified for this location.

- **Days of week**—Specify which days of the week you want Notes to replicate with the server. You may elect to have Notes replicate every day of the week, in which case you would select all seven days. However, if you work at this location only on weekends, you may want to specify Fri, Sat, and Sun, as those are most likely the only days in which you want Notes to try to call.

> **Note**
>
> Notes uses the replication information to replicate databases located on the Replicator tab of your workspace. You learn more about this tab in Chapter 21, "Working Remote."

Advanced Settings. You have two settings available to you if you select the section indicator next to the Advanced section in the locations document:

- **Local time zone**—Select the time zone that is typically used for your location. For example, if you typically use this location profile when you are working in Georgia, you would choose Eastern Standard Time. This selection changes the time/date information that Lotus Notes uses during the work session to meet that of the local time zone.

- **Daylight savings time**—Select Observed Here if you want daylight savings time observed for this location. Notes will automatically change the time stamp it uses to match daylight savings time. Otherwise, select Not Observed Here.

- **Only for user**—If you are using a shared workstation, and this location profile is to be used only by a particular person or group, specify the names of the users in this field exactly as they are named in the Public Name & Address Book. Otherwise, leave the asterisk (*) in this entry to indicate that anyone can use this location setting.

- **User ID to switch to**—Click the flashlight icon to select a new user ID to switch to whenever you are working at this location. For example, if you are a Notes developer and maintain a separate Notes ID for testing, you can create a Location called Testing and specify a Notes test ID in this field. Whenever you switch to this location, Notes will switch your user ID and prompt you for that ID's password.

- **Load images**—To facilitate your working with the Web, you have the capability to tell Notes when you want it to load an image in the document when you first open the document. You can have Notes always load the images when the document is loaded, or load the images only On request.

- **Java Applet Security**—This section of the Advanced settings tells Notes how you want to work with Java applets that appear in Notes. You will learn more about these features in Chapter 25, "Lotus Notes and the Web."

Administration Settings. The Administration section of the location document is used to identify individuals that are allowed to make changes to this document. Make the following entries in this section, if applicable:

- **Owner**—Type the full name of the individual allowed to modify this location document exactly as it is spelled in the Public Name & Address Book. If you leave this field blank, any user can modify this document. If you are the only person using this workstation, you do not need to use this field.

- **Administrators**—Enter the full name of any groups or individuals allowed to edit this document. If you leave this field blank, any user can modify this document. If you are the only person using this workstation, you do not need to use this field.

Switching and Editing Locations

You can easily switch between locations at any time by selecting the Location box in the status bar at the bottom of the Notes window, as shown in Figure 20.10. Click once on the Locations box to open the list of defined locations, and then select the location you want to use.

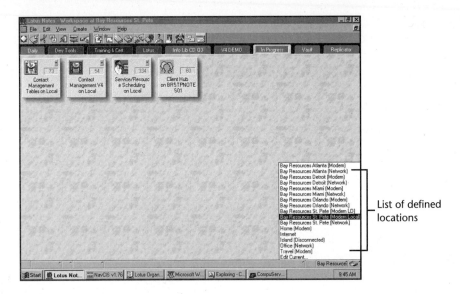

Fig. 20.10 You can switch locations from the status bar.

You can edit a current location by selecting Edit Current from the list of options. The current location document will open in edit mode for you to modify. The changes occur when you exit and save the entries. (You can also edit a location by opening its document in your Personal Name & Address book in the Locations view.)

Setting Up Connections Records

To specify the server(s) you want to use, add their entries to your Personal Address Book as Server Connections.

> **Note**
>
> When your PC was set up initially for remote use, an entry for your Mail server (where your Mail database is located) was created automatically in your Personal Address Book.

To add the server entries to your address book, follow these steps:

1. Open your Personal Address Book. (For information on using Notes address books, see Chapter 5.)

2. Select the indicator next to Servers in the navigator, and then select Connections.

   If you have had a connection previously set up for you, you will see the connections document appear in this view. The view looks similar to the one in Figure 20.11. This view indicates that three servers and an Internet location have been set up with connections records: BRSTPNOTES01/BAY RESOURCES, BRSTPNOTES02/BAY RESOURCES, BRORLNOTES01/BAY RESOURCES, and home/notes/net.

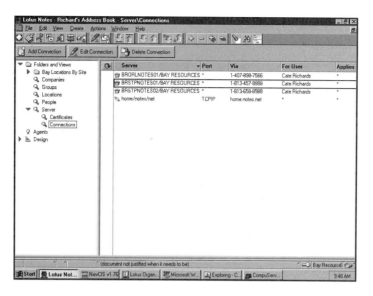

Fig. 20.11   The Server Connections records view lists your defined connections.

To view the connections record and make edits as necessary, highlight the connections record and press Ctrl+E, or open the document and double-click anywhere within the document to place it in edit mode; then make the necessary changes as described below. If you do not have the server connections document you need, you must create a new one as indicated in step 3.

3. Choose Create, Server Connection. The Server Connection form opens as shown in Figure 20.12.

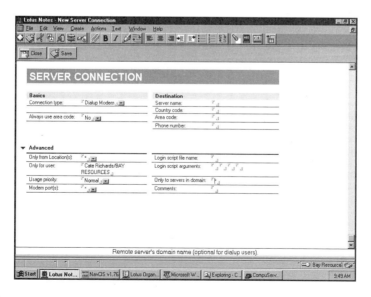

Fig. 20.12   Use this form to create a new connections record.

4. Enter the necessary information. (The list following these steps describes the information needed.)

5. Close the window and choose <u>Y</u>es to save the connections record.

Repeat this process for each remote connection you want to make.

In the Server Connection form, you need to provide the following basic information:

■ **Connection type**—Select Dialup Modem to indicate that you will be accessing this server via a modem.

■ **Always use area code**—Select Yes if you will always use an area code to reach a server and you want Notes to dial the area code—even if it is the same as the area code entered in the Location document. Otherwise, enter **No**. If you enter **No**, you will reference your Location document for an area code to use.

You must also make some Destination settings, as follows:

■ **Server name**—Type the exact name of the server you are connecting to. You need to include all hierarchical naming in this entry. You can determine the exact server entry you need to enter by opening the Public Name & Address Book and viewing the server connections.

■ **Country code**—Select the country (or type in the country code) in which this server is located. Notes will automatically list the country code for the server if its country location is defined in the list of countries.

■ **Area code**—If necessary, enter an area code for this server phone number. You may want to leave this field blank in this document, and enter the area code via the location document as defined previously in the section "Setting Up Locations." Leaving this field blank allows you to use this server connection's definition in all of your locations, without having to individually edit the phone number each time you set up a location.

■ **Phone number**—Type the unique part of the phone number that must be dialed to connect to the Notes server. The unique part of the phone number is that portion you have to dial no matter where you are calling from. When you dial the server, an entry box enables you to enter a prefix for the server you dial so you can include any numbers that you need to get an outside line. You can also specify the non-unique part of the server phone number when you set up locations, as defined previously in "Setting Up Locations."

You can use hyphens between numbers; hyphens don't affect the dialing. However, if your modem does not support entering a long string of numbers, you may want to exclude entering hyphens.

To include pauses in the dialing, type a comma between numbers for each two seconds you want the modem to pause—each comma translates to two seconds. For example, typing **9,,,** (with three commas) causes a six-second pause after you dial the 9. You may need to experiment with the number of commas you need to dial successfully.

If your server has multiple modems with their own phone numbers and they are not set up in a hunt group (where you call one number, and a hunt group automatically switches you to each of several server numbers until it finds one that is open), separate the phone numbers with a semicolon (;). If the first number is busy, the next one is tried, and so on.

Advanced Connection Settings

To enter advanced settings for a connection record, select the section indicator next to the Advanced section heading in the Remote Connections form. A group of advanced settings will appear. Make entries for any of the following settings as needed:

- **Only From Location(s)**—Select the locations in which you want this connections document to be used. Typing an asterisk (*) in this field allows this connections document to be used for all locations.

- **Only for user**—By default, the document author's name is entered in this field. If you want to enter additional users for this connections record if you are sharing a workstation, enter their full Notes names here.

- **Usage priority**—Select Low priority if you plan to use the priority settings of the database to create a replication schedule for accessing a server based on the importance in which a database must send or receive information, and you don't place an importance on this database replicating on a frequent basis. Select Normal for routine scheduling of database replications with the server. You can also elect to replicate High priority databases through the Replicator tab, as you will learn in Chapter 21, "Working Remote."

  Typically, this setting is made for connections between servers, rather than between remote workstations and servers. However, you can use this option to control the number of times your database replicates with the server during a scheduled replication by using these settings.

- **Modem port(s)**—Select which modem ports can use this connections record. Typing an asterisk (*) in this field allows all modem ports to use this record.

- **Login Script file name**—If applicable, enter the file name for the login script that you need to use to connect to your server. Contact your Notes administrator for information on any script files that may be required.

- **Login Script Arguments**—If you use a login script, and you must pass unique arguments to the script as you connect to the server (for example, passwords, name, and so on), type those arguments in the four fields provided in the order in which they are requested by the login script. Contact your Notes administrator for additional information on these entries.

- **Only to servers in domain**—If you want to connect only to particular remote domain servers, specify their names in this field. This entry is optional for remote users. Typing an asterisk (*) in this field enables this connections record to connect to servers in all domains.

- **Comments**—Specify any additional comments in this field to document the connections record.

Setting Up for Background Replication

Notes enables you to schedule calls to a server to perform background exchanges of information by making setup selections in the location document as defined in the earlier section "Setting Up Locations." A background exchange enables you to continue working in Notes remotely as your modem (if it's on) dials and performs an exchange with the server. It also allows you to schedule calls while you are not working so that you can have up-to-date information when you next begin to work.

Meeting the Requirements for Background Replication

You may want to take advantage of the background replication feature if you are traveling and want to have Notes update the information in your databases while you are out of your hotel room. You can set up Notes to call the server at 5:00 P.M. to exchange information so that you will be working with the latest updates when you return to your room at 6:00 P.M.

You can take advantage of the scheduled calling while you are asleep, at meetings, or possibly at times when the calling costs are lower. You may also want to check with your Notes administrator, or check the Phone Calls view in the server's Notes Log database to determine times when the server modems are usually not as busy. Schedule your calls during their slack time, particularly if you are continuously getting busy signals when you call the server during regular work hours.

Keep in mind that you can always force a call to the server outside of the times set in this section when you want to make contact at an unscheduled time.

Lotus Notes performs the background replication if the following conditions are met:

- You have Lotus Notes running.

- You have your modem plugged into an analog jack.

- You have switched to a location that has enabled background replication.

When you start Lotus Notes, Notes checks the replication schedule defined in the location setup and performs the next background replication according to that location's settings. You can follow the progress of the background replication by switching to your Replicator tab. You will learn more about the Replicator in Chapter 21.

Setting Up Windows for *SHARE.EXE*

If you work on a DOS/Windows workstation and you want to take advantage of the background replication option, you must first load the DOS SHARE.EXE program before you try to run a background replication. (SHARE is often already loaded on your system, but if it isn't, you will need to load it.) To load the program, exit Windows and Notes, and then type **SHARE** at the DOS prompt. Restart Notes and Windows and proceed to run a background replication.

To automatically load the SHARE program every time you start your PC, follow these steps at the DOS prompt:

1. Type **EDIT C:\AUTOEXEC.BAT**.

2. Insert the following line in the AUTOEXEC.BAT file—typically about three to four lines down:

```
LOADHIGH C:\DOS\SHARE.EXE
```

3. Exit and save the modified AUTOEXEC.BAT file.

When you restart your computer, the SHARE program will load automatically.

Caution

When you use the background replication method, Notes will keep trying to call the server within the time parameters you set, which ties up your phone line for any incoming calls that you may receive.

Also, if you begin a database exchange using background exchange with the server, and something happens to terminate the connection, Notes will keep trying to call the server to continue completing the task until the replication is fully completed.

If you have a large document, perhaps one that contains several attachments and is over 1 or 2M in size, you may continuously be disconnected before the replication successfully completes because large documents often have difficulty making it over phone lines in one piece, particularly if you connect at a low baud. Notes will keep trying and will tie up your phone line, as well as the server's, for as long as it takes to be successful, unless you terminate the process manually!

Be careful using this feature unsupervised unless you take precautions to not replicate large documents or attachments.

From Here...

If you have followed the instructions in this chapter, your PC and modem should now be configured to successfully use Notes remotely, and you should have at least one location and connection record set up to use when working remote. Often, your Notes administrator has already configured your system for you. It is still wise to scan through this chapter though so that you are familiar with the configuration of your equipment. It will help you if you ever have trouble while working remote. Don't forget to review the CD-ROM for any troubleshooting you may need to do!

For information on topics that relate to getting set up to work remote, you may want to review some of the following chapters:

■ Chapter 5, "Using the Address Book," provides an understanding of how the Name & Address Book works in Notes.

■ Chapter 21, "Working Remote," teaches you the procedures to work remote and communicate with the server. You will also learn many tips on how to work smart when you are working remote.

■ Chapter 24, "Notes: Under the Hood," provides more information on how Notes servers work and how you work with them.

Chapter 21

Working Remote

If you followed the procedures in Chapter 20, "Setting Up to Go Remote," your PC and connections should be all set up to begin working with Notes remote. As described at the beginning of Chapter 20, working remote involves some different equipment and procedures than when you are working on the network and are directly connected to the server.

This chapter briefly describes the process involved in working remote.

Understanding Remote Access

When you connect to a Notes server through a local area network, you work with the most current database information and have continuous access to databases stored on a server. As you edit documents, create new documents, or delete documents, Notes instantly updates the database on the server. Notes transfers mail instantly, too, so that mail you send is routed immediately through the server to the destination you specify.

Notes works quite differently, however, when you work remote. When you set up Notes on your remote PC, you must create replica (you will learn more about this term shortly) copies of all the databases you want to use on your PC's hard disk (unless you are working strictly via Interactive Connection—discussed later in this chapter in the "Using the Interactive Connection Method" section). When you first begin to work with Notes remote, the database copies on your PC match the databases on the server. They don't match for long, however. As you travel, you edit, delete, and create new documents in the databases stored on your hard disk. Back at the office, other users are doing the same to the original databases. Soon you have documents on your PC that aren't on the server, and vice versa.

Every so often you connect your PC to a phone line and tell Notes to perform a replication. Notes calls one or more of your servers, and your PC and the server determine what changes have taken place since the last time you exchanged information. If you have created new documents, Notes transfers

Some of the main topics in this chapter are

- Setting up your mail to work remote

- Setting up the Calendaring and Scheduling system to check free time while working remote

- Creating replicas of your databases

- Working interactively

- Replicating information

them to the server; if you have deleted documents, Notes deletes them from the server. Similarly, any changes that other people have made to the server databases are transferred to your PC. If you are working with Notes mail, you may also be transferring e-mail when you call the server.

After the exchange is complete, Notes disconnects the phone line, and again the database copies on your PC match the databases on the server. As a result, the information in these local copies is only as current as the last time you performed an exchange with Notes.

You can work remote in two ways:

- Replication means that you work disconnected from the server in replica copies of databases, dial the server, exchange information, hang up, and then continue working disconnected from the server.

- Interactive means that you dial the server and then work connected on the server in network copies of the databases, as though you were on a network. With this method, the information you have added to, or read in, the server copies is not copied to your hard drive and therefore is not available to you when you hang up.

Each method is discussed in detail in the following sections.

Understanding How Mail Works Remote

How you set up your Notes mail while working remote depends on how you plan to work with the server. You can use replication, work interactively, or use a combination of the two methods. To understand why it is important to prepare your Notes mail, it is necessary to understand how Notes works with Mail both on and off the network.

A mail message is a Notes document that is composed using a special form. This form contains a field titled SendTo (CopyTo and BlindCopyTo also work this way) that tells Notes to send the document to the recipients. Your standard e-mail memo form, reply forms, and so forth all contain this field to alert Notes that the document is to be treated as mail. You can put this field in any form design to create a mail document. An application developer must take a few additional steps to turn the form into mail; if you are interested in learning about form design, check out Chapter 11, "Designing Forms."

When you are working connected to a network and you mail a document with a SendTo field, you send it to a Notes mail router for delivery to the recipients listed in the field. The mail router runs on a Notes server and carries messages from your workstation to the destination (much like the post office handles paper mail) by looking up the names and groups listed in the To, cc, and bcc fields of your message and comparing them to the names and groups listed in the company's Name & Address Book, which is located on every server. The router verifies that each individual name is valid, and if it is not, the router will try to find people with similar names in the address book and will then prompt you to make a selection. Names can be considered invalid if you have misspelled them, the individual listed has been denied access to Notes by the Notes administrator, or you have otherwise gotten the name wrong.

Once the router has reconciled the names in your memo with the names in the address book, it delivers the message to the recipient's mail database anywhere in the network. If the recipient's mail database is located on the same server as yours, the message is delivered immediately. If the recipient is located on another server, the router finds the path to that server based on the information stored along with your recipient's name in the Name & Address Book.

When you are working disconnected from the server, however, you turn on a switch that tells Notes to store any documents to be mailed in a holding database titled Outgoing Mail. This database's filename is `MAIL.BOX` (which performs the same service as the mailbox outside your home). When you send messages, Notes looks up the names and groups in your Personal Name & Address Book (and Public Name & Address Book if you have created a replica copy of it) stored on your hard drive. If the message is addressed to any groups, Notes substitutes the names in the group listing for the group name in your memo.

Notes also checks to see whether individuals listed in your memo have forwarding addresses associated with their names in the address books stored on your hard drive, and then substitutes the forwarding names for the names listed in the memo. Notes then uses the Outgoing Mail database to store the messages because you have no mail router available to you until you call the server.

Notes does not prompt you if you have misspelled a name or otherwise have it incorrect when you are working remote because you are not required to carry the company Name & Address Book, which is the official listing, on your hard drive. It is the Public Name & Address Book listing that tells Notes where to deliver mail—if the name you type does not match the names listed in this book, Notes will not know where to route the mail.

When you call the server and replicate your Mail database (you learn more about this process later), your workstation transfers all of the messages you have stored in your Outgoing Mail database to the router on the server in one batch. Because all the memos are dumped on the server at one time, the server receiving the memos does not check to see whether the addresses are valid at that time. As a result, remote users are not prompted if any names are wrong. If the names are wrong, remote users receive a Delivery Failure report the next time they call the server to exchange database information.

Once your outgoing mail is transferred to the server, Notes will begin to update your mail database with any incoming mail that has been sent to you. Notes will also update the server copy of your mail database with any mail you saved in your local copy of your mail database. If you selected any other databases to update that have replicas on the server, Notes will update them during the session as well.

Settings for Mail

When you are working remote and plan to use Mail, you must first decide how you are going to communicate with the server. If you are working using the replication method, choose the Local mail option in the location document you're using in order to signal Notes to hold all of the mail you are sending in the Outgoing Mail database until you call the server. If you plan to use the interactive method, select the On Server Mail option to signal Notes to immediately transfer the mail to the recipients in the memos you send. When you use the replication method, you work in a replica of your Mail database that is stored on your hard drive. When you work interactively, you typically use the network copy of your Mail database stored on the server. (The section "Preparing a Replica of a Database," which comes later in this chapter, discusses how to create a replica of your Mail database.)

Interactive Mail Setup. To set up your workstation to work remote using the interactive method, verify that the On Server option is selected in the location document you are using for this session. To check whether this option is set, select the Locations box in the status bar at the bottom of the Notes window (see Figure 21.1).

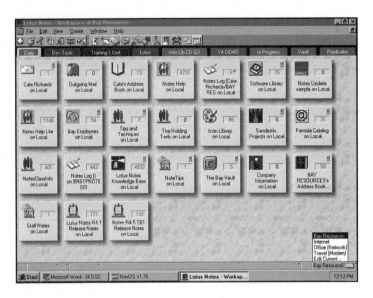

Fig. 21.1   Select a location to edit or review settings.

Select Edit Current from the pop-up list to view the current location document. Check to verify that the setting in the Mail File Location field is set to On Server. If it is not, place the cursor in that field and press the spacebar to change the setting. You learn more about working with the interactive method in the section titled "Using the Interactive Connection Method" toward the end of this chapter.

Note

On Server is the Mail File Location selection that is used when you are working on the network. When On Server mail is selected, your Outgoing Mail database is turned off, and the Public Name & Address Book is referenced first when you send mail. When you send a mail message, the server immediately routes it to the recipient's mailbox.

If you select Local as the Mail File Location, your Outgoing Mail database is turned on, and your Personal Name & Address Book is used for addressing messages. If the recipients you enter are not listed in your Personal Name & Address Book, Notes allows you to mail your message, but it doesn't verify the name until the message is sent to the server for routing.

Replication Mail Setup. If you choose to work using the replication method, you must have a replica of your Mail database stored on your hard drive. If you installed Lotus Notes as remote (or network/remote), a replica of your Mail database was created for you at that time. To check whether you have a replica of your Mail database on your workstation, select View, Show Server Names from your Notes workspace, and then look at the database icons on your workspace for a database titled *Your Name* on Local (see Figure 21.2).

Fig. 21.2 Locating your local Mail database is easy when the icons are not stacked, but your workspace may otherwise begin to get quite cluttered.

If your icons are stacked, select the icon indicator in the upper right corner of the database icon, and check to see whether the Local selection is present, as shown in Figure 21.3. If you see the Local selection, you already have a remote Mail database installed on your workspace. Otherwise, follow the procedures in "Preparing a Replica of a Database" later in this chapter to create a replica of your Mail database on your workspace.

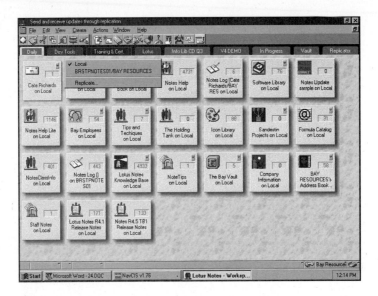

Fig. 21.3 Usually, your local mail database icon will be positioned on top when working at a remote location. However, if you need to switch to the local database, click the small down arrow in the upper right corner of your mail database icon, and then select Local.

Switching Between Local and On Server Mail

If you frequently switch between Local and On Server mail, you should define separate location documents for these options, as described in Chapter 20, "Setting Up to Go Remote." When you first begin a work session, switch to the appropriate location so that the correct mail settings are activated. You can switch locations at the beginning of a work session or any time during a work session by selecting the Locations box in the status bar at the bottom right corner of the Notes window or by selecting File, Mobile, Choose Current Location, as shown in Figure 21.4. The Choose Location dialog box appears (see Figure 21.5). Select the location you want to use in this dialog box, and then click OK.

Fig. 21.4 You can use menu commands to switch locations.

Fig. 21.5 Choose the location you want from the Choose Location dialog box.

IV

Going Mobile

When You Work Both on and off the Network

If you frequently work on and off the network, choose File, Tools, User Preferences, Prompt for Location to have Notes ask you what location you are working from each time you start Notes. Your location must have the Local option selected for you to work remote, or you will be prompted to call the server each time you send mail.

Specifying the Local option turns on the Outgoing Mail database and tells Notes to look only in your Personal Name & Address Book. If your location specifies Local mail while you are working on the server, however, all mail that you send is still held in the Outgoing Mail database until you perform the next replication with the server instead of being routed immediately to the addressees specified in the memo.

If you travel across time zones frequently, check your Date and Time each time you start Notes by selecting the Prompt for Time/Date/Phone option in the location document as described in Chapter 20, "Setting Up to Go Remote." Selecting this option ensures that any scheduled replications that you may have set up in your server locations (see Chapter 20 for further information on scheduled replications) and any timed agents are running at their proper times (see Chapter 16, "Buttons and Agents," for further information on agents).

Setting Up to Check Free Time

You can set up Notes to check the free time available for selected individuals in your company while you are working remote. In Chapter 9, "Lotus Notes Group Calendaring and Scheduling," you learned how to schedule appointments and check on the free time for each person you were inviting to a meeting. However, when you are working remote, you typically do not have access to each user's free time unless you tell Notes to replicate their information to your remote workstation.

When Notes 4.5 was installed on your workspace, a database entry for checking free time was automatically entered on your Replicator tab (you will learn more about this feature shortly) as displayed in Figure 21.6. When you click the replicator arrow (the blue arrow next to the database icon), you may be prompted to call the server to check free time. To set up free time, however, you do not need to call the server, so select No if prompted. The Local free time settings dialog box will appear, as shown in Figure 21.7.

Make the following settings in the Local free time settings dialog box:

■ Type or select the users' names for which you want to replicate free time schedules. Make sure your name is in this list. Click the down arrow next to the Keep local free time information field to open the Name & Address Books you have access to if you want to select the users' names (recommended).

■ Select the Amount of free time information to keep local from the keyword list. For example, if you want to keep up to a month's worth of free time information for scheduling purposes, select One Month from the selection list.

■ Select the length of time you want Notes to wait before checking for free time again with the server in the Do not refresh free time information more often than: list box. For example, select Once every eight hours if you want Notes to check for free time only once during the workday.

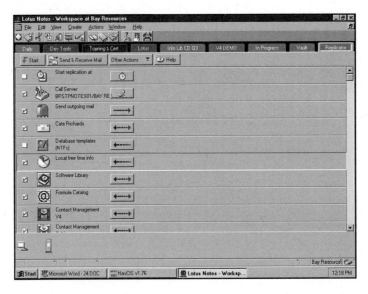

Fig. 21.6 Notes 4.5 automatically adds the Local free time information replication entry to your workspace. Place a checkmark next to its icon if you want to poll the server for free time information when you replicate.

Select OK to save your settings. Notes is now configured to keep track of the free time for those individuals you have selected.

Note

Keep in mind that keeping track of users' free time will take up space on your hard drive and increase the amount of time it will take to replicate with the server. Set up only those users in which it is important to keep track of free time—or you may find yourself short on disk space pretty quickly! Also, limit the amount of time you want to keep the free time information to further reduce the amount of disk space used. Finally, limit the number of times you poll the server to check free time to eliminate several calls to the server while you are working remote.

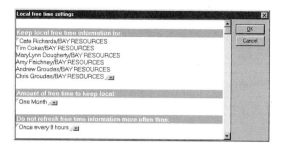

Fig. 21.7 You can tell Notes whose free time schedules you want to maintain while working on the road.

Replicating a Database

Replication is the process of updating replica copies, referred to as replicas, of a database. After you create a replica of a server database on your hard drive, you work in that copy and then dial the server to exchange new, modified, and deleted documents in the databases.

To work with a replica of a database (one stored on your hard drive), it is helpful to understand how to tell a local copy of a Notes database from a server copy. The icon for a local copy of a database includes the name Local with the database title, whereas a server icon displays the server name. To verify which databases are local and which are on the server, select View and make sure that the Show Server Names option is selected. If a server name is present below the title of the database, it is a server copy of the database; otherwise, it is a local database.

Double-clicking a server copy's icon when you are working disconnected from the server results in a prompt for you to call a server in order to open the database. Double-clicking a local database icon opens the database from your hard drive when you are working remote. Figure 21.8 shows examples of network and local database icons for the same database.

If your database icons are stacked (you selected View, Stack Replica Icons), click the icon indicator in the right corner of the database icon to view a list of where each copy of the database is referencing. If Local is one of the options in that list, then you have a local copy of the database stored on your hard drive. You may also see multiple server names listed in the drop-down box if you have added the same network copy of the database icon from multiple servers, as shown in Figure 21.9.

Having multiple database icons for the same database that is stored on multiple servers is common for many remote users, and is often convenient for updating purposes (see Figure 21.9). Databases (like the database catalog) that users access frequently may be located on all servers in an organization to facilitate users accessing them—from the network or when calling in from a remote location. Having a popular database stored on many servers often reduces the number of phone calls a remote user needs to make to update all of their databases.

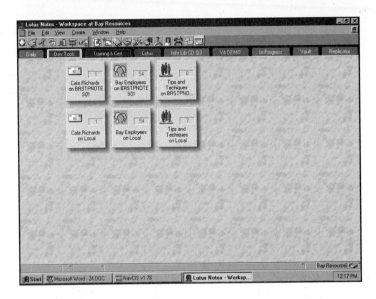

Fig. 21.8 These are examples of local and network database icons.

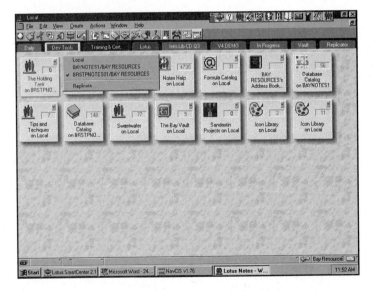

Fig. 21.9 This is an example of stacked icons referencing multiple servers.

To replicate a database, follow these steps:

1. Prepare a first-time replica of a database.

2. Choose appropriate replica options.

3. Verify access levels.

4. Replicate the database.

The following sections discuss these steps in detail.

Preparing a Replica of a Database

Before you use the replication method, you must prepare a replica icon of each database that you plan to use. Replicas of server databases are duplicates of the server databases, including the identification numbers, called Replica IDs, that distinguish the database from all others. When you exchange or access a Notes database, Notes looks at the Replica ID, not the name of the database, to determine what database you are trying to access. If the numbers don't match, Notes will not access the server's copy of the database during replication.

> ### Caution
>
> If you do not create replicas of databases when you work remote, your databases will not be able to exchange information with the server! Don't confuse creating replicas (File, Replication, New Replica) of a database with creating copies (File, Database, New Copy). Copies of databases contain all of the database's design and documents, but not the same Replica ID—which is what the Notes server looks for when exchanging information with a database. If the Replica ID between your database and the server do not match, you will not be able to replicate the database.

To create a replica of a database, follow these steps:

1. Select the database icon you want to use to create a replica. You may need to connect to the server and add the database icons you want to use to create replicas.

2. Choose File, Replication, New Replica to display the New Replica dialog box (see Figure 21.10).

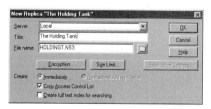

Fig. 21.10 Use this dialog box to create replicas.

3. In the Server list box, select the server where you want to store the replica database—Local in this case as that is the name given for databases stored on your local hard drive.

4. Type the Title of the database as you want it displayed on your replica. By default, Notes enters the network title of the database you selected. You can edit this title if you want to.

5. Type the <u>F</u>ile name of the database to include its path as you want it stored on your hard drive or floppy disk. By default, Notes enters the filename as it is stored on the network.

Note

Be sure to name replicas of any database the same as they're named on the server. Although this practice isn't mandatory, naming databases this way helps eliminate confusion. If you highlight a copy of a database that you want to make a replica of, Notes automatically fills in the appropriate server and filenames for you when you select <u>F</u>ile, <u>R</u>eplication, <u>N</u>ew Replica.

If you are making a replica of your Mail database, always give the replica the same name as the original database on the server, including any subdirectory names (for example, MAIL\CRICHARD). Otherwise, Notes may not be able to find your Mail database when you switch from On Server mail (on-site) to Local mail (off-site) operations.

---

6. Select either or both of the following options:

   - The Copy <u>A</u>ccess Control List (recommended) option copies the original database's Access Control List to the new replica. If you do not select this option, you will be listed as the Manager of the database, but servers may not be listed, which will create problems when you try to replicate later.

   - The <u>C</u>reate full text index for searching option automatically creates a full text index at the time you make the replica of the database so that the Full Text Search option is immediately available. If you do not select this option now, you can always create an index at a later date. Depending on the size of your database, creating an index may take some time—keep this in mind when selecting this option.

7. Choose <u>I</u>mmediately to immediately create a replica of the database that is initialized and filled with the contents (or a subset) of the original database, or choose <u>N</u>ext scheduled replication to create a shell of the database that will be filled with the contents the first time you perform an exchange.

Tip

Select the First Replication option if you plan to make several replica copies of databases or you expect that the initial replication of the database will be lengthy. You can then replicate with the server once to fill all the database shells at the same time.

---

8. Make any <u>E</u>ncryption, Si<u>z</u>e Limit, or <u>R</u>eplication Settings desired for this replica database. Each of these options is discussed in the following sections.

9. Choose <u>O</u>K to create the replica database.

> **Note**
>
> If you don't have a copy of the network database icon available on your workstation when you want to make a replica copy to take on the road, choose File, Database, Open to add the database icon to your workstation before following the preceding steps to make a replica copy. If you are working remote and do not have a copy of the icon, you can select File, Mobile, Call Server and call, or select File, Replication, New Replica and select the Server name where the database is located. Notes will prompt you to call the server.
>
> Once you are connected with the server, the Choose database dialog box is opened for you. Choose the database you want to create a replica of, and then choose Select. Notes will display the New Replica dialog box with the relevant information entered for you. Complete the settings as mentioned previously to create your replica.

Setting Database Encryption Options

You can set the security of your local database so that only someone with your Notes ID and password can open it. Follow these steps:

1. Select the Encryption button in the New Replica dialog box. The Encryption dialog box appears (see Figure 21.11).

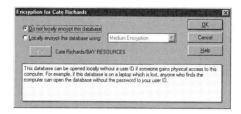

Fig. 21.11 Use this dialog box to encrypt a local database.

2. Select Locally encrypt this database using.

3. Select Simple, Medium, or Strong Encryption from the drop-down list box. Simple Encryption enables you to open the database much quicker than you can with Medium or Strong encryption, so unless you must carry a higher level of security on the database, choose Simple.

4. Select the For button to open a list of names from the Address book if you want to encrypt the database for someone other than yourself. Encrypting the database for someone else will make it inaccessible to you—so make sure this is a setting you want to make!

5. Click OK to return to the New Replica dialog box.

Notes uses the public portion of your Notes ID encryption key to secure this database from other people accessing it without your Notes ID and password. Keep in mind, however, that if you are sharing a public workstation and encrypt a database locally that others also need to use, they will not be able to access the database with their IDs. For more information on encryption, read Chapter 22, "Security and Encryption."

Identifying a Size Limit

You can specify the maximum size for this database by selecting the Size Limit button in the New Replica dialog box. The Size Limit dialog box appears (see Figure 21.12).

Fig. 21.12 Use this dialog box to set the size limit of a local database.

Size limits are set in gigabytes, so you will most likely be able to leave the default (1G) as your entry. Click OK to exit and save your selection. Chances are your remote PC will not be able to host databases larger than this amount anyway.

> **Note**
>
> You can also set limits on the size of the database (to make limits less than 1G) through the Administration pane.

 ▶▶ See "Accessing System Database Information," p. 968

Choosing Replication Settings

To conserve space, speed up replication time, control what is sent to the server, or make any other settings that affect the way a replica database replicates with a server, or servers, you can select the Replication Settings button while creating a new replica of a database. You can also modify replication settings at a later date by highlighting a replica of a database and selecting File, Replication, Settings to display the Replication Settings dialog box shown in Figure 21.13.

To set or change replication settings for a database, perform the following steps:

1. Select the database whose replication settings you want to change.

2. Select the File Replications Settings SmartIcon if you are creating a new replica, or select File, Replication, Settings while highlighting an existing replica database icon to display the Replication Settings dialog box shown in Figure 21.13.

3. Choose all options that meet your needs, and then choose OK.

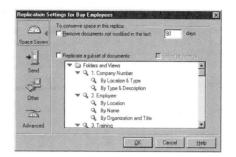

Fig. 21.13 Use the Replication Settings dialog box to control different aspects of the replication process.

The Replication Settings dialog box offers four panels to facilitate making all of the replication settings for the database; the following sections describe the options available in each panel.

Saving Space. The first panel to appear when you open the Replication Settings dialog box is the Space Savers panel. You may select from any of the following options:

- **Remove documents not modified in the last ___ days**—This option purges documents that have not been edited within the specified time period. If your database has documents meeting the criteria specified in this option, you will be prompted each time you open the database until you answer Yes to remove the documents, change the number of days, or disable this option. The purging process removes all references to the deletion stub from this replica that can be copied to other replicas of the database. This option is a great way to save space and is discussed in more detail in the later section "Working Smart Remote." Selecting this option in your *remote* copy of the database does not remove documents from the *server* copy of the database.

- **Replicate a subset of documents**—This option lets you specify the criteria that will define the specific documents you receive from the server during replication. You can select particular views of documents to replicate, or specify a formula to use to limit the documents you replicate with the server. You will learn more about this feature in the section titled "Selective Replication" later in this chapter.

Limiting What Is Sent to the Server. Just as you can limit what information is received from the server, you can also limit what information is sent to the server by selecting the Send icon in the Replication Settings dialog box. The Send panel of the Replication Settings dialog box appears (see Figure 21.14).

You can make any of the following selections:

- **Do not send deletions made in this replica to other replicas**—When you have this option selected, you can delete documents from your local copy of the database without worrying about passing those deletions on to other replicas on the server. This selection is handy if you cannot define a particular selective replication setting (date created, author name, subject matter, etc.) to limit the documents in your local database, and you need to reduce the size of the database you are storing locally. Your deletions will not be passed on to the server.

This option is also handy in case you accidentally delete documents from a local copy and you do not want to risk passing those deletions to the server. If you have the correct access to delete documents from the server copy of the database, you could delete all instances of a particular document if this option is not selected.

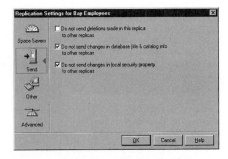

Fig. 21.14 Use the Send panel to limit the information that is sent to the server.

- **Do not send changes in database title & catalog info to other replicas—** Select this option if you want to make changes to the title of your local replica of the database and update the catalog information without having the change replicate to the server copy of the database. This setting is primarily used by managers or designers of applications that want to work with them locally. You must have at least Designer level access on the server copy of the database to change database titles on the server copy and catalog information.

- **Do not send changes in local security property to other replicas—**Select this option if you want to change Access Control information for this replica of the database without changing the Access Control information in other replicas. This setting is primarily used by managers of applications that want to work with them locally. You must have Manager level access to change Access Control settings on the server copy of the database.

Other Replication Settings. You can temporarily disable replication, assign replication priority, limit documents received during replication according to a specified date, or identify a CD-ROM publishing date. Select the Other icon in the Replication Settings dialog box to display the Other panel shown in Figure 21.15.

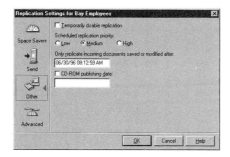

Fig. 21.15 Use this panel to further control replication.

Select from any of these options:

■ **Temporarily disable replication**—When this option is selected, the database will not be included in any replications with other replicas, even if it is selected when you schedule a replication. This option is ideal if you think your application may be corrupted, and you don't want to risk passing on corrupt data to another copy of the database. You can also use this option to disable a database that changes infrequently so that the server won't spend time trying to read it during a scheduled replication. You can later deselect this option when you want to begin replication again.

■ **Scheduled replication priority**—With this option, select Low, Medium, or High to indicate the level at which this database will replicate during scheduled replications. Notes provides options that enable you to opt only to replicate databases with a particular priority setting during a session. The Replicator will let you elect to replicate only High priority databases as an option to limit the number of databases replicated during a scheduled replication. This is particularly useful if you are in a hurry and only want to receive information from databases you have indicated as being highly important.

■ **Only replicate incoming documents saved or modified after**—In this option, enter the cutoff date you want to use to limit the documents you want replicated. This option lets you minimize the number of documents you are replicating to only those created or edited on or before the date specified so that you can reduce the amount of hard disk space that's used and the length of replication time. This setting is ideal if you only want to get the latest information from a database while working remote, particularly if you typically access this database on a frequent basis when you are connected to the network.

> **Tip**
>
> Selecting the Only replicate incoming documents saved or modified after option is a great feature to use if, for some reason, there is a very high volume of documents being added to a database and you go on vacation. This will enable you to replicate only a small subset of the documents rather than everything (which could take a long time).

- **CD-ROM publishing date**—If you are creating a CD-ROM in which you are publishing a replica of this database, you can tell Notes to specify the publishing date for the replica with this option. The recipient of the CD-ROM copy of the database can then copy the CD-ROM file to his or her local drive (or server), and then replicate with the original database without having to perform a full replication—only the documents created after the publishing date will have to be replicated.

Advanced Replication Options. If you want to get really sophisticated with your replication strategies, select the Advanced icon in the Replication Settings dialog box to open the Advanced panel shown in Figure 21.16.

Fig. 21.16 The Advanced panel contains more replication options.

If more than one server contains a replica of a database, you can select the server your replica receives. If you receive from more than one server, you can select different documents or different parts of a database's design to receive from each. To select only particular servers to replicate with, do the following:

1. Leave the When computer option at the default, which is your Notes name.

2. Click the server indicator (the computer icon) next to the Receives from box, and then select the server you want to replicate with in the Servers dialog box that appears (see Figure 21.17). Click OK.

> **Tip**
>
> You can also use this dialog box to remove servers that you want to exclude replication with by highlighting their names and selecting the Delete Server option before clicking OK.

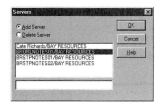

Fig. 21.17   You can specify which servers you want to receive from in the Servers dialog box.

3. To receive only selected documents from the server, select the Replicate a subset of documents option, and do one of the following:

  • Select the folders and views you want.

  • Select the Select by formula option and specify a formula.

4. To receive only selected parts of a database's design, do one or more of the following:

  • Select Forms, views, and so on, to receive a database's basic design.

  • Select Agents to receive a database's agents.

  • Select Replication formula to receive the formula a database uses to select the documents it receives.

  • Select Access control list to receive a database's Access Control List (ACL).

  • To prevent receiving document deletions from the server copy, deselect Deletions.

  • Select Fields, and then select the Define button if you only want to replicate particular fields in the database with the server. When you select the Define button, you will be able to select All Fields or Custom from the drop-down list box. If you select Custom, you will see a list of all fields that are present in the database that you can see (see Figure 21.18).

Fig. 21.18   You can tell Notes to only replicate information in specific fields when you exchange information with the server.

5. Select those fields that you want to replicate (a checkmark is put next to the names of selected fields), and then click <u>O</u>K.

6. Click <u>O</u>K to exit the Replication Settings dialog box.

Caution

Be careful using this option in Notes. If you are not familiar with the design of the database, you could end up replicating the wrong information and have views that do not sort because the correct fields of information were not brought down, and so on. While this option can substantially reduce the amount of information that you replicate over the phone lines, it can cause problems.

Note

You learn more about using the selective replication sections of the Space Savers and Advanced panels in the "Selective Replication" section later in this chapter.

Verifying Access Levels

When you first make a replica of a server database, you must verify, and possibly modify, the access level for you and for the server(s) you will dial into to perform an exchange. To do so, follow these steps:

1. Select the replica of the database you want to verify.

2. Choose <u>F</u>ile, <u>D</u>atabase, <u>A</u>ccess Control (or select the File Database Access Control SmartIcon). The Database Access Control List dialog box appears (see Figure 21.19).

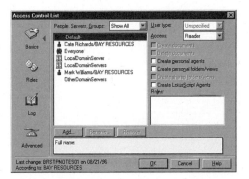

Fig. 21.19 Use this dialog box to verify the Access Control List settings.

3. Select your name in the People, Servers, <u>G</u>roups list box. If your name is not listed, click on the A<u>d</u>d button to enter your name—exactly as it is defined in Notes. You may either type your name (including any hierarchical naming conventions), or select the person icon to open the Name & Address Book where you can select your name from the list of users.

4. Choose Person from the <u>U</u>ser type list box if it is not already selected.

5. Choose Manager from the <u>A</u>ccess level list box if it is not already selected.

6. Go through the list box to find the Notes server name(s) where the database is located. Select the server name(s) with which you will replicate this database.

7. Choose Server from the <u>U</u>ser type list box if it is not already selected.

8. Choose Manager in the <u>A</u>ccess list box for each server to ensure that they can read, write, and modify the databases you replicate.

> **Tip**
>
> You should also have two server entries in your database access list titled LocalDomainServers and OtherDomainServers. If you access the same database on multiple servers in your domain (the more likely case) or across multiple domains (not quite as common), grant one or both of these entries Manager level access as well.
>
> If your company maintains only one domain, you can update the access for LocalDomainServers only and feel safe in removing access for the OtherDomainServers setting. Making these updates helps eliminate the possibility of replication problems if the database is moved to another server and that server's name is not entered in this access list.
>
> For these server group names to work in your remote environment, you must have their entries in the group list of your Public Name and Address Book, or have made a replica copy of the Public Name and Address Book on your hard drive.

9. Repeat steps 6 through 8 for each server you dial to update this database.

10. Choose <u>O</u>K to exit the dialog box and save your changes.

Repeat the preceding process for each replica database on your desktop.

> **Caution**
>
> If the server name isn't present, you must enter the name in the text box directly below the People, Servers, <u>G</u>roups list box. The spelling of the server name must be exactly as the Notes administrator designated; Notes is case-sensitive about this spelling. (To avoid misspellings, select the name of the server by clicking the A<u>d</u>d button, and then select the person icon next to the Person, Server, or Group text entry box to select the server name from the Name & Address Book.)
>
> Identify the server as Server in the <u>U</u>ser type list box, assign the server Manager access, and choose A<u>d</u>d User. If the server isn't listed in the ACL, it cannot update your replica of the database after you create it the first time.

Setting Up the Replicator

Notes 4.x provides a feature called the Replicator. With Replicator, you can replicate multiple databases with different servers with a single command. You also can do other work while Notes replicates in the background.

To display the Replicator, click the Replicator tab in your workspace. When you switch to the Replicator, the workspace appears as shown in Figure 21.20.

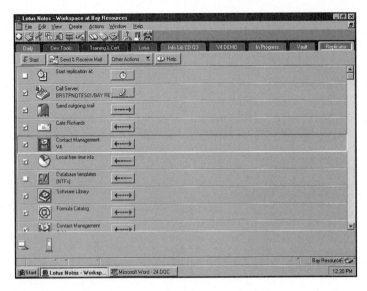

Fig. 21.20   The Replicator enables you to manage the replication of your local databases in one place.

When you use Notes away from the office, you can have Replicator call each server you want to replicate with automatically. If you're using a passthru server or a remote LAN server, you can have Replicator make a single call and replicate all of your local databases at one time, even if they're on different servers. Replicator also lets you customize replication based on the location you are working from. Replicator also provides additional ways to replicate; for example, you can assign High priority to selected databases and replicate only those databases. The following sections describe the Replicator.

Understanding the Replicator Page. Replicator is always the last page on your workspace; you cannot delete it. Replicator automatically contains the following types of entries:

- **Database**—Replicator contains a database entry for each local replica you have unless you deleted the entry from the Replicator page. When you add replicas of databases to your workstation, they are automatically added to the Replicator. To remove replicas of databases that you do not want on your Replicator, highlight the database entry and press Delete. Select Yes to indicate that you want to remove the entry.

- **Start replication at**—Use this entry to specify a replication schedule and enable scheduled replication. The replication schedule used is dependent on the location you are using and the settings you made in its location document. If you want to modify the time at which you start replication, click the clock icon displayed on the Start replication at entry, and Notes will open your current location document (see Figure 21.19). After you have made any necessary changes, press Esc and select Yes to save your changes. If you are not using scheduled replication, this option will be blank. To replicate, you will need to press the Start button manually, as described in "Performing a Replication," later in this chapter.

The Start replication at entry is always first and cannot be deleted (refer to Figure 21.20).

- **Database templates**—You can use this entry to refresh the designs of template-based databases. You cannot delete the Database templates entry (refer to Figure 21.20).

- **Send outgoing mail**—You can use this entry to send all pending messages from your Outgoing Mail database (MAIL.BOX). You cannot delete the Send outgoing mail entry (refer to Figure 21.20).

You can also create the following types of entries for mobile locations (such as Home and Travel):

- **Call**—When you create a Call entry, you specify the server you want to call, and the Replicator uses the information from the Server Connection record, along with any special location prefix and suffix numbers that may have been defined, when it dials. You can use a Call entry to connect to a server (refer to Figure 21.20).

- **Hangup**—You can use a Hangup entry to end a connection with a server. The Hangup entry tells Notes to end a call with the current server (refer to Figure 21.20).

To set up the Replicator, perform any of the tasks described in the following sections.

Moving a Replicator Entry. Except for the Start Replication At entry, which always comes first, you can arrange Replicator entries in any order that you want. For example, you may want to group Replicator entries according to the server on which you want to replicate so that the Replicator only has to call that server one time to exchange all databases in common. To move a Replicator entry, follow these steps:

1. Click and hold the left mouse button over the entry you want to move. Be careful not to drag over the actual button, or you may start the procedure for that button!

2. Drag the entry to its new position.

3. Release the left mouse button.

Creating a Replicator Entry. You can create entries that automatically connect and disconnect from servers when you replicate over a modem. You can create a Call entry or Hangup entry as explained in the following steps.

> **Note**
>
> The Replicator automatically adds Database entries when you create replicas of databases. However, if you have deleted a database replication entry and you want to add it to the Replicator again, perform the following steps:
>
> 1. Switch to the workpage that has the replica of the database, and click the replica's icon.
>
> 2. Hold down the left mouse button and drag the icon to the Replicator tab.
>
> 3. Release the mouse button when the mouse cursor is positioned over the tab.
>
> Notes adds the Database entry to the Replicator again.

To make a Call entry, perform the following steps:

1. If necessary, switch to the location where you use your modem to connect to the Notes servers.

2. On the Replicator tab, click where you want the Call entry to be located. Notes places the Call entry directly above the entry you click.

3. Select Create, Call Entry. Notes automatically creates the entry for your Home server by default.

4. If you want to create a Call entry to a server other than your Home server, double-click the new Call entry's action button (it has a small, yellow phone on its icon). Select the server you want to call, and then click OK.

When creating Call entries, keep the following tips in mind:

- If you have set up a server connection for a passthru server or a remote LAN server, create a single Call entry for this server on the Replicator tab. When you do this, the Replicator can make just one phone call to replicate with all of the servers. You will need to ask your Notes administrator about pass-through and remote LAN server connections particular to your company.

- When Replicator calls a server, it stays connected to the server until it reaches another Call entry or a Hangup entry. You don't need to create a Hangup entry for each Call entry, just the last one.

- If you create two or more Call entries next to each other, Replicator tries each call in turn. When Replicator makes a connection to a server, it then skips to the first entry that is not a Call entry.

- You can replicate over a modem without Call entries. If you don't have Call entries created, Replicator tries to call the last server that the first Database entry replicated with.

You can create a Hangup entry so that the Replicator automatically disconnects from a server when you replicate over a modem. To create a Hangup entry, follow these steps:

1. On the Replicator tab, click where you want the Hangup entry. Notes adds the Hangup entry immediately above the entry you click.

2. Select Create, Hangup Entry. Notes adds a new Hangup entry to the Replicator directly above the entry you clicked.

If you want to make the Hangup entry the last entry in the list, click and hold the left mouse button over the Hangup entry and drag it to the last position. Remember, you only need one Hangup entry, even if you have more than one Call entry. When Replicator reaches a new Call entry, it automatically hangs up the current call!

Specifying Replicator Options. Replicator entries contain action buttons, which you can use to specify Replicator options. The following options are available (refer to Figure 21.20):

- You can click the clock action button on a Start Replication At entry to specify a replication schedule for the current location. The current location document opens in Edit mode for you to make any changes you want to make. Press Esc and then Yes to save your new settings.

- You can click the arrow action buttons on a Database entry to specify whether you want to send and/or receive documents from a server. If you select the Receive Documents from Server option, you can reduce the length of time it takes for replication by also selecting to receive full documents, document summaries and the first 40K of rich text only, or document summaries only.

Note

The Receive summary and 40K of rich text option only enables you to shorten a document by removing bitmaps, other large objects, and all attachments from the document copies received from the server. When you select this option, Notes only retrieves the document summary (basic document information, such as author and subject) and the first 40K of information. Notes doesn't remove the large objects and attachments from the documents stored on the server, however—just from the copies you receive. This option helps reduce long exchange times and saves valuable disk space by keeping file size low. If you later decide that you want to get the information you excluded during replication, you can deselect this option or work interactively in the server copy of the database to review the entire document.

The following are a few things that you need to keep in mind, however, when selecting this option:

- When you open a shortened document, Notes displays (TRUNCATED) as part of the document's title in the title bar.

- You cannot categorize or edit shortened documents.

- Agents do not work on shortened documents.

(continues)

(continued)

- Notes does not send shortened documents to another replica unless the replica has the Receive summary and 40K of rich text only option selected.

- If you elect to shorten documents, you can retrieve the entire document by selecting Actions, Retrieve Entire Document while reading the document. Notes will dial the server and retrieve the rest of the document for you to review.

Tip

If you find errors in your replication with a server and are either not receiving or not sending documents during a session, check to see if the arrow action button is set to send (arrow pointing to the right), receive (arrow pointing to the left), or send and receive (arrow pointing both ways). Make changes as necessary.

If you are still having difficulty, check the access control to make sure both you and the server you are replicating with have the appropriate access level for the database. Finally, check to make sure your database is a replica of the one located on the server, and not just a plain copy.

- You can click any Call entry action button to specify a different server to call. Select the server from the pop-up list that appears when you click this action button. In this list, Notes displays the servers for which you have already defined phone numbers.

 ◀◀ See "Setting Up Connections Records," p. 818

Deleting a Replicator Entry. You can easily delete Replicator entries by clicking the entry you want to remove and pressing the Delete key. Select Yes to confirm the deletion.

Replicating with the Server

When you are ready to replicate with the server, either to fill the database shells you may have created in the previous section or to exchange information with the server on an ongoing basis, you will need to plug your modem into your PC and connect the modem to the telephone jack. You can either carry your own telephone cable with you when working on the road or unplug the cable from the connection in back of the phone (if possible) and plug it into your modem jack. Make sure the other end of the cable is plugged into the telephone jack in the wall!

It is recommended that you carry a telephone cable with you. In the United States, the telephone jack connector is commonly referred to as an RJ-11; you may need to verify the appropriate cable connector you will need if working internationally as it varies by country. If you need to dial manually (where you must dial through an operator to get an outside line), if the closest phone cable is permanently attached to the phone, or if the phone cable you are trying to use is damaged, you will be thankful you have a spare.

> **Note**
>
> Some phones have data ports located in the back of the phone; in which case, you run a telephone cable from your modem to the back of the phone, rather than directly to the jack. You will need a second cable in this case. When it's possible, running the telephone cable directly from your modem into the wall jack is the preferable option. This setup makes your replications much smoother.

Performing a Replication. You can replicate information between the server and one (or many) of the replica databases located on your workspace. When you perform an exchange (replication), you dial the server, send and receive database information, and hang up. There are two ways to replicate with a server:

- Replicate selected databases in the foreground
- Replicate selected databases with the Replicator

The following sections describe both options.

Replicating in the Foreground. You can replicate with a server in the foreground. Follow these steps:

1. Select the database you want to replicate.

2. Select File, Replication, Replicate, or select the File Replication Replicate SmartIcon. The Replicate dialog box appears (see Figure 21.21).

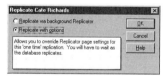

Fig. 21.21   The Replicate dialog box appears when you replicate in the foreground.

3. Select Replicate with options, and then select OK. The Replicate dialog box displays additional new settings, as shown in Figure 21.22.

Fig. 21.22   You can choose additional settings in this Replicate dialog box.

4. Select a different server to replicate with by clicking the down arrow next to the with drop-down list box, if necessary.

5. Select one or both of the following:

- Send documents to server.

- Receive documents from server. If you select this option, you may also specify whether you want to receive full documents, document summaries and the first 40K of rich text only, or document summaries only.

6. Select OK. Notes prompts you for permission to dial the server you selected. Select Yes to begin the replication.

When you use the Replicate with options setting to replicate databases, Notes calls the server and performs the replication in the foreground; you will have to wait until the replication is complete before you can continue working. If you want to continue to work while Notes is replicating, you must use the Replicator (background replication) as discussed in the following section.

> **Tip**
>
> If you work on-site and off-site, you can decrease the amount of time required to perform remote database exchanges. While you are still connected on-site to the server, perform a database exchange for all your local replicas, as described earlier. You leave the office with the most recent database information and decrease the amount of time needed to perform a remote replication because you don't need to send and receive as many documents. Database replication with the server is also a great deal faster to perform when you do it on the network.

Replicating Databases with the Replicator. You can replicate databases in the background with Replicator by switching to the Replicator tab and selecting Start (recommended), or by selecting File, Replication, Replicate, Replicate via background Replicator. When you replicate in the background, you can continue to do other work while Notes replicates. If your modem is connected to a phone line, Notes begins calling the first server identified on the Replicator tab and replicates information until it handles the last replication entry.

> **Note**
>
> If your current location is set up for scheduled replication, you don't need to do anything to have Replicator begin background replication when the replication settings criteria is met. When the criteria for replication is met, Notes will automatically begin the replication sequence set up on the Replicator tab.

Watch the bottom of the Replicator tab to determine the status of each database as it replicates (see Figure 21.23). Notes communicates each step in the replication process to you, as well as the estimated time it will take for the replication of each database to be complete. Notice that a hand points to each entry on the Replicator tab as it becomes active.

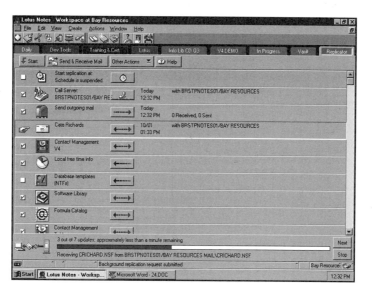

Fig. 21.23 This is how a replication in progress looks when you use the Replicator.

If you select Next, Notes stops replicating the current database and moves to the next entry. Select Stop if you want to completely end the current replication. Notes stops replicating the current database and ignores the remaining entries on the Replicator tab—but does not hang up the connection. If you want to hang up manually, select File, Mobile, Hang Up.

Note

If you work off-site and on a network, keep in mind that any information you have entered into your local replicas doesn't appear on the server copy of the database when you return to the office unless you performed a database exchange after your last entry. To update the server copy of the database, perform a background replication as soon as you connect back on the network.

Using Some Special Actions with Replicator. Often, when working remote, you may want to replicate mail, replicate only one database, replicate only selected databases or with a selected server, or replicate high priority databases only. The Send and Receive Mail Only and the Other Actions buttons enable you to perform the following actions during a replication:

- Select the Send and Receive Mail Only button if you only want to replicate mail during a particular replication. Notes immediately calls your Home/Mail server and exchanges Mail databases. It also transfers all the mail you may have created and stored in your Outgoing Mail database.

- Select Other Actions, Replicate High Priority Databases to begin replicating only those databases whose replication settings indicate high priority (see "Other Replication Settings" earlier in this chapter for information on setting database priorities).

- Select the databases you want to replicate by clicking in the boxes next to their entries. Select Other Actions, Replicate with Server, and then select the server you want to replicate with. Select <u>O</u>K to begin the replication. Notes calls only that server to replicate with. Keep in mind that if the database(s) you select do not have replicas on that particular server, and you are not calling a passthru server, your database(s) will not be updated.

- Select the database you want to replicate by clicking its entry in the Replicator. Select Other Actions, Replicate Selected Database Only. Notes calls the server and replicates only that database.

- Select the databases you want to replicate by clicking the box next to their entries (make sure you deselect those you don't want to replicate as well). Select Other Actions, Replicate Selected Databases Only. Notes calls and replicates only the selected databases.

- To only send your outgoing mail, select Other Actions and then Send Outgoing Mail. Notes will call your server and only transfer your outgoing mail to the server. You will not receive any updates or send any updates to other server databases.

Monitoring Replication History. After you replicate using the Replicator, you see how many documents you sent and received logged directly on each database entry that was selected for replication. However, you may want to see the history of past replications to see who replicated with a particular database and when. You can do so by highlighting the database you are interested in on the regular workpage, and then selecting <u>F</u>ile, Replication, <u>H</u>istory. The Replication History dialog box appears (see Figure 21.24).

Fig. 21.24 You can view the replication history of a database in this dialog box.

You can Copy the information to the Clipboard to paste into a report, <u>C</u>lear the history, or change the way you view the information (by <u>S</u>erver name or by <u>D</u>ate). Select Do<u>n</u>e when you are ready to exit the Replication History dialog box. This technique is ideal for database managers who need to review database activity!

Tip

If you do not think you are replicating correctly with the server, for instance, you are not receiving all of the documents that you should be getting, you can elect to <u>C</u>lear the history of the replication. The next time Notes calls the server, it will begin to replicate as though it is the first time,

---

rather than perform an incremental replication of only those items in the database that changed since the last time you replicated. Keep in mind though that if the database is large, it may take a long time to perform your next replication.

More About Using Mail Remote

Notes makes sending and receiving mail documents easy while operating remote. A few areas about using mail remote warrant further discussion, however. In the following sections, you learn more about using the Outgoing Mail database (MAIL.BOX) and working remote with the Notes address books.

Understanding the Outgoing Mail Database

When you use mail remote, Notes stores all mail that you send (including any return receipt reports for documents you received and opened) in a special Outgoing Mail database named MAIL.BOX. The Outgoing Mail database automatically appears on your workspace if you set up Notes for remote use when you first installed Lotus Notes. If you installed Notes as a network only user and later created a replica of your Mail database, Notes automatically created the Outgoing Mail database at that time.

If you think the Outgoing Mail database is present, but don't see its icon on your workspace, select File, Database, Open and with Local highlighted in the servers list, type **MAIL.BOX** in the Filename text box. Select Add Icon and then select Done. If an error message appears indicating that the file does not exist, create a new one by performing the following steps:

1. Select File, Database, New. The New Database dialog box appears (see Figure 21.25).

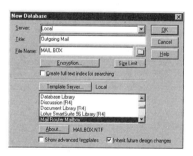

Fig. 21.25 Use the New Database dialog box to create an Outgoing Mail database.

2. Select Local for the Server entry.

3. Type Outgoing Mail in the Title box.

4. Edit the File Name to read MAIL.BOX.

Caution

You must name the Outgoing Mail database MAIL.BOX in the File Name field, or Notes will not recognize the filename when trying to store sent mail remote.

5. Select Mail Router Mailbox from the Template list box. If you do not see the Mail Router Mailbox template, enable the Show advanced templates option in the lower left corner of the dialog box to display additional templates to choose from.

6. Select OK. Notes creates the Outgoing Mail database, and adds its icon to your workspace.

If you want to verify whether you sent a mail document from your Mail database (you may not remember whether you chose to mail a document you were working on or you may suspect that your remote mail capabilities are not working correctly), open the Outgoing Mail database. If the mail document title is displayed, the message will transfer to the server the next time you perform a database exchange when you replicate your Mail database. If you decide that you don't want to mail the document, you can delete the document from this database before you perform an exchange.

Likewise, to make sure that all the mail you send is transferred to the server during the last exchange, open the Outgoing Mail database. No documents display in the Mail view if your exchange was performed successfully.

Note

Do not compose memos from the Outgoing Mail database. This database is used only as a holding tank for mail waiting to be transferred to the server! Notes treats this database specially, and you may find that your messages are not being delivered, or otherwise have problems if you try to compose messages from this database.

Caution

Do not open the Outgoing Mail database while you are in the process of transferring mail to the server. This database must be closed during replication for mail to successfully transfer!

Using Address Books Remote

For mail to be routed properly, the recipients listed in the To, cc, and bcc fields must be spelled exactly as they are in the server's address book. Usually, only users listed in the server's address book can receive Notes mail because the server's address book displays all Notes users set up to receive mail on your network. The exception is if special gateways are installed to work with Notes on your network to route mail to other foreign Notes domains or other types of e-mail systems. (Refer to Chapter 6, "Advanced Mail," for additional information on this exception.)

As previously discussed, Notes looks in your Personal Name & Address Book first to find recipients. If the recipient isn't listed there, Notes transfers the document to the server anyway during a database exchange. The server then looks for the recipient in the Public Name & Address Book. If the server cannot find the name, it sends a non-delivery report to your mail file on the server. You aren't aware of the delivery failure until the next time you perform a database exchange.

If you are a remote-only user, you can use the interactive connection method to connect to your Notes server to update your Personal Name & Address Book with other Notes users' names so that you have their names available to you when you address mail. There is an alternative method: replicating the Public Address Book to your hard drive (recommended), also discussed in this section. This first method is used mainly for users that, for some reason, cannot replicate a copy of the Public Name and Address Book to their hard drives.

To update your Personal Name & Address Book with users' names, follow these steps:

1. Open your Personal Name & Address Book.

2. Choose View, People.

3. Choose Edit, Select All.

> ### Caution
>
> If you follow this procedure, you will delete all of your current entries from the database—including any unique entries (people you have defined that are not in your company). If you use your Personal Name & Address Book to maintain unique entries, then you may want to select only those names that are in your group/company. Be careful when following these procedures so that you do not lose any of your personal, unique names.

4. Delete all the selected documents.

5. Choose File, Mobile, Call Server, and follow the steps in the following section "Using the Interactive Connection Method" to connect to the server.

6. Open the Public Name & Address Book on the server.

7. Choose View, People.

8. Choose Edit, Select All (or you can select each individual name that you want to copy to your Personal Name & Address Book instead). Keep in mind that if you have a large number of users defined in your Public Name & Address Book, your Personal Name & Address Book is going to grow quite large if you copy all user names.

9. Choose Edit, Copy. Notes begins copying all the documents to the Clipboard. (This process can take a while, depending on the number of names that must be copied.)

> **Caution**
>
> If you did not remove all of the names that are in common with the Public Name & Address Book prior to pasting all of the new names into the book, you will have duplicate entries of user names, which will cause Notes to prompt you with error messages when you try to send to the user. Delete all duplicate names from the list.

10. After the copying is complete, exit the Public Name & Address Book.

11. Open your Personal Address Book and choose Edit, Paste. Notes pastes all the names into your Personal Name & Address Book.

12. Choose File, Mobile, Hangup and select the appropriate COM port, and then choose Hangup to end the connection with the server.

If you use this method, you may want to compact your database after you update the database to remove any "white space" which takes up unnecessary disk space (you learn more about compacting your database in "Working Smart Remote," later in this chapter.

Rather than cut and paste documents from the server's address book to your personal one or going without Notes users' names available to you, follow these steps for a simpler, recommended, alternative method:

> **Caution**
>
> Although the following information works for most Notes users, check with your Notes administrator to make sure that carrying a replica of the Public Address Book for your company does not interfere with any special setup or policy the administrator may have made.
>
> Also, depending on the number of users you have on your network, this database can be quite large, and therefore may be impractical to carry on your hard drive.
>
> Finally, users can make changes to the network copy of this database several times a day, and you may find it too time-consuming to replicate this database frequently. Turn off replication or limit replication to a few times a month.

1. Make a replica stub of the Public Address Book in your local directory (refer to the section "Preparing a Replica of a Database" earlier in this chapter). Enter any filename other than NAMES.NSF because that is being used by your Personal Name & Address Book. For our example, enter the filename NAMES2.NSF.

2. In the Space Savers settings of the Replications Settings dialog box, select the option to Replicate a subset of documents (you will learn more about this feature shortly).

3. Select the people and groups views below the Folders and Views icon, as shown in Figure 21.26.

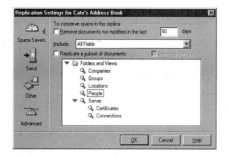

Fig. 21.26   You can set up selective replication for the Public Name & Address Book.

4. Select <u>O</u>K.

When Notes replicates with the Public Address Book, it only replicates group lists and person documents.

You also need to add a line to your NOTES.INI file to tell Notes that you have another address book to use when addressing mail remote. You can do this by choosing <u>F</u>ile, <u>T</u>ools, <u>U</u>ser Preferences, Mail and selecting the name of the new Address Book (for example, NAMES2.NSF) from the list. Click OK to exit the User Preferences dialog box. Notes will update the NOTES.INI setting for you. For details on updating NOTES.INI for multiple Address Books and in setting User Preferences, see Chapter 2, "Customizing Notes."

After modifying your NOTES.INI file, you should be able to switch between your Personal and Public Address Books while working remote. You can update your replica of the address book by replicating it just like any other database. For more information on using the Address Books, read Chapter 5, "Using the Address Book."

You now have a replica of the Public Address Book to use with the mail address feature when you are working remote. To access the names in the list remote, follow the instructions in Chapter 5. All of the addressees appear in your Public Address Book.

(continued)

to your hard drive to successfully use the Public Address Book remotely to address mail. Selecting this option will replicate only the necessary fields in the Person and Group documents that you need to address messages remotely. This option can save considerable hard disk space if your company's Public Address Book is large.

You can also expand the amount of information you replicate by selecting in the Person documents beyond the minimal information it takes to address mail messages:

- "Minimal Address Book, Encryption," which includes the Encryption key information for that person as well as the address information.

- "Minimal Address Book, Person Info," which includes the personal information like phone number, address, and so on, as well as the address information.

- "Minimal Address Book, Person Info, Encryption," which includes both the encryption and personal information in the Person document as well as the address information.

Keep in mind, however, that the more you elect to replicate, the more hard disk space you will require.

Using the Interactive Connection Method

An interactive connection establishes a direct link between your remote station and the server, requiring a constant telephone connection. Although your PC is connected to the server by telephone lines rather than LAN cables, you can use the databases stored on the server and receive the most up-to-date information in the databases just as though you were working on-site. You receive mail directly from the mail router, and the mail you send is transferred through the mail router directly to the recipient you specify as soon as you send it.

Interactive connections, however, tie up the server for a longer period of time, resulting in higher phone costs. Plan to use an interactive connection only when you work with a very large database and you don't have the resources to install the database on your remote PC or when you are adding a database so that you can create a replica of it. An interactive connection also can be useful if you don't use the database frequently.

Caution

If you use an interactive connection, save documents often. Otherwise, if your connection with the server is discontinued before you complete and save an entry, you may lose the information. If you lose the connection, keep the document you are trying to work with open on your desktop until the connection can be reestablished. Save the file when you are connected back with the server.

To work interactively, you must first call the server. Once you are connected, you can work in the databases on that server as though you were connected on a LAN.

> **Note**
>
> If the databases you want to work in are on different servers, you must repeat this process for each server after you complete the work on one unless you are connecting to a passthru server.

To call the server, follow these steps:

1. Choose File, Mobile, Call Server or press the File Mobile Call Server SmartIcon. The Call Server dialog box shown in Figure 21.27 appears.

Fig. 21.27   Use this dialog box to call the server directly.

2. Select a server from the server list. The servers listed are the ones for which you have connection documents in your Personal Address Book.

3. Specify any prefix or suffix options you want to use.

4. Choose Auto Dial to have the computer dial the server immediately, or choose Manual Dial if you want Notes to prompt you to pick up the phone to dial manually.

5. Select File, Mobile, Hang up when you are through working with the server.

If you are unsuccessful in connecting to the server, Notes prompts you with the appropriate message. Try to dial the server again. If you still are unsuccessful, refer to "Remote Troubleshooting" on the CD-ROM.

> **Caution**
>
> If you plan to use NotesMail and want to have the memos routed immediately upon sending, make sure you have selected a location that is set up for On Server mail. Use your network copy of your Mail database while working interactively.

◀◀ See "Setting Up Locations," p. 806

You now are connected to the server and can open any database on the server for which you have been granted access. (It's just like a network connection at this point, only slower and less reliable!) If you don't have the server's database icon already on your desktop (it will have the server's name on the icon if you have View, Show Server Names selected), you can add it. If you have stacked your replica icons, click the icon indicator on the database you want to use, and highlight the server name you have just connected with from the drop-down list.

> **Note**
>
> When you use the interactive connection method, you may lose connection with the server on several occasions. An interruption in the phone line causes this problem most often; the problem also may be caused when you don't perform an activity for a long time (for example, if you are reading a long document) and the Hangup if Idle for time expires. If this problem occurs too frequently, increase the Hangup if Idle for setting.

◀◀ See "Setting Up Your Modem," p. 800

Working Smart Remote

This section has a wide variety of tips and techniques you can use while working remote to take advantage of Notes capabilities, reduce the amount of hard disk space you are using, minimize the amount of time you are spending on the network, and otherwise work smart!

Transporting Databases on a Floppy Disk

If you work away from the office and use a different remote computer than on the network, you can reduce the cost and time involved in performing an off-site database exchange for the first time by copying a database to a floppy disk while you are on-site, and then copying it to your remote computer off-site. This process takes much less time to perform than setting up a remote replica off-site and then dialing in to perform the first exchange to fill the database with documents.

To copy a database to a floppy disk and then install it on your remote PC, follow these steps:

1. While on-site, make a full replica of the database you want to install on your remote system to your C:\NOTES\DATA directory. (You will want to delete this copy after the procedure, so take note of the icon's location.)

2. Check the database file size by choosing File, Database, Properties, and switching to the Information tab (marked by a small *i*). Write this size down for future reference.

3. Using your operating system's commands, copy the database to a floppy disk. Once the database is copied to the floppy disk, delete the copy on your hard drive—unless you have other reasons for keeping it there.

   At the remote site, copy the replica of the database on your floppy disk to your remote C:\NOTES\DATA directory (or whichever directory you have specified as your Notes data directory) by using your operating systems commands.

4. Launch Lotus Notes.

5. Add the newly copied database to your workspace.

> **Caution**
>
> Keep in mind that you must maintain replica copies of databases on your local hard drive if you want to replicate with the server. Using the operating system commands to copy a database to and from a disk will maintain the replica copy status of the database. If you copy the database to or from the floppy disk using Notes' commands, make sure you select File, Replication, New Replica to make the copies—this method is actually slower than using the operating system commands.

If the replica is too large to fit on a single floppy disk (check the file size you found in step 2), use one of the following methods:

- Make only a partial replica of a database (as discussed in "Preparing a Replica of a Database" earlier in this chapter). Restrict the number of documents in the database replica by selecting the Only Replicate Incoming Documents Saved or Modified After Days option in the Replication Settings dialog box when you create the new replica.

- Use compression programs (such as PKZIP) to reduce a database's size. Your local software dealer can recommend several programs that can help you. PKZIP can often have tremendous returns on compression due to the database structure of Notes. However, should the size of the database when zipped still exceed more than the space available on the disk, you can tell PKZIP to compress onto multiple disks by including the -& command when zipping the file.

- Use your operating system's Backup command to create a backup copy of the replica database in your C:\NOTES\DATA directory onto multiple floppy disks. Then use the operating system's Restore command to load the database onto your remote PC. (Refer to your operating system's manual for details on backup and restore procedures.)

- Use any of the other space-saving replication settings, such as Selective replication (discussed later in this section), to reduce the size of the database being copied as a new replica.

Maintaining Replica Databases

You can use the options in the Replication Settings dialog box (refer to "Choosing Replication Settings" earlier in this chapter) and a few other techniques to clean out your off-site replica databases from time to time. These options enable you to purge (delete) documents automatically from a database replica, delete documents from a database replica manually without copying the deletions back to the network, reduce the size of a database replica through selective replication, compact a database, and delete a database replica from your system. The following sections discuss these techniques in more detail.

Deleting Documents from Replicas. You can remove older documents by deleting them from your database without deleting them from other replicas. This option is usually used when you cannot automatically remove documents based on the date they were last saved/modified (described in the next section). Follow these steps:

1. Select the database from which you want to remove documents. Display the Replication Settings dialog box by choosing File, Replication, Settings or selecting the File Replication Settings SmartIcon. Select Send to display the Send panel.

2. Choose the Do Not Send Deletions Made in This Replica to Other Replicas option if you don't want to copy any deletions made in this database to the server.

3. Select OK, and then delete any documents that you want from the database without worrying that the documents will also be removed from other replicas. See Chapter 3, "Using Databases," if you need instructions on deleting documents manually.

> **Caution**
>
> If you don't select the Do Not Send Deletions Made in This Replica to Other Replicas option and you have the access on the server copy of the database to delete documents, you will delete all of the documents from the server copy that you delete in your local copy. The server, in turn, will delete all of these same documents from other users' replica copies the next time they replicate with the server. Be careful and make sure you have the selection checked.

Automatically Reducing the Number of Documents. You can have Notes automatically reduce the number of documents in a database by filling out the Remove Documents Not Modified in the Last ___ Days option. Notes automatically removes the documents from your replica that were saved/last edited prior to the cutoff date without deleting the documents from the server or leaving deletion identifiers (which take up space!) in your database.

This method is preferable to deleting documents for most databases because you don't have to constantly manage the deletions; however, it is not always feasible. Some databases (such as library databases and the Name & Address Book documents) may contain information that is important because of its topic (or other classification) rather than the date it was created or modified. For these types of databases, you may want to either delete the unwanted documents or set up a selective replication formula (as described later in this section) to limit the database to only those documents you want.

Compacting the Database. Although deleting documents may reduce the number of documents in the database, the document deletion identifiers take up space within the database. Also, after you use a database for a while, your database begins to contain an increasing amount of "white space," just as your hard drive begins to get fragmented over a period of time.

You can remove the white space by highlighting the database icon and selecting File, Database, Properties, and then selecting the Information tab (marked by a small *i*). Select the Compact button to begin compacting your database. Notes begins to compact the database (squeeze out the white space).

It is usually only necessary to compact a database about once a month or when there is about ten percent to 15 percent unused space in the database. You can find out how much space is used by selecting File, Database, Properties, and then selecting the Information tab (marked by a small *i*). Select the %Used button to show how much space is being used. Subtract the amount of space used from 100 percent.

> **Note**
>
> Compacting may take a while if the database is large. When Notes compacts a database, it makes a temporary copy of the active or selected database and copies it over the original file, preserving the original Read/Unread markers while removing unused space. If you try to open the database during the copying process, you see the message `Database is in use by you or another user`.

> **Caution**
>
> If you wait until you have very little free disk space available before you try to compact your databases, you may not have enough free space to perform this function! Be diligent in performing your housekeeping tasks.
>
> If you do find that you do not have enough disk space free to compact a large database, try compacting smaller ones first to see whether you can free up enough space for the larger ones. You may also need to consider deleting databases (or other files) from your hard disk that you no longer use.

Maintaining Special Databases. When working remote, pay special attention to your Mail, Notes Log, and Outgoing Mail databases. The following tips give guidance for maintaining these databases in particular, but they can apply to others as well:

- Your Mail database will most likely be the most active database while working remote and will therefore require compacting quite frequently. Consider carrying only the last week or two of mail in your database by following the instructions in the previous section "Automatically Reducing the Number of Documents." (You can always access older mail documents by working interactively with the server in the network copy of your Mail database, as long as you haven't deleted them.) You may also consider making an Archive Mail database to store documents that you want to carry with you that are older than the specified replication cutoff date. (Refer to Chapter 10, "Creating New Databases," for further information on creating databases.)

- If you have received and detached attachments in e-mail documents, delete the memo containing the attachments (or if you need to retain the memo, place it in Edit mode and remove the attachments). You may also be able to use the attachments you receive without detaching them (if you only need to read the attachment) from the memo by selecting Launch, which would allow you to read the attachment information without having to save it on your hard drive. For further information on using attachments, refer to Chapter 6, "Advanced Mail."

■ If you selected Log Modem I/O when you set up your modem, Notes creates a document every time you call the server. Even if this selection is not made, your Notes Log database will grow over time and must be cleaned out. You can either set a purge interval as previously discussed in this section; open each view of the Notes Log database, manually delete the documents, and then compact the database; or simply delete the entire database (if you don't need any of the Log history anymore). If you delete the database, you must then re-create it using the Notes Log template available to you. Make sure you name the new database LOG.NSF and store it in your local data directory. (Refer to Chapter 10, "Creating New Databases," for additional information on creating databases from templates.)

■ If you do not have enough disk space available to compact any databases, deleting the Notes Log database and then re-creating it after you have compacted all the other databases may be the best way to go. Also, you may get an error message if you try to compact your Log database because Notes may be accessing it for a background process. If you want to reduce your Log file size under this circumstance, you either have to set a purge interval or delete and re-create the database.

■ Over time, your Outgoing Mail database will grow just like other databases, even though documents are only being stored here temporarily. Make it a habit to compact this database whenever you compact your Mail database. You may occasionally receive an error message indicating that your Outgoing Mail file is in use and cannot be compacted. This message is primarily caused if background replication is underway. It is typically easier to find a time to compact this database when you first start Notes.

If you do not have enough space to compact the Outgoing Mail database (or others), you can permanently delete the database and then re-create it.

Deleting a Database Replica. You may want to delete a database replica permanently from your hard disk. (Removing a replica file from your hard disk doesn't affect other replicas of the database on the server.) The steps to delete a replica are the same as deleting any other database:

1. Select the database icon.

2. Choose File, Database, Delete.

3. Select Yes to acknowledge the deletion of this database.

> **Caution**
>
> You will lose all the information stored in any database replica you elect to delete that you have not replicated to the server. Make sure that any information you want to keep is replicated with the server or copied and stored in another database before deleting the database.

Selective Replication. Selective replication allows you to control what type of information will transfer from the source database on the server to a replica of a database. You can identify particular folders or views of documents to replicate or use replication formulas to limit the number of documents replicating from the server. Replication settings are a part of the database in which they're created, but they only apply to replication with a particular server. The default is Any Server.

Replication formulas are very similar to the View Selection formulas you may write when designing a view in a database. For example, if you had a Sales Tracking database for all of the regions in which your company does business, and your Western Sales Manager, Bill Moore, only wants to receive the documents in his replica of the database that are for the Western region, you can create a replication selection formula in Bill's replica of the database that tells Notes to receive only the documents that contain the criteria specified in the formula. The selection formula would appear as follows:

```
Select SalesRegion = "Western"
```

Where `SalesRegion` is the field name used in the database form design to specify the sales regions for this company and `Western` is the name of Bill's region. This selection formula limits the data Bill receives to only those forms in which there is a field titled SalesRegion and the entry in the documents with this field is Western. For more information on writing formulas, refer to Chapter 14, "Working with Formulas."

You automatically have Manager level access for all local replicas of databases, so you have the correct access level to set up selective replication on those databases. You must, however, have Designer or Manager level access to create replication formulas on the server copies of the database because those formulas may affect all database users.

The following information provides you with the steps to follow to set up selective replication for a database. Refer to Part II, "Designing Applications," for further information on formulas and database design.

> **Note**
>
> Keep in mind that selective replication formulas can only work if the design of the database allows you to select the information in the manner in which you want. For example, if there were no fields distinguishing the Sales Region in Bill's database, he would not be able to select on that criteria. If you are designing databases that will be replicated to users or other servers, keep this fact in mind as you proceed.

To take advantage of selective replication, follow these steps:

1. Highlight the database you want to set up, and then select File, Replication, Settings. The Replication Settings dialog box appears (see Figure 21.28).

2. In the Space Savers panel, you must first decide whether you want to create a selective replication by highlighting folders and/or views available in the database design or whether you need to write a formula to provide you with the selective replication you need.

3. If you want to replicate based on the folders and/or views available to you in the database design, select Replicate a subset of documents by clicking the box next to this option. A checkmark should appear. Then select the folders or views you want

to replicate to your hard drive. This method is by far the simplest, particularly for novice users, so if the view or folder definitions will provide you with the subset of information you want, choose this method.

Fig. 21.28   Use this dialog box to set up selective replication.

4. If you cannot get the subset of information you require by selecting folders or views to replicate, click the Select by formula option. Enter the selective replication formula in the text entry box below this setting. The default formula is SELECT @All, which tells Notes to copy all of the documents from the server. Notes adds the word SELECT to all selection formulas when they are saved, so you don't have to type it. Enter the selection formula just as you would any other Notes formula (refer to Chapter 14, "Working with Formulas," for assistance with formulas).

5. Select OK to save your settings and exit the dialog box.

Notes will now limit the number of documents you replicate from the server based on the criteria you have chosen.

Note

You also can create selective replication formulas in the Advanced panel of the Replication Settings dialog box to have Notes selectively replicate information based on specific servers you replicate with. You could set up replication formulas to replicate all documents with one server, but only documents meeting specific criteria from another server, for example.

Follow the preceding instructions for creating the subset replication settings. Refer to the "Choosing Replication Settings" section in this chapter for additional information on the Advanced panel settings.

Replication formulas that the source database Manager writes and applies to a database take precedence over all formulas written and applied to local copies of a database. For example, if the source database Manager creates a selective replication formula telling Notes to replicate only those documents created by the user, the user of a replica cannot use a selective replication formula to replicate all documents—Notes will ignore it. The user can, however, create formulas to further restrict the documents received, as Bill did in the previous example.

From Here...

The capability to effectively work remote can prove to be a distinct advantage to businesses today as the need to communicate between the home office and the field becomes critical. As you have seen, Lotus Notes makes this capability quite easy whether you always work as a remote user or work on-site part of the time. This chapter has explained what remote communication entails and how to work remote. It has also provided you with many tips for successfully working with Notes remote.

For more information on the topics discussed in this chapter, refer to the following:

- Chapter 5, "Using the Address Book," provides you with more information on the functions and features of the Name & Address Books, which control how you communicate with Notes.

- Chapter 6, "Advanced Mail," provides further information on working with many of the features in NotesMail that you will use while working remote.

- Chapter 20, "Setting Up to Go Remote," gives you instructions on setting up your system to work from a remote location.

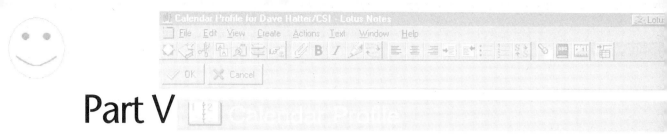

Part V

Advanced Notes Topics

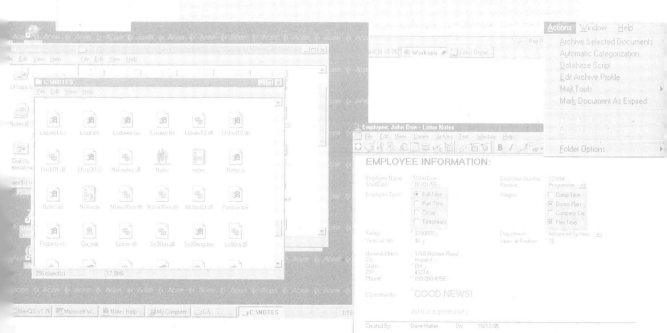

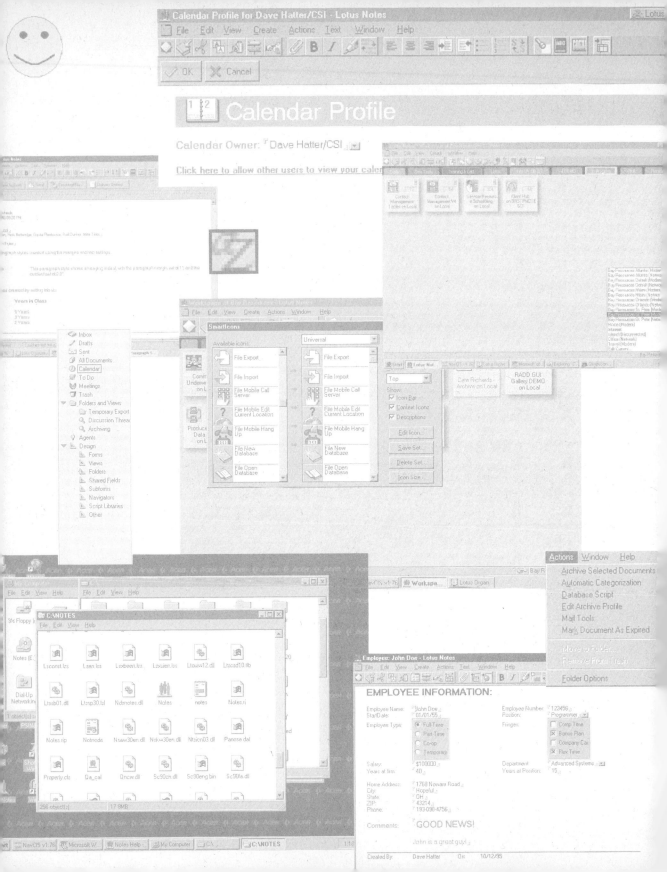

Chapter 22

Security and Encryption

Anytime people store and distribute data, there is always the danger that prying eyes will want to intercept or even alter that data. Some data may be subject to simple nosy snooping—perhaps an employee that wants to examine personal records of other employees. Other data may be critical to a project's success, making it attractive to corporate spies.

Whatever the reason, much of the information passed around inside companies is secret from somebody.

The designers of an information system such as Notes must consider the following security issues:

- The system must include security features that can protect information from even knowledgeable snoops. Simple, unsophisticated measures may stop nosy employees or hackers who are just casually curious. However, more sophisticated features are necessary to thwart the corporate spy who may be well-versed in computer security systems and how to defeat them.

- The system must protect data from being altered or forged. For example, when you receive a mail message, you should be confident that the message was sent to you by the person listed in the From field and that the contents of the message were not altered after it was sent.

- Security features must be easy to use, or people won't use them. You never think corporate spies are after your information, and it's all too easy in the crush of crucial deadlines to forget about the safety of your data.

Notes provides several features to protect information in various ways, and you learn about these features in this chapter.

Four Levels of Security

Notes offers significant control when it comes to securing your data. By implementing several varying levels of security, Lotus clearly kept the integrity of

Some of the main topics in this chapter are

- Understand the varying levels of Notes security

- Request Certificates to allow access to a Notes Server

- Request and send public keys to other Notes users

- Create encryption keys to encrypt fields of a Notes document

- Understand Execution Control Lists and when to use them

your databases in mind when developing Notes. There are several security options available to you, ranging from protecting a Notes server from unwanted eyes to verifying the author of a single field of information to prevent forgery. The following list introduces you to the four levels of Notes security available to you:

- **Server-Level Security**—Before users can access a database on a server, they must have access to the server. Server access is controlled by the server administrator through the use of certificates attached to users' ID files and server access lists. This is the first and most general layer of security.

- **Database-Level Security**—Database security for any database on a server is handled by the database access control list (ACL). The ACL lists users and servers and assigns them rights to the database. Access levels range from Manager—who has total access to the database—to No Access. The database manager creates and controls the ACL. An additional database-level security feature is local encryption, which encrypts local databases so that only specified users can access them.

- **Document-Level Security**—Document security consists of the document's read access list. The read access list is defined by the form's read access list, any reader names fields in the document, and the read access list in the Document Properties InfoBox. The read access list refines the ACL for that document—meaning that if someone has Reader access or better in the ACL but is not listed in any read access list, he or she cannot read the document. If they are not readers in the ACL, they cannot read the document even if they are listed in the document's read access list.

- **Field-Level Security**—Certain fields on a form can be encrypted using encryption keys, so only users with the correct key can read those fields. The database designer specifies that fields are encryptable, and when a key is associated to the document, all encryptable fields are encrypted with the key.

Your Notes ID

The key to protecting your information in Notes is your Notes ID file. All security features in Notes work through the information contained in your ID file. Through your ID file, Notes grants you access to the information you're supposed to see and keeps you out of documents and databases that are off-limits to you.

Your Notes ID file contains the following information:

- Your name

- Your Lotus Notes license, which gives you permission to use Lotus Notes

- Your private and public encryption keys, which Notes uses to encrypt and decrypt messages

- Your password

- Encryption keys and certificates

The name of your Notes ID file usually consists of your first initial and last name with an ID extension. For example, Steve Smith's ID file would be SSMITH.ID. You can usually find your ID file in the Notes Data directory, but some users keep their ID file on a floppy disk as extra security because it can be locked up at night, they can take the file with them when they travel, or they can place it in their home directory on their LAN, so it can be accessed from any workstation on the LAN.

Note

On your computer, Notes may have named your personal ID file USER.ID instead of using your first and last name as previously described.

Safeguarding Your Password

If your ID file is your gateway to Notes, then your password is your key to your ID file. Notes will not allow you to use the information stored in your ID file until you have entered your correct password. By requiring you to enter your password, Notes can ensure that only you can use your ID file and the information it contains.

It is crucial that no one but you knows your password. Every security feature found in Notes works under the assumption that no one else knows your password. With your password and access to your ID file, someone else can access your mailbox, read and compose documents in databases that you have access to, send messages with your name, and decrypt messages you receive.

When your system administrator installs Lotus Notes on your PC, he or she creates an ID file that contains your initial password. You should immediately select a new password and store the new password in your ID file. The following sections explain how.

Selecting a New Password. Your choice of passwords plays an important role in determining the security of the information you store in Notes; yet, too many Notes users put more effort into picking this morning's parking space. The privacy of your mailbox and all the databases you have access to depends on the fact that only you know your password, and therefore only you can use your Notes ID file. You must select a password that no one else can discover but that is easy for you to type and remember. Choose your new password carefully, and consider these points when making your decision:

- Anyone attempting to guess your password is likely to try the names of your pets, spouse, parents, children, and other relatives, as well as number combinations that represent your birthday, Social Security number, and anniversary. Similarly, do not pick words that reflect your interests, such as the name of your favorite sports team. People who know you can guess such passwords.

- A password such as starshine491 is much harder to guess than simply starshine.

- Thus StarsHinE491 is an even more secure password than starshine491 because it expands the realm of characters used.

- Pick a password that is at least eight characters long. Notes will allow you to select passwords as long as 31 characters.

- For example, you might recall the line "Three rings for the eleven kings under the sky" (from *The Lord of the Rings* by J.R.R. Tolkien) and from it construct the password 3r4tekuts. It is very unlikely that anyone else could guess such a password, and yet you can remember it easily by recalling that famous phrase.

Once you have selected your password, follow these rules to protect it:

- Never write down your password. Someone may find it.

- Never tell anyone your password. (Possible exception: a secretary who processes the boss' mail.)

Changing Your Password. Once you have selected a new password, you can use this procedure to change your Notes password:

1. Choose File, Tools, User ID. Notes asks you to type in your current password before you can access any of your user options.

2. Once you've typed your password, click OK to display the User ID dialog box (see Figure 22.1). You'll be working with this screen a lot because this is where many security options can be selected.

Fig. 22.1   Notes lets you change your password from here.

3. Click the Set Password button to change your Notes password.

4. Notes prompts you for your current password to make sure that it is really you trying to change your password.

5. Next, notes displays the Set Password dialog box (see Figure 22.2). The dialog box reminds you that Notes passwords are case-sensitive, which means that if you capitalize any letters in your new password, you must capitalize those same letters each time you use your password in the future. Enter your new password and choose OK.

Fig. 22.2   All the Xs hide your password so people can't read it while you type.

6. Notes displays another Set Password dialog box. Enter your new password again, and choose <u>O</u>K. By making you repeat your password, Notes ensures you didn't mistype your password the first time. If your two attempts to enter your new password don't match, Notes will make you repeat steps 3 and 4.

Troubleshooting

Why do I get more Xs than what I typed?

As you type your password you may notice that a random number of Xs appears for every letter or number you typed. This is so that anyone looking over your shoulder can't tell how many characters are in your password simply by counting the Xs.

If You Forget Your Password. If you can possibly avoid it, try not to forget your password. If you do, ask your system administrator to create a new ID file for you with a new password.

Forgetting your password can cause some difficulty because there is unique encryption information that is stored within each ID file that cannot be re-created. You will lose access to information encrypted by your user ID permanently. Check with your system administrator for his or her recommended ID backup procedures.

Understanding Certificates

One of the crucial components in your ID file is your certificate. You can think of your certificate as your company's seal of approval on your Notes ID. The certificate is the electronic equivalent of a notary's seal, telling the Notes servers throughout your company that your ID was properly created by an authorized administrator within your company. Certificates play a key role in preventing hackers and spies from creating bogus ID files and infiltrating your company's Notes system.

Note

Most users have a single certificate in their ID file, but some people have several. If you regularly access databases that belong to other companies—perhaps you provide technical support for your clients—you might have a certificate in your ID file from each one of those companies. Each server wants to see a certificate that it trusts before you can access that server.

Much like your driver's license, certificates have an expiration date, usually two years from the date they were issued. As the expiration date on your certificate approaches (within 60 days), Notes displays a dialog box warning you that your certificate is about to expire.

When you receive this message, you must have your certificate recertified, just as you must get your driver's license renewed from time to time. To request recertification, you must first mail a "safe copy" of your ID to your system administrator, using the following procedure (a safe copy of your ID is simply a shell of a normal ID file that lets you send, request, and obtain certificates—just think of it as a secure courier system that is protected by your personal password):

V

Advanced Notes Topics

1. Before you begin, make sure you know the name of the person in your company who certifies IDs.

2. Choose File, Tools, User ID to bring up the User ID dialog box. Select the Certificate pane, and click Request Certificate. Notes displays the Mail Certificate Request dialog box (see Figure 22.3).

Fig. 22.3   Request a certificate via e-mail through the Mail Certificate Request dialog box.

3. Enter the name of the person in your company who certifies IDs in the To text box. If you're unsure of the spelling, you can choose Address to access the company Name & Address Book.

4. Choose Send. Notes sends a mail message to your system administrator with the safe copy of your Notes ID attached and a message requesting that he or she recertify your ID.

Your system administrator will recertify your ID and send it back to you by mail. (You hope he or she accomplishes this task before your certificate expires. Otherwise, you may need to make a few phone calls.)

To accept the new certificate, follow this procedure:

1. Choose File, Tools, User ID to access the User ID dialog box.

2. Notes prompts you first for your Notes password. Enter your password and choose OK.

3. Choose the More Options pane shown in Figure 22.4.

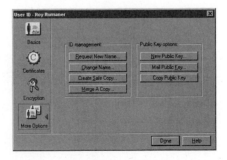

Fig. 22.4   Control your advanced Notes ID options from this pane.

4. Click the Merge a Copy button and select the ID file to merge. Notes copies your new certificate into your Notes ID file, and you're good for another two years.

Although the process outlined describes how to update a Notes certificate, you follow the same steps to request a new certificate. You've just got to ensure that you are mailing the safe copy of your ID file to the correct individual who can certify you.

Understanding Database Security

Each time you access a database, Notes applies various security features to determine which operations you are allowed to perform. In this section, you come to understand how Notes decides who can perform various database operations and how you can change how people can access databases.

Access Levels

Whenever you attempt to access a Notes database, Notes classifies you into one of several access levels that determines what you are allowed to do while working with that database. Your access level is different for each database you access and is determined by the manager of the database.

The seven possible access levels are the following:

- **No Access**—You cannot access the database in any way.

- **Depositor**—You can create new documents in the database but cannot read any documents stored in the database, even if you created them.

- **Reader**—You can read documents but cannot create new documents or modify documents already stored in the database.

- **Author**—You can create new documents and read existing documents. You can modify documents if you created them.

- **Editor**—Same privileges as Author, except that you can modify documents created by other people as well as by you.

- **Designer**—All the privileges of Editor. In addition, you can modify the design (such as forms and views) of the database.

- **Manager**—You are allowed to perform any operation in the database. Only the Manager can delete the database and can control what others can do to the database. Every database must have at least one Manager.

If you have any permissions other than Manager, your only exposure to database security involves learning what you and your coworkers are allowed to do. However, if you are the Manager of a database, you are responsible for deciding what others can do. In the following section, you learn how to control access to the database.

The Access Control List

Associated with every database is an ACL that specifies who can access a database and what they're allowed to do with the database. Anyone who has access to the database can view the ACL, but only someone with Manager access can modify the ACL.

To display the ACL for a database, select or open the database and choose File, Database, Access Control. Notes displays the Access Control List dialog box (see Figure 22.5).

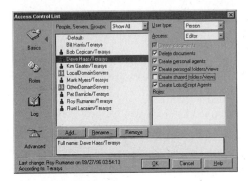

Fig. 22.5 Check the database's ACL settings here.

The People, Servers, Groups combo box lists the names all the people, servers, and groups for which the Manager wants to specify access. Whenever the Access Control List dialog box is displayed and one of the names is selected, the remainder of the dialog box shows the access permissions for the name. You can change the selected name just like you change the selected item in any combo box.

In Figure 22.5, Dave Haas' name is selected. The Access combo box shows that Dave has Editor privileges for this database, and the User type combo box shows that this is a Person entry in the list. Notice the six checkboxes to the right of the list box; they allow you to further refine the creation and deletion rights of the individual.

If you select a different name from the People, Servers, Groups combo box, the Access combo box, the User type combo box, and the checkboxes change to reflect the permissions for the newly selected name.

The six checkboxes at the right of the dialog box only apply to names with certain privileges. For example, if the selected name has Editor access, Notes grays out the Create documents checkbox so that it is always marked because all Editors can always create documents.

In addition to the names of people, the ACL can contain the names of groups. Every member of that group then receives the same privileges.

The ACL can contain both the name of a group, and the name of one or more people in that group. When deciding what permissions should apply to a specific user, Notes first looks for the person's name. If the person's name is not found, Notes then looks for a group to which that person belongs. This feature enables you to override group permissions for a specific person by making an entry for that person. Remember that using groups to define your ACL requires that your company's Name & Address Book is secure; otherwise, individuals could be added to groups and have access to databases they shouldn't.

Every ACL also has an entry for Default. Notes applies these permissions for anyone not listed by name and not a member of any group.

Two predefined names always appear in the ACL:

- **LocalDomainServers**—The access level for this entry determines the access for other servers within your domain, which probably represents your company. For databases that are replicated on other servers within your company, LocalDomainServers must be Reader access or better.

- **OtherDomainServers**—The access level for this entry determines the access for servers outside your domain (probably company). You will probably want to set this entry to No Access unless you are building databases that can be accessed by other companies.

If you have Manager privileges for the database, you will be able to change the permissions for a name in the ACL. Simply select the name you want to change and click the button that represents the access you want that name to have.

Roles

Notes security includes the concept of roles, which can help you organize the people who need to access the forms and views in a database. A role is any group of people you define who need to have similar access to the forms and views within a database.

A role is most useful when you can identify a group of people who all need to perform the same operations on a database and will therefore need the same privileges. By creating a role for this group you are simply adding and removing privileges for the entire group.

You can add to the list of roles for a database by selecting the Roles pane from the Access Control List dialog box. Notes displays the list of roles (see Figure 22.6). In this example, three roles—Trainers, Managers, and Developers—have been defined.

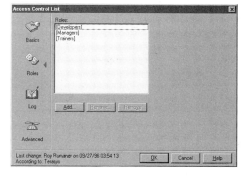

Fig. 22.6 Set your Notes roles from the Access Control List dialog box.

To create a new role, click Add. Notes prompts you for the name of the new role and adds it to the list. To delete a role, select the role from the list and then click Remove. To rename a role, click Rename.

To control which users are included in a role, click the Basics icon to return to the Basics pane and select a name. Any roles that person belongs to are marked in the Roles box. To add another role to the person, click the role in the Roles box. The role will appear with a checkmark next to it. To remove someone from a role, uncheck the role in the Roles box. Figure 22.7 shows Mark Myers assigned to the Trainers role.

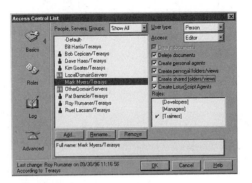

Fig. 22.7   Mark Myers is assigned to the Trainers role.

Once you have created a role, you can specify the role in place of a user name in the Read Access Control List dialog box and Compose Access Control List dialog box for forms and views. If you specify that the Supervisor role can access a particular form, all the users you placed in the Supervisor role can access that form. Later, if you decide they no longer have need to access the form, you simply remove the role and none of those users has access.

Understanding Encryption

You may think that because your company is not building nuclear warheads or involved in national security (then again, maybe they are), you really don't have much need for privacy. However, in even the most mundane of businesses, you may encounter sensitive information that you must protect at all costs. Encryption enables you to keep your secrets secret.

If you have no concerns about who sees your data—if you deal exclusively with information that is not particularly private—then Notes' database security is probably all the security you'll ever need, and you can skip the rest of this chapter. But even so, if you want to know how the cloak-and-dagger folks hide their information, read on. This is fascinating stuff!

A Quick History of Encryption

Throughout history people have constantly sought ways to store and convey information in ways that kept it secret from enemies who might try to intercept the information. The oldest technique for sending secret information was concealment, in which the sender might simply try to hide the secret information. The sender might send a package that contains a secret compartment or bury a secret message in a letter among otherwise innocent-looking text.

More commonly in recent times, people rely upon encryption to conceal information, a process in which the sender scrambles the message in some way to make it unreadable. The receiver then performs a related operation, known as decryption, that converts the scrambled message back to its original form. An enemy who intercepts the message along the way sees only the scrambled message.

The earliest forms of encryption relied on keeping the decryption technique secret. The sender encrypted information using a complex technique that they hoped an enemy couldn't figure out. In Roman times, simply substituting one letter for another (A=B, B=C, C=D, and so on) was good enough, but today many newspapers routinely publish such encrypted messages on their puzzles page, and amateur cryptographers crack them in minutes.

Before the 20th century, there was a practical limit to how complex an encryption technique could be. The more complex an encryption system was, the greater the chance that the person encrypting or decrypting the message would make a mistake. Also, quite often encrypted messages are needed in a hurry, such as on a battlefield. If an encryption technique is too complex, people can't use it quickly.

Computers changed everything. They could handle complex encryption and decryption techniques flawlessly and quickly. However, they also enabled code-breakers to crack very complex encrypted messages. The techniques that let you securely encrypt your messages today are very sophisticated, and in the following sections, you'll come to understand the basics of how they work.

Understanding Encryption Keys

Of all the things to learn about Notes, possibly few topics are less understood by users than encryption. Perhaps that's because most users don't feel that their information is sensitive enough to require such secrecy. But like a lot of features, once you know encryption is available, you'll probably find opportunities to use it.

Most encryption schemes today involve some type of scrambling that is controlled by a key. The sender selects a secret phrase, word, or number—the key—and uses the key along with some process to encrypt the information. The receiver, who must know the key, applies a reverse process using the same key to decrypt the message and retrieve the original information. If an enemy intercepts the message (and the encryption technique is sophisticated enough), he or she cannot recover the information without the key, even if he or she knows how the technique works for encrypting and decrypting.

This technique is known as single-key encryption. Lotus Notes has the ability to encrypt a message using a single key and later decrypt the message back into its original form. In fact, single-key encryption plays an important part in Lotus Notes (see "Using Encryption Keys" later in this chapter).

However, single-key encryption is not well-suited for exchanging e-mail because of an important drawback: both the sender and the receiver must have the same key, but they must manage to keep the key secret from the rest of the world. You must figure out some way to exchange the key ahead of time, and if an enemy should intercept the key, he or she can read your secret messages as easily as the intended receiver.

One of the greatest advances in modern cryptography is the development of a technique that does not require you to exchange keys in secret. This technique is the focus of Notes encryption and of most modern encryption systems.

Understanding Public-Key Encryption. The most recent innovation and the central technique in Lotus Notes is called *public-key encryption*. In this technique, you (and all users) have two keys. Public-key encryption is based on the fact that the keys are related in such a way that a message encrypted with either one of the keys can be decrypted only with the other key.

In any public-key encryption system (including Lotus Notes), you create two keys. (In the case of Notes, Notes performs this operation for you.) You keep one of the keys—known as your private key—secret, but the other key—known as your public key—can be widely distributed and given to anyone.

If someone wants to send you a secret message, they use your public key, which you have distributed to all your friends and coworkers, to encrypt the message. When you receive the message, you use your private key to decrypt the message. Remember that messages encrypted with one key can be decrypted only with the other key. The crucial feature of public-key encryption is that messages cannot be decrypted with the same key that was used to encrypt them. Thus, an enemy cannot decrypt your message even if he or she knows your public key. Because your public key only lets others encrypt messages for you, you can distribute your public key through normal means without worrying about unfriendlies intercepting it.

How Safe Is Encryption?

Your public and private keys are always related in such a way that messages encrypted with one key can only be decrypted with the other. However, the relationship between the two keys is so complex that the chances of anyone figuring out your private key, even if they know your public key, is virtually nil.

How safe is public-key encryption? Cryptographers widely believed that a good public-key system was virtually uncrackable. In 1977, three leading cryptographers encrypted a short message using a public-key technique, and jokingly offered a $100 prize to anyone who could crack the message. The public-key technique they used was very similar to the technique used by Lotus Notes. They believed that the calculations needed to determine the private key and thus uncover the message would require more time than the lifetime of the universe.

Imagine their surprise when the code was cracked in eight months.

Arjen Lenstra at Bellcore (the research and development outfit jointly owned by the regional Bell telephone companies) couldn't resist the challenge, and organized a team of codebreakers at Iowa State, MIT, and Oxford, along with 600 codebreaker-wannabes on the Internet. After a massive effort that required eight months and a lot of mainframe and supercomputer time, Lenstra and his team cracked the code.

For us mere mortals, this exercise probably doesn't mean much. The effort that Lenstra and his team devoted to cracking the message was enormous, and probably no one is willing to devote such an enormous amount of effort and equipment to cracking anything you or I are likely to send through e-mail. And having cracked this one message doesn't lessen the effort Lenstra has to expend to crack a different message encrypted with a different key.

> However, it does illustrate that given enough time and money, nothing is ever 100 percent secure. Oh, and the message? It turned out to be, "The magic words are squeamish ossifrage."

Lotus Notes creates your private and public keys for you. Both are extremely huge numbers (hundreds of digits each) that Notes selects at random. You do not need to know the specific numbers that Notes selects for your keys; what's important is that they are available for Notes to use when encrypting and decrypting messages and that they have that crucial relationship: messages encrypted with one key can be decrypted only with the other key. Your private key is stored in your ID file, and your public key is stored in the Notes Name & Address Book along with your other public information. In this way, everyone can access your public key because everyone has access to the Name & Address Book, but only you have access to your private key because only you can access your ID file.

Encrypting Outgoing Mail. If a determined spy really wants to intercept e-mail, he or she can find lots of opportunities. As your electronic message travels from your machine to your recipients, it may pass through numerous machines, miles of network cable, and possibly thousands of miles of public telephone lines. With the proper equipment, your message can be intercepted anywhere along the way.

You can ensure the privacy of an outgoing mail message by encrypting it. Sending encrypted mail is easy with Lotus Notes, and most of the work happens automatically without any action on your part. You can encrypt a message simply by selecting the Delivery Options button at the top of the screen when composing a mail memo. This brings up the Delivery Options dialog box (see Figure 22.8). To encrypt, select the Encrypt option before selecting <u>O</u>K.

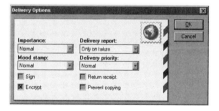

Fig. 22.8 Change your delivery options in the Delivery Options dialog box.

Note

If you usually want to encrypt your mail, you can choose <u>F</u>ile, <u>T</u>ools, <u>U</u>ser Preferences to bring up the User Preferences dialog box. Click the Mail pane, and select <u>E</u>ncrypt sent mail. From then on, Notes marks the Encrypt option for you each time you send mail. If you do not want to encrypt a particular message, you can turn the option off for that message by clicking E<u>n</u>crypt when you send the message.

When you tell Lotus Notes to encrypt a message, Notes locates your recipient in the Notes Name & Address Book and retrieves his or her public key. It uses the public key to encrypt the body of the message and then sends the message as it does any other message. When the recipient retrieves the message, Notes recognizes that the message is encrypted, and automatically decrypts the message using the recipient's private key, which is stored in his or her ID file.

If you send an encrypted message to several recipients, Notes encrypts the message in such a way that it can be decrypted using the private key of each of the recipients.

Caution

When you encrypt a message, Notes encrypts only the body of the message—not the other fields, such as the subject, date, sender, or recipient's name. You defeat the purpose of encryption if you convey too much information in these fields, especially the subject. For example, if the subject of your message, which is not encrypted, is "Hostile corporate takeover is on for tomorrow," then if your message is intercepted, it won't matter that the body of the message is encrypted—the subject gives it all away!

Obtaining Missing Public Keys. For outgoing mail encryption to work correctly, Notes must know the recipient's public key. As you sit at your desk at work sending mail to your coworkers, you shouldn't have a problem. Notes will retrieve recipients' public keys from your company's Name & Address Book, and you can happily encrypt any mail you want.

However, in the following two situations you may find that Notes doesn't have your recipient's public key:

- If you send a message to someone outside your company, they won't have an entry in your company's Name & Address Book.

- If you are using Notes remote and composing mail for later replication (see Chapter 21, "Working Remote"), Notes doesn't have access to your company's Name & Address Book.

If Notes doesn't have access to the public keys it needs, and therefore can't encrypt your message, Notes warns you by displaying the Mail Encryption Failure dialog box. You can select OK to Send to tell Notes to send the message even though it cannot be encrypted. Otherwise, select Cancel Sending if you are not willing to send the note without encryption.

Because Notes can't find the entry it needs in the company Name & Address Book in these situations, you can enable Notes to encrypt messages by placing an entry for the recipient in your personal Name & Address Book along with the public key. The following two sections describe procedures you can use to accomplish this task.

Finding the Public Key for Someone Inside Your Company. You can get the public key for someone inside your company from your company's Name & Address Book. If you are a remote user, you can copy the entry from your company's Name & Address

Book into your Personal Name & Address Book by following this procedure (remember, you will not need to perform this procedure if you are not a remote user because Notes will be able to access the Name & Address Book automatically when you send encrypted mail):

1. Dial in to your home server by selecting File, Mobile, Call Server.

2. If your company's Name & Address Book is not already on your workspace, choose File, Database, Add Workspace Icon.

3. Open your company's Name & Address Book database.

4. If the People view is not already showing, choose View, People to display it.

5. Locate the document describing your recipient and select it by clicking it or moving the selection bar to it. (Do not open it by double-clicking it.)

6. Choose Edit, Copy to copy your recipient's entry to your Clipboard.

7. Close your company's Name & Address Book database, and open your personal Name & Address database.

8. Choose Edit, Paste to copy your recipient's entry from your Clipboard into your personal Name & Address database.

Getting the Public Key for Someone Outside Your Company. If you want to be able to send encrypted mail to someone outside your company, you must have the recipient give you his or her public key. Suppose you want to exchange encrypted mail with your friend at another company. She will need to send you her public key, which she can do using this procedure:

1. Choose File, Tools, User ID. Notes prompts for a password, and then displays the User ID dialog box.

> **Note**
>
> Many of the techniques you learn in this chapter involve the User ID dialog box. You will undoubtedly notice that every time you access this dialog box, Notes prompts you for your Notes password. Because working with encryption is such a sensitive activity, Notes needs to ensure whenever you access this dialog box that it really is you typing commands at the keyboard and not someone who happened to sit down at your desk while you were away. You may find it annoying to have to type your password each time you work with this dialog box, but be thankful that Notes is looking out for your security.

2. Choose the More Options icon.

3. Click Mail Public Key. Note displays the Mail Public Key dialog box (see Figure 22.9). Your friend should enter your name in the To field. (If she wants to use the Name & Address Book to help with the addressing, she can select Address.) Notes supplies an appropriate subject for the memo.

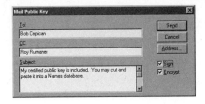

Fig. 22.9   Choose the recipient of your public key from this dialog box.

    4. Choose Se_n_d. Notes will send you a mail message containing her public key.

    5. Select D_o_ne to close the User ID dialog box.

Recall that you do not need to worry about someone intercepting this message. If an enemy intercepts her message containing her public key, she has only intercepted something that she wants to make public anyway. Remember, having your friend's public key will enable someone only to send encrypted mail to her, but not read her encrypted mail.

When you receive the message containing her public key, the subject of the message will explain what the message contains. The body of the message appears as a huge, seemingly meaningless number.

When you receive your friend's message, follow this procedure to extract the key:

    1. Open the message.

    2. The body of the message will contain your friend's public key and nothing else. Select the body of the message—all 500 or so digits.

    3. Choose _E_dit, _C_opy to copy the key to your Clipboard.

    4. Close the message and your mailbox, and open your Personal Address Book.

    5. Choose _C_reate, Person to create a document describing your recipient.

    6. Complete the first two sections that contain the information about your recipient's name and location.

    7. Later in the document, in the section labeled Advanced, there is a field available called Public Key. Place the insertion point there.

    8. Choose _E_dit, _P_aste to paste your recipient's public key into the field.

    9. Close and save the document by pressing Esc.

Once you complete this procedure, Notes can access your friend's public encryption key, and you can send encrypted mail to your friend. If she wants to send encrypted mail to you, you must perform the first procedure described earlier to send her your public key, and she must perform the second procedure when she receives your message to insert the key into her Name & Address database.

Sending Encrypted Mail Internationally

The U.S. State Department considers encryption technology to be a matter of national security and won't permit the export of the most sophisticated encryption software outside North America. Lotus provides three versions of Notes: one for sale in North America, an international version for sale elsewhere, and a third version which combines security features for the whole world. The three versions work identically, except that the North American version can use either of two encryption methods: a very secure method, which is restricted by the State Department, and a different, slightly less secure method, which is not restricted. The international version includes only the less secure method. The third version (North American Worldwide Security) uses a combination of the other two versions of Notes to maintain its security.

Similarly, each Notes user purchases one or both types of licenses: a North American license or an international license. The North American version grants you permission to use the more secure North American encryption scheme, while the international version does not. Your license is included in your ID file. You can tell which type of license you have by displaying the User ID dialog box (choose File, Tools, User ID).

Regardless of which type of license you have, you can use any version of Lotus Notes either within North America or internationally. However, if you send encrypted mail, Notes will only use the more secure North American encryption method if you are using the North American version of Notes and you have a North American license.

Note that if you are using the North American version of Notes and have a North American license, you cannot send encrypted mail to an international user. Your version of Notes will use the robust North American encryption method to encrypt your message, but your international recipient won't be able to decrypt the message with its international version. In this case, you'll want to use the North American Worldwide Security version of Notes, which is ideal for companies who are international Notes users or require their employees to travel out of the country.

However, an international user can send encrypted mail to a North American user. The North American version of Notes will be able to decrypt the message because it includes the ability to use either decryption method.

Note

With Notes 4.0, Lotus reached a compromise with the United States government so it didn't have to support three versions of security for a single product. Notes now uniformly incorporates the stronger North American security in all versions sold worldwide.

This security uses 64 random bits to ensure that a message is properly encrypted. According to U.S. restrictions, encryption using a maximum of 40 bits (significantly less secure) could be exported. To reach a compromise, Lotus had to give the U.S. a "key" to the last 24 bits of the encryption key. Although this might seem like a security risk, Lotus now offers full 64-bit security (extremely secure) across the world, and only the U.S. government has the 24-bit key.

Don't worry, though; the government would still have to crack the other 40 bits in an encrypted message to break Notes' code. Besides, the government can only use their 24-bit key when investigating criminal activity.

Encrypting Incoming and Saved Mail

In the previous sections, you learned to encrypt mail that you send to others so that it is unreadable as it makes its way to your recipient's mailbox. Another option, encrypting saved mail, enables you to tell Notes that all mail, whether sent in encrypted form or not, should be encrypted when stored in your mailbox. This feature is particularly useful if you store sensitive messages—both sent and received—in your mailbox for long periods of time because it ensures that no one can look through your mailbox.

> **Note**
>
> Your system administrator can configure Notes so that all mail messages arriving in mailboxes on a particular server are encrypted, regardless of the users' settings. This option might be appropriate in a high-security environment, such as a defense contractor or for a server in a company's human resources department, which naturally deals with sensitive issues.

You can encrypt your saved copy of mail that you send to others. Choose File, Tools, User Preferences. Notes displays the Preferences dialog box. Click the Mail icon, and check the Encrypt Saved Mail checkbox. Even when you send mail that is not encrypted, the copy you store in your own mailbox will be encrypted. This feature will also encrypt incoming mail, but only after you have read the mail.

Confidentiality of Personal Mail

If you get along well with the people you work with, it's natural that some of the communication that goes on at work is not strictly business-related. Officially, most companies frown on using the company's e-mail system for personal messages, but realistically everybody knows that some small fraction of any company's e-mail traffic is not about department budgets and sales proposals. As long as everybody keeps the personal messages to a minimum, most companies look the other way.

However, you should understand that your right to privacy on your company's e-mail system is virtually nonexistent. Consider this excerpt from a large company's corporate policy document:

"Electronic mail systems such as Lotus Notes are not public electronic communications services as defined by 28 USC 2510. They are the property of the company that you work for, are restricted to use solely by authorized users for business purposes, and the contents of any such systems are subject to random or periodic monitoring and disclosure by management without notification to users."

People in most Western countries have come to expect complete privacy of mail sent through the postal service, but do not be fooled into thinking that this privacy extends to your company's e-mail system. In the U.S., at least, the courts have upheld the right of your company to peruse your mailbox and to insist that you decrypt encrypted mail for their examination. If one of your Lotus Notes messages contains evidence of inappropriate or illegal behavior, and a company administrator should happen to see the message in your mailbox, you will not be able to claim that the company illegally searched your personal mail as some employees have tried to do. Unless you work in a country where the rules are different, your mail belongs to your company.

So give a little thought to what you send through Lotus Notes. If you work in a particularly sensitive environment (such as the defense industry), you can bet your company does occasional spot checks in employees' mailboxes. Your plans for a palace coup are best reserved for the U.S. mail.

Encryption and Performance

Should you encrypt all your mail? Is there any disadvantage to encryption? Just one.

Encryption takes time. Every time you encrypt a message, there is a delay of a few seconds while Notes encrypts your message. The larger the message, the longer it takes to encrypt it. Similarly, when your recipient reads your message it takes a few seconds for Notes to decrypt the message. When deciding whether or not to use encryption, you must weigh the extra privacy encryption provides against the slight increase in time it takes Notes to process the encrypted message.

Encrypting Documents

In the preceding sections, you learned how to encrypt mail. However, Notes includes a second type of encryption, unrelated to the public-key encryption technique you saw earlier in this chapter. This second type of encryption lets you encrypt data not only in mail messages, but in other types of documents as well. You can encrypt fields within almost any kind of document if the database designer has enabled this feature. Using encrypted fields, you can ensure that sensitive data stored in databases is as secure as the data you exchange through mail messages.

> **Note**
>
> Many beginning Notes users, struggling to learn about Notes encryption, never realize that Notes contains two separate schemes for encrypting things: public-key encryption and single-key encryption. Although they share some characteristics and can often be used together in some combination, keep in mind as you read this section that you are learning about a completely new technique.

Understanding Single-Key Encryption

Public-key encryption is used almost exclusively to encrypt mail. When using e-mail, one person encrypts the message and sends it to a recipient who decrypts it. But what if you want to encrypt a document that is stored in a database, and you want to make sure only certain people can decrypt it? Single-key encryption is a better choice.

Unlike public-key encryption, which involves a public and private key, the scheme Notes uses for encrypting fields involves only a single key, known simply as an encryption key. As with public-key encryption, you use a key to encrypt data, but unlike public-key encryption, you use the same key to decrypt the data.

As a Notes user, you can create any number of encryption keys, which Notes stores in your ID file. You can use these keys to encrypt data so that only you can read it, or you can distribute any of these keys to other users so that they, too, can decrypt the data.

V

Advanced Notes Topics

You can think of your ID file as an electronic version of a key ring. Your key ring can contain keys that you create, as well as copies of keys that other people create and give to you. You can lock (encrypt) data with one of the keys, and other Notes users can unlock (decrypt) the data if they have a copy of the same key. Similarly, they can encrypt data with their keys, which you can read if you have a copy of the same key.

You can have any number of keys on your key ring, and you will probably share different keys with different groups of people. For example, you might have one key that you use to encrypt data that you expect to share with folks in the sales department. Each member of the sales department would have a copy of that key and will thus be able to read any data encrypted with that key. Others outside the sales group cannot read the information because they don't possess the key.

You might create another key and use it to encrypt data that you want to share with people in your Seattle office, and of course you will need to give a copy of that key to everyone in the Seattle office. The sales group and the Seattle group will not be able to read one another's data because members of one group do not possess the key that members of the other group use to encrypt data. You will be able to read both sets of data because you possess both keys. (Obviously, a salesperson in the Seattle office will also possess both keys and will be able to read data from both groups.)

Finally, you might have a key that you use to encrypt data that you do not want to share with anyone and therefore you would not give a copy of the key to anyone.

Thus, by knowing who has a copy of a particular key, you can control exactly who can read any data you encrypt.

You learned that one of the characteristics of public-key encryption is that you can freely distribute your public key to anyone because this key can be used only for encrypting data but not decrypting. By contrast, you must carefully control who possesses a particular key in single-key encryption. If the wrong person obtains a key, he or she will be able to read anything that was encrypted with that key.

Table 22.1 summarizes the differences between public-key encryption and single-key encryption.

Table 22.1 Public-Key Encryption versus Single-Key Encryption	
Public-Key Encryption	**Single-Key Encryption**
Each user has only two keys: one public and one private.	Each user can create as many encryption keys as they like.
Your public and private keys are created by Notes when your Notes ID file is created.	You create encryption keys whenever you want, using the procedure described in this chapter.
Notes uses the public key to encrypt messages and the private key to decrypt messages.	Notes uses the same key to encrypt and decrypt messages.

Public-Key Encryption	Single-Key Encryption
Each user keeps his or her private key secret but can distribute the public key to anyone.	The key's creator must carefully consider who receives a key.
Only the person with the private key can decrypt data.	Anyone with the key can decrypt data that was encrypted with the same key.

Using encryption keys depends on various people performing these procedures:

- Creating encryptable fields

- Creating encryption keys

- Distributing the keys to other users with whom you want to share encrypted data

- Encrypting and decrypting data

In the following sections, you learn how to perform these procedures.

Creating Encryptable Fields

When someone designs a database form (see Chapter 3, "Using Databases," for more information about designing forms), he or she can specify that specific fields are encryptable, which means that they can contain encrypted data. (The data in an encryptable field doesn't have to be encrypted; giving a field this attribute simply gives users the option of storing encrypted information in the field.)

You can spot an encryptable field by the corners that surround the field when you compose a document. For most fields the corners are white, but for encryptable fields they are red.

If you are a database designer, you can make a field encryptable with the following procedure:

1. Enter edit mode for the form if you have not already done so. In the database's navigator pane, choose Design and then Forms. In the document selection window (on the right side of the screen), select the form that the field resides on.

2. Double-click the field you want to make encryptable. Notes displays the field's Properties InfoBox (see Figure 22.10).

Fig. 22.10   You can enable a field to be encrypted from this InfoBox.

3. Select the Options tab.

4. Click the Security options combo box and choose Enable encryption for this field.

5. Close the Field Properties InfoBox.

Creating Encryption Keys

To encrypt fields within a document, you must use an encryption key, which you or someone else must create. Typically, you create a new key when you identify a group of people that want to be able to share encrypted data. Once you create a key, you distribute that key among the members of that group. For example, when a member of the word processing department realizes that it would be nice for the members of her department to share encrypted data, she creates a key and distributes it to everyone in the word processing department.

To create an encryption key, follow this procedure:

1. Choose File, Tools, User ID.

2. Notes prompts you for your Notes password. Enter your password and choose OK. Notes displays the User ID dialog box (see Figure 22.11).

Fig. 22.11   Set your User Preferences in the User ID dialog box.

3. Click the Encryption icon. Notes displays a list showing all the keys currently stored in your ID file (see Figure 22.12). The first key is selected. The Comment box shows a comment for the selected key if there is one. The dialog box also shows the date the selected key was created and restrictions on the key (explained later in this chapter).

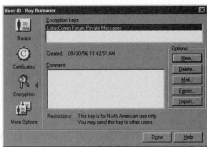

Fig. 22.12   The User ID dialog box shows your available encryption keys.

4. Choose <u>V</u>iew to create a new encryption key. Notes displays the Add Encryption Key dialog box (see Figure 22.13).

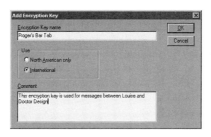

Fig. 22.13   Type your new encryption key's name here.

5. Enter a name for your key in the <u>E</u>ncryption Key name field. You should select a name that describes who will use the key or what kind of data will be encrypted using the key.

6. Choose either North <u>A</u>merican or <u>I</u>nternational use. As with public-key encryption, Notes has two schemes for single-key encryption. If you select North <u>A</u>merican only, Notes uses its more secure encryption method, but you cannot share the key with coworkers outside North America. If you select <u>I</u>nternational, you may share the key with anyone, but Notes uses a less secure encryption method.

7. In the <u>C</u>omment text box, enter any additional information that you may want to keep with the key for your future reference. Your comments can help you remember what a particular encryption key should be used for.

8. Choose <u>O</u>K. Notes returns to the User ID dialog box.

9. If you want to create more keys, repeat this procedure from step 3. Otherwise, select D<u>o</u>ne to close the User ID dialog box. Notes adds the keys that you created to your ID file.

Caution

Notice that the User ID dialog box contains a <u>D</u>elete button, which you can use to delete keys from your ID file; simply select the key you want to delete, and choose <u>D</u>elete. However, once you delete a key, you will not be able to read any data encrypted with that key without getting another copy from someone. Worse, if everyone who has a copy of that key deletes his or her copy, all data encrypted with that key is forever unreadable. Even though someone can create another key with the same name, it is not the same key and cannot be used to decrypt data that was encrypted by the old key. So think twice—or three times—before deleting a key.

Creating an encryption key is only the first step in making it useful. Unless you intend to use the key to encrypt data that you do not want to share, you next must distribute the key to other people. The next two sections tell you how to distribute encryption keys.

V

Advanced Notes Topics

Distributing Encryption Keys by E-Mail

Most often, you will distribute encryption keys to other users through Notes mail. To mail one of your encryption keys to another user, follow this procedure:

1. Display the User ID dialog box by choosing File, Tools, User ID. Notes prompts you for your password.

2. Click the Encryption icon. Notes displays the list of encryption keys in the Encryption pane (see Figure 22.14).

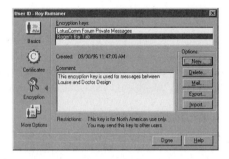

Fig. 22.14 Here are your encryption options again.

3. Click Mail. Notes displays the Mail Address Encryption Key dialog box (see Figure 22.15).

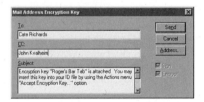

Fig. 22.15 Send your encryption keys to the users indicated on the Mail Address Encryption Key dialog box.

4. Enter the names of the people that you want to mail the key to. You can access the Name & Address Book to help with the addressing, just as with any mail message, by choosing Address. Note that this dialog box doesn't allow you to deselect the Sign and Encrypt checkboxes. All mail messages containing encryption keys must be signed and encrypted.

5. When you have entered all the names, select Send.

6. Notes displays a dialog box asking if you want your recipient to be able to send the encryption key to other people. If you want to be sure that no one has the key other than the people you send it to, choose To. If you choose Yes, people who receive the key from you may pass it on to other users. After you choose Yes or No, Notes sends a message containing the encryption key to the people you specified.

Now, consider the recipient of a mail message containing an encryption key. Fortunately, when someone sends you an encryption key, the subject of the mail message explains what the message contains and tells you what to do.

The encryption key itself appears as an attachment with a strange-looking filename. However, do not use the usual technique (described in Chapter 5, "Using the Address Book") to extract this attachment. Instead, follow this procedure:

1. Choose <u>A</u>ction, Accept Encryption <u>K</u>ey. The second item is new to this menu.

2. Notes prompts you for your Notes password. Enter your password and choose <u>O</u>K.

3. Notes displays the Accept Encryption Key dialog box, which shows the name of the key, the date it was created, and what restrictions the key carries (where it can be used and whether or not you can pass the key on to others) (see Figure 22.16). The dialog box also displays the comment that was entered (if any) when the key was created. You can modify or add to this comment if you want.

Fig. 22.16   Accept encryption keys while reading e-mail.

4. To insert the key into your ID file, choose <u>A</u>ccept.

Distributing Encryption Keys by File

Most often, you will distribute encryption keys to other users by mail, but occasionally you may need an alternate method. For example, consider these situations:

■ Perhaps one of your client companies uses Lotus Notes, but people in that company cannot send or receive mail outside the company. You have made a copy of a database that you want to send them (using the procedure you learned in Chapter 3 for copying a database) onto a floppy disk, but some of the data in the database is encrypted, and you want to send them the encryption key as well.

■ As secure as NotesMail is, a floppy disk in your shirt pocket is even more secure. You know your encryption key hasn't been intercepted if you put it on a floppy disk, take it to a coworker, and put it on his or her machine.

Notes enables you to create a file which contains an encryption key. You can write this file onto a floppy disk or onto a network drive, and from there distribute it to other people. You can also make a copy of such a file for safekeeping to ensure that you don't lose an important encryption key.

To create a copy of an encryption key on floppy disk, follow these steps:

1. Display the User ID dialog box by choosing File, Tools, User ID. Notes prompts you for your password.

2. Click the Encryption icon. Notes displays the list of encryption keys.

3. Select the key you want to write to floppy disk, and select Export. Notes lets you type in a password to protect this encryption key should it fall in the wrong hands (see Figure 22.17).

Fig. 22.17   Enter a password to protect your encryption key.

4. Notes lets you place restrictions on the encryption key you write to the floppy disk. If you choose Restrict Use, Notes displays the Encryption Key Restrictions dialog box, shown in Figure 22.18, and provides you with a text box in which you can specify the name of a single user. Notes will not allow anyone except that user to extract the encryption key stored on the floppy disk. In addition, a checkbox (marked by default) allows that user to pass the encryption key on to other users. If you uncheck the checkbox, the user cannot pass the key on to other users.

Fig. 22.18   Give specific control over who can use this encryption key.

5. After you have entered a user's name and optionally unchecked the checkbox, choose OK and Notes returns to the User ID Encryption Key Export dialog box.

6. The Password and Confirmation text boxes enable you to enter a password to protect your encryption key. No one will be able to read the encryption key from the floppy disk into his or her ID file without this password. This feature provides protection against the floppy disk falling into the wrong hands. Choose a password and enter it in both the Password and Confirmation boxes (the password does not appear on-screen), and choose OK. If you are willing to forego the safety of password-protecting the key (say, if your coworker is just down the hall), you can bypass entering the password by selecting To Password instead of OK.

7. Notes displays a dialog box so that you can enter the name of the file you want to create. To write the file to a floppy disk, enter a filename that begins with A: or B: (depending on which drive you want to access) followed by a name ending in *KEY*. For example, if the key is used by the sales department, you might name the file A:SALES.KEY.

8. Choose OK and Notes writes the key to the floppy disk.

Instruct your recipient to use the following procedure for importing the key from the floppy disk into his or her ID file, or perform this procedure yourself if you receive a floppy disk containing an encryption key:

1. Display the User ID dialog box by choosing File, Tools, User ID. Notes prompts you for your password.

2. Click the Encryption icon. Notes displays the list of encryption keys.

3. Choose Import. Notes displays a dialog box asking you for the name of the file that contains the key you want to import. Type the name of the file. Alternatively, type **A:** or **B:** to produce a list of all the files on the floppy disk, and select the proper file from the list. Choose OK.

4. If a password was assigned to the encryption key, Notes asks you to type it in. Then, Notes displays the Accept Encryption Key dialog box (refer to Figure 22.16). As before, it displays the name of the key, the date it was created, and what restrictions the key carries (where it can be used and whether or not you can pass the key on to others). To add this key to your ID file, choose Accept.

Tip

When you import an encryption key, the original is not removed from the disk you used. Use Windows Explorer to remove the encryption key from your disk. You may even want to format the disk to ensure that file recovery tools cannot recover the encryption key should the disk used fall in the wrong hands.

Encrypting Data with Encryption Keys

You can use any of your encryption keys, whether you created them yourself or someone else sent them to you, to encrypt data in any document or editing the document:

1. Choose File, Document Properties. Notes displays the Properties InfoBox for the document.

2. Click the tab with the icon key to display the document's security information.

3. Click the Encryption keys combo box. Notes shows all the encryption keys stored in your ID file, any of which you can use to encrypt the document. If the document is currently encrypted, a checkmark appears next to the keys currently in use.

4. Select any of your keys from the Encryption keys list. After selecting one or more keys, close the list by clicking the checkmark that you used to open the list.

5. Close the Document Properties InfoBox.

When you encrypt a document, only the encryptable fields—the ones with the red corners—are encrypted. All other fields are still viewable by anyone. As you're entering sensitive information into a document, be sure that you don't enter anything private into a field that is not encryptable (has white corners).

You can remove encryption keys from an encrypted document using the same dialog box. You might want to remove a key if a document is encrypted with several keys, and you later realize that the group that shares a particular key shouldn't be allowed to access the document. Follow the same procedure you used previously to select encryption keys. If you click a key that is currently in use (and has a checkmark next to it), the checkmark disappears and Notes no longer uses the key to encrypt the document. If you deselect all of the encryption keys used to encrypt a document, the document is no longer encrypted.

Note

If you design databases, you sometimes may want all documents within a database to be encrypted. You can specify one or more keys to use by default for encryption. While editing a form in a database's design, choose File, Document Properties. Notes displays a Properties InfoBox similar to the Properties InfoBox you see for individual documents. As before, select the tab with the key icon, and select one or more encryption keys from the Encryption keys combo box. When users create new documents, Notes automatically uses those keys to encrypt the documents. If the users want to specify other keys to use, or if they want to specify that some of the default keys are not to be used, they display the Document Properties InfoBox to add or remove any keys they want.

Accessing Encrypted Documents

To access a document that contains encrypted fields, you don't need to do anything out of the ordinary. When you attempt to open an encrypted document, Notes looks in your ID file to see if you have a copy of any of the encryption keys that were used to encrypt the document. As long as you have at least one of the keys, you can read or edit the document as you normally would.

If you do not have a copy of any of the keys, your access to the document is restricted. If you open the document for viewing, you see only the unencrypted fields. If you attempt to edit the document, Notes displays a dialog box explaining that the document is encrypted and that you cannot edit it unless you have a copy of one of the keys.

Understanding Electronic Signatures

In Chapter 4, "Getting Started with Electronic Mail," you learned that you can sign e-mail by marking the Sign checkbox when you send the mail. Now that you have learned how encryption works, you can understand how an electronic signature works.

Encryption enables you to prevent an enemy from intercepting and reading or altering the body of your message. An electronic signature prevents an enemy from forging the other fields in a message. Without electronic signatures, an enemy who is knowledgeable about Notes could produce a message that he or she wrote, but by forging the From field can make the message appear to be from you. Electronic signatures prevent such tampering.

When you sign a message, Notes attaches a hidden electronic code that proves to the receiver that you are the sender of the message and that the message has not been altered along the way. The electronic signature is possible through a curious twist involving public-key encryption.

Earlier in this chapter, in the section "Understanding Public-Key Encryption," you learned that each Notes user has a private encryption key (known only to that user and stored in his or her ID file) and a public encryption key (known to everyone, and stored in the Notes Name & Address Book). You also learned that the key characteristic of public-key encryption is that data encrypted with one key can be decrypted only with the other.

As you've seen, when someone sends you encrypted mail, Notes uses your public key to encrypt the data. When you receive the mail, Notes uses your private key to decrypt the data. At first, you would think that for public-key encryption to be useful, the public key is always used to encrypt data and the private key is always used to decrypt data. But recall the definition of public-key encryption: The keys are related in such a way that a message encrypted with either one of the keys can be decrypted only with the other key.

This definition doesn't say that you must use the public key for encryption and the private key for decryption; it says that either key can be used to encrypt data, and the other key used to decrypt the data. That is, it's possible to encrypt data with your private key, and decrypt the data with your public key. At first blush, that doesn't appear to be a very useful thing to do because the whole world knows your public key, and thus anyone can read the data that's encrypted with your private key. But in the case of electronic signatures, that's exactly what we want.

In constructing an electronic signature, Notes uses your public and private keys in a technique that's backward from the usual encryption scheme. When you send signed mail, Notes builds a 16-byte block of data, called a fingerprint, from your message's recipient name, your name, cc field, domain name, and subject. Notes then encrypts the fingerprint with your private key and attaches it to the message.

When your recipient receives your mail, Notes spots the encrypted fingerprint and uses your public key to decrypt the data. Notes then checks the fingerprint against the message's recipient name, sender name, and other fields. If it still matches, Notes can be sure that the message has not been altered along the way because only you (with your private key) could have encrypted the fingerprint in such a way that it could be decrypted correctly with your public key. As your recipient opens your message, Notes displays a message on the status line that reassures your recipient that all is well:

```
Signed by Roy Rumaner on 9/30/96 10:32:34, according to Terasys
```

V

Advanced Notes Topics

Cases can arise where Notes cannot verify the validity of a signature, even though the message was properly signed. Most often, problems in verifying a signature occur when you receive mail from outside your company. Depending on how your system administrator has set up the connection with the other company, Notes may not be able to ensure the validity of the sender's public key. In such a case, Notes displays a message telling you that it cannot verify the signature. This message does not mean that Notes has detected anything wrong with the message, merely that Notes doesn't have the information it needs to ensure a proper signature.

Encryption Hazards

Using encryption to secure your data seems like a good idea, and something you would want to always do. But there are hazards to using encryption:

- **Risk of losing a key**—If you lose an encryption key, your data is lost. This seems like an unlikely occurrence, but all it takes is a disk to go bad, and you could lose the key.

- **Risk of losing your ID**—If you lose your ID, you lose your private key, meaning that you cannot read your encrypted mail. Also if you forget your password, it's as good as losing your ID.

- **Difficulty in administering keys**—If you are using encryption keys, you have to make sure you distribute them to all users who need the data. This can become difficult once you get past a few users.

For these reasons, use encryption with care. If an application absolutely requires encryption, use it; but, otherwise, use it sparingly.

Execution Control Lists

The *Execution Control List (ECL)* enables users to protect their data against the threats of mail bombs, viruses, Trojan horses, or unwanted application intrusions encountered when navigating the Internet. Execution Control Lists provide a mechanism for managing whether such executable files should be allowed to execute, and what level of access the program should be permitted.

ECLs are managed on a per user basis via the User Preferences panel and can be controlled to a granular level in the Execution Control List (see Figure 22.19). For example, a user may stipulate that when a document is digitally signed by a certain trusted colleague, programs executed by that document can access documents and databases as well as modify environment variables, but cannot access the file system or external programs.

> **Tip**
>
> It is a good idea to leave the Default options blank. This helps reduce the chances of someone causing damage to your system.

Fig. 22.19 The Execution Control List dialog box.

Password Expiration and Reuse

Passwords protect and ensure the security of the Notes system by preventing other users from using a person's ID file. Lotus recommends that all users password-protect their ID files and keep passwords private. The Password Expiration feature was designed to protect the Notes system from situations in which a malicious user obtains the ID file and password of a user and impersonates that user. The feature enables Notes administrators to specify and enforce an expiration period/date on passwords for user ID files. During the authentication dialog, the user is notified that his or her password has expired and is required to supply a new one. A list of previous passwords prevents users from reusing any of their previous passwords.

From Here...

If you have an interest in learning more about encryption, you'll find no shortage of books in your public library that describe the rich history of the art. Books and magazine articles that discuss public-key encryption will help increase your understanding of Notes encryption (even if they don't mention Notes specifically).

For more information on the topics discussed in this chapter, refer to the following:

- Chapter 10, "Creating New Databases," teaches you the basics of designing a Lotus Notes database.

- Chapter 12, "Designing Views," teaches you how to design views, and more about creating folders within the design of a database.

- Chapter 24, "Notes: Under the Hood," continues your study of Notes' advanced topics and shows you how replication works and describes the various Notes platforms.

Chapter 23

Case Study: Taking Advantage of Lotus Notes Features

So far, you have reviewed many new features for the application development in Lotus Notes 4. These features enable you to develop richer applications that offer more functionality to your users. This enhanced functionality improves ease of use of your applications. R4 takes the next step toward making Lotus Notes a full-featured application development environment.

In this chapter, you learn how to take the next steps to upgrade your Notes R3 application to utilize R4 features. You will watch and learn as an R3 application is converted to R4. The R3 to R4 conversion uses a real-life application that is currently in production with over 1,000 users worldwide. In each example, you see the application design in R3 and the corresponding enhanced design in R4 via actual screen shots of the design.

The application example is a Data Integration application, called the Sentinel.

What Does the Sentinel Application Do?

Composing Notes forms allows users to bulk import and export data to and from Notes databases. The Sentinel Data Integrator uses a Notes form from the Sentinel Notes Database to initiate, organize, document, and schedule data loading tasks. The Sentinel Engine performs the actual data loading.

The Sentinel Data Integrator is a comprehensive utility tool that enables Notes Developers, administrators, and data warehouse managers to initialize, organize, and schedule data transport and extract tasks in the convenient and easy-to-use Notes interface.

The Sentinel Data Integrator automatically transports and updates legacy or warehouse data into Notes applications without the use of script language or the Notes API toolkit.

Sentinel is useful for Notes application developers and designers who need to initialize and update Notes applications quickly and easily with data from any ASCII or ODBC data source.

Some of the main topics in this chapter are

- Form and View Action Buttons

- Using Hide When in forms design

- Inserting collapsible sections in your documents

- Creating user folders to organize your documents

- Using subforms to simplify the design

- Creating navigators to help users move around the application

The CD-ROM in the back of this book includes an evaluation copy of the Sentinel Data Integrator. The Sentinel application has 24 forms and 15 views. This is a complex application that is typical of the kinds of applications you can deploy using R4.

Note

R3 designs are fully compatible with R4. No work is required to make them run under R4. However, there are changes made to the application's design that you should be aware of. The Migration database (`MIGRATE.NSF`) is installed in the data directory with the Server install of Notes. This database provides an overview of the migration process, to include changes made to applications when you move from Notes 3.x to Notes 4.x. Open this database and review the design changes that are made to your Notes application when it is converted from Notes 3.x to Notes 4.x. This chapter covers how to exploit new R4 features for better, more exciting R4 applications.

On the flip side, Notes 4.x designs are not compatible with Notes 3.x—unless you save the Notes database with an .NS3 extension. Notes 3.x users will not be able to use any of the Notes 4 new functionality (like graphical navigators). If you are working in a mixed environment of Notes 3.x and Notes 4.x users, you should keep your application design as Notes 3.x. Refer to the Migration database on your server for further details on moving from Notes 3.x to Notes 4.x.

Adding the Example Databases to Your Notes Workspace

Both the original R3 Sentinel Database and the final R4 design, with the changes outlined in the rest of this chapter, exist on the CD-ROM attached to this book. You may follow along with these examples to actually perform these changes on the R3 databases. Check your work with the completed R4 design. Do not worry if your changes do not exactly match the R4 design. The goal of the exercise is to demonstrate features that you can use immediately on your R3 applications.

To follow along electronically with the provided NSF files on the CD-ROM, copy these files to your Notes working directory (usually `C:\NOTES` or `C:\NOTES\DATA`). Files copied from CD-ROMs generally remain read-only on your hard drive. Because you are detaching or launching these files from the Notes database in which they are stored, the read-only constraint should not be in effect. However, if you do find problems opening the files and accessing the information, use the Explorer in Windows 95, or File Manager in Windows 3.1 to fix the selections. Select each file and choose File, Properties. In the Attributes section, deselect the Read-only flag. To add these databases to your workspace, use File, Database, Open. Open the subdirectory in which you detached the databases (if you elected to launch the database, then you can ignore this step) and select one of the following databases:

- Integration Tasks 3.5 (`R3TASKS.NSF`): The R3 Sentinel Database.

- Integration Tasks 4.0 (`R4TASKS.NSF`): The R4 Sentinel Database with the changes from this chapter.

> **Note**
>
> Even if you do not choose to follow along electronically, the examples in this chapter contain numerous screen pictures that demonstrate each new design feature, and allow you to follow the progression of the application changes from R3 to R4.

Overview of the R3 to R4 Conversion

The Sentinel database has 13 main forms, many of which have portions in common. Some initial analysis work allows you to select the options that will make your R4 design functional for the intended business purpose, as well as aesthetically appealing. There is no right answer or way to perform this conversion. As mentioned earlier, R4 does not require any additional work to make an application run. R3 is completely compatible with R4. That being said, if you do not take advantage of the new features available, your application designs will not be working as hard for you and the end user as you want them to work.

Maintainability. R4 has added some features to make your applications more maintainable. Maintenance of an application can cost as much or more than the original design work. R4 offers new shared design features like subforms that enable you to completely reuse entire portions of a subform across many forms. Just as shared fields enabled R3 designers to reuse a field across all forms, subforms are a common design element that allow all forms to immediately reflect any changes made to inserted subforms. This reduces the maintenance effort substantially, while producing more consistent applications designs.

Layout. Deciding on the layout of the conversion is the hardest part of the task. R3 to R4 conversions require some trial and error to verify which features best utilize the R4 technology while also satisfying the business purpose of the Notes database. Specific rules do not exist to walk you through the process. You must experiment with different styles and design features until you complete a design that fulfills the business objectives of the database with a maintainable application design.

Using Subforms to Standardize Design

Take a minute to review a standard Sentinel form, shown in Figure 23.1.

Of the Sentinel's 24 database forms, 13 perform similar functionality. These 13 specify to the Sentinel Engine parameters of data movement. All 13 forms have many sections, or design elements, in common.

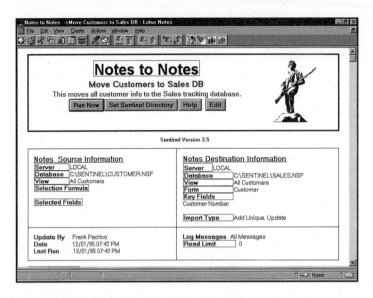

Fig. 23.1   This is a sample R3 Sentinel form before conversion to Notes R4.

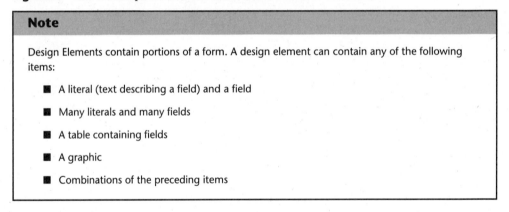

> **Note**
>
> Design Elements contain portions of a form. A design element can contain any of the following items:
>
> ■ A literal (text describing a field) and a field
>
> ■ Many literals and many fields
>
> ■ A table containing fields
>
> ■ A graphic
>
> ■ Combinations of the preceding items

Design Analysis of Common Design Elements

In the Sentinel R3 database, each form contains a design element listing information about the data source, as well as a design element listing information about the data destination. Sources and destination databases can be ASCII, ODBC, or Notes. Performing an analysis of forms that have common design elements reveals that ten forms contain identical design elements whenever Notes is listed as the destination database.

Further analysis of the R3 Sentinel database reveals that 11 of the 13 forms have design elements in common. The first major simplification of this R3 to R4 database conversion is to eliminate duplicate elements of the form. The resulting R4 database requires very little maintenance. Table 23.1 shows the results of the analysis of design elements.

Type	Number of Occurrences
Form Heading	13
Notes Source	7
Notes Destination	10
ASCII Source	2
ASCII Destination	1
ODBC Source	1
ODBC Destination	1
Run Now Button	13
Edit Button	13
Save Button	13
Set Sentinel Directory Button	13
Help Button	13
Log Messages	13
Notes Formula	13
User Comments	13

Table 23.1   Common Design Elements

This table shows that changes to one design element in a Notes source impact seven different forms. Changes in one design element in a Notes destination impact ten different forms. ASCII and ODBC sources and destinations are not significant, as they occur in only one or two forms. The Form Heading, listing Task Name and Task Description, appears in all 13 forms. Therefore, the first design change to the Sentinel database is to create a subform for the Task Heading. This immediately reduces maintenance of these 13 forms.

For this example, you will use the Notes to Notes form. See Figure 23.2 to review the R3 design of the form.

Open the Integration Tasks 3.5 (R3TASKS.NSF) file by double-clicking the icon.

The first task is to select Design Forms from the view pane and click the form "1. Data Integration\4. Notes to Notes" in the forms pane (right pane). Your screen should look similar to Figure 23.2.

Note

Figure 23.2 has the programmer pane minimized to show more of the form. When appropriate, the figures in this chapter show the programmer pane. You do not have to change your default design settings to follow these examples.

V

Advanced Notes Topics

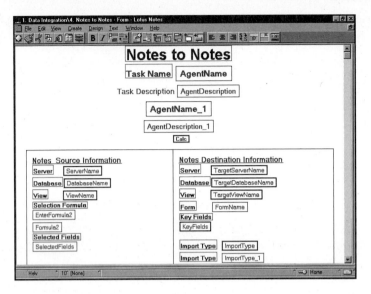

Fig. 23.2   This displays the R3 Design of the Notes to Notes form.

Creating a Subform TaskHeading

This section of the chapter shows you how to create your first subform and insert it into the main form.

Note

The use of subforms means the elimination of some of the tables in the form, as subforms are not allowed within tables. This is not as bad as it first seems, as collapsible sections, discussed later in this chapter, replace some of the need for tables.

You must now cut and paste the design elements from the main form to the Clipboard. All 13 forms require a unique Task Name and Task Description. This is an obvious place to create a subform across all documents. Start by copying the Notes to Notes pop-up to the very top of the screen, above the table from which you cut it.

Next, cut the design elements starting from the green literal Task Name until the Run Now button. Create a subform and paste these design elements into the new subform. Select Create, Design, Subform, and paste the selection into the subform. Choose File, Save and save this subform as TaskHeading.

Tip

Make sure to check the Include in Insert Subform dialog checkbox. If you do not, the Insert Subform menu choice will not show this subform.

Move to the top of the form, underneath the Notes to Notes pop-up, and select Create, Insert Subform from the menu. Select TaskHeading from the Insert Subform picklist that appears. The entire subform TaskHeading appears in the subform box (see Figure 23.3). Notice the box around the subform area.

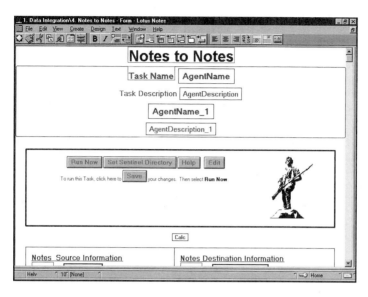

Fig. 23.3   Form redesign by attaching the first subform.

You have now created your first reusable design element. You can insert this into any form in this database. Whenever you change the subform, all documents into which that subform is inserted immediately reflect that change. If you decided to change the color of the Task Name from green to blue, all 13 forms that use this subform would immediately show the newly changed blue field.

Creating Form Action Buttons

Notice the buttons in Figure 23.3. Buttons "float" in the window, meaning they may or may not appear on the visible portion of the screen.

You can place Action Buttons on the always visible Action Bar (located below the Search Bar and spanning the entire top of the screen, just like the Search Bar). In R3, buttons are placed on the form wherever is most convenient for the application design. These form buttons still work in R4, of course. The problem with the buttons being placed on the form is that they may not be on the part of the form displayed on the screen. R4 lets you put the buttons always at the top, in the Action Bar.

You can convert R3 applications to R4 by moving the button logic to new Action Buttons on the Action Bar. You must do this form by form. Each form has its own Action Bar. This allows the Action Bar to change as you move from one document to a different document.

V

Advanced Notes Topics

Moving a Form Button to the Action Bar

The Sentinel for R3 has a Run Now button that starts the data importing. This button may or may not be on the part of the form displayed when the user wants to execute the Run Now command. Moving this button to the action bar solves that problem.

Select Create, Action to create a new Action, with the Title initially provided by Notes in the Properties InfoBox as (Untitled). The Sentinel needs to call this action button Run Now, which you can type into the Title bar in the Properties InfoBox. Select a Button Icon from the same window. You can select Blank for a text-only button. Pick the icon of a person running (see Figure 23.4).

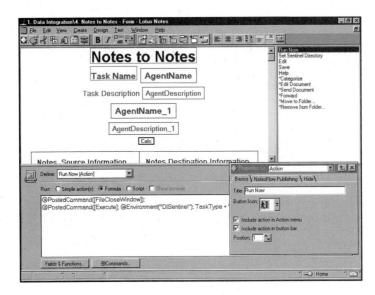

Fig. 23.4   This displays the design of the first action button, Run Now.

Next, select the formula from the on-form button. Move to the on-screen form button Run Now and copy the formula that appears in the programmer pane to the Clipboard. Select the Run Now action from the Action pane and paste the formula into the formula section of the programmer pane.

Hiding the Action Button in Edit Mode

To perform Run Now, the Sentinel wants the document to be open in display mode. An unsaved document may not have passed all the edit checks that are necessary to properly import data. Therefore, on the Properties InfoBox, under the tab Hide, select Previewed for editing and Opened for editing to disable the button during edit mode.

Tip

Once the Action is created, you can copy it to the Clipboard for later reuse in other forms. For the Sentinel, this button needs to be copied and pasted 13 times, once for each form in the database.

Creating Edit and Save Buttons

Four other buttons need to be created, to remove them from the form and place them in the Action Bar.

Two common buttons are the Edit and Save buttons (see Figures 23.5 and 23.6). You can use edit buttons and save buttons during read mode and edit mode, respectively. Make sure to check Hide when editing in the Action Properties InfoBox.

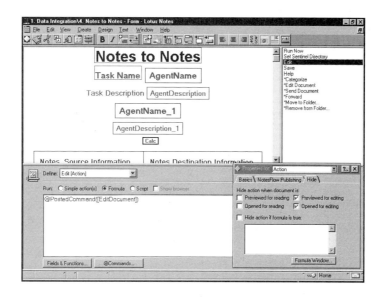

Fig. 23.5   Edit button parameters are shown here.

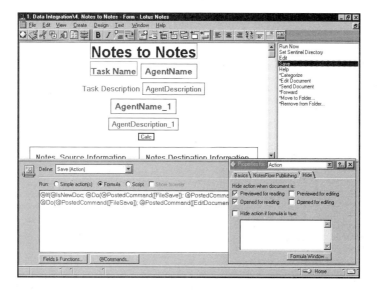

Fig. 23.6   Save button parameters are shown here.

Notice that the Edit button, in the top right pane, can be modified simultaneously with modifying the Notes form. This can be initially confusing. With practice, the ability to "jump around" the various design elements becomes a great time-saver.

Creating a Help Button

The Help button opens the <u>H</u>elp, Using This Database document. The Sentinel includes a separate database of user documentation. The <u>H</u>elp, <u>U</u>sing This Database document contains doclinks to this database. On your own, copy the formula from the on-form help button to a newly created action button.

> **Tip**
>
> If you have built user documentation, create a table of doclinks in your <u>H</u>elp, <u>U</u>sing This Database document to guide users to more advanced topics. This lets the user quickly doclink to a pertinent subject in much greater detail than available in form pop-ups. You can also store information about your organization's policies and procedures. This helps maintain uniform usage of the database across the organization.

Cleaning Up the Form

Finally, let's eliminate the entire box (which is actually a Notes table of just one row and one column) containing the buttons that are no longer needed, and the Sentinel logo, simplifying and cleaning up the form's overall appearance. Figure 23.7 shows a document composed using the Simplified form.

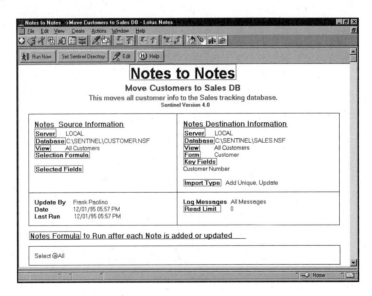

Fig. 23.7 This figure displays a document composed with the R4 Simplified Sentinel form, using a subform and form action buttons.

Summary of Changes

Save this form by selecting File, Save. Switch to the default view, "1. Task \1. Destination Notes Database Name." Double-click the task Move Customers to Sales DB. Your form should look similar to Figure 23.7.

The following is the summary of changes so far:

- Created a subform comprised of the Task Name and Task Description design elements. This subform is inserted into the main form.

- Created the following five action buttons:

  - Run Now

  - Set Sentinel Directory

  - Edit (hidden when editing)

  - Save (hidden when reading)

  - Help

- Performed hide when on two of the buttons, edit and save. Edit is hidden when editing and save is hidden when reading.

- Deleted on-form buttons.

- Deleted Table holding all these design elements.

Making Four More Subforms

In the Sentinel, as referenced in Table 23.1, there are seven forms that use Notes as a source to move data. There are ten forms that use Notes as a destination. This section covers creating four more subforms, which will eventually be enhanced to collapsible sections (covered later in this chapter). Figure 23.8 shows four parts of the form that must be converted to sections.

You must move all four of the areas of this form out of the table. Remember, you cannot create subforms within a table.

Creating the Subform NotesSource

From the top left area of the form (Notes Source Information), highlight the common design elements, which is the entire contents of that cell of the table, and copy these design elements to the Clipboard. Select Create, Design, Subform to create a new subform. Paste the design elements into the subform. Name the subform NotesSource in the Properties InfoBox. Make sure to check the Include in Insert Subform dialog checkbox. If you do not, the Insert Subform menu choice will not show this subform. Select File, Save to save this new subform. Select File, Close to close this subform design window. Figure 23.9 shows the subform NotesSource, after pasting in the design elements from the top left area of the form.

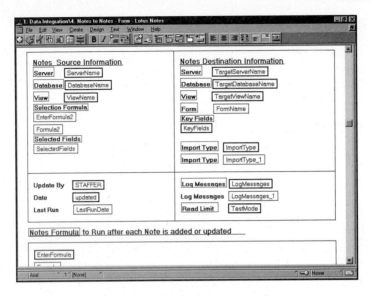

Fig. 23.8   Create four subforms from these four areas.

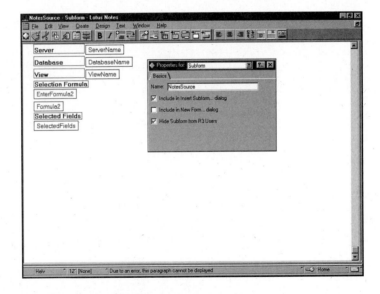

Fig. 23.9   This displays the design of the Subform NotesSource.

Creating the Subform NotesDestination

From the top right area of the form (Notes Source Destination), highlight the common design elements, which is the entire contents of that cell of the table, and copy these design elements to the Clipboard. Select Create, Design, Subform to create a new subform. Paste the design elements into the subform. Name the subform NotesDestination in the Subform Properties InfoBox. Make sure to check the Include in Insert Subform dialog checkbox. Select File, Save to save this new subform. Select File,

Close to close this subform design window. Figure 23.10 shows the design of the Subform NotesDestination.

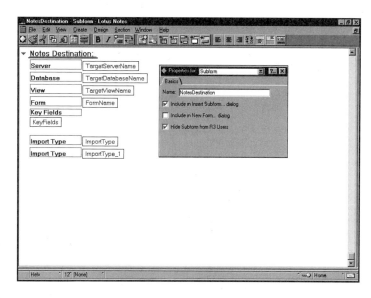

Fig. 23.10 This displays the design of the Subform NotesDestination.

Creating the Subform LogMessages

From the bottom right area of the form (Log Messages), highlight the common design elements, which are the entire contents of that cell of the table, and copy these design elements to the Clipboard. Select Create, Design, Subform to create a new subform. Paste the design elements into the subform. Name the subform LogMessages in the Properties InfoBox. Make sure to check the Include in Insert Subform dialog checkbox. Select File, Save to save this new subform. Select File, Close to close this subform design window. Figure 23.11 shows the design of the Subform LogMessages.

Creating the Subform UpdateInformation

From the bottom left area of the form (UpdateInformation), highlight the common design elements, which are the entire contents of that cell of the table, and copy these design elements to the Clipboard. Select Create, Design, Subform to create a new subform. Paste the design elements into the subform. Name the subform UpdateInformation in the Subform Properties InfoBox. Make sure to check the Include in Insert Subform dialog checkbox. Select File, Save to save this new subform. Select File, Close to close this subform design window. Figure 23.12 shows the design of the Subform.

V

Advanced Notes Topics

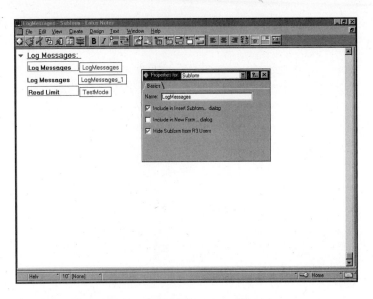

Fig. 23.11 This displays the design of the Subform LogMessages.

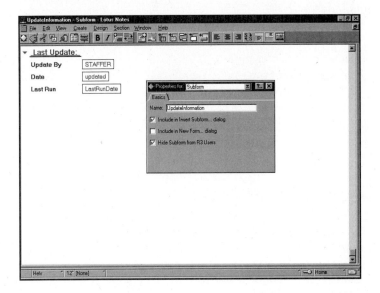

Fig. 23.12 This displays the design of the Subform UpdateInformation.

Inserting the New Subforms into the Notes to Notes Form

If you have not closed the Notes to Notes design window, switch to it using the Window menu choice. If it is not one of the choices, open it for design using the view pane.

Because we have made four new subforms, the table with four areas is no longer necessary. Delete the entire table, and the fields contained within it.

Now you can insert the first subform. Select <u>C</u>reate, Insert S<u>u</u>bform from the menu. Select NotesSource from the picklist. The entire subform NotesSource appears in the subform box (see Figure 23.13).

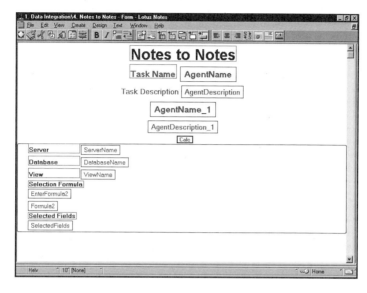

Fig. 23.13   Notes to Notes with Inserted NotesSource subform NotesSource.

Repeat this process for each of the other three subforms:

1. Select <u>C</u>reate, Insert S<u>u</u>bform from the menu. Select NotesDestination from the picklist. The entire subform NotesDestination appears in the subform box.

2. Select <u>C</u>reate, Insert S<u>u</u>bform from the menu. Select LogMessages from the picklist. The entire subform LogMessages appears in the subform box.

3. Select <u>C</u>reate, Insert S<u>u</u>bform from the menu. Select UpdateInformation from the picklist. The entire subform UpdateInformation appears in the subform box.

To review our progress, you have created five subforms. They are the following:

- TaskHeading
- NotesSource
- NotesDestination
- LogMessages
- UpdateInformation

Building Collapsible Sections

Now that the tables are removed from this form, there needs to be a way to look at summary information on the form without being overwhelmed with multiple pages of fields

V

Advanced Notes Topics

and data. Sections are a very nice feature that make Notes forms work harder. R4 of Notes allows sections to collapse into a single title, marked with solid arrows (or twisties) that point right if collapsed or point down if expanded. Users click the twisties to expand and collapse the section, just as they already know how to do in R3 Notes to expand and collapse a section of a view.

In the Sentinel form, you can collapse the Notes source section into one line on the form that appears as NotesSource. In this way, you can put a whole lot more on every form, without it appearing too crowded.

The NotesSource section is a subform, meaning it is a shared design feature across the database. You can make the section collapsible by making the changes on the subform, not the main form. In changing the subform to make the NotesSource section collapse into one line, all current and future forms that use this subform will automatically reflect this change.

Edit the NotesSource subform by selecting Design Subforms from the view pane. The first task is to create a new section on this form. Move the cursor to the top of the form, where you want to create the new section. Select Create, Section, Standard from the menu. This puts a new section with the name Untitled Section on the top of the form. The fields below are not automatically inserted into the section. You must cut and paste them into the section.

> **Tip**
>
> Sometimes it is difficult to know where the section ends. Type END into the section. Click the twistie, and make sure END disappears when collapsed. You now know the boundaries of the section. Paste your fields or text from the Clipboard between the Section Title and the END mark. Either delete the word END when completed, or hide it when reading and editing (so only form designers can see it). This makes your updates easier in the future.

Expand/Collapse Options

Select the Expand/Collapse tab on the Section Properties InfoBox. The database designer must decide whether to show these sections as expanded or collapsed. In this case, there is quite a lot of data. Initially collapsing the sections makes the form easier to read in one glance. Figure 23.14 sets the Expand and Collapse rules to Auto-collapse in both read modes.

> **Tip**
>
> As a general rule, select Auto-expand when Printed. Otherwise, users of a printed form cannot see the underlying data.

Using Text as a Section Title

You can title sections as either Text or Formula. You could use the simple section title: NotesSource Information. The user would know by this title to expand this section to see more information about the Notes source.

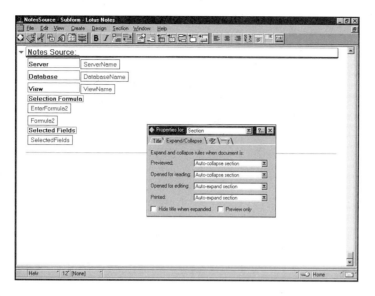

Fig. 23.14 The Section Properties InfoBox for Expand/Collapse.

Tip

Spending a few minutes to carefully select this section title can save hours of training and questions later, and result in a more usable application.

Using a Formula as a Section Title

If a section is collapsed when opened for reading, users want to know some of the basic elements in that section without expanding the entire section. A formula for a section title helps users to "peek" beneath the section. Selecting one or two critical fields for display in the section title accomplishes the goal of a more informational title without expanding the section. In the Sentinel, the formula is the following:

```
"Notes Source: " + DatabaseName
```

Figure 23.15 shows the Section Properties InfoBox with the title formula.

Making a Title Formula in a Collapsible Section. This displays the literals "Notes Source:" plus the database name. This makes the form easy to read when opened for reading. The user can see pertinent information without expanding the section. This "at-a-glance" approach is excellent for previewing forms because the entire form can be summarized in six to eight lines.

Finishing Up the Sections

Now, the remaining task is to create collapsible sections on the other three subforms: NotesDestination, LogMessages, and UpdateInformation. The objective is to make the overall form readable, without overwhelming the users with multiple pages of data when opening the form. Figure 23.16 shows the new Notes to Notes form, after modifying the NotesDestination, LogMessages, and UpdateInformation forms.

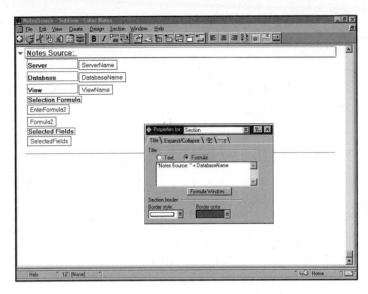

Fig. 23.15 Making a Title formula in a collapsible section.

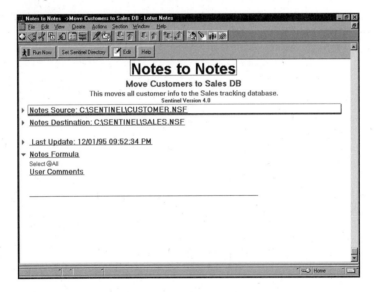

Fig. 23.16 Sample document created with the enhanced Notes to Notes form with sections.

The form has a clean, crisp appearance while presenting summary information to the user. Compare this R4 enhanced design to the original R3 Notes to Notes form shown in Figure 23.17.

These collapsed sections also work well with the preview pane. Figure 23.17 shows Move Customers to Sales DB in a preview pane. Notice how the user can see the most significant document information from the following four newly added subforms:

- TaskHeading

- NotesSource

- NotesDestination

- LastUpdate

You can, of course, decide what significant document information to display in your collapsed sections of forms that you design using Notes R4.

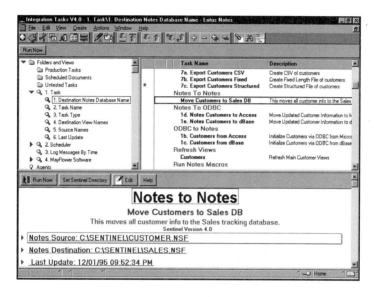

Fig. 23.17 Notes to Notes form using the preview pane.

Using the Hide When Feature

Of all the new features in Notes R4, the Hide When feature has the most utility for applications development. The reason is that there is always a need for forms to serve multiple purposes for multiple users in multiple situations. In other programming languages, a simple `if` statement allows a new section or window to appear to allow additional data to be entered if certain conditions are true. Notes R4 allows similar functionality. In Notes R3, the application designer had to swap forms and shuffle fields around trying to please everyone under all circumstances. R4 has greatly expanded Hide When functionality beyond the R3 Hide When. Instead of just Reading and Editing, you can Hide When based on an evaluation of a formula.

A simple way of thinking of this is to look at an example. When a Hide When formula such as `@Username = "Frank Paolino` is evaluated, a section of the form could disappear. In addition to the obvious practical jokes that could be played using this feature (such as fields not appearing on the screen for certain users), Hide When is extremely useful for dynamic forms that transform themselves based on dynamically changing conditions.

Let's apply this feature to the Sentinel database. Looking at the Notes Destination Subform, there is a field PKeyFields that is necessary only if the user is importing response documents. It confuses users if it appears unnecessarily, as they assume they must fill it in. In Notes R3, you had to use field help and pop-up boxes to train the users. Now, you can hide the field PKeyFields if the field DocType is Document. Figure 23.18 shows the design of the form. Notice that Hide paragraph if formula is true is checked, and the formula in the formula window.

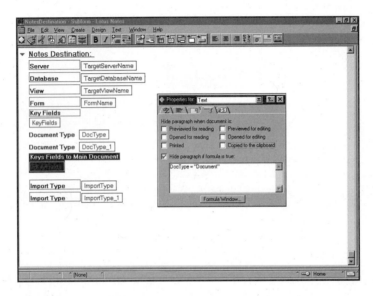

Fig. 23.18   A Notes form, using the feature Hide when a condition is true.

It is important to understand that the field PKeyFields will not appear or disappear until the document fields are refreshed. A simple way to accomplish this without refreshing all fields after each field edit is to select the DocType field. Switch to the Properties InfoBox. Select the second tab. Put a checkmark next to the item Refresh fields on keyword change. This will cause the field PKeyFields to appear or disappear properly, without slowing the overall form performance due to unnecessary field refreshes.

Tip

Make all "triggers" to Hide When fields or sections based on fields of Field Type Keywords. This will make the Hide When fields appear and disappear on cue.

Testing the Form

The next job is testing the form. Select Design, Test Form, and Notes lets you simulate actual use of the form. This saves the cycle time of saving the form, switching views, and creating another form, only to discard it, switch view, and return to design mode.

Figure 23.19 shows that the literal Key Fields to Main Document and the field PKeyFields do not appear when the Document Type is Document.

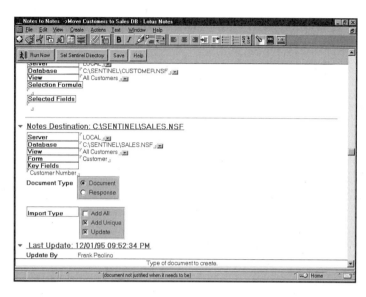

Fig. 23.19   Form Notes to Notes with hidden literal key fields to main document.

Clicking the field Document Type to change the value from Document to Response makes the literal Key Fields to Main Document and the field PKeyFields appear immediately on the form. Figure 23.20 shows that exact same form after selecting Response.

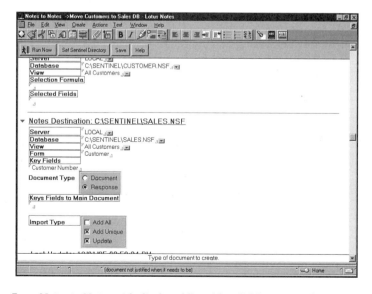

Fig. 23.20   Form Notes to Notes with displayed literal key fields to main document.

Now the form dynamically presents information and fields to the user. This feature represents a major step forward in application design capability in Lotus Notes.

Applying the Subforms to the Other Forms

The last job is modifying the other seven forms that contain the exact same Notes Source design elements. This is simply a cut-and-paste operation, repeated seven times. The long-term time saving benefit is that you need to perform maintenance on only one subform. All other forms into which you have inserted subforms do not need to be updated after you have made changes to the subform.

Adding Action Buttons to the View

A very similar feature to Action Buttons is placed at the top of the view. They are similar to the Form Action Buttons. Each view can have its own set of Action Buttons. These are handy to Add, Edit, or Delete documents in a view, as well as to move them among folders.

To place the Run Now button on the View Action Bar, you create it in the same manner as for the Form Action Buttons. Switch to the view pane. Select Design Views. Double-click the default view "1. Task\1. Destination Notes Database Name."

Select Create Action to create a new Action, with the Title initially provided by Notes in the Properties InfoBox as (Untitled). The Sentinel needs to call this Action Button Run Now, which you can type into the Title bar in the Properties InfoBox. Select a Button Icon from the same window. Pick the icon of a person running.

View buttons can interrogate the document and behave differently depending on the values of certain fields. In the Sentinel database, users who upgrade must edit and save the document to recalculate new form fields. This also interrogates a field called VersionNumber, which is calculated in a shared field. If that value is not 4.0, the form prompts the user to edit and save the document before the action is completed. This is the essence of good programming: To check whether an operation will be successful before attempting to proceed. The formula is as follows:

```
@If(VersionNumber != "4.0";
@Prompt([OK];"Error";"This document created with a previous version of the
_Sentinel. Please Edit and Save before Run Now.");
@PostedCommand([Execute]; @Environment("DISentinel"); TaskType + "-" +
_AgentName))
```

Figure 23.21 shows the design of the view with the formula of the action button Run Now.

This capability to interrogate a document before attempting an operation is essential to better management of creating response documents. In the Sentinel R3 database, users could mistakenly attempt to compose a response document against a parent or main document that made no sense whatsoever. As R3 allowed you to compose any of the available forms, you had to know which form was the correct form to compose in any situation. This invariably leads to increased training and user frustration.

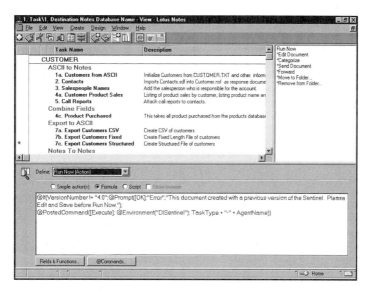

Fig. 23.21   Creating a button with a user prompt from View Action Bar.

In R4 View Action Buttons, each button can first check that the form is correct under the circumstances. For example, in a customer tracking database, there are certain business facts that are fundamental:

- Companies have contacts.

- Contacts have call reports.

- Call reports have follow-ups.

In Notes, that means that Company is a main document, Contact is a response document, and Call Reports and Follow-up items are response-to-response documents. In R3, it was possible to mistakenly compose a call report against a customer. This invariably confuses users, while frustrating them. R4 View Action Buttons lets you put four buttons on the View Action Bar:

- Company (Main Document)

- Contact Person (response)

- Call Report (response)

- Follow-Up Item (response)

Each button, when clicked, interrogates the database to determine which form (Note) that the cursor is highlighting. If the cursor is pointing to a valid document, the operation can proceed. If it is not pointing to the appropriate form, the user receives an error message. For example, the Contact button first asks if the document form name is Customer. If not, it prompts the user with a message, and aborts the attempted document creation. Call reports can only be created against contacts in the same way. This guarantees proper field inheritance from main document to response document.

Organizing Views and Folders

In designing applications, have you ever wondered when the number of views that the customer requires will ever end? If you design Notes applications long enough, you know that the requests for more views never end. The biggest request is for special purpose views. If you've tried categories, you know that they help, but do not close the gap to what the user wants. Enter folders. It may take you a couple of minutes to understand the difference between folders and views, but when it hits you, you will be impressed. At first glance, folders appear to be renamed views, and in some ways they are. However, folders are basically ad hoc views, allowing the user to drag documents into another view (actually into a folder) based on some user opinion of the document's importance.

In R3 Sentinel, we put numerous status fields on the form. This enables the user to categorize certain task documents as one of the following categories:

- Production Tasks

- Scheduled Documents

- Untested Tasks

Different users can work on different tasks. Like all software endeavors, Sentinel tasks must be tested to ensure that the user set all the parameters correctly. During testing, the user may want these documents to appear in the Untested Tasks view, for quick reference. These documents are always a subset of all documents in the database. Most importantly, they are individually selected by the user, based on personal criteria that do not have to be set jointly by committee. Figure 23.22 shows the new folder, Untested Tasks, containing two documents.

You can create a new folder by selecting Create, Folders from the view pane. The initial Folder name is Untitled. Type Untested Tasks as the Folder name. Selecting the Options button lets you choose a view or folder from which to inherit the design of this folder. This is a private folder, which means only you can place documents into it. Checking the Shared box allows other users to place documents into this folder. The Untested Tasks folder is a private folder for your personal Sentinel tasks.

Sales Management's Use of Hot Follow-Ups

In the sales force application, there is a view of Hot Follow-Up items. What makes an item "hot?" No one could decide even after interminable meetings. In reality, a follow-up is hot if the user thinks it is, based on interpretation. With folders, the user simply drags a document from a view into a folder. That document is, in a sense, "categorized" by the user. Now, a hot follow-up is hot if a user says it is, without a view committee meeting. This saves hours of view programming that users may not perceive as valuable. This will slow view proliferation.

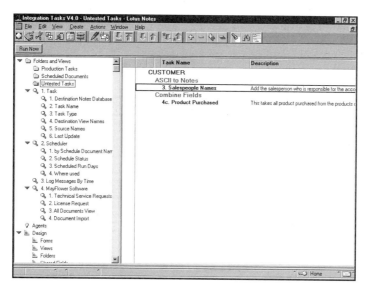

Fig. 23.22   Creating user folder for Untested Tasks.

Adding Navigators

As discussed in Chapter 3, "Using Databases," navigators are an interesting new feature of Notes R4. They offer the possibility of guided tours through databases by clicking "hot" sections of a graphical form. The common example of this feature is a geographical map, showing sales territories. Clicking specific areas of the map moves the user to sales information concerning that territory. This makes navigation through the Notes databases more visually oriented.

Certain databases lend themselves to navigators better than others. Generally, databases where the material is static (that is, where the material changes infrequently) better utilize navigators. Databases where creation of new documents occurs frequently offer more difficult design challenges in utilizing navigators for the application designer.

Good Database Candidates for Navigators

Following is a list of databases that take better advantage of navigators:

- **Help databases**—These databases change infrequently. You can build doclinks from a navigator to already existing documents. Usually one person or department controls database content. This enables that department to fix some hotspots to other documents.

- **Training and How-To databases**—These databases also have fixed content, controlled by one person or department. These are excellent candidates for navigators, as there can be multiple navigator screens moving from basic techniques to more advanced techniques. These databases generally do not have Create options, as users do not participate in their content. All of the content is already established, so the navigators do not have to contemplate additional information, or changes to current information.

- **Bulletin Board databases**—As with Help and Training databases, the content is generally static. An example of a bulletin board database is a list of company policies concerning employees, such as vacation time, sick time, benefits plans, and family leave. Again, all of the content is controlled and managed by one department, so the navigators can be assigned in advance.

The underlying criteria for good to excellent candidates for navigators is a static database controlled by one person or department.

Other Uses for Navigators

In dynamically changing databases, navigators cannot point to specific documents, as that document may not exist, or may not be created yet. Therefore, navigators must primarily point to views that the user might want to visit. However, if this were their only purpose, they would not be adding much value over the view pane to a developer. You can, however, put other buttons on a navigator that point to static information that a user might like. Following is a list of uses for a navigator in a dynamically changing database:

- **Help text**—As in help databases, specific navigators can point to more detailed help information.

- **Another navigator**—Here is where the navigators become powerful. One navigator hotspot can point to another navigator. In this example, that second navigator could be a table of contents of help topics. At this point, you are dealing with static text, and you can place many links within the navigator.

- **User instructions**—This allows simple user instructions to appear in the navigator. R3 is very light on functions that let the application developer guide the user through the application. Pop-ups and the Help Using document are the main facilities. R4 Navigators allow more detailed guidance throughout the application.

- **Create Form buttons**—Using nested navigators and compose buttons, you can guide a user around the database, and offer form creation (R3 compose) buttons at the correct locations. This generally involves hiding all Create form choices from the user and hiding the menu choices for each of the forms from the user. This enables the developer to fully control the user's navigation of the database, allowing form creation via action buttons only, while offering direction and help throughout.

- **View pane replacement**—Navigators can replace the view pane with more graphical representations of folders.

Designing Navigators into the Sentinel

From a designer's perspective, navigators force some difficult decisions. Do you hide the view pane completely? Which views should be in the navigator? How do you let users create private folders and then access them?

The Sentinel database is a dynamic database with some static help information. Earlier in this chapter, we built a View Action Button pointing to the Help Using screen, which pointed to the help database. In this section, you will learn how to upgrade an R3 database design to incorporate a navigator for a dynamically changing database. The navigator will contain hotspots for views, as well as a hotspot to switch back to folders.

From the menu, select Create, Design Navigator. A blank screen appears. You should name this navigator first. As this is the Sentinel database's first navigator, call it Home. Set the background color to red, and select Auto adjust panes at runtime. This allows all navigator buttons to be seen on the screen.

Using Graphics in Navigators. Navigators take excellent advantage of graphics. The Sentinel uses a "Swiss Army Knife" to demonstrate its versatility in moving data from source to destination. To insert graphics into a navigator, you must first copy it to the Clipboard. Once that is done, select Create, Graphic Background. Notes automatically pastes the graphic background onto the screen. Figure 23.23 shows the beginning of the Sentinel's first navigator.

Fig. 23.23   Home Navigator with graphic.

Creating Text to Be Used as Navigation Hotspots. The next task is to create text to be used as navigation hotspots. From the menu, select Create, Text. Using the mouse, click and hold the left button. Drag the rectangle to a size sufficient to hold two or three words.

The next task is to create four hotspot text buttons, one for each major view. Although the Sentinel has 15 views, only one button per major view is necessary.

Create four text box rectangles, one for each view. You can copy and paste these rectangles once you set the properties on the first text rectangle to your liking. Each text caption should be as follows:

- By Destination Name
- Schedule Tasks
- Log Messages
- License Forms

Figure 23.24 shows the Navigator with four action text boxes.

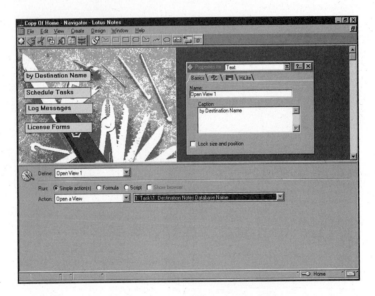

Fig. 23.24   Home Navigator with four action text boxes.

Creating a Way Back to the View Pane via Hotspot Rectangles. Now that we have a navigator, we need a way to get back to the view pane. Once in the navigator, there is no way back to the view pane unless programmed by you, the developer. In the Sentinel example, you can create a text box and a graphic of a folder. Wrapping all of that in a hotspot rectangle makes a hotspot to the view pane.

To do this, first create another text box, as before. Make the Text caption view pane. The Action in the programmer pane should be (none). Copy a graphic of a file folder (or whatever you feel represents the view pane window) to the Clipboard. Paste this to the Navigator by selecting Create, Graphic Button. The Action in the programmer pane for the Graphic Button should also be (none). Drag this next to the text that says view pane.

You can create a Hotspot Rectangle just as you did to create a Text Rectangle. From the menu, select Create, Hotspot Rectangle. Using the mouse, click and hold the left button. Drag the rectangle to a size approximately the size of the view pane text plus the graphic. A little larger will not cause any problems. Drag this hotspot rectangle on top of the view pane and File Folder graphic. In the programmer pane, type in the formula shown in Figure 23.25, which will enable the user to navigate back to the view pane when clicked.

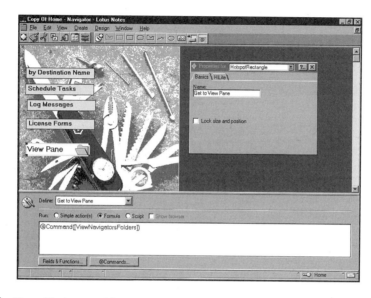

Fig. 23.25   Home Navigator with view pane hotspot rectangle.

Adding a Navigator Button to the Default View

To enable the user to switch to the navigator, place a button on the default view. This button opens the navigator Home.

Select Design Views from the View Pane. Double-click the default view "1. Task \1. Destination Notes Database Name." Select Create, Action. Call this Action Button Navigator in the Properties InfoBox. The formula is as follows:

```
@PostedCommand([OpenNavigator];"Home";"0")
```

Figure 23.26 shows the Navigator with a button using this formula to open the Home Navigator.

When clicked, this button opens the Home Navigator that you created. The parameter 0 means that Home is opened in the view pane (left side of the screen). The parameter 1 opens the navigator in its own window, filling the screen. The second choice is desirable if you want the navigator to be the sole method of moving around the database. This insulates the user from the details of the database design. Figure 23.27 shows the default database view with the Home Navigator appearing in the Action Bar.

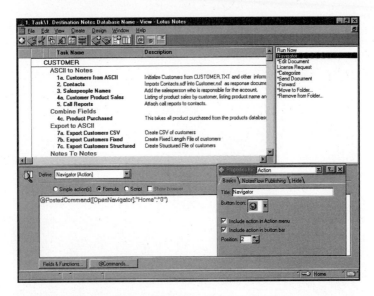

Fig. 23.26   Placing a button on the default view to open the Home Navigator.

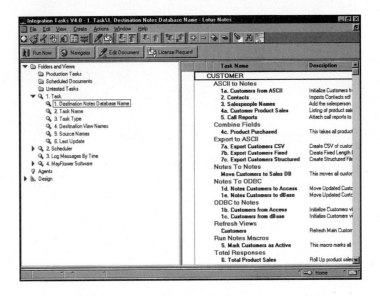

Fig. 23.27   Default view with Home Navigator button.

You can optionally open the navigator as soon as the user opens the database. To do this, switch to the Properties InfoBox. In the top field marked Properties for, select Database. Click the tab marked Launch (see Figure 23.28). Notes offers two choices in the On Database Open list box:

■ **Open designated Navigator**—This initially opens the navigator. Users can move from the navigator to other views or folders in the database.

■ **Open designated Navigator in its own window**—This initially opens the navigator. When users press Escape (or choose File, Close), they always return to the navigator. This makes the navigator truly a "home page" for the database.

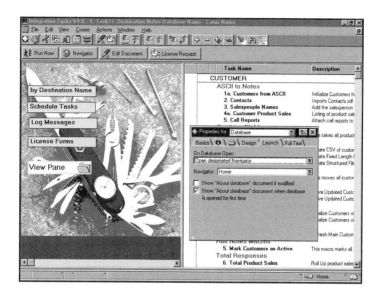

Fig. 23.28 Setting Launch parameters, on Database Open, to reference the Home Navigator.

From Here...

In this chapter, you participated in migrating a complicated Notes application from R3 Notes to R4 Notes. For more information on the topics discussed in this chapter, refer to the following:

■ Chapter 11, "Designing Forms," describes how to create and design forms in Notes R4.

■ Chapter 24, "Notes: Under the Hood," continues your study of Notes advanced topics and shows you how replication works and describes the various Notes platforms.

Chapter 24

Notes: Under the Hood

Millions of Notes users now know that Notes has many powerful and unique services that allow it to deliver in ways no competing product can. Understanding what these services do and how they work is crucial to having a happy and healthy Notes installation. This chapter is written with the Administrator in mind as it takes an in-depth look at how Notes works its magic.

Understanding Notes Replication

In today's business environment as teams become the prevalent work force model and the need to share information across time and geographic boundaries increases, the ability to synchronize databases so that users in disparate locations can share information on a timely basis is becoming more and more critical in order to maintain a competitive advantage. One of the most powerful and complicated features of Notes is its ability to synchronize multiple copies of Notes databases stored on different servers or client workstations. This process, known as *replication*, enables users on different networks—even in different time zones or in different countries—to share the same information in a timely and effective manner.

Some of the main topics in this chapter are

- How replication works

- The role of Notes servers

- Notes network topology

- The new Notes Admin Agent

- Supporting multiple licenses and Notes servers

- Notes and the Internet: an overview

V

Advanced Notes Topics

> **Note**
>
> Lotus Notes was the first product on the market that supports true client/server replication, and many companies now claim that their product supports replication. This claim must be scrutinized very carefully because most of these products are file-system based, meaning they must transfer an entire file or are messaging-based, meaning they must send messages that contain data between "replicas." As of this writing, Lotus Notes is the only product that supports client/server replication, and Lotus has taken it a step further in Notes 4.5: now replication can be done at the field level. Currently, no other product can make this claim.

The primary reason to use replication is to enable users who do not have direct access to the server where a database resides to work collaboratively with the information it contains. For instance, people who don't have a persistent connection to the LAN, such as salespeople, people who work from home, or people who use a server in a different location, can work with a replica of the database and have their replica synchronized with the original database through the replication process.

A good example of the need for replication is demonstrated by users configured for workstation-based mail. When mail messages are delivered to you, they are placed in your mailbox on the server. Workstation-based mail dictates that you will have a replica of your mailbox on your workstation. Each time you replicate with your Notes server, the Replicator will synchronize the local copy of your mailbox with the copy on the server.

Replication is not merely a file system-based process where an entire file is copied from one machine to another, but is a true client/server based process that bidirectionally synchronizes each replica of the database with changes from the other copy. In Notes 3.x, this was a document-level process. If any changes were made to a document, the entire document was replicated. In Notes 4.5, replication is a field-level process. If only one field in a document changes, only the information contained in that field is sent to the other database.

To illustrate the importance of field-based replication, consider this example. Company XYZ has a Marketing Encyclopedia database used to store PowerPoint and Freelance Graphics presentations, video, and sound files as file attachments in a rich text field. In Notes 3.x, when a user edited a document and changed the Presentation Format field from PowerPoint to Freelance, the entire document—including the large presentation stored as an attachment—was replicated to all replica databases. This can consume a vast amount of time and system resources.

If the same scenario took place in a Notes 4.5 database, only the fields that actually changed—in this case, the Presentation Format field—would be replicated, thus saving a tremendous amount of time and system resources, particularly for dial-up users.

> **Note**
>
> In some cases, field-based replication may not be desirable. It adds overhead on the front end of the process because each database must be searched more thoroughly to determine which fields have changed. If a particular database has frequent changes to large documents, field-based replication can be very useful; otherwise, it might actually take slightly more time.

For the replication process to be efficient and effective, Notes must track several pieces of information at the database level, such as the Replica ID and Replication History; and at the document level, such as the Document ID, Created date, Modified date, and Added to file Date. I will now examine each of these in detail.

As you will see in the following sections, replication is a very powerful but very compli-cated feature of Notes, and I can only scratch the surface in this chapter. In most in-stances, the Notes Administrator will configure your workstation and you will need not worry about these issues. On the other hand, if you need more information, refer to your Notes manuals and online Help database.

> **Note**
>
> Much of the replication process is controlled by database-specific settings accessible through the Replication Settings dialog box. To access this dialog box, right-click the database icon and choose Database Properties to display the Database Property InfoBox. Click the Replication Settings button to display the Replication Settings dialog box. For details on how to use and change these settings, see the section, "Choosing Replication Settings" in Chapter 21, "Working Remote."

Replica ID

Each Notes database, when it is first created (when the File, Database, New operation is performed), gets assigned a unique Replica ID. When two or more databases share the same Replica ID, this is the signal to the Notes server that these databases are linked and should be synchronized. Only databases that have identical Replica IDs will be synchro-nized.

To see the Replica ID of any database, choose File, Database, Properties right click the database icon and choose Properties, or select the database and click the Properties SmartIcon.

Either of these actions will display the Database Properties InfoBox. You can then click the i tab to see the Replica ID of the database. Figure 24.1 displays the i tab of the proper-ties for my mail database.

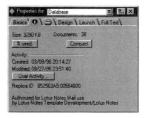

Fig. 24.1 You can use the Database Property InfoBox to quickly and easily view the Replica ID.

When a new replica of a database is created by choosing File, Replication, New Replica, the new database will be assigned the same Replica ID, and replication between the two databases can begin.

> ### Caution
>
> If you have the capability to create replica databases on your server (which can be limited by the Notes Administrator), it is very important that you understand the distinction between a replica database and a database copy. A copy of a database made by choosing File, New Copy, assigns a new Replica ID to the copy. Although the database looks the same and contains the same data, a new Replica ID will be assigned to the database.
>
> This means that the database will *not* replicate with the original database. If you want to make a copy of a database that will *not* replicate with the original, such as a Mail Archive database, this is the method you should use.

Replication History

The first time a database is replicated successfully, a *Replication History* is created that tracks the time, date, username or servername, and actions of that last replication. To access the Replication History of a database, select it and choose File, Replication, History, or right-click the database icon and choose History; the Replication History dialog box shown in Figure 24.2 will be displayed.

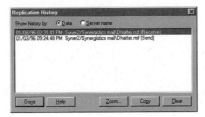

Fig. 24.2   When a database replicates successfully, the Notes server will examine the Replication History to determine when the database last replicated successfully.

Only successful replications will be logged in the Replication History for a database. For instance, if you are a dial-up user and initiate a replication session while the server's lines are busy, the Replication History will not be updated until the database actually replicates.

Once the Notes server knows the date and time of the last successful replication, it will use special time and date information stored in each document to determine which documents have been added, modified, or deleted since the last successful replication. This is known as *incremental replication* and can drastically reduce the time needed to replicate. If the last successful replication time and date cannot be determined, which could happen if the Replication History was cleared or if the database in question is a brand-new replica, a full replication will be performed. This will take much longer and consume more resources because each document in each database must be examined for changes.

Tip

The Replication History can be a valuable troubleshooting tool for experienced Notes Administrators because you can quickly determine when a database last replicated, with whom it replicated, and whether information was sent, received, or both. In addition, some replication problems can be solved by clearing the Replication History of a database. For example, if a user's time or date get out of synch with the time and date of the server, replication may no longer work properly. Once the time and date are properly set, clearing the replication history gets the process back on track. If you have Manager access to a server database or are working with a local copy of a database, you can use the <u>C</u>lear button on the Replication History dialog box shown in Figure 24.2 to delete the Replication History of the database and ensure a full replication when the next replication takes place.

Document ID

Much like the Replica ID of a database, each Notes document has a unique *document ID*. Each document actually has three different IDs that Notes uses to provide varying levels of identification and uniqueness. The value displayed in the Document Property InfoBox for the ID is all three of the following values concatenated:

- The primary identifier is the Document ID, which can be used to distinguish a document within a database.

- The Universal ID is unique between replica databases, but is the same for all replicas of the same document.

- The highest level identifier is the Originator ID, which is unique among all documents in all replica copies of a database.

In addition, Notes keeps track of several time/date values that it uses for replication and auditing purposes. The five time/date values it tracks are Created, Modified, Added to this file, Modified in this file, and Accessed in this file. You can view these dates with the information tab of the Document Properties InfoBox. In order to do so, select any document and choose <u>F</u>ile, Docume<u>n</u>t Properties, right-click a document in a view or folder and choose Document Properties, or select a document and click the Properties SmartIcon. Figure 24.3 displays the Document Properties InfoBox that appears and shows these dates and the document's unique ID.

Fig. 24.3 The Document Properties InfoBox displays pertinent document-level replication information.

The following sections describe the individual date values.

Created. Every Notes document will have a Created date associated with it. This is the date document that was originally created (regardless of the replica it was created in) and is database-independent. The Created date value will be the same in each replica copy of a document in each database and will never change.

The dates associated with a document such as the Created, Modified, and Added to File dates, as well as dates associated with a database, are dependent upon the system date of the workstation or server in use when a document is added, updated, or replicated. If the system date is inaccurate, it can cause replication problems. You should occasionally check your system time and date to ensure that it is correct. To easily check or edit the system time and date, simply choose File, Mobile, Edit Current Time/Phone, which will launch the dialog box shown in Figure 24.4. You can edit as needed.

Fig. 24.4   The Time and Phone Information dialog box—use this dialog to change your location related time, date, and dialing information.

Modified. Each time a document is modified after its creation, the Modified date is updated. The Modified date is crucial for replication because Notes uses this date in conjunction with the Replication History to perform incremental replication. The Modified date can vary for replicas of the same document because a user may update a copy of the document in a replica of the original, or vice versa. During replication, Notes views the differences in the dates as a signal that the document has changed and at least one of the field needs to be replicated. After the databases have replicated, the Modified date should be the same in each copy of the document until the next edit takes place.

Added to File Date. The Added to file date is database-dependent in that it reflects the date that a particular document was placed into the copy of the database you are using. For example, if a document originates in the server copy of a database, the Added to file date will reflect the date the document was saved in that database. When the database next replicates and that document is transferred to the replica, the Added to file date of the document in the replica will display the date it was placed into the replica.

Modified in This File. The Modified in this file date is also database-dependent. It displays the date on which a particular document was last modified in the current database. In any given document, this date changes when a user updates a document or the replicator updates a document that was changed in a replica copy.

Accessed in This file. The Accessed in this file date is database-dependent. As its name implies, it displays the date the selected document was last accessed.

The Replication Process

The ABC Company, for example, maintains a database named Marketing Discussion on Server_A in the Atlanta office. When a new office opens in Chicago, a new replica of the database is made on the Server_B in Chicago, which copies all of the documents in the database from Server_A to Server_B. When the initial replication is completed, the Replication History in the Marketing Discussion database on Server_A should look something like this:

```
Server_B/ABC Company DATA\MDISCUSS.NSF 10/19/96 08:25:16 PM (Send)
```

From this Replication History, you can see that Server_A sent data from this database to its replica on Server_B on 10/19/96 at 8:25 P.M. No data was received from the new database because it was a Replica Stub and contained no data.

> **Note**
>
> A Replica Stub is a new replica database that has not been initialized, meaning that it shares a Replica ID with another database, but it has yet to actually replicate.

The Replication History of the replica database on Server_B should look something like this:

```
Server_A/ABC Company DATA\MDISCUSS.NSF 10/19/96 08:26:38 PM (Receive)
```

This Replication History tells you that the replica database received data from the Marketing Discussion database on Server_A and took just over a minute to transmit the data. As you have probably guessed, the amount of time required for replication will depend on the size of the data being transmitted and the volume of changes transmitted.

In most instances, if replication is functioning correctly, you will see two distinct entries in the Replication History of each database that replicates with another database. One indicates that data was sent to the other database (Send), and the other indicates that data was received from the other database (Receive).

As users begin to use the new database on Server_B, new documents get added and existing documents get updated or deleted. As an example, follow six documents through the process. Table 24.1 shows the two databases as they exist after the replication on 10/19/96 at 8:25:55 P.M.

Table 24.1 Replication Example 1

Doc #	Doc ID*	Created	Modified	Added to File	Server	Delete
1	ABC234:364VBC	10/20/96 7:22:40 a.m.	10/20/96 9:31:56 a.m.	10/21/96 6:22:11 a.m.	Server_A	
2	AB1X42:BN456X	10/20/96 12:45:32 p.m.	10/21/96 3:44:11 p.m.	10/20/96 12:45:32 p.m.	Server_B	
3	AXV567:CBV768	10/19/96 7:20:45 a.m.		10/19/96 7:20:45 a.m.	Server_A	

(continues)

Advanced Notes Topics

V

Doc #	Doc ID*	Created	Modified	Added to File	Server	Delete
Table 24.1 Continued						
4	AXV567:CBV768	10/19/96 7:20:45 a.m.	10/21/96 6:55:11 p.m.	10/19/96 8:25:55 p.m.	Server_B	
5	C2SD34:681S45	10/19/96 7:59:08 a.m.	10/21/96 4:25:22 p.m.	10/19/96 7:59:08 a.m.	Server_A	Yes
6	C2SD34:681S45	10/19/96 7:59:08 a.m.		10/19/96 8:26:57 p.m.	Server_B	

The document IDs in this example have been shortened in order to save space.

Document 1 was created in another replica (by a remote user perhaps) of the Marketing Discussion database on 10/20/96 and was modified on 10/20/96, but did not get replicated into the copy on Server_A until 10/21/96. (This is a good example of what happens when you have users with local replicas of a database that do not replicate daily.)

Document 2 was created in the replica of the Marketing Discussion database on Server_B on 10/20/96 (which is why the Created date and Added to file dates are the same), and it was modified on 10/21/96.

Document 3 was created in the Server_A copy of the Marketing Discussion database on 10/19/96 and has not been modified in this copy.

Document 4 is a replica of Document 3 that was placed into the Marketing Discussion database on Server_B during the initial replication (notice that the Document IDs and Created dates are the same). Document 4 was modified on 10/21/96 at 6:55:11 P.M.

Document 5 was created in the Server_A copy of the Marketing Discussion database on 10/19/96 and was deleted from the Server_A database on 10/21/96.

Document 6 is a replica of Document 5 that was placed in the Marketing Discussion replica on Server_B during the initial replication.

Table 24.2 shows the states of the two replica databases after Server_A and Server_B replicate on 10/22/96 at 6:00:00 A.M.

Doc #	Doc ID*	Created	Modified	Added to File	Server	Delete
Table 24.2 Replication Example 2						
1	ABC234:364VBC	10/20/96 7:22:40 a.m.	10/20/96 9:31:56 a.m.	10/21/96 6:22:11 a.m.	Server_A	
2	AB1X42:BN456X	10/20/96 12:45:32 p.m.	10/21/96 3:44:11 p.m.	10/20/96 12:45:32 p.m.	Server_B	
3	AXV567:CBV768	10/19/96 7:20:45 a.m.	10/21/96 6:55:11 p.m.	10/22/96 6:00:45 a.m.	Server_A	
4	AXV567:CBV768	10/19/96 7:20:45 a.m.	10/21/96 6:55:11 p.m.	10/19/96 8:25:55 p.m.	Server_B	

Doc #	Doc ID*	Created	Modified	Added to File	Server	Delete
5	C2SD34:681S45	10/19/96 7:59:08 a.m.	10/21/96 4:25:22 p.m.	10/19/96 7:59:08 a.m.	Server_A	Yes
6	C2SD34:681S45	10/19/96 7:59:08 a.m.	10/21/96 4:25:22 p.m.	10/22/96 6:05:12 a.m.	Server_B	Yes
7	ABC234:364VBC	10/20/96 7:22:40 a.m.	10/20/96 9:31:56 a.m.	10/22/96 6:05:56 a.m.	Server_B	
8	AB1X42:BN456X	10/20/96 12:45:32 p.m.	10/21/96 3:44:11 p.m.	10/22/96 6:01:32 p.m.	Server_A	

After the scheduled replication on 10/22/96 at 6:00:00 A.M., the replication history of the Marketing Discussion database on Server_A would look something like this (the actual times will vary based on the size of the documents being replicated):

```
Server_A/ABC Company DATA\MDISCUSS.NSF 10/22/96 06:04:23 AM (Receive)

Server_A/ABC Company DATA\MDISCUSS.NSF 10/22/96 06:01:34 PM (Send)
```

After the scheduled replication on 10/22/96 at 6:00:00 A.M., the replication history of the Marketing Discussion database on Server_B would look something like this (the actual times will vary based on the size of the documents being replicated):

```
Server_B/ABC Company DATA\MDISCUSS.NSF 10/22/96 06:00:15 AM (Send)

Server_B/ABC Company DATA\MDISCUSS.NSF 10/22/96 06:05:32 PM (Receive)
```

As you can see in Table 24.2, the databases have been synchronized. The Replicator has created a new instance of Document 1 in Server_B's database (Document 7) because Document 1 was added to Server_A's copy after the first replication with Server_B on 10/19/96.

Likewise, Document 8 in Server_A's copy of the database is a new instance of Document 2 because Document 2 was added to Server_B's copy of the database after the first replication on 10/19/96.

In our example, Document 4 in Server_B's copy was a replica of Document 3 created in Server_B's copy during the initial replication on 10/19/96. On 10/21/96 at 6:55:11 P.M., Document 4 was modified in Server_B's copy. During the replication on 10/22/96, the modifications made to Document 4 were made to Document 3 in Server_A's copy. Notice that in Table 24.2, Document 3 and Document 4 now have the same Created and Modified dates; however, the Added to file dates reflect the dates each of these documents were added into their respective databases.

Handling Deleted Documents. Document 5 and Document 6 require some special attention because Document 5 has been deleted. Document 6 in Server_B's database is a replica of Document 5 in Server_A's copy. On 10/21/96 at 4:25:22 P.M., Document 5 was deleted from the database on Server_A. If Document 5 was actually physically deleted, then the Replicator process would see that Document 6 exists in Server_B's database and does not exist in Server_A's copy after the next replication. It would then create a new replica of Document 6 in Server_A's database.

To solve this problem, Notes handles deletions in a special way. When a document is deleted, a *deletion stub* is created to act as a flag for the Replicator. During the next replication, the Replicator sees the deletion stubs and knows that the documents that have the same Document IDs should be deleted and deletion stubs should be created in their places (this is necessary so that the deletion stubs are populated throughout all replicas of the database).

In our example, when the replication takes place on 10/22/96, the Replicator will see the deletion stub for Document 5 and will delete Document 6 from Server_B's database. Table 24.2 shows that both documents have been deleted.

Changing the Purge Interval. Deletion stubs are relatively small and contain only enough information for the Replicator task to find the corresponding document in each replica of a database. However, over time, deletion stubs can waste a significant amount of space. Notes enables you to set a *purge interval* so that deletion stubs can be physically removed from the database after a specified period of time.

The purge interval for a database is one-third the number of days specified in the Remove documents not modified in the last X days setting of each database (where X is a numeric value that you supply). The default value for this setting is 90 days. If you do not change this value, then all deletion stubs will be removed from the specified database every 30 days.

To access this setting, choose File, Database, Properties, and click the Replication Settings button on the Database Property InfoBox that appears, or right-click a database, choose Properties, and click the Replication Settings button on the Database Property InfoBox. Either of these methods will launch the Replication Settings dialog box shown in Figure 24.5.

◀◀ See "Choosing Replication Settings," p. 838

Fig. 24.5 Use the Replication Settings dialog box to control replication options for each database.

Be aware that if the purge interval for a database is more frequent than the Replication Schedule, documents that you have deleted will reappear in your copy of the database. This happens because the deletion stubs are removed from your copy of the database before they are sent to the server copy of the database. When the Server copy next replicates with your copy (whether it's local or another server copy), it will re-create each of the deleted documents.

The moral of this story is to ensure that the frequency of replication between replicas of the database is greater than the purge interval for those databases.

> **Tip**
>
> The Do not send deletions made in this replica to other replicas checkbox enables you to delete documents in your database without creating deletion stubs, which means the deletions will not be sent to other replicas. To enable this setting, click the Send icon on the Replication Settings dialog box.

◄◄ See "Limiting What Is Sent to the Server," p. 839

Preventing Replication or Save Conflicts. At this point, Server_A and Server_B have identical copies of the Marketing Discussion database. Any other replicas of this database that replicate with Server_A or Server_B will also be synchronized.

If you are familiar with relational databases, by now you are most likely thinking, "But what if you and I edit replicas of the same document in different databases between scheduled replication?" When this happens—and it inevitably will—a *replication*, or save conflict, occurs. Take, for example, a database on Server_A and its replica on Server_B. If you examine Table 24.3 with the knowledge that the two servers last replicated on 10/23/96 at 12:30:01 P.M. and will next replicate on 10/25/96 at 12:30:00 P.M., you can see from the Modified date of the two documents that each was edited in its respective database between scheduled replications.

Table 24.3 Replication Example 3

Doc #	Doc ID*	Created	Modified	Added to File	Server	Delete
1	C34VB1:98D345	10/23/96 7:22:40 a.m.	10/24/96 10:37:46 a.m.	10/23/96 7:22:40 a.m.	Server_A	
2	C34VB1:98D345	10/23/96 7:22:40 a.m.	10/24/96 3:24:12 p.m.	10/23/96 12:30:32 p.m.	Server_B	

The document IDs in this example have been shortened in order to save space.

By default (and design), the Replicator does not overwrite one user's changes to a replica of a document with the other's changes. Instead, the Replicator chooses a "winner" and makes it the *main*, or *parent*, *document*. The "loser" becomes a *response*, or *child*, *document* of the "winner" and is marked as a Replication or Save conflict. (The document will contain a $Conflict field.) The document that has been edited and saved most frequently becomes the winner. If both documents have been edited and saved the same number of times, the document that was saved most recently becomes the winner.

V

Advanced Notes Topics

However, Lotus realizes that handling this process manually for a large number of databases with many documents and many replica copies would be unbearable. They implemented a way, at the form level of each database, to effectively handle these conflicts automatically. Figure 24.6 shows the versioning options available in the Form Properties InfoBox.

Fig. 24.6   The document versioning options for Notes forms allows you to automatically merge conflicts, saving you time and effort.

There are three options you can use to help reduce or eliminate Replication or Save conflicts. You can enable the New versions become responses, and the New versions become siblings versioning options to help reduce conflicts. You can also enable the Merge replication conflicts options to put all of the conflicts into one document to ease the task of determining what to keep.

> **Note**
>
> Replication or save conflicts can be resolved manually by editing and saving the child document. This will remove the conflict status and elevate the document from a response document to a main (parent) document. You can then decide which document has the most correct information and delete the others. In addition, replication or save conflicts can be handled programmatically. For more information regarding this topic, consult the Lotus Notes Help database or Lotus Notes documentation.

How the ACL Affects Replication. Replication is not the all-or-nothing process it may appear to be from the prior example. In fact, the replication process is highly customizable, and the information that's actually replicated will depend on several factors, such as selective replication settings, database ACLs, and Read Access Lists.

First and foremost, replication is subordinate to the database ACL. For instance, if you have two servers in your organization, ABC_1 and ABC_2, and ABC_2 has a replica of a database on ABC_1, the data that replicates between these two servers is wholly dependent upon the access level each server has been granted to the other's copy of the database. Table 24.4 briefly demonstrates the effect that various access levels have on the replication process between servers.

Table 24.4   Database Access Levels

ABC_1 Access Level in ABC_2's Database	ABC_2 Access Level in ABC_1's Database	Effect
Manager	Reader	ABC_1 can send ALL changes (data, design, and ACL) to ABC 2. ABC_1 will accept no changes from ABC_2. Generally speaking, a server should have Manager access to all databases that reside on that server; however, certain security needs may merit lower access levels.
Designer	Author	ABC_1 can send data and design changes to ABC_2. ABC_2 can only send new documents created on ABC_2 and modifications to those documents.
Editor	Editor	ABC_1 can only send new documents and modifications to existing documents. (If the Can Delete Documents option is enabled for Editor access, deletions will also be accepted.) ABC_2 will not accept design or ACL changes from ABC_1. Likewise, ABC_2 can send data changes, but cannot alter the design or ACL of the database ABC_1.

Note

If your changes don't seem to be replicating between replicas of a database, check your Notes Log for messages that indicate that the access level is set in the database in question to disallow replication from the other database. The following is an example of a message you might see:

```
Access control is set in DATA\DISCUSS.NSF not to allow
replication from ABC_1\DATA\DISCUSS.NSF
```

This message indicates that server ABC_1 does not have sufficient access rights to replicate with the local database. If this is the case, have your Administrator grant you the required access level in the database's ACL.

If you have a local replica of a database, you most likely have Manager access (ACLs can now be enforced locally in Notes 4.5, so it's possible that the database manager would enable this feature and change your local access. If you do not have manager access to a local database, see your Administrator) to that database. With Manager access, you not only can create new documents and edit or delete existing documents, you can make changes to the design of the database. However, your access level in the server's copy of the database dictates what changes the server will accept from you. If you make changes to the local copy that you are not authorized to make to the server copy, then the server will overwrite your changes during the next replication.

◄◄ See " Understanding Database Access," p. 405

V

Advanced Notes Topics

Limiting Read Access. Another security feature of Notes is the ability to add Read Access Lists to forms, views, folders, and documents. By adding a Read Access List to any of these elements, access is limited exclusively to those users, servers, or groups explicitly named in the list.

What this means in terms of replication is that if a server or user's name is not in the list, that user or server will not have that element replicated to it. For example, if you work on a local replica of a database and create a document that has a ReaderNames field in it, you must specify the names of all users, servers, and groups who can access this document. If you were to accidentally omit the name of the server where the database is stored, that document would not be replicated to the server and, therefore, would not be accessible to other users. (Normally, if ReaderNames fields are implemented in a form, the database designer will write code to automatically populate the field with the server's name so that the document will replicate with the server.)

◀◀ See " Names Fields," p. 108

> **Note**
>
> Read Access Lists and ReaderNames fields can be very powerful security devices. However, they should not be implemented without a thorough understanding of how replication works and the effect these features have on the replication process. Please see the Lotus Notes Help database or Lotus Notes documentation for more information on ReaderNames fields and Read Access Lists.

Selective Replication. Using the Replicate a subset of documents checkbox in the Replication Settings dialog box enables you to pull only documents that meet criteria you define. This *selective replication* can greatly reduce the amount of data replicated, thereby reducing the amount time and disk space required.

Many people think that selective replication is a security feature because you can limit the documents a workstation or server can replicate. However, as Lotus clearly states in the Notes manuals, this is not a security feature because users with only a rudimentary knowledge of Notes can change the selection formula. If you want to limit the documents that certain users can see, consider using ReaderNames fields in the documents and enforce database ACLs locally.

◀◀ See "Understanding the Data Types," p. 454
◀◀ See "Selective Replication," p. 866

The Role of Notes Servers

Lotus Notes is a client/server application that relies on networking technology to enable groups of people to collaborate. It consists of two primary components: the Notes server and the Notes workstation. By now, you most likely have worked with the Notes client software extensively and are quite familiar with its functions and features, but becoming familiar with the server is critical if you are responsible for developing Notes applications, administering Notes, or want to have a thorough understanding of how Notes does its magic. The Notes server is the glue that holds a Notes installation together because it provides mail routing, replication, authentication, communication services, and a plethora of other services to users and other servers. Accessing a Notes server requires very little knowledge on the part of the user (this is by design, as the hard stuff is left to the Notes Administrator). This section explains the role of the Notes server in your Notes installation.

The Notes server is not a file server. A *file server* is a machine that is connected to a network and is running a network operating system (NOS), such as Novell NetWare or Microsoft Windows NT, that provides access to shared resources, such as applications, printers, disk storage, modems, scanners, and other peripherals.

A *Notes server,* on the other hand, is application software running on a machine that is connected to a network. Notes servers are built around the client/server model and provide service for Notes users and other Notes servers. Although it is possible to run a Notes server on the same machine that acts as a file server, Lotus recommends that the Notes server software be run on a separate machine. The Notes server can consume a good amount of resources, and the extra overhead of running on a file server can seriously hamper performance.

The Notes server is essential to any Notes installation because it provides the communication mechanism for the workstations. You can think of it as the glue that holds the whole system together. The Notes server provides the following services to Notes clients and other Notes servers:

- Storage and replication of databases
- Directory services
- Mail routing
- Security
- MTA/Gateway interface
- HTTP Services/Web Publishing
- Calendaring & Scheduling Services
- Custom server tasks
- Add-ins

The first half of this chapter explored replication; the following sections discuss the other services provided by the server.

Directory Services

If you have read Chapter 5, "Using the Address Book," you are already familiar with the directory services role that the Notes server plays in a Notes installation. All users and servers in a domain (also see Chapter 5 for more information about domains) share a common Public Name & Address Book (N & A Book). The Public N & A Book stores information about all valid Notes users, servers, groups, MTAs, and gateways in the domain as well as foreign domains and makes this information available to users, servers, and server processes.

Mail Routing

As you are probably aware from Chapter 4, "Getting Started with Electronic Mail," and Chapter 6, "Advanced Mail," Notes sports a powerful, integrated, client/server-based store-and-forward mail system built around the cc:Mail interface. The server plays a pivotal role in the mail system for the following reasons:

- It provides a connection point for Notes clients and other servers.

- The *router* is a server task responsible for mail routing and delivery.

- Each mailbox resides on the user's home server.

In most installations, the router runs constantly on each server, continuously checking for new mail messages in the server's MAIL.BOX database. When the router encounters a new mail message, it examines the recipients' addresses to determine whether this server is the home server of any of the recipients. If it is, then a copy of the document will be placed into the mailboxes of the recipients on the server.

If the mailbox of any recipient is on another server or in a different domain, the router task will determine the best route for the mail message and transfer it to a MAIL.BOX file on the next server. Once there, the process is repeated until the message has been delivered to all recipients or an error condition is encountered.

> **Note**
>
> Notes 4.5 has a very powerful new mail feature named Shared Mail. Shared mail, when enabled (by default it is not enabled), provides a central object store for mail messages so that when multiple recipients are specified for a mail message, only one complete copy is stored on the server, and the recipients receive only the envelope of the mail with a link to the body (this is unknown to the user). The real benefit of this technology is the amount of space that can be saved on the server's hard disk. For example, if a user mails a 5M WordPro document as an attachment to 10 users, in the non-shared model, 50M of disk space would be consumed because a copy to the mail message would be stored in each user's mailbox. Using the shared mail model, only one 5M copy is stored in the mail object store and the header (probably no more than 64-100K) is stored in the user's mail files.

Security

From its inception, Lotus Notes was designed as a very secure system that is independent of the platform and operating system. The client/server computing model is, by nature, more secure than file system-based systems because access to data is tightly controlled by the server. In addition, Notes utilizes RSA encryption technology, which enables user authentication, certification, encryption, and digital signatures to provide substantial security.

> **Note**
>
> The Rivest, Shamir, and Adleman (RSA) public key encryption scheme is *the* leading public key scheme. In this system, each user has two 512-bit keys: one private key, which only the user holds, and one public key, which is made available to other users. Security is then provided by encrypting messages with the recipient's public key, which can be decrypted only with the recipient's private key. This method is extraordinarily secure because it encrypts data in 64-bit blocks. The potential key combinations that would have to be tested to break just one key number is somewhere in the quadrillions.

Notes servers provide essentially four types of security, as follows:

- Authentication
- Access control
- Digital signatures
- Encryption

These features are discussed in the following sections.

Authentication. *Authentication* is a bidirectional verification process that is invoked anytime a user and a server or two servers communicate. A good illustration of authentication is the process of logging in to your Notes server.

> **Note**
>
> When the first Notes server in an organization is installed, a special "master" ID known as the *Certifier ID* (CERT.ID) is created. When a new ID file is created for use in a Notes installation, it must be certified by the Certifier ID. During the certification process, an electronic "stamp" known as a *certificate* is generated based on the private key in the Certifier ID and is placed into each new ID file. The certificate verifies that the public key associated with the new ID file is valid.
>
> For a workstation to communicate with a server, it *must* have certificates derived from a common or ancestral Certifier ID. In layman's terms, this means that to access a Notes server, your ID file must have been created by the certifier ID for the organization you are trying to access, or one of its descendants, or must have been cross-certified. For more information on certificates and certification, see the online Help database and the Lotus Notes documentation.

The server will generate a random number and encrypt it using the public encryption key stored in the Person document (in the Public N & A Book) that corresponds to the user ID in use during the login. The workstation software will then use the matching private encryption key stored in your user ID to decrypt the number and return it to the server. If your workstation returns the correct number (which can happen only if the matching private encryption key is used), you are authenticated as a valid user on this server. If the correct number is not returned, the server will not grant access. The process is then reversed, and your workstation software attempts to authenticate the server.

Access Control. *Access control* should be a familiar concept by this point. Each database, document, form, view, and folder can employ access control to grant or deny very specific, well-defined user privileges to individual users, servers, and groups. Server access can also be granted or denied to specific users, servers, and groups through the Access server and Not Access server fields in the Server document. For more information on access control and Access Control Lists, see Chapter 3, "Using Databases."

Electronic Signatures. *Electronic signatures* are also based on the RSA encryption scheme. They can be used to guarantee that a message is actually from the sender it claims to be from and guarantees that the message has not been altered while being transmitted. For more in-depth coverage of this feature, please see Chapter 22, "Security and Encryption."

Encryption. *Encryption* is essentially the scrambling of data by applying an encryption key so that if the data is accessed by unauthorized users, they will not be able to understand it. The data can only be unscrambled with the appropriate key. As mentioned earlier in this section, Notes uses the RSA Public Key encryption scheme. Lotus Notes supports three levels of encryption, as follows:

- First, at the network level, data can be encrypted so that if it is intercepted during transfer, it contains no intelligence without the appropriate key.

- At the message level, mail messages can be encrypted so that only recipients with the appropriate key can decrypt them.

- Finally, Notes supports field level encryption so that information within a document can be encrypted.

> **Caution**
>
> Although encryption is a very powerful security measure, it should be used judiciously and only when absolutely necessary for two reasons. First, encryption and decryption consume resources and time. The second and more important reason is that all of your encryption keys are stored in your user ID file. If that file became corrupted, got accidentally deleted, or otherwise became unavailable, you would no longer be able to access any of the information that was encrypted using that ID.
>
> There are no "backdoors" to this system; in fact, not even Lotus can help you if you lose your ID. This is especially critical with field and message level encryption. If this is enabled in your system, you should frequently back up your user ID file and keep it protected.

As you can see, Notes provides a security-rich environment that can protect even the most sensitive data from prying eyes. But be aware that many or all of these security features can be circumvented if your user ID or a server ID is compromised. If someone has physical access to an ID file and can crack the password for that ID, then he or she can assume that identity and see and do anything your ID permits.

To prevent unauthorized access, important ID files such as the Certifier ID and server IDs should be physically secured. Further, all passwords should be difficult to guess. (Your wife's name or your son's birthday make poor passwords.) In that regard, long passwords are better than short ones, and a mixture of numeric and text characters in a password makes it even harder to crack. Nonetheless, all passwords should be changed frequently.

Server Programs and Add-In Programs

The Notes server software was designed in a highly modular fashion so that it is easy for the Notes Administrator to configure a server to perform any or all of the tasks shown in Table 24.5. Many of these tasks are automatically loaded on the server by default settings in the NOTES.INI file. Any server program can be loaded or unloaded at any time without shutting down the Notes server. Also, you can create Program documents in the Public N & A Book to launch a server program at a specified time.

To load a server program that is not currently running, at the server console, type the following:

```
LOAD <programname> [argument1],[argumentn]
```

where the *<programname>* is the name of the Notes server program to load, and *argument* is the command line parameters this program accepts. Table 24.5 shows the standard Notes server programs.

Table 24.5 Common Server Tasks

Task Name	Program Name to Load	Description
Administration	ADMINP	Performs global name changes and deletions. Useful for maintaining access control lists.
Agent Manager	AMGR	Runs agents on one or more databases.
Billing	BILLING	Collects all generated billing information.
Cataloger	CATALOG	Updates the Database Catalog database.
Database Compactor	COMPACT	Compacts all databases on the server, which removes white space and frees disk space.
Database Fixup	FIXUP	Checks databases for corruption, such as truncated documents. Fixes problems when possible.
Designer	DESIGN	Synchronizes the design of any database that has a Design Template with the template.
Event	EVENT	Starts and performs server event logging.
Indexer	UPDATE	Updates all opened views in a specific database or when other tasks such as the Replicator have changes waiting.

(continues)

V

Advanced Notes Topics

Table 24.5   Continued

Task Name	Program Name to Load	Description
Indexer	UPDALL	Updates all changed views or full text indexes for all databases on the server. This program accepts several command line parameters.
Login	LOGIN	Listens to enabled ports for requests from users of add-in programs.
Object Store	OBJECT	Performs maintenance on data-bases and mail files that use shared mail.
POP3	POP3	Enables a Notes server to act as a maildrop for POP3 clients.
Chronos	CHRONOS	Runs background macros and any other time-related tasks. This is always loaded by default; there is no program file to load.
Replicator	REPLICA	Replicates databases with other servers.
Router	ROUTER	Routes mail to other servers.
Statistics	STATLOG	Updates database statistics in the Server's log file.
Web Retriever	Web	Implements the HTTP protocol to retrieve Web pages and convert them into Notes documents.

For more information about Notes server programs, consult the Help database or the Lotus Notes documentation.

If your server is not running the Designer process and you want to load it, then at the server console or by using the Remote Console icon in the Notes Administration dialog box (which can be accessed by choosing File, Tools, Administration), enter the following command:

```
LOAD DESIGN
```

> **Note**
>
> Your ability to interact with the Server Console or load any of these tasks might be limited by your access level or a console password.

Notes also enables you to load and run add-in tasks, which are other programs written specifically to run on a Notes server. Your organization, for example, might have a C programmer write an API program to archive Notes databases at 3:00 A.M. each day. In the next section on gateways, you will see that most of the gateways for Notes are actually Notes add-in tasks. The capacity to create custom programs for the Notes server provides tremendous expansion capabilities.

Gateways

To further expand the capabilities of Lotus Notes and provide easy integration with existing systems, Lotus has developed a wide array of gateways. According to the *LAN Times Encyclopedia of Networking,* a gateway is "a computer system or other device that acts as a translator between two systems that do not use the same communication protocols, data formatting structures, languages, and/or architecture."

Some of the gateways that are currently available for Notes are described in the following sections. As you will see from the large number of gateways, Lotus has made a commitment to connectivity and will continue to provide excellent connectivity with other popular systems.

Incoming/Outgoing Fax Gateway. The Lotus Fax Server (LFS) is additional software that enables Notes users to send e-mail messages as faxes and receive faxes as e-mail. When faxes are received, the actual fax (which is graphical as opposed to text) is stored as an attachment in the TIFF format. This software comes with the Lotus Image Viewer (LIV) so that the TIFF files can easily be viewed.

Sky-Tel Pager Gateway. The Lotusv pager gateway is an OS/2 server add-in task that enables Notes mail messages to be sent to Sky-Tel pagers. This gateway requires a free COM port and modem so that these messages can be sent immediately.

Microsoft Mail Gateway. This gateway requires a dedicated PC and enables your Notes mail users to transparently communicate via e-mail with Microsoft mail users.

MHS Gateway. The MHS Gateway software is an OS/2 server add-in task that enables Notes mail users to communicate with Novell NetWare messaging services using Novell's Message Handling Server format.

Lotus Connect for X.25 Gateway. This is an OS/2-based add-in task that enables users to connect to an X.25 network.

DEC Message Router. This gateway runs on VAX/VMS and enables Notes mail users to communicate with DEC mail users.

Ca-email+ Gateway. This gateway enables Notes mail users to communicate with Ca-email+ users. It is a CICS-based application for IBM host machines.

Dedicating Servers by Task

When planning your Notes network, if you envision multiple servers, consider dedicating each server to a specific task, which can increase performance and greatly simplify the administration of the network. Some suggested dedicated server types to consider are described in the following sections.

Mail Server. Mail servers store users' mail databases and route mail. Some of the benefits of a dedicated mail server are as follows:

- When the database server is down, users can still access their mail database, and vice versa.

■ Administration is simplified because all of the mail databases reside on one server, and network traffic is reduced because the vast majority of all messages will not route across the LAN.

■ The amount of mail databases you could reasonably expect to store on one server is dependent upon the number of concurrent users you expect at any given time as well as the server platform you are running.

Database Server. A database server could be used to store only application databases. The following are some of the benefits of setting up a dedicated database server:

■ The administration is easier because databases can be grouped by type, replication, or security needs.

■ It's easier for users to find a database when it's only on a limited number of servers.

■ A dedicated server can be "tuned" to achieve optimal performance without considering mail routing, and as the system expands, it's easy to add more database servers.

Dial-Up Server. A dial-up server can be set up to provide a single, secure point of entry into your network for all remote users. Some benefits of a dedicated dial-up server are the following:

■ Security is enhanced because remote users connect with only one server that can provide access to other servers.

■ LAN traffic can be decreased by putting all of the databases that remote users need on the dial-up server.

■ Call tracking and logging is simplified due to single point of entry.

■ Call costs can be monitored and tuned more easily due to single entry point.

Passthru Server. A passthru is a server set up to enable other Notes servers or users running different LAN protocols to communicate with each other through the passthru server. This of course dictates that the passthru server run all of the protocols needed to connect to each network.

After a passthru server has been configured, it can be used as a stepping stone to get to other servers. Users can go through the passthru server to other servers without needing to know all of the routing steps required to make the connection. In addition, dial-up users can call the passthru server and then access other servers on the network from the passthru server.

Some of the benefits of a dedicated passthru server are as follows:

■ Dial-up users can connect to multiple servers with a single phone call.

■ Users on different LANs can communicate with one another through the passthru server.

The passthru server feature is new to Notes 4.5. To set up a passthru server, you must create a Passthru Connection document in the Public Name & Address Book. See Chapter 5, "Using the Address Book," for more information on Passthru Connection documents.

Gateway Servers. A dedicated gateway server can reduce the overhead required to run a gateway as an add-in on a production server. For instance, if you wanted to run the Lotus Fax Server software, it may behoove your company to purchase a separate machine to run it on, as this would reduce the overhead on the Notes server and provide faster performance for the Notes server and the Fax gateway.

Hub Server. A hub server is usually set up as the central server that controls replication and mail routing in a hub-and-spoke Notes network. Hub servers are generally not accessed by end users.

Hot-Swap (Backup) Server. A hot-swap server is a server that is fully configured and ready to go in the event that another, mission-critical, server fails. Users can be redirected to the hot-swap server while the other server is down.

Message Transfer Agent Server (MTA). If your organization runs several MTAs, such as the SMTP and the X,400 MTA, or you will have a large volume of messages passing through an MTA, you should consider setting up an MTA server that does nothing but handle the messaging demands of your installation.

Notes Server Topology Overview

Notes servers can be configured to replicate and route in a variety of ways depending on a number of factors, such as the servers' locations, the number of servers, the frequency with which the servers need to be updated, and the goals of the Administrator (to make administration easier or reduce costs).

Based on these factors, there are three common replication topologies: hub-and-spoke, binary tree, and peer-to-peer, and it's very important to understand the distinction between the Notes network topology as opposed to your actual LAN topology. Notes Network topology determines how servers will replicate and route mail, and is not tied to your actual network topology in any way. For example, your actual network might be comprised of NT servers with a multiple domain model running TCP/IP over Internet in a bus topology, while your Notes servers (running on the NT servers) are configured in a hub-and-spoke scheme. The following sections examine the pros and cons of each of the three Notes topologies.

Hub-and-Spoke Replication

In the hub-and-spoke replication scheme, the hub server initiates all connections, based on scheduled connections (defined in connection documents in the Public N & A Book on the server), and controls replication and mail routing with the spokes (see Figure 24.7). As an example, Table 24.6 displays a subset of four connection documents from the Public N & A Book on the hub.

A Simple Hub-and-Spoke Replication Scheme

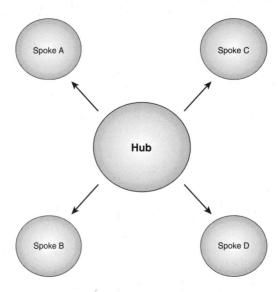

Fig. 24.7 A graphic representation of a small hub-and-spoke network.

Table 24.6	An Example of Hub-and-Spoke Connection Documents			
From Computer	**To Call Computer**	**Call at Times**	**Tasks**	**Use Port**
Hub	Spoke A	11:00 P.M.	Replication, Routing	LAN0
Hub	Spoke B	12:30 A.M.	Replication, Routing	COM1
Hub	Spoke C	2:00 A.M.	Replication, Routing	LAN0
Hub	Spoke D	3:30 A.M.	Replication, Routing	LAN0

This very simple example assumes that all of the servers are in the same domain; that scheduled calling is enabled in each of these connection documents; and that the hub will attempt to call each server only once a day at the specified time.

Based on the connection documents in Table 24.6, the hub first calls Spoke A for replication and mail routing. Exactly 90 minutes later, the hub calls Spoke B for replication and mail routing. Every 90 minutes, the hub calls the next spoke. When all of the spokes have replicated with the hub, the hub then replicates with other hubs, if any exist.

> **Note**
>
> When using the hub-and-spoke replication model, be sure that the connection documents have enough time between scheduled calls to enable the hub to finish replication with one spoke before calling the next. Otherwise, all of the changes may not get transferred correctly.

In this model, all of the necessary connection documents are maintained in the Public N & A Book on the hub server. The following are some of the advantages of this model:

- It enables centralized administration of the Public N & A Book.

- A hub can be used to "bridge" two LANs running different protocols if the hub supports both protocols.

- Most transactions within the domain are a maximum of two "hops" away, mail routing is peer-to-peer in the same domain, and all mail servers are only one hop away. This helps to drastically reduce the amount of network traffic generated on the LAN.

- The hub-and-spoke model scales well as the installation grows. In other words, as new servers are added to the network, the hub-and-spoke model makes it easy to integrate these new servers into the network because you need to add only a small number of connection documents.

Binary Tree Replication

In the binary tree method of replication, one server replicates with two servers at a lower level in the tree, and they in turn replicate with two servers at lower levels until all of the databases have been replicated. Then the servers at the top level replicate with one another (see Figure 24.8).

A Simple Binary Tree Replication Scheme

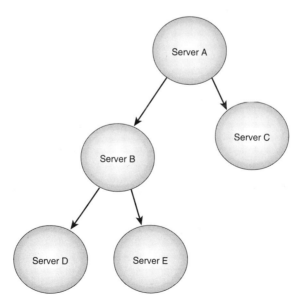

Fig. 24.8 A graphic representation of a simple Binary Tree Replication model.

Because it can take a long time for information to move from the top of the tree to the bottom, this method is generally not as efficient as the hub-and-spoke method.

The binary tree method is often used in large international corporations due to the distances between locations and because of political issues.

Peer-to-Peer Replication

The peer-to-peer method of replication dictates that each server in a domain replicate with every other server in the domain (see Figure 24.9).

A Simple Peer-to-Peer Replication Scheme

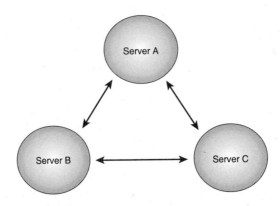

Fig. 24.9   A simple peer-to-peer replication model.

Based on Figure 24.9, the Public N & A Book for the domain needs two connection documents for each database because each database must call all other databases. Peer-to-peer replication is highly inefficient and needs additional administration due to the greater number of connection documents required. This method should be used only in installations that have very few servers.

Notes Named Networks

Another unique, but important, Notes concept is Notes named networks. A Notes named network identifies a group of servers that share a common network protocol and can communicate directly with one another using that protocol.

In a large LAN environment, it is very common to run a number of network protocols such as TCP/IP and SPX/IPX or NetBIOS as certain protocols provide specific advantages over others. For example, NetBIOS is easy to implement and has a very small memory footprint, but it cannot be routed. TCP/IP, on the other hand, has a relatively large memory footprint, but it can be routed and allows easy connections to the Internet.

Because Notes is platform-independent and protocol-independent, you can choose the protocol(s) that best suit the needs of your users. Once you have selected your LAN protocols, you simply need to tell your Notes server which protocol(s) it should use, for example, TCP/IP on the NIC and X.PC (this is the native Notes protocol for serial communications) on COM1. Each individual protocol that a server runs dictates that the server be added to a Notes named network for that protocol.

The name you choose for a particular Notes named network is completely up to you; however, using a descriptive name, particularly in a large Notes installation, can make administration easier. The following are some naming suggestions: Use a network name that reflects the location of the servers, such as Cincinnati. Use a name that indicates the location and network type, such as Lexington TCP/IP. Or just identify the network protocol, such as XPC.

One important reason to group servers in a Notes named network is that users, by default, will see the servers only in their Notes named network. This is by design so as to encourage users to access servers that are close to them, as opposed to accessing servers that are more remote and therefore more expensive to access and slower. For example, when a user in the named network Cincinnati TCP/IP chooses File, Open Database, the list of servers contains only those located in Cincinnati and running TCP/IP.

Tip

Although Notes will not display the names of servers outside your Notes named network in operations such as File, Open Database, if you have been granted access to those servers and a physical path exists, you can access those servers by typing the server's name directly into the servername field.

To view or edit the Notes named network a particular server is in, simply open that server's server document in the Public Name and Address Book and expand the server's Network section, which will display a table indicating the Notes named networks the server belongs to.

Configuring a Notes named network is simple. The server Mars has two ports configured, SPX (running SPX/IPX on one NIC) and TCP (running TCP/IP on a second NIC). Each port is then added to a Notes named network. I arbitrarily chose the names SPX and TCP/IP respectively for the Notes named networks and as I add new servers running these protocols into the network, I'd add them to the aforementioned groups. For each port, a network address can be specified to help other servers find this server. The final step is to then enable or disable the port through the use of the Enable/Disable radio buttons.

Tip

You can put multiple Network Interface Cards (NICs) into a server and bind different protocols to each card. This allows you to use the server to "bridge" the different protocols so that users can access servers and databases outside their Notes named network. For example, you can bind TCP/IP to one card and SPX to another card in the same server which would allow users running SPX to get to Notes resources on the TCP/IP side.

V

Advanced Notes Topics

Understanding Notes named networks is key to successfully implementing Notes. For more in-depth information, please refer to the *Lotus Notes System Administration Guide,* or see the Notes Administration Help database.

The Admin Agent

The Admin Agent in Notes 4.5 is a great boon to Notes Administrators because it helps eliminate the tedious and time-consuming task of cleaning up the Public N & A Book and database ACLs when a user is deleted, recertified, or renamed.

In Notes 3.x, when a user was deleted, recertified, or renamed, the Administrator had to try to ferret out all of the groups that the user's or server's name was in, as well as all database ACLs that might have been affected by the change. The Admin Agent will do the searching for you and automatically take the following actions:

- If a user has been deleted, the Admin Agent will remove that user from all Public N & A Book entries and will remove that user from all database ACLs.

- If a user has been recertified or renamed, the Admin Agent will update all documents in the Public N & A Book related to that user and all affected database ACLs so that the user's new information is reflected.

The Notes Administrator Interface

In Notes 3.x, the Administrator had to use several different levels of non-intuitive menus to accomplish administrative tasks. The Notes 4.5 workstation software now has a new and vastly improved administrative interface that consolidates most administrative functions in one window. To access this new interface, choose File, Tools, Server Administration, which will launch the Lotus Notes Administration window shown in Figure 24.10.

> **Note**
>
> Remember that your ability to use these features will be determined by your server access level. If you are not named in the Administrator field in the server document, you will not be able to use the Server Administration tool.

When the Administration window is displayed, you will see the Choose a server to administer field (and the corresponding list box below it that displays the servers in your Notes Named Network). You will also see several large buttons that enable you to quickly and easily administer certain key aspects of the server.

> **Note**
>
> Notice that some of the buttons have small down arrows displayed on them. When one of those buttons is pressed, you are presented with a menu that displays additional choices. Buttons that do not have the down arrow launch directly into another screen.

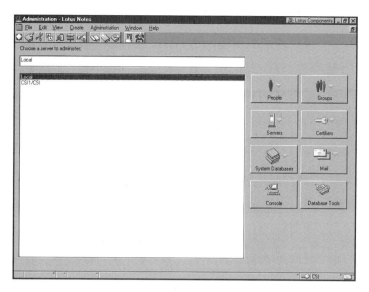

Fig. 24.10 The super cool new Notes 4.5 System Administrator Interface.

Under the Choose a server to administer field, you will see a list box that should display all of the Notes servers in your Public Name & Address Book. You can select any of the servers from the list, and the name of the server should be displayed in the Choose a server to administer field. When you have selected a server, you can click any of the eight buttons described below to begin administrative tasks.

> **Tip**
>
> If you want to access a server that is not displayed in the list and you know the fully distinguished name, you can simply type the server's name in the Choose a server to administer field and press enter. Remember, to access that server with the Server Administrator, you must have been named in the server's Administrators field.

Each of the eight buttons—People, Groups, Servers, Certifiers, System Databases, Mail, Console, and Database Tools—are covered in detail throughout the remainder of this section.

Changing the List of Users

The People button, when pressed, will present the pop-up menu shown in Figure 24.11.

Fig. 24.11 You can use the People button to easily add or maintain Notes users in your installation.

The first option, People View, launches the People view in the Public Name & Address Book so that you can quickly and easily find users.

The second option, Register Person, enables the Administrator to register a new Notes user (which creates a new Person document in the Public Name & Address Book and creates a new User ID file).

The last option, Register From File, allows the Administrator to automate the registration process by registering new Notes users from a previously created text file. The text file requires a certain format for this to work correctly. If you intend to use this feature, be sure to read the Notes documentation.

Changing the Groups

The Groups button presents the pop-up menu shown in Figure 24.12.

Fig. 24.12   You can use the Groups button to add or maintain Notes user groups.

The first option, Groups View, launches the Groups view in the Public Name & Address Book.

The second option, Create Group, enables the Administrator to create a new Group document in the Public Name & Address Book.

Changing the Server Settings

The Servers button displays the pop-up menu show in Figure 24.13.

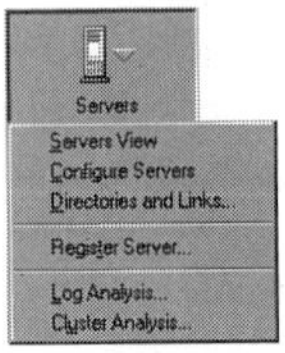

Fig. 24.13   Use the servers button to configure or analyze your servers.

The first option, Servers View, launches the Servers view in the Public Name & Address Book.

The second option, Configure Servers, opens the Public Name & Address Book and launches the Configuration view.

The third option, Directories and Links, launches the directory and link management interface shown in Figure 24.14. This is an extremely handy new feature of Notes 4.5 that makes it easy to view, create, modify, and delete directories and directory links. It also shows you the actual directory each link points at and enables you to add users to the directory links. In the old days, the creation and maintenance of directory links had to be done manually with a text editor and, even worse, there was no way to see what links existed or where they pointed without going out to the OS and looking for them.

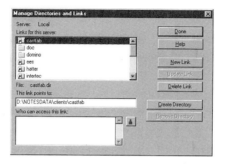

Fig. 24.14   Use the Directories and Links option to launch the Manage Directories and Links dialog box.

The fourth option, Register Server, enables the Administrator to register a new Notes server (which creates a Server document in the Public Name & Address Book and a new Server ID).

The fifth option, Log Analysis, displays a dialog box that enables the Administrator to configure analysis parameters and run an analysis on the Notes Log. This can be extremely useful when doing troubleshooting because it does the searching for you. You no longer have to open the log and manually scan it for specific information. When the analysis is complete, the data is written into the database you specify.

The sixth and final option, Cluster Analysis, displays a dialog box that enables you to perform several types of analysis on servers within a server cluster. When the analysis is complete, the data is written into the database you specify.

Controlling Certification

The Certifiers button displays the pop-up menu shown in Figure 24.15.

Fig. 24.15   The Certifiers button can be used to perform certification and registration tasks from your workstation.

The Certify ID File option enables the Administrator to "stamp" a certificate into an ID file.

The Cross Certify ID file option enables the Administrator to place a cross certificate into an ID file.

Edit Multiple Passwords allows you to perform maintenance on the User ID files that have multiple passwords associated with them.

Register Organizational Unit enables the Administrator to certify an organizational unit ID.

Register Organization enables the Administrator to register an organization ID.

Register Non-Hierarchical enables the Administrator to register a Non-Hierarchical ID.

Accessing System Database Information

The System Databases button drops System Databases on the chosen server and Configure statistics reporting for a given server. The system databases include the Public N & A Book, the server's Notes Log, the Database Catalog, the Statistics Reporting Database, the Administration Requests Database, the Certification Log, and the server's Outgoing Mailbox (see Figure 24.16).

> **Note**
>
> Statistics Reporting is a powerful Notes server administration feature that enables you to track a wide variety of Notes server statistics and thresholds in a special Notes database. If you are responsible for the administration of a Notes installation, look into the features of statistics reporting.

Fig. 24.16   The system databases include the Public N&A Book, the server's Notes Log, the Database Catalog, the Statistics Reporting Database, the Administration Requests Database, the Certification Log, and the server's Outgoing Mailbox.

Mail Options

The Mail button displays the pop-up menu shown in Figure 24.17.

Fig. 24.17   The Mail button can be used to perform key mail-related tasks on the server.

The Open Outgoing Mailbox option opens the server's Outgoing Mailbox (MAIL.BOX) and launches the view that was opened last.

The Send Mail Trace option launches a dialog box that enables you to send a Mail Trace to track a mail message's routing path. This is very useful for troubleshooting mail routing problems.

Controlling the Server with the Remote Server Console

The Console button launches the Remote Server Console dialog box shown in Figure 24.18.

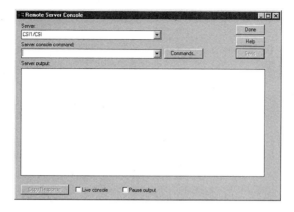

Fig. 24.18   The Remote Server console window can be used to send commands to a server from your workstation.

The Remote Sever Console window enables the administrator to choose a server and send commands to it remotely. This is a very useful tool because an Administrator can troubleshoot or "tweak" a server from a remote location. In order to use the remote console, you must be named an administrator in the server document on the server you want to administer.

Database Information

The last button, Database Tools, displays the dialog box shown in Figure 24.19.

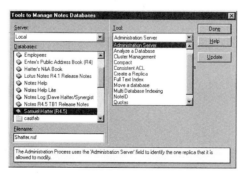

Fig. 24.19   The database-related tools available from the Databases button.

From this dialog box, you can perform a number of administrative tasks. The Server combobox lets you choose the server that hosts the database you are interested in. After you have selected a server, the Database list box presents you with a list of databases on that server. You can then select a database and use the Tools combobox to select an action to perform on the selected database from the following list:

- **Administration Server**—This option lets you set the server that will perform administrative tasks (run the Admin agent), such as updating the ACL when the address book changes.

- **Analyze a Database**—This option enables you to choose a series of things to scan a database for, such as user writes. It also enables you to indicate the time frame for the scan and a database into which the output should be written. This is a very powerful feature because the system can do the searching for you, and present you with a summary.

- **Cluster Management**—If you are using server clusters, this option lets you tell the cluster about the status of a database.

- **Compact**—You can select any database and use the compact feature to free up the white space it contains and even discard the view indexes, which can also free up a tremendous amount of space.

- **Consistent ACL**—This option lets you make a database enforce consistent ACLs across all copies of a database. You must have manager access to the selected database to perform this action.

- **Create a Replica**—This option lets you create a replica copy of the selected database on one or more servers. You must be in the Create Replicas field in the server document of the servers you want to create a replica on.

- **Full Text Index**—This option enables you to set the parameters and create a full text index for the selected database.

- **Move a Database**—If you are using server clusters, you can use this option to move a database from one server in the cluster to another.

- **Multi Database Indexing**—This option lets you include this database in an index that spans multiple servers or databases. You must have manager access to implement this option.

- **NoteID**—This option enables you to enter the NoteID of a document and search a database for the specified document. If the document is found, you can then view the document's fields and properties. This search method works on only one database at a time.

- **Quotas**—This option lets you set various parameters that control the size of database on the server.

■ **Replication**—This option acts as a toggle to enable or disable replication for the specified database. You must have manager access to implement this option.

Notes Server Platforms

Lotus Notes is truly a cross-platform application that is capable of running most popular operating systems. Notes server software is available for Windows 95, Windows NT, OS/2, various flavors of UNIX, and as Novell Netware servers (NLM). Lotus gives you the flexibility to choose the platform that is the best fit for your organization, depending on the networks and operating systems in use at your company. Notes was originally developed for an OS/2 server and the OS/2 server software still provides the most functionality and flexibility, although the other server platforms are rapidly catching up.

Supporting Multiple Licenses

Although a Notes installation can quickly provide a high return on investment, a large Notes installation can be costly. Lotus realized that many Notes users did not need to have access to the full Notes workstation functionality, such as the design tools, and therefore could use a subset of the full client to meet their needs at a reduced cost.

Based on the varying need for access to Notes functionality, Lotus responded by developing three types of licenses that provide different degrees of access to Notes features and functionality. The three types of licenses are the following:

■ **Full Lotus Notes License** —While being the most costly of the three, it enables each user ID created with this type full access to all of Notes core services. Most users, unless they will be doing database design, will not need the full client.

■ **Lotus Notes Desktop License**—This is actually a less costly version of the Full License that has had the database design tools disabled. This license gives users the legal authority to use any Notes database.

■ **Lotus NotesMail License**—This supports the least number of features and is the least costly of the three types of licenses. In fact, users who have been given the Express License are legally obliged to use only the five databases that ship with this license.

Notes supports a heterogeneous mixture of different license types within a Notes installation. For instance, you might be using a Notes Desktop License while your coworker in the next cubicle is using an Express License.

To find out what type of license you have been issued, choose File, Tools, User ID. You will then be prompted for your password. After you enter your password and click enter, you will see the User ID dialog box (see Figure 24.20).

V

Advanced Notes Topics

Fig. 24.20 The License field displays the type of license that you have been granted.

Notes and the Internet: An Overview

By now, you've surely felt the shockwave the Internet has sent through the business world. In fact, if you were to believe the hype surrounding it, you'd most likely not be reading this book as industry pundits have predicted that the Internet will be the death of Notes. However, people who have used the Internet know that it is just not ready for the mission-critical applications that you can build with Notes. In fact, people who truly understand the power of Notes know that Notes and the Internet are complementary, rather than competing, technologies, and Lotus has capitalized on this fact by creating world-class, industry-leading applications than can leverage the Internet to extend the reach of Notes. Lotus has accomplished this through three technologies: The Simple Mail Transport Protocol (SMTP) Message Transfer Agent (MTA), Domino (Hypertext Transport Protocol [HTTP] Services), and the InterNotes Web Publisher. This section will cover each of these services briefly and point to other chapters for detailed information.

The SMTP MTA

Internet mail has become incredibly pervasive both in the business world and in the consumer world. In fact, it's estimated that over 30 million people have Internet connectivity and that number is increasing very rapidly. Lotus saw the need to allow NotesMail users to send Internet mail and provides a powerful native solution in the form of the SMTP MTA.

The SMTP MTA is a powerful, full-featured Message Transfer Agent that not only converts NotesMail messages to SMTP messages and vice versa, but also supports Multi-Part Internet Mail Extensions (MIME), which enables users to send and receive file attachments just as they would in NotesMail, making life easy.

Implementing the SMTP MTA requires several things. First, you must choose a server on which to run the SMTP MTA tasks and configure your Public N & A Book so that mail destined for the Internet is routed to the SMTP MTA server. Second, the server running the SMTP MTA must have a connection to an Internet Service Provider. Once these things are in place, sending a mail message to an Internet user is as simple as sending mail to a Notes user. For example, if your company configures the SMTP MTA and has a connection to the Internet, you can use Notes to drop me a line by composing a new mail message and entering **Dhatter@one.net** in the To: field and then just sending the mail message. Notes will route the mail to the SMTP MTA, which will convert the mail message into the SMTP format and then will route the mail to the ISP who will put the mail "out on the wire."

If you are considering an SMTP solution for your company, the Notes SMTP MTA is an excellent choice.

The InterNotes Web Publisher

The World Wide Web (WWW) is probably the hottest and most exciting of the Internet services and has been one of the primary reasons for the Internet's explosive growth. Lotus also was quick to realize that the WWW is a powerful system that can extend Notes capabilities and was the first company in the industry to develop a Web solution like InterNotes. InterNotes is a series of server tasks that runs on a Notes server and converts selected databases to Hypertext Markup Language (HTML) that can be accessed through the Internet with Web browsers such as Netscape Navigator or Microsoft Internet Explorer.

The way InterNotes works is relatively simple. You install the InterNotes software on a Notes server and ensure that the Notes server starts the InterNotes tasks. Once InterNotes is running, you use the Web Publisher Configuration database to tell InterNotes which databases to publish and how often they should be published. Once this is configured, Notes will "publish" (convert the database into HTML files) on the intervals you define into a subdirectory that you specify. The HTML files can then be propagated ("served-up") to the Internet or an intranet through a Web server such as Microsoft Internet Information Server.

> **Note**
>
> Once the HTML files have been generated, you can edit the file and tweak the HTML to get whatever functions you need. For more on HTML, Que publishes several excellent books on HTML development, such as *HTML by Example* and *Special Edition Using HTML*.

If you want to set up a Web site that requires very little maintenance and contains relatively static information, InterNotes is an excellent solution. This is especially true as you can leverage existing Notes development experience in your organization to build the Notes database, because InterNotes handles the hard stuff for you.

Domino

Domino (Hypertext Transport Protocol services for Notes) is one of the most exciting things to happen in the Internet world for some time. Domino is a series of Notes server tasks that, once installed, convert Notes databases into HTML dynamically as requested by a browser; this is as opposed to InterNotes, which is a more static process.

In a nutshell, this means that you can use a Web browser to not only read information in a Notes database (and see updates to it almost immediately), but also use a Web browser to enter information directly into a Notes database. You can actually create Notes applications that can be accessed over the Web (either over the Internet or an intranet) with a browser or through Notes with a Notes client.

The following scenario demonstrates a typical Domino session based on the following assumptions: Your Notes server is running Domino; the server has a connection to the Internet; and the user has a Web browser.

John Doe is a "road warrior" with Windows 95 dial-up networking and a Netscape Navigator on his notebook. John connects to the ISP from his hotel room and launches Navigator. He enters the URL **http://www.acmecompany.com**, which points to the home page on your Domino server. He clicks the C & S region on the imagemap (which is really a hotspot on a Notes Navigator), which prompts him for a Username and password. Once he is authenticated, he is taken to his Mailbox and his Calendar is displayed. He schedules two new meetings and then checks his mail and accepts an invitation to a meeting next week—all through his browser!

Not only can Domino convert Notes databases to HTML as a browser makes requests (ensuring the most current data is displayed), but it also supports the HTML 3.0 spec (and you can code HTML directly into the database to tweak it), and supports native Notes ACL level security over the Internet. If you want to build a dynamic, high-performance, low-maintenance Web site, there is NO better solution than Domino. For more detailed information on Domino, please see Chapter 27, "Using Domino Server's HTTP Service."

From Here...

In this chapter, we discussed much of the advanced functionality and features of Notes. After reading this chapter, other chapters that you might find interesting and useful include the following:

- Chapter 3, "Using Databases," discusses the Replica ID and database replication further.

- Chapter 5, "Using the Address Book," covers the Public Name & Address Book.

- Chapter 27, "Using Domino Server's HTTP Service," explains how to use Notes with Domino to get the most out of the Internet.

Part VI

Working with the Web

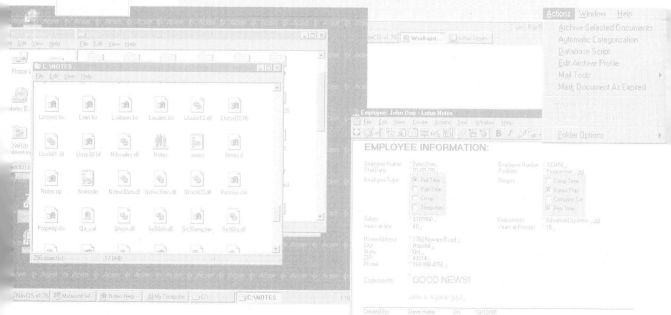

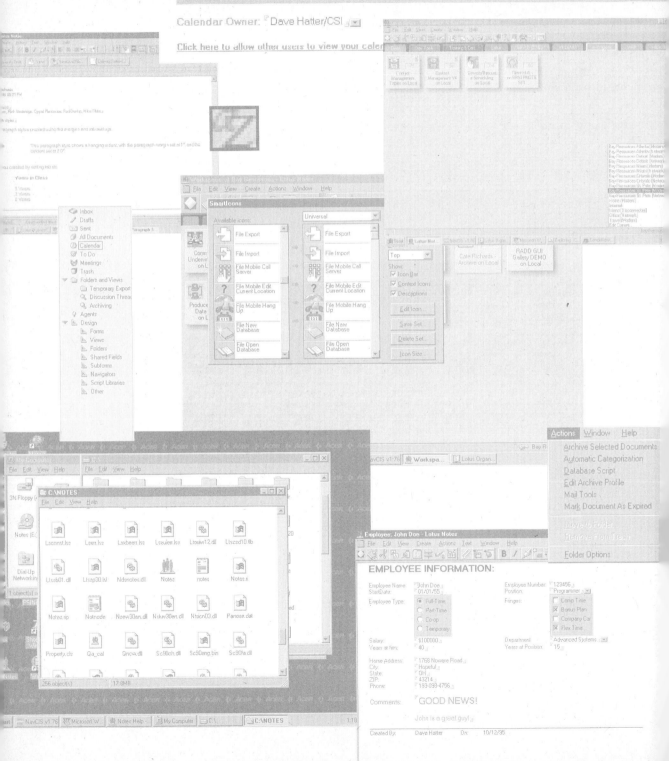

Chapter 25

Lotus Notes and the Web

The next three chapters introduce the Internet enhancements to Lotus Notes/Lotus Domino. This chapter provides an overview of those enhancements. For the reader who is not familiar with the Internet, this chapter provides an overview of the Internet.

A Brief Overview of the Internet

Over the last few years, the Internet has become an inescapable presence in our world. It has been around, in one form or another, since the late sixties, growing slowly over most of that time. But in the last few years, it has caught the imagination of the general public; and its growth has become explosive as the number of people using the Internet has doubled and redoubled and redoubled again in a very short period of time. Now you can barely turn on the television or open a magazine without seeing advertisers' Internet addresses plastered across the screen or page.

The original purpose of the Internet was to encourage communication and collaboration among people doing, first, government research, and later, general academic research. Over most of its duration, the Internet was a ho-hum, text-only medium. Early on, the tools available for using it were hard to master. These things limited the audience and the appeal of the Internet.

As time passed, the usefulness of the Internet for long-distance communication and collaboration caught the attention of more and more people. Users of the Internet added new and better tools and protocols to the tool set. Computer technology became widely and cheaply available.

A few years ago, these trends converged to fuel the Internet's present, explosive growth. Programmers at CERN (European Laboratory for Particle Physics) in Switzerland developed a new kind of research tool that involved rich text documents with links to related documents embedded right in the body of a document. This tool became the World Wide Web. The documents were not just plain text. They were formatted text and they could include embedded objects, such as pictures.

Some of the main topics in this chapter are

- What the Internet is— an overview

- Significant Internet protocols and tools

- Intranets

- Lotus' Internet strategy

Later, programmers at the National Center for Supercomputing Applications (NCSA) created a graphical tool for viewing documents on the World Wide Web. They called this new tool *Mosaic,* and they distributed it for free to anyone who wanted to use it and further develop it.

Mosaic allowed the user to see not only the text of a Web document on-screen, but also the embedded objects—the pictures, the animations, the videos clips, and the sound bites (well, you could only hear the sound bites). Mosaic turned the World Wide Web into a multimedia version of the Internet. By the time this happened, computers that could use Mosaic—Macintoshes, PCs running Windows, and computers running graphical versions of UNIX—were sitting on millions of desks in universities, offices, and homes all over the world. The computers were the tinder. Mosaic was the flint. Together, they sparked the phenomenon that the Internet is today—a fire that consumes the imagination of marketers, programmers, computer makers, and users all over the world.

Mosaic and the World Wide Web are not the sole catalysts that transformed the Internet. UseNet newsgroups, Internet Relay Chat, and Internet-based sound and video transmission have all contributed new ways to use the Internet. Along with the Web, these new technologies have turned the Internet into not merely a handy communication medium and research library, but also a marketplace, a playground, and a hotbed of experimentation in new ways to use networked computers.

Furthermore, the growth of networking in general has fed the popularity of the Internet. At bottom, the Internet is simply a computer network based on standard network communication protocols. Even if you don't have a use for all the newfangled communication and research tools that have been popping up, you can still connect two computers—say two Notes servers—to the Internet, and they will communicate with each other as if they were both on your office LAN. This allows replication and mail routing between your Notes servers.

To companies in the computer industry, the Internet is a huge opportunity, a huge risk, and a threat to their livelihoods. Someone will make a lot of money selling products that power the Internet, many people will lose a lot of money trying, and many others will wake up one morning to discover that their products no longer have a market because they aren't Internet products.

Thus, we are witness to the browser wars. The programmers who wrote Mosaic later left the NCSA and formed a company, Netscape, where they wrote and released Netscape Navigator, an enhanced version of the Mosaic Web browser. Netscape Navigator (commonly referred to as just "Netscape") quickly gained a dominant market position of maybe 80 percent penetration.

Microsoft woke up one day and realized the Internet boat was about to leave the dock without them. Microsoft has managed, through its monopoly on the PC operating system market, to become dominant in all of the desktop software markets. When they realized they were about to be stranded on the DOS/Windows island as the whole world embarked for the "new world" of the Internet, Microsoft transformed themselves overnight into an Internet products vendor and hopped on board. Microsoft has since made it its goal to knock Netscape off its perch. As a result, throughout 1996, Netscape and Microsoft released new versions of their Web browsers—Netscape Navigator and Microsoft Internet Explorer—every three months or so, adding bells and whistles at a furious pace, and all but giving the products away.

The Internet—What It Is

The Internet is the granddaddy of all internetworks. Its defining characteristic is the TCP/IP protocol suite.

People who work with computer networks define them as follows: Two or more computers connected to each other on a single, shared segment of cable (through which they communicate) constitute a *local area network* (*LAN*). Two or more LANs connected to each other by an internetworking device such as a bridge or a router constitute an *internetwork*. If two LANs are so physically distant from each other that you could not practically wire them to each other directly, but must use the resources of the telephone company to connect them—and you do so—the resulting internetwork constitutes a *wide area network* (*WAN*). Any network that exists primarily so that other networks can connect to it is a *backbone* network. The Internet is thousands of networks, all over the world, connected to each other primarily through the telephone networks, which constitute backbone networks.

A *protocol* is a set of rules. A *computer networking protocol* defines how computers on a network will communicate with each other. A *protocol suite* is a set of protocols that are related to each other and build on each other. There are many protocol suites, including TCP/IP, IPX/SPX, NetBEUI, SNA, AppleTalk, and others. Most protocol suites were developed by corporate enterprises and are, therefore, proprietary. The evolution of the Internet from the Defense Department experiment included, among other things, the development of the TCP/IP protocol suite; therefore, TCP/IP is not proprietary. For any computer to be considered "on the Internet," it must use TCP/IP. If your computer does not use TCP/IP, it can still communicate, via a *proxy server*, with computers on the Internet; but your computer is not itself *on the Internet* if it does not itself use TCP/IP.

The TCP/IP suite includes scores of protocols, most of which are acronyms like TCP and IP, but some of which are more cleverly named, like *gopher*. Some of the Internet protocols that are important to your understanding of Notes and its relationship to the Internet include the following:

- **Internet Protocol (IP)**—This is the basic communication protocol that computers use when they transfer information back and forth. All the other Internet protocols rely and build on IP. Some programs use only IP when transferring information to another computer.

    Among other things, IP defines Internet addressing. Every computer on the Internet must have a unique address. IP addresses consist of 32 bits of information that is usually presented in dotted-decimal format—that is, as a series of four decimal numbers, separated from each other by periods. Each number may be from one to 254. So, an IP address might look like this: 123.123.123.123

- **Serial Line Internet Protocol (SLIP) and Point-to-Point Protocol (PPP)**—These are the versions of IP that you will use if your computer is not connected to a LAN and you have to connect to the Internet by dial-up telephone. You will use one or the other, not both. PPP is a later, more powerful version of SLIP.

- **Transmission Control Protocol (TCP)**—Adds reliability to IP data transmissions, among other things. Notes uses TCP, not just IP, to transfer data to other Notes computers.

- **Domain Name Service (DNS)**—Since most human beings (not including system administrators) don't want to bother with remembering numeric computer addresses (see previous IP addressing bullet), the Internet also permits you to give your computer a host name under the Domain Name system.

  Under this system, every computer (or host) belongs to a super domain, which may be one of the three-letter domains such as **gov** (government), **mil** (military), **edu** (educational institution), **org** (non-profit organization), and **com** (commercial enterprise). Or it may be a two-letter country code such as **us**, **uk**, **jp**, **au**—the list goes on.

  Within the super domain, your computer belongs to a private domain, which may in turn have sub-domains defined. Thus, a computer named **www.lotus.com** has host name **www**, and is a member of the **lotus** domain, which is in turn part of the **com** super-domain. When sending information to that computer, you can address its **host.domain** name instead of its IP address. Domain name servers that exist in each domain work together to resolve the host name of each computer to its IP address.

- **HyperText Transfer Protocol (HTTP)**—World Wide Web servers and browsers communicate with each other and transfer files to each other using this protocol. It, too, builds and relies on IP. A Notes server running Domino Web Publisher understands both HTTP and Notes' proprietary method of transferring data to Notes clients and other Notes servers.

- **HyperText Markup Language (HTML)**—This is the set of codes and syntax rules that define the formatting of documents on the World Wide Web. A document written in HTML is called an *HTML document*. If you look at the document with a Web browser, it appears to be fully formatted. If you look at it with a text editor, you see that it is just plain text with some strange looking codes tossed in here and there. The codes are enclosed in angle brackets (< and >). HTML also encompasses the embedding of hypertext links into HTML documents. A hypertext link is a pointer to another document. When you click a hypertext link, your Web browser will send an HTTP message to the computer named in the link, requesting the document named in the link.

- **Uniform Resource Locators (URLs)**—These are addresses of computers and the files on them. The format of an URL for a computer is ***protocol://hostname.domainname.superdomain*** where ***protocol*** is a protocol that the computer named in the URL should use to interpret the accompanying message, and ***hostname.domainname.superdomain*** are the DNS host name of the target computer.

The format of an URL for a file is ***protocol://hostname.domainname.superdomain/dirname/filename***, where **dirname/filename** is the location of the file on the target computer. An example of an URL for a computer would be **http://www.lotus.com**. This indicates that the computer, **www.lotus.com**, should interpret the accompanying message using HTTP. It could only do so if it has Web server or client software running on it.

- **File Transfer Protocol (FTP)**—This is the original Internet protocol that defines how files will be transferred from one computer to another. Nowadays, you can transfer files using either FTP or HTTP.

- **Simple Message Transfer Protocol (SMTP)**—This is the protocol that defines how e-mail messages will be formatted, addressed, and delivered. SMTP does not provide for rich text messages, attached files, or hypertext links. As such, SMTP is what some refer to as a *first-generation mail system* (where file attachment capability defines a second-generation mail system, rich—or formatted—text defines a third-generation mail system, and hypertext links define a fourth-generation mail system, such as Lotus Notes).

- **Multipurpose Internet Multimedia Extensions (MIME)**—A mail program that complies with MIME can send and receive messages with file attachments and with rich text content. In other words, MIME extends SMTP and other protocols. Your MIME-compliant mail program is effectively a third-generation mail program.

- **Post Office Protocol, version 3 (POP3)**—If your computer does not remain connected to the Internet around the clock, then a computer that is constantly connected must hold your incoming mail for you until you do connect and then receive your mail. POP3 defines a way for this whole transaction to take place.

- **Network News Transfer Protocol(NNTP)**—UseNet newsservers use this protocol to transfer data back and forth.

- **Gopher**—This protocol defines how Gopher servers store and organize information.

- **Secure Sockets Layer (SSL)**—The Internet is notoriously insecure. The early Internet protocols took security considerations pretty lightly, because the Internet, at that time, was a closed system available only to insiders. As the Internet has become a public network accessible to anyone, the lack of security features has become its Achilles heel. The great promise of the Internet, in particular the World Wide Web, to commercial entities is that it will become a huge marketplace where you will shop for and buy their products.

But everyone knows that you can't risk sending your credit card information over the Net. Various entities have been working on this problem. Several security schemes have been proposed. One, SSL, proposed and implemented by Netscape, seems to be gaining wide acceptance (including an implementation by Lotus in Domino Server) and may become an Internet standard for implementing secure financial transactions. SSL works much like Notes security. You and the party you want to do business with both receive certificates that identify you from a trusted third party. That way, no impostor can pretend to be the second party that you think you are dealing with. Then you use public key/private key encryption to authenticate each other and protect your data transmissions from eavesdroppers.

Internet Tools

Since the Internet has from its earliest days served as a medium of communication and research, the first available user tools served those purposes. Over time, Internet users have developed more sophisticated tools but, generally, they still serve the purposes of enabling electronic communication, research, and collaboration. The earliest Internet tools still in use include the following:

- **Terminal Emulation**—The Telnet protocol allows a person sitting at one computer to control and run programs on a remote computer.

- **E-Mail**—Electronic messaging, in the form of the Simple Message Transfer Protocol (SMTP), allows people remote from each other in time and place to carry on long-term conversations.

- **File Transfer**—File transfer, in the form of the File Transfer Protocol (FTP), allows collaborators in research projects to more easily work together and share the results of their work with each other.

As time has passed, the original communications and research tools have been augmented with newer and better tools. Some, certainly not all of them, are listed here.

The communication tools are as follows:

- **Internet Mailing Lists**—These are list servers, or computers that maintain mailing lists of people's e-mail addresses. If you are on a mailing list, you can send a message to the list server that maintains it, and the list server will broadcast your message to all the other people on the list. These provide a great way to hold ongoing, special interest discussions among people who can't easily get together face-to-face.

- **UseNet Newsgroups**—These are Internet-based discussion groups, or bulletin boards. You can post messages on newsservers. Others can reply to your messages. Everyone can read and follow the resulting conversations. This is another good way to hold discussions among widely dispersed people.

- **Internet Relay Chat (IRC)**—These are "live" discussion rooms. You type a short message and hit Enter. Your message appears on the screens of everyone in your "chat room." Their messages appear when they hit enter. Live conversation.

- **Internet telephone programs**—This is one-to-one, live voice conversation. Just like real telephones, it is cheaper for long-distance calls but has much lower voice quality and reliability.

- **CU-SeeMe**—This is one-to-one, live voice conversation with video. You can watch each other as you talk to each other.

- **Internet radio and television**—Live or recorded, this is voice or video transmission via Internet into your computer.

- **PointCast Network**—This is customized news feeds via the World Wide Web right to your browser.

The research tools are as follows:

- **Archie Servers**—These servers maintain searchable lists of computer-based documents. Need to find research documents about Elvis sightings? Search for them on Archie servers, which will return lists of documents that meet your search criteria.

- **Wide Area Information Servers (WAIS)**—These are like Archie servers, except they maintain full-text indexes of their libraries, so you can search the bodies of the documents, not just their titles and keyword lists.

- **Gopher**—Gopher servers let you browse their contents, and the contents of other Gopher servers, in a menu interface. Choose an item on a Gopher menu. It may open to a deeper menu or a document. The menu or document that it opens to could be on the same or a different Gopher server. The universe of Gopher servers interconnected in this way is sometimes called *Gopher-space*. You might call the menus *hyper-menus* because they transport you instantly across space to another server entirely.

- **World Wide Web**—This is mostly what has caught the imagination of the world and fueled the phenomenal growth of the Internet. Documents in Web servers are connected to each other with hyperlinks. That is, embedded in one Web document are pointers to other Web documents that relate to the first one contextually. You research a topic by activating the hyperlinks and scrolling down page after page until you find the one(s) that have the information you need.

- **Finger**—You can use Finger to find the names of people in a specific domain, so that you can send e-mail to them.

The World Wide Web

The World Wide Web is a system of servers and clients. The Web servers store documents, called *Web pages*, in HTML format, and send them to Web clients on request. The more advanced Web servers, like the Lotus Domino Web Server, may also store pages in database format and convert them to HTML when sending them to requesters. The clients, called Web browsers, request and receive the pages from the servers, format them according to the embedded formatting codes, and display them to you. The browsers request documents from the servers by sending a document's URL to the server. If a browser sends an URL that only names the Web server and not a specific page, then the server sends a default page, known as the *home page*, to the browser. The server sends pages to the browser, or sends a reply if the page is unavailable, using the HTTP protocol.

The most capable Web browsers can do lots more than just request and receive HTML pages from Web servers. They can also retrieve Gopher menus from Gopher servers, directory listings and documents from FTP servers, and articles from newsservers. They can send Finger requests. They include a POP3 mail reader. It used to be that you needed different programs to do all of these things. The day may soon arrive when your Web browser does it all.

Like Lotus Notes documents, HTML documents can store virtually any kind of information. They consist of plain text plus embedded formatting codes, or *tags*, that look something like this: *<HTMLCODE>*, where *HTMLCODE* is some actual text string that has a specific meaning to a Web browser. A given code might tell the browser to italicize (<I>) the text that follows or to center (<CENTER>) the paragraph that follows. It might tell the browser to insert a horizontal rule at this point (<HR>). It might tell the browser to retrieve a graphics file from the server and insert it at this location (<IMG SRC="image.location">).

That last example is significant. The browser interprets the code to mean that it should retrieve another file. The example specified a graphics file. But similar codes can specify any kind of file. Among the kinds of files that a browser might retrieve are programs that the browser might execute on the spot. Or, when the file arrives, it might be accompanied by a MIME specification that tells the browser which helper application it should start up that can execute the program properly or otherwise handle the data file correctly. Thus your browser might start up a program that can play an audio or video file. If your browser can execute Java or ActiveX or programs, then you might see an animated graphic right in a Web page displayed on your screen, or a spreadsheet might pop up so that you could calculate, say, a mortgage payment. The possibilities are endless.

Intranets

The Internet is a public network, available to anyone who wants to connect to it, virtually anywhere in the world. An intranet is a *private* network that uses Internet protocols.

Many companies have realized how the Internet and the World Wide Web can enhance communication and collaboration in teams of people scattered all over the world. These companies would like to take advantage of the Internet but are afraid of opening their internal computer networks to the lawlessness of the Internet. A popular compromise has been to borrow the technology of the Internet—the IP, HTTP, HTML, FTP, and other protocols—and use them internally but without any connection to the Internet, per se. The result is an intranet. Notes and its Internet extensions work just as well on the Internet or a corporate intranet.

Lotus' Internet Thrust—Toward Total Integration

Like everyone else in the computer industry, Lotus is scrambling to establish its presence and identity in the Internet. For Lotus, the rise of Internet hysteria is an especially great opportunity. In case you haven't noticed, the core purposes of the Internet and of Lotus Notes are nearly the same. Both the Internet and Notes were originally developed to promote communication and collaboration among groups of people who need to work together but who are rarely if ever in the same room at the same time.

It must have been vexing to Lotus to watch the World Wide Web steal Notes' fire, especially since the Web can do many, but not all of the things Notes has been doing for years. On the other hand, Notes is better poised than any other product, by far, to become *the* killer Internet application. If Lotus can just play its cards right—if it can properly integrate Notes with the Internet, and if it can get the attention of all the people who are so excited about the potential of the Internet and convince them that Notes is the obvious tool for realizing the Internet's potential—then Lotus could be the dark horse that wins the race for Internet dominance.

Lotus' strategy is to offer Notes/Domino as an Internet applications server—that is, a Web server that incorporates Notes functionality. Lotus' two main thrusts in accomplishing this goal have been, first, to integrate core Internet protocols right into Notes and, second, to develop a series of add-on products that enhance the value of Domino as an Internet applications server. Significant Internet-related enhancements to Notes and add-on Notes products include the following:

- **Built-In Internet protocols**—For years, Notes servers and clients have been able to communicate with others using the TCP/IP protocol suite. Beginning with Release 4.0, Lotus began incorporating extended Internet protocols, including HTML/HTTP into Notes. Release 4.5 includes HTML/HTTP, FTP, Gopher, MIME, and finger protocols in the Notes client and HTML/HTTP, SMTP/MIME, and POP3 in the Domino server.

- **Combined Notes/Web Server**—Domino Server is both a Web and a Notes server. It stores data both in Notes databases and, optionally, as HTML documents in an HTML data directory. It serves up Notes documents to Notes clients and to Web clients, HTML documents, or Notes documents converted to HTML format.

- **Internet Mail Server**—Because the Domino Server complies with the SMTP, MIME, and POP3 protocols, it can serve as a post office for SMTP/MIME mail clients and as an SMTP message transfer agent. Domino Server can also act as post office for MAPI mail clients.

- **Server Clustering**—This is part of Domino Advanced Services, which is an extra-cost add-in to the Domino Server. Server clustering permits configuring multiple Domino servers to replicate with each other in real time and to appear to the user as a single server. It provides fault-tolerance, load balancing, and fail over.

- **Server Partitioning**—This is also part of Domino Advanced Services. You can create multiple server partitions on one computer, which causes the computer to appear to users as multiple Domino servers. This is useful if you want to host multiple Web sites on one computer or if you want to host multiple Domino applications on one computer.

- **Usage Tracking and Billing**—This is also part of Domino Advanced Services. You can track and compile system usage and use the information to bill users or to monitor trends.

VI

Working with the Web

■ **Web Navigator**—This is a Web browser built right into Notes. If a Notes user has access to the Internet (or an intranet), he/she can use Notes to browse Web sites, Gopher sites, and FTP servers. Retrieved pages are stored in the Web Navigator database. See Chapter 26, "Using the Web Navigator," for details about this product.

■ **Lotus Weblicator**—This brings Notes functionality, including the Notes object store, replication, and agents, to non-Notes Web browsers. In effect, it turns third-party Web browsers, such as Netscape Navigator and Microsoft Internet Explorer, into "Notes Lite." With Weblicator running alongside them, they can retrieve Web pages into a Notes database on the browser computer. You can then use the browser like a Notes client to view the downloaded Web pages off-line. Since they are stored in a Notes database, you can index and search through them; you can sort and categorize them various ways; you can edit them or fill in CGI forms off-line. Then you can reconnect to Domino servers and replicated back to them any pages you edited. Or you can reconnect to a third-party Web server any CGI forms you filled in off-line. Weblicator also includes agents that will automate the retrieval of Web pages.

■ **Web Publisher**—This is Lotus' first Notes-to-Web product. With it, you can publish selected Notes databases to a third-party Web server and, under some circumstances, retrieve information from Web users back into a Notes database. See "Working with the Web Publisher" on the CD-ROM for details about this product.

■ **Notes News**—This is a gateway between Notes/Domino servers and UseNet newsgroups. Since newsservers are simply a form of bulletin board or discussion forum, they are analogous to Notes discussion databases. Notes News converts selected newsgroups to Notes discussion databases. The articles posted in the newsgroups become Notes documents in the Notes discussion databases. Notes users can then follow the newsgroup discussions without ever having to access the newsservers directly. If a Notes user contributes to the discussion, Notes News converts the user's contribution to a News article and submits it to the newsserver.

■ **Notes Network Information Center (NotesNIC)**—This is a service provided on the Internet by Lotus (actually by its subsidiary Iris Development Corporation, the developers of Notes) to all Notes-using organizations. It is a Notes domain that resides on the Internet. You can set up a Notes server of your own in the NotesNIC domain. Being your server, you control what databases reside on it and all access control lists.

Being in the NotesNIC domain, the server's public address book includes the servers of all other organizations that have joined the NotesNIC domain—in other words, hundreds of other Notes organizations. You can set up easy mail delivery and database replication between your organizations by going through your respective NotesNIC servers.

■ **NetApps**—To make it as easy as possible for a Notes organization to quickly set up a powerful, Domino-based Web site, Lotus has developed NetApps. These are templates from which you can, by filling in a series of forms, generate a whole, interactive Web application. You don't have to develop the applications or create the databases yourself. Just fill in the forms and NetApps does all the programming for you. The purpose of filling in the forms is so you can customize the resulting applications to your own needs, using your own names and vocabulary.

The templates available with NetApps include the following:

- **Notes:Newsstand**, available since January 1996, lets you design and publish electronic newsletters, newspapers, and magazines as pages in short order as pages on your Web site. Notes provides the page design and populates the pages with the content you specify.

- **Domino.Action** is bundled with Domino Server. Use it to bring up a full-service Web site, including home page, corporate information pages, user registration database, discussion/feedback database, and more.

- **Domino.Marketing**, announced but not yet released, will generate a Notes/Web marketing application. It will include a catalog builder, a payment mechanism, and SSL security.

- **Domino.Service**, announced but not yet released, will generate a Web-based customer support application.

- **Domino.Broadcast for PointCast** will use Domino Server and PointCast I-Server software to allow you to set up a news feed by which you can pipe company news via PointCast to any PointCast subscriber.

In essence, what Lotus is trying to accomplish here is to make Notes and Domino Server indispensable to anyone who wants to accomplish anything more elaborate on the Web than simple publishing. By marrying Notes technology to Web technology, Lotus gives you the tools to create powerful, interactive Internet applications with ease. Then Lotus makes it even easier by offering application generators that do all the work for you. All you have to do is set up Notes and Domino on a server, connect the server to the Internet, and fill in a series of questionnaires. The application generator then creates all the Notes databases for you.

From Here...

Lotus has set forth and largely implemented a powerful strategy for integrating Notes with the Internet. The following chapters discuss several Notes Internet features in detail:

- Chapter 26, "Using the InterNotes Web Navigator," examines the setup, use, and advanced features of Notes' integrated Web browser.

- Chapter 27, "Using Domino Server's HTTP Service," examines a Lotus-to-Web piece of Lotus Notes.

VI

Working with the Web

Chapter 26

Using the Web Navigator

With the huge rise in popularity of the Internet over the past couple of years, Lotus realized that it had to incorporate Internet connectivity into Notes. With the release of Notes 4.0 in January 1996, Lotus incorporated a World Wide Web browser into Notes. Called Web Navigator, the Web browser in Notes 4.0 worked through the Notes server.

Starting with Notes 4.5, Lotus has enhanced Web Navigator so that now you can browse through the Notes server, as before, or directly from your workstation. You no longer have to be attached to a Notes server to browse the Web. Also, you can use Notes to browse the Web or Notes will call your favorite Web browser for you. Please note that *Navigator* and *browser* are used interchangeably in this chapter.

Understanding Web Navigator

Web Navigator is a Web browser built into Notes, along with a companion Notes database that stores the Web pages retrieved by the browser. Actually, there are two versions of Web Navigator—the server version and the personal version. In the server version, the browser and the database, named Web Navigator, both reside on a Notes server (although you can put a replica copy of the database on your workstation, if you want). The server that they reside on is called the Notes server. In the personal version, the browser and the database (this one is named Personal Web Navigator) both reside on the Notes client.

The user can browse the World Wide Web, or the corporate intranet, by either entering an URL into a dialog box or clicking an URL in a Notes document. Whether the server or client does the actual browsing—and whether browsing occurs at all—depends on a setting in the user's current Location document. This allows the user to use the server version sometimes, the personal version other times, and no browser at yet other times.

Some of the main topics in this chapter are

- How Web Navigator works

- How to set up Web Navigator

- How to search the Web with the Server and Personal Web Navigators

- How to share Web pages with Notes users

- How to store and use stored documents in the Server and Personal Web Navigators

VI

Working with the Web

For example, Jane, an ace account rep, works all morning at her New York City office, preparing for tomorrow's meeting with her client in San Francisco. She flies there during the afternoon and spends the night in a hotel. While in the office, her Office Location document specifies that she use the server version of Web Navigator. On the plane, she has no Internet connection and so cannot browse, not online at least. However, if she has a Personal Web Navigator database or a replica copy of the Server Web Navigator database on her laptop, she can browse within the database. Her Island Location document specifies No Retrievals in the Retrieve/open pages field, so if she clicks the URL of a document not in the database, Notes displays an error message. In the hotel, she switches to a Travel Location document, which specifies From Notes Workstation in the Retrieve/open pages field. She dials out to the Internet with her modem and, when she opens an URL, Notes automatically uses the Personal Web Navigator to browse.

Working with Web Navigator

When you enter an URL in Notes, or click one in a Notes or Web document in Notes, exactly what happens depends on what choices you have made in your current Location document. There you can choose to browse indirectly through a Notes server, directly from your Notes client, from a third-party Web browser, or not at all.

If you have chosen to browse with the Server Web Navigator, then your copy of Notes forwards the URL to your designated server. A server task called Web Retriever forwards the URL to the destination server. If the destination server returns a page, Web Retriever converts it to Notes format. Then the Database Server task stores it in the Server Web Navigator database and forwards a copy to you, which your copy of Notes displays on your screen (see Figure 26.1).

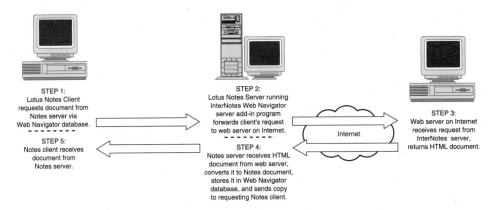

Fig. 26.1   When you use the Server Web Navigator, your server retrieves pages for you.

If you have chosen to browse with the Personal Web Navigator, then your own copy of Notes sends the URL to the computer named in it. If the other computer responds by sending a Web page back to you, Notes converts that Web page to Notes format, stores it in the Personal Web Navigator database, and displays it to you on-screen (see Figure 26.2).

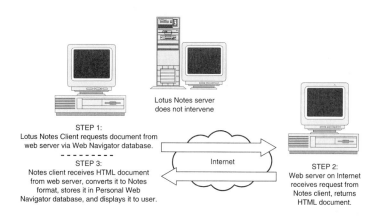

STEP 1:
Lotus Notes Client requests document from
web server via Web Navigator database.

Lotus Notes server
does not intervene

Internet

STEP 3:
Notes client receives HTML document
from web server, converts it to Notes
format, stores it in Personal Web
Navigator database, and displays it to user.

STEP 2:
Web server on Internet
receives request from
Notes client, returns
HTML document.

Fig. 26.2   When you use the Personal Web Navigator, your own computer retrieves Web pages directly, without intervention by a Notes server.

Actually, when you enter or click an URL, Notes may not forward the URL to another computer at all. If you ask for a page that Web Navigator has retrieved recently, it may simply return to you the copy sitting in its database.

This is one of the advantages of using Notes to browse the Web. You can quickly download a whole series of Web pages into your Web Navigator database without spending much time in them. Then you can disconnect and read the pages more carefully offline, at your leisure, without accumulating connect charges.

Notes works a little differently when you browse the Web than it works when you explore non-Web-related Notes databases. When you open standard Notes documents, each document appears in its own window. However, when you browse with Web Navigator, your Web pages all appear in the same window. They designed Notes to browse this way because Notes can only open nine sub-windows at most. When you browse the Web, you tend to open so many Web documents so quickly that, if Notes opened a window for each one, you would quickly reach the maximum number of windows and then would have to stop and close a window every time you want to jump to a new one. No fun.

As you browse, Notes maintains a history of the pages you view. You can see the pages listed in the History dialog box. You can open this by clicking the History button that appears whenever you view a Web page. You can jump directly to any listed page by double-clicking its title in the History dialog box.

Setting Up Web Navigator

You don't have to install Web Navigator. It is part of Notes and was installed along with Notes. To use it, however, you have to do a bit of setup. The setup requirements are not the same for Personal Web Navigator and Server Web Navigator.

Setting Up Personal Web Navigator

To use Personal Web Navigator, you have to take the following steps to set it up:

1. Meet system requirements for running Notes on your system. See the Notes Workstation Install Guide and the Notes 4.5 Release Notes for more information on Notes system requirements.

2. Use a Location document that specifies From Notes Workstation in the Retrieve/open pages field. All of the Location documents that come with a plain vanilla installation of Notes default to From Server, so you must change the field before you can use Personal Web Navigator. The Notes administrator can set this up before or after installing Notes on your computer, or you can do it yourself at any time.

3. Open an URL, either from the menu by choosing File, Open URL, or from a Notes document by clicking an embedded URL, which appears underlined in green. This causes Notes to create the Personal Web Navigator database. The database receives the default name of `perweb45.nsf`, is based on the `perweb45.ntf` design template, and receives and stores all pages retrieved by the Personal Web Navigator.

System Requirements for Personal Web Navigator. The system requirements for Personal Web Navigator, over and above those for the Notes client itself, are the following:

- A connection to the Internet or intranet
- TCP/IP running on your workstation
- 500M free hard disk space

The last one isn't really a requirement, but a recommendation by Lotus. Lotus knows that you tend to accumulate Web pages fast when you surf the Web, and your Personal Web Navigator database is likely to get big. There is no specific minimum amount of disk space necessary to run Personal Web Navigator. But remember the axiom: You can never have too much disk space (or RAM or processing power or video resolution or network bandwidth or, well, you get the picture).

If you are connecting to the Internet, there are three possible ways:

- A direct connection, via your Local Area Network (LAN) or leased telephone line, to an Internet Service Provider (ISP)
- A direct connection, via modem, to an ISP
- An indirect connection to an ISP, via a proxy server, to which you will probably connect by LAN

When you are connected to your company's LAN, you probably connect to the Internet across the LAN, either directly to an ISP or indirectly through a proxy server. If you are at home or in a hotel room, you connect directly to an ISP using your modem.

If you are connecting to your company's intranet, you either connect directly across the LAN or, if you are out of the office, directly by modem or indirectly by proxy server. Because proxy servers protect your LAN from unauthorized access by outsiders, there is no need for you to use a proxy server when you are on the LAN. But going through a proxy server may be the only way to get to your intranet when you are on the outside.

In any event, you must have the TCP/IP protocol stack in your computer's memory to use the Personal Web Navigator. The TCP/IP protocol stack is the hallmark of the Internet and intranets. Without it, you are not on the Internet/intranet.

Setting Up a Location Document for Personal Web Navigator. To browse with Personal Web Navigator, you must be using a Location document that specifies From Notes Workstation in the Retrieve/open pages field. All of the Location documents that come with a plain vanilla installation of Notes default to From Server. Notes interprets this to mean it should use the Server Web Navigator, so someone must change the field before you can use Personal Web Navigator. The Notes administrator can set this up before or after installing Notes, or the user can set it up before using Personal Web Navigator for the first time.

If you are a Notes administrator and you intend for your users to use Personal Web Navigator rather than Server Web Navigator, the most efficient way to set them up is to create and assign a Profile document to new users when you register them. In the Profile document, you can specify From Notes Workstation in the Retrieve/open pages field. When you set up the user's workstation, the Location documents inherit that setting (see Figure 26.3).

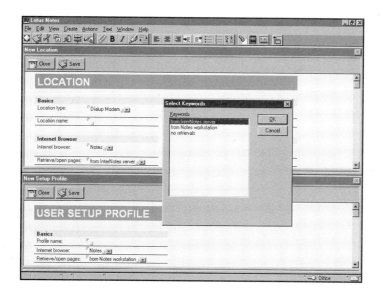

Fig. 26.3 Both Location documents and User Setup Profile documents have a Retrieve/Open pages field. Clicking the button in the field opens the displayed dialog box.

If users will use a proxy server to reach the Internet, you can also enter the proxy server addresses into the Profile document. The user Location documents will inherit those settings too.

Finally, you can set forth in the Profile document what actions Notes will take when it receives a Web page that includes a Java applet. A Java applet is a program, and can potentially damage your software and data. Or, it can make network connections to other hosts and give them access to your system and data. Notes allows you to list trusted hosts—computers from which you are reasonably sure you will never receive damaging Java applets—and specify what degree of access to your computer's resources are permitted to Java applets from either trusted or untrusted hosts (see Figure 26.4).

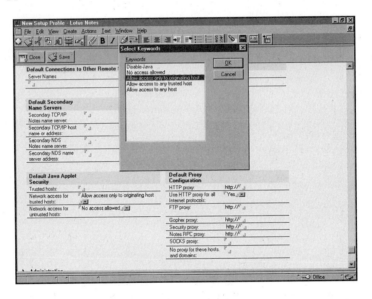

Fig. 26.4   Here are the Default Proxy Configuration and Default Java Applet Security sections of a User Setup Profile form. The dialog box shows the choices available in the Network access for trusted hosts field.

The choices for the Network access for trusted hosts fields include the following five choices. The choices for the Network access for untrusted hosts field include the first three of the following choices:

- **Disable Java**—Notes does not run Java applets.

- **No access allowed**—Notes does not permit a Java applet to expose your computer's resources to any computer.

- **Allow access only to originating host**—Notes permits the Java applet to expose your computer's resources only to the computer from which it obtained the Java applet.

- **Allow access to any trusted host**—Notes permits the Java applet to expose your computer's resources to any computer in your list of trusted hosts. This is the default setting.

- **Allow access to any host**—Notes permits the Java applet to expose your computer's resources to any other computer.

If the Notes administrator did not have the opportunity or foresight to set up the location document using a User Setup Profile document, then either the administrator or the user will have to make changes to the appropriate Location documents themselves. In addition to the Retrieve/open pages field, the proxy server fields, and the Java security fields that were duplicated in the User Profile Setup document, the following are some other fields that may affect your Web browsing:

- **Internet browser**—Choose your Web browser here. Defaults to Notes, but you can choose to have Notes display Web pages in another Web browser whenever you open an URL.

- **Web Retriever Configuration Section**—In this section of the Location document, you control several aspects of the behavior of the Personal Web Navigator. They include the following five fields:

  - **Web Navigator database**—Holds the file name of the Personal Web Navigator database. If you ever decide to rename or change the location of the database, enter its new path name here.

  - **Concurrent retrievers**—This is the number of retriever processes that can reside in memory concurrently. If you want to browse more intensively than you can with four retrievers, increase this number. Be sure to increase your RAM as well, 2M for each additional retriever.

  - **Retriever log level**—Notes logs retrieval activity to your Notes log by default. You can reduce the logging or turn it off entirely here.

  - **Update cache**—The default is Never. The first time the Web Navigator receives a request for a page, it gets it from the designated Web server. It stores the page in the Web Navigator database and displays a copy to you. Thereafter, when you request that page again, the Web Navigator delivers the cached copy of the page instead of retrieving it anew from the Web server. By the default of this field, Web Navigator never checks with the Web server to discover whether the page has been updated since first retrieved. You can change this to Once per Session or Every Time. If you choose Once per Session, the Web Retriever does not check with the Web server if you ask for the same page again in the same browsing session, but it does check with the Web server if you ask for the page again in a future browsing session. If you choose Every Time, then every time you ask for a cached page, before the Web Retriever delivers the cached copy of the page, it queries the originating Web server to see whether a new version of the document is on the server.

VI

Working with the Web

- **Accept SSL site certificates**—The default is No. Change it to Yes to accept Secure Sockets Layer (SSL) certificates from computers with which you do not otherwise share a certificate issued by a third-party Certification Authority (CA). Then, if you do accept a certificate from a computer, you have to take it on faith that the computer you are talking to is really the computer it claims to be, because by accepting a certificate from the computer, you have no way of knowing who issued its public and private keys. However, you still get the other two benefits of SSL security—encryption of data transmissions between the two computers and assurance that no tampering with any secured message has occurred en route. See Chapter 27, "Using Domino Server's HTTP Service," for more information about SSL.

■ **Java Applet Security Section**—In this section of the Location document, you control the way Personal Web Navigator handles incoming Java applets. The first three fields in this section are the same as the ones in the User Setup Profile document described earlier. If a certifier assigns a User Profile Document to a user at registration time, the entries in those fields in this Location document are inherited from the User Setup Profile when the new user's workstation is set up.

This section has one additional field, Trust HTTP Proxy, that was not in the Java security section of the User Setup Profile. This field is only relevant if you access the Internet through an HTTP proxy server. The default is No, meaning that your computer makes its own determination of whether the host from which a Java applet is received is a trusted host. If you cannot run a Java applet, it may be because your computer cannot resolve the Web server's host name to its IP address. Changing this field to Yes tells your computer to assume that the HTTP proxy server successfully resolved the host name with the IP address, and to go ahead and run the applet according to the Trusted host/Untrusted host settings of the other fields in this section.

Creating the Personal Web Navigator Database. The last step of setting up the Personal Web Navigator is to create the Personal Web Navigator database. You don't have to do this yourself. All you have to do is retrieve a Web document. Do this any of several ways: choose File, Open URL in the menu and entering an URL; click the Open URL SmartIcon and enter an URL; or click an URL embedded in any Notes document. You will recognize an embedded URL because it looks like an URL (for example, **http:// www.lotus.com**) and it is underlined in green.

Tip

If URLs in your Notes documents are not underlined in green and Notes doesn't try to retrieve the document when you click the URL, it is probably because you have not enabled the automatic conversion of URLs to Notes hotspots. To enable automatic conversion, follow these steps:

1. Choose File, Tools, User Preferences in the Notes menu. The User Preferences dialog box appears.

> **2.** In the <u>A</u>dvanced Options field of the User Preferences dialog box, add a checkmark to the list next to Make Internet URLs (**http://...**) into Hotspots.
>
> **3.** Click OK to accept the change.
>
> Next time you see an URL in a Notes document, it should appear and act as a Notes hotspot.

When you retrieve that first Web document, Personal Web Navigator creates the Personal Web Navigator database in the Notes data directory on your computer, then tries to retrieve the Web page. If it retrieves it successfully, it puts the page into the new database.

At this time, the Personal Web Navigator database also sets up a configuration document called Internet Options that you can use to fine tune the way the database works. The Internet Options document has generally acceptable default settings, and you may never have to change it. However, the first time you open the Personal Web Navigator database, a dialog box will appear presenting you with the opportunity to review the Internet Options document and make any changes in it that you want. Except for that last step, the setup of Personal Web Navigator is now complete, and you can retrieve Web documents to your heart's content.

Setting Internet Options in the Personal Web Navigator Database

Startup Options. Here you can specify what happens when you open the Personal Web Navigator database. By default, it opens to a standard Notes three-pane interface in which you see a list of views in the upper-left corner, the documents in the currently selected view in the lower-left corner, and the currently selected document previewed on the right. You can instead open to a home page. To do so, you edit the following two fields:

- Put a checkmark in the box labeled Open Home Page on Database Open.

- Optionally, enter the URL of the home page to which you want to open in the Home Page field. It defaults to **www.notes.net**, which is the home page of Lotus's InterNIC Web site.

Search Options. A preferred method to locate information on the Web is to use a search engine to search indexes of documents. This field permits you to choose a default search engine from several popular ones. It defaults to Yahoo!, but you can choose Alta Vista, Excite, Lycos, or enter the name of any other search engine you prefer. Whichever search engine you choose, it is not the one you will use to search your Web Navigator database; for that you will use Notes' own search engine.

Web Ahead Agent Preferences. In the Preload Web pages field, you can choose to retrieve pages one, two, three, or four levels ahead of the current page. If you have not enabled Web Ahead, a button labeled Enable Web Ahead also appears in this section. If the button does not appear, Web Ahead has been enabled. For more information on the Web Ahead feature, see the section "Using the Web Ahead Agent in Personal Web Navigator to Retrieve Multiple Related Pages" later in this chapter.

VI

Working with the Web

Page Minder Agent Preferences. Page Minder is an agent that watches for updates to chosen Web pages and notifies you when it finds them. It runs only when your Notes workstation is running, and it can function only when you are connected to the Internet, but it can keep you up-to-date on important events effortlessly. For details on how to use the Page Minder agent, see the section "Using the Page Minder Agent in the Personal Web Navigator" later in this chapter.

Following are the fields in Page Minder agent preferences:

- **Search for updates every**—You can choose to search every hour, every four hours, every day, or every week. The default is every day.

- **When updates are found**—By default, the agent mails you a summary notifying you that the page has changed. In this field, you can change that to Send Me the Actual Page and receive the updated page in your mail.

- **Send to**—This automatically lists you as the addressee for change notices. You can add or substitute other addressees if you want.

Database Purge Options. With all these agents (not to mention enthusiastic humans) gathering pages from all over the Net and dropping them conveniently into your Personal Web Navigator database, you can imagine how quickly it takes over your hard disk. To combat this cancer, you can set up automatic purging of old files in the database. By default, this is enabled. But you can change this to Reduce Full Pages to Links If Not Read Within, or Remove Pages from Database If Not Read Within, and then set a time limit. The time limit defaults to 30 days. You can change that to 60 or 90 days. Reduce Full Pages to Links means that the pages are purged from the database, but their URLs are retained. You will still see the purged pages in the Personal Web Navigator database and, if you click one, Personal Web Navigator retrieves it anew for you.

You can also have Notes warn you when the Personal Web Navigator database exceeds 5, 10, 25, or 50 megabytes in size.

Collaboration Options. One of the drawbacks of using the Personal Web Navigator instead of the Public Web Navigator is that you do not get the benefit of other people's browsing experience. The Public Web Navigator database holds not only your pages but also those of other people browsing through the Public Web Navigator. When other people think a page is particularly useful, beneficial, just plain cool, or, for that matter, really bad, they can rate the pages. Public Web Navigator averages together the ratings that different people give to a page. Over time, you can really benefit from one another's experiences and opinions.

While you cannot benefit in this way from others' experiences when you use Personal Web Navigator, you can give them the benefit of your experiences by sharing Web pages you have found, as well as your ratings of them. To do that, enter the name of a Notes server in the Server field and a Public Web Navigator database in the Databasefield in the Collaboration Options section of the Internet Options document.

Then, when you encounter a page that you especially want to bring to others' attention, click the Share button in the Action bar. A dialog box, shown in Figure 26.5, appears from which you can choose one of the following three options:

- **Forward only the URL**—This mails the URL to whomever you specify.

- **Copy page to shared Web Navigator database**—This copies the page to the database specified in the fields in the Internet Options document.

- **Create Rating in shared Web Navigator database**—When you select this, a rating form appears in the dialog box. Rate the document from one to five, choose a category for it, write your comments, and click OK. Notes forwards the page to the Public Web Navigator database and creates a Rating document there as well.

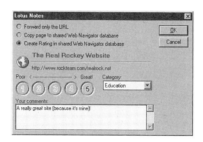

Fig. 26.5   This dialog box permits you to share Web pages with others. You can even share your opinion of a Web page.

Presentation Preferences. Web documents are made up of plain text and embedded codes. The codes are part of the Internet protocol known as HyperText Markup Language (HTML), and they define the formatting of the document. Web browsers interpret the codes and replace them with formatting, so that you and I see a formatted document, not a bunch of inscrutable codes. You can affect how Web Navigator interprets the codes by altering the contents of the following fields:

- **Anchors**—These are the URL links that appear on HTML pages. They appear, by default, underlined and in blue. You can change this.

- **Body Text**—This defaults to 11pt Times. You can change it to 10 or 12pt and to Helvetica or Courier.

- **Fixed**—This is the typeface (defaulting to Courier) used within code pairs that begin with <CODE>, <KBD>, <SAMPLE>, and <TT>.

- **Plain**—This is the typeface (defaulting to Courier) used within code pairs that begin with <PLAINTEXT>, <PRE>, and <EXAMPLE>.

- **Address**—This is the typeface (defaulting to Times) used within the <ADDRESS> code pair.

- **Listing**—This is the typeface (defaulting to Courier) used within the `<LISTING>` code pair.

- **Save HTML in Note**—Notes converts HTML documents to Notes format, then saves them in this database. By default, Notes discards the HTML source code. Checking the box in this field causes the server to save the HTML source code in a field called HTMLSource.

Network Preferences. This last section of the Internet Options document includes a button that, when you click it, loads the current Location document so you can edit it and change your network preferences.

Setting Up Server Web Navigator

Before you can use Server Web Navigator, take the following steps to set it up:

1. Meet system and network requirements and those for running the Notes server.

2. On the Notes server, load the Web Retriever into memory.

3. In the Server documents of the Home/Mail servers of the users who will be using a given Notes server, enter the server's fully distinguished name in the Notes server field.

4. Notify and train your users.

System Requirements for Server Web Navigator. System requirements for the server running Server Web Navigator, over and above those for a standard Notes server, include the following:

- Potential additional memory and disk space requirements

- Specific network requirements necessary to connect the server to the Internet or company intranet

Whether you need additional RAM or disk space on the Notes server depends on how much demand your users will make on Web Navigator. You can assume that the Web Navigator database will grow very large; you should reserve at least 500M of disk space for it; that is the default maximum size for it.

Beyond that, the general rule is that for each additional Web Retriever process (over the default number of 25), you add in the Concurrent Retrievers field of the Notes server's Server document, the following:

- 2M RAM to the base RAM requirements for your server platform

- 10M disk space to the default page file size for your server platform

Second, you must have access of some sort to the Internet or a company intranet; otherwise, there is no Web to browse on. You obtain access to the Internet through an Internet service provider (ISP). ISPs are connected to the Internet and they are in the business of extending their Internet connections to "the rest of us."

There are several ways to classify connections to the Internet. One distinction is between direct and indirect connections. You have a direct connection if your computer has an IP address issued by the InterNIC and can communicate directly with all the other direct-connected computers on the Net. You have an indirect connection if, IP address or not, you can only communicate with the computers on the Internet through a proxy server. That is, you send an URL to the proxy server and it sends the URL to the Web server on your behalf. The proxy server receives the page back from the Web server and forwards it to you.

Sounds sort of like browsing the Web with the Public Web Navigator, doesn't it? In fact, the Public Web Navigator *is* a proxy server. It, in turn, may be using yet another proxy server. And you may have the capacity to connect directly to the Internet. But, when you are using Public Web Navigator, you are connecting indirectly. In fact, one of the most attractive features of the Public Web Navigator is that you don't have to connect every-one in the office to the Internet; you can connect just the Notes server and let all the users connect indirectly through it.

You may very well have both direct and indirect connections. You may have a direct connection when you are dialing in from home and an indirect connection when you are in the office. The Internet is an infamously insecure and lawless place. (Or is it an *un*-place?) Network administrators are famously skittish about the security of their data. So it is not at all uncommon for company local area networks (LANs) to be insulated from the Internet by firewalls and proxy servers.

Another distinction is between LAN-based connections and dial-up connections. Your computer may be connected to a LAN that is, in turn, connected to the Internet through a Router. Or, you may have to dial in to the Internet using your computer's modem or maybe a shared modem on the LAN.

LAN-based computers typically have more or less permanent access to the Internet. They also may have very high-speed access to the Internet. Say you are sitting in your office, reading your Notes mail, and a message arrives with an URL in it. You click the URL and the page arrives in your computer in about three finger-snaps. Either the page was in the Web Navigator database already, or you have a LAN-based connection to the Internet. Except, if the page was already in the Web Publisher database, then it would have arrived in *one* finger-snap. Having the page already in the database is unquestionably the fastest way to retrieve it to your screen.

With dial-up access, you click the URL, then a message appears asking if you want to dial a certain phone number. You answer yes, then you wait while the computer dials and handshakes with the other computer (unless you have ISDN phone service, in which case dialing and handshaking are almost instantaneous). Then you play a little Solitaire, read your snail mail, get a cup of coffee—or you watch the numbers climb slowly as the page arrives, bit-by-bit, over the phone line. Modem access to the Internet is not fast.

VI

Working with the Web

> **Tip**
>
> Get the fastest modem available. If ISDN isn't too prohibitively expensive in your area, and if you can find an Internet Service Provider (ISP) that provides it, get ISDN. It is four to eight times faster than the fastest analog modem.

If your computer is connected to a LAN and you are not connecting to the Internet through a proxy server, then you probably have a permanently assigned IP address. If you dial in to an ISP, your IP address is probably assigned to you at the beginning of the call and reassigned to another caller after you hang up.

If you actually have to set up all this stuff yourself, and you don't already have a pretty good idea how to do it, you may want to hire an ISP or a network/communications consultant to help you out. Meanwhile, refer to the documentation and help databases that come with the Notes server, especially the Web Navigator Administrator's Guide, which is available as both a printed book and a Notes database located in the doc subdirectory of the Notes data directory. See also several databases available on Lotus's Web site, including The Internet Cookbook and Notes and the Internet. Lotus's Web site is located at **http://www.lotus.com**.

Starting and Stopping the Web Retriever. Notes servers all come with Web Navigator installed. But they don't run it automatically. You connect it to the Internet/intranet (see preceding section) and you run the Web Retriever server task. To run the Web Retriever manually, you enter the following command at the server console or remote server console:

```
load web
```

Pretty hard, eh? To unload the Web Retriever, you enter the following command:

```
tell web quit
```

To set up a server so that the Web Retriever starts automatically whenever the server starts, edit the server's NOTES.INI file by adding the word Web to the ServerTasks variable. When you finish, the ServerTasks variable looks something like this:

```
ServerTasks=Replica,Router,Update,Stats,AMgr,Adminp,Sched,CalConn,Web
```

If the server is running when you edit NOTES.INI, you must bring the server down and restart it before it recognizes the change. Instead of doing that, however, you simply load the Web Retriever manually with the load web command.

Configuring the Server Web Navigator. The one thing you have to do to enable the Public Web Navigator, other than start it up, is tell the users about it. By that, I mean not only that you should inform your users, but also that you tell their copies of Notes that this is the server they should go to when the user requests a Web page. When that happens, the Notes client program is going to look around for the identity of the designated server.

First, the Notes client looks in the current location document at the server field. If a server is identified there, the Notes client tries to send the URL there. If that server is unavailable or refuses for any reason to play, or if the server field in the Location document is empty, then the Notes client looks to the Server document of the user's Home/Mail server, and looks in the server field there. If that field is empty, or the server named there won't play, then the request for the page fails.

So, the administrator's first job is to enter the name of the Notes server in one or both of those fields. Because it is a whole lot easier to fill in one field on one or a few server documents than it is to fill them in on, say, hundreds of Location documents scattered all over creation, the administrator adds the server's fully distinguished name to the Server documents of the Home/Mail servers of the users who should use that server. You don't really have to worry about the Location documents after that, except to override the Home server document. An example of when you would do that is the traveling employee. She spends most of her time in the New York City office. Her Home server is in that office. But when she is visiting clients in L.A., San Francisco, and Seattle, she switches to Location documents for each of those cities. Among other things, those Location documents name Notes servers in those cities, so that she doesn't have to reach all the way back to New York to surf the Net.

The administrator *can* predefine the entries to key fields in the Location documents for people he/she registers in the future as Notes users. That is, the administrator can create one or more User Setup Profile documents in the Public Address Book. User Setup Profile documents set forth a series of default entries that Notes can use when it sets up a new user workstation. At that time, Notes creates a Personal Address Book for the user and generates and adds to it several Location and Connection documents. Notes uses the settings in the User Setup Profile document to set up the Location and Connection documents properly.

The User Setup Profile Document Settings. Several settings in the User Setup Profile document are relevant to Web Navigator. These settings are as follows:

- **Internet browser**—The default is Notes, but the user can specify another browser instead. Here the administrator can define the default browser.

- **Retrieve/open pages**—The default is From the Notes Workstation. In other words, by default, when people want to retrieve Web pages, they use their Personal Web Navigator to do it. If the administrator wants users to use the Server Web Navigator instead, or wants to disable Web browsing, he should change this field to either From Server or No Retrievals.

- **The Default Java Applet Security fields**—These are three fields that define how the Notes client handles pages that have Java applets embedded in them. Because Java applets are actual programs that the Notes client can run, the potential exists that they could damage the software and data on the computer or open network connections to other computers, thereby exposing your computer's and network's resources to outsiders. These fields let you define what computers Notes accepts or does not accept Java applets from, and how it handles them when it does. See the section "Setting Up a Location Document for Personal Web Navigator," earlier in this chapter, for more information about these fields and their settings.

■ **The Default Proxy Configuration fields**—These fields let the administrator define the URL of any proxy servers the users will be using.

For more information regarding the use of User Setup Profile documents, see the section "Setting Up a Location Document for Personal Web Navigator," earlier in this chapter.

The Server Document Settings. The server document also governs how the Web Retriever runs. This time it is the Notes server's Server document that governs. The following fields are located in the Web Retriever Administration section of the Server document:

■ **Web Navigator database**—This is the filename of the Public Web Navigator database. If you want to change the name of the actual database, you have to change it here as well.

■ **Services**—Web Navigator supports five Internet services, including HTTP, HTTPS, FTP, Gopher, and Finger. Here you control which ones are available to users. By default, only HTTP, FTP, and Gopher are available.

■ **Concurrent retrievers**—The default is 25, meaning the server services up to 25 simultaneous requests for documents. If the server sees heavy Web usage and slow responses to Web retrieval requests, increase this number. But remember to increase the amount of server RAM by 2M and the size of the page file by 10M for every retriever added.

■ **Retriever log level**—The default is None; there is no logging of Web Retriever activity. If you want to log this activity to the server console and the LOG.NSF file, change this to Terse or Verbose.

■ **Update cache**—The default is Never. The first time the Web Navigator receives a request for a page, it gets it from the designated Web server. It stores the page in the Web Navigator database and sends a copy to the requesting user. Thereafter, whenever someone requests that page again, the Web Navigator delivers the cached copy of the page instead of retrieving it anew from the Web server. By the default of this field, Web Navigator never checks with the Web server to discover if the page has been updated since first retrieved. You can change this to Once Per Session or Every Time. If you choose Once Per Session, the Web Retriever does not check with the Web server if you ask for the same page again in the same browsing session, but it does check with the Web server if you ask for the page again in a future browsing session, or if some other user asks for it. If you choose Every Time, then every time anyone asks for a cached page, before the Web Retriever delivers the cached copy of the page, it queries the Web server to see if a new version of the document is on the server.

■ **SMTP Domain**—When a user clicks a mailto URL on a Web page, Notes composes a new mail message addressed to the person named in the URL. The person's address looks like ***personsname@domainname.xxx***. If your organization uses the Lotus SMTP Mail Gateway to route mail to the Internet, you must append that to your gateway's foreign domain name. Let's say you always mail to the Internet by addressing to ***personsname@domainname.xxx@internet***, where ***internet*** is the gateway's foreign domain name. Notes appends ***@internet*** to the mailto address if you enter ***internet*** into this field.

■ **Allow access to these Internet sites**—By default, you can access all Internet sites. If you enter site domain names or IP addresses into this field, you are, in effect, saying, "Allow access to only the listed sites and no others." Administrators can use this field to severely restrict the number of Web sites users can visit when using the Public Web Navigator.

■ **Deny access to these Internet sites**—By default, no sites are denied to the user. If you enter site domain names or IP addresses into this field, you are saying, "Allow access to all sites except those listed here." Administrators can use this field to keep users out of a relatively small number of sites.

The Web Navigator Administration Document Settings. Finally, the Web Navigator database itself has a configuration document called Administration that further governs the way Web Navigator works. The trick here is to figure out how to find the Administration document. You won't find it in any views. The only way to open it is as follows:

1. Open the Web Navigator database. The Home Navigator appears.

2. In the menu, choose File, Database, Access Control. If your name appears in the list, select it. If not, but a group appears that you are a member of, select that group. If you are not named individually and you do not belong to any groups that are listed here, then select Default. In the lower-right, note whether a checkmark appears next to the Role called [WebMaster]. If no checkmark appears, then you do not occupy that Role and you are not able to open the Administration document. Sorry.

3. Click Database Views in the lower-left corner of the Navigator. The Database Views Navigator appears.

4. Choose All Documents, then open the Actions menu. If you are a member of the [WebMaster] role, then Administration should appear there. Click it. The Administration document opens at last.

In the Web Navigator Administration document, the following fields appear.

Server Basics. This section includes basic information about the Notes server. It includes the following four fields:

VI

Working with the Web

- **Server name**—This is the fully distinguished, canonical name of the server that populates this database. The database could be replicated onto other servers, but only the server named in this field adds documents to it.

- **Maximum database size**—This is the maximum size this database is permitted to reach. The default is 500M.

- **Save author information**—By default, the server does not save the identity of the user who originally retrieved a page from the Internet. Add a checkmark to the box to cause the server to start saving that information in a field called Save_Author. If you do save author information, then you must create a view to see the information.

- **Save HTML in Notes**—Notes converts HTML documents to Notes format, then saves them in this database. By default, Notes discards the HTML source code. Checking the box in this field causes the server to save the HTML source code in a field called HTMLSource.

Purge Agent Settings. The Web Navigator database has a built-in agent, called the Purge agent, intended to help the administrator manage the size of the database. The Purge agent purges old and large documents from the database. You can configure how it works by setting the following variables:

- **Purge agent action**—By default, it purges by reducing a document, which means it throws out the document but keeps the URL. As a result, the page continues to appear in views and, if anyone chooses to open it in the view, Web Retriever goes and gets a fresh copy of it. You can change this field to Delete page, which deletes the page from the database entirely.

- **Purge to what % of maximum database size**—When the purge agent runs, it purges enough documents to reduce the database to, by default, 80 percent of its maximum size as set in the Maximum database size field. At 500M, by default, in that field, 80 percent reduces to 400M. Because the purge agent runs nightly, the defaults give the Web Navigator database 100M of leeway for new documents in any one day.

- **Purge documents older than**—The purge agent purges the oldest documents first, and, by default, looks for documents older than 30 days.

- **Purge documents larger than**—The purge agent also purges the largest documents first, looking, by default, at documents larger than 256K.

- **Purge Private documents**—When a user retrieves pages from a Web site that requires authentication, the retrieved pages are not placed in the general views of the database for all to see. Rather, they are encrypted with the requester's public key, so that only the requester can open them, and they are placed in a folder that is private to the requester, so that other users don't even know the pages are in the database. This field allows the administrator to tell the purge agent to delete these private documents, which the purge agent would not do by default.

HTML Preferences. These are the same preferences that appear in the Internet Options document in the Personal Web Navigator database. They were described earlier in the section "Presentation Preferences."

Using Web Navigator

You can retrieve Web pages from almost anywhere in Notes. But the pages almost always end up in one or the other of the Web Navigator databases. So surfing the Web in Notes is largely a matter of understanding how the Web Navigator databases work and what you can do with them. While they both act as repositories of Web pages, they look different from each other and have different features and capabilities. This arises largely from their different goals and audiences.

Public Web Navigator

Public Web Navigator has been around since Notes 4.0 arrived in January 1996. It was designed with the goals of introducing the World Wide Web to groups of people who might not have previously experienced it, of extracting synergies from the Web surfing experiences of groups of people, so that individual members of the group might benefit from the collective experiences of the whole group, and of letting employers limit the amount and kind of surfing employees do on company time. Public Web Navigator has a Navigator front end that invites the novice user to explore the unknown terrain of the Web by clicking hotspots and discovering where they lead. Also, Public Web Navigator has tools that allow you to share good and bad Web surfing experiences with each other. Finally, because the Notes server actually does the Web browsing for you, you can only surf where and when the server is willing.

The first time you open the Public Web Navigator, you will probably see the Home Navigator, as shown in Figure 26.6. It consists of a bunch of hotspots that, when you click them, load a Web page, open another Navigator, or open a dialog box.

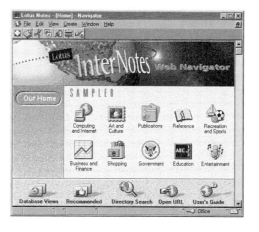

Fig. 26.6   With Public Web Navigator, you get a flashy Navigator. Click one of the icons and see where it takes you.

One hotspot, called Our Home, takes you to the home page of the Notes Network Information Center (NotesNIC), unless someone has customized the Web Navigator database, in which case it may take you to your own company's home page.

The hotspots in the Sampler section of the Home Navigator all take you to another Navigator. The name of the Navigator varies, depending on which hotspot you click. They all look alike, though, showing you hotspots that open three of the more popular Web search engines. Alongside this Navigator, you see a view that displays the documents in the Web Navigator database that fall in the chosen category. Thus, you can browse the database for documents of the chosen type, or you can search the Web for more such documents. In Figure 26.7, the Entertainment appears.

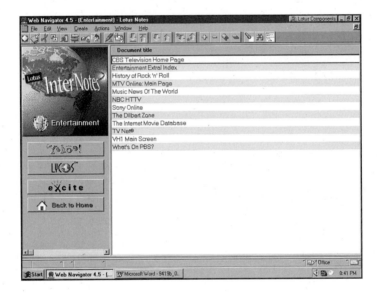

Fig. 26.7 The Entertainment Navigator appears when you click the Entertainment Hotspot in the Sampler section of the Home Navigator.

The icons along the bottom of the Home Navigator have the following functions:

- **Database Views**—Opens the View Navigator, which lists various Views of the Web pages already stored in the database

- **Recommended**—Opens the Recommended Navigator where you can see the Rated documents

- **Directory Search**—Displays a search form that lets you perform searches with Internet search engines

- **Open URL**—Displays a dialog box in which you enter the URL of a Web page in order to open it

- **User's Guide**—Opens the online Web Navigator User's Guide database

When you click Database Views in the Home Navigator, the View Navigator opens. Here each hotspot opens a particular View of the contents of the Web Navigator database. Table 26.1 describes each button in the View Navigator.

Table 26.1 The View Navigator Buttons	
Button	**Click This Button to...**
My Bookmarks	Open pages you saved in your Bookmarks folder. To add a page to the Bookmarks folder, drag and drop the page onto this button. You add pages to the Bookmarks folder from the Web by clicking Bookmarks, selecting My Bookmarks in the Move to Folder dialog box, and clicking Add.
Folders	Open a standard Folders Navigator.
All Documents	Display all the Web pages stored in this database.
By Host	Display all Web pages sorted by their host site.
File Archive	Display all file attachments and their sizes.
Web Tours	Display all the saved Web Tours.
Recommended	Open the Recommended Navigator.
Back to Home	Return to the Home Navigator.

The Server Web Navigator Action Bar. When you open a document stored in the Web Navigator database, an action bar appears. It is unlike the action bars in other Notes databases (except the Personal Web Navigator database). Rather, it emulates the action bars that you see in Web browsers such as Mosaic, Netscape Navigator, and Microsoft's Internet Explorer. This action bar helps you browse the Web (see Figure 26.8).

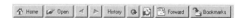

Fig. 26.8   The action bar of the Public Web Navigator emulates the action bar you see in Web browsers.

The buttons in the action bar serve the functions listed in Table 26.2.

Table 26.2 Action Buttons	
Button	**Click This Button to...**
Home	Go back to the Home Page Navigator
Open	Open the Open URL dialog box
Previous	Go to the previous page in the History file
Next	Go to the next page in the History file
History	Open the History dialog box to save pages to the History or go to other pages listed in the History
Reload	Reload the current Web page from the Internet server
Recommend	Open the dialog box to enter your rating of the current Web page
Forward	Forward the Web page to someone by e-mail
Bookmarks	Store the current Web page in the Bookmarks folder

The Server Web Navigator Search Bar. The Search Bar in Notes 4.5 is actually a dual purpose tool. You can use it to enter an URL and retrieve a Web page, or you can search the Web Navigator database for text you enter in the Search Bar. You toggle between the two modes by clicking the icon at the left end of the Search Bar.

In the Web Navigator databases, the Search Bar appears when you are in a View or when a Web document is open; however, when a document is open, you can only use the Search Bar to retrieve Web pages. In other databases, the Search Bar only appears when you are in a View, not when a document is open. The Search Bar appears by default only in databases that have been full-text indexed. If you don't see the Search Bar, select View, Search Bar.

The two versions of the Search Bar are potentially confusing (see Figures 26.9 and 26.10). Make sure the proper icon is showing for the type of search you want to perform. When you want to retrieve a Web page, you may need to click the Search icon to switch to Open URL mode. When you want to search for text within the pages of the database, you may need to click the Open URL icon to switch to Search mode.

Fig. 26.9   Here the Search Bar is in Web retrieval mode. Note which icon appears on the left. Note what words appear in the buttons on the right and compare to Figure 26.10.

Fig. 26.10   Here the Search Bar is in full-text search mode. Note which icon appears on the left. Note what words appear in the buttons on the right and compare to Figure 26.9.

The buttons on the Open URL Search Bar are described in Table 26.3. The buttons in the Full Text Search Bar are described in Table 26.4.

Table 26.3   The Buttons on the Open URL Search Bar

Button	Description
Open URL	Sets which type of Search Bar you're using.
Text box	Enter the URL you want here.
Open	Click to open the specified URL.
Reset	Click to clear the URL name.
History	If you are connected to the Internet/intranet when you click this button, Notes displays the History dialog box, from where you can go directly to any page you have visited during the current session. If you are not connected to the Web, nothing happens when you click this box.

Table 26.4 The Buttons on the Text Search Bar	
Button	**Description**
Search	Sets the Search Bar to search for text in the database.
Text	Enter the word or phrase you're looking for.
Create Index	This button only appears if the database is not indexed. Click it to start the index creation process.
Add Condition	The Create Index button becomes the Add Condition button after you create the index. Use it to display the Search Builder dialog box, where Notes does most of the work of building your search query.
Search	Click here to activate the search.
Reset	Click here to clear the search results from the View pane. The query that produced the search remains in the Search Bar for you to edit.
Search Menu	Drops down a menu of search options. The programmers couldn't think of a short description (like, say, "menu") for the button, so, in the spirit of "one word is worth 1,000 pictures," they used an inscrutable diagram instead.

To search for text, your database must be full-text indexed. If it is not, the first button in the Search Bar is Create Index. Click it to open the Database Properties InfoBox to the Full Text panel. There you can set options, and then begin the index creation process. If you create an index for a Local database, you may have to wait around while Notes creates it. If you have not enabled local background indexing in User Preferences, you will have to wait around. If you have enabled local background indexing, you will still have to wait for Notes to create the index, but you can read your mail or something while waiting because Notes will create the index in the background. If it is a large database and Notes is making you wait, go get a cup of coffee or something.

Personal Web Navigator

The Personal Web Navigator was introduced with Notes 4.5 in response to the need of people to surf at times when they might not have an server handy. It is intended primarily to meet the needs of individuals, not groups. Therefore, it does not have a fancy front end like Public Web Navigator. It opens to the standard Notes split-screen—except that, in this case, the preview pane is open by default and it takes up most of the screen when it is open, so that we see a three-pane screen (see Figure 26.11). Personal Web Navigator has tools to enable the individual Notes user to gather information on the Web and keep up with changes in it; and it lacks the restrictive features included in the Public Web Navigator, which makes sense.

The default list of views and folders includes the following:

- **All Documents**—Shows all the Web pages in the database.

- **Bookmarks**—Use this folder to save your favorite Web pages for quick access later. To add a page to the Bookmarks folder, drag and drop the page onto this folder. When you're on the Web, add pages to the Bookmarks folder by clicking the Move to Folder action button, select Bookmarks as the folder, and choose Add.

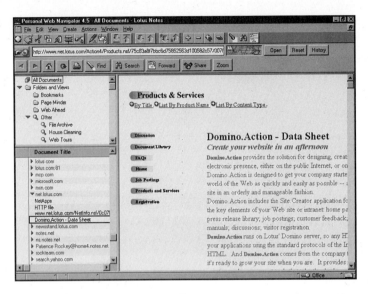

Fig. 26.11   Unlike Public Web Navigator, Personal Web Navigator opens up to the standard Notes three-pane window.

- ■ **Page Minder**—When you put a page in this folder, the Page Minder agent (if it is enabled) periodically checks its original site for updates. If it has been updated since you downloaded it, the agent notifies you. See the sections "Page Minder Agent Preferences" and "Using the Page Minder Agent in the Personal Web Navigator" in this chapter for more details.

- ■ **Web Ahead**—When you put a page in this folder, the Web Ahead agent (if it is enabled) retrieves in the background all the pages that it points to. Depending on how you have configured the agent, it may also retrieve all the pages pointed to by those pages, all by those, and all by those—that is, up to four levels of pages. A really good way to fill up a hard disk fast. See the section "Web Ahead Agent Preferences" in this chapter for more details.

- ■ **File Archive**—Displays all file attachments and their sizes.

- ■ **House Cleaning**—Displays Web pages sorted by size so you know which ones to reduce to their URLs.

- ■ **Web Tours**—Displays all the Web Tour documents you've made.

The Personal Web Navigator Action Bar. The Personal Web Navigator has both View and Form action bars. They are nearly identical to each other, but they are different from the action bar that appears in the Public Web Navigator (see Figure 26.12). As with the Public Web Navigator, these action bars emulate those you see in Web browsers. They help you browse the Web.

Fig. 26.12 The action bar of the Personal Web Navigator emulates those in Web browsers.

The actions in the action bar are described in Table 26.5.

Table 26.5	Action Buttons
Button	**Click This Button to...**
Previous	Go to the previous page in the History list.
Next	Go to the next page in the History list.
Home	Go to the page you defined in Internet Options as your home Web page.
Reload	Reload the current Web page from the Internet server.
Print	Print the current page.
Find	Find pages from any of the views or finds text in any of the documents in the Personal Web Navigator database.
Search	Search for pages on the Web using the Internet search engine you specified in Internet Options.
Forward	Forward the Web page to someone via e-mail.
Share	Share the Web page according to the specifications you made in Internet Options. This opens a dialog box in which you can choose to forward the page to someone, copy it to the Public Web Navigator database, or rate it and copy it and your rating to the Server Web Navigator database.
Reduce	Save space in your database by reducing the Web page to its URL only.
Zoom	Open the Web page. This action appears in the View Action Bar only.
Move to Folder	Display the Move to Folder dialog box, where you can choose a folder for the page. This Action appears in the Form Action Bar only.

The Personal Web Navigator Search Bar. The Search Bar works the same way in the Personal Web Navigator database as it does in the Public Web Navigator database. See details about its use in the earlier section "The Public Web Navigator Search Bar."

Using Internet Search Engines

Up until now, you worked your way around the Web by typing in an URL to go to a specific site. But what if you don't know the URL of a site you want to visit? Or, what if you don't know what site would have information of the type you need? For example, what if you want to search for information about The King? You know, Elvis. You could try typing **www.elvis.com**. Is this a real Web site? Well, type it and find out. Of course, even if you get lucky and guess right on the name of a site, how do you know what other sites might also have valuable information about Elvis in them?

A more efficient way to locate information on the Web, when you don't know where to look, is to use an Internet search engine. With an Internet search engine, you can type in a search term, such as **Elvis**, and the search engine searches one or more Web indexes for entries that contain the word *Elvis*. Then it returns a list of links to the sites that it found. Most search engines will list the sites with the most hits at the top of the list.

Searching for Elvis might return an awful lot of hits— perhaps thousands, certainly hundreds, and probably more than you need. So, to narrow your search and find a better match, you can supply additional information to the search engine. For example, **Elvis AND Sands AND Las Vegas AND October 1966** is bound to return a few less hits.

Different search engines maintain different lists of Web pages, and after working with a few, you'll find one you like best. Or, if you need to do a really exhaustive search, you might run the same search with different search engines. When you select a search engine to use, Web Publisher takes you to the home page of that search engine where you can type your search criteria. Although you can use any search engine, makes it easy for you to choose Yahoo!, Lycos, AltaVista, or Excite.

Searching the World Wide Web with the Public Web Navigator

To access the search engines in the Public Web Navigator, follow these steps:

1. Open the Public Web Navigator database.

2. Click the Directory Search icon (see Figure 26.13).

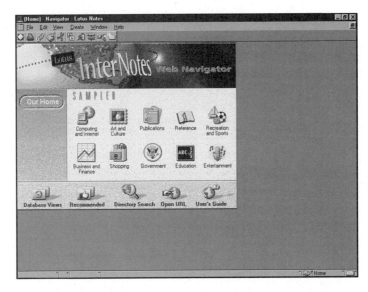

Fig. 26.13   The Directory Search icon appears on the Public Web Navigator home page.

3. Enter your topic to search in the text box, as shown in Figure 26.14.

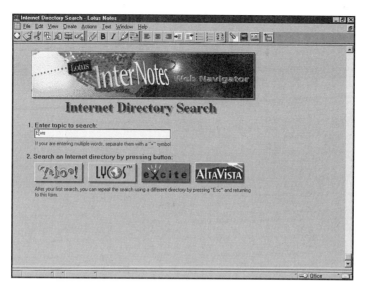

Fig. 26.14   Here, we have entered *Elvis* in the search field.

   4. Click the search engine you want to use (Yahoo!, or Lycos).

   5. Web Navigator takes you to the site you requested (Yahoo!, AltaVista, Excite, or Lycos), and the results of your search are displayed on your screen. Figure 26.15 shows the results of searching Yahoo! for *Elvis*.

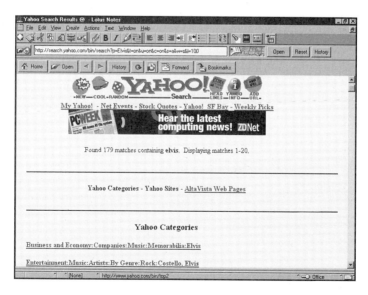

Fig. 26.15   Yahoo! found 179 references to *Elvis*.

6. Scrolling down the Yahoo! page, you see some of the links to Elvis sightings, as shown in Figure 26.16.

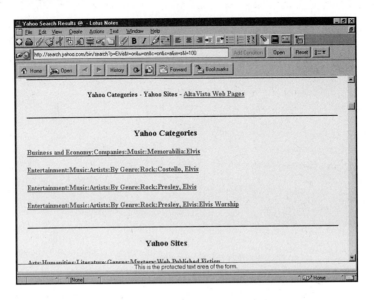

Fig. 26.16   Yahoo! displays the URLs of the Elvis references.

7. You can now scroll through the Elvis list. When you find a page you want to read, click the underlined text.

Searching the World Wide Web with the Personal Web Navigator

The Personal Web Navigator allows you to select your preferred search engine, but using a search engine isn't quite as intuitive as it is in the Public Web Navigator. To access a search engine, you can either type in the search engine's URL, or you can set a preferred search engine in your Internet Options document. To set a preferred search engine, follow these steps:

1. From the workspace, select the Personal Web Navigator and choose <u>A</u>ctions, <u>I</u>nternet Options from the menu.

2. In the Search Options section, select the search engine you prefer in the Preferred Search Engine field. If you select AltaVista, Excite, Lycos, or Yahoo!, save and close this document. If you choose Other, a new field appears and you must provide an URL in the new text field, as shown in Figure 26.17. Then save and close this document.

To use the search engine you just selected, follow these steps:

1. Open the Personal Web Navigator.

2. Click the Search icon on the Action Bar.

3. The Web Navigator retrieves the search engine Web page. Enter your search.

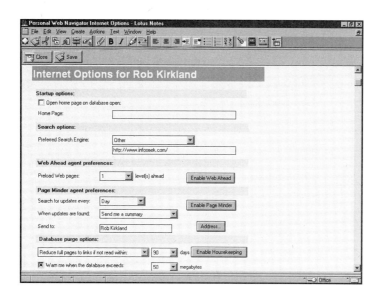

Fig. 26.17   Choose a preferred search engine in the Search Options section of the Internet Options document.

Tip

You can perform searches on some Web pages. If a Web page is indexed, Web Navigator displays a search button on the Action Bar. Often a Web page that is indexed indicates that it is indexed. Visit **http://www.sec.gov/cgi-bin/srch-edgar** to see an example of an indexed Web page.

Using Bookmarks

Have you had this frustrating experience? You initiate a search and drill deeper and deeper down through layer after layer of information. The address of the page you have reached is
http:\\www.bongo.biz\technotes\dir_423\idea\ohno\iamlost\littlefeat.

The phone rings, the system goes down, you get distracted, and did not make note of the address of this very important document. How do you ever find it again?

You could have saved the page in the Bookmarks folder. Both the Personal Web Navigator and the Public Web Navigator have them. The My Bookmarks folder in the Public Web Navigator is a private folder, stored on the Notes server; its contents are accessible only by you. If your Notes administrator has elected to periodically purge the Server Web Navigator database, the contents of the My Bookmarks folder and any subfolders you create under it are not, by default, deleted during the purge (although the Database Manager can override the default).

Saving Bookmarks in the Public Web Navigator

To add an open page to the My Bookmarks folder while using the Public Web Navigator, click the Folder button of the Action Bar. Select the Bookmarks folder and choose Add.

To add a page to the My Bookmarks folder from the view pane of the database, drag and drop the page into the Bookmarks folder icon in the navigation pane.

Saving Bookmarks in the Personal Web Navigator

To add an open page to the Bookmarks folder while using the Personal Web Navigator, click the Move to Folder button in the Action Bar. The Move to Folder dialog box appears. Select the Bookmarks folder and choose Add.

To add a page to the My Bookmarks folder from the view pane of the database, drag and drop the page into the My Bookmarks Navigator button or folder icon.

Reducing a Page to an URL in Personal Web Navigator

After you save a page in the Bookmark folder, you may want to save space in your database by reducing the page to an URL. If you choose this option, the only thing that is saved is the URL and not the page itself. When you open a reduced page, the address appears in the Open URL box, and no part of the page is visible. You can see the page by reloading it from the Internet server. You can do this only in the Personal Web Navigator. (In Public Web Navigator, it is an option in the Purge agent.) To reduce a page to an URL, follow these steps:

1. Open the page from the view pane of the database.

2. Click the Reduce button on the Action Bar.

3. To view this page again, select the page and click the Reload button on the Action Bar.

Downloading Files from the Web

Some Webpages may have one or more files attached to them. The attached files sometimes appear as embedded icons with file names beneath them. To retrieve such a file from a Web page, follow these steps:

1. Double-click the filename listed in the Web page, click the Download option on the Web page, or follow the instructions for downloading that appear on the page. The Attachment Properties InfoBox appears, as shown in Figure 26.18. This InfoBox displays details about the file and offers three options: View, Launch, and Detach.

2. Select Detach. The Save Attachment dialog box appears (see Figure 26.19).

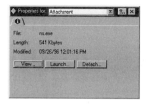

Fig. 26.18   The Attachment Properties box shows the filename, size, and date and time of last modification of a file. You can view, launch, or detach a file.

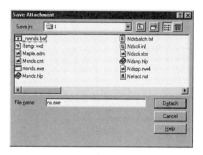

Fig. 26.19   Choose a drive, directory, and filename under which to save your file in the Save Attachment dialog box. Notes will offer to save under the file's original name.

   3. Select a drive, directory, and filename under which to save the file. Click Detach. Notes will save the file. It doesn't actually detach the file but just detaches a copy. You can detach another copy later if you want.

Sharing Information

You can share Web pages with others by e-mailing them or by making recommendations in the Public Web Navigator. *How* you share is slightly different in the Personal Web Navigator versus the Public Web Navigator.

Recommending Web Pages in the Public Web Navigator

The Public Web Navigator allows you to make recommendations about useful or interesting Web pages to others within your company who are also Notes users. Because the Public Web Navigator is a shared database, everyone can see each other's recommendations just by looking in the database, so recommending a page is a relatively simple procedure.

To recommend a Web page while using the Public Web Navigator, follow these steps:

   1. Open the Web page you want to recommend.

   2. Click the Recommend button in the Action Bar.

   3. A dialog box appears, as shown in Figure 26.20.

Fig. 26.20   In the Recommend dialog box, you can rate and categorize Web pages.

4. Select a rating from 1 to 5 for this page.

5. Add your comments about this page in the comments text field.

6. Select a category for your recommendation.

7. Click OK to save this recommendation.

Recommending or Sharing a Document in the Personal Web Navigator

In the Personal Web Navigator, you can either share or recommend a Web page. Because the Personal Web Navigator database is your own personal database—not shared with others—it takes a little more effort than with the Public Web Navigator to share the fruits of your labors with others.

To recommend a Web page using the Personal Web Navigator, you first need to supply the name of your Notes server in your Internet Options document as explained in the previous section "Setting Internet Options in the Personal Web Navigator Database" in this chapter. Then you must either forward the page's URL to people by mail or you must copy the page to the Public Web Navigator database. Notes automates both of these procedures, as follows:

1. Open the Personal Web Navigator.

2. Click a document in the Navigator pane, or open a document.

3. Click the Share button in the Action Bar.

4. A dialog box appears, as shown in Figure 26.21. This dialog box is different from the one the Public Web Navigator displays, and gives you the following three options:

Fig. 26.21   In this dialog box, you can forward a document's URL to someone, copy the document to the Public Web Navigator database, or copy it and recommend it.

- **Forward only the URL**—Forwards the URL to others via e-mail. When you select this option, you are prompted for addressee names. You can fill in the name or click the address icon to select a name from your Personal Address Book. When you click OK, Notes sends a message to your addressee(s) in which the subject of the message is the title of the Web page as it appears in your database, and the body of the message is the URL of the database. If you are not connected to an server, this is the only option you can choose.

- **Copy page to shared Web Navigator Database**—This copies the page to the All Documents view of the Public Web Navigator. You must be connected to the server to choose this option.

- **Create Rating in shared Web Navigator Database**—This prompts you to create a rating as you would in the Public Web Navigator database and sends the page with its rating to the Recommended views of the Server Web Navigator. You must be connected to the server to choose this option.

5. Click OK to send the document (or its URL), and close the dialog box.

Viewing Recommended Web Pages

To view the Web pages you and others have recommended in the Public Web Navigator, follow these steps:

1. Open the Public Web Navigator.

2. Click the Recommended button in the Navigator home page.

3. The Recommended Navigator appears on the left of the screen. It allows you to view the contents of the recommended Web pages in the following three ways:

- **By Category**—A list of classifications chosen when Web page ratings were created. A good view for finding pages by topics.

- **By Reviewer**—Sorted by the person who rated the Web page.

- **Top Ten**—Shows the top ten pages with the highest cumulative ratings.

Forwarding Web Pages to Other Users

You can e-mail a Web page to other Notes users from any view or any open document in the Web Navigator databases. Choose Actions, Forward in the menu, click the Actions Forward SmartIcon, or, if a document is open, click the Forward action in the Action Bar. Notes will open a mail memo. The Web page appears in the body of the memo, and the subject line is automatically filled in with the title of the Web page. Figure 26.22 shows a Web page ready to be forwarded. Address the memo, add your comments, and click Send.

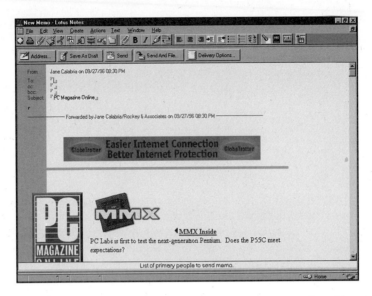

Fig. 26.22   You can forward a Web page just like any other document. When the recipient opens the forwarded page, the links in it will be live.

Viewing Java Applets

Java is a programming language that allows you to build small, cross-platform programs called *applets*. You can embed an applet in a Web page by including its URL in an HTML code with the <APPLET> tag. When Notes encounters the <APPLET> tag during interpretation of the page, it retrieves the applet itself from its location on the Web and copies it into memory. Then the Java interpreter that comes with Notes runs the Java applet.

Allowing Java applets to run on your computer raises questions of security. Because these applets are actual programs, they can harm your PC. Worse, they can expose your PC's resources and, by extension, the rest of your network to an outside computer. They pose a real security threat.

Lotus Notes allows you to decide if you want to enable Java applets and from whom (which hosts) you will allow Java applets to be received. Additionally, you can instruct Notes not to permit any outside host access to any of your system resources (files, environment variables, password files, and so on). For example, you may feel confident that Lotus corporation isn't going to send you any viruses, and you can decide to trust the Lotus host. On the other hand, Elvis from Bulgaria may not be as trustworthy and you can decide to put him on your untrusted list, either not allowing him to send you applets or disabling some of the functionality of the ones you receive from him. If you don't enable applets, you still see the Web pages minus the applets.

Earlier in this chapter, we discussed most of the parameters that affect the performance of Java applets in Notes. Here is a short recap:

- Enable Java applets on each computer by checking the Enable Java applets option under Advanced options in User Preferences. In the menu, choose File, Tools, User Preferences.

- Configure Java performance by filling in the fields in the Java Applet Security section of the Location document you will be using when browsing the Web. If you are a Notes administrator setting up new users, you can set most of these fields in a User Setup Profile document, which will then apply the settings to new users automatically.

Viewing HTML Code

If you ever do any HTML programming, then you might occasionally visit a Web page and say to yourself, "How did they do that?" Really cool colors, formatting, and graphics help entice people to your site. In Chapter 26 of this book, you learn about building Notes applications and optimizing those applications for publication to the Web, and you learn about HTML code.

Here, you can learn how to view the HTML code behind Web pages. So, if you see a cool Web page and you want to know more about the design of the page, you can view the HTML code on that page and get ideas for your own Web site.

To see the code underlying the HTML documents Notes retrieves, you must enable the Save HTML in Note? option for the Web Navigator database. In the Public Web Navigator, do this in the Administration document, which you open from the Actions menu when the All Documents view appears. In the Personal Web Navigator, do it in the Internet Options page, also reachable in the Action menu.

By default, when Notes converts a retrieved HTML page to Notes format, it discards the HTML source code. After you enable the Save HTML in Note? option, Notes will save the HTML source code of newly retrieved pages in a hidden field called HTMLSource. You can view the HTML source code only in the Document Properties box of a Web page (see Figure 26.23). It is a little difficult to read in that confined space, however. To ease the pain, copy the HTML source code from the Document Properties box to a text editor or a text field in a Notes document.

Viewing HTML Source Code in Notes Documents in a Usable Form

You might think Lotus would provide a form that displays the HTML source code in a field. But Lotus has not yet done so, and you cannot create such a form. The HTMLSource field is of data type HTML, which is not a data type you can choose when you create a field in a form. So, even if you create a form with a field in it called HTMLSource, and switch to that form when viewing a document, the HTML source code will not appear in that field.

What you *can* do is select the contents of the HTMLSource field in the Document Properties box, copy the selected text to the Clipboard, and paste it into a text editor or a text field in a Notes document.

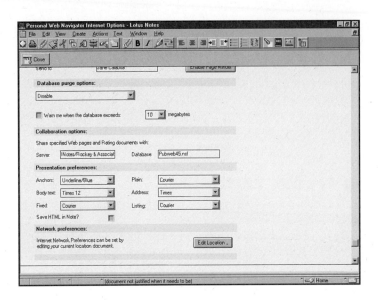

Fig. 26.23 If you check off the Save HTML in Note? field, Notes will store the HTML code of a Web page in a hidden field called HTMLSource.

To view HTML code, follow these steps:

1. Select the Web page in either the Public or Personal Web Navigator.

2. Choose File, Document Properties from the menu.

3. Go to the Fields tab.

4. Select the HTMLSource field in the left column to see the HTML code in the right column.

5. Select the HTML code in the right column with your mouse, and then copy it to the Clipboard.

6. Paste the HTML code into a text editor or a text field in any Notes document. Print a copy if you like.

Streamlining Web Page Retrieval

In general, Web Navigator is a slower Web browser than the mainstream stand-alone Web browsers, such as Netscape Navigator and Microsoft Internet Explorer. However, what Web Navigator offers that those browsers do not is delivery of Web pages into the Web Navigator databases. What this allows you to do is collect pages in these databases, then bring the power of Notes to bear on them. For example, you could retrieve a mass of pages, then go off-line (say, because you are getting on a plane to fly to a client site) and read the retrieved documents at your leisure.

If you do want to collect a lot of information from the Web in a hurry, there are two ways to do it. First, you can initiate retrieval of several Web pages at the same time.

That is, you don't have to wait for one page to finish downloading before you start downloading a second, third, or fourth. Second, you can use the Web Ahead agent to retrieve whole groups of pages from the Web while you do something else.

Multiple, Simultaneous Web Retrievals

The Personal Web Navigator allows you to retrieve up to six pages simultaneously. To allow multiple Web retrievals, follow these steps:

1. Edit your Location Document by clicking the Location on the status bar and selecting Edit Current.

2. In the Concurrent Retrievers field, select the number of pages you want to be able to retrieve simultaneously. You can choose from two to six.

3. Save your changes and close the document.

After you have edited your Location Document, you can retrieve multiple Web pages at one time. For each Web page you want to open, choose File, Open URL from the menu, complete the fields in the Open URL dialog box, and click OK. Or, enter successive URLs into the Open URL Search Bar. Personal Web Navigator opens a new Window for each Open URL command and retrieves the requested pages into the separate windows simultaneously. To see the pages, select Window from the menu and move from page to page from the Window menu, or choose Window, Cascade or Window, Tile to see all of your Web pages.

Using the Web Ahead Agent in Personal Web Navigator to Retrieve Multiple Related Pages

Web Ahead is a Notes agent that automatically retrieves into the Personal Web Navigator database all the pages pointed to by URLs on a given page. You can configure Web Ahead to retrieve up to four levels of pages. That is, you can pull in just the pages pointed to by URLs on the current page, or all of those plus all of the pages pointed to by the second level of pages, or plus the third level, or plus the fourth level.

Caution
You better have a lot of free disk space if you plan to choose level four.

The idea here is that, instead of manually (and tediously) retrieving all the pages and having to wait around while they arrive, you can start the agent running, go off and do something else, and then come back and browse at your pace (not the Web's) through the copies of the pages waiting in your database.

To use the Web Ahead agent, you must first enable it. To do so, follow these steps:

1. Choose File, Tools, User Preferences to open the User Preferences dialog box.

2. In the User Preferences dialog box, place a checkmark in the box labeled Enable Scheduled Local Agents. Then click OK to close this dialog box.

VI

Working with the Web

3. Open the Internet Options document in the Personal Web Navigator database. Click the Enable Web Ahead button. If asked what server to run it on, choose Local. Click OK. If the Enable Web Ahead button does not appear in the Internet Options document, it is because Web Ahead has already been enabled.

   You can verify this by checking the Agents view of the Web Navigator database. A checkmark should appear in the checkbox next to the Web Ahead listing.

4. Set the number of levels ahead that you want Web Ahead to retrieve. Set this in the Internet Options document in the Personal Web Navigator database.

5. To use the Web Ahead agent, just drag a page into the Web Ahead folder. The agent does the rest automatically. You do, of course, have to have an active connection to the Internet for Web Ahead to be able to do its job.

Viewing the Most Current Version of a Web Page

Web pages are updated constantly. When you visit a Web site, you want current information, not last week's news. So, there is a chance that a Web page stored in your database could be out-of-date a day later. On the other hand, opening a Web page from the Notes database is a lot faster than opening a Web page on the Web! So, how can you balance between opening pages from the Web or the database?

The following are three ways you can make sure you are looking at a relatively recent version of a Web page:

- You can manually refresh any page when you are looking at it by clicking the Reload button on the Action Bar. (The Reload button is the circular blue arrow.) This causes the Web Retriever to get a new copy of the page from the original source on the Web. It displays the new copy and overwrites the old copy in the Web Navigator database with the new copy.

  Also, when you retrieve a page in the Open URL dialog box, you can force Web Navigator to ignore any copy of the page that might already be in the Web Navigator database, and to overwrite that page—if it does exist—with a new copy from the Web, by selecting the Reload from Internet Server option before clicking OK.

- You can set the Web Retriever cache options so that, under certain circumstances, the Web Retriever will retrieve a fresh copy of a page when you open it, even though a copy of the page already resides in the Web Navigator database. The drawback of this method is that it updates all pages indiscriminately, even pages that are strictly archival and unchanging by nature.

- Best of all, in the Personal Web Navigator database you can activate the Page Minder agent, which will refresh pages that you designate on a scheduled basis. The really nice thing about this method is that the Page Minder will tell you when it has updated a page in the Web Navigator database. You don't have to affirmatively remember to check for updates.

Setting Web Retriever Cache Options

You set Web Retriever cache options for the Public Web Navigator by changing the settings of the Update Cache field in the Web Retriever Administration section of the server's Server document in the Public Address Book. (Of course, not just anybody can do that; you have to have adequate access rights to the database and that document.)

You set Web Retriever cache options for the Personal Web Navigator by changing the settings of the same field—the Update Cache field. But in this case, the field is located in the Web Retriever Configuration section of the appropriate Location document in your Personal Address Book. The appropriate Location document is, of course, the one that is current whenever you browse with the Personal Web Navigator.

The choices in the Update Cache field are the same, whether you are changing the one in the Public Address Book or the one in the Personal Address Book. They are as follows:

- **Never**—This is the default setting. Select Never if you do not want your Web pages indiscriminately refreshed when you open them. With Never as your choice, you have to click the Reload button on the Action Bar to refresh your Web pages.

- **Once per session**—Select this option to refresh your Web page at the time you open it from the database, and not again during your current Notes session. If you are using the Public Web Navigator, Notes will give you a fresh reload even if some other Notes user opened the same page one second before you did.

- **Every time**—Select this option to refresh a Web page every time you open it from the database, even if the last time you (or anyone else) opened it was just a minute earlier during the same Notes session.

Using the Page Minder Agent in the Personal Web Navigator

To use the Page Minder agent in the Personal Web Navigator, do the following:

1. Enable background agents in User Preferences. Choose File, Tools, User Preferences in the menu.

2. On the Basics page, under Startup Options, enter a checkmark next to Enable scheduled local agents. Click OK.

3. Enable the Page Minder agent in the Personal Web Navigator database. You can do this in one of two ways:

   - In the Page Minder agent preferences section of the Internet Option document of the Personal Web Navigator database, click the Enable Page Minder button. (If the button doesn't appear there, you have already enabled the agent.)

   - In the Agents view of the Personal Web Navigator database, put a checkmark in the checkbox next to the Page Minder agent listing.

4. Set Page Minder options in the Page Minder agent preferences section of the Internet Options document in the Personal Web Navigator database. You can set

VI

Working with the Web

the frequency of updates to every hour, every four hours, every day, or every week. You can tell it whether to mail the updated page to you or to just mail you a notice that the page has been updated in the Web Navigator database. And you can designate the addressees of the new page or notice. See the earlier section "Page Minder Agent Preferences" in this chapter for more information about the Page Minder option fields in the Internet Options document.

5. Choose which Web pages should be updated by Page Minder. This is the easy part. If you want Page Minder to update a given page for you, just find the page in the Web Navigator database and put a copy of it in the Page Minder folder.

From Here...

Web Navigator is a powerful adjunct to the overall functionality of Notes. By allowing you to extend Notes' reach to the far corners of the Internet, Web Navigator truly enhances Notes' role as a repository of information of all kinds.

For related information, see the following chapters:

■ Chapter 25, "Lotus Notes and the Web," provides a general introduction to the Internet, the World Wide Web, and intranets; introduces Lotus' Internet products; and discusses Lotus' overall Internet strategy.

■ Chapter 27, "Using Domino Server's HTTP Service," examines the Web functionality side of Lotus Notes.

Chapter 27

Using Domino Server's HTTP Service

Lotus Notes has always consisted of two components: the client and the server. In past Notes releases, they were known as the Notes client and the Notes server. In the summer of 1996, Lotus released a product that turned the Notes server into a combination Notes/Web server. Lotus alternately called this product the *HTTP Service for Lotus Notes and the Domino Web Server*. With the release of Notes 4.5, Lotus folded the Web server add-on so completely into the Notes server that Lotus renamed the Notes server; it is now the Lotus Domino server.

In this chapter, we examine in detail the add-on from which the Lotus Domino server took its new name. To differentiate between the general server functions of the Domino server and the Web-related functions, we refer to the Web-server function as the *HTTP service*.

What Is Domino Server's HTTP Service?

HTTP Service is a Lotus Domino server task that adds Web server capabilities to the Domino server. It incorporates several Internet protocols into the Domino server, including HTTM, HTML, URL syntax, CGI, and SSL. (See Chapter 25, "Lotus Notes and the Web," for definitions of these terms.) In effect, Domino is both a Notes server and a Web server. More important, HTTP Service extends to Web users both read and write access to Notes databases. This means that Web users can add to and update Notes databases just as though they were using the Notes client. This brings Notes' power as a workflow automation tool directly to the Web. In the words of Lotus, this makes Notes with Domino not just another Web server, but an Internet applications server.

How HTTP Service Works

The HTTP server task adds complete HTTP services to the Domino server. The HTTP side of the server stores HTML files just as any HTTP server does.

Some of the main topics in this chapter are

- What the Domino HTTP Service is and how it works

- How to set up and configure a Domino Web site

- Domino database security and the World Wide Web

- How to modify and develop Notes applications to take best advantage of Domino's Internet features

The Notes side of the server maintains Notes databases. When a Notes client requests services, the "Notes" server provides them. When a Web client requests documents, the HTTP server either provides them itself from its store of HTML files, or it requests the documents from the Notes server; then it converts them from Notes format to HTML, and delivers them to the requesting Web client. If a Web client submits a form or a query, the HTTP service converts it to Notes format and submits it to the Notes server, which processes it appropriately (see Figure 27.1).

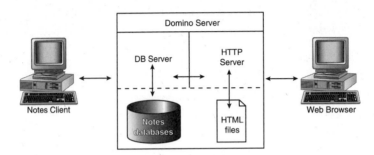

Fig. 27.1   The Notes database server and the HTTP Web server coexist in the Domino server memory space. One services Notes clients. The other services Web clients.

System Requirements

The HTTP service was an add-in to earlier versions of Notes. You had to download it from the Internet (at no charge, of course), and then carefully follow a set of installation instructions to get it running with Notes. But starting with Notes Release 4.5, the HTTP service is included with the Domino server as a standard server task and setup is much easier than before.

If you put the HTTP service to use on a server, it does increase the load on the processor, RAM, and disk space, although precisely how much depends on how heavily you use the HTTP service. Lotus recommends that a Domino server running the HTTP service have 64M RAM and 1G disk space. However, I have been running a lightly-used Domino/HTTP server successfully now for several weeks with only 48M RAM, and I have run tests of various Domino HTTP functions on a computer with only 32M RAM. But I recommend that you run a production server with 64M RAM if you expect a steady stream of users from the Web.

Of course, as an HTTP server, your Domino server must run the TCP/IP protocol suite, and be accessible to Web users either on the Internet or on your intranet. Notes clients can use any protocol available under Notes to access the server. But Web users, by definition, must use TCP/IP.

Configuring Your Site

The server installation process performs most of the setup necessary to implement the HTTP service. To finish configuring it, all you have to do is set it to start up when the Domino server starts, and edit (or at least review) several sections of the server document.

When you perform a Domino 4.5 server installation, the Install program automatically installs the HTTP files and creates a set of data directories beneath the Notes data directory. These include a directory called HTML, intended as the location of any HTML files maintained by Domino; CGI-BIN, the location of CGI scripts to be executed by Domino; and ICONS, where Domino stores .GIF versions of Notes icons to be substituted for them when a Notes page is converted to HTML—see the directory structure in Figure 27.2. Domino creates a fourth subdirectory, CACHE, after you run it for the first time, and a possible fifth directory if and when you enable logging.

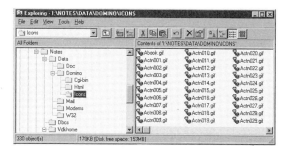

Fig. 27.2 The Domino server installation process automatically creates the data directories that Domino will use, and populates the ICONS subdirectory with bitmap files.

Running the HTTP Service

The server installation and configuration process does not configure the HTTP service to start up when Domino starts. You have to do that yourself, by editing the ServerTasks variable in the NOTES.INI file. Immediately after server installation, the variable is set as follows:

```
ServerTasks=Replica,Router,Update,Stats,AMgr,Adminp,Sched,CalConn
```

Edit this line by adding HTTP to it. When edited properly, ServerTasks looks like this:

```
ServerTasks=Replica,Router,Update,Stats,AMgr,Adminp,Sched,CalConn,HTTP
```

When you start Domino, this statement causes the HTTP service to start up at that time, along with all the other Domino server tasks listed. Another way to edit this line is by entering the following command at the server console:

```
set configuration
"ServerTasks=Replica,Router,Update,Stats,AMgr,Adminp,Sched,CalConn,HTTP"
```

VI

Working with the Web

This statement commands Domino to insert the quoted text into NOTES.INI itself, substituting it for the existing ServerTasks variable. By entering this command, you save yourself the trouble of opening, saving, and closing the NOTES.INI file. However, I prefer to edit NOTES.INI directly, because if I mistype a single character of the Set Configuration command, I can really impair the functioning of the server. There is less opportunity for typos if I have to add one word to the end of the statement in a text editor than if I have to retype the whole, long statement in the Notes server console.

You can also start the HTTP server task manually. To do so, enter the following command at the server console:

```
load http
```

Stop the HTTP server task manually by entering the following command at the server console:

```
tell http quit
```

The other thing you have to do is review and possibly change a multitude of parameters in the server document in the Public Name & Address Book.

Server Document Variables

Two sections of the Server document control the actions of the HTTP service: Security and HTTP Server. We look at the HTTP Server parameters here and discuss the Security parameters in the section "Domino Security Features," later in this chapter.

The HTTP Server section of the Server document has five parts: Basics, Mapping, Timeouts, Operational Information, and Logging. Initially, you only have to make a few decisions. Later, you can go back and perhaps fine-tune Domino's settings. The fields you must look at up front include those in Table 27.1.

Table 27.1   Essential HTTP Server Settings

Part	Field	Description
Basics	TCP/IP port number	Default is 80. You only need to change it if you are running a third-party Web server on the same computer, so that both servers don't try to use port 80.
	Host name	Default is blank, which means that the HTTP server will get the host name from the TCP/IP stack in the server's memory. If you have registered an alias with your Domain Name Server, enter the alias here. Or enter the server's IP address, so that Web users can access the server by typing the IP address.
Mapping	Home URL	Default is /?Open, which causes the server to send a list of Notes databases as the site home page. If you want to create a real home page, enter its filename here or clear this field. If you want to designate a home page database, enter its filename here.

> ### Caution
>
> Whenever you make a change in the HTTP Server section of the server document, remember to stop and restart the HTTP server task (if it was running). Otherwise, your changes do not take effect.

The rest of the fields are listed as follows, grouped by subsection. Many of them you should never have to change. You may be able to improve the performance of your server by changing some of them.

HTTP Server Basics. This is the first subsection of the HTTP Server part of the Server document. It covers—you guessed it—the basics:

- **TCP/IP port number**—The default is 80, which is the standard HTTP port. You only need to change it if you are running more than one HTTP server on this computer—that is, you are running some other HTTP server in addition to Domino. If you do have to change it, you must change it to a port number greater than 1024, and you might prefer to change it to 8008 or 8080, which are commonly used as alternate HTTP port numbers. If you use a port number other than 80, users have to enter it as part of your URL, in the form **http://domino.chestnet.com:8080**.

- **TCP/IP port status**—The default is Enabled. You disable this only if you want to force users to use the SSL (Secure Sockets Layer) port. If both ports are disabled, the HTTP service will not function properly. See the section "Domino and the SSL Protocol" later in this chapter.

- **Host name**—By default, this field is blank, which means that Domino will get the host name from the TCP/IP stack in the server's memory. If you have registered an alias with your Domain Name Server, you can enter the alias here. Or, if the server is not registered with a Domain Name Server, enter the server's IP address, which enables users to access the server by typing the IP address in the form **http://192.192.192.11**.

- **DNS lookup**—This is disabled by default. If enabled, Domino attempts to retrieve the host name of all requesting clients. If disabled, Domino only gets the client's IP address. Because enabling this function requires the server to do more work, it degrades overall server performance. If the server obtains clients' host names, they will be recorded in the Domino log files and filter.

- **Default home page**—This defaults to default.htm. When a client makes a request that does not specify a page name, this is the page that Domino serves up.

- **Maximum active threads and Minimum active threads**—These default to 40 and 20, respectively. Domino always keeps at least the minimum number of threads open, even when idling. If it reaches the maximum number, it puts any additional requests on hold until threads become free. The more RAM your server has, the higher you should set these values. If your computer seems to spend a lot of time and effort swapping memory to disk, reduce these values.

Mapping. The fields in this subsection of the Server document specify the physical and mapped locations of Domino's HTML-related data directories. The mapped values are shorthand values that conform to UNIX/URL syntax rules (meaning that they use forward instead of backslashes). Web users enter the mapped locations. The server uses the entries in these fields to translate from the mapped to the actual locations of these directories. As long as you do not change the default setup of the server, you need not change most of these values. If you do decide to designate other data directories than the system defaults, you must change the entries in the path fields in this section.

The default data directories, as subdirectories of the Notes data directory, are designated by their relative path names. If you move the data directories out of the Notes data subdirectory tree, enter full versions of the new path names.

The fields in the Mapping subsection are as follows:

- **HTML directory**—By default, it is set to domino\html. If the Notes data directory path is c:\notes\data, then this partial path name translates to c:\notes\data\domino\html. If you move the HTML data files to, say, c:\domino\html, then you change this field to c:\domino\html. There is no corresponding mapped path for this directory, because to users seeking static HTML pages from the Domino server, this is the root data directory. That is, if a user asks for **http://domino.chestnet.com/pagename.htm**, the Domino server translates that to c:\notes\data\domino\html\pagename.htm.

- **Home URL**—This defaults to /?open, which causes the server to send a list of Notes databases as the site home page (sort of like when a Notes user chooses File, Database, Open from the menu). If you want to create a static home page that users see when they enter your host name, put it in the HTML directory and enter its filename in this field; or clear this field for the same effect. If you want to designate a home page database that users will open when they enter your host name, enter its filename here.

- **CGI URL path and CGI directory**—The CGI URL path is the name users enter to reach the actual directory identified in the CGI directory field. This is where CGI scripts are located.

- **Icon URL path and Path to icons**—The Icon URL path is the name users enter to reach the directory identified in the Path to Icons field. These are the graphics files that Domino substitutes for the actual icons when translating from Notes to HTML file format.

Timeouts. All of the system timeout variables appear in this subsection. They are as follows:

- **Idle thread timeout**—This is the same thread referred to in the Maximum and Minimum active threads fields listed in the previous section "HTTP Server Basics." As used here, a thread is an independent process that the server maintains to serve up requested documents. Multiple threads are available so that the server can service multiple simultaneous requests. Upon startup, Domino creates the number of threads set in the Minimum active threads field. If enough simultaneous page requests come in that the server needs to activate more threads, it will do so on an as-needed basis. Under no circumstances, however, will Domino open more threads than the number in the Maximum active threads field.

It takes some time and effort for the computer to establish a new thread, so there is some benefit to keeping inactive threads alive even though there is no work for them to do. On the other hand, they use up memory and processor time, so there is also benefit to killing inactive threads. This field dictates how long after it finishes servicing a request a thread will hang around idle before dying. The default setting of zero minutes means that it never dies. In effect, the number of threads ratchets up, never dropping back down. This favors performance over memory conservation.

- **Input timeout**—When one computer transfers a file to another computer, the computers typically establish a *session* or *connection* with each other and maintain that session/connection until the transaction is complete. Some types of servers maintain the connection for a long period of time even though there is no activity with the client. Web servers, impatient beings that they are, and in eager anticipation of receiving requests from large numbers of strangers, typically drop connections after very short periods of inactivity. Domino is configurable in this regard. This field (which defaults to two minutes) dictates how long the server waits for a request after a client first connects. If no request is forthcoming within the time limit, the server drops the connection.

- **Output timeout**—This field dictates how much time Domino has to fulfill a request before it drops the connection with the requester. The default is 20 minutes, which means, in effect, that Domino is never able to deliver anything that takes longer than that to download. It also ensures that a malfunctioning delivery does not hang forever. If Web users will be downloading large files from your server, files that, in the real world of congested Internet pathways, might take more than 20 minutes to transfer to a user through his 14.4kbps modem, then maybe you should increase the value of this field.

- **CGI timeout**—This determines the maximum amount of time (defaulting to five minutes) that any CGI script has to get its job done. Among other things, this kills a program that has gotten trapped in a perpetual loop.

Operation Information. When Domino receives a request for a Notes document that includes embedded images or attached files, Domino converts the images to GIF-formatted files and delivers these and the attached files to the requester. It stores copies of both the newly created GIF files and the attachment files in a cache directory. When Domino receives another request for the same document, it is able to deliver it faster the second time because it does not have to regenerate the GIFs or redetach the attached files; it retrieves them from the cache, instead. This increases performance at the expense of disk space.

The fields in this subsection determine how, where, and for how long Domino stores these cached files. You can also set default graphics file settings and HTML output settings here:

- **Cache directory (for GIFs and file attachments)**—This is the location on disk of the file cache directory. It defaults to domino\cache. Domino creates this directory the first time it runs.

- **Garbage collection**—This is the process Domino uses to delete cached files in order to keep the size of the cache directory within its maximum size (see Maximum cache size, two bullets down). Domino deletes least accessed files first. Disable this *only if you also disable caching*. If you disable garbage collection without also disabling caching, the cache is able to grow beyond its maximum size, eventually to take over all of the server's disk space.

- **Garbage collection interval**—Specifies how often the garbage collection process runs, and defaults to every 60 minutes. If the size of the cache exceeds its maximum, garbage collection does not wait until the next scheduled runtime, but runs immediately.

- **Maximum cache size**—This is the maximum amount of disk space the files in the cache directory are permitted to occupy. By default, this is set to 50M. If you have lots of free disk space, consider increasing this number. The benefit is faster delivery of documents to requesters.

- **Delete cache on shutdown**—This is disabled by default. If you enable it, Domino deletes all files from the cache directory whenever you shut Domino down.

- **Image conversion format**—By default, Domino converts images embedded in Notes documents to GIF files. Here you can change that to JPEG, if you want.

- **Interlaced rendering**—This field appears in the server document only if you have selected GIF in the Image conversion format field. Interlaced rendering is enabled by default. When enabled, Domino delivers GIFs interlaced—that is, it delivers every eighth line, then every fourth line, then every second line, then the remaining lines. The effect is that the receiver is able to discern what the image will look like before it is entirely rendered on-screen. This cuts down on the user's frustration factor.

- **Progressive rendering**—This field appears in the server document only if you have selected JPEG in the Image conversion format field. Progressive rendering is enabled by default. When enabled, the image is rendered at first blurry, then, with each pass, more clearly. Like interlaced GIF rendering, this enables the user to tell how the image will look before it is fully rendered.

- **JPEG image quality**—This field appears in the server document only if you have selected JPEG in the Image conversion format field. JPEG files are compressed in a way that causes them to lose fidelity with the original copy when decompressed. This is known as lossy compression; the other kind, used by GIF among other formats, is lossless compression, in which, when decompressed, the image retains 100 percent fidelity with the original. The benefit of using lossy compression is that you can obtain higher compression ratios and thus use less disk space when storing files and less time when transmitting them.

In this field, you can specify just how tightly JPEGs will compress or, to put it the other way, just how much fidelity they will lose when decompressed. A high number in this field means less compression, more fidelity. The default is 75; the range is zero to 100.

- **Default lines per view**—If a Notes view has more than the number of rows set in this field (default is 30), then Domino divides the view up into multiple view pages for delivery to the requester. Each view page has the number of rows dictated by this field. Every database is affected by this setting.

GIF versus JPEG

You have to decide whether to use GIF or JPEG when converting embedded images in Notes documents into graphics files that Web users will be able to see in their browsers. The factors are these:

- GIF (Graphics Interchange Format) files:

    Are compressed using a lossless compression scheme. This means that the decompressed image is identical to the original.

    Can display a maximum of 256 colors.

    Are better than JPEG for computer-generated art.

- JPEG (Joint Photographic Experts Group) files:

    Are compressed using a lossy compression scheme. This means that, when decompressed, the resulting image loses some of the detail that the original image had. The trade-off is higher compression ratios. With JPEG compression, you can also specify ahead of time just how much compression/loss you will get. That is, at compression time you can specify 100 percent fidelity with no compression or progressively less fidelity with correspondingly greater compression. You may wonder why anyone would want to lose fidelity with the original image. Well, it turns out that, with photographic images, the losses aren't particularly noticeable to the human eye. By sacrificing barely noticeable detail, you may be able to reclaim lots of disk space and transmission time. Considering that most video monitors are going to degrade a photographic image anyway, the trade-off may be well worthwhile.

    Can display upwards of 16 million colors.

    Cannot be displayed by some older browsers.

    Are better than GIF for photographic art.

(continues)

VI

Working with the Web

(continued)

So, which one should you choose? It depends on what types of images you are storing in your Notes databases—photographs or computer-generated art. If your Notes databases include pre-dominantly photographs, choose JPEG; if computer-generated art, choose GIF. Sorry, you can't choose database-by-database. You could, however, alter the way you store images in a given database if you want to give viewers the benefits of both image types. For example, if your data-bases store mostly computer art, but one database stores photographs, you can choose GIF as the default graphics conversion format, but then store JPEG copies of embedded photographs as attachments to the documents in which the photographs appear.

Logging. Domino optionally maintains Web access and error log files. Enable logging by entering into the Access log and Error log fields the path names of the directories where access and error logs will be stored. You can enter directory and filenames if you also want to specify the file names Domino will use when it creates log files. Then stop the HTTP server task if it was running and restart it. On restart, Domino creates the directo-ries you specified, then the files. The files increase in size fast. Each day at midnight Domino closes the previous day's log files and creates new files for the new day. Don't enable logging without good reason; the log files will gradually take over your disk space. If you do enable logging, delete old log files when you no longer need them.

If you enable access logging, Domino creates two log files. If you did not specify a log file name, Domino creates files named agent_log.*mmmddyy*, and referer_log.*mmmddyy*, where *mmmddyy* is the month, day, and year of the file. Domino records an entry into the current copy of each log whenever it receives a request for a document from a Web user. It enters the identity of the browser program in the agent log and either the IP address or the host name of the requesting computer in the referer log. It enters host names *only if you have enabled DNS lookup.* Otherwise, it enters IP addresses. See "HTTP Server Basics," earlier in this chapter, for the details about DNS lookup.

Tip

Because Domino appends *mmmddyy* to log filenames, it becomes a little awkward to read the files in a text editor. If you try to double-click the log file, Windows reports that it does not recognize the extension. If you open your text editor, the log files do not appear in any Open File dialog boxes unless you tell it to display all types of files.

A good way to open the file in Notepad under Windows NT 3.5x is to select the log file in File Manager; choose File, Run, enter **Notepad** in front of the name of the file, and click OK.

In Windows 95 or Windows NT 4.x, select the file in Windows Explorer (My Computer, Network Neighborhood), choose File, Open with, and choose Notepad from the list of files that appears. Better yet, add Notepad to the Send To fly-out menu that appears in Explorer's File menu. Then select the file and choose File, Send To, Notepad.

To add Notepad to the Send To menu, add a shortcut to it to the Send To folder, which appears either in the Windows folder or in your personal folder under the Profiles folder in the Windows folder. (Inhale!) Got that? If not, look it up in Explorer Help by searching for the word *send*.

If you enable error logging, Domino creates three log files: access.*mmmddyy*, errors.*mmmddyy*, and cgi_error.*mmmddyy*. Domino records internal errors in the first two log files and CGI errors in the last. When an internal error occurs, Domino records the identity of the requesting computer and the text of the request in the access log, and it records the Domino-generated error message in the errors log.

The actual field descriptions follow:

- **Access log**—Leave this blank to disable access logging. Enter a directory path name to enable access logging. Restart the HTTP server task after changing this entry.

- **Error log**—Leave this blank to disable error logging. Enter a directory path name to enable access logging. Restart the HTTP server task after changing this entry.

- **Time stamp**—This defaults to using Domino's local time when making entries in the logs. You can change it so that it uses Greenwich Mean Time.

- **No log**—Use this field to filter entries into the access logs. Enter here templates of either IP addresses or host/domain names. By templates, I mean you can use wildcards. For example, you can enter **192.192.*.***, or ***.chestnet.com**. Accesses to your server would not be logged if the accessing host has an IP address that begins with **192.192**, or has a host name ending in **chestnet.com**. Separate entries in this field with spaces. You can use host names in this field *only if you have enabled DNS lookup*. Otherwise, you can only use IP addresses. See "HTTP Server Basics," earlier in this chapter, for the details about DNS lookup.

Domino Security Features

An amazing thing happens when you start up the HTTP server for the first time. A server that previously would have guarded its databases with all the zeal of a mother bear protecting her cubs suddenly lets almost anyone in the world have entry to them (the databases, not the cubs). Lotus Notes is renowned for its robust security. The typical Domino server requires positive identification of anyone coming to it with a request for data. Even after you identify yourself to it, chances are you will either be turned away or given only the most proscribed access to the data you seek.

Every Notes administrator knows that you *can* disable the authentication function in Lotus Notes. But they know that you have to do so positively, by changing a field in the server document. Now comes along this server task that, by the mere act of loading it, disables the requirement of authentication. If you're new to Notes, you may be thinking right about now, "Okay, so what?" But people who have spent some time with traditional Notes servers tend to react to this discovery with shock. The really ironic part is that, while loading the HTTP service into memory opens the Domino server's secrets up to any Web surfer who wants to come poking around, the Notes server continues to jealously protect that same data whenever a legitimate Notes user comes around. Notes users have to authenticate with the server, while mere Web users can have anonymous access. Makes me lightheaded just to think about it.

If this still doesn't make *you* lightheaded, let's step back and examine Domino's security features from the ground up. To gain access to databases on a standard (non-HTTP) Domino server, a Notes user must first *authenticate* with the server, then must survive the server's access list, then get past a layered series of access lists in each database—view access lists, form access lists, document access lists, section access lists, and encrypted fields. One roadblock anywhere along the way, and the user is stopped cold.

In the authentication process, both the user and the server have to prove to each other that they are members of *trusted* organizations and they have to prove their identities. This involves a series of encryptions and decryptions of information using public and private keys. After the server has authenticated the user, the server can still refuse the user access to the server if the user is in the Not Access Server field or is not in the Access Server field in the Server's server document.

If the user gets past this checkpoint, the server considers any user request to access a database. The server consults the database's Access Control List, where the user may be listed, either individually or as a member of a group, as having Manager access, Designer access, Editor access, Author access, Reader access, Depositor access, or No access. Or, the user may not be listed at all, in which case the user is granted the Default level of access, which could be any of the listed levels. The rights that each access level grants are in Table 27.2.

Table 27.2   Lotus Notes Database Access Rights

Access Level	Activities Allowed
Manager	The database manager can do anything in a database, including change the Access Control List.
Designer	Database designers can do anything in a database, including making changes in the database design, but excluding making changes in the Access Control List.
Editor	Database editors can add data documents to a database and can make changes in any data document in the database, regardless of the document's authorship. Editors cannot change database design or the Access Control List.
Author	Database authors can create new data documents and they can edit documents they originally created. With certain exceptions, they cannot edit documents not authored by themselves. Nor can they make changes in the database design or Access Control List.
Reader	Database readers can read data documents and views but cannot make changes of any kind in the database.
Depositor	Database depositors can create and save new data documents, but they cannot read any document, including their own after they close it. Nor can they make changes of any kind in the database.
No Access	Users with no access are not allowed to open a database at all.

Assuming a user has some degree of access that allows him to at least read documents, the user may further be restricted by the following:

- View access lists, which forbid the use of a particular view to see what documents are in the database

- Form access lists, which forbid the use of a particular form when creating, editing, or reading documents

- Readers fields and $Readers fields, which can forbid the viewing of a particular document

- Authors fields, which can forbid the editing of a particular document

- Section access lists, which can forbid the reading or editing of a section of a document

- Encrypted fields, which can forbid the reading of those fields in a document

In Notes Release 4.5, you can relax Notes' security by allowing unauthenticated users to access a given server and its databases. An unauthenticated user is one whose identity the server has not ascertained and who, therefore, is essentially *anonymous* to the server. You permit anonymous access by setting the Allow Anonymous Notes Connections field in the Security section of the Server document in the Public Address Book to Yes; it defaults to No. You can control the degree of access such users have to given databases by adding Anonymous to each database's Access Control List and specifying the degree of access that Anonymous should have. If you don't add Anonymous to a database Access Control List, anonymous users are granted Default access.

Web Users and Domino Security

When you load the HTTP server task into the server's memory, you permit (by default) unauthenticated Web users to access your server and its databases. As a result, whether you like it or not, Web users now have access to your databases. They have Anonymous access to any database in which Anonymous appears in the database's Access Control List. They have Default access to all other databases.

You can tighten up the security of the databases on your Domino server in the following several ways:

- Remove from the Domino server any databases that don't need to be there.

- Altogether deny Web users anonymous access to your server, just the way the server denies access to unauthenticated Notes users, by resetting several fields in the Security section of the server document.

- Hide databases from view by resetting fields in each database's Properties InfoBox.

■ Review the Access Control List of every database on the server and ensure either that there is an entry in it for Anonymous, with the appropriate degree of access assigned, or that the degree of access assigned to Default is appropriate for unauthenticated Web users.

■ Deny anonymous access to a given database, then require Web users who want access to it to register with you. This is known as *basic authentication*. It is a standard Web authentication technique, and it gives a Web user individualized access to your site. That is, after registering with you, they are no longer anonymous. They tell you their names and passwords, and then you let them in—just like Notes users.

■ Activate Secure Sockets Layer (SSL) security for Web-based transactions.

Limiting Web Access at the Server Level. The Security section of the Server document has several fields that apply to Web security. By default, they permit wide open access to your Notes server. The fields are as follows:

■ **Allow anonymous HTTP connections**—Defaults to Yes. Setting it to No allows only authenticated Web users to access the databases on your site. All Web users, when they request a document from your site, must first enter their name and password in a dialog box. The server denies access if the name and password submitted do not match those in a Person document in the Public Name & Address Book.

■ **Allow HTTP clients to browse databases**—Defaults to Yes. By default, anyone who can access your site can retrieve a list of databases there by entering the /?open command. That is, they could enter something like this: **http:// domino.chestnet.com/?Open**. Setting this field to No forces users to authenticate before they can browse in this way.

Limiting Web Access at the Database Level. The fields described in the preceding section limit the types of access that anonymous Web users can gain to your server. You can do the same things on a database level. You can make it difficult for a Web user to locate a database on your server by changing two settings in the Database Properties InfoBox. You can control the types of things a Web user can do in a database by adding a user named Anonymous to the database's Access Control List.

You may not want to altogether disallow browsing with the /?open command. Instead, you can stop a database from appearing in the list that the /?open command procures. You do this in that database's Properties InfoBox, in the Design panel. Remove the checkmark from the box labeled Show in 'Open Database' Dialog (see Figure 27.3). You can also make sure the checkbox labeled List in Database Catalog is not checked, so that a user cannot browse in the Database Catalog database for the database you are trying to hide.

However, even if you hide a file so that a user cannot discover it by browsing, the user can still open any database whose filename he knows with the following command:

```
http://domino.chestnet.com/dbfilename.nsf/?OpenDatabase
```

Fig. 27.3   Two fields in the Database Properties InfoBox affect people's ability to find databases on the Domino server.

Ultimately, you control user access to databases with the Database Access Control List (ACL). Domino controls anonymous access to databases with two ACL entries: Anonymous and Default. If you add the name Anonymous to a database's ACL, anonymous users have the level of access that you assign to Anonymous. If you don't want anonymous Web users poking around in your Public Name & Address Book, gathering the names and phone numbers of your most valued employees, add Anonymous to the ACL and assign No Access.

If you neglect to add Anonymous to the ACL of a database, not to worry. Anonymous users still only get the level of access assigned to Default. Assign No Access to Default in the ACLs of your most sensitive databases, and only named users are able to open them.

You can further control user access at the view, form, and document levels. Every view, form, and document in a database has an Access List, located in the object's Properties InfoBox, which defaults to permitting use by everyone with appropriate ACL access. You can limit the membership of any Reader Access List. Notes documents can include Readers or Authors fields. If a user with Author ACL access is included in an Authors field, that user can edit the document even though he did not create the document. If a user with Reader ACL access is excluded from a Readers field, he is not able to read the document. Anonymous users may be included in or excluded from any of these Access Lists or fields. Anonymous users may be members of groups which are, in turn, included in or excluded from any of these Access Lists.

The only sub-database-level access limiters that do not function the same for Web users as for Notes users are signed and encrypted fields. Field signatures and encryption do not function when Web users view a document.

Setting Up Basic Authentication. You can give a Web user individualized database access if you create a Person document for that user entering data in two fields. First, you must enter the user's name in the User Name field. Second, you must enter a password into the HTTP Password field. The password is encrypted as soon as you save the Person document.

Tip

What? You don't feel like personally creating a Person document for every Web user who wants access to your restricted databases? Sounds like a blast to me. But, hey, that's okay, because you can set up a Notes registration application that allows Web users to register themselves. Lotus provides a sample registration application at **domino.lotus.com**. A user fills in a form and submits it; then a LotusScript agent creates a Person document for him in the Public Name & Address Book and adds him to a group in the Public Name & Address Book called Domino Users. Really cool application! Lotus uses it to register users at its own Web sites. Download it. Use it as is, customize it, or borrow pieces of it and create your own registration application. Lotus won't mind. They want you to take it. So, go for it. Better yet, look for it on the CD-ROM in the back of this book. The application is called Domino Registration Application. It is located at **http:// domino.lotus.com/domsite/domdown.nsf**.

After a Person document exists for a Web user, you can treat the user individually in database ACLs. You can set the access level of Anonymous in a database to No Access, and the access level of the registered user—or more realistically, of a group to which the registered user belongs—to Reader or some higher access level. When the registered Web user tries to access the database, he has to identify himself by name and password. Notes verifies the information entered against the information in the Public Name & Address Book, and then gives appropriate access to the database.

Here's another example: In a database ACL, you can give Reader access to Anonymous and Author access to your registered user (or a group of which he is a member). When the registered user opens the database, Notes goes along and opens it. When the user tries to add a document to the database, the server asks the user to identify himself.

You can also give your registered Notes users Web access to the server by adding a password to the HTTP Password field in their Person documents. Actually, if Default access in the Public Name & Address Book ACL is set to Author, then your users can do this for themselves. Thereafter, your Notes users are able to access the Notes server using either their Notes client or their Web browser.

There's one little catch here, though. Your users have to enter their fully distinguished names when prompted by their Web browser for name and password. The reason for this is that each Notes user's fully distinguished name appears first in the Full Name field of his/her Person document. You can remedy this by reordering the versions of each user's name in the Full Name field of his/her Person document, so that the user's common name (first name, optional middle initial, and last name only) appears first, on a line by itself. The resulting entry in the field looks like this:

```
User name:     Bob Dobbs
               Bob Dobbs/Sales/AcmeCorp
```

Thereafter, your users will be able to enter their common names when prompted by their Web browsers.

There is yet another safeguard in the ACL of each database that applies to Web users. On the Advanced page of the database ACL, the Maximum Internet browser access field defaults to No Access. You can set it to any ACL access level. It defines the maximum level of access that any non-Notes user will have to that database, no matter what access is shown for the user (or for Anonymous) on the Basics page. For example, if Maximum Internet browser access is set to Author, and a Web user is a member of a group that has Editor access on the Basics page, the Web user still only has Author access. The ACL access level in Maximum Internet browser access prevails over any higher access level granted on the Basics page.

Domino and the SSL Protocol

Domino supports the Secure Sockets Layer (SSL) security protocol for further securing Domino access by Web users. SSL is a public/private key encryption system that supports the following features:

- Encryption of data transferred between the Domino server and Web clients
- Validation that messages between the Domino server and Web clients were not tampered with en route
- Digital signatures

This, in turn, permits you to establish true user/server authentication between Web users and your Domino Web server, not just the pale imitation that basic Web authentication represents.

The SSL system works like other public/private key systems, such as Notes' own security system. In fact, both Notes and SSL use the RSA (Rivest, Shamir, Adleman) cryptosystem to create their encryption keys. Each user and server possesses both a private key and a public key. The user or server then makes the public key available to the world and keeps the private key to him/her/itself.

Only the private key can decrypt data that was encrypted with the public key. Only the public key can decrypt data that was encrypted with the private key. If I want to encrypt a message to you, I do so with your public key. Only you have possession of your private key, so only you can decrypt the message. If I want to assure you that a message is really from me and not some impostor, I can sign the message with my private key. If you can decrypt the signature with my public key, you can assume it came from me, because (presumably) nobody but me has access to my private key.

The weakness of public/private key encryption systems is that I can send you a public key and tell you it is from anyone in the world—say, for example, Bill Clinton. Then I can send out all sorts of politically damaging statements, sign them with Bill Clinton's private key, and you might say, "I know Bill Clinton said these things because he signed his name to them!" (Sure you would. And I have a bridge for sale, cheap, in Brooklyn.)

VI

Working with the Web

How do you verify that the public key I send you really isn't from Bill Clinton at all? You establish positive identification of me, that's how. Either you have to get the public key from me personally, satisfying yourself at that time that I am who I say I am. Or, you have to get someone that you trust to vouch for me and the public key I am offering you. In SSL parlance, this trusted third party is a Certification Authority (CA). It is the equivalent of the Certifier in Notes.

The CA establishes who I am and issues me a certificate, signed by the CA, declaring that I am me. The CA does the same for you. (Under SSL, we store our certificates, along with our private public keys, in a password-protected file called a *keyring* file. In Notes, we store our certificates in our ID files.) When you and I, total strangers until now, want to establish a confidential relationship, we can establish each other's identity by presenting to each other the certificates issued to us by the CA. We can trust each other's certificate because they were both signed using the same private key (that belonging to the CA). We each know the difficulty we had to undergo to get the certificate; we assume the other had to go through the same ordeal. Each can assume the other is the person the CA certifies him to be.

In the future, anytime we want to communicate with each other, we can reestablish each other's identity the same way. We never have to worry that we are talking to an impostor (unless someone stole one of our private keys, of course).

Notes' implementation of SSL allows great flexibility in establishing a certification scheme. You can self-certify for testing purposes or if you don't need the assurance of certification by a CA. You can become a CA and issue certificates to others. You can contract with a commercial CA. For example, if you want to set up secure transactions within your own intranet, you can set yourself up as the company CA. Your office issues the certificates to your Domino server and to all of the secured users. If you want to set up secure transactions outside your company—say, to conduct sales on the Internet— you can contract with a commercial CA, such as VeriSign (**www.verisign.com**), to certify you and all users who want to do business with you.

Domino comes with a Notes application, Domino SSL Administration, that automates the establishment of SSL security. It guides you through the process of either self-certifying or submitting a request for a certificate to either your own internal CA or VeriSign. It also guides you through the process of merging the resulting certificate into your keyring file. Finally, if you want to become a CA yourself, it guides you through that process as well as the process of issuing certificates to others. We don't have enough space to describe these processes in detail, but you can obtain more information in two databases that come with the Notes server: the Domino Documentation database, Chapter 5, "Security (SSL)," and the Domino SSL Administration database. You can also download the Notes and the Internet database from **domino.lotus.com**.

The Domino Site as Seen from a Browser

As soon as the HTTP server task is running, you can reach the Domino server from a Web browser. At first, your Domino-based Web site does not look like much to Web users. But you can change the default settings in the Server document and redesign your databases to take advantage of the features of HTML. You can use a variety of techniques to improve the appearance and usefulness of your Web site.

When you look at a brand new, unrefined Domino Web site through a browser, the first thing you see is a list of the databases stored on the Domino Notes server. Each database appears as an HTML hyperlink (see Figure 27.4).

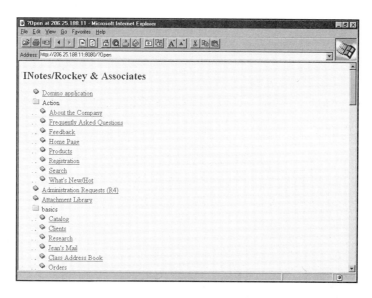

Fig. 27.4   The unadorned Domino Web site displays a list of available databases instead of a home page.

When you click a database hyperlink, by default Domino sends you a list of available views in that database. Each view appears as an HTML hyperlink (see Figure 27.5). If a database is designed to open a graphic navigator when you open it in Notes, that navigator appears instead of the list of views when you open the database in a browser.

Click a view hyperlink to see the contents of the view—a list of documents, each appearing as an HTML hyperlink (see Figure 27.6). At the top of the view, you see one or possibly two action bars. The action bar you see is a row of five navigation graphics that Domino inserts in every view automatically. The first two graphics take you to the previous and next views, respectively. The next two graphics either expand or collapse a view category. (Yes, Domino supports collapsible views.) The last takes you to a search screen. If the Notes version of the view has an action bar associated with it, the action bar items may appear as a row of buttons across the top of the HTML version of the list of views. Scroll to the bottom of the view and you see the row of navigation graphics again, duplicated at the bottom of the view.

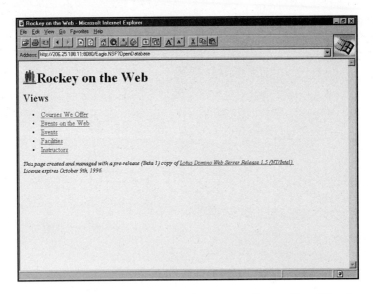

Fig. 27.5   When you click one of the databases, Domino sends you a list of the views in the database.

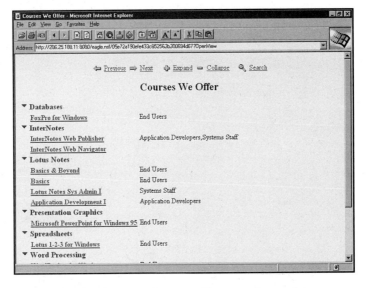

Fig. 27.6   Domino adds an action bar to the top and bottom of every view page.

Click a document in the view and, you guessed it, the document appears. To see other documents, views, or databases, you can back up to a previous level high enough to display it, then move down that branch.

In addition to browsing the views, you can perform a full-text search of any database on the site that has been full-text indexed. When you click the Search icon in the action bar of a view, you see a Full Text Search screen that looks like the one in Figure 27.7. You might recognize that the fields in this screen are the same choices that you have when defining a full-text search in Notes. If the Domino server has been set up for multi-database searching, you may see another search form, and when you use it to perform a search, Domino will search multiple databases.

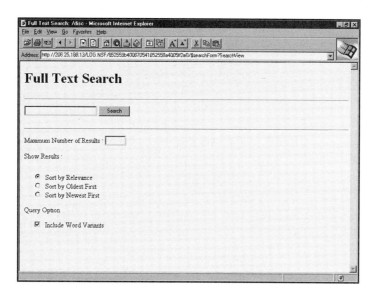

Fig. 27.7   Enter a Boolean (AND, OR, NOT) query in the search window. Notes returns a list of links to documents in the database that meet the terms of your query.

If the Webmaster of a Domino Web site has had an opportunity to modify the parameters of the Server document and the databases on the server, then your first look at the site will probably not be a list of databases. Instead, you see a real home page. The home page may be a file residing in the Domino server's HTML directory, designed by some artist to knock your socks off when you first see it, in hopes that you will come back again and again to the site and tell all your friends and associates about it. Or, the home page might be the About This Database document or an opening graphical navigator for one of the databases on the server. Considering what you can do with graphics in Notes, this might knock your socks off, too.

If the Webmaster has gone to the trouble of creating a home page for you, there undoubtedly will be links on it to other documents at the site and perhaps other sites. The links may take you to database home pages, database view pages, document pages, form pages, or HTML files.

If you follow a link to a form page, you see a series of fields into which you can enter data (see Figure 27.8). The form also has at least one Submit button which, when you click it, returns the filled-in form to the Domino server. Submitting a form to Domino in a Web browser is basically the same process that it is in Notes. The form looks different than a typical Notes form. It may not have all the functionality of the same form under Notes. But it does have the same kinds of fields. Most standard Notes @functions work in it just as in Notes forms. After you hit the Submit button, Domino treats the resulting document like a document that any Notes user might have created. That is, it executes any input translation or input validation formulas. It creates a new Notes document based on the form. Any agents that process other documents will act on this one, too.

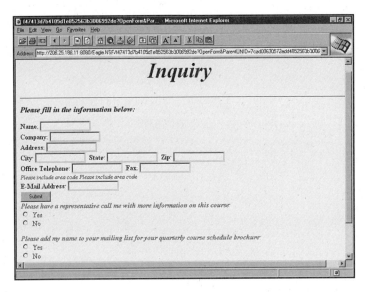

Fig. 27.8   When a Web user submits a form, Domino turns it into a standard Notes document and stores it in a database on the Domino server.

Developing Applications for the Domino Web Site

The unmodified Domino Web site is a perfectly serviceable but not especially exciting site. It makes the information available, but does not exactly send shock waves out over the Internet. What you really want is to modify your Notes databases so that they pack a little punch. Instead of seeing an undifferentiated list of database names and exploring them at random, the Web user can see an attractive and informative home page that focuses his attention on the things you want him to see. Instead of browsing your site more or less aimlessly, the user can see on the home page what is available, what is interesting, and how to get there. Your user doesn't waste time getting the information he needs, and he is less likely to try to get into databases you don't want him in.

More important than making your site inviting is making it interactive. The big advantage that Notes has over the World Wide Web is that Notes was designed from the bottom up to be interactive. The users both create the data and retrieve it. The World Wide Web started out as a one-way information publishing scheme. To get information from the users back into the vanilla Web server, you have to build what amount to kludges by writing scripts in CGI. Because the Web is not inherently a two-way information tool, browsers don't typically provide tools for users to add, edit, or delete documents on Web servers. To provide that functionality, you have to add those capabilities to the views, forms, and documents in your Notes databases.

To make your Domino Web site both more appealing and more interactive, you can do the following:

- Designate and create a home page document or home page database containing links to all the other pages and databases you want to make available to Web users

- Add actions to forms and views to enhance interactivity

- Redesign forms to minimize the text formatting limitations of HTML

- Consider the differences in how Notes and HTML handle graphics

- Consider enhancing views, forms, and documents with embedded HTML codes

- Consider enhancing views and forms with special Notes fields designed specifically for Web-enhancing your databases

- Use Notes graphics navigators as HTML image maps

- Add CGI variables to input forms to gather information automatically from Web users

- Use MIME type mappings to inform the Web user's browser what program to open an attached file with

Text-Formatting Considerations

When designing any form—whether an About Database form that Web users will view as a home page, or a form that will act as a template for documents in a database—you need to be aware of the limitations of HTML text formatting. You don't want to use Notes' text-formatting features that do not translate well into HTML.

Notes' text-formatting features that are supported by HTML include the following:

- Left-aligned, centered, and right-aligned paragraphs

- Inter-paragraph spacing

- Table column alignment (but not column widths)

- Extra space characters (preserved only if using a platform's default monospace font—for example, Courier in Windows)

- Font styles (bold, italic, underline, and so on, but not Shadow, Emboss, or Extrude)

- Font colors

- Bulleted and numbered lists

- Named styles

Notes' text-formatting features that are not supported by HTML include the following:

- Paragraph indentation (whether using tabs or the indentation markers on the ruler)

- Inter-line spacing

- Tab spacing

- Extra space characters (are removed on translation to HTML except when using a platform's default monospace font—for example, Courier in Windows)

- Fully justified and no-wrap paragraphs (they become left-aligned)

- Font sizes (they are mapped to predefined HTML heading styles)

The upshot here is that HTML eliminates white space from paragraphs, no matter how you insert the white space, except for one way—using tables. Inter-line spacing within a paragraph is reduced to single-spacing. Indents disappear, whether they were created using tabs, spaces, or the indent markers on the ruler. With one exception, white space between words disappears, all but one space, whether put there with spaces or tabs.

On the other hand, centered and right-aligned paragraphs are supported. Inter-paragraph spacing is preserved, whether inserted with carriage returns or by using the Spacing Above/Below fields in the Text Properties InfoBox. Column alignments are preserved in a table. And if you use your computer platform's default monospace font (in Windows, that is Courier, not Courier New), then white space inserted using the space bar is preserved.

The Notes formatting features that Domino does support, it supports by inserting equivalent HTML codes into the text at the time it delivers a form or document to the Web user.

Text Tables. If you want to set up text in columns that translate into HTML columns, there are two ways to do it: using HTML tables or using extra spaces with your operating system's default monospace font. Use Notes tables if your Web audience uses graphical browsers that support HTML tables. That includes most of the world. If a large number of the Web users that you cater to (and this should be a dwindlingly small number) use text-based browsers or any browser that does not support HTML tables, you can use manually spaced tables formatted in your computer platform's default monospace font. In Windows, that is Courier, not Courier New.

When you use Notes tables, the border settings of the top, left cell become the border settings of the whole table in HTML. And you can choose whether to have cell borders or not.

Font Sizes. Font sizes in Notes map to HTML header styles as shown in Table 27.3. The HTML header styles in turn map to font sizes on a Web browser according to the browser's configuration. What that boils down to is there is not a one-to-one correlation between the font sizes Notes uses to display a document and the font sizes a Web browser uses to display the same document.

Table 27.3 Notes Font Sizes versus HTML Header Styles	
Notes Font Point Sizes Less Than or Equal To	**HTML Header Style**
8pt	H1
10pt	H2
12pt	H3
14pt	H4
18pt	H5
24pt	H6
Larger than 24pt	H7

Graphics Formatting Considerations

You can transfer graphic images from Notes documents to HTML documents in two ways. First, Domino automatically converts embedded graphics of all kinds into files in either GIF or JPEG format {depending on your choice in the HTTP Server section of the Server document) and sends the resulting graphic file to the Web user along with the HTML document, which has a reference in it to the graphic file.

Second, you can insert *passthru HTML code* into a form or document. Passthru HTML is a reference to an existing file on your server. When Domino converts the Notes document to HTML and sends it to the user, the reference is passed, unchanged, through to the HTML document. The user receives both the document and the referenced graphics file. A passthru HTML code looks something like this:

```
[<IMG SRC="http://domino.chestnet.com/filename.gif" WIDTH=240 HEIGHT=120>]
```

In the preceding code, IMG SRC means image source, *filename* is the name of the file, and the WIDTH and HEIGHT commands tell the browser the size of the image in pixels. For absolute fidelity to the original image, use the same width and height sizes as the actual image. If you use different sizes, some browsers resize the image accordingly (and, naturally, other browsers ignore the size parameters). If you do resize in any way other than multiplying the original measurements by integers (original measurement ×2 or ×3 or ×4, and so on), the resulting image may look distorted or have moiré patterns.

Domino servers store embedded graphics in two forms, a platform-dependent metafile (Windows Metafile in Windows), and a platform-independent bitmap. When you view the document in Notes, you may be looking at either the metafile or the bitmap (depending on a choice made by the person who embedded the file originally). Notes ships the bitmap, not the metafile, to the Web user. Because the metafile and the bitmap may not look exactly alike, the graphic that Notes users and Web users see might be slightly different.

Navigators as Image Maps

An image map is a graphic image, included in an HTML document, that has hotspot links associated with different parts of it. If you click this portion of the image, you are requesting one document; if you click that portion of the image, you are requesting another document. Well-designed image maps are attractive and make it easy for a Web user to navigate around in your Web site.

Domino converts graphics navigators in Notes databases into image maps in the resulting HTML documents. Domino-created image maps are both *client-side* and *server-side* image maps, meaning that all browsers support them.

To create an image map, you create a graphic navigator, paste the graphic image you want to use into it as a graphic background, and then add hotspots to it that link to other navigators, views, documents, other databases, and so on.

There are two caveats. First, any graphics that you paste onto the navigator as anything other than a graphic background disappear from the image map upon translation to HTML. Second, any text that you add in Notes to the navigator also disappears on translation. Therefore, you need to create the entire graphic image, including all graphical and text components, in a graphics program external to Notes. The only thing you do in Notes is paste the image in the navigator as a graphic background, add the hotspots to it, and program the hotspots.

To create a navigator, follow these steps:

1. Create or open in a paint or drawing program the graphic image that will become the image map.

2. Copy the image (or the portion of it that you want) to the Clipboard. Most programs allow you to do this by selecting the image (or part of it) and then choosing Edit, Copy in the menu. You may also be able to select the image, and then press Ctrl+C.

3. Return to Notes. Open the database in which you intend to create the navigator.

4. Create a new navigator by choosing Create, Design, Navigator in the menu. A new Navigator design window appears.

5. In the menu, choose Design, Navigator Properties. The Navigator Properties InfoBox appears.

6. Enter a name for the navigator in the Name field of the InfoBox. You can give it an alias as well as a name by naming it in the format Navigator Name ¦ Alias.

7. Paste the Clipboard image into the navigator by choosing Create, Graphic Background in the menu. Do not paste the image using Edit, Paste; it doesn't work that way.

8. Assign URL links to different portions of the image. To learn how, see the sections "Creating a Hotspot Rectangle," "Creating a Hotspot Polygon," "Defining Hotspot Properties," and "Assigning an URL to a Hotspot Rectangle or Polygon," later in this chapter.

9. Save and close the navigator.

To define an URL link in a graphical navigator, create a hotspot rectangle or hotspot polygon and assign the @URLOpen ("*URLname*") @function to it (see Figure 27.9).

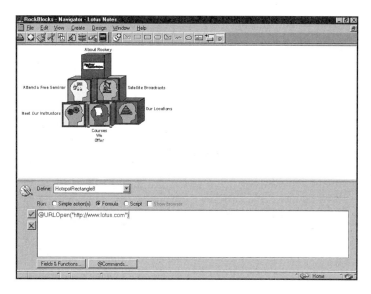

Fig. 27.9   This is a Navigator in Design mode. Note the @URLOpen @function in the formula pane.

Creating a Hotspot Rectangle. To create a hotspot rectangle, choose Create, Hotspot Rectangle in the menu or click the red rectangle icon in the Toolbar. Your mouse pointer becomes a crosshair. Place the crosshair at one corner of the area to be covered by the rectangle, and then, holding the mouse button down, drag the crosshair to the opposite corner. You see a black rectangle appear as you draw. When you release the mouse button, it becomes a red rectangle.

If you are not happy with the resulting rectangle, you can resize it by dragging the corner handles. If no corner handles appear, click anywhere on the rectangle to make them appear.

Creating a Hotspot Polygon. Use the hotspot polygon to define a non-rectangular portion of the graphic image. To create a Hotspot Polygon, choose Create, Hotspot Polygon in the menu; or choose the red polygon icon in the toolbar. Your mouse pointer becomes a crosshair.

Place the crosshair at one apex of the area to be defined. Click the mouse button to anchor a line at that point. Move the mouse pointer to an adjacent apex. A line connects the first apex to your mouse pointer.

At the second apex, click the mouse again to anchor the other end of the first line and create an anchor for your next line. Move the mouse pointer to the third apex. Click to create the third line.

Continue until you have reached the last unconnected apex. There you double-click, which creates the second-to-last line and the last line between the last apex and the first apex. The secret to using the Hotspot Polygon tool is to remember to double-click the last apex to close the polygon.

When you finish creating the hotspot polygon, the lines turn red, and corner handles appear when the hotspot polygon is selected. If you want to adjust the shape of the polygon, drag the handles.

Defining Hotspot Properties. After you have created a hotspot rectangle or polygon, you can define its properties in the HotspotRectangle/Polygon Properties InfoBox. You can rename it in the Name field. You can lock or unlock its size and position. You can define whether the outline of the hotspot appears either when you touch it with the mouse pointer or when you click it. Finally, you can define the weight and color of the outline.

Assigning an URL to a Hotspot Rectangle or Polygon. To assign an URL to a hotspot rectangle or hotspot polygon in a graphic navigator, select the rectangle or polygon while in Design mode. Handles appear at the corners of the object when it is selected. Or, you can select the name of the hotspot from the list in the Define field in the Formula pane of the design window. Then, in the Run field, choose Formula. In the formula pane, enter @URLOpen ("*URLname*"), where *URLname* is the URL of the page that this hotspot should point to.

For example, if the hotspot should point to the Lotus Domino Web site, the formula should read: @URLOpen("http://domino.lotus.com"). To point to the home page of your own site, the formula could read: @URLOpen("/").

Attachments and MIME

If you attach files to Notes documents, they appear in the documents as representative icons. When you double-click the icon in Notes, an Attachment Properties InfoBox appears. On the first tab of the InfoBox, three buttons appear: View, Launch, and Detach. Clicking one allows you to view the contents of the file, run the program that created the file, or make a copy of the file on disk.

When Domino sends a Notes document with attachments to a Web user, it does two things. First, it copies the attached file to the cache directory. Second, it converts the icon representing the file to a GIF image and turns the GIF into a link hotspot that points to the location on the Domino server of the file. The code behind the link looks something like this:

```
http://www.planetnotes.com/DatabaseName.nsf/ViewUNID/
DocumentUNID/Attachments/CachedFileName/
OriginalAttachmentFileName.ext?OpenElement
```

In the preceding code, *DatabaseName* is the name of the database in which the HTML document originated. *ViewUNID* is Notes' unique identifier (a very long number) of the view in which the document was located. *DocumentUNID* is Notes' unique identifier of the original document. *CachedFileName* is the filename under which Domino stored the cached version of the attached file. *OriginalAttachmentFileName.ext* is the original filename of the attachment before it was attached to the Notes document. *?OpenElement* is the HTTP command to send the attachment to the browser.

If the user clicks the GIF hotspot, the browser retrieves the file and attempts to view it or run it as a program. If the browser cannot figure out how to do either of those things, it presents the viewer with a dialog box offering the options of either saving the file or telling the browser what helper application it should use to launch or view the file. If the user decides to save the file, the browser uses the *OriginalAttachmentFileName.ext* as the default filename.

The way the browser figures out how to handle a downloaded file is by referring to a file in the Notes data directory, an HTTP configuration file called HTTPD.CNF, placed there by the installation program when the server was installed (or by the Domino install program if Domino was installed separately from Notes 4.5). HTTPD.CNF is a text file that contains line after line of MIME type mappings as well as lots of other interesting and/or mystifying lines of text.

MIME is an acronym that stands for *Multipurpose Internet Multimedia Extensions*. MIME is an Internet protocol that defines a set of rules for attaching files of all kinds to mail messages and other files (such as HTML files) that computers send to each other across the Net. The early Internet messaging protocols, such as *SMTP* (*Simple Message Transfer Protocol*), defined how to format and e-mail a message but did not provide for attaching files to messages. In the early days of the Internet, you didn't attach files to messages. You sent the messages by SMTP and you transferred the files by a separate process called *FTP* (*File Transfer Protocol*). As time passed, people came up with various ways to attach files to mail messages, but it was always a chore until MIME established a standard way of doing it.

A MIME *type mapping* is a line of text that defines a file type and equates its filename extension to a program that can be used to open the file or run the program, if that is what the file is. MIME-compliant programs, such as modern Internet mail programs like Eudora and modern Web browsers, can receive a file attached to or embedded in another file, and then process the attached/embedded file or hand it off to another program to process. The way a MIME-compliant browser knows how to do this is by obtaining the file type from the HTTPD.CNF file.

If you get in the habit of attaching a particular type of file to your Notes documents, and you would like Web users to be able to process the files automatically, you can add a type-mapping row to the `HTTPD.CNF` file to represent your file type. When the user downloads a file, Domino sends the information from the type-mapping line to the user along with the file. If the user has the program needed to process the file, the processing takes place automatically.

The syntax for a MIME type-mapping line is the following:

```
Addtype .extension type/subtype/ encoding [quality[ character-set]] # Comment
```

`Addtype` is the MIME keyword identifying this as a type-mapping line. `.extension` is the file extension used to identify the file type. `Type/subtype` identifies the file type. Examples of types are application, audio, image, and text. `Encoding` tells how the file is encoded. Types of encoding include binary, 7-bit bytes, and 8-bit bytes. `Quality` and `character set`, both optional, identify the file yet further. The pound sign (#) identifies the text that follows it as a comment.

A sample of type mappings appears in Figure 27.10.

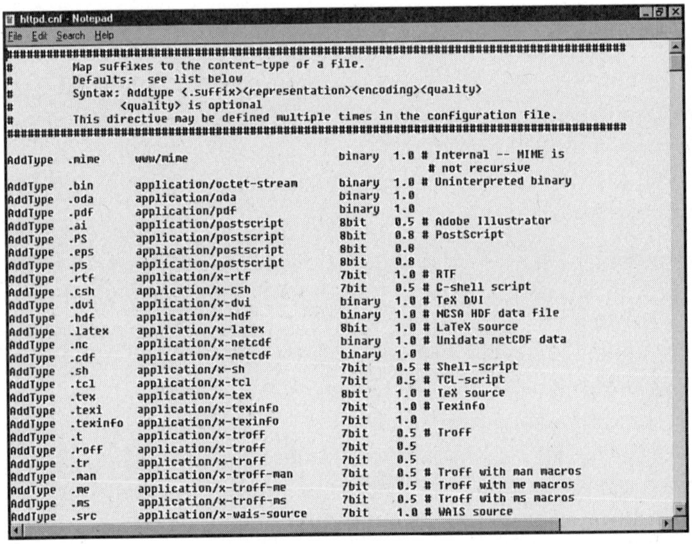


```
################################################################################
#        Map suffixes to the content-type of a file.
#        Defaults:  see list below
#        Syntax: Addtype <.suffix><representation><encoding><quality>
#                <quality> is optional
#        This directive may be defined multiple times in the configuration file.
################################################################################

AddType  .mime      www/mime                     binary  1.0 # Internal -- MIME is
                                                             # not recursive

AddType  .bin       application/octet-stream     binary  1.0 # Uninterpreted binary
AddType  .oda       application/oda              binary  1.0
AddType  .pdf       application/pdf              binary  1.0
AddType  .ai        application/postscript       8bit    0.5 # Adobe Illustrator
AddType  .PS        application/postscript       8bit    0.8 # PostScript
AddType  .eps       application/postscript       8bit    0.8
AddType  .ps        application/postscript       8bit    0.8
AddType  .rtf       application/x-rtf            7bit    1.0 # RTF
AddType  .csh       application/x-csh            7bit    0.5 # C-shell script
AddType  .dvi       application/x-dvi            binary  1.0 # TeX DVI
AddType  .hdf       application/x-hdf            binary  1.0 # NCSA HDF data file
AddType  .latex     application/x-latex          8bit    1.0 # LaTeX source
AddType  .nc        application/x-netcdf         binary  1.0 # Unidata netCDF data
AddType  .cdf       application/x-netcdf         binary  1.0
AddType  .sh        application/x-sh             7bit    0.5 # Shell-script
AddType  .tcl       application/x-tcl            7bit    0.5 # TCL-script
AddType  .tex       application/x-tex            8bit    1.0 # TeX source
AddType  .texi      application/x-texinfo        7bit    1.0 # Texinfo
AddType  .texinfo   application/x-texinfo        7bit    1.0
AddType  .t         application/x-troff          7bit    0.5 # Troff
AddType  .roff      application/x-troff          7bit    0.5
AddType  .tr        application/x-troff          7bit    0.5
AddType  .man       application/x-troff-man      7bit    0.5 # Troff with man macros
AddType  .me        application/x-troff-me       7bit    0.5 # Troff with me macros
AddType  .ms        application/x-troff-ms       7bit    0.5 # Troff with ms macros
AddType  .src       application/x-wais-source    7bit    1.0 # WAIS source
```

Fig. 27.10 The `HTTPD.CNF` file includes line after line of MIME type mappings.

HTML Tags

You don't need to use HTML tags in your databases, but they do offer a handy set of tools for improving the look of your databases when viewed in a Web browser. You can add them in the following three ways:

- Embed them in any field by enclosing them in square brackets
- Place them in a rich text paragraph assigned a style named HTML
- Place them in a rich text field named HTML

Using Bracketed HTML Codes. Because HTML codes are already enclosed in angle brackets, when you embed them in a field by enclosing them in square brackets, they end up being double-bracketed, like this: [<*HTMLcode*>] (where *HTMLcode* is the actual code). When Domino translates the document into HTML, it strips off the square brackets and passes the enclosed code, unchanged, through to the HTML document, so that the code appears like this: <*HTMLcode*>.

Using a Paragraph Style Named HTML. The key to using a paragraph style named HTML is that you need not use the square brackets at all. Domino assumes that any text within the paragraph that is enclosed in angle brackets is an HTML code, and acts accordingly. Thus, the paragraph style called HTML is just an alternative to enclosing codes in a double set of brackets. If you have a lot of HTML codes you want to embed, you can save yourself the hassle of entering all those square brackets.

To create a paragraph style in Notes, follow these steps:

1. In Notes, place the text insertion point either in a rich text field or in the design pane of a form in Design mode. This causes the Text menu item to appear in Notes' menu bar. A quick way to get to a rich text field is to compose a mail memo, and put the insertion point into the Body field, which is a rich text field.

2. Format a paragraph of text (any text will do, including nonsense text) the way you want the style to be defined. If you are creating an HTML style, you don't much care about the Notes formatting, because the purpose of this style is to inform the Domino HTTP service that this paragraph consists of HTML tags, which should be passed through unaltered to the Web client.

3. In the menu, choose Text, Text Properties. The Text Properties InfoBox opens.

4. Click the last tab in the Text Properties InfoBox. The tab looks like a tag with the letter S in it. The paragraph style panel appears.

5. Click the Create Style button. The Create Named Style dialog box appears.

6. Enter **HTML** in the Style name field.

7. Check the boxes in the other three fields according to your own preferences. For most styles, I prefer to check all three boxes. Click the Help button to learn more about each field. Click OK when finished.

The new style appears in the list of available styles in the Text Properties InfoBox and in the status bar at the bottom of the Notes program window. Apply the HTML style to a paragraph by placing the insertion point anywhere in the paragraph, then selecting HTML in either style list (the one in the Text Properties InfoBox or the one in the status bar). Or assign the style by cycling to it with repeated presses of the Cycle key (F11). While our goal here is to save ourselves the trouble of entering square brackets around every HTML tag in this paragraph, you might just take note that paragraph styles are also a great, fast, easy way to apply formatting to any Notes paragraph.

VI

Working with the Web

By the way, if you don't want Notes users scratching their heads over all the chicken scratchings in an HTML paragraph, use Hide When properties to hide it from them. To do this, do the following:

1. Go into the document in Edit mode.

2. Put the insertion point anywhere in the paragraph. You need not select the whole paragraph because Hide When properties always affect whole paragraphs, whether you like it or not.

3. Choose Text, Text Properties. The Text Properties InfoBox appears.

4. Click the window shade tab in the InfoBox. The hide-paragraph properties appear.

5. Check the boxes marked Preview for reading and Opened for reading.

6. Close the InfoBox and save and close the document.

Using a Text or Rich Text Field Named HTML. Finally, let's say you have a bunch of existing HTML documents. Maybe they are currently being stored on the third-party Web server that you plan to retire just as soon as you get your Domino Web server running smoothly. You don't want to lose those documents.

Well, you can just move them over to the HTML directory on the Domino server. But then you can't track them with Notes. You still have to manage them manually. What you really want to do is import them into one or more Notes databases. That way, Notes can keep track of them for you.

The question is: How can you take these existing HTML documents and store them in Notes documents in such a way that they pass, entire and unchanged, through Domino's translation process to Web users?

The answer is: You can create a form that contains a text or rich text field that you name HTML. If the HTML field is rich text, you should also include at least one other text field, so that the document can appear in a view (rich text fields do not appear in view columns). The form can also include other fields, as many (and of whatever data types) as you want. Next, create documents based on the form, paste or import your HTML documents into the HTML field of each new document, and save the new documents.

Whenever Domino translates such a document, it not only passes the imported HTML document through unaltered to the Web user, but—and this is the cool part—it ignores all other fields in the document. It passes *only* the contents of the HTML field to the Web user.

The other fields are important. They can include all sorts of information about the contents of the HTML field, so that you can classify the document. Most important, a year or two after you have forgotten altogether that the document exists, you can go back and draw some clue from the other fields what the document is all about.

Input Forms

Notes was designed from day one, from the ground up, to receive information from Notes users, then give it back to them. Domino's HTTP service was designed from day one, from the ground up, to extend the functionality of Notes to non-Notes users out on the Internet. Not only can Domino get information in Notes databases out to the non-Notes world, but non-Notes users can, almost transparently, put information back into Notes and, by natural extension, participate in Notes applications. As Lotus puts it, Domino is the world's first Internet Application Server. It is Notes for the Internet.

When I say Web users can participate almost transparently in Notes applications, I mean the following two things:

- Notes forms are not as accessible to Web users as they are to Notes users.

- Notes forms are not as fully functional on the Web as they are in Notes.

Making Input Forms Accessible to Web Users. The first problem is that, when you, the Web user, want to create, edit, or delete a Notes document from within a browser, you can't just pull down the menu and choose a command. The database designer must make the commands available to you in one of the following three ways:

- As an action on a view or form action bar

- As an action hotspot anywhere in a document or form

- As an HTML link anywhere in a document or form

These all appear as clickable buttons, text, or graphics. The user clicks it and a form appears. The user completes the form, clicks the Submit button that appears automatically at the bottom of the form, and Domino takes the form, translates it back into Notes format, and stores it in the database.

Actions. Actions are buttons that appear in an action bar at the top of the screen whenever a view or document that has an action bar is present on the screen. When viewed in a Web browser, action bar actions look like cells in a bordered table. The text inside each cell is a link that, when you click it, performs the defined action. In your case, you might want it to do any number of things: create a new document, open an existing document in Edit mode, move a document to a folder, or delete a document.

To create an action that creates a new document, you can use @Command([Compose]). The steps for creating such an action are as follows:

1. Open in Design mode the view or form in whose action bar the action should appear.

2. Make the action pane appear. Choose <u>V</u>iew, <u>A</u>ction Pane in the menu. Or drag the action pane border out from the right side of the screen. Or double-click the action pane border. Or click the Action Pane SmartIcon (third from the right in a Form window, rightmost in a View window).

The action pane displays a list of all currently defined actions for the current view or form. There are six Default Actions, recognizable because their names begin with an asterisk.

3. Create another action by choosing Create, Action in the menu. The word (Untitled) appears in the action pane and the Action Properties InfoBox for that action appears on the screen.

4. Name the new action in the Title field of the Action Properties InfoBox. The name should be descriptive but short, because it will be the text that appears in the action bar in both Notes and the browser.

5. Optionally, choose an icon from the array in the Button Icon field. The icon appears to the left of the actions title in the action bar both in Notes and the browser. Don't skip this step; it's the neatest part of creating an action, and may be the hardest. (Choosing just the right icon is tough.)

6. Check the box labeled Include Action in Button Bar.

7. Change the action's horizontal position in the action bar (and its vertical position in the Action Menu) by changing the number in the Position field. Number one is the leftmost (topmost) position.

8. If this form is to be used only by Web users, go to the Hide When panel by clicking the window shade icon. Check the box labeled Hide action if formula is true. Enter the following formula in the formula field:

```
!@IsMember("$$WebClient";@Userroles)
```

9. Close the Action Properties InfoBox. Make sure the design pane appears in the bottom half of the screen. If it does not, choose View, Design Pane in the menu. Or drag the design pane border up from the bottom of the screen. Or double-click the design pane border. Or click the Design Pane SmartIcon (fourth from right in a Form window, second from right in a View window).

10. In the design pane, make sure the Define field says *ActionName*(Action), where *ActionName* is the title of your action. Make sure the Formula radio button is selected. Enter the following formula in the formula window:

```
!@Command([Compose]; "FormName")
```

11. Save, close, and test the form or view.

If you did everything correctly, your new action should appear in the action bar when the view or form to which you added it is open on the screen. That is, if you did not hide the action from Notes users, it should appear when the form or view is open in Notes and when it is open in a browser. If you hid the form from Notes users, then the action should appear only in a Web browser.

The first formula in step 8, of the preceding steps, is interpreted in the next few paragraphs.

@UserRoles returns any Roles that the current user fulfills. These are the Roles that appear in the database ACL, mostly. However, if a user is coming in from the Web, @UserRoles returns $$WebClient.

@IsMember asks if $$WebClient is a member of the list of Roles returned by @UserRoles. If it *is* a member, as it would be if the user is coming from the Web, then @IsMember returns 1, true. If it is not a member, as it would not be if the user is coming in from a Notes client, then @IsMember returns 0, false. The exclamation point that precedes @IsMember means *NOT*. The whole thing taken together is true if the user is not a member of $$WebClient (and is therefore a Notes user, not a Web user), in which case the action is hidden from that user.

The second formula, in step 10, says compose a form called *FormName*, where *FormName* is the name of the form the user wants to compose.

To create an action that performs some act upon an existing document, you have to add your action to the action bar of the form with which the document is displayed. You cannot put this kind of action in a view action bar because there is no way in a Web browser to tell the action which document in the view it should act upon.

To add an action that opens an existing document in Edit mode, perform the same preceding steps, but use this formula in step 10:

```
@Command([EditDocument])
```

You can also hide this action when the document is being edited, because the action doesn't do anything in Edit mode when in a Web browser. Interestingly, one of the Default Actions (the ones whose names begin with an asterisk) is Edit Document. You can't use it, however, because the Default Actions do not show up in the action bar when viewed in a Web browser; you have to make your own @command and duplicate the functionality of the Default Action. (Oh, well. Maybe in the next release...)

To add an action that deletes a document, use the following formula:

```
@Command([EditClear])
```

Notes provides a Simple Action that deletes documents. But (like Default Actions), Simple Actions do not show up in the action bar when viewed in a Web browser.

By now, maybe you can see the pattern. To add an action that affects an existing document, you have to add it to the form action bar not to the view action bar. And you have to use an @command formula even though a Default Action or a Simple Action would do the same thing in Notes that you want your action to do in a Web browser.

Action Hotspots. An *action hotspot* is a block of text—usually surrounded by a box so that it stands out from surrounding text—programmed so that, when you double-click it, some action takes place. It is a Notes equivalent to a text hotspot in an HTML document, and you can program it to open a form in Compose mode, open a document in Edit mode, delete a document, and all the other things you can do with the action bar as discussed in the preceding section.

To create an action hotspot, you select the block of text that will be clickable. Then you choose Create, Hotspot, Action Hotspot in the menu. The HotSpot Button Properties InfoBox appears, but you don't have to do anything in it. All you have to do next is, in the design pane, choose Formula and enter the following formula where *FormName* is the name of the form to be composed:

```
@Command([Compose]; "FormName")
```

In a browser, the hotspot text appears as a standard, different color, underlined HTML link. When you point to it, the mouse pointer changes to a hand. When you click it, a new document, based on the Notes form *FormName*, opens in Edit mode.

If you want to perform some other action, just substitute the appropriate @command.

HTML Links. Finally, you can open a form (but not perform any other action) with an HTML link. This is an HTML code. That is, it is text and it can appear anywhere on a form in Design mode, or you can even add it to a text field in a document. It appears as follows:

```
[<A HREF="/databasename/formname?OpenForm">Click here to create formname</a>]
```

A HREF is the HTML tag that means "add a hypertext reference." *databasename* and *formname* are the names of the database and form to be opened, respectively. /*databasename*/*formname*?OpenForm is the command to open the named Notes form in the named Notes database. Click here to create *formname* is the text that becomes the hotspot. </A> denotes the end of the opening <A> reference (<A> and </A> being a paired code).

The resulting link appears and performs as a standard text link in a browser.

Making Input Forms Functional. The second problem with forms in Web browsers is that they behave differently in a Web browser than in Notes. For that reason, you may need to redesign a form so that it is usable in a browser. Or you may decide to create two sets of forms, one for use in Notes, the other for use in Web browsers.

Of course, most of the features of Notes that you apply to forms work the same whether the form appears in a Notes client or a Web browser. For example, Default Value, Input Translation, and Input Validation formulas work the same on both platforms. All types of Computed fields work on both platforms. All data types are available in Web-based forms, with a minor exception. The types of keyword fields that are unique to layout regions are not available in Web-based forms, because layout regions themselves do not work at all in Web-based forms.

Field inheritance works slightly differently in Web-based forms. Rich text fields cannot inherit from another document. Also, you cannot select a document in a Web-based view, so if you compose a document by clicking a view action, no inheritance takes place. You have to compose a document from within another document for inheritance to work.

Forms on the Web have some features that forms in Notes do not. In particular, you can use HTML tags in Web-based forms to control field input.

For example, you can control the width and maximum characters in a text field by entering a tag similar to the following into the Help Description field of a Field Properties InfoBox: [<SIZE=30 MAXLENGTH=50>]. This example sets the width of the field as displayed in a browser at 30 characters, and permits entry of up to 50 characters into the field.

You can control how many keywords appear in the browser display of a keyword file by putting a tag similar to the following into the Help Description field of the Field Properties InfoBox: [<SIZE=4>]. This tag would cause a scrollbar to appear in the field if more than four keywords are available.

You can control the size and wrap characteristics of a text field with the following tag: [<ROWS=12 COLS=75 WRAP=VIRTUAL>]. This causes the text field to display in the browser as a 12-row by 75-column text entry area, and your text wraps within the confines of this space but is transmitted as long, unbroken lines. WRAP=PHYSICAL would cause lines to wrap and be transmitted with breaks at wrap points. WRAP=OFF (you guessed it) turns word wrap off, so that the typist has to press Enter to force wrapping.

The Submit Button. Another way forms perform differently on the Web is that they have a Submit button. Domino automatically adds a Submit button to the bottom of any form that a Web user opens. The default Submit button has the word Submit on it. You can move the Submit button or change the words that appear on its face. But you cannot alter its behavior. You cannot put more than one Submit button on a form. And you cannot put any other kind of button on a Web-based form.

To move or change the Submit button on a form intended for use by Web users, do the following:

1. Open the form in Design mode.

2. Place the text cursor where you want the Submit button to appear.

3. In the menu, choose <u>C</u>reate, <u>H</u>otspot, <u>B</u>utton. A button appears on your form and the Button Properties InfoBox opens.

4. In the Button Properties InfoBox, enter the desired button text into the button label field. If you leave this blank, the word Submit will appear when Web users open the form.

5. Save and close the form.

Don't bother trying to program an action for the button. Domino ignores your programming. The only button it recognizes in Web-based forms is the Submit button.

Customizing Responses to User Submissions with the $$Return Field. When you do submit a form on the Web, a default message, Form processed, appears on the screen. You can customize this response with the $$Return field. For example, you can cause Domino to respond: Thank you, Rob. One of our representatives will reply to you within one business day.

You do this by adding a computed field to the form that users submit and naming the field $$Return. In the formula pane, you enter a formula defining the response message.

The formula that responds with the Thank You message looks something like this:

```
@Return("<H2>Thank you, " + FirstName + ". One of our representatives will
reply to you within one business day.</H2>")
```

The following formula says Thank you, Rob. and displays, on the following line, a hotspot back to the site home page:

```
@Return("<H2>Thank you, " + FirstName + ".</H2><BR><H4><a href=/</a>")
```

You can also use $$Return to run a CGI script or to display a selected HTML page.

Returning Information with CGI Variables. Finally, there is a set of fields you can put in a form that only have meaning and function in Web-based forms. These are the fields named after CGI variables. CGI variables are a set of standard variables that CGI programmers can use when writing scripts. CGI variables carry information about the server and client that a CGI script refers to when executing. If fields named for CGI variables appear in an input form, the Web browser automatically enters the values of those variables into the fields. Notes could then use the information when processing a form received from a Web user. See Figure 27.11 for an example of each field name and a corresponding value.

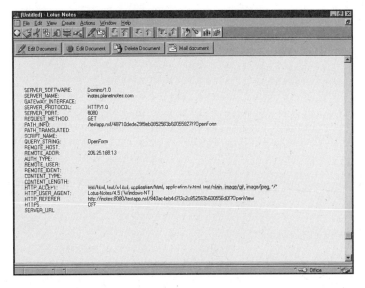

Fig. 27.11 These are sample values that would appear in the CGI variable fields of a Web input form.

If you add CGI variable fields, they should be text fields. Name them with the CGI variable names whose data you want to collect. Because the user submitting the form will not fill in these fields manually, you should mark them as hidden. To do so, open the Field Properties InfoBox for each such field. Display the Hide When panel by clicking the window shade tab. Mark the fields Hide When Editing.

The CGI variable names that Web Publisher recognizes include those in Table 27.4.

Table 27.4 CGI Environment Variables	
Variable	**Description**
Auth_Type	Returns the protocol-specific authentication method used to validate the user, but only if the server supports user authentication and the script is protected
Content_Length	Returns the length of the content, if and as reported by the browser
Content_Type	Returns the content type of the data For queries that have attached information, such as PUT and HTTP POST queries
Gateway_Interface	Returns the server's CGI version number
HTTP_Accept	Returns the MIME types that the client will accept
HTTP_Referer	Returns the URL of the page from which the user opened this form
HTTP_User_Agent	Returns the name and version of the browser used to create this form
HTTPS	Returns On if the server is running the SSL protocol; otherwise, returns Off
Path_Info	Returns the portion of an URL that trails the name of the HTTP server
Path_Translated	Returns the same Path_Info, but in terms of the physical path name not the virtual path name
Query_String	Returns the portion of an URL that trails the question mark
Remote_Addr	Returns the IP address of the browser's host
Remote_Host	Returns the host name of the browser's host
Remote_Ident	Returns the user name of the browser's host
Remote_User	Returns the name by which a Web user authenticated
Request_Method	Returns the HTTP command the browser used to make the current request
Script_Name	Returns the virtual path name of the script being executed
Server_Name	Returns the server's host name or IP address
Server_Port	Returns the server's HTTP port number
Server_Protocol	Returns the name and version number of the protocol being used by the browser to make this request
Server_Software	Returns the name and version of the HTTP server program
Server_URL	Returns the version of CGI with which the server complies

For more information about CGI variables, see Special Edition Using CGI, *published by Que.*

Links

The World Wide Web *is* hyperlinks. It is a super-document, made up of lots and lots of documents, all of which are connected to each other by hyperlinks. Notes is not merely hyperlinks; it is certainly a whole lot more. But Notes supports hyperlinks in the form of document links, view links, and database links, as well as various kinds of hotspots that can link you to navigators, views, forms, and documents. Notes and the Web are a natural fit. Domino automatically converts Notes links into Web hyperlinks. It automatically turns lists into lists of hyperlinks. That is, the list of databases that appears as the default home page is really a list of hyperlinks to the databases. The list of views that appears when you click one of the databases is a list of hyperlinks to the listed views. The views are lists of hyperlinks to the listed documents.

The vast majority of links on a Domino server are forged automatically. You only have to create a few of them yourself. If you replace the default home page, you have to add links to your home page by hand. You may also want to add links to other Web sites. You may want to put links in documents that shortcut you back to a view or a home page. Occasionally, you might want to set up a special relationship between two otherwise unlinked documents.

Most of the links you have to create by hand you will do with Notes linking techniques. Some—mostly to pages at other Web sites—you will do with HTML linking techniques. The linking techniques that Domino recognizes include the following:

- Notes document, view, and database links

- Link hotspots

- Action hotspots

- Actions on action bars

- Passthru HTML

The question remains: When should you choose one type of link instead of another? As a general rule, you should use links that Notes maintains whenever possible. These include document, view, and database links, and link hotspots. When you use passthru HTML, or an action bar action or action hotspot with @URLOpen, you enter a static URL. Notes cannot automatically update the URL if the address of the resource that it points to changes; you have to change it manually.

Document, View, and Database Links. You can link Notes documents to other Notes documents with document links, to Notes views with view links, or to other Notes databases with database links. You create Notes links as follows:

1. Navigate to the document, view, or database icon that you want to link to and select or open it.

2. With the target selected, choose Edit, Copy as Link, and then Document Link, View Link, or Database Link.

3. Navigate back to the document that will contain the link, and place the insertion point where you want the link to appear.

4. Choose Edit, Paste. A link icon appears.

Link Hotspots. Link hotspots act like document, view, and database links but look like boxed text. You create link hotspots the same as standard Notes links, except that in step 4 (of the procedure listed in the preceding section), instead of choosing Edit, Paste, you select a block of text, then choose Create, Hotspot, Link Hotspot. The selected text appears to be outlined by a box.

Actions, Action Hotspots, and Passthru HTML Links. Instructions for making actions, action hotspots, and passthru HTML links appear in Making Input Forms Accessible to Web Users, earlier in this chapter. To refresh your memory, you use the @OpenURL @function in actions and action hotspots. A passthru HTML link to another document would look something like this in a Notes document or form:

```
[<A HREF="url.address">clickable text</A>]
```

In the preceding reference, *url.address* is the actual URL of the page to which this reference points, and *clickable text* is the text that, in the HTML page as it appears in a Web browser, is highlighted and, when clicked with the mouse, causes the browser to retrieve *url.address*.

Customizing Database Elements for Viewing on the Web

When you look at a standard Notes database from a Web browser, you see a bare list of views. When you go to a view, you see a bare list of documents. When you open a document, you see a bare document. If you are looking at a navigator, you see nothing else on the screen. If you perform a search, the results come back in a bare screen.

Notes provides a series of tools that allow you to enhance Notes databases so that lists of views, lists of documents, navigators, and search results appear as elements on a page, along with other text and graphics elements. In effect, you can merge views, navigators, and search results with forms.

You can approach this merger of Notes elements in two ways. One approach is to add special fields to forms so that, when a user opens any document created with the form, the user sees, embedded in the document where you placed a special field, a list of views, a list of documents (i.e., a view), or a navigator. The other approach is to create forms that are templates for views, navigators, or search results, so that when a user opens a view or a navigator or performs a search, the resulting page includes textual and graphic enhancements that normally appear only on forms.

The difference between the two approaches is a little subtle. The first approach enhances forms (therefore documents) by embedding views, view lists, and navigators in them. The second approach enhances views, navigators, and search results with elements that normally appear only on forms.

Embedding Views, View Lists, and Navigators in Forms. You can embed a list of views, a view, or a navigator in a form by creating fields using the following reserved field names:

■ **$$ViewList**—Returns a list of available views and folders in the database. They appear as they do in the standard Folders navigator.

VI

Working with the Web

- **$$ViewBody**—Returns the contents of a specific view in the database. You may only use one $$ViewBody field per form.

- **$$NavigatorBody** or **$$NavigatorBody_n**—Returns a specific navigator in the database. You may use more than one $$NavigatorBody field in a form; if you do use more than one, name them $$NavigatorBody_1, $$NavigatorBody_2, and so on.

These fields may be Editable, Computed, Computed for display, or Computed when composed. They should be of data type text. $$ViewBody and $$NavigatorBody field definitions must include a string value equal to the name of a view or navigator; or they must include a formula that resolves to the name of a view or navigator. $$ViewList field definitions need not include any value.

Create the field where you want the element to appear. You may place these fields in collapsible sections or in tables. These fields have no effect when viewing the resulting document from within Notes; they only affect documents seen from a Web browser.

Creating Custom Views, Navigators, and Search Results Pages. You may create custom views, navigators, or search results pages by creating forms that use the following reserved form names:

- **$$ViewTemplate for *viewname***—Where *viewname* is the alias or name of a view. This form must include a $$ViewBody field for *viewname*.

- **$$ViewTemplateDefault**—All views not associated with a specific form using $$ViewTemplate for *viewname* will be displayed using this form.

- **$$NavigatorTemplate for *navigatorname***—Where *navigatorname* is the alias or name of a navigator. This form must include a $$NavigatorBody field for *navigatorname*.

- **$$NavigatorTemplateDefault**—All navigators not associated with a specific form using $$ViewTemplate for *navigatorname* will be displayed using this form.

- **$$SearchTemplate for *viewname***—Where *viewname* is the alias or name of a view. This form must include a $$ViewBody field for *viewname*; the search results will appear in the $$ViewBody field.

- **$$SearchTemplateDefault**—All search results from views not associated with a specific search results form using $$SearchTemplate for *viewname* will be displayed using this form.

- **$$SearchSiteTemplate**—If you create this form in a site search database, all results of all site searches from this database will display using this form. For more information, see the section "Domino Site Searches" later in this chapter.

The effect of creating these forms is that, whenever someone opens a view or navigator that is affected by the form, the view or navigator will appear on-screen framed in the form. Whenever someone conducts a search that is affected by one of these forms, the search results will appear framed by the form. So you can include custom text, graphic elements, or anything you want in these forms; the resulting Web pages will look customized, not generic.

Domino Site Searches

When you conduct searches in Lotus Notes, you normally search within individual databases. When you conduct a search on the World Wide Web, you normally search an entire Web site. You can set up Notes to emulate standard Web site searches by having Notes search multiple databases with a single search query.

Notes' site-search capability is actually more powerful, in a way, than that of a standard Web server, because you can configure it so that different subsets of databases get searched in different circumstances. For example, a search conducted from a site home page might involve every site-related database on the server, but a search conducted from within a product information page might only search product-related databases.

To set up site-search capability, you complete the following process:

1. Enable the Include in multi database indexing option for the databases to be included in site searches. Do this one of two ways. Either select each database, open its Database Properties InfoBox, go to the Design panel, and enable the option. Or, if you want to enable the option for many databases, do it from the Server Administrations screen. There, you can open the Tools to Manage Notes Databases dialog box either by choosing <u>A</u>dministration, <u>D</u>atabase Tools in the menu or by clicking the Database Tools icon. In the dialog box, you can choose the Web site server in the <u>S</u>erver field, choose a database in the <u>D</u>atabases field, and choose Multi Database Indexing in the <u>T</u>ool field. After you have enabled multi-database indexing for all the databases you want, click Done.

2. On the Web site server, create one or more site-search databases, using the Web Site Search (`websrch.ntf`) design template. Create one site-search database for each multi-database search you want to define.

3. In each site-search database that you create, define the scope of the search by creating a Search Scope Configuration document. This document includes the following fields:

    -   **Scope**: Choose Database, Directory, Server, or Domain. For a Web site search, you would normally choose Server. For a partial site search, you might choose Database or Directory.

    -   **Domain**: For searches of Domain scope, enter the name of the Notes domain.

    -   **Server**: For searches of Server or less scope, enter the name of the Web site server. If you leave this field blank, the search takes place on the server conducting it.

    -   **Filename**: For searches of Directory scope, enter the names of one or more directories. For searches of Database scope, enter the names of one or more databases.

    -   **Full Text Index options**: Enter No Index, Index Summary Data (not rich text fields), Index Full Document, or Index Full Document and Attachments.

4. Create a full-text index for each site search database that you created in step 2. After the database is indexed, go to the Database By Title view to verify that the databases included in multi-database indexing in step 1 appear in the view.

5. To the forms and documents in your Web site, databases add URLs that bring up the search forms from the site-search databases. The URLs should be in the following format:

http://*SiteName*/*SiteSearchDBName*/$SearchForm?SearchSite

where ***SiteName*** is the Internet domain name or intranet host name of your Web site server and ***SiteSearchDBName*** is the Notes title (not file name) of the site-search database to be queried.

The URL in step 5 retrieves a search form from the database named in the URL. The preceding query returns the Simple search form to the Web user. This form appears in Figure 27.12. The Web user can click a link in the form which then returns the Advanced search form, pictured in Figure 27.13.

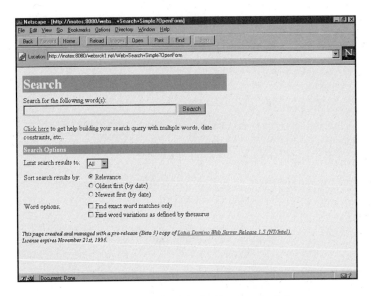

Fig. 27.12 By default, you start a site search with the Simple search form.

You can also enter a site search manually using an URL in the following form:

**http://*SiteName*/*SearchSiteDBName*?SearchSite&Query=*SearchString1*
+AND+*SearchString2*...**

where the plus signs represent the space character and ***SearchString1*** and ***SearchString2*** are search strings separated by the logical AND. In other words, this query searches for all documents that include both ***SearchString1*** and ***SearchString2***.

When a Web user fills in and submits one of the search forms, or when a user enters a manual search query like the one in the previous paragraph, Domino performs a search of the databases defined in the Databases By Title view of the site-search database.

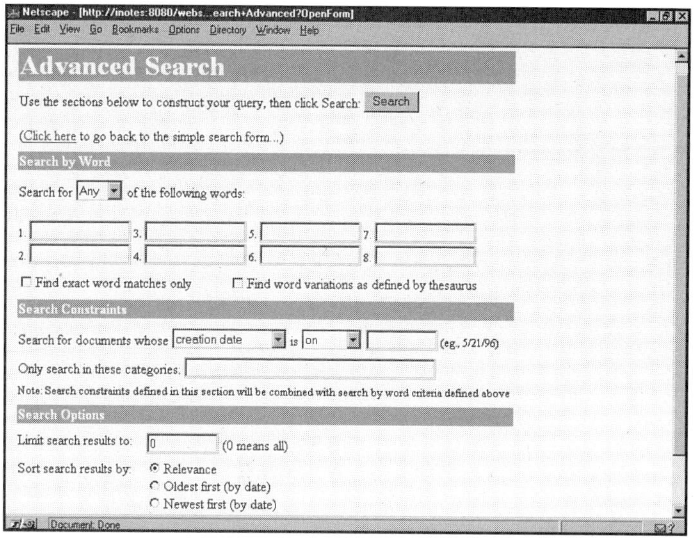

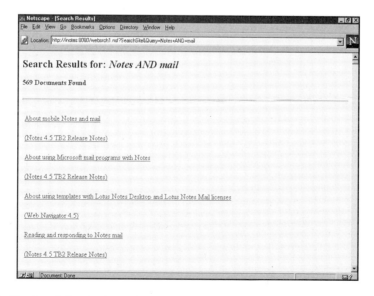

Fig. 27.13 You can then click a link to retrieve the Advanced search form.

When Domino returns the results of a search, it uses the Results form from the site-search database. This is a bare-bones form: Its title shows the query that produced it; it indicates the number of documents found by the search; and it lists the documents in the order specified in the search (see Figure 27.14).

Fig. 27.14 The Search Results form shows the search query, the number of documents found by the search query, and a list of links to the documents found.

If you prefer, Domino will return the search results on a custom search results form, $$SearchSiteTemplate. See the sections "Creating Custom Views," "Navigators," and "Search Results Pages," earlier in this chapter, for instructions on creating this form.

From Here...

This single chapter cannot possibly provide you with all the information available about Domino's HTTP service. This is especially true because of the constantly evolving nature of the World Wide Web and the applications that run on it. Additional sources of information about Domino's HTTP service are available at the following Lotus Web sites: **http://www.lotus.com**, **http://domino.lotus.com**, and **http://www.notes.net.** Look especially for document updates, sample databases, references to other Domino-based Web sites, and a Notes discussion database devoted to Domino HTTP issues. You may also want to read the following:

- Chapter 25, "Lotus Notes and the Web," is an overview of the Internet and Notes' relationship with the Internet.

- Chapter 26, "Using the Web Navigator," describes in detail the Web browser functions of Lotus Notes.

Chapter 28

Using Domino.Action

Domino.Action is a Lotus Notes application that creates and maintains a whole, Domino-based World Wide Web site. It simplifies the creation of a Web site by working from preset designs into which you plug your information and graphics. *Domino.Action* leads you through the design process in a step-by-step manner in which you enter your company information and choose the functions your site will perform, how you want your site to look, and how you want your users to work with the site. Then, Domino.Action generates your Web site as a set of databases that can be used both in Notes and on the Web.

Domino.Action lets you take advantage of Notes' workflow, security, and document-management features for your Web site. When you use Domino.Action, you can control who can author, edit, and approve Web pages for your site; and you can distribute the authoring, editing, and approval tasks.

Installing Domino.Action

The Domino.Action application consists of two database templates—SiteCreator (SiteAct.ntf) for configuring and generating the databases that make up your site and Library (LibAct.ntf), which stores the design elements SiteCreator uses to build the site. You may install these two templates locally (on your own computer) or on a server. However, once Domino.Action generates the databases that make up your Web site, the generated databases must be located on the Domino server for the Web site to work.

To install Domino.Action:

1. Copy the ActProg11e.exe file into the \Notes directory on your computer or on your server, depending on where you want to do your development work. ActProg11e.exe is a self-extracting compressed file that contains the program components of Domino.Action.

2. Run the ActProg11e.exe file to extract the three program files (appassmn.exe, Foundact.dat, and W32htapi.dll).

Some of the topics covered in this chapter are

- How to install Domino.Action

- How to set up the appearance, organization and content-approval options for your site

- How to configure multiple areas using the site areas such as Registration, About the Company, and Discussion

- How to generate the site using the SiteCreator

3. Copy the `ActTempl11e.exe` file into the `Notes\Data` subdirectory on your computer or server. This self-extracting compressed file contains the database templates.

4. Run the `ActTempl11e.exe` file (by double-clicking the file) to extract the two template files, `SiteAct.ntf` and `LibAct.ntf`.

The SiteCreator database lets you select and configure the elements of your site. You can decide where you want your site to be, how you want it to appear, and how you want visitors to interact with your site. When you have set it up the way you want, SiteCreator generates your Web site as a set of Notes databases which you can use either in Notes or in a Web browser.

To create the SiteCreator database for your Web site:

1. Choose File, Database, New. The New Database dialog box appears (see Figure 28.1).

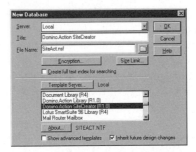

Fig. 28.1 The New Database dialog box uses the template Domino.Action SiteCreator. You will only find this template on the server on which you executed the `Action8.exe` file.

2. Specify the server (Local or the Domino server) in the Server drop-down list box.

3. Enter a title for the database in the Title box. This is the title that appears on the database icon. You can choose SiteCreator if this is the only site you're going to make using the SiteCreator template, or make up a title that is specific to your Web site.

4. In the File Name box, enter the name of the database (with an `.NSF` file extension) or accept the name Notes generated.

5. From the list of templates, find and highlight the Domino.Action SiteCreator template (`SiteAct.ntf`).

6. Leave Inherit future design changes selected.

7. Click OK.

The second database you need is the Library, which includes forms, subforms, views, and other design elements that may be used to build your site. During the site generation process, the SiteCreator looks to the Library for the design elements you selected during your setup. When SiteCreator generates the site, several databases are created by marrying the information you supply in the Site Configuration document to the resources of the Domino.Action Library.

To create the Library database, follow these steps:

1. Choose File, Database, New. The New Database dialog box appears.

2. Specify the server (Local or the Domino server) in the Server drop-down list box.

3. Enter a title for the database in the Title box. This is the title that appears on the database icon. You can choose Library if you're only making one Web site; or make up a title that is specific to your Web site.

4. In the File Name box, enter the name of the database (with an .NSF file extension), or accept the name Notes generated.

5. From the list of templates, find and highlight the Domino.Action Library template (LibAct.ntf).

6. Leave Inherit future design changes selected.

7. Click OK.

Now you can open the SiteCreator database and begin building your Web site.

How SiteCreator Works

You configure your Web site in the SiteCreator database by making a series of choices in a profile document. Then you make a series of design decisions about how your site should look and act. The design elements that will make up the Web site are stored in the Library database. As part of the Web site creation process, you install the AppAssembler module, which pulls together the design elements and your configuration choices to generate the databases that will make up your Web site. Finally, you set the access controls and the approval process.

The Action View

When you double-click the SiteCreator database icon and open the database, you'll see a screen that is split into three panes (see Figure 28.2). The lower left pane displays the contents of the Action view. There are four categories in the view. Under the Quick Start:Site Creator category are five documents—the SiteCreator Overview document, one document for each of the three steps necessary to create a site, and one to Finish Your Site. The documents under the User's Guide category provide valuable information on putting your site together, and you should refer to Before You Begin for pointers on what information you'll need to gather prior to starting Step 1. Administration Tasks provides instructions or suggestions you may need after you have set up the Web site. The Release Notes—Release 1.0 document contains information on this particular release of Domino. Action.

The preview pane (right side of the screen) displays the currently selected document in preview mode. The first time you open the database in this view, the currently selected document is the SiteCreator Overview. This document explains how SiteCreator works, what will happen during each phase of the site creation process, and what additional steps you must take at the end of the process. You can read the document when it's in this preview mode, but you must double-click the name of the document in the view to open the document.

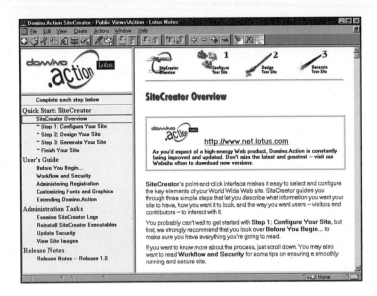

Fig. 28.2   The opening screen of the SiteCreator database provides an overview of Domino.Action and includes a view for the User's Guide.

At the bottom of the SiteCreator Overview document is a hotspot labeled "Launch Step 1" (see Figure 28.3). Once you've read the document, click this hotspot, which will return you to the Action view to begin the process of creating your Web site.

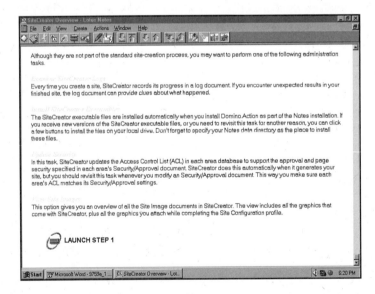

Fig. 28.3   The "Launch Step 1" hotspot is the button to press when you are ready to begin the site creation process.

The Site Creation Process

As you go through the steps involved in creating your site, SiteCreator will offer you suggestions, so you don't need to have decided ahead of time how you want the site to appear and work. However, you should have goals in mind for what you want to accomplish with your site. Then you should collect any information or graphics you want to include on your Web pages; and you should know where on your system such files are stored.

The site creation process steps you through the following:

- **Step 1: Configure Your Site**. You supply information about your company, where the Domino.Action Library is located, the name and location of your Web site, who's in charge of your Web site, and so on. You'll also select the areas you want to have for your site. An *area* is a portion of the site containing related information, such as descriptions of your services or products. An area becomes a separate database when SiteCreator generates the site.

- **Step 2: Design Your Site**. You'll work with a series of documents that control the appearance, organization, and approval settings for each of the areas you've selected for your site. This is where you set the page layout, select background colors and/or images, choose categories, and specify who is authorized to compose, approve, and read the pages in the area. A Quick Design option lets you reduce your design time by using default settings. You can always go back later if you change your mind.

- **Step 3: Generate Your Site**. Using the design decisions you made and the data you included in the configuration information, SiteCreator retrieves the needed design elements from the Library database and creates a new database for each site area you specified in the site configuration.

- **Step 4: Finish Your Site**. Once you've completed the three important steps toward building your site, including building all the site areas, you refresh all the documents and establish all the links between the site areas.

Completing the Site Configuration Document

You specify the "backbone" information for your Web site in the Site Configuration document. In this document, you enter data on the name and location of the Library database, the name of your site, who's in charge of the site, what types of information you want included in the site, and information about your company. Much of this information will appear on your home page, as well as in the area databases the SiteCreator will make.

To open the Site Configuration document:

1. Open the SiteCreator database.

2. In the SiteCreator Overview document, click the Launch Step 1 hotspot. Alternately, in the Action view, double-click Step 1: Configure Your Site to open that document (see Figure 28.4). This document briefly explains what will happen in this first step of the process.

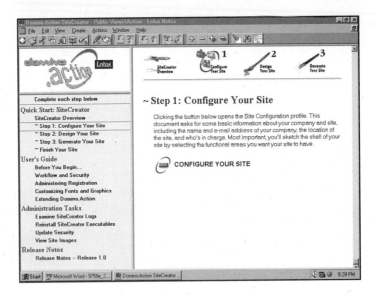

Fig. 28.4   Step 1: Configure Your Site explains the beginning of the site configuration process. Click the button labeled Configure Your Site to begin the process.

3. To continue the process, click the Configure Your Site button at the bottom of the document. This opens the Site Configuration view.

4. The Set up Site Configuration document is automatically selected. Click the Edit hotspot on the preview pane to change the default settings on the Site Configuration form (see Figure 28.5).

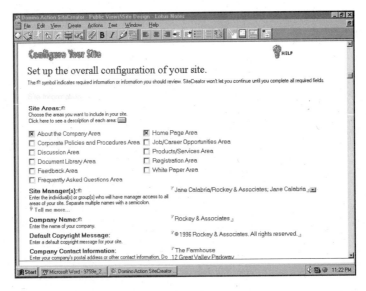

Fig. 28.5   The Site Configuration form contains some required fields and you need to scroll down the page to see the entire form.

5. Complete the fields in the Site Configuration form using the following guidelines. Then save the form and close it. A checkmark appears in front of Step 1 in the Action view to indicate that this step is complete:

- **Site Areas**—You can select up to 11 areas, each of which will become a database serving a particular purpose (see Figure 28.6). The choices are explained in Table 28.1.

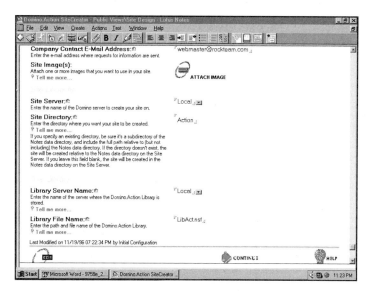

Fig. 28.6 The bottom portion of the Site Configuration form contains the site area choices and a separate database is created for each of the site areas you select.

- **Site Manager(s)**—The Site Manager is the person or group who will have Manager access to all areas of your site and is the equivalent of the Webmaster for your site. SiteCreator assumes the person filling in this form will be the Site Manager, but you may enter the names of any person or group that appears in your Public Address Book (click the list button to open a browser that allows you to select people or groups from the Public Address Book). Because the databases you are creating can be accessed from both Notes and the Internet, all names must appear in both hierarchical (Bob Dobbs/Planet Notes) and flat (Bob Dobbs) format. Separate multiple names with semicolons. In the group and person documents in the Public Address Book, be sure to enter the flat format name in each person document or for each participant in each group. This is a required field.

- **Company Name**—This is the name of the company that the site will serve. This is a required field.

- **Default Copyright Message**—Enter a copyright notice here that will appear throughout the site. You'll have the opportunity to change this message

VI

Working with the Web

on specific pages later. If you're working on a private intranet site, you can leave this field blank.

- **Company Contact Information**—Enter the company postal address or any other contact information that you want, such as telephone or fax numbers. Don't include the company name.

- **Company Contact E-Mail Address**—Enter an e-mail address where you will receive requests for information. This is a required field.

- **Company Image(s)**—Click the Attach Image button to open the Site Design form, with which you can create an image library document. The GIF and JPEG images you attach will be available to use as you design your site. See the section "Attaching a Company Image" in this chapter for more details.

- **Site Server**—Enter the name of the Domino server where you want to create your site. SiteCreator defaults to Local. Leave the selection at Local if the Library database is located on the computer where you are working. This is a required field.

- **Site Directory**—Enter the directory where you want to create the site. It must be a subdirectory of the \Notes\Data directory, so you need only enter the path relative to that directory. If the directory doesn't exist, SiteCreator will create it for you. The default setting is the \Action subdirectory. This is a required field.

- **Library Server Name**—This is the name of the server where the Library database is located. SiteCreator defaults to Local. Leave the selection at Local if the Library database is located on the computer where you are working. Otherwise, enter the name of the server where the Library database is located. This is a required field.

- **Library File Name**—This is the path and name of the Library database, relative to the Notes data directory. If you stored the Library file in c:\notes\data, enter just the filename of the Library database. If you stored the Library database in a subdirectory of the Notes data directory, list both the subdirectory in which the Library database is located and the filename of the Library database (for example, \website\ourweb.nsf). This is a required field.

Table 28.1   Site Areas and Their Purposes

Area	Purpose
About the Company	General information about the company and its products and services.
Home Page	The site home page. The starting point from which users can reach all other areas of the site.
Frequently Asked Questions	List of the questions and answers most often handled by customer service, marketing, corporate communications, or technical support personnel.

Area	Purpose
Feedback	Provides a questionnaire that visitors to your site can complete. You define the questions and answer choices that appear in the questionnaire.
Product/Services	Descriptions of your products and services and pricing information.
Registration	Visitors to the site can register here.
Discussion	Visitors to this area can exchange information and ideas with one another and with company personnel who moderate the discussion.
Document Library	Stores reference documents in this area.
White Paper	Stores white papers in this area.
Job Postings/ Career Opportunities	List of current employment opportunities in your company. This area would be appropriate for a company's internal site.
Corporate Policies and Procedures	Policy and procedure guides, employee manuals, and human resources information. This area would be appropriate for a company's internal site.

Attaching a Site Image. A *site image* is a graphic file that contains a drawing or photograph that you intend to include in your Web pages. This might be your company logo, a photograph of your building, the map showing directions to your store, or a picture of the president of the company or of your product. For each image that you want to include in your site, you have to create a Site Image document (see Figure 28.7). Here you name the image, describe it, categorize it, and attach a copy of it. A new Site Design document appears when you click the Attach Image button in the Site Image(s) field of the Site Configuration document. Images must be in GIF or JPEG format.

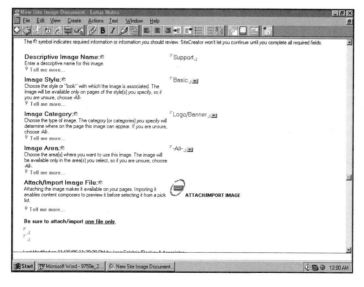

Fig. 28.7 You can attach a graphic file in the Site Design form. The file must be in GIF or JPEG format.

Complete the fields of the Site Design document as follows:

- **Descriptive Image Name**—Enter a brief name to identify the image. This name will appear on the drop-down lists when you select images for your pages.

- **Image Style**—Select a "look" with which to associate the image. The choices include All, Basic, Corporate, and Contemporary. If you are not going to mix and match looks in your site, select All.

- **Image Category**—Select a category from the keyword list which will appear when you click in the Image Category field. The category determines where the SiteCreator will place the image on your Web pages. The available categories are the following:

  - **All.** An image that can fit in any of the categories below, or not quite in any one of them.

  - **Logo/Banner.** Your company logo is an important image for your site. Lotus suggests that you capture your logo in more than one size or have differently colored logos for use on different types of pages. A banner image stretches across the top of a page. Both the Discussion and Feedback pages have banners on them so visitors can easily identify them. Domino.Action provides banner options for those pages but you can substitute your own graphics by customizing the pages.

  - **Background.** A background image fills the entire background of a Web page. If your image is not large enough to fill that space, it will be repeated, or *tiled*, to fill the page. Background images should be light in color with a simple pattern so the text on top can be easily read by a visitor to the site. Typically, backgrounds have a textured look.

  - **Person Image.** If you want to display photos of employees or company officials in your About Company area or of authors in the White Paper area, place the photos in this category.

  - **Product Image.** If you've included a product/services area, you may want to include pictures of your products.

- **Image Area**—If you want to use an image only in a specific site area, select that area. Otherwise, specify All.

- **Attach/Import Image**—To attach/import an image, click the Attach/Import Image button. In the Create Attachment dialog box, select the file you want to attach and then click Create. When the Import dialog box appears, select the same file and then click Import. Below the Attach/Import Image button, the attachment icon appears in the first available field and then the picture of the image appears in the second available field.

> ### Caution
>
> You must save your image in a graphics file format that can be published on the Web, either GIF or JPEG. Also, make sure your image is saved in the same size you want it to appear on the Web page. You cannot resize it.

Save and close this document to return to the Site Configuration page. Click the Attach/ Import Image button on the Site Configuration form and fill in a Site Design form for each image you need to store for your site.

Once you've completed the Site Configuration document, click the Exit or Continue hotspot at the bottom of the page. Click Exit if you do not intend to continue at this time with site configuration. Click Continue if you want to go to Step 2 now. This will return you to the navigator and place a checkmark in front of Step 1.

Starting the Site Design. When you click the Continue hotspot at the bottom of the completed Site Configuration document, the SiteCreator returns you to the Action view. Click Step 2: Design Your Site in the Action view pane (lower left of screen). This displays the Step 2: Design Your Site document in the preview pane (right side of screen).

As the Design Your Site document explains, this step of the site creation process will lead you through setting the appearance, organization, and content approvals for your pages.

You have two options at this point—click the Quick Design hotspot at the bottom of the document to accept the Domino.Action defaults for fast site setup, or click the Custom Design hotspot if you want to review each document as you go along. If you choose the Quick Design method, you should still review the documents that have a star in front of them.

If you choose the Custom Design option, the Site Design view appears, where you will see listed all the site areas that you selected in the Site Configuration form (see Figure 28.8). For each site area, there are several documents listed that you must complete to build your site.

The most logical procedure is to start with the home page area and then work through the other site areas from the top and going down the list.

The home page is the first page visitors see when they look at your site, so it's important that it be attractive, informative, easy to use, and have valid links to your other pages.

There are four documents listed under the Home Page Area category. The first document is Set Up Home Page Area. Double-click this document to open it.

The first field on the form is Create this Area? Select Create so that the SiteCreator will later create a home page area for your site.

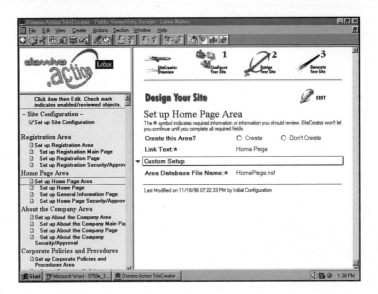

Fig. 28.8 The Site Design view displays all of the documents you'll need to complete to configure your site, based upon selections you made in the Site Configuration document.

Note

The Create radio button must be selected for every page type you want to use in your site.

The second field is Link Text. As visitors to your site view different pages, they may want to return to your home page so they can start in a different direction. On each page, you'll want to include a link that visitors may click to return automatically to the home page. Enter the text for the Home Page link in the Link Text field. Alternately, accept the default text.

Click the Custom Setup section head to expand the section if you want to enter a name for the database that contains your home page area in the Area Database File Name field, such as HomePage.nsf. You can also accept the default name given here.

When the Set Up Home Page Area form is complete, click the Continue hotspot at the bottom of the page to return to the Site Design view.

Setting Up the Home Page. From the Site Design view, double-click the Set Up Home Page document to open it (see Figure 28.9).

In this document, you will provide information about page layout, background color, background image, and copyright information for the home page. Remember that the home page is the page all visitors to your Web site will see first, so it is important to establish the "look" for your site here. This document actually prepares a home page form in the home page database that you will later use to add your own information for site visitors.

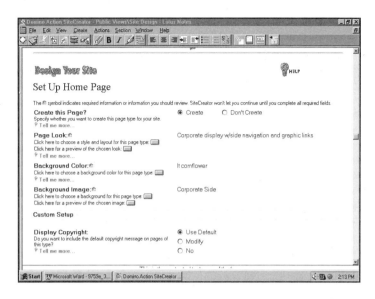

Fig. 28.9 The Set Up Home Page form creates a template for your home page. After you finish the SiteCreator process, you'll return to the Home Page form in your Home Page database to complete the text you want to appear on your home page.

To complete this form, follow these steps:

1. To have the SiteCreator create this page (not now—but during Step 3), select the Create radio button in the Create this Page? field.

2. Click the button next to the Page Look field to select one of the following available layouts from the dialog list. This includes Basic, Contemporary, and Corporate layouts, with navigation information in different positions on the page. You can preview the selection before choosing it.

   To preview a selection, click the button labeled Click here for a preview of the chosen layout. A screen similar to Figure 28.10 will appear.

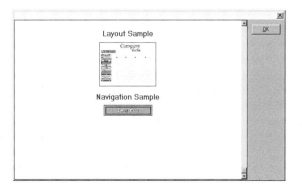

Fig. 28.10 You can preview the layout selection for basic Web pages. This allows you to determine your preferences for your Web page appearances.

3. Click the Background Color button to choose a color for your page. Even if you are planning to use a background image, you should still select a color, since quite a few Web browsers offer their users the option to turn off backgrounds.

4. If you plan to use an image in the background (you should attach the file in the Site Configuration document), click the Background Image button and select the image from the dialog list. You can preview your images by clicking the preview button.

5. Click the Custom Setup section to expand it if you want to change the copyright settings you made in the Site Configuration form. There are three choices: None, Use Default (which uses the one you already specified), or Modify (which lets you change the copyright text just for this page).

6. Click the Continue hotspot. This returns you to the Site Design view.

Setting Up General Information Pages. You use General Information pages for documents that apply to your entire site, such as extended copyrights, licenses, and legal information. A By Title link on the home page gives you access to these documents.

To set up a General Information page, follow these steps:

1. Click Set Up General Information Page in the Site Design view.

2. Click the Edit hotspot to modify the existing document.

3. Choose the Create option under Create This Page?.

4. Select a style and look for the page from the dialog list that appears when you click the button under Page Look. To see what your choice looks like, click the preview button.

5. Click the Background Color button to choose a color for your page.

6. If you plan to use an image in the background, click the Background Image button and select the image name from the dialog list. To see what your selection looks like, click the preview button.

7. Click the Custom Setup section to expand it if you want to change the copyright settings you made in the Site Configuration form. There are three choices: None, Use Default (which uses the one you already specified), or Modify (which lets you change the copyright text just for this page).

8. Click the Continue hotspot. This returns you to the Site Design view.

Setting Up the Home Page Approval Process. The next step is to set up your home page security/approval process. Double-click Set up Home Page Approval Process in the navigator. It is on this page that you specify who will be authorized to compose pages in the home page area, who will be authorized to approve the pages before they become available on the site, and who will be authorized to read pages in this area of the site (see Figure 28.11).

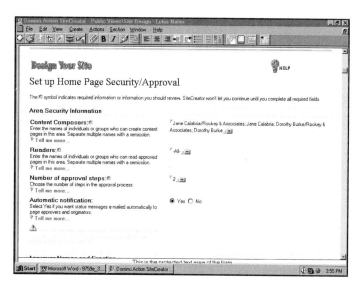

Fig. 28.11 The Home Page Security/Approval Process form is a long form, so be certain to scroll down to view the rest of the document.

To complete this document, follow these steps:

1. In the Content Composers field, enter or select the names of the people or groups who may compose pages in this site area. If you click the down arrow, a browser opens that lets you choose names from the Public Address Book. If you leave the field empty, anyone will be able to compose pages. Multiple names must be separated by semicolons. For each person, both the hierarchical (Jim Harkin/Hamilton-Beaks) and the common name (Jim Harkin) must appear.

2. In the Readers field, specify the people or groups who may read the pages in this site area. The default is All, which means everyone will be able to read the pages. You would not ordinarily limit the readers of your home page, but you may very well limit the readers of pages in other site areas.

3. If you want to establish an approval process where people or groups approve the contents of the page, enter the number of steps (up to five) you want in the Number of Approval Steps field. Otherwise, enter **0** for none.

4. If you entered a number of approval steps greater than zero, the Automatic Notification field appears. When you select Yes, e-mail is automatically sent to the approver alerting him or her that a page needs approval. Likewise, the composer of the page and the WebMaster are alerted when the page is accepted or rejected.

5. If you entered a number of approval steps greater than zero, the Approver Names and Function section appears (see Figure 28.12). Under Approver Names, you'll see fields for Step 1 Approvers, Step 2 Approvers, and so on, depending on the number of steps you specified. In each of these fields, enter or select the names of people or groups who will be involved in that level of approval. Then, under Approver Function, you may optionally enter a brief description of what an approver at that level must do.

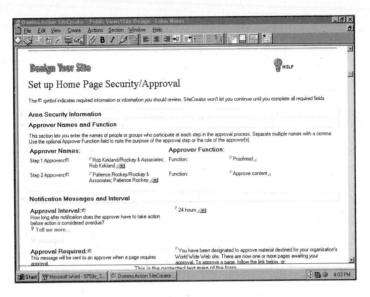

Fig. 28.12 The Approver Names and Function section of the Set up Home Page Security/ Approval Process will appear only if you have entered a number greater than zero in the Number of Approval Steps field.

6. If you set Notification to Yes, the Notification Messages and Interval section appears (see Figure 28.13). You need to enter a time limit in the Approval Interval field to indicate how long after receiving notification the Approver will have to approve or reject. If the Approver does not reply within that time interval, the system sends out an overdue alert to the tardy Approver.

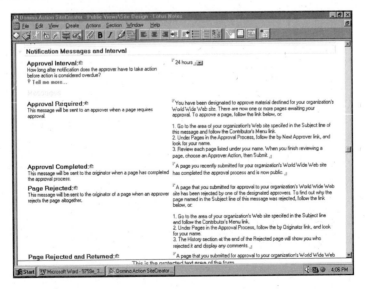

Fig. 28.13 The Notification Messages and Interval section determines the workflow process and routing for approvals.

7. Also, in the Notification Messages and Interval section there are four fields in which appears the text of the messages that will go out to people during the approval process. You may edit the messages. The four fields are the Approval-Required Message field, the Approval-Completed Message field, the Page-Rejected field, and the Page-Rejected and Returned field.

8. When you have completed this form, click the Continue hotspot to return to the Site Design view.

Setting Up a Site Area. For each of the areas you selected on the Site Configuration document, you'll be setting up a Site Design document. You created a Site Design document for the home page area in a previous section. The Site Design document asks if you want to create the site, what link text you want to use to bring visitors to this area of the site, and what name you want to give to the database that SiteCreator will generate for this area (see Figure 28.14).

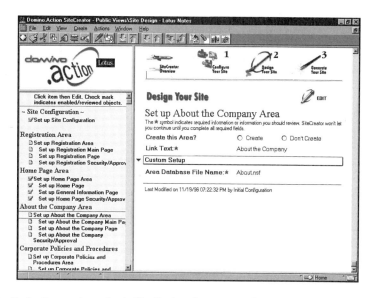

Fig. 28.14 Each site area has a basic Site Design document. This figure displays the Site Design document for the About the Company Area.

To complete the Site Design document, follow these steps:

1. From the Site Design view, select the first document under the category heading for that area. For example, if you chose to create an About the Company area, the document is called "Set up About the Company Area."

2. Click the Edit hotspot in the preview pane to modify the document. In the Create field, select Create to have the SiteCreator create the site area.

3. When visitors come to your Web site and want to learn about your company, they will click a hyperlink to go immediately to that area of your site. In the Link Text field, enter the text the visitors will click to go to this area. For example, to send a

visitor to the About the Company area, you might enter **Learn more about our company**.

4. If you want to set the name of the database for this site area, click the Custom Setup section head and enter the filename in the Area Database File Name field.

5. Click the Continue hotspot to save the document and return to the Site Design view.

Creating the Area Main Page. Once you set up an area, you need to create an area main page. This is the introductory page users see when they jump to a site area. Normally, this page contains information about the site area plus links to other pages in the area.

To create an area main page, follow these steps:

1. From the Site Design view, Select the set up main page document (for example, in the About the Company area, this document is called "Set Up About the Company Main Page") (see Figure 28.15).

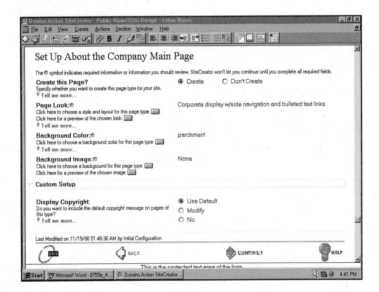

Fig. 28.15   Every area site has a main page that acts as an opening page for that database. This figure shows the About the Company Main Page document.

2. To have the SiteCreator create the page, select Create in the Create this Page? field.

3. Click the Page Look button and select one of the available page layouts (click the preview button to see what the layout looks like).

   To gain some idea what any one of these layouts looks like, you can choose it from the list, and then click the button Click here for a preview of the chosen layout (see Figure 28.16).

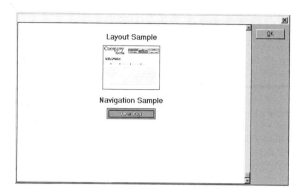

Fig. 28.16 You can preview the layout of main pages in the same way you can preview the layout of a home page.

4. Click the Background Color button and select a color for the background of the page from the list of colors.

5. If you want to use a Background Image, select the name of the background image you attached when you created the Site Configuration document.

6. Click the Custom Setup section head if you want to change the copyright or not use one on this page. From the Display Copyright field, choose No, Use Default (the one you set in the Site Configuration document), or Modify (which gives you the ability to enter new text or correct the existing copyright).

7. Click the Continue hotspot to save the document and return to the Site Design view.

Setting Up a Page. The next step is to set up pages for your site area. These pages can contain a variety of information, but the set-up document lets you establish categories for the types of pages you make for that particular site area.

To set up pages for the site area, follow these steps:

1. From the Site Design view, select the page set-up document to display it in the preview pane. For the About the Company area, this document is called "Set Up About the Company Page" (see Figure 28.17).

2. To have the SiteCreator create the page, select Create in the Create this Page? field.

3. In the Page Look field, click the buttton and select one of the available page looks from the dialog list.

4. Click the Background Color button to select a color for the background of the page from the list of colors.

5. If you want to use a Background Image, select the name of the background image you attached when you created the Site Configuration document. You can also use one of the predesigned background images provided by Domino.Action.

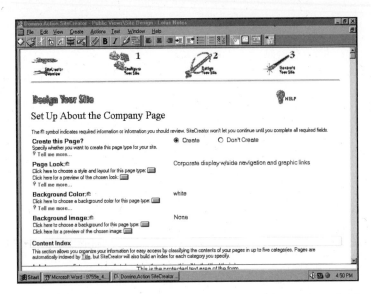

Fig. 28.17   Every area site has one or more page templates. The Set Up About the Company Page document provides you the opportunity to categorize your Web pages.

6. To set up the categories for your pages, click the Content Index section head (see Figure 28.18). You can sort your pages into five categories that you specify. For each category, enter a Label (descriptive title) for the category and Choices (set the options a user can select). Then click Yes or No in the Choices field. If you select No, users will be able to select only from the categories listed in the Choices field. If you select Yes, users will be able to add categories other than those in the Choices field.

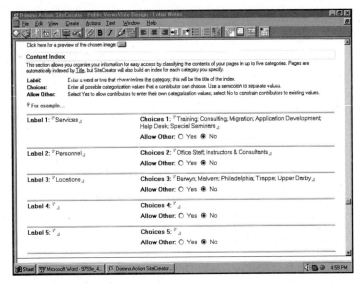

Fig. 28.18   Once you have provided information in the Content Index section, users who are authorized to provide content to your Web site will use the categories when they are creating new Web pages.

7. Click the Custom Setup section head if you want to eliminate or change the default copyright notice on this page. From the Display Copyright field, choose No, Use Default (the one you set in the Site Configuration document), or Modify (which gives you the ability to enter new text or correct the existing copyright).

8. Click the Continue hotspot to save the document and return to the Site Design view.

Specifying the Approval Process. On the Security/Approval page, you specify who will be authorized to compose pages in the area, who will be authorized to approve the pages before they become available on the site, and who will be authorized to read pages in this area of the site. If you enable an approval process, you have to specify the details of how it will work.

Follow these steps to complete the Set Up Security/Approval process document:

1. Click the set-up security/approval document to display it in the preview pane (for example, in the About the Company site area, the document is called "Set up About the Company Security/Approval," as shown in Figure 28.19).

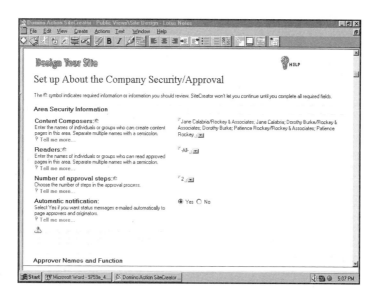

Fig. 28.19 The Approval Process for the site area works like the approval process for the home page.

2. For the Content Composers field, enter or select the names of the people or groups who may compose pages in this site area. If you click the down arrow button to the right of the field, a browser opens that lets you choose names from the Public Address Book. Use semicolons to separate multiple names, and be sure to use both the hierarchical (Joan Blossom/Blossom Fragrance) and common (Joan Blossom) names.

3. In the Readers field, specify the people or groups who may read the pages in this site area. Leave it set to All if you want everyone to read the pages.

4. If you want to establish an approval process where people or groups approve the contents of newly composed pages before they become available to readers, enter the number of steps (between one and five) you want in the Number of Approval Steps field. To disable the approval process, enter **0** for no steps.

5. If you entered a number of approval steps greater than zero, the Automatic Notification field appears. When you select Yes, e-mail is automatically sent to the approver alerting him or her that a page needs approval. Likewise, the composer of the page and the WebMaster are alerted when the page is accepted or rejected.

6. If you set up approval steps, the Approver Names and Function section appears. Under Approver Names, you'll see fields for Step 1 Approvers, Step 2 Approvers, and so on, depending on the number of steps you specified. In each of these fields, enter or select the names of people or groups who will be involved in that level of approval. Then under Approver Function, you may optionally enter a brief description of what that level approver must do.

7. If you set Notification to Yes, the Notification Messages and Interval section appears. You need to enter a time limit in the Approval Interval field to indicate how long after receiving notification does the Approver have to reply. If the Approver does not reply within that time interval, an overdue alert is sent.

8. Also in the Notification Messages and Interval section there are four fields in which appear the text of the messages that will go out to people during the approval process. You may optionally edit the messages. The four fields are the Approval-Required Message field, the Approval-Completed Message field, the Page-Rejected field, and the Page-Rejected and Returned field.

9. Once you have completed the form, click the Continue hotspot to return to the Site Design view.

Working with Site Areas

Most site area setups follow the procedures outlined in the section "Setting Up a Site Area." However, there may be some customization involved in certain site areas. For example, the Registration area requires that you work with agents.

In this section, each of the site areas is described and if customization is appropriate, it is defined.

About the Company. This is a very straightforward site to set up using the procedures outlined in the section "Setting Up a Site Area." It provides the visitor to your site with information about the company, its goals, its products and services, its officers, its locations, and so on.

Corporate Policies and Procedures. This site area is geared more toward an intranet site rather than an Internet site. It is where users would find an employee manual, benefits information, vacation and sick leave policies, office procedures, and so on. You can easily set it up using the procedures outlined in the "Setting Up a Site Area" section.

Discussion. The Discussion area is where users can comment on your company and services, ask questions, make suggestions, complain, and share information with one another. It is a Notes discussion database, but is available to Web users.

Banners. To make the Discussion area more inviting and identifiable, Domino.Action adds a design feature to this site area main page. In the Set Up Discussion Main Topic Page document, there is an additional field called Banner where you may specify the banner you want to use on the page by clicking the Banner button and selecting one from the dialog box. A *banner* is a graphic that usually goes across the top of the page from left margin to right margin. Domino.Action has several graphics available for you to use (see the list in Figure 28.20), but if you attached an image file as a banner in the Site Configuration document, you may specify the name of that file in the Banner field.

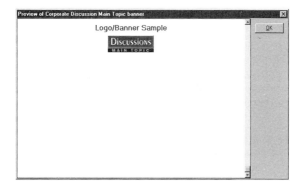

Fig. 28.20   The Banner selection dialog box lists pre-built banners. To preview the banners, click the preview button located under Banner on the Site Design form.

Domino.Action also adds a banner to the Main Topic and Response pages in the Discussion site area. Pick a Main Topic banner or a Response banner in the Banner field of the setup document for each of these kind of pages.

Categorization. Making the discussion area easy to use is important, and one way to do it is to index the pages. Each page in a discussion area is automatically indexed by author, date, and title. The Set Up Discussion Main Topic document has a Content Index collapsible section that allows you to further index discussions by category (see Figure 28.21).

In the Label field, accept the default label of Categories or enter a label that better defines the categorization choices. Enter the categorization choices in the Choices field if you want to narrow the categories to a select few. Select Yes under Allow Other if you want the users to be able to add new categories on their own; in which case, any categories you entered in Choices are just to get the ball rolling. Don't allow other categories if you want to narrow the areas of discussion.

Discussion Response Page. The discussion site area provides an additional page type for users to respond to questions or comments posted by others. This page type also features a banner in its design. In all other ways, it sets up in the same way as other page types. In usage, as a response document, it inherits information from the document to which it responds.

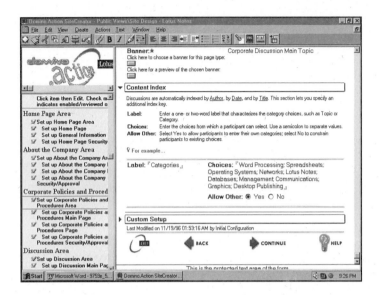

Fig. 28.21   The Content Index section of a Discussion Site differs from the categorization in the About the Company form. These categories will be made available to Web browsers who participate in the Web discussion database to categorize their Main Topics in the database.

Security/Approval

There are two additional fields in the Security/Approval page for the Discussion area. If you select Yes in the Allow Anonymous Access field, you are permitting any visitor to view the pages in this area without entering a user name or password. Selecting No restricts visitors to registered users or specified names or groups.

Selecting Yes in the Allow Anyone to Author field permits visitors to author documents in this area. However, they will not be able to edit documents, not even the ones they created. Choosing No restricts authoring of documents to the individuals and groups specified in the Content Composers field.

Document Library. The Document Library provides an area where you can store documents for shared use or files for download. On the Set Up Document Library Page, there is a Content Index section similar to the one in the Discussion site area (see Figure 28.22). Although the pages are automatically categorized by title, you may specify five additional categories.

In the Label field, enter a label that better defines the categorization choices (such as Class Manuals). Enter the categorization choices in the Choices field if you want to narrow the categories to a select few (Introductory, Intermediate, Advanced, and so on). Select Yes under Allow Other if you want the users to be able to add categories in addition to the ones you entered in the Choices field.

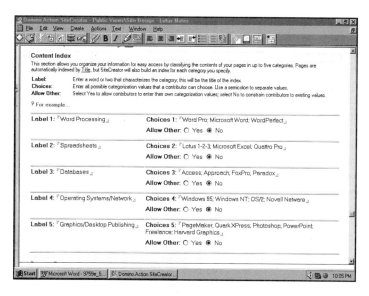

Fig. 28.22 The Content Index section of the Set Up Document Library Page document allows for additional categories.

Feedback. The Feedback site area provides users with a feedback form to fill out and submit. The Banner choices allow you to set up either a user feedback (for your site) or a customer feedback page; although you can use a banner you attached to the Site Configuration document or no banner to create a different type of feedback page. The unique portion of setting up this site area is the Feedback Custom Questions section of the Set Up Feedback Page document. In this section, you can specify up to five feedback questions to include on the feedback form (see Figure 28.23).

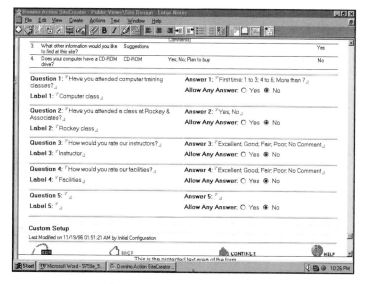

Fig. 28.23 The Feedback Custom Questions section allows you to receive feedback from Web browsers.

VI

Working with the Web

In the Question field, enter the question you want users to answer (such as Did you find this site helpful?).

Enter a brief label that characterizes the question in the Label field to help index the database information (such as Rating). You don't need to use date, author, or title because feedback is automatically indexed by those categories (author information is automatically collected, so Feedback pages don't need an author field).

In the Answer field, enter all the possible answers to the question (such as Extremely, Somewhat, Not much, or Not at all). Separate multiple entries with a comma or semicolon. Leave the field blank if you want the users to supply their own answers, or choose Yes under Allow Any Answer to encourage user comments.

Frequently Asked Questions. You can publish frequently asked questions and their answers in this area of your Web site and save yourself the trouble of answering the same, repetitive questions over and over again, while providing useful information to visitors to your site.

Like several of the other site areas, the pages in the Frequently Asked Questions area are automatically indexed by title. You may specify additional indexing categories in the Content Index section of the Set Up FAQs Page document (see Figure 28.24).

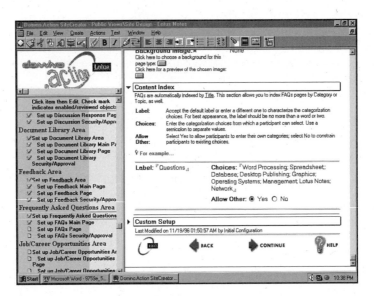

Fig. 28.24   The pages for this site area do not display a banner area, but you do have a full range of page layout choices.

Specify an indexing category in the Label field (such as Company) and then enter possible options in the Choices field (Directions, Experience, and so on). If you want users to add their own categories, select Yes in the Allow Other field.

Job /Career Opportunities. Whether you're running an intranet or an Internet site, offering job opportunities will attract many users looking to improve their current positions, make career advancements, or start new jobs.

Pages in this site area are automatically indexed by title, but you can specify up to five categories in the Content Index section of the Set Up Job Posting Page document (see Figure 28.25).

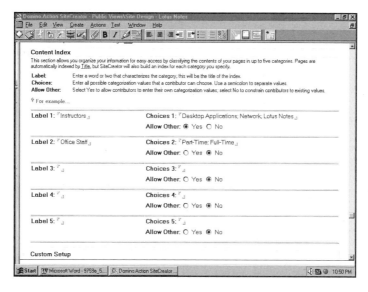

Fig. 28.25   This page provides an inexpensive way to widely advertise your job openings.

Specify an indexing category in the Label field (such as Administrative Support) and then enter possible options in the Choices field (like Secretary, Data Entry, and so on). If you want users to add their own categories, select Yes in the Allow Other field.

Product/Services. The Product/Services area gives you a chance to sell, either by displaying your products or explaining your services. This site involves three types of pages—Product Information, Product Review, and Product Specification.

Product Information pages are automatically indexed by title, but you may specify five additional categories in the Content Index section of the Set Up Product Information Pages document.

Because the Product Review pages are responses to the Product Information documents, setting up these pages is straightforward and without categorization. Instead, these pages inherit the categories from their parent documents (the Product Information pages).

The Product Specification pages only have the standard fields and no categorization questions, as they inherit their category from their parent documents (the Product Information pages).

Registration. The Registration site area lets you collect information about visitors to your site and store it in a database. Once a visitor is registered, you can let him have greater privileges in your Web site. The registration process automatically adds newly registered users to a registered users group. By adding this group to database access control lists, you can give registered users rights different from those accorded to anonymous (non-registered) visitors to your site.

The Set Up Registration Page document has some unique fields for you to complete. There are two collapsible sections on this document. The first one is called Registration and contains the administrative information for collecting and storing information on users (see Figure 28.26).

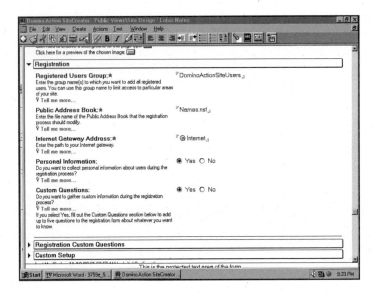

Fig. 28.26   The Registration section.

Complete the following fields in this section:

- **Registered Users Group**—Enter the name of the group or groups in the Public Address Book to which you want to add all the registered users.

- **Public Address Book**—Enter the filename of the address book to which the registration information will be added. Names.nsf is the name of your company's Public Address Book, but you may want to create a new address book for testing purposes. The Public Address Book must reside on the Domino server and must be located in the Domino data directory. Always include the path in the filename if the file is located in a subdirectory.

- **Gateway Address**—Enter the address of your Internet mail gateway here. By default, @ Internet appears in this field. If your Domino server has direct access to the Internet gateway domain, use the SMTP gateway domain name. If not, enter all the mail routing hops necessary to get e-mail to your company's Internet gateway domain.

■ **Personal Information**—Select Yes if you want to collect personal information about your users during the registration process, such as company name, address, and phone number.

■ **Custom Questions**—Select Yes to ask up to five custom questions during the registration process and then fill out the Registration Custom Questions section of the Set Up Registration Pages document.

In the Registration Custom Questions section, you can add up to five specific questions you want users to answer (see Figure 28.27). Enter each question in the Question field and then add a selection of possible answers in the Answer field. If you want users to add their own answers, select Yes in the Allow Other field.

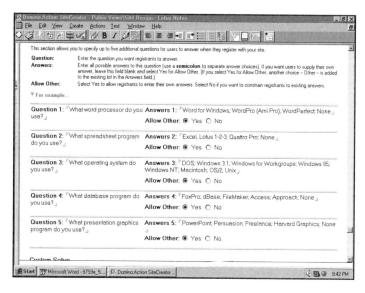

Fig. 28.27   The Registration Custom Questions section.

Once you have created the Registration site area database, be sure that the default access in the access control list is Author access with the ability to create documents only. Make roles for Readers, Approvers, Composers, and WebMaster. Composer and Reader roles should also be given default access. Add the name of the Domino server to the Access Control List and assign it Manager access.

In the creation process, SiteCreator makes two agents for the Registration site area. The Handle Requests agent processes registration requests and password-change requests submitted by site visitors. Every time a visitor to your site submits a registration request, this agent creates a Person record in the Public Address Book on the server, then adds the person to the registered users group you specified in the Set Up Registration Page document (the default group name is DominoActionSiteUsers). When a password change is requested, the agent replaces the old password with the new password in the existing Person document. The Handle Requests agent must be enabled and set up to run on the Domino server, or registration won't work. To set the agent up to run on the Domino server, click the Schedule button and select the Domino server's name from the Run only on list box. You must also enable the Send Mail agent. This agent automatically sends e-mail to users when the following occurs:

- **A registration request has been processed.** A thank you message is sent saying `Thank you for registering with` **`http://siteURL`**`. Your username is` **`username`**`. Please remember that your password is case-sensitive.`

- **A password change request is received.** The agent sends the message `Your password has successfully been changed. Your username is` **`username`**`. You may now log in with your new password. Please remember that your password is case-sensitive.`

- **A registration or password change request cannot be processed.** The following message is sent: `There was a problem with your registration request. The error returned was:` `error`. `Try resubmitting your request. If you get another error notification, contact the Webmaster. Include the text of this message and describe the problems you are experiencing.`

Although the two agents operate automatically, you must enable them by opening the Notes client on the Domino server (using the server ID) and adding the Registration database (`Registra.nsf`, by default) to the workspace.

White Paper. The White Paper site area lets you store white papers for user reference. The pages are indexed by title, but as with many of the other site areas you can add up to five categories in the Content Index section of the Set Up White Paper Page document. You could skip setting up the White Paper area entirely and include white papers as a category of document in the Document Library area of your site.

Generating Your Site

The generation process begins with the AppAssembler, which combines information you entered in SiteCreator with templates and other design elements from the Library to generate the components of your site. These components are Lotus Notes databases that can be used in Notes or published to the Web for viewing from a Web browser.

To begin generating the site, follow these steps:

1. Go to Step 3: Generate Your Site (see Figure 28.28).

2. Click the Generate Your Site hotspot to begin the generation process.

3. Once the processing of documents is complete, the Run AppAssembler document appears in the preview pane (see Figure 28.29).

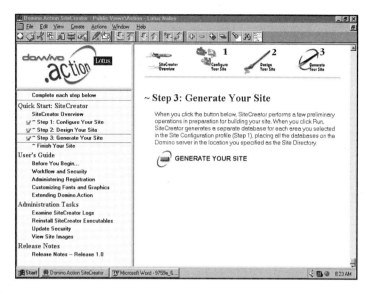

Fig. 28.28   The Step 3: Generate Your Site document begins the generation process for the site.

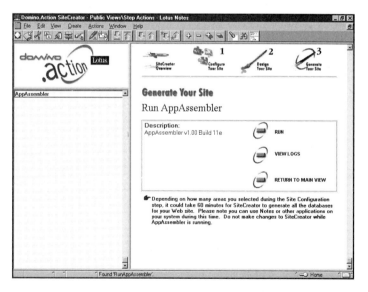

Fig. 28.29   Notice the message at the bottom of the page. AppAssembler could take up to 60 minutes to generate all of the databases in your Web site.

4. Click the Run button to begin assembling the application. The process may pause for you to enter your password before it completes the task. While the AppAssembler is running, you may run Notes or other applications in the background but do not change any of the SiteCreator documents.

5. When the process is complete, click the Return to Action View button.

Finishing Your Site

The Finish Your Site step in the site creation process refreshes your database documents and establishes all the links between the documents. To finish your site, do the following:

1. From the Action view, select the Finish Your Site document (see Figure 28.30).

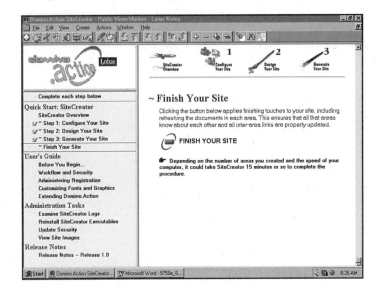

Fig. 28.30 The process of finishing a site can take 15 minutes or so to complete.

2. Click the Finish Your Site button.

3. SiteCreator resets all the access control lists for each of the databases you created and updates them. You may want to manually review them once this operation is complete and make sure that the names defined as Content Composer, Site Manager, and Approver are in the Public Address Book and in the same format as in the Security/Approval documents of each database.

Getting Your Site Up and Working

The area databases now exist in the `\Notes\Data\Action` directory. You can open these databases or add their icons to your workspace. However, before your site is up and running, there are a few finishing touches you must make.

Replicate any local databases to your Domino server, making certain that you change the Site Configuration document to specify the location of your databases as being on your Domino server instead of your local computer.

Specify your home page database as the default home page (or have the Notes Administrator do this for you) by opening the Server document in the Public Address book. Under the HTTP section, enter the filename of your home page database (unless you changed it, the filename is `Homepage.nsf`) in the Default Home Page field.

To add content to your pages (or have the Content Composer do it if you are not the designated Content Composer), start your Web browser, go to the specific area to which you want to add content, and click Edit/Approve This Page. Then add a title and other content to the page, and select Process and Submit. If the Security/Approval profile for the area calls for one or more approval steps, each Approver must accept the content.

To approve pages if you are in the approval cycle, go to the main page for the site menu. From the Contributor's menu, select one of the Approval Process views and find the pages that need approval. Click Edit/Approve This Page, review the document, and select an Approver Action. Submit the form.

Remember to Full Text Index each area database. Now your site should be fully functional.

Updating the Site

To change the design of your area databases, make your changes to the area's Site Design documents in SiteCreator and then regenerate the site. To do so, follow these steps:

1. Select all the Site Design documents in all the unaffected areas by highlighting each one and then pressing the spacebar. Once the unaffected documents are all selected, choose Actions, Public, Disable Creation. This disables any areas you are not changing.

2. Run Step 3 Generate Your Site again. Once the generation process is complete, click Finish Your Site.

3. From the workspace, select each database with changes and then choose Actions, Update Existing Documents.

Replacing Graphics

To replace the graphic from the Web (you must use a Web browser that supports file upload, such as Netscape Navigator), follow these steps:

1. Go to the main page of the area where you want to replace the graphic.

2. Click the link to the Contributor's menu.

3. Click the File Library's By Category link to see a list of all the GIF files.

4. Click Edit Page next to the graphic you want to replace.

5. A File Upload document opens. Scroll down the page and click Edit This Page.

6. Check Mark attachments for deletion.

7. Click Submit.

8. Once you see "You successfully submitted this page," click the Go to link for the page you just submitted.

9. Click Edit this page. Use the Browse button to locate the new GIF file.

10. Click Submit.

You must follow these steps for each GIF file you want to replace, and you must upload a file in each area in which it will be used.

To replace the graphic from Notes, you need to edit the Site Image documents. To do so, follow these steps:

1. From the main view of the SiteCreator, open the View Site Images document and click the button.

2. Select the image you want to replace and click the Edit icon.

3. Delete the existing GIF file and image.

4. Click the Attach/Import Image button.

5. Use the Browser to locate the new GIF file and then click Create.

6. Locate the image file and then click Import.

7. Save and close the document.

From Here...

Domino.Action is the first of numerous Web development applications to be offered by Lotus for the Domino 4.5 server. The next scheduled application will be Domino.Merchant, designed to support Internet-based sales of your company product line. Visit the Lotus Web site at **www.lotus.com** often to keep abreast of new offerings. You might want to use the Page Minder feature of Notes to automate the process of retrieving the latest updates from the Lotus Web site.

For more information on the association between Lotus Notes and the Web, turn to the following chapters:

- Chapter 25, "Lotus Notes and the Web," is an overview of the Internet and Notes' relationship with the Internet.

- Chapter 26, "Using the Web Navigator," describes in detail the Web browser functions of Lotus Notes.

- Chapter 27, "Using Domino Server's HTTP Service," describes in detail the building of Web applications without the use of Domino.Action.

VI

Working with the Web

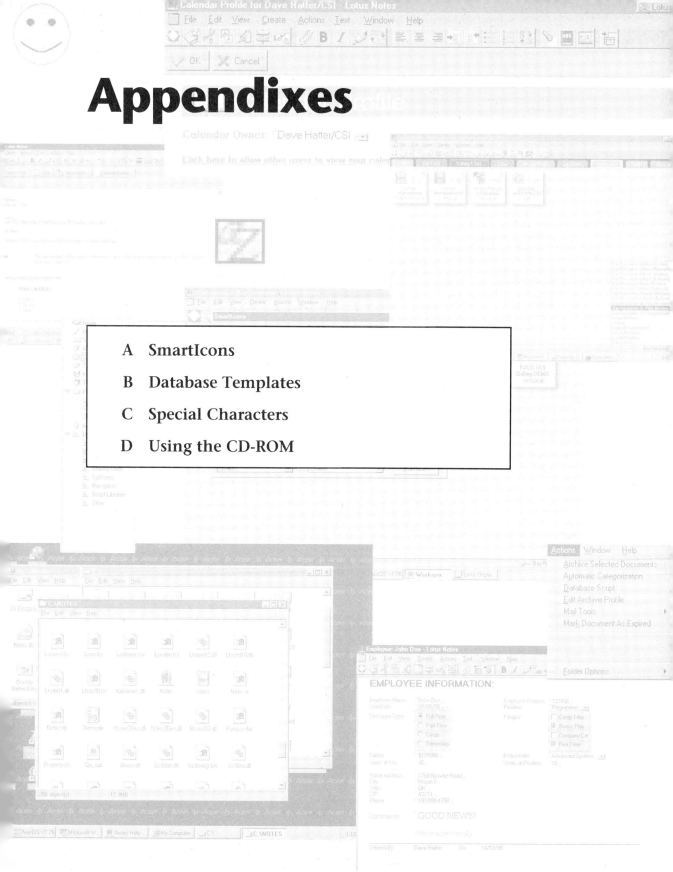

Appendixes

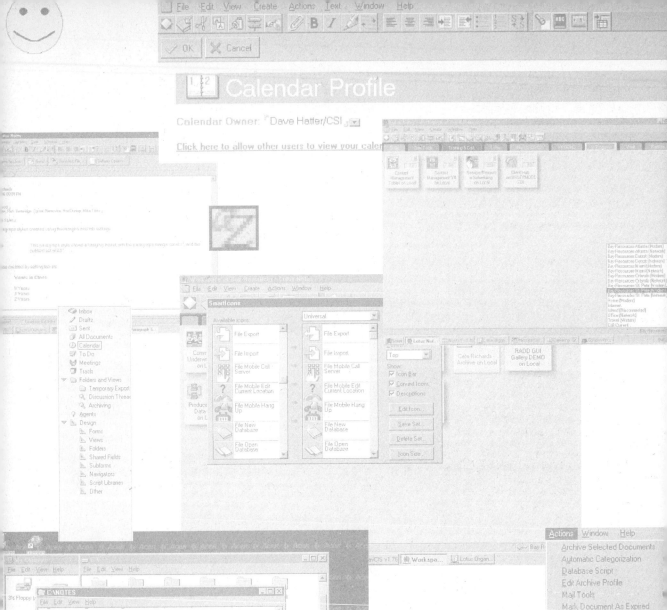
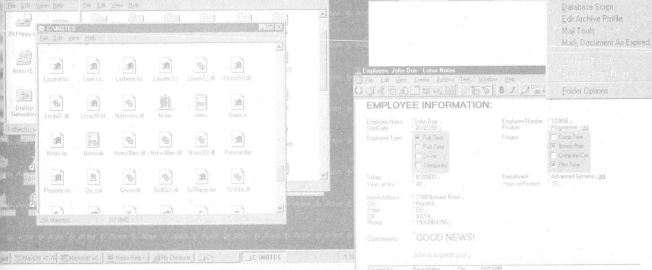

Appendix A

SmartIcons

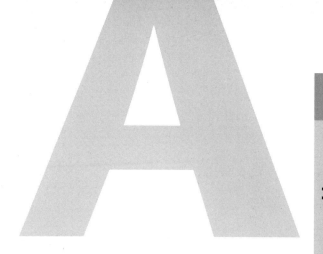

This appendix lists all the SmartIcons available in Notes Release 4.5 and the equivalent menu command.

Tip

If you forget the meaning of any SmartIcon displayed on the SmartIcon bar, click and hold the right mouse button while pointing to the icon. Notes displays the description of the icon at the top of the screen. You can also get icon "bubble help" descriptions when you place your mouse pointer over the icon. If this doesn't happen, make sure that this option is enabled by selecting File, Tools, SmartIcons and checking the Show Descriptions checkbox.

SmartIcon	Name
	Actions Categorize
	Actions Edit Document
	Actions Forward
	Create Agent
	Create Ellipse
	Create Field
	Create Folder
	Create Form
	Create Graphic Button
	Create Hotspot Button

(continues)

(continued)

SmartIcon	Name
	Create Hotspot Polygon
	Create Hotspot Rectangle
	Create Hotspot Text Popup
	Create Insert New Column
	Create Insert Shared Field
	Create Insert Subform
	Create Layout Region
	Create Mail Memo
	Create Navigator
	Create Object
	Create Page Break
	Create Polygon
	Create Polyline
	Create Rectangle
	Create Rounded Rectangle
	Create Shared Field
	Create Subform
	Create Table
	Create Textbox
	Design Bring to Front
	Design Column Properties
	Design Field Properties
	Design Form Properties

SmartIcon	Name
	Design Icon
	Design Send to Back
	Design View
	Design View Properties
	Design View Form Formula
	Design View Selection Conditions
	Edit Check Spelling
	Edit Clear
	Edit Copy
	Edit Copy As Link
	Edit Cut
	Edit External Links
	Edit Find Next
	Edit Find/Replace
	Edit Mark All Read
	Edit Mark All Unread
	Edit Mark Selected Read
	Edit Mark Selected Unread
	Edit Paste
	Edit Paste Special
	Edit Scan Choose
	Edit Scan Unread Choose Preferred
	Edit Scan Unread Mail

(continues)

(continued)

SmartIcon	Name
	Edit Select All
	Edit Undo
	File Attach
	File Database Access Control
	File Database Design Synopsis
	File Database Full Text Create Index
	File Database Full Text Info
	File Database Full Text Update Index
	File Database Header Footer
	File Database New Copy
	File Database Properties
	File Database Publish
	File Document Properties
	File Exit Notes
	File Export
	File Import
	File Mobile Call Server
	File Mobile Edit Current Location
	File Mobile Hang Up
	File New Database
	File Open Database
	File Page Setup
	File Preferences Mail

SmartIcon

SmartIcon	Name
	File Preferences Ports
	File Print
	File Print Setup
	File Replication New Replica
	File Replication Replicate
	File Replication Settings
	File Save
	File Switch User ID
	File Tools Server Administration
	File Tools SmartIcons
	Help Guide Me
	Help Topics
	Lock ID
	Mail Address
	Mail Open
	Mail Send Document
	Navigate Next
	Navigate Next Highlight
	Navigate Next Main
	Navigate Next Selected
	Navigate Next Unread
	Navigate Previous
	Navigate Previous Highlight

(continues)

(continued)

SmartIcon

(continued)

SmartIcon	Name
	View Expand
	View Expand All
	View Go Up Level
	View Refresh
	View Ruler
	View Show/Hide Action Pane
	View Show/Hide Design Pane
	View Show/Hide Preview Document Links
	View Show/Hide Preview Pane
	View Show/Hide Preview Parent
	View Show/Hide Search Bar
	View Show Page Breaks
	View Show Server Names
	View Show Unread
	Window Workspace
	Window Cascade
	Window Tile
	User-customizable icon
	User-customizable icon
	User-customizable icon
	User-customizable icon
	User-customizable icon
	User-customizable icon

SmartIcon	Name
	User-customizable icon
	User-customizable icon
	User-customizable icon
	User-customizable icon
	User-cutsomizable icon
	User-customizable icon
	User-customizable icon
	User-customizable icon

Appendixes

Appendix B

Database Templates

Lotus Notes comes with a selection of database templates that can be used as the foundation for creating new databases. Database templates are identified by their unique NTF (Notes Template File) file extension. Several of the templates are designed to take advantage of new functionality available in Release 4. This appendix provides you a brief description of the database templates included with Release 4 and 4.5 that will assist you in designing applications.

> **Tip**
>
> The Lotus Web Site (**http://www.lotus.com**) has a download section in the Lotus Notes area where updated templates are posted.

◄◄ See "Using Templates," p. 396

You will also see a brief description of those applications used to facilitate the administration of Notes. Listed directly below the template description is the template filename, and the design template name used when creating an application in which you want to control updates to the design through the design template. You can read more about designing applications in Chapter 10, "Creating New Databases."

Application Templates

Here are the application templates included in Release 4 that you can use when you begin designing applications in Notes. Application templates speed up your development process by providing a starting point in your application design—for which you can later customize to further meet your business needs:

- **Approval Cycle**—Companies can use this database to manage their electronic approval requirements. Based on a flexible design, forms can be created to cater to a variety of approval types, yet designers only need to maintain one set of approval logic. The approval logic, stored in the ApprovalLogic subform, can be modified quickly when a company's approval cycle changes.

Template filename: APPROVE4.NTF

Design template name: StdR4Approval

■ **Discussion**—Discussion databases are one of the most common Lotus Notes application types. A workgroup can use a discussion database as a meeting place to collect and share ideas without having to be physically present. Nearly all workgroups can take advantage of the benefits discussion databases have to offer. Financial planners can use them to discuss annual budgets, sales managers can use them to discuss targets, and social committees can use them to plan events. Users have the ability to simply follow discussion threads or to take a more active role and contribute to discussions. Users can also make anonymous contributions.

Discussion databases have a number of key elements. First, discussion thread hierarchies are easy to maintain through the use of main topic, response, and response-to-response forms. Second, the form layouts are designed to be simple to use, making it an ideal application for first-time Lotus Notes users. Third, views are designed to enable users to quickly navigate contributions by category, author, or favorite documents. Users can even set up interest profiles and be notified via the Newsletter Agent when conditions they specify are met. For example, users may want to be notified when their name appears in a discussion thread. In addition, there are full archiving capabilities in place to store documents in a separate database when they become obsolete.

Template filename: DISCUSS4.NTF

Design template name: StdR4Disc

■ **Document Library**—The document library is a database used to capture and store documents. It is an electronic filing cabinet with document review and archiving functions. A document library might contain all the product specifications for an electronic components manufacturer or all drug study information for a pharmaceutical company.

Template filename: DOCLIB4.NTF

Design template name: StdR4DocLib

■ **Lotus SmartSuite 96 Library (R4)**—This Document Library template is designed specifically for Lotus SmartSuite 96 applications. Forms are included for creating 1-2-3 worksheets, freelance presentations, and WordPro documents. Document review and archiving functions are included. (This template is not designed for backward compatibility with previous versions of Lotus SmartSuite.)

Template filename: DOCLIBL4.NTF

Design template name: StdR4DocLibLS

- **Microsoft Office Library (R4)**—This Document Library template is designed specifically for Microsoft Office applications. Forms are included for creating Excel worksheets, Paintbrush pictures, PowerPoint presentations, and Word documents. Document review and archiving functions are included.

  Template filename: DOCLIBM4.NTF

  Design template name: StdR4DocLibMS

- **Personal Address Book**—The Personal Address Book is the replacement for the full Name & Address Book from prior versions of Lotus Notes. This address book is tailored to the personal use of a Lotus Notes user. Information about a contact's work, home, and e-mail systems is stored in this database. Connection records to other Lotus Notes servers are stored in this database, as are location documents which store information about the different locations from which you use Notes. Notes creates three locations for you the first time you start it: Office, Home, and Disconnected.

  Template filename: PERNAMES.NTF

  Design template name: StdR4PersonalAddressBook

- **Personal Journal**—The Personal Journal is a database designed to store private documents. Users can elect to encrypt this database to add further security to entries. A personal journal could be used to store documents in draft form, thoughts, ideas, or just about anything a user wants to record.

  Template filename: JOURNAL4.NTF

  Design template name: StdR4Journal

- **Room Reservations (R4)**—This database is used for booking and tracking reservations for rooms and other resources for an organization. Resource forms are completed for each entity and users complete booking forms to reserve the resources.

  Template filename: RESERVE4.NTF

  Design template name: StdR4Room

Administration Templates

These are templates designed for use by the Notes Setup program, server software, and Notes administrators:

- **Master Address Book**—This template is used to create a server database that is used by Notes for monitoring users, servers, and groups in a Notes community. It is the full version of the Lotus Notes Name & Address Book, containing all of the forms and views required to successfully administer both Notes Servers and users—where the Personal Name & Address Book contains only forms and views pertaining to the individual user.

Template filename: MAB45.NTF

Design template name: None

■ **Public Address Book**—This template is used to create a server database that is used by Notes for monitoring users, servers, and groups in a Notes community. It is the full version of the Lotus Notes Name & Address Book, containing all of the forms and views required to successfully administer both Notes Servers and users—where the Personal Name & Address Book contains only forms and views pertaining to the individual user.

Template filename: PUBNAMES.NTF

Design template name: StdR4PublicAddressBook

■ **Administration Requests**—This template is used to create a server database that is used by the Notes Administration Agent to keep track of requests and processes against the server.

Template filename: ADMIN4.NTF

Design template name: StdR4AdminRequests

■ **Agent Log**—This template is used to create a server log that provides an easy way to review actions and errors that occur during execution of a LotusScript program that uses the NotesLog class.

Template filename: ALOG4.NTF

Design template name: StdR4AgentLog

■ **Certification Log**—This template is used to create a server database that maintains records of certified Notes IDs in a Notes community.

Template filename: CERTLOG.NTF

Design template name: StdNotesCertificationLog

■ **Cluster Analysis**—This template is used to create a server database that maintains cluster test data in a Notes Cluster. A Notes Cluster is a Notes Server topology that contains two to six servers sharing the same network protocol(s) and where special event driven replication is used. You can view test results by cluster, by date, or by test.

Template filename: CLUSTA4.NTF

Design template name: StdR4ClusterAnalysis

■ **Cluster Directory (R4)**—This template is used to automatically create a server database that maintains information on databases within Notes Clusters. Users cannot create documents in this database—they are created and updated by a Notes Server Cluster Database Directory (CLDBDIR) add-in task.

Template filename: CLDBDIR4.NTF

Design template name: StdR4ClusterDirectory

- **Database Analysis**—You can run an analysis against a single database to determine specifics about its design and other application settings. This template is used to create a server database for storing the results of a single database analysis. Note that this database template is not intended to be used to create a new database, but is designed solely for use with the database analysis available from the Server Administration window.

Template filename: DBA4.NTF

Design template name: StdR4DBAnalysis

- **Database Catalog**—This template is used to create a server reference database that records and stores information about the databases on a Notes server. Information is added to the Database Catalog by the Catalog process that runs on a Notes server. Database designers or administrators have the option to exclude a database from the Database Catalog.

Template filename: CATALOG.NTF

Design template name: StdNotesCatalog

- **Database Library**—Similar to the Database Catalog, this template is used to create a database that contains a list of public databases to which users can request access. The main difference between the two applications is that entries are not automatically placed in the Database Library—the database manager must specify that a particular database be listed. This Database Library is ideal for users who may want to create a library of the databases they have stored on their particular hardware, or which they manage. Databases are published to a Database Library using the menu command File, Database, Publish.

Template filename: DBLIB4.NTF

Design template name: StdR4DatabaseLib

- **Local Free Time Info**—This template is used to create a server database used by the Calendaring and Scheduling features in Release 4.5.

Template filename: BUSYTIME.NTF

Design template name: BusyTime

- **Mail (R4)**—The Mail template is used to create a database for managing the use, storage, and routing of electronic mail between Notes users. The template contains forms for creating mail, replies, and tasks. Forms for creating out of office profiles and archive criteria assist with mail management.

Template filename: MAIL4.NTF

Design template name: StdR4Mail

■ **Mail (R4.5)**—The Mail template is the same as the Mail (R4) template but also contains new Calendaring and Scheduling features that can be used to manage personal time more effectively, create and track appointments and meetings, or to delegate tasks to other people. The Calendar View provides a desktop calendar to view appointments.

Template filename: `MAIL45.NTF`

Design template name: StdR45Mail

■ **Mail Router Mailbox**—This template is used to create a server or local database that stores mail from a user that is en route to another user. This database acts as a holding tank for all mail that is to be transferred to other users.

Template filename: `MAILBOX.NTF`

Design template name: StdNotesMailbox

■ **Notes Group Analysis**—This template is used to create a server database for storing the results for a group of logs.

Template filename: `GROUP45.NTF`

Design template name: StdR4GroupAnalysis

■ **Notes Log**—This template is used to create the Notes Log database, a special and important database used for capturing a plethora of Notes server and workstation activity information. The Notes Log tracks activities like server errors, database usage, replication events, database sizes, memory usage, communication information, and miscellaneous events.

Template filename: `LOG.NTF`

Design template name: StdNotesLog

■ **Notes Log Analysis**— The Log Analysis database is designed to hold Results documents created by the Log Analysis tool. Note that this database template is not intended to be used to create a new database, as the Log Analysis Tool creates this database.

Template filename: `LOGA4.NTF`

Design template name: StdR4LogAnalysis

■ **Search Results**—This template is used to create a database for creating and submitting simple or advanced queries that can search for information in multiple databases on multiple servers. Users can build queries including single or multiple words, exact words, word variations, and date criteria. Results can be sorted in a variety of ways.

Template filename: `SRCHSITE.NTF`

Design template name: StdNotesSearchSite

- **Statistics & Events**—This template is used to create a server database that stores configuration records for statistics reporting and monitoring tools, as well as a listing of server messages.

  Template filename: EVENTS4.NTF

  Design template name: StdR4Events

- **Statistics Reporting**—This template is used to create a database that records information about the activity on one or more Notes servers.

  Template filename: STATREP.NTF

  Design template name: StdR4StatReport

- **Personal Web Navigator 4.5**—This template is used to create a database that records information about the activity on one or more Notes servers.

  Template filename: PERWEB45.NTF

  Design template name: StdR45PersonalWebNavigator

- **Web Navigator**—This template is used by the server add-in program WEB.EXE to create the server navigator database that gives Notes users access to the World Wide Web. It also stores Internet documents before they are retrieved by workstations.

  Template filename: WEB.NTF

  Design template name: StdR4WebNavigator

- **Web Navigator 4.5**—This is an update to the Web Navigator template.

  Template filename: PUBWEB45.NTF

  Design template name: StdR45WebNavigator

Appendix C

Special Characters

Special characters—usually not found on your keyboard—represent foreign language letters, foreign currency symbols, copyright and trademark characters, and mathematical symbols. By pressing a key combination, you can use special characters in Notes anywhere you can enter text.

Notes uses the keyboard combination Alt+F1 plus special codes to create special characters. For example, to enter the cent symbol (¢), press Alt+F1, then C, then /. Listed in this appendix are the special characters and key combinations for the Windows, OS/2, and UNIX platforms. Macintosh users can look in the Notes Online help under LMBCS (Lotus Multibyte Character Set) for the help document containing characters and codes for the Macintosh.

> **Note**
>
> Notes provides several codes for many common characters. You can use whichever seems easiest to type or remember.

Press Alt+F1 Plus...	To Get This Character	Character Description
C,	Ç	C cedilla
u"	ü	u umlaut
e'	é	e acute
a^	â	a circumflex
a"	ä	a umlaut
a`	à	a grave
a*	å	a angstrom
c,	ç	c cedilla
e^	ê	e circumflex
e"	ë	e umlaut
e`	è	e grave

(continues)

(continued)

Press Alt+F1 Plus...	To Get This Character	Character Description
i"	ï	i umlaut
i^	î	i circumflex
i`	ì	i grave
A"	Ä	A umlaut
A*	Å	A angstrom
E'	É	E acute
ae	æ	ae diphthong
AE	Æ	AE diphthong
o^	ô	o circumflex
o"	ö	o umlaut
o`	ò	o grave
u^	û	u circumflex
u`	ù	u grave
y"	ÿ	y umlaut
O"	Ö	O umlaut
U"	Ü	U umlaut
o/	ø	o slash
L= or l= or L- or l-	£	Pound sign
O/	Ø	O slash
xx or XX	×	Multiply
a'	á	a acute
i'	í	i acute
o'	ó	o acute
u'	ú	u acute
n~	ñ	n tilde
N~	Ñ	N tilde
a_ or A_	ª	Feminine ordinal indicator
O_ or o_	º	Masculine ordinal indicator
??	¿	Inverted ?
RO or R0 or r0	®	Registered
-]		Start of line
12	½	Half
14	¼	Quarter
!!	¡	Inverted exclamation
<<	«	Left Angle quotes
>>	»	Right Angle quotes
A'	Á	A acute
A^	Â	A circumflex

Press Alt+F1 Plus...	To Get This Character	Character Description
A`	À	A grave
CO or co or C0 or c0	©	Copyright
cl or c/ or Cl or C/	¢	cent
Y= or y= or Y- or y-	¥	Yen
a~	ã	a tilde
A~	Ã	A tilde
XO or xo or X0 or x0	¤	International Currency
d-	ð	Eth lower
D-	Ð	Eth upper
E^	Ê	E circumflex
E"	Ë	E umlaut
E`	È	E grave
I'	Í	I acute
I^	Î	I circumflex, uppercase
I"	Ï	I umlaut, uppercase
/<space>	¦	Vertical line, broken
I`	Ì	I grave
O'	Ó	O acute, uppercase
ss	ß	German sharp, lowercase
O^	Ô	O circumflex, uppercase
O`	Ò	O grave, uppercase
o~	õ	o tilde, lowercase
O~	Õ	O tilde, uppercase
/u	µ	Greek mu, lowercase
p-	þ	Icelandic Thorn, lowercase
P-	Þ	Icelandic Thorn, uppercase
U'	Ú	U acute, uppercase
U^	Û	U circumflex, uppercase
Ù	Ù	U grave, uppercase
y'	ý	y acute, lowercase
Y'	Ý	Y acute, uppercase
_^		Overline
spacebar then '	´	Acute
-=	–	Hyphen
+-	±	Plus/Minus
34	¾	3 quarters
!p	¶	Paragraph symbol
so	§	Section symbol

(continues)

(continued)

Press Alt+F1 Plus...	To Get This Character	Character Description
:-	÷	Division
''	,	Cedilla
^0	°	Degree
spacebar then "	¨	Umlaut
^.	·	Center dot
^1	1	1 Superscript
^2	2	2 Superscript
^3	3	3 Superscript

Appendix D

Using the CD-ROM

The CD-ROM enclosed with this manual has been provided to give you the entire *Special Edition Using Lotus Notes and Domino 4.5* book online, with demo applications, troubleshooting databases, and additional information on Lotus Business Partners, companion products, and third-party applications. You will find a host of screencams, applications, technical documents, and more—all stored within a single Notes database on the CD-ROM. You simply have to open the Notes database on the CD-ROM, read through the documents to see what is attached, and then detach and/or launch the file attachments to use them. Each document in the database that contains a file attachment provides instructions on how you might want to work with that file, as well as a brief description of the application.

In addition to this book being provided to you in its entirety, the following table provides you a sneak peek into what is available on the CD-ROM.

Program/File	Contributor
GroupShield Evaluation Copy	McAfee
GroupScan Evaluation Copy	McAfee
Notes Network-Based Training Demo	ReCor Corporation
R4 Update Flash Cards	Avalon Consulting, Inc.
Remind Project Management Demo	Changepoint Corporation
Instant I-Net Evaluation Copy	InfoImage
Lotus Notes Advisor Premier Magazine	Advisor Publications
SmartForm Modem Doctor	Lotus Development Corporation
WorldCom's Help & Services Database	WorldCom
WorldCom's Setup Database	WorldCom
Sentinel	Mayflower Software
Notes Update Magazine Sample Articles	Xephon
ViP for Lotus Notes	Revelation Technologies

(continues)

(continued)

Program/File	Contributor
EtQ Solutions	EtQ Management Consultants, Inc.
GroupFocus	Business Evolution, Inc.
Acrobat Reader	Adobe Systems Incorporated
ScreenCam Player 2.0	Lotus Development Corporation
Mobile Survivor's Kit	Lotus Development Corporation
Formula Catalog	Author Supplement Database
Icon Library	Author Supplement Database
Recipe Tracker	Author Supplement
Video/CD Tracker	Author Supplement
Administrator's Guidebook	Author Supplement

All of this is included and more!

Working with the Database

All of the files on this CD, with the exception of the electronic versions of *Special Edition Using Lotus Notes and Domino 4.5* and *Special Edition Using JavaScript,* are located in a single Notes database; accessing these files is as easy as opening any other Notes database. Perform the following steps to access the *Special Edition Using Lotus Notes and Domino 4.5* database:

1. Select File, Database, Open. The Open Database dialog box appears (see Figure D.1).

Fig. D.1   Open the database from the CD-ROM to begin exploring the wealth of information contributed from a wide range of sources.

2. Type **D:\QUEBOOK.NSF** in the Filename box as shown in Figure D.1. (Substitute your CD-ROM drive designation for *D:*, if necessary, to access your CD-ROM drive.) You can also use the Browse feature in the Open Database dialog box to open the CD-ROM and locate the QUEBOOK.NSF file.

3. Select Open.

Notes will open the *Special Edition Using Lotus Notes and Domino 4.5* database for you to review its contents. Instructions for using specific files attached to the documents in this database are provided within each document in the "Using This Demo" section. Read through this section to understand how to work with a particular file.

When you exit the database, Notes will leave its icon on your workspace for future use of the database—double-click the icon to open all subsequent accesses to this database. Keep in mind that you will need the CD-ROM accompanying this book in your CD-ROM drive when accessing the database—unless you copied the database to your workspace.

Using the Electronic Book

Special Edition Using Lotus Notes and Domino 4.5 is available to you as an HTML document that can be read from any World Wide Web browser that you may have currently installed on your machine (such as the Domino Web browser, Internet Explorer, or Netscape Navigator). If you don't have a Web browser, we have included Microsoft's Internet Explorer for you.

Reading the Electronic Book as an HTML Document

To read the electronic book, you will need to start your Web browser and open the document file INDEX.HTML located on the \EBOOK subdirectory of the CD-ROM. Alternatively, you can browse the CD-ROM directory using any file manager and double-click INDEX.HTML.

Once you have opened the INDEX.HTML page, you can access all of the book's contents by clicking the highlighted chapter number or topic name. The electronic book works like any other Web page; when you click a hot link, a new page is opened or the browser will take you to the new location in the document. As you read through the electronic book, you will notice other highlighted words or phrases. Clicking these cross-references will also take you to a new location within the electronic book. You can always use your browser's forward or backward buttons to return to your original location.

Installing the Internet Explorer

If you don't have a Web browser installed on your machine, you can use Microsoft's Internet Explorer 3.0, included on this CD-ROM.

The Microsoft Internet Explorer can be installed from the self-extracting file in the \EXPLORER directory. Double-click MSIE30M.EXE or use the Control Panel's Add/Remove Programs option and follow the instructions in the install routine. Please be aware that you must have Windows 95 installed on your machine to use this version of Internet Explorer. Other versions of this software can be downloaded from Microsoft's Web site at **http://www.microsoft.com/ie**.

Index

X-Z

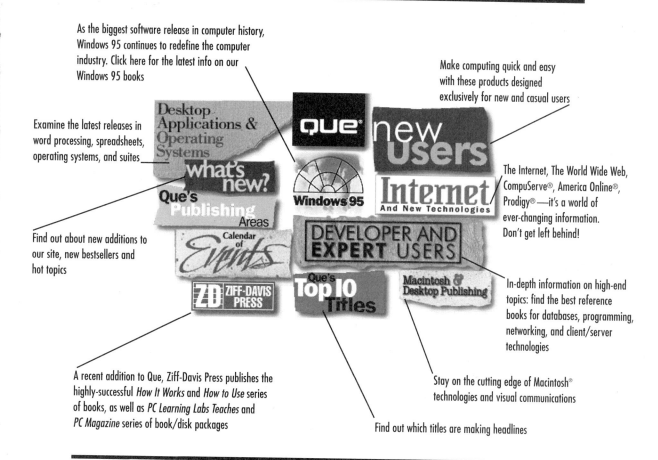

Licensing Agreement

By opening this package, you are agreeing to be bound by the following:

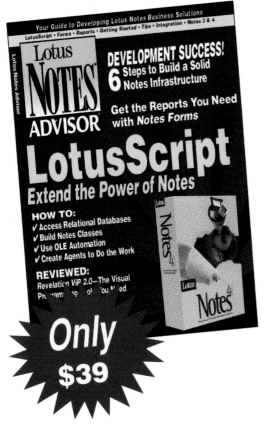

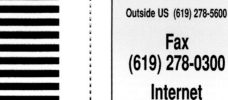